This edition of the Club's record book is dedicated to those ethical, responsible bowhunters among us, faceless men and women who pursue their quarry fairly and legally, accepting their occasional successes with humility and heartfelt appreciation. They understand that the challenge of the chase is all important, that there is satisfaction to be found in attempting as well as achieving. May their ranks multiply!

———————————————

The Official Pope and Young Club Conservation print, *"The King Speaks,"* 24 x 36 inches, Oil/Stretched Linen

Prepared and edited by the:
Book Editorial Committee

M. R. James, Editor	Harv Ebers
G. Fred Asbell	Ron Sherer
Dr. Donald Ace Morgan	Glenn Hisey
Dr. C. Randall Byers	Scott Showalter
Stan Rauch	Bill Krenz
Jim Dougherty	Larry Streiff
Dr. David Samuel	Glenn St. Charles

Library of Congress Catalog Card Number: 93-083450
ISBN Number: 0-936531-07-X
Published April, 1993

Produced and Published in the United States of America by:
The Pope and Young Club
P. O. Box 548, Chatfield, MN 55923

Designed by Lisa M. Wayand

BOWHUNTING

BIG GAME RECORDS
OF NORTH AMERICA

Fourth Edition

POPE AND YOUNG CLUB

CONTENTS

CONTENTS

ACKNOWLEDGEMENTS

This Fourth Edition of the Club's big game record book is the result of a genuine interest and sincere effort by many talented people who deserve public recognition for combining their talents to create this volume.

Special thanks go to the Pope and Young Book Committee whose leadership role saw the project through from rough draft to published volume. Committee members include Editor M. R. James, G. Fred Asbell, Stan Rauch, Glenn Hisey, Don Morgan, Jim Dougherty, Scott Showalter, Bill Krenz, Ron Sherer, Larry Streiff, Dave Samuel, Harv Ebers, Randy Byers and Glenn St. Charles.

Additional kudos are due contributors Frank "Rit" Heller, Joe St. Charles and Bill McCrary whose joint writing effort resulted in the chapter tracing the early day history of hunting heads. Thanks, too, go to Judd Cooney whose photographs capably illustrate this book, and to Leon Parson whose wildlife art graces these pages. Finally, sincere thanks to the Ishi Award recipients — Del Austin, Mel Johnson, Ray Alt, Art Kragness, Dr. Michael Cusack, B. G. Shurtleff, Ray Cox, Jerry James, Bill Barcus, Gary Laya, James Ludvigson and James Decker — for writing brief versions of their hunts and sharing them with readers.

Also, Charles A. Young earns deserved thanks for providing the "Hunting Big Game with a Bow and Arrow" chapter from his grandfather's collection of writings.

As always, a note of appreciation is due the Boone and Crockett Club for permission to adapt and reproduce B&C scoring forms for use by the Pope and Young Club.

Executive Secretary Glenn Hisey, mentioned above, deserves additional recognition for his work with Records Chairman Randy Byers in checking the listings of more than 22,000 big game trophies and ensuring the accuracy of the information. And Kevin Hisey earns a heartfelt note of thanks for his proofing efforts.

Finally, no book such as this can be produced without a production team that is responsible for typesetting, layout design and proofreading. Extra special thanks go to Lisa Wayand, **Bowhunter** Magazine Art Director, who created the book's overall appearance; to Club member Steve Ashley for his efforts in adding the touches of color to this volume; and to Banta ISG/Viking Press for its considerable assistance.

FOREWORD

THIS IS THE FOURTH EDITION of the Pope and Young Club's record book. Like the three previous editions, it is a continuing compilation of trophy class North American big game animals taken with the bow and arrow.

Immediately obvious should be the size of this publication when compared to the First and Second Editions — published in 1975 and 1981, respectively — and, to a lesser degree, to the Third Edition published in 1987. This Fourth Edition of Bowhunting Big Game Records of North America, published 18 years after the Club's first record book, contains 22,417 entries with 5,696 of these new entries from the 1991-1992 recording period.

The initial record book, published 17 years after our Club's first competition as the age of modern bowhunting was dawning, contained some 2,400 total entries. Compare that modest number, collected over more than a decade and a half, with approximately 19,000 big game trophies recorded over the past 18 years. That is an increase so large it is almost incomprehensible to me. I am unaware of anything in the annals of modern day hunting which has experienced such growth.

Each record book, in its own right, serves as a historic documentation of the evolution of hunting with the bow and arrow. Each book is a testimonial to the efficiency of the bow and arrow as a hunting weapon and is a chronicle of the fantastic growth of trophy bowhunting — as well as the appeal of this wonderful pastime.

Interestingly enough, the formation of the Pope and Young Club arose from a need to show the world that the bow was an effective, viable hunting tool. Most hunters and most state game agencies of the 1940s and 1950s believed the bow was little more than a toy and few had interest in recognizing it as a serious hunting weapon. It was Glenn St. Charles and a small group of dedicated bowhunters who conceived the idea of pulling together all the nationwide bowhunting successes they could locate and document, bringing everything together in one place so this information could be held up to those who believed bowhunting to be ineffective, saying, in

effect, "Look, see how big these animals are. These big animals were taken with the bow and arrow. The bow works just fine, thank you." Then, later, the message would be, "You can see the bow and arrow works exceptionally well as a hunting weapon — but it is a lot more difficult and takes more time. How about giving us a few days in the woods ahead of the rifle season?"

The rest, as they say, is history. Today the hunting bow is accepted by every game agency in the country and droves of hunters continue answering its romantic call. The size of this book testifies, beyond the shadow of any doubt, to the trophy-taking ability of the bow and arrow. It has succeeded, as Glenn St. Charles is fond of saying, "...beyond our wildest dreams." Bowhunting and trophy bowhunting are moving forward almost faster than the eye can follow. The growth of this record book is only one indicator. One only has to look around to find dozens more.

But this isn't time to sit back and rest on our laurels. Hunting is under serious attack at every turn today. Of course, hunting has always been under attack — probably since about a week after the first pound of meat was commercially sold to someone. But today's attacks are continuous and serious. Probably media-use, a worldwide instant audience and its craving for news — especially of the negative type — have been the biggest factors in what seems like unrelenting bad press for hunters. Modern hunters are being depicted at every turn as unsavory, bloodthirsty, unwashed, insensitive louts. The public image of the hunter these days may be at its lowest point ever. Bowhunting, because it represents a smaller group within the hunting community, has been targeted by our enemies as the most vulnerable. Indeed, we are seeing intensive efforts to stop, completely, the hunting of animals with the bow and arrow. Indeed, this certainly is no time for the Pope and Young Club to sit back and tell ourselves that we've accomplished what we set out to do.

The underlying principle behind the formation of the Pope and Young Club was its goal of helping bowhunting and the bowhunter. It would seem that improving the image of today's hunter is the most important task before us, along with the need to communicate the fact that hunters are America's most concerned conservationists. These tasks may loom every bit as large and challenging as those we faced 35 years ago.

Few people in the non-hunting world think of the hunter as a conservationist, yet he has always been that. The hunter was one of the first conservationists, long before it was the socially acceptable thing to do. Aldo Leopold, the father of the modern conservation ethic, was a bowhunter and an advocate of stewardship of the land. And, of course, it was Theodore Roosevelt who conceived the idea of the Boone and Crockett Club — the organization served as a model for our own — and who initiated the national park system. Roosevelt, an avid hunter, was a conservationist of the first magnitude. Again, the truth is hunters have had more positive influence on the conservation of our world's environment and its wildlife than any other segment of society — and that most certainly includes all of the anti-hunting/ animal rights advocates.

Hunters have always been concerned about perpetuating and protecting the ancient relationship between man and animal. Hunters have a firsthand knowledge of the fragile environment, just as they have always understood the complex intertwining of man and nature. Unfortunately, hunters haven't been very successful conveying their message to the non-hunting public. We've taken too much for granted. We've probably become somewhat insensitive to the fact that much of today's urban population does not understand what we do, or why we do it. There are those who only know that hunters kill things — and some believe we do it only to hang trophies on our walls. You and I know that trophy hunting is good conservation. But few others know that — and won't know unless you and I tell them. It is in the best interests of all of us who hunt to begin a concerted effort to change public misconceptions.

The day of the casual, uncommitted hunter is rapidly passing. The day of concerned, dedicated, ethical hunters is here. Our beliefs, our activities and our tenacity will all be sorely tested in the years ahead.

Each line in this book represents a hunter and an animal and a special moment in time involving man and the natural environment. As hunters, we know our place in this world. As hunters, we understand it is impossible to return from a day afield and not be richer for the experience.

— G. Fred Asbell

THE FUTURE *of* BOWHUNTING

by Dr. Dave Samuel

IT IS AMAZING how differently people view bowhunting. We hunters see it as a beautiful way to go back in time, to participate in nature, to hunt in a traditional and challenging way. Anti-hunters see bowhunting as something cruel and inhumane. Our perceptions and values are very different.

For many of us bowhunting began when we were very young with a simple desire to shoot the bow and arrow. In early days some of us got that desire from watching films of Howard Hill shooting the bow in extraordinary ways. In the late 1940s it was common for movie theaters to show newsy or entertaining "short subjects" before the feature film. Howard Hill made numerous such "shorts" and seeing him shoot the bow was captivating.

I'm sure some were also intrigued by the Robin Hood films featuring Errol Flynn. No question, he stimulated my imagination and desire to make and shoot a bow when I was a kid. Others probably go back even further to the namesakes of our Club and the other early adventurers who shot the bow and arrow. More modern converts to bowhunting emulated the legend, Fred Bear. This thin man in the Borsalino hat led hundreds of thousands of men and women into bowhunting.

We cannot minimize the role of parents in introducing young people into bowhunting. I know in my case my dad made it possible for me to first shoot the bow. He bought me a bow when I was ten and took me to a local archery range several times a week. Shooting was a family affair involving my brothers, mother and dad. This early bow shooting led to bowhunting and opened up a whole new world for me. What experiences!

Will today's children get the same opportunities we had to learn about nature through the eyes of a hunter? Maybe not. Society is changing, attitudes are changing and the paths many of us followed that naturally led us into the woods are disappearing. Let's look at some of the changes and attempt to determine their impacts on our sport.

NUMBERS OF HUNTERS

In recent years the number of hunters has slowly declined. However, this decrease is not exactly the huge drop some newspaper writers claim. Let's look at the real numbers.

In 1965 there were 14.2 million hunters. Numbers climbed steadily until 1977 when the total reached 16.5 million hunters. Next, from 1977 until 1983 the numbers rose and fell with a high of 16.7 million in '83. Since then numbers have slowly fallen to around 15.8 million where they've remained since 1988. The pro-hunters might say that we now have more hunters than we did in 1965; the anti-hunters might say that we now have fewer hunters than we did in 1983. Both statements are true.

If we consider the percent of the population that hunts, we find the following:

In 1965, 9.6 percent of the population hunted and by 1975 the percentage had climbed to 9.9. By 1980, 8.9 percent of the population hunted and by 1985 the percentage had fallen to 8.3. I have no figures for recent years; however, they likely have dropped a bit more since 1985. The conclusion is that overall hunter numbers — as a percentage of the total population — have dropped slightly (about 1.5 percent in the past 30 years) while total hunter numbers have risen since 1965 though dropping slightly in recent years.

THE FUTURE FOR NUMBERS OF HUNTERS

Though the above figures appear fairly optimistic, recent demographic studies show that the numbers of hunters will not increase in the near future — and probably not ever. Consider these data collected by Dan Decker and his cohorts at Cornell University.

In 1987 in New York the male population aged 13 through 23 (the age category from which two-thirds of hunters are recruited) was 88 percent of what it was in 1981. Consider also that since 1970 the number of single-parent households has doubled. One estimate is that 90 percent of 15 million children under the age of 19 live with their mother. In most such cases these children will not be exposed to hunting. Thus, not only is the pool of potential hunters decreasing, but divorces are also creating situations that essentially will not create any new hunters.

Can we recruit new hunters from older age categories? As a matter of fact more older people are taking up the sport of hunting. In 1978 in New York some 30 percent of the state's new hunters were 20 years of age or older. Five years later that percentage jumped to 43 percent. At first glance it appears this recruitment of older people into hunting is a good thing. But Dr. Decker points out problems.

Consider that hunters who take up the sport as post adolescents are twice as likely to drop out of hunting (maybe 40 percent drop out during the first two to three years). Also consider that in New York between 1978 and 1983 the population of new hunting recruits living in urban/suburban vs. rural areas increased from one-third to one-half. Survivorship of urban-raised hunters is likely lower than for rural-raised hunters, too. So we have more hunters starting at older ages and we have more hunters coming from urban areas — both groups having higher dropout rates than hunters living in the country and starting at a younger age.

We also know that hunters stay in the sport longer when their families have roots in hunting. In such families it is typical for the father to teach the son or daughter to hunt and these children begin hunting when younger. When there is no family hunting role model, friends teach people to hunt (with obvious problems compared to the father/son or father/daughter hunting lessons). But as already noted, hunters starting later in life tend to drop out at a faster rate. Also, there are fewer internalized hunting values taught and this can lead to problems with hunter ethics and a less consistent hunting activity pattern. None of these signs, frankly, is good for the future of hunting. Each dramatically points out the need for surrogate father training programs which teach interested youngsters to hunt.

A CHANGING PUBLIC

Eighty-five percent of our population approves of hunting for meat while 67 percent approves of hunting for meat and recreation. Although most members of society support harvest as a part of wise management of natural resources, other sincere individuals have emerged from our urban society to oppose such views. A small but growing segment of the population believes that animals should have rights. When it comes to the use of animals for man's benefit, these "animal rightists" are on one polarized end of the spectrum with hunters at the other end.

In between we find the vast silent majority, yet with each successive generation this group moves further from the realities of death and nature than it once had while living on the farm. Consider your own family. How many generations off the farm are your children? The trend toward an urban/suburban society will likely continue.

Surveys of youngsters today show a widening gap between realities learned when living close to the land and artificial knowledge learned living in a concrete and asphalt environment. A 1992 study at Michigan State University showed cartoons strongly influenced children's perceptions about animals. Many such cartoons are anti-kill, anti-hunting. Still another study showed that television had a major influence on how children think about wildlife. How many pro-hunting TV shows do children see?

Teachers play a major role in the attitude of children. A recent Missouri study showed some 37 percent of public school teachers cared more for the suffering of individual animals than for the overall population of that species. It's little wonder the animal rightists have targeted public school teachers with their propaganda.

WILL THE MEDIA HELP US?

If we think that the television and newspaper reporters will help educate our children — and the general public — about real nature and death in the wild, we are mistaken. The typical national media representative is young, educated, liberal and urban with no rural experience — and obviously no hunting experience or interest. Do not expect help from the media.

The Discovery Channel reaches 56 million people and it would be wonderful if game and fish agencies could do as well. None comes close. A recent report showed that the Louisiana Department of Wildlife and Fisheries reached only 10 percent of that state's population with its messages. As state agencies go, this result is pretty darn good; however, the problem is the 10

percent reached is likely people who already are sold on hunting and fishing. Game agencies are not reaching the non-hunters and the media have no positive interest in pro-hunting messages. The potential is there but hunting is not something that urban America is interested in. Game and fish agencies — and the hunters and fishermen of America — have a lot to learn about dealing with today's media.

"ANIMAL RIGHTS" VALUE SYSTEM

The most common criticism of bowhunting is that it is cruel and violates the rights of the animals being hunted. In recent years the Fund for Animals has made bow-wounding a major issue. However, science has countered this issue and in the future you will see major study reports refuting the reported bowhunting losses. Wounding losses reported in the 50-to 80-percent range have already been refuted. New research shows losses below five to eight percent.

Even though most bow-wounded animals either die immediately or recover from their wounds, bowhunters must make every effort to reduce wounding rates. Today's ethical bowhunter is highly sensitive to the possible suffering of any animal. Most of us attempt to keep pain to a minimum and we must continue to improve in this area. But we do this because it's the thing to do, not because animal rightists demand it.

Animal rightists say that wounding is why they are upset with bowhunters. That probably is untrue. They also say pain is the issue; however, that likely is not the

real issue, either. The real issue for animal rightists is that they feel animals should have the same moral standing and legal rights as people. That means animals cannot be used by people for any purpose — not for meat, not for medical research, not as pets and obviously not for hunting or fishing. It is a value system that the general public will not buy.

Robert Bidinotto, a writer for **Reader's Digest**, spoke to the Northeast Fish and Wildlife Conference in Norfolk, Virginia in May, 1992. He stated that the non-hunting public was not particularly predisposed to the anti-hunting message — but they were confused. He stated that game agencies and sportsmen needed to let the public know about the twisted, illogical animal rights value system seeking to give animals the same rights people enjoy. "Uphold the moral rightness of human intervention in nature," Bidinotto said. "Focus on philosophical issues. Critics of hunting and our system of wildlife management do not care that it is the most successful system in the world. They are radical and uncompromising. That is why we must focus on their value system. Force them to defend a value system that the public cannot understand. Put them on the defensive."

Bidinotto and others believe that the general public should understand the difference between the terms "animal rights" and "animal welfare." Animal welfarists are concerned about the humane treatment of animals and such people may well include hunters, non-hunters and anti-hunters. They support humane treatment of animals and using animals in a humane way to benefit man (e.g., through medical research) and unlike "animal rightists" do not support the total elimination of such uses. Some animal welfarists feel it is morally wrong for humans to hunt for sport; others do not feel that way.

There is also the growing question on the ethics of hunting. Such issues usually are spawned by "animal rightists" who question the morality of hunting by modern man. Even though many papers and books describe the evolution of man as a hunting animal, the antis feel modern man is somehow supposed to turn off such evolutionary instincts. Ann Causey, in a classic paper "On the Morality of Hunting," stated that "...it is not morally wrong to take pleasure in killing game, nor is it morally right. It is simply not a moral issue at all..."

Over the coming years we will see certain forms of hunting — and bowhunting — attacked because they are perceived to be "unethical" by some segments of the general public. Watch for the continuing questioning of the morality of hunting.

THE ECONOMICS OF HUNTING

However right we feel our motives are, there is a growing segment of society that does not relate to wild nature at all. With an increasing urbanization of this continent, with a decreasing number of people involved in agriculture, with a greater empowerment of women (who generally are more anti-hunting than males) and with the reduced recruitment of hunters, it is obvious that hunting faces an uphill battle. How can we possibly win?

Mike Hayden, former wildlife biologist and governor of Kansas, addressed this issue at the North American Wildlife and Natural Resources Conference in Charlotte, North Carolina in March, 1992. He stated that public education should "...start with what is on everybody's mind nowadays — the economy. The fact is that supporting wildlife makes good economic sense. Supporting wildlife means jobs...economic growth...and a better life for every American." He went on to point out that hunters spent $10 billion in 1991 in pursuit of game. Fishermen spent another $28 billion.

Hayden also gave an example of what can happen when these recreations are threatened. When the red drum fisheries declined off the Texas coast in the late 1970s, the state spent $647,000 a year to stock hatchery-raised drum. The result of such management? Red drum populations soared and by 1992 they were worth an estimated $178 million per year. Now there is a business investment that any person can understand.

THE FUTURE OF BOWHUNTING

Even though there have been several anti-bowhunting victories in recent years, most anti-bow

actions have not been successful. Bowhunting has proven to be a valuable management tool. In quite a few states bowhunters harvest more than 20 percent of the total deer taken each year during all hunting seasons. And in urban/suburban situations, bowhunting is expanding as a method to control deer numbers. It is safe, quiet and effective. Thus, even though much of the preceding information might lead one to be pessimistic about our future, I do not believe that there will be an outright ban of bowhunting in the next 30 to 40 years. The rightness of bowhunting is far too strong for that.

Tom Heberlein, in a 1991 paper in the **Wildlife Society Bulletin** titled "Changing Attitudes and Funding for Wildlife Preserving the Sport Hunter," (Volume 19, pages 523-534) agrees but has other concerns. Heberlein says that "...if wildlife...is to be preserved...[then] those of us in the profession must change how we do business." He believes that even if there were major declines in hunter numbers, which there are not, this will "...not seriously affect the funding base for wildlife management." The reason is that hunters are willing to pay more to hunt.

Be ready to do this. It is vital to the continuation of our present system of wildlife management.

Heberlein also pointed our that future hunters will need more hunter education. Thus, I see the role of the International Bowhunter Education Program expanding even more than it has in recent years. This is a plus for the future of our sport.

Bowhunters must take on new responsibilities if our sport is to survive. And there are several things you can do. First, get your hunting club involved with "good citizen" projects. Such projects send positive messages to your non-hunting neighbors and friends that bowhunters are good people who are concerned about their community. Second, prepare to pay more to bowhunt. Regardless of increasing costs, it remains a very inexpensive form of recreation. Third, support bowhunter education programs and get involved in the IBEP. Educating hunters and getting young people into archery/bowhunting will be vital in the future. Improving the image of bowhunters is something that every bowhunter must do. And fourth, help law enforcement arrest those who violate our game laws. We hunters cannot afford to allow any unethical or illegal activities to continue.

Finally, all bowhunters must become more informed and more involved if our sport is to survive. Aldo Leopold once wrote that as we become more knowledgeable about something, it will have more intrinsic value to us. It's true for the game we hunt and it should be true for bowhunting as well. Read, learn, get involved and give the future of bowhunting a new meaning for yourself and the generations that follow.

THE GOOD OLD DAYS?

The Time is Now!

by Dr. C. Randall Byers

I WAS TALKING with Ed this past summer. Obviously, our conversation focused on bowhunting. The season was only a few short months away! And as our conversation progressed, I mentioned that the previous fall I had seen as many deer in one evening as I used to see in the good old days. As our conversation continued and the details — all factual, of course — of that hunt and other fall sorties unfolded, it occurred to me that the hunt had been every bit as good as ones I'd enjoyed in the good old days.

More reflection on this matter causes me to wonder if the good old days aren't right now. True, hunting is under attack and the habitat base is shrinking. Yet modern game practices coupled with changing hunting ethics and practices are combining to produce some of the finest trophy hunting ever enjoyed by bowhunters.

What are the facts to back up such a statement? Consider the growth of the bowhunting records maintained by the Pope and Young Club. This Fourth Edition of the **Bowhunting Big Game Records of North America** lists 22,417 trophies. The very first listing, prepared in 1961, recorded a total of 244 trophies. In this, the Eighteenth Recording Period, 5,696 trophies were accepted for the records. These 5,696 animals represent over 23 percent of the total entries in the Club records for all time! All but a few of these 5,696 entries were taken in the 1990s. For this reason alone it is easy to argue that the good old days are now.

Other factors support this argument as well. If we look at the quality of the animals in the Club records, we see that many of the highest scoring trophies ever entered were taken in recent times. The Pope and Young Club recognizes World Record entries in 32 categories. Due to ties, 35 World Record animals are recorded. Five of these records were taken in the last two years and a whopping 22 in the past decade. Of the 8,869 whitetail deer listed in the records, the fourth largest was shot in 1991. All in all, quality hunting is right now.

From an organizational perspective the records program is on solid ground. The number of entries continues to increase with each recording period. Still, things are changing. It is clear that pressure is on the hunting sports despite the remarkable accomplishments and successes of modern game management. Hunting ethics are changing, too, in part in response to some of these pressures but in a larger part due to maturation by sport hunters. Yet this change in hunting ethics is desirable and supports the notion that the good old days are now.

Consider the following passage from an account of hunting in Africa in the 1850s taken from **A Hunter's Life in South Africa** by R. Gordon Cumming:

It was now quite dark, and hard to tell what sort of game we were going to fire at. Strydom, however, whispered to me that they were quaggas, and they certainly appeared to be such. His gun snapped three times at the wildebeast, upon which they all set off at a gallop. Strydom, who was riding my stallion, let go his bridle when he ran in to fire, taking advantage of which the horse set off at a gallop after them. I then mounted "The Cow," and after riding hard for about a mile I

came up to them. They were standing still, and the stallion was in the middle of them. I could make him out by his saddle; so, jumping off my horse in a state of intense excitement, I ran forward and fired both barrels of my two-grooved rifle into the quaggas, and heard the bullets tell loudly. They then started off, but the stallion was soon once more in the middle of them. I was astonished and delighted to remark how my horse was able to take up their attention, so they appeared heedless of the reports of my rifle.

In haste I commenced loading, but to my dismay I found that I had left my loading rod with Hendrick. Mounting "The Cow," I rode nearer the quaggas, and was delighted to find they allowed my horse to come within easy shot. It was now very dark, but I set off in the hope to fall in with Hendrick on the wide plain, and galloped along shouting with all my might, but in vain. I then rode across the plain for the hill to try to find some bush large enough to make a ramrod. In this, by the greatest of chance, I succeeded, and, being provided with a knife, I cut a good ramrod, loaded my rifle, and rode off to seek the quaggas once more. I soon fell in with them, and, coming within shot, fired at them right and left, and heard both tell, upon which they galloped across the plains with the stallion still after them. One of them, however, was very hard hit, and soon dropped astern. The stallion remained to keep him company.

About this time the moon shown forth faintly. I galloped on after the troop, and, presently coming up with them, rode on one side, and dismounting, and dropping on my knee, I sent a bullet through the shoulder of the last quagga; he staggered, fell to the ground with a heavy crash, and expired. The rest of the troop charged wildly around him, snorting and prancing like wild horses in Mazeppa, and then set off at full speed across the plain. I did not wait to bleed the quagga, but, mounting my horse, I galloped on after the troop, but could not, however, overtake them. I now returned and endeavored to find the quagga which I had last shot, but owing to the darkness, and to my having no mark to guide me on the plain, I failed to find him. I then set off to try for the quagga which I had dropped astern with the stallion; Having searched some time in vain, I dismounted and laid my head on the ground, when I made out two dark objects which turned out to be what I thought. On my approaching, the quagga tried to make off, when I sent a ball through his shoulder, which laid him low. On going up to him in the full expectation of inspecting for the first time one of these animals, what was my disappointment and vexation to find a fine brown gelding, with two white stars on his forehead! The truth now flashed upon me; Strydom and I had both been mistaken; instead of quaggas, the wagon-team of a neighboring Dutchman had afforded me my evening's shooting!

I caught my stallion and rode home, intending to pay for the horses which I had killed and wounded; but on telling my story to Strydom, with which he seemed quite amused, he told me not to say a word about it, as the owners of the horses were very avaricious, and would make me pay treble their value, and that if I kept quiet it would be supposed they had been killed either by lions or wild Bushmen.

Cumming was a noted lion hunter and respected sportsman of his time. His account of his African adventure was widely read and he was popular on the lecture curcuit. Likewise his description of the hunt and chase parallels many that I have read from that era. However, riding about at night and shooting without regard to shot selection at neighbors' horses certainly would not fall within today's perception of ethical hunting practices.

In a similar fashion if one reads accounts of the Club's namesakes, Dr. Saxton Pope and Art Young, from their hunts 50 years later, one sees stark contrasts to the picture painted by today's bowhunting authors. Many readers of this edition are familiar with the thrilling account of Pope and Young's bowhunt for grizzly bears in the Yellowstone area. A more complete version of this hunt was published in the Third Edition of our Club's record book. A portion of that account follows:

We went to the blind about an hour before midnight, feeling surely this evening the big fellow would come. After two hours of frigidity and immobility, we heard the velvet foot-falls of bear coming up the canyon. There came our patrician and her royal family. The little fellows pattered up the trail before their mother. They came within range. I signalled Young and we shot together at the cubs. We struck. There was a squeak, a roar, a jumble of shadowy figures and the entire flock of bears came tumbling in our direction.

At that very moment the big grizzly appeared on the scene. There were five bears in sight. Turning her head from side to side, trying to find her enemy, the she-bear came towards us. I whispered to Young, "Shoot the big fellow." At the same time, I drew an arrow to the head and drove it at the oncoming female. It struck her full in the chest. She roared; threw herself sidewise, bellowed with rage, staggered and fell to the ground. She rose again, weakened, stumbled forward, and with great gasps she died. In less than half a minute it was all over. The little ones ran up the hill past us, one later returned and set upon its mother's head, then disappeared in the dark forever.

While all this transpired, the monster grizzly was romping back and forth in the shaded forest not more than sixty-five yards away. With deep booming growls like distant thunder, he voiced his anger and intent to kill. As he flitted between the shadows of trees, the moonlight glinted on his massive body; he was enormous.

Young dispatched three arrows at him. I shot two. We should have landed, he was so large. But he galloped off and I saw my last arrow at the point blank range of seventy-five yards, fall between his legs.

I have read this account numerous times. The best of the painters with words couldn't begin to capture the emotion and feelings of these two men as they faced an enraged sow and a 1,000 pound boar with their bows on that dark night in Yellowstone Park. I still read with great amusement Pope's account, "I whispered to Young, 'Shoot the big fellow'," as the sow bore down on him. Somehow there was more to that statement than words will ever express.

Fair chase? Yes! Ethical? By the standards of that day and age, no doubt. Permissible today? No. Times, techniques and hunting practices change.

Consider, too, these passages from **The Adventurous Bowmen** by Saxton Pope which details accounts of his African safari with Art Young. The passages describe their encounters with lions.

We went slowly up to 85 yards and decided by his actions and low growl that this was just about his charging distance; another five paces and he would come at us with a roar and a rush. We set ourselves, adjusting our quivers for easy access to the arrows.

One flight and we got his range. We hit him, once in the head and once in the shoulder. He reared and struck at the arrow in his forehead and savagely bit the shaft in two, at his shoulder. As he stood up on his hind legs and lunged at the shafts, he was a noble sight; a lion rampant! We shot again and drove an arrow deep in his side.

Now hitting a lion at eighty yards, as he lies head on in the grass is not an easy thing with a bow. It is about the same as hitting an oil can at the length of a city block. And after you hit him you have not done him much damage, even with a bullet, much less an arrow, because he is so heavily armored by bone in his head and masses of muscles in his shoulders.

But what does happen when we send an arrow whizzing and strike him in the forehead or in the wide open mouth; he rises and turns, throws himself, rears in a most dramatic way, trying to dislodge the offending shaft. Then we shoot to get at his heart or chest cavity.

The longest shot made by any of us with the bow was one by Art Young on this recent safari. He hit a gazelle at 155 yards and downed it.

Long distance shots with unsure arrow placement are things of the past. Just as hunting practices and laws change, so does the accepted hunting ethic. Pope, Young and others were the pioneers early in this century. As more hunters adopted the bow as the weapon of choice, hunting changed. Now as we close out the twentieth century, different conditions exist. Today's bowhunter

The purpose and objectives of the Club shall be:

2.1 To establish and maintain a scientific system of classification of North American big game animals taken with bow and arrow under sportsmanlike conditions under the rules of Fair Chase as specifically designated by this Club.

2.2 To collect and maintain scientific data and accurate scientific records pertaining to bowhunting and North American big game trophies taken with bow and arrow; to establish and maintain scientific methods and formulas for measuring, checking and classifying such big game trophies; to maintain a repository of such scientific data and records pertaining to such trophies, including the size and condition of the animals and location and habitat, where taken and to make such data and records available to all interested parties on a nondiscriminatory basis.

2.3 To publish and disseminate information in relation to such North American big game trophies to all interested persons on a nondiscriminatory basis, including, but not limited to other conservation groups, sporting groups and game departments.

2.4 To promote the welfare and conservation of North American big game and their habitat.

2.5 To promote bowhunting as a healthy and satisfying outdoor, recreational sport and to encourage the selective taking of mature trophy animals.

2.6 To publish and disseminate to any interested person, on a nondiscriminatory basis, information and scientific data collected by the Club pertaining to bowhunting.

2.7 To encourage, above all, good sportsmanship; respect for the animals one hunts; respect for the game laws; and a deep and sincere regard for the natural beauties of our planet.

2.8 To establish, maintain and enforce from time to time such rules and regulations as the Club feels necessary or desirable to accomplish its objects and purposes.

2.9 To be an organization not actively engaged in the approval, defeat or repeal of public legislation or the election of public legislators and officials.

From the Club Bylaws

must be aware of his or her limitations and confine shots to self-imposed limits. Arrow placement and shot selection are as much a part of today's archer's hunting approach as are tree stands and scents.

Nor did this evolution in hunting ethic occur early in this century. Only a few short years ago accounts of hunters shooting at caribou while the herds swam the rivers and lakes of northern Canada were all too common. A tradition of party hunting is slowly dying out. Filling bag limits is still too much a mark of success among some; too bad they have not fully developed an appreciation for the aesthetics of the hunt and the chase. While we, as hunters, may have disagreed with the portrayal of the sport in the CBS television program, **The Guns of Autumn**, we should have recognized its message.

As a record keeping organization, the Pope and Young Club has an obligation to play a part in this evolution. Currently the Club receives over 2,000 entries annually. Questions are raised on some. In every case we attempt to sort out the details to find out whether the concerns were legitimate or simply smoke blowing in the wind. If the concerns are legitimate, we drop that entry and all others for that "hunter." If they are not, we close the file. However, until we check out the questions, we cannot tell which action is appropriate.

If we do not attempt to police the records and allowed all entries to go unquestioned, then the criticisms that are raised by some against the keeping of records would have some basis. The one action that I don't believe to be appropriate is to "bury our heads in the sand" when a concern is raised. To do so would only serve to promote unethical and illegal activity.

We have dropped entries where the animal was taken while swimming, where the hunter purchased the head, where the hunter altered the antlers, where game laws were violated. If we ignored such "questions," we would be remiss as keepers of the **Bowhunting Records**.

The Club has taken an active role in insisting that ethical, legal behavior be followed by those wishing to enter animals into the records. When a hunter signs the Fair Chase Affidavit, he or she is attesting that they have met all of the conditions listed on the Affidavit.

The Pope and Young Club Fair Chase Affidavit states: "To be entered into the Pope & Young Club Records, the animal must meet the minimum scoring requirements, and must be taken in complete compliance with the controlling game laws and the Rules of Fair Chase." This statement is the Club's position. All bowhunters should be aware of this statement and its meaning. Acceptance of animals into the record book goes beyond these explicit requirements and the conditions of fair chase further defined on the Affidavit.

Certain actions may be legal but unethical. For example, in one zone in Alaska it is not illegal to shoot swimming caribou. Still that does not make an animal taken in that manner acceptable for entry as such a method of harvest clearly constitutes unfair chase.

It is legal to shoot big game with a rifle or crossbow in many areas; these animals well may have been taken under conditions deemed to be fair chase. Obviously, however, such trophies are not listed in the **Bowhunting Records**. Sometimes antlers and horns are altered to enhance the score. Such action may not be illegal; it is not explicitly precluded on the Fair Chase Affidavit. But, again, it is a condition that will lead to rejection of the animal for entry into the records. When an entry is rejected or removed for one of these reasons, all other entries for that individual are removed. We simply are saying that we no longer wish to be associated with that person. As entries are removed, we make the name of the person known to our membership. We want you to know who they are, as well.

This policy helps affect the changes that are coming about in today's hunter. And if we think about these changes, they too support the idea that the good old days are now. Many prior hunting practices should make

modern hunters blanch. Early hunters were much more interested in shooting than hunting. There is a difference! As archers, we are very aware of this difference.

I enjoy game meat as much as anyone but it is a poor rationalization to say that I hunt "for the meat." I don't; rather, I hunt for the hunt itself. This may make me a trophy hunter. I have no problem with that. A "trophy" takes on many material forms. It may be a 160 class whitetail or a mule deer doe or an arrow just passing over the back of some bruin as he feeds along. Saxton Pope said it well in **The Adventurous Bowmen**:

Man never had a more perfect weapon than the bow and arrow, from the standpoint of charm and intimate response. The bow becomes part of his mood; member of his faculties, yielding service and direct action in proportion to the throbbing life placed in it. The very sinews of the huntsman are implicated in his weapon. The poise and nicety of his mental state is made manifest in the flight of his arrow. The serenity and steadfast nature of his nerves are registered in its true flight.

The bow is part of man, and when by painful effort he has conquered its untamed spirit, it becomes a companion in the fields and woods, a light burden when he climbs the winding trails, a prop and stay as he runs and risks limbs, a protector against harmful beasts, sweet company in camp when he tends its simple wants with wax for the string and oil for the timber. He gives it soft shelter from inclement weather, and at night it lies by his side, when both may rest from the chase.

Every arrow in his quiver is a messenger, blithe and gay, singing as it goes, keen in service, when well sped, striking home and slaying humanely and cleanly. When careless prompting from its master lets it wander from the mark, there you will find it calling in the grass where its bright colors send an appeal to your questioning eye. Back it goes with its fellows, ever a cheerful philosopher and optimist: "better luck next time!" it murmurs softly as it rustles in the quiver. And your marks need not be living things. Your shafts are ever ready to leap forth in flight. There is no noise or smoke, no waste or harm. Shoot at yonder dandelion and sink your arrows into the sweet grass. On all sides are little targets for your aim. Cautiously you view the field, then pick out a pine cone on the waving tree top. That is a good mark: now shy an arrow at that and see it fly swift and close, then circle slowly in the air and with perfect grace wing its way home to mother earth. No harm in that!

Or there squawks a naughty jay, and just to chide him, and hardly hoping to hit him you loose an arrow at the rascal. A close miss is better than a hit, and off he flies confounded by your magic.

So the day is none too long for the archer. And when he really wants to slay and capture his quarry, he

can do it with the bow. It is no puerile toy, but a man's weapon, honored by our ancestors and worthy of respect today. To prove this, that's why we came to Africa.

For myself I would rather some other disciple of Toxophilis had taken the burden of this African adventure. I do not like to travel these long irksome miles. The sweet forests and purple mountains of California give me all I want in sport. The bounding deer, the panther, the lumbering bear, all are meat for my shafts and those hearty lads who have fared with me in the greenwood: Will Compton, Arthur Young, Cassius Styles, Donnan Smith, John Graves, Keith Evans, Monte the Indian, and many another worthy archer.

As the twentieth century draws to a close and we look to the twenty-first, I wonder what the future holds for bowhunters. Pope's words describe the essence of what we, as bowhunters, are all about. History has shown that there will be vast change. Today's game herds are at all time highs in many regions. Entries into the records continue to grow; that too will continue. And Pope's words will remain as relevant for tomorrow's sylvan stalker.

One too can look at the stated objectives of the Pope and Young Club on the previous page as a guide to where we have been, where we are and where we are going.

To these ends we have done well. The Pope and Young Club is the recognized authority on record keeping for North American game animals. Likewise, the Club has taken a very proactive stand in defense of bowhunting as a modern game management tool. Consistent with item 2.7 of the Bylaws, we encourage sportsmanship, respect for animals and respect for game laws. These objectives will serve us well in the next century.

In the Second Edition of our record book, two prime responsibilities to the Club were stated:

First, we maintain the **Bowhunting Big Game Records of North America**. We are responsible for the authenticity and accuracy of these records. We appoint and maintain official measurers across the North American continent. These measurers score, for the records, outstanding specimens of big game taken with a bow and arrow.

Our second responsibility is the enhancement of the bowhunter's image. We must, by example, promote the principles of fair chase. We must strive to maintain the wildlife heritage so dear to us all. Our cause is far better served by members who adhere to the principles described here than those who have enjoyed exceptional hunting success.

These responsibilities are as appropriate today as then and will be as we enter the twenty-first century. With these responsibilities, we, the hunting public, incur certain obligations. The Club's founder, Glenn St. Charles, spoke of our obligation in his contribution to the Second Edition titled, " Tomorrow: Much More To Do." His challenge is worth reiterating again today:

The uphill struggle for bowhunters from the era of Saxton Pope and Art Young has been difficult. We have come a long way. We have reached our initial goal of proving that the bow and arrow is effective in the harvesting of big game animals. Bowhunters are now respected; surely, the Pope and Young Club's conservation program and its impressive record lists of trophy animals have been factors.

We must consolidate our position and that of all bowhunters by treating our success with reserve and humility. There is much more to do. As the balance of nature becomes increasingly fragile, there will be extreme environmental concern. We share in this concern and, wherever possible, provide help through our conservation program.

It appears that bowhunting has a bright future. However, it is not an unclouded future. As the human population increases, animal habitat decreases. Western states also have the added factor of many diverse groups, all concerned over the available land. Timber, cattle and other interests have to be served.

The time has come when states must face up to the fact that big game herds in some parts of the continent can withstand little, if any, increased pressure.

There is much pushing and pulling between various hunting groups, all vying for the same hunting times and places. Some things will change. States will take longer looks at hunting methods and styles, taking into consideration their impacts on animal resources. Bowhunters could play a larger role in big game hunting as long as our success ratio remains relatively low and bowhunting equipment remains reasonably primitive. Some sort of balance must be struck, but it should not become a tug of war between the supporters of various styles of hunting in the quest for a place to hunt and game to harvest.

All hunters must face the problem together. There are others waiting in the wings to impose their solutions should we falter in this responsibility, and they would take it (all hunting) from us. We must continue to seek ways to educate the nonhunting public in the importance of game and habitat preservation and the vitally important role the hunter plays in game management and conservation. The future of big game hunting lies in our abilities to persuade the nonhunting public.

The obligations of which Glenn spoke also remain with us today — maybe even more so now than then. We, too, must strive to make the needed commitment to fulfill these obligations in the next era of bowhunting. The challenge is clearly there. I, for one, think we can successfully address it. We must if we wish, for tomorrow's days to be the good old days for future generations of hunters. The good old days of bowhunting may well be now. Let us hope through our collective efforts the good old days will still be there tomorrow.

THE TRUTH *About* TROPHY HUNTING

by Bill Krenz

TROPHY HUNTING IS undoubtedly the most misunderstood segment of a widely misunderstood sport.

Certainly, a significant segment of today's non-hunting public misunderstands trophy hunting. To them, the very idea of selectively hunting for trophy animals seems, looks and feels questionable.

Surprisingly though, this group — the non-hunting portion of our population — is not the only group to misunderstand the concept of trophy hunting. Tucked away within the very ranks of hunters are also a few who apparently misunderstand.

For either group, the non-hunters or the few misunderstanding hunters, the path to understanding trophy hunting can be uncovered by first grasping the concept that trophy hunting is a philosophy and not a science. The differences between the two are crucial.

On one hand a science is an accumulation of data gained through observation and experimentation. It is a collection of facts and figures that can be studied and learned — and used to create external profit or reward.

On the other hand a philosophy is a search for a general understanding of values and reality by chiefly speculative rather than observational (scientific) means. It becomes a collection of fundamental beliefs, a code, a standard of conduct that comprises the personal ethics of an individual.

It is also helpful to note that one of the key differences between a philosophy and a science lies in the nature of the rewards that can be derived from each. A science typically yields external rewards; the rewards of a philosophy are generally internal. For example, use science to design a better automobile tire and the world will pay you (external reward) for the technology. For your scientific accomplishment, you may even be

promoted, glorified in trade or popular journals or praised in public (more external rewards).

In direct contrast, the rewards of a philosophy are fundamentally internal. With a philosophy there is no hard product to be outwardly sold, no end commodity to be marketed and no notoriety to be had. Instead, the proceeds become highly personal, internal ones. The yield of a philosophy, including the philosophy of trophy hunting, is in the likes of personal conviction, personal morality, personal respect and personal honor.

It seems clear that much of the misunderstanding that surrounds trophy hunting comes from the erroneous assumption that trophy hunting is a science. This false assumption supposes that trophy hunting is merely a collection of data designed to facilitate the killing of exceptionally large big game animals. But, in reality, trophy hunting is something quite different.

Trophy hunting is an all-encompassing hunting philosophy. In detail it is a philosophy comprised of two parts. The first part, as might be expected, addresses trophy size. That is undeniable. But the second part, the higher priority part, deals clearly with how these trophies are to be hunted and taken.

For the true trophy hunter nothing is more important than this second part. How the hunter conducts himself or herself. How the hunt is experienced, felt and endured. How the animal is finally brought to bag. In the philosophy of trophy hunting, these things override all other concerns — even the first concern, the concern of trophy size.

The relative importance of trophy size is another area that is frequently misunderstood by those attempting to comprehend trophy hunting.

Too often the incorrect assumption made is that the trophy hunter is overly — even solely — concerned with trophy size. This misconception holds that the trophy hunter will do anything for the next, the bigger trophy. Absolutely nothing could be further from the truth of trophy hunting.

With trophy hunting it is crystal clear that the primary concern is much more with the nature of the effort than it is with the goal of trophy size.

The real magic of the trophy hunting philosophy, the thing that makes it so worthwhile, is that it so artfully and yet so forcefully fuses the secondary goal of trophy size with the primary goal of proper and acceptable effort. Fused in this manner, in the proper proportion and with the correct priority, these goals and these efforts have become the two solid cornerstones of the philosophy of trophy hunting.

Over the years the Pope and Young Club has based its trophy hunting convictions around these carefully prioritized cornerstones. Animals are entered into the record books but only if the code of effort has been adhered to. In the case of the Pope and Young Club, a distinct set of written Fair Chase

guidelines has been developed. These guidelines are continually reviewed and updated. These are the codes of conduct. In the eyes of the Club, nothing — absolutely nothing — is more important than these guidelines. Also, nothing is more serious in the Club's mind than a transgression of these codes. For such infractions individuals have been removed from Pope and Young Club membership for life and their entire collection of previously recorded big game trophies stricken from the official records.

Clearly, the individuals involved in such transgressions are among those who do not understand trophy hunting. They have ignored or refused to accept trophy hunting's comprehensive, two-part goal and effort philosophy. They have placed trophy size ahead of acceptable effort. They have failed to grasp the concept that trophy hunting, while goal driven, is undeniably honor bound. They have confused the philosophy of trophy hunting with what to them has become the science of killing. These individuals, ego-driven and generally demanding external recognition and gains, only take from hunting. Trophy hunters, comfortable with their stringent priorities, strive only to give to hunting. Fortunately, for all hunters and for the game they pursue, such misguided individuals are few and far between.

The philosophy of trophy hunting continues to grow. It aspires to make hunting more perfect. It pushes hunters to reach for lofty trophy goals. Yet it holds to a clear priority schedule of conduct and honor over trophy size.

Trophy hunting is a true philosophy of challenge and ethics and internal rewards. Like all philosophies, it takes what it finds and attempts to make it better. In our opinion, it is succeeding in doing just that.

THE VALUE *of* TROPHY HUNTING

by Jim Dougherty

I N TODAY'S SOCIAL CLIMATE those of us who hunt seem to find ourselves being more frequently reviewed and scrutinized by a modern urban society that has no true understanding of what we do — or why. With each passing year we slide increasingly upward on the scale of its (society's) concerns, another chapter in its insatiable book of "issues." The question of hunting — whether or not it is acceptable, necessary or possessive of any moral value — is becoming a major topic of some public and political dialogue, the outcome of which, quite frankly, is very much up in the air.

Unfortunately, trophy hunting is becoming increasingly perceived as one of the most abhorrent elements of our (hunters') "barbaric rituals." All of us who hold the pages of this book in almost reverent contemplation have heard the critics' comments a thousands times:

"Modern man does not need to hunt."

"Animals have rights, too."

"Hunting may be all right for food but hunting for antlers (trophies) is wrong."

"Killing off the best animals damages the herd."

"The babies won't have their daddies."

Is there any truth to such emotional comments? Certainly there are some minor threads of truth in the words. Indeed modern man does not need to hunt to survive in our society — although there still are human societies that do. And wildlife does have certain rights — and man has done a generally remarkable job protecting those rights. For example, the animals we hunt deserve to be treated with dignity and respect and maintained in the proper place in both the world of the hunter and non-hunter alike. We would all agree with that, those of us who hunt as emphatically as those who do not. The difference has to do with a matter of perspective: Are animals equal or inferior to man? We hunters look upon

animals as the **Bible** tells us God intended, a renewable resource provided for the well being of our health and spirit. That's a severe difference of opinion with those radical groups who believe animals deserve equal rights with humans.

Truthfully, we hunters have proven that we do more and give more — and quite likely care more, too — about wildlife than does the bulk of contemporary society. Interestingly, our society is comprised mostly of non-hunters for whom wildlife rarely gets a casual passing thought except when someone, somewhere — cast under that all-encompassing title of "a hunter," makes the news with some evil deed and thereby provides room for exaggeration by a distressingly biased anti-hunting media. Seldom, if ever, do we see or read of the many good, positive things we do. The deck has been stacked and in that deck are few cards left to be dealt to the trophy hunter!

Trophy hunting today is big business. Being a successful trophy hunter can be big business for an individual. The selling of trophy heads has become a significant industry. While there is a value in such things, is this the real picture, the true meaning of trophy hunting?

The need to succeed in the eyes of our peers, to feed individual egos and even fabricate reputations has spawned all too many indecent acts that have demeaned hunting in general and trophy hunting in particular. This damages the image of the true trophy hunter. And this is sad; for in my lifetime, and perhaps in yours, there is no better mantle to wear than when we occasionally don the cloak of success among peers — if the chase has been fair and the trophy honestly won. Such moments represent victory and winning at something — be it bowhunting, billiards or business — is the very essence of the challenge of life. We can talk of all the honest, subliminal reasons why we hunt all we want; but in truth we all want to win, to wear the mantle of success at times.

Every bowhunter wants a trophy. We spend countless restless nights, time and dollars often beyond our practical means in pursuit of our sport with the dream always whispering through our thoughts that

maybe the Big One will be over the next ridge or under the next stand. For most of us it seldom, if ever, happens. But the dream is there. It remains. And the dream is as much a part of trophy hunting as the rare reality of success.

Is this a legitimate value of trophy hunting? Probably so, for if man does not dream he does not excel. And if he does not excel, he seldom wins at anything.

Trophy hunting is about winning — winning over adversity, winning under strain both mental and physical. It is about hardship and commitment, too. Finally, successful trophy hunting is about being lucky. All of these values make life, in any endeavor, worth living.

Trophies themselves are more a matter of personal choice; however, if success is achieved at the particular level of individual commitment, the results are equally satisfying whether the trophy earns a "book" listing or merely the hunter's satisfied admiration. Truly, size is a matter of arbitrary opinion.

We are all to some extent trophy hunters. True, some of us are more committed than others but we all share in the understanding of what life and what hunting are all about. Our reverence and appreciation of the more outstanding big game trophies binds us more tightly together. In the frequently hostile climate today, there is a great deal of value in this.

Can or will hunting endure? Does the issue of trophy hunting loom as the gallows pole for hunting itself? Some say it is so and urge less emphasis on trophies, withdrawing recognition and dimming the public spotlight surrounding it. It seems as if some believe such actions would remove hunting from the public consciousness. But that, too, is a dream though not nearly so honest as the dream of the trophy seeker. Rather, it is simply wishful thinking.

Trophy hunting will endure for as long as there is any hunting. Trophy hunting is the heartbeat of hunting today. No greater effort is expended than that of today's trophy hunters and their organizations in supporting the foundations of wise and proper stewardship of our wildlife resources — or in the individual efforts supporting the honest and time honored values of hunting itself.

HUNTING BIG GAME

with a Bow and Arrow

by Arthur H. Young

Originally published in The Olympian, June 1921. Reprinted with permission of Charles A. Young

Now let us move to a district where larger game may be found.

Naturally our paraphernalia contained our best arrows with steel heads one and one-quarter inches wide and three inches long. Two bows for each man, as there is a possiblity of one breaking. Three men W. J. Compton, Dr. Pope and myself anticipating a good time and some game. Compton had killed large game before with the arrow, and knew what to expect. Doc and I could only be presumptuous enough to believe that a buck would grace our firearmless camp. Not a powderburning instrument of any kind was in our kit. Doc and I were going to have nothing get away after we managed to get in a shot, so poisoned our arrows. This, we thought, was the only advantage we were taking of the game, as we had our "doots" about doing the trick as thoroughly as we wished.

This was five or six years ago.

Scarcely had we reached our camping place and unpacked our horses when an evening hunt was on. We were anxious and a most peculiar feeling came over me as I ventured out on my first deer hunt with a bow substituted for a gun. Confident, still not with the feeling of assurance I desired.

Not more than two hundred yards from camp, when I surprised an old doe by making a sneak to within easy shooting distance. With no intention to shoot, I was simply trying something that was not required with the gun, as a bullet is let drive from any distance.

No bucks were seen that evening, although Compton said he could have thrown his hat over the head of a little spike.

It was fun, and not much short of exciting just to walk or "Injun" around with bow anticipating a shot at a buck.

For deer hunting we use no dogs, and still-hunting or "Injun" hunting is resorted to. The deer have a big advantage over the hunter. This animal is alertness personified, and unless found feeding, is most always careful to protect himself, and there is not much lacking in his ears, eyes and nose. He is a specialist to be sure.

After a couple days' hard hunting Doc shot a buck at 40 yards. The first arrow missed, but the deer never moved. The second shaft caught him in the ribs and the arrow passed clear through, landing on the ground several yards beyond. The deer traveled but 20 yards after being hit. Arrows passing through in this manner deposit no poison, therefore no more was used.

Shortly after this Compton made a fine shot and pinned a buck through the shoulders. My three-pointer was shot in the flank and the arrow came out the shoulder.

Venison galore, and all secured without the aid of dogs and leaving the happy hunting grounds undisturbed.

The following year found us in Northern California after black bear. Our first bear was shot several times in as many seconds, and only one arrow failed to pass clear through. This hit a heavy shoulder bone.

Later we were again after deer and brown bear — and successful.

Eventually we wanted a mountain lion, but as this venison destroyer is quite hard to get without the aid of dogs, we made arrangements accordingly.

The strange characteristic of this animal to jump from any height when hit was demonstrated. The instant he was pricked with an arrow he flashed out and landed 60 feet below. His jump was made in the direction he was headed, so Doc and I stepped aside to give him room to land. After regaining his feet from the impact and before we could draw another arrow, he made off through the jack pines.

The dogs having been held, and almost uncontrollable with excitement, were kicking up a great fuss. After a few seconds they were released, and in their anxiety rushed off depending altogether on their sight and making no attempt to use their track organs. Doc and I followed and had gone but a few yards when we almost stumbled over the lion — nearly dead. The dogs soon learned of their blunder and joined us. Ely, the best dog, took possession of the lion and the rest of the dogs asked no compromise — for the time being.

Doc held a general anatomical diagnosis, while I was content to learn what the animal's stomach contained. As usual — venison.

Lions, black, brown and grizzly bear have fallen before our arrows, yet of the animals shot, all succumbed surprisingly quickly. A statement that five grizzly bears were killed with one arrow each (five arrows in all) will no doubt be discredited by not a few; however, this is the fact. One of these animals dropped only a few feet from where she was hit. In most cases only one arrow is employed to kill an animal, and I have known of only one large animal that escaped wounded. Not a bad record to be sure.

I am not advising the shooting fraternity to hastily throw away their shooting irons and take up the use of the bow and arrow. To become a successful archer requires much practice and patience and for most hunters the securing of game would be too infrequent.

Ned Frost, after having witnessed the shooting by Dr. Pope and myself of both large and small game with the arrow, has appeared in print as follows: "I am converted to the bow after hunting grizzly last spring. I never had so much excitement in my life before. It took only one arrow for each of them — all clean, quick kills, but one I had to stop within eight steps, though she would have been dead in five seconds; but that would not do in this case. It is the real thing from a real sporting standpoint, and is less apt to cause suffering than the average hunter with a high-power rifle, and far more fair to the game. I am for it strong. I hope you will also be for it, and believe you will when you see it in a different light and understand it better. I think there is far less chance wounding game than with the rifle. You have no idea the wounds these arrows make.

"They are as sure death as anything going, but of course lack the knockdown of the high-power rifle bullet. But think of the real hunting ability necessary to get within range of your game, and of the far smaller number of game animals that would be killed. I tell you I would rather have the pleasure of stalking an old ram, even though I missed him, with an arrow, than to kill a dozen with a rifle."

I might add that Frost's experience has been practically nothing but hunting and trapping.

I have made it a practice never to kill wantonly. The game destroying birds and animals I give no quarter.

After a day's outing with the smokewagon, I usually have cause to feel for the wounded.

EDITOR'S NOTE: Art Young's candid admission of his doubts about the effectiveness of the bow and arrow — and his references to using "poison" on his hunting heads — underscore the skepticism held by many individuals unfamiliar with bowhunting. Referring to their initial deer hunt, he later wrote: "Dr. Pope, my hunting companion, and I had so little faith in the effectiveness of the arrow that we smeared strychnine on the steel points. This was not a last minute preparation for considerable time had been given to trying to find the best poison to use and the glue which would dissolve the quickest, thus permitting the poison to take effect in the shortest time possible. What happened? We secured three deer on this first bow-and-arrow trip... Each buck — and they were buck — was killed with one arrow and in each case the shaft went entirely through the deer. Two of these arrows after passing through the animal, struck the ground on the opposite side. The bucks being from 25 to 45 yards from us. None of the deer traveled over 40 yards after being hit. Of course, there was no chance for the glue to dissolve and deposit the poison as the arrow passed through the animal too quickly. We found that the arrowhead was effective enough so that was the last of any thought to have poison assist us."

A WALK *in the* WOODS

by Glenn St. Charles

THE USUAL HUNTING TALK is beginning to subside — how they passed up shots — they're waiting for the big one. Hey, I've hunted with these guys for the last 30 years. Bob Kelly, Bill Jardine, Bob Arvine are all my cronies — and a man's gotta have cronies. We're all trophy hunters — until something else comes along. The chattering has stopped and judging from the noise level that is beginning to rise, yes, they are asleep.

From the rattling of pans in the living quarters below, it is obvious that the resident field mice have taken over, all vying for the goodies left over from the table. That won't take long. Next they'll be back up here bouncing back and forth across our sleeping bags, looking for a warm place to snuggle — occasionally inside.

This two-story chalet, a crude cedar shake structure about 12 x 14 feet, is our hunting camp. Vintage 1952, it is completely hidden in dense timber and sits astride the best doggone migration route of mule deer coming from the far reaches of the Canadian border.

I am wide awake on my back, looking at the rafters above, brushing an occasional mouse off my chest. I am planning tomorrow's hunt. The sound of a bubbling creek outside is trying to put me to sleep. But no. I keep asking myself where will those critters be. A light snow is falling, adding to the some four inches that are already out there. This is the first snow, the one that triggers the rut and tells the animals that it is time to get out of the high country and prepare for the winter. The first snowfall will disappear and allow time for the energies

Bob Arvine (left) and Glenn St. Charles with their "Walk in the Woods" deer, 1952.

of the rutting animals to be restored before the real winter hits. If it's still snowing in the morning, I reason that I should look under the cedars. If it's wind and rain they'll be in the aspen and vine maple thickets. Sun and melting snow, the sunny slopes will be the place to look. Yes, if I were a deer, just where would I be? It's the answer I'm looking for. I'm ready. I have already checked off all the preliminaries. I've seen several deer. Lord only knows why I can never shoot the first one. I guess I just don't have my juices up. The clatter of the first underfoot grouse has scared the living daylights out of me. The first squirrel chattered away any shot that I might have had at a nice buck two days ago. Even a marmot has seen fit to give me a whistle — probably my plaid shirt. Yes, I've honed my senses to all the sights and sounds of the woods. It's time.

Long before daylight I wake to the crackling of a wood fire in the black iron "toad" below. Some of the aroma of fresh brewed coffee sifts through the cracks in the loft floor and if the snorts and blows of the other two still up here mean anything, that coffee aroma will soon be overpowered. As we peel down the ladder to the deck below, we are greeted by a cup and Kelly's favorite — bacon, eggs and pancakes.

The sting of the ice cold water from the washpan really sharpens one's appetite. The cakes are flipping and flapping. Bill's and Arvine's stomachs are very accommodating. A morning constitution later, I'm polishing off the last of the cakes. I am pouring syrup out of the chimney of a Log Cabin syrup can. Lo and behold, out comes a long gray tail.

"Egad! We've got to do something about these mice!"

"Yeah," Kelly remarks, "let me know when you figure out how to take care of 10 million acres of them."

"Let's keep the lid on that can, fellows," I plead. "I guess this furry little guy was sacrificed to get even for the rubber blunt thumping we've been giving them off the walls."

Kelly, having done his chores for the morning, heads out the door with bow in hand. "I'm headed for Marty's Corner. See ya."

Arvine, our so-called second cook, is gathering up the dishes. The mice will clean up the table scraps. Bill, never in a hurry, is contemplating over another cup of coffee. I'm gone.

"I'll be up at the saddle," I say as I go out the door. "Got a hunch, with this clearing sky, there'll be critters on the sunny south slopes close to the vine maples."

––––––––

A thought: How would you readers like to go with me to the mountain? It's early and if you have the time I don't mind taking a little detour to a lookout about the 6,000 foot level. There you can get a pretty good handle on the whole Nason Creek Reserve. It's a climb, about 1,500 feet higher than the cabin — won't take long if we're not interrupted by a critter along the way. Bring your field glasses and you'll need a flashlight part of the way. It looks like there's about six inches of snow.

We'll head up along this open hillside parallel to the cedar flat where we got our shakes and material for the chalet. Beyond that is a spring feeding the creek that runs right by the cabin. The three inches of fresh snow deadens the sound of the crusty stuff underneath. Look out for the snow that will be falling from the willow branches as we plow through. The big buckbrush wall you see up ahead is the east side of the saddle that rises 25 or 30 yards above the slope that we are on. The flat of the saddle is where I generally start looking for the critters. It will be daylight about the time we reach the top.

Traversing that wall was not too bad. There is nothing in sight so let's proceed right on out to the Lake Julius switchback trail. This is where I'll really begin the day's hunt. I'd like to get back here about the time that sunball breaks over the horizon and brings this flat awash. It will bring the deer out from under the snow-covered cedar trees that ring this area. We'll be gaining a little altitude and more snow, but the view will be worth it. See that rotten stump up ahead? I'll have to take a couple of cracks at it. Got to get in tune with the environment. I never take the first shot of the day at an animal.

Left handed? Yes, shooting the bow is the only thing I do left handed. I switched about five years ago because of a problem. How did I cope with my right master eye? An instinctor doesn't worry about that — you shoot with both eyes open. Anything to the contrary is a myth. Fred Bear and Jim Dougherty both switched and so did Col. Milan Elott who later wrote about it in his book.

Let's go slow now, blow ourselves a little before we ease over that little rise. Got to be ready — you never know. Okay. All clear. Here's where it's at — where the ponderosa pines and clouds join with the sky. God's country. Look at the colors, even in this early light. It's that time of year. Julius and Eileen are the lakes nestled in the rock potholes below. Their waters are deep, cold and harbor lots of fine trout. Many have felt the bend of the fly rod. Some even made it to the fry pan.

The furthest lake away is Eileen — the big rock on the far side. I leaned a bow against that hunk one day and while scrounging firewood on the hillside beyond I dislodged a boulder that rolled down the hill and all but demolished my bow. Another string made it usable, but barely.

There's momma bear and a little guy down there on the snowline, sucking up the last of the blueberries. Use your glasses. They are really fueling their winter gas tanks — I do mean literally. Lake Ethel lies on the other side of that ridge beyond Lake Eileen. You can't see it but I know it's there. The tall rock pinnacles on the far side of Ethel are like a dam holding back the waters from spilling out the east side of the area. Those boulders along the horizon gather the sun's rays and, on occasion, harbor some nice bucks that like the warmth they find there. From here, walking along the top of that wall looks easy, but don't you believe it! The trail is treacherous; you dislodge a pebble from the off side and it will wind up an avalanche 2,000 feet below.

That big mountain of rocks over there sits on the southwest corner, the highest point in the area, about 7,400 feet — not a blade of grass the last 500 feet. I had to see what was on the other side one day. While nearing the top a pint-sized pika rabbit ran down to greet me like he was going to eat me alive. Had me worried for a few seconds. There is nothing on the other side but more rocks which taper off into brushy slopes and benches that end up at Wild Horse Creek, 5,000 feet below, the west boundary of the Reserve. Those were the days I was known as "Ridgerunner George." I had to climb over everything just to see what was on the other side. I don't do that anymore. I know what's on the other side.

Back of us, off to the left, southeast — that big stand of ponderosa pine on the horizon — is Marty's Corner. Kelly is going through it now like a fine tooth comb. We've taken a few nice deer out of there and he knows where they hang out.

Glenn St. Charles,
Club founder, views
his hunting area.

Well, that's about it — an hour into daylight. I have to get on with today's hunt. I'm sure you know your way back. Perhaps our paths will cross again one day. Stay here as long as you like. You'll really see the autumn colors when the sun reaches the hollow below. Drink in all the good stuff you can. You'll not find another place much closer to the Guy above.

The deer pasture that I'm going to doesn't need any witnesses. I want to be alone, if and when the once in a lifetime comes along. Everytime is a once in a lifetime experience — all different.

Back down to the saddle, the sun is just breaking over the horizon. It will soon warm the nearby cedars. Deer should be hiding under their branches. As I traverse through this area, a slight breeze at my back isn't helping much but I have no choice in getting to the wide domed ridge that will take me to the lower slopes where all the deer seem to be headed. Tracks are everywhere. Now I have a quartering wind in my face and it will be a long haul to traverse from one side of the ridge to the other. Huge ponderosa pines dot the slopes, snow drifts piled at their base. There are a couple of deer off to my left, just going out of sight. The sun is now beginning to wash this ridge. The deer seem to be feeding on a broadleaf plant that pops up through the melting snow. The pine branches are beginning to unload their covering of fresh fluff. There is still enough crunch left in the old snow to dictate that I stop once in a while, for 10 or 15 minutes, to allow time for a wandering critter to walk into me

without hearing. From my perch now I can see the stand of timber around the chalet off to my right about three quarters of a mile away. The sun is just getting to the slope above the chalet where I took a nice heavy buck last year.

Yes, it appears that I am pushing deer out ahead of me. It's about 10:00 a.m. I have reached the lower part of the ridge where it spreads out into the willow and vine maple flat about the size of a football field. The southeast side tapers off into the slope above the chalet. From the number of tracks going into this flat, things could get interesting. However, for now, it's time for a candy bar.

A nice big granite rock accommodates the seat of my pants as I anticipate the sweets. Gad, does that wrapper make a lot of noise. Sounds like someone stuffing a wastepaper basket. Next, an apple. Noisy, you bet. I have a feeling there're critters around. You probably know the feeling. Like you're being watched. Like something else might have heard the candy wrapper and crunch of apple. Foreign sounds competing with the falling chunks of snow. My head slowly pivots. Yes, my bow is ready, arrow nocked — it's always ready when I'm lookin', listenin', eatin' and sittin'.

Did I see a glint off to my left at the edge of that flat? Yes, my field glasses confirm it. Horns! Fragile looking horns and the dark horseshoe above the eyes facing right at me. He not only heard, he sees. Okay. No use getting excited. Don't make any fast moves or moves indicating I see him. Don't try to get out of sight. As long as he sees me and doesn't know I see him, there are possibilities.

Sounds complicated, doesn't it? Not really. A shot, there isn't. He's way too far. A close encounter in terms of the whole area and a lot of fun and games ahead if he likes the area and I don't push him out. So, I'm sounding like a wishful thinker — anything but realistic. Surely he'll spook any second now. Okay, but that's what it's all about — the unknown.

You start with the bare necessities. A loaded bow across your knees. You are sitting on a rock with an half-eaten apple in your lap and a pair of field glasses glued to your head, a deer standing, in snow, partly hidden by willows — out of range. Is this just a sighting or a possibility of a happening? It won't take long to find out. I stand up, in full view, looking away, toss the apple aside, jostle my quiver of arrows back into place on my shoulder, stuff the arrow in and out, all as if I don't see, oblivious to anything unusual.

Trying to be nonchalant, I observe out of the corner of my eye that he is still there, watching. He turns away like he's about to bolt, but no — seems like he's preoccupied with something else of more concern; perhaps it's another buck, a doe, whatever. Could be the rut. There's a well-used trail and a definite scent of musk in the air. Possibly he has a set migration direction in mind and I'm in the way.

As we continue to watch each other, he nuzzles a willow sapling and starts walking diagonally, as if to go around. I counter by appearing to move away, but get behind some cover and sneak a little closer to what could be an ambush. However, conditions are still not right as he continues by. As he is about to go off the flat and down the slope, he looks back at me, makes a couple of bounds — probably winded me — and is gone. I tiptoe to the edge, only to be caught flat footed. There he is, squared away, looking right at me like he was expecting. There we are eyeball to eyeball, neither making a move until I begin to cramp up. In such a situation it is very difficult for me to look ho-hum. Difficult for both of us really, because I know my own dog can tell when I'm thinking about a bath for him, even when he's not in the same room. I can only back off and give the buck lots of space. I wait in ambush with the remote possibility he will come back. Yes, 15 minutes or so later he is slowly entering the flat. Of course, I am in the wrong place. Like my dog, this buck knows. He's looking and listening as he heads right back to where he was when first sighted. Such behavior, the likes of which I've never encountered before!

Obviously, scent-sound-sight is not a factor. Well, this cat and mouse operation lasts for three or four more hours until a well defined oval trail is worn in the snow. At times I wonder who is following who. Rarely do I catch him broadside. I am either looking at his rear or front end. The gap is closing, however. He is getting used to my presence. At times I wonder if maybe he likes me! He certainly appears in no hurry to bring this episode to a head and I am beginning to wonder how much more of this fun I can stand. I'll have to figure out something. There has to be a way. Next time around I'll try something different.

At the lower part of the loop, where the buck jumped down the slope, there is a little mound sparsely covered with waist-high buckbrush. It is about 20 feet higher than the trail. If, in following the buck as he goes down the slope, I could cross over to that mound, I would be able to observe the lower trail and the buck coming back up the other side onto the flat. Surely there would be enough cover, one way or another, for an ambush at very close range. We'll check this out on this round.

I'm trailing him, but not too close, as he heads down the trail. I sneak over to the mound and get high enough so I can see where he will turn the corner below and, hopefully, head back up to the flat and past the mound. He occasionally looks back. I have scooped up some snow and I toss it down the slope where I would most probably be. He looks back at the sound, and, yes, he is coming back up the slope toward my position. All the while I am looking for the place a shot can be made. Not this time, I think — the next time, if there is a next time, if he doesn't figure out what I'm up to. I'll let him go by and and note the brush and the openings with possibilities. The shot will be downhill about four bow lengths, at most.

He appears to be stopping more often and listening. Perhaps he suspects because he is not hearing everything the same. I hold my position until he is clear out of sight. Meanwhile, I want to get behind again to assure him that I am still there. If all goes well and nothing changes, I have about 30 minutes to decide what to do.

Now it has become a question: If given the opportunity, do I really want to take my friend? He has given me a great hunt already — excitement, unknowns — one on one. Patience has allowed me to get his guard down, like moves in a chess game when you make moves anticipating your opponent's moves. I guess I'm just trying to justify what I am about to try to do. Yes, after all, this is what it's all about. Even if I don't make the shot, what happened today will never leave my mind (as even now, about 40 years later, I am emotionally writing it). No matter what, I assure myself, I'll never have regrets.

Why couldn't I have just jumped the critter, real close, shot and had it over with? The better part of the hunt is history. To culminate it is agonizing. Maybe this will make up for the doe I surprised in a brush patch earlier. I had just separated a small herd of deer from an aspen thicket. Something out of the corner of my eye got my attention and then I found my broadhead right on the nose of a doe which had hung back to care for her fawn that couldn't keep up. It was a very happy feeling to see her bound away with the little guy in tow.

Well, while the decision is still being made, the buck and I slowly head back to the ambush area. He goes over the end, down the trail. I gather up a snowball, crawl over to the mound, toss the snow down to where I should be. He's on the way back up and now I must pick the right patch of brush that he will be up against when he goes by. He stops, looks back, starts up — this is it! The bright coloring, where the arrow enters the snowbank beyond, tells me that it's over. There will be no need for another arrow. There will be no trailing, no lingering anguish and no beating of drums. I know why I wanted the Guy up there as my only witness. He knows my feelings and understands the contest between the hunted and the hunter. The buck has slid down the snowy slope into a little hollow. He's a beautiful animal — heavy — neck a little swollen; the rut could have dulled his sense of survival.

With legs bunched and tied together, the animal is ready for the slide down through the snow to the cabin. My bow is slung over my shoulder freeing my hands for the task of dragging the critter over logs, bumps and hollows. The camp robbers are already on the scene as I make my way down the hill. I hear a raven sounding off across the slope. He knows and will be here shortly.

It's 3:00 p.m. Where did the time go? Five hours! It was as if time stood still. A wisp of white smoke is threading its way out of the cabin area. Somebody's back catching up on the chores. Sure, I could go for help, but no, I need to spend more time reflecting on the day. Besides, there is a lot of daylight left. I need to unwind and be alone with my thoughts. I recall that I had two other such encounters where migration-bent deer would not turn back, insist on going through, but never have I had one go by and return. A walk in the woods — an animal — what a hunt! And you can be sure the story will be one day put to print.

It wasn't long before all the logs and brush patches had been negotiated and I found myself close enough to call for the guys. And what followed is another real part of what it is all about. Whoops and hollers, a pat on the back, sharing with friends. With the critter secure under the cedar canopy, things finally quieted down. You knew we were back to normal when Kelly, cook extra-ordinaire, asked, "Where is the liver?" Yes, it will be liver and onions tonight.

With our dinner over and all stories of the day told in detail — near encounters, four grouse that had fallen to arrows — all in all it was a great day with more to follow. The season isn't over yet.

"Okay, guys, ante up. It's jacks or better. Bill, will you please disturb that gray critter that's sitting on the window sill next to you? I can't concentrate with that piercing stare... Which reminds me, we'll have to open up another can of syrup in the morning."

the FANG

A handcrafted hunting head (top left) on one of Will Thompson's arrows rests atop a copy of his brother's book. An assortment of Ben Pearson broadheads (middle left) is pictured with a 1942 company catalog. A Mickey Finn head (below right), shot by Club founder Glenn St. Charles, stopped this British Columbia black bear in 1954. Also pictured are broadhead ads published in magazines during the late 1930s and early 1940s.

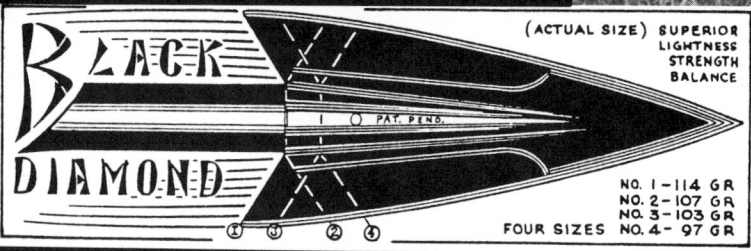

BROADHEADS —

The First 50 Years

by Rit Heller, Bill McCrary *and* Joe St. Charles

BROADHEAD. That word alone is synonymous with bowhunting. You can't think of one without thinking of the other. Say "broadhead" and somehow you think of Robin Hood, cool days spent in field and forest, woolen clothing and leaves changing color. It also conjures thoughts of old friends, past adventures and future hunts. And perhaps nothing in our sport fascinates the bowhunter's eye like broadhead designs.

The broadhead is one of the most important pieces of equipment — maybe the most important piece — carried by the bowhunter. We know that even after a successful stalk and shot all could be lost if the broadhead fails to perform. Our suspicion is that we are not alone in these thoughts; they have been shared by thousands of hunting archers across the centuries.

Most of us would agree that a well-sharpened broadhead of almost any design, shot into the right place, will do its intended job quickly. Then why so many choices in broadheads over the years? Apparently it's only because the human mind knows no limits to what it can conceive and create when facing the task of trying to improve something, even something seemingly simple in design and shape.

This chapter's focus is on the first 50 years of steel hunting point development. It spotlights broadheads used for hunting big game primarily from 1920 to 1970. We will not even try to complicate matters by explaining the origins of Stone Age or Bronze Age heads. All that has

been well documented in other writings over the years.

Of course, it is impossible in a single short chapter to tell the entire story or to show all of the photos necessary to trace the development of steel broadheads — but we will try. Understand that many heads made an impact on the development of modern broadheads; likewise, many did not. Some heads were truly unique; other heads were simply designed by famous people in our sport. In general, a variety of all sorts of design ideas showed up.

This is not a complete listing of the history of broadheads but rather a general overview. It is intended to present a bit of background and to show some of the heads envisioned, made and used between the years of 1920 and 1970.

First came the simple flat-pointed piece of steel, usually attached to the front of the shaft through a slot sawed into the wood. Such heads had to be tied on or pinned or glued on somehow. Next, people tried a small piece of tubing, sized to fit the shaft with the other end of the tubing generally flattened and attached to the blade by drilling, pinning or soldering. Still later high powered rifle shell jackets were slotted with a hacksaw and soldered to blades.

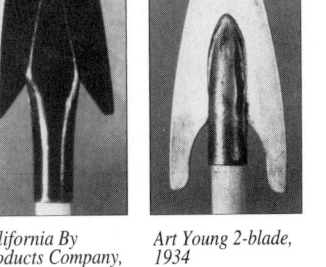

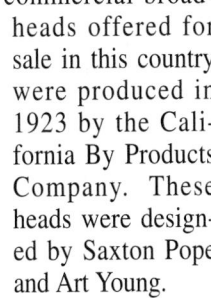

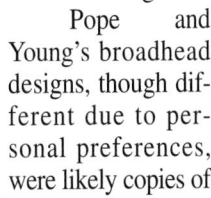

California By Products Company, 1923

Art Young 2-blade, 1934

The first commercial broadheads offered for sale in this country were produced in 1923 by the California By Products Company. These heads were designed by Saxton Pope and Art Young.

Pope and Young's broadhead designs, though different due to personal preferences, were likely copies of old English broadheads combined with a bit of Will "Chief" Compton's styling. Compton and Ishi, the Yana Indian, taught Pope and Young how to make archery tackle and shoot their bows.

Pope's **Hunting With the Bow and Arrow**, published in 1923, detailed his group's bowhunting adventures and offered instructions for making a number of different types and sizes of both big game and small game hunting arrowheads. Undoubtedly, many novice bowhunters of that day profited from the equipment-making instructions provided by Dr. Pope.

In the 1920s, with the growing interest in archery and bowhunting thanks in large part to Pope's book, a number of archery equipment manufacturing companies came into existence. Prior to this time most purchased equipment had come from small workshops scattered around the country. The new, larger companies offered all types of archery and bowhunting tackle, including a small but growing number of broadheads.

The American Broadhead Collector's Club, founded in 1974, currently recognizes nearly 2,000 different broadheads. The earliest of these dates from the 1920s and all of them were commercially produced by a bona fide manufacturer. They rank as either a prototype, experimental, special order or normal production model broadhead. Their sizes range from a diminutive one-half inch by three-quarters inch up to a giant three-by-four inch head! Grain weights run from just over 50 to nearly 400 grains. These broadheads come in two, three, four, five, six and eight blades in barbed and barbless styles. Some are one-piece construction; others have as many as 10 distinct components. Their cutting edges feature either a concave, straight or convex profile with either a rough burr edge, a razor edge and a light or heavily serrated edge. Some were designed as one-shot disposables while others are virtually indestructible. They feature ferrules whose interior diameter measurements range from one-quarter to three-eighths inches in either tapered or parallel versions. Other ferrule designs include those made to be glued or screwed into hollow fiberglass or aluminum shafts.

Stemmler Big Game 2-blade, 1935

Ropers Indian arrowhead 2-blade, 1954

Sportsman Archery 2-blade, 1926

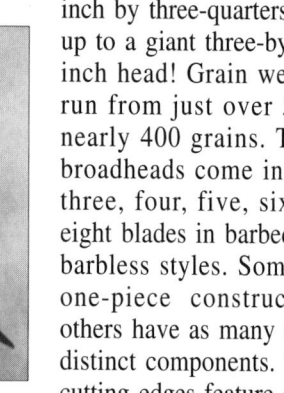

Geronimo 4-blade

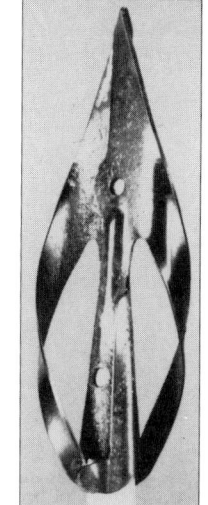

Excaliber .45 2-blade, 1958

Most early broadheads have fixed blades but a few feature blades which expand upon impact to offer increased cutting action. Some blades have solid surfaces while others have one or more cut-out sections. Most blades are flat but a few have a helical or spiral twist which supposedly works with the arrow's normal rotation to increase penetration. There also have been commemorative models produced by various archery companies and organizations, models for big and small game hunting and some models designed expressly for practice. They have come from one-man basement workshops, precision machine shops and large archery companies looking to expand and increase their product line. Some lasted a single season; others have been successfully manufactured and sold for many years.

As should be evident, a great variety of styles and models have been produced for bowhunters by a variety of manufacturers. The full array of broadhead design is fascinating.

During the 1920s and 1930s — even into the 1940s — many heads were wicked looking barbed models. Soon, however, various state fish and game agencies began banning broadheads that allowed the shaft and broadhead to remain in wounded animals.

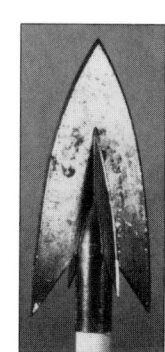

Hillcraft barbed 4-blade, 1944

When barbed heads started to disappear, something else happened. Many bowhunting machinists and tool and die makers began to refine heads, giving them smoother lines. They cut holes through them to allow air passage in flight. They also tried different types of metal — steel, magnesium, beryllium, copper, bronze and combinations with plastics (just beginning to come on the scene in the early '40s). They also began to mass produce heads with the aid of dies. They also began to have their designed heads patented so no one could copy them (with more than a few lawsuits filed as a result of the infringement by copycats).

Bloodtrail 2-blade, 1956

Back in the 1920s and 1930s archers often copied head designs. If someone had a good looking broadhead or killed something with one, he passed the information along to his friends since most early day archers

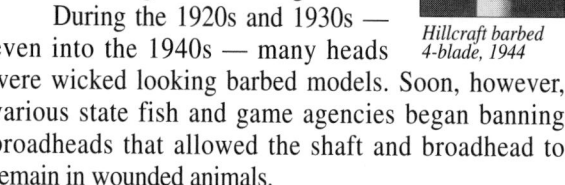

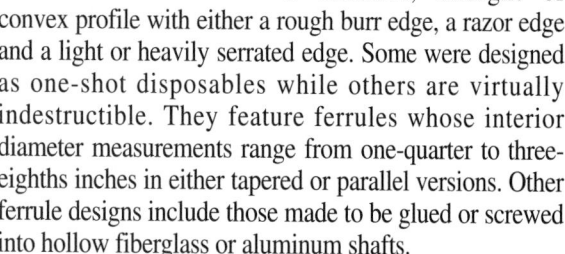

made their own equipment. But people who designed heads saw a demand for manufactured broadheads and a way to make extra money during hard times. Protecting broadhead design became important.

By now heads could be truly aligned and ferrules pressed right into the broadhead. After World War II, during the late '40s and early '50s, came the working idea of attaching razor blades to the broadhead in a variety of ways. But the idea was slow to catch on since veteran bowhunters seemed to feel such heads were too flimsy and too delicate to be used properly on big game.

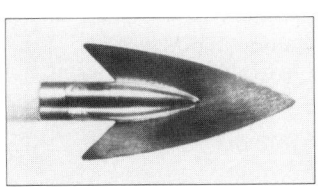

Case Kiska 2-blade, 1927

Fred Bear likely did the most during this period to prove that razor heads were quite deadly. Through his field testing on big game hunts, through his movies of actual hunts shown to audiences of eager archers and through his own promotion and dedication, most bowhunters began to understand the idea was a good one.

The broadheads shown here illustrate only a small portion of the kinds of heads available from the 1920s through 1970.

Roy Case, who arrowed his first deer in Wisconsin in 1930, is generally credited with coining the term "bowhunter." Case designed, developed and sold many heads with which his name was connected. His heads were inexpensive and available in parts that allowed archers to solder together — facts which appealed to the do-it-yourselfer during the hard economic times of the '30s. The Case Kiska model head, first introduced in 1927, featured a barbed blade fifteen-sixteenths of an inch wide soldered into either a .30 or .35 caliber bullet jacket ferrule. Case ordered the bullet jackets from ammunition companies in lots of 1,000 especially for broadhead use. Each was slotted by hand with a hacksaw to accept the blade.

By the way, Case used a Kiska-tipped shaft to down the Vilas County spike buck in 1930 and become the first Wisconsin bowhunter in modern times to legally take a whitetail deer with bow and arrow.

The Kiska also deserves notoriety because in the 1930s it was used as a model by the Wisconsin Conservation Department to set broadhead size requirements. Since the Kiska broadhead was a popular broadhead at this time and its reduced size after sharpening was seven-eighths of an inch, this became the minimum legal width. In later years other states looked to Wisconsin for guidance in establishing their own bowhunting regulations and copied some laws verbatim. So Wisconsin's minimum size requirement, developed from the Kiska, was adopted almost universally and in many states this size regulation remains unchanged

Mahler Interchangeable 2-blade, 1936

today. Thus the diminutive Kiska broadhead, first introduced during the 1920s, continues to influence bowhunting into the 1990s.

Case went on to produce well over a dozen different broadhead models with sales of select designs lasting into the 1950s. With the exception of the tapered ferrule "Last Case," all models used the bullet jacket.

Forest Nagler, on his two well documented trips to British Columbia in 1931 and 1932, hunted moose, caribou, deer, bear and grouse with bow, arrows and broadheads which he made. He used five different types of heads with some degree of success.

In 1936 J. H. Mahler of Hartsdale, New York introduced his "Mahler Interchangeable" broadheads. Two sizes were offered: the larger blade style featured a ferrule for a three-eighth inch shaft while the small model would fit a five-sixteenth inch shaft. Each was composed of a blade riveted to a tapered ferrule and a male, threaded shank. This then screwed into an appropriately sized shaft adapter. The broadhead blade could be unscrewed from the adapter on the arrow shaft and replaced with either a target or roving style point.

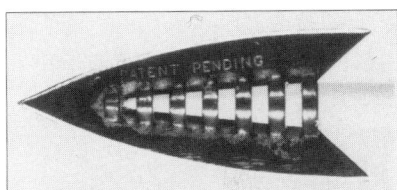

Ben Pearson 2-blade, Skelton Ferrel, 1939

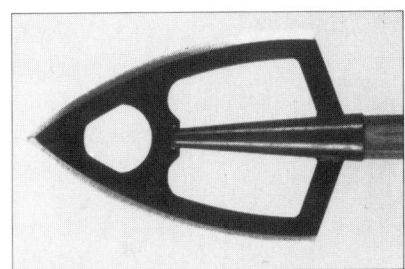

Ben Pearson Deadhead 2-blade, 1964

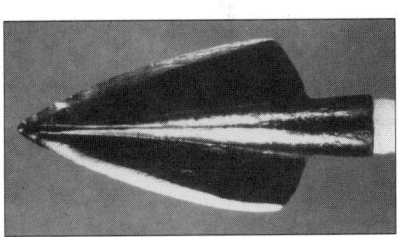

Easton 2-blade, 1932

Today, nearly all bowhunters are aware of the screw-in or the screw-on broadhead/practice point systems. Most arrowheads currently being made use it. Yet few archers know that a variation of the current system was first tried

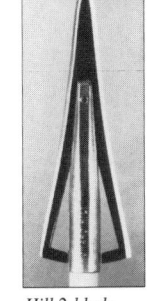

Hill 2-blade improved, 1958

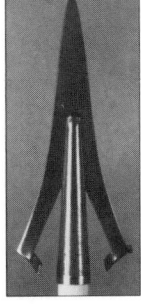

Pinecrest ST-X-100 2-blade, 1962

back in the 1930s. Unfortunately, the idea was ahead of its time. The concept never really caught on and it is believed that relatively few Mahler interchangeable broadheads were produced or sold.

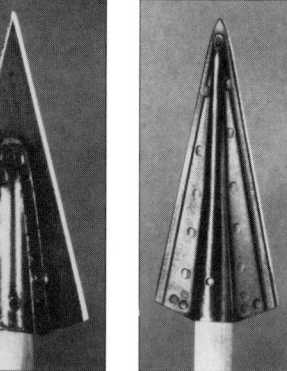

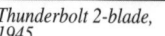
Thunderbolt 2-blade, 1945
Mickey Finn 2-blade, 1953

Ben Pearson made, marketed and hunted with a vast array of skeleton ferrule heads from 1938 through the 1950s. He also made a splendid group of solid forged heads and later still his famous Deadhead.

James D.Easton, founder of Easton Aluminum shafts, also made a very nice two-blade forged head in 1932. He even made a unique forged fish point with a barb. It was the first commercial broadhead with a five-degree taper.

(Above) Gus Atkins BF-1 copperhead and (below) BF-2 copperhead

Howard Hill, the archer well remembered for all his contributions to hunting with the bow and arrow, designed and mass produced several broadheads, first with barbs and later without. He worked closely with Ben Pearson for some time and they jointly mass produced Hill heads. Later Hilbre, Bowlo and Pinecrest made similar looking points with minor variations.

Glenn St. Charles, our Club's founder and Past President, designed and sold two well known heads in the Pacific Northwest — the Thunderbolt, made between 1945 and 1946, and the Mickey Finn, made between 1953 and 1959. He used them with considerable success, too.

In 1945 Gus Adkins from Richmond, Virginia came up with a unique set of five original two-blade broadheads which he labeled Copperheads. He added two more uniquely different heads later and his broadhead advertisements were eye-catching.

Back in 1939 Cliff Zwickey came out with his first ever barbed Black Diamond. The design was quickly changed to barbless. These were among the first heads to use a five degree-taper

Zwickey Black Diamond barbed 2-blade, 1939

on their ferrules and in 1942 Zwickey did something no one else had done: he punched a small triangular section from each side of the ferrule and bent it perpendicular to the main blade, and by sharpening the front edges he created the first commercial four-blade broadhead design.

Meanwhile, Ole La Fond of Michigan was working on his Lightning Ripper which featured serrated blade edges.

The 1930s, 1940s and 1950s saw many more innovations in heads. Veteran bowhunters will remember some by name and photos; others likely will go unrecognized.

In late 1946 the L. C. Whiffen Archery Company of Milwaukee introduced its first "BodKin" three-blade broadhead. This was the second three-blade design to come on the market and differed from the earlier Krieger model in that it featured a tapered ferrule and three-piece laminated construction. In later

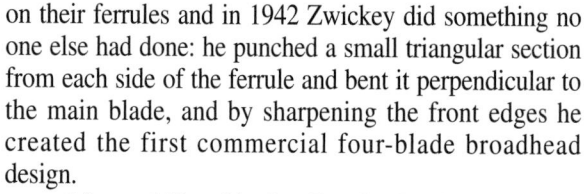
Bo' n Arrer Shop Rocket 4-blade, 1955

years the Whiffen Company would go on to produce a wide variety of sizes and models of three-blade heads. The tradition continues today and the company is now into its fifth decade of producing broadheads for bowhunters.

As the 1950s began, the stage was set for further growth and progress in the sport of archery. The hobby was becoming increasingly popular and gaining new advocates daily. Many states had established archery-only seasons and areas. And the manufacturing of archery equipment was becoming firmly entrenched as a growing industry. These factors combined to act as a catalyst for additional changes in broadhead design and manufacture.

The first was the "Bo' n Arrer Rocket" broadhead designed by W. W. Rice of Leeds, New York. Introduced in October of 1955, the broadhead featured a parallel ferrule body that accepted four razor style blades in milled slots. Once positioned in the slots, the blades were secured with a screw-on, cone shaped tip. As desired, the bowhunter could disassemble the unit and repair or replace the component sections. The head could be shot without the blades for practice or used as a small game point if the special blunt tip was added.

LaFonds Lightning Ripper 2-blade, 1955

Without anyone realizing it at the time, this broadhead set the stage for what would eventually become an entirely new direction for broadhead design. The Bo' n Arrer Rocket was the very first commercial

48

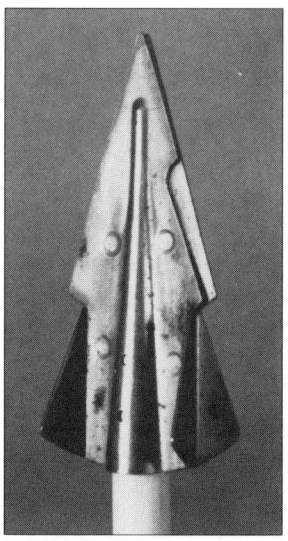

Ishi 6-blade, 1953

razor insert style broadhead available to bowhunters. Today razor insert styles are common and hundreds of such models have been introduced. Though some newer models may shoot faster, fly straighter and cut deeper than the Rocket, none can claim a share of its unique historical niche as the first of its kind.

There is even an Ishi Broadhead made by Jim Ramsey of Arizona, an inventor and designer with a rich Indian heritage. He designed a six-blade steel head called the "Ishi" that sold in 1953. Ramsey later was asked by Fred Bear and Charlie Kroll to make obsidian spear points for the Pope and Young Club's Ishi Award.

Fred Bear, inventor of one of the most famous broadheads of all time — the Bear Razorhead — came out with his original marketed head in 1956. It went through a series of changes to evolve into the head of today. Not only did the main blade and ferrule change, the razor insert was redesigned at least six times. Undoubtedly, one of the best things that Bear's heads had going for them from the very beginning, was Fred Bear himself. He personally hunted

Flying Dutchman 4-blade, 1968

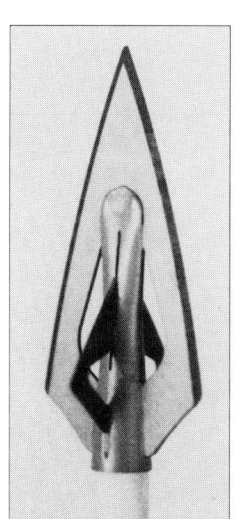

Bear Razorhead 4-blade, 1956 (This is a 1968 model)

with his broadheads, produced promotional movies of his hunts and then made the movies available to members of almost any archery club or organization wanting to view them. Many personal friends who hunted with him were given Razorheads to use on their hunts. Evaluations were taken and minor changes began to occur every few years. His promotional genius made Bear Razorheads the ones that most bowhunters used for many years — and the heads remain popular today.

In the 1960s Homer "Dutch" Wambold, a well known archery personality of the '50s and '60s who authored **Bowhunting for Deer**, was involved designing his "Flying Dutchman," a large, heavy double-bladed head created for the largest big game species. It never got into production due to Wambold's untimely death.

Today we have a vast array of broadheads from which to choose. Look closely at them. You may see something borrowed from a head designed some years ago. Regardless, one of the very best things about many of the newer heads is that most use razor insert, replaceable blades in some form. Used and treated properly, these heads are practical, humane and hard to beat.

Someone coming along later may feel compelled to write a history of the second 50 years of broadhead development. Judging from the number of new heads coming onto the market lately, the written account will probably have to be a longer piece than this one.

EDITOR'S NOTE: *Readers interested in delving further into the research of broadheads — and perhaps even becoming a collector — should begin by contacting The American Broadhead Collector's Club (ABCC) at 12516 West Youth Camp Road, Columbus, IN 47201.*

The three co-authors of this chapter are all bowhunters as well as active collectors of broadheads and members of the ABCC. Each has had a lot of fun locating old, rare broadheads — often found on arrows in an old quiver somewhere. The heads turn up in all parts of the country — forgotten in basements, garages, old archery shops and the personal hunting gear of veteran bowhunters.

If you are a bowhunter yourself, you may have unknowingly started your own miniature broadhead collection. Check out the different versions of broadheads you may have bought and tried over the last few seasons. You just may be surprised with what you find.

*I*shi,
the
Last
Yana
Indian.

THE ISHI HUNTS

THE ISHI AWARD is the highest honor that can be bestowed by the Pope and Young Club. Only one Ishi Award may be presented for any Recording Period and then only if a truly outstanding North American big game trophy animal is judged worthy of such recognition. There have been a dozen Ishi Awards presented during the history of the Pope and Young Club. Following are brief accounts, told in each hunter's own words, of the bowhunts that resulted in Ishi presentations:

◆ ◆ ◆ ◆ ◆

4th Recording Period (1963-1964)
Non-Typical Whitetail Deer
Score: 279 7/8
taken in Nebraska by Del Austin (1962)

MOSSY HORNS

To take a trophy such as this one naturally takes a certain amount of skill — but patience and luck were deciding factors.

Al Dawson, a friend and hunting partner, had hunted this very buck for several years. He was the one who told me of a large island where the deer stayed and his approximate bedding area.

I had hunted this Platte River area in central Nebraska for three years and knew the wise old buck did not leave the dense island cover until after dark, except for periods during the rutting season. With this in mind, I started putting up my stand some distance from his bedding area.

On Halloween evening of 1962 I grabbed my bow, razor sharp broadheads, portable tree stand and headed for the island. I mounted my stand on a tree some 10 feet off the ground and about 30 feet from a well used deer trail. Rut was in full swing and I did not spare the buck lure, splashing some of the evil-smelling stuff on bushes around the tree I was in.

Time dragged and it appeared to be another fruitless hunt when suddenly a huge buck came charging

out of the brush directly downwind and stopped broadside 25 yards away. The sight of him was unnerving but I managed to drive an arrow home and put my tag on a buck that had almost become a legend.

◆ ◆ ◆ ◆ ◆

6th Recording Period (1967-1968)
Typical Whitetail Deer
Score 204 4/8
taken in Illinois by Mel Johnson (1965)

BEANFIELD BUCK

The year was 1965. I was hunting the edge of a soybean field near Peoria, Illinois. Deer, including a big buck, fed here nightly.

I had no blind in this area so I quickly cleared the oak leaves from a brushy spot, nocked an arrow and settled back. My camouflage clothing blended nicely with the background and the wind was in my face. Everything seemed right for the evening wait.

I had just started relaxing when a deer appeared at the far corner of the field, walking in my direction. My breath caught in my throat at the sight of the large rack that swung gently with every step. I realized if he kept coming he would pass directly in front of my stand. My hand grasped the bow.

The buck cautiously made his way along the field's edge, stopping to check for danger from time to time. The wind was still in my favor as he moved nearer. After what seemed to be an entire deer season, the big whitetail was directly in front of me and my heart almost stopped as he turned and stared right through me. But a moment later he casually turned his massive head and walked on.

One step. Two steps. In one continuous motion I raised slightly, came to full draw and released my arrow. It sliced through his middle and he jumped forward, running toward the center of the field. There was a slight rise in the beanfield and I lost sight of him as he bounded over it. I automatically nocked another arrow and when I looked up he was standing near the rise, looking back in my direction. Then he turned and disappeared again.

I got to my feet and started after him. Soon I saw my arrow on the ground and I placed it back in my quiver. A few more steps and I could see him lying just beyond the rise.

7th Recording Period (1969-1970)
Bighorn Sheep
Score: 176 3/8
taken in Montana by Ray Alt (1968)

MONTANA MONARCH

I first caught sheep fever back in 1968 on my very first bighorn hunt. I was living in Montana at the time and I got a permit to hunt the Sweet Grass Primitive Area. Not many people hunted sheep with a bow in those days and you had to share the area with rifle hunters. I was 28 — young, eager and determined — and Lady Luck really smiled on me that initial season.

I had a new 60-inch recurve pulling 60 pounds at 28 inches. I'd bought 100 wooden shafts and a gross of broadheads from Glenn St. Charles, the founder of the Pope and Young Club, who owned an archery shop in Seattle. I made up my own hunting arrows and practiced with my bow until I felt I was ready.

That year we got a lot of early snow and the Fish and Game decided to leave the sheep season open until mid-December. I hunted long and hard, battling the cold and wading through deep snow, and finally, on December 2, 1968 I took my ram in a mountain snowstorm. Visibility was very bad at times, a fact that helped the sheep in some ways — but it also helped this bowhunter get close enough to a big ram that turned out to be the World Record bighorn.

8th Recording Period (1971-1972)
Barren Ground Caribou
Score: 446 6/8
taken in Alaska by Art Kragness (1970)

KING CARIBOU

I was hunting just south of the Meshik River on the Alaska Peninsula after being ferried by airboat from our island camp to shore where we'd begin the day's hunt.

My hunting buddy, Bill Carlos, and I had been hunting the large herds by spotting from high points, glassing the enormous muskeg flats below. When we sighted a likely herd we'd plan ambushes — most of which

didn't work, of course. But both Bill and I each managed to fill one of two tags in only four days of hunting.

Hunting the large herds made stalking difficult since there were so many eyes looking at once. My plan was to hunt an area where I always seemed to see singles and small groups. I wanted to give stalking a try.

I'd glassed only half an hour when I spotted a lone bull — and he was huge. Over the next five hours of following him around, I never saw another animal. At the time I had no idea how good a trophy he was since I didn't have other bulls nearby to compare him with.

During those five hours he bedded down several times. It was then that I gained the most ground on him and I managed to stay within 100 yards or so. Finally during one of his catnaps I crept within 30 yards. I could plainly see his double shovels and a heap of points. I really had to force myself to take my time. Buck fever was getting to me.

My shot was good. He jumped to his feet and looked in all directions. Then he did the most surprising thing — he began to feed on nearby willows. The bull died on his feet, never suspecting there was a hunter within 100 miles of him.

12th Recording Period (1979-1980)
Black Bear
Score: 22 4/16
taken in Colorado by Ray Cox (1978)

BACKCOUNTRY BRUISER

On August 16, 1978 my son Jamie and I left Paonia for a bear hunt north of Paradox, Colorado. We met a close friend, Willis Butolph, at a lake north of Paradox and the following day we found an old track that the dogs worked for several hours before abandoning the trail.

The next morning Jamie and I found a track in the road but it was in a part of the road that was hardpacked and I couldn't tell how big it was. I called Willis. We turned the dogs out but they couldn't smell a thing.

I finally took old Pistol and got off the road down in the timber. We made a big circle and he hit the track and started cold trailing it. The other dogs went to Pistol and as they went down the canyon the trail got hotter. Two hours later they were barking treed in the bottom of a canyon.

When Jamie and I got down to the bottom we found the bear bayed under a big ledge. The dogs were under the rock, fighting the bear. He finally ran and I was right in his path when he came out from under the ledge. I jumped up on a rock. The bear reared up not four feet away and started flailing at the dogs. He then ran about 40 yards and climbed a big yellow pine that had limbs all the way to the ground.

I shot the bear three times before he fell out. We still didn't realize what a big bear we had until we walked up to him. It took us five hours to climb out of that canyon with the skull and hide, trailed by a pack of tired dogs.

9th Recording Period (1973-1974)
Alaska-Yukon Moose
Score: 248 0/8
taken in Alaska by Dr. Michael Cusack (1973)

THE LARGEST ANTLERS

In 1973, the moose season in the area of Alaska that I hunted ran from August 20 to January 1. Living as I do in Anchorage, there was a great opportunity to hunt on weekends after a one-hour commercial flight to King Salmon. I would generally be in the hunting area along Bear Creek on most weekends.

For a few years now I had been chasing rumors of huge moose. Only the week before I lucked out, I had spooked a giant bull while on a stalk. All I saw was his antlers moving above the brush as he crashed away.

Then, in early December of '73, my chance came when everything worked out well. The moose was bedded in a little draw with heavy alders surrounding him. The snow was crunchy and I didn't think I would be able to get close enough for the shot. After stalking for over an hour, I was 30 yards away from the broadside bull. I drew, held and released. My arrow entered behind his ribs and angled into his chest. He made it only 50 yards and fell. He was much bigger than I had imagined, easily the World Record.

11th Recording Period (1977-1978)
Columbian Blacktail Deer
Score: 172 2/8
taken in Oregon by B. G. Shurtleff (1969)

THE BIGGEST BLACKTAIL

My best trophy was taken on October 2, 1969 on a one-day hunt near home. I drove a short distance into the hills on the east side of the Willamette Valley. The brush in this area is so thick you can hardly get through it, so trail-watching is the only answer. I had found a good trail near a creek under a rocky bluff and this was where I planned to sit. I was on my stand by first light.

After what seemed like a very long time I was tempted to leave, quite sure nothing was going to come by. Then I saw antlers — and what a set of antlers! He

was coming my way.

I was so excited I had to tell myself, "Cool it. Let him walk past before you move."

As he walked by I drew, aimed and released all in one motion. It was a good hit. Talk about buck fever! I really had it now.

After working my way down the bluff to where I'd last seen the deer, I found a blood trail — and the deer was a short distance beyond.

Getting him out was an ordeal. I had to cut him up and make several trips. But even the hard work didn't dampen the thrill of taking one of the largest deer I've ever seen.

13th Recording Period (1981-1982)
Cougar
Score: 15 11/16
taken in Idaho by Jerry James (1982)

KING CAT

It was a long trail to bagging my World Record cougar. I had hunted two years unsuccessfully as there had been no snow for tracking. On my third hunt, however, snow conditions were ideal but I was still blessed with bad luck.

I was hunting with Bob Smith of Kooskia, Idaho, and the majority of our hunt was spent in the Selway River area. During the first six days of my hunt we found three different cougar tracks but none was fresh enough to run. The seventh day was perfect with two inches of fresh snow. We spent part of the morning in an area where a cougar had been sighted by a truck driver. We found tracks but they were too old to follow. We spent some time listening for ravens, which might indicate a kill, but that also drew a blank so we started to drive our usual route.

After some time we found the track of a large cat that had crossed the road and headed up the mountain. The track was filled with snow but we knew it had been made during the night. We took two of Bob's best cat dogs, Chief and Ralph. Bob kept Ralph on a leash while Chief was allowed to run ahead. Chief is half Airedale and half Bluetick and he'll only run the trail if Bob gives the command or he jumps the cougar. We trailed the cat up the side of the mountain and into a small canyon. All of a sudden Chief started barking. He'd jumped the cat and was on its trail.

Bob turned Ralph loose and soon both dogs were barking treed. We hurried over and there was the most beautiful sight I've ever seen. The big tom looked golden brown against the green of the pines. Bob tied the dogs while I positioned myself for a shot. I only had a small hole to shoot through and my arrow deflected, hitting the cat. He snarled and started down the tree, breaking branches as he came. I nocked another arrow and took a quick shot just before the cat jumped from the tree. My arrow hit right behind the front leg and he was down before he went 20 yards. Later when we laid his hide on the floor it measured eight feet and seven inches. We estimated his weight at 160 pounds.

14th Recording Period (1983-1984)
Typical Mule Deer
Score: 203 1/8
taken in Colorado by Bill Barcus (1979)

AWESOME ANTLERS

I made my first bowhunt in 1972. It took five seasons before I managed to arrow my first deer — a muley doe. By the time the 1979 Colorado archery season rolled around, I had bowhunted seven consecutive years with just that one deer to show for it. That season I wanted to fill my tag with a buck. In fact, my first buck EVER.

The season had been open a week before I could get away for a two-week hunt. My parents joined me a few days later, after checking out the fishing in some of the nearby lakes.

Dawn was still more than an hour away as I started the climb up the ridge. Just at daylight, I reached a small clearing on the crest where I began hunting. Almost instantly I saw four bucks feeding along the fringe of aspens on the other side of the clearing, about 80 yards away. Any one of them would make a great "first buck," but two of them carried awesome antlers! After they moved into the aspen, I made a try at getting close enough for a shot but blew it. The rest of the morning passed uneventfully.

I had been moving easterly most of the morning and decided to cut over a small saddle to the north and hunt my way back to the clearing. On a particularly steep part of the hill, I came to a game trail that paralleled the ridgetop. Turning west on the trail, I began still-hunting again.

It was more of a "I thought I saw it" than real movement that drew my attention to some thick weeds and grass on the lip of a small terrace about 85 yards below. Through my binoculars I finally picked out the dark, fuzzy tine of an antler, then a second. At first I thought there were two bucks bedded together; the portions of antler I could make out were too far apart to belong to the same animal. But that impression didn't last long as the antler pieces moved in unison! The longer I looked, the more obvious it became that one buck belonged to both antlers!

An hour — maybe more — passed before I found myself 15 yards slightly uphill from the unsuspecting deer. I had to force myself not to look at the buck's awesome headgear. As the sight pin hovered on the aiming point, I was a bit startled to see the feathers of an arrow magically appear, then vanish in the spot. I had completed the shot without really knowing it.

As I reached the lip of the terrace, I saw the giant — down for the count — 30 yards lower on the slope. The "hunting" part of the season was over and the "work" part was about to begin.

Even with the help of my parents, getting the deer two miles back to camp was all of the ordeal I knew it would be. As incredible as it may sound, I actually thought about leaving the cumbersome antlers behind!

"That's nonsense! I'll carry them," Mom insisted.

Taking the saw, she removed the antlers from the skull and patiently steered them through the brush, trees and downfall all the way to camp. To think, if it hadn't been for my mother, the seven-by-seven antlers might have been left behind on that ridgetop.

15th Recording Period (1985-1986)
Dall Sheep
Score: 164 5/8
taken in the Northwest Territories by Gary Laya (1986)

BACKPACK BOWHUNT

Wow! What a trip this was going to be. In August of 1986 I was headed for parts unknown on a Beaver float plane, somewhere over the Northwest Territories. It was my first hunt this far north — a backpack hunt with outfitter Greg Williams.

The first day out we hiked for nine hours with 10 days of provisions on our backs. As we unzipped the tent on the second morning and peered out across a canyon, there on the next ridge over stood two good Dall rams. Out came the spotting scope and my guide, Al Barvir, said one of the rams was exceptional. For the next seven days we chased that ram from one end of the mountain range to the other and back.

The first day I saw the ram I got within 40 yards of him but he offered me no shot. The third day brought a near vertical shot at 25 yards that just went over his back. I had little interest in any other. I guess that's the only reason why I looked over 25 other rams and passed up a dozen of them. But after the sixth day of hunting that old ram, I was beginning to believe he was truly a white ghost.

On the seventh day out I decided to go after him just one more time. If things didn't work out this time, I would try for another sheep. I spotted him in a small drainage and watched him for over two hours before he bedded down where I could stalk him.

When I was well within good bow range, he saw me and bolted up the other side of the ravine. As he came to a stop, my arrow was on its way and found the spot I had been hoping for. The beautiful white trophy ram was finally mine.

16th Recording Period (1987-1988)
Non-Typical Yellowstone Elk
Score: 419 5/8
taken in Arizona by James L. Ludvigson (1985)

A MAGNIFICENT BULL

Just south of the Grand Canyon, on Friday the 13th, the Arizona archery elk season started and a very lucky season it was for me.

On the first day I sat by a little trickle tank and as the morning progressed I tried my bugle. I got an answer from up the canyon. The bull would not come to me, so I slowly stalked my way closer to him, bugling occasionally. I ended up in a stand of trees across a little clearing. Nothing.

On the way back to camp I found a fresh wallow and rebuilt a ground blind I had placed there two years before. On the second morning I approached the blind at the wallow and whistled to make sure no one else was there first. To my surprise I got an answer to my whistle from what sounded like the bull I had been bugling the previous day. I slipped into the blind and sat quietly waiting.

Then from a trail leading to the wallow came a magnificent elk with antlers that seemed to be coming out all over the place. He stopped and watched the wallow before coming in. As he moved closer, I got on my knees and readied for the shot. He stopped and started to throw mud with his antlers. I had a shot but decided not to take it because there were a few small oak branches I might have hit with my arrow.

I waited and he moved farther out into the wallow, turned and gave me a broadside shot at 25 yards. All I had to do was just miss the ends of some pine needles hiding part of his shoulder. My heart was pounding but to my surprise when I glanced down at my hands they were not shaking. I drew back my 72 pound bow and put the 25-yard pin a third of the way up his chest, behind the shoulder. I said a little prayer asking God to guide the arrow to where I wanted it to go. Then I released my four-fletched arrow.

The shaft hit the chest four inches from the point of aim and penetrated to the skin on the far side. The bull bolted away from the wallow, going through a barbed wire fence and laying one post over on the ground. I waited 45 minutes to start trailing him and it seemed like an eternity. I had an easy trailing job. He ran 300 yards and then walked another 100 yards before keeling over.

When I got to him I thought, "He's big and he's mine." I made a fast trip back to camp to where my dad was waiting for me. On the way I met up with hunting friends Wayne Holt and Dave Deason. After pictures were taken and the gutting/boning finished, the meat was on its way to a processing plant in Flagstaff. I received several awards for this animal and I can say after 30 years of practicing and hunting with a bow, it has all paid off for me with this truly magnificent bull elk I will never forget.

17th Recording Period (1989-1990)
Non-Typical Blacktail Deer
Score: 194 4/8
taken in Oregon by James Decker (1988)

A SEASON TO REMEMBER

The 1988 season started off with me hunting the high Cascades for Roosevelt elk. I've always been a meat hunter and I shot a nice five-pointer that provided 375 pounds of meat for the freezer. Now I could be a little picky on the size of the deer I tagged this year.

Late season came in and I was ready. This year was good for rattling. Lots of bucks came in and it was hard to pass up a big buck at 15 yards but I was waiting for a monster.

On the last evening of the season I saw a nice four-by-four some 70 yards away. He had two does with him. I rattled and raked the ground. He'd look my way but wouldn't come any closer. Finally, the does came within 20 yards but soon grazed back to the buck.

I grew tired of messing with the buck so I slipped away without spooking the deer. I hunted up to a strip of pines surrounded by oaks. Suddenly I focused on a big buck standing down the hill. He was looking right at me so I kept on walking, acting like I'd not seen him. When I passed behind the next big tree, I nocked an arrow, drew my bow and eased into view. I let go of the string. The arrow struck. He bucked and ran off.

I sat down and waited for a time before walking down to where he'd been standing. I didn't really need a blood trail because he left tracks anyone could have followed — and he went down only 75 yards away. When I walked up, my eyes nearly popped out of my head. I could not believe the size of the rack. It had 12 points on each side and bits of bark clung to its burrs. My arrow had penetrated both lungs.

Being in the right place at the right time made it all possible.

POPE & YOUNG TROPHY BRONZES

by Scott Showalter

IN 1990 THE CLUB'S BOARD OF DIRECTORS approved the latest in its series of ongoing art projects, limited edition bronze sculptures representing bowhunting's World Record big game animals.

The Club has two objectives in mind. First, it seeks to create and offer outstanding artwork with lasting value and beauty, artwork representing the Club and its record-keeping function, artwork that has universal appeal to the bowhunter, trophy hunter and all hunters in general. Second, it seeks creation of a program that provides both moral support and financial assistance to protect bowhunting and the rights of bowhunters.

To meet this end the Pope and Young Club has pledged $100 of the purchase price of each sculpture to support bowhunting.

Whitetail deer were chosen as the initial subjects. Each sculpture is a one-third lifesize replica of the World Record whitetails mounted on an elliptical walnut plaque with an inset Pope and Young Club medallion.

First cast was "Old Mossy Horns," the unique and much photographed buck taken in Nebraska by Del Austin in 1962. It became and currently remains bowhunting's World Record non-typical whitetail deer. It was the recipient of the first Ishi Award presented by the Pope and Young Club.

The second casting was the World Record typical whitetail. Called the "Beanfield Buck" by some admirers, this trophy was taken in Illinois by Mel Johnson in 1965. It still reigns as the World Record typical whitetail and was recipient of the Club's second Ishi Award. The buck also received the Boone and Crockett Club's Sagamore Hill Award and today remains the Number Three all-time trophy whitetail.

Each sculpture in the Pope and Young series is limited to an edition of 252 pieces including two artist's proofs owned by the Club. Two hundred of the remaining castings, featuring the Pope and Young medallion, are offered to members and to the general public while the artist, Charlie Norton, retains rights to the remaining 50 pieces.

Club officials encourage members to examine the trophy bronzes and to consider investing in the future of bowhunting. Each purchase offers quality artwork of exceptional value plus the assurance that funds generated by this project are going directly to support bowhunting.

ABOUT THE ARTIST

Art, history and hunting are an inborn part of Charlie Norton's life. "I can't remember a time when I wasn't hunting, sketching or learning about history. I think a person has to be very realistic and honest with himself about his work. Creating sculpture is one of the most everlasting statements a man can make."

Each Norton sculpture or painting is a historical statement. To ensure its authenticity, he carefully researches his work and draws from a lifelong interest in art, history, hunting and archaeology to give his art its realism.

Born in Scott City, Kansas in 1942, Norton grew up near the small agricultural community of Leoti and started sketching while still in school. Following a stint in the Army, he returned to Kansas and took his turn at ranching, rodeoing and hammering out a living shoeing horses. He became a full-time artist in 1973.

A lifelong hunter, Norton today shares his passion for archery and art with his entire family. He receives numerous commissions and his art has earned him honors as well as a way of life that is the envy of his peers. Norton's artwork is found in private collections, museums across the country and in our nation's capitol.

LEON PARSON

Of Form and Feeling

by M.R. James

*These excerpts were originally published in the August/September 1991 issue of **Bowhunter Magazine**.*

LIKE MOST BOWHUNTERS, Leon Parson is fond of recalling the sights and sounds and events of each day's hunting experience. But unlike most bowhunters, this talented Idaho wildlife artist routinely captures certain special outdoor moments on canvas or linen, preserving forever his private memories — and then sharing them with appreciative hunters nationwide.

Whether you realize it or not, chances are good you've already seen dozens of Parson's paintings. His art regularly graces the covers or inside pages of **Outdoor Life** and other hunting magazines — **Petersen's Hunting, North American Hunter, Game Coin, Bugle** — as well as being featured on the cover of this record book. In all he has some 60 outdoor magazine covers to his credit, plus hundreds of book, magazine, catalog and calendar illustrations.

Parson the hunter cannot be separated from Parson the artist. He explains:

"The hunting experiences I've had are an integral part of my art. It's one thing to claim to be a wildlife artist and then open up **Bowhunter** or **National Geographic**, look at a picture and then do a painting. It's quite a different thing to be there when the sun goes up or goes down...or to watch a rut-swollen buck chase a doe around and around...or to smell the rank odor of elk as you move through the timber...or hear the spine-tingling bugles of rutting bulls. If I'm not out there living it, how can I say it honestly and accurately in art? Anybody can copy a photograph!"

Artistic honesty and accuracy are constant Parson goals. But he wants more. He wants each painting to stir special feelings and memories in those who see it. He wants hunters to recognize a mood as well as a visual image. To him, one of the highest compliments he can be paid is to have a fellow hunter say the look and feel of a painting is "just right."

Parson's painting style is best described as realistic with a trace of impressionism mixed in.

"I paint the way I believe we see things — that is, areas of interest are sharp, focused while less important surroundings receive less emphasis. For example, the average viewer pays very little attention to the grass under a deer or elk's belly. But as a painter I have to make sure it's there, that it's the right value, the right size, the right color and that it's applied with a brush in such a way so as to feel in harmony with the rest of the paint on the canvas. All that just for something that will hardly be noticed. However, if I fail on any of the above characteristics, it will be noticed — too much."

Although proficient in virtually every medium of painting and drawing — from pastel to scratchboard and oil to egg tempera — Parson prefers oil paint on stretched linen. He smiles at the admission.

"A few years back, as I was struggling to learn how to control paint, I once stated, 'I hate oils! They are greasy, hard to control and smell bad.' Now I love oil painting and look forward to that weird artistic sensory feedback achieved from pushing paint around on canvas."

Pushing paint on canvas began for Parson some 32 years ago when, as an eight-year-old, he received an oil paint set for Christmas. It was a gift from his father, himself an artist,

Leon Parson poses with trophy-class mountain caribou in the Northwest Territories.

who had viewed the youngster's initial artistic efforts and commented, "That's fine, Leon. Now go and draw something else."

Young Leon took his dad's suggestion to heart. He arranged some rubber animal toys — gifts from Santa — and produced his very first wildlife painting, a composition depicting three deer, bears eating salmon and a squirrel in a tree.

Leon bought his first bow, a recurve, when he was 12. He used money earned from milking cows to make the purchase and he promptly began perforating hay bales in his rural Idaho neighborhood.

"I developed some good instinctive shooting skills," he recalls, "along with a lot of the bad habits that go with just picking up a bow and shooting. It wasn't until 10 years later, when I started teaching college art, that I took advantage of an indoor archery class and began to define and correct the bad habits. I first bowhunted at age 17 but it was about a dozen years later before I started getting serious about the sport."

Among Parson's boyhood heroes were a mix of outdoorsmen and artists.

"I cut my teeth on Jack O'Connor hunting stories," he says. "Obviously, the legend of Fred Bear intrigued me and kindled my fascination with archery hunting. Bob Kuhn sparked my interest in wildlife art. I was overwhelmed by one of his **Outdoor Life** covers and said to myself, 'Someday I want to do this.'"

Ironically, each of these boyhood heroes was to play a supporting role in the adult life of artist Leon Parson. In due time Parson's paintings were used to illustrate **Outdoor Life** features by O'Connor, the publication's longtime Shooting Editor and a man many hail, even years after his death, as the "Dean of Outdoor Writers." The same magazine commissioned a portrait of Papa Bear to illustrate a feature about the legendary bowhunter and later presented the Parson drawing to Bear on the occasion of his 80th birthday. Parson, the artist, once visited Bob Kuhn's Connecticut studio and recalls the meeting with one of the world's best wildlife artists as "a cherished privilege."

But ask Leon Parson who is his favorite and he will be quick to answer: "My all-time favorite hero is hunter/artist/ naturalist Karl Runguis. He is, in my opinion, the best there ever has been. He loved the out-of-doors and loved to hunt. I did my master's thesis on him and have traveled from Oklahoma to Alberta to study his originals. They are awesome! I'd love to have gone hunting with him, staying up all night in a tent or under the stars and talking about hunting and art.

"I've hunted big game with rifles and black powder, bows and cameras from Canada to Mexico, New Jersey to Alaska," he says. "I still do. Archery equipment allows me to get started earlier and hunt longer. My favorite time to hunt, other than when the bucks are still in velvet, is in November after the snow and rut have put the big mule deer with the does."

Several seasons ago Parson took a Boone and Crockett muley buck with his rifle, fulfilling a life-long hunting goal and creating the basis for yet another painting, "Snow Buck." His big buck, by the way, has a gross score exceeding 207 B&C points and has an official measurement of 196 ⅞ after deductions.

Parson's most vivid hunting memories often are woven into his paintings. One morning he sneaked within 20 yards of a bedded four-point muley and then watched two huge four-pointers thrash it out. "I was only 40 yards away when the fight started," he recalls, "and was as close as 15 yards at one time. The painting, 'Backside of No-Tellum Ridge,' is a partial result of that hunting experience."

His most memorable bowhunting experience occurred in 1989 while on a mountain caribou/Dall sheep hunt in the Northwest Territories with outfitters Duane and Darrel Nelson.

"After a 250-mile one-way bush plane flight, we took another 100-mile round trip ride on horseback," Parson remembers. "We saw plenty of game including five grizzlies, one of which backed my guide and me up to our tent. I have photos of the bear that fill the view frame and although the camera was on a tripod, the photos are still a bit shaky.

"We spotted my bull the first day in our final camp. After watching him through the spotting scope for a couple of hours, I decided to turn him down and continue hunting. My guide, Tom, said I might want to take a closer look, that he'd only seen four bulls that big in this area all during the previous season. The caribou was probably half a mile away, across a canyon, and I told Tom if I walked all the way over there and got within shooting range I was going to take the bull. Tom laughed. I believe he thought I was a little naive.

"The caribou was out of sight from the minute I dropped over the edge of the canyon. But 45 minutes later, thanks to some good hand signals from my guide, I was within 35 yards. As I inched toward a shooting lane and the bull fed along, my arrow fell off the rest and made a little click. In a heartbeat we were staring at each other nose to nose. I drew, released and watched my arrow sail just over his back as he turned to run. He ran out a few steps and then paused broadside. By then I had another arrow on the string. I remember thinking, 'Right about there' and releasing. This time I watched my arrow's orange and blue fletching disappear — then whack! He ran 70 yards, stopped, tripped over and rolled down the mountain stone dead."

That bull's antlers were large enough to qualify for the Pope and Young records. And speaking of the Pope and Young Club, Leon Parson was commissioned by the

record keep-
ing organization
to create its first Con-
servation Print. His elk painting, "The King Speaks,"
was completed in March of 1990 and limited edition
prints went on sale at the Pope and Young Club's 30th
Anniversary Meeting and Awards Banquet in Seattle.

A prolific artist, Parson has a growing list of fans
and collectors which includes a broad, eclectic
representation of men and women, some of whom know
nothing whatsoever about hunting. He is often asked,
"How can you paint such beautiful animals and then
hunt them?" Parson considers this a valid question. He
also believes that answering the questioner is his
responsibility as both a hunter and sportsman.

"My short version of the answer is that I enjoy
hunting...my family and I eat the harvested animal...I use
my hunting time for field research... and I do indepth, on
the spot studies of animals with my camera and
structural studies at home.

"My long answer includes acknowledgement that
it is a serious action to take the life of anything and never
should be regarded lightly. I believe that animals were
put here on earth for the benefit and use of man. I also
believe we ultimately will be accountable to God for the
lives of every animal we take. Every hunter must be
responsible for his actions and answer to his or her own
conscience. Honestly, I would have to say I have killed
some animals that I cannot justify. Therefore I am far
more selective today than I used to be."

Whether hunter or non-hunter, study any of Leon
Parson's paintings and perhaps you can better understand
what the artist means when he says he always seeks both
form and feeling in what he paints.

"I feel that true art and the goals of true art should
be visual, intellectual and emotional communication. To
be successful that communication must stimulate the
emotions of the viewer, not just the intellect. Any painter
who just copies photos will always be able to
communicate subject matter, an intellectual stimuli. But
once the intellectual response is made, if there is not any
feeling created, the painting is dead.

"Emotions are what makes art 'live.' True art must
stir the heart and reach deep into the soul of the viewer if
it is going to last. Achieving that is hard. In addition to
possessing all the artistic technical skills and a good
selection of reference material, it requires the artist must
already have the emotional understanding himself before
he can hope to stir another. The quality can only come
from personal firsthand experience. The best wildlife
artists are people who have 'been there.'"

People, for example, like Leon Parson.

BIG GAME PAINTINGS

by Leon Parson

"The Veteran"

"Migration Time"

"Clearcut Bonanza"

"Masters of the High Country"

71

"Midday Repose"

"Looking Over the Menu"

"The King Speaks"

"Snow Buck"

"Lord of the Rimrock"

"Taking 25"

"Catching Some Sun"

"The Gleaners"

"Twilight on Springcreek"

"Crest of No-Tellum Ridge"

"Sir"

"Into the Silence"

THE RECORDS

World Record Alaska Brown Bear
Score: 28 7/16
Unimak Island, Alaska - 1985
Hunter: John D. Frost

ALASKA BROWN BEAR

Ursus arctos middendorffi
and certain related subspecies

MINIMUM SCORE 20

Score	Greatest Length	Greatest Width	Sex	Area	State/ Province	Hunter's Name	Date	Rank
28 7/16	17 11/16	10 12/16	M	Unimak Island	AK	John D. 'Jack' Frost	1985	1
28 0/16	17 15/16	10 1/16	M	Wide Bay, AK Pen.	AK	Fred Bear	1960	2
27 1/16	16 15/16	10 2/16	M	Bear Bay	AK	Fred Bear	1962	3
27 1/16	17 2/16	9 15/16	M	Dog Salmon River	AK	Chuck Adams	1989	3
26 13/16	17 0/16	9 13/16	M	Wide Bay	AK	Archie Nesbitt	1991	5
25 5/16	15 14/16	9 7/16	M	Lake Clark	AK	Richard L. Busk	1991	6
25 2/16	16 2/16	9 0/16	M	Chichagof Island	AK	Kenneth T. Wotring	1982	7
24 10/16	15 4/16	9 6/16	M	Kodiak Island	AK	Dean Stebner	1991	8
24 1/16	14 12/16	9 5/16	M	Admiralty Island	AK	Richard J. Callahan	1991	9
23 10/16	15 2/16	8 8/16	F	Port Heiden	AK	George P. Mann	1989	10
23 6/16	14 6/16	9 0/16	M	Kodiak Island	AK	Gordon Longville	1961	11
23 4/16	14 11/16	8 9/16	M	Admiralty Island	AK	John R. Thiele	1984	12
23 4/16	15 3/16	8 1/16	F	Joshua Green River	AK	John Koldeway	1985	12
22 15/16	14 2/16	8 13/16	F	Sheepcreek-Valdez	AK	Gerald R. Gold	1966	14
22 7/16	14 2/16	8 5/16	F	Merrill Pass	AK	Ralph Ertz	1975	15
22 6/16	14 4/16	8 2/16	M	Kodiak Island	AK	Buddy Watson	1965	16
22 5/16	14 9/16	7 12/16	M	Portage Creek	AK	John "Jack" C. Culpepper	1991	17
21 15/16	14 7/16	7 8/16	M	Kajulik Bay	AK	Thomas J. Hoffman	1983	18
21 13/16	13 15/16	7 14/16	F	Merrill Pass	AK	Dan Hollingsworth	1975	19
21 13/16	13 4/16	8 9/16	F	Dana Glacier	AK	Dan W. Morrison	1975	19
21 10/16	13 14/16	7 12/16	F	Alaska Peninsula	AK	Bill Van Houten	1961	21
21 9/16	14 4/16	7 5/16	M	Alaska Peninsula	AK	Kurt Lepping	1989	22
21 8/16	13 9/16	7 15/16	M	Hoonah	AK	Len Cardinale	1979	23
21 7/16	13 8/16	7 15/16	F	Fidalgo Bay	AK	Joseph West	1966	24
21 7/16	14 1/16	7 6/16	M	Chichagof Island	AK	Ray Keenan	1984	24
21 7/16	13 11/16	7 12/16	M	Clear Creek	AK	Eric Colledge	1992	24
21 6/16	13 13/16	7 9/16	F	Imuya Bay	AK	J. Dale Hale	1991	27
21 2/16	13 14/16	7 4/16	M	Anachuck River	AK	Martin Hanson	1958	28
21 1/16	13 12/16	7 5/16	F	Mat-Su Borough	AK	Rickie D. Snell	1985	29
20 15/16	13 4/16	7 11/16	M	Admiralty Island	AK	Allen L. Grierson	1985	30
20 12/16	13 8/16	7 4/16	F	King Salmon	AK	Rhonda Baker	1977	31
20 11/16	13 9/16	7 2/16	M	Talkeetna Mtns.	AK	L.M. Peppers	1983	32
20 1/16	12 14/16	7 3/16	M	Fog Lakes	AK	Dennis L. Lattery	1984	33

World Record Black Bear
Score: 22 8/16
Kanawha County, West Virginia - 1991
Hunter: Glenn Murphy/Victor Ryan

BLACK BEAR

Ursus americanus americanus
and related subspecies

SCORE	GREATEST LENGTH	GREATEST WIDTH	SEX	AREA	STATE/ PROVINCE	HUNTER'S NAME	DATE	RANK
22 8/16	14 1/16	8 7/16	M	Kanawha County	WV	G. Murphy / V. Ryan	1991	1
22 6/16	13 12/16	8 10/16	M	Gronlid	SAS	Floyd Forster	1992	2
22 4/16	13 7/16	8 13/16	M	Sinbad Ridge	CO	Ray Cox	1978	3
22 0/16	13 11/16	8 5/16	M	Lincoln County	WI	Bob Faufau	1981	4
22 0/16	13 12/16	8 4/16	M	Prince of Wales Island	AK	George P. Mann	1991	4
22 0/16	13 10/16	8 6/16	M	Bronson Lake	SAS	Roger Fournier	1992	4
21 15/16	13 13/16	8 2/16	M	Prince of Wales Island	AK	Stanley L. Parkerson	1991	7
21 14/16	13 7/16	8 7/16	M	Prince of Wales Island	AK	Jim Ponciano	1990	8
21 13/16	13 9/16	8 4/16	M	Idaho County	ID	Harold Boyack	1976	9
21 13/16	13 1/16	8 12/16	M	Dog Lake	ONT	Larry Murray	1990	9
21 13/16	14 4/16	7 9/16	M	Rossburn	MAN	Barry Minshull	1990	9
21 12/16	13 5/16	8 7/16	M	Price County	WI	Robert Brotske	1981	12
21 12/16	13 6/16	8 6/16	M	Big River	SAS	Bill Dear	1985	12
21 12/16	13 3/16	8 9/16	M	Prince of Wales Island	AK	Mark Robecker	1991	12
21 12/16	13 10/16	8 2/16	M	Alonsa	MAN	Cory Mozdzen	1991	12
21 12/16	13 6/16	8 6/16	M	Peace River	ALB	Mike Scott	1992	12
21 11/16	13 9/16	8 2/16	M	Nipawin	SAS	Ray Mastel	1974	17
21 11/16	13 7/16	8 4/16	M	Sevier County	UT	Robert F. Fitzgerald	1984	17
21 10/16	13 6/16	8 4/16	M	Hudson Bay	SAS	Craig Richardson	1985	19
21 10/16	13 5/16	8 5/16	M	Grande Prairie	ALB	Blair Trout	1989	19
21 10/16	13 10/16	8 0/16	M	Prince of Wales Island	AK	James E. Hodson	1991	19
21 10/16	12 15/16	8 11/16	M	Winifred Lake	ALB	Cornel Yarmoloy	1992	19
21 9/16	13 5/16	8 4/16	M	Iron County	WI	Gary Johnson	1982	23
21 9/16	13 9/16	8 0/16	M	Bay Tree	ALB	David E. Samuel	1990	23
21 8/16	13 6/16	8 2/16	M	Hudson Bay	SAS	Garry Benson	1976	25
21 8/16	13 2/16	8 6/16	M	Kern County	CA	Dean M. Lutge	1981	25
21 7/16	13 7/16	8 0/16	M	Nipawin	SAS	Don Adams	1975	27
21 7/16	13 7/16	8 0/16	M	Mendocino County	CA	Jim Oliver	1984	27
21 7/16	13 0/16	8 7/16	M	Garfield County	CO	Norman J. O'Bryan	1985	27
21 6/16	13 6/16	8 0/16	M	Bayfield County	WI	Larry L. Frye	1975	30
21 6/16	13 6/16	8 0/16	M	Grant County	WV	Carnie Carr, Sr.	1988	30
21 6/16	13 4/16	8 2/16	M	North Hudson Bay	SAS	Malcolm Garratt	1991	30
21 6/16	13 2/16	8 4/16	M	York County	NBW	Kenneth J. Fluck	1991	30
21 5/16	13 5/16	8 0/16	M	Ministikwan	SAS	Gary Mutter	1985	34
21 5/16	13 0/16	8 5/16	M	Kenora	ONT	Robert Svoboda	1986	34
21 5/16	13 2/16	8 3/16	M	Swan River	MAN	Richard C. Weber	1991	34
21 5/16	12 14/16	8 7/16	M	Sawyer County	WI	Mark Heath	1991	34
21 5/16	13 4/16	8 1/16	M	Prince of Wales Island	AK	Rick Schikora	1992	34
21 5/16	12 12/16	8 9/16	M	Terrace	BC	Wayne Topolewski	1992	34
21 5/16	13 8/16	7 13/16	M	Sawyer County	WI	Steve Bouton	1992	34
21 4/16	13 7/16	7 13/16	M	Tehama County	CA	Jim Cox	1980	41
21 4/16	13 5/16	7 15/16	M	Cass County	MN	Myles Keller	1980	41
21 4/16	13 4/16	8 0/16	M	Duck Mtn.	MAN	Dave Cordes	1984	41
21 4/16	13 8/16	7 12/16	M	Spiritwood	SAS	Ron Schira	1985	41
21 4/16	13 4/16	8 0/16	M	Mille Lacs County	MN	Timothy J. Dusbabek	1987	41
21 4/16	13 1/16	8 3/16	M	Catron County	NM	Gary L. Raney	1988	41
21 4/16	13 0/16	8 4/16	M	Ketchikan	AK	Doug Miller	1989	41
21 4/16	13 5/16	7 15/16	M	Flatbush	ALB	Dave Falls	1990	41
21 4/16	13 4/16	8 0/16	M	Flotten Lake	SAS	Michael S. Meier	1991	41
21 3/16	13 0/16	8 3/16	M	Eaglehead Lake	ONT	Ty Sweeney	1986	50
21 3/16	12 15/16	8 4/16	M	Lane County	OR	Ray Cross	1989	50
21 3/16	13 3/16	8 0/16	M	Prince of Wales Island	AK	George P. Mann	1990	50
21 3/16	13 7/16	7 12/16	M	Assinaboine River	SAS	Rodney S. Petrychyn	1991	50
21 3/16	13 1/16	8 2/16	M	Catron County	NM	John M. Burton, Jr.	1991	50
21 2/16	13 2/16	8 0/16	M	Madera County	CA	Clarke Merrill	1963	55
21 2/16	13 7/16	7 12/16	M	Hubbard County	MN	Dean Como	1974	55
21 2/16	13 4/16	7 14/16	M	Hudson Bay	SAS	Sam Qualls	1981	55
21 2/16	13 10/16	7 8/16	M	Langlade County	WI	Mike Steliga	1981	55
21 2/16	13 6/16	7 12/16	M	Rockingham County	VA	Roger O. Wyant	1984	55
21 2/16	13 1/16	8 1/16	M	Caribou County	ID	Ronald J. Thompson	1986	55
21 2/16	12 14/16	8 4/16	M	Herkimer County	NY	John Palmer	1986	55
21 2/16	13 4/16	7 14/16	M	Glaslyn	SAS	Tony L. Johnson	1989	55
21 2/16	13 0/16	8 2/16	M	Jackson County	OR	Brian Day	1989	55
21 2/16	13 9/16	7 9/16	M	Prairie River	SAS	Tom White	1991	55
21 1/16	13 1/16	8 0/16	M	Hubbard County	MN	Darrell Magnussen	1974	65
21 1/16	13 2/16	7 15/16	M	Quetico Provincial Park	ONT	Robert Filbrandt	1981	65
21 1/16	13 1/16	8 0/16	M	Cass County	MN	John Hughes	1987	65
21 1/16	13 1/16	8 0/16	M	Lincoln County	WI	Daniel Lemke	1987	65
21 1/16	12 13/16	8 4/16	M	Siskiyou County	CA	Jules Pacheco	1987	65
21 1/16	13 1/16	8 0/16	M	Charlevoix County	MI	Gerald L. Fuller	1988	65

SCORE	GREATEST LENGTH	GREATEST WIDTH	SEX	AREA	STATE/ PROVINCE	HUNTER'S NAME	DATE	RANK
21 1/16	13 0/16	8 1/16	M	Kanawha County	WV	Brian Petty	1991	65
21 0/16	12 13/16	8 3/16	M	Sioux Narrows	ONT	R. B. Cooley	1960	72
21 0/16	12 14/16	8 2/16	M	Uncompahgre N.F.	CO	Dr. James Emerson	1974	72
21 0/16	13 3/16	7 13/16	M	Shasta County	CA	Norman Mallonee	1974	72
21 0/16	13 3/16	7 13/16	M	Ashland County	WI	Bryan C. Anderson	1980	72
21 0/16	13 2/16	7 14/16	M	Yavapai County	AZ	Mike Whelan	1981	72
21 0/16	13 2/16	7 14/16	M	Riding Mtn.	MAN	James A. Carson	1982	72
21 0/16	13 2/16	7 14/16	M	Sawyer County	WI	John G. Bohmann	1982	72
21 0/16	12 15/16	8 1/16	M	Kosciusko Island	AK	Michael C. Fezatte	1982	72
21 0/16	13 3/16	7 13/16	M	Langlade County	WI	Michael Steliga	1982	72
21 0/16	13 4/16	7 12/16	M	Hudson Bay	SAS	Archie Lovelace	1983	72
21 0/16	12 10/16	8 6/16	M	Echouani Lake	QUE	Collins F. Kellogg	1985	72
21 0/16	13 3/16	7 13/16	M	Debden	SAS	Allan Sykes	1986	72
21 0/16	13 1/16	7 15/16	M	Carrot River	SAS	Demetry Procyk	1987	72
21 0/16	13 0/16	8 0/16	M	Carbon County	UT	Lonnie K. Bell	1989	72
21 0/16	12 13/16	8 3/16	M	Iron County	WI	Todd J. Braver	1989	72
21 0/16	13 0/16	8 0/16	M	Le Domaine	QUE	Tony Beceiro	1990	72
21 0/16	12 14/16	8 2/16	M	Lake County	MT	Colin L. Andrews	1990	72
21 0/16	12 12/16	8 4/16	M	Herkimer County	NY	Glen Stedman	1990	72
21 0/16	13 0/16	8 0/16	M	Ventura County	CA	Jeff Prentice	1991	72
21 0/16	13 1/16	7 15/16	M	Peace River	ALB	Doug Walker	1991	72
21 0/16	13 1/16	7 15/16	M	Prince of Wales Island	AK	Rick M. Young	1992	72
20 15/16	13 4/16	7 11/16	M	Sequoia National Forest	CA	Robert Shilling	1971	93
20 15/16	12 12/16	8 3/16	M	Lincoln County	WI	Jay Manthei	1980	93
20 15/16	13 1/16	7 14/16	M	Nipawan	SAS	Glen Sellsted	1981	93
20 15/16	12 14/16	8 1/16	M	Goodsoil	SAS	Ralph Clarke	1982	93
20 15/16	12 11/16	8 4/16	M	Routt County	CO	Mark A. Chapman	1982	93
20 15/16	13 0/16	7 15/16	M	Monominto	MAN	Erik Thienpondt	1983	93
20 15/16	12 15/16	8 0/16	M	Meadow Lake	SAS	Bruce Stieber	1986	93
20 15/16	12 11/16	8 4/16	M	Washago	ONT	Chris Marsh	1992	93
20 14/16	12 10/16	8 6/16	M	Mesa County	CO	Richard A. Schreiber	1973	101
20 14/16	13 0/16	7 14/16	M	Prince of Wales Island	AK	Gary G. Smith	1978	101
20 14/16	12 8/16	8 6/16	M	Red Lake	ONT	George Law	1981	101
20 14/16	13 2/16	7 12/16	M	Cass County	MN	Craig Enervold	1982	101
20 14/16	13 6/16	7 8/16	M	Duck Mtn.	MAN	John 'Jack' Cordes	1984	101
20 14/16	12 9/16	8 5/16	M	Routt County	CO	Lonny Vanatta	1984	101
20 14/16	12 12/16	8 2/16	M	Thunder Bay	ONT	Tim Walters	1985	101
20 14/16	12 15/16	7 15/16	M	Camas County	ID	Ed Cushman	1986	101
20 14/16	12 13/16	8 1/16	M	Prince of Wales Island	AK	Kevin Robinson	1988	101
20 14/16	13 2/16	7 12/16	M	Edmonton	ALB	Bruce Nederveld	1990	101
20 14/16	13 0/16	7 14/16	M	Prince of Wales Island	AK	Thomas Chadwick	1991	101
20 14/16	13 2/16	7 12/16	M	Ministikwan Lake	SAS	Brent Maxwell	1992	101
20 13/16	12 12/16	8 1/16	M	Marrns Creek	ID	Joe Schreideler	1977	113
20 13/16	12 11/16	8 2/16	M	Langlade County	WI	Eugene Strong	1978	113
20 13/16	12 14/16	7 15/16	M	Humboldt County	CA	Calvin Farner	1983	113
20 13/16	13 4/16	7 9/16	M	Meadow Lake	SAS	D. Mitch Kottas	1988	113
20 13/16	12 15/16	7 14/16	M	Carrot River	SAS	Mike Palmer	1989	113
20 13/16	12 14/16	7 15/16	M	Pine County	MN	Steven J. Gardas	1989	113
20 13/16	12 15/16	7 14/16	M	Prince of Wales Island	AK	George P. Mann	1992	113
20 13/16	12 13/16	8 0/16	M	Davidson	QUE	Jack Satterfield, Jr.	1992	113
20 12/16	12 12/16	8 0/16	?	Apache County	AZ	Dr. C. G. Clare	1967	121
20 12/16	12 5/16	8 7/16	M	Emmet County	MI	Hawley H. Rhew	1974	121
20 12/16	12 12/16	8 0/16	M	Douglas County	WI	Robert J. Schmidt	1975	121
20 12/16	12 15/16	7 13/16	M	Armstrong	ONT	Paul Mahaney	1977	121
20 12/16	13 0/16	7 12/16	M	San Miguel County	CO	John W. Rowe	1978	121
20 12/16	12 15/16	7 13/16	M	Bonneville County	ID	John Hill	1983	121
20 12/16	12 11/16	8 1/16	M	Prince of Wales Island	AK	Jack Williams	1985	121
20 12/16	12 12/16	8 0/16	M	Carbon County	WY	Steve Powell	1985	121
20 12/16	12 11/16	8 1/16	M	Plumes County	CA	Kevin Hull	1986	121
20 12/16	13 0/16	7 12/16	M	Aitkin County	MN	Merrill D. Holm	1986	121
20 12/16	12 14/16	7 14/16	M	Prince of Wales Island	AK	Kevin Robinson	1988	121
20 12/16	13 0/16	7 12/16	M	Douglas County	WI	Harold Halverson	1990	121
20 12/16	12 11/16	8 1/16	M	Ketchican	AK	Greg Munther	1991	121
20 12/16	12 12/16	8 0/16	M	Lloydminster	SAS	Steve Preziosi	1991	121
20 12/16	13 0/16	7 12/16	M	Athabasca River	ALB	Larry Oppe	1992	121
20 12/16	12 7/16	8 5/16	M	Fort McMurray	ALB	Darrin West	1992	121
20 11/16	12 13/16	7 14/16	M	Thunder Bay	ONT	Mel Johnson	1974	137
20 11/16	12 14/16	7 13/16	M	Pitkin County	CO	Dale W. Gray	1975	137
20 11/16	13 2/16	7 9/16	M	Rio Blanco County	CO	Walter Krom	1976	137
20 11/16	13 2/16	7 9/16	M	Rockingham County	VA	Roger O. Wyant	1982	137

MINIMUM SCORE 18 *(Continued)*

SCORE	GREATEST LENGTH	GREATEST WIDTH	SEX	AREA	STATE/ PROVINCE	HUNTER'S NAME	DATE	RANK
20 11/16	13 2/16	7 9/16	M	Quesnel	BC	Russell Thornberry	1987	137
20 11/16	12 10/16	8 1/16	M	Sunbury County	NBW	Raymond Faulknor	1987	137
20 11/16	12 14/16	7 13/16	M	Chuit River	AK	George P. Mann	1987	137
20 11/16	13 3/16	7 8/16	M	Rappahannock County	VA	Jeff S. Good	1987	137
20 11/16	13 2/16	7 9/16	M	Prince of Wales Island	AK	Tracy Lucas	1989	137
20 11/16	13 0/16	7 11/16	M	Douglas County	WI	Roger W. Hansen	1990	137
20 11/16	13 2/16	7 9/16	M	Prince of Wales Island	AK	Ken A. Vorisek	1991	137
20 11/16	12 15/16	7 12/16	M	Douglas County	WI	Steve Wittke	1992	137
20 10/16	13 1/16	7 9/16	M	Rio Blanco County	CO	Frank 'Rit' Heller	1969	149
20 10/16	12 10/16	8 0/16	M	Sierra County	CA	Ervin K. McMakin	1971	149
20 10/16	12 14/16	7 12/16	M	Ft. Francis	ONT	George Geisert	1973	149
20 10/16	12 10/16	8 0/16	M	Crawford Park	MAN	Brent Mills	1981	149
20 10/16	12 10/16	8 0/16	M	Tweed	ONT	John E. Lawson	1983	149
20 10/16	12 14/16	7 12/16	M	Cass County	MN	James D. Zahalka	1987	149
20 10/16	12 12/16	7 14/16	M	Prince of Wales Island	AK	Danny Moore	1990	149
20 10/16	12 8/16	8 2/16	M	Ravalli County	MT	John C. Locke	1990	149
20 10/16	12 11/16	7 15/16	M	Nairn Township	ONT	Ron Hergott	1990	149
20 10/16	12 13/16	7 13/16	M	Iron County	WI	Jeff Ott	1990	149
20 10/16	13 0/16	7 10/16	M	Stone Lake	ONT	Jack A. Vos	1991	149
20 10/16	12 15/16	7 11/16	M	Pine County	MN	Thomas Behrends	1991	149
20 9/16	12 12/16	7 13/16	M	Lake County	MN	Art A. Heinze	1970	161
20 9/16	12 12/16	7 13/16	M	Prince of Wales Island	AK	Roy C. Ewen	1973	161
20 9/16	12 7/16	8 2/16	M	Grand County	CO	Curt Lynn	1973	161
20 9/16	12 12/16	7 13/16	M	Wawa	ONT	Robert C. McGuire	1975	161
20 9/16	12 11/16	7 14/16	M	Aitkin County	MN	Myles Keller	1977	161
20 9/16	13 1/16	7 8/16	M	Thunder Bay	ONT	Lester W. Jass	1979	161
20 9/16	12 13/16	7 12/16	M	Delta County	CO	Steve McCarthy	1982	161
20 9/16	12 9/16	8 0/16	M	Franklin County	NY	Edward M. Odell	1982	161
20 9/16	12 11/16	7 14/16	M	Missaukee County	MI	Gregory Korkoske	1983	161
20 9/16	12 10/16	7 15/16	M	Northwest of Dryden	ONT	Larry Bauman	1984	161
20 9/16	13 1/16	7 8/16	M	Durban	MAN	David H. Boland	1985	161
20 9/16	12 7/16	8 2/16	M	Thunder Bay	ONT	Daniel Schuttler	1985	161
20 9/16	13 1/16	7 8/16	M	Florence County	WI	Daniel G. Villenauve	1986	161
20 9/16	12 9/16	8 0/16	M	Custer County	ID	Doug Burkman	1987	161
20 9/16	12 10/16	7 15/16	M	Prince of Wales Island	AK	Richard L. Westervelt	1988	161
20 9/16	12 15/16	7 10/16	M	McAdams	NB	David F. Baldwin	1988	161
20 9/16	12 13/16	7 12/16	M	Aroostook County	ME	Danny Corey	1988	161
20 9/16	13 3/16	7 6/16	M	Douglas County	WI	Steve Peterson	1988	161
20 9/16	12 10/16	7 15/16	M	Marinette County	WI	Perry Kosek	1988	161
20 9/16	13 1/16	7 8/16	M	Poplarfield	MAN	John C. Collins	1991	161
20 9/16	13 0/16	7 9/16	M	Catron County	NM	Patty Foley	1991	161
20 9/16	13 1/16	7 8/16	M	Summit County	UT	Maury Butterfield	1992	161
20 9/16	13 6/16	7 3/16	M	Sudbury	ONT	Vinnie Pisani	1992	161
20 8/16	12 13/16	7 11/16	M	Queen Charlotte Islands	BC	Peter Halbig	1960	184
20 8/16	12 14/16	7 10/16	M	Shawano County	WI	Bud Wiesman	1974	184
20 8/16	12 14/16	7 10/16	M	Kamsack	SAS	Steve Boychuk	1977	184
20 8/16	12 14/16	7 10/16	M	Tehama County	CA	Anthony P. Davi	1980	184
20 8/16	12 11/16	7 13/16	M	Strathnaver	BC	Dan Wicks	1981	184
20 8/16	12 13/16	7 11/16	M	Valley County	ID	Dave Scott	1982	184
20 8/16	12 1/16	8 7/16	M	Ignace	ONT	Jerry Klinesmith	1983	184
20 8/16	13 2/16	7 6/16	M	Cass County	MN	Anne M. Zahalka	1988	184
20 8/16	12 15/16	7 9/16	M	Dryden	ONT	Robert J. Crane	1990	184
20 8/16	12 15/16	7 9/16	M	Nolalu	ONT	Billy Roy Leach	1991	184
20 8/16	12 8/16	8 0/16	M	Tehama County	CA	Kim Cooper	1991	184
20 8/16	12 11/16	7 13/16	M	Pitkin County	CO	Stanley E. Lauriski	1992	184
20 8/16	12 10/16	7 14/16	M	Mendocino County	CA	James W. Rutledge	1992	184
20 7/16	13 9/16	6 14/16	M	Nenana	AK	Robert Dunn	1968	197
20 7/16	12 10/16	7 13/16	M	Price County	WI	Bob Eckarot	1974	197
20 7/16	12 14/16	7 9/16	M	Montezuma County	CO	Bryan C. Neeley	1974	197
20 7/16	12 7/16	8 0/16	M	Whiteshell	MAN	Ken Warkentin	1978	197
20 7/16	12 11/16	7 12/16	M	Mille Lacs County	MN	Milt Zernechel	1980	197
20 7/16	12 6/16	8 1/16	M	Marquette County	MI	Thomas Benak	1982	197
20 7/16	12 11/16	7 12/16	M	Mat-Su Borough	AK	Jack V. Rouse	1983	197
20 7/16	12 10/16	7 13/16	M	St. Louis County	MN	Ken Lenk	1983	197
20 7/16	12 12/16	7 11/16	M	Garfield County	CO	Roger Bolander	1985	197
20 7/16	12 14/16	7 9/16	M	Arran	SAS	Bill Clink	1986	197
20 7/16	12 14/16	7 9/16	M	Valleyview	ALB	Stan Walchuk, Jr.	1986	197
20 7/16	12 11/16	7 12/16	M	Routt County	CO	Bill Grammer	1987	197
20 7/16	12 4/16	8 3/16	M	Atikokan	ONT	Kenny Stoner	1988	197
20 7/16	12 12/16	7 11/16	M	Iron County	WI	Brian Tessmann	1989	197

SCORE	GREATEST LENGTH	GREATEST WIDTH	SEX	AREA	STATE/ PROVINCE	HUNTER'S NAME	DATE	RANK
20 7/16	12 7/16	8 0/16	M	Rappahannock County	VA	Collis W. Dodson, Jr.	1989	197
20 7/16	12 12/16	7 11/16	M	Madera County	CA	James Joseph Doherty,Jr.	1991	197
20 7/16	12 12/16	7 11/16	M	Spirit River	ALB	Jim Stinson	1992	197
20 7/16	12 11/16	7 12/16	M	Fort McMurray	ALB	James Pike	1992	197
20 7/16	12 7/16	8 0/16	M	San Bernardino County	CA	Allen Davis	1992	197
20 7/16	13 0/16	7 7/16	M	Douglas County	WI	Mark P. Haan	1992	197
20 6/16	12 11/16	7 11/16	M	Tulare County	CA	Quentin M. Boutch	1967	217
20 6/16	12 11/16	7 11/16	M	Garfield County	CO	Steve Bergman	1970	217
20 6/16	12 15/16	7 7/16	M	Kern County	CA	Leo Farley	1973	217
20 6/16	12 8/16	7 14/16	M	Shasta County	CA	Susan Mallonee	1974	217
20 6/16	12 6/16	8 0/16	M	Saguache County	CO	Ed Wiseman	1975	217
20 6/16	12 11/16	7 11/16	M	Reindeer Lake	SAS	James Buchanan	1976	217
20 6/16	12 12/16	7 10/16	M	Flower Station	ONT	Richard H. Shoup	1977	217
20 6/16	12 9/16	7 13/16	M	Ear Falls	ONT	Terry R. Fletcher	1978	217
20 6/16	12 11/16	7 11/16	M	St. Louis County	MN	Russell Wimberly	1979	217
20 6/16	12 11/16	7 11/16	M	Reserve	SAS	Richard Loffler	1984	217
20 6/16	12 14/16	7 8/16	M	Bayfield County	WI	Paul Deckert	1984	217
20 6/16	12 9/16	7 13/16	M	Ignace	ONT	Randy J. Tylke	1985	217
20 6/16	13 2/16	7 4/16	M	Meadow Lake	SAS	Craig Larson	1986	217
20 6/16	12 5/16	8 1/16	M	Spiritwood	SAS	Robert W. Peet	1987	217
20 6/16	12 8/16	7 14/16	M	Wrangel Island	AK	Bob Smith	1987	217
20 6/16	12 13/16	7 9/16	M	Athabasca	ALB	John Visscher	1988	217
20 6/16	12 14/16	7 8/16	M	Hudson Bay	SAS	Kendall Haberstroh	1988	217
20 6/16	12 8/16	7 14/16	M	Rochester	ALB	Dave Gerber	1988	217
20 6/16	12 13/16	7 9/16	M	Wandering River	ALB	Warren Witherspoon	1988	217
20 6/16	12 10/16	7 12/16	M	Wallowa County	OR	Russell McCall	1989	217
20 6/16	12 15/16	7 7/16	M	Pine County	MN	Thomas Behrends	1989	217
20 6/16	12 14/16	7 8/16	M	Ashland County	WI	James A. Liermann	1989	217
20 6/16	12 9/16	7 13/16	M	Lac Forant	QUE	Harold Shepard	1990	217
20 6/16	12 10/16	7 12/16	M	La Plata County	CO	Paul Nichols	1991	217
20 6/16	12 10/16	7 12/16	M	Clearwater County	ID	Steve Stajkowski	1991	217
20 6/16	12 11/16	7 11/16	M	Iron County	MI	Jeff Fontecchio	1991	217
20 6/16	12 7/16	7 15/16	M	Missoula County	MT	Rick L. Stone	1991	217
20 6/16	12 6/16	8 0/16	M	Plumas County	CA	Bill Graves	1991	217
20 6/16	13 0/16	7 6/16	M	Hubbard County	MN	Hal Dickelman	1992	217
20 5/16	12 14/16	7 7/16	M	Shasta County	CA	Harv Ebers	1964	246
20 5/16	12 12/16	7 9/16	M	St. Louis County	MN	Jay Deones	1970	246
20 5/16	12 13/16	7 8/16	M	Buncombe County	NC	Robert T. Austin	1971	246
20 5/16	13 0/16	7 5/16	M	Emma Lake	SAS	Ernie Johnston	1972	246
20 5/16	12 4/16	8 1/16	M	Montezuma County	CO	Stanley A. Coval	1975	246
20 5/16	12 11/16	7 10/16	M	Montrose County	CO	Jack Cassidy	1976	246
20 5/16	12 11/16	7 10/16	M	Lemhi County	ID	Richard R. Smith	1977	246
20 5/16	12 10/16	7 11/16	M	Lincoln County	NM	Tom Mitchell	1978	246
20 5/16	12 12/16	7 9/16	M	Marquette County	MI	Bernard E. Stiritz	1980	246
20 5/16	12 9/16	7 12/16	M	Hudson Bay	SAS	Sam Qualls	1981	246
20 5/16	12 13/16	7 8/16	M	Bonneville County	ID	Michael Ferraro	1981	246
20 5/16	12 3/16	8 2/16	M	Presque Isle County	MI	William C. Green III	1981	246
20 5/16	12 9/16	7 12/16	M	Deviin Lake	ONT	J. E. Abhold	1982	246
20 5/16	12 5/16	8 0/16	M	Meagher County	MT	Richard M. Campbell	1982	246
20 5/16	12 12/16	7 9/16	M	Otero County	NM	Michael Crabb	1984	246
20 5/16	12 7/16	7 14/16	M	Atikokan	ONT	Greg Morehead	1985	246
20 5/16	12 8/16	7 13/16	M	Archuleta County	CO	Ronald J. Murphy	1985	246
20 5/16	12 6/16	7 15/16	M	Jackson County	OR	David Greisen, Jr.	1985	246
20 5/16	12 10/16	7 11/16	M	Ontonagon County	MI	Dale W. Gray	1986	246
20 5/16	12 9/16	7 12/16	M	Siskiyou County	CA	Bob Jensen	1986	246
20 5/16	12 7/16	7 14/16	M	Gila County	AZ	Eric Pierce	1987	246
20 5/16	12 10/16	7 11/16	M	Douglas County	WI	William T. Solie	1987	246
20 5/16	12 12/16	7 9/16	M	Prince of Wales Island	AK	Mike Taylor	1989	246
20 5/16	12 4/16	8 1/16	M	Okanogan County	WA	D. Kirk Sapp	1989	246
20 5/16	12 10/16	7 11/16	M	Lincoln County	WI	Gerald O. Arndt	1989	246
20 5/16	13 0/16	7 5/16	M	Mesa County	CO	Paul Alan Seidelman	1989	246
20 5/16	12 12/16	7 9/16	M	Lac La Biche	ALB	Ronald H. Haver	1990	246
20 5/16	12 9/16	7 12/16	M	Prince of Wales Island	AK	Timothy Putnam	1991	246
20 5/16	12 6/16	7 15/16	M	Shasta County	CA	Douglas Trouette	1991	246
20 5/16	12 7/16	7 14/16	M	Skownan	MAN	Walt Krom	1992	246
20 4/16	12 6/16	7 14/16	M	Oceana County	MI	William Benson	1967	276
20 4/16	12 11/16	7 9/16	M	Somerset County	ME	Felix Nosewicz	1968	276
20 4/16	12 10/16	7 10/16	M	Mesa County	CO	M. R. James	1971	276
20 4/16	12 12/16	7 8/16	M	Los Alamos County	NM	Kenneth A. Meyer	1971	276
20 4/16	12 12/16	7 8/16	M	Sawyer County	WI	George Geisert	1972	276

Score	Greatest Length	Greatest Width	Sex	Area	State/ Province	Hunter's Name	Date	Rank
20 4/16	12 7/16	7 13/16	M	Madison County	MT	Bob Savage	1977	276
20 4/16	12 5/16	7 15/16	M	Kashabowie	ONT	Hans C. Forssell	1978	276
20 4/16	12 7/16	7 13/16	M	Valora	ONT	Elmer R. Luse, Jr.	1981	276
20 4/16	12 8/16	7 12/16	M	Siskiyou County	CA	Bill Waters	1981	276
20 4/16	12 8/16	7 12/16	M	Mesa County	CO	Larry A. McIntosh	1982	276
20 4/16	12 5/16	7 15/16	M	Nez Perce County	ID	Hubert M. Sims, Jr.	1982	276
20 4/16	12 7/16	7 13/16	M	Trinity County	CA	Rodney A. York	1983	276
20 4/16	12 8/16	7 12/16	M	Rockingham County	VA	Charles Larry Danner	1984	276
20 4/16	12 12/16	7 8/16	M	Carrot River	SAS	William Jorgensen	1985	276
20 4/16	12 8/16	7 12/16	M	Swan River	MAN	Marc N. Shaft	1985	276
20 4/16	12 11/16	7 9/16	M	Waterhen River	SAS	Pink Atkins	1986	276
20 4/16	12 10/16	7 10/16	M	Mat-Su Valley	AK	Bill Parker	1987	276
20 4/16	12 6/16	7 14/16	M	Wrangel Island	AK	Bob Smith	1987	276
20 4/16	12 10/16	7 10/16	M	Canoe Lake	SAS	Richard Robert Ritzel	1988	276
20 4/16	12 10/16	7 10/16	M	Prince of Wales Island	AK	Danny Moore	1989	276
20 4/16	12 5/16	7 15/16	M	Cranberry Portage	MAN	Dean K. Reidt	1989	276
20 4/16	12 14/16	7 6/16	M	King County	WA	Greg Winters	1989	276
20 4/16	12 12/16	7 8/16	M	Olha	MAN	Tim Stahman	1990	276
20 4/16	12 12/16	7 8/16	M	Lanark	ONT	Ben Graham	1990	276
20 4/16	12 7/16	7 13/16	M	Caramat	ONT	Rick Stump	1990	276
20 4/16	12 4/16	8 0/16	M	Dorion	ONT	Bruce Hudalla	1991	276
20 4/16	12 8/16	7 12/16	M	Ignace	ONT	Thomas C. Klinesmith	1991	276
20 4/16	12 10/16	7 10/16	M	Howley	NFL	Roger Lewis	1991	276
20 4/16	12 9/16	7 11/16	M	Lewis County	WA	Kevin R. Amos	1991	276
20 4/16	12 11/16	7 9/16	M	Lane County	OR	Dave Smith	1991	276
20 4/16	12 7/16	7 13/16	M	Madison County	MT	Larry Stackhouse	1992	276
20 3/16	12 13/16	7 6/16	M	Prince Rupert	BC	Frank Huneck	1960	307
20 3/16	12 6/16	7 13/16	M	Ignace	ONT	Jerry Ulrich	1968	307
20 3/16	12 4/16	7 15/16	M	Adams County	ID	Joe Adams	1971	307
20 3/16	12 8/16	7 11/16	M	Coos County	OR	Robert L. Wegand	1971	307
20 3/16	12 3/16	8 0/16	M	Boise County	ID	Mark W. Powell	1975	307
20 3/16	12 12/16	7 7/16	M	Smoke Lake	ALB	Kenneth Szgatti	1975	307
20 3/16	12 6/16	7 13/16	M	Dolores County	CO	Randy E. Dossey	1979	307
20 3/16	12 5/16	7 14/16	M	Dolores County	CO	Marvin Reichenau	1979	307
20 3/16	12 10/16	7 9/16	M	Itasca County	MN	Gerald N. Rivetts, Jr.	1980	307
20 3/16	12 12/16	7 7/16	M	Burnett County	WI	Dan McElfresh	1982	307
20 3/16	12 8/16	7 11/16	M	Foxford	SAS	Brian Acton	1982	307
20 3/16	12 14/16	7 5/16	M	Loon Lake	SAS	Dennis Meyer	1984	307
20 3/16	12 13/16	7 6/16	M	Catron County	NM	John R. Caminiti	1984	307
20 3/16	12 3/16	8 0/16	M	Marquette County	MI	Kurt Funk	1985	307
20 3/16	12 13/16	7 6/16	M	Red Lake	ONT	Gerald Dykin	1986	307
20 3/16	12 12/16	7 7/16	M	Sioux Lookout	ONT	Tom Rosenthal	1986	307
20 3/16	12 12/16	7 7/16	M	McMunn	MAN	Rod Black	1987	307
20 3/16	12 11/16	7 8/16	M	Canterbury	NBW	David G. Cote	1987	307
20 3/16	12 4/16	7 15/16	M	Schefferville	QUE	Charles L. Buechel, Jr.	1987	307
20 3/16	12 7/16	7 12/16	M	Iron County	WI	Mike Lutz	1987	307
20 3/16	12 13/16	7 6/16	M	Ft. Assiniboine	ALB	Wes Skakun	1988	307
20 3/16	12 8/16	7 11/16	M	Pine County	MN	Ed Nielsen	1989	307
20 3/16	12 8/16	7 11/16	M	Houghton County	MI	Loren G. Baker	1989	307
20 3/16	13 2/16	7 1/16	M	Chisago County	MN	Dennis Jaworski	1989	307
20 3/16	12 8/16	7 11/16	M	Coconino County	AZ	William Bedlion	1989	307
20 3/16	12 10/16	7 9/16	M	Goodsoil	SAS	Larry H. Hoyt	1990	307
20 3/16	12 5/16	7 14/16	M	Lac La Biche	ALB	Jesse Meyer	1991	307
20 3/16	12 10/16	7 9/16	M	LaLoche	SAS	Robert Bramlett	1992	307
20 3/16	12 11/16	7 8/16	M	Wabasca River	ALB	Greg Duncan	1992	307
20 3/16	12 4/16	7 15/16	M	Chapleau	ONT	J. R. Mester	1992	307
20 2/16	12 9/16	7 9/16	M	St. Louis County	MN	James Harwood	1966	337
20 2/16	12 9/16	7 9/16	M	St. Louis County	MN	Ron Johnson	1968	337
20 2/16	12 6/16	7 12/16	M	Bayfield County	WI	Clarence J. Biddle	1973	337
20 2/16	12 6/16	7 12/16	M	Iron County	WI	Chuck Ramsay	1973	337
20 2/16	12 9/16	7 9/16	M	Delta County	CO	Bill Izon	1976	337
20 2/16	12 10/16	7 8/16	M	Montrose County	CO	John Brandt	1978	337
20 2/16	12 1/16	8 1/16	M	Del Norte County	CA	Fred D. Davis, Jr.	1978	337
20 2/16	12 12/16	7 6/16	M	Montezuma County	CO	Floyd H. Hicks	1978	337
20 2/16	12 8/16	7 10/16	M	Mesa County	CO	Dennis Behn	1979	337
20 2/16	12 9/16	7 9/16	M	Delta County	CO	Scott Dillon	1981	337
20 2/16	12 6/16	7 12/16	M	Mendocino County	CA	Kenneth Marquardt	1981	337
20 2/16	12 12/16	7 6/16	M	Tehama County	CA	Randy Rehse	1981	337
20 2/16	12 2/16	7 6/16	M	Hudson Bay	SAS	Randy Lorenz	1982	337
20 2/16	12 7/16	7 11/16	M	Iron County	MI	George J. Hronkin III	1982	337

BLACK BEAR

(Continued)

Score	Greatest Length	Greatest Width	Sex	Area	State/ Province	Hunter's Name	Date	Rank
20 2/16	12 10/16	7 8/16	M	Douglas County	WI	Ron Ekstrand	1983	337
20 2/16	12 6/16	7 12/16	M	Kuiu Island	AK	William F. Burgess	1984	337
20 2/16	12 7/16	7 11/16	M	Meadow Lake	SAS	Richard W. Theurer	1984	337
20 2/16	12 8/16	7 10/16	M	Nipigon	ONT	Richard Scorzafava	1985	337
20 2/16	12 4/16	7 14/16	M	Sudbury	ONT	Ben L. Staponski	1986	337
20 2/16	13 1/16	7 1/16	M	Sudbury	ONT	Frank Calabro	1986	337
20 2/16	12 13/16	7 5/16	M	Chisago County	MN	Mark Piel	1986	337
20 2/16	12 6/16	7 12/16	M	Mendocino County	CA	Patrick M. Griffin	1986	337
20 2/16	12 8/16	7 10/16	M	Lake of the Woods	ONT	Karen Raasch	1987	337
20 2/16	12 8/16	7 10/16	M	Duchesne County	UT	Kenneth M. Labrum	1988	337
20 2/16	12 6/16	7 12/16	M	El Paso County	CO	Russ Nily	1988	337
20 2/16	12 14/16	7 4/16	M	Pine County	MN	Brian D. Scarnegie	1988	337
20 2/16	12 7/16	7 11/16	M	Crawford County	MI	Jerry D. Pratt	1988	337
20 2/16	12 8/16	7 10/16	M	Meadow Lake	SAS	Ian Twidale	1989	337
20 2/16	13 0/16	7 2/16	M	Beltrami County	MN	James Luverne Johnson	1989	337
20 2/16	12 7/16	7 11/16	M	Marathon County	WI	Daniel Auner	1989	337
20 2/16	12 9/16	7 9/16	M	Sullivan County	NY	John P. Dise	1989	337
20 2/16	12 8/16	7 10/16	M	Rabun County	GA	Terry Tyler	1989	337
20 2/16	12 8/16	7 10/16	M	Catron County	NM	Larry Joe Cearley	1990	337
20 2/16	12 10/16	7 8/16	M	Latah County	ID	Mick McCullough	1990	337
20 2/16	12 7/16	7 11/16	M	Fort McMurray	ALB	Ron LeBreton	1990	337
20 2/16	12 11/16	7 7/16	M	Kuiu Island	AK	Joe Miguel	1991	337
20 2/16	12 8/16	7 10/16	M	Fort McMurray	ALB	Fred Joseph	1991	337
20 2/16	12 8/16	7 10/16	M	Fort McMurray	ALB	Margaret Whittle Hice	1991	337
20 2/16	12 8/16	7 10/16	M	Rabun County	GA	Chuck Conner	1991	337
20 2/16	12 10/16	7 8/16	M	Otero County	NM	Beto Gutierrez	1991	337
20 2/16	12 12/16	7 6/16	M	Monds Township	ONT	Jeff Standafer	1992	337
20 2/16	12 4/16	7 14/16	M	Square Lake	ALB	Dave Stull	1992	337
20 2/16	12 6/16	7 12/16	M	Peace River	ALB	John Lindell	1992	337
20 1/16	12 9/16	7 8/16	M	Shasta County	CA	Robert G. Sinclair	1967	380
20 1/16	12 5/16	7 12/16	M	Nipigon	ONT	Wilfred J. Ritchie, Jr.	1968	380
20 1/16	12 6/16	7 11/16	M	Vilas County	WI	Ben Jones	1972	380
20 1/16	11 15/16	8 2/16	M	Deep Creek, Ruby	AK	Harry Copeland	1976	380
20 1/16	12 10/16	7 7/16	M	Cowlitz County	WA	Smokey Crews	1976	380
20 1/16	12 10/16	7 7/16	M	Kitsap County	WA	Bud Jones	1977	380
20 1/16	12 4/16	7 13/16	M	Montrose County	CO	Mike Barber	1978	380
20 1/16	12 10/16	7 7/16	M	E. Braintree	MAN	Ed Beamish	1979	380
20 1/16	12 0/16	8 1/16	M	Vilas County	WI	Peter J. Leder	1979	380
20 1/16	12 10/16	7 7/16	M	Grand County	UT	Thomas W. Newman	1979	380
20 1/16	12 4/16	7 13/16	M	Archuleta County	CO	Len Cardinale	1980	380
20 1/16	12 3/16	7 14/16	M	Archuleta County	CO	Judd Cooney	1980	380
20 1/16	12 10/16	7 7/16	M	Mistatim	SAS	Gregory Simoneau	1980	380
20 1/16	12 5/16	7 12/16	M	Fremont County	ID	Nancy Atwood	1981	380
20 1/16	12 6/16	7 11/16	M	Clark County	ID	Garry James Kite	1981	380
20 1/16	12 6/16	7 11/16	M	Hudson Bay	SAS	Jerry Bien	1982	380
20 1/16	12 9/16	7 8/16	M	Glenn County	CA	Ron Fonseca	1982	380
20 1/16	12 6/16	7 11/16	M	Hudson Bay	SAS	Craig Richardson	1982	380
20 1/16	13 0/16	7 1/16	M	Bladen County	NC	R. G. Harris	1983	380
20 1/16	12 8/16	7 9/16	M	Fergus County	MT	Tom Storm	1984	380
20 1/16	12 1/16	8 0/16	M	Powell County	MT	Gene Coughlin	1984	380
20 1/16	12 4/16	7 13/16	M	Lost Lake	ONT	Gunter Lemke	1985	380
20 1/16	12 7/16	7 10/16	M	Lewis County	WA	Keith Heldreth	1985	380
20 1/16	12 5/16	7 12/16	M	Siskiyou County	CA	Stan Allison	1985	380
20 1/16	12 10/16	7 7/16	M	Hudson Bay	SAS	Bill Zahradka	1987	380
20 1/16	12 5/16	7 12/16	M	Ft. McMurray	ALB	Reg Adair	1987	380
20 1/16	12 4/16	7 13/16	M	Sevier County	UT	Tom Dale Harrison	1988	380
20 1/16	12 7/16	7 10/16	M	Carbon County	WY	Bill McEwen	1988	380
20 1/16	12 8/16	7 9/16	M	Ft. McMurray	ALB	Darrin West	1989	380
20 1/16	12 3/16	7 14/16	M	Williams Lake	BC	Don Davidson	1989	380
20 1/16	12 8/16	7 9/16	M	Sioux Lookout	ONT	Jim Graf	1989	380
20 1/16	12 8/16	7 9/16	M	Dryden	ONT	Alan E. Forbes	1989	380
20 1/16	12 11/16	7 6/16	M	Clatsop County	OR	David Soyars	1989	380
20 1/16	12 11/16	7 6/16	M	Keweenaw County	MI	Fred Embry Pickett	1989	380
20 1/16	12 11/16	7 6/16	M	Flatbush	ALB	Steve Neuberger	1990	380
20 1/16	12 8/16	7 9/16	M	Glenfell	ONT	Lucien Fecteau	1990	380
20 1/16	12 9/16	7 8/16	M	Prince of Wales Island	AK	Dennis Sturgis, Jr.	1990	380
20 1/16	12 6/16	7 11/16	M	Aitkin County	MN	William Gene Kuhlman	1990	380
20 1/16	12 10/16	7 7/16	M	Tulare County	CA	Dean Grommet	1991	380
20 1/16	12 9/16	7 8/16	M	Union County	OR	Gregg Hargett	1991	380
20 1/16	12 2/16	7 15/16	M	Prince of Wales Island	AK	Don Davidson	1991	380

Score	Greatest Length	Greatest Width	Sex	Area	State/ Province	Hunter's Name	Date	Rank
20 1/16	12 7/16	7 10/16	M	Harney County	OR	Marti Boatman	1991	380
20 1/16	12 15/16	7 2/16	M	Whitemouth Lake	MAN	Serge L. Proulx	1991	380
20 0/16	12 10/16	7 6/16	M	Oneida County	WI	Fred Felbab	1964	423
20 0/16	12 4/16	7 12/16	M	Shasta County	CA	Jim Dougherty	1970	423
20 0/16	13 4/16	6 12/16	M	Cumberland County	TN	Louis Wix	1970	423
20 0/16	12 11/16	7 5/16	M	Fremont County	ID	Earl Peterson	1978	423
20 0/16	12 4/16	7 12/16	M	Kalkaska County	MI	Doug Daniels	1978	423
20 0/16	12 9/16	7 7/16	M	Adams County	ID	Jack Arbaugh	1979	423
20 0/16	12 10/16	7 6/16	M	Tehama County	CA	Jim Dueval	1980	423
20 0/16	12 7/16	7 9/16	M	Prince George	BC	Ron F. McKay	1980	423
20 0/16	12 10/16	7 6/16	M	Ear Falls	ONT	Richard Eldridge	1981	423
20 0/16	12 6/16	7 10/16	M	Red Lake	ONT	Donald Schram	1981	423
20 0/16	12 5/16	7 11/16	M	Grand County	CO	Randy O. Vineyard	1981	423
20 0/16	12 6/16	7 10/16	M	Bobcaygeon	ONT	Arthur H. Whitney	1982	423
20 0/16	12 7/16	7 9/16	M	Sierra County	NM	Ray Hatfield	1983	423
20 0/16	12 5/16	7 11/16	M	Otter Lake	QUE	C. Roger Jerzerick	1983	423
20 0/16	12 3/16	7 13/16	M	Wallowa County	OR	Bill Lancaster	1983	423
20 0/16	12 7/16	7 9/16	M	Itasca County	MN	Roger Millard	1984	423
20 0/16	12 6/16	7 10/16	M	Apache County	AZ	Robert E. David	1984	423
20 0/16	12 8/16	7 8/16	M	Langlade County	WI	Jeff Traska	1984	423
20 0/16	12 2/16	7 14/16	M	Cowlitz County	WA	Annette Crews	1985	423
20 0/16	12 12/16	7 4/16	M	Meadow Lake	SAS	Robert Bain	1986	423
20 0/16	12 3/16	7 13/16	M	Thunder Bay	ONT	Bob Vrbsky	1986	423
20 0/16	12 8/16	7 8/16	M	Caribou County	ID	Coby Tigert	1986	423
20 0/16	12 15/16	7 1/16	M	Aitkin County	MN	Scott H. Mogen	1986	423
20 0/16	12 12/16	7 4/16	M	Rockingham County	VA	Roger Wyant	1986	423
20 0/16	12 8/16	7 8/16	M	Cold Lake	ALB	Glenn Moir	1987	423
20 0/16	12 6/16	7 10/16	M	Pinehurst Lake	ALB	Jay Stewart	1988	423
20 0/16	12 11/16	7 5/16	M	King County	WA	Brent R. Perschon	1988	423
20 0/16	12 11/16	7 5/16	M	Lake of the Woods Co.	MN	Dallas Vanden Einde	1988	423
20 0/16	12 5/16	7 11/16	M	Gogebic County	MI	Ted Nugent	1988	423
20 0/16	12 6/16	7 10/16	M	Elmore County	ID	Mark E. Zastrow	1989	423
20 0/16	12 5/16	7 11/16	M	Graham Area	ONT	Ian Robinson	1989	423
20 0/16	12 5/16	7 11/16	M	Carbon County	UT	Dave Scott	1989	423
20 0/16	12 4/16	7 12/16	M	Sudbury	ONT	Ray Hatfield	1989	423
20 0/16	12 8/16	7 8/16	M	High Prairie	ALB	Thomas Hlinka	1989	423
20 0/16	12 8/16	7 8/16	M	Wallowa County	OR	Terry Garbacik	1989	423
20 0/16	12 5/16	7 11/16	M	Iron County	WI	R. Joe Maciejewski	1989	423
20 0/16	12 9/16	7 7/16	M	Crawford County	MI	Jerry D. Pratt	1989	423
20 0/16	12 8/16	7 8/16	M	Catron County	NM	Dr. Dale Mansfield	1989	423
20 0/16	12 10/16	7 6/16	M	Ile-a-LaCrosse	SAS	Michael D Tofte	1990	423
20 0/16	12 6/16	7 10/16	M	Kenora	ONT	Steven G. Dennis	1990	423
20 0/16	12 0/16	8 0/16	M	Seibert Lake	ALB	Keith Dana	1990	423
20 0/16	12 6/16	7 10/16	M	Garfield County	CO	Gus Sexauer	1990	423
20 0/16	12 12/16	7 4/16	M	Fraser River	BC	Dave Hannas	1990	423
20 0/16	12 3/16	7 13/16	M	Cowlitz County	WA	Edward H. Soyars	1991	423
20 0/16	12 6/16	7 10/16	M	Catron County	NM	Bruce Carlisle	1991	423
20 0/16	12 12/16	7 4/16	M	Douglas County	WI	Philip Stener	1991	423
20 0/16	12 7/16	7 9/16	M	Bissett	MAN	David Harris	1992	423
20 0/16	12 12/16	7 4/16	M	Red Earth	ALB	Dave Bathke	1992	423
19 15/16	11 15/16	8 0/16	F	Iron County	WI	Robert W. Blair	1967	471
19 15/16	12 0/16	7 15/16	M	Bayfield County	WI	Gary P. Kalal	1973	471
19 15/16	12 7/16	7 8/16	M	Blind River	ONT	John Lee	1973	471
19 15/16	12 8/16	7 7/16	M	Dryden	ONT	Robert C. Kirschner	1974	471
19 15/16	12 3/16	7 12/16	M	Conejos County	CO	Joseph Strasser, Jr.	1978	471
19 15/16	12 4/16	7 11/16	M	Grande Praire	ALB	Wolf Hoffman	1979	471
19 15/16	12 1/16	7 14/16	M	Gunnison County	CO	Arthur Pace	1980	471
19 15/16	12 8/16	7 7/16	M	Florence County	WI	Peter H. Kortenhorn	1981	471
19 15/16	12 7/16	7 8/16	M	Dolores County	CO	Stanley A. Coval	1981	471
19 15/16	12 2/16	7 13/16	M	Ear Falls	ONT	Mike Woolman	1981	471
19 15/16	11 14/16	8 1/16	M	Penobscot County	ME	Henry C. Williams III	1983	471
19 15/16	12 3/16	7 12/16	M	Sandoval County	NM	James M. Finn	1984	471
19 15/16	12 9/16	7 6/16	M	Burnett County	WI	Jerry Strese	1984	471
19 15/16	12 8/16	7 7/16	M	Baker County	OR	Steven E. Lewis	1986	471
19 15/16	12 0/16	7 15/16	M	Dryden	ONT	Lane Foosee	1987	471
19 15/16	12 4/16	7 11/16	M	Pine County	MN	Randy Broz	1987	471
19 15/16	12 7/16	7 8/16	M	Carrot River	SAS	Ron Gunwall	1988	471
19 15/16	12 1/16	7 14/16	M	Pickerel River	ONT	Walter L. Douglas	1988	471
19 15/16	12 10/16	7 5/16	M	Garfield County	CO	James Bowerman	1988	471
19 15/16	12 13/16	7 2/16	M	Douglas County	WI	Timothy E. Freid	1988	471

SCORE	GREATEST LENGTH	GREATEST WIDTH	SEX	AREA	STATE/ PROVINCE	HUNTER'S NAME	DATE	RANK
19 15/16	12 9/16	7 6/16	M	Chippewa County	MI	Edwin A. Armentrout	1988	471
19 15/16	12 5/16	7 10/16	M	Clearwater County	ID	John H. Dyche	1989	471
19 15/16	12 4/16	7 11/16	M	Grande Prairie	ALB	Ron Jungwirth	1990	471
19 15/16	12 9/16	7 6/16	M	Wahkiakum County	WA	Brandon Casey	1990	471
19 15/16	12 9/16	7 6/16	M	Jackson County	OR	Joe Holland	1990	471
19 15/16	12 9/16	7 6/16	M	Bayfield County	WI	Jeffrey Tuescher	1990	471
19 15/16	12 12/16	7 3/16	M	Rockingham County	VA	Roger O. Wyant	1990	471
19 15/16	12 4/16	7 11/16	M	Torrance County	NM	Eric Montoya	1990	471
19 15/16	12 7/16	7 8/16	M	Prince of Wales Island	AK	Chuck Lynde	1991	471
19 15/16	12 5/16	7 10/16	M	Kenora	ONT	Gary Liebsch	1991	471
19 15/16	12 3/16	7 12/16	M	La Ronge	SAS	James E. Hummel	1992	471
19 15/16	12 7/16	7 8/16	M	Prince of Wales Island	AK	Don Vernay	1992	471
19 15/16	12 2/16	7 13/16	M	Matagami	QUE	Jacques Harvey	1992	471
19 15/16	12 8/16	7 7/16	M	Riding Mtn.	MAN	Robert J. Wech	1992	471
19 15/16	12 8/16	7 7/16	M	Price County	WI	Gary L. Hintz	1992	471
19 14/16	12 2/16	7 12/16	M	Routt County	CO	Ronald C. Gravenkemper	1962	506
19 14/16	12 2/16	7 12/16	M	Colcord Mountain	AZ	Hugh Pearson	1963	506
19 14/16	12 5/16	7 9/16	M	Rio Blanco County	CO	H. R. 'Dutch' Wambold	1969	506
19 14/16	12 4/16	7 10/16	M	La Plata County	CO	Wayne E. Knisley	1971	506
19 14/16	12 12/16	7 2/16	M	Tulare County	CA	Ronald J. Wade	1972	506
19 14/16	12 0/16	7 14/16	M	Mesa County	CO	Clint Johnston	1973	506
19 14/16	12 4/16	7 10/16	M	Ignace	ONT	Thomas Tietz	1977	506
19 14/16	12 6/16	7 8/16	M	Missoula County	MT	Dwayne Garner	1978	506
19 14/16	12 3/16	7 11/16	M	Thunder Bay	ONT	Lester W. Jass	1978	506
19 14/16	12 4/16	7 10/16	M	Routt County	CO	Mark Chapman	1979	506
19 14/16	12 2/16	7 12/16	M	Gunnison County	CO	Robert Feller	1979	506
19 14/16	12 5/16	7 9/16	M	Marinette County	WI	Paul B. Pelzek	1979	506
19 14/16	12 12/16	7 2/16	M	Hudson Bay	SAS	Jerry Bien	1980	506
19 14/16	12 7/16	7 7/16	M	Sandoval County	NM	Mark Johnson	1980	506
19 14/16	12 6/16	7 8/16	M	Baraga County	MI	Thomas G. Young	1981	506
19 14/16	12 6/16	7 8/16	M	Glenn County	CA	Guy W. Foster	1982	506
19 14/16	12 8/16	7 6/16	M	Duck Mtn.	MAN	John 'Jack' Cordes	1983	506
19 14/16	12 5/16	7 9/16	M	Mesa County	CO	Raymond Roussett, Jr.	1983	506
19 14/16	12 5/16	7 9/16	M	Ear Falls	ONT	Brent Allen Poindexter	1985	506
19 14/16	12 11/16	7 3/16	M	Kootenai County	ID	John S. Thomson, Jr.	1986	506
19 14/16	12 4/16	7 10/16	M	Boise County	ID	Scott Privette	1986	506
19 14/16	12 8/16	7 6/16	M	Little Susitna River	AK	Brett Blessing	1986	506
19 14/16	12 5/16	7 9/16	M	Elmore County	ID	Ed Sweet	1988	506
19 14/16	12 3/16	7 11/16	M	Dolores County	CO	Bill Corley	1988	506
19 14/16	12 5/16	7 9/16	M	Warren	ONT	Gary Lawrence Harding	1988	506
19 14/16	12 14/16	7 0/16	M	Douglas County	WI	Dale Jaworski	1988	506
19 14/16	12 4/16	7 10/16	M	Delta County	CO	Rick L. Gillenwater	1989	506
19 14/16	12 7/16	7 7/16	M	Dryden	ONT	Jeffrey R. Beilke	1989	506
19 14/16	12 4/16	7 10/16	M	Green Lake	SAS	Fortunato Cuevas	1989	506
19 14/16	12 7/16	7 7/16	M	Fredericton	NBW	Edward J. Bleau	1989	506
19 14/16	12 4/16	7 10/16	M	Deep River	ONT	Rand J. Moore	1989	506
19 14/16	12 1/16	7 13/16	M	Luce County	MI	Terry L. Cook	1989	506
19 14/16	12 10/16	7 4/16	M	Clearwater County	ID	John M. Ramsey	1990	506
19 14/16	12 7/16	7 7/16	M	Cumberland House	SAS	Jim Jarvis	1991	506
19 14/16	12 4/16	7 10/16	M	Grand County	UT	Royce Carroll	1991	506
19 14/16	12 7/16	7 7/16	M	Dryden	ONT	Bruce E. Crocker	1991	506
19 14/16	12 7/16	7 7/16	M	Frog Lake	ALB	Mark Stevens	1992	506
19 14/16	12 9/16	7 5/16	M	Pine County	MN	Kirk D. Grupa	1992	506
19 14/16	12 8/16	7 6/16	M	Sawyer County	WI	Daniel T. Seibert	1992	506
19 13/16	12 7/16	7 6/16	M	Shasta County	CA	Stan L. McIntyre	1968	545
19 13/16	12 4/16	7 9/16	M	Dolores County	CO	Daryl Tieben	1976	545
19 13/16	12 11/16	7 2/16	M	Wawa	ONT	Robert C. McGuire	1977	545
19 13/16	12 7/16	7 6/16	M	Estaire	ONT	David L. Roose	1980	545
19 13/16	12 5/16	7 8/16	M	Bonneville County	ID	Tom Edwards	1981	545
19 13/16	12 6/16	7 7/16	M	Humboldt County	CA	Bill Hofferber	1981	545
19 13/16	12 7/16	7 6/16	M	Douglas County	WI	Richard Peterson	1982	545
19 13/16	12 9/16	7 4/16	M	Tucker County	WV	Robert B. Golightly	1982	545
19 13/16	12 2/16	7 11/16	M	Beardmore	ONT	Mike Mooney	1984	545
19 13/16	12 11/16	7 2/16	M	Hudson Bay	SAS	Craig Richardson	1985	545
19 13/16	12 4/16	7 9/16	M	Graham	ONT	Todd Henck	1985	545
19 13/16	12 5/16	7 8/16	M	Gallatin County	MT	LaVern Rucker	1985	545
19 13/16	12 6/16	7 7/16	M	Calvin Twp.	ONT	Bob Foulkrod	1986	545
19 13/16	12 3/16	7 10/16	M	Snohomish County	WA	Greg Winters	1986	545
19 13/16	12 8/16	7 5/16	M	Revillagigedo Island	AK	Michael Edwards	1987	545
19 13/16	12 0/16	7 13/16	M	Adies Pond	NFL	Ernest Libby	1988	545

SCORE	GREATEST LENGTH	GREATEST WIDTH	SEX	AREA	STATE/ PROVINCE	HUNTER'S NAME	DATE	RANK
19 13/16	12 4/16	7 9/16	M	Ear Falls	ONT	Rickey L. Morley	1988	545
19 13/16	12 3/16	7 10/16	M	Sexsmith	ALB	Oral Murphy	1989	545
19 13/16	12 5/16	7 8/16	M	Cranberry Portage	MAN	Ron Rogers	1989	545
19 13/16	12 1/16	7 12/16	M	Caramat	ONT	Steven Fowler	1990	545
19 13/16	12 5/16	7 8/16	M	Rio Arriba County	NM	Dwayne Sargent	1990	545
19 13/16	12 8/16	7 5/16	M	Frog Lake	ALB	Darrell Pinske	1991	545
19 13/16	12 13/16	7 0/16	M	Riding Mtn.	MAN	Dean A. Toth	1991	545
19 13/16	12 5/16	7 8/16	M	Utikamu	ALB	Donald L. DeLong	1992	545
19 13/16	11 15/16	7 14/16	M	Brace Bridge	ONT	David D. Williams	1992	545
19 13/16	12 8/16	7 5/16	M	Spokane County	WA	Rob Culp	1992	545
19 13/16	12 8/16	7 5/16	M	Ashland County	WI	Steven D. Pfaff	1992	545
19 12/16	12 4/16	7 8/16	M	Kenora	ONT	Noel Feather	1964	572
19 12/16	12 2/16	7 10/16	M	Chapleau	ONT	Lawrence Gallagher	1966	572
19 12/16	11 14/16	7 14/16	M	Lake County	MT	Joe Lawrence	1966	572
19 12/16	12 7/16	7 5/16	M	Grand County	UT	Edmund H. Auffhammer	1968	572
19 12/16	12 3/16	7 9/16	M	Chapleau	ONT	Anne M. Fiaschetti	1971	572
19 12/16	12 7/16	7 5/16	M	Catron County	NM	Joe E. Stroube	1971	572
19 12/16	12 4/16	7 8/16	F	Colfax County	NM	Bill Conn, Jr.	1973	572
19 12/16	12 4/16	7 8/16	M	Itasca County	MN	James R. Kroupa	1973	572
19 12/16	12 2/16	7 10/16	M	Conejos County	CO	Michael Miller	1974	572
19 12/16	12 3/16	7 9/16	M	Siskiyou County	CA	Wayne Haley	1975	572
19 12/16	12 6/16	7 6/16	M	Garfield County	CO	David Freeman	1976	572
19 12/16	12 1/16	7 11/16	M	Killarney	ONT	Ken Barnhart	1979	572
19 12/16	12 13/16	6 15/16	M	Crow Wing County	MN	Dave A. Engholm	1980	572
19 12/16	12 8/16	7 4/16	M	Riding Mtn.	MAN	James Carson	1980	572
19 12/16	12 0/16	7 12/16	M	North Bay	ONT	Ronald Gerrits	1980	572
19 12/16	12 5/16	7 7/16	M	Lewis & Clark County	MT	James L. Marlen	1980	572
19 12/16	12 8/16	7 4/16	M	Beluga	AK	John Moline	1980	572
19 12/16	12 4/16	7 8/16	M	Caribou County	ID	Alan G. Smith	1981	572
19 12/16	11 14/16	7 14/16	M	San Juan County	UT	Rick Collard	1982	572
19 12/16	12 7/16	7 5/16	M	The Pas	MAN	Ken Evenson	1983	572
19 12/16	12 3/16	7 9/16	M	Koochiching County	MN	Mike Little	1983	572
19 12/16	12 8/16	7 4/16	M	Gogebic County	MI	Steven D. Baker	1983	572
19 12/16	12 4/16	7 8/16	M	Madison County	MT	John Lantow	1984	572
19 12/16	12 10/16	7 2/16	M	Game Area #23	MAN	Gary Kaluzniak	1984	572
19 12/16	12 1/16	7 11/16	M	St. Louis County	MN	Clancy Lindvall	1984	572
19 12/16	12 8/16	7 4/16	M	Union County	OR	Brad Hathaway	1984	572
19 12/16	12 5/16	7 7/16	M	Ignace	ONT	Raymond Nowak, Jr.	1986	572
19 12/16	12 5/16	7 7/16	M	Cass County	MN	Lauren Brorby	1986	572
19 12/16	12 4/16	7 8/16	M	Mesa County	CO	Larry Shoop	1987	572
19 12/16	12 6/16	7 6/16	M	Mesa County	CO	Stephen K. Meredith	1987	572
19 12/16	12 10/16	7 2/16	M	Swan River	MAN	Harrey Bergen	1987	572
19 12/16	12 4/16	7 8/16	M	Westbank	BC	Robert McCulley	1987	572
19 12/16	12 6/16	7 6/16	M	Chaffee County	CO	Bob Merciez	1988	572
19 12/16	12 6/16	7 6/16	M	Miles Bay	ONT	Kenneth Rader	1988	572
19 12/16	12 6/16	7 6/16	M	Bear Paw Landing	QUE	Lonnie Rumley	1988	572
19 12/16	12 5/16	7 7/16	M	St. Louis County	MN	Scott Gruhlke	1988	572
19 12/16	12 0/16	7 12/16	M	Amos	QUE	Simon Harvey	1989	572
19 12/16	12 0/16	7 12/16	M	Aitkin County	MN	Scott Dirkes	1989	572
19 12/16	12 1/16	7 11/16	M	Sioux Lookout	ONT	Daniel J. Riegelman	1989	572
19 12/16	12 10/16	7 2/16	M	St. Louis County	MN	Dr Eugene T Altiere	1989	572
19 12/16	12 4/16	7 8/16	M	Coos County	OR	Russell McCall	1989	572
19 12/16	11 13/16	7 15/16	M	Vilas County	WI	Gary F. Robinson	1989	572
19 12/16	12 11/16	7 1/16	M	Langlade County	WI	Stanley WilliamJanusiewi	1989	572
19 12/16	12 9/16	7 3/16	M	Prince of Wales Island	AK	Dyrk Eddie	1990	572
19 12/16	12 6/16	7 6/16	M	Athabasca	ALB	Ryk Visscher	1990	572
19 12/16	12 6/16	7 6/16	M	Columbia County	WA	Kenneth Fuller	1990	572
19 12/16	12 4/16	7 8/16	M	Atikokan	ONT	Rick Grooms	1991	572
19 12/16	12 11/16	7 1/16	M	Iron County	MI	Michael A. Samuels	1991	572
19 12/16	12 10/16	7 2/16	M	Newton County	AR	Joel Phillips	1991	572
19 12/16	12 0/16	7 12/16	M	Harcourt Park	ONT	Henry Quittard	1991	572
19 12/16	12 1/16	7 11/16	M	Las Animas County	CO	Garry Woodman	1992	572
19 12/16	12 8/16	7 4/16	M	La Plata County	CO	John L. Gardner	1992	572
19 12/16	12 8/16	7 4/16	M	Vermette Lake	SAS	Eric Erickson	1992	572
19 12/16	12 3/16	7 9/16	M	Lac Kipawa	QUE	Ken Taylor	1992	572
19 12/16	12 11/16	7 1/16	M	Sawyer County	WI	Rodney Pearson	1992	572
19 11/16	12 3/16	7 8/16	M	Atikokan	ONT	Dennis Gregory	1967	627
19 11/16	12 2/16	7 9/16	M	Montezuma County	CO	Marvin Reichenau	1972	627
19 11/16	12 3/16	7 8/16	M	La Plata County	CO	Robert L. Everett	1973	627
19 11/16	12 4/16	7 7/16	M	Larimer County	CO	Lee Kline	1974	627

BLACK BEAR

(Continued)

Score	Greatest Length	Greatest Width	Sex	Area	State/Province	Hunter's Name	Date	Rank
19 11/16	11 15/16	7 12/16	M	Chapleau	ONT	Donald E. Meushaw	1975	627
19 11/16	12 9/16	7 2/16	M	Montezuma County	CO	Marvin Reichenau	1976	627
19 11/16	12 11/16	7 0/16	M	Garfield County	CO	C. David Wix	1976	627
19 11/16	12 4/16	7 7/16	M	Somerset County	ME	Anthony Carratura	1977	627
19 11/16	12 4/16	7 7/16	M	Washington County	ME	Charles Hardish	1977	627
19 11/16	12 0/16	7 11/16	M	Ignace	ONT	John Dmytryka	1978	627
19 11/16	12 6/16	7 5/16	M	Itasca County	MN	Daniel "Boone" Bell	1979	627
19 11/16	11 11/16	8 0/16	M	Washington County	ME	Gary Farquhar	1979	627
19 11/16	12 1/16	7 10/16	M	Boise County	ID	Michael Sherer	1981	627
19 11/16	12 5/16	7 6/16	M	Prince of Wales Island	AK	Doug Miller	1982	627
19 11/16	12 3/16	7 8/16	M	Gunflint Lake	ONT	Kelly Wilhelmi	1982	627
19 11/16	12 1/16	7 10/16	M	Routt County	CO	Guenter Hackl	1983	627
19 11/16	12 11/16	7 0/16	M	Boise County	ID	L. Dean Goodner	1983	627
19 11/16	12 5/16	7 6/16	M	Dickinson County	MI	Mike Vandeven	1983	627
19 11/16	12 0/16	7 11/16	M	Archuleta County	CO	Britton F. Kelley, Jr.	1984	627
19 11/16	12 0/16	7 11/16	M	Sioux Lookout	ONT	James E. Tiefenthaler	1984	627
19 11/16	11 7/16	8 4/16	M	Gogama	ONT	Frank E. Brinton IV	1985	627
19 11/16	11 15/16	7 12/16	M	Cascaden	ONT	Ronnie Long	1985	627
19 11/16	12 6/16	7 5/16	M	Garfield County	CO	Paul B. Walker	1986	627
19 11/16	12 0/16	7 11/16	M	Sudbury	ONT	Wendell L. DeWitt	1987	627
19 11/16	12 7/16	7 4/16	M	Nestor Falls	ONT	Martin J. Weber	1987	627
19 11/16	12 3/16	7 8/16	M	Valley County	ID	Jon Vanderhoef	1987	627
19 11/16	12 7/16	7 4/16	M	Marinette County	WI	Tim H. Boucher	1988	627
19 11/16	12 3/16	7 8/16	M	Forest County	WI	Tim B. Olk	1988	627
19 11/16	12 5/16	7 6/16	M	Carbon County	UT	Bill Mamales	1989	627
19 11/16	12 8/16	7 3/16	M	Ester Passage	AK	Don Williams	1989	627
19 11/16	12 6/16	7 5/16	M	Grand County	UT	Paul Ensz	1989	627
19 11/16	12 5/16	7 6/16	M	Dryden	ONT	Jack T. Wolf	1989	627
19 11/16	12 5/16	7 6/16	M	Blair	ONT	Douglass J. Street	1989	627
19 11/16	12 6/16	7 5/16	M	Alcona County	MI	Fred Eugene Upperstrom	1989	627
19 11/16	12 7/16	7 4/16	M	Cynthia	ALB	Bert Skulmoski	1990	627
19 11/16	12 1/16	7 10/16	M	Thadious Lake	ONT	Gary R. Ziesmer	1990	627
19 11/16	12 12/16	6 15/16	M	Green Lake	SAS	Richard P. Smith	1991	627
19 11/16	12 2/16	7 9/16	M	Fort McMurray	ALB	Edward Smith	1991	627
19 11/16	12 4/16	7 7/16	M	Prince of Wales Island	AK	Don Youngblood	1992	627
19 11/16	12 7/16	7 4/16	M	Fort McMurray	ALB	Steve Swinhoe	1992	627
19 11/16	12 1/16	7 10/16	M	Harvey Station	NBW	Dennis Hayden	1992	627
19 11/16	12 2/16	7 9/16	M	Sideburn Lake	ONT	David Jerome Miller	1992	627
19 10/16	12 0/16	7 10/16	M	Lincoln County	NM	David B. Terk	1964	669
19 10/16	12 6/16	7 4/16	M	Iron County	WI	William Tutt	1966	669
19 10/16	12 10/16	7 0/16	M	Madera County	CA	John D. Faulconer	1971	669
19 10/16	12 2/16	7 8/16	M	Nez Perce County	ID	Bob Gulman	1972	669
19 10/16	12 4/16	7 6/16	M	Forest County	WI	James L. Rablin	1972	669
19 10/16	12 7/16	7 3/16	M	Boise County	ID	Jimmie DeSaro, Jr.	1975	669
19 10/16	12 4/16	7 6/16	M	LaRonge	SAS	David L. Miller	1976	669
19 10/16	11 13/16	7 13/16	M	El Paso County	CO	Billy Mulholland	1976	669
19 10/16	12 6/16	7 4/16	M	Sandilands	MAN	Jerry Parizek	1976	669
19 10/16	12 4/16	7 6/16	M	Gunnison County	CO	Travis L. Wakefield	1977	669
19 10/16	12 2/16	7 8/16	M	St. Louis County	MN	Richard G. Butters	1979	669
19 10/16	12 6/16	7 4/16	M	Grand County	UT	Sam Nesi, Jr.	1979	669
19 10/16	12 12/16	6 14/16	M	Itasca County	MN	Gordon Steffen	1979	669
19 10/16	12 3/16	7 7/16	M	Trinity County	CA	Willis Duhon	1981	669
19 10/16	11 12/16	7 14/16	M	Fort Frances	ONT	Ron Carlson	1982	669
19 10/16	12 2/16	7 8/16	M	Vermillion Bay	ONT	Dean Hamilton	1983	669
19 10/16	12 2/16	7 8/16	M	Siskiyou County	CA	Jerry Martinez	1983	669
19 10/16	12 11/16	6 15/16	M	Iron County	MI	Leslie Vorpahl	1983	669
19 10/16	12 6/16	7 4/16	M	Langlade County	WI	Thomas Radtke	1984	669
19 10/16	12 5/16	7 5/16	M	Archuleta County	CO	Joel L. Duncan	1986	669
19 10/16	12 1/16	7 9/16	M	Lanark	ONT	Elmer M. Hagood, Jr.	1986	669
19 10/16	12 4/16	7 6/16	M	Sudbury	ONT	Richard W. Dohm	1987	669
19 10/16	12 3/16	7 7/16	M	Woody Lake	SAS	L. 'Andy' Anderson	1987	669
19 10/16	12 2/16	7 8/16	M	Gallatin County	MT	Frank W. Holland	1987	669
19 10/16	12 4/16	7 6/16	M	Siskiyou County	CA	Jeff Buck	1987	669
19 10/16	13 1/16	6 9/16	M	Limestone Lake	ONT	Steve Schwarzkopf	1988	669
19 10/16	12 5/16	7 5/16	M	Squaw Rapids	SAS	Phillip M. Revering	1988	669
19 10/16	12 8/16	7 2/16	M	Oxford County	ME	Richard Grannis	1988	669
19 10/16	12 5/16	7 5/16	M	Clearwater River	BC	Michael H. Ritcey	1988	669
19 10/16	12 4/16	7 6/16	M	Valley County	ID	Robert Dowen	1989	669
19 10/16	12 9/16	7 1/16	M	Archuleta County	CO	Ron R. Maez	1989	669
19 10/16	12 4/16	7 6/16	M	Sneaton	SAS	Gene A. Welle	1990	669

SCORE	GREATEST LENGTH	GREATEST WIDTH	SEX	AREA	STATE/ PROVINCE	HUNTER'S NAME	DATE	RANK
19 10/16	12 2/16	7 8/16	M	Vivian	MAN	Erik Thienpondt	1990	669
19 10/16	12 4/16	7 6/16	M	Grande Prairie	ALB	Tom Zimmerman	1990	669
19 10/16	12 2/16	7 8/16	M	Wawa	ONT	Edwin L. DeYoung	1990	669
19 10/16	12 2/16	7 8/16	M	Troy Lake	MAN	Derek McCarthy	1990	669
19 10/16	12 5/16	7 5/16	M	Canterbury	NBW	Don Rahe	1990	669
19 10/16	12 2/16	7 8/16	M	Gila County	AZ	Amos Culbert	1990	669
19 10/16	12 2/16	7 8/16	M	La Plata County	CO	John L. Gardner	1990	669
19 10/16	12 6/16	7 4/16	M	Gila County	AZ	Warren Mark Smith	1990	669
19 10/16	12 8/16	7 2/16	M	Cordova	AK	Tony Casagrande	1990	669
19 10/16	12 2/16	7 8/16	M	Kosciusko Island	AK	Rob Seelye	1991	669
19 10/16	12 7/16	7 3/16	M	The Pas	MAN	Marvin Weible	1991	669
19 10/16	12 5/16	7 5/16	M	Thompson	MAN	Thomas P. Rabette	1991	669
19 10/16	12 1/16	7 9/16	M	Athabasca River	ALB	Bruce R. Schoeneweis	1991	669
19 10/16	12 3/16	7 7/16	M	Taylors Brook	NFL	Thomas Spero	1991	669
19 10/16	12 8/16	7 2/16	M	Clinton County	NY	Jim Provost	1991	669
19 10/16	12 8/16	7 2/16	M	Beluga River	AK	James R. Bussell	1992	669
19 10/16	12 2/16	7 8/16	M	Dryden	ONT	Mike Barkac	1992	669
19 10/16	12 2/16	7 8/16	M	St. Louis County	MN	Kenneth G. Larsen	1992	669
19 10/16	12 3/16	7 7/16	M	Delta County	MI	Ronald J. Sharkey	1992	669
19 9/16	12 10/16	6 15/16	M	Douglas County	WI ·	Edwin Fitzgerald	1966	720
19 9/16	12 6/16	7 3/16	M	Grand County	CO	Judd Cooney	1967	720
19 9/16	12 0/16	7 9/16	M	Ignace	ONT	Gordon Bentley	1968	720
19 9/16	11 15/16	7 10/16	M	Idaho County	ID	Kenneth Wallenberg	1970	720
19 9/16	11 9/16	8 0/16	M	Boise County	ID	Ronald L. Sherer	1971	720
19 9/16	12 1/16	7 8/16	M	Blount County	TN	Gary Jordan	1973	720
19 9/16	12 5/16	7 4/16	M	Franklin County	ME	Ralph Pfister	1977	720
19 9/16	11 9/16	8 0/16	M	Boise County	ID	Susan D. Sherer	1978	720
19 9/16	12 4/16	7 5/16	M	Idaho County	ID	Bob Jacobsen	1979	720
19 9/16	12 4/16	7 5/16	M	Valley County	ID	L. Dean Goodner	1979	720
19 9/16	11 11/16	7 14/16	M	Sandilands	MAN	Ron Derlago	1979	720
19 9/16	12 4/16	7 5/16	M	Grand County	CO	Leonard L. Kohan	1980	720
19 9/16	12 0/16	7 9/16	M	Pitkin County	CO	Judy Nielsen	1981	720
19 9/16	11 11/16	7 14/16	M	Bobcaygeon	ONT	Dale W. Gray	1982	720
19 9/16	12 4/16	7 5/16	M	Ear Falls	ONT	Grant A. Poindexter	1982	720
19 9/16	12 0/16	7 9/16	M	Ft. Wainwright	AK	Gregory Dean Royse	1983	720
19 9/16	12 4/16	7 5/16	M	Coconino County	AZ	Dale H. Long	1983	720
19 9/16	12 5/16	7 4/16	M	Sawyer County	WI	Richard Carolfi	1983	720
19 9/16	12 3/16	7 6/16	M	Mesa County	CO	Jeff Tedore	1984	720
19 9/16	12 8/16	7 1/16	M	Beluga River	AK	Chad Burris	1984	720
19 9/16	12 5/16	7 4/16	M	Itasca County	MN	Dennis K. Fideldy	1984	720
19 9/16	12 6/16	7 3/16	M	Uintah County	UT	John C. Matejov	1985	720
19 9/16	12 6/16	7 3/16	M	La Tuque	QUE	John C. Hutchinson	1986	720
19 9/16	12 5/16	7 4/16	M	Bonneville County	ID	Larry Cross	1986	720
19 9/16	12 7/16	7 2/16	M	Washington County	ME	Cliff Wiseman	1986	720
19 9/16	12 7/16	7 2/16	M	Hudson Bay	SAS	Bill Zahradka	1987	720
19 9/16	12 1/16	7 8/16	M	Kenora	ONT	Scott A. Lamphier	1987	720
19 9/16	12 5/16	7 4/16	M	Atikokan	ONT	Lawrence A. Meyers	1987	720
19 9/16	12 5/16	7 4/16	M	Fort Coulonge	QUE	Harvey D. Garrett	1988	720
19 9/16	12 1/16	7 8/16	M	Barron County	WI	Dennis O. Freid	1988	720
19 9/16	12 10/16	6 15/16	M	Taylor County	WI	Rick Smith	1988	720
19 9/16	12 4/16	7 5/16	M	Emmet County	MI	Randall J. McCune	1988	720
19 9/16	12 1/16	7 8/16	M	Prince of Wales Island	AK	Carl E. Brent	1989	720
19 9/16	11 11/16	7 14/16	M	Las Animas County	CO	R. L. Erdmann	1989	720
19 9/16	12 4/16	7 5/16	M	Killala Lake	ONT	Orrin Malick	1989	720
19 9/16	12 9/16	7 0/16	M	Saint John	NBW	Mike L. LaVan	1989	720
19 9/16	11 15/16	7 10/16	M	Fort Coulonge	QUE	J. J. Fegan	1989	720
19 9/16	12 7/16	7 2/16	M	Prince of Wales Island	AK	Dan E. Hiltz	1989	720
19 9/16	12 11/16	6 14/16	M	Messines	QUE	Charles L. Hart III	1989	720
19 9/16	12 6/16	7 3/16	M	Kings County	NBW	Ernest Sperl	1989	720
19 9/16	12 5/16	7 4/16	M	Mowat Township	ONT	Ricky McDaniel	1990	720
19 9/16	12 1/16	7 8/16	M	Boise County	ID	James L. Sullivan	1990	720
19 9/16	12 5/16	7 4/16	M	Madison County	ID	Rita Harris	1990	720
19 9/16	11 15/16	7 10/16	M	Lac Flavrian	QUE	Eric Grandbois	1990	720
19 9/16	12 5/16	7 4/16	M	Somerset County	ME	Gregory A. Bonecutter,Sr	1990	720
19 9/16	12 1/16	7 8/16	M	Lake of the Woods Co.	MN	Brian McGregor	1990	720
19 9/16	12 0/16	7 9/16	M	Sudbury	ONT	Jim Bratton	1991	720
19 9/16	12 0/16	7 9/16	M	High Level	ALB	R. E. Smith	1991	720
19 9/16	12 4/16	7 5/16	M	St. Louis County	MN	Edwin John Durushia	1991	720
19 9/16	12 4/16	7 5/16	M	Dolores County	CO	Jay Jaburg	1991	720
19 9/16	12 2/16	7 7/16	M	Routt County	CO	Bob Sanders	1991	720

SCORE	GREATEST LENGTH	GREATEST WIDTH	SEX	AREA	STATE/ PROVINCE	HUNTER'S NAME	DATE	RANK
19 8/16	12 3/16	7 5/16	M	Chapleau	ONT	Bob Sharpe	1959	771
19 8/16	12 4/16	7 4/16	M	Presque Isle County	MI	Eugene W. McKechnie	1964	771
19 8/16	12 6/16	7 2/16	M	Forest County	WI	Jerad Dittrich	1965	771
19 8/16	12 1/16	7 7/16	M	Piscataquis County	ME	James Matulis	1967	771
19 8/16	12 6/16	7 2/16	M	Crow Wing County	MN	James L. Beard	1975	771
19 8/16	11 12/16	7 12/16	M	Boise County	ID	Jack Arbaugh	1976	771
19 8/16	11 11/16	7 13/16	M	Atikokan	ONT	David Graves	1978	771
19 8/16	12 2/16	7 6/16	M	Ear Falls	ONT	Grant Poindexter	1978	771
19 8/16	12 5/16	7 3/16	M	Archuleta County	CO	Robert Hoague	1981	771
19 8/16	12 3/16	7 5/16	M	Broadwater County	MT	Jan Hamer	1982	771
19 8/16	12 3/16	7 5/16	M	Remigny	QUE	Joe Hopwood	1982	771
19 8/16	11 15/16	7 9/16	M	Madison County	MT	Shep Lantow	1982	771
19 8/16	12 7/16	7 1/16	M	Loon Lake	SAS	Brian Acton	1984	771
19 8/16	12 6/16	7 2/16	M	Hudson Bay	SAS	Bill Zahradka	1984	771
19 8/16	12 0/16	7 8/16	M	Las Animas County	CO	Sam Durham	1984	771
19 8/16	11 11/16	7 13/16	M	Converse County	WY	Neil Hymas	1984	771
19 8/16	12 8/16	7 0/16	M	Sioux Narrows	ONT	Kenneth E. Krahn	1985	771
19 8/16	12 2/16	7 6/16	M	Grant County	OR	Mike E. Billman	1985	771
19 8/16	11 14/16	7 10/16	M	Siskiyou County	CA	Richard L. Westervelt	1985	771
19 8/16	12 6/16	7 2/16	M	One Portage Lake	MAN	Paolo Strapazzon	1986	771
19 8/16	12 4/16	7 4/16	M	Minden	ONT	William J. Davi	1986	771
19 8/16	12 8/16	7 0/16	M	Lincoln County	MT	Jim Eff	1986	771
19 8/16	12 4/16	7 4/16	M	Custer County	ID	Richard D. Stocking	1986	771
19 8/16	12 5/16	7 3/16	M	Huerfano County	CO	Randy Wright	1987	771
19 8/16	11 13/16	7 11/16	M	Essex County	NY	Paul Durling	1987	771
19 8/16	12 5/16	7 3/16	M	Hancock County	ME	John R. Mitchell	1987	771
19 8/16	12 0/16	7 8/16	M	Maniwaki	QUE	Aldo Bonacasta, Jr.	1989	771
19 8/16	12 10/16	6 14/16	M	Duchesne County	UT	Jerry B. Reynolds	1989	771
19 8/16	11 15/16	7 9/16	M	La Ronge	SAS	Robert D. Lingo	1989	771
19 8/16	12 1/16	7 7/16	M	San Fernando Island	AK	Kurt Goesch	1989	771
19 8/16	12 0/16	7 8/16	M	Zec Maganasipi	QUE	Stephen Kotz	1989	771
19 8/16	12 2/16	7 6/16	M	Bigoray River	ALB	Gunter Lemke	1990	771
19 8/16	12 11/16	6 13/16	M	Fort McMurray	ALB	Mike Menke	1990	771
19 8/16	12 5/16	7 3/16	M	Archuleta County	CO	Roger DeGroat	1990	771
19 8/16	12 4/16	7 4/16	M	Clackamas County	OR	Ben R. Cook	1990	771
19 8/16	11 14/16	7 10/16	M	Custer County	ID	David J. McPherson	1990	771
19 8/16	12 5/16	7 3/16	M	Forest County	WI	Mark Gaffke	1990	771
19 8/16	12 3/16	7 5/16	M	Rio Arriba County	NM	Robert J. Seeds	1990	771
19 8/16	12 7/16	7 1/16	M	Mons Township	ONT	Russell Trusty	1991	771
19 8/16	12 1/16	7 7/16	M	Atikokan	ONT	Jim Aebel	1991	771
19 8/16	11 14/16	7 10/16	M	Thunder Bay	ONT	Dave McKenzie	1991	771
19 8/16	12 4/16	7 4/16	M	Zec Dumoine	QUE	John K. Deveney	1991	771
19 8/16	12 0/16	7 8/16	M	Routt County	CO	Joel Anderson	1992	771
19 8/16	12 4/16	7 4/16	M	Fort McMurray	ALB	Mark A. Balavender	1992	771
19 8/16	12 0/16	7 8/16	M	Fort McMurray	ALB	Jim Trafford	1992	771
19 8/16	12 5/16	7 3/16	M	Zec St. Patrice	QUE	Ted Brilhart	1992	771
19 8/16	11 14/16	7 10/16	M	Obatogamau Lake	QUE	Zig Kertenis, Jr.	1992	771
19 7/16	12 3/16	7 4/16	M	Kenora	ONT	Norman Pint	1964	818
19 7/16	12 5/16	7 2/16	M	Caribou County	ID	Ronald S. Curtis	1969	818
19 7/16	11 10/16	7 13/16	M	St. Louis County	MN	Don Dvoroznak	1970	818
19 7/16	11 15/16	7 8/16	M	Moffat County	CO	Louis Preba	1972	818
19 7/16	12 0/16	7 7/16	M	Nestor Falls	ONT	Dennis Bartness	1974	818
19 7/16	12 0/16	7 7/16	M	Haddo Township	ONT	Paul Sorke	1974	818
19 7/16	12 0/16	7 7/16	M	La Plata County	CO	Mike Dunaway	1975	818
19 7/16	12 7/16	7 0/16	M	Somme	SAS	Phil Patchin	1975	818
19 7/16	12 3/16	7 4/16	M	Garfield County	UT	Lee G. Stoddard	1975	818
19 7/16	12 7/16	7 0/16	M	Snohomish County	WA	Charles J. Bartlett	1976	818
19 7/16	12 1/16	7 6/16	M	Roscommon County	MI	Roger Maeder	1976	818
19 7/16	12 0/16	7 7/16	M	Larimer County	CO	Ron Breitsprecher	1977	818
19 7/16	12 2/16	7 5/16	M	Costilla County	CO	Dr. Thomas I. LaValle	1978	818
19 7/16	12 5/16	7 2/16	M	Byers Lake	AK	Eugene Smith, Jr.	1978	818
19 7/16	11 11/16	7 12/16	M	Fremont County	CO	Ronald E. Sniff	1978	818
19 7/16	12 4/16	7 3/16	M	Idaho County	ID	Ray Koenig	1979	818
19 7/16	12 11/16	6 12/16	M	Tehama County	CA	Roy B. Cartwright	1980	818
19 7/16	12 7/16	7 0/16	M	Cass County	MN	Wayne Enger	1980	818
19 7/16	12 2/16	7 5/16	M	Starkey Unit	OR	Bill Lancaster	1980	818
19 7/16	11 15/16	7 8/16	M	Wolf Lake Road	ONT	Gary Johnston	1981	818
19 7/16	12 0/16	7 7/16	M	Huerfano County	CO	Kent Connally	1983	818
19 7/16	11 14/16	7 9/16	M	Bayfield County	WI	Steve Finn	1983	818
19 7/16	12 0/16	7 7/16	M	Dryden	ONT	Alan Koester	1984	818

SCORE	GREATEST LENGTH	GREATEST WIDTH	SEX	AREA	STATE/ PROVINCE	HUNTER'S NAME	DATE	RANK
19 7/16	11 8/16	7 15/16	M	Caramat	ONT	Robert D. DuBois	1984	818
19 7/16	12 3/16	7 4/16	M	Hudson Bay	SAS	Bill Zahradka	1986	818
19 7/16	12 3/16	7 4/16	M	Archuleta County	CO	Richard M. Young, Jr.	1986	818
19 7/16	11 8/16	7 15/16	M	Sioux Narrows	ONT	Richard Sapp	1986	818
19 7/16	11 15/16	7 8/16	M	Mine Centre	ONT	Lonnie Johnson	1987	818
19 7/16	12 3/16	7 4/16	M	Siskiyou County	CA	John E. Koblos	1987	818
19 7/16	12 5/16	7 2/16	M	Lac La Biche	ALB	Daniel J. Hungle	1988	818
19 7/16	12 3/16	7 4/16	M	Catron County	NM	Parris Nottingham	1988	818
19 7/16	12 0/16	7 7/16	M	Mayerthorpe	ALB	Dan Perez	1989	818
19 7/16	12 5/16	7 2/16	M	Kimowin Lake	ALB	Thomas Schneider	1989	818
19 7/16	12 4/16	7 3/16	M	Buffalo Narrows	SAS	Matt Curry	1990	818
19 7/16	12 3/16	7 4/16	M	Cadillac	QUE	Bob Drumm	1990	818
19 7/16	12 8/16	6 15/16	M	Prince of Wales Island	AK	Doy Curtis	1990	818
19 7/16	12 8/16	6 15/16	M	Bayfield County	WI	George Herold	1990	818
19 7/16	12 5/16	7 2/16	M	Baraga County	MI	Mark Savic	1990	818
19 7/16	12 3/16	7 4/16	M	Otter Creek	SAS	L. H. King, MD	1991	818
19 7/16	12 1/16	7 6/16	M	Ear Falls	ONT	Joseph E. Church	1991	818
19 7/16	12 6/16	7 1/16	M	Goodsoil	SAS	Charles Ranua	1991	818
19 7/16	11 10/16	7 13/16	M	Apisko Lake	MAN	Karl Teitt	1991	818
19 7/16	12 5/16	7 2/16	M	Boise County	ID	Russ Meyer	1991	818
19 7/16	12 0/16	7 7/16	M	Roseau County	MN	Rick Hill	1991	818
19 7/16	12 1/16	7 6/16	M	Elk River	BC	Alan Williams	1991	818
19 7/16	12 0/16	7 7/16	M	Garfield County	CO	Stace Strouse	1991	818
19 7/16	12 5/16	7 2/16	M	Wallowa County	OR	Tony Piper	1991	818
19 7/16	12 4/16	7 3/16	M	Meadow Lake	SAS	Matthew Curry	1992	818
19 7/16	11 11/16	7 12/16	M	Williams Lake	ONT	Eric Matheson	1992	818
19 7/16	11 9/16	7 14/16	M	Alpine County	CA	Kevin L. Hall	1992	818
19 7/16	12 0/16	7 7/16	M	Florence County	WI	Steven J. Woulf	1992	818
19 6/16	12 7/16	6 15/16	M	Shasta County	CA	L. Dale Towery	1965	869
19 6/16	11 14/16	7 8/16	M	Atikokan	ONT	Dennis Gregory	1969	869
19 6/16	11 14/16	7 8/16	M	Mesa County	CO	Charles Leidheiser	1971	869
19 6/16	12 2/16	7 4/16	M	Franklin County	ME	Walter Seville	1971	869
19 6/16	12 6/16	7 0/16	F	Sawyer County	WI	Ronald Curry, Jr.	1972	869
19 6/16	12 3/16	7 3/16	M	Uncompahgre N.F.	CO	Thomas J. Hentrick	1975	869
19 6/16	12 2/16	7 4/16	M	Ashland County	WI	Jim Keim	1977	869
19 6/16	12 2/16	7 4/16	M	Atikokan	ONT	Earle K. Gray	1979	869
19 6/16	11 14/16	7 8/16	M	Wabigoon Lake	ONT	Gary W. Shaffer	1979	869
19 6/16	11 13/16	7 9/16	M	Cascade County	MT	H. Richard Long	1981	869
19 6/16	12 4/16	7 2/16	M	Lewis & Clark County	MT	Donald K. MacCallum	1982	869
19 6/16	12 0/16	7 6/16	M	Aroostook County	ME	Frank 'Rit' Heller	1982	869
19 6/16	12 2/16	7 4/16	M	Hampshire County	MA	James 'Boomer' Hayden	1982	869
19 6/16	12 4/16	7 2/16	M	Hudson Bay	SAS	David Tofte	1983	869
19 6/16	12 4/16	7 2/16	M	Sioux Lookout	ONT	Ray Ryan	1983	869
19 6/16	12 2/16	7 4/16	M	Beluga River	AK	Christine Koldeway	1984	869
19 6/16	12 9/16	6 13/16	M	Kitsap County	WA	Betty Jones	1984	869
19 6/16	11 15/16	7 7/16	M	Lemhi County	ID	Ron Scherer	1985	869
19 6/16	11 14/16	7 8/16	M	Heathcote	ONT	Joseph A. Lasch	1985	869
19 6/16	11 14/16	7 8/16	M	Drury Twp.	ONT	John Wyszynski	1985	869
19 6/16	11 10/16	7 12/16	M	Kenora	ONT	Mark D. Moss	1985	869
19 6/16	12 1/16	7 5/16	M	Bighorn County	WY	Joel D. Prickett	1985	869
19 6/16	12 0/16	7 6/16	M	Shasta County	CA	Larry Mork	1985	869
19 6/16	12 1/16	7 5/16	M	Teton County	ID	Marc S. Johnson	1986	869
19 6/16	11 12/16	7 10/16	M	Herkimer County	NY	Patrick Niznik	1986	869
19 6/16	12 0/16	7 6/16	M	Trinity County	CA	Robert Pearce	1986	869
19 6/16	12 0/16	7 6/16	M	Washago	ONT	James E. Doberstein	1987	869
19 6/16	12 0/16	7 6/16	M	Clearwater County	ID	Dennis Blackford	1987	869
19 6/16	12 2/16	7 4/16	M	Graham County	AZ	Jeffrey Keith Volk	1987	869
19 6/16	12 3/16	7 3/16	M	Oneida County	WI	James J. Wallack	1987	869
19 6/16	11 14/16	7 8/16	M	Hillsport	ONT	Richard Shive	1988	869
19 6/16	11 15/16	7 7/16	M	Valley County	ID	William R. Vanderhoef	1988	869
19 6/16	12 4/16	7 2/16	M	Madera County	CA	Ken Woolsey	1988	869
19 6/16	12 4/16	7 2/16	M	Fresno County	CA	DeeAnn Robinson	1988	869
19 6/16	12 3/16	7 3/16	M	Bayfield County	WI	Daniel L Snider	1989	869
19 6/16	12 3/16	7 3/16	M	Colfax County	NM	Steven A. Leyh	1990	869
19 6/16	12 2/16	7 4/16	M	Fraser Lake	BC	Stanley D. Moore	1990	869
19 6/16	11 14/16	7 8/16	M	Aulneau Peninsula	ONT	Mike Koska	1990	869
19 6/16	12 3/16	7 3/16	M	Peace River	ALB	Mike Conroy	1990	869
19 6/16	11 12/16	7 10/16	M	Franklin County	ME	Peter L. Shippee	1990	869
19 6/16	12 1/16	7 5/16	M	Colfax County	NM	Daniel Hurd	1990	869
19 6/16	11 14/16	7 8/16	M	Prince of Wales Island	AK	Mark Robecker	1990	869

Score	Greatest Length	Greatest Width	Sex	Area	State/Province	Hunter's Name	Date	Rank
19 6/16	12 5/16	7 1/16	M	Prince of Wales Island	AK	David Rue	1991	869
19 6/16	12 2/16	7 4/16	F	Lac La Biche	ALB	Bruce Nederveld	1991	869
19 6/16	12 0/16	7 6/16	M	Fort McMurray	ALB	Galen F. Shinkle	1991	869
19 6/16	12 6/16	7 0/16	M	Bruce County	ONT	Dean Adams	1991	869
19 6/16	12 4/16	7 2/16	M	Minto Flats	AK	James Wayne Dillard	1991	869
19 6/16	11 15/16	7 7/16	M	Falconbridge	ONT	Daniel Ralich	1991	869
19 6/16	12 4/16	7 2/16	M	Darlens	QUE	Dennis L. Blankenship	1991	869
19 6/16	12 7/16	6 15/16	M	Leaf River	QUE	Joseph Testerman	1991	869
19 6/16	11 14/16	7 8/16	M	Lake County	MN	David Ruzek	1991	869
19 6/16	12 1/16	7 5/16	M	Bancroft	ONT	Jeffrey C. Fretz	1991	869
19 6/16	12 2/16	7 4/16	M	Hood River County	OR	Michael L. Tollen	1991	869
19 6/16	12 1/16	7 5/16	M	Marathon County	WI	John J. Fischer	1991	869
19 6/16	12 3/16	7 3/16	M	Hearst	ONT	Russell V. Riese	1992	869
19 6/16	11 15/16	7 7/16	M	Sheridan County	WY	Lee Jernigan	1992	869
19 5/16	11 13/16	7 8/16	M	Clearwater County	ID	William R. Vanderhoef	1959	925
19 5/16	11 12/16	7 9/16	M	Upper Peninsula	MI	Donald Schram	1961	925
19 5/16	12 0/16	7 5/16	M	Gunnison County	CO	James Jarvis	1976	925
19 5/16	11 12/16	7 9/16	M	Las Animas County	CO	Barry Powell	1976	925
19 5/16	12 3/16	7 2/16	M	Raith	ONT	Jon K. Young	1976	925
19 5/16	12 1/16	7 4/16	M	Mesa County	CO	T. J. Colburn	1977	925
19 5/16	11 11/16	7 10/16	M	Franklin County	ME	Al Del Greco	1978	925
19 5/16	11 11/16	7 10/16	M	Ear Falls	ONT	Michael Mealey	1978	925
19 5/16	12 0/16	7 5/16	M	Washington County	ME	Dan Paugh	1978	925
19 5/16	12 6/16	6 15/16	M	Dolores County	CO	Marv Reichenau	1979	925
19 5/16	12 1/16	7 4/16	M	Oneida County	NY	Ronald J. Beerhalter	1980	925
19 5/16	12 2/16	7 3/16	M	Tulare County	CA	Fred R. Cisneros	1981	925
19 5/16	11 14/16	7 7/16	M	White Lake	ONT	Daniel B. Johnson	1981	925
19 5/16	11 15/16	7 6/16	M	Bonneville County	ID	Richard K. Russell	1981	925
19 5/16	12 2/16	7 3/16	M	Dryden	ONT	Craig A. Swenson	1982	925
19 5/16	12 1/16	7 4/16	M	Sudbury County	ONT	William Doczy	1983	925
19 5/16	12 4/16	7 1/16	M	St. Louis County	MN	Kimberley Anne McGurren	1983	925
19 5/16	12 1/16	7 4/16	M	King County	WA	Larry Jensen	1983	925
19 5/16	11 13/16	7 8/16	M	Smeaton	SAS	Gene Welle	1984	925
19 5/16	11 14/16	7 7/16	M	Caribou County	ID	Coby Tigert	1984	925
19 5/16	12 1/16	7 4/16	M	Snohomish County	WA	Mathew Hayvaz	1984	925
19 5/16	12 1/16	7 4/16	M	Plumes County	CA	Dr. Ronald H. Thole	1984	925
19 5/16	12 1/16	7 4/16	M	Parry Sound	ONT	Ronald D. Lundy	1985	925
19 5/16	12 4/16	7 1/16	M	Cass County	MN	Brad Blanchard	1985	925
19 5/16	12 8/16	6 13/16	M	Caldwell County	NC	Danny K. Adams	1986	925
19 5/16	12 8/16	6 13/16	M	Grand County	UT	David Snyder	1986	925
19 5/16	12 5/16	7 0/16	M	Valley County	ID	Brian Hunter Heck	1986	925
19 5/16	11 9/16	7 12/16	M	Flathead County	MT	Jay Vojta, Jr.	1987	925
19 5/16	12 1/16	7 4/16	M	Garfield County	WA	David Jansen	1987	925
19 5/16	12 3/16	7 2/16	M	Catron County	NM	Stan Rauch	1988	925
19 5/16	12 0/16	7 5/16	M	Rocky Lake	MAN	Cecil Tharp	1988	925
19 5/16	12 3/16	7 2/16	M	Rocky Lake	MAN	Tim Finley	1988	925
19 5/16	11 11/16	7 10/16	M	Fort Coulonge	QUE	David Keith Burchette	1988	925
19 5/16	11 14/16	7 7/16	M	North Bay	QUE	Jeff Anderson	1988	925
19 5/16	12 1/16	7 4/16	M	High Prairie	ALB	Joseph F. Petti	1989	925
19 5/16	12 4/16	7 1/16	M	Montrose County	CO	Clint Hovey	1989	925
19 5/16	11 15/16	7 6/16	M	Sioux Lookout	ONT	Stan Godfrey	1989	925
19 5/16	12 1/16	7 4/16	M	Zec Maganasipi	QUE	F. Edward Campbell	1989	925
19 5/16	11 14/16	7 7/16	M	Cold Lake	ALB	Glenn Moir	1989	925
19 5/16	11 10/16	7 11/16	M	Las Animas County	CO	David Brooks	1990	925
19 5/16	12 3/16	7 2/16	M	Fawcett	ALB	Garfield Vikse	1990	925
19 5/16	11 15/16	7 6/16	M	Stranger Lake	ONT	Mitchell S. Thorpe	1990	925
19 5/16	12 1/16	7 4/16	M	Oconto County	WI	James A. Krouse	1990	925
19 5/16	11 15/16	7 6/16	M	MacNeil Twp.	ONT	Ted Whittle	1990	925
19 5/16	11 15/16	7 6/16	M	High Level	ALB	Bobby G. Williams	1991	925
19 5/16	12 1/16	7 4/16	M	Rio Arriba County	NM	Tim J. Mariner	1991	925
19 5/16	12 6/16	6 15/16	F	Boise County	ID	Scott T. Doxey	1991	925
19 5/16	12 2/16	7 3/16	M	Idaho County	ID	Charles R. Whitfield	1991	925
19 5/16	12 3/16	7 2/16	M	Pitkin County	CO	James P. Krasinski, Sr.	1991	925
19 5/16	12 0/16	7 5/16	M	Colfax County	NM	Stephen W. Long	1991	925
19 5/16	12 1/16	7 4/16	M	Athabasca River	ALB	Casmir S. Domurat, Jr.	1991	925
19 5/16	12 7/16	6 14/16	M	Cranberry Portage	MAN	John Beardslee	1992	925
19 5/16	11 12/16	7 9/16	M	Saguache County	CO	Dennis Reid	1992	925
19 5/16	11 15/16	7 6/16	M	Skagit County	WA	Rick W. Giles	1992	925
19 5/16	12 5/16	7 0/16	M	Catron County	NM	David H. Boland	1992	925
19 4/16	12 4/16	7 0/16	M	Ashland County	WI	Herbert H. Lange	1961	980

SCORE	GREATEST LENGTH	GREATEST WIDTH	SEX	AREA	STATE/ PROVINCE	HUNTER'S NAME	DATE	RANK
19 4/16	12 4/16	7 0/16	M	Murphy Dome	AK	Thomas Clark	1963	980
19 4/16	11 15/16	7 5/16	M	Jackson County	OR	Bob Jacobs	1964	980
19 4/16	12 0/16	7 4/16	M	Idaho County	ID	Dick Gulman	1967	980
19 4/16	12 3/16	7 1/16	M	L'Ascension	QUE	Michael L. Kaluszka	1971	980
19 4/16	11 8/16	7 12/16	M	Idaho County	ID	Harold Boyack	1973	980
19 4/16	11 12/16	7 8/16	M	Wasco County	OR	John Higgins	1974	980
19 4/16	11 11/16	7 9/16	M	Wanapitei River	ONT	Ken Barnhart	1976	980
19 4/16	11 11/16	7 9/16	M	Gunnison County	CO	Roger Reinbold	1976	980
19 4/16	12 1/16	7 3/16	M	Saguache County	CO	Richard Baumfalk	1977	980
19 4/16	11 14/16	7 6/16	M	Pigeon Mtn.	ALB	David R. Coupland	1977	980
19 4/16	12 4/16	7 0/16	M	Bayfield County	WI	Bruce Eggenberger	1977	980
19 4/16	11 15/16	7 5/16	M	Capreol	ONT	Bobby Clenney	1978	980
19 4/16	12 0/16	7 4/16	M	Franklin County	ME	Harry Feaster	1978	980
19 4/16	11 13/16	7 7/16	M	Thessalon	ONT	Robert R. Rider	1979	980
19 4/16	12 4/16	7 0/16	M	Ontonagon County	MI	Daniel F. Stiltner	1979	980
19 4/16	11 12/16	7 8/16	M	Bayfield County	WI	Dave Tabbert	1979	980
19 4/16	12 1/16	7 3/16	M	Price County	WI	Glenn E. Gaulke	1980	980
19 4/16	11 12/16	7 8/16	M	Shoshone County	ID	Bill Hoffman, Sr.	1980	980
19 4/16	11 14/16	7 6/16	M	Dryden	ONT	Gerald T. Flynn	1981	980
19 4/16	11 12/16	7 8/16	M	Idaho County	ID	Ray Koenig	1981	980
19 4/16	12 2/16	7 2/16	M	Archuleta County	CO	Denny Lane Williamson	1981	980
19 4/16	11 14/16	7 6/16	M	St. Lawrence County	NY	Henry P. Bouchard	1982	980
19 4/16	12 1/16	7 3/16	M	Park County	MT	Gary Hartman	1982	980
19 4/16	12 8/16	6 12/16	M	Burnett County	WI	David Hess	1982	980
19 4/16	12 4/16	7 0/16	M	Mackinac County	MI	Dale H. Betcher	1983	980
19 4/16	11 14/16	7 6/16	M	Emo	ONT	Hal McClelland	1983	980
19 4/16	12 5/16	6 15/16	M	Game Area #23	MAN	Gary Kaluzniak	1984	980
19 4/16	12 0/16	7 4/16	M	Susitina River	AK	Patricia A. Stewart	1984	980
19 4/16	11 14/16	7 6/16	M	Touchwood Lake	ALB	Warren Witherspoon	1984	980
19 4/16	12 0/16	7 4/16	M	Game Area #23	MAN	Gary Kaluzniak	1984	980
19 4/16	11 12/16	7 8/16	M	Rollet	QUE	George Ollert	1984	980
19 4/16	11 11/16	7 9/16	M	Siskiyou County	CA	Greg Nichols	1984	980
19 4/16	11 14/16	7 6/16	M	Wawa	ONT	James C. Hicks	1984	980
19 4/16	12 1/16	7 3/16	M	Archuleta County	CO	Lisa Cooney	1985	980
19 4/16	12 2/16	7 2/16	M	Cheboygan County	MI	Steve E. Hutchinson	1985	980
19 4/16	12 4/16	7 0/16	M	Madison County	MT	John Ralph	1985	980
19 4/16	12 2/16	7 2/16	M	Siskiyou County	CA	Bruce Kipley	1985	980
19 4/16	12 6/16	6 14/16	M	Turtle River	ONT	Al Haines	1986	980
19 4/16	12 2/16	7 2/16	M	Archuleta County	CO	David Swanson	1986	980
19 4/16	12 1/16	7 3/16	M	Keeley Lake	SAS	Bruce E. Menz	1986	980
19 4/16	12 0/16	7 4/16	M	Delay River	QUE	Benjamin O. Brookhart III	1986	980
19 4/16	11 13/16	7 7/16	M	La Plata County	CO	Karen Stevens	1987	980
19 4/16	12 3/16	7 1/16	M	Fort Coulonge	QUE	David W. Wachter	1987	980
19 4/16	12 0/16	7 4/16	M	Wawa	ONT	Bruce Waterman	1987	980
19 4/16	12 0/16	7 4/16	M	Shining Tree	ONT	Alan J. Skowron	1988	980
19 4/16	11 11/16	7 9/16	M	Canterbury	NB	David G. Cote	1988	980
19 4/16	12 2/16	7 2/16	M	Iron County	MI	Douglas Wagner	1988	980
19 4/16	11 14/16	7 6/16	M	Iron County	WI	Roger Adamavich	1988	980
19 4/16	11 15/16	7 5/16	M	Herkimer County	NY	Paul Tomeo	1988	980
19 4/16	12 1/16	7 3/16	M	Grand County	UT	Jay Wick	1989	980
19 4/16	11 15/16	7 5/16	M	High Level	ALB	Stuart Sinclair-Smith	1989	980
19 4/16	12 0/16	7 4/16	M	Mitehell	QUE	Bruce D. Trapp	1989	980
19 4/16	11 14/16	7 6/16	M	San Fernando Island	AK	Kurt Goesch	1989	980
19 4/16	12 0/16	7 4/16	M	Dryden	ONT	Kreg A. Elmer	1989	980
19 4/16	12 2/16	7 2/16	M	Douglas County	WI	Dennis Nicholson	1989	980
19 4/16	11 14/16	7 6/16	M	Ravalli County	MT	Travis E. Proctor	1989	980
19 4/16	12 2/16	7 2/16	M	Sandoval County	NM	James O. Marquis	1989	980
19 4/16	11 11/16	7 9/16	M	River Valley	ONT	Jim D. Mullins	1990	980
19 4/16	12 2/16	7 2/16	M	East Bull Lake	ONT	Gerald A. Dick II	1990	980
19 4/16	12 1/16	7 3/16	M	Sheridan County	WY	Dennis F. Craft	1990	980
19 4/16	12 2/16	7 2/16	M	Delta County	MI	Bob Bouck	1990	980
19 4/16	12 7/16	6 13/16	M	Schoolcraft County	MI	Dennis W. Kleeman	1990	980
19 4/16	11 12/16	7 8/16	M	Archuleta County	CO	Grant Adkisson	1991	980
19 4/16	12 0/16	7 4/16	M	Lincoln County	OR	Chad Fletcher	1991	980
19 4/16	12 5/16	6 15/16	M	Chippewa County	WI	William E. Gladitsch	1991	980
19 4/16	12 0/16	7 4/16	M	Yukon River	AK	Bruce A. Haas	1992	980
19 4/16	12 2/16	7 2/16	M	Davidson	QUE	Brian I. King	1992	980
19 3/16	11 12/16	7 7/16	M	Mineral County	CO	Edward Wintz	1960	1,048
19 3/16	12 2/16	7 1/16	M	Rio Arriba County	NM	Dan Ward	1964	1,048
19 3/16	11 13/16	7 6/16	M	Iron Bridge	ONT	Philip L. Hawkins	1965	1,048

Score	Greatest Length	Greatest Width	Sex	Area	State/ Province	Hunter's Name	Date	Rank
19 3/16	11 12/16	7 7/16	M	Shasta County	CA	Michael D. Combs	1967	1,048
19 3/16	11 11/16	7 8/16	M	Sudbury District	ONT	Floyd Eccleston	1970	1,048
19 3/16	11 13/16	7 6/16	M	Uncompahgre N.F.	CO	Charles Bojarski	1971	1,048
19 3/16	11 14/16	7 5/16	M	Sequoia National Forest	CA	Martin Szekeresh, Jr.	1973	1,048
19 3/16	11 11/16	7 8/16	M	Powell County	MT	Gary L. Wilson	1975	1,048
19 3/16	11 13/16	7 6/16	M	Fremont County	ID	Roger Atwood	1977	1,048
19 3/16	12 3/16	7 0/16	M	Dryden	ONT	Bill Rose	1978	1,048
19 3/16	11 14/16	7 5/16	M	Saguache County	CO	Ross M. Clark	1979	1,048
19 3/16	11 13/16	7 6/16	M	Roscommon County	MI	Roger J. Maeder	1979	1,048
19 3/16	11 15/16	7 4/16	M	Bonneville County	ID	Fred Huffman	1980	1,048
19 3/16	11 14/16	7 5/16	M	Conejos County	CO	Frank Scott	1980	1,048
19 3/16	12 1/16	7 2/16	M	Iron County	WI	Frank Rasch	1982	1,048
19 3/16	11 15/16	7 4/16	M	Las Animas County	CO	Tom Nelson	1983	1,048
19 3/16	12 1/16	7 2/16	M	Delta County	CO	Doug McCauley	1983	1,048
19 3/16	12 1/16	7 2/16	M	Graham	ONT	Michael Perrott	1983	1,048
19 3/16	11 12/16	7 7/16	M	Grand County	CO	Jim Williams	1983	1,048
19 3/16	11 14/16	7 5/16	M	Kenora	ONT	Kenneth Gilb	1983	1,048
19 3/16	12 2/16	7 1/16	M	Hubbard County	MN	Omar Maggard	1984	1,048
19 3/16	11 13/16	7 6/16	M	Black Sturgeon Lake	ONT	Clarence 'Bud' Mrozek	1985	1,048
19 3/16	12 2/16	7 1/16	M	Durban	MAN	Bill Clink	1985	1,048
19 3/16	12 2/16	7 1/16	M	Whitemud Creek	ALB	Paul St. Laurent	1986	1,048
19 3/16	11 11/16	7 8/16	M	Caramat	ONT	Burley Hall	1986	1,048
19 3/16	11 15/16	7 4/16	M	Thunder Bay	ONT	Ron K. Serwa	1986	1,048
19 3/16	11 15/16	7 4/16	M	Bending Lake	ONT	John Lamp	1986	1,048
19 3/16	11 12/16	7 7/16	M	Park County	CO	Robert Wright	1987	1,048
19 3/16	11 12/16	7 7/16	M	Sussex	NB	Roger W. Kerry	1987	1,048
19 3/16	11 11/16	7 8/16	M	Sioux Narrows	ONT	Todd Gebert	1987	1,048
19 3/16	11 15/16	7 4/16	M	Clearwater County	ID	Don Larson	1987	1,048
19 3/16	11 9/16	7 10/16	M	Black River	ONT	E. L. Boyd III	1987	1,048
19 3/16	12 2/16	7 1/16	M	Custer County	CO	Rod Niles	1987	1,048
19 3/16	11 15/16	7 4/16	M	Boise County	ID	Curtis B. Wiker	1987	1,048
19 3/16	11 12/16	7 7/16	M	Franklin County	ME	Jim Roy	1987	1,048
19 3/16	12 4/16	6 15/16	M	Itasca County	MN	Cary Dalton	1987	1,048
19 3/16	12 1/16	7 2/16	M	Durban	MAN	Mike Delfino, Jr.	1987	1,048
19 3/16	12 3/16	7 0/16	M	Siskiyou County	CA	Clifford Mosley	1987	1,048
19 3/16	11 14/16	7 5/16	M	Boise County	ID	Dave Scott	1988	1,048
19 3/16	11 9/16	7 10/16	M	Siskiyou County	CA	William Payne	1988	1,048
19 3/16	11 15/16	7 4/16	M	High Prairie	ALB	Stephen Ebel	1989	1,048
19 3/16	12 0/16	7 3/16	M	Latah County	ID	Steve Krier	1989	1,048
19 3/16	11 11/16	7 8/16	M	Carbon County	UT	Hugh H. Hogle	1989	1,048
19 3/16	11 10/16	7 9/16	M	Lac Le Truite Territory	QUE	Brian Hendricks	1989	1,048
19 3/16	12 8/16	6 11/16	M	Extall River	BC	Larry H. Hill	1990	1,048
19 3/16	12 4/16	6 15/16	M	Wawang Lake	ONT	Todd A. Sturgul	1990	1,048
19 3/16	12 2/16	7 1/16	M	High Level	ALB	David Petet	1990	1,048
19 3/16	11 12/16	7 7/16	M	Lane County	OR	Dave Elliott	1990	1,048
19 3/16	12 2/16	7 1/16	M	Fort Chipwan	ALB	Patrick H. Aucoin	1991	1,048
19 3/16	12 6/16	6 13/16	M	Nancy Lake	AK	Mark R. Daum	1991	1,048
19 3/16	12 4/16	6 15/16	M	Beluga River	AK	Dr. Robert Edward Speegle	1991	1,048
19 3/16	12 2/16	7 1/16	M	High Level	ALB	Gino Giannetti	1991	1,048
19 3/16	12 4/16	6 15/16	M	Sheridan County	WY	Scott Runde	1991	1,048
19 3/16	12 5/16	6 14/16	M	Latuque	QUE	Bernard E. Beaudin	1991	1,048
19 3/16	12 1/16	7 2/16	M	Grand Rapids	MAN	James R. Kramp	1991	1,048
19 3/16	12 3/16	7 0/16	M	Montezuma County	CO	Paula R. Morton	1992	1,048
19 3/16	11 12/16	7 7/16	M	Edmonton	ALB	Keith Morris	1992	1,048
19 3/16	12 2/16	7 1/16	M	Idaho County	ID	Charles R. Whitfield	1992	1,048
19 3/16	12 3/16	7 0/16	M	Duchesne County	UT	Hal R. Stauff	1992	1,048
19 3/16	11 13/16	7 6/16	M	Raleigh Lake	ONT	Jeffrey Rueth	1992	1,048
19 2/16	11 9/16	7 9/16	M	Sudbury	ONT	Clarence Grandt	1963	1,108
19 2/16	11 12/16	7 6/16	M	Blount County	TN	Don Dvoroznak	1968	1,108
19 2/16	11 13/16	7 5/16	M	Chapleau	ONT	Gerald E. Taft	1968	1,108
19 2/16	11 12/16	7 6/16	M	Trinity County	CA	Fred M. Frakes	1970	1,108
19 2/16	12 3/16	6 15/16	M	Shasta County	CA	Gerald P. Doyle	1971	1,108
19 2/16	11 14/16	7 4/16	M	Vilas County	WI	William L. Yessa	1971	1,108
19 2/16	11 11/16	7 7/16	M	Kormak	ONT	Marvin E. Davis	1972	1,108
19 2/16	11 15/16	7 3/16	M	Uncompahgre N.F.	CO	Ed Bonardi	1973	1,108
19 2/16	11 13/16	7 5/16	M	Lemhi County	ID	Curley Keadle	1973	1,108
19 2/16	12 0/16	7 2/16	M	Dolores County	CO	Marvin Reichenau	1973	1,108
19 2/16	11 14/16	7 4/16	M	Archuleta County	CO	Judd Cooney	1974	1,108
19 2/16	11 13/16	7 5/16	M	Vancouver Island	BC	F. Guillon/A.Klopfenstei	1974	1,108
19 2/16	12 1/16	7 1/16	M	Dryden	ONT	Ken Horton	1977	1,108

Score	Greatest Length	Greatest Width	Sex	Area	State/ Province	Hunter's Name	Date	Rank
19 2/16	12 4/16	6 14/16	M	Vilas County	WI	Michael Gapa	1979	1,108
19 2/16	11 14/16	7 4/16	M	Skamania County	WA	John H. Wahl	1979	1,108
19 2/16	11 11/16	7 7/16	M	Shasta County	CA	Mark David Broadhead	1980	1,108
19 2/16	11 14/16	7 4/16	M	Douglas County	CO	Thomas P. Grainger	1980	1,108
19 2/16	12 1/16	7 1/16	M	Chetwynd	BC	Ron F. McKay	1980	1,108
19 2/16	12 0/16	7 2/16	M	Bayfield County	WI	William F. Schutte	1980	1,108
19 2/16	11 15/16	7 3/16	M	Las Animas County	CO	David S. Bunce	1981	1,108
19 2/16	12 4/16	6 14/16	M	Whitecourt	ALB	Wade Johnson	1981	1,108
19 2/16	12 4/16	6 14/16	M	St. Louis County	MN	Charlie Paine	1981	1,108
19 2/16	12 2/16	7 0/16	M	Flathead County	MT	Owen Weaver	1981	1,108
19 2/16	12 0/16	7 2/16	M	Boise County	ID	Larry Hoff	1982	1,108
19 2/16	11 12/16	7 6/16	M	Las Animas County	CO	Bill R. Lopatta	1982	1,108
19 2/16	12 0/16	7 2/16	M	Moose Creek	AK	Robert T. Thomason, Jr.	1983	1,108
19 2/16	11 10/16	7 8/16	M	Gallatin County	MT	Pat Sinclair	1983	1,108
19 2/16	11 14/16	7 4/16	M	Savant Lake	ONT	Mark Milford	1983	1,108
19 2/16	12 4/16	6 14/16	M	Grassy Narrows	ONT	Mike Jacobs	1983	1,108
19 2/16	11 12/16	7 6/16	M	Caramat	ONT	Thomas Hlinka	1983	1,108
19 2/16	12 3/16	6 15/16	M	Aulneau Peninsula	ONT	Mike Koska	1984	1,108
19 2/16	11 14/16	7 4/16	M	Atikokan	ONT	Roger L. Hensley	1984	1,108
19 2/16	11 12/16	7 6/16	M	Mackinac County	MI	Carson D. McMullen	1984	1,108
19 2/16	12 2/16	7 0/16	M	Grand County	UT	Diane Snyder	1985	1,108
19 2/16	11 11/16	7 7/16	M	Valley County	ID	Kenneth A. Hyde	1985	1,108
19 2/16	12 3/16	6 15/16	M	Sanpete County	UT	Terry Casper	1986	1,108
19 2/16	12 1/16	7 1/16	M	Rocky Lake	MAN	Dennis Jacobson	1986	1,108
19 2/16	12 0/16	7 2/16	M	French River	ONT	Mike Bishop	1986	1,108
19 2/16	11 14/16	7 4/16	M	Boise County	ID	Gary Titus	1986	1,108
19 2/16	12 0/16	7 2/16	M	Durban	MAN	David H. Boland	1986	1,108
19 2/16	12 2/16	7 0/16	M	Duck Mtn.	MAN	Chris Switzer	1987	1,108
19 2/16	12 0/16	7 2/16	M	Hearst	ONT	Paul David Forquer	1987	1,108
19 2/16	12 0/16	7 2/16	M	King County	WA	Irvin E. Harris, Jr.	1987	1,108
19 2/16	12 0/16	7 2/16	M	Catron County	NM	Perry D. Harper	1987	1,108
19 2/16	12 7/16	6 11/16	M	Cass County	MN	Philip M. Scott	1987	1,108
19 2/16	12 2/16	7 0/16	M	Haywood County	NC	Michael Treadway	1987	1,108
19 2/16	11 15/16	7 3/16	M	Greenbrier County	WV	Billy J. Hutchinson	1987	1,108
19 2/16	12 6/16	6 12/16	M	Taylor County	WI	Allen K. Beard	1988	1,108
19 2/16	12 4/16	6 14/16	M	Price County	WI	Randall J. Johnson	1988	1,108
19 2/16	11 13/16	7 5/16	M	Rio Arriba County	NM	James H. Miller	1989	1,108
19 2/16	12 2/16	7 0/16	M	Knouff Lake	BC	Steve Zelisko	1989	1,108
19 2/16	11 10/16	7 8/16	M	Caramat	ONT	Chris Hile	1989	1,108
19 2/16	12 1/16	7 1/16	M	Starr Lake	MAN	Brian Gross	1989	1,108
19 2/16	11 14/16	7 4/16	M	Thunder Bay	ONT	E. Alex Gouthro	1989	1,108
19 2/16	11 15/16	7 3/16	M	Jim Lake	AK	Tom Hocking	1989	1,108
19 2/16	11 13/16	7 5/16	M	La Tuque	QUE	Ronald T. Kinnas	1989	1,108
19 2/16	11 12/16	7 6/16	M	Prince of Wales Island	AK	Steve Martin	1989	1,108
19 2/16	11 14/16	7 4/16	M	Thunder Bay	ONT	Dale Miller	1990	1,108
19 2/16	12 2/16	7 0/16	M	Christopher Lake	SAS	Lance W. McCrary	1990	1,108
19 2/16	11 15/16	7 3/16	M	Kenora	ONT	Jeffrey C. Dais	1991	1,108
19 2/16	11 13/16	7 5/16	M	High Level	ALB	R. E. Smith	1991	1,108
19 2/16	11 12/16	7 6/16	M	Le Domaine	QUE	Steven J. Niedzielski	1991	1,108
19 2/16	12 0/16	7 2/16	M	Cook County	MN	John Truebenbach	1991	1,108
19 2/16	11 14/16	7 4/16	M	Sullivan County	NY	Larry Micera	1991	1,108
19 2/16	12 0/16	7 2/16	M	Beauville	SAS	Don Lindsay	1992	1,108
19 2/16	12 2/16	7 0/16	M	Cranberry Lake	ALB	Terry C. Parkinson	1992	1,108
19 1/16	11 1/16	8 0/16	M	Jackson County	OR	Leander Lowel	1959	1,174
19 1/16	11 12/16	7 5/16	M	Mineral County	CO	Ed Wintz	1959	1,174
19 1/16	11 15/16	7 2/16	M	Gogebic County	MI	Margaret R. Cooley	1961	1,174
19 1/16	11 5/16	7 12/16	M	Upper Peninsula	MI	Jerry D. Anderson	1967	1,174
19 1/16	12 1/16	7 0/16	M	Red Lake	ONT	Don Ellett	1969	1,174
19 1/16	11 15/16	7 2/16	M	Langlade County	WI	Roland Mantzke	1969	1,174
19 1/16	11 14/16	7 3/16	M	Archuleta County	CO	Maurice Chambers	1973	1,174
19 1/16	11 15/16	7 2/16	M	Marquette County	MI	Pete Hillesheim	1974	1,174
19 1/16	11 4/16	7 13/16	M	Vancouver Island	BC	Klaus Schultz	1974	1,174
19 1/16	12 1/16	7 0/16	M	Itasca County	MN	William Biggs	1976	1,174
19 1/16	12 3/16	6 14/16	M	Garfield County	CO	Michael D. Dickess	1976	1,174
19 1/16	11 11/16	7 6/16	M	St. Louis County	MN	Gerry Benson	1977	1,174
19 1/16	12 0/16	7 1/16	M	Kitsap County	WA	Larry A. Martin	1977	1,174
19 1/16	11 10/16	7 7/16	M	Oxford County	ME	James P. Wellever	1978	1,174
19 1/16	12 2/16	6 15/16	M	Oneida County	WI	Douglas A. Severson	1979	1,174
19 1/16	12 1/16	7 0/16	M	Lincoln County	WY	Ronell Skinner	1979	1,174
19 1/16	11 12/16	7 5/16	M	Marquette County	MI	Jeff Apel	1980	1,174

SCORE	GREATEST LENGTH	GREATEST WIDTH	SEX	AREA	STATE/ PROVINCE	HUNTER'S NAME	DATE	RANK
19 1/16	12 2/16	6 15/16	M	Cass County	MN	Robert M. Burtch	1980	1,174
19 1/16	11 13/16	7 4/16	M	Coos County	NH	James 'Boomer' Hayden	1980	1,174
19 1/16	12 0/16	7 1/16	M	Terrace	BC	Bill Coburn	1981	1,174
19 1/16	11 12/16	7 5/16	M	Caribou Snare Creek	AK	Bill Krenz	1981	1,174
19 1/16	11 14/16	7 3/16	M	Franklin County	ME	Albert J. Kolatac	1982	1,174
19 1/16	12 2/16	6 15/16	M	Bayfield County	WI	Larry Frye	1982	1,174
19 1/16	11 15/16	7 2/16	M	Kenora	ONT	Ray Hawver	1982	1,174
19 1/16	11 14/16	7 3/16	M	Nestor Falls	ONT	Larry Streiff	1982	1,174
19 1/16	11 12/16	7 5/16	M	Espanola	ONT	Donald W. Taylor	1982	1,174
19 1/16	11 15/16	7 2/16	M	Bonneville County	ID	Ronnel J. Stacey	1983	1,174
19 1/16	11 15/16	7 2/16	M	Jellicoe	ONT	Ed Herzog	1983	1,174
19 1/16	12 1/16	7 0/16	M	Pitkin County	CO	Perry Smith	1983	1,174
19 1/16	12 4/16	6 13/16	M	Rockingham County	VA	Roger O. Wyant	1983	1,174
19 1/16	12 3/16	6 14/16	M	Hudson Bay	SAS	Warren Buss	1984	1,174
19 1/16	11 15/16	7 2/16	M	Plumes County	CA	Mike Holley	1984	1,174
19 1/16	12 1/16	7 0/16	M	Coos County	OR	Rick Gabbard	1984	1,174
19 1/16	11 14/16	7 3/16	M	Redditt	ONT	Jim Christman	1985	1,174
19 1/16	11 15/16	7 2/16	M	Little Bear Lake	SAS	Michael J. Ward	1986	1,174
19 1/16	12 2/16	6 15/16	M	Terrance Lake	ONT	Jerry Krolik	1986	1,174
19 1/16	12 6/16	6 11/16	M	Nez Perce County	ID	Steve Marcell	1986	1,174
19 1/16	11 15/16	7 2/16	F	Sanpete County	UT	Judy Hallman	1986	1,174
19 1/16	12 2/16	6 15/16	M	Plumes County	CA	Mike Holley	1986	1,174
19 1/16	12 3/16	6 14/16	M	Alpine County	CA	Rick Lund	1986	1,174
19 1/16	12 2/16	6 15/16	M	Carbon County	UT	Hugh Hogle	1987	1,174
19 1/16	11 13/16	7 4/16	M	Fremont County	CO	Cheryl Ray	1987	1,174
19 1/16	11 15/16	7 2/16	M	Atikokan	ONT	Paul Maas	1987	1,174
19 1/16	11 15/16	7 2/16	M	Grand County	UT	O. Clair Adams	1988	1,174
19 1/16	11 15/16	7 2/16	M	Zone 67	SAS	Ivan Buss	1988	1,174
19 1/16	12 0/16	7 1/16	M	Dryden	ONT	Terry C. Arndt	1988	1,174
19 1/16	11 14/16	7 3/16	M	Bryson Lake	QUE	Stephen P. Pointer	1988	1,174
19 1/16	11 10/16	7 7/16	M	Inyo County	CA	Jim Voges	1988	1,174
19 1/16	11 15/16	7 2/16	M	Millville	NBW	Lamar M. Shafer	1988	1,174
19 1/16	12 0/16	7 1/16	M	Smokey Lake	ALB	Greg Reynolds	1989	1,174
19 1/16	11 14/16	7 3/16	M	Horn Payne	ONT	Paul R. Chaffee	1989	1,174
19 1/16	11 14/16	7 3/16	M	Larimer County	CO	Ed Bennett	1989	1,174
19 1/16	11 6/16	7 11/16	M	Dryden	ONT	Troy S. Lowrey	1989	1,174
19 1/16	12 2/16	6 15/16	M	Porcupine Mtns.	SAS	Dave McKenzie	1989	1,174
19 1/16	11 10/16	7 7/16	M	Warren	ONT	Gary Lawrence Harding	1989	1,174
19 1/16	11 13/16	7 4/16	M	Kenora	ONT	Chuck Harris	1989	1,174
19 1/16	11 15/16	7 2/16	M	Sudbury	ONT	Randolph J. Hempton	1989	1,174
19 1/16	11 14/16	7 3/16	M	Fort McMurray	ALB	Jim Trafford	1990	1,174
19 1/16	11 14/16	7 3/16	M	Kenora	ONT	Shawn A. Wahl	1990	1,174
19 1/16	12 1/16	7 0/16	M	Duchesne County	UT	Roger Cyfers	1990	1,174
19 1/16	11 15/16	7 2/16	M	Marathon	ONT	David Weerstra	1990	1,174
19 1/16	11 12/16	7 5/16	M	Stevens County	WA	Robert M. Larson	1990	1,174
19 1/16	12 1/16	7 0/16	M	Prince of Wales Island	AK	Bernie Weisgerber	1990	1,174
19 1/16	11 11/16	7 6/16	M	Wallowa County	OR	Dick Dohm	1990	1,174
19 1/16	12 1/16	7 0/16	M	Prince of Wales Island	AK	Dan Moore	1991	1,174
19 1/16	11 3/16	7 14/16	F	Riding Mtn.	MAN	Cory A. Pardon	1991	1,174
19 1/16	12 4/16	6 13/16	M	High Level	ALB	Gino Giannetti	1991	1,174
19 1/16	11 12/16	7 5/16	M	Sandoval County	NM	Wayne C. Wendel	1991	1,174
19 1/16	12 1/16	7 0/16	M	Beltrami County	MN	Charles W. Gahagan	1991	1,174
19 1/16	12 3/16	6 14/16	M	Smokey Lake	ALB	Andy Melnychuk	1991	1,174
19 1/16	12 0/16	7 1/16	M	Preston County	WV	Robert Peddicord	1991	1,174
19 1/16	11 15/16	7 2/16	M	Grand County	CO	Cary Laman	1992	1,174
19 1/16	12 0/16	7 1/16	M	Montrose County	CO	Johnnie R. Walters	1992	1,174
19 1/16	11 15/16	7 2/16	M	Trinity County	CA	Edward Bianchi	1992	1,174
19 1/16	12 2/16	6 15/16	M	Prince of Wales Island	AK	Kelly Norskog	1992	1,174
19 0/16	12 6/16	6 10/16	M	Iron County	WI	Charles Kroll	1966	1,249
19 0/16	11 9/16	7 7/16	M	Sioux Narrows	ONT	Walter J. Sawicki	1967	1,249
19 0/16	11 13/16	7 3/16	M	Kamloops	BC	Terry J. Haines	1968	1,249
19 0/16	11 12/16	7 4/16	M	Chapleau	ONT	Kenneth R. Larson	1968	1,249
19 0/16	11 15/16	7 1/16	M	Ignace	ONT	Stanley Olson	1968	1,249
19 0/16	11 10/16	7 6/16	M	Kenora	ONT	Barry Englehardt	1969	1,249
19 0/16	11 12/16	7 4/16	M	Armstrong	ONT	James Mahoney	1969	1,249
19 0/16	11 8/16	7 8/16	M	Shasta County	CA	Patrick J. Marley	1969	1,249
19 0/16	11 11/16	7 5/16	M	Skamania County	WA	Dennis E. DesJardins	1970	1,249
19 0/16	11 11/16	7 5/16	M	Skamania County	WA	Dennis E. DesJardins	1970	1,249
19 0/16	11 7/16	7 9/16	M	Grand County	UT	C. Donald Lechner	1970	1,249
19 0/16	11 9/16	7 7/16	M	Lemhi County	ID	Douglas Kittredge	1971	1,249

SCORE	GREATEST LENGTH	GREATEST WIDTH	SEX	AREA	STATE/ PROVINCE	HUNTER'S NAME	DATE	RANK
19 0/16	11 11/16	7 5/16	M	Saguache County	CO	Gary Ginther	1973	1,249
19 0/16	11 14/16	7 2/16	M	Cloyne	ONT	Tom Erkinger	1976	1,249
19 0/16	11 14/16	7 2/16	M	Lanark	ONT	Guy Pointer	1977	1,249
19 0/16	11 14/16	7 2/16	M	St. Louis County	MN	Jimmy F. Rogers	1978	1,249
19 0/16	11 8/16	7 8/16	M	Wawa	ONT	Don LaDuke	1980	1,249
19 0/16	12 5/16	6 11/16	M	Sullivan County	NY	John Nasuta	1980	1,249
19 0/16	11 9/16	7 7/16	M	Boise County	ID	Richard C. Nichols	1981	1,249
19 0/16	11 14/16	7 2/16	M	North Bay	ONT	Grant R. Beattie	1981	1,249
19 0/16	12 1/16	6 15/16	M	Fort St. John	BC	Duane Hicks	1981	1,249
19 0/16	11 11/16	7 5/16	M	Ravalli County	MT	Rod Osburn	1981	1,249
19 0/16	11 8/16	7 8/16	M	Coos County	NH	Edward Silva	1981	1,249
19 0/16	11 14/16	7 2/16	F	San Juan County	UT	Sheldon Anderson	1982	1,249
19 0/16	12 1/16	6 15/16	M	Las Animas County	CO	Bob Lopatta	1982	1,249
19 0/16	11 14/16	7 2/16	M	Pacific County	WA	Annette Crews	1983	1,249
19 0/16	11 13/16	7 3/16	M	Siskiyou County	CA	Fred Searle	1983	1,249
19 0/16	11 14/16	7 2/16	M	Fort Frances	ONT	Kerry Ella	1984	1,249
19 0/16	11 9/16	7 7/16	M	Chapeau	QUE	Joseph D. Maddock	1984	1,249
19 0/16	11 13/16	7 3/16	M	Meadow Lake	SAS	Gary Bauer	1984	1,249
19 0/16	12 1/16	6 15/16	M	Fremont County	ID	Joe Bronson	1984	1,249
19 0/16	11 15/16	7 1/16	M	York County	NBW	Daniel L. Shaffer	1984	1,249
19 0/16	11 13/16	7 3/16	M	Bingham County	ID	Mike Lee Wohlschlegel	1984	1,249
19 0/16	12 1/16	6 15/16	M	Lincoln County	WI	Jim Wurster	1984	1,249
19 0/16	11 14/16	7 2/16	M	Vilas County	WI	Mike Eidson	1984	1,249
19 0/16	11 13/16	7 3/16	M	Mine Centre	ONT	Bob Roulet	1985	1,249
19 0/16	12 2/16	6 14/16	M	Ear Falls	ONT	Brent Allen Poindexter	1985	1,249
19 0/16	11 8/16	7 8/16	M	Chelan County	WA	Leroy E. House	1986	1,249
19 0/16	11 14/16	7 2/16	M	Ravalli County	MT	John Locke	1987	1,249
19 0/16	11 14/16	7 2/16	M	Grays Harbor County	WA	Mark Tupper	1987	1,249
19 0/16	12 0/16	7 0/16	M	Tulare County	CA	Don Reid	1987	1,249
19 0/16	12 0/16	7 0/16	M	Smeaton	SAS	Gene Welle	1988	1,249
19 0/16	12 7/16	6 9/16	M	Cranbrook	BC	Jasper Kenneth White, Jr.	1988	1,249
19 0/16	11 10/16	7 6/16	M	Sioux Lookout	ONT	Steve Schmidt	1988	1,249
19 0/16	12 4/16	6 12/16	M	Langlade County	WI	Jeff Traska	1988	1,249
19 0/16	12 0/16	7 0/16	M	Hardy County	WV	Clarence W. Houck	1988	1,249
19 0/16	11 12/16	7 4/16	M	Cold Lake	ALB	Ron R. Dixon	1989	1,249
19 0/16	11 9/16	7 7/16	M	Cochrane	ONT	Ed Rogalski	1989	1,249
19 0/16	12 2/16	6 14/16	M	Ft. McMurray	ALB	James Pike	1989	1,249
19 0/16	12 0/16	7 0/16	M	Chapleau	ONT	Dennis D. Wentz	1989	1,249
19 0/16	11 14/16	7 2/16	M	Drury Twp.	ONT	Marty Masek	1989	1,249
19 0/16	11 13/16	7 3/16	M	Foleyet	ONT	Mike Schmidt	1989	1,249
19 0/16	11 10/16	7 6/16	M	Sandoval County	NM	Noble Sinclair	1989	1,249
19 0/16	11 12/16	7 4/16	M	Kitsap County	WA	Gary A. Bell	1989	1,249
19 0/16	11 11/16	7 5/16	M	Pierce County	WA	Warren L. Byrd	1989	1,249
19 0/16	11 15/16	7 1/16	M	Aroostook County	ME	Louis J. Lorenzo	1989	1,249
19 0/16	12 1/16	6 15/16	M	Langlade County	WI	Glen A. Rutten	1989	1,249
19 0/16	11 11/16	7 5/16	M	Bella Coola	BC	J. Dale Hale	1989	1,249
19 0/16	12 0/16	7 0/16	M	Sheridan County	WY	Larry O. Burtis	1990	1,249
19 0/16	11 8/16	7 8/16	M	Chelmsford	ONT	Timothy C. Shock	1990	1,249
19 0/16	11 13/16	7 3/16	M	Chapleau	ONT	Dennis Dawson	1990	1,249
19 0/16	12 2/16	6 14/16	M	Minaki	ONT	Carroll Cunningham	1990	1,249
19 0/16	11 12/16	7 4/16	M	Wallowa County	OR	Eugene Smith, Jr.	1990	1,249
19 0/16	12 1/16	6 15/16	M	Bayfield County	WI	Randall O. Nash	1990	1,249
19 0/16	12 0/16	7 0/16	M	Sawyer County	WI	Kim Lemke	1990	1,249
19 0/16	11 9/16	7 7/16	M	Manitouwadge	ONT	Rick Buchanan	1991	1,249
19 0/16	11 14/16	7 2/16	M	Hearst	ONT	Steven B. Karel	1991	1,249
19 0/16	11 15/16	7 1/16	M	Remigny	QUE	Max Reagin	1991	1,249
19 0/16	11 10/16	7 6/16	M	Matagami	QUE	Jacques Harvey	1991	1,249
19 0/16	12 5/16	6 11/16	M	Sevier County	UT	Dennis Nielsen	1991	1,249
19 0/16	12 0/16	7 0/16	M	Ontonagon County	MI	Carl R. Birely	1991	1,249
19 0/16	11 12/16	7 4/16	M	Oxford County	ME	Gary J. Russell	1991	1,249
19 0/16	12 0/16	7 0/16	M	Custer County	ID	Pascal Perrin	1992	1,249
19 0/16	11 9/16	7 7/16	M	Hollinshead Lake	ONT	John E. Larsen	1992	1,249
19 0/16	11 9/16	7 7/16	M	Grande Prairie	ALB	Les Baird	1992	1,249
19 0/16	11 4/16	7 12/16	M	Wanless	MAN	Tim Finley	1992	1,249
19 0/16	11 9/16	7 7/16	M	Mammeville	QUE	George A. Kearns	1992	1,249
19 0/16	12 0/16	7 0/16	M	Goodsoil	SAS	Carol Hathaway	1992	1,249
18 15/16	11 9/16	7 6/16	M	King George IV Lake	NFL	Frank M. Davis	1958	1,327
18 15/16	11 15/16	7 0/16	M	Flathead County	MT	Danny Moore	1976	1,327
18 15/16	12 1/16	6 14/16	M	Pitkin County	CO	Sharon Payne	1976	1,327
18 15/16	12 0/16	6 15/16	M	St. Louis County	MN	Roy Kahabka	1978	1,327

Score	Greatest Length	Greatest Width	Sex	Area	State/ Province	Hunter's Name	Date	Rank
18 15/16	12 2/16	6 13/16	M	Hubbard County	MN	Dr. James Schubert	1978	1,327
18 15/16	11 14/16	7 1/16	M	Delta County	CO	Bob Gulman, Jr.	1979	1,327
18 15/16	11 4/16	7 11/16	M	Kalkaska County	MI	Gregory Korkoske	1979	1,327
18 15/16	12 0/16	6 15/16	M	Pough Lake	ONT	Jozset Vass	1979	1,327
18 15/16	11 11/16	7 4/16	M	Roscommon County	MI	Lloyd B. Beebe	1980	1,327
18 15/16	11 15/16	7 0/16	M	Sandilands	MAN	Fred Hay	1981	1,327
18 15/16	12 1/16	6 14/16	M	Boise County	ID	Jack Arbaugh	1981	1,327
18 15/16	12 0/16	6 15/16	M	San Miguel County	NM	Dick McClain	1981	1,327
18 15/16	12 1/16	6 14/16	M	Espanola	ONT	Martin Masek	1982	1,327
18 15/16	12 0/16	6 15/16	M	Valley County	ID	Bob Dawson	1982	1,327
18 15/16	11 15/16	7 0/16	M	Larimer County	CO	Douglas Beck	1982	1,327
18 15/16	11 9/16	7 6/16	M	Pontiac	QUE	Chuck Wade	1983	1,327
18 15/16	11 10/16	7 5/16	M	Warren	ONT	Clarence Keaton	1983	1,327
18 15/16	11 14/16	7 1/16	M	Coos County	NH	Greg White	1984	1,327
18 15/16	12 2/16	6 13/16	M	Little Sturge Lake	ONT	David F. Martinek	1985	1,327
18 15/16	11 15/16	7 0/16	M	Delta County	CO	Terry Bridgman	1985	1,327
18 15/16	11 9/16	7 6/16	M	Renfrew	ONT	Jeffrey Tucker	1985	1,327
18 15/16	11 14/16	7 1/16	M	Timiskaming	ONT	Gary F. Greene	1985	1,327
18 15/16	11 8/16	7 7/16	M	Poitras	ONT	Robert H. Pavlovic	1985	1,327
18 15/16	12 2/16	6 13/16	M	Mine Centre	ONT	Larry Looman	1986	1,327
18 15/16	11 12/16	7 3/16	M	Hudson Bay	SAS	Bruce Balerud	1986	1,327
18 15/16	12 4/16	6 11/16	M	Espanola	ONT	Terry J. Gerber	1986	1,327
18 15/16	11 14/16	7 1/16	M	Cygnet Lake	ONT	Greg Roufs	1986	1,327
18 15/16	12 0/16	6 15/16	M	Sioux Lookout	ONT	Dr. Joe Nilsson	1986	1,327
18 15/16	11 12/16	7 3/16	M	Findlay Lake	QUE	Paul Bertrand	1986	1,327
18 15/16	11 13/16	7 2/16	M	King County	WA	Steven Jackl	1986	1,327
18 15/16	11 11/16	7 4/16	M	Lincoln County	WY	Vaughn Ballard	1987	1,327
18 15/16	11 14/16	7 1/16	M	Coos County	OR	G. Julie Woodman	1987	1,327
18 15/16	11 7/16	7 8/16	M	Herkimer County	NY	Daniel R. Walters	1987	1,327
18 15/16	12 1/16	6 14/16	M	Rockingham County	VA	Donald G. Hodges	1987	1,327
18 15/16	11 12/16	7 3/16	M	Cold Lake	ALB	Joseph R. Weber	1988	1,327
18 15/16	11 12/16	7 3/16	M	Latah County	ID	David B. Silcock	1988	1,327
18 15/16	11 14/16	7 1/16	M	Iron County	WI	Henry J. Lindberg	1988	1,327
18 15/16	11 14/16	7 1/16	M	Lemhi County	ID	Randy Lee Davidson	1988	1,327
18 15/16	11 6/16	7 9/16	M	Elmore County	ID	John Turner	1989	1,327
18 15/16	11 10/16	7 5/16	M	Caramat	ONT	Charles P. Morgan, Jr.	1989	1,327
18 15/16	11 8/16	7 7/16	M	Boise County	ID	Julian Salutregui	1989	1,327
18 15/16	11 7/16	7 8/16	M	Zec Restigo	QUE	Clade St. Amour	1989	1,327
18 15/16	12 1/16	6 14/16	M	Fayette County	WV	Michael D. King	1989	1,327
18 15/16	11 10/16	7 5/16	M	Tucker County	WV	Robert McGee	1989	1,327
18 15/16	12 6/16	6 9/16	M	Beltrami County	MN	Ronald Alan Lemire	1990	1,327
18 15/16	11 14/16	7 1/16	M	Tucker County	WV	Randall Lee Marsh	1990	1,327
18 15/16	12 1/16	6 14/16	M	Lincoln County	NM	Jack Berger	1990	1,327
18 15/16	12 1/16	6 14/16	M	Kenora	ONT	David Johnson	1991	1,327
18 15/16	11 12/16	7 3/16	M	Valley County	ID	David R. Heck	1991	1,327
18 15/16	11 11/16	7 4/16	M	Fort McMurray	ALB	Wes Whenham	1992	1,327
18 15/16	11 13/16	7 2/16	M	Siebert Lake	ALB	Orest Popil	1992	1,327
18 14/16	11 6/16	7 8/16	M	Vermillion Bay	ONT	Wayne I. Munkel	1966	1,378
18 14/16	12 7/16	6 7/16	M	Vanderhoof	BC	Cecil Raphael	1967	1,378
18 14/16	11 2/16	7 12/16	M	Cranberry Portage	MAN	Carl Anderson	1968	1,378
18 14/16	11 11/16	7 3/16	M	Orleans County	VT	James Gilman	1969	1,378
18 14/16	11 12/16	7 2/16	M	Idaho County	ID	Peter Eremo	1970	1,378
18 14/16	12 2/16	6 12/16	M	Mesa County	CO	Jerry Cunningham	1972	1,378
18 14/16	12 3/16	6 11/16	M	Madera County	CA	Duane A. Whittle	1973	1,378
18 14/16	11 12/16	7 2/16	M	Lake County	MN	Art Heinze	1974	1,378
18 14/16	12 2/16	6 12/16	M	Vermillion Bay	ONT	Myles Keller	1974	1,378
18 14/16	11 13/16	7 1/16	M	Lincoln County	OR	Stanley D. Miles	1974	1,378
18 14/16	12 0/16	6 14/16	M	Wabigoon	ONT	Keith Olson	1975	1,378
18 14/16	11 14/16	7 0/16	M	Minaki	ONT	Greg Stezenski	1975	1,378
18 14/16	11 10/16	7 4/16	M	Nipigon	ONT	Vickery Frederick	1976	1,378
18 14/16	11 13/16	7 1/16	M	Prince George	BC	Jim Jackson	1976	1,378
18 14/16	11 14/16	7 0/16	M	Somerset County	ME	John J. Sweeney	1976	1,378
18 14/16	11 13/16	7 1/16	M	Custer County	CO	William Henderson	1978	1,378
18 14/16	11 12/16	7 2/16	M	Bighorn Mountains	WY	David M. Nahrgang	1978	1,378
18 14/16	12 0/16	6 14/16	M	Washington County	ME	Raymond Olson	1979	1,378
18 14/16	11 14/16	7 0/16	M	Bob Marshall Wilderness	MT	James Dean	1980	1,378
18 14/16	11 10/16	7 4/16	M	Sandilands	MAN	Larry Kraynyk	1980	1,378
18 14/16	11 11/16	7 3/16	M	Marquette County	MI	William Robert Baltrip	1981	1,378
18 14/16	11 9/16	7 5/16	M	Grant County	NM	Ross Johnson	1981	1,378
18 14/16	12 0/16	6 14/16	M	Ignace	ONT	Robert I. Mussey	1981	1,378

MINIMUM SCORE 18

(Continued)

SCORE	GREATEST LENGTH	GREATEST WIDTH	SEX	AREA	STATE/ PROVINCE	HUNTER'S NAME	DATE	RANK
18 14/16	11 14/16	7 0/16	M	Dryden	ONT	Gary J. O'Donnell	1981	1,378
18 14/16	11 9/16	7 5/16	M	Kootenai County	ID	Stanley Leake	1982	1,378
18 14/16	11 12/16	7 2/16	M	Chapleau	ONT	Robert J. Davis	1982	1,378
18 14/16	11 15/16	6 15/16	M	Sioux Lookout	ONT	Michael R. Traub	1982	1,378
18 14/16	11 14/16	7 0/16	M	Montezuma County	CO	William C. Shuster	1983	1,378
18 14/16	11 9/16	7 5/16	M	Aulneau Peninsula	ONT	Michael F. Koska	1983	1,378
18 14/16	11 13/16	7 1/16	M	Thunder Bay	ONT	Todd Gilb	1983	1,378
18 14/16	11 13/16	7 1/16	M	Park County	MT	Cecil Hendricks	1983	1,378
18 14/16	11 12/16	7 2/16	M	Mine Centre	ONT	Al Haines	1984	1,378
18 14/16	11 9/16	7 5/16	M	Jackson County	CO	Kurt Keskimaki	1984	1,378
18 14/16	11 12/16	7 2/16	M	Tatalina River	AK	Timothy J. Barber	1984	1,378
18 14/16	11 6/16	7 8/16	M	Fort Frances	ONT	Lloyd R. Branchcomb	1984	1,378
18 14/16	11 13/16	7 1/16	M	Wallowa County	OR	Jerry Jensen	1984	1,378
18 14/16	11 12/16	7 2/16	M	Scoop Lake	BC	Ronald Montross	1984	1,378
18 14/16	11 8/16	7 6/16	M	Mine Centre	ONT	Gary Schuler	1985	1,378
18 14/16	11 12/16	7 2/16	M	Fremont County	CO	Leroy Miller	1985	1,378
18 14/16	12 1/16	6 13/16	M	Ignace	ONT	Ken Terry	1985	1,378
18 14/16	11 10/16	7 4/16	M	Atikokan	ONT	Eugene Francisco	1985	1,378
18 14/16	11 12/16	7 2/16	M	San Miguel County	NM	Dick McClain	1986	1,378
18 14/16	12 0/16	6 14/16	M	Grant County	OR	Don D. Litts	1986	1,378
18 14/16	11 10/16	7 4/16	M	Park County	CO	Mike Boland	1987	1,378
18 14/16	11 8/16	7 6/16	M	Ignace	ONT	Robert James Lewis	1987	1,378
18 14/16	12 2/16	6 12/16	M	Archuleta County	CO	H. Kitchener Layland,Jr.	1987	1,378
18 14/16	11 9/16	7 5/16	M	Ear Falls	ONT	Daniel J. Mercer	1988	1,378
18 14/16	11 11/16	7 3/16	M	Green Lake	SAS	Steven Kent Camburn	1988	1,378
18 14/16	12 0/16	6 14/16	M	Winefred Lake	ALB	Danny Moore	1988	1,378
18 14/16	11 11/16	7 3/16	M	Fort Coulonge	QUE	Hubert L. Norfleet, Jr.	1988	1,378
18 14/16	11 9/16	7 5/16	M	Idaho County	ID	Ron Smith	1988	1,378
18 14/16	11 13/16	7 1/16	M	Saddle Hills	ALB	Ben White	1988	1,378
18 14/16	11 12/16	7 2/16	M	Water Hen River	SAS	Pink Atkins	1988	1,378
18 14/16	12 0/16	6 14/16	M	Koochiching County	MN	Matt Barry	1988	1,378
18 14/16	12 1/16	6 13/16	M	Luce County	MI	Terry L. Cook	1988	1,378
18 14/16	11 12/16	7 2/16	M	Mann River	SAS	David P. Heinselman II	1989	1,378
18 14/16	11 10/16	7 4/16	M	Prince William Sound	AK	Richard Moran	1989	1,378
18 14/16	11 15/16	6 15/16	M	Sioux Lookout	ONT	Tom Nebbs	1989	1,378
18 14/16	11 13/16	7 1/16	M	Pelican Narrows	SAS	Doug Otte	1989	1,378
18 14/16	12 4/16	6 10/16	M	Rocky Lake	MAN	Cecil Tharp	1989	1,378
18 14/16	11 12/16	7 2/16	M	Fort Coulonge	QUE	Barry J. Horton	1989	1,378
18 14/16	11 8/16	7 6/16	M	Coos County	NH	Mark Milne	1989	1,378
18 14/16	11 15/16	6 15/16	M	Sanders County	MT	Greg L. Munther	1989	1,378
18 14/16	11 10/16	7 4/16	M	Le Club Trout Lake	QUE	Kenneth Augsburger	1990	1,378
18 14/16	11 15/16	6 15/16	M	Trois Rivers	QUE	Lee Libbey	1990	1,378
18 14/16	11 8/16	7 6/16	M	Boise County	ID	Julian Salutrequi	1990	1,378
18 14/16	11 11/16	7 3/16	M	Minaki	ONT	Joe Devlin	1990	1,378
18 14/16	11 5/16	7 9/16	M	Elmore County	ID	John Turner	1990	1,378
18 14/16	12 2/16	6 12/16	M	Chippewa County	WI	Donald J. Lunemann	1990	1,378
18 14/16	11 15/16	6 15/16	M	Forest County	WI	Douglas R. Oswald	1990	1,378
18 14/16	12 0/16	6 14/16	M	Lincoln County	NM	Rocky Drake	1991	1,378
18 14/16	11 7/16	7 7/16	M	Lynn Lake	MAN	Steve Gorr	1991	1,378
18 14/16	11 14/16	7 0/16	M	Grays Harbor County	WA	Alex Langbell	1991	1,378
18 14/16	12 0/16	6 14/16	M	Beltrami County	MN	Brian Aune	1991	1,378
18 14/16	11 14/16	7 0/16	M	Stevens County	WA	Michael R. Brunson	1991	1,378
18 14/16	11 12/16	7 2/16	M	Ignace	ONT	Tony Dickerson	1992	1,378
18 13/16	11 11/16	7 2/16	M	Iron County	MI	John E. Lawson	1971	1,454
18 13/16	11 8/16	7 5/16	M	Washington County	ME	Norman Jolliffe	1973	1,454
18 13/16	11 6/16	7 7/16	M	Jefferson County	CO	Chuck Hutton	1974	1,454
18 13/16	11 11/16	7 2/16	M	Colfax County	NM	Jerry R. Wood	1974	1,454
18 13/16	11 10/16	7 3/16	M		ONT	Lee Murphy	1975	1,454
18 13/16	11 8/16	7 5/16	M	Pemberton	BC	Dr. Michael R. Cummings	1976	1,454
18 13/16	11 8/16	7 5/16	M	Sanders County	MT	Jay Gunter	1976	1,454
18 13/16	11 7/16	7 6/16	M	Messines	QUE	Larry R. Scott, Sr.	1977	1,454
18 13/16	11 12/16	7 1/16	M	Dryden	ONT	Dr. Bill Young	1977	1,454
18 13/16	12 0/16	6 13/16	M	Gem County	ID	DeLoy Desaro	1978	1,454
18 13/16	11 10/16	7 3/16	M	Somerset County	ME	Ray King	1978	1,454
18 13/16	11 14/16	6 15/16	M	Chapleau	ONT	Maurice Perrault	1978	1,454
18 13/16	11 13/16	7 0/16	M	Koochiching County	MN	Mark A. Andrist	1979	1,454
18 13/16	11 11/16	7 2/16	M	Smokey Mountain	WA	Ronald D. Hopkins	1979	1,454
18 13/16	11 12/16	7 1/16	M	Wawa	ONT	Robert C. McGuire	1979	1,454
18 13/16	12 4/16	6 9/16	M	Lincoln County	WI	Bob Faufau	1980	1,454
18 13/16	11 11/16	7 2/16	M	Thunder Bay	ONT	David Manthei	1980	1,454

SCORE	GREATEST LENGTH	GREATEST WIDTH	SEX	AREA	STATE/ PROVINCE	HUNTER'S NAME	DATE	RANK
18 13/16	11 14/16	6 15/16	M	Armistice Lake	ONT	Cliff Buland, Jr.	1982	1,454
18 13/16	12 4/16	6 9/16	M	Price County	WI	Gary Berg	1982	1,454
18 13/16	12 3/16	6 10/16	M	Tulare County	CA	Bill Sweetser	1982	1,454
18 13/16	11 15/16	6 14/16	M	Kenora	ONT	John L. Angel	1982	1,454
18 13/16	12 1/16	6 12/16	M	Hudson Bay	SAS	Mark Hughes	1982	1,454
18 13/16	12 0/16	6 13/16	M	The Pas	MAN	Scott Lang	1983	1,454
18 13/16	11 12/16	7 1/16	M	Iron County	MI	John O. Cowell	1983	1,454
18 13/16	11 5/16	7 8/16	M	Caramat	ONT	Robert A. Boyer	1984	1,454
18 13/16	12 1/16	6 12/16	M	Sunbury County	NBW	Burchel Blevins	1984	1,454
18 13/16	12 1/16	6 12/16	M	Dist. 21	ONT	Ron Harger	1985	1,454
18 13/16	11 7/16	7 6/16	M	Otter Lake	QUE	Dana P. Calhoun	1985	1,454
18 13/16	12 2/16	6 11/16	M	St. James Bay	AK	John Gary Price	1985	1,454
18 13/16	12 0/16	6 13/16	M	Sierra County	NM	Kendall Doyle	1985	1,454
18 13/16	11 11/16	7 2/16	M	Thunder Bay	ONT	Howard Leopold	1985	1,454
18 13/16	11 14/16	6 15/16	M	Kenora	ONT	Ron Books	1986	1,454
18 13/16	11 8/16	7 5/16	M	Gallatin County	MT	Stephen Lockington	1986	1,454
18 13/16	11 11/16	7 2/16	M	Archuleta County	CO	Lonnie Draper	1986	1,454
18 13/16	12 3/16	6 10/16	M	Wasilla	AK	Ted Grover	1986	1,454
18 13/16	12 0/16	6 13/16	M	Atikokan	ONT	Steve Weekly	1987	1,454
18 13/16	11 10/16	7 3/16	M	Sundridge	ONT	Abby Lape	1987	1,454
18 13/16	11 8/16	7 5/16	M	Archuleta County	CO	Mark Charles Petersen	1987	1,454
18 13/16	12 2/16	6 11/16	M	Fox Creek	ALB	Ryk Visscher	1987	1,454
18 13/16	11 14/16	6 15/16	M	Crook County	OR	Jeff Carver	1987	1,454
18 13/16	11 12/16	7 1/16	M	Teton County	MT	Ron Carpenter	1987	1,454
18 13/16	11 7/16	7 6/16	M	Hampshire County	MA	Raymond H. Moulton, Jr.	1987	1,454
18 13/16	11 14/16	6 15/16	M	Wawa	ONT	Dale Rohrbeck	1988	1,454
18 13/16	12 1/16	6 12/16	M	Pine County	MN	Arnold F. Ostgarden	1988	1,454
18 13/16	12 0/16	6 13/16	M	Iron County	WI	Gary G. Johnson	1988	1,454
18 13/16	11 15/16	6 14/16	M	Bayfield County	WI	William F. Schutte	1988	1,454
18 13/16	12 0/16	6 13/16	M	Las Animas County	CO	Richard J. Racioppi	1989	1,454
18 13/16	11 7/16	7 6/16	M	Mine Centre	ONT	Willard L. Voight	1989	1,454
18 13/16	11 12/16	7 1/16	M	Cowan	MAN	Vito Benedetto	1989	1,454
18 13/16	11 9/16	7 4/16	M	Nestor Falls	ONT	Robert E. Grainger	1989	1,454
18 13/16	11 10/16	7 3/16	M	La Tuque	QUE	Bernard E. Beaudin, Jr.	1989	1,454
18 13/16	11 12/16	7 1/16	M	Cadillac	QUE	Jerry Woodrum	1989	1,454
18 13/16	12 2/16	6 11/16	M	Aitkin County	MN	David Emmen	1989	1,454
18 13/16	11 10/16	7 3/16	M	Fayette County	WV	James E. Grey	1989	1,454
18 13/16	11 14/16	6 15/16	M	Fawcett	ALB	Troy Dzioba	1990	1,454
18 13/16	11 14/16	6 15/16	M	Gowganda	ONT	Bob E. Collins	1990	1,454
18 13/16	11 11/16	7 2/16	M	Wawa	ONT	Pauly Paul	1990	1,454
18 13/16	11 15/16	6 14/16	M	Augusta County	VA	Raymond Leverock	1990	1,454
18 13/16	12 4/16	6 9/16	M	Apache County	AZ	Stephen D. Hornady	1991	1,454
18 13/16	11 9/16	7 4/16	M	Fauquier	ONT	Bradley I. Anderson	1991	1,454
18 13/16	11 15/16	6 14/16	M	Asotin County	WA	Brady Olson	1991	1,454
18 13/16	11 11/16	7 2/16	M	St. Louis County	MN	Jeffrey C. Minske	1991	1,454
18 13/16	11 13/16	7 0/16	M	Baker County	OR	Tom Christakos	1991	1,454
18 13/16	10 14/16	7 15/16	M	Madison County	MT	Tom L. Miller	1991	1,454
18 13/16	12 0/16	6 13/16	M	Montezuma County	CO	Jerry Rush	1992	1,454
18 13/16	11 14/16	6 15/16	M	Camas County	ID	Dallas Smith	1992	1,454
18 13/16	11 15/16	6 14/16	M	Caribou County	ID	Russell Clark	1992	1,454
18 12/16	12 1/16	6 11/16	M	Shasta County	CA	Harv Ebers	1964	1,521
18 12/16	11 11/16	7 1/16	M	Carbon County	UT	Marvin Tye	1965	1,521
18 12/16	11 9/16	7 3/16	M	Manowam Lake	QUE	Dennis H. Driscoll	1969	1,521
18 12/16	11 5/16	7 7/16	M	Siskiyou County	CA	W. E. Cates	1972	1,521
18 12/16	11 13/16	6 15/16	M	Franklin County	ME	Bob Kuhar	1973	1,521
18 12/16	11 14/16	6 14/16	M	Trinity County	CA	Daniel Higuera	1974	1,521
18 12/16	11 13/16	6 15/16	M	Uncompahgre N.F.	CO	Anthony Keeling	1975	1,521
18 12/16	12 1/16	6 11/16	M	Hubbard County	MN	Jack Smythe	1977	1,521
18 12/16	12 2/16	6 10/16	M	Lesser Slave Lake	ALB	Gene Solyntjes	1978	1,521
18 12/16	11 14/16	6 14/16	M	Fremont County	ID	Dennis L. Shirley	1979	1,521
18 12/16	11 10/16	7 2/16	M	Franklin County	ME	Len Cardinale	1980	1,521
18 12/16	12 2/16	6 10/16	M	Gunnison County	CO	James F. Dougherty	1980	1,521
18 12/16	11 3/16	7 9/16	M	Franklin County	ME	John Janelli	1980	1,521
18 12/16	11 14/16	6 14/16	M	Lake County	MN	Herbert O. Lundberg	1980	1,521
18 12/16	11 15/16	6 13/16	M	Sandy Bar Creek	CA	Dale H. Bracken	1981	1,521
18 12/16	11 12/16	7 0/16	M	Warren County	VA	Joseph A. Ramey	1981	1,521
18 12/16	11 12/16	7 0/16	M	Clear Creek County	CO	David L. Skiff	1981	1,521
18 12/16	12 0/16	6 12/16	M	Lemhi County	ID	Bob Ulshafer	1981	1,521
18 12/16	11 14/16	6 14/16	M	Remingy	QUE	Richard L. Jackson	1982	1,521
18 12/16	12 1/16	6 11/16	M	Idaho County	ID	Robert Dale Evans	1982	1,521

BLACK BEAR

(Continued)

SCORE	GREATEST LENGTH	GREATEST WIDTH	SEX	AREA	STATE/ PROVINCE	HUNTER'S NAME	DATE	RANK
18 12/16	11 14/16	6 14/16	M	Madoc	ONT	Mel Johnson	1982	1,521
18 12/16	11 6/16	7 6/16	M	Archuleta County	CO	Steve Vittetow	1982	1,521
18 12/16	12 0/16	6 12/16	M	Kenmount	ONT	James D. Murray	1983	1,521
18 12/16	11 8/16	7 4/16	M	McAdam	NBW	David W. Peltier	1983	1,521
18 12/16	12 3/16	6 9/16	M	Langlade County	WI	Michael Steliga	1983	1,521
18 12/16	12 2/16	6 10/16	M	Langlade County	WI	Larry Petts	1983	1,521
18 12/16	11 13/16	6 15/16	M	Graham	ONT	Joe Neal Walters	1984	1,521
18 12/16	11 6/16	7 6/16	M	Boise County	ID	Gary Kinney	1984	1,521
18 12/16	11 14/16	6 14/16	M	Koochiching County	MN	Daniel Krasean	1984	1,521
18 12/16	11 12/16	7 0/16	M	Koochiching County	MN	Larry Hillman	1984	1,521
18 12/16	12 0/16	6 12/16	M	Dryden	ONT	Mark Guelzow	1985	1,521
18 12/16	12 0/16	6 12/16	M	Riverside County	CA	Paul Persano	1985	1,521
18 12/16	11 11/16	7 1/16	M	Capreol	ONT	Lawrence M. Sowders	1986	1,521
18 12/16	11 9/16	7 3/16	M	Pitkin County	CO	Gary B. McClure	1986	1,521
18 12/16	11 12/16	7 0/16	M	Wawa	ONT	Thomas May	1986	1,521
18 12/16	11 14/16	6 14/16	M	Savant Lake	ONT	Marlo G. Sloan	1987	1,521
18 12/16	11 14/16	6 14/16	M	Thunder Bay	ONT	Eugene M. Tonk II	1987	1,521
18 12/16	12 0/16	6 12/16	M	Cumberland House	SAS	Dave Kapanke	1987	1,521
18 12/16	11 6/16	7 6/16	M	Killaloe Station	ONT	Norman J. Roy	1987	1,521
18 12/16	12 1/16	6 11/16	M	Ft. McMurray	ALB	James Pike	1987	1,521
18 12/16	12 6/16	6 6/16	M	Otero County	NM	Ronnie B. Hall	1987	1,521
18 12/16	11 10/16	7 2/16	M	King County	WA	Curtis A. Geise	1987	1,521
18 12/16	11 5/16	7 7/16	M	Marquette County	MI	Alvin Meadows	1987	1,521
18 12/16	11 10/16	7 2/16	M	Spokane County	WA	Tracy Kenworthy	1987	1,521
18 12/16	11 15/16	6 13/16	M	Peers	ALB	Kevin Hehn	1988	1,521
18 12/16	11 13/16	6 15/16	M	Yaremko Twp.	ONT	Ed Oplinger	1988	1,521
18 12/16	11 13/16	6 15/16	M	Oxford County	ME	Robert Grannis	1988	1,521
18 12/16	11 10/16	7 2/16	M	Marquette County	MI	Dale B. Parish	1988	1,521
18 12/16	12 1/16	6 11/16	F	Rio Arriba County	NM	Kelley B. Ward	1989	1,521
18 12/16	11 10/16	7 2/16	M	Snow Lake	MAN	Dick Pugh	1989	1,521
18 12/16	11 9/16	7 3/16	M	Eagle Lake	ONT	Allan Marohn	1989	1,521
18 12/16	11 10/16	7 2/16	M	Rapides des Joachims	QUE	Ron Bice	1989	1,521
18 12/16	11 8/16	7 4/16	M	Zec Dumoine	QUE	Paul J. Sisz	1989	1,521
18 12/16	11 8/16	7 4/16	M	Aitkin County	MN	Dr. Ken Nordberg	1989	1,521
18 12/16	11 10/16	7 2/16	M	Shoshone County	ID	Randy Huber	1989	1,521
18 12/16	11 14/16	6 14/16	M	Ferry County	WA	Bob Conyers	1989	1,521
18 12/16	11 8/16	7 4/16	M	Mesa County	CO	Ricky R. Lowery	1990	1,521
18 12/16	11 9/16	7 3/16	M	Highwinds Lake	ONT	John E. Larsen	1990	1,521
18 12/16	11 15/16	6 13/16	M	Black River	ONT	James S. Nowakowski	1990	1,521
18 12/16	11 14/16	6 14/16	M	LacLarouge	SAS	Randy G. Cook	1990	1,521
18 12/16	11 11/16	7 1/16	M	Clearwater County	ID	Stan Bocian	1990	1,521
18 12/16	11 7/16	7 5/16	M	Atikokan	ONT	Roger Carpenter	1990	1,521
18 12/16	11 12/16	7 0/16	M	Mystery Lake	MAN	Lois Monteath	1991	1,521
18 12/16	11 11/16	7 1/16	M	Idaho County	ID	Dr. Andrew F. Jones	1991	1,521
18 12/16	11 9/16	7 3/16	M	Kapuskasing	ONT	Harold A. Eichorn	1991	1,521
18 12/16	11 15/16	6 13/16	M	Wassilla	AK	Sam J. Smith	1991	1,521
18 12/16	12 0/16	6 12/16	M	Kootenai County	ID	Mark Jones	1992	1,521
18 12/16	12 0/16	6 12/16	M	Prince of Wales Island	AK	Dave Rue	1992	1,521
18 12/16	12 1/16	6 11/16	M	Shoshone County	ID	Craig R. Anderson	1992	1,521
18 12/16	11 15/16	6 13/16	M	Fort Assinobane	ALB	Brian R. Burrows	1992	1,521
18 12/16	11 13/16	6 15/16	M	Flatbush	ALB	Kevin Wilson	1992	1,521
18 12/16	11 8/16	7 4/16	M	Butler	ONT	Robert H. Pavlovic	1992	1,521
18 12/16	11 9/16	7 3/16	M	Terrace Bay	ONT	Alvin Anderson	1992	1,521
18 12/16	11 11/16	7 1/16	M	Temiscaming	ONT	Jerry Boudreault	1992	1,521
18 12/16	11 12/16	7 0/16	M	Coconino County	AZ	James Q. Anderson	1992	1,521
18 12/16	11 10/16	7 2/16	M	Wawa	ONT	Peter G. Dykstra	1992	1,521
18 11/16	11 12/16	6 15/16	M	Presque Isle County	MI	Herbert Miller	1957	1,597
18 11/16	11 8/16	7 3/16	M	Chirvakum Creek	WA	Joe Zuend	1962	1,597
18 11/16	11 13/16	6 14/16	M	Iron County	MI	Donald Schram	1965	1,597
18 11/16	11 7/16	7 4/16	M	Shawano County	WI	Kenneth Karbon	1970	1,597
18 11/16	11 10/16	7 1/16	M	Lac Cayamant	QUE	Charles Shaffner	1971	1,597
18 11/16	11 9/16	7 2/16	M	Grand County	UT	Dennis Schoenick	1972	1,597
18 11/16	11 7/16	7 4/16	M	San Miguel County	NM	Dr. Rick H. Jackson	1975	1,597
18 11/16	11 12/16	6 15/16	M	Nestor Falls	ONT	Greg Roach	1977	1,597
18 11/16	11 11/16	7 0/16	M	Estaire	ONT	Donnie Evans	1978	1,597
18 11/16	11 10/16	7 1/16	M	Lake Nipigon	ONT	Gary L. Smith	1978	1,597
18 11/16	11 7/16	7 4/16	M	Clearwater County	ID	John Wagner	1978	1,597
18 11/16	11 15/16	6 12/16	M	Itasca County	MN	Harold Whitt	1979	1,597
18 11/16	11 9/16	7 2/16	M	Huerfano County	CO	Patricia J. Matarazzo	1980	1,597
18 11/16	11 10/16	7 1/16	M	Franklin County	ME	Jeff Roberts	1980	1,597

Score	Greatest Length	Greatest Width	Sex	Area	State/ Province	Hunter's Name	Date	Rank
18 11/16	11 11/16	7 0/16	M	Gogebic County	MI	Edward Burley	1981	1,597
18 11/16	11 10/16	7 1/16	M	Itasca County	MN	Tom Brudeli	1981	1,597
18 11/16	11 11/16	7 0/16	M	Iron County	MI	Tom A. Longnecker	1981	1,597
18 11/16	11 12/16	6 15/16	M	Washington County	ME	Lincoln Michaud	1981	1,597
18 11/16	11 11/16	7 0/16	M	Dryden	ONT	Harry L. Stalter	1981	1,597
18 11/16	11 8/16	7 3/16	M	Franklin County	MA	George Holmes, Jr.	1982	1,597
18 11/16	11 9/16	7 2/16	M	Chapleau	ONT	Jim Grooters	1982	1,597
18 11/16	11 11/16	7 0/16	M	Atikokan	ONT	Al Taylor	1983	1,597
18 11/16	11 15/16	6 12/16	M	Dorset	ONT	Daryll E. Smith	1983	1,597
18 11/16	11 5/16	7 6/16	M	Lynn Lake	MAN	Gord Monteath	1983	1,597
18 11/16	11 12/16	6 15/16	M	Valley County	ID	George Wadsworth	1983	1,597
18 11/16	11 6/16	7 5/16	M	Klamath County	OR	Jeffery K. Russell	1983	1,597
18 11/16	11 13/16	6 14/16	M	Rio Arriba County	NM	William Rule	1983	1,597
18 11/16	11 10/16	7 1/16	M	North of Fort Frances	ONT	Kerry Ella	1984	1,597
18 11/16	11 7/16	7 4/16	M	Muskoka	ONT	Alexander Button	1984	1,597
18 11/16	11 9/16	7 2/16	M	Bonner County	ID	Brian T. Farley	1984	1,597
18 11/16	11 14/16	6 13/16	M	Franklin County	ME	Harold Osborne	1984	1,597
18 11/16	11 15/16	6 12/16	M	Spokane County	WA	David Lossett, Sr.	1984	1,597
18 11/16	11 11/16	7 0/16	M	Smeaton	SAS	Randy Modin	1985	1,597
18 11/16	11 9/16	7 2/16	M	Opasatika	ONT	Rob J. Smith	1985	1,597
18 11/16	11 12/16	6 15/16	M	Huerfano County	CO	Jerry Barth	1985	1,597
18 11/16	11 13/16	6 14/16	M	Sioux Lookout	ONT	Todd Koelzer	1986	1,597
18 11/16	11 15/16	6 12/16	M	Lost Lake	ONT	Richard Martin	1986	1,597
18 11/16	11 10/16	7 1/16	M	Fort Coulonge	QUE	Kevin Ball	1986	1,597
18 11/16	12 2/16	6 9/16	M	Duck Mts.	MAN	Terry Schar	1986	1,597
18 11/16	12 0/16	6 11/16	M	Aroostook County	ME	Gilbert P. Verwey	1986	1,597
18 11/16	11 14/16	6 13/16	M	Oconto County	WI	James S. Nowakowski	1986	1,597
18 11/16	11 10/16	7 1/16	M	Routt County	CO	Lonny Vanatta	1987	1,597
18 11/16	11 12/16	6 15/16	M	Ear Falls	ONT	Jeff Knights	1987	1,597
18 11/16	11 5/16	7 6/16	M	Fremont County	WY	Pat Eastes	1987	1,597
18 11/16	11 12/16	6 15/16	M	Delay River	QUE	W. R. "Tony" Dukes	1987	1,597
18 11/16	11 14/16	6 13/16	M	Ashland County	WI	Joe VyVyan	1987	1,597
18 11/16	11 12/16	6 15/16	M	Gila County	AZ	Paul Neill	1987	1,597
18 11/16	11 9/16	7 2/16	M	Boise County	ID	Troy M. Miller	1988	1,597
18 11/16	11 10/16	7 1/16	M	Zec Maganasipi	QUE	Shawn P. Harrington	1988	1,597
18 11/16	11 12/16	6 15/16	M	Valley County	ID	Jim Wilson	1988	1,597
18 11/16	11 9/16	7 2/16	M	Coos County	NH	Gerard D. Theriault	1988	1,597
18 11/16	11 7/16	7 4/16	M	Franklin County	ME	Jim Roy	1988	1,597
18 11/16	11 10/16	7 1/16	M	Madison County	MT	Ricky Huffstetler	1988	1,597
18 11/16	12 3/16	6 8/16	M	Carrot River	SAS	Kurt Schroeder	1988	1,597
18 11/16	11 15/16	6 12/16	M	Larimer County	CO	James Little	1989	1,597
18 11/16	11 11/16	7 0/16	M	Idaho County	ID	Ronald Smith	1989	1,597
18 11/16	11 7/16	7 4/16	M	McAdam	NBW	Joseph Khan	1989	1,597
18 11/16	11 11/16	7 0/16	M	Coos County	NH	David G. Cote	1989	1,597
18 11/16	11 5/16	7 6/16	M	Manitowadge	ONT	Charles W. Haertel	1990	1,597
18 11/16	11 11/16	7 0/16	M	Owl River	ALB	Thomas J. Papoutsis	1990	1,597
18 11/16	12 2/16	6 9/16	M	Coos County	NH	Gary J. Russell	1990	1,597
18 11/16	11 15/16	6 12/16	M	Mesa County	CO	Ron A. Stover	1990	1,597
18 11/16	11 12/16	6 15/16	M	Rocky Mountain House	ALB	Randy Bernier	1991	1,597
18 11/16	11 15/16	6 12/16	M	Remigny	QUE	Steve Reedy	1991	1,597
18 11/16	11 15/16	6 12/16	M	Wanless	MAN	Louis Raimondi	1991	1,597
18 11/16	11 15/16	6 12/16	M	Thompson	MAN	Richard E. Davis	1991	1,597
18 11/16	11 14/16	6 13/16	M	Chulitna River	AK	Karen L. Schwanke	1991	1,597
18 11/16	11 13/16	6 14/16	M	Maple Leaf	ONT	Kurt M. Zurawski	1992	1,597
18 11/16	11 8/16	7 3/16	M	Wabigoon	ONT	John H. Rosenstock	1992	1,597
18 11/16	11 10/16	7 1/16	M	Wanless	MAN	Damon Finley	1992	1,597
18 11/16	11 6/16	7 5/16	M	Thunder Bay	ONT	Randy Adkins	1992	1,597
18 11/16	11 7/16	7 4/16	M	McNeil Township	ONT	Archie Mackinnon	1992	1,597
18 11/16	12 0/16	6 11/16	M	Rusk County	WI	Douglas Bleecker	1992	1,597
18 10/16	11 8/16	7 2/16	M	Iron County	WI	Carl Hulbert	1963	1,670
18 10/16	11 8/16	7 2/16	M	Montreal River	ONT	S. Robinson/J. Beach	1966	1,670
18 10/16	11 7/16	7 3/16	M	Rio Grande County	CO	Ron Wintz	1967	1,670
18 10/16	11 11/16	6 15/16	M	Vermillion Bay	ONT	Thomas L. A. Pucci	1968	1,670
18 10/16	11 12/16	6 14/16	M	Idaho County	ID	Randolph Coleman	1970	1,670
18 10/16	12 2/16	6 8/16	M	McLeod Lake	BC	Ron McKay	1973	1,670
18 10/16	11 8/16	7 2/16	M	Las Animas County	CO	Dr. John Adams	1974	1,670
18 10/16	11 5/16	7 5/16	M	Madison County	ID	Bruce W. Baird	1974	1,670
18 10/16	11 0/16	7 10/16	M	Marinette County	WI	Dan Stencel	1974	1,670
18 10/16	11 8/16	7 2/16	M	Franklin County	ME	Mark Checki	1976	1,670
18 10/16	11 13/16	6 13/16	M	Starkey Unit	OR	Timothy D. Palmore	1976	1,670

MINIMUM SCORE 18

(Continued)

SCORE	GREATEST LENGTH	GREATEST WIDTH	SEX	AREA	STATE/ PROVINCE	HUNTER'S NAME	DATE	RANK
18 10/16	11 5/16	7 5/16	M	Grand County	CO	Lyle Willmarth	1976	1,670
18 10/16	11 10/16	7 0/16	M	Clearwater County	ID	Tom Cummings	1977	1,670
18 10/16	11 11/16	6 15/16	M	Lewis & Clark County	MT	Scott Koelzer	1977	1,670
18 10/16	12 1/16	6 9/16	M	Palmer	AK	John F. Sumrall	1977	1,670
18 10/16	11 8/16	7 2/16	M	Uncompahgre N.F.	CO	William Hendricks	1978	1,670
18 10/16	11 12/16	6 14/16	M	Stone Creek	BC	Larry McKay	1978	1,670
18 10/16	11 10/16	7 0/16	M	Chaffee County	CO	Frank A. Morminello	1978	1,670
18 10/16	11 10/16	7 0/16	M	Mendocino County	CA	Russell L. Browning	1979	1,670
18 10/16	11 14/16	6 12/16	M	Dolores County	CO	Stanley A. Coval	1979	1,670
18 10/16	11 14/16	6 12/16	M	Pipe Lake	ONT	Richard Colby	1980	1,670
18 10/16	11 5/16	7 5/16	M	Boise County	ID	Richard C. Nichols	1981	1,670
18 10/16	11 2/16	7 8/16	M	Judith Basin County	MT	Don Davidson	1981	1,670
18 10/16	11 7/16	7 3/16	M	Thunder Bay	ONT	Roberta Byerly	1982	1,670
18 10/16	11 7/16	7 3/16	M	Warren County	NY	Ernie Ahr	1982	1,670
18 10/16	12 0/16	6 10/16	M	Susitna Valley	AK	Matt Jones	1982	1,670
18 10/16	11 12/16	6 14/16	M	Gunnison County	CO	Mike Miller	1982	1,670
18 10/16	11 10/16	7 0/16	M	Meagher County	MT	John Levison	1983	1,670
18 10/16	11 14/16	6 12/16	M	Clearwater County	ID	Tim Newbold	1983	1,670
18 10/16	11 9/16	7 1/16	M	Ear Falls	ONT	Ron Marion	1983	1,670
18 10/16	11 14/16	6 12/16	M	Douglas County	OR	Ralph Burt	1983	1,670
18 10/16	11 2/16	7 8/16	M	Rouyn-Noranda	QUE	Claude St. Amour	1983	1,670
18 10/16	12 0/16	6 10/16	M	Mine Centre	ONT	Edwin John Durushia	1984	1,670
18 10/16	11 13/16	6 13/16	M	Lemhi County	ID	Clint Bevins	1984	1,670
18 10/16	11 13/16	6 13/16	M	Beluga River	AK	Dennis Redden	1984	1,670
18 10/16	12 2/16	6 8/16	M	Fremont County	WY	Jerry Bodar	1984	1,670
18 10/16	12 1/16	6 9/16	M	Valley County	ID	Gary Angell	1985	1,670
18 10/16	11 11/16	6 15/16	M	Hudson Bay	SAS	Warren Buss	1985	1,670
18 10/16	11 6/16	7 4/16	M	Huerfano County	CO	Michael Beckwith	1985	1,670
18 10/16	11 7/16	7 3/16	M	Jellicoe	ONT	John Paul McKown	1985	1,670
18 10/16	11 13/16	6 13/16	M	Las Animas County	CO	Tom Storr	1985	1,670
18 10/16	11 10/16	7 0/16	F	Sanpete County	UT	C. Danny Butler	1986	1,670
18 10/16	11 14/16	6 12/16	M	Nestor Falls	ONT	Byron Korby	1986	1,670
18 10/16	11 12/16	6 14/16	M	Fort Coulonge	QUE	Glenn R Noel	1986	1,670
18 10/16	11 4/16	7 6/16	M	Papineau Twp.	ONT	Fred Law	1986	1,670
18 10/16	11 10/16	7 0/16	M	Fort Coulonge	QUE	F. Edward Campbell	1986	1,670
18 10/16	11 6/16	7 4/16	M	Carlton County	MN	Donald Schleicher	1986	1,670
18 10/16	11 14/16	6 12/16	M	Long Lake	ALB	Dave Gerber	1987	1,670
18 10/16	11 14/16	6 12/16	M	Sturgeon Landing	SAS	Jeff Scherr	1987	1,670
18 10/16	11 13/16	6 13/16	M	Black River	QUE	Robert L. Brilhart	1987	1,670
18 10/16	12 0/16	6 10/16	M	Price Creek	ONT	Rick Candos	1987	1,670
18 10/16	11 10/16	7 0/16	M	Sudbury	ONT	William F. Boggess	1987	1,670
18 10/16	12 3/16	6 7/16	M	Ignace	ONT	Donald W. Goers	1987	1,670
18 10/16	11 13/16	6 13/16	M	Sioux Lookout	ONT	Mike Prokop	1987	1,670
18 10/16	11 11/16	6 15/16	M	Fort Coulonge	QUE	James E. Turner,Jr.	1987	1,670
18 10/16	11 12/16	6 14/16	M	Lemhi County	ID	Art C. Hrabec	1988	1,670
18 10/16	11 10/16	7 0/16	M	Dryden	ONT	Tony Mollus	1988	1,670
18 10/16	11 10/16	7 0/16	M	Perrault Falls	ONT	Ronald R. Mower	1988	1,670
18 10/16	11 12/16	6 14/16	M	Black River	QUE	Ronald E. Whitfield	1988	1,670
18 10/16	11 8/16	7 2/16	M	Bathurst	NB	Thomas J. Liguori	1988	1,670
18 10/16	12 2/16	6 8/16	M	Tulare County	CA	Bill Sweetser	1988	1,670
18 10/16	11 12/16	6 14/16	M	Florence County	WI	Richard J. Gohr	1988	1,670
18 10/16	11 13/16	6 13/16	M	Coos County	OR	Rick Gabbard	1988	1,670
18 10/16	11 10/16	7 0/16	M	Bathurst	NBW	Larry D. Benedict	1989	1,670
18 10/16	11 15/16	6 11/16	M	King County	WA	David B. Young	1989	1,670
18 10/16	11 13/16	6 13/16	M	Ashland County	WI	Wilbur C. Kuecker	1989	1,670
18 10/16	11 12/16	6 14/16	M	Poplarfield	MAN	Karl Dunich	1990	1,670
18 10/16	11 12/16	6 14/16	M	Smokey River	ALB	Chris G. Sanford	1990	1,670
18 10/16	11 2/16	7 8/16	M	Boise County	ID	Gary C. Gapp	1990	1,670
18 10/16	11 9/16	7 1/16	M	Chibougamau	QUE	Brian R. Brochu	1990	1,670
18 10/16	11 12/16	6 14/16	M	King County	WA	Donald H. Hubble	1990	1,670
18 10/16	11 10/16	7 0/16	M	Blind River	ONT	Thomas M. Losiewski	1990	1,670
18 10/16	11 15/16	6 11/16	M	Perry Sound	ONT	Robert Hill, Jr.	1990	1,670
18 10/16	12 1/16	6 9/16	M	Prince of Wales Island	AK	Ken A. Vorisek	1991	1,670
18 10/16	11 11/16	6 15/16	M	Zec Capitachouane	QUE	Jay A. Mengel	1991	1,670
18 10/16	11 11/16	6 15/16	M	Idaho County	ID	Stephan S. Jones	1991	1,670
18 10/16	11 6/16	7 4/16	M	Los Alamos County	NM	David R. Aikin	1991	1,670
18 10/16	11 11/16	6 15/16	M	Chapleau	ONT	Linda S. Schwochert	1991	1,670
18 10/16	11 13/16	6 13/16	M	Barrier Lake	SAS	Ray Fredin	1991	1,670
18 10/16	11 12/16	6 14/16	M	Coos County	NH	Harry Bodenrader	1991	1,670
18 10/16	11 10/16	7 0/16	M	Millville	NBW	Stephen Buck	1991	1,670

SCORE	GREATEST LENGTH	GREATEST WIDTH	SEX	AREA	STATE/ PROVINCE	HUNTER'S NAME	DATE	RANK
18 10/16	11 11/16	6 15/16	M	Wallowa County	OR	Brett Duane Monaghan	1991	1,670
18 10/16	11 6/16	7 4/16	M	French River	ONT	Kenneth E. Briggs	1992	1,670
18 10/16	11 12/16	6 14/16	M	Terrace Bay	ONT	Paul J. Paiser	1992	1,670
18 10/16	11 10/16	7 0/16	M	Yukon River	AK	Timothy J. Barber	1992	1,670
18 10/16	11 14/16	6 12/16	M	Price County	WI	Daniel E. Kester	1992	1,670
18 10/16	11 13/16	6 13/16	M	Aitkin County	MN	Donald K. Olson	1992	1,670
18 10/16	11 11/16	6 15/16	M	Wallowa County	OR	Jeff Matson	1992	1,670
18 9/16	11 5/16	7 4/16	M	Chelan County	WA	Wayne Hathaway	1960	1,758
18 9/16	11 6/16	7 3/16	M	Olsen Bay	AK	Don Daniels	1963	1,758
18 9/16	11 10/16	6 15/16	M	Iron County	MI	Don Schram	1964	1,758
18 9/16	11 10/16	6 15/16	M	Mattawa	ONT	Dr. Max G. Menefee	1966	1,758
18 9/16	11 5/16	7 4/16	M	St. Louis County	MN	Ron Johnson	1967	1,758
18 9/16	11 5/16	7 4/16	M	Blue Jay Ridge	CA	Delbert Allmon	1972	1,758
18 9/16	11 6/16	7 3/16	M	Nez Perce County	ID	Betty Gulman	1972	1,758
18 9/16	11 12/16	6 13/16	M	Rio Arriba County	NM	Curtis W. McClahan	1973	1,758
18 9/16	12 0/16	6 9/16	M	Swan Hills	ALB	Gerald L. Egbert	1976	1,758
18 9/16	11 7/16	7 2/16	M	Franklin County	ME	John G. Morningstar	1977	1,758
18 9/16	11 9/16	7 0/16	M	Ottawa River	QUE	Roger D. Davis	1978	1,758
18 9/16	11 12/16	6 13/16	M	Fremont County	ID	Tom Savage	1979	1,758
18 9/16	11 13/16	6 12/16	M	Wabigoon	ONT	Jon Helgason	1979	1,758
18 9/16	11 4/16	7 5/16	M	Caramat	ONT	John LaForge	1979	1,758
18 9/16	11 5/16	7 4/16	M	Idaho County	ID	Darrel Howard	1980	1,758
18 9/16	11 13/16	6 12/16	M	Sawyer County	WI	Joe Gohres	1980	1,758
18 9/16	11 6/16	7 3/16	M	Catron County	NM	Cornie P. Intveld	1980	1,758
18 9/16	11 11/16	6 14/16	M	Ravalli County	MT	Mike F. Bartz	1981	1,758
18 9/16	11 9/16	7 0/16	M	Marquette County	MI	Gary Lohman	1981	1,758
18 9/16	11 7/16	7 2/16	M	Idaho County	ID	Darrell Howard	1982	1,758
18 9/16	11 11/16	6 14/16	M	Marquette County	MI	Keith B. Putnam	1982	1,758
18 9/16	11 13/16	6 12/16	M	Dryden	ONT	Dennis L. Havey	1982	1,758
18 9/16	11 7/16	7 2/16	M	Nipigon	ONT	James P. Kina	1982	1,758
18 9/16	11 8/16	7 1/16	M	Susitna Valley	AK	Patrick McKay	1982	1,758
18 9/16	12 3/16	6 6/16	M	Game Area #23	MAN	Gary Kaluzniak	1983	1,758
18 9/16	12 5/16	6 4/16	M	Carlton County	MN	Larry H. Hoyt	1983	1,758
18 9/16	11 10/16	6 15/16	M	Ear Falls	ONT	Scott J. Strook	1984	1,758
18 9/16	11 8/16	7 1/16	M	Temiscaminque	QUE	Joe G. Hopwood	1984	1,758
18 9/16	11 9/16	7 0/16	M	Cedar Lake	ONT	Brad Wiehr	1984	1,758
18 9/16	11 9/16	7 0/16	M	Idaho County	ID	Ronald J. Larson	1984	1,758
18 9/16	11 9/16	7 0/16	M	Shasta County	CA	Peter Esposito	1984	1,758
18 9/16	11 8/16	7 1/16	M	Sudbury	ONT	Vinnie Pisani	1985	1,758
18 9/16	11 9/16	7 0/16	M	Dryden	ONT	James F. Hendricks	1985	1,758
18 9/16	11 10/16	6 15/16	M	Pancake Bay	ONT	Brad L. Rogers	1985	1,758
18 9/16	11 10/16	6 15/16	M	Mendocino County	CA	Charles Verne	1985	1,758
18 9/16	11 7/16	7 2/16	M	Lemhi County	ID	Thomas Fuller	1985	1,758
18 9/16	11 12/16	6 13/16	M	Cass County	MN	Larry Fischer	1985	1,758
18 9/16	11 6/16	7 3/16	M	Missoula County	MT	Terry See	1985	1,758
18 9/16	11 12/16	6 13/16	M	Sudbury	ONT	David L. Willis	1986	1,758
18 9/16	11 11/16	6 14/16	M	Boundary County	ID	Walt Dinning	1986	1,758
18 9/16	11 11/16	6 14/16	M	Clearwater County	ID	Ronnie Larson	1986	1,758
18 9/16	11 2/16	7 7/16	M	Caramat	ONT	Scott A. Atton	1986	1,758
18 9/16	11 9/16	7 0/16	M	Fort Coulonge	QUE	Westley Keller	1986	1,758
18 9/16	11 10/16	6 15/16	M	Washington County	ME	Marty Kane	1986	1,758
18 9/16	12 2/16	6 7/16	M	Burnett County	WI	Duane Hoefs	1986	1,758
18 9/16	11 9/16	7 0/16	M	Mine Centre	ONT	Stan H. Myers	1987	1,758
18 9/16	11 13/16	6 12/16	M	Monominto	MAN	Erik Thienpondt	1987	1,758
18 9/16	11 10/16	6 15/16	M	Montreal River	ONT	Thomas Hlinka	1987	1,758
18 9/16	12 1/16	6 8/16	M	Clearwater County	MN	Kevin Anderson	1987	1,758
18 9/16	11 5/16	7 4/16	M	Puperville	ONT	John DeWyse	1987	1,758
18 9/16	11 8/16	7 1/16	M	Los Alamos County	NM	Robert Hand	1987	1,758
18 9/16	11 9/16	7 0/16	M	Jackson County	OR	Jeff S. Cleveland	1987	1,758
18 9/16	11 10/16	6 15/16	M	Kenora	ONT	James G. Aldrich	1988	1,758
18 9/16	11 10/16	6 15/16	M	Wanless	MAN	Jon P. Thomas	1988	1,758
18 9/16	11 9/16	7 0/16	M	Kenora	ONT	John E. Larsen	1988	1,758
18 9/16	11 6/16	7 3/16	M	Clearwater County	ID	Gregg Tanner	1988	1,758
18 9/16	11 8/16	7 1/16	M	Temiscaming	QUE	Daniel E. Wallace	1988	1,758
18 9/16	11 13/16	6 12/16	M	Oneida County	WI	Tim Johnson	1988	1,758
18 9/16	11 14/16	6 11/16	M	Oneida County	WI	Greg L. Reed	1988	1,758
18 9/16	11 11/16	6 14/16	M	Rockingham County	VA	Roger O. Wyant	1988	1,758
18 9/16	11 14/16	6 11/16	M	Prince of Wales Island	AK	Dyrk Eddie	1989	1,758
18 9/16	11 12/16	6 13/16	M	Lane County	OR	Steven T Jones	1989	1,758
18 9/16	11 6/16	7 3/16	M	Clericy	QUE	Roger Stricklen	1989	1,758

SCORE	GREATEST LENGTH	GREATEST WIDTH	SEX	AREA	STATE/ PROVINCE	HUNTER'S NAME	DATE	RANK
18 9/16	11 10/16	6 15/16	M	Swift Creek	BC	Dan Yalowega	1989	1,758
18 9/16	11 11/16	6 14/16	M	Waterhen Lake	MAN	Walt Krom	1989	1,758
18 9/16	11 8/16	7 1/16	M	San Miguel County	NM	Harold Wallace	1989	1,758
18 9/16	11 10/16	6 15/16	M	Idaho County	ID	Monty Moravec	1990	1,758
18 9/16	11 8/16	7 1/16	M	Campbell River	BC	Don Quackenbush	1990	1,758
18 9/16	11 9/16	7 0/16	M	Pluto Lake	ONT	John D. Schmidt	1990	1,758
18 9/16	11 10/16	6 15/16	M	King County	WA	G. Dan Feighner	1990	1,758
18 9/16	11 11/16	6 14/16	M	Lincoln County	NM	Charlie C. Bing	1990	1,758
18 9/16	11 15/16	6 10/16	M	Marinette County	WI	Jeffrey J. Zepnick	1990	1,758
18 9/16	11 12/16	6 13/16	M	Holinshead Lake	ONT	Jack Leschner	1991	1,758
18 9/16	11 5/16	7 4/16	M	Clearwater County	ID	Johnny Watson	1991	1,758
18 9/16	11 6/16	7 3/16	M	County #1	ALB	Douglas E. Erickson	1991	1,758
18 9/16	11 12/16	6 13/16	M	Grand County	UT	Kim Tatman	1991	1,758
18 9/16	11 3/16	7 6/16	M	Haileybury	ONT	Dean G. Bartolomucci	1991	1,758
18 9/16	12 2/16	6 7/16	M	Lewis County	WA	Ronald D. Amrine	1991	1,758
18 9/16	11 11/16	6 14/16	M	Somerset County	ME	Corey Sibbio	1991	1,758
18 9/16	11 15/16	6 10/16	M	Roscommon County	MI	Elmer E. Clemson	1991	1,758
18 9/16	11 12/16	6 13/16	M	Gila County	AZ	Mark Ovitt	1991	1,758
18 9/16	12 2/16	6 7/16	M	Warren County	VA	John B. Stewart	1991	1,758
18 9/16	10 14/16	7 11/16	M	Nicholas County	WV	Steve A. Antoline	1991	1,758
18 9/16	11 13/16	6 12/16	M	Erickson	MAN	Glen Newton	1992	1,758
18 9/16	11 13/16	6 12/16	M	Emo	ONT	Steven J. Snyder	1992	1,758
18 8/16	11 8/16	7 0/16	M	Whatcom County	WA	Jack Fish	1961	1,843
18 8/16	11 13/16	6 11/16	M	Prince William Sound	AK	Bob Snelson	1962	1,843
18 8/16	11 8/16	7 0/16	M	Iron County	WI	Maynard Peck	1963	1,843
18 8/16	11 6/16	7 2/16	M	Clearwater County	ID	Robert J. Kreisher	1965	1,843
18 8/16	11 11/16	6 13/16	M	Sapawe	ONT	Dennis Gregory	1967	1,843
18 8/16	11 4/16	7 4/16	M	Mineral County	CO	Ron Wintz	1967	1,843
18 8/16	11 12/16	6 12/16	M	Siskiyou County	CA	Lyle L. Stroble	1968	1,843
18 8/16	11 7/16	7 1/16	M	Franklin County	ME	John Miterko	1970	1,843
18 8/16	12 0/16	6 8/16	M	Forest County	WI	Vilas Backhaus	1972	1,843
18 8/16	11 4/16	7 4/16	M	Messines	QUE	John W. Redmond	1973	1,843
18 8/16	11 10/16	6 14/16	M	Somerset County	ME	John D. Bonargo	1974	1,843
18 8/16	11 7/16	7 1/16	M	La Plata County	CO	Ronald C. Gaines	1975	1,843
18 8/16	11 0/16	7 8/16	M	Messines	QUE	Arthur R. Litschewski	1975	1,843
18 8/16	11 7/16	7 1/16	M	Hopetown	ONT	Dale Bailey	1976	1,843
18 8/16	11 6/16	7 2/16	M	Dryden	ONT	Jim Dyer	1977	1,843
18 8/16	11 6/16	7 2/16	M	Sioux Narrows	ONT	David Bailey	1978	1,843
18 8/16	11 8/16	7 0/16	M	Cook County	MN	Paul Smith	1978	1,843
18 8/16	11 6/16	7 2/16	M	Sandoval County	NM	Johnny R. Trujillo	1978	1,843
18 8/16	11 4/16	7 4/16	M	Franklin County	ME	John Janelli	1979	1,843
18 8/16	11 13/16	6 11/16	M	Lincoln County	WI	James Lechleitner	1981	1,843
18 8/16	12 0/16	6 8/16	M	Burnett County	WI	Gary K. Roholt	1981	1,843
18 8/16	11 6/16	7 2/16	M	Atikokan	ONT	Larry Stewart	1982	1,843
18 8/16	11 12/16	6 12/16	M	Kanabec County	MN	Raymond J. Altman	1982	1,843
18 8/16	11 10/16	6 14/16	M	Bancroft	ONT	Dean J. Farkas	1982	1,843
18 8/16	11 3/16	7 5/16	M	Love	SAS	David M. Tofte	1982	1,843
18 8/16	11 7/16	7 1/16	M	Terrace Bay	ONT	William J. Ernst	1983	1,843
18 8/16	11 7/16	7 1/16	M	McAdam	NBW	David Baldwin	1983	1,843
18 8/16	12 1/16	6 7/16	M	Ear Falls	ONT	Ernest C. Boser	1983	1,843
18 8/16	11 12/16	6 12/16	M	Langlade County	WI	Raymond Juedes	1983	1,843
18 8/16	11 11/16	6 13/16	M	Vilas County	WI	Alan L. Black	1983	1,843
18 8/16	11 8/16	7 0/16	M	Park County	CO	Larry A. Welchlen	1984	1,843
18 8/16	11 2/16	7 6/16	M	Carbon County	WY	Vaughn Cross	1984	1,843
18 8/16	11 10/16	6 14/16	M	Swan River	MAN	Kevin Hisey	1984	1,843
18 8/16	11 6/16	7 2/16	M	Spokane County	WA	Kenneth R. Wengert	1984	1,843
18 8/16	11 11/16	6 13/16	M	Iron County	WI	Gary Johnson	1984	1,843
18 8/16	11 9/16	6 15/16	M	Ft. McMurray	ALB	Darrin West	1985	1,843
18 8/16	11 12/16	6 12/16	M	Kootenai County	ID	Kenneth R. Wengert	1985	1,843
18 8/16	11 10/16	6 14/16	M	Susitna River	AK	Roger Stewart	1985	1,843
18 8/16	11 9/16	6 15/16	M	Fremont County	ID	Doug Burkman	1985	1,843
18 8/16	11 10/16	6 14/16	M	Penobscot County	ME	G. Kent Tableman	1985	1,843
18 8/16	11 14/16	6 10/16	M	Shasta County	CA	Larry Walkley	1985	1,843
18 8/16	11 6/16	7 2/16	M	Pitkin County	CO	Richard E. Davis	1986	1,843
18 8/16	11 4/16	7 4/16	M	Lemhi County	ID	Art Hrabec	1986	1,843
18 8/16	11 6/16	7 2/16	M	White River	ONT	Daniel B. Meece	1986	1,843
18 8/16	11 11/16	6 13/16	M	St. James Bay	AK	Ronald Callahan	1986	1,843
18 8/16	11 7/16	7 1/16	M	Jones	ONT	Hank Denowski	1986	1,843
18 8/16	11 5/16	7 3/16	M	Palfrey Lake	NBW	Lou Probo	1986	1,843
18 8/16	11 8/16	7 0/16	M	Cook County	MN	Kevin Cook	1986	1,843

SCORE	GREATEST LENGTH	GREATEST WIDTH	SEX	AREA	STATE/ PROVINCE	HUNTER'S NAME	DATE	RANK
18 8/16	11 10/16	6 14/16	M	Augusta County	VA	W. Thurman Hensley	1986	1,843
18 8/16	12 0/16	6 8/16	M	Siskiyou County	CA	Larry Holmes	1986	1,843
18 8/16	11 10/16	6 14/16	M	Rusagonis	NB	Stephen Buckingham	1987	1,843
18 8/16	11 12/16	6 12/16	M	Atikokan	ONT	Dean M. Westby	1987	1,843
18 8/16	11 12/16	6 12/16	M	Mine Centre	ONT	Terry Hadd	1987	1,843
18 8/16	11 12/16	6 12/16	M	Hartland	NBW	Frank Cinquemani	1987	1,843
18 8/16	11 5/16	7 3/16	M	Oliver	BC	A. R. Bryant	1987	1,843
18 8/16	11 6/16	7 2/16	M	Caramat	ONT	William M. Long	1987	1,843
18 8/16	11 4/16	7 4/16	F	Grassy Narrows	ONT	Mike Jacobs	1987	1,843
18 8/16	11 9/16	6 15/16	M	Pennhorwood Twp.	ONT	Harry A. Weishaar	1987	1,843
18 8/16	12 4/16	6 4/16	M	National Mills	MAN	T. J. Kearns	1987	1,843
18 8/16	11 9/16	6 15/16	M	Lincoln County	NM	Jon R. Reid	1987	1,843
18 8/16	11 13/16	6 11/16	M	Iron County	MI	Andy Holinga	1987	1,843
18 8/16	11 11/16	6 13/16	M	Unit 66	SAS	Donald Goracke	1987	1,843
18 8/16	11 8/16	7 0/16	M	Dryden	ONT	Tommy M. Brown	1988	1,843
18 8/16	12 0/16	6 8/16	M	Wallowa County	OR	William Kevin McCadden	1988	1,843
18 8/16	11 14/16	6 10/16	M	Mesa County	CO	Ron A. Stover	1988	1,843
18 8/16	11 13/16	6 11/16	M	Houghton County	MI	Daniel Glinn	1988	1,843
18 8/16	11 6/16	7 2/16	M	Ravalli County	MT	John Locke	1988	1,843
18 8/16	11 6/16	7 2/16	M	Douglas County	OR	Tom E. Tipton	1988	1,843
18 8/16	11 11/16	6 13/16	M	Rocky Mtn. House	ALB	Andrew Wiese	1989	1,843
18 8/16	11 13/16	6 11/16	M	Wapawekka Hills	SAS	Ronald J. Collier	1989	1,843
18 8/16	11 12/16	6 12/16	M	Archuleta County	CO	Michael G. Morton	1989	1,843
18 8/16	11 1/16	7 7/16	M	Webbwood	ONT	Jim Norris	1989	1,843
18 8/16	11 11/16	6 13/16	M	Red Lake	ONT	Donald Tjader	1989	1,843
18 8/16	11 10/16	6 14/16	M	Shining Tree	ONT	Bernard J. Higley	1989	1,843
18 8/16	11 10/16	6 14/16	M	Las Animas County	CO	Joe Johnston	1989	1,843
18 8/16	11 9/16	6 15/16	M	Baraga County	MI	Randy I Lee	1989	1,843
18 8/16	11 12/16	6 12/16	M	Douglas County	OR	Stephen Herrera	1989	1,843
18 8/16	11 6/16	7 2/16	M	Atikokan	ONT	Robert M. Jurica	1990	1,843
18 8/16	11 8/16	7 0/16	M	Ft. McMurray	ALB	James Pike	1990	1,843
18 8/16	11 12/16	6 12/16	M	Peace River	ALB	Roy M. Goodwin	1990	1,843
18 8/16	11 9/16	6 15/16	M	Highland Grove	ONT	Bob Capece	1990	1,843
18 8/16	11 9/16	6 15/16	M	Rocky Lake	MAN	Morris McManus	1990	1,843
18 8/16	11 14/16	6 10/16	M	Doaktown	NBW	Scott E. Komaridis	1990	1,843
18 8/16	11 10/16	6 14/16	M	St. Alexis Des Monts	QUE	Mike Hammond	1990	1,843
18 8/16	11 15/16	6 9/16	M	Swan River	MAN	Joseph S. Holiday	1990	1,843
18 8/16	11 2/16	7 6/16	M	Somerset County	ME	Bob Eisele	1990	1,843
18 8/16	11 9/16	6 15/16	M	Shawano County	WI	Ricky R. Kauffman	1990	1,843
18 8/16	11 6/16	7 2/16	M	Zec Rapides Des Joachins	QUE	Ken Dwyer	1990	1,843
18 8/16	11 10/16	6 14/16	M	Graham County	AZ	Dave Bushell	1991	1,843
18 8/16	11 14/16	6 10/16	M	Peace River	ALB	Bruce McRae	1991	1,843
18 8/16	11 13/16	6 11/16	M	Fawcett	ALB	James W. Thomson	1991	1,843
18 8/16	11 8/16	7 0/16	M	Braice Township	ONT	Timothy A. Salisbury	1991	1,843
18 8/16	11 10/16	6 14/16	M	Hythe	ALB	Rex Dacus	1991	1,843
18 8/16	11 9/16	6 15/16	M	Brown Bear Lake	ONT	Mark Kayser	1991	1,843
18 8/16	11 15/16	6 9/16	M	Lewis County	WA	Wayne A. Grasseth	1991	1,843
18 8/16	11 10/16	6 14/16	M	Grand County	UT	Pat Snyder	1991	1,843
18 8/16	11 14/16	6 10/16	M	Doak Town	NBW	George Louis	1991	1,843
18 8/16	11 14/16	6 10/16	M	Sioux Lookout	ONT	John Shields	1991	1,843
18 8/16	11 14/16	6 10/16	M	Remigny	QUE	Tom Mundy	1991	1,843
18 8/16	11 4/16	7 4/16	M	Ear Falls	ONT	Steve Jancar	1991	1,843
18 8/16	11 12/16	6 12/16	M	Pine County	MN	Brandon R. Johnson	1991	1,843
18 8/16	11 6/16	7 2/16	M	Forest County	WI	Steven W. Kluth	1991	1,843
18 8/16	11 8/16	7 0/16	M	Linn County	OR	Rick Kopf	1991	1,843
18 8/16	11 14/16	6 10/16	M	Cold Lake	ALB	Ron Dixon	1992	1,843
18 8/16	11 12/16	6 12/16	M	Barrier Lake	SAS	Ray Fredin	1992	1,843
18 8/16	11 14/16	6 10/16	M	Fischer Branch	MAN	Fred W. Lambley	1992	1,843
18 8/16	11 9/16	6 15/16	M	Wabigoon	ONT	Charles Drerup	1992	1,843
18 7/16	11 11/16	6 12/16	M	Oneida County	WI	Tim Johnson	1967	1,950
18 7/16	11 5/16	7 2/16	M	Franklin County	ME	Ed Hall	1968	1,950
18 7/16	11 11/16	6 12/16	M	Larimer County	CO	Ronald M. Breitsprecher	1975	1,950
18 7/16	11 8/16	6 15/16	M	Piscataquis County	ME	John Kuhar	1975	1,950
18 7/16	11 9/16	6 14/16	M	Clearwater County	ID	Edward Russell	1976	1,950
18 7/16	11 12/16	6 11/16	M	Cass County	MN	Walter L. Lash	1976	1,950
18 7/16	11 13/16	6 10/16	M	Albemarle County	VA	J. C. Locke	1976	1,950
18 7/16	11 11/16	6 12/16	M	Atikokan	ONT	John Carlson	1977	1,950
18 7/16	11 9/16	6 14/16	M	Lake County	MN	W. Dan Williams, Jr.	1977	1,950
18 7/16	11 7/16	7 0/16	M	English Bay	AK	Roger Stewart	1978	1,950
18 7/16	12 1/16	6 6/16	M	Iron County	WI	Douglas R. Parrott	1979	1,950

MINIMUM SCORE 18

SCORE	GREATEST LENGTH	GREATEST WIDTH	SEX	AREA	STATE/ PROVINCE	HUNTER'S NAME	DATE	RANK
18 7/16	11 1/16	7 6/16	M	Phelps Twp.	ONT	Robert C. Precious	1979	1,950
18 7/16	11 10/16	6 13/16	M	Almonte	ONT	Thomas S. Gerstner	1980	1,950
18 7/16	11 9/16	6 14/16	M	Franklin County	ME	Bob Spano	1980	1,950
18 7/16	11 6/16	7 1/16	M	Meagher County	MT	Gary H. Thompson	1980	1,950
18 7/16	11 12/16	6 11/16	M	Beluga	AK	Tom Atkins	1981	1,950
18 7/16	11 4/16	7 3/16	M	El Paso County	CO	Max Tallent	1981	1,950
18 7/16	11 15/16	6 8/16	M	Archuleta County	CO	James P. Mitchell	1982	1,950
18 7/16	11 8/16	6 15/16	M	Kenora	ONT	Floyd McDanell	1982	1,950
18 7/16	11 10/16	6 13/16	M		ONT	Bill Stonebraker	1982	1,950
18 7/16	11 12/16	6 11/16	M	Sierra County	NM	James N. Amlong, Jr.	1983	1,950
18 7/16	11 10/16	6 13/16	M	Kirkland Lake	ONT	Michael Hogan	1983	1,950
18 7/16	11 7/16	7 0/16	M	Nipigon	ONT	Wayne Beltz, Jr.	1983	1,950
18 7/16	11 9/16	6 14/16	M	Timmins	ONT	Paul Eldridge	1983	1,950
18 7/16	11 10/16	6 13/16	M	Tatalina River	AK	Timothy J. Barber	1983	1,950
18 7/16	11 6/16	7 1/16	M	Clackamas County	OR	Robert L. Smitherman	1983	1,950
18 7/16	11 9/16	6 14/16	M	Sudbury	ONT	Terry William Polkinghorn	1984	1,950
18 7/16	11 1/16	7 6/16	M	Sioux Lookout	ONT	Steve Sherry	1984	1,950
18 7/16	11 9/16	6 14/16	M	Skeleton Lake	ALB	Dwayne Alton	1984	1,950
18 7/16	11 8/16	6 15/16	M	Devlin	ONT	Jim Leqve	1984	1,950
18 7/16	11 11/16	6 12/16	M	Luce County	MI	Terry L. Cook	1984	1,950
18 7/16	11 13/16	6 10/16	M	Marquette County	MI	Randy Clark	1984	1,950
18 7/16	11 2/16	7 5/16	M	Lemhi County	ID	Dennis Derrer	1985	1,950
18 7/16	11 7/16	7 0/16	M	Kenora	ONT	Steven Duerksen	1985	1,950
18 7/16	11 2/16	7 5/16	M	Adams County	ID	Rick Clinton	1985	1,950
18 7/16	11 13/16	6 10/16	M	Las Animas County	CO	Kelly Williams	1985	1,950
18 7/16	11 9/16	6 14/16	M	Douglas County	OR	Jim Nielsen	1985	1,950
18 7/16	11 7/16	7 0/16	M	Gallatin County	MT	Terry L. Anderson	1985	1,950
18 7/16	11 9/16	6 14/16	M	Mine Centre	ONT	Bob Roulet	1986	1,950
18 7/16	11 10/16	6 13/16	M	Emo	ONT	Bruce Eggenberger	1986	1,950
18 7/16	11 12/16	6 11/16	M	Savant Lake	ONT	Daniel J. Gartner	1986	1,950
18 7/16	11 9/16	6 14/16	F	Smith	ALB	Dave Gerber	1986	1,950
18 7/16	12 0/16	6 7/16	M	Porcupine Plain	SAS	Peter Reimer	1987	1,950
18 7/16	11 5/16	7 2/16	M	Perrault Falls	ONT	Larry Gohlke	1987	1,950
18 7/16	11 7/16	7 0/16	M	Thunder Bay	ONT	Larry H. Hoyt	1987	1,950
18 7/16	11 11/16	6 12/16	M	Victoria County	ONT	William H. Guile	1987	1,950
18 7/16	11 9/16	6 14/16	M	Dryden	ONT	Richard E. Kohles	1987	1,950
18 7/16	11 8/16	6 15/16	M	Halfway River	BC	Dave Hannas	1987	1,950
18 7/16	11 7/16	7 0/16	M	Highland Valley	BC	Kenneth A. Brown	1987	1,950
18 7/16	11 9/16	6 14/16	M	Chelmsford	ONT	Bernard Langhorne	1987	1,950
18 7/16	11 7/16	7 0/16	M	Manitouwadge	ONT	Robert Mitchell	1988	1,950
18 7/16	11 13/16	6 10/16	M	Ft. McMurray	ALB	James Pike	1988	1,950
18 7/16	11 7/16	7 0/16	M	Geraldton	ONT	Gary E. Mayle	1988	1,950
18 7/16	11 10/16	6 13/16	M	Kootenai County	ID	Linda Leake	1988	1,950
18 7/16	11 11/16	6 12/16	M	Sublette County	WY	Keith Dana	1988	1,950
18 7/16	11 11/16	6 12/16	M	Susitna River	AK	Dave Hyrb	1988	1,950
18 7/16	11 12/16	6 11/16	M	King County	WA	David A. Emery	1988	1,950
18 7/16	11 10/16	6 13/16	M	Somerset County	ME	David James Obuchowski	1988	1,950
18 7/16	11 10/16	6 13/16	M	Kenora	ONT	Joe Devlin	1989	1,950
18 7/16	11 15/16	6 8/16	M	Zec Restigo	QUE	Joseph Sabo	1989	1,950
18 7/16	11 4/16	7 3/16	M	Wawa	ONT	Michael J. Klaeser	1989	1,950
18 7/16	11 9/16	6 14/16	M	Esther Island	AK	Tim Fritzler	1989	1,950
18 7/16	11 10/16	6 13/16	M	Jefferson County	WA	Wayne Haag	1989	1,950
18 7/16	12 1/16	6 6/16	M	Sawyer County	WI	John H. Henriksen	1989	1,950
18 7/16	11 6/16	7 1/16	M	Rockingham County	VA	Roger O. Wyant	1989	1,950
18 7/16	11 11/16	6 12/16	M	Belleterre	QUE	Terry Gaudlip	1990	1,950
18 7/16	11 11/16	6 12/16	M	Lincoln County	WY	John Trout, Jr.	1990	1,950
18 7/16	11 4/16	7 3/16	M	Rollet	QUE	Claude St' Amour	1990	1,950
18 7/16	11 12/16	6 11/16	M	Cumberland House	SAS	Mike Lewandowski	1991	1,950
18 7/16	11 6/16	7 1/16	M	Latah County	ID	Daniel D. Davenport	1991	1,950
18 7/16	11 10/16	6 13/16	M	La Ronge	SAS	Brian Hummel	1991	1,950
18 7/16	11 6/16	7 1/16	M	Caramet	ONT	Kelly Russell	1991	1,950
18 7/16	11 8/16	6 15/16	M	Moon Beam	ONT	John Meyers	1991	1,950
18 7/16	11 3/16	7 4/16	M	Zec Dumoine	QUE	Joseph Arkuszeski	1991	1,950
18 7/16	11 11/16	6 12/16	M	Terrace Bay	ONT	Greg Huffman	1991	1,950
18 7/16	11 13/16	6 10/16	M	Lake of the Woods	ONT	Bob Wickler	1991	1,950
18 7/16	11 11/16	6 12/16	M	Livengood	AK	Todd A. Wolf	1991	1,950
18 7/16	11 12/16	6 11/16	M	Idaho County	ID	Dan Hiltz	1991	1,950
18 7/16	11 13/16	6 10/16	M	Carbon County	WY	Damon Handley	1991	1,950
18 7/16	11 9/16	6 14/16	M	Temiscaming	QUE	Louis Seville	1991	1,950
18 7/16	11 9/16	6 14/16	M	Delta County	MI	James S. Stankowski	1991	1,950

SCORE	GREATEST LENGTH	GREATEST WIDTH	SEX	AREA	STATE/ PROVINCE	HUNTER'S NAME	DATE	RANK
18 7/16	11 12/16	6 11/16	M	Houghton County	MI	Tony E. La Pratt	1991	1,950
18 7/16	11 8/16	6 15/16	M	Spirit River	ALB	Paul Deme	1992	1,950
18 7/16	11 2/16	7 5/16	M	Sudbury	ONT	Phillip Wilkinson	1992	1,950
18 7/16	11 10/16	6 13/16	M	Fort McMurray	ALB	Jon P. Thomas	1992	1,950
18 7/16	11 8/16	6 15/16	M	Nemegauche	ONT	Lawrence Lee Wilbur	1992	1,950
18 6/16	11 9/16	6 13/16	M	Mariposa County	CA	Douglas Walker	1965	2,036
18 6/16	11 8/16	6 14/16	M	Fulton County	NY	Peter Mertens	1966	2,036
18 6/16	11 8/16	6 14/16	M	Clear Creek County	CO	Jim Dougherty	1970	2,036
18 6/16	11 12/16	6 10/16	M	Franklin County	ME	Joe Melchiore	1970	2,036
18 6/16	11 10/16	6 12/16	M	Yancey County	NC	Jerry Rushing	1970	2,036
18 6/16	11 2/16	7 4/16	M	Chetwynd	BC	Lee E. Hansel	1973	2,036
18 6/16	11 4/16	7 2/16	M	Valley County	ID	Charles F. Maloney	1973	2,036
18 6/16	11 8/16	6 14/16	M	Becker County	MN	Gordon Swenson	1973	2,036
18 6/16	11 6/16	7 0/16	M	Dryden	ONT	John L. Dykes	1974	2,036
18 6/16	11 12/16	6 10/16	M	Flathead County	MT	Dr. Barry Wensel	1974	2,036
18 6/16	11 8/16	6 14/16	M	Archuleta County	CO	Judd Cooney	1975	2,036
18 6/16	12 0/16	6 6/16	M	Snohomish County	WA	Jim Gregory	1975	2,036
18 6/16	11 0/16	7 6/16	M	Larimer County	CO	Michael Lewis	1975	2,036
18 6/16	11 10/16	6 12/16	M	Saguache County	CO	Sandra Scheid	1975	2,036
18 6/16	11 6/16	7 0/16	M	Somerset County	ME	Anthony Ciletti	1976	2,036
18 6/16	11 12/16	6 10/16	M	Rio Blanco County	CO	Brad Cook	1978	2,036
18 6/16	11 5/16	7 1/16	M	Lemhi County	ID	Roy Auwen	1979	2,036
18 6/16	11 8/16	6 14/16	M	Marinette County	WI	William Brunette	1979	2,036
18 6/16	11 14/16	6 8/16	M	Thunder Bay	ONT	Neil E. Gilles	1980	2,036
18 6/16	11 10/16	6 12/16	M	Red Lake	ONT	Leon L. Miller	1981	2,036
18 6/16	11 4/16	7 2/16	M	Espanola	ONT	Ronald E. Hergott	1982	2,036
18 6/16	11 5/16	7 1/16	M	Siskiyou County	CA	Dave S. Semple	1982	2,036
18 6/16	11 7/16	6 15/16	M	Uintah Countyn	UT	Bill Dunstan IV	1982	2,036
18 6/16	11 14/16	6 8/16	M	Game Area #23	MAN	Gary Kaluzniak	1983	2,036
18 6/16	11 8/16	6 14/16	M	McAdam	NBW	Donald R. Shipley	1983	2,036
18 6/16	11 5/16	7 1/16	M	Ramsey Twp.	ONT	Robert H. Pavlovic	1983	2,036
18 6/16	11 12/16	6 10/16	M	Cheboygan County	MI	Roger A. Greve	1983	2,036
18 6/16	11 15/16	6 7/16	M	Sawyer County	WI	Kevin Capelle	1983	2,036
18 6/16	11 8/16	6 14/16	M	Chelan County	WA	Edward M. Beitner	1983	2,036
18 6/16	11 15/16	6 7/16	M	Greene County	NY	Bob Spina	1983	2,036
18 6/16	11 4/16	7 2/16	M	Douglas County	OR	Tim O'Kelly	1984	2,036
18 6/16	11 15/16	6 7/16	M	Cass County	MN	James D. Zahalka	1984	2,036
18 6/16	11 8/16	6 14/16	M	Marquette County	MI	George M. Barosko	1984	2,036
18 6/16	11 10/16	6 12/16	M	Luce County	MI	Norman E. Bell	1984	2,036
18 6/16	11 2/16	7 4/16	M	Bathurst	NBW	Daryl Labarron	1985	2,036
18 6/16	11 4/16	7 2/16	M	Pontiac	QUE	Loren L. Fish	1985	2,036
18 6/16	11 3/16	7 3/16	M	Carroll County	NH	Donald W. Murdock	1985	2,036
18 6/16	11 8/16	6 14/16	F	Spirtwood	SAS	Kent W. Brigham	1986	2,036
18 6/16	11 10/16	6 12/16	M	Rio Arriba County	NM	Terry Sanders	1986	2,036
18 6/16	11 8/16	6 14/16	M	Thunder Bay	ONT	Gene Anderson	1986	2,036
18 6/16	11 3/16	7 3/16	M	Valley County	ID	Larry Hoff	1986	2,036
18 6/16	10 15/16	7 7/16	M	Fremont County	ID	Blair R. Jones	1986	2,036
18 6/16	11 14/16	6 8/16	M	Hudson Bay	SAS	C. Randall Byers	1987	2,036
18 6/16	11 3/16	7 3/16	M	Wabigoon	ONT	Robert Barrie	1987	2,036
18 6/16	11 10/16	6 12/16	M	St. Louis County	MN	Loren Slette	1987	2,036
18 6/16	11 9/16	6 13/16	M	Oxford County	ME	Patrick Ferrie	1987	2,036
18 6/16	11 15/16	6 7/16	M	Lincoln County	WI	James G. Gouger	1987	2,036
18 6/16	11 10/16	6 12/16	M	Wolf Lake	ALB	Keith Baker	1988	2,036
18 6/16	11 15/16	6 7/16	M	Hudson Bay	SAS	Kent Brandt	1988	2,036
18 6/16	11 15/16	6 7/16	M	Emo	ONT	Robert John Brown	1988	2,036
18 6/16	11 6/16	7 0/16	M	Gull River	ONT	Larry R. Brosamle	1988	2,036
18 6/16	11 7/16	6 15/16	M	Kenora	ONT	Dean M. Westby	1988	2,036
18 6/16	11 11/16	6 11/16	M	Chelsea	QUE	Jim Ray	1988	2,036
18 6/16	11 1/16	7 5/16	M	Jocko River	ONT	Gary Boals	1988	2,036
18 6/16	12 1/16	6 5/16	M	Susitna River	AK	Richmon R. Schumann	1988	2,036
18 6/16	11 8/16	6 14/16	M	La Plata County	CO	Dale Sunblom	1988	2,036
18 6/16	11 6/16	7 0/16	M	Chibougamau	QUE	Dale R. Walburger	1988	2,036
18 6/16	11 1/16	7 5/16	M	Okanogan County	WA	Duane N. Fink	1988	2,036
18 6/16	11 4/16	7 2/16	M	Delay River	QUE	Dennis N. Ballweg	1988	2,036
18 6/16	11 6/16	7 0/16	M	Ashland County	WI	Thomas J. Mischo	1988	2,036
18 6/16	11 12/16	6 10/16	M	Coconino County	AZ	Richard Dawe, Jr.	1988	2,036
18 6/16	11 11/16	6 11/16	M	Saguache County	CO	Sid Strzok	1989	2,036
18 6/16	11 10/16	6 12/16	M	Mens Twp.	ONT	Jon T. Wente	1989	2,036
18 6/16	11 7/16	6 15/16	M	Emo	ONT	Leo Hazelton	1989	2,036
18 6/16	11 7/16	6 15/16	M	Peace River	ALB	John Peruchini	1990	2,036

Score	Greatest Length	Greatest Width	Sex	Area	State/ Province	Hunter's Name	Date	Rank
18 6/16	11 10/16	6 12/16	M	Dolores County	CO	Duain Morton	1990	2,036
18 6/16	12 0/16	6 6/16	M	Buffalo Narrows	SAS	David M Tofte	1990	2,036
18 6/16	11 4/16	7 2/16	M	Messines	QUE	Charles L. Hart III	1990	2,036
18 6/16	11 7/16	6 15/16	M	Meadow Lake	SAS	Tonnie Elwood Davis	1990	2,036
18 6/16	11 13/16	6 9/16	M	Bayfield County	WI	Gary J. Ader	1990	2,036
18 6/16	11 14/16	6 8/16	M	Iron County	WI	Thomas R. Hujet	1990	2,036
18 6/16	11 6/16	7 0/16	M	Clatsup County	OR	William H. Stevens	1991	2,036
18 6/16	11 12/16	6 10/16	M	Plevna	ONT	Brant Bergstrome	1991	2,036
18 6/16	11 12/16	6 10/16	M	Itasca County	MN	Shawn E. Eyre	1991	2,036
18 6/16	11 4/16	7 2/16	M	Colfax County	NM	Rodrigo Cruz	1991	2,036
18 6/16	11 12/16	6 10/16	M	Caribou County	ID	Trent McBride	1991	2,036
18 6/16	11 10/16	6 12/16	M	Savant Lake	ONT	Dean Wells	1992	2,036
18 6/16	11 12/16	6 10/16	M	Thunder Bay	ONT	Michael Kemp	1992	2,036
18 5/16	11 3/16	7 2/16	M	Iron Bridge	ONT	Philip L. Hawkins	1965	2,114
18 5/16	11 9/16	6 12/16	M	Gogebic County	MI	LaVern Miller	1971	2,114
18 5/16	11 6/16	6 15/16	M	Florence County	WI	Jim Thimmig	1971	2,114
18 5/16	11 3/16	7 2/16	M	Forest County	WI	Ernie V. Hutchinson	1972	2,114
18 5/16	11 4/16	7 1/16	M	St. Louis County	MN	Art Heinze	1973	2,114
18 5/16	11 9/16	6 12/16	M	Coconino County	AZ	Stan Nordell	1975	2,114
18 5/16	11 7/16	6 14/16	M	Gunnison County	CO	Rick Hunckler	1976	2,114
18 5/16	11 7/16	6 14/16	M	Montezuma County	CO	Stanley A. Coval	1977	2,114
18 5/16	11 7/16	6 14/16	M	Ear Falls	ONT	John Brandt	1980	2,114
18 5/16	11 9/16	6 12/16	M	Park County	MT	Charles Burdette	1980	2,114
18 5/16	11 3/16	7 2/16	M	E. Braintree	MAN	Chester Surma	1980	2,114
18 5/16	11 2/16	7 3/16	M	Douglas County	OR	Dan Viles	1980	2,114
18 5/16	11 5/16	7 0/16	M	Gogebic County	MI	Donald E. Thompson, Jr.	1981	2,114
18 5/16	11 7/16	6 14/16	M	Blind River	ONT	Cleve Roush	1982	2,114
18 5/16	11 11/16	6 10/16	M	Iron County	WI	Keith Kaat	1982	2,114
18 5/16	11 11/16	6 10/16	M	Alatna River	AK	John D. 'Jack' Frost	1982	2,114
18 5/16	11 4/16	7 1/16	M	Missoula County	MT	Tom Storm	1983	2,114
18 5/16	11 9/16	6 12/16	M	Sundridge	ONT	Abby Lape	1983	2,114
18 5/16	11 9/16	6 12/16	M	Kootenai County	ID	Larry M. Leake	1985	2,114
18 5/16	11 8/16	6 13/16	M	Thunder Bay	ONT	Bob Kraus	1985	2,114
18 5/16	11 11/16	6 10/16	M	Hudson Bay	SAS	Clark Jenner	1985	2,114
18 5/16	11 8/16	6 13/16	M	Cold Lake	ALB	Orest Popil	1985	2,114
18 5/16	11 6/16	6 15/16	M	Atikokan	ONT	Bruce Wynn	1985	2,114
18 5/16	11 12/16	6 9/16	M	Lake County	MT	Don Davidson	1986	2,114
18 5/16	11 14/16	6 7/16	M	Grand County	CO	Lyle Willmarth	1986	2,114
18 5/16	11 8/16	6 13/16	M	Massey	ONT	Jim Hunsaker	1986	2,114
18 5/16	11 11/16	6 10/16	M	Sudbury	ONT	Richard Dohm	1986	2,114
18 5/16	11 4/16	7 1/16	M	Park County	CO	Gary Christoffersen	1986	2,114
18 5/16	11 13/16	6 8/16	M	Rocky Lake	MAN	Tim Finley	1986	2,114
18 5/16	11 5/16	7 0/16	M	Blaine County	ID	Larry R. Newton	1986	2,114
18 5/16	11 11/16	6 10/16	M	Iron County	MI	Richard Seasword	1986	2,114
18 5/16	11 5/16	7 0/16	M	Kootenai County	ID	Linda Leake	1987	2,114
18 5/16	11 10/16	6 11/16	M	Algonquin	ONT	Stephen Michael Carroll	1987	2,114
18 5/16	11 8/16	6 13/16	M	Saint James Bay	AK	Richard J. Callahan	1987	2,114
18 5/16	11 11/16	6 10/16	M	Lemhi County	ID	Mike Lopez	1987	2,114
18 5/16	11 7/16	6 14/16	M	Plumes County	CA	Steven Demello	1987	2,114
18 5/16	11 2/16	7 3/16	M	Somerset County	ME	Al Cresci	1987	2,114
18 5/16	11 5/16	7 0/16	M	Placer County	CA	Kenneth Braden	1987	2,114
18 5/16	11 10/16	6 11/16	M	Athabasca River	ALB	Archie J. Nesbitt	1988	2,114
18 5/16	11 13/16	6 8/16	M	Sundre	ALB	David R. Coupland	1988	2,114
18 5/16	11 11/16	6 10/16	M	Ignace	ONT	Joel Breitung	1988	2,114
18 5/16	11 9/16	6 12/16	M	Bonneville County	ID	Terri L. Stephens	1988	2,114
18 5/16	11 9/16	6 12/16	M	San Miguel County	CO	LaJuan Huare	1989	2,114
18 5/16	11 12/16	6 9/16	M	Manitouwadge	ONT	Stuart Hazard III	1989	2,114
18 5/16	11 10/16	6 11/16	M	Boise Franc Rd.	Que	August S. Gray	1989	2,114
18 5/16	11 8/16	6 13/16	M	Pierce County	WA	Howard L. Harding	1989	2,114
18 5/16	11 6/16	6 15/16	M	Aroostook County	ME	Tad David Proudlove	1989	2,114
18 5/16	11 7/16	6 14/16	M	Powell Lake	ONT	Michael J. Goza	1989	2,114
18 5/16	11 3/16	7 2/16	M	MacNeil Twp.	ONT	Ted Whittle	1989	2,114
18 5/16	11 4/16	7 1/16	M	Lemhi County	ID	Al Youman	1990	2,114
18 5/16	11 14/16	6 7/16	M	Gravel Lake Cabins	ONT	James D. Smith	1990	2,114
18 5/16	11 1/16	7 4/16	M	Prince of Wales Island	AK	Gordon Diehl	1990	2,114
18 5/16	11 3/16	7 2/16	M	Ashland County	WI	Kenneth A. Johnson	1990	2,114
18 5/16	11 10/16	6 11/16	M	Oconto County	WI	Chuck D. Peterson	1990	2,114
18 5/16	11 11/16	6 10/16	M	Telegraph Creek	BC	Rick Simonson	1990	2,114
18 5/16	11 12/16	6 9/16	M	Crimson Lake	ALB	Dale Peters	1991	2,114
18 5/16	11 6/16	6 15/16	M	Chipmunk Creek	BC	Ken Scheer	1991	2,114

SCORE	GREATEST LENGTH	GREATEST WIDTH	SEX	AREA	STATE/ PROVINCE	HUNTER'S NAME	DATE	RANK
18 5/16	11 8/16	6 13/16	M	Atikokan	ONT	Judy Grooms	1991	2,114
18 5/16	11 6/16	6 15/16	M	Las Animas County	CO	H. Brian Jackson	1991	2,114
18 5/16	11 6/16	6 15/16	M	Sandoval County	NM	Noble Sinclair	1992	2,114
18 5/16	11 5/16	7 0/16	M	Grafton County	NH	Dana E. Plourde	1992	2,114
18 5/16	11 8/16	6 13/16	M	Swan River	MAN	Richard C. Weber	1992	2,114
18 4/16	10 14/16	7 6/16	M	Latah County	ID	Don Lawrence	1962	2,176
18 4/16	11 7/16	6 13/16	M	Curry County	OR	Gerald Rimbey	1962	2,176
18 4/16	11 4/16	7 0/16	M	Shawano County	WI	Peter Erickson	1967	2,176
18 4/16	11 12/16	6 8/16	M	Ft. Frances	ONT	Wayne Keefer	1968	2,176
18 4/16	11 6/16	6 14/16	M	Idaho County	ID	Larry W. Gehre	1972	2,176
18 4/16	11 12/16	6 8/16	M	Itasca County	MN	Lonny Herrick	1973	2,176
18 4/16	11 10/16	6 10/16	M	La Plata County	CO	Kenneth L. Biegel	1974	2,176
18 4/16	11 7/16	6 13/16	M	Tuolumne County	CA	Willis Chapman	1974	2,176
18 4/16	11 6/16	6 14/16	M	Harcourt	ONT	Robert M. Sweisthal	1977	2,176
18 4/16	11 7/16	6 13/16	M	Boise County	ID	Richard C. Nichols	1978	2,176
18 4/16	11 12/16	6 8/16	M	Caribou County	ID	Randy J. Stephens	1978	2,176
18 4/16	11 7/16	6 13/16	M	Vermillion Bay	ONT	Daniel D. Carlson	1979	2,176
18 4/16	11 6/16	6 14/16	M	Lily Lake	BC	Stanley Moore	1979	2,176
18 4/16	11 8/16	6 12/16	M	Mesa County	CO	David E. Samuel	1979	2,176
18 4/16	11 9/16	6 11/16	M	Beltrami County	MN	Greg Siekaniec	1979	2,176
18 4/16	11 7/16	6 13/16	M	Piscataquis County	ME	Mark Sutherly	1979	2,176
18 4/16	11 7/16	6 13/16	M	Essex County	VT	James 'Boomer' Hayden	1980	2,176
18 4/16	11 12/16	6 8/16	M	Tehama County	CA	Gerald McKenzie	1980	2,176
18 4/16	11 7/16	6 13/16	M	St. Louis County	MN	Mike Schullo	1981	2,176
18 4/16	11 8/16	6 12/16	M	Dryden	ONT	Alan E. Forbes	1982	2,176
18 4/16	11 12/16	6 8/16	M	Susitna River	AK	Mel Hein	1983	2,176
18 4/16	11 6/16	6 14/16	M	Seine River	ONT	George David Shelton	1983	2,176
18 4/16	11 4/16	7 0/16	M	Cloud Bay	ONT	Ronald C. Maikranz	1983	2,176
18 4/16	11 10/16	6 10/16	M	Iron County	MI	Jim Johnson	1983	2,176
18 4/16	11 10/16	6 10/16	M	Mistatim	SAS	Jeff Grewe	1984	2,176
18 4/16	11 8/16	6 12/16	M	Saguache County	CO	Jerry Barth	1984	2,176
18 4/16	10 14/16	7 6/16	M	Idaho County	ID	James Jay Hill	1984	2,176
18 4/16	11 4/16	7 0/16	M	Langlade County	WI	Edward R. Jenelewicz	1984	2,176
18 4/16	11 8/16	6 12/16	M	Oxford County	ME	Gary Russell	1984	2,176
18 4/16	11 12/16	6 8/16	M	Sudbury	ONT	Nancy A. Guisbert	1985	2,176
18 4/16	11 10/16	6 10/16	M	Fawcett Lake	ALB	David R. Coupland	1985	2,176
18 4/16	11 8/16	6 12/16	M	Bell Lake	ONT	Dale D. Conley	1985	2,176
18 4/16	11 8/16	6 12/16	M	Jellicoe	ONT	Mike Mooney	1985	2,176
18 4/16	11 0/16	7 4/16	M	Oxford County	ME	Allen Baker	1985	2,176
18 4/16	11 6/16	6 14/16	M	Lemhi County	ID	Mark Neer	1985	2,176
18 4/16	12 0/16	6 4/16	M	Ft. Assiniboine	ALB	Jim Dahlberg	1985	2,176
18 4/16	11 10/16	6 10/16	M	Siskiyou County	CA	Arthur M. Cain	1985	2,176
18 4/16	11 5/16	6 15/16	M	Smeaton	SAS	Renee Welle	1986	2,176
18 4/16	11 8/16	6 12/16	M	Standard Creek	AK	William B. Childress	1986	2,176
18 4/16	11 10/16	6 10/16	M	Fort Coulonge	QUE	Anthony G. Horrell	1986	2,176
18 4/16	11 2/16	7 2/16	M	Dryden	ONT	Gene Rokus	1986	2,176
18 4/16	11 10/16	6 10/16	M	Beaconsfield	NBW	William Clark	1986	2,176
18 4/16	11 8/16	6 12/16	M	Fergus	ONT	David L. Reeves	1986	2,176
18 4/16	11 11/16	6 9/16	M	Lac du Bonnet	MAN	Russell R. Popp	1987	2,176
18 4/16	11 3/16	7 1/16	M	Grand County	CO	Jerry L. Novak	1987	2,176
18 4/16	11 5/16	6 15/16	M	Boise County	ID	Jim Wilson	1987	2,176
18 4/16	11 15/16	6 5/16	M	Canoe Lake	SAS	Kim Steven Hussong	1988	2,176
18 4/16	11 12/16	6 8/16	M	Slave Lake	ALB	Kevin Hehn	1988	2,176
18 4/16	11 4/16	7 0/16	M	Felix	ONT	Bradley C. Chamberlain	1988	2,176
18 4/16	11 5/16	6 15/16	M	Kenora	ONT	Greg Zirbel	1988	2,176
18 4/16	11 14/16	6 6/16	M	Jackson County	OR	Jim Turcke	1988	2,176
18 4/16	11 7/16	6 13/16	M	Duchesne County	UT	Dirk B. Watrous	1989	2,176
18 4/16	11 11/16	6 9/16	M	Sioux Lookout	ONT	Manfred Gehrlein	1989	2,176
18 4/16	11 8/16	6 12/16	M	Lake Manitou	QUE	Keith Mitchell	1989	2,176
18 4/16	11 5/16	6 15/16	M	Lincoln County	MT	Robert W. "Bill" Armstrong	1989	2,176
18 4/16	11 2/16	7 2/16	M	Ravalli County	MT	James Patenaude	1989	2,176
18 4/16	11 4/16	7 0/16	M	Gallatin County	MT	Andy Locker	1989	2,176
18 4/16	11 10/16	6 10/16	M	Conejos County	CO	Rick Ivers	1990	2,176
18 4/16	11 7/16	6 13/16	M	Unit 9A	ONT	Dave Steinhorst	1990	2,176
18 4/16	11 12/16	6 8/16	M	Rainy River	ONT	Michael Judas	1990	2,176
18 4/16	11 7/16	6 13/16	M	Green Lake	SAS	Herb B. Merkert, Jr.	1990	2,176
18 4/16	11 2/16	7 2/16	M	Biscotasing	ONT	Thomas Hlinka	1990	2,176
18 4/16	11 8/16	6 12/16	M	Sultan	ONT	Daniel A. Phillips	1990	2,176
18 4/16	11 8/16	6 12/16	M	Chibougamau	QUE	Alfred Bergeron	1990	2,176
18 4/16	11 7/16	6 13/16	M	Wawa	ONT	Mark R. Sherman	1990	2,176

SCORE	GREATEST LENGTH	GREATEST WIDTH	SEX	AREA	STATE/ PROVINCE	HUNTER'S NAME	DATE	RANK
18 4/16	11 6/16	6 14/16	M	Border Lake	BC	Dean Stebner	1990	2,176
18 4/16	11 5/16	6 15/16	M	Moon Beam	ONT	Dick Clark	1991	2,176
18 4/16	11 6/16	6 14/16	M	Boise County	ID	Richard R. Larrivee	1991	2,176
18 4/16	11 10/16	6 10/16	M	Buffalo Narrows	SAS	Bernard J. Garcarz	1991	2,176
18 4/16	11 2/16	7 2/16	M	Kapuskasing	ONT	Jim Melton	1991	2,176
18 4/16	11 9/16	6 11/16	M	Longlac	ONT	Douglas C. Arnold	1991	2,176
18 4/16	11 6/16	6 14/16	M	Temiscaming	QUE	Fred Wallace	1991	2,176
18 4/16	11 5/16	6 15/16	M	La Plata County	CO	Perry Howell	1991	2,176
18 4/16	11 8/16	6 12/16	M	Kalkaska County	MI	David L. Roose	1991	2,176
18 4/16	11 9/16	6 11/16	M	Saddle Hills	ALB	Ken Baker	1992	2,176
18 4/16	11 5/16	6 15/16	M	Mink Lake	ONT	David Kennedy	1992	2,176
18 4/16	11 4/16	7 0/16	M	Rouyn-Noranda	QUE	Daniel K. Shivery	1992	2,176
18 4/16	11 11/16	6 9/16	M	Manitouwadge	ONT	Douglas E. McGuire	1992	2,176
18 4/16	11 8/16	6 12/16	M	Lac La Biche	ALB	Tom L. Nelson	1992	2,176
18 4/16	11 8/16	6 12/16	M	Fort McMurray	ALB	Bill Thompson	1992	2,176
18 4/16	11 5/16	6 15/16	M	Mine Center	ONT	David Wolf	1992	2,176
18 4/16	11 12/16	6 8/16	M	Boise County	ID	Bruce Capes	1992	2,176
18 4/16	11 5/16	6 15/16	M	Clearwater County	ID	Jim Bradford	1992	2,176
18 4/16	11 10/16	6 10/16	M	Zec Restigo	QUE	William E. Lockwood, Jr.	1992	2,176
18 3/16	11 1/16	7 2/16	M	Penobscot County	ME	Charles A. Kronyak	1965	2,260
18 3/16	11 0/16	7 3/16	M	Custer County	ID	C. Randall Byers	1966	2,260
18 3/16	11 4/16	6 15/16	M	Franklin County	ME	Philip Copp	1967	2,260
18 3/16	11 6/16	6 13/16	M	Florence County	WI	Elaine S. Peck	1967	2,260
18 3/16	11 15/16	6 4/16	M	Garfield County	CO	Bob Swinehart	1967	2,260
18 3/16	11 3/16	7 0/16	M	Douglas County	CO	Larry Baker	1975	2,260
18 3/16	11 8/16	6 11/16	M	Penobscot County	ME	Neil Zullo	1975	2,260
18 3/16	11 6/16	6 13/16	M	Slave Lake	ALB	Gordon Roline	1976	2,260
18 3/16	11 8/16	6 11/16	M	Targhee National Forest	ID	Thomas Pinkston	1978	2,260
18 3/16	11 3/16	7 0/16	M	Sudbury	ONT	Alvin Lybarger	1979	2,260
18 3/16	10 15/16	7 4/16	M	St. Louis County	MN	George Sheets	1979	2,260
18 3/16	11 9/16	6 10/16	M	Anchorage	AK	Ronald Arch	1980	2,260
18 3/16	11 10/16	6 9/16	M	Renfrew	ONT	Walter Cymbal	1980	2,260
18 3/16	11 11/16	6 8/16	M	Fremont County	ID	Doug M. Chase	1981	2,260
18 3/16	11 6/16	6 13/16	M	Thunder Bay	ONT	Sharon Larsen	1981	2,260
18 3/16	11 7/16	6 12/16	M	Fort Frances	ONT	Pam Baird	1982	2,260
18 3/16	11 3/16	7 0/16	M	Baraga County	MI	Jim Humber III	1982	2,260
18 3/16	11 2/16	7 1/16	M	Meagher County	MT	Chuck Adams	1982	2,260
18 3/16	11 6/16	6 13/16	M	Sierra County	CA	Robert Smith	1982	2,260
18 3/16	11 8/16	6 11/16	M	Dryden	ONT	Richard Stock	1983	2,260
18 3/16	11 6/16	6 13/16	M	Fremont County	CO	Al Weaver	1983	2,260
18 3/16	11 1/16	7 2/16	M	Echouani Lake	QUE	Collins F. Kellogg	1983	2,260
18 3/16	11 12/16	6 7/16	M	Burnett County	WI	Daniel D. Clayton	1983	2,260
18 3/16	11 10/16	6 9/16	M	Otter Lake	QUE	Dana P. Calhoun	1984	2,260
18 3/16	11 10/16	6 9/16	M	Moose River	ONT	Bob Duncan	1984	2,260
18 3/16	11 5/16	6 14/16	M	Standard Creek	AK	James A. Jones	1984	2,260
18 3/16	11 2/16	7 1/16	M	Idaho County	ID	David Gename	1984	2,260
18 3/16	11 11/16	6 8/16	M	Langlade County	WI	Dan Buss	1984	2,260
18 3/16	11 2/16	7 1/16	M	Wallowa County	OR	Mike Tyrholm	1984	2,260
18 3/16	11 3/16	7 0/16	M	Valley County	ID	Douglas Bunch	1984	2,260
18 3/16	11 6/16	6 13/16	M	Douglas County	WI	Dennis Plantenberg	1984	2,260
18 3/16	11 10/16	6 9/16	F	Augusta County	VA	W. Thurman Hensley	1984	2,260
18 3/16	11 6/16	6 13/16	M	Bear Paw Landing	ONT	Gordan Rabetski	1985	2,260
18 3/16	11 3/16	7 0/16	M	Larimer County	CO	Doug O'Herron	1985	2,260
18 3/16	11 7/16	6 12/16	M	English River	ONT	Richard Nielsen	1985	2,260
18 3/16	11 3/16	7 0/16	M	Ignace	ONT	Walter E. Hammerling	1985	2,260
18 3/16	12 1/16	6 2/16	M	Durban	MAN	Bill Wright, Jr.	1985	2,260
18 3/16	11 6/16	6 13/16	M	Ear Falls	ONT	James C. Gates	1986	2,260
18 3/16	11 15/16	6 4/16	M	Loon Lake	SAS	Harvey McNalley	1986	2,260
18 3/16	11 4/16	6 15/16	M	Idaho County	ID	David Gename	1986	2,260
18 3/16	11 6/16	6 13/16	M	King County	WA	Charles D. Singh	1986	2,260
18 3/16	11 12/16	6 7/16	M	Catron County	NM	Stan Rauch	1987	2,260
18 3/16	11 9/16	6 10/16	M	Minaki	ONT	Donald Schram	1987	2,260
18 3/16	11 9/16	6 10/16	M	Webbwood	ONT	Stephen P. Turay	1987	2,260
18 3/16	11 6/16	6 13/16	M	Gogama	ONT	Tom P. Kidwell	1987	2,260
18 3/16	11 6/16	6 13/16	M	Jims Lake	QUE	David A. Shepard	1987	2,260
18 3/16	11 5/16	6 14/16	M	Bonneville County	ID	Ron Stacey	1987	2,260
18 3/16	11 2/16	7 1/16	M	Washington County	ME	Norman R. Gulbransen	1987	2,260
18 3/16	11 11/16	6 8/16	M	Goodsoil	SAS	John Kalbfleisch	1987	2,260
18 3/16	11 3/16	7 0/16	M	Oxford County	ME	Patrick Abalsamo	1987	2,260
18 3/16	11 3/16	7 0/16	M	Ravalli County	MT	Shaun Twardoski	1987	2,260

SCORE	GREATEST LENGTH	GREATEST WIDTH	SEX	AREA	STATE/ PROVINCE	HUNTER'S NAME	DATE	RANK
18 3/16	11 6/16	6 13/16	M	Chippewa Falls	ONT	Christopher J. Hodyna	1988	2,260
18 3/16	11 13/16	6 6/16	M	Cordova	AK	Jack E. Lape	1988	2,260
18 3/16	11 6/16	6 13/16	M	Sled Lake	SAS	Thomas C. Phillips	1988	2,260
18 3/16	11 8/16	6 11/16	M	Dryden	ONT	Stanley M. Eddy	1988	2,260
18 3/16	11 8/16	6 11/16	M	Idaho County	ID	Howard Holmes	1988	2,260
18 3/16	11 1/16	7 2/16	M	Oxford County	ME	Jack Smith	1988	2,260
18 3/16	11 12/16	6 7/16	M	Washburn County	WI	Edward Peterson	1988	2,260
18 3/16	11 3/16	7 0/16	M	Lemhi County	ID	Dennis N. Minnich	1989	2,260
18 3/16	11 7/16	6 12/16	M	Keg River	ALB	David W. Williams	1989	2,260
18 3/16	11 5/16	6 14/16	M	Boise County	ID	Robert Barrow	1989	2,260
18 3/16	11 8/16	6 11/16	M	Cass County	MN	Mike Honek	1989	2,260
18 3/16	11 2/16	7 1/16	F	Prince of Wales Island	AK	Rickie D. Snell	1990	2,260
18 3/16	11 10/16	6 9/16	M	Elk Point	ALB	C. B. Farnsworth	1990	2,260
18 3/16	11 7/16	6 12/16	M	Long Lac	ONT	David L. Fuller	1990	2,260
18 3/16	11 11/16	6 8/16	M	Kenora	ONT	Wayne D. May	1990	2,260
18 3/16	12 2/16	6 1/16	M	Beltrami County	MN	Evelyn Johnson	1990	2,260
18 3/16	11 12/16	6 7/16	M	Bonnyville	ALB	Glen Garton	1991	2,260
18 3/16	11 2/16	7 1/16	M	Algoma	ONT	Patrick W. Farrow	1991	2,260
18 3/16	11 6/16	6 13/16	M	Fairbanks	AK	Randolph M.S. Galloway	1991	2,260
18 3/16	11 10/16	6 9/16	M	Grand County	UT	Dave Justmann	1991	2,260
18 3/16	11 0/16	7 3/16	M	Dowling	ONT	Lawrence Fillhard	1991	2,260
18 3/16	11 10/16	6 9/16	M	La Ronge	SAS	Roger Wintle	1991	2,260
18 3/16	11 10/16	6 9/16	M	Fort McMurray	ALB	Len Cardinale	1991	2,260
18 3/16	11 5/16	6 14/16	M	Latuque	QUE	William R. Lewis	1991	2,260
18 3/16	11 5/16	6 14/16	M	Zec Rapides des Joachims	QUE	John Neal, Jr.	1992	2,260
18 3/16	11 7/16	6 12/16	M	Saddle Hills	ALB	Wilf Lehners	1992	2,260
18 3/16	11 13/16	6 6/16	M	Zec Domion	QUE	James R. Battreall	1992	2,260
18 3/16	11 12/16	6 7/16	F	Forest County	WI	Scott P. Allen	1992	2,260
18 2/16	11 8/16	6 10/16	M	Murphy Dome	AK	Richard Cooper	1955	2,339
18 2/16	11 2/16	7 0/16	M	Sudbury	ONT	Floyd Eccleston	1961	2,339
18 2/16	11 4/16	6 14/16	M	Penobscot County	ME	Bill L. Carlos	1963	2,339
18 2/16	11 8/16	6 10/16	M	Penobscot County	ME	Dennis H. Driscoll	1967	2,339
18 2/16	11 8/16	6 10/16	M	Franklin County	ME	Kenneth Rapp	1969	2,339
18 2/16	11 5/16	6 13/16	M	Chapleau	ONT	Ed Helgason	1970	2,339
18 2/16	11 6/16	6 12/16	M	Chetwynd	BC	Lee E. Hansel	1973	2,339
18 2/16	11 9/16	6 9/16	M	La Plata County	CO	Rose Neeley	1975	2,339
18 2/16	11 6/16	6 12/16	M	Waupaca County	WI	Neil Pietenpol	1975	2,339
18 2/16	10 14/16	7 4/16	M	Flathead County	MT	Paul P. Schafer	1976	2,339
18 2/16	11 12/16	6 6/16	M	Iron County	MI	Harry W. Squibb	1976	2,339
18 2/16	11 6/16	6 12/16	M	Madison County	ID	Paul Beesley	1977	2,339
18 2/16	11 10/16	6 8/16	M	King County	WA	Stephen C. Zabransky	1978	2,339
18 2/16	11 7/16	6 11/16	M	Kootenai County	ID	Stanley Leake	1979	2,339
18 2/16	11 8/16	6 10/16	M	Powell County	MT	Paul Brunner	1979	2,339
18 2/16	11 9/16	6 9/16	M	St. Louis County	MN	James D. Coakley	1979	2,339
18 2/16	11 4/16	6 14/16	M	Whitney	ONT	Doug Merkel	1979	2,339
18 2/16	11 11/16	6 7/16	F	Fremont County	ID	Paul Phillips	1979	2,339
18 2/16	11 7/16	6 11/16	M	Boise County	ID	Larry Spiva	1979	2,339
18 2/16	11 14/16	6 4/16	M	Boise County	ID	Larry Hoff	1980	2,339
18 2/16	11 10/16	6 8/16	M	Gunnison County	CO	Holt Dougherty	1980	2,339
18 2/16	11 11/16	6 7/16	M	Chichester	QUE	Don Marin	1981	2,339
18 2/16	11 4/16	6 14/16	M	Piscataquis County	ME	Daniel E. Reznik	1981	2,339
18 2/16	11 4/16	6 14/16	M	Ear Falls	ONT	Robert J. Roach	1981	2,339
18 2/16	10 15/16	7 3/16	M	Coos County	NH	Phillip E. Williams	1981	2,339
18 2/16	11 8/16	6 10/16	M	Ignace	ONT	Elmer R. Luce, Jr.	1982	2,339
18 2/16	11 4/16	6 14/16	M	Washington County	ME	Richard Manchur	1982	2,339
18 2/16	11 10/16	6 8/16	M	Clearwater County	ID	Dan J. Martin	1983	2,339
18 2/16	11 4/16	6 14/16	M	Longlac	ONT	Bill Zaepfel	1983	2,339
18 2/16	11 10/16	6 8/16	M	Algonquin	ONT	Walter F. Dotson, Jr.	1983	2,339
18 2/16	11 8/16	6 10/16	M	Dwight	ONT	Walt Krom	1983	2,339
18 2/16	11 5/16	6 13/16	M	Sundridge	ONT	Jack Lape	1983	2,339
18 2/16	11 2/16	7 0/16	M	Haliburton	ONT	John Dawson	1983	2,339
18 2/16	11 1/16	7 1/16	M	Boise County	ID	Larry Spiva	1983	2,339
18 2/16	11 8/16	6 10/16	M	Oneida County	WI	Don Ries	1983	2,339
18 2/16	11 7/16	6 11/16	M	Ontonagon County	MI	Greg M. Ebel	1983	2,339
18 2/16	11 4/16	6 14/16	M	Latah County	ID	Marcus B. Caudill	1984	2,339
18 2/16	11 2/16	7 0/16	M	Cumberland House	SAS	Wayne Muth	1984	2,339
18 2/16	11 6/16	6 12/16	M	Latah County	ID	Robert Walter Brooks	1984	2,339
18 2/16	11 10/16	6 8/16	M	Clearwater County	ID	Mark McMurray	1984	2,339
18 2/16	11 6/16	6 12/16	M	Pontiac	QUE	Russ Kay	1984	2,339
18 2/16	11 8/16	6 10/16	M	Fiddler Twp.	ONT	Mike Johnson	1984	2,339

MINIMUM SCORE 18

SCORE	GREATEST LENGTH	GREATEST WIDTH	SEX	AREA	STATE/ PROVINCE	HUNTER'S NAME	DATE	RANK
18 2/16	11 9/16	6 9/16	M	Valley County	ID	Kenneth Hyde	1984	2,339
18 2/16	11 7/16	6 11/16	M	Sunbury County	NBW	Mike Lamade	1985	2,339
18 2/16	11 4/16	6 14/16	M	Fort Coulonge	QUE	Wm. Fred Stone	1985	2,339
18 2/16	11 6/16	6 12/16	M	Penobscot County	ME	Gary Thorne	1985	2,339
18 2/16	11 6/16	6 12/16	M	Riverside County	CA	Jim Wagner	1985	2,339
18 2/16	11 6/16	6 12/16	M	Jackson County	OR	Lou Probo	1985	2,339
18 2/16	11 8/16	6 10/16	M	Eagle Lake	ONT	Paul Sieg	1986	2,339
18 2/16	11 7/16	6 11/16	M	Fort Frances	ONT	Randy Durushia	1986	2,339
18 2/16	11 9/16	6 9/16	M	Wabigoon	ONT	Robert Barrie	1986	2,339
18 2/16	11 15/16	6 3/16	M	Duck Mtn.	MAN	Bill Clink	1986	2,339
18 2/16	10 10/16	7 8/16	M	Thaddeus Lake	ONT	Robert Brodhagen	1986	2,339
18 2/16	11 10/16	6 8/16	M	Grant County	NM	Dr. Douglas R. Hahn	1986	2,339
18 2/16	11 1/16	7 1/16	M	Siskiyou County	CA	Kirk Westervelt	1986	2,339
18 2/16	11 6/16	6 12/16	M	Atikokan	ONT	Jim Holdenried	1987	2,339
18 2/16	11 12/16	6 6/16	M	Hudson Bay	SAS	Billy Ellis III	1987	2,339
18 2/16	11 5/16	6 13/16	M	Ignace	ONT	Richard Nielsen	1987	2,339
18 2/16	11 4/16	6 14/16	M	Clearwater County	ID	Timothy A. King	1987	2,339
18 2/16	11 7/16	6 11/16	M	Teton County	ID	Frank W. Sparkman	1987	2,339
18 2/16	11 6/16	6 12/16	M	Graham County	AZ	Michael E. Duperret	1987	2,339
18 2/16	11 11/16	6 7/16	F	Duck Mtn.	MAN	Richard W. Sage	1987	2,339
18 2/16	11 4/16	6 14/16	M	Marathon	ONT	Robert W. Russell	1987	2,339
18 2/16	11 2/16	7 0/16	M	Essex County	NY	John Douglas Durling	1987	2,339
18 2/16	11 15/16	6 3/16	M	King County	WA	Mark A. Graham	1987	2,339
18 2/16	11 2/16	7 0/16	M	Baker County	OR	Scott Reed	1988	2,339
18 2/16	11 7/16	6 11/16	M	Latah County	ID	Kirk T. Byers	1988	2,339
18 2/16	11 6/16	6 12/16	M	Wabigoon	ONT	Albert J. Smith	1988	2,339
18 2/16	11 6/16	6 12/16	M	Bear Lake County	ID	Rick Bergholm	1988	2,339
18 2/16	11 7/16	6 11/16	M	La Tuque	QUE	Tracey S. Goodrich	1988	2,339
18 2/16	11 6/16	6 12/16	M	Wawa	ONT	Donald L. Cox	1988	2,339
18 2/16	11 8/16	6 10/16	M	Valley County	ID	Phil Barton	1988	2,339
18 2/16	11 1/16	7 1/16	M	Sandoval County	NM	Derek A. Tierney	1988	2,339
18 2/16	11 5/16	6 13/16	M	Atikokan	ONT	Marc Headington	1988	2,339
18 2/16	11 13/16	6 5/16	M	Loon Lake	SAS	Daniel J. Robertson	1988	2,339
18 2/16	11 8/16	6 10/16	M	Whitefish Bay	ONT	Walter Skic	1989	2,339
18 2/16	11 7/16	6 11/16	M	Caviar Lake	ONT	Glen Bohl	1989	2,339
18 2/16	11 2/16	7 0/16	M	Clearwater County	ID	Dr Christopher L Allen	1989	2,339
18 2/16	11 8/16	6 10/16	M	King County	WA	Kenneth Bean	1989	2,339
18 2/16	11 12/16	6 6/16	M	Valley County	ID	Larry Hoff	1989	2,339
18 2/16	11 10/16	6 8/16	M	Lincoln County	WI	William J. Niehaus	1989	2,339
18 2/16	11 6/16	6 12/16	M	San Miguel County	NM	Dick McClain	1989	2,339
18 2/16	11 6/16	6 12/16	M	Lane County	OR	Jay P. Marcott	1989	2,339
18 2/16	11 2/16	7 0/16	M	Dryden	ONT	Robert J. Crane	1990	2,339
18 2/16	11 8/16	6 10/16	M	Cumberland House	SAS	Denny Raper	1990	2,339
18 2/16	11 2/16	7 0/16	M	Lake Ascension	QUE	Michael Stone	1990	2,339
18 2/16	11 4/16	6 14/16	M	Folette	ONT	Richard A. Bugher	1990	2,339
18 2/16	11 2/16	7 0/16	M	Zec Restigo	QUE	Michael P. Murphy	1990	2,339
18 2/16	11 8/16	6 10/16	M	Stevens County	WA	Allen J. Thrush	1990	2,339
18 2/16	11 2/16	7 0/16	M	Lake Kipawa	QUE	Billy Feltman	1991	2,339
18 2/16	11 8/16	6 10/16	M	Holinshead Lake	ONT	Linda Turek	1991	2,339
18 2/16	11 8/16	6 10/16	M	Lebel Township	ONT	Mike Hartling	1991	2,339
18 2/16	11 2/16	7 0/16	M	Aroostook County	ME	Charles Stulz	1991	2,339
18 2/16	11 4/16	6 14/16	M	Gift Lake	ALB	Ronald C. Putzler	1992	2,339
18 2/16	11 11/16	6 7/16	M	Grand County	CO	Barry J. Smith	1992	2,339
18 2/16	11 9/16	6 9/16	M	Savant Lake	ONT	Jerry G. Marchant	1992	2,339
18 2/16	11 6/16	6 12/16	M	Margo Lake	ONT	Dean V. Ashton	1992	2,339
18 1/16	11 8/16	6 9/16	M	Chelan County	WA	Dick Smethvrst	1965	2,436
18 1/16	11 4/16	6 13/16	M	Clearwater County	ID	Jess Stinichcome	1965	2,436
18 1/16	11 0/16	7 1/16	M	Somerset County	ME	Raymond Benedetto	1970	2,436
18 1/16	11 7/16	6 10/16	M	Archuleta County	CO	A. H. Gutierrez, Jr.	1971	2,436
18 1/16	11 7/16	6 10/16	M	Franklin County	ME	Walter Krom	1972	2,436
18 1/16	11 3/16	6 14/16	M	Blackwater River	BC	Ron McKay	1974	2,436
18 1/16	11 3/16	6 14/16	M	Delta County	MI	Rick Moudry	1975	2,436
18 1/16	11 12/16	6 5/16	M	Itasca County	MN	Charles W. Schultz	1976	2,436
18 1/16	11 4/16	6 13/16	M	Franklin County	ME	Bernard Caruso	1977	2,436
18 1/16	11 1/16	7 0/16	M	Saguache County	CO	Robert Faris II	1977	2,436
18 1/16	11 8/16	6 9/16	M	Kalkaska County	MI	Jerome H. Lubbers	1978	2,436
18 1/16	11 3/16	6 14/16	M	Fremont County	CO	Robert Andrew	1978	2,436
18 1/16	11 9/16	6 8/16	M	Cooper Landing	AK	Richard A. Hoag	1979	2,436
18 1/16	11 6/16	6 11/16	M	Clearwater County	ID	George P. Mann	1980	2,436
18 1/16	11 0/16	7 1/16	M	Oxford County	ME	Michael Matoushek	1980	2,436

SCORE	GREATEST LENGTH	GREATEST WIDTH	SEX	AREA	STATE/ PROVINCE	HUNTER'S NAME	DATE	RANK
18 1/16	11 10/16	6 7/16	M	Kenora	ONT	Ervin Wagner	1980	2,436
18 1/16	11 8/16	6 9/16	M	Iron County	MI	George Hronkin III	1981	2,436
18 1/16	11 9/16	6 8/16	M	Dryden	ONT	Anne M. Fancher	1982	2,436
18 1/16	11 5/16	6 12/16	M	Idaho County	ID	Brad L. Johnson	1982	2,436
18 1/16	11 9/16	6 8/16	M	Archuleta County	CO	Stephen E. Kennedy	1982	2,436
18 1/16	11 8/16	6 9/16	M	Mineral County	MT	Greg L. Munther	1982	2,436
18 1/16	11 8/16	6 9/16	M	Dwight	ONT	Michael D. Moore	1983	2,436
18 1/16	10 10/16	7 7/16	M	Fort Coulonge	QUE	Curtis A. Peterman	1983	2,436
18 1/16	11 5/16	6 12/16	M	Park County	CO	Dan Tekavec	1983	2,436
18 1/16	11 2/16	6 15/16	M	Colfax County	NM	Dean Oatman	1983	2,436
18 1/16	11 10/16	6 7/16	M	Ignace	ONT	Kenneth C. Kaufmann	1984	2,436
18 1/16	11 13/16	6 4/16	M	Price County	WI	Tom Gouger	1984	2,436
18 1/16	11 5/16	6 12/16	M	Clackamas County	OR	Bob Smitherman	1984	2,436
18 1/16	11 8/16	6 9/16	M	Marinette County	WI	James L. Behn	1984	2,436
18 1/16	11 3/16	6 14/16	M	Ashland County	WI	Tony D. Snow	1984	2,436
18 1/16	11 9/16	6 8/16	M	McBride Lake	SAS	John Rook	1985	2,436
18 1/16	11 3/16	6 14/16	M	Clearwater County	ID	Gene Kiele	1985	2,436
18 1/16	11 11/16	6 6/16	M	Nass River	BC	John Jones	1985	2,436
18 1/16	11 9/16	6 8/16	M	King County	WA	Greg Winters	1985	2,436
18 1/16	11 6/16	6 11/16	M	Payette County	ID	Gary Kinney	1986	2,436
18 1/16	11 6/16	6 11/16	M	Lemhi County	ID	Anthony S. Winterer	1986	2,436
18 1/16	11 5/16	6 12/16	M	Bird River	MAN	Dale Selby	1986	2,436
18 1/16	11 2/16	6 15/16	M	Lemhi County	ID	Cathy Lee Jordan	1986	2,436
18 1/16	11 5/16	6 12/16	M	Josephine County	OR	Terry Garbacik	1986	2,436
18 1/16	11 9/16	6 8/16	M	Becker County	MN	Richard Enger	1986	2,436
18 1/16	11 9/16	6 8/16	M	Wallowa County	OR	Michael Crawford	1986	2,436
18 1/16	11 11/16	6 6/16	M	Delta County	CO	Jon P. Thomas	1986	2,436
18 1/16	10 13/16	7 4/16	M	Pitkin County	CO	T. Michael Casey	1987	2,436
18 1/16	11 6/16	6 11/16	M	Natal Twp.	ONT	Terry D. Colescott	1988	2,436
18 1/16	11 6/16	6 11/16	M	Maganasipi Lake	QUE	Gerard Mascellino	1988	2,436
18 1/16	11 3/16	6 14/16	M	Timmins	ONT	Allen G. Hughes	1988	2,436
18 1/16	11 4/16	6 13/16	M	Idaho County	ID	John Zawaski	1988	2,436
18 1/16	11 9/16	6 8/16	M	Lemhi County	ID	Tim Kanapeckas	1988	2,436
18 1/16	11 12/16	6 5/16	M	Houghton County	MI	John Knieper	1988	2,436
18 1/16	11 7/16	6 10/16	M	Skamania County	WA	Annette Crews	1988	2,436
18 1/16	11 11/16	6 6/16	M	Huerfano County	CO	Jim Witcombe	1989	2,436
18 1/16	11 11/16	6 6/16	M	Mayerthorpe	ALB	Rudy Wilkison	1989	2,436
18 1/16	11 7/16	6 10/16	M	Ignace	ONT	Gordan A. Etris	1989	2,436
18 1/16	11 7/16	6 10/16	M	Ear Falls	ONT	Larry Sparks	1989	2,436
18 1/16	11 8/16	6 9/16	M	Terrace Bay	ONT	Troy D. Huffman	1989	2,436
18 1/16	11 1/16	7 0/16	M	Idaho County	ID	Monty Moravec	1989	2,436
18 1/16	11 4/16	6 13/16	M	Rapides des Joachims	QUE	Pete Karels	1989	2,436
18 1/16	11 8/16	6 9/16	M	McKerrow	ONT	Terry Walton	1989	2,436
18 1/16	11 0/16	7 1/16	M	Custer County	ID	Patrick Patterson	1989	2,436
18 1/16	11 3/16	6 14/16	M	Zec Dumoine	QUE	Richard E. Lockwood, Sr.	1989	2,436
18 1/16	11 3/16	6 14/16	M	Lewis & Clark County	MT	Ronald Parker	1989	2,436
18 1/16	11 9/16	6 8/16	M	Houston	BC	Michael Whited	1990	2,436
18 1/16	11 3/16	6 14/16	M	Apisko Lake	MAN	Jerry Stroot	1990	2,436
18 1/16	11 5/16	6 12/16	M	Ear Falls	ONT	Mark Zink	1990	2,436
18 1/16	11 7/16	6 10/16	M	Nipigon	ONT	Fred W. Achilles	1990	2,436
18 1/16	11 8/16	6 9/16	M	Green Lake	SAS	William Smith	1990	2,436
18 1/16	11 7/16	6 10/16	M	Huerfano County	CO	Robert L. Beckwith	1990	2,436
18 1/16	11 9/16	6 8/16	M	Lake of the Woods	ONT	Scott J. Simons	1991	2,436
18 1/16	11 9/16	6 8/16	M	Geraldton	ONT	Clark M. Vickers	1991	2,436
18 1/16	11 1/16	7 0/16	M	Pacific County	WA	Brandy Knight	1991	2,436
18 1/16	11 8/16	6 9/16	M	Riding Mtn.	MAN	Ryan J. Dorak	1991	2,436
18 1/16	11 6/16	6 11/16	M	Kelvington	SAS	Ross Meyer	1992	2,436
18 1/16	11 10/16	6 7/16	M	Poplarfield	MAN	Dan Dietrich	1992	2,436
18 1/16	11 9/16	6 8/16	M	Kelvington	SAS	Robert C. McCardell	1992	2,436
18 1/16	11 3/16	6 14/16	M	Hornepayne	ONT	David M. Lakich	1992	2,436
18 1/16	11 8/16	6 9/16	M	Dalton Highway	AK	Thomas Chadwick	1992	2,436
18 0/16	11 0/16	7 0/16	M	Polk County	OR	H. Dale Overholser	1959	2,512
18 0/16	11 9/16	6 7/16	M	Prince William Sound	AK	Bob Snelson	1962	2,512
18 0/16	11 12/16	6 4/16	M	Franklin County	ME	John Iannuzzo	1966	2,512
18 0/16	11 6/16	6 10/16	M	Jackson County	OR	Pat Mastan	1970	2,512
18 0/16	11 2/16	6 14/16	M	Franklin County	ME	Donald R. Pyne	1970	2,512
18 0/16	11 0/16	7 0/16	M	Franklin County	ME	John Fedor	1973	2,512
18 0/16	11 8/16	6 8/16	M	Igitna River	AK	George Faerber	1974	2,512
18 0/16	11 4/16	6 12/16	M		ONT	Larry Kuskie	1974	2,512
18 0/16	11 10/16	6 6/16	M	Franklin County	ME	Michael P. Murphy	1974	2,512

Score	Greatest Length	Greatest Width	Sex	Area	State/ Province	Hunter's Name	Date	Rank
18 0/16	11 6/16	6 10/16	F	Taylor County	WI	Christopher A. Jeffords	1976	2,512
18 0/16	11 9/16	6 7/16	M	Marathon County	WI	Jay Schultz	1977	2,512
18 0/16	11 12/16	6 4/16	M	Boise County	ID	Clae Kress	1978	2,512
18 0/16	11 6/16	6 10/16	M	Franklin County	ME	James E. Roy	1978	2,512
18 0/16	11 8/16	6 8/16	F	Hubbard County	MN	George Arimond	1979	2,512
18 0/16	11 6/16	6 10/16	M	Siskiyou County	CA	John Grochowski, Jr.	1979	2,512
18 0/16	11 10/16	6 6/16	M	Bonneville County	ID	Paul M. Kniss	1980	2,512
18 0/16	11 1/16	6 15/16	M	Somerset County	ME	Albert Buonanno	1980	2,512
18 0/16	11 3/16	6 13/16	M	Almonte	ONT	Stephen Van Zile	1981	2,512
18 0/16	11 8/16	6 8/16	M	Red Lake	ONT	Bernie Pawlaser	1981	2,512
18 0/16	11 5/16	6 11/16	M	St. Lawrence County	NY	Richard Hurteau	1981	2,512
18 0/16	11 4/16	6 12/16	M	Custer County	CO	Leonard Moore	1981	2,512
18 0/16	11 7/16	6 9/16	M	Thunder Bay	ONT	Rob J. Smith	1981	2,512
18 0/16	11 8/16	6 8/16	M	Hatcher Pass	AK	Roger Stewart	1981	2,512
18 0/16	11 6/16	6 10/16	M	Susitina River	AK	Roger G. Stewart	1984	2,512
18 0/16	11 7/16	6 9/16	M	Archuleta County	CO	Roy S. Marlow III	1984	2,512
18 0/16	11 10/16	6 6/16	M	Little Susitna River	AK	Gary G. Wall	1984	2,512
18 0/16	11 5/16	6 11/16	M	Beluga Mtn.	AK	Dick Carlson	1984	2,512
18 0/16	11 6/16	6 10/16	M	Sublette County	WY	Randy Erye	1984	2,512
18 0/16	11 6/16	6 10/16	M	Messines	QUE	Howard 'Butch' Malone	1984	2,512
18 0/16	11 1/16	6 15/16	M	North Bay	ONT	John R. Rexroad	1984	2,512
18 0/16	11 2/16	6 14/16	M	Kechika Range	BC	Wade L. Carstens	1984	2,512
18 0/16	11 7/16	6 9/16	M	Iron County	WI	Floyd J. Vancil	1984	2,512
18 0/16	11 7/16	6 9/16	M	Gilpin County	CO	Bryon Scott Johnson	1985	2,512
18 0/16	11 3/16	6 13/16	M	Anchorage	AK	Ronald D. Mills	1985	2,512
18 0/16	11 5/16	6 11/16	M	Idaho County	ID	Ed Vallee	1985	2,512
18 0/16	11 9/16	6 7/16	M	Clearwater County	MN	Kyle Bauman	1985	2,512
18 0/16	11 7/16	6 9/16	M	Wayne County	PA	Mike B. Lamade	1985	2,512
18 0/16	11 10/16	6 6/16	M	Brandon	MAN	Gary Kaluzniak	1986	2,512
18 0/16	11 6/16	6 10/16	M	Pasquia Hills	SAS	Marcus Vogel	1986	2,512
18 0/16	11 1/16	6 15/16	M	Missoula County	MT	John L. Wozniak	1986	2,512
18 0/16	11 6/16	6 10/16	F	Rouyn-Noranda	QUE	Roy Cucuzza	1986	2,512
18 0/16	11 2/16	6 14/16	M	Breckenridge Twp.	ONT	John A. Bogucki	1986	2,512
18 0/16	11 8/16	6 8/16	F	Duck Mtn.	MAN	Marty Stubstad	1986	2,512
18 0/16	11 5/16	6 11/16	M	Idaho County	ID	Jay J. Bowman	1986	2,512
18 0/16	11 8/16	6 8/16	M	Durban	MAN	Jerry V. Finley	1986	2,512
18 0/16	11 5/16	6 11/16	M	Oxford County	ME	Christopher Scott Harrima	1986	2,512
18 0/16	11 7/16	6 9/16	M	Cook County	MN	Richard P. Smith	1986	2,512
18 0/16	11 9/16	6 7/16	M	Dryden	ONT	Jeff Duhrkopf	1986	2,512
18 0/16	11 4/16	6 12/16	M	Clearwater County	ID	Christopher B. Holmes	1987	2,512
18 0/16	11 8/16	6 8/16	M	Vermillion Bay	ONT	Jerry Podratz	1987	2,512
18 0/16	11 5/16	6 11/16	M	Dryden	ONT	Kevin Smaby	1987	2,512
18 0/16	11 10/16	6 6/16	M	Capreol	ONT	Tony Willwerth	1987	2,512
18 0/16	11 8/16	6 8/16	M	Cowlitz County	WA	David Soyars	1987	2,512
18 0/16	11 4/16	6 12/16	M	Muldrew Township	ONT	Daniel P. Wieske	1987	2,512
18 0/16	11 11/16	6 5/16	M	Crow Wing County	MN	Ron Snyder	1987	2,512
18 0/16	11 5/16	6 11/16	M	Conejos County	CO	Joseph E. Marrinan, Jr.	1988	2,512
18 0/16	11 0/16	7 0/16	M	Dorion	ONT	Larry D. Paulsen	1988	2,512
18 0/16	11 12/16	6 4/16	M	Talkeetna	AK	Beverly Hajenga	1988	2,512
18 0/16	11 4/16	6 12/16	M	Fort Coulonge	QUE	Terry Lee Summey	1988	2,512
18 0/16	11 9/16	6 7/16	M	Susitna River	AK	Tom Orbison	1988	2,512
18 0/16	11 6/16	6 10/16	M	Valley County	ID	Julie E. Johnston	1988	2,512
18 0/16	10 14/16	7 2/16	M	Atikokan	ONT	Matthew Andersen	1988	2,512
18 0/16	11 11/16	6 5/16	M	Athabasca River	ALB	Grant Adkisson	1989	2,512
18 0/16	11 4/16	6 12/16	M	Algoma	ONT	Denis Belcourt	1989	2,512
18 0/16	11 6/16	6 10/16	M	Sexsmith	ALB	Ted Brown	1989	2,512
18 0/16	11 9/16	6 7/16	M	Dryden	ONT	Albert J. Smith	1989	2,512
18 0/16	11 6/16	6 10/16	M	Lac Nilgaut	QUE	John S. Ashe	1989	2,512
18 0/16	11 8/16	6 8/16	M	Flotten Lake	SAS	Paul Prochaska	1989	2,512
18 0/16	11 2/16	6 14/16	M	Rollet	QUE	Douglas E. Ott	1989	2,512
18 0/16	11 9/16	6 7/16	M	Zec Restigo	QUE	David Dibblee	1989	2,512
18 0/16	11 4/16	6 12/16	M	Beurling River	QUE	Philippe Galley	1989	2,512
18 0/16	11 7/16	6 9/16	M	Saddle Hills	ALB	Dr. Michael D. Pickering,	1990	2,512
18 0/16	11 4/16	6 12/16	M	Cranberry Portage	MAN	Bob Beardsley	1990	2,512
18 0/16	11 5/16	6 11/16	M	Sturgeon Landing	SAS	Kay Lang	1990	2,512
18 0/16	11 6/16	6 10/16	M	Red Lake	ONT	Fred Sprague	1990	2,512
18 0/16	11 4/16	6 12/16	M	Echo Bay	ONT	Ralph W. Fairbanks	1990	2,512
18 0/16	11 10/16	6 6/16	M	Latuque	QUE	Ronald T. Kinnas	1990	2,512
18 0/16	11 12/16	6 4/16	M	Lake County	MN	John Koschmeder	1990	2,512
18 0/16	11 6/16	6 10/16	M	Delta County	MI	Rob Horwitz	1990	2,512

Minimum score 18

Score	Greatest Length	Greatest Width	Sex	Area	State/ Province	Hunter's Name	Date	Rank
18 0/16	11 6/16	6 10/16	M	Caldwell County	NC	Teddy Adams	1990	2,512
18 0/16	11 9/16	6 7/16	M	The Pas	MAN	George G. Wilson, Jr.	1991	2,512
18 0/16	11 10/16	6 6/16	M	Biscotasing	ONT	Everett W. Ayers	1991	2,512
18 0/16	11 2/16	6 14/16	M	Norman Wells	NWT	Lyndon Walker	1991	2,512
18 0/16	11 11/16	6 5/16	M	Gunnison County	CO	Robert Kuntz	1991	2,512
18 0/16	11 10/16	6 6/16	M	Tobin Lake	SAS	Kirk Winters	1991	2,512
18 0/16	11 1/16	6 15/16	M	Chippewa County	WI	Larry Paulsen	1991	2,512
18 0/16	11 5/16	6 11/16	M	Ravalli County	MT	David H. Stalling	1991	2,512
18 0/16	11 9/16	6 7/16	M	Mesa County	CO	Steven R. Hickok	1992	2,512
18 0/16	11 5/16	6 11/16	M	Lake Caviar	ONT	Roger E. Wendorf	1992	2,512
18 0/16	11 9/16	6 7/16	M	Lincoln County	WY	Jim Fowler	1992	2,512
18 0/16	11 0/16	7 0/16	M	Idaho County	ID	T. J. Conrads	1992	2,512
18 0/16	10 14/16	7 2/16	M	Widdifield Township	ONT	Cliff O'Donnell	1992	2,512
18 0/16	11 8/16	6 8/16	M	La Plata County	CO	Dennis L. Howell	1992	2,512

World Record Grizzly Bear
Score: 25 13/16
Moose Lake, British Columbia - 1987
Hunter: Derril Lamb

GRIZZLY BEAR

MINIMUM SCORE 19   *Ursus arctos horribilis*

SCORE	GREATEST LENGTH	GREATEST WIDTH	SEX	AREA	STATE/ PROVINCE	HUNTER'S NAME	DATE	RANK
25 13/16	16 1/16	9 12/16	M	Moose Lake	BC	Derril Lamb	1987	1
25 6/16	16 0/16	9 6/16	M	Anzac River	BC	Harley Tison	1972	2
25 3/16	15 13/16	9 6/16	M	Stevens Lakes	BC	Dr. Rex Hancock	1968	3
24 14/16	15 10/16	9 4/16	M	Yellowstone National Park	WY	Art Young	1920	4
24 11/16	15 2/16	9 9/16	M	Stevens Lakes	BC	Dr. R. L. Hambrick	1965	5
24 9/16	15 13/16	8 12/16	M	Bella Coola	BC	William P. Mastrangel	1956	6
23 13/16	15 6/16	8 7/16	M	Gulkana River	AK	Art Kragness	1973	7
23 12/16	14 15/16	8 13/16	M	Kotzebue	AK	James P. Jacobson	1981	8
23 7/16	14 14/16	8 9/16	M	Kakwa River	ALB	Rick Michalski	1981	9
22 13/16	14 3/16	8 10/16	M	Kingcome Inlet	BC	Peter Halbig	1982	10
22 12/16	14 6/16	8 6/16	M	Brazeua River	ALB	Curt Lynn	1973	11
22 7/16	13 15/16	8 8/16	M	Earn Lake	YUK	Dr. R. D. Keeler	1986	12
22 1/16	14 0/16	8 1/16	M	Galena	AK	Larry Spiva	1992	13
21 8/16	13 15/16	7 9/16	F	Bella Coola	BC	J. Dale Hale	1989	14
21 1/16	13 3/16	7 14/16	F	Tolovana	AK	Larry Edward Townsend	1990	15
21 0/16	13 11/16	7 5/16	M	Little Tok River	AK	Don Davidson, Jr.	1987	16
20 10/16	13 3/16	7 7/16	F	Rivers Inlet	BC	Chuck Adams	1988	17
20 9/16	13 1/16	7 8/16	F	Meziadin Lake	BC	Glenn Hisey	1992	18
20 7/16	13 0/16	7 7/16	F	Kispiox	BC	Dr. Rex Hancock	1965	19
20 6/16	12 14/16	7 8/16	F	Scoop Lake	BC	Ronald Montross	1984	20
20 3/16	13 2/16	7 1/16	M	Galbraith Lake	AK	Maxallen D. Jackson	1981	21
20 1/16	13 1/16	7 0/16	M	Stevens Lakes	BC	Fred Bear	1961	22
20 0/16	12 14/16	7 2/16	F	Yellowstone National Park	WY	Saxton T. Pope	1920	23
20 0/16	12 13/16	7 3/16	M	Ivishak River	AK	Jeff Lindeman	1988	23
19 15/16	12 11/16	7 4/16	M	Dalton Hwy.	AK	Thomas Chadwick	1984	25
19 14/16	12 8/16	7 6/16	F	Ptarmigan Creek	AK	Donald O. Smith	1964	26
19 14/16	13 0/16	6 14/16	M	Atigun Pass	AK	Alan Richey	1984	26
19 10/16	12 5/16	7 5/16	F	Stevens Lakes	BC	G. Fred Asbell	1969	28
19 8/16	12 8/16	7 0/16	M	Tangle Lakes	AK	John Musacchia	1972	29
19 8/16	12 10/16	6 14/16	M	Whitehorse	YUK	Scott Koelzer	1977	29
19 5/16	11 15/16	7 6/16	F	Stevens Lakes	BC	Walter Krom	1968	31
19 0/16	12 10/16	6 6/16	M	Kispiox River	BC	Charles Kroll	1960	32
19 0/16	12 8/16	6 8/16	M	Brooks Range	AK	Ronald W. Lang, Jr.	1992	32

World Record Polar Bear
Score: 26 6/16
Cape Lisburne, Alaska - 1958
Hunter: Richard McIntyre

POLAR BEAR

MINIMUM SCORE 20

Ursus maritimus

SCORE	GREATEST LENGTH	GREATEST WIDTH	SEX	AREA	STATE/ PROVINCE	HUNTER'S NAME	DATE	RANK
26 6/16	16 4/16	10 2/16	M	Cape Lisburne	AK	Richard McIntyre	1958	1
26 0/16	16 2/16	9 14/16	M	Resolute Bay	NWT	Gary F. Bogner	1989	2
25 14/16	16 3/16	9 11/16	M	Chukchi Sea	AK	Larry Jones	1965	3
25 1/16	15 5/16	9 12/16	F	Baffin Island	NWT	Arthur Young	1926	4
25 0/16	15 12/16	9 4/16	M	Resolute Bay	NWT	George P. Mann	1991	5
24 4/16	15 5/16	8 15/16	F	Baffin Island	NWT	Arthur Young	1926	6
23 13/16	14 13/16	8 14/16	M	Bathurst Island	NWT	Archie Nesbitt	1989	7

World Record Bison
Score: 115 6/8
Garfield County, Utah - 1991
Hunter: Pete Shepley

BISON

Bison bison bison
and *Bison bison athabascae*

MINIMUM SCORE 100

SCORE	LENGTH OF R HORN L		CIRCUMFERENCE OF R BASE L		GREATEST SPREAD	AREA	STATE/ PROVINCE	HUNTER'S NAME	DATE	RANK
115 6/8	16 4/8	17 7/8	13 2/8	14 0/8	29 0/8	Garfield County	UT	Pete Shepley	1991	1
112 2/8	18 4/8	18 0/8	14 1/8	14 1/8	29 6/8	Farewell Lake	AK	George A. Moerlein	1972	2
111 0/8	18 0/8	17 6/8	13 3/8	13 4/8	27 2/8	Garfield County	UT	Craig Bonham	1983	3
110 6/8	19 0/8	18 7/8	12 7/8	12 6/8	27 2/8	Garfield County	UT	Jim Ryan	1989	4
110 4/8	16 2/8	15 2/8	14 1/8	14 1/8	26 7/8	Garfield County	UT	Paul B. Brunner	1979	5
108 6/8	18 5/8	18 7/8	12 2/8	12 2/8	26 2/8	Garfield County	UT	Mike Poynor	1987	6
108 4/8	16 3/8	17 7/8	12 6/8	12 7/8	30 0/8	Davis County	UT	Troy M.Miller	1991	7
106 6/8	17 2/8	16 4/8	13 0/8	12 7/8	25 0/8	Garfield County	UT	Chuck Adams	1986	8
105 6/8	18 0/8	18 2/8	12 6/8	12 7/8	28 5/8	Delta Junction	AK	David Ray Western	1990	9
105 2/8	16 2/8	16 3/8	13 0/8	12 7/8	27 4/8	Delta Junction	AK	Scott Schultz	1986	10
105 0/8	17 4/8	17 4/8	12 2/8	12 3/8	23 0/8	Delta Junction	AK	Tony Russ	1992	11
102 4/8	15 3/8	15 3/8	12 6/8	12 6/8	24 2/8	Garfield County	UT	Dale Drilling	1991	12
102 2/8	15 6/8	15 5/8	12 4/8	12 4/8	23 5/8	Garfield County	UT	Hugh H.Hogle	1992	13
101 4/8	16 7/8	16 6/8	12 4/8	12 4/8	25 0/8	Delta Junction	AK	John Sarvis	1991	14
100 6/8	16 1/8	16 1/8	12 1/8	12 0/8	24 1/8	Garfield County	UT	Max Park	1989	15
95 4/8	15 7/8	15 5/8	11 4/8	11 4/8	24 0/8	Farewell	AK	Rick D. Snell	1992	16
83 0/8	15 6/8	15 3/8	8 5/8	8 5/8	22 6/8	Garfield County	UT	Vaughn Ballard	1988	17

World Record Barren Ground Caribou
Score: 448 6/8
Lake Clark Region, Alaska - 1984
Hunter: Dennis Burdick

BARREN GROUND CARIBOU

Minimum score 300

Rangifer tarandus granti,
Rangifer tarandus stonei and
Rangifer tarandus arcticus

SCORE	LENGTH OF MAIN BEAM R	L	INSIDE SPREAD	NUMBER OF POINTS R	L	AREA	STATE/ PROVINCE	HUNTER'S NAME	DATE	RANK
448 6/8	48 4/8	48 5/8	40 3/8	17	20	Lake Clark	AK	Dennis Burdick	1984	1
446 6/8	55 0/8	55 6/8	40 5/8	23	19	Meshik River	AK	Art Kragness	1970	2
424 4/8	50 1/8	49 7/8	45 2/8	15	13	Naknek River	AK	Jack Wood	1990	3
424 0/8	52 7/8	51 1/8	41 6/8	21	12	Delta River	AK	Bill Brown	1960	4
419 6/8	51 1/8	49 0/8	35 0/8	15	15	Pilot Point	AK	Scott Atton	1987	5
417 2/8	60 2/8	60 2/8	39 0/8	11	11	Dog Salmon River	AK	John S. Alley	1987	6
417 0/8	50 5/8	52 3/8	33 6/8	13	17	Little Delta River	AK	Fred Bear	1959	7
416 1/8	53 5/8	53 2/8	44 2/8	14	18	Kipchuk River	AK	Roy Humphires	1986	8
415 3/8	45 0/8	46 0/8	31 1/8	17	18	Ugashik River	AK	Ron Madsen	1987	9
414 6/8	48 3/8	47 1/8	39 7/8	13	12	Aleutian Range	AK	Robert Smith	1983	10
414 3/8	62 1/8	63 6/8	51 7/8	14	10	King Salmon	AK	Larry Spiva	1983	11
412 5/8	53 3/8	54 3/8	37 3/8	15	21	Lake Iliamna	AK	Don Wells	1982	12
407 4/8	54 3/8	55 3/8	51 4/8	20	14	Lake Becharof	AK	Larry Jones	1969	13
407 4/8	57 3/8	52 6/8	29 3/8	10	15	White Fish Lake	AK	Ron Lehmann	1984	13
406 7/8	50 3/8	49 7/8	49 3/8	12	12	Salmon River	AK	Gary R. Haske	1987	15
406 2/8	56 5/8	58 2/8	37 3/8	11	23	Port Heiden	AK	Art Heinze	1973	16
405 3/8	47 2/8	48 3/8	38 4/8	15	14	Chanuk Creek	AK	Roger O. Wyant	1989	17
405 0/8	61 4/8	62 5/8	47 0/8	13	13	Bonanza Hills	AK	Dan Hollingsworth	1982	18
404 7/8	51 2/8	50 6/8	40 0/8	13	14	Franklin Bluffs	AK	Rickie D. Snell	1989	19
404 2/8	46 6/8	47 7/8	34 0/8	18	16	Mulchatna River	AK	Steven B Novy	1987	20
401 3/8	53 4/8	52 6/8	42 0/8	14	16	Glenn Highway	AK	Harv Ebers	1959	21
401 2/8	50 3/8	50 2/8	37 7/8	13	13	Lake Clark	AK	Pat Breen	1986	22
400 2/8	51 6/8	51 6/8	43 2/8	14	14	Upper Noatak River	AK	Patrick Campanella	1989	23
400 0/8	53 1/8	53 1/8	37 0/8	9	19	Lake Louise	AK	George Moerlein	1962	24
399 5/8	55 3/8	57 6/8	46 6/8	12	8	Swan River	AK	Dr. Steven G. Hammons	1992	25
399 0/8	50 5/8	51 2/8	40 2/8	16	14	Clemmons	AK	Bob Lee	1960	26
397 4/8	46 4/8	46 3/8	34 2/8	15	15	Telaquana Lake	AK	John Moline	1971	27
397 4/8	48 2/8	49 0/8	44 1/8	12	14	Muddy River	AK	Roger O. Wyant	1990	27
397 1/8	55 0/8	55 4/8	42 7/8	15	16	Ugashik River	AK	Jim McCain	1986	29
396 6/8	50 1/8	49 5/8	49 1/8	12	15	Aleutian Range	AK	Chuck Adams	1984	30
396 6/8	52 4/8	50 4/8	42 4/8	9	11	Fishtrap Lake	AK	Allen L. Dougal	1986	30
396 5/8	57 7/8	55 1/8	49 4/8	13	11	Tyone Lake	AK	James Moline	1961	32
396 5/8	50 0/8	46 6/8	40 5/8	13	16	Telaquana Lake	AK	Eldon W. Zeller	1972	32
396 2/8	55 3/8	53 0/8	33 3/8	18	19	Little Delta River	AK	Keith R. Clemmons	1958	34
394 5/8	51 0/8	48 7/8	27 6/8	13	19	Susitna	AK	Ron Mason	1980	35
394 0/8	53 6/8	53 7/8	36 2/8	8	9	Port Alsworth	AK	Vince Shepherd	1989	36
392 2/8	51 3/8	55 4/8	32 6/8	13	15	Aleutian Range	AK	Chuck Adams	1983	37
391 7/8	53 6/8	50 5/8	45 6/8	11	14	Glenn Highway	AK	Joe West	1965	38
391 7/8	57 0/8	56 3/8	31 4/8	11	14	Lake Clark	AK	Jim Jarvis	1982	38
391 0/8	49 3/8	53 0/8	41 6/8	11	13	Ugashik River	AK	Dr. Robert Roland-Smith	1986	40
391 0/8	56 0/8	53 7/8	53 0/8	12	10	Kenai	AK	David L. Hawkins	1988	40
390 5/8	53 2/8	52 7/8	42 0/8	11	10	Hook River	AK	William Elfland	1990	42
390 0/8	58 7/8	57 1/8	37 5/8	15	16	Whitefish Lake	AK	Charles C. Smith	1988	43
389 7/8	47 3/8	49 1/8	40 7/8	16	14	Mulchatna River	AK	Greg L. Munther	1987	44
389 4/8	48 0/8	49 2/8	34 0/8	22	19	Mother Goose Lake	AK	Dennis L. Smythe	1975	45
388 5/8	52 0/8	53 2/8	32 6/8	18	18	Delta River	AK	Dick Bolding	1957	46
388 2/8	56 5/8	57 1/8	47 2/8	18	16	Ugashik River	AK	George Moerlein	1972	47
388 2/8	50 7/8	55 7/8	30 5/8	14	15	Atigun Pass	AK	Alan Richey	1984	47
387 7/8	42 0/8	40 6/8	31 5/8	23	25	McGrath	AK	Robert Barrie	1975	49
387 5/8	60 2/8	59 1/8	45 4/8	8	10	Atigun Pass	AK	David E. Rankin	1989	50
387 1/8	53 2/8	55 6/8	36 3/8	13	13	Baffin Island	NWT	Randall J. Kiessel	1986	51
387 0/8	52 2/8	62 4/8	51 3/8	10	10	Lake Iliamna	AK	Jon Vanderhoef	1983	52
386 7/8	48 4/8	44 5/8	43 4/8	19	18	Little Delta	AK	Dale K. Marcy	1964	53
386 6/8	50 2/8	52 0/8	32 3/8	12	12	Nushagak River	AK	Richard Mazol	1991	54
385 3/8	51 2/8	53 5/8	40 0/8	13	11	King Salmon	AK	Tom Daley	1984	55
385 2/8	58 5/8	57 0/8	38 0/8	14	17	Talkeetna Mtns.	AK	Harvey Matz	1959	56
384 6/8	40 1/8	37 5/8	41 2/8	19	21	Yanert River	AK	E. Donnall Thomas, Jr.	1984	57
384 5/8	47 2/8	47 5/8	37 5/8	16	15	Talkeetna Mtns.	AK	Dr. Rex Hancock	1962	58
384 3/8	49 2/8	49 1/8	34 6/8	15	18	Alaska Peninsula	AK	Betty Gulman	1968	59
384 0/8	55 3/8	57 3/8	40 6/8	12	9	Mulchatna River	AK	Carl E. Brent	1990	60
382 7/8	46 2/8	44 5/8	33 7/8	22	17	Wide Bay	AK	Archie Nesbitt	1991	61
382 4/8	50 2/8	51 3/8	39 2/8	17	27	King Salmon River	AK	Eugene Smith, Jr.	1978	62
381 5/8	51 1/8	47 1/8	39 1/8	14	19	Ugu River	AK	Stanley J. Rogers, Jr.	1974	63
381 2/8	51 4/8	53 2/8	41 1/8	11	13	Ugashik River	AK	Craig Richardson	1988	64
381 1/8	52 4/8	50 7/8	43 2/8	12	17	Galbraith Lake	AK	Edward L. Russell	1981	65
380 7/8	46 1/8	47 7/8	36 7/8	13	15	Delta Creek	AK	Wayne Trimm	1960	66
380 5/8	61 2/8	62 2/8	36 5/8	8	9	King Salmon	AK	Glenn Hisey	1984	67
380 2/8	49 1/8	50 3/8	40 0/8	11	13	MacKay Lake	NWT	Richard Martin	1990	68
380 0/8	48 1/8	49 1/8	30 2/8	14	18	Cutler River	AK	Jay Deones	1990	69
379 6/8	49 5/8	53 0/8	39 1/8	13	12	Shotgun Hill	AK	Joe Ellithorpe	1987	70

SCORE	LENGTH OF MAIN BEAM R	L	INSIDE SPREAD	NUMBER OF POINTS R	L	AREA	STATE/ PROVINCE	HUNTER'S NAME	DATE	RANK
379 5/8	46 2/8	48 4/8	33 2/8	20	19	Alatna River	AK	Don D. Seward	1975	71
378 7/8	45 5/8	45 0/8	36 7/8	12	11	Moose Creek	AK	Richard Moran	1989	72
378 1/8	47 3/8	47 3/8	40 4/8	10	10	Lake Clark	AK	Neil K. Hymas	1984	73
377 7/8	55 7/8	57 0/8	40 0/8	11	11	Ugashik River	AK	Douglas A. Smythe	1986	74
377 6/8	52 0/8	51 4/8	35 6/8	13	19	Dawn Lake	AK	Bob Kroll	1963	75
376 7/8	50 2/8	45 4/8	40 2/8	14	13	Alaska Peninsula	AK	Bob Gulman	1968	76
376 7/8	52 6/8	50 5/8	49 4/8	16	14	Alaska Peninsula	AK	Roger O. Iveson	1976	76
376 4/8	51 6/8	53 7/8	38 6/8	12	15	Little Underhill Creek	AK	Gary L. Stephens	1992	78
376 0/8	58 3/8	52 3/8	44 0/8	9	10	Lake Clark	AK	Joe Ball	1986	79
376 0/8	54 0/8	53 6/8	33 1/8	14	12	MacKay Lake	NWT	John D. Totemeier	1990	79
374 3/8	57 2/8	51 4/8	33 4/8	11	12	Hohlitna River	AK	Rick Tollison	1978	81
374 3/8	51 1/8	51 1/8	32 6/8	15	13	McKay Lakes	NWT	Duane Hicks	1987	81
374 0/8	48 0/8	49 7/8	40 5/8	10	8	Dog Salmon River	AK	Bob Holzberger	1991	83
373 6/8	47 5/8	47 5/8	40 2/8	11	17	Delta Creek	AK	Dwight Guynn	1980	84
373 5/8	46 6/8	46 7/8	39 5/8	18	15	Devil Creek	AK	Douglas Walker	1966	85
372 5/8	44 6/8	44 6/8	25 5/8	11	11	Atigun River	AK	James W. Black, Jr.	1988	86
372 2/8	46 0/8	48 4/8	30 0/8	14	14	Area 1	MAN	Don McCrea	1992	87
372 0/8	56 7/8	58 5/8	38 6/8	9	11	Lake Iliamna	AK	Gary Wright	1991	88
371 7/8	47 4/8	49 1/8	46 1/8	16	17	Prudhoe Bay	AK	Randy Richardson	1986	89
371 6/8	46 4/8	48 6/8	33 0/8	12	13	Cutler River	AK	Randy Doyle	1985	90
371 5/8	40 1/8	40 1/8	34 1/8	17	28	Maclaren River	AK	Dick Cooley	1962	91
371 5/8	48 5/8	49 1/8	41 6/8	20	15	Port Heiden	AK	Jim Dougherty	1968	91
371 3/8	51 5/8	51 6/8	39 5/8	11	17	Cinder River	AK	Keith Pilz	1976	93
371 1/8	50 3/8	48 4/8	44 0/8	13	13	MacKay Lake	NWT	Dan Brockman	1990	94
370 7/8	56 3/8	56 1/8	42 6/8	11	12	Arctic Coastal Plain	AK	Robin D. Johnson	1987	95
370 6/8	47 7/8	46 5/8	30 2/8	12	12	MacKay Lake	NWT	Greg Leroux	1990	96
370 6/8	53 3/8	55 5/8	37 1/8	10	10	King Salmon River	AK	Ed Evans	1990	96
370 5/8	45 3/8	48 3/8	39 2/8	11	15	Lake Iliamna	AK	John Meschko	1981	98
370 4/8	46 4/8	47 7/8	34 5/8	12	11	Dog Salmon River	AK	Gary Thompson	1991	99
370 3/8	48 7/8	49 7/8	32 3/8	10	12	Shenjek Lake	AK	J. Keith Chastain	1984	100
370 2/8	55 3/8	54 5/8	38 5/8	9	9	Mulchatna River	AK	William A. Sheka, Jr.	1984	101
370 1/8	54 0/8	52 6/8	34 5/8	10	13	North Slope	AK	Ronald L. Sherer	1983	102
370 1/8	49 6/8	49 6/8	43 4/8	9	11	Lake Clark	AK	Ron Crouch	1989	102
369 6/8	42 4/8	42 0/8	46 5/8	13	15	Lake Iliamna	AK	David L. Wolf	1988	104
369 5/8	44 0/8	44 4/8	34 4/8	13	14	Ugashik River	AK	William J. Stonebraker	1987	105
369 3/8	47 7/8	49 4/8	40 1/8	12	12	Mulchatna River	AK	Jeffrey L. Rentzel	1990	106
369 1/8	52 0/8	51 4/8	34 1/8	12	9	Fairbanks	AK	Keith Jensen	1986	107
368 7/8	46 6/8	47 1/8	40 7/8	16	17	Prudhoe Bay	AK	Calvin Farner	1985	108
368 4/8	58 2/8	55 6/8	40 1/8	12	11	Ambler	AK	Rick Kinmon	1983	109
368 2/8	51 1/8	53 6/8	44 1/8	12	12	Swift River	AK	Rolf J. Sandberg	1986	110
368 2/8	49 7/8	49 7/8	41 1/8	10	12	King Salmon	AK	David Isom	1987	110
368 0/8	51 5/8	46 4/8	36 3/8	14	19	Port Heiden	AK	John E. Lawson	1970	112
368 0/8	55 1/8	54 5/8	38 3/8	14	10	King Salmon River	AK	Rick Grooms	1979	112
367 4/8	50 2/8	52 1/8	49 7/8	12	13	Lake Iliamna	AK	David Niehaus	1991	114
367 2/8	55 0/8	57 5/8	41 5/8	12	12	Tundra Lake	AK	Jim Garant	1988	115
366 5/8	49 5/8	48 0/8	28 7/8	13	14	Carlos Creek	AK	Braun Kopsack	1989	116
366 3/8	45 0/8	47 7/8	41 6/8	12	10	Hohlitna River	AK	Vance Henry	1988	117
366 2/8	47 6/8	47 3/8	35 3/8	12	17	Stoney River	AK	Craig E. Thomas	1989	118
366 0/8	54 1/8	53 5/8	47 7/8	10	12	Upper Stuyahok River	AK	Jim Bradford	1989	119
365 4/8	47 3/8	45 7/8	27 0/8	12	12	Cutler River	AK	Larry Streiff	1990	120
364 6/8	53 5/8	51 5/8	26 3/8	12	19	Sagavanirktok River	AK	Judd Cooney	1982	121
364 6/8	46 3/8	47 2/8	28 2/8	11	8	Courageous Lake	NWT	Steve Crooks	1990	121
364 5/8	45 6/8	45 5/8	32 7/8	14	11	Cantwell	AK	Rick D. Snell	1991	123
364 2/8	48 3/8	48 0/8	30 6/8	11	11	Cinder River	AK	Jack Dykstra	1991	124
363 0/8	53 4/8	52 6/8	37 5/8	10	9	King Salmon	AK	Kent D. Keenlyne	1982	125
363 0/8	47 0/8	47 0/8	39 5/8	8	10	Aleutian Range	AK	H. Richard Long	1984	125
362 6/8	54 3/8	52 0/8	37 6/8	7	9	Lake Clark	AK	John Thomas Cruger	1987	127
362 6/8	49 3/8	48 6/8	36 2/8	10	11	Ugashik Lake	AK	Kyle Culver	1989	127
362 4/8	44 3/8	47 2/8	34 4/8	17	18	Egegik River	AK	Walter Eslinger	1970	129
362 2/8	51 1/8	51 1/8	36 0/8	14	11	Sourdough	AK	Dan Jordan	1965	130
361 7/8	57 4/8	57 0/8	34 1/8	13	13	White Hills	AK	Dick Carlson	1984	131
361 3/8	54 4/8	54 0/8	46 1/8	9	10	Kajulik Bay	AK	Thomas J. Hoffman	1983	132
361 3/8	51 6/8	52 5/8	44 2/8	13	12	Brooks Range	AK	John Ribic	1986	132
361 0/8	49 2/8	48 4/8	41 2/8	11	11	Mulchatna River	AK	James W. Southworth	1983	134
360 7/8	51 7/8	50 2/8	41 2/8	14	16	Iliamna	AK	Scott Halbert	1992	135
360 6/8	52 7/8	52 3/8	36 4/8	10	8	Lake Clark	AK	John W. Rose	1986	136
359 6/8	45 5/8	46 3/8	43 7/8	17	16	Mulchatna River	AK	Ralph Ertz	1982	137
359 6/8	51 3/8	51 1/8	40 1/8	15	14	Kujulik Bay	AK	Norman Stahlman	1987	137
359 3/8	52 7/8	53 4/8	29 7/8	10	9	Lake Clark	AK	Mark Buehrer	1985	139
358 5/8	49 2/8	34 6/8	40 5/8	13	14	Becharof Lake	AK	Joseph O. Fogleman	1986	140

BARREN GROUND CARIBOU

(Continued)

SCORE	LENGTH OF MAIN BEAM R	L	INSIDE SPREAD	NUMBER OF POINTS R	L	AREA	STATE/ PROVINCE	HUNTER'S NAME	DATE	RANK
358 4/8	50 0/8	51 0/8	34 1/8	13	12	Alaska Peninsula	AK	Chris Cassidy	1982	141
358 2/8	54 7/8	57 1/8	35 5/8	13	10	Tyone Lake	AK	Jake Sonnentag	1961	142
358 2/8	53 5/8	54 5/8	41 0/8	13	13	Maclaren River	AK	George Moerlein	1963	142
358 1/8	51 6/8	51 7/8	34 2/8	9	11	Lake Providence	NWT	Gerry Backhaus	1988	144
358 0/8	48 4/8	49 3/8	36 5/8	9	11	King Salmon	AK	Norm Epperson	1983	145
358 0/8	46 4/8	46 5/8	34 6/8	14	13	MacKay Lake	NWT	Mike Wheeler	1991	145
357 5/8	48 6/8	49 0/8	45 3/8	11	12	Deadhorse	AK	George P. Mann	1986	147
357 3/8	48 0/8	48 3/8	39 7/8	11	13	King Salmon	AK	Gerry C. Stinski	1986	148
355 7/8	54 7/8	53 7/8	26 7/8	10	10	Mulchatna River	AK	Dan L. Carroll	1987	149
355 6/8	43 5/8	42 4/8	28 2/8	12	14	Deadhorse	AK	Jim Hodson	1985	150
355 6/8	47 0/8	48 6/8	40 3/8	15	14	McKay Lakes	NWT	Stan Godfrey	1988	150
355 6/8	49 3/8	50 0/8	33 3/8	14	14	Noatak River	AK	Roger A. Rasmussen	1990	150
355 5/8	57 0/8	56 0/8	44 0/8	15	16	Sagaranirktok River	AK	David D. Bestul	1986	153
354 7/8	46 0/8	46 0/8	36 0/8	10	10	Sagaranirktok River	AK	Kevin R. Wiley	1986	154
354 6/8	49 4/8	51 4/8	44 6/8	10	14	Kuktuli River	AK	Neil Summers	1982	155
354 6/8	47 1/8	45 0/8	44 1/8	12	13	Mulchatna River	AK	Richard LeBlond	1985	155
354 6/8	51 7/8	51 1/8	33 4/8	10	12	King Salmon	AK	Bruce A. Bouley	1987	155
354 1/8	49 0/8	50 6/8	39 1/8	10	9	Alaska Range	AK	Roger Wintle	1985	158
354 0/8	44 2/8	44 3/8	34 1/8	9	8	Lime Hills	AK	Bernard G. Norton	1990	159
353 6/8	52 5/8	52 4/8	47 1/8	12	10	Ugashik Lake	AK	Scott Lang	1988	160
353 5/8	48 1/8	46 7/8	37 4/8	14	12	Kotzebue	AK	Larry Welchlen	1988	161
353 3/8	48 2/8	46 6/8	36 7/8	17	13	Caribou Creek	AK	H. R. 'Dutch' Wambold	1964	162
353 3/8	54 4/8	53 7/8	43 2/8	11	12	Telaquana Lake	AK	Jake Sonnentag	1971	162
353 1/8	45 4/8	46 2/8	37 4/8	13	14	Richardson Highway	AK	Donald O. Smith	1963	164
352 3/8	48 2/8	46 5/8	30 1/8	14	14	Lacabana Lake	AK	O. Dale Porter	1986	165
352 2/8	54 1/8	54 0/8	45 1/8	9	10	Pilot Point	AK	John D. 'Jack' Frost	1980	166
351 5/8	48 4/8	52 6/8	38 5/8	10	11	Ugashik Lake	AK	Diane Snyder	1984	167
351 2/8	62 4/8	59 5/8	36 2/8	13	12	Ugashik Lake	AK	John Amundson	1986	168
351 2/8	46 1/8	48 6/8	38 1/8	14	14	Prudhoe Bay	AK	James R. Sanders, Jr.	1988	168
351 2/8	50 0/8	50 6/8	36 4/8	12	8	Ugashik River	AK	David A. Widby	1988	168
351 2/8	49 3/8	48 5/8	40 4/8	12	12	Port Heiden	AK	Mike Traub	1989	168
351 1/8	50 6/8	49 6/8	40 2/8	13	11	Lake Clark	AK	Bob Schwanke	1988	172
351 1/8	44 5/8	45 1/8	40 2/8	13	14	Ugashik River	AK	Joe P. Twitchell, Jr.	1988	172
350 7/8	51 3/8	49 0/8	27 2/8	20	21	Big Delta	AK	Bill Brown	1958	174
350 6/8	55 1/8	56 0/8	31 4/8	9	8	Lake Clark	AK	Stacy M. Tompkinson	1986	175
350 6/8	46 7/8	47 1/8	37 2/8	9	10	Lime Hills	AK	John Crum	1988	175
350 5/8	51 1/8	47 6/8	43 4/8	9	11	Selawik River	AK	Kirk Westervelt	1985	177
350 3/8	51 3/8	44 0/8	41 3/8	11	14	Meshik River	AK	Art Kragness	1970	178
350 3/8	47 5/8	47 1/8	25 5/8	12	12	40 Mile River	AK	Stan Parkerson	1984	178
350 3/8	42 0/8	45 6/8	38 6/8	9	11	Fish Lake	AK	Vikki Gross	1991	178
350 0/8	50 2/8	48 0/8	36 1/8	13	10	Sag River	AK	Guy Doyle	1991	181
349 7/8	52 2/8	45 3/8	35 1/8	15	11	Pilot Point	AK	Rolf J. Sandberg	1976	182
349 7/8	48 1/8	49 3/8	28 7/8	10	12	Franklin Bluffs	AK	Craig Kulchak	1982	182
349 6/8	51 2/8	53 0/8	43 5/8	9	10	Koktuli River	AK	Kristine Staffeldt	1992	184
349 5/8	47 7/8	47 3/8	44 6/8	11	8	Alaska Peninsula	AK	Vee F. Hanks	1990	185
349 4/8	55 7/8	57 3/8	39 2/8	9	11	Prudhoe Bay	AK	Rick Grooms	1986	186
349 2/8	52 4/8	51 5/8	36 4/8	13	8	Kobuk River	AK	Rick Kinmon	1986	187
349 1/8	47 2/8	50 4/8	34 1/8	11	9	Deadhorse	AK	James M. Young	1980	188
348 6/8	43 6/8	44 6/8	42 0/8	13	14	Putilick Mt.	AK	Gary B. Gingerich	1986	189
348 1/8	44 0/8	44 0/8	39 1/8	16	15	Warburton Bay	NWT	David R. Coupland	1992	190
348 0/8	51 1/8	49 2/8	37 3/8	10	13	Alaska Range	AK	Salvatore J. Scaltrito	1983	191
348 0/8	48 3/8	49 6/8	43 7/8	10	8	Kaskanac Foothills	AK	Jeffrey S. Stevens	1988	191
348 0/8	50 4/8	50 0/8	29 0/8	13	12	Galbraith Lake	AK	Stan Parkerson	1990	191
348 0/8	46 0/8	47 6/8	36 6/8	14	14	Lake Providence	NWT	Ron Books	1991	191
348 0/8	47 4/8	46 0/8	32 7/8	16	18	Kotzabue	AK	Carl H. Spaeth	1991	191
347 6/8	55 6/8	59 0/8	42 0/8	10	10	Stuyahok River	AK	Marlon Clapham	1989	196
347 5/8	46 4/8	47 6/8	37 6/8	20	16	Colville River	AK	John D. 'Jack' Frost	1982	197
347 4/8	46 2/8	45 2/8	41 7/8	12	14	Ogilvie Range	YUK	Emile Gele	1965	198
347 3/8	46 7/8	52 4/8	37 0/8	9	9	Mulchatna River	AK	Ray Roussett, Jr.	1986	199
347 1/8	52 0/8	50 1/8	39 0/8	14	13	Dog Salmon River	AK	Gary H. Thompson	1989	200
347 1/8	45 4/8	47 2/8	33 0/8	12	10	King Salmon River	AK	John "Rosey" Roseland	1991	200
346 7/8	50 4/8	50 2/8	32 0/8	10	19	Telaquana Lake	AK	Gary Wall	1974	202
346 5/8	50 0/8	48 6/8	36 5/8	10	12	Little Delta	AK	Herb Lindsay	1964	203
346 5/8	49 1/8	48 2/8	35 2/8	17	17	Sagavanirktok River	AK	Judd Cooney	1982	203
345 5/8	49 5/8	49 5/8	35 6/8	12	12	Alaska Range	AK	Lon E. Lauber	1988	205
345 3/8	47 5/8	49 0/8	37 4/8	16	22	Kuskokwim Mtn.	AK	Robert K. Paulson	1977	206
345 3/8	54 0/8	48 1/8	36 5/8	12	14	Cutler River	AK	Doug Strecker	1985	206
345 2/8	47 3/8	48 6/8	32 4/8	11	10	Port Heiden	AK	Dennis G. Goldbach	1979	208
345 2/8	46 4/8	48 7/8	34 4/8	10	11	Alaskan Pennisula	AK	Calvin Farner	1987	208
345 2/8	56 3/8	57 0/8	37 7/8	9	9	Lake Clark	AK	Mel Tenneson	1988	208

Score	Length of Main Beam R	L	Inside Spread	Number of Points R	L	Area	State/ Province	Hunter's Name	Date	Rank
345 2/8	56 7/8	52 2/8	31 3/8	12	10	Yellowknife	NWT	Gil Gilbertson	1990	208
345 1/8	51 4/8	53 4/8	43 1/8	9	8	Lake Lach Buna	AK	Bob Ebert	1983	212
345 1/8	47 2/8	45 5/8	42 1/8	10	12	Mulchatna River	AK	E. Donnall Thomas, Jr.	1985	212
345 0/8	56 0/8	52 1/8	39 2/8	14	9	Wrench Creek	AK	Richard L. Westervelt	1991	214
344 7/8	51 4/8	50 4/8	34 0/8	13	12	Lake Clark	AK	Troy Hymas	1984	215
344 6/8	52 5/8	51 1/8	29 4/8	15	11	Susitna Valley	AK	Ronald D. Hopkins	1974	216
344 4/8	49 7/8	51 6/8	38 6/8	13	16	Mirror Lake	AK	Robert E. Speegle, MD	1990	217
344 2/8	46 1/8	43 6/8	27 7/8	11	13	Franklin Bluffs	AK	Matthew A. Jones	1987	218
344 1/8	49 2/8	50 0/8	33 2/8	11	10	Happy Valley	AK	Tim J. Mariner	1991	219
343 6/8	45 2/8	46 3/8	30 6/8	14	14	Mulchatna Drainage	AK	Christopher G. Hixson	1990	220
343 6/8	53 3/8	51 7/8	33 1/8	13	11	Tagg River	AK	Gayland Jones	1991	220
343 3/8	53 2/8	52 0/8	37 5/8	9	10	MacKay Lake	NWT	Carolyn Godfrey	1990	222
343 1/8	51 6/8	53 2/8	38 6/8	8	13	Taylor Highway	AK	Jae Beardon	1961	223
343 1/8	52 2/8	51 2/8	34 4/8	10	9	333 Dalton Highway	AK	Robert A. Chadwick	1987	223
343 1/8	47 4/8	48 5/8	37 5/8	12	12	Lake Providence	NWT	Ron Books	1991	223
343 0/8	49 4/8	48 2/8	40 7/8	9	14	Wrench Creek	AK	Kirk Westervelt	1991	226
343 0/8	47 7/8	50 2/8	32 7/8	8	9	Nodinka Narrows	NWT	Gunter Lemke	1991	226
342 4/8	50 7/8	53 4/8	38 0/8	9	10	Dalton Highway	AK	Tom Chadwick	1991	228
342 0/8	45 7/8	49 3/8	40 7/8	13	16	Imuya Bay	AK	Archie Nesbitt	1989	229
341 6/8	58 2/8	56 3/8	39 6/8	11	14	McGrath	AK	Jim Holdenried	1982	230
341 5/8	48 5/8	47 6/8	33 4/8	12	13	Alaska Peninsula	AK	Edward L. Russell	1980	231
341 4/8	53 3/8	52 2/8	43 4/8	14	12	Franklin Bluffs	AK	Dr. Jack Harvey	1984	232
341 4/8	43 3/8	45 0/8	30 4/8	14	11	Brooks Range	AK	Jeff Lindeman	1988	232
341 2/8	49 2/8	49 7/8	29 1/8	9	8	Toolik Lake	AK	Judy Watson	1988	234
341 0/8	49 2/8	49 0/8	37 2/8	14	13	King Salmon	AK	Reggie Callender	1971	235
340 6/8	49 2/8	49 3/8	27 1/8	12	13	Brooks Range	AK	Roger G. Stewart	1983	236
340 2/8	48 2/8	46 4/8	30 4/8	14	14	Lake Providence	NWT	Doug Walker	1988	237
340 2/8	49 6/8	45 5/8	28 0/8	18	14	Lake Providence	NWT	Doug Walker	1988	237
340 0/8	49 0/8	51 0/8	36 2/8	14	14	Franklin Bluffs	AK	John T. Toenes	1985	239
340 0/8	45 0/8	44 6/8	32 6/8	13	14	Lac Rendez-vous	NWT	Richard A. Hjort	1989	239
339 7/8	48 3/8	43 4/8	36 3/8	14	12	Prudhoe Bay	AK	John Bilek	1986	241
339 7/8	51 4/8	52 0/8	32 4/8	15	12	Sagavanirktok River	AK	Ron Serwa	1987	241
339 6/8	44 4/8	47 4/8	32 4/8	12	9	Prudhoe Bay	AK	Wayne Piersol	1987	243
339 5/8	50 6/8	48 4/8	34 5/8	10	10	Humphy Lake	NWT	Johnnie R. Walters	1992	244
339 4/8	46 0/8	45 0/8	29 0/8	12	13	Port Heiden	AK	Dennis G. Goldbach	1980	245
339 4/8	49 5/8	51 7/8	41 0/8	12	10	Franklin Bluffs	AK	Roger E. Wheelock	1982	245
339 1/8	52 5/8	53 4/8	38 4/8	10	12	Little Delta	AK	Dr. Judd Grindell	1959	247
339 0/8	45 3/8	51 5/8	34 4/8	18	13	Tyone Lake	AK	Jake Sonnentag	1963	248
338 6/8	58 5/8	61 0/8	39 1/8	10	9	MacKay Lake	NWT	Stan Godfrey	1990	249
338 4/8	49 4/8	47 7/8	35 1/8	11	16	Bonanza Hills	AK	Larry Langston	1974	250
338 4/8	46 6/8	47 2/8	30 7/8	14	12	Brooks Range	AK	Lyle Willmarth	1984	250
338 3/8	52 4/8	49 1/8	29 3/8	9	10	Tundra Lake	AK	Carl Handyside	1991	252
338 0/8	53 3/8	55 4/8	40 0/8	12	10	Adak Island	AK	Lon E. Lauber	1984	253
338 0/8	48 7/8	48 7/8	38 6/8	13	14	Ugashik Lake	AK	Dave Scott	1989	253
337 7/8	50 7/8	51 7/8	39 6/8	16	11	Cold Bay	AK	John Sarvis	1985	255
337 5/8	49 7/8	49 1/8	41 6/8	12	14	Cinder River	AK	Francis Hosch	1966	256
337 3/8	47 4/8	47 3/8	32 2/8	13	14	Maclaren River	AK	George Moerlein	1963	257
337 1/8	50 6/8	51 2/8	29 1/8	19	18	Dry Creek	AK	Russell Kucinski	1983	258
337 1/8	49 3/8	50 2/8	37 7/8	9	9	Lime Hills	AK	Clifford R. Neville, Sr.	1990	258
336 6/8	55 2/8	51 1/8	42 0/8	12	14	Featherly Pass	AK	Dale DeBoer	1987	260
336 2/8	45 5/8	47 1/8	27 3/8	13	9	MacKay Lake	NWT	Stan Godfrey	1990	261
336 0/8	42 7/8	45 2/8	35 0/8	13	9	Lake Iliamna	AK	Todd F. Lewis	1988	262
335 7/8	50 2/8	47 1/8	42 0/8	12	16	Port Heiden	AK	Noel Feather	1973	263
335 6/8	49 6/8	49 2/8	37 0/8	7	7	Nodinka Narrows	NWT	Marc Nyrose	1991	264
335 4/8	43 6/8	45 5/8	36 4/8	15	12	Sag River	AK	Stan Parkerson	1986	265
335 2/8	42 3/8	43 4/8	27 3/8	14	17	MacKay Lake	NWT	R. E. Smith	1992	266
335 1/8	47 3/8	48 3/8	22 5/8	9	10	Colville River	AK	Bob Gulman	1984	267
334 7/8	52 7/8	54 0/8	34 0/8	14	10	Squirrel River	AK	James Borron	1992	268
334 6/8	44 6/8	46 0/8	41 2/8	9	11	Sandy River	AK	Roger O. Wyant	1988	269
334 5/8	43 6/8	42 3/8	33 0/8	15	11	Carlos Creek	AK	Braun Kopsack	1988	270
334 5/8	51 1/8	50 1/8	32 7/8	12	14	Wrench Creek	AK	Kirk Westervelt	1991	270
334 4/8	43 1/8	45 3/8	33 6/8	13	9	Franklin's Bluffs	AK	John F. Gilmore	1991	272
334 2/8	45 2/8	43 6/8	31 6/8	10	12	MacKay Lake	NWT	Michael J. Underhill	1990	273
334 1/8	45 7/8	50 0/8	35 1/8	7	10	Nikabuna Lake	AK	Timothy J. Conrads	1988	274
334 0/8	45 3/8	45 5/8	30 0/8	15	13	Happy Valley	AK	Michael Chadwick	1992	275
333 7/8	54 4/8	56 0/8	47 2/8	10	8	Selawik River	AK	Kirk Westervelt	1985	276
333 5/8	47 2/8	47 2/8	32 5/8	15	11	Ugashik	AK	Stanley Winslow	1973	277
333 5/8	47 7/8	48 4/8	32 0/8	12	17	Happy Valley	AK	Troy Graziadei	1984	277
333 1/8	44 0/8	44 6/8	35 0/8	12	12	Sagavanirktok River	AK	Steven M. Stroka	1991	279
333 0/8	41 5/8	43 1/8	22 1/8	13	13	MacKay Lake	NWT	Jay St. Charles	1992	280

SCORE	LENGTH OF MAIN BEAM R	LENGTH OF MAIN BEAM L	INSIDE SPREAD	NUMBER OF POINTS R	NUMBER OF POINTS L	AREA	STATE/ PROVINCE	HUNTER'S NAME	DATE	RANK
332 7/8	53 0/8	54 3/8	36 2/8	18	15	Denali Hwy.	AK	Junie Moll	1961	281
332 6/8	49 5/8	50 7/8	30 4/8	12	9	Squirrel River	AK	Charles Kuss	1992	282
332 5/8	48 1/8	47 2/8	35 7/8	18	13	Caribou River Drainage	AK	Al Reay	1981	283
332 4/8	47 2/8	47 3/8	40 3/8	10	11	Mulchatna River	AK	Skip Koske	1986	284
332 3/8	45 3/8	46 1/8	29 1/8	9	10	Mulchatna River	AK	Mike Barrett	1987	285
332 3/8	46 4/8	47 4/8	26 7/8	13	11	Yellowknife	NWT	Bruce R. Schoeneweis	1990	285
332 2/8	52 5/8	53 0/8	26 1/8	9	9	Kukaklek Lake	AK	Jay Kuhre	1989	287
332 1/8	44 6/8	43 7/8	33 2/8	13	15	Mulchatna River	AK	Richard R. Schnell	1990	288
332 1/8	44 7/8	46 1/8	41 0/8	10	10	Non Dalton	AK	Gary L. Wilford	1992	288
331 7/8	54 3/8	55 0/8	35 6/8	9	16	Port Heiden	AK	John E. Lawson	1970	290
331 5/8	45 5/8	48 1/8	35 6/8	12	11	High Lakes	AK	Doug Walker	1970	291
331 5/8	50 3/8	50 5/8	39 3/8	12	11	Ugashik River	AK	Terry Sanders	1988	291
331 5/8	48 1/8	47 6/8	37 1/8	14	16	Brooks Range	AK	James L. Behn	1991	291
331 4/8	53 2/8	54 0/8	29 0/8	11	11	Point Lake	NWT	Cam Wilson	1987	294
331 2/8	44 6/8	46 1/8	28 6/8	14	15	MacKay Lake	NWT	David Emken	1990	295
331 1/8	47 6/8	46 1/8	28 7/8	12	14	Bonanza Hills	AK	Dan Klebenow	1990	296
331 0/8	49 2/8	49 3/8	29 4/8	14	11	MacKay Lake	NWT	Charles L. Hunt	1990	297
330 5/8	51 1/8	51 5/8	35 6/8	15	10	Tangle Lakes	AK	R. Glen Williams	1966	298
330 2/8	47 7/8	49 7/8	34 3/8	13	10	Franklin's Bluffs	AK	Eudane Vicenti	1991	299
330 0/8	54 2/8	55 0/8	37 7/8	13	12	Atigun Pass	AK	Keith K. Appel	1984	300
330 0/8	52 0/8	50 6/8	31 6/8	9	9	MacKay Lake	NWT	Manfred Gehrlein	1990	300
329 7/8	47 4/8	47 3/8	31 0/8	10	15	Dawn Lake	AK	Chuck Kroll	1963	302
329 7/8	56 4/8	53 7/8	40 3/8	9	12	Little Delta	AK	Bill Tutt	1964	302
329 7/8	52 2/8	50 0/8	35 0/8	9	11	Jolly River	NWT	Jay St. Charles	1987	302
329 6/8	49 6/8	49 4/8	33 1/8	6	8	Sagavanirktok River	AK	Patricia A. Stewart	1983	305
329 4/8	57 6/8	53 2/8	41 3/8	8	9	Chandler River	AK	Chuck Roady	1986	306
329 4/8	46 0/8	46 1/8	37 7/8	15	12	Ugashik River	AK	Stan Rauch	1988	306
329 4/8	49 3/8	50 2/8	36 0/8	17	14	MacKay Lake	NWT	Terry Tabor	1990	306
329 1/8	49 0/8	48 4/8	40 2/8	11	8	Ambler	AK	Dean Bergman	1986	309
329 0/8	46 4/8	46 4/8	40 4/8	9	6	Denali Hwy.	AK	Gordon Spidle	1988	310
328 7/8	49 3/8	48 7/8	37 6/8	10	7	Tutna Lake	AK	Gene Clark	1987	311
328 4/8	42 6/8	44 3/8	31 5/8	18	12	Little Delta	AK	Roy Bryan	1964	312
328 4/8	47 6/8	47 7/8	35 3/8	11	13	Sagavanirktok River	AK	Paul G. Barclay	1981	312
328 4/8	49 7/8	49 0/8	39 2/8	12	9	MacKay Lake	NWT	Ryk Visscher	1991	312
328 3/8	50 2/8	49 1/8	30 3/8	9	9	Prudhoe Bay	AK	Denver Perry	1981	315
328 2/8	42 0/8	39 7/8	27 2/8	8	9	Prudhoe Bay	AK	Gene Barcak	1985	316
327 7/8	47 0/8	45 1/8	29 0/8	11	11	MacKay Lake	NWT	Charles L. Hunt	1990	317
327 6/8	40 7/8	41 3/8	36 7/8	15	12	Galbraith Lake	AK	G. Stevens Abdoe	1983	318
327 6/8	39 7/8	40 0/8	37 3/8	12	11	Sagaranirktok River	AK	Roger Stewart	1989	318
327 5/8	47 3/8	49 3/8	40 0/8	13	13	North Slope	AK	Susan D. Sherer	1983	320
327 5/8	45 5/8	46 4/8	36 1/8	11	10	Prudhoe Bay	AK	Dennis Redden	1992	320
327 3/8	46 1/8	47 0/8	40 0/8	8	9	Selawik River	AK	Richard L. Westervelt	1985	322
327 2/8	45 6/8	48 5/8	35 6/8	12	12	Noatak River	AK	Donald R. Powers	1987	323
327 2/8	48 6/8	47 3/8	30 6/8	11	11	Kobuk River	AK	Niels Knudsen	1990	323
326 7/8	47 6/8	51 2/8	27 3/8	15	13	Dago Creek	AK	Don Davidson	1980	325
326 7/8	49 1/8	47 1/8	30 7/8	11	10	MacKay Lake	NWT	Tom Taylor	1992	325
326 6/8	49 1/8	47 3/8	41 0/8	12	18	Anchorage	AK	Roy Bryan	1964	327
326 5/8	43 0/8	45 0/8	38 3/8	12	12	Galena	AK	Larry Spiva	1992	328
326 4/8	47 7/8	49 7/8	31 7/8	10	11	Brooks Range	AK	Roger Stewart	1985	329
326 3/8	47 6/8	49 0/8	39 0/8	11	13	King Salmon	AK	Glenn Hisey	1983	330
326 3/8	51 0/8	53 1/8	41 1/8	11	10	Yellow Creek Hill	AK	Don Poole	1992	330
325 6/8	49 0/8	46 1/8	21 1/8	14	13	Atigun Pass	AK	Maxallen D. Jackson	1980	332
325 4/8	52 4/8	52 3/8	31 0/8	13	15	Galbraith Lake	AK	Maxallen D. Jackson	1981	333
325 0/8	46 6/8	48 5/8	30 5/8	8	9	Ugashik River	AK	Bob "Jake" Jacobsen	1988	334
324 2/8	52 5/8	50 6/8	35 3/8	7	9	Wrench Creek	AK	Richard L. Westervelt	1991	335
324 1/8	51 1/8	44 6/8	24 0/8	11	10	Brooks Range	AK	Robert D. Warpack	1985	336
323 7/8	47 4/8	51 2/8	38 7/8	13	8	Squirrel River	AK	Larry Spiva	1985	337
323 7/8	47 2/8	48 2/8	30 2/8	12	12	Chilikadrotna River	AK	Mike Cockcroft	1987	337
323 7/8	55 3/8	52 1/8	29 4/8	10	11	Dalton Hwy Mile 357	AK	Ken Vorisek	1988	337
323 5/8	44 4/8	45 0/8	26 4/8	12	16	Wejalini Lake	MAN	Gord Monteath	1991	340
323 2/8	46 7/8	46 5/8	40 3/8	13	13	King Salmon	AK	Howard Wille	1972	341
323 2/8	48 7/8	52 4/8	39 4/8	10	11	Franklin Bluffs	AK	Roger G. Stewart	1987	341
323 1/8	42 0/8	45 0/8	31 2/8	8	9	High Lake	AK	Clarence Bowers, Jr.	1970	343
322 5/8	48 6/8	49 3/8	35 1/8	13	14	King Salmon River	AK	Harold Stam	1976	344
322 4/8	48 0/8	48 2/8	35 5/8	10	17	Brooks Range	AK	Patricia Stewart	1982	345
322 4/8	54 3/8	53 4/8	37 6/8	9	8	Caribou Creek	AK	Braun Kopsack	1990	345
321 7/8	50 7/8	50 1/8	32 3/8	11	8	Squirrel River	AK	Timothy J. Conrads	1986	347
321 7/8	51 0/8	50 5/8	31 3/8	10	11	Brooks Range	AK	Carl H. Spaeth	1992	347
321 6/8	48 5/8	48 4/8	30 3/8	7	11	De Long Mtns.	AK	Dan White	1981	349
321 6/8	44 7/8	44 6/8	29 5/8	13	12	Brooks Range	AK	Larry E. Townsend	1992	349

SCORE	LENGTH OF MAIN BEAM R	L	INSIDE SPREAD	NUMBER OF POINTS R	L	AREA	STATE/ PROVINCE	HUNTER'S NAME	DATE	RANK
321 4/8	49 3/8	48 3/8	32 6/8	12	13	Sagavanirktok River	AK	Guy Doyle	1988	351
321 3/8	60 6/8	60 6/8	38 4/8	9	10	Toolik River	AK	Bill Krenz	1984	352
321 2/8	45 0/8	45 6/8	34 1/8	11	12	Alaska Peninsula	AK	Curt Lynn	1977	353
321 2/8	48 5/8	47 3/8	40 0/8	13	14	Selawick River	AK	Kirk Westervelt	1984	353
321 2/8	45 7/8	46 1/8	47 7/8	7	6	Port Heiden	AK	George P. Mann	1989	353
320 4/8	45 7/8	42 4/8	29 1/8	11	11	Lime Village	AK	Dale Drilling	1979	356
320 4/8	53 4/8	54 4/8	30 3/8	7	7	MacKay Lake	NWT	Ryk Visscher	1991	356
320 2/8	38 4/8	38 4/8	34 6/8	8	10	Ugashik Lake	AK	Richard E. Davis	1986	358
320 2/8	38 7/8	40 1/8	28 5/8	15	15	Dry Creek	AK	Eric Colledge	1989	358
320 2/8	52 2/8	54 2/8	35 2/8	8	11	MacKay Lake	NWT	Manfred Gehrlein	1990	358
320 0/8	46 5/8	46 2/8	29 5/8	13	11	Ugashik Narrows	AK	Richard D. Thomas	1983	361
320 0/8	41 6/8	42 0/8	30 2/8	13	14	Lake Clark	AK	Sam Weatherford	1989	361
319 5/8	43 7/8	44 1/8	43 4/8	7	8	Franklin Bluffs	AK	Keith K. Appel	1984	363
319 4/8	46 3/8	44 5/8	35 6/8	11	15	Chulitna	AK	Keith Johnson	1964	364
319 4/8	42 3/8	43 3/8	39 3/8	9	9	Kuichich River	AK	Jim Weiman	1987	364
318 5/8	51 4/8	52 0/8	34 2/8	9	12	Crosswinds Lake	AK	Ray Uhl, Sr.	1964	366
318 5/8	54 6/8	50 0/8	39 6/8	11	8	Last Lake	AK	Donald Gansch	1983	366
318 5/8	45 5/8	46 0/8	37 3/8	11	9	Noatak River	AK	Donald R. Powers	1987	366
318 4/8	42 6/8	43 1/8	37 0/8	16	14	Meshik River	AK	Scott M. Showalter	1974	369
318 0/8	49 6/8	52 0/8	34 6/8	8	11	Prudhoe Bay	AK	Joe Redden	1992	370
318 0/8	45 6/8	46 2/8	28 2/8	12	10	Humphy Lake	NWT	Johnnie R. Walters	1992	370
317 4/8	48 5/8	46 0/8	34 3/8	13	14	Squirrel River	AK	Randy Martin	1992	372
317 3/8	43 1/8	44 5/8	31 5/8	11	8	Lake Clark	AK	Scott Lower	1988	373
316 7/8	44 6/8	44 0/8	31 2/8	16	15	Delta River	AK	Glenn St. Charles	1957	374
316 5/8	46 6/8	47 4/8	46 0/8	10	13	Alaska Peninsula	AK	David G. Snyder	1979	375
316 5/8	46 6/8	48 6/8	37 0/8	7	7	MacKay Lake	NWT	Howard L. Harding	1992	375
316 0/8	44 2/8	44 5/8	34 3/8	9	9	Lake Clark	AK	Dale Schimmoeller	1987	377
315 6/8	46 6/8	50 0/8	28 4/8	11	11	MacKay Lake	NWT	Jim Visscher	1990	378
315 6/8	43 2/8	46 5/8	35 1/8	9	8	Warburton Bay	NWT	David R. Coupland	1992	378
315 5/8	45 7/8	48 6/8	33 6/8	8	7	Mulchatna River	AK	Michael J. Schneider	1984	380
314 7/8	48 3/8	50 5/8	34 1/8	5	5	Lake Clark	AK	G. William Buxton	1990	381
314 6/8	48 0/8	48 4/8	34 4/8	15	10	Nueman Creek	AK	Paul Brunner	1973	382
314 3/8	43 1/8	39 4/8	36 1/8	10	11	Lake Clark	AK	Michael D. Lewis	1986	383
314 2/8	46 7/8	48 7/8	35 5/8	19	12	Stoney River	AK	Bruce D. Kipley	1981	384
314 2/8	50 2/8	48 5/8	38 4/8	9	11	Featherly Pass	AK	Floyd McElroy	1987	384
314 1/8	45 2/8	45 7/8	38 6/8	12	11	Sagavanirktok River	AK	Judd Cooney	1982	386
314 1/8	42 4/8	46 4/8	33 4/8	8	8	Alaskan Pennisula	AK	Calvin Farner	1989	386
313 7/8	43 5/8	42 2/8	31 3/8	9	10	Sagavanirktok River	AK	David J. Towne	1990	388
313 6/8	47 2/8	49 5/8	26 0/8	11	10	Jolly River	NWT	Ty Martin	1987	389
313 6/8	51 5/8	49 6/8	25 6/8	11	10	MacKay Lake	NWT	James Kelter	1992	389
313 3/8	47 4/8	45 5/8	30 6/8	8	11	Deadhorse	AK	Kurt Lepping	1986	391
313 3/8	44 2/8	46 2/8	34 2/8	12	13	Yellow Creek Hill	AK	William C. Shuster	1992	391
313 0/8	46 0/8	46 0/8	24 4/8	15	14	Atigun Pass	AK	Maxallen D. Jackson	1980	393
313 0/8	47 0/8	47 4/8	37 0/8	10	10	Cutler River	AK	Randy Deones	1990	393
312 7/8	51 6/8	49 4/8	37 1/8	10	12	Dry Creek	AK	Eric Colledge	1988	395
312 6/8	45 7/8	42 1/8	36 5/8	9	10	Lake Clark	AK	Art Cracraft	1977	396
312 6/8	54 2/8	50 2/8	37 2/8	9	10	Needle Lake	AK	Daniel T. Bertalan	1986	396
312 5/8	41 0/8	41 7/8	28 6/8	13	12	Whitehorse	YUK	Scott Koelzer	1977	398
312 2/8	47 0/8	46 0/8	38 6/8	10	10	MacKay Lake	NWT	Dennis G. Hicks	1990	399
312 0/8	51 4/8	44 5/8	24 4/8	14	17	McKay Lakes	NWT	Duane Hicks	1988	400
311 7/8	51 1/8	46 6/8	37 2/8	8	9	Dalton Highway	AK	James F. Wright	1992	401
311 6/8	44 2/8	49 5/8	36 0/8	9	10	David River	AK	Melvin E. Putnam	1983	402
311 6/8	46 2/8	44 5/8	33 6/8	7	9	Kobuk River	AK	Dean Bergman	1987	402
311 4/8	50 1/8	48 3/8	28 0/8	8	11	MacKay Lake	NWT	Marc Nyrose	1991	404
311 0/8	48 2/8	47 4/8	40 7/8	10	10	MacKay Lake	NWT	John Visscher	1991	405
310 7/8	51 0/8	52 2/8	25 1/8	13	8	MacKay Lake	NWT	Ryk Visscher	1990	406
310 5/8	38 6/8	47 3/8	41 4/8	9	12	Port Heiden	AK	Paul R. Shannon	1974	407
310 4/8	44 6/8	47 7/8	35 0/8	11	9	Stoney River	AK	Craig E. Thomas	1990	408
310 4/8	46 5/8	48 4/8	37 0/8	9	10	Prudhoe Bay	AK	Jermi Redden	1992	408
310 2/8	50 2/8	48 5/8	38 4/8	8	7	Featherly Pass	AK	Floyd McElroy	1987	410
310 0/8	42 2/8	45 6/8	21 4/8	9	11	MacKay Lake	NWT	John Visscher	1990	411
309 7/8	47 0/8	49 0/8	32 3/8	10	13	Sagavanirktok River	AK	Jack V. Rouse	1984	412
309 6/8	40 1/8	42 1/8	26 6/8	12	12	Lake Clark	AK	Jim Walton	1988	413
309 3/8	46 4/8	47 0/8	38 3/8	11	11	Chandler River	AK	Walt Dinning	1986	414
309 2/8	46 6/8	45 6/8	36 4/8	9	6	Toolik River	AK	Patricia Stewart	1989	415
308 7/8	34 2/8	37 1/8	26 0/8	15	14	Unit 13D	AK	Dayle Paulson	1971	416
308 7/8	48 1/8	46 7/8	39 4/8	10	10	Prudhoe Bay	AK	Daniel D. Bestul	1984	416
308 7/8	48 0/8	46 3/8	40 4/8	9	12	Happy Valley	AK	Peyton Merideth	1992	416
308 1/8	54 0/8	54 0/8	30 5/8	13	10	Little Delta River	AK	Dr. Judd Grindell	1959	419
308 1/8	48 2/8	46 2/8	29 1/8	12	15	Lake Chandalar	AK	George Moerlein	1966	419

BARREN GROUND CARIBOU

Minimum score 300

(Continued)

Score	Length of Main Beam R	Length of Main Beam L	Inside Spread	Number of Points R	Number of Points L	Area	State/ Province	Hunter's Name	Date	Rank
308 0/8	47 4/8	47 3/8	36 3/8	8	8	White Fish Lake	AK	David Fowler	1984	421
308 0/8	51 1/8	53 5/8	45 3/8	7	7	Mulchatna River	AK	Mark A. Kruse	1989	421
307 2/8	43 4/8	41 6/8	31 7/8	10	9	Brooks Range	AK	Roger Stewart	1988	423
307 0/8	48 0/8	46 0/8	30 7/8	7	8	Kuparuk River	AK	Michael J. Lettis	1989	424
307 0/8	50 1/8	47 3/8	32 3/8	13	10	Selawik River	AK	Stephen Kotz	1989	424
306 6/8	47 6/8	46 4/8	31 6/8	9	10	Lake Iliamna	AK	Duane "Corky" Richardson	1988	426
306 6/8	41 4/8	43 3/8	34 4/8	5	5	Adak Island	AK	Lon E. Lauber	1990	426
305 5/8	46 0/8	44 4/8	24 0/8	11	10	Cutler River	AK	Eugene Arndt	1991	428
305 4/8	50 5/8	50 2/8	28 0/8	8	8	MacKay Lake	NWT	Dan Brockman	1990	429
305 1/8	48 7/8	50 7/8	28 5/8	8	6	Cold Bay	AK	John Sarvis	1983	430
305 0/8	40 7/8	41 6/8	35 4/8	10	14	Brooks Range	AK	John Hale	1980	431
304 7/8	48 1/8	48 3/8	29 7/8	9	8	MacKay Lake	NWT	David R. Coupland	1991	432
304 6/8	45 3/8	46 0/8	25 2/8	13	11	MacKay Lake	NWT	Howard L. Harding	1992	433
304 5/8	44 5/8	49 6/8	38 3/8	11	10	Toolik River	AK	Bill Krenz	1984	434
303 4/8	45 5/8	45 0/8	37 6/8	13	14	Port Heiden	AK	Jon G. Koshell	1964	435
303 1/8	46 7/8	49 5/8	35 6/8	13	11	Galbraith Lake	AK	Mark Wayne Smith	1990	436
302 7/8	48 4/8	47 5/8	44 4/8	8	8	Brooks Range	AK	Ted Hysell	1986	437
302 6/8	45 5/8	47 3/8	30 0/8	7	8	Prudhoe Bay	AK	Guy C. Doyle	1990	438
302 6/8	44 6/8	44 2/8	29 0/8	11	9	MacKay Lake	NWT	Les Malsch	1990	438
302 4/8	46 1/8	46 2/8	33 5/8	9	14	Courageous Lake	NWT	William R. Vanderhoef	1987	440
302 2/8	53 2/8	50 2/8	34 4/8	14	16	Sagwon	AK	Stephen E. Russell	1986	441
302 1/8	50 7/8	50 7/8	30 2/8	7	10	MacKay Lake	NWT	Russ Tye	1992	442
301 5/8	50 0/8	51 5/8	33 4/8	13	13	Walik River	AK	Todd F. Kluth	1992	443
301 4/8	38 4/8	38 2/8	26 6/8	10	11	Lime Hills	AK	Robert F. Norton	1990	444
300 6/8	40 4/8	39 7/8	30 4/8	10	15	MacKay Lake	NWT	Dale Holpainen	1992	445
300 3/8	48 2/8	45 5/8	34 0/8	10	9	Tangle Lakes	AK	R. Glen Williams	1966	446
300 3/8	38 2/8	38 3/8	30 0/8	19	16	Alaska Peninsula	AK	Curt Lynn	1977	446
300 3/8	40 7/8	41 4/8	27 6/8	13	11	Cutler River	AK	Larry Streiff	1990	446

World Record Mountain Caribou
Score: 410 2/8
Cassiar Mountains, British Columbia - 1978
Hunter: Thomas B. Frye

MOUNTAIN CARIBOU

Rangifer tarandus osborni,
Rangifer tarandus fortidens and
Rangifer tarandus montanus

MINIMUM SCORE 265

SCORE	LENGTH OF R MAIN BEAM L		INSIDE SPREAD	NUMBER OF R POINTS L		AREA	STATE/ PROVINCE	HUNTER'S NAME	DATE	RANK
410 2/8	54 0/8	55 6/8	46 0/8	15	12	Cassiar Mtns.	BC	Thomas B. Frye	1978	1
390 1/8	55 2/8	51 6/8	34 1/8	15	11	Firesteel River	BC	Melvin K. Wolf	1970	2
387 6/8	44 3/8	42 7/8	36 0/8	15	14	Cold Fish Lake	BC	Steve Gorr	1976	3
378 2/8	49 3/8	47 4/8	37 0/8	11	10	O'Grady Lake	NWT	C. Randall Byers	1988	4
378 0/8	42 1/8	44 1/8	31 7/8	12	11	Tahltan River	BC	Arthur Harlow	1988	5
374 6/8	55 4/8	55 6/8	40 2/8	10	8	Thutade Lake	BC	Edward C. Pawinski	1984	6
374 1/8	43 6/8	47 1/8	35 0/8	16	16	Duti River	BC	Dr. Lowell Eddy	1967	7
373 3/8	45 5/8	43 7/8	31 0/8	13	17	June Lake	NWT	Dennis Palmer	1988	8
373 2/8	45 4/8	44 7/8	37 7/8	10	13	Natla River	NWT	Chuck Adams	1990	9
371 7/8	48 1/8	47 1/8	39 1/8	15	13	Tatlatui Lake	BC	Larry Alma	1979	10
371 7/8	46 0/8	46 0/8	36 4/8	14	12	Divide Lake	NWT	Mike Parsons	1988	10
371 3/8	38 7/8	39 3/8	30 3/8	16	15	Thutade Lake	BC	Bob Brill	1980	12
370 1/8	45 1/8	45 2/8	29 6/8	12	16	Cassiar Mtns.	BC	Ray Wilson	1988	13
370 1/8	45 5/8	48 4/8	40 6/8	8	10	Russell Lake	YUK	Bob Fromme	1990	13
370 0/8	46 4/8	44 5/8	30 4/8	14	14	Natla River	NWT	Janice J. Traub	1985	15
368 0/8	43 1/8	45 0/8	30 0/8	13	13	Keel River	NWT	Jay Brown	1991	16

MOUNTAIN CARIBOU

(Continued)

SCORE	LENGTH OF MAIN BEAM R	LENGTH OF MAIN BEAM L	INSIDE SPREAD	NUMBER OF POINTS R	NUMBER OF POINTS L	AREA	STATE/ PROVINCE	HUNTER'S NAME	DATE	RANK
365 7/8	49 0/8	49 6/8	34 0/8	12	12	O'Grady Lake	NWT	R. Brian Oates	1990	17
365 2/8	47 4/8	48 5/8	32 1/8	14	13	Horseshoe Lake	NWT	Mike Parsons	1989	18
361 2/8	49 4/8	53 2/8	31 7/8	12	10	O'Grady Lake	NWT	G. Fred Asbell	1988	19
356 5/8	38 7/8	40 5/8	32 0/8	15	16	Horseshoe Lake	NWT	Don Davidson	1989	20
354 3/8	41 3/8	42 4/8	28 6/8	10	10	O'Grady Lake	NWT	C. Randall Byers	1991	21
353 5/8	45 3/8	44 5/8	35 0/8	11	13	Whitehorse	YUK	Guy-Maurice Algier	1992	22
351 6/8	46 4/8	45 0/8	37 4/8	11	11	Watson Lake	YUK	Pete Shepley	1985	23
350 6/8	41 0/8	42 0/8	30 1/8	8	8	Caribou Lake	NWT	John W. Borlang	1989	24
350 5/8	46 7/8	46 5/8	33 7/8	12	13	Mountain River	NWT	Tom D. Slusser	1991	25
348 3/8	52 4/8	55 3/8	48 5/8	12	9	O'Grady Lake	NWT	Marc N. Shaft	1988	26
347 5/8	33 4/8	32 5/8	31 4/8	14	11	O'Grady Lake	NWT	Don Davidson	1991	27
347 1/8	44 6/8	46 6/8	37 6/8	14	12	Stikine River	BC	Claudio Canonica	1988	28
345 0/8	51 5/8	49 1/8	33 7/8	13	11	Divide Lake	NWT	Al Reay	1982	29
344 4/8	57 3/8	56 2/8	38 6/8	10	9	O'Grady Lake	NWT	Steven R. Hohensee	1992	30
343 3/8	48 2/8	50 6/8	35 4/8	15	11	Serpentine Mt.	BC	Randolph P. Wilson	1976	31
342 2/8	47 6/8	47 1/8	34 4/8	10	9	Divide Lake	NWT	Stanley Walchuk, Jr.	1984	32
340 7/8	46 4/8	45 3/8	37 3/8	9	12	Horseshoe Lake	NWT	Jerry Keller	1990	33
339 6/8	42 7/8	44 6/8	20 0/8	20	18	Tatlatui Lake	BC	G. Fred Asbell	1975	34
339 4/8	47 1/8	48 6/8	37 0/8	10	11	Divide Lake	NWT	Dan Brockman	1991	35
336 7/8	45 1/8	47 4/8	29 2/8	8	10	June Lake	NWT	Mike Zech	1989	36
336 1/8	46 6/8	47 2/8	36 3/8	7	9	Summit Lake	YUK	Gregory White	1989	37
335 4/8	43 7/8	43 4/8	32 0/8	13	10	Divide Lake	NWT	Mark Zastrow	1991	38
334 2/8	40 7/8	40 0/8	36 5/8	15	11	Wolverine Creek	NWT	Stan Godfrey	1988	39
334 1/8	40 4/8	41 1/8	33 7/8	13	17	Firesteel River	BC	Walter Krom	1971	40
333 5/8	45 1/8	47 2/8	31 0/8	12	11	Firesteel River	BC	Jay Deones	1978	41
332 1/8	40 0/8	40 4/8	32 5/8	10	12	Firesteel River	BC	Larry Alma	1984	42
328 3/8	41 2/8	40 6/8	26 5/8	12	10	Divide Lake	NWT	Chuck Adams	1992	43
327 0/8	41 2/8	40 1/8	31 4/8	15	15	Moontair River	NWT	Mike Barrett	1990	44
321 7/8	48 4/8	47 3/8	32 4/8	13	14	Kitchener Lake	BC	Stephen E. Mitchell	1970	45
320 6/8	43 6/8	44 4/8	31 7/8	11	12	Thutade Lake	BC	Jack W. Kriener	1974	46
319 3/8	45 0/8	45 2/8	40 5/8	10	12	Kitchener Lake	BC	Doug Strecker	1979	47
319 1/8	44 3/8	48 5/8	24 7/8	13	10	Cold Fish Lake	BC	Steve Gorr	1975	48
318 7/8	38 2/8	40 0/8	35 4/8	9	9	Mackenzie Mtns.	NWT	Steven Weekly	1987	49
317 3/8	43 1/8	45 5/8	29 0/8	11	11	Keele River	NWT	Ron Serwa	1988	50
315 5/8	43 3/8	44 3/8	29 1/8	11	12	Kitchener Lake	BC	Dick Crowder	1976	51
314 7/8	42 6/8	46 0/8	33 5/8	10	10	Divide Lake	NWT	Dale Drilling	1989	52
314 5/8	44 7/8	47 6/8	32 7/8	10	9	Ittlemit Lake	YUK	Chuck Buchanan	1979	53
314 3/8	43 7/8	43 3/8	30 7/8	9	12	Divide Lake	NWT	Duane Zemliska	1991	54
314 2/8	42 7/8	44 0/8	28 3/8	10	10	O'Grady Lake	NWT	Don Davidson, Jr.	1988	55
313 4/8	40 2/8	45 1/8	32 7/8	10	8	Mackenzie Mtns.	NWT	John 'Jack' Cordes	1985	56
309 2/8	43 3/8	41 2/8	27 2/8	10	13	Thutade Lake	BC	Harold H. Vander Horst	1974	57
307 7/8	46 6/8	47 4/8	29 7/8	9	9	Thutade Lake	BC	Kim S. Ades	1984	58
306 2/8	43 4/8	43 2/8	29 2/8	11	10	Tatlatui Lake	BC	Robert Pitt	1975	59
304 2/8	37 2/8	40 7/8	27 1/8	10	10	O'Grady Lake	NWT	P. Tod Byers	1991	60
303 6/8	42 4/8	42 4/8	25 2/8	9	12	Tatlatui Lake	BC	Rick Gilley	1983	61
298 4/8	40 5/8	41 2/8	24 2/8	12	15	Tatlatui Lake	BC	Curtis W. Lynn	1974	62
297 6/8	38 2/8	37 7/8	21 5/8	13	12	Whitehorse	YUK	A. M. Oakes, Jr.	1980	63
295 0/8	36 4/8	38 3/8	22 1/8	7	11	Bucking Horse River	BC	Robert Zseder	1990	64
293 5/8	35 7/8	39 0/8	24 2/8	11	9	Tanzilla River	BC	Don St. Jean	1988	65
292 3/8	42 2/8	41 4/8	35 7/8	12	9	Area 21	BC	Harold H. Vander Horst	1972	66
291 7/8	35 4/8	37 1/8	30 6/8	13	14	Keele River	NWT	Dennis Potter	1987	67
290 0/8	42 3/8	45 2/8	25 0/8	10	9	Cotty Plateau	BC	Pink Atkins	1984	68
289 3/8	47 0/8	49 6/8	25 6/8	10	7	Stalk Lakes	BC	Chester J. Thompson	1977	69
288 2/8	37 1/8	36 7/8	27 0/8	10	11	Stony Saddle	BC	Peter L. Halbig	1968	70
288 1/8	36 3/8	39 3/8	27 0/8	11	12	Cold Fish Lake	BC	Dennis Behn	1976	71
278 3/8	36 0/8	40 2/8	27 0/8	11	9	Cold Fish Lake	BC	Fred Bear	1957	72
272 2/8	39 4/8	44 2/8	36 0/8	13	9	Kechika River	BC	Scott L. Koelzer	1976	73

World Record Quebec Labrador Caribou
Score: 434 0/8
Tunulik River, Quebec - 1984
Hunter: Carol Ann Mauch

152

QUEBEC LABRADOR CARIBOU

MINIMUM SCORE 300

SCORE	LENGTH OF R MAIN BEAM L		INSIDE SPREAD	NUMBER OF R POINTS L		AREA	STATE/ PROVINCE	HUNTER'S NAME	DATE	RANK
434 0/8	53 6/8	56 1/8	46 1/8	17	12	Tunulik River	QUE	Carol Ann Mauch	1984	1
429 1/8	52 2/8	52 1/8	45 1/8	15	17	Delay River	QUE	Bob Foulkrod	1985	2
416 6/8	51 2/8	49 6/8	50 0/8	13	14	Lake Consigny	QUE	Ricardo L. Garza	1989	3
416 5/8	45 3/8	47 7/8	47 4/8	28	27	George River	QUE	Collins F. Kellogg	1978	4
415 7/8	51 5/8	55 3/8	53 0/8	16	16	Ungava Bay	QUE	Dr. Woodallen G. Snyder	1984	5
412 7/8	52 7/8	53 0/8	49 3/8	17	18	LG4	QUE	Gary Robbins	1990	6
411 4/8	56 4/8	57 0/8	52 0/8	16	14	Ungava Region	QUE	Richard S. Neely	1977	7
410 2/8	52 4/8	51 6/8	48 4/8	15	16	Pons Island	QUE	Don Young	1988	8
410 0/8	56 0/8	55 6/8	52 1/8	13	11	Schefferville	QUE	Charles L. Buechel, Jr.	1987	9
407 5/8	50 3/8	50 0/8	45 3/8	13	15	Delay River	QUE	Jeff Baker	1988	10
403 7/8	51 3/8	50 3/8	43 5/8	14	16	Delay River	QUE	Dr. James J. Barnes	1987	11
402 3/8	59 4/8	57 7/8	56 6/8	13	14	Ungava Bay	QUE	Leonard J. Letendre	1989	12
401 3/8	49 4/8	49 0/8	51 1/8	14	14	Lac Pon's	QUE	Gordon Demeritt	1988	13
399 7/8	52 3/8	53 1/8	49 6/8	12	12	Whiskey Lake	QUE	D.F.Baldwin & T. Barta	1985	14
398 5/8	52 2/8	54 2/8	51 1/8	20	17	George River	QUE	Richard Mielke	1981	15
398 5/8	54 4/8	54 5/8	52 4/8	10	11	Caniapiscau River	QUE	Henry O. Fromm	1987	15
398 1/8	51 4/8	52 2/8	48 3/8	11	11	Lac Otelnuk	QUE	Rudy Tremain	1989	17
396 1/8	51 6/8	51 2/8	48 1/8	14	15	Weymouth Inlet	QUE	Tink Nathan	1986	18
395 6/8	59 4/8	55 4/8	47 7/8	18	16	George River	QUE	Paul Brunner	1980	19
392 4/8	52 4/8	53 4/8	44 7/8	15	13	Caniapiscau River	QUE	Mike Ingold	1988	20
392 0/8	51 4/8	50 6/8	48 2/8	18	27	Lac Cananee	QUE	Brad L. Johnson	1981	21
391 0/8	55 6/8	56 2/8	39 4/8	17	15	George River	QUE	Jim McCrory	1980	22
388 3/8	49 2/8	51 6/8	40 5/8	12	12	Delay River	QUE	Richard E. Davis	1987	23
388 2/8	46 0/8	45 4/8	42 6/8	11	11	Delay River	QUE	William G. Mason	1988	24
387 6/8	62 1/8	60 7/8	53 7/8	12	11	Delay River	QUE	Roy M. Goodwin	1987	25
387 6/8	50 1/8	49 4/8	45 6/8	12	14	Pons River	QUE	Louis J. Lorenzo	1991	25
387 4/8	42 2/8	39 5/8	47 7/8	24	16	Delay River	QUE	Larry Smith	1987	27
387 1/8	52 0/8	53 5/8	48 4/8	9	12	Schefferville	QUE	Tom Kayser	1986	28
387 1/8	47 0/8	44 5/8	46 6/8	14	13	Weeks Lake	QUE	Donald L. Stout	1990	28
386 4/8	56 2/8	54 4/8	57 7/8	15	20	George River	QUE	John Kuhar	1972	30
385 5/8	50 2/8	52 2/8	50 7/8	16	18	Pons Island	QUE	James C. Walters	1987	31
384 7/8	50 6/8	50 0/8	50 0/8	15	18	Whale River	QUE	David L. Willis	1986	32
384 4/8	46 4/8	46 5/8	42 4/8	15	16	Schefferville	QUE	Elmer R. Luce, Jr.	1987	33
384 2/8	45 2/8	46 6/8	49 0/8	19	19	Schefferville	QUE	Elmer R. Luce, Jr.	1987	34
384 0/8	46 0/8	44 3/8	43 0/8	17	13	Weymouth Inlet	QUE	Jules Pacheco	1986	35
383 7/8	47 3/8	49 5/8	46 7/8	14	17	Lake Loudin	QUE	Roger M. Schmitt	1988	36
381 6/8	50 4/8	52 0/8	50 2/8	13	13	Delay River	QUE	Robert G. McCulley	1988	37
381 4/8	51 0/8	51 6/8	41 2/8	17	19	Wedge Hill Lodge	QUE	John Janelli	1980	38
381 3/8	52 0/8	49 2/8	48 0/8	13	14	Ungava Region	QUE	Wayne A. Vanstratten	1986	39
381 2/8	48 3/8	50 4/8	39 1/8	13	14	Caniapiscau River	QUE	David C. Arndt	1986	40
381 0/8	51 0/8	52 1/8	44 3/8	14	13	LG4	QUE	Stephen Kotz	1990	41
380 6/8	56 0/8	52 1/8	40 4/8	12	12	Oltanook Lake	QUE	Ken Mowerson	1986	42
380 5/8	57 6/8	53 5/8	56 7/8	11	16	Ungava Region	QUE	Donald Schram	1982	43
379 7/8	49 0/8	50 2/8	51 2/8	15	13	Schefferville	QUE	Michael C. Dysh	1990	44
379 6/8	49 4/8	49 2/8	42 5/8	11	12	Schefferville	QUE	Ted Jaycox	1986	45
379 0/8	55 6/8	55 4/8	48 2/8	12	13	Delay River	QUE	Paul Rigsby	1988	46
378 7/8	54 2/8	54 2/8	54 3/8	11	12	Tunulik River	QUE	Jay G. St. Charles	1986	47
378 4/8	49 5/8	49 0/8	44 3/8	14	15	Fort Chimo	QUE	Robert Pyne	1989	48
377 3/8	51 6/8	55 2/8	52 4/8	12	13	Schefferville	QUE	Frank 'Rit' Heller	1978	49
377 0/8	53 6/8	55 7/8	36 7/8	15	15	Delay River	QUE	Dale Underwood	1990	50
376 7/8	48 1/8	49 6/8	51 0/8	17	13	Lake Lac Hine	QUE	Edward A. Mertins	1990	51
376 5/8	50 4/8	50 4/8	57 0/8	13	11	Ungava Bay	QUE	Ed Riley	1985	52
376 2/8	49 2/8	48 2/8	49 4/8	17	18	Fort Chimo	QUE	David Bailey	1985	53
375 7/8	46 2/8	47 6/8	37 2/8	24	25	Ungava Region	QUE	Jose Rivero	1979	54
375 1/8	60 3/8	59 6/8	42 0/8	15	16	George River	QUE	Robert M. Sweisthal, Jr.	1980	55
374 7/8	49 5/8	52 1/8	59 2/8	11	15	Ungava Region	QUE	Bob Frank	1979	56
374 6/8	47 5/8	48 7/8	43 6/8	13	12	Weeks Lake	QUE	Raymond Villeneuve	1990	57
374 4/8	54 0/8	59 2/8	34 7/8	9	12	Schefferville	QUE	Brian L. Johnson	1988	58
374 4/8	51 0/8	47 4/8	39 1/8	14	13	George River	QUE	David A. Spacek	1990	58
374 3/8	60 2/8	59 0/8	52 5/8	14	13	Schefferville	QUE	Bill Heather	1979	60
373 3/8	53 2/8	51 1/8	40 0/8	15	13	Fort Chimo	QUE	Scott M. Showalter	1982	61
372 7/8	44 2/8	45 2/8	37 7/8	17	17	Delay River	QUE	Ray Moulton	1986	62
372 7/8	46 6/8	47 4/8	47 6/8	15	13	Henrys Lake	QUE	Kip Boten	1990	62
372 4/8	55 7/8	53 1/8	43 2/8	13	13	Ungava Bay	QUE	David Dunnigan	1984	64
372 4/8	53 0/8	58 7/8	43 4/8	11	10	Lac LeFrancois	QUE	Raymond W. Murray III	1990	64
372 4/8	45 6/8	45 5/8	41 1/8	16	16	LG4	QUE	Paul J. Sisz	1991	64
372 1/8	52 6/8	53 2/8	52 4/8	17	15	Ungava Bay	QUE	Roy M. Goodwin	1989	67
371 6/8	48 7/8	50 1/8	42 6/8	17	16	Fort Chimo	QUE	Robert Pyne	1989	68
371 5/8	48 6/8	47 3/8	42 4/8	16	13	Maricourt Lake	QUE	James Kingsley	1992	69
370 7/8	46 6/8	44 5/8	41 2/8	5	6	Schefferville	QUE	Elmer R. Luce, Jr.	1986	70

Score	Length of R Main Beam L		Inside Spread	Number of R Points L		Area	State/Province	Hunter's Name	Date	Rank
370 5/8	45 0/8	48 0/8	37 5/8	20	14	Caniapiscau River	QUE	Gregory White	1987	71
370 2/8	46 0/8	46 7/8	55 1/8	12	13	Delay River	QUE	Mike Iuzzolino	1991	72
369 1/8	53 6/8	52 4/8	50 5/8	14	12	Jack's Lake	QUE	Denis Weisensel	1989	73
368 6/8	51 3/8	52 6/8	51 7/8	11	14	Kuujjacq River	QUE	Glen Ogle	1988	74
368 5/8	52 0/8	46 1/8	44 4/8	21	15	Fort Chimo	QUE	Joseph A. Borgna	1989	75
368 5/8	47 2/8	46 2/8	46 0/8	15	16	LG4	QUE	Claude St' Amour	1990	75
368 4/8	53 0/8	51 4/8	43 4/8	13	12	Fort Chimo	QUE	Jerry Schauer	1990	77
367 4/8	54 7/8	52 0/8	43 3/8	11	14	George River	QUE	Lee Kline	1980	78
367 1/8	50 6/8	51 5/8	39 7/8	13	11	Schefferville	QUE	Raymond A. Guay	1988	79
367 0/8	47 0/8	48 0/8	44 7/8	12	12	Fort Chimo	QUE	James E. Doberstein	1989	80
366 4/8	53 1/8	55 5/8	44 6/8	15	14	Fort Chimo	QUE	Larry DeVormer, Sr.	1988	81
366 2/8	54 7/8	52 3/8	55 0/8	20	16	Ungava Region	QUE	Joe Caruso	1979	82
366 1/8	48 0/8	48 2/8	38 2/8	21	14	Mistinibi Lake	QUE	Dieter Foerst	1981	83
365 6/8	49 0/8	49 3/8	39 5/8	20	17	Pons River	QUE	Thomas Mathews	1988	84
364 5/8	49 0/8	51 0/8	34 4/8	13	11	George River	QUE	Gary L. Fritzler	1983	85
364 4/8	54 6/8	54 1/8	53 6/8	10	9	Delay River	QUE	W. R. "Tony" Dukes	1987	86
364 3/8	53 4/8	53 1/8	48 0/8	12	10	George River	QUE	Billy Ellis	1980	87
364 3/8	50 5/8	50 6/8	41 5/8	11	17	Ungava Bay	QUE	Stephen Michael Carroll	1988	87
364 2/8	49 5/8	47 3/8	41 0/8	16	16	Big Island Lake	QUE	Jim Ponciano	1985	89
364 2/8	57 7/8	58 5/8	55 2/8	13	14	Delay River	QUE	Bob Watkins	1987	89
363 7/8	50 3/8	50 1/8	49 1/8	12	11	Delay River	QUE	Robert Bain	1987	91
363 4/8	52 6/8	52 2/8	34 2/8	14	15	Ungava Bay	QUE	Steve Bruggeman	1990	92
363 0/8	48 6/8	47 5/8	48 6/8	13	14	Tunulik River	QUE	Rick Morgan	1986	93
363 0/8	45 5/8	48 0/8	44 3/8	10	14	Ungava Bay	QUE	James Norvell	1989	93
362 4/8	53 7/8	47 1/8	53 1/8	10	16	River De Paz	QUE	David F. Baldwin	1981	95
362 4/8	55 7/8	53 6/8	45 5/8	12	11	Fort Chimo	QUE	William H. Moyer	1988	95
362 3/8	47 6/8	48 3/8	41 4/8	13	12	Tunulik River	QUE	David J. Hell	1986	97
362 2/8	53 0/8	52 1/8	47 6/8	11	12	Saglek Bay	LAB	Charles Allen Poole	1990	98
362 0/8	60 2/8	57 5/8	49 4/8	11	14	Delay River	QUE	Richard V. McKeown	1990	99
361 4/8	48 2/8	47 2/8	40 4/8	11	14	Fort Chimo	QUE	Dave Seidelman	1985	100
361 4/8	54 6/8	55 0/8	53 4/8	11	11	Akuliak	QUE	Perry Merkes	1988	100
361 3/8	54 4/8	55 6/8	42 0/8	12	11	Schefferville	QUE	Elmer R. Luce, Jr.	1986	102
361 3/8	47 7/8	48 6/8	41 5/8	14	14	Delay River	QUE	John Akkerman	1990	102
361 0/8	52 2/8	51 1/8	36 5/8	15	12	Delay River	QUE	Jerry Costanza	1991	104
360 3/8	50 0/8	51 0/8	42 1/8	14	12	Schefferville	QUE	Robert M. Burtch	1988	105
360 1/8	46 3/8	48 4/8	53 0/8	14	11	Schefferville	QUE	Steven H. Byerly	1989	106
360 0/8	57 2/8	58 4/8	43 6/8	10	10	Fort Chimo	QUE	Linda Berkompas	1989	107
359 7/8	50 4/8	51 2/8	47 0/8	15	17	George River	QUE	Cecil Tharp	1982	108
359 7/8	50 0/8	50 1/8	42 2/8	11	11	Ribero Lake	QUE	Rick Bolin	1986	108
359 7/8	51 3/8	52 2/8	42 1/8	13	14	Delay River	QUE	Edward G. Gilkes	1988	108
359 7/8	53 6/8	53 6/8	40 7/8	13	20	Ungava Bay	QUE	Greg Strait	1989	108
359 6/8	49 6/8	50 5/8	35 4/8	13	12	Schefferville	QUE	Steven P. Salmieri	1989	112
359 5/8	54 2/8	55 5/8	58 0/8	13	12	Ricky Lake	QUE	William A.S. Heuer, Sr.	1987	113
359 4/8	53 7/8	54 0/8	42 0/8	13	17	Weymouth Inlet	QUE	David C. Smart	1988	114
359 3/8	44 7/8	46 1/8	37 1/8	18	15	Fort Chimo	QUE	Roger Schwarz	1988	115
359 3/8	49 1/8	47 5/8	51 6/8	9	11	Lake Sammy	QUE	Chuck Adams	1989	115
359 0/8	47 4/8	51 3/8	42 4/8	9	10	Maricourt River	QUE	Evan Steinhorst	1990	117
358 6/8	50 6/8	53 1/8	42 2/8	18	23	George River	QUE	Dale Selby	1980	118
358 2/8	41 5/8	42 1/8	34 7/8	15	18	Delay River	QUE	Ray Moulton	1986	119
358 1/8	52 1/8	50 4/8	48 0/8	14	17	Pons Island	QUE	Harold B. "Pat" Clark	1987	120
358 1/8	49 2/8	54 0/8	51 2/8	16	12	Jack's Lake	QUE	Raymond A. Luce	1989	120
358 0/8	52 4/8	52 0/8	41 7/8	15	17	Ungava Region	QUE	Carl G. Esterly	1983	122
357 5/8	56 1/8	52 4/8	43 3/8	17	15	Delay River	QUE	Steve Beilgard	1989	123
357 4/8	50 4/8	50 6/8	32 6/8	14	12	Naskapis Lake	QUE	Guy-Maurice Algier	1988	124
357 0/8	48 2/8	50 4/8	42 2/8	17	13	Lake Narcy	QUE	Roy Hampton	1988	125
356 6/8	49 1/8	49 3/8	41 6/8	13	13	Fort Chimo	QUE	Chris W. Taylor	1989	126
356 4/8	51 5/8	53 3/8	44 6/8	11	10	Ungava Bay	QUE	Larry Nirk	1983	127
356 4/8	46 0/8	47 5/8	42 0/8	17	20	Schefferville	QUE	William A.S. Heuer, Jr.	1987	127
356 4/8	54 2/8	53 2/8	38 6/8	9	12	Fort Chimo	QUE	Roy Javenkowski	1989	127
356 4/8	48 7/8	46 1/8	50 2/8	15	13	Jack's Lake	QUE	William F. Jackson	1989	127
356 1/8	47 3/8	47 2/8	45 0/8	16	12	Lake Cambrian	QUE	Clyde Doolittle	1988	131
356 0/8	55 4/8	56 4/8	49 4/8	17	23	Schefferville	QUE	Gregory G. Justus	1980	132
356 0/8	54 3/8	54 0/8	45 6/8	10	8	Schefferville	QUE	Nicholas J. Gray	1981	132
355 5/8	55 6/8	58 0/8	50 4/8	10	14	George River	QUE	Charles E. Spreeman	1985	134
355 4/8	47 0/8	47 2/8	36 3/8	17	18	Sixteen-Island-Lake	QUE	W. Bruce Nicolls	1987	135
355 1/8	55 7/8	56 0/8	48 0/8	10	13	Tunulik River	QUE	Tom Paluso	1988	136
355 1/8	49 6/8	50 2/8	39 7/8	9	9	Schefferville	QUE	Jerry Keller	1991	136
355 0/8	58 3/8	54 1/8	35 4/8	9	10	Fort Chimo	QUE	Lewis Miller	1990	138
354 6/8	48 4/8	48 7/8	49 6/8	13	14	Schefferville	QUE	Tom Hlinka	1990	139
354 4/8	47 5/8	48 0/8	48 0/8	15	12	Lake Otelnuk	QUE	Steve Vanzile	1986	140

MINIMUM SCORE 300

Score	Length of Main Beam R	L	Inside Spread	Number of Points R	L	Area	State/ Province	Hunter's Name	Date	Rank
354 4/8	48 1/8	43 5/8	45 3/8	10	9	Doreen Lake	QUE	Eugene Arndt	1990	140
354 2/8	50 2/8	50 1/8	41 5/8	9	10	Big Island	QUE	Fred C. Church	1985	142
354 1/8	59 2/8	61 5/8	51 4/8	13	7	Ungava Bay	QUE	Joe Prinzi	1985	143
354 1/8	44 3/8	45 2/8	40 1/8	10	12	Schefferville	QUE	Robert Pyne	1985	143
354 0/8	50 3/8	50 1/8	48 2/8	13	13	Lake Des Bergere	QUE	Ronald L. Musser	1988	145
353 7/8	57 0/8	53 6/8	45 0/8	12	14	Fort Chimo	QUE	David Samuel	1991	146
353 4/8	52 7/8	51 2/8	39 6/8	14	12	Schefferville	QUE	Robert J. Lewis	1986	147
353 2/8	61 5/8	58 2/8	47 5/8	12	10	Tunulik River	QUE	Jon Vanderhoef	1984	148
353 0/8	50 4/8	49 2/8	46 2/8	13	9	Ungava Region	QUE	Casimir Leknius	1977	149
352 6/8	44 2/8	48 0/8	38 5/8	16	15	Delay River	QUE	Val S. Schmaus, Jr.	1989	150
352 3/8	51 1/8	48 2/8	40 4/8	11	12	Caniaspiscau River	QUE	Jimmy J. Meadows	1990	151
352 0/8	55 4/8	54 6/8	44 3/8	11	11	Ungava Bay	QUE	Tink Nathan	1984	152
352 0/8	48 1/8	47 7/8	41 7/8	12	12	Mistinibi Lake	QUE	John Anthony Jerome	1987	152
351 6/8	44 0/8	43 6/8	35 1/8	20	20	Schefferville	QUE	Steven P. Salmieri	1989	154
351 5/8	51 4/8	49 1/8	48 1/8	15	14	George River	QUE	Frank Charette	1982	155
351 5/8	50 3/8	51 0/8	41 1/8	11	12	Loudin Lake	QUE	Steven J. Lepic	1988	155
351 3/8	44 2/8	41 5/8	39 3/8	15	16	Ricky Lake	QUE	William A.S. Heuer, Jr.	1987	157
351 2/8	48 5/8	48 3/8	42 2/8	10	10	Delay River	QUE	Fred J. Ward	1988	158
351 0/8	53 2/8	52 7/8	36 6/8	20	15	Dihourse Lake	QUE	Kenneth W. Lohr	1982	159
351 0/8	48 0/8	51 2/8	48 0/8	12	12	Delay River	QUE	Robert Bain	1987	159
350 6/8	55 5/8	56 2/8	45 3/8	14	12	Tunulik River	QUE	Henry F. Rauch	1982	161
350 6/8	38 3/8	38 2/8	31 7/8	12	13	Jack's Lake	QUE	Tony Odhner	1989	161
350 6/8	56 7/8	55 5/8	35 5/8	16	14	Schefferville	QUE	John W. Offord	1990	161
350 5/8	46 2/8	46 6/8	38 7/8	12	13	Schefferville	QUE	Greg Seymour	1986	164
350 5/8	43 6/8	46 6/8	44 6/8	14	12	Ungava Bay	QUE	Alan Niemeyer	1989	164
350 3/8	49 5/8	49 6/8	46 0/8	16	14	Desbergere	QUE	Lee Burnett	1989	166
350 2/8	55 7/8	52 0/8	46 6/8	13	14	Weymouth Inlet	QUE	Tom Taylor	1991	167
349 7/8	43 5/8	41 5/8	34 3/8	13	14	Kenny Lake	QUE	Ross Trujillo, Jr.	1991	168
349 6/8	47 0/8	44 1/8	37 4/8	20	15	George River	QUE	Charlie Kroll	1980	169
349 6/8	45 7/8	49 5/8	44 7/8	16	15	Ungava Peninsula	QUE	Bill VyVyan	1988	169
349 4/8	51 0/8	51 3/8	37 0/8	12	13	Caniapiscau River	QUE	Henry O. Fromm	1987	171
349 4/8	46 5/8	46 2/8	43 2/8	17	13	Harold Lake	QUE	Don Davidson	1990	171
349 4/8	51 3/8	50 3/8	48 4/8	11	9	Delay River	QUE	Bob Mussey	1990	171
349 4/8	49 1/8	43 6/8	42 6/8	16	12	Ungava Bay	QUE	Steve Bruggeman	1990	171
349 3/8	48 6/8	52 4/8	44 0/8	8	11	Delay River	QUE	Roger Gipple	1988	175
349 2/8	49 5/8	49 0/8	37 5/8	10	11	Fort Chimo	QUE	James E. Doberstein	1989	176
349 0/8	49 3/8	49 1/8	35 7/8	12	9	Tunulik River	QUE	Ty Martin	1986	177
349 0/8	46 7/8	45 6/8	45 4/8	10	13	Pons River	QUE	Wayne A. Lamoreux	1991	177
348 7/8	46 6/8	49 4/8	31 4/8	17	20	Mulay River	QUE	Don Keady	1987	179
348 5/8	52 0/8	51 7/8	45 0/8	9	10	Lac Coulounge	QUE	John W. Borlang	1987	180
348 5/8	49 6/8	52 2/8	48 3/8	11	14	LG4	QUE	Donald W. Hoffman	1991	180
348 3/8	53 0/8	49 7/8	40 4/8	11	14	Jack's Lake	QUE	William F. Jackson	1989	182
348 1/8	52 4/8	55 3/8	28 7/8	18	14	George River	QUE	Bob Goodall	1980	183
348 1/8	49 0/8	50 2/8	44 2/8	14	9	George River	QUE	Phillip J. Taylor	1984	183
347 7/8	53 1/8	54 1/8	49 6/8	15	14	Wayne Lake	QUE	Jay J. Kaster	1988	185
347 5/8	52 3/8	52 2/8	49 0/8	12	12	Ungava Region	QUE	Charles R. Leidheiser	1977	186
347 5/8	44 6/8	45 3/8	41 7/8	13	12	Kenny Lake	QUE	Matt Lamoreux	1991	186
347 1/8	51 4/8	53 6/8	47 1/8	11	11	Schefferville	QUE	Ronnie Everett	1986	188
346 7/8	54 4/8	58 4/8	41 0/8	10	11	Akuliak	QUE	Lauri Johnson	1985	189
346 6/8	48 2/8	47 2/8	49 2/8	9	12	Delay River	QUE	Gregory J. Fries	1987	190
346 6/8	55 1/8	56 4/8	43 7/8	13	11	Delay River	QUE	Robert Pastor	1988	190
346 6/8	46 7/8	47 5/8	41 5/8	12	10	Jack's Lake	QUE	Curt Christensen	1989	190
346 3/8	47 5/8	47 3/8	40 6/8	11	10	Maricourt Lake	QUE	Jerry W. Huffaker	1990	193
346 2/8	50 5/8	49 1/8	44 3/8	11	13	Ungava Bay	QUE	Lou Kindred	1986	194
346 2/8	46 3/8	43 5/8	38 6/8	14	14	Lake Otelnuk	QUE	Eddie Cooper	1988	194
346 1/8	55 0/8	55 0/8	37 3/8	12	17	River Lac Cambrien	QUE	Kent W. Brigham	1987	196
346 1/8	41 0/8	42 5/8	39 5/8	17	15	Schefferville	QUE	Edward Faucher	1990	196
346 1/8	42 4/8	46 2/8	40 4/8	13	13	LG4	QUE	Mark D. Mishinski	1991	196
346 0/8	48 6/8	50 6/8	45 7/8	13	14	George River	QUE	William E. Bullock	1982	199
346 0/8	51 6/8	52 4/8	43 2/8	12	10	Delay River	QUE	Dennis N. Ballweg	1988	199
345 7/8	52 6/8	54 1/8	45 2/8	11	13	Ungava Bay	QUE	John Musacchia	1978	201
345 7/8	52 3/8	51 7/8	44 2/8	13	17	Schefferville	QUE	Barry J. Smith	1988	201
345 3/8	51 4/8	53 5/8	36 1/8	14	11	Maricourt River	QUE	Michael J. Churchill	1990	203
345 2/8	47 2/8	48 7/8	41 5/8	11	18	Fort Chimo	QUE	Bob Jensen	1982	204
345 2/8	43 2/8	48 0/8	48 0/8	10	12	Delay River	QUE	William "Ted" Bennett	1988	204
345 1/8	56 5/8	52 5/8	42 3/8	11	10	Ungava Bay	QUE	Richard Gamache	1988	206
344 7/8	45 0/8	48 7/8	37 7/8	16	14	Mulay River	QUE	Don Keady	1987	207
344 6/8	51 0/8	50 5/8	38 6/8	10	11	Schefferville	QUE	Gregg Tanner	1985	208
344 6/8	53 6/8	55 3/8	41 5/8	15	18	16 Islands	QUE	Chris McDonnell	1990	208
344 4/8	45 6/8	46 7/8	45 0/8	12	10	Ungava Bay	QUE	David Baldwin	1986	210

MINIMUM SCORE 300

SCORE	LENGTH OF MAIN BEAM		INSIDE SPREAD	NUMBER OF POINTS		AREA	STATE/ PROVINCE	HUNTER'S NAME	DATE	RANK
	R	L		R	L					
344 4/8	44 4/8	47 6/8	41 4/8	14	12	Ungava Bay	QUE	James Norvell	1989	210
344 2/8	43 2/8	43 0/8	43 2/8	13	13	Melezes River	QUE	G. Fred Asbell	1990	212
343 7/8	54 2/8	51 1/8	39 3/8	13	13	Lake Nullualuk	QUE	Clifford White	1992	213
343 6/8	48 0/8	48 0/8	38 4/8	11	14	Akuliak	QUE	Barry Dyar	1985	214
343 6/8	52 2/8	51 1/8	48 3/8	12	12	Schefferville	QUE	Gregory V. Pilot	1992	214
343 3/8	48 0/8	47 0/8	44 7/8	14	12	George River	QUE	Leonard L. Kohan	1981	216
343 3/8	49 2/8	50 1/8	43 5/8	9	10	Ungava Bay	QUE	L. Dan Neebe	1988	216
343 1/8	51 3/8	48 6/8	48 4/8	17	18	Kuujjuak River	QUE	Arthur J. Pelon	1985	218
342 7/8	53 4/8	52 6/8	39 5/8	14	14	George River	QUE	Frank Hogan	1980	219
342 6/8	43 3/8	47 1/8	40 7/8	17	17	Kuujjuac River	QUE	Steven Sendek	1985	220
342 5/8	47 4/8	50 3/8	46 1/8	15	10	Tuktu Camp	QUE	Martin G. Billeri	1977	221
342 5/8	37 2/8	34 5/8	40 2/8	14	15	Ricky Lake	QUE	William A.S. Heuer, Sr.	1987	221
342 5/8	50 5/8	51 0/8	46 4/8	14	14	LG4	QUE	Gregory A. Bonecutter, Sr	1991	221
342 4/8	43 1/8	45 4/8	44 0/8	11	13	DeLay River	QUE	William Bos	1990	224
342 2/8	47 5/8	50 3/8	42 0/8	13	10	Ungava Bay	QUE	Rayot A. DiFate	1988	225
341 6/8	47 4/8	47 5/8	44 1/8	10	13	Ungava Bay	QUE	Steve Crooks	1988	226
341 6/8	46 1/8	45 0/8	52 0/8	12	18	Delay River	QUE	Jim E. Roe	1988	226
341 3/8	48 5/8	48 6/8	47 4/8	14	15	George River	QUE	William B. Bullock, Jr.	1982	228
341 2/8	50 4/8	49 6/8	50 2/8	15	12	Pons River	QUE	Walter F. Dotson, Jr.	1987	229
341 2/8	49 3/8	44 6/8	48 6/8	13	11	Schefferville	QUE	Robert J. Lewis	1987	229
341 0/8	51 3/8	45 7/8	44 4/8	14	12	Ungava Region	QUE	Glenn Reno	1980	231
341 0/8	45 0/8	43 5/8	35 0/8	14	16	May Lake	QUE	Larry M. Peterson	1990	231
340 5/8	54 7/8	57 7/8	51 0/8	14	13	Tunulik River	QUE	Jean-Claude Duff	1985	233
340 5/8	46 4/8	46 1/8	34 0/8	17	14	Schefferville	QUE	Pat Vincenti	1990	233
340 3/8	39 2/8	48 7/8	31 5/8	18	15	George River	QUE	Craig Richardson	1982	235
340 2/8	41 6/8	44 6/8	46 7/8	16	12	Shirley Lake	QUE	Duane Zemliska	1990	236
340 1/8	46 4/8	47 3/8	37 7/8	17	13	LG4	QUE	Fred Johnston III	1991	237
339 7/8	49 1/8	49 0/8	44 1/8	17	15	Weymouth Inlet	QUE	Chuck Adams	1991	238
339 6/8	45 4/8	47 3/8	43 3/8	15	13	Ungava Bay	QUE	Dean M. Westby	1986	239
339 6/8	50 3/8	49 5/8	42 5/8	12	12	Ungava Peninsula	QUE	Bill Vyvyan	1988	239
339 6/8	42 2/8	41 5/8	51 1/8	13	13	Delay River	QUE	Robert Hermann	1989	239
339 6/8	48 1/8	48 3/8	46 0/8	11	11	Martha's Lake	QUE	Mark Zastrow	1992	239
339 4/8	47 7/8	48 2/8	44 6/8	13	15	Audiepure Lake	QUE	Stan Godfrey	1983	243
339 3/8	46 0/8	46 1/8	44 2/8	14	16	Tunulik River	QUE	David Quong	1992	244
339 0/8	56 4/8	55 0/8	45 5/8	12	11	Tuktu Camp	QUE	John C. Mitchell	1984	245
339 0/8	47 6/8	47 6/8	51 3/8	12	10	Long Lake	QUE	Mark Gerhard	1990	245
338 4/8	54 4/8	56 3/8	36 4/8	15	12	Potier River	QUE	Lawrence R. Gibbons	1990	247
338 3/8	47 1/8	46 1/8	38 0/8	19	20	George River	QUE	Len Cardinale	1971	248
338 3/8	54 0/8	53 3/8	32 0/8	13	16	Schefferville	QUE	Kenneth C. Kaufman	1987	248
338 1/8	48 4/8	47 4/8	40 6/8	17	13	Ungava Bay	QUE	Alan Niemeyer	1989	250
338 0/8	40 3/8	45 0/8	34 7/8	15	16	Echo Lake	QUE	Matthew J. Luxem	1989	251
337 7/8	48 3/8	47 2/8	45 5/8	14	12	De Pas & George River	QUE	Fred F. Potts	1974	252
337 7/8	44 0/8	45 3/8	42 3/8	13	11	Schefferville	QUE	Dale Drilling	1987	252
337 7/8	52 3/8	53 1/8	41 6/8	13	14	Whiskey Lake	QUE	Thomas Ippolito	1987	252
337 6/8	52 0/8	51 7/8	45 4/8	9	10	Tunulik River	QUE	Jay E. Johnson	1985	255
337 6/8	51 0/8	51 5/8	48 4/8	8	9	Pons River	QUE	Bradford Higson	1986	255
337 4/8	46 4/8	46 5/8	45 1/8	15	12	Wayne Lake	QUE	Randall L. Schoenly	1987	257
337 0/8	52 5/8	52 2/8	39 7/8	13	12	Jack's Lake	QUE	Greg Odhner	1989	258
336 6/8	48 2/8	46 5/8	34 7/8	17	16	Delay River	QUE	W.R. "Tony" Dukes	1987	259
336 4/8	53 4/8	52 2/8	41 0/8	10	10	George River	QUE	David Tofte	1982	260
336 1/8	53 0/8	52 0/8	51 0/8	15	19	Twin Lake	QUE	Jon P. Thomas	1982	261
336 0/8	42 3/8	41 7/8	45 3/8	13	13	Lake Leopard	QUE	Robert B. Seger II	1989	262
335 5/8	51 7/8	52 1/8	41 3/8	10	12	Tunulik River	QUE	DeeAnn Robinson	1992	263
335 4/8	48 1/8	50 0/8	40 2/8	10	14	Pons River	QUE	Thomas Hopkins	1987	264
335 3/8	49 1/8	46 2/8	49 1/8	16	17	Ungava Peninsula	QUE	Tony Snow	1988	265
335 2/8	44 0/8	45 6/8	47 7/8	19	12	Lake Otelnuk	QUE	John L. Wagner	1989	266
335 0/8	51 2/8	50 2/8	42 4/8	9	12	Tunulik River	QUE	Robert A. Shank	1988	267
334 7/8	44 5/8	44 0/8	40 0/8	14	18	Pons River	QUE	Joe Hoffman	1991	268
334 6/8	49 5/8	47 7/8	41 4/8	13	14	Shirley Lake	QUE	Jerry E. Burt	1990	269
334 2/8	48 7/8	46 7/8	34 3/8	13	14	Dugue River	QUE	Lee A. Heath	1990	270
334 1/8	40 5/8	43 3/8	38 4/8	17	13	Serigny River	QUE	Howard T. Isenberg, Jr.	1990	271
334 1/8	47 5/8	47 6/8	38 0/8	17	13	Lake Anonyme	QUE	Dennis Hayden	1992	271
333 5/8	53 2/8	52 7/8	41 6/8	12	13	Tunulik River	QUE	Gregory G. Kilby	1985	273
333 4/8	51 3/8	53 0/8	45 1/8	7	7	Delay River	QUE	Robert H. Pavlovic	1988	274
333 3/8	45 3/8	48 2/8	45 3/8	12	13	Lake Loudon	QUE	Jim Gompf	1990	275
333 2/8	55 4/8	52 6/8	47 5/8	13	15	Schefferville	QUE	Al Reay	1978	276
333 2/8	51 6/8	53 1/8	46 1/8	11	10	Whiskey Lake	QUE	Glenn R. Kuklick	1986	276
333 1/8	51 3/8	52 5/8	49 7/8	5	8	Schefferville	QUE	Robert James Lewis	1987	278
332 7/8	47 6/8	48 4/8	48 6/8	11	8	Schefferville	QUE	Darwin L. Damp	1988	279
332 6/8	49 1/8	46 2/8	40 4/8	10	12	Agnew Lake	QUE	James P Loughran	1989	280

QUEBEC LABRADOR CARIBOU

MINIMUM SCORE 300

(Continued)

Score	Length of Main Beam R	L	Inside Spread	Number of Points R	L	Area	State/Province	Hunter's Name	Date	Rank
332 4/8	51 6/8	51 1/8	36 3/8	10	11	Tunulik River	QUE	Glenn St. Charles	1984	281
332 3/8	56 2/8	51 2/8	39 6/8	9	12	Kuujjuak River	QUE	Mark Thompson	1987	282
332 3/8	48 3/8	48 4/8	43 4/8	12	12	Riviere aux Melezes	QUE	David R. Rogers	1987	282
332 0/8	53 4/8	48 5/8	52 2/8	8	10	Ungava Bay	QUE	Richard J. Chobot, Jr.	1986	284
332 0/8	50 4/8	50 2/8	43 0/8	12	11	Weymouth Inlet	QUE	Kenneth M. Beno	1988	284
331 7/8	46 0/8	42 6/8	43 7/8	14	12	Fort Chimo	QUE	Harold Halverson	1991	286
331 6/8	52 0/8	52 6/8	45 4/8	15	14	Schefferville	QUE	Thomas E. Smith	1981	287
331 6/8	46 7/8	47 3/8	38 0/8	14	13	Cedar Lake	QUE	Anders J. Meyer	1989	287
331 5/8	55 5/8	55 4/8	39 1/8	14	9	Pons River	QUE	Robert Amaral	1986	289
331 3/8	47 0/8	47 1/8	47 1/8	9	9	Whiskey Lake	QUE	Peter L. Halbig	1986	290
331 3/8	45 3/8	47 1/8	35 4/8	14	16	Fort Chimo	QUE	Gene Culver	1989	290
331 3/8	45 7/8	48 0/8	50 4/8	10	9	Fort Chimo	QUE	John Leo Hojan	1990	290
331 0/8	56 3/8	58 5/8	47 5/8	9	7	Waymouth Inlet	QUE	Edwin DeYoung	1989	293
330 7/8	49 4/8	48 0/8	42 4/8	12	10	LG 4	QUE	Frank Kozielec, Jr.	1992	294
330 6/8	45 5/8	47 1/8	36 0/8	13	14	Pons Island	QUE	Lou Edelis	1987	295
330 5/8	49 4/8	48 6/8	36 6/8	14	15	LG4	QUE	Charles Moore	1991	296
330 2/8	49 1/8	49 4/8	37 5/8	16	16	Delay River	QUE	Roy Goodwin	1986	297
330 2/8	46 0/8	48 7/8	37 0/8	14	11	Delay River	QUE	James Kingsley	1990	297
330 0/8	49 5/8	45 6/8	31 0/8	12	10	Fort Chimo	QUE	Larry Hayes	1986	299
330 0/8	50 2/8	49 4/8	43 0/8	11	8	Harold Lake	QUE	Ron Haver	1992	299
329 2/8	47 0/8	48 0/8	42 3/8	14	10	Schefferville	QUE	Jerry W. Robertson	1988	301
329 1/8	52 5/8	48 7/8	43 7/8	16	13	George River	QUE	Jerry V. Finley	1981	302
329 0/8	42 6/8	39 5/8	40 2/8	13	15	Rogers Lake	QUE	Joe Powroznik	1988	303
329 0/8	51 5/8	55 2/8	37 7/8	8	7	Melaise River	QUE	A. Owen Shifflett	1989	303
328 6/8	55 4/8	56 7/8	42 3/8	9	11	Ungava Region	QUE	David L. Cook	1982	305
328 6/8	43 0/8	42 4/8	38 5/8	17	13	Schefferville	QUE	Michael J. Kennedy	1992	305
328 5/8	49 1/8	52 4/8	45 2/8	13	12	Pons River	QUE	Jim Ellis	1986	307
328 5/8	44 5/8	44 3/8	33 0/8	16	14	Schefferville	QUE	Kenneth C. Kaufmann	1987	307
328 4/8	44 6/8	43 0/8	39 0/8	16	16	Long Lake	QUE	David J. Stanislawski	1990	309
328 2/8	49 6/8	49 1/8	48 1/8	8	9	Pons Island	QUE	Gary Reich	1987	310
328 2/8	42 2/8	43 3/8	49 5/8	13	8	Delay River	QUE	August S. Gray	1988	310
328 0/8	47 6/8	47 1/8	41 5/8	11	10	Big Island	QUE	Ralph Willits	1989	312
328 0/8	51 6/8	48 7/8	44 6/8	12	8	Melezes River	QUE	Peter L. Bucklin	1990	312
328 0/8	54 4/8	56 0/8	44 7/8	12	15	Maricourt Lake	QUE	Doug Kerska	1990	312
327 6/8	52 0/8	53 0/8	45 3/8	15	19	Schefferville	QUE	Irv Plotz	1981	315
327 6/8	49 3/8	48 5/8	48 6/8	14	17	Weymouth Inlet	QUE	David L. Stull	1989	315
327 5/8	43 0/8	44 4/8	45 3/8	11	18	LG 4	QUE	Stephen Kotz	1992	317
327 0/8	47 3/8	47 0/8	44 3/8	12	15	Lake Martine	QUE	Tom Nelson	1990	318
326 7/8	45 7/8	45 6/8	50 2/8	11	6	Schefferville	QUE	Joseph Strasser, Jr.	1988	319
326 6/8	53 6/8	54 3/8	44 0/8	8	10	Tunulik River	QUE	Ty Martin	1986	320
326 6/8	44 0/8	47 0/8	34 1/8	12	13	Delay River	QUE	Douglas Kerska	1988	320
326 2/8	46 1/8	45 1/8	32 7/8	13	15	Lake Leopard	QUE	Wes Seaver	1989	322
326 2/8	45 0/8	46 6/8	47 7/8	7	7	Schefferville	QUE	Jerry Parsons	1990	322
326 1/8	59 3/8	57 0/8	43 6/8	10	17	Ungava Region	QUE	Gary L. Snyder	1977	324
326 1/8	48 0/8	49 2/8	46 7/8	8	8	Delay River	QUE	Roger Gipple	1988	324
325 6/8	49 4/8	48 3/8	53 0/8	8	9	Delay River	QUE	Paul Converse	1991	326
325 3/8	45 3/8	47 5/8	48 4/8	9	7	Lac Louis	QUE	Alan J. Rhinerson	1991	327
325 1/8	60 1/8	60 5/8	49 3/8	7	4	Tunulik River	QUE	Ron Carpenter	1982	328
325 1/8	42 0/8	46 4/8	40 4/8	11	11	Lake Narcy	QUE	Kenny E. Leo	1988	328
324 5/8	51 4/8	53 4/8	44 3/8	13	15	George River	QUE	Emanuele Baron	1972	330
324 5/8	50 7/8	49 4/8	42 2/8	7	8	George River	QUE	Ray Daniels	1987	330
324 5/8	48 4/8	47 7/8	43 0/8	11	11	Ronald Lake	QUE	Timothy Silha	1992	330
324 4/8	48 7/8	48 0/8	34 1/8	12	12	Melezes River	QUE	Quinn Poll	1992	333
324 1/8	52 1/8	55 5/8	39 0/8	8	6	Caniaspiscau River	QUE	Larry Cross	1988	334
323 7/8	44 7/8	46 0/8	40 2/8	11	9	Lake Ageneav	QUE	Dan Bertalan	1990	335
323 4/8	44 6/8	44 7/8	46 7/8	16	10	LG4	QUE	Charles Moore	1992	336
323 3/8	44 4/8	43 1/8	37 6/8	19	22	De Pas & George River	QUE	Walter L. Seville	1971	337
323 3/8	56 2/8	52 5/8	39 7/8	12	14	Schefferville	QUE	Rick L. Remme	1988	337
323 3/8	42 2/8	41 3/8	42 2/8	10	11	Delay River	QUE	Robert Hermann	1989	337
323 1/8	45 0/8	47 0/8	40 2/8	15	11	Delay River	QUE	C. Eugene Jordan	1992	340
322 7/8	50 3/8	50 0/8	35 7/8	14	17	Lake Sabrina	QUE	Chuck Adams	1990	341
322 6/8	50 2/8	49 0/8	43 4/8	14	15	Fort Chimo	QUE	David E. Stepp	1990	342
322 6/8	46 5/8	45 6/8	45 4/8	12	10	Leaf River	QUE	Joseph Testerman	1991	342
322 4/8	39 1/8	40 7/8	35 4/8	12	13	Barbara's Lake	QUE	Michael L. Warner	1991	344
322 3/8	45 1/8	41 7/8	50 2/8	10	14	Lac Weeks	QUE	Ronald Arthur Schaefer	1990	345
321 6/8	50 6/8	46 0/8	47 4/8	12	12	Lake Otelnuk	QUE	Ms. Charlie White	1988	346
321 0/8	49 7/8	47 5/8	37 6/8	13	13	Lake Otelnuk	QUE	Ms. Charlie White	1988	347
320 7/8	49 4/8	50 3/8	34 5/8	13	11	Harold Lake	QUE	Don Davidson	1990	348
320 7/8	47 5/8	48 3/8	37 6/8	9	10	Maricourt Lake	QUE	Bryan Miller	1990	348
320 6/8	45 7/8	43 7/8	43 4/8	16	17	Lake Otelnuk	QUE	Bob Westerfield	1988	350

QUEBEC LABRADOR CARIBOU

SCORE	LENGTH OF MAIN BEAM R	L	INSIDE SPREAD	NUMBER OF POINTS R	L	AREA	STATE/ PROVINCE	HUNTER'S NAME	DATE	RANK
320 6/8	53 4/8	51 4/8	30 5/8	13	13	Maricourt Lake	QUE	Colburn Dick	1990	350
320 5/8	46 1/8	46 0/8	39 0/8	17	16	Fort Chimo	QUE	Mark Gies	1989	352
320 5/8	48 1/8	48 0/8	43 2/8	9	8	LG4	QUE	James E. McCloskey, Jr.	1991	352
320 3/8	46 7/8	47 2/8	41 7/8	12	11	Jack's Lake	QUE	Dennis Klemick	1989	354
320 2/8	51 2/8	50 1/8	44 4/8	11	9	Fort Chimo	QUE	Richard L. Smith	1990	355
320 2/8	48 2/8	49 1/8	40 5/8	15	14	Fort Chimo	QUE	Joseph D. Maddock	1990	355
320 0/8	46 5/8	50 1/8	37 2/8	10	11	Schefferville	QUE	Charles L. Buechel, Jr.	1987	357
320 0/8	53 1/8	51 2/8	45 6/8	9	10	Fort Chimo	QUE	Raymond Goff	1990	357
319 7/8	45 3/8	44 4/8	36 5/8	12	13	Schefferville	QUE	Christian S. Janusiewicz	1991	359
319 6/8	48 1/8	48 2/8	48 0/8	8	8	Tunulik River	QUE	Glenn St. Charles	1982	360
319 6/8	39 2/8	40 0/8	39 2/8	14	18	Delay River	QUE	Gerri Achtenberg	1987	360
319 5/8	54 0/8	53 0/8	46 2/8	13	11	Schefferville	QUE	Dennis Groebner	1981	362
319 4/8	46 1/8	43 7/8	44 3/8	10	12	Lac Montgenault	QUE	Richard Christman	1991	363
319 3/8	50 2/8	49 5/8	43 1/8	11	11	Weymouth Inlet	QUE	Scott Neuman	1991	364
318 6/8	47 6/8	48 7/8	45 0/8	9	9	Long Lake	QUE	Craig E. Garbrecht	1988	365
318 6/8	40 2/8	39 3/8	31 1/8	14	15	Martha's Lake	QUE	John E. Anderson	1992	365
318 5/8	48 3/8	48 0/8	37 2/8	11	10	Schefferville	QUE	Jeff Lindeman	1986	367
318 5/8	47 3/8	44 1/8	44 4/8	11	14	Delay River	QUE	Simon Harvey	1990	367
318 4/8	48 1/8	48 0/8	38 3/8	12	16	Lake Otelnuk	QUE	George W. Mullen, Jr.	1988	369
318 4/8	46 6/8	46 1/8	49 1/8	11	9	Caniapiscau River	QUE	Richard D. Mencl	1988	369
318 1/8	45 1/8	46 0/8	41 0/8	14	10	Lac Rigouville	QUE	Doug Clayton	1991	371
318 0/8	57 0/8	56 2/8	41 0/8	9	8	Ungava Bay	QUE	Greg Strait	1989	372
318 0/8	48 1/8	49 6/8	37 3/8	10	11	Delay River	QUE	Bob Mussey	1990	372
317 7/8	56 7/8	58 2/8	50 5/8	7	5	Nouveau	QUE	Richard Kling	1990	374
317 4/8	58 5/8	56 4/8	55 4/8	7	7	Tunulik River	QUE	Jack Joseph	1984	375
317 3/8	48 4/8	49 5/8	42 0/8	12	12	Pons Island	QUE	John Manarte	1986	376
316 4/8	48 7/8	51 1/8	31 4/8	12	14	Portage Lake	QUE	Mike Palmer	1990	377
316 3/8	43 4/8	44 4/8	45 4/8	9	10	LG 4	QUE	Wolf Gengaro	1992	378
316 1/8	48 1/8	47 3/8	38 7/8	10	13	George River	QUE	Michael Shaughnessy	1980	379
316 1/8	45 7/8	47 5/8	47 4/8	13	10	Leif Lake	QUE	Rick Simonson	1987	379
315 7/8	50 3/8	52 2/8	40 0/8	10	11	Harold Lake	QUE	Dave Brummond	1990	381
315 6/8	44 6/8	46 0/8	43 3/8	11	10	Ungava Bay	QUE	John M. McAteer	1986	382
315 6/8	50 5/8	47 6/8	41 4/8	9	14	Maricourt Lake	QUE	Bryan Miller	1990	382
315 5/8	42 1/8	41 5/8	38 0/8	15	14	Maricourt River	QUE	Mark T. Jacobson	1990	384
315 4/8	49 4/8	46 6/8	39 0/8	11	9	Martha's Lake	QUE	Steve Kiene	1992	385
315 3/8	48 1/8	46 3/8	59 6/8	13	9	Fort Chimo	QUE	David L. Butler	1988	386
315 3/8	43 6/8	47 0/8	35 1/8	9	11	Delay River	QUE	Richard V. McKeown	1990	386
315 1/8	46 2/8	47 4/8	37 2/8	14	14	Delay River	QUE	Robert L. Kampen	1989	388
314 7/8	50 6/8	51 2/8	44 4/8	5	10	George River	QUE	Stanley Skorch	1980	389
314 7/8	49 3/8	49 7/8	39 3/8	13	12	Schefferville	QUE	Tom Hlinka	1990	389
314 4/8	48 3/8	43 7/8	53 0/8	9	13	George River	QUE	Dean Farkas	1980	391
314 4/8	43 1/8	43 1/8	44 5/8	9	10	Delay River	QUE	Robert H. Pavlovic	1988	391
314 4/8	46 2/8	47 6/8	32 6/8	17	14	Lac Weeks	QUE	Ronald Arthur Schaefer	1990	391
314 3/8	50 0/8	52 6/8	35 0/8	10	15	Schefferville	QUE	Barry J. Blaskowski	1991	394
314 0/8	51 1/8	50 4/8	41 0/8	7	9	Audiepure Lake	QUE	Ryk Visscher	1983	395
314 0/8	47 7/8	47 6/8	42 0/8	19	11	Delay River	QUE	Jerry Laurino	1988	395
313 6/8	45 2/8	45 0/8	44 0/8	13	12	LG4	QUE	Stephen A. Kotz	1991	397
313 4/8	49 3/8	51 6/8	47 0/8	10	10	Delay River	QUE	Gordie Rieber	1990	398
313 3/8	49 0/8	49 6/8	50 2/8	10	11	Martha's Lake	QUE	Mark Buehrer	1992	399
312 7/8	48 2/8	47 1/8	50 0/8	10	10	Pothier River	QUE	Theodore Dzienis	1989	400
312 7/8	46 4/8	47 0/8	39 1/8	12	12	Maricourt River	QUE	Michael J. Churchill	1990	400
312 6/8	41 3/8	41 6/8	35 5/8	14	15	Schefferville	QUE	John Quinn	1990	402
312 5/8	45 7/8	46 6/8	38 1/8	12	10	Doreen Lake	QUE	Terry Krahn	1990	403
312 0/8	50 4/8	50 1/8	40 4/8	7	7	Rouge Mont	QUE	Dave Norman	1992	404
311 7/8	46 3/8	47 6/8	42 6/8	14	15	George River	QUE	Hayden Allen, Jr.	1980	405
311 6/8	44 3/8	47 7/8	51 3/8	12	16	De Pas & George River	QUE	William L. Winter	1974	406
311 6/8	47 0/8	49 4/8	40 0/8	11	11	Pons Island	QUE	Roger Balogh	1987	406
311 5/8	51 4/8	52 3/8	48 5/8	4	7	Fort Chimo	QUE	Jack Olson	1989	408
311 4/8	45 5/8	47 7/8	42 7/8	10	9	Delay River	QUE	M. R. James	1990	409
311 2/8	52 2/8	53 3/8	43 6/8	13	12	Doreen Lake	QUE	Nathan L. Andersohn	1990	410
311 0/8	45 0/8	47 4/8	44 4/8	9	14	Chateauguay River	QUE	Robert Lucius	1991	411
310 7/8	46 6/8	44 5/8	41 2/8	5	6	Schefferville	QUE	Elmer R. Luce, Jr.	1986	412
310 6/8	45 5/8	46 2/8	47 0/8	12	11	LG 4	QUE	Stephen Kotz	1992	413
310 5/8	45 6/8	44 5/8	42 0/8	11	10	Consigne Lake	QUE	Randall Eigenbrode	1990	414
309 7/8	49 3/8	46 4/8	40 3/8	13	12	Delay River	QUE	Roy Goodwin	1986	415
309 7/8	52 0/8	52 0/8	44 6/8	13	7	Ungava Area	QUE	Charles Eichelberger	1989	415
309 7/8	44 4/8	42 6/8	40 6/8	12	13	Dunphy Lake	QUE	Ed Lanske	1990	415
309 5/8	45 0/8	44 2/8	41 0/8	10	10	Tunulik River	QUE	Kenneth Bean	1982	418
309 5/8	44 5/8	47 3/8	32 2/8	15	13	Rigouville Lake	QUE	Raymond G. Fair	1991	418
309 4/8	50 1/8	50 2/8	40 5/8	9	9	Delay River	QUE	Peter Hartley	1989	420

Quebec Labrador Caribou

(Continued)

Score	Length of Main Beam R	L	Inside Spread	Number of Points R	L	Area	State/ Province	Hunter's Name	Date	Rank
309 3/8	54 7/8	56 1/8	41 6/8	13	11	George River	QUE	John 'Jack' Cordes	1981	421
309 2/8	35 3/8	35 4/8	32 4/8	15	14	Lake Sammy	QUE	Chuck Adams	1989	422
309 2/8	45 4/8	46 0/8	42 2/8	14	17	Imbault Lake	QUE	William A. Rusch	1991	422
309 0/8	44 2/8	44 2/8	36 6/8	9	10	Tunulik River	QUE	William R. Vanderhoef	1984	424
308 5/8	46 0/8	45 3/8	44 7/8	9	14	Otelnuk Lake	QUE	Randy Durushia	1989	425
308 5/8	40 2/8	40 2/8	31 0/8	12	13	Sir James Lake	QUE	Edd Clack	1992	425
308 4/8	54 2/8	51 7/8	47 6/8	10	9	DeLay River	QUE	Daniel "Boone" Bell	1990	427
308 2/8	44 2/8	44 4/8	39 2/8	12	15	Ungava Region	QUE	James Dobay	1974	428
308 2/8	47 6/8	46 0/8	38 3/8	9	9	Weymouth Inlet	QUE	Denise Laux	1986	428
308 1/8	40 6/8	41 3/8	39 0/8	14	16	Tunulik River	QUE	Tom Paluso	1988	430
308 0/8	51 7/8	52 2/8	40 5/8	8	8	Delay River	QUE	G. D. Malone	1988	431
307 6/8	49 0/8	46 5/8	38 4/8	11	12	Fort Chimo	QUE	James A. Fink	1990	432
307 4/8	40 4/8	39 5/8	50 2/8	12	8	Schefferville	QUE	Larry Cornett	1988	433
307 1/8	48 1/8	47 2/8	37 3/8	11	9	Sir James Lake	QUE	Ben G. Bishop	1990	434
306 7/8	41 5/8	44 1/8	30 2/8	9	9	Tunulik River	QUE	Kenneth G. Straub	1989	435
306 5/8	48 0/8	48 6/8	42 4/8	11	10	Fort Chimo	QUE	Kenneth M. Thompson	1990	436
306 2/8	42 1/8	42 5/8	43 0/8	10	12	Melezes River	QUE	G. Fred Asbell	1990	437
306 1/8	49 6/8	51 4/8	40 1/8	6	9	Maricourt Lake	QUE	Bruce Scheehle	1992	438
306 0/8	41 1/8	43 4/8	26 7/8	12	15	Schefferville	QUE	Burt Thompson, Jr.	1987	439
305 7/8	41 2/8	39 4/8	52 1/8	9	12	Schefferville	QUE	Darwin L. Damp	1988	440
305 7/8	45 7/8	44 1/8	46 6/8	12	13	Saglek Bay	LAB	Bruce R. Schoeneweis	1990	440
305 4/8	49 3/8	47 3/8	47 6/8	6	8	Weymouth Inlet	QUE	Denise Laux	1986	442
305 1/8	48 4/8	49 5/8	43 7/8	10	11	Fort Chimo	QUE	George R. Garman	1985	443
304 7/8	55 1/8	52 3/8	40 6/8	13	8	George River	QUE	Byron Knutson	1980	444
304 6/8	45 3/8	46 0/8	51 7/8	8	7	Delay River	QUE	Douglas Kerska	1988	445
304 6/8	51 6/8	53 4/8	44 0/8	7	7	Caniaspiscau River	QUE	Larry Cross	1988	445
304 6/8	51 0/8	36 3/8	38 6/8	16	12	Schefferville	QUE	Ron Sherer	1990	445
304 6/8	44 1/8	44 3/8	37 7/8	11	10	Maricourt Lake	QUE	Jim Leqve	1991	445
304 5/8	44 3/8	46 3/8	45 1/8	10	8	Martha's Lake	QUE	Jerry E. Burt	1992	449
304 3/8	41 7/8	46 0/8	44 2/8	15	14	Delay River	QUE	Simon Harvey	1990	450
304 3/8	50 4/8	49 3/8	35 4/8	9	12	Schefferville	QUE	Grady Brantley	1992	450
304 3/8	41 3/8	42 1/8	34 7/8	8	11	Delay River	QUE	John Zawaski	1992	450
303 7/8	45 3/8	43 3/8	48 6/8	8	8	Maricourt Lake	QUE	Jerry W. Huffaker	1990	453
303 5/8	47 4/8	47 0/8	48 3/8	10	9	George River	QUE	George A. Kearns	1985	454
303 5/8	48 2/8	53 2/8	38 2/8	12	13	16 Islands Lake	QUE	Kevin Parker	1990	454
303 4/8	38 4/8	37 2/8	28 5/8	18	18	Tunulik River	QUE	Larry Hoff	1984	456
303 4/8	46 2/8	46 0/8	35 4/8	14	13	Delay River	QUE	Chuck Williams	1990	456
303 3/8	37 4/8	40 1/8	32 2/8	16	18	Lake Briscan	QUE	John P. Renwick	1989	458
303 1/8	47 2/8	42 6/8	36 5/8	8	13	Consigne Lake	QUE	Jerry Leair	1990	459
302 0/8	44 0/8	43 2/8	43 6/8	13	17	Lake Nullualuk	QUE	William German	1992	460
301 6/8	43 5/8	44 4/8	43 0/8	12	13	Fort Chimo	QUE	Joanne D. Adams	1990	461
301 2/8	49 0/8	48 6/8	47 1/8	12	12	Serigny River	QUE	Edd Clack	1988	462
300 4/8	54 0/8	55 7/8	45 4/8	6	8	Martha's Lake	QUE	Gary Angell	1992	463
300 3/8	40 1/8	43 0/8	45 0/8	13	11	L. Sierra	QUE	John R. Ahrens	1990	464
300 1/8	44 1/8	44 0/8	35 7/8	7	8	Whiskey Lake	QUE	Ronald J. Watt	1986	465
300 1/8	41 4/8	42 0/8	29 5/8	13	13	LG4	QUE	Stephen A. Kotz	1991	465
300 0/8	45 3/8	50 2/8	54 3/8	6	8	Delay River	QUE	Chuck Williams	1990	467

World Record Woodland Caribou
Score: 345 2/8
Victoria River, Newfoundland - 1966
Hunter: Demsey Cape

WOODLAND CARIBOU

MINIMUM SCORE 220

Rangifer tarandus caribou
from Nova Scotia, New Brunswick,
and Newfoundland

SCORE	R MAIN BEAM L		INSIDE SPREAD	R POINTS L		AREA	STATE/ PROVINCE	HUNTER'S NAME	DATE	RANK
345 2/8	46 6/8	46 4/8	27 3/8	11	12	Victoria River	NFL	Dempsey Cape	1966	1
324 0/8	42 7/8	42 3/8	26 6/8	10	11	Sitdown Pond	NFL	Ed J. Bowser	1966	2
310 1/8	41 0/8	41 0/8	29 2/8	10	12	Millertown	NFL	Gerhart Huber	1966	3
287 4/8	35 0/8	34 1/8	27 6/8	9	10	Dashwood Pond	NFL	Kerry K. Kammer	1990	4
286 4/8	37 0/8	37 0/8	29 5/8	9	11	Rocky Pond	NFL	Chuck Adams	1988	5
276 7/8	42 3/8	43 0/8	25 2/8	10	9	King George IV Lake	NFL	Mark McCarty	1966	6
275 6/8	35 4/8	33 4/8	25 6/8	10	9	Alex Pond	NFL	Paul Locey	1988	7
274 7/8	38 5/8	39 4/8	29 0/8	8	8	Caribou Creek	NFL	Dan Bertalan	1992	8
272 1/8	33 2/8	33 0/8	25 2/8	13	10	Buchans Plateau	NFL	Eddie Smith	1988	9
270 6/8	33 4/8	33 6/8	34 2/8	9	10	Atikonak Lake	NFL	Dr. James L. Emerson	1973	10
269 1/8	37 1/8	37 4/8	23 4/8	15	13	Corner Brook	NFL	Al Reay	1980	11
267 0/8	35 4/8	34 2/8	22 7/8	8	7	Alex Pond	NFL	James Pike	1991	12
262 6/8	39 4/8	41 6/8	34 4/8	6	7	Buchans Plateau	NFL	Fred A. Turner	1984	13
260 3/8	35 2/8	35 3/8	27 5/8	9	11	Buchans Plateau	NFL	William R. Vanderhoef	1986	14
259 5/8	37 6/8	32 2/8	34 7/8	10	11	Buchans Plateau	NFL	John 'Jack' Cordes	1982	15
259 0/8	31 1/8	27 4/8	27 0/8	12	16	Saddler Pond	NFL	Stan Godfrey	1989	16
258 7/8	40 4/8	37 6/8	33 1/8	6	7	Lloyds River	NFL	Harold A. Hill	1964	17
258 5/8	33 6/8	33 0/8	25 6/8	10	9	Howley	NFL	Ken Mowerson	1989	18
258 1/8	36 7/8	33 6/8	25 4/8	10	11	Atikonak Lake	NFL	Bill L. Carlos	1972	19
253 7/8	37 4/8	35 5/8	32 1/8	10	8	Buchans Plateau	NFL	Steve D. Munier	1990	20
249 3/8	36 5/8	37 2/8	26 4/8	9	9	Millertown	NFL	Cliff Wiseman	1962	21
248 0/8	40 7/8	36 7/8	34 0/8	7	7	Sitdown Pond	NFL	Dr. Ed Bowser	1965	22
247 3/8	34 5/8	37 4/8	28 4/8	7	7	King George IV Lake	NFL	Bill Hirst	1966	23
246 2/8	32 4/8	29 0/8	27 0/8	10	9	Alex Pond	NFL	Darrin West	1991	24
243 6/8	34 6/8	34 6/8	27 7/8	7	6	Greys Island	NFL	Terry Krahn	1991	25
241 3/8	33 2/8	30 6/8	29 2/8	9	11	Buchans Plateau	NFL	Glenn Hisey	1982	26
241 2/8	33 2/8	34 6/8	25 1/8	11	11	Interior District	NFL	Bill Goff	1965	27
237 2/8	35 0/8	36 2/8	29 7/8	7	8	Saddler Pond	NFL	Carolyn Godfrey	1989	28
237 1/8	35 1/8	35 2/8	24 6/8	10	7	Buchans Plateau	NFL	Doug Strecker	1990	29
236 3/8	36 0/8	35 0/8	25 3/8	12	9	Princess Lake	NFL	John Musacchia	1967	30
233 2/8	38 0/8	37 0/8	27 5/8	7	4	Gull Lake	NFL	M. W. Bowser	1958	31
232 6/8	34 2/8	31 2/8	32 7/8	7	5	Millertown	NFL	Tom Taylor	1992	32
232 5/8	33 3/8	35 0/8	24 5/8	6	7	Deer Lake	NFL	Douglas L. Buchler	1984	33
232 4/8	35 5/8	34 7/8	26 7/8	6	6	Buchans Plateau	NFL	Terrence H. Estes	1984	34
227 7/8	36 1/8	33 0/8	27 1/8	10	9	Princess Lake	NFL	Ken Rapp	1966	35
225 4/8	34 2/8	34 5/8	27 6/8	7	8	Bruce's Pond	NFL	Randy Doyle	1990	36
225 0/8	38 0/8	40 3/8	25 1/8	5	8	Victoria River	NFL	Clarence Bowers, Jr.	1966	37
224 1/8	36 0/8	35 0/8	27 4/8	8	9	Lloyds River	NFL	Harold A. Hill	1965	38
221 0/8	32 6/8	30 2/8	27 2/8	11	8	Saddler Pond	NFL	Paul Locey	1982	39
220 2/8	37 6/8	40 7/8	24 0/8	7	14	Alex Pond	NFL	Dr. James J. Schubert	1980	40

World Record Cougar *(Tie)*

Score: 15 11/16	Score: 15 11/16	Score: 15 11/16
Idaho, County, Idaho - 1982	Idaho, County, Idaho - 1985	Ferry County, Washington - 1986
Hunter: Jerry J. James	Hunter: Mike McCall	Hunter: Bill Buckingham

Cougar *(Mountain Lion)*

MINIMUM SCORE 13 8/16

Felis concolor hippolestes

Score	Greatest Length	Greatest Width	Sex	Area	State/ Province	Hunter's Name	Date	Rank
15 11/16	9 2/16	6 9/16	M	Idaho County	ID	Jerry J. James	1982	1
15 11/16	9 4/16	6 7/16	M	Idaho County	ID	Mike McCall	1985	1
15 11/16	9 7/16	6 4/16	M	Ferry County	WA	Bill Buckingham	1986	1
15 10/16	9 0/16	6 10/16	M	Unit 5-5	BC	Harold J. Coult	1986	4
15 8/16	9 1/16	6 7/16	M	Lemhi County	ID	Doug Kittredge	1971	5
15 8/16	8 15/16	6 9/16	M	Clearwater County	ID	John R. Bridwell	1988	5
15 8/16	8 15/16	6 9/16	M	Gila County	AZ	Stephen D. Hornady	1991	5
15 7/16	9 2/16	6 5/16	M	Huerfano County	CO	J. D. Dodge	1971	8
15 7/16	9 0/16	6 7/16	M	Idaho County	ID	William Egner	1972	8
15 7/16	9 4/16	6 3/16	M	Sandoval County	NM	Tom David	1980	8
15 7/16	9 2/16	6 5/16	M	Rio Arriba County	NM	Dick Ray	1985	8
15 7/16	9 2/16	6 5/16	M	Uintah County	UT	John M Mc Ateer	1985	8
15 7/16	9 0/16	6 7/16	M	Idaho County	ID	Steven Anderson	1986	8
15 7/16	8 15/16	6 8/16	M	Ferry County	WA	John Peruchini	1989	8
15 7/16	9 8/16	5 15/16	M	Catron County	NM	Guy-Maurice Algier	1991	8
15 7/16	8 14/16	6 9/16	M	Shoshone County	ID	Eugene L. Lewis	1991	8
15 7/16	9 0/16	6 7/16	M	Clearwater County	ID	Dennis L. Butler	1992	8
15 6/16	9 4/16	6 2/16	M	Grand County	UT	Art Kragness	1969	18
15 6/16	8 11/16	6 11/16	M	Taos County	NM	George P. Mann	1981	18
15 6/16	9 2/16	6 4/16	M	Water Valley	ALB	Don Ferguson	1983	18
15 6/16	9 0/16	6 6/16	M	Idaho County	ID	Ralph L. Hatter	1987	18
15 5/16	8 15/16	6 6/16	M	Mesa County	CO	John Lamicq, Jr.	1969	22
15 5/16	8 15/16	6 6/16	M	Mineral County	MT	Dennis Moos	1976	22
15 5/16	8 15/16	6 6/16	M	Larimer County	CO	Glenn Schmidt	1976	22
15 5/16	8 13/16	6 8/16	M	Madison County	MT	Don Schaufler	1982	22
15 5/16	9 0/16	6 5/16	M	Idaho County	ID	A. M. Oakes, Jr.	1985	22
15 5/16	9 2/16	6 3/16	M	Rio Blanco County	CO	Rob Raley	1985	22
15 5/16	9 0/16	6 5/16	M	Clearwater County	ID	Daniel J. Greve	1985	22
15 5/16	9 0/16	6 5/16	M	Idaho County	ID	Drexel Schilling	1987	22
15 5/16	9 1/16	6 4/16	M	Clearwater County	ID	Rudy Marmelo, Jr.	1990	22
15 5/16	9 0/16	6 5/16	M	Lindsey Lake	BC	Harvey J. Surina	1991	22
15 4/16	9 0/16	6 4/16	M	Gila County	AZ	Dr. James L. Smith	1958	32
15 4/16	8 15/16	6 5/16	M	Ogden County	UT	Royce Ross	1971	32
15 4/16	9 0/16	6 4/16	M	Uintah County	UT	Albert L. Farace	1986	32
15 4/16	9 2/16	6 2/16	M	San Juan County	UT	Diane Snyder	1986	32
15 4/16	9 0/16	6 4/16	M	Madison County	MT	Pat Connell	1986	32
15 4/16	8 14/16	6 6/16	M	Clearwater County	ID	Elwood Schultz	1986	32
15 4/16	9 1/16	6 3/16	M	San Miguel County	CO	G. Merrill Jones	1987	32
15 4/16	9 0/16	6 4/16	M	Porcupine Hills	ALB	John Visscher	1990	32
15 3/16	8 13/16	6 6/16	M	Ventura County	CA	Warren C. Johnston	1953	40
15 3/16	9 0/16	6 3/16	M	Fremont County	CO	Art Heinze	1976	40
15 3/16	8 14/16	6 5/16	M	Douglas County	CO	Donald R. Looper	1977	40
15 3/16	8 13/16	6 6/16	M	Rio Arriba County	NM	Anderson Bakewell, S.J.	1978	40
15 3/16	8 4/16	6 15/16	M	Cassia County	ID	Ronald C. Ward	1984	40
15 3/16	8 13/16	6 6/16	M	Clallam County	WA	Ron W. Cram	1984	40
15 3/16	8 14/16	6 5/16	M	Huerfano County	CO	Bob Sigman	1987	40
15 3/16	8 14/16	6 5/16	M	Clearwater County	ID	Mike T. McCain	1988	40
15 3/16	8 14/16	6 5/16	M	Lincoln County	MT	Jon Greeno Clark	1989	40
15 3/16	9 1/16	6 2/16	M	Ravalli County	MT	Mario Locatelli	1990	40
15 3/16	9 2/16	6 1/16	M	Archuleta County	CO	Charles T. Ames	1991	40
15 3/16	8 15/16	6 4/16	M	Idaho County	ID	Steve B. Schilling	1992	40
15 3/16	8 15/16	6 4/16	M	Daggett County	UT	John Richardson	1992	40
15 2/16	8 15/16	6 3/16	M	Rio Blanco County	CO	Leonard Cardinale	1963	53
15 2/16	9 0/16	6 2/16	M	Grand County	UT	Richard Oakleaf	1967	53
15 2/16	8 12/16	6 6/16	M	Flathead County	MT	Jerry Almos	1971	53
15 2/16	8 14/16	6 4/16	M	Wallowa County	OR	Terrell Buchanan	1973	53
15 2/16	9 0/16	6 2/16	M	Utah County	UT	Max F. Park	1975	53
15 2/16	8 14/16	6 4/16	M	Sanders County	MT	Conrad Anderson	1984	53
15 2/16	8 14/16	6 4/16	M	Meagher County	MT	Gene Clark	1985	53
15 2/16	8 12/16	6 6/16	M	Teton County	WY	Craig Richardson	1986	53
15 2/16	8 14/16	6 4/16	M	Wallowa County	OR	Thomas C. Ashcroft	1986	53
15 2/16	8 14/16	6 4/16	M	Daggett County	UT	Franco DiPietro	1987	53
15 2/16	8 14/16	6 4/16	M	Conejos County	CO	Wayne Miller	1987	53
15 2/16	9 0/16	6 2/16	M	Mesa County	CO	Frank P. Alameno	1987	53
15 2/16	8 15/16	6 3/16	M	Clearwater County	ID	Michael J. Kennedy	1987	53
15 2/16	8 13/16	6 5/16	M	Pincher Creek	ALB	Duane B. Schultz	1988	53
15 2/16	8 12/16	6 6/16	M	Iron County	UT	Bob Spina	1989	53
15 2/16	8 15/16	6 3/16	M	Park County	CO	Jack P. Van Vianen	1990	53
15 2/16	8 13/16	6 5/16	M	Shoshone County	ID	Pat D. Jerald	1991	53
15 1/16	8 13/16	6 4/16	M	Iron County	UT	William P. Mastrangel	1964	70

162

COUGAR (*Mountain Lion*)

MINIMUM SCORE 13 8/16

(Continued)

SCORE	GREATEST LENGTH	GREATEST WIDTH	SEX	AREA	STATE/ PROVINCE	HUNTER'S NAME	DATE	RANK
15 1/16	8 12/16	6 5/16	M	Nez Perce County	ID	Pete Baughman, Jr.	1979	70
15 1/16	8 15/16	6 2/16	M	Rio Arriba County	NM	Joe Strasser, Jr.	1980	70
15 1/16	8 13/16	6 4/16	M	Archuleta County	CO	Judd Cooney	1982	70
15 1/16	9 1/16	6 0/16	M	Lincoln County	MT	Gary C. Cargill	1986	70
15 1/16	8 15/16	6 2/16	M	Clearwater County	ID	Charles "Smitty" Smith	1987	70
15 1/16	8 11/16	6 6/16	M	Sundre	ALB	Fred Houtstra	1987	70
15 1/16	9 1/16	6 0/16	M	Valley County	ID	Douglas L. Petty	1987	70
15 1/16	8 14/16	6 3/16	M	Ouray County	CO	Steven A. Rider	1989	70
15 1/16	9 0/16	6 1/16	M	Millard County	UT	Edwin A. Lewis	1990	70
15 1/16	8 14/16	6 3/16	M	Rio Blanco County	CO	Dr. Gerald L. Dowling	1990	70
15 1/16	9 0/16	6 1/16	M	Taos County	NM	Bill Porteous	1990	70
15 1/16	8 15/16	6 2/16	M	Mineral County	MT	Gerg Balzum	1990	70
15 1/16	8 12/16	6 5/16	M	Eagle County	CO	Richard E. Davis	1990	70
15 0/16	8 11/16	6 5/16	M	Elko County	NV	Earl Dudley	1959	84
15 0/16	8 13/16	6 3/16	M	Utah County	UT	Richard C. Smith	1968	84
15 0/16	8 11/16	6 5/16	M	Mizzezula Mtns.	BC	Bengt G. Bjalme	1969	84
15 0/16	8 12/16	6 4/16	M	Columbia Lake	BC	Ray Lundstrom	1979	84
15 0/16	8 14/16	6 2/16	M	Madison County	MT	George A. Dieruf	1980	84
15 0/16	8 12/16	6 4/16	M	Lemhi County	ID	Roy Auwen	1981	84
15 0/16	8 11/16	6 5/16	M	Sandoval County	NM	Ernest C. Torres	1981	84
15 0/16	8 11/16	6 5/16	M	Rio Arriba County	NM	Mike Ray	1982	84
15 0/16	8 11/16	6 5/16	M	Mineral County	MT	Grover L. Hedrick	1983	84
15 0/16	8 10/16	6 6/16	M	Sanders County	MT	Joe Schaefer	1984	84
15 0/16	8 10/16	6 6/16	M	Wallowa County	OR	Chuck Warner	1985	84
15 0/16	9 0/16	6 0/16	M	Rio Grande County	CO	Richard J. Dugas	1986	84
15 0/16	8 12/16	6 4/16	M	San Juan County	NM	Richard M. Young, Jr.	1987	84
15 0/16	8 10/16	6 6/16	M	Sanpete County	UT	Craig Adams	1988	84
15 0/16	9 0/16	6 0/16	M	Elmore County	ID	Ed Strayhorn	1989	84
15 0/16	8 14/16	6 2/16	M	Rio Arriba County	NM	Robert J. Seeds	1989	84
15 0/16	8 13/16	6 3/16	M	Pillar Lake	BC	Kent Michie/TerryWasylys	1989	84
15 0/16	8 12/16	6 4/16	M	Cache County	UT	Gino Giannetti	1990	84
15 0/16	8 14/16	6 2/16	M	Carbon County	UT	Roy Wheeler, Jr.	1990	84
15 0/16	8 12/16	6 4/16	M	Camas County	ID	Andy Moore	1990	84
15 0/16	8 12/16	6 4/16	M	Shoshone County	ID	Buster Karrer	1991	84
15 0/16	8 11/16	6 5/16	M	Fergus County	MT	Chuck Taylor	1991	84
15 0/16	8 14/16	6 2/16	M	Garfield County	UT	Gregory Nixon	1992	84
14 15/16	8 12/16	6 3/16	M	Lincoln County	MT	Allen Apling	1959	107
14 15/16	8 11/16	6 4/16	M	Boundary County	ID	Rick Furniss	1968	107
14 15/16	8 14/16	6 1/16	M	Rio Blanco County	CO	Jack Pawlak	1971	107
14 15/16	8 13/16	6 2/16	M	Rio Blanco County	CO	Stanley R. Winslow	1971	107
14 15/16	8 14/16	6 1/16	M	Carbon County	UT	Larry Wright	1975	107
14 15/16	8 11/16	6 4/16	M	Idaho County	ID	Dick Gulman	1976	107
14 15/16	8 12/16	6 3/16	M	Piute County	UT	Douglas Wagner	1976	107
14 15/16	8 11/16	6 4/16	M	Deer Lodge County	MT	Scott Koelzer	1979	107
14 15/16	8 15/16	6 0/16	M	Montezuma County	CO	Roy Keefer	1984	107
14 15/16	8 14/16	6 1/16	M	Cascade County	MT	Charles A. Vande Hei	1984	107
14 15/16	8 13/16	6 2/16	M	Sevier County	UT	Chuck Morger	1988	107
14 15/16	8 11/16	6 4/16	M	Park County	MT	Patrick Gilligan	1988	107
14 15/16	8 13/16	6 2/16	M	Ouray County	CO	Doug McCauley	1988	107
14 15/16	8 14/16	6 1/16	M	Garfield County	CO	Bruce R. Schoeneweis	1989	107
14 15/16	8 13/16	6 2/16	M	Bear Lake County	ID	Rick Berghelm	1990	107
14 15/16	8 12/16	6 3/16	M	Missoula County	MT	Mike Miller	1990	107
14 15/16	8 12/16	6 3/16	M	San Miguel County	CO	Monroe A. Hare	1991	107
14 15/16	8 12/16	6 3/16	M	Idaho County	ID	Mark Jacobson	1991	107
14 15/16	8 12/16	6 3/16	M	Missoula County	MT	Kenneth B. Scobie	1991	107
14 14/16	8 14/16	6 0/16	M	Lincoln County	MT	Dr. B. L. Lundberg	1958	126
14 14/16	8 11/16	6 3/16	M	Flathead County	MT	Jack Whitney	1967	126
14 14/16	8 10/16	6 4/16	M	Lemhi County	ID	Ray Torrey	1969	126
14 14/16	8 10/16	6 4/16	M	Granite County	MT	John Lawler	1972	126
14 14/16	8 13/16	6 1/16	M	Elmore County	ID	Dan F. Hackney	1973	126
14 14/16	8 15/16	5 15/16	M	Lemhi County	ID	Jim Dougherty	1980	126
14 14/16	8 11/16	6 3/16	M	Utah County	UT	Kelly R. Clements	1981	126
14 14/16	8 12/16	6 2/16	M	Lemhi County	ID	Jay Meyers	1982	126
14 14/16	8 12/16	6 2/16	M	Iron County	UT	Craig R. White	1983	126
14 14/16	8 12/16	6 2/16	M	Montezuma County	CO	Ms. Charlie White	1983	126
14 14/16	8 12/16	6 2/16	M	Madison County	MT	Cecil I. Tharp	1984	126
14 14/16	8 14/16	6 0/16	M	Rio Blanco County	CO	Calvin Farner	1986	126
14 14/16	8 10/16	6 4/16	M	Flathead County	MT	Bruce Whitaker	1988	126
14 14/16	8 13/16	6 1/16	M	Utah County	UT	Daniel M. Taylor	1989	126
14 14/16	8 13/16	6 1/16	M	Clearwater County	ID	Reva Anne Hyde	1990	126

163

SCORE	GREATEST LENGTH	GREATEST WIDTH	SEX	AREA	STATE/PROVINCE	HUNTER'S NAME	DATE	RANK
14 14/16	8 11/16	6 3/16	M	Grand County	UT	Joseph A. Segaria	1991	126
14 14/16	8 13/16	6 1/16	M	North Fork	ALB	Victor Lawson	1991	126
14 13/16	8 11/16	6 2/16	M	Chelan County	WA	Dr. R. Congdon	1951	143
14 13/16	8 11/16	6 2/16	M	Ferry County	WA	R. O. Hilderbrant	1965	143
14 13/16	8 12/16	6 1/16	F	Duchesne County	UT	Larry Jones	1967	143
14 13/16	8 13/16	6 0/16	M	Garfield County	CO	Albert L. Heise	1971	143
14 13/16	8 13/16	6 0/16	M	Chaffee County	CO	Phillip B. Grable	1973	143
14 13/16	8 10/16	6 3/16	M	Huerfano County	CO	William F. Eikleberry	1974	143
14 13/16	8 12/16	6 1/16	M	Emery County	UT	Rex Peterson	1975	143
14 13/16	8 11/16	6 2/16	M	Uintah County	UT	Ronald D. Shank	1976	143
14 13/16	8 12/16	6 1/16	M	Warner	BC	John 'Jack' Cordes	1977	143
14 13/16	8 10/16	6 3/16	M	Stevens County	WA	Tim C. Boyd	1979	143
14 13/16	8 10/16	6 3/16	M	Elmore County	ID	Dr. Robert T. Laughery	1979	143
14 13/16	8 14/16	5 15/16	M	Mesa County	CO	Jim R. Lewis	1981	143
14 13/16	8 13/16	6 0/16	M	Idaho County	ID	Ray Keenan	1982	143
14 13/16	8 12/16	6 1/16	M	Moffat County	CO	John A. Lee	1982	143
14 13/16	8 11/16	6 2/16	M	McGuire Creek	BC	William Morley	1983	143
14 13/16	8 12/16	6 1/16	M	Sanders County	MT	Gil Gilbertson	1984	143
14 13/16	8 11/16	6 2/16	M	San Miguel County	CO	David E. Smith	1985	143
14 13/16	8 12/16	6 1/16	M	Albany County	WY	R.D. Keeler, D.C.	1985	143
14 13/16	8 13/16	6 0/16	M	Camas County	ID	Larry R. Newton	1987	143
14 13/16	8 11/16	6 2/16	M	Fish Creek	ALB	Ken Maier	1987	143
14 13/16	8 9/16	6 4/16	M	Montezuma County	CO	Richard Kimball	1987	143
14 13/16	8 11/16	6 2/16	M	Clearwater County	ID	Thomas A. Kayser	1988	143
14 13/16	8 11/16	6 2/16	M	Clearwater County	ID	Ralph Albright	1989	143
14 13/16	8 12/16	6 1/16	M	Emery County	UT	Sam Raby	1989	143
14 13/16	8 12/16	6 1/16	M	Dolores County	CO	Robert R. Hoffa, Jr.	1990	143
14 13/16	8 10/16	6 3/16	M	Black Mountain	ALB	Udo Kerber	1991	143
14 13/16	8 10/16	6 3/16	M	Elko	BC	Gordon Mailey	1991	143
14 13/16	8 11/16	6 2/16	M	Carbon County	UT	Tracy Jacobsen	1992	143
14 13/16	8 13/16	6 0/16	M	Archuleta County	CO	Sam B. Ray	1992	143
14 12/16	8 14/16	5 14/16	M	Chelan County	WA	Dr. R. Congdon	1952	172
14 12/16	8 12/16	6 0/16	M	Clallam County	WA	Lloyd Beebe	1953	172
14 12/16	8 11/16	6 3/16	M	Rio Blanco County	CO	LeRoy Wood	1965	172
14 12/16	8 12/16	6 0/16	M		CO	Clyde Hector	1967	172
14 12/16	8 13/16	5 15/16	M	Garfield County	UT	Harold Boyack	1968	172
14 12/16	8 11/16	6 1/16	M	Valley County	ID	John Buford Reese	1976	172
14 12/16	8 10/16	6 2/16	M	Maguire Creek	BC	William Morley	1979	172
14 12/16	8 10/16	6 2/16	M	Boulder County	CO	Doug Beck	1984	172
14 12/16	8 10/16	6 2/16	M	Larimer County	CO	Jim Johnson	1985	172
14 12/16	8 14/16	5 14/16	M	Moffat County	CO	Michael B. Moline	1985	172
14 12/16	8 11/16	6 1/16	M	Cache County	UT	Ed Lawlor	1985	172
14 12/16	8 9/16	6 3/16	M	Madison County	MT	Ken Hoehn	1985	172
14 12/16	9 0/16	5 12/16	M	Custer County	CO	David Waldrop	1986	172
14 12/16	8 12/16	6 0/16	M	Emery County	UT	Ricky Schroder	1986	172
14 12/16	8 11/16	6 1/16	M	Rio Arriba County	NM	Robert John Seeds	1988	172
14 12/16	8 11/16	6 1/16	M	Utah County	UT	Blake A. Ryan	1988	172
14 12/16	8 12/16	6 0/16	M	Saguache County	CO	Mark Wuerthle	1988	172
14 12/16	8 10/16	6 2/16	M	Wallowa County	OR	Paul Turcke	1988	172
14 12/16	8 10/16	6 2/16	M	Saguache County	CO	Roger Maurice Tyler	1989	172
14 12/16	8 11/16	6 1/16	M	Flathead County	MT	Gary A. Crowe	1989	172
14 12/16	8 10/16	6 2/16	M	Mesa County	CO	Kerry Kammer	1990	172
14 12/16	8 10/16	6 2/16	M	Sevier County	UT	James Schade	1991	172
14 12/16	8 13/16	5 15/16	M	Rio Blanco County	CO	Ross L. Talbott	1991	172
14 12/16	8 13/16	5 15/16	M	Elk River	BC	Doug Scott	1991	172
14 12/16	8 11/16	6 1/16	M	Duchesne County	UT	Kent E. Smith	1992	172
14 12/16	8 9/16	6 3/16	M	Lewis & Clark County	MT	Mike Knapstad	1992	172
14 12/16	8 10/16	6 2/16	M	Nakasp	BC	Edwin L. DeYoung	1992	172
14 12/16	8 11/16	6 1/16	M	Kootenay River	BC	Brian Schuck	1992	172
14 12/16	8 11/16	6 1/16	M	Lincoln County	NV	Stephen L. Geller	1992	172
14 11/16	8 10/16	6 1/16	M	Sundre	ALB	Tom Decker	1966	201
14 11/16	8 8/16	6 3/16	M	Custer County	ID	Ralph V. Pehrson	1969	201
14 11/16	8 9/16	6 2/16	M	Boise County	ID	Harlow D. Austad	1971	201
14 11/16	8 8/16	6 3/16	M	Kettle River	BC	Irvin Plotz	1976	201
14 11/16	8 12/16	5 15/16	M	Lincoln County	MT	Ronald J. Wade	1976	201
14 11/16	8 10/16	6 1/16	M	Garfield County	UT	Bradford L. Sheltrown	1977	201
14 11/16	8 10/16	6 1/16	M	Middle Fork	ID	Robert Frank	1978	201
14 11/16	8 10/16	6 1/16	M	Flathead County	MT	Dr. James J. Shubert	1978	201
14 11/16	8 14/16	5 13/16	M	Custer County	CO	Philip Stegenga	1979	201
14 11/16	8 12/16	5 15/16	M	Columbia County	WA	John Wahl	1979	201

COUGAR (*Mountain Lion*)

(Continued)

MINIMUM SCORE 13 8/16

SCORE	GREATEST LENGTH	GREATEST WIDTH	SEX	AREA	STATE/ PROVINCE	HUNTER'S NAME	DATE	RANK
14 11/16	8 9/16	6 2/16	M	Ravalli County	MT	Bill Mitchell	1980	201
14 11/16	8 10/16	6 1/16	M	San Miguel County	CO	Judd Cooney	1981	201
14 11/16	8 12/16	5 15/16	M	Utah County	UT	Fred Tarran	1982	201
14 11/16	8 8/16	6 3/16	M	Chaffee County	CO	Reggie Spiegelberg	1983	201
14 11/16	8 10/16	6 1/16	M	Washakie County	WY	Nelson Scherrer	1986	201
14 11/16	8 7/16	6 4/16	M	Socorro County	NM	Chuck Sherwin	1986	201
14 11/16	8 10/16	6 0/16	M	Montezuma County	CO	Carla D. Coval	1987	201
14 11/16	8 7/16	6 4/16	M	Elko County	NV	Robert Pyne	1987	201
14 11/16	8 12/16	5 15/16	M	Owyhee County	ID	Gladwin F. Mills	1988	201
14 11/16	8 11/16	6 0/16	M	Valley County	ID	Tom Augustine	1988	201
14 11/16	8 10/16	6 1/16	M	Washakie County	WY	Ron Books	1989	201
14 11/16	8 12/16	5 15/16	M	Teton County	WY	Joseph P. Furlong	1989	201
14 11/16	8 10/16	6 1/16	M	Park County	MT	Patrick Gilligan	1989	201
14 11/16	8 12/16	5 15/16	M	Lemhi County	ID	Randy Lee Cooley	1989	201
14 11/16	8 12/16	5 15/16	M	Montezuma County	CO	Phil M. Elmore	1990	201
14 11/16	8 12/16	5 15/16	M	Humboldt County	NV	Dean Knoles	1990	201
14 11/16	8 8/16	6 3/16	M	Clearwater County	ID	Thomas Storr	1990	201
14 11/16	8 12/16	5 15/16	M	Lemhi County	ID	Bill Connors	1990	201
14 11/16	8 10/16	6 1/16	M	San Juan County	UT	Aaron Bronson	1991	201
14 11/16	8 12/16	5 15/16	M	Coconino County	AZ	George N. Davies	1991	201
14 10/16	8 10/16	6 0/16	M	Lincoln County	MT	Dr. Lowell L. Eddy	1967	231
14 10/16	8 10/16	6 0/16	M	Idaho County	ID	C. Bruce Peeples, Jr.	1970	231
14 10/16	8 9/16	6 1/16	M	Carbon County	UT	Paul E. Nottingham	1972	231
14 10/16	8 8/16	6 2/16	M	Rio Blanco County	CO	Paul Janke	1976	231
14 10/16	8 10/16	6 0/16	M	Flathead County	MT	Jerry Karsky	1976	231
14 10/16	8 10/16	6 0/16	M	Pincher Creek	ALB	Theo Mitchell	1977	231
14 10/16	8 8/16	6 2/16	M	Madison County	MT	Don Schaufler	1977	231
14 10/16	8 10/16	6 0/16	M	Sevier County	UT	Harold Hugelen	1979	231
14 10/16	8 10/16	6 0/16	M	Fremont County	CO	Pete J. Santi	1979	231
14 10/16	8 11/16	5 15/16	M	Las Animas County	CO	Glenn R. Kuklick	1980	231
14 10/16	8 9/16	6 1/16	M	Elmore County	ID	L. Dean Goodner	1981	231
14 10/16	8 10/16	6 0/16	M	Fremont County	CO	Johnny J. Lama	1981	231
14 10/16	8 13/16	5 13/16	M	Fremont County	CO	Carolyn E. Lama	1981	231
14 10/16	8 10/16	6 0/16	M	Carbon County	UT	Claude A. Flippin	1982	231
14 10/16	8 8/16	6 2/16	M	Sanders County	MT	Scott Lennard	1982	231
14 10/16	8 9/16	6 1/16	M	Box Elder County	UT	Jerry Mason	1982	231
14 10/16	8 13/16	5 13/16	M	San Miguel County	CO	James Yuds	1982	231
14 10/16	8 10/16	6 0/16	M	Montezuma County	CO	Mike Morgan	1983	231
14 10/16	8 10/16	6 0/16	M	Piute County	UT	James C. Hicks	1983	231
14 10/16	8 15/16	5 11/16	M	Chaffee County	CO	Tom Bowman	1983	231
14 10/16	8 9/16	6 1/16	M	San Juan County	NM	Gary Weber	1984	231
14 10/16	8 9/16	6 1/16	M	Douglas County	NV	Kirk Westervelt	1986	231
14 10/16	8 8/16	6 2/16	M	Flathead County	MT	Dyrk Eddie	1986	231
14 10/16	8 9/16	6 1/16	M	Montrose County	CO	David Ernest Nesler	1987	231
14 10/16	8 11/16	5 15/16	M	Sevier County	UT	Kelly Poulsen	1987	231
14 10/16	8 13/16	5 13/16	M	Alamosa County	CO	Tim Walters	1987	231
14 10/16	8 10/16	6 0/16	M	Owyhee County	ID	Richard Fritz	1988	231
14 10/16	8 9/16	6 1/16	M	Nye County	NV	Arrah C. Curry	1988	231
14 10/16	8 10/16	6 0/16	M	Carbon County	UT	Dennis G. McElvain	1988	231
14 10/16	8 9/16	6 1/16	M	Gilpin County	CO	Garry V. Woodman	1988	231
14 10/16	8 12/16	5 14/16	M	Montezuma County	CO	Steven J. Vittetow	1989	231
14 10/16	8 9/16	6 1/16	M	Wheatland County	MT	Albert W. Winter	1989	231
14 10/16	8 10/16	6 0/16	M	Umatilla County	OR	Javier Garcia	1989	231
14 10/16	8 10/16	6 0/16	M	Judith Basin County	MT	John Rosey Roseland	1989	231
14 10/16	8 7/16	6 3/16	M	Lander County	NV	Jack Dykstra	1990	231
14 10/16	8 11/16	5 15/16	M	Swan Lake	ALB	Dave Gerber	1990	231
14 10/16	8 10/16	6 0/16	M	Arrow Lake	BC	Jim Ryan	1990	231
14 10/16	8 10/16	6 0/16	M	Missoula County	MT	Monty Moravec	1990	231
14 10/16	8 12/16	5 14/16	M	Carbon County	UT	Paul Martinez	1991	231
14 10/16	8 12/16	5 14/16	M	Kane County	UT	Glen C. Ames	1991	231
14 10/16	8 9/16	6 1/16	M	Morgan County	UT	Brian Dam	1992	231
14 9/16	8 5/16	6 4/16	M	Gila County	AZ	Ben Pearson	1958	272
14 9/16	8 10/16	5 15/16	M	Idaho County	ID	Keith N. Johnson	1966	272
14 9/16	8 8/16	6 1/16	M	Grand County	UT	Henry 'Hank' Frey	1974	272
14 9/16	8 8/16	6 1/16	M	Lemhi County	ID	Richard E. Vail	1974	272
14 9/16	8 8/16	6 1/16	M	Sandoval County	NM	John W. Rose	1979	272
14 9/16	8 11/16	5 14/16	M	Garfield County	UT	Al Schweitzer	1979	272
14 9/16	8 8/16	6 1/16	M	San Miguel County	NM	Richard McClain	1980	272
14 9/16	8 9/16	6 0/16	M	Jefferson County	CO	Lee Veldhouse	1984	272
14 9/16	8 6/16	6 3/16	M	Idaho County	ID	LeRoy West	1984	272

COUGAR (*Mountain Lion*)

(*Continued*)

SCORE	GREATEST LENGTH	GREATEST WIDTH	SEX	AREA	STATE/ PROVINCE	HUNTER'S NAME	DATE	RANK
14 9/16	8 7/16	6 2/16	M	Elmore County	ID	Susan D. Sherer	1984	272
14 9/16	8 10/16	5 15/16	M	Rio Blanco County	CO	Don Waechtler	1984	272
14 9/16	8 9/16	6 0/16	M	Douglas County	CO	Wayne Kraft	1986	272
14 9/16	8 9/16	6 0/16	F	Wheatland County	MT	Jim Bouchard	1986	272
14 9/16	8 10/16	5 15/16	M	Fremont County	CO	Bill Goodspeed	1986	272
14 9/16	8 10/16	5 15/16	M	Clearwater County	ID	Jeffrey S. Stevens	1986	272
14 9/16	8 9/16	6 0/16	M	Asotin County	WA	Bill Meyers, Jr.	1987	272
14 9/16	8 9/16	6 0/16	M	Grand County	UT	Wes Walton	1987	272
14 9/16	8 10/16	5 15/16	M	Barnes Lake	BC	Kenneth Arthur Brown	1988	272
14 9/16	8 11/16	5 14/16	M	Chaffee County	CO	David Douty	1988	272
14 9/16	8 8/16	6 1/16	M	Jefferson County	CO	Steve Fausel	1989	272
14 9/16	8 10/16	5 15/16	M	Kane County	UT	Jeff Buck	1989	272
14 9/16	8 9/16	6 0/16	M	Owyhee County	ID	Bernard Langhorne	1990	272
14 9/16	8 10/16	5 15/16	M	Sanpete County	UT	Larry Mathis	1990	272
14 9/16	8 9/16	6 0/16	M	Duchesne County	UT	Don Keady	1991	272
14 9/16	8 8/16	6 1/16	M	Madison County	MT	Fred Richter	1991	272
14 9/16	8 9/16	6 0/16	M	Sanders County	MT	William A. Kaminski	1991	272
14 9/16	8 10/16	5 15/16	M	Valley County	ID	Bob Dawson	1991	272
14 9/16	8 9/16	6 0/16	M	Catron County	NM	Dwight E. Moser	1992	272
14 9/16	8 10/16	5 15/16	M	Water Valley	ALB	Steve Ouwerkerk	1992	272
14 8/16	8 9/16	5 15/16	F	Latah County	ID	Charles Kelso	1965	301
14 8/16	8 8/16	6 0/16	M	Ventura County	CA	Betty Gulman	1967	301
14 8/16	8 10/16	5 14/16	M	Catron County	NM	Ed Schaub	1970	301
14 8/16	8 8/16	6 0/16	M	Weber County	UT	Norm Goodwin	1971	301
14 8/16	8 9/16	5 15/16	M	Lemhi County	ID	Dr. Henry C. McDonald	1971	301
14 8/16	8 9/16	5 15/16	M	Emery County	UT	Terry Molneux	1972	301
14 8/16	8 9/16	5 15/16	M	Kane County	UT	Charles F. Maloney, Jr.	1973	301
14 8/16	8 6/16	6 2/16	M	Lincoln County	MT	Jerry Brown	1975	301
14 8/16	8 6/16	6 2/16	M	Duchesne County	UT	Roland Mantzke	1976	301
14 8/16	8 10/16	5 14/16	M	Elmore County	ID	Ronald L. Sherer	1979	301
14 8/16	8 9/16	5 15/16	M	Boise County	ID	Richard C. Nichols	1981	301
14 8/16	8 12/16	5 12/16	M	Saguache County	CO	J. Keith Chastain	1982	301
14 8/16	8 7/16	6 1/16	M	Utah County	UT	Dell J. Christensen	1982	301
14 8/16	8 8/16	6 0/16	M	Eagle County	CO	Stephen W. Nottingham	1982	301
14 8/16	8 8/16	6 0/16	M	Sheep River	ALB	Bob Toothill	1984	301
14 8/16	8 10/16	5 14/16	M	Grand County	UT	Harold Lee Schuerman	1984	301
14 8/16	8 10/16	5 14/16	M	Washoe County	NV	Jerry Pennington	1984	301
14 8/16	8 8/16	6 0/16	M	Garfield County	CO	Douglas Starks	1984	301
14 8/16	8 10/16	5 14/16	M	Union County	OR	Ken Richter	1984	301
14 8/16	8 9/16	5 15/16	M	Archuleta County	CO	Howard Payne	1985	301
14 8/16	8 7/16	6 1/16	M	Idaho County	ID	William A.S. Hever, Sr.	1985	301
14 8/16	8 9/16	5 15/16	M	Fremont County	CO	Oney Cole	1985	301
14 8/16	8 9/16	5 15/16	M	Iron County	UT	Patrick Barwick	1985	301
14 8/16	8 7/16	6 1/16	M	Elmore County	ID	Chris Koldeway	1985	301
14 8/16	8 10/16	5 14/16	M	Larimer County	CO	David Skiff	1987	301
14 8/16	8 9/16	5 15/16	M	Sweet Grass County	MT	Dwight Wagner	1987	301
14 8/16	8 7/16	6 1/16	M	Flathead County	MT	Chris Switzer	1987	301
14 8/16	8 8/16	6 0/16	M	Lane County	OR	Larry D. Jones	1987	301
14 8/16	8 5/16	6 3/16	M	Caribou County	ID	Eric De Clark	1987	301
14 8/16	8 8/16	6 0/16	M	Chaffee County	CO	Scott Pelino	1987	301
14 8/16	8 8/16	6 0/16	M	Saguache County	CO	William Larry Wray	1987	301
14 8/16	8 9/16	5 15/16	M	Garfield County	CO	Roy M. Goodwin	1988	301
14 8/16	8 12/16	5 12/16	M	Webb County	TX	Daniel Juarez, Jr.	1988	301
14 8/16	8 7/16	6 1/16	M	Sheridan County	WY	Bill Roberts	1988	301
14 8/16	8 9/16	5 15/16	M	Elko County	NV	Donald Thompson	1988	301
14 8/16	8 9/16	5 15/16	M	Missoula County	MT	Bob Lussier	1988	301
14 8/16	8 10/16	5 14/16	M	Custer County	ID	Chip Palmer	1989	301
14 8/16	8 8/16	6 0/16	M	Boise County	ID	Curtis Wiker	1989	301
14 8/16	8 8/16	6 0/16	M	Larimer County	CO	John D. Lindell	1989	301
14 8/16	8 9/16	5 15/16	M	Montrose County	CO	Jimmy C. Garner	1990	301
14 8/16	8 6/16	6 2/16	M	Linn County	OR	Wayne Mathews	1990	301
14 8/16	8 11/16	5 13/16	M	Judith Basin County	MT	Kelly Norskog	1990	301
14 8/16	8 10/16	5 14/16	M	Montezuma County	CO	Mark D. Thomson	1991	301
14 8/16	8 9/16	5 15/16	M	Sevier County	UT	Mayben Crane	1991	301
14 8/16	8 9/16	5 15/16	M	San Miguel County	CO	Dewayne Mullins	1992	301
14 8/16	8 10/16	5 14/16	M	Garfield County	CO	Carroll Thomas Roach	1992	301
14 8/16	8 6/16	6 2/16	M	Idaho County	ID	Rick A. Albers	1992	301
14 8/16	8 7/16	6 1/16	M	Nakusp	BC	Dave Richardson	1992	301
14 8/16	8 9/16	5 15/16	M	Gallatin County	MT	Kevin Conners	1992	301
14 8/16	8 10/16	5 14/16	M	Terrell County	TX	E. Josh Isbell	1992	301

MINIMUM SCORE 13 8/16   *(Continued)*

SCORE	GREATEST LENGTH	GREATEST WIDTH	SEX	AREA	STATE/ PROVINCE	HUNTER'S NAME	DATE	RANK
14 7/16	8 9/16	5 14/16	M	Elmore County	ID	William R. Vanderhoef	1966	351
14 7/16	8 11/16	5 12/16	M	Range Creek	UT	Gordy J. Longville	1967	351
14 7/16	8 6/16	6 1/16	M	White Pine County	NV	Barry L. May	1975	351
14 7/16	8 8/16	5 15/16	M	Lemhi County	ID	Wally Rueger	1975	351
14 7/16	8 9/16	5 14/16	M	Carbon County	UT	Rick Hunckler	1977	351
14 7/16	8 9/16	5 14/16	M	Duffy Lake	BC	Wilfred Klingsat	1977	351
14 7/16	8 9/16	5 14/16	M	Ravalli County	MT	Kim Engelbert	1978	351
14 7/16	8 6/16	6 1/16	M	Custer County	ID	Jim L. McCrory	1978	351
14 7/16	8 7/16	6 0/16	M	San Miguel County	CO	Bob Mays, Sr.	1979	351
14 7/16	8 6/16	6 1/16	M	Sevier County	UT	Lee Jernigan	1980	351
14 7/16	8 10/16	5 13/16	M	Lemhi County	ID	Daniel M. Alegre	1983	351
14 7/16	8 9/16	5 14/16	M	Sanders County	MT	Jerry V. Finley	1983	351
14 7/16	8 8/16	5 15/16	M	Franklin County	ID	Clair J. Buxton	1983	351
14 7/16	8 9/16	5 14/16	M	Judith Basin County	MT	Kay Davidson	1984	351
14 7/16	8 9/16	5 14/16	M	Duchesne County	UT	Jerry Ippolito	1984	351
14 7/16	8 8/16	5 15/16	M	Lemhi County	ID	Dennis N. Minnich	1984	351
14 7/16	8 6/16	6 1/16	M	Dolores County	CO	Ms. Charlie White	1984	351
14 7/16	8 8/16	5 15/16	M	Lander County	NV	David P. Lindman	1985	351
14 7/16	8 9/16	5 14/16	M	Catron County	NM	Stan Rauch	1986	351
14 7/16	8 8/16	5 15/16	M	Mesa County	CO	Sandy Vancourt	1987	351
14 7/16	8 7/16	6 0/16	M	Emery County	UT	Clark James Stokes	1987	351
14 7/16	8 8/16	5 15/16	M	Meagher County	MT	Sandra L. Gratz	1987	351
14 7/16	8 8/16	5 15/16	M	Skagit County	WA	Jerry Solie	1987	351
14 7/16	8 9/16	5 14/16	M	Sanpete County	UT	Don M. Markus	1988	351
14 7/16	8 6/16	6 1/16	M	Garfield County	CO	Doug Starks	1988	351
14 7/16	8 9/16	5 14/16	M	San Miguel County	CO	Robert Bain	1989	351
14 7/16	8 6/16	6 1/16	M	Cascade County	MT	Gene Henck	1989	351
14 7/16	8 12/16	5 11/16	M	Carbon County	UT	Stanley W. Biltz	1989	351
14 7/16	8 7/16	6 0/16	M	Lemhi County	ID	John Henry Smith	1989	351
14 7/16	8 4/16	6 3/16	M	Madison County	MT	Stephen P. (Pat) Connell	1990	351
14 7/16	8 9/16	5 14/16	M	Wasatch County	UT	E. Duane Park	1990	351
14 7/16	8 9/16	5 14/16	M	Rio Arriba County	NM	Jim Marquis	1990	351
14 7/16	8 6/16	6 1/16	M	Wallowa County	OR	William K. McCadden	1990	351
14 7/16	8 8/16	5 15/16	M	Fremont County	CO	Steve Sylvia	1991	351
14 7/16	8 9/16	5 14/16	M	Rio Arriba County	NM	Vito Benedetto	1991	351
14 7/16	8 7/16	6 0/16	M	Millard County	UT	Phillip R. Brown	1992	351
14 7/16	8 9/16	5 14/16	M	Rio Blanco County	CO	Tim Cuthriell	1992	351
14 7/16	8 11/16	5 12/16	M	Sanpete County	UT	J. Seth Kunz	1992	351
14 6/16	8 7/16	5 15/16	M	Sequoia National Forest	CA	Douglas Walker	1960	389
14 6/16	8 7/16	5 15/16	M	Elmore County	ID	C. Randall Byers	1966	389
14 6/16	8 8/16	5 14/16	M	Missoula County	MT	John Hershey	1969	389
14 6/16	8 7/16	5 15/16	M	Lemhi County	ID	Ray Torrey	1971	389
14 6/16	8 6/16	6 0/16	M	Falkland	BC	W. Klingsat	1974	389
14 6/16	8 7/16	5 15/16	M	Colfax County	NM	Richard A. Meyer	1974	389
14 6/16	8 8/16	5 14/16	M	Huerfano County	CO	Douglas E. Miller	1974	389
14 6/16	8 7/16	5 15/16	M	Clearwater County	ID	Oscar Levingston	1975	389
14 6/16	8 7/16	5 15/16	M	Carbon County	UT	Thomas W. Pinkston	1977	389
14 6/16	8 8/16	5 14/16	M	Uintah County	UT	Donald Redfox	1978	389
14 6/16	8 5/16	6 1/16	M	Fremont County	CO	Russell Hull	1979	389
14 6/16	8 9/16	5 13/16	M	Dry Wash Creek	UT	Mark J. Checki	1981	389
14 6/16	8 6/16	6 0/16	M	Chaffee County	CO	Judy Clyncke	1981	389
14 6/16	8 8/16	5 14/16	M	Ravalli County	MT	Dean Irwin	1982	389
14 6/16	8 6/16	6 0/16	M	Colfax County	NM	Joseph Wambach	1982	389
14 6/16	8 8/16	5 14/16	M	San Juan County	NM	Mike Ray	1983	389
14 6/16	8 8/16	5 14/16	M	Wasatch County	UT	Kendall Julander	1983	389
14 6/16	8 7/16	5 15/16	M	Clearwater County	ID	Tim Newbold	1983	389
14 6/16	8 9/16	5 13/16	M	Walla Walla County	WA	Winford Bradford	1983	389
14 6/16	8 3/16	6 3/16	M	Caribou County	ID	Rhett Bradford	1984	389
14 6/16	8 6/16	6 0/16	M	Lemhi County	ID	Donald L. Minnich	1984	389
14 6/16	8 8/16	5 14/16	M	Lemhi County	ID	Phil R. Ginochio	1985	389
14 6/16	8 5/16	6 1/16	M	Boise County	ID	David W. Peltier	1985	389
14 6/16	8 8/16	5 14/16	M	Cochise County	AZ	John Holcomb	1985	389
14 6/16	8 6/16	6 0/16	M	Flathead County	MT	Earl W. Weaver	1986	389
14 6/16	8 8/16	5 14/16	M	Missoula County	MT	Vinnie Pisani	1987	389
14 6/16	8 8/16	5 14/16	M	Summit County	UT	Jeffrey W. Potter	1988	389
14 6/16	8 10/16	5 12/16	M	Fremont County	CO	Daniel Daly	1988	389
14 6/16	8 7/16	5 15/16	M	Sanders County	MT	Harold R. Anderson	1988	389
14 6/16	8 6/16	6 0/16	M	Lincoln County	MT	Rich Hjort	1989	389
14 6/16	8 11/16	5 11/16	M	Josephine County	OR	Brian Day	1990	389
14 6/16	8 9/16	5 13/16	M	Garfield County	CO	Johnnie R. Walters	1991	389

COUGAR (*Mountain Lion*)

(Continued)

SCORE	GREATEST LENGTH	GREATEST WIDTH	SEX	AREA	STATE/ PROVINCE	HUNTER'S NAME	DATE	RANK
14 6/16	8 7/16	5 15/16	M	Elmore County	ID	William C. MacCarty III	1991	389
14 6/16	8 6/16	6 0/16	M	Mesa County	CO	James Bornman	1992	389
14 5/16	8 6/16	5 15/16	M	Esmeralda County	NV	Don Schram	1965	423
14 5/16	8 9/16	5 12/16	M	Tatla Lake	BC	William L. Nickerson	1966	423
14 5/16	8 8/16	5 13/16	M	Garfield County	UT	H. R. 'Dutch' Wambold	1966	423
14 5/16	8 8/16	5 13/16	M	Garfield County	UT	Robert K. Paulson	1968	423
14 5/16	8 10/16	5 11/16	M	Carbon County	UT	M. R. James	1970	423
14 5/16	8 8/16	5 13/16	M	Chaffee County	CO	Michael Ballard	1975	423
14 5/16	8 7/16	5 14/16	M	White Pine County	NV	James L. Beard	1975	423
14 5/16	8 8/16	5 13/16	M	Beaver County	UT	Bruce Post	1975	423
14 5/16	8 7/16	5 14/16	M	Las Animas County	CO	Barry L. Powell	1975	423
14 5/16	8 8/16	5 13/16	M	Daggett County	UT	Bob Butler	1976	423
14 5/16	8 9/16	5 12/16	M	Elmore County	ID	L. Dean Goodner	1978	423
14 5/16	8 10/16	5 11/16	M	Grand County	UT	Terry L. Benzine	1978	423
14 5/16	8 9/16	5 12/16	M	Fire Mtn.	BC	John 'Jack' Cordes	1978	423
14 5/16	8 7/16	5 14/16	M	Custer County	CO	William Henderson	1979	423
14 5/16	8 7/16	5 14/16	M	Judith Basin County	MT	Don Davidson	1981	423
14 5/16	8 7/16	5 14/16	M	Montezuma County	CO	Marvin Reichenau	1981	423
14 5/16	8 10/16	5 11/16	M	Dolores County	CO	Mike Gleason	1982	423
14 5/16	8 6/16	5 15/16	M	Lemhi County	ID	Stephen N. Bean	1983	423
14 5/16	8 8/16	5 13/16	M	Custer County	ID	Robert L. Hudman	1984	423
14 5/16	8 5/16	6 0/16	M	Jefferson County	CO	Jeff Fulkner	1984	423
14 5/16	8 8/16	5 13/16	M	Rio Blanco County	CO	Michael Ingold	1984	423
14 5/16	8 7/16	5 14/16	M	Sanders County	MT	Alan Gaston	1984	423
14 5/16	8 8/16	5 13/16	M	Sanpete County	UT	Judy Hallman	1985	423
14 5/16	8 5/16	6 0/16	M	Colfax County	NM	Jim Stauft	1985	423
14 5/16	8 7/16	5 14/16	M	Idaho County	ID	Jay D. Stringer	1985	423
14 5/16	8 8/16	5 13/16	M	Judith Basin County	MT	Joseph R. 'Bob' Fabian	1986	423
14 5/16	8 9/16	5 12/16	M	Dona Ana County	NM	Larry M. Sellers	1986	423
14 5/16	8 9/16	5 12/16	M	Kane County	UT	Allan Dangerfield	1986	423
14 5/16	8 5/16	6 0/16	M	Sanders County	MT	Byron E. Wates, Jr.	1986	423
14 5/16	8 10/16	5 11/16	M	Pend Oreille County	WA	Leonard F. Rock	1986	423
14 5/16	8 8/16	5 13/16	M	Daggett County	UT	Jeff Schneider	1987	423
14 5/16	8 9/16	5 12/16	M	Grand County	UT	James S. Saunoris	1987	423
14 5/16	8 7/16	5 14/16	M	Elmore County	ID	Alfred John Gemrich	1988	423
14 5/16	8 5/16	6 0/16	M	Idaho County	ID	Daniel R. Hooper	1988	423
14 5/16	8 6/16	5 15/16	M	Lane County	OR	John Stone	1988	423
14 5/16	8 6/16	5 15/16	M	Madison County	MT	Scott T. Smolen	1988	423
14 5/16	8 7/16	5 14/16	M	Idaho County	ID	Doug Hawkins	1989	423
14 5/16	8 8/16	5 13/16	M	Sanders County	MT	Charles R. Gallo	1990	423
14 5/16	8 8/16	5 13/16	M	Broadwater County	MT	Mike Parsons	1990	423
14 5/16	8 7/16	5 14/16	M	West Kettle River	BC	Lyndon Walker	1990	423
14 5/16	8 5/16	6 0/16	M	San Miguel County	CO	Roger Degroat	1991	423
14 5/16	8 7/16	5 14/16	M	Montezuma County	CO	Jerry Rush	1991	423
14 5/16	8 7/16	5 14/16	M	Garfield County	CO	Marvin Weible	1991	423
14 5/16	8 7/16	5 14/16	M	Garfield County	CO	Terry C. Parkinson	1992	423
14 4/16	8 8/16	5 12/16	M	Stoneman Lake	AZ	Dr. C. L. Clare	1962	467
14 4/16	8 8/16	5 12/16	M	Lincoln County	MT	Dale McNutt	1964	467
14 4/16	8 10/16	5 10/16	M	Elmore County	ID	Don Bennett	1968	467
14 4/16	8 4/16	6 0/16	M	Missoula County	MT	Tony Dumay	1968	467
14 4/16	8 6/16	5 14/16	M	Elmore County	ID	John E. Anderson	1972	467
14 4/16	8 6/16	5 14/16	M	Lemhi County	ID	Kenneth Anselmi	1972	467
14 4/16	8 6/16	5 14/16	M	Nye County	NV	Ken Viles	1972	467
14 4/16	8 4/16	6 0/16	M	Salmon River	ID	Bob Tucker	1974	467
14 4/16	8 6/16	5 14/16	M	Lemhi County	ID	H. R. 'Rusty' Neely	1975	467
14 4/16	8 4/16	6 0/16	M	Mesa County	CO	Robert Tobias	1975	467
14 4/16	8 6/16	5 14/16	M	Custer County	ID	Gerald Conway	1978	467
14 4/16	8 8/16	5 12/16	M	McMullen County	TX	James E. Jordan	1978	467
14 4/16	8 4/16	6 0/16	M	Washington County	UT	Richard L. Mobilio	1979	467
14 4/16	8 8/16	5 12/16	M	Garfield County	UT	George Holfeltz	1980	467
14 4/16	8 3/16	6 1/16	M	Colfax County	NM	Stephen 'Don' Hornady	1980	467
14 4/16	8 4/16	6 0/16	M	Garfield County	CO	T. Michael Casey	1982	467
14 4/16	8 6/16	5 14/16	M	Salt Lake County	UT	William L. Randles	1982	467
14 4/16	8 8/16	5 12/16	M	Lincoln County	NV	David A. Widby	1982	467
14 4/16	8 6/16	5 14/16	M	Clearwater County	ID	Ralph Ertz	1983	467
14 4/16	8 5/16	5 15/16	M	Elmore County	ID	Brad L. Johnson	1983	467
14 4/16	8 6/16	5 14/16	M	Lemhi County	ID	Bob Hudson	1984	467
14 4/16	8 6/16	5 14/16	M	Spokane County	WA	Kenneth R. Wengert	1984	467
14 4/16	8 7/16	5 13/16	M	Lander County	NV	Peter Esposito	1984	467
14 4/16	8 8/16	5 12/16	M	Sanpete County	UT	C. Danny Butler	1985	467

SCORE	GREATEST LENGTH	GREATEST WIDTH	SEX	AREA	STATE/ PROVINCE	HUNTER'S NAME	DATE	RANK
14 4/16	8 7/16	5 13/16	M	Lander County	NV	Leonard Ruimveld	1985	467
14 4/16	8 5/16	5 15/16	M	Montrose County	CO	Tony Hoza	1986	467
14 4/16	8 6/16	5 14/16	M	Colfax County	NM	John L. Chapman	1986	467
14 4/16	8 8/16	5 12/16	M	Eureka County	NV	Marty Pawelek	1986	467
14 4/16	8 6/16	5 14/16	M	Jackson County	OR	Jon Updegraff	1986	467
14 4/16	8 6/16	5 14/16	M	Coconino County	AZ	Todd Rice	1986	467
14 4/16	8 4/16	6 0/16	M	Nakusp	BC	Len Surina	1987	467
14 4/16	8 5/16	5 15/16	M	Benewah County	ID	William N. Latshaw	1988	467
14 4/16	8 8/16	5 12/16	M	Colfax County	NM	Robert L. Pagel	1988	467
14 4/16	8 6/16	5 14/16	M	Ravalli County	MT	Erik "Rick" Aslesen	1988	467
14 4/16	8 8/16	5 12/16	M	White Pine County	NV	Archie Nesbitt	1988	467
14 4/16	8 8/16	5 12/16	M	Iron County	UT	Bernie E. Belfrage	1988	467
14 4/16	8 5/16	5 15/16	M	Douglas County	OR	Stanley Myers	1988	467
14 4/16	8 7/16	5 13/16	M	Yavapai County	AZ	Roy Ruiz	1989	467
14 4/16	8 7/16	5 13/16	M	Carbon County	UT	Mike Hillis	1990	467
14 4/16	8 8/16	5 12/16	M	Converse County	WY	James P. Smith	1990	467
14 4/16	8 8/16	5 12/16	M	Sweet Grass County	MT	Roger A. Greve, Jr.	1990	467
14 4/16	8 5/16	5 15/16	M	Coconino County	AZ	H. Gordon Purl	1990	467
14 4/16	8 6/16	5 14/16	M	Rio Blanco County	CO	Kenton Meyers	1990	467
14 4/16	8 7/16	5 13/16	M	Ouray County	CO	Randy Caspersen	1991	467
14 4/16	8 9/16	5 11/16	M	Freemont County	CO	Bill Hartman	1991	467
14 4/16	8 4/16	6 0/16	M	Wasatch County	UT	Karl Hirst	1991	467
14 4/16	8 8/16	5 12/16	M	Boise County	ID	Larry Hoff	1991	467
14 4/16	8 7/16	5 13/16	M	Boise County	ID	William James TuffieldII	1991	467
14 4/16	8 8/16	5 12/16	M	Clearwater County	ID	Patrick L. Hovey	1992	467
14 4/16	8 9/16	5 11/16	M	Mesa County	CO	Alan Parkerson	1992	467
14 4/16	8 4/16	6 0/16	M	Judith Basin County	MT	Don Davidson	1992	467
14 3/16	8 6/16	5 13/16	M	Nye County	NV	Dick Gulman	1968	518
14 3/16	8 7/16	5 12/16	M	Ferry County	WA	Tom Smith	1968	518
14 3/16	8 5/16	5 14/16	M	Grand County	UT	John B. Baughman	1969	518
14 3/16	8 6/16	5 13/16	M	Douglas County	NV	Bill Fuller	1972	518
14 3/16	8 7/16	5 12/16	M	Huerfano County	CO	Marvin C. Clyncke	1973	518
14 3/16	8 9/16	5 10/16	M	Juab County	UT	Samuel McCarty	1975	518
14 3/16	8 7/16	5 12/16	M	Stevens County	WA	Ronald A. Carpenter	1977	518
14 3/16	8 8/16	5 11/16	M	Chaffee County	CO	John C. Dekker	1977	518
14 3/16	8 8/16	5 11/16	M	Sevier County	UT	Claude Flippin	1980	518
14 3/16	8 7/16	5 12/16	M	Adams County	ID	Rube Powell	1982	518
14 3/16	8 4/16	5 15/16	M	Mesa County	CO	William G. Padilla	1982	518
14 3/16	8 6/16	5 13/16	M	Judith Basin County	MT	Stan Colton	1983	518
14 3/16	8 5/16	5 14/16	M	Madison County	MT	Tony Schaufler	1983	518
14 3/16	8 4/16	5 15/16	M	Flathead County	MT	Gary A. Crowe	1983	518
14 3/16	8 6/16	5 13/16	M	Sierra County	NM	Kendall Doyle	1985	518
14 3/16	8 4/16	5 15/16	M	Montezuma County	CO	Duain Morton	1985	518
14 3/16	8 5/16	5 14/16	F	Shuswap River	BC	Mark Siegmueller	1985	518
14 3/16	8 5/16	5 14/16	M	Sanders County	MT	Jim Clark	1985	518
14 3/16	8 4/16	5 15/16	M	Clearwater County	ID	Dexter Siler	1986	518
14 3/16	8 5/16	5 14/16	M	Lemhi County	ID	Ben L. Fahnolz	1987	518
14 3/16	8 6/16	5 13/16	M	Idaho County	ID	G. Sam Cloninger	1987	518
14 3/16	8 7/16	5 12/16	M	Elmore County	ID	Joe Blake	1987	518
14 3/16	8 8/16	5 11/16	M	Elko County	NV	Charles Lee Pemble	1989	518
14 3/16	8 8/16	5 11/16	M	Tooele County	UT	Dale G. Kelson	1989	518
14 3/16	8 6/16	5 13/16	M	Fremont County	CO	R. E. Smith	1989	518
14 3/16	8 5/16	5 14/16	M	Lemhi County	ID	Richard Smith	1990	518
14 3/16	8 7/16	5 12/16	M	Rivalli County	MT	Jim Loughran	1990	518
14 3/16	8 14/16	5 5/16	M	Eagle County	CO	Cary Laman	1991	518
14 2/16	8 6/16	5 12/16	M	Okanogan County	WA	Dr. Russell Congdon	1950	546
14 2/16	8 6/16	5 12/16	M	Kane County	UT	William P. Mastrangel	1957	546
14 2/16	8 4/16	5 14/16	M	Fresno County	CA	John Faulconer	1964	546
14 2/16	8 6/16	5 12/16	M	Garfield County	CO	Phillip C. Durr	1970	546
14 2/16	8 4/16	5 14/16	M	Uintah County	UT	Larry Jones	1970	546
14 2/16	8 5/16	5 13/16	M	Fremont County	CO	Noel Feather	1975	546
14 2/16	8 6/16	5 12/16	M	Rio Blanco County	CO	James L. Emerson	1976	546
14 2/16	8 4/16	5 14/16	M	Lane County	OR	Eugene W. Gramzow	1978	546
14 2/16	8 5/16	5 13/16	M	Saguache County	CO	John T. Rauch	1979	546
14 2/16	8 4/16	5 14/16	M	Ravalli County	MT	Dean Irwin	1980	546
14 2/16	8 3/16	5 15/16	M	Montrose County	CO	Hoyte Driggers	1981	546
14 2/16	8 4/16	5 14/16	M	Greenlee County	AZ	Fred L. Smith	1982	546
14 2/16	8 8/16	5 10/16	M	Duchesne County	UT	Bill Painter	1982	546
14 2/16	8 9/16	5 9/16	M	Duchesne County	UT	Michael Wieck	1983	546
14 2/16	8 6/16	5 12/16	M	Garfield County	UT	Carl D. Winton	1984	546

SCORE	GREATEST LENGTH	GREATEST WIDTH	SEX	AREA	STATE/ PROVINCE	HUNTER'S NAME	DATE	RANK
14 2/16	8 4/16	5 14/16	M	Sweet Grass County	MT	David W. Sorensen	1984	546
14 2/16	8 2/16	6 0/16	M	Catron County	NM	Dean Hamilton	1985	546
14 2/16	8 8/16	5 10/16	M	Ravalli County	MT	John L Wozniak	1985	546
14 2/16	8 3/16	5 15/16	M	Mesa County	CO	David A. Schroeder	1986	546
14 2/16	8 6/16	5 12/16	M	Sanpete County	UT	Joe Johnston	1986	546
14 2/16	8 5/16	5 13/16	M	Larimer County	CO	Jerry L. Novak	1987	546
14 2/16	8 6/16	5 12/16	M	Mesa County	CO	Norm Stahlman	1987	546
14 2/16	8 6/16	5 12/16	M	Grand County	UT	J. Dale Hale	1988	546
14 2/16	8 4/16	5 14/16	M	Lemhi County	ID	Kent Brandt	1988	546
14 2/16	8 7/16	5 11/16	M	Dolores County	CO	Ernest N. Schroch	1988	546
14 2/16	8 6/16	5 12/16	M	Garfield County	CO	James "Boomer" Hayden	1988	546
14 2/16	8 4/16	5 14/16	M	Cranbrook	BC	Paul Deme	1989	546
14 2/16	8 6/16	5 12/16	M	Mesa County	CO	Tom Nelson	1989	546
14 2/16	8 9/16	5 9/16	M	Nye County	NV	Jesse Andrew Westby	1989	546
14 2/16	8 4/16	5 14/16	M	Greenlee County	AZ	Brian Davis	1989	546
14 2/16	8 1/16	6 1/16	M	Box Elder County	UT	Ellis Wall	1990	546
14 2/16	8 6/16	5 12/16	M	Mesa County	CO	Don Marascalco	1990	546
14 2/16	8 7/16	5 11/16	M	Custer County	ID	Trent Haberstroh	1990	546
14 2/16	8 6/16	5 12/16	M	Park County	CO	Bryon Scott Johnson	1991	546
14 2/16	8 6/16	5 12/16	M	Arrow Lakes	BC	Glenn Dreger	1991	546
14 2/16	8 11/16	5 7/16	M	Wayne County	UT	Charles M. Moore	1991	546
14 2/16	8 7/16	5 11/16	M	Sevier County	UT	Jack W. Powell	1991	546
14 2/16	8 4/16	5 14/16	M	Elmore County	ID	Jon Brockfeld	1992	546
14 1/16	8 14/16	5 3/16	M	Garfield County	CO	Jack Peters	1964	584
14 1/16	8 7/16	5 10/16	M	Rio Blanco County	CO	Charles Kohler	1969	584
14 1/16	8 7/16	5 10/16	M	Chaffee County	CO	Frank B. Parrish	1969	584
14 1/16	8 6/16	5 11/16	M	Elmore County	ID	Jerry E. Burt	1971	584
14 1/16	8 3/16	5 14/16	M	Mesa County	CO	Cary E. Weldon	1972	584
14 1/16	8 5/16	5 12/16	M	Carbon County	UT	David K. Elliot	1973	584
14 1/16	8 5/16	5 12/16	M	Butte County	ID	Ken Anselmi	1975	584
14 1/16	8 5/16	5 12/16	M	Rio Blanco County	CO	Chris Christian	1976	584
14 1/16	8 5/16	5 12/16	M	Wayne County	UT	C. Duane Kerr	1979	584
14 1/16	8 5/16	5 12/16	M	Cache County	UT	Val D. Larsen	1980	584
14 1/16	8 5/16	5 12/16	M	Coconino County	AZ	Fred McDonald	1980	584
14 1/16	8 5/16	5 12/16	M	Elko County	NV	Don Tripp	1980	584
14 1/16	8 5/16	5 12/16	M	Lemhi County	ID	Jim Jungk	1981	584
14 1/16	8 4/16	5 13/16	M	Adams County	ID	Dennis Atwater	1982	584
14 1/16	8 9/16	5 8/16	M	Coconino County	AZ	Dale Tasa	1982	584
14 1/16	8 5/16	5 12/16	M	Douglas County	CO	Gary James Morrow	1982	584
14 1/16	8 4/16	5 13/16	M	Madison County	MT	Dick Curtis	1983	584
14 1/16	8 6/16	5 11/16	M	Madison County	MT	John E. Larsen	1984	584
14 1/16	8 5/16	5 12/16	M	Tooele County	UT	Dennis L. Shirley	1984	584
14 1/16	8 6/16	5 11/16	M	Flathead County	MT	Dean F. Bergman	1984	584
14 1/16	8 5/16	5 12/16	M	Lander County	NV	Louis Probo	1984	584
14 1/16	8 4/16	5 13/16	M	Gilpin County	CO	Kurt W. Keskimaki	1985	584
14 1/16	8 4/16	5 13/16	M	Idaho County	ID	William J. Bowen	1986	584
14 1/16	8 5/16	5 12/16	M	Lincoln County	MT	Ben Rossetto	1986	584
14 1/16	8 8/16	5 9/16	M	Millard County	UT	Dave Scott	1987	584
14 1/16	8 5/16	5 12/16	M	Lemhi County	ID	Bobby A. Berg	1987	584
14 1/16	8 2/16	5 15/16	M	White Pine County	NV	Perry W. Greene, Jr.	1987	584
14 1/16	8 5/16	5 12/16	M	Conejos County	CO	Mike Boland	1987	584
14 1/16	8 5/16	5 12/16	M	Elmore County	ID	Mark Zastrow	1988	584
14 1/16	8 5/16	5 12/16	M	Coconino County	AZ	Don Flagel	1988	584
14 1/16	8 6/16	5 11/16	M	Montrose County	CO	Joe Garvey	1988	584
14 1/16	8 5/16	5 12/16	M	Alamosa County	CO	Dan Call	1989	584
14 1/16	8 6/16	5 11/16	M	Sevier County	UT	William G. Cummard II	1989	584
14 1/16	8 5/16	5 12/16	M	Meagher County	MT	Michael A. Blase, Jr.	1990	584
14 1/16	8 4/16	5 13/16	M	Custer County	ID	David Hotten	1991	584
14 1/16	8 5/16	5 12/16	M	Eureka County	NV	Gilbert Hernandez	1991	584
14 1/16	8 4/16	5 13/16	M	Garfield County	CO	Roger Wintle	1992	584
14 1/16	8 4/16	5 13/16	M	Pueblo County	CO	Tim Rose	1992	584
14 0/16	8 4/16	5 12/16	M	Uintah County	UT	Dr. Quentin F. Mangion	1962	622
14 0/16	8 4/16	5 12/16	M	Gila County	AZ	Hugh Pearson	1963	622
14 0/16	8 4/16	5 12/16	M	Flathead County	MT	Dorn L. Brinker	1969	622
14 0/16	8 3/16	5 13/16	M	Valley County	ID	Ronald N. Kolpin	1972	622
14 0/16	8 1/16	5 15/16	M	Yavapai County	AZ	Louis A. Vohs	1973	622
14 0/16	8 5/16	5 11/16	M	Lemhi County	ID	T. A. Low IV	1977	622
14 0/16	8 2/16	5 14/16	M	Duchesne County	UT	James Sot	1977	622
14 0/16	8 4/16	5 12/16	M	Blacktail Mountain	UT	Jerry Dittrich	1978	622
14 0/16	8 5/16	5 11/16	M	Fremont County	CO	Gary Fisher	1979	622

SCORE	GREATEST LENGTH	GREATEST WIDTH	SEX	AREA	STATE/ PROVINCE	HUNTER'S NAME	DATE	RANK
14 0/16	8 4/16	5 12/16	M	San Juan County	UT	Gary Paluszcyk	1979	622
14 0/16	8 4/16	5 12/16	M	Boise County	ID	Paul Anderson	1980	622
14 0/16	8 3/16	5 13/16	M	Coconino County	AZ	Larry Almaraz	1981	622
14 0/16	8 3/16	5 13/16	M	San Miguel County	CO	Robert Finelli	1981	622
14 0/16	8 5/16	5 11/16	M	Madison County	MT	Leland S. Speakes, Jr.	1984	622
14 0/16	8 4/16	5 12/16	M	Wasatch County	UT	Vicki Mamales	1985	622
14 0/16	8 2/16	5 14/16	M	Madison County	MT	Pat Sinclair	1985	622
14 0/16	8 8/16	5 8/16	M	Rio Grande County	CO	Tom Tietz	1985	622
14 0/16	8 2/16	5 14/16	M	Madison County	MT	Carl Spaeth	1986	622
14 0/16	8 3/16	5 13/16	M	Coconino County	AZ	George Richardson	1987	622
14 0/16	8 2/16	5 14/16	M	San Juan County	NM	Keith Hardy	1987	622
14 0/16	8 6/16	5 10/16	M	Judith Basin County	MT	Noel J. Poux	1988	622
14 0/16	8 4/16	5 12/16	M	San Miguel County	CO	Jack Downing	1988	622
14 0/16	8 4/16	5 12/16	M	Idaho County	ID	David A. Shupp	1989	622
14 0/16	8 7/16	5 9/16	M	Millard County	UT	Norman Bradley	1990	622
14 0/16	8 4/16	5 12/16	M	Tooele County	UT	Merrill Clarke	1990	622
14 0/16	8 6/16	5 10/16	M	Elmore County	ID	Julian Salutrequi	1990	622
14 0/16	8 7/16	5 9/16	M	Iron County	UT	Ken Wilson	1990	622
14 0/16	8 4/16	5 12/16	M	Lemhi County	ID	Larry Dockery	1990	622
14 0/16	8 6/16	5 10/16	M	Union County	OR	Jeff Carver	1990	622
14 0/16	8 5/16	5 11/16	M	Coconino County	AZ	Kenneth Meadors	1991	622
14 0/16	8 3/16	5 13/16	M	Stoney Lake	BC	Gregory White	1991	622
14 0/16	8 2/16	5 14/16	M	Granite County	MT	Richard E. LaCrone	1992	622
13 15/16	8 3/16	5 12/16	M	Gila County	AZ	Hugh Pearson	1963	654
13 15/16	8 5/16	5 10/16	M	Rio Blanco County	CO	Joel Hogan	1967	654
13 15/16	8 6/16	5 9/16	M	Okanogan County	WA	Stuart Irwin	1971	654
13 15/16	8 5/16	5 10/16	M	Lemhi County	ID	John Mascellino	1972	654
13 15/16	8 3/16	5 12/16	M	San Miguel County	CO	Ken Grandow	1979	654
13 15/16	8 6/16	5 9/16	M	Elmore County	ID	Richard C. Nichols	1980	654
13 15/16	8 3/16	5 12/16	M	Judith Basin County	MT	Ed Evans	1981	654
13 15/16	8 5/16	5 10/16	M	Las Animas County	CO	David S. Bunce	1982	654
13 15/16	8 5/16	5 10/16	M	Piute County	UT	Lynn Kuhlmann	1984	654
13 15/16	8 3/16	5 12/16	M	Boise County	ID	William Atkinson, Jr.	1985	654
13 15/16	8 4/16	5 11/16	M	Lemhi County	ID	James S. Disalvo	1985	654
13 15/16	8 2/16	5 13/16	M	Elko County	NV	Donald Pyne	1987	654
13 15/16	8 3/16	5 12/16	M	Elmore County	ID	Carolyn Godfrey	1987	654
13 15/16	8 5/16	5 10/16	M	Sevier County	UT	Philippe Lantagne	1988	654
13 15/16	8 6/16	5 9/16	M	Washington County	UT	Gerald Laurino	1988	654
13 15/16	8 2/16	5 13/16	M	Carbon County	UT	Gail B. Raby	1989	654
13 15/16	8 4/16	5 11/16	M	Nye County	NV	Charles Pat Walker, Jr.	1990	654
13 15/16	8 4/16	5 11/16	M	Carbon County	UT	Roger Cyfers	1990	654
13 15/16	8 5/16	5 10/16	M	Chaffee County	CO	Scott Pelino	1990	654
13 15/16	8 5/16	5 10/16	M	Beaverhead County	MT	Lynn Lamphiear	1991	654
13 15/16	8 4/16	5 11/16	M	Lincoln County	MT	Dennis L. Kari	1991	654
13 14/16	8 4/16	5 10/16	M	Flathead County	MT	Jerry Almos	1970	675
13 14/16	8 6/16	5 8/16	F	Coconino County	AZ	Midge Dandridge	1972	675
13 14/16	8 1/16	5 13/16	M	Mesa County	CO	Stan Bocian	1974	675
13 14/16	8 5/16	5 9/16	M	Chaffee County	CO	Ben Cuadra	1975	675
13 14/16	8 2/16	5 12/16	M	Boise County	ID	Robert L. Bevan	1976	675
13 14/16	8 6/16	5 8/16	M	Lemhi County	ID	James C. Costopoulos	1976	675
13 14/16	8 1/16	5 13/16	M	Garfield County	CO	Lou Kindred	1977	675
13 14/16	8 4/16	5 10/16	M	Lemhi County	ID	Dan E. Hershberger	1979	675
13 14/16	8 4/16	5 10/16	M	Rio Blanco County	CO	Wayne Watson, Sr.	1979	675
13 14/16	8 3/16	5 11/16	M	Uintah County	UT	Dan Darrell Boy	1980	675
13 14/16	8 9/16	5 5/16	M	Washington County	UT	Scott Petersen	1982	675
13 14/16	8 3/16	5 11/16	M	Grand County	UT	Henry 'Hank' Frey	1982	675
13 14/16	8 3/16	5 11/16	M	Archuleta County	CO	Ronald Murphy	1983	675
13 14/16	8 1/16	5 13/16	M	Lemhi County	ID	Wendell L. Seelig	1983	675
13 14/16	8 2/16	5 12/16	M	Sevier County	UT	John Alden Brown, Jr.	1984	675
13 14/16	8 3/16	5 11/16	M	Sanpete County	UT	Bob Fitzgerald	1984	675
13 14/16	8 5/16	5 9/16	M	Chaffee County	CO	Raymond Roussett, Jr.	1985	675
13 14/16	8 5/16	5 9/16	M	Elmore County	ID	John Koldeway	1985	675
13 14/16	8 2/16	5 12/16	M	Gilpin County	CO	Lyle Willmarth	1986	675
13 14/16	8 6/16	5 8/16	M	San Miguel County	CO	Ronald J. Collier	1986	675
13 14/16	8 2/16	5 12/16	M	Sheridan County	WY	Mike Pilch	1987	675
13 14/16	8 4/16	5 10/16	M	Coconino County	AZ	Cindi Richardson	1987	675
13 14/16	8 5/16	5 9/16	M	Lincoln County	MT	Kenneth Mamatz	1988	675
13 14/16	7 15/16	5 15/16	M	Sheridan County	WY	Harold Carnell	1988	675
13 14/16	8 4/16	5 10/16	M	White Pine County	NV	Randy Bennett	1989	675
13 14/16	8 4/16	5 10/16	M	Idaho County	ID	Kenny Holliday	1990	675

SCORE	GREATEST LENGTH	GREATEST WIDTH	SEX	AREA	STATE/PROVINCE	HUNTER'S NAME	DATE	RANK
13 14/16	8 3/16	5 11/16	M	Elmore County	ID	Stan Godfrey	1991	675
13 14/16	8 2/16	5 12/16	M	Grand County	UT	Dale Bigger	1991	675
13 14/16	8 3/16	5 11/16	F	Clearwater County	ID	Russ A. Van Rite	1991	675
13 14/16	8 5/16	5 9/16	M	Elmore County	ID	Richard A. Schreiber	1991	675
13 14/16	8 3/16	5 11/16	M	Catron County	NM	G. David Moser	1992	675
13 13/16	8 2/16	5 11/16	M	Esmeralda County	NV	George Hooker	1961	706
13 13/16	7 15/16	5 14/16	M	Lemhi County	ID	Vern Herman	1969	706
13 13/16	8 2/16	5 11/16	M	EL Paso County	CO	L. Clark Kiser	1984	706
13 13/16	8 4/16	5 9/16	M	Mesa County	CO	Edgar Bobo	1984	706
13 13/16	8 1/16	5 12/16	M	Sandoval County	NM	David Taylor	1985	706
13 13/16	8 1/16	5 12/16	M	San Juan County	UT	David Snyder	1985	706
13 13/16	8 3/16	5 10/16	M	Johnson County	WY	Terry Krahn	1986	706
13 13/16	8 3/16	5 10/16	M	Cochise County	AZ	Randy Hall	1987	706
13 13/16	8 5/16	5 8/16	M	Boulder County	CO	Jerry Souders	1987	706
13 13/16	8 0/16	5 13/16	M	Greenlee County	AZ	Eugene Fritsky	1989	706
13 13/16	8 2/16	5 11/16	M	San Juan County	UT	Ronald D. Kirk	1990	706
13 13/16	8 5/16	5 8/16	M	Garfield County	CO	Neil Smith	1990	706
13 13/16	8 3/16	5 10/16	M	Chaffee County	CO	David Spacek	1990	706
13 13/16	8 5/16	5 8/16	M	San Miguel County	CO	Evans V. Brewster	1991	706
13 13/16	8 4/16	5 9/16	M	Coconino County	AZ	Stephen A. Kotz	1991	706
13 13/16	8 1/16	5 12/16	M	San Juan County	UT	Daniel Willems	1992	706
13 12/16	8 4/16	5 8/16	M	Shasta National Forest	CA	Harv Ebers	1963	722
13 12/16	8 0/16	5 12/16	M	Swan R. Valley	MT	Joe Lawrence	1965	722
13 12/16	7 11/16	6 1/16	M	Garfield County	UT	Robert E. Todd	1969	722
13 12/16	8 2/16	5 10/16	M	Pima County	AZ	Sherwin Lipsitz	1976	722
13 12/16	8 3/16	5 9/16	M	Lemhi County	ID	Ray Torrey	1978	722
13 12/16	8 3/16	5 9/16	M	Custer County	ID	Larry Bonetti	1979	722
13 12/16	8 4/16	5 8/16	M	Lemhi County	ID	Buck Farni	1979	722
13 12/16	8 3/16	5 9/16	M	Carbon County	UT	Claude Flippin	1981	722
13 12/16	8 4/16	5 8/16	M	Uintah County	UT	Ken Labrum	1985	722
13 12/16	8 2/16	5 10/16	M	Grand County	UT	Robert Jacobsen	1986	722
13 12/16	8 0/16	5 12/16	M	Gallatin County	MT	Carmine Agostinelli	1986	722
13 12/16	8 4/16	5 8/16	M	Clearwater County	ID	George J. McCuster	1986	722
13 12/16	8 2/16	5 10/16	M	San Miguel County	CO	Joe Wright	1987	722
13 12/16	8 2/16	5 10/16	M	Powell County	MT	Thomas W. Moore	1987	722
13 12/16	8 3/16	5 9/16	M	Carbon County	UT	Jim Saunoris, Jr.	1987	722
13 12/16	8 3/16	5 9/16	M	Lemhi County	ID	Dan L. Moultrie	1988	722
13 12/16	8 2/16	5 10/16	M	Douglas County	OR	Rick Gabbard	1988	722
13 12/16	8 3/16	5 9/16	M	Rio Blanco County	CO	Tom Brakke	1990	722
13 12/16	8 3/16	5 9/16	M	Beaverhead County	MT	Jeff D. Wingard	1991	722
13 12/16	8 3/16	5 9/16	M	St. Mary's River	BC	Richard Kirkvold	1991	722
13 12/16	8 6/16	5 6/16	M	Sandoval County	NM	Thomas W. Dunn	1991	722
13 12/16	8 3/16	5 9/16	M	Montrose County	CO	Gregory Hise	1992	722
13 12/16	8 4/16	5 8/16	M	Summit County	UT	Tony Park	1992	722
13 11/16	8 3/16	5 8/16	M	Valley County	ID	Clarence Grandt	1972	745
13 11/16	8 3/16	5 8/16	M	Mesa County	CO	William J. Vincent	1972	745
13 11/16	8 2/16	5 9/16	M	Carbon County	UT	Bernard R. Giacoletto	1975	745
13 11/16	8 6/16	5 5/16	M	San Juan County.	UT	James Karlovec	1975	745
13 11/16	7 15/16	5 12/16	M	Grand County	UT	David Seidelman	1975	745
13 11/16	8 0/16	5 11/16	M	Garfield County	CO	Darlene Frye	1976	745
13 11/16	8 4/16	5 7/16	M	Boise County	ID	Fred Sanders	1981	745
13 11/16	7 15/16	5 12/16	M	Missoula County	MT	Blair Hamer	1983	745
13 11/16	8 3/16	5 8/16	M	Gilpin County	CO	John Rhine	1984	745
13 11/16	8 3/16	5 8/16	M	Clearwater County	ID	Mike I. Powers	1984	745
13 11/16	8 3/16	5 8/16	F	Socorro County	NM	Paul Persano	1986	745
13 11/16	8 3/16	5 8/16	M	Pima County	AZ	Ernest R. Allen	1987	745
13 11/16	8 4/16	5 7/16	M	Boise County	ID	Raymond A. Guay	1987	745
13 11/16	8 1/16	5 10/16	M	Nye County	NV	Ronald W. Lindquist	1987	745
13 11/16	8 4/16	5 7/16	M	Washington County	UT	Jules Pacheco	1989	745
13 11/16	8 0/16	5 11/16	F	Clearwater County	ID	Colin G. Crook	1989	745
13 11/16	8 1/16	5 10/16	M	Asotin County	WA	Mark Kolowith	1990	745
13 11/16	8 3/16	5 8/16	M	Fremont County	CO	Travis Todd	1990	745
13 11/16	8 3/16	5 8/16	M	Jackson County	OR	Florian Davis	1990	745
13 11/16	8 5/16	5 6/16	M	Uintah County	UT	Robert G. Petersen	1991	745
13 11/16	8 4/16	5 7/16	M	Saguache County	CO	Roger M. Tyler	1992	745
13 10/16	8 2/16	5 8/16	F	Moffat County	CO	Roland C. Gravenkemper	1959	766
13 10/16	8 0/16	5 10/16	F	Sana Arroya Canyon	UT	Edward Collins	1967	766
13 10/16	7 14/16	5 12/16	M	Fremont County	CO	Jeffrey D. McKnight	1970	766
13 10/16	7 15/16	5 11/16	M	Boise County	ID	Robert B. Braswell	1971	766
13 10/16	7 12/16	5 14/16	M	Lemhi County	ID	Richard R. Smith	1976	766

SCORE	GREATEST LENGTH	GREATEST WIDTH	SEX	AREA	STATE/ PROVINCE	HUNTER'S NAME	DATE	RANK
13 10/16	8 2/16	5 8/16	M	Grand County	UT	Karen Jacobsen	1980	766
13 10/16	8 3/16	5 7/16	M	Sevier County	UT	Robert C. McGuire	1980	766
13 10/16	8 0/16	5 10/16	M	Coconino County	AZ	Les Shelton	1981	766
13 10/16	8 2/16	5 8/16	M	Garfield County	UT	William B. McGuire, Jr.	1983	766
13 10/16	8 2/16	5 8/16	M	Sevier County	UT	Kenneth L. Jackson	1984	766
13 10/16	8 0/16	5 10/16	M	Flathead County	MT	Charles J. Williams	1986	766
13 10/16	8 4/16	5 6/16	M	Colfax County	NM	I. Lionel Kelley	1986	766
13 10/16	7 15/16	5 11/16	M	Beaver County	UT	David L. Welch	1987	766
13 10/16	8 2/16	5 8/16	M	Fergus County	MT	John "Rosey" Roseland	1987	766
13 10/16	8 1/16	5 9/16	M	Millard County	UT	Roy Evans	1988	766
13 10/16	8 1/16	5 9/16	M	Washington County	UT	Ken Mowerson	1988	766
13 10/16	8 1/16	5 9/16	M	Lincoln County	NV	Glen R. Cousins	1988	766
13 10/16	8 3/16	5 7/16	M	Blairmore	ALB	Larry Vayro	1990	766
13 10/16	8 2/16	5 8/16	M	Elmore County	ID	Mike Ambur	1990	766
13 10/16	8 1/16	5 9/16	M	Jackson County	OR	Randy D. Peyton	1990	766
13 10/16	7 15/16	5 11/16	M	Iron County	UT	Jeryl F. Williams	1991	766
13 10/16	8 1/16	5 9/16	M	Teller County	CO	Dennis R. Bader	1991	766
13 10/16	8 0/16	5 10/16	M	Custer County	ID	Phil Sullivan	1991	766
13 9/16	8 0/16	5 9/16	M	Carbon County	UT	Tom Kludy	1965	789
13 9/16	8 1/16	5 8/16	M	Elmore County	ID	Larry Bergmann	1972	789
13 9/16	8 0/16	5 9/16	F	Custer County	ID	John Kuhar	1975	789
13 9/16	7 15/16	5 10/16	M	Rio Blanco County	CO	John Horstman	1977	789
13 9/16	8 0/16	5 9/16	M	Saguache County	CO	Ed R. Wiseman	1977	789
13 9/16	8 3/16	5 6/16	M	Peachland	BC	Roger Gipple	1983	789
13 9/16	7 15/16	5 10/16	M	Hot Springs County	WY	John Backs	1983	789
13 9/16	8 5/16	5 4/16	M	Monroe County	UT	Peter Esposito	1984	789
13 9/16	7 14/16	5 11/16	M	Sanders County	MT	Fred J. Hoppe	1984	789
13 9/16	8 3/16	5 6/16	M	Beaver County	UT	Joseph Drover	1985	789
13 9/16	8 2/16	5 7/16	M	San Juan County	UT	Charles R. Horvath	1985	789
13 9/16	8 0/16	5 9/16	M	Lemhi County	ID	Ed Montouri	1985	789
13 9/16	8 0/16	5 9/16	M	Sanders County	MT	Dr. Eugene T. Altiere	1985	789
13 9/16	8 1/16	5 8/16	M	Juab County	UT	Kirt Prestwich	1986	789
13 9/16	8 2/16	5 7/16	M	Clearwater County	ID	Terry L. Sochor	1987	789
13 9/16	8 1/16	5 8/16	M	Garfield County	UT	George E. Wright	1987	789
13 9/16	8 0/16	5 9/16	M	White Pine County	NV	Robert S. Price	1987	789
13 9/16	8 3/16	5 6/16	M	Rio Blanco County	CO	Steven J. Lepic	1987	789
13 9/16	8 0/16	5 9/16	M	Fremont County	CO	Chuck Anderson, Jr.	1987	789
13 9/16	8 1/16	5 8/16	M	Garfield County	CO	Steven W. Kluth	1988	789
13 9/16	8 2/16	5 7/16	M	Granite County	MT	Rocky Drake	1989	789
13 9/16	8 4/16	5 5/16	M	Mesa County	CO	Steve Haberland	1990	789
13 9/16	8 2/16	5 7/16	M	Mesa County	CO	Troy James	1991	789
13 9/16	8 0/16	5 9/16	M	Duchesne County	UT	Roy Hampton	1992	789
13 9/16	7 15/16	5 10/16	F	Chaffee County	CO	Dave Luko	1992	789
13 8/16	8 0/16	5 8/16	M	Uintah County	UT	Creetie Kerr	1964	814
13 8/16	8 2/16	5 6/16	M	Uintah County	UT	Dr. George A. Waldriff	1965	814
13 8/16	7 12/16	5 12/16	F	Lincoln County	MT	G. H. Malinoski	1967	814
13 8/16	8 8/16	5 0/16	F	Churchill County	NV	Quentin P. Nightingale	1971	814
13 8/16	8 1/16	5 7/16	M	Coconino County	AZ	Tim Kennedy	1974	814
13 8/16	8 2/16	5 6/16	M	Coconino County	AZ	Robert West	1974	814
13 8/16	8 0/16	5 8/16	M	Carbon County	UT	John Brandt	1978	814
13 8/16	8 0/16	5 8/16	M	Cassia County	ID	Leon Peterson	1978	814
13 8/16	8 2/16	5 6/16	M	Penticton	BC	Dale W. Gray	1979	814
13 8/16	8 0/16	5 8/16	M	Lemhi County	ID	John A. McCarthy	1979	814
13 8/16	8 1/16	5 7/16	M	Fremont County	CO	Steve Byerly	1981	814
13 8/16	8 2/16	5 6/16	M	Clearwater County	ID	Donita K. Powers	1982	814
13 8/16	7 10/16	5 14/16	M	Park County	WY	David C. Gordon, Sr.	1983	814
13 8/16	8 1/16	5 7/16	F	Wallowa County	OR	Jim Turcke	1983	814
13 8/16	8 1/16	5 7/16	M	Washington County	UT	Nic Blake	1984	814
13 8/16	8 1/16	5 7/16	M	Alamosa County	CO	Barry J. Smith	1985	814
13 8/16	7 13/16	5 11/16	M	Madison County	MT	Jim Ellis	1985	814
13 8/16	8 3/16	5 5/16	M	Sevier County	UT	Greg Strait	1986	814
13 8/16	8 0/16	5 8/16	M	Coconino County	AZ	Mike T. Miller	1988	814
13 8/16	7 15/16	5 9/16	M	Fergus County	MT	Lisa Roseland	1988	814
13 8/16	8 0/16	5 8/16	M	Fergus County	MT	John Fleharty	1988	814
13 8/16	8 0/16	5 8/16	M	Montrose County	CO	Gene Mathias	1988	814
13 8/16	8 3/16	5 5/16	M	Boise County	ID	Gerard J. Gareri	1990	814
13 8/16	8 0/16	5 8/16	M	Lincoln County	MT	Jon Clark	1991	814
13 8/16	8 2/16	5 6/16	M	Sevier County	UT	Raymond J. Francingues, Jr.	1992	814

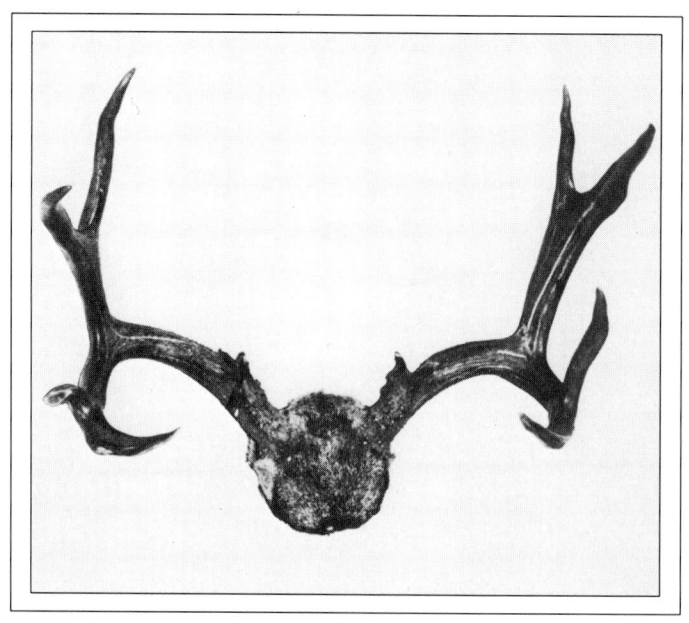

World Record Columbian Blacktail Deer (Typical Antlers)
Score:172 2/8
Marion County, Oregon - 1969
Hunter: B.G. Shurtleff

COLUMBIAN BLACKTAIL *(Typical Antlers)*

MINIMUM SCORE 90

Odocoileus hemionus columbianus

SCORE	LENGTH OF R MAIN BEAM L		INSIDE SPREAD	NUMBER OF R POINTS L		AREA	STATE/ PROVINCE	HUNTER'S NAME	DATE	RANK
172 2/8	26 3/8	25 7/8	20 4/8	7	7	Marion County	OR	B. G. Shurtleff	1969	1
172 0/8	26 4/8	25 5/8	22 6/8	4	4	Multnomah County	OR	Dave Brill	1985	2
164 7/8	23 6/8	23 3/8	19 7/8	5	5	Marion County	OR	B. G. Shurtleff	1977	3
160 7/8	23 0/8	23 4/8	19 4/8	6	5	Jackson County	OR	Dr. G. Scott Jennings	1972	4
156 7/8	23 5/8	24 1/8	23 1/8	5	5	Trinity County	CA	Steve Bradford	1986	5
152 6/8	22 2/8	22 2/8	18 0/8	5	5	Clackamas County	OR	Phillip L. Severson	1991	6
150 4/8	23 4/8	23 1/8	20 2/8	5	5	Jackson County	OR	E. C. Brittsan	1976	7
146 6/8	20 0/8	20 0/8	17 6/8	5	5	Marion County	OR	Jim Brackenbury	1990	8
144 5/8	21 2/8	20 3/8	16 6/8	6	7	Jackson County	OR	Leroy Bedingfield	1970	9
143 7/8	21 0/8	20 6/8	21 0/8	5	5	Shasta County	CA	Dave Swenson	1968	10
142 4/8	21 4/8	21 5/8	17 4/8	5	5	Lane County	OR	Vernon King, Sr.	1988	11
142 2/8	19 1/8	19 7/8	19 0/8	5	5	Lake County	OR	Don Chandler	1968	12
141 7/8	20 7/8	21 0/8	17 3/8	5	5	Jackson County	OR	Chester Stevenson	1917	13
140 6/8	21 3/8	20 4/8	16 2/8	3	3	Jackson County	OR	Art W. Lee	1965	14
140 6/8	22 6/8	22 5/8	15 4/8	4	5	Jackson County	OR	Dr. G. Scott Jennings	1973	14
138 4/8	22 5/8	22 4/8	18 5/8	5	5	Siskiyou County	CA	John Bridgewater	1980	16
137 6/8	20 3/8	22 0/8	15 6/8	5	5	Jackson County	OR	John Schauble	1986	17
137 2/8	20 2/8	19 7/8	16 1/8	6	5	Jackson County	OR	Steve Wirth	1983	18
137 1/8	21 2/8	20 1/8	16 1/8	4	6	Linn County	OR	Scot E. Lafond	1991	19
137 0/8	20 3/8	20 1/8	14 5/8	4	4	Mendocino County	CA	Russell L. Browning	1980	20
137 0/8	21 1/8	21 2/8	15 7/8	4	5	Linn County	OR	Charlie Endicott	1985	20
136 7/8	21 0/8	20 7/8	15 3/8	6	6	Skamania County	WA	Melvin W. Berry	1991	22
136 6/8	21 0/8	21 1/8	18 2/8	5	5	Linn County	OR	Tom Nichols	1985	23
136 5/8	21 1/8	22 1/8	17 1/8	4	5	Linn County	OR	Rebecca Saunders	1986	24
136 4/8	21 4/8	21 6/8	16 4/8	4	6	Clackamas County	OR	Craig Hyatt	1990	25
135 0/8	22 0/8	21 2/8	18 7/8	6	4	Jackson County	OR	Bob Staten	1964	26
134 5/8	21 0/8	16 0/8	16 2/8	5	4	Jackson County	OR	Milton L. Cady	1968	27
134 5/8	21 7/8	21 7/8	17 0/8	7	5	Trinity County	CA	Bob Auser	1981	27
134 4/8	22 5/8	21 4/8	15 6/8	4	4	Glenn County	CA	Steve Bashaw	1989	29
133 7/8	20 6/8	20 6/8	18 7/8	4	4	Jackson County	OR	Donald R. Pritchett	1966	30
133 7/8	19 4/8	21 6/8	13 7/8	7	7	Linn County	OR	J. C. James	1984	30

SCORE	LENGTH OF MAIN BEAM R	L	INSIDE SPREAD	NUMBER OF POINTS R	L	AREA	STATE/ PROVINCE	HUNTER'S NAME	DATE	RANK
133 2/8	20 1/8	20 2/8	17 0/8	5	5	Jackson County	OR	Chester Stevenson	1921	32
133 1/8	18 7/8	17 6/8	15 3/8	5	5	Lane County	OR	Matt Dodson	1990	33
133 0/8	20 5/8	21 0/8	14 6/8	5	5	Benton County	OR	Robert W. Worthean	1982	34
132 7/8	20 0/8	20 0/8	14 7/8	5	5	Lane County	OR	Clyde Romero, Jr.	1991	35
132 6/8	20 1/8	20 6/8	18 0/8	4	5	Jackson County	OR	Stanley Moore	1962	36
132 5/8	22 0/8	21 0/8	16 1/8	7	7	Clackamas County	OR	Charlie Medlicott	1983	37
132 3/8	18 6/8	19 4/8	16 7/8	5	5	Jackson County	OR	Donald R. Pritchett	1966	38
132 1/8	20 2/8	19 6/8	18 4/8	5	7	Jackson County	OR	John Schauble	1985	39
131 7/8	22 0/8	21 6/8	16 7/8	4	4	Douglas County	OR	Jim Hodson	1987	40
131 4/8	21 5/8	22 0/8	17 3/8	6	4	Multnomah County	OR	Dennis Thorud	1985	41
131 3/8	20 0/8	20 0/8	15 5/8	5	5	Jackson County	OR	Joe Williamson	1965	42
131 3/8	20 1/8	20 2/8	17 3/8	5	5	Douglas County	OR	Ken French	1988	42
131 2/8	19 6/8	19 3/8	22 2/8	5	5	Linn County	OR	David F. Scheid	1968	44
131 2/8	21 2/8	21 4/8	18 2/8	5	4	Clatsop County	OR	B. G. Shurtleff	1979	44
131 1/8	19 4/8	19 4/8	14 5/8	5	5	Kitsap County	WA	Dale Axtman	1983	46
130 7/8	22 2/8	21 4/8	15 2/8	6	7	Benton County	OR	Chuck Warner	1991	47
130 1/8	19 0/8	18 7/8	15 1/8	5	5	Linn County	OR	Duane Etherington	1983	48
129 5/8	18 7/8	18 5/8	17 7/8	5	5	Colusa County	CA	Jay Overholtzer	1988	49
129 3/8	26 1/8	25 3/8	19 2/8	5	3	Klamath County	OR	Troy Fennel	1964	50
129 3/8	21 4/8	21 1/8	16 7/8	5	5	Siskiyou County	CA	Daniel Franks	1991	50
129 1/8	20 4/8	20 4/8	16 3/8	4	4	Douglas County	OR	Tom E. Tipton	1988	52
128 7/8	18 2/8	18 2/8	16 3/8	5	5	Lane County	OR	Dave E. Jarrett	1982	53
128 5/8	19 1/8	18 7/8	15 7/8	5	5	Lake County	CA	Joe Emmons	1989	54
128 2/8	19 3/8	19 4/8	14 4/8	8	5	Clackamas County	OR	John Christiansen	1981	55
128 2/8	20 1/8	20 3/8	15 2/8	6	5	Linn County	OR	Steve Richards	1983	55
127 7/8	19 2/8	20 3/8	18 7/8	5	5	Linn County	OR	Chuck Warner	1987	57
127 5/8	22 0/8	22 1/8	16 3/8	6	5	Josephine County	OR	Frank Sanders	1991	58
127 5/8	21 1/8	20 1/8	16 1/8	5	5	Douglas County	OR	Joe Hulburt	1991	58
127 4/8	21 3/8	21 1/8	19 6/8	5	5	Linn County	OR	John Stone	1981	60
127 3/8	21 4/8	20 2/8	19 7/8	4	4	Mendocino County	CA	Lawrence Christensen	1991	61
127 2/8	20 2/8	19 6/8	14 6/8	5	5	Trinity County	CA	George Flournoy, Jr.	1986	62
127 1/8	18 7/8	19 5/8	16 1/8	6	5	Mendocino County	CA	James Buffum	1965	63
126 5/8	18 2/8	17 4/8	13 7/8	5	5	Douglas County	OR	Kenneth A. French	1989	64
126 4/8	17 1/8	18 5/8	14 6/8	5	5	Linn County	OR	Dennis H. Wessels	1985	65
125 7/8	19 1/8	19 4/8	13 7/8	5	5	Marion County	OR	Doug Harris	1985	66
125 6/8	19 3/8	18 5/8	14 2/8	4	4	Siskiyou County	CA	Cliff Dewell	1969	67
125 4/8	19 7/8	21 6/8	19 6/8	6	6	Josephine County	OR	Dave Hall	1983	68
125 3/8	22 0/8	23 4/8	19 3/8	5	4	Lane County	OR	Joe Lilley	1992	69
124 7/8	19 2/8	19 2/8	14 1/8	4	4	Humboldt County	CA	Mike Taylor	1987	70
124 7/8	18 0/8	19 0/8	15 3/8	5	4	Alameda County	CA	Eugene Damron	1988	70
124 6/8	20 7/8	19 0/8	16 6/8	4	5	Clackamas County	OR	Joseph Suire	1983	72
124 2/8	20 0/8	20 6/8	16 4/8	4	5	Lewis County	WA	Sandy Tyler	1957	73
124 2/8	19 0/8	19 5/8	17 2/8	4	5	Lane County	OR	David Wright Bucknum	1989	73
123 7/8	17 3/8	17 4/8	15 1/8	5	5	Siskiyou County	CA	Bill Collinsworth	1983	75
123 6/8	19 5/8	20 0/8	16 2/8	5	5	Lane County	OR	Steve Rogers	1990	76
123 5/8	19 0/8	19 0/8	15 1/8	5	5	Lewis County	WA	Bob Eisele	1991	77
123 4/8	21 3/8	21 7/8	16 2/8	4	4	Thurston County	WA	Al Kowalski	1978	78
123 4/8	19 0/8	20 0/8	14 4/8	4	5	Lewis County	WA	Randal E. White	1990	78
123 3/8	18 6/8	19 1/8	17 3/8	5	5	Trinity County	CA	Glen S. Ceccon	1987	80
123 0/8	20 0/8	21 0/8	14 4/8	6	5	Klickitat County	WA	Larry Ramsey	1977	81
123 0/8	18 6/8	18 7/8	14 6/8	6	6	Jackson County	OR	Larry Frost	1984	81
123 0/8	21 0/8	20 6/8	15 0/8	5	5	Clackamas County	OR	Alan M. Taylor	1991	81
122 7/8	19 1/8	20 4/8	16 1/8	4	4	Trinity County	CA	Loran G. August	1981	84
122 5/8	17 7/8	18 1/8	15 3/8	5	5	Trinity County	CA	Ted Lohse	1985	85
122 5/8	19 0/8	19 1/8	15 1/8	5	4	Mendocino County	CA	Mark Masamori	1992	85
122 1/8	19 5/8	19 5/8	17 4/8	5	6	Jackson County	OR	Richard G. Speer	1965	87
122 0/8	19 7/8	20 4/8	15 6/8	4	4	Contra Costa County	CA	Donald M. Graves	1990	88
121 7/8	20 5/8	20 6/8	15 7/8	5	5	Lewis County	WA	Robert E. Hill	1988	89
121 4/8	20 6/8	20 5/8	17 4/8	5	4	Lane County	OR	Bradley M. Dorsing	1991	90
121 3/8	15 5/8	15 2/8	14 0/8	5	5	Humboldt County	CA	Doug Walker	1965	91
121 3/8	19 7/8	18 7/8	16 4/8	7	5	Trinity County	CA	Mark Greving	1982	91
121 2/8	22 4/8	22 4/8	22 2/8	4	4	Humboldt County	CA	Arthur Cain	1991	93
121 1/8	20 3/8	20 6/8	18 2/8	4	3	Yamhill County	OR	Ray Kelton	1981	94
121 0/8	18 0/8	17 0/8	14 4/8	5	5	Benton County	OR	Larry D. Jones	1966	95
120 6/8	18 5/8	19 0/8	15 4/8	5	5	Humboldt County	CA	Joe Henry	1980	96
120 6/8	20 0/8	19 6/8	18 2/8	4	3	Linn County	OR	Jim R. Brown	1987	96
120 3/8	17 1/8	18 1/8	12 7/8	5	5	Santa Cruz County	CA	Douglas G. Bonetti	1987	98
120 3/8	19 2/8	18 7/8	18 1/8	6	6	Glenn County	CA	Jim Alves	1987	98
120 1/8	18 3/8	18 4/8	15 5/8	5	5	Lane County	OR	Dale Drilling	1990	100
119 6/8	20 0/8	20 3/8	16 2/8	4	4	Pacific County	WA	John Higgins	1973	101

SCORE	LENGTH OF MAIN BEAM		INSIDE SPREAD	NUMBER OF POINTS		AREA	STATE/ PROVINCE	HUNTER'S NAME	DATE	RANK
	R	L		R	L					
119 5/8	21 2/8	21 2/8	19 6/8	6	7	Wasco County	OR	Cecil Shuler	1967	102
119 4/8	20 5/8	20 4/8	16 2/8	5	4	Mendocino County	CA	Edward V. Moore	1989	103
119 3/8	21 5/8	21 4/8	17 3/8	4	3	Humboldt County	CA	Art Young	1918	104
119 0/8	20 6/8	19 2/8	15 6/8	5	5	Kitsap County	WA	Bob Devine	1986	105
118 6/8	20 4/8	20 2/8	14 6/8	4	5	Skamania County	WA	Frank Adkins	1967	106
118 6/8	18 4/8	17 7/8	14 4/8	4	4	Santa Clara County	CA	Eugene Damron	1987	106
118 5/8	19 0/8	19 5/8	19 5/8	4	4	Sonoma County	CA	Paul Fiedorek	1987	108
118 4/8	20 3/8	19 7/8	19 2/8	4	5	Slesse Creek	BC	Ken Davidson	1987	109
117 7/8	18 0/8	18 1/8	15 7/8	5	4	Benton County	OR	Chuck Warner	1992	110
117 4/8	18 0/8	18 2/8	14 1/8	5	5	Benton County	OR	Chris Reed	1970	111
117 3/8	18 1/8	18 3/8	16 3/8	4	4	Humboldt County	CA	Dennis A. McClelland	1989	112
117 3/8	18 3/8	19 7/8	16 3/8	4	4	Lincoln County	OR	Dianna Rorie	1991	112
116 7/8	18 6/8	18 2/8	13 7/8	5	5	Kitsap County	WA	Don D. Axtman	1990	114
116 5/8	19 5/8	20 3/8	12 5/8	4	5	Pacific County	WA	Smokey Crews	1969	115
116 5/8	20 1/8	20 7/8	17 3/8	4	4	Lincoln County	OR	Fred Rorie	1990	115
116 2/8	18 7/8	19 7/8	19 0/8	4	4	Jackson County	OR	Ray Gibson	1962	117
116 2/8	18 6/8	18 4/8	16 6/8	5	4	Trinity County	CA	Mike Lindley	1983	117
116 2/8	17 4/8	17 2/8	14 0/8	5	4	Clackamas County	OR	W. Troy Stevens	1988	117
116 1/8	19 0/8	19 4/8	15 3/8	5	4	King County	WA	John Martin	1983	120
115 6/8	19 6/8	19 6/8	16 6/8	5	4	Clackamas County	OR	Jack Smith	1981	121
115 6/8	19 2/8	18 2/8	18 0/8	5	5	Siskiyou County	CA	Fred Searle	1983	121
115 5/8	17 4/8	17 4/8	13 7/8	5	5	Siskiyou County	CA	Mike Garretson	1981	123
115 5/8	17 0/8	17 1/8	14 5/8	5	5	Polk County	OR	Randy Gunn	1981	123
115 4/8	22 2/8	21 7/8	19 2/8	5	3	Lane County	OR	Ken Holland	1988	125
115 2/8	19 4/8	19 4/8	16 2/8	4	4	Humboldt County	CA	J. E. Grundman	1963	126
115 2/8	16 6/8	16 4/8	15 4/8	5	5	Douglas County	OR	Kevin Dicke	1989	126
115 1/8	16 6/8	16 3/8	15 7/8	5	5	Sumas Mtn.	BC	Peter L. Halbig	1985	128
115 1/8	17 4/8	18 0/8	14 3/8	5	4	Marion County	OR	Ronald J. Miller	1989	128
115 0/8	21 2/8	21 0/8	17 1/8	6	4	Marion County	OR	Chuck Lynde	1989	130
114 1/8	20 1/8	19 3/8	15 5/8	5	5	Kitsap County	WA	Boyd Shelby	1989	131
114 0/8	17 3/8	16 6/8	16 0/8	5	4	Clackamas County	OR	Dave Showerman	1982	132
113 6/8	17 3/8	15 6/8	15 0/8	5	5	Benton County	OR	Gregory M. McHuron	1966	133
113 4/8	18 1/8	17 5/8	15 2/8	4	4	Mendocino County	CA	Jeff S. Spangler	1982	134
113 4/8	19 2/8	19 2/8	19 0/8	4	5	Linn County	OR	John Stone	1986	134
113 2/8	18 2/8	17 5/8	16 0/8	4	4	King County	WA	Vick Stevens	1984	136
113 2/8	17 0/8	16 7/8	12 2/8	4	4	Lane County	OR	Neil Summers	1991	136
112 7/8	19 1/8	17 6/8	14 1/8	4	5	Skagit County	WA	J. B. Bright	1986	138
112 5/8	21 2/8	20 4/8	14 1/8	5	5	King County	WA	Greg Tedlund	1984	139
112 4/8	16 0/8	15 1/8	13 4/8	5	5	Trinity County	CA	Dennis Schroer	1982	140
112 4/8	18 6/8	17 6/8	14 2/8	5	5	Lane County	OR	Steve Rogers	1989	140
112 3/8	16 7/8	16 3/8	13 7/8	5	5	Snohomish County	WA	Jack Davis	1975	142
112 3/8	17 4/8	19 2/8	13 6/8	4	5	Douglas County	OR	Ken French	1980	142
112 2/8	18 5/8	19 1/8	15 2/8	4	4	Pacific County	WA	Leon Poindexter	1968	144
112 1/8	17 1/8	17 4/8	13 3/8	5	5	Benton County	OR	Gary Nyden	1986	145
112 0/8	18 4/8	19 2/8	16 4/8	4	4	Lane County	OR	Ken Kalinowski	1988	146
111 7/8	17 7/8	17 0/8	14 5/8	4	4	Pacific County	WA	Smokey Crews	1967	147
111 5/8	20 0/8	19 4/8	15 5/8	5	5	Pierce County	WA	Randy Cole	1989	148
111 5/8	16 4/8	15 5/8	12 3/8	5	5	Lincoln County	OR	Jeffrey D. Messmer	1989	148
111 3/8	16 0/8	17 3/8	17 4/8	5	4	Linn County	OR	Chuck Warner	1985	150
111 3/8	19 5/8	19 6/8	16 3/8	5	4	Lane County	OR	David Chapman	1986	150
111 0/8	19 2/8	18 4/8	14 4/8	4	3	Skagit County	WA	Sam Ingram	1988	152
110 7/8	18 3/8	17 0/8	16 3/8	4	4	Jackson County	OR	Dale K. Marcy	1966	153
110 7/8	17 5/8	18 3/8	14 5/8	4	5	Marion County	OR	David Conway	1991	153
110 6/8	18 4/8	17 7/8	17 0/8	4	4	Del Norte County	CA	Michael Penn	1979	155
110 6/8	20 6/8	21 5/8	19 4/8	3	3	Contra Costa County	CA	Richard L. Westervelt	1987	155
110 5/8	19 7/8	20 3/8	13 4/8	4	6	Jackson County	OR	Dr. G. Scott Jennings	1979	157
110 4/8	17 1/8	17 3/8	13 6/8	4	4	Clark County	WA	Larry D. Nahrstedt	1968	158
110 4/8	17 0/8	18 7/8	17 4/8	4	4	Marin County	CA	Howard C. Gold	1976	158
110 4/8	18 4/8	18 4/8	15 6/8	4	4	Pierce County	WA	Greg Paige	1990	158
110 3/8	16 1/8	15 1/8	15 7/8	5	5	Wild Deer Lake	BC	Guy Anttila	1970	161
110 3/8	19 3/8	20 0/8	13 6/8	6	5	North Vancouver	BC	Fred Day	1970	161
110 2/8	19 6/8	20 0/8	17 4/8	5	5	Lane County	OR	Richard M. Cook	1982	163
109 7/8	22 0/8	21 3/8	14 5/8	5	5	Linn County	OR	Steve Gilbert	1982	164
109 6/8	21 1/8	20 7/8	16 4/8	3	4	Lewis County	WA	Barney Johnson	1974	165
109 6/8	17 4/8	18 2/8	18 2/8	4	4	Santa Cruz County	CA	Robert Alan Nottingham	1992	165
109 5/8	20 4/8	19 4/8	15 3/8	5	4	Douglas County	OR	Teddy Rainville	1980	167
109 5/8	19 1/8	21 0/8	14 5/8	3	3	Lake County	CA	Paul W. Farina	1983	167
109 5/8	16 2/8	16 2/8	14 5/8	4	4	Siskiyou County	CA	Ralph Atkinson	1984	167
109 5/8	17 1/8	17 2/8	15 7/8	4	4	Clackamas County	OR	Randy Teeney	1985	167
109 5/8	18 4/8	18 6/8	15 5/8	4	4	Lane County	OR	Wm E. Sweetland	1985	167

Score	Length of Main Beam R	L	Inside Spread	Number of Points R	L	Area	State/ Province	Hunter's Name	Date	Rank
109 5/8	21 4/8	19 7/8	19 5/8	3	3	Santa Clara County	CA	Eugene Damron	1991	167
109 4/8	19 6/8	19 7/8	14 2/8	6	5	Pierce County	WA	Don Axtman	1989	173
109 4/8	16 5/8	16 4/8	12 6/8	5	5	Clackamas County	OR	Nick G. Kathrein	1991	173
109 3/8	17 0/8	17 5/8	14 4/8	6	5	Lane County	OR	Mark Klein	1982	175
109 3/8	18 3/8	17 2/8	16 7/8	4	4	Clackamas County	OR	Stanley P. Stagl	1989	175
109 3/8	17 0/8	17 7/8	17 5/8	4	4	Cowlitz County	WA	Tom Heltemes	1990	175
109 2/8	17 5/8	16 5/8	14 2/8	5	5	Lane County	OR	Brandy Knight	1991	178
109 1/8	19 7/8	19 7/8	14 1/8	5	4	Lewis County	WA	Glen Marquis	1990	179
109 0/8	20 0/8	20 0/8	15 6/8	4	3	Josephine County	OR	Sam Burten	1987	180
108 7/8	17 6/8	19 1/8	13 7/8	5	5	Jackson County	OR	Joe Williamson	1963	181
108 7/8	16 7/8	17 0/8	13 5/8	5	5	Josephine County	OR	Michael Penn	1983	181
108 5/8	19 2/8	18 4/8	16 3/8	3	3	Douglas County	OR	Rick Gabbard	1984	183
108 4/8	16 1/8	16 2/8	11 6/8	5	4	Clackamas County	OR	Ed Franzen	1985	184
108 4/8	18 0/8	17 7/8	16 2/8	5	4	Lane County	OR	Jim Howell	1988	184
108 3/8	19 1/8	19 2/8	13 1/8	4	3	Mendocino County	CA	Gaylen Kessel	1988	186
108 1/8	19 1/8	18 4/8	15 2/8	6	6	Skagit County	WA	Charles Kager	1988	187
108 1/8	18 0/8	17 5/8	17 5/8	4	4	Sonoma County	CA	Robert Larson	1992	187
108 0/8	18 3/8	19 5/8	16 0/8	4	4	Trinity County	CA	Michael Hopper	1989	189
107 7/8	20 6/8	20 7/8	19 7/8	3	3	Sonoma County	CA	Michael Bradeen	1992	190
107 6/8	18 2/8	18 4/8	19 3/8	3	4	Trinity County	CA	Dennis Alan Betts	1980	191
107 6/8	17 2/8	17 4/8	13 0/8	4	3	Lane County	OR	James A. Conway	1988	191
107 6/8	18 1/8	18 0/8	15 4/8	4	4	Douglas County	OR	Joe Cordonier	1989	191
107 5/8	17 5/8	18 5/8	14 1/8	5	4	Clackamas County	OR	Bob Manley	1982	194
107 4/8	21 4/8	22 3/8	19 4/8	2	2	Trinity County	CA	John R. Sample	1989	195
107 1/8	15 7/8	15 4/8	13 7/8	4	4	Lincoln County	OR	Ray Kelton	1982	196
106 7/8	18 3/8	18 2/8	16 3/8	4	3	Skamania County	WA	Steve Shipp	1984	197
106 6/8	19 3/8	20 0/8	19 6/8	4	3	Contra Costa County	CA	Frank Sanders	1990	198
106 2/8	17 1/8	16 3/8	13 6/8	5	4	Lewis County	WA	Mike Mussman	1984	199
106 1/8	19 4/8	19 0/8	12 7/8	3	4	Trinity County	CA	Mike Lindley	1981	200
106 0/8	17 4/8	17 6/8	17 7/8	4	5	Trinity County	CA	Chuck Adams	1982	201
106 0/8	17 5/8	17 5/8	14 2/8	4	4	Skamania County	WA	Jeffrey L. Kujala	1984	201
106 0/8	17 6/8	17 7/8	14 6/8	5	4	Lane County	OR	Dan Rogers	1989	201
105 3/8	17 3/8	17 3/8	15 5/8	3	4	Coos County	OR	Gary Scorby	1971	204
105 1/8	18 6/8	19 2/8	15 7/8	3	3	Stanislaus County	CA	Harold Arnold	1970	205
105 1/8	18 1/8	18 1/8	18 4/8	3	3	San Mateo County	CA	John Grochowski	1985	205
104 6/8	17 3/8	17 2/8	13 6/8	5	4	Coos County	OR	Darryl S. Herndon	1989	207
104 5/8	16 2/8	16 2/8	12 7/8	4	4	King County	WA	Ken Gettman	1987	208
104 3/8	18 5/8	18 3/8	15 3/8	4	4	Polk County	OR	Tim Nolan	1987	209
104 3/8	17 4/8	18 2/8	16 5/8	4	4	Lane County	OR	Cameron Hanes	1990	209
104 2/8	16 4/8	17 0/8	16 2/8	4	4	Lake County	CA	Phil Phillips	1991	211
104 2/8	17 2/8	17 4/8	16 2/8	5	4	Mendocino County	CA	Michael Christensen	1991	211
104 1/8	15 4/8	15 6/8	13 3/8	5	5	Clackamas County	OR	Ben Cook	1988	213
104 0/8	18 6/8	21 6/8	15 1/8	5	5	Trinity County	CA	Chuck Adams	1982	214
103 6/8	15 7/8	16 4/8	12 2/8	5	5	Linn County	OR	Doug Bashor	1986	215
103 5/8	17 7/8	18 3/8	15 5/8	3	3	Linn County	OR	Gary Burns	1981	216
103 4/8	19 0/8	19 5/8	13 2/8	3	3	Lane County	OR	Randy Cook	1988	217
103 4/8	16 6/8	17 1/8	13 7/8	5	4	Lane County	OR	Neil Summers	1989	217
103 3/8	16 7/8	16 6/8	17 0/8	3	4	Sonoma County	CA	Arnie Dado	1986	219
103 2/8	17 7/8	17 7/8	15 0/8	4	4	Lewis County	WA	Charles L. Hunt	1990	220
103 0/8	15 5/8	15 0/8	14 0/8	5	5	Mendocino County	CA	Gregg L. Welch	1982	221
103 0/8	19 2/8	19 0/8	14 4/8	5	3	Clark County	WA	W. R. "Rick" Hassler	1988	221
103 0/8	16 6/8	17 2/8	12 4/8	4	4	Santa Clara County	CA	Thomas L. Liston	1990	221
102 6/8	17 4/8	17 4/8	17 4/8	3	3	Polk County	OR	Robert L. Ball	1975	224
102 5/8	16 7/8	16 6/8	14 5/8	4	4	Deschutes County	OR	Steve L. Stilwell	1976	225
102 3/8	18 4/8	19 1/8	16 5/8	4	4	Siskiyou County	CA	Terry Proctor	1988	226
102 2/8	17 7/8	16 5/8	12 0/8	3	4	Clackamas County	OR	A. Corey Heath	1980	227
102 0/8	17 2/8	17 0/8	13 6/8	4	4	Jackson County	OR	George Miller	1966	228
101 4/8	18 5/8	17 5/8	15 1/8	5	5	King County	WA	Mike D. Dunham	1987	229
101 3/8	17 0/8	17 4/8	15 3/8	4	3	Jackson County	OR	Dr. G. Scott Jennings	1959	230
100 7/8	17 1/8	17 2/8	14 7/8	4	4	Marshall Creek	BC	Ken Scheer	1988	231
100 6/8	15 6/8	15 5/8	15 4/8	4	5	Klamath County	OR	Dr. George Miller	1964	232
100 5/8	17 0/8	17 4/8	13 7/8	5	4	Clackamas County	OR	Stanley P. Stagl	1990	233
100 1/8	16 7/8	16 6/8	13 7/8	4	4	Douglas County	OR	James F. Rayner	1988	234
100 0/8	18 2/8	18 5/8	14 2/8	3	4	Kitsap County	WA	Boyd E. Shelby, Jr.	1990	235
99 6/8	20 6/8	20 0/8	14 0/8	2	2	Pacific County	WA	Robert A. Brown	1965	236
99 6/8	17 1/8	17 2/8	14 6/8	5	4	Humboldt County	CA	Greg Gottschalk	1990	236
99 5/8	17 3/8	18 1/8	12 7/8	4	4	Lewis County	WA	Eric H. Ames	1989	238
99 5/8	16 5/8	17 0/8	13 7/8	5	4	Clackamas County	OR	Tim Streight	1990	238
99 3/8	17 5/8	18 0/8	15 1/8	3	3	Siskiyou County	CA	Dave S. Semple	1984	240
99 1/8	19 2/8	18 5/8	11 3/8	4	3	Lincoln County	OR	Fred Rorie	1988	241

SCORE	LENGTH OF MAIN BEAM R L	INSIDE SPREAD	NUMBER OF POINTS R L		AREA	STATE/ PROVINCE	HUNTER'S NAME	DATE	RANK
99 0/8	16 3/8	16 5/8	14 0/8	5	5	Lincoln County	OR	Charles M. Roeser	1974	242
99 0/8	21 2/8	19 7/8	15 6/8	4	5	Santa Clara County	CA	Mike Walker	1979	242
99 0/8	16 6/8	16 6/8	12 6/8	4	4	Mendocino County	CA	Russell L. Browning	1983	242
99 0/8	17 0/8	16 3/8	13 2/8	4	4	Contra Costa County	CA	Richard L. Westervelt	1985	242
99 0/8	16 2/8	16 5/8	14 6/8	4	5	Kitsap County	WA	Cecil McConnell	1986	242
99 0/8	16 7/8	15 7/8	15 4/8	4	4	Clackamas County	OR	Darrell Scheffer	1991	242
98 7/8	20 2/8	19 4/8	14 1/8	3	2	Pacific County	WA	William V. Mishler	1968	248
98 5/8	19 2/8	19 2/8	14 5/8	3	3	Mendocino County	CA	Joseph A. Wyman	1990	249
98 3/8	16 1/8	16 3/8	14 3/8	4	4	Sonoma County	CA	Ray Torrey	1967	250
98 3/8	16 3/8	16 1/8	17 0/8	4	4	Lane County	OR	Gary R. Swan	1990	250
98 1/8	16 0/8	16 3/8	12 7/8	4	4	Rogue Unit	OR	Barbara Richardson	1964	252
98 1/8	17 3/8	17 1/8	17 1/8	4	4	Clackamas County	OR	Blake M. Bartley	1988	252
98 0/8	19 7/8	19 6/8	14 6/8	4	2	Pacific County	WA	Morris Wolters	1967	254
97 7/8	16 3/8	15 5/8	16 1/8	5	5	Benton County	OR	Harold Stice	1957	255
97 5/8	20 2/8	19 7/8	16 7/8	3	3	Marin County	CA	Mike Taylor	1985	256
97 5/8	17 4/8	17 6/8	13 5/8	3	3	Siskiyou County	CA	Randy Root	1987	256
97 4/8	18 6/8	18 2/8	18 6/8	3	3	Whatcom County	WA	Steve Holland	1963	258
97 4/8	18 1/8	18 4/8	15 6/8	3	3	Marion County	OR	Ken Kalinowski	1981	258
97 4/8	20 3/8	19 7/8	15 4/8	4	3	Trinity County	CA	Rodney A. York	1987	258
97 3/8	19 1/8	18 4/8	20 0/8	3	3	Marin County	CA	Joe Checchio	1985	261
97 3/8	17 2/8	18 0/8	14 5/8	3	3	Linn County	OR	Michael A. Cramblit	1989	261
97 2/8	16 7/8	17 0/8	12 2/8	4	3	Pacific County	WA	Todd Hubble	1980	263
97 2/8	17 4/8	17 4/8	13 4/8	4	4	King County	WA	Jay E. Tinker	1986	263
97 0/8	16 7/8	16 4/8	12 0/8	4	4	Pacific County	WA	Lawrence Rogers	1972	265
97 0/8	18 0/8	18 3/8	14 4/8	3	2	Mendocino County	CA	Wayne Piersol	1991	265
96 7/8	17 2/8	17 2/8	14 7/8	4	4	Glenn County	CA	Joe Williams	1977	267
96 6/8	16 5/8	16 3/8	12 0/8	4	4	Benton County	OR	John W. Shipley	1991	268
96 1/8	15 4/8	15 0/8	13 3/8	4	4	Pacific County	WA	Lynne Sharp	1965	269
96 0/8	16 0/8	15 7/8	12 6/8	4	4	Soda Springs	OR	Harold Benson	1961	270
96 0/8	15 5/8	16 2/8	13 6/8	4	5	Clackamas County	OR	Robert Oxley	1989	270
95 5/8	17 5/8	15 2/8	14 3/8	5	5	Siskiyou County	CA	Thomas V. Sieverding	1971	272
95 5/8	16 1/8	17 2/8	12 1/8	4	4	Humboldt County	CA	Calvin Farner	1983	272
94 7/8	17 7/8	18 2/8	16 3/8	2	2	Santa Cruz County	CA	Robert Alan Nottingham	1984	274
94 7/8	15 7/8	16 1/8	14 1/8	4	4	Shasta County	CA	Danny R. Shurtleff	1987	274
94 7/8	18 4/8	18 2/8	16 3/8	2	2	Sonoma County	CA	Wayne Piersol	1992	274
94 6/8	16 3/8	17 1/8	14 2/8	5	4	Lewis County	WA	Daniel A. Yirka	1987	277
94 6/8	18 7/8	19 3/8	17 2/8	3	2	Sonoma County	CA	Mike Taylor	1989	277
94 5/8	15 6/8	15 3/8	10 7/8	4	4	Benton County	OR	Raymond E. Root	1970	279
94 5/8	15 7/8	15 5/8	16 1/8	4	4	Sonoma County	CA	Russell L. Browning	1980	279
94 4/8	18 0/8	17 5/8	13 2/8	4	3	Mendocino County	CA	Chuck Adams	1983	281
94 3/8	18 0/8	16 2/8	16 5/8	2	4	Klamath County	OR	Don Pritchett	1964	282
94 0/8	16 7/8	18 4/8	12 0/8	4	4	Capitol Forest	WA	C. N. Pickle	1960	283
94 0/8	17 6/8	17 5/8	11 4/8	3	4	Benton County	OR	Edward U. Tobler	1970	283
94 0/8	16 6/8	16 5/8	18 0/8	3	3	Humboldt County	CA	Craig Coolahan	1989	283
93 7/8	18 2/8	16 4/8	16 5/8	4	5	Sonoma County	CA	Sean Dunn	1992	286
93 6/8	18 3/8	18 5/8	13 6/8	2	4	Lewis County	WA	Floyd Gregg	1962	287
93 6/8	15 6/8	15 5/8	12 6/8	4	4	Mendocino County	CA	Chuck Adams	1979	287
93 3/8	18 5/8	18 5/8	15 4/8	5	5	Clackamas County	OR	Randy Teeney	1987	289
93 2/8	17 0/8	16 7/8	12 4/8	4	3	Linn County	OR	Joe Mengore	1983	290
93 2/8	16 2/8	17 2/8	17 3/8	3	3	Humboldt County	CA	Monty Clemmer	1986	290
93 0/8	17 3/8	17 6/8	14 0/8	4	3	Clallam County	WA	Wayne Haag	1987	292
92 6/8	16 0/8	16 3/8	13 4/8	5	5	Marion County	OR	Larry Jones	1986	293
92 3/8	18 0/8	18 2/8	15 1/8	3	2	Mendocino County	CA	Wilfred Willis	1982	294
92 0/8	18 4/8	18 4/8	19 2/8	2	2	Josephine County	OR	Joe White	1986	295
92 0/8	16 4/8	16 5/8	16 0/8	3	3	Santa Cruz County	CA	H. Brian Malsbury	1987	295
91 5/8	15 1/8	15 2/8	13 1/8	5	5	King County	WA	Vic Stevens	1986	297
91 3/8	17 3/8	17 0/8	16 3/8	2	2	Mendocino County	CA	Joseph Wyman	1991	298
91 2/8	18 0/8	17 4/8	13 4/8	5	3	Yamhill County	OR	R. Keith Potter	1990	299
91 1/8	17 1/8	18 0/8	13 1/8	3	3	Benton County	OR	Jim Nielsen	1981	300
91 1/8	15 3/8	16 5/8	13 1/8	3	4	Lane County	OR	Ken Kalinowski	1986	300
91 1/8	15 4/8	16 1/8	16 3/8	3	3	Sonoma County	CA	Ernie Fechter	1990	300
90 7/8	15 5/8	15 1/8	12 3/8	3	3	Clallam County	WA	Renny Mason	1989	303
90 5/8	16 7/8	17 1/8	15 1/8	2	2	Santa Clara County	CA	Sandee Cox	1989	304
90 4/8	14 6/8	14 3/8	12 3/8	4	4	Whatcom County	WA	Jack Fish	1956	305
90 4/8	16 4/8	16 7/8	15 0/8	2	2	Merced County	CA	Jim Walton	1980	305
90 3/8	16 6/8	15 6/8	14 3/8	4	5	Mendocino County	CA	Chuck Adams	1977	307
90 2/8	14 5/8	15 1/8	12 0/8	4	4	Pacific County	WA	Leonard Bray	1965	308
90 0/8	15 0/8	14 6/8	12 6/8	4	4	Benton County	OR	Tom Ronchetti	1990	309

World Record Columbian Blacktail (Non-Typical Antlers)
Score: 194 4/8
Jackson County, Oregon - 1988
Hunter: James Decker

COLUMBIAN BLACKTAIL *(Non-Typical Antlers)*

MINIMUM SCORE 110

Odocoileus hemionus columbianus

SCORE	LENGTH OF R MAIN BEAM L		INSIDE SPREAD	NUMBER OF R POINTS L		AREA	STATE/ PROVINCE	HUNTER'S NAME	DATE	RANK
194 4/8	23 3/8	23 4/8	19 1/8	8	10	Jackson County	OR	James Decker	1988	1
146 0/8	19 2/8	19 0/8	15 7/8	7	7	San Mateo County	CA	John Grochowski	1984	2
139 5/8	18 6/8	18 6/8	15 7/8	5	8	Siskiyou County	CA	Kurt Case	1980	3
131 6/8	22 7/8	22 6/8	18 3/8	7	4	Douglas County	OR	Jerry R. De Loach	1975	4
123 4/8	20 5/8	19 2/8	16 0/8	4	7	Douglas County	OR	Thomas E. Tipton	1983	5

World Record Sitka Blacktail Deer
Score: 116 3/8
Prince of Wales Island, Alaska - 1987
Hunter: Charles Hakari

SCORE	R LENGTH OF MAIN BEAM L		INSIDE SPREAD	R NUMBER OF POINTS L		AREA	STATE/ PROVINCE	HUNTER'S NAME	DATE	RANK
116 3/8	18 4/8	18 2/8	13 1/8	5	5	Prince of Wales Island	AK	Charles Hakari	1987	1
115 6/8	17 1/8	16 3/8	14 6/8	5	5	Prince of Wales Island	AK	Kirt O. Marsh	1988	2
114 3/8	18 5/8	18 7/8	18 1/8	5	5	Kodiak Island	AK	Jim Ryan	1986	3
112 2/8	19 0/8	19 2/8	16 4/8	4	4	Kodiak Island	AK	John D. "Jack" Frost	1987	4
110 5/8	17 3/8	17 1/8	15 5/8	6	5	Kodiak Island	AK	Bill Krenz	1988	5
108 4/8	16 4/8	15 6/8	15 0/8	5	5	Kodiak Island	AK	Chuck Adams	1986	6
107 6/8	17 2/8	16 2/8	14 2/8	5	5	Kodiak Island	AK	Chuck Adams	1986	7
107 4/8	17 3/8	17 4/8	14 4/8	5	5	Kodiak Island	AK	Chuck Adams	1987	8
107 4/8	17 3/8	17 1/8	14 4/8	5	5	Prince of Wales Island	AK	Danny Moore	1988	8
107 2/8	15 3/8	15 1/8	13 6/8	5	5	Kodiak Island	AK	Chris Dau	1986	10
106 4/8	17 3/8	16 6/8	16 5/8	5	6	Kodiak Island	AK	Douglas G. Bonetti	1985	11
105 3/8	16 3/8	16 4/8	15 1/8	5	6	Kodiak Island	AK	John T. Toenes	1988	12
104 5/8	18 0/8	17 5/8	17 7/8	4	5	Kodiak Island	AK	Richard L. Westervelt	1987	13
103 5/8	18 4/8	17 2/8	15 7/8	4	5	Kodiak Island	AK	Chuck Adams	1987	14
102 2/8	18 4/8	16 6/8	13 4/8	4	5	Kodiak Island	AK	Brad H. Parker	1989	15
102 0/8	18 0/8	18 0/8	16 2/8	5	4	Kodiak Island	AK	John D. 'Jack' Frost	1986	16
101 6/8	15 4/8	16 2/8	13 6/8	5	5	Kodiak Island	Ak	Gary G. Wall	1986	17
101 3/8	15 6/8	16 3/8	14 3/8	5	5	Kodiak Island	AK	Lon E. Lauber	1991	18
101 0/8	19 0/8	19 0/8	17 0/8	5	5	Kodiak Island	AK	Gene Coughlin	1984	19
101 0/8	18 1/8	17 7/8	16 4/8	5	4	Kodiak Island	AK	Danny Moore	1986	19
100 5/8	17 7/8	17 0/8	16 3/8	4	5	Ugak Bay	AK	Thomas Chadwick	1987	21
99 4/8	17 4/8	17 7/8	16 0/8	4	5	Kodiak Island	AK	Danny Moore	1984	22
99 0/8	14 1/8	15 5/8	13 4/8	5	5	Kodiak Island	AK	Al Besch	1984	23
98 7/8	16 6/8	16 6/8	14 5/8	5	4	Kodiak Island	AK	Danny Moore	1986	24
98 5/8	16 6/8	16 2/8	16 5/8	4	4	Kodiak Island	AK	Craig D. Morrow	1987	25
98 4/8	16 4/8	14 2/8	14 0/8	4	5	Kodiak Island	AK	Michael L. Nunn	1984	26
98 4/8	14 4/8	17 0/8	17 1/8	5	4	Kodiak Island	AK	Tom Chadwick	1985	26
98 2/8	14 7/8	14 7/8	13 4/8	5	5	Kodiak Island	AK	Philip F. Nuechterlein	1985	28
98 2/8	15 0/8	14 7/8	13 2/8	5	5	Kodiak Island	AK	Glenn Vandergaw	1988	28
97 7/8	18 2/8	18 4/8	14 1/8	4	4	Larson Bay	AK	Carol Kindred	1989	30
97 6/8	18 1/8	18 0/8	18 0/8	4	3	Kodiak Island	AK	Patricia A. Stewart	1983	31
97 5/8	16 4/8	17 4/8	16 7/8	4	5	Prince of Wales Island	AK	Marvin H. Walter	1987	32
97 5/8	16 7/8	17 2/8	16 3/8	4	4	Kodiak Island	AK	Roger Stewart	1988	33
97 2/8	15 0/8	13 6/8	13 0/8	5	5	Kodiak Island	AK	Chuck Adams	1986	34
96 4/8	18 1/8	18 2/8	15 6/8	4	5	Prince of Wales Island	AK	Glen R. Shepard	1987	35
96 3/8	16 1/8	16 6/8	15 5/8	4	4	Kodiak Island	AK	Gary G. Wall	1986	36
96 2/8	17 5/8	17 0/8	15 6/8	3	4	Kodiak Island	AK	Dick McClain	1990	37
96 1/8	17 1/8	16 3/8	13 7/8	4	4	Kodiak Island	AK	Don Rossiter	1985	38
95 6/8	17 5/8	17 4/8	17 0/8	3	3	Kodiak Island	AK	Paul Persano	1986	39
95 3/8	17 4/8	17 3/8	15 5/8	4	4	Kodiak Island	AK	John D. "Jack" Frost	1990	40
94 7/8	16 7/8	16 7/8	13 1/8	5	6	Kodiak Island	AK	Chuck Adams	1984	41
94 3/8	16 1/8	15 5/8	16 1/8	4	4	Kodiak Island	AK	Dyrk Eddie	1986	42
94 3/8	16 4/8	16 1/8	15 5/8	4	4	Kodiak Island	AK	Doug Keller	1988	42
93 4/8	15 2/8	15 4/8	15 4/8	5	4	Kodiak Island	AK	Paul Persano	1986	44
93 3/8	15 2/8	15 4/8	13 3/8	5	5	Kodiak Island	AK	Herman J. Griese	1982	45
93 3/8	17 4/8	15 4/8	13 5/8	4	4	Kodiak Island	AK	Chuck Adams	1987	45
93 2/8	16 0/8	15 6/8	15 0/8	4	4	Kodiak Island	AK	John Toenes	1987	47
93 2/8	18 0/8	17 1/8	14 0/8	4	4	Kodiak Island	AK	Russell M. Kucinski	1989	47
92 7/8	16 3/8	15 6/8	15 1/8	4	4	Kodiak Island	AK	John Sarvis	1987	49
92 1/8	14 7/8	14 0/8	15 0/8	4	4	Kodiak Island	AK	Richard Moran	1988	50
92 0/8	16 5/8	16 0/8	13 4/8	4	4	Kodiak Island	AK	Chuck Adams	1986	51
92 0/8	15 2/8	16 2/8	13 4/8	6	5	Larson Bay	AK	Lou Kindred	1989	51
91 7/8	16 1/8	16 5/8	14 7/8	4	4	Afognak Island	AK	Edward L. Russell	1980	53
91 7/8	14 4/8	15 0/8	12 3/8	4	4	Queen Charlotte Islands	BC	Grant Janczyn	1991	53
91 5/8	14 2/8	14 2/8	14 5/8	4	4	Afognak Island	AK	Ray Ryan	1984	55
91 5/8	14 4/8	15 1/8	12 7/8	5	5	Kodiak Island	AK	Danny Moore	1986	55
91 4/8	14 6/8	14 4/8	13 0/8	5	5	Kodiak Island	AK	Chuck Adams	1986	57
91 2/8	12 4/8	16 2/8	13 2/8	5	4	Kodiak Island	AK	Randy Mannix	1984	58
91 2/8	15 2/8	16 0/8	14 4/8	4	4	Kodiak Island	AK	Tim Stelzer	1988	58
90 7/8	15 4/8	15 3/8	15 1/8	4	4	Kodiak Island	AK	Kirk Westervelt	1987	60
90 7/8	15 6/8	15 4/8	13 1/8	4	4	Kodiak Island	AK	John Sarvis	1987	60
90 7/8	15 5/8	15 6/8	14 3/8	4	4	Kodiak Island	AK	Jon Vanderhoef	1989	60
90 4/8	15 3/8	15 3/8	13 3/8	5	5	Kodiak Island	AK	Reggie Spiegelberg	1986	63
90 2/8	16 4/8	16 5/8	15 6/8	5	3	Kodiak Island	AK	Mike Fenton	1988	64
90 0/8	14 2/8	14 2/8	14 0/8	4	4	Kodiak Island	AK	Patricia Stewart	1989	65
89 7/8	17 1/8	16 7/8	15 7/8	4	3	Kodiak Island	AK	John Sarvis	1991	66
89 6/8	15 1/8	14 3/8	12 4/8	5	4	Kodiak Island	AK	John Sarvis	1984	67
89 1/8	17 2/8	16 4/8	16 3/8	3	2	Kiliuda Bay	AK	Rick Tollison	1978	68
89 0/8	16 3/8	16 4/8	18 3/8	4	3	Kodiak Island	AK	Roger Stewart	1987	69
89 0/8	15 7/8	15 0/8	13 2/8	4	4	Kodiak Island	AK	George A. Moerlein	1990	69

Score	Length of Main Beam R	L	Inside Spread	Number of Points R	L	Area	State/ Province	Hunter's Name	Date	Rank
88 7/8	15 7/8	15 5/8	16 4/8	3	4	Kodiak Island	AK	Kirk Westervelt	1987	71
88 6/8	14 7/8	15 0/8	12 6/8	5	4	Kodiak Island	Ak	John Sarvis	1986	72
88 5/8	14 5/8	15 2/8	12 7/8	4	4	Queen Charlotte Islands	BC	Atley Lovelace	1984	73
88 5/8	17 0/8	16 4/8	15 5/8	3	4	Kodiak Island	AK	Larry Spiva	1986	73
88 4/8	14 3/8	14 0/8	14 2/8	5	4	Afognak Island	AK	Edward L. Russell	1983	75
88 2/8	16 0/8	15 4/8	14 2/8	4	4	Kodiak Island	AK	Michael Menke	1986	76
88 2/8	16 0/8	16 0/8	15 2/8	3	3	Kodiak Island	AK	Reggie Spiegelberg	1986	76
88 0/8	16 7/8	16 0/8	15 0/8	3	4	Kodiak Island	AK	Richard L. Westervelt	1987	78
87 2/8	16 6/8	16 5/8	17 1/8	4	2	Kodiak Island	AK	Lon E. Lauber	1990	79
86 7/8	15 0/8	14 4/8	14 3/8	4	4	Kodiak Island	AK	Jim Hodson	1985	80
86 7/8	15 1/8	15 2/8	14 3/8	4	4	Kodiak Island	AK	Stan Parkerson	1990	80
86 6/8	16 2/8	14 7/8	14 2/8	4	4	Kodiak Island	AK	Matt Jones	1985	82
86 5/8	16 1/8	15 5/8	16 3/8	4	3	Admiralty Island	AK	Charles R. Hakari	1983	83
86 4/8	13 7/8	15 0/8	14 0/8	5	5	Kodiak Island	AK	Emron A. Yancey	1986	84
86 2/8	16 0/8	15 1/8	14 0/8	4	4	Kodiak Island	AK	Troy Graziadei	1989	85
86 1/8	15 0/8	13 7/8	12 7/8	4	4	Kodiak Island	AK	John Toenes	1987	86
85 6/8	15 6/8	15 2/8	13 6/8	4	3	Kodiak Island	Ak	Bob Hayes	1986	87
85 3/8	16 3/8	16 0/8	15 5/8	3	3	Afognak Island	AK	Roger Stewart	1980	88
85 2/8	15 4/8	15 0/8	14 0/8	3	4	Afognak Island	AK	Ralph Ertz	1983	89
85 2/8	15 7/8	14 6/8	13 4/8	4	4	Kodiak Island	AK	Marv Walter	1989	89
85 0/8	14 6/8	14 5/8	15 7/8	4	4	Kodiak Island	AK	John Sarvis	1985	91
85 0/8	13 1/8	14 4/8	15 1/8	4	4	Kodiak Island	AK	Roger Stewart	1987	91
84 2/8	14 6/8	14 1/8	14 7/8	4	3	Kodiak Island	AK	Bill Krenz	1988	93
84 1/8	16 2/8	16 6/8	15 1/8	4	3	Kodiak Island	AK	Ralph Ertz	1984	94
84 0/8	16 0/8	16 1/8	15 2/8	3	3	Kodiak Island	AK	Lon E. Lauber	1990	95
83 6/8	14 1/8	14 4/8	11 6/8	4	4	Kodiak Island	AK	Russell M. Kucinski	1989	96
83 2/8	15 4/8	15 2/8	15 4/8	3	3	Montague Island	AK	Ray Uhl	1978	97
83 2/8	14 4/8	14 0/8	13 2/8	6	6	Afognak Island	AK	Ralph Ertz	1981	97
83 0/8	14 3/8	13 3/8	12 4/8	4	4	Kodiak Island	AK	Rich Biehl	1992	99
82 7/8	15 3/8	15 1/8	14 5/8	4	3	Kodiak Iskand	AK	John Sarvis	1991	100
82 4/8	12 6/8	14 0/8	12 6/8	5	5	Afognak Island	AK	Ralph Ertz	1980	101
82 4/8	14 4/8	13 7/8	14 5/8	4	4	Kodiak Island	AK	Richard L. Westervelt	1986	101
82 4/8	14 4/8	15 4/8	14 6/8	3	3	Kodiak Island	AK	Kirk Westervelt	1986	101
82 2/8	14 3/8	14 2/8	12 4/8	4	4	Kodiak Island	AK	Kurt Keskimaki	1986	104
81 7/8	15 4/8	14 2/8	13 7/8	3	3	Kodiak Island	Ak	Dyrk Eddie	1986	105
81 6/8	14 4/8	14 5/8	13 4/8	4	4	Kodiak Island	AK	Roger Stewart	1988	106
81 3/8	12 7/8	13 3/8	13 6/8	4	3	Kodiak Island	AK	Lon E. Lauber	1991	107
81 2/8	15 0/8	11 7/8	13 4/8	4	4	Kodiak Island	AK	Richard L. Westervelt	1986	108
80 6/8	14 2/8	13 0/8	13 0/8	4	4	Kodiak Island	AK	Roger Stewart	1988	109
80 4/8	14 2/8	15 7/8	13 2/8	4	3	Kodiak Island	AK	Steve Gorr	1989	110
80 1/8	13 2/8	13 1/8	13 1/8	4	4	Kodiak Island	AK	Jim Hodson	1985	111
80 0/8	15 6/8	14 5/8	14 2/8	3	4	Afognak Island	AK	Charlie Kroll	1984	112
80 0/8	13 4/8	13 6/8	13 0/8	4	4	Kodiak Island	AK	Tony Russ	1990	112
79 7/8	15 0/8	12 6/8	13 7/8	4	4	Ugak Bay	AK	Carl E. Brent	1988	114
79 5/8	14 5/8	15 0/8	12 7/8	4	3	Kodiak Island	AK	Richard L. Westervelt	1988	115
79 4/8	15 0/8	13 5/8	14 0/8	3	3	Kodiak Island	AK	Jim Hodson	1986	116
79 4/8	13 7/8	14 0/8	15 4/8	3	3	Kodiak Island	AK	Richard Gibson	1988	116
79 3/8	16 1/8	16 1/8	17 0/8	4	3	Kodiak Island	AK	Chad Doell	1991	118
79 2/8	14 7/8	15 1/8	14 4/8	4	3	Kodiak Island	AK	Lon E. Lauber	1990	119
79 2/8	15 0/8	14 4/8	12 2/8	3	4	Kodiak Island	AK	John Sarvis	1990	119
79 0/8	14 7/8	14 0/8	13 4/8	3	4	Kodiak Island	AK	Jim Hodson	1987	121
78 6/8	13 7/8	14 3/8	13 0/8	4	4	Kodiak Island	AK	John Sarvis	1990	122
78 6/8	14 1/8	15 1/8	11 2/8	4	3	Kodiak Island	AK	Shawn McCrosky	1991	122
78 5/8	15 7/8	15 7/8	19 0/8	2	3	Kodiak Island	AK	Roger Stewart	1987	124
78 5/8	14 5/8	14 2/8	13 7/8	3	4	Kodiak Island	AK	Tim Moerlein	1988	124
78 1/8	14 3/8	15 1/8	12 3/8	3	3	Kodiak Island	AK	Danny Moore	1984	126
78 1/8	14 4/8	14 7/8	13 5/8	4	4	Kodiak Island	AK	Len Cardinale	1986	126
78 1/8	14 3/8	13 4/8	13 7/8	4	4	Kodiak Island	AK	Michael V. Frost	1990	126
78 0/8	13 1/8	12 6/8	12 6/8	3	3	Kodiak Island	AK	David A. Widby	1988	129
78 0/8	16 3/8	15 3/8	16 4/8	4	3	Kodiak Island	AK	Lon E. Lauber	1992	129
77 7/8	14 4/8	14 0/8	14 3/8	3	3	Kodiak Island	AK	Stan Parkerson	1991	131
77 4/8	14 3/8	14 2/8	13 0/8	4	3	Kodiak Island	AK	Craig E. Scarbrough	1990	132
77 4/8	14 6/8	15 3/8	15 0/8	4	3	Kodiak Island	AK	David A. Widby	1990	132
77 3/8	13 4/8	13 0/8	12 1/8	4	4	Kodiak Island	AK	John Sarvis	1990	134
77 3/8	15 1/8	14 7/8	15 1/8	2	2	Prince of Wales Island	AK	Don Davidson	1991	134
77 2/8	15 2/8	15 2/8	13 2/8	3	3	Kodiak Island	AK	Chuck Adams	1984	136
76 7/8	14 0/8	13 3/8	10 7/8	4	4	Kodiak Island	AK	John Sarvis	1987	137
76 6/8	13 6/8	13 6/8	14 7/8	3	3	Kodiak Island	AK	Patricia Stewart	1988	138
76 5/8	12 7/8	13 1/8	13 5/8	4	3	Kodiak Island	AK	Tony Russ	1990	139
76 0/8	15 4/8	14 6/8	14 2/8	3	3	Kodiak Island	AK	Lyle Willmarth	1986	140

MINIMUM SCORE 65

SCORE	LENGTH OF MAIN BEAM		INSIDE SPREAD	NUMBER OF POINTS		AREA	STATE/ PROVINCE	HUNTER'S NAME	DATE	RANK
	R	L		R	L					
75 6/8	13 5/8	13 7/8	12 0/8	3	4	Afognak Island	AK	H. Richard Long	1984	141
75 4/8	12 4/8	12 2/8	11 4/8	4	4	Kodiak Island	AK	John Sarvis	1987	142
75 4/8	13 0/8	12 5/8	12 4/8	4	4	Kodiak Island	AK	John Sarvis	1988	142
75 2/8	13 5/8	13 1/8	12 6/8	3	4	Kodiak Island	AK	Gary G. Wall	1985	144
75 2/8	13 4/8	13 0/8	13 7/8	3	4	Kodiak Island	AK	Lon E. Lauber	1991	144
75 0/8	14 2/8	14 2/8	12 2/8	4	3	Kodiak Island	AK	Richard Moran	1988	146
74 7/8	11 3/8	10 7/8	12 4/8	4	4	Kodiak Island	AK	Patricia A. Stewart	1987	147
74 5/8	12 3/8	13 0/8	12 5/8	4	3	Kodiak Island	AK	Richard L. Westervelt	1988	148
74 5/8	12 7/8	12 5/8	11 1/8	3	4	Prince of Wales Island	AK	Robert L. Cunningham	1991	148
73 4/8	13 2/8	13 1/8	13 4/8	3	3	Kodiak Island	AK	Dennis L. Smythe	1980	150
73 4/8	14 0/8	13 4/8	14 3/8	4	4	Kodiak Island	AK	Lon E. Lauber	1990	150
72 6/8	11 5/8	12 6/8	14 5/8	3	4	Douglas Island	AK	Keith Mickelsen	1991	152
72 5/8	12 7/8	13 1/8	12 5/8	4	4	Kodiak Island	AK	Larry Spiva	1986	153
72 4/8	13 2/8	11 6/8	13 0/8	3	4	Kodiak Island	AK	Marc N. Shaft	1987	154
72 1/8	13 3/8	13 7/8	15 0/8	3	3	Admiralty Island	AK	Ron Callahan	1986	155
72 0/8	12 4/8	11 6/8	11 6/8	4	4	Kodiak Island	AK	Ken Vorisek	1989	156
71 6/8	12 4/8	13 2/8	13 6/8	3	4	Kodiak Island	AK	Donald R. Rossiter	1984	157
71 5/8	12 7/8	13 7/8	12 3/8	4	3	Kodiak Island	AK	Craig Scarbrough	1988	158
71 5/8	13 6/8	12 6/8	11 7/8	2	5	Kodiak Island	AK	Jerry Karsky	1989	158
71 4/8	13 1/8	13 0/8	12 0/8	3	3	Kodiak Island	AK	Ralph Ertz	1982	160
71 3/8	13 0/8	12 6/8	10 5/8	3	4	Kodiak Island	AK	Chuck Adams	1984	161
71 1/8	12 1/8	13 3/8	11 7/8	4	4	Kodiak Island	AK	Richard Gibson	1988	162
70 0/8	13 2/8	12 2/8	11 0/8	4	4	Kodiak Island	AK	John Sarvis	1989	163
69 5/8	12 2/8	13 3/8	11 7/8	3	4	Kodiak Island	AK	Kirk Westervelt	1986	164
68 4/8	12 6/8	12 3/8	15 0/8	3	3	Kodiak Island	AK	Shawn C. Joyce	1988	165
68 0/8	13 4/8	12 5/8	12 6/8	3	2	Kodiak Island	AK	Robert T. Thomason, Jr.	1985	166
68 0/8	12 6/8	13 6/8	12 2/8	2	2	Kodiak Island	AK	Richard Moran	1989	166
66 6/8	13 2/8	12 7/8	11 6/8	4	2	Kodiak Island	AK	Roger Stewart	1983	168
66 3/8	12 3/8	12 0/8	12 1/8	3	2	Kodiak Island	AK	Dick McClain	1990	169
66 1/8	13 5/8	12 4/8	13 5/8	3	2	Kodiak Island	AK	Kirk Westervelt	1986	170
65 1/8	13 4/8	12 3/8	11 7/8	3	3	Kodiak Island	AK	Patricia A. Stewart	1987	171

World Record Coues Deer (Typical Antlers)
Score: 113 0/8
Cochise County, Arizona - 1991
Hunter: Dennis Eaton

COUES DEER *(Typical Antlers)*

MINIMUM SCORE 65

Odocoileus virginianus couesi

SCORE	LENGTH OF R MAIN BEAM L		INSIDE SPREAD	NUMBER OF R POINTS L		AREA	STATE/ PROVINCE	HUNTER'S NAME	DATE	RANK
113 0/8	19 2/8	19 2/8	15 6/8	4	4	Cochise County	AZ	Dennis Eaton	1991	1
110 5/8	19 5/8	19 2/8	16 1/8	4	4	Pinal County	AZ	Chuck Adams	1989	2
110 4/8	19 0/8	19 2/8	13 4/8	4	5	Pima County	AZ	Mike J. Frey	1991	3
106 1/8	17 5/8	18 5/8	14 3/8	5	5	Cochise County	AZ	Harlon Wilson	1982	4
105 7/8	17 5/8	17 2/8	11 7/8	4	6	Pima County	AZ	Harold Boyack	1985	5
104 2/8	18 2/8	17 7/8	15 0/8	4	4	Gila County	AZ	Larry Peterson	1978	6
103 5/8	17 7/8	17 5/8	16 1/8	5	5	Sonora	MEX	Jim Velazquez	1991	7
103 2/8	16 7/8	17 2/8	14 4/8	4	4	Grant County	NM	Daryl Tow	1990	8
102 7/8	17 1/8	15 5/8	13 3/8	5	5	Grant County	NM	Daniel Morningstar	1988	9
101 7/8	15 6/8	17 0/8	15 6/8	5	4	Grant County	NM	Peter LaScala	1989	10
100 6/8	16 6/8	16 3/8	12 6/8	4	4	Graham County	AZ	Hugh H. Hamman	1966	11
100 4/8	17 5/8	16 5/8	12 4/8	4	5	Cochise County	AZ	Dallas Scherck	1971	12
100 2/8	17 0/8	16 0/8	14 5/8	4	5	Cochise County	AZ	Ray Edwards	1984	13
99 6/8	16 6/8	17 0/8	14 0/8	4	4	Pima County	AZ	Tracy Gene Hardy	1982	14
99 3/8	16 7/8	16 0/8	13 3/8	4	4	Gila County	AZ	David B. Hatch	1988	15
99 1/8	16 3/8	16 2/8	13 5/8	4	4	Pima County	AZ	Jim Walton	1992	16
98 7/8	15 7/8	15 5/8	14 5/8	4	5	Gila County	AZ	Darryl Kessler	1978	17
98 5/8	13 0/8	13 4/8	12 3/8	6	4	Graham County	AZ	John A. Holcomb	1983	18
98 5/8	16 6/8	16 2/8	14 3/8	4	5	Pima County	AZ	George G. Alcorta	1989	18
98 3/8	17 1/8	17 0/8	13 7/8	4	4	Cochise County	AZ	David Schied	1973	20

(Continued)

SCORE	LENGTH OF MAIN BEAM R	L	INSIDE SPREAD	NUMBER OF POINTS R	L	AREA	STATE/ PROVINCE	HUNTER'S NAME	DATE	RANK
98 2/8	16 5/8	16 5/8	14 0/8	4	4	Grant County	NM	Larry M. Looman	1991	21
97 7/8	16 0/8	16 3/8	12 3/8	4	4	Cochise County	AZ	Randy Breland	1989	22
97 6/8	16 2/8	16 2/8	11 4/8	4	4	Santa Cruz County	AZ	Brian Ham	1992	23
97 4/8	16 0/8	15 0/8	14 1/8	4	5	Pima County	AZ	Steve Fossman	1989	24
96 3/8	16 6/8	17 1/8	15 6/8	6	5	Graham County	AZ	Maurice Holthaus	1984	25
96 3/8	16 3/8	16 6/8	12 7/8	5	4	Grant County	NM	Duane Beenblossom	1992	25
95 5/8	15 7/8	16 2/8	13 5/8	4	4	Santa Cruz County	AZ	Bill Krenz	1984	27
95 3/8	17 2/8	17 6/8	15 3/8	5	4	Maricopa County	AZ	Bob Fromme	1986	28
94 3/8	15 6/8	15 4/8	12 3/8	4	4	Cochise County	AZ	Randy Breland	1987	29
94 1/8	15 0/8	16 0/8	13 6/8	5	4	Greenlee County	AZ	John T. Skeen	1975	30
94 1/8	14 3/8	15 2/8	13 3/8	4	4	Cochise County	AZ	Daniel Staples	1981	30
94 0/8	16 6/8	16 1/8	14 0/8	4	4	Greenlee County	AZ	Jack Sartain	1983	32
93 1/8	14 3/8	15 0/8	14 3/8	4	4	Pima County	AZ	Jerry Muir	1982	33
92 6/8	16 0/8	17 0/8	13 4/8	4	4	Pima County	AZ	Peter C. Knagge	1986	34
92 4/8	15 6/8	16 1/8	13 2/8	4	5	Pima County	AZ	Rick Forrest	1991	35
92 2/8	16 1/8	16 2/8	14 2/8	4	5	Santa Cruz County	AZ	Rowland J. Robinson	1985	36
91 6/8	15 1/8	15 4/8	14 4/8	4	4	Cochise County	AZ	Randy Breland	1981	37
91 2/8	15 2/8	14 6/8	12 2/8	4	4	Santa Cruz County	AZ	Perry Schaal	1983	38
91 1/8	14 5/8	14 4/8	14 6/8	4	5	Yavapai County	AZ	Kyle Brock	1986	39
91 0/8	16 2/8	15 5/8	12 6/8	4	4	Gila County	AZ	John Radford	1972	40
90 6/8	17 0/8	17 5/8	14 6/8	4	4	Cochise County	AZ	Richard E. 'Dick' Johnson	1986	41
90 0/8	15 5/8	14 6/8	10 4/8	4	4	Cochise County	AZ	Bob Ramirez	1990	42
89 0/8	15 3/8	16 5/8	13 2/8	4	4	Sierra County	NM	Perry Harper	1989	43
88 4/8	15 6/8	17 1/8	11 6/8	4	5	Cochise County	AZ	R. Ertz	1991	44
88 0/8	13 7/8	13 4/8	11 2/8	4	4	Grant County	NM	Al Haines	1991	45
87 7/8	15 4/8	13 1/8	12 7/8	4	4	Cochise County	AZ	Dan Gwaltwey	1989	46
86 2/8	15 1/8	16 3/8	14 4/8	4	4	Grant County	NM	Bill Elmer	1992	47
86 1/8	14 7/8	15 6/8	14 3/8	4	3	Pinal County	AZ	Steve E. Allen	1979	48
85 5/8	13 4/8	13 3/8	12 7/8	4	4	Hidalgo County	NM	John D. "Jack" Frost	1992	49
85 4/8	13 6/8	16 0/8	12 2/8	5	4	Santa Cruz County	AZ	Brad Wedding	1990	50
85 0/8	15 0/8	14 6/8	12 0/8	5	5	Graham County	AZ	Dennis L. Shirley	1991	51
84 7/8	13 0/8	12 2/8	10 3/8	4	4	Cochise County	AZ	Dave Rhodes	1976	52
84 6/8	14 4/8	14 5/8	12 6/8	4	4	Pima County	AZ	Bill Thompkins	1988	53
84 2/8	15 0/8	13 4/8	13 2/8	4	4	Pima County	AZ	Robert W. Ledbetter	1989	54
84 1/8	13 4/8	13 7/8	12 5/8	4	4	Maricopa County	AZ	Ed Matteson	1963	55
82 6/8	15 3/8	15 7/8	13 3/8	4	4	Coconino County	AZ	Carl Vance	1973	56
82 5/8	14 3/8	15 2/8	13 1/8	4	4	Gila County	AZ	Mike Mahoney	1976	57
81 6/8	13 1/8	13 1/8	12 0/8	4	4	Pima County	AZ	Jack R. Frazier	1984	58
81 5/8	14 3/8	14 4/8	12 3/8	4	4	Greenlee County	AZ	David L. Willis	1992	59
81 2/8	12 4/8	12 1/8	13 0/8	4	4	Graham County	AZ	Bill Cross	1967	60
81 1/8	16 1/8	14 7/8	12 3/8	4	4	Pima County	AZ	Robert Forrest	1991	61
81 0/8	14 5/8	14 0/8	13 2/8	4	4	Grant County	NM	Bob J. Brown	1960	62
80 7/8	14 2/8	14 3/8	14 3/8	4	4	Gila County	AZ	Gary H. Behrends, Jr.	1989	63
80 6/8	15 2/8	15 5/8	14 6/8	3	4	Grant County	NM	George M. Ratliff	1992	64
80 1/8	13 4/8	13 4/8	10 3/8	4	4	Pima County	AZ	Dave Snyder	1983	65
79 2/8	16 0/8	13 7/8	13 5/8	4	4	Pima County	AZ	David C. Durkee	1987	66
78 2/8	14 0/8	14 1/8	12 4/8	4	4	Pima County	AZ	Jim Walton	1990	67
77 7/8	15 3/8	14 7/8	12 5/8	3	3	Gila County	AZ	Tom Hashem	1964	68
77 6/8	14 2/8	14 1/8	9 6/8	5	5	Pima County	AZ	Richard Dawe, Jr.	1964	69
77 4/8	14 4/8	13 7/8	10 4/8	4	5	Sierra County	NM	Charles E. Franzoy	1972	70
76 6/8	12 7/8	13 3/8	12 0/8	4	3	Cochise County	AZ	Robert G. Ables	1989	71
75 4/8	13 1/8	12 7/8	12 0/8	4	4	Coconino County	AZ	Les Shelton	1987	72
75 2/8	13 2/8	13 7/8	10 2/8	4	4	Cochise County	AZ	Russell L. Gann	1987	73
75 2/8	14 4/8	14 6/8	12 0/8	4	4	Graham County	AZ	Chuck Adams	1989	73
75 2/8	12 7/8	13 0/8	10 6/8	4	4	Cochise County	AZ	R. Ertz	1990	73
74 5/8	14 5/8	14 6/8	10 5/8	3	4	Sierra County	NM	Jim Ryan	1988	76
74 2/8	12 6/8	12 1/8	9 4/8	4	4	Grant County	NM	Mike W. Leonard	1992	77
73 6/8	12 6/8	13 1/8	10 4/8	4	4	Pima County	AZ	Howard Cooper	1980	78
73 6/8	12 2/8	13 5/8	11 2/8	4	3	Pima County	AZ	William E. Dickinson	1982	78
73 5/8	12 2/8	12 7/8	13 4/8	5	4	Hidalgo County	NM	Larry Behrends	1969	80
73 4/8	15 0/8	14 4/8	13 2/8	2	4	Pima County	AZ	Michael L. Henrikson	1979	81
73 2/8	13 0/8	13 0/8	10 6/8	4	4	Gila County	AZ	Jim Mercer	1958	82
72 4/8	11 6/8	11 6/8	11 4/8	4	4	Gila County	AZ	Gary H. Behrends	1969	83
71 2/8	13 2/8	12 7/8	13 2/8	4	3	Pima County	AZ	Stephen E. Johnson	1979	84
68 6/8	13 2/8	12 7/8	10 0/8	3	4	Atasco Mtns.	AZ	Peter C. Knagge	1978	85
68 6/8	12 5/8	12 7/8	12 0/8	4	4	Cochise County	AZ	Daniel Staples	1980	85
67 4/8	13 0/8	13 3/8	13 0/8	4	3	Graham County	AZ	Chuck Adams	1988	87
66 6/8	12 1/8	11 7/8	10 6/8	4	4	Pima County	AZ	Steve Neuberger	1989	88
66 4/8	12 3/8	12 4/8	8 6/8	3	3	Pima County	AZ	Larry Rogge	1984	89
66 2/8	12 3/8	12 5/8	10 0/8	3	3	Grant County	NM	Chuck Schultz	1991	90

World Record Coues Deer (Non-Typical Antlers)
Score: 124 0/8
Coconino County, Arizona - 1987
Hunter: John George Evans

COUES DEER *(Non-Typical Antlers)*

MINIMUM SCORE 75

Odocoileus virginianus couesi

SCORE	LENGTH OF R MAIN BEAM L		INSIDE SPREAD	NUMBER OF R POINTS L		AREA	STATE/ PROVINCE	HUNTER'S NAME	DATE	RANK
124 0/8	17 7/8	17 0/8	16 3/8	5	6	Coconino County	AZ	John George Evans	1987	1
119 5/8	19 3/8	18 6/8	13 0/8	6	6	Pima County	AZ	Art Gonzales	1987	2
116 7/8	16 7/8	17 0/8	11 5/8	6	8	Santa Cruz County	AZ	John F. May	1991	3
112 4/8	18 4/8	18 6/8	13 2/8	5	5	Pima County	AZ	David G. Snyder	1984	4
96 4/8	15 4/8	13 2/8	15 5/8	6	7	Gila County	AZ	Larry Behrends	1989	5

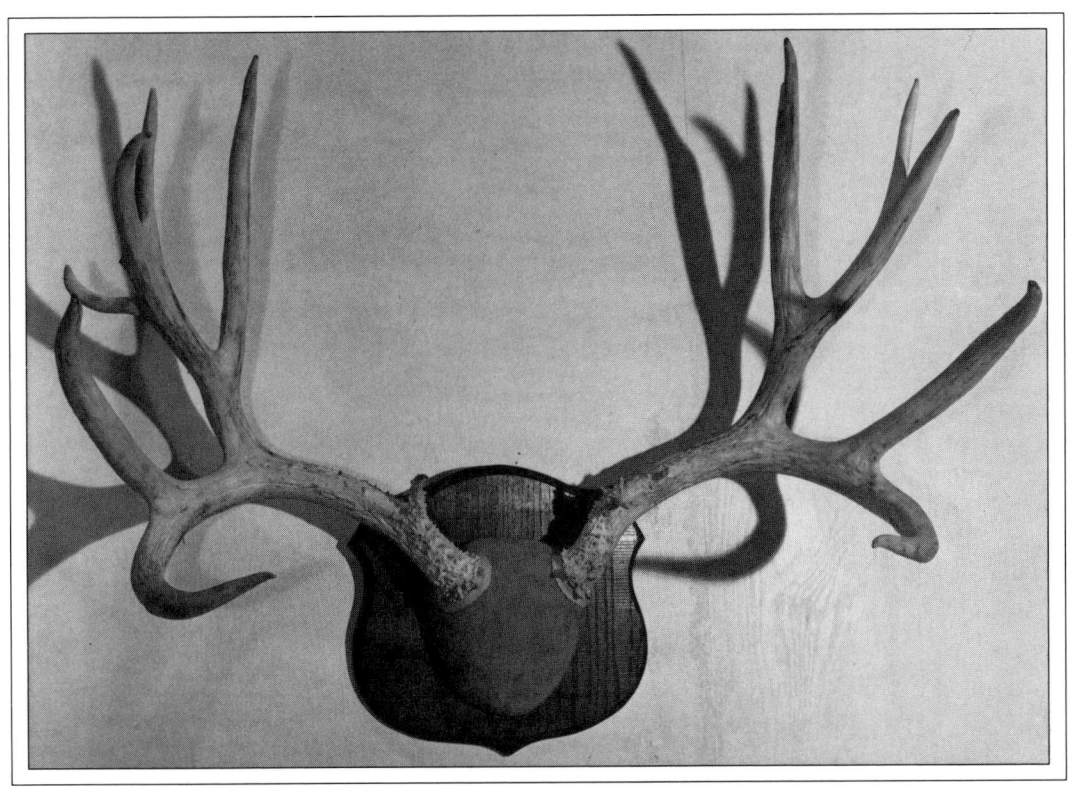

World Record Mule Deer (Typical Antlers)
Score: 203 1/8
White River National Forrest, Colorado - 1979
Hunter: Bill Barcus

MULE DEER *(Typical Antlers)*

MINIMUM SCORE 145

Odocoileus hemionus
and certain related subspecies

SCORE	R LENGTH OF MAIN BEAM L		INSIDE SPREAD	R NUMBER OF POINTS L		AREA	STATE/ PROVINCE	HUNTER'S NAME	DATE	RANK
203 1/8	28 5/8	27 6/8	30 2/8	7	7	White River N.F.	CO	Bill Barcus	1979	1
202 6/8	26 7/8	26 2/8	26 7/8	7	6	Gove County	KS	Carl Ghan, Jr.	1992	2
198 4/8	28 0/8	26 0/8	32 2/8	7	7	Apache County	AZ	William T. Rose	1985	3
197 6/8	24 1/8	24 7/8	23 3/8	5	6	Dolores County	CO	Jim Horneck	1988	4
197 1/8	24 2/8	22 4/8	21 4/8	6	6	Beaver County	UT	David Snyder	1982	5
197 0/8	24 6/8	27 7/8	23 6/8	5	5	Park County	CO	Ronald E. Sniff	1969	6
196 5/8	25 0/8	25 6/8	23 4/8	5	6	Coconino County	AZ	Jim Wagner	1986	7
195 7/8	29 7/8	29 7/8	30 2/8	6	7	Crook County	OR	Gidion "Hop" Jackson	1990	8
193 5/8	27 0/8	30 1/8	23 1/8	6	5	Cibola County	NM	Kenny R. Bruton	1987	9
192 7/8	24 6/8	23 3/8	23 0/8	6	5	San Isabel National Forest	CO	Donald D. Garrison	1972	10
192 1/8	25 3/8	26 2/8	23 0/8	6	5	Lemhi County	ID	Mike Nelson	1978	11
192 0/8	25 6/8	26 4/8	22 0/8	7	5	Uncompahgre Plateau	CO	Donald Click	1973	12
190 6/8	27 4/8	27 4/8	25 7/8	9	8	Mesa County	CO	Allen Personious	1976	13
190 5/8	26 2/8	26 2/8	22 4/8	7	8	Teller County	CO	Dan Mersman	1982	14
190 1/8	25 3/8	24 6/8	25 3/8	6	5	Moffat County	CO	Glenn Pritchard	1990	15
190 0/8	25 1/8	23 4/8	24 4/8	5	5	Utah County	UT	John Edwards	1967	16
189 3/8	27 0/8	27 0/8	24 1/8	6	5	Tooele County	UT	Ken Davis	1963	17
189 1/8	23 6/8	23 7/8	23 6/8	5	8	Chelan County	WA	R. Early/D. Davies, Jr.	1983	18
189 0/8	24 4/8	23 5/8	25 6/8	5	6	Montezuma County	CO	Al Newkirk	1983	19
188 7/8	25 2/8	26 3/8	21 1/8	6	6	Settlement Canyon	UT	Derald R. Evans	1965	20
188 6/8	24 5/8	24 6/8	21 2/8	5	5	Mesa County	CO	Bob Jensen	1974	21
188 4/8	25 6/8	26 6/8	24 3/8	6	5	Abbey	SAS	Barry Minor	1979	22
188 2/8	24 3/8	24 4/8	23 2/8	6	6	Mesa County	CO	John Lamicq, Jr.	1967	23
187 7/8	23 7/8	24 7/8	22 5/8	5	6	Duck Creek	UT	Gerald Clark	1966	24
187 5/8	23 2/8	22 5/8	18 3/8	5	5	Moffat County	CO	Leonard Jefferson	1971	25
187 5/8	25 0/8	25 1/8	28 3/8	8	5	Boulder County	CO	Jeff Biemiller	1991	25

MULE DEER *(Typical Antlers)*

SCORE	LENGTH OF MAIN BEAM		INSIDE SPREAD	NUMBER OF POINTS		AREA	STATE/ PROVINCE	HUNTER'S NAME	DATE	RANK
	R	L		R	L					
187 2/8	24 3/8	22 3/8	22 2/8	5	5	Dawes County	NE	Kirk Peters	1989	27
187 1/8	23 6/8	25 6/8	25 2/8	7	7	Milk River	ALB	Robin Tremblay	1992	28
187 0/8	20 1/8	22 1/8	22 0/8	6	5	Boise County	ID	Ricky D. Addison	1984	29
186 7/8	25 3/8	25 0/8	20 1/8	5	6	Eagle County	CO	Dr. J. D. Jones	1963	30
186 7/8	26 3/8	26 0/8	22 0/8	6	8	Uncompahgre Plateau	CO	Jerry Click	1973	30
186 6/8	24 5/8	25 2/8	24 2/8	5	5	Cassia County	ID	Pat Miller	1965	32
186 5/8	25 1/8	25 6/8	19 2/8	5	6	Elbert County	CO	Loren Dellinger	1984	33
186 4/8	24 2/8	23 1/8	24 4/8	5	5	White River N.F.	CO	Walt Seville	1977	34
186 2/8	26 4/8	26 0/8	27 4/8	6	9	Gunnison County	CO	Don E. Lampert	1973	35
186 1/8	24 1/8	24 0/8	21 3/8	5	5	Cassia County	ID	Bill Shockey	1965	36
186 1/8	25 3/8	24 0/8	25 4/8	5	5	Humboldt County	NV	Tim Bray	1984	36
185 6/8	24 1/8	24 4/8	24 0/8	5	5	Imperial County	CA	Gilbert Clement	1982	38
185 5/8	24 2/8	25 4/8	27 0/8	7	6	Mesa County	CO	Art Cook	1962	39
185 4/8	22 0/8	22 3/8	20 4/8	5	5	Coconino County	AZ	Ronald Hollamon	1978	40
185 0/8	26 0/8	26 2/8	26 3/8	5	6	Larimer County	CO	Don Lampert	1969	41
185 0/8	26 1/8	25 1/8	24 0/8	5	5	Montrose County	CO	Darryl L. Coe	1988	41
184 7/8	25 7/8	25 4/8	21 7/8	5	5	Mesa County	CO	James L. Peterson	1983	43
184 7/8	24 2/8	24 4/8	25 1/8	6	5	Maricopa County	AZ	Timothy Gibson	1987	43
184 6/8	23 0/8	23 2/8	23 3/8	5	5	Mesa County	CO	David L. Myers	1976	45
184 3/8	24 4/8	23 3/8	28 4/8	6	5	Caribou County	ID	Coby Tigert	1983	46
184 2/8	25 2/8	24 3/8	22 7/8	5	6	Teton County	WY	Donald R. Williamson	1991	47
184 1/8	24 3/8	24 6/8	24 6/8	5	6	Delta County	CO	Scott Kolb	1963	48
184 1/8	27 5/8	27 0/8	25 3/8	5	4	Bernalillo County	NM	Gregory A. Gwash	1970	48
184 0/8	24 1/8	25 1/8	24 2/8	5	6	Boise County	ID	Joseph Greenley	1984	50
183 7/8	25 0/8	24 3/8	23 7/8	5	5	Moffat County	CO	Joel Hogan	1966	51
183 6/8	26 4/8	27 3/8	27 0/8	5	4	Iron County	UT	Ted Garrett	1963	52
183 5/8	26 6/8	25 7/8	25 5/8	5	5	Sanpete County	UT	Weldon Noland	1965	53
183 5/8	20 2/8	19 3/8	20 2/8	6	6	Rio Arriba County	NM	Billy Terrazas	1985	53
183 4/8	29 0/8	26 5/8	23 6/8	5	4	Kiowa County	CO	Dave Moyer	1988	55
183 3/8	25 7/8	26 1/8	22 4/8	7	5	Sevier County	UT	Kyle Johnson	1970	56
183 2/8	25 5/8	26 5/8	22 7/8	6	9	Wasatch County	UT	Blake Spenser	1963	57
183 1/8	25 0/8	25 1/8	24 5/8	5	6	White Pine County	NV	Robert Price	1986	58
183 0/8	25 1/8	25 5/8	25 2/8	5	6	Lincoln County	MT	John C. Bartlett	1982	59
182 7/8	23 3/8	22 0/8	21 7/8	5	5	Caribou County	ID	Neil Dursteler	1967	60
182 7/8	24 4/8	25 1/8	24 1/8	5	5	Cache County	UT	Robert Bronson	1985	60
182 6/8	22 0/8	22 2/8	20 2/8	5	7	Chelan County	WA	Glenn St. Charles	1959	62
182 6/8	23 3/8	23 4/8	20 3/8	7	5	Moffat County	CO	Glenn Pritchard	1987	62
182 5/8	26 4/8	25 4/8	21 5/8	5	5	Lincoln County	WY	Laei Eddins	1978	64
182 4/8	25 2/8	24 2/8	25 0/8	5	5	Humboldt County	NV	George Rajnus	1985	65
182 4/8	24 5/8	24 3/8	21 4/8	5	5	Mesa County	CO	Charles C. Perry	1985	65
182 4/8	25 0/8	25 5/8	21 2/8	5	5	Mesa County	CO	David M. Gant	1986	65
182 4/8	23 5/8	25 4/8	20 4/8	5	5	Cypress	ALB	James Drader	1992	65
182 2/8	25 6/8	24 2/8	25 2/8	6	5	Mesa County	CO	Robert C. Dawson	1974	69
182 2/8	25 1/8	25 2/8	24 0/8	6	5	Caribou County	ID	Eric Bowman	1983	69
182 2/8	25 4/8	26 1/8	23 6/8	7	9	Graham County	KS	Phillip L. Kirkland	1988	69
181 7/8	21 7/8	21 1/8	22 6/8	5	5	Power County	ID	Austin Cummins	1970	72
181 5/8	24 3/8	24 0/8	21 5/8	5	5	Wakely	CO	Lynn Grace	1964	73
181 4/8	24 4/8	23 2/8	25 6/8	5	5	Garfield County	CO	Henry Wichers	1967	74
181 4/8	23 6/8	23 3/8	24 7/8	5	5	Butte County	ID	Richard A. Southwell	1980	74
181 3/8	26 0/8	26 5/8	26 3/8	5	5	Montrose County	CO	John Lamb	1981	76
181 2/8	22 1/8	22 6/8	20 5/8	5	6	Larimer County	CO	Wayne Eberhard	1972	77
181 1/8	24 3/8	25 4/8	19 3/8	6	6	Union County	OR	Thomas Mussatto	1968	78
181 0/8	24 7/8	22 7/8	23 0/8	6	6	Rio Arriba County	NM	Charles Tapia	1965	79
181 0/8	26 0/8	25 5/8	24 4/8	5	5	Boise County	ID	Tom D'Aquino	1991	79
180 7/8	25 2/8	24 7/8	22 7/8	5	5	Washoe County	NV	Donald E. Callen	1984	81
180 6/8	23 6/8	24 6/8	20 4/8	5	5	La Plata County	CO	Ralph RePola	1988	82
180 4/8	24 1/8	25 1/8	21 6/8	4	4	Mesa County	CO	Jack Kruckenburg	1958	83
180 4/8	24 0/8	24 7/8	21 0/8	6	6	Fremont County	ID	Steven M. Jones	1979	83
180 4/8	24 6/8	25 3/8	24 0/8	6	5	Ravalli County	MT	Gary Habeck	1984	83
180 4/8	22 6/8	22 2/8	21 7/8	7	6	Montezuma County	CO	Marvin Reichenau	1987	83
180 3/8	24 0/8	25 5/8	27 5/8	5	5	Boise County	ID	Benton K. Wetzel	1970	87
180 2/8	24 5/8	24 7/8	25 7/8	8	5	Garfield County	CO	Michael R. Allen	1967	88
180 2/8	23 1/8	24 0/8	23 2/8	5	5	Lincoln County	NV	Fred B. Allen III	1974	88
180 2/8	23 2/8	24 2/8	24 0/8	5	5	Humboldt County	NV	Robert A. Ashby	1980	88
180 1/8	22 0/8	22 4/8	19 3/8	5	5	Dawson County	MT	Gordon M. Quilling	1957	91
180 1/8	24 6/8	24 4/8	21 5/8	5	5	Grant County	OR	Kim C. Theile	1989	91
179 6/8	25 0/8	25 7/8	20 0/8	5	5	Umatilla County	OR	Dannie W. Crawley	1991	93
179 6/8	22 7/8	24 5/8	21 1/8	6	6	Okotoks	ALB	Harvey Paddock	1991	93
179 5/8	26 4/8	27 1/8	27 2/8	5	7	Union County	NM	Ronnie Williams	1984	95
179 4/8	24 3/8	23 0/8	21 4/8	5	8	Ada County	ID	Vance Gardner	1971	96

MULE DEER (*Typical Antlers*)

(Continued)

SCORE	LENGTH OF R MAIN BEAM L		INSIDE SPREAD	NUMBER OF R POINTS L		AREA	STATE/ PROVINCE	HUNTER'S NAME	DATE	RANK
179 4/8	22 2/8	24 3/8	19 6/8	5	5	Garfield County	CO	Ed Downard	1984	96
179 2/8	24 2/8	24 1/8	24 6/8	5	4	Illinois Creek Drainage	unk	Gordon E. Scott	1964	98
179 0/8	19 1/8	19 4/8	21 4/8	5	6	Sandoval County	NM	D. J. Heckler, Jr.	1969	99
179 0/8	23 6/8	23 4/8	24 1/8	5	5	Lake County	CO	Sam E. Adkins	1978	99
179 0/8	23 5/8	24 4/8	22 4/8	5	5	Elko County	NV	Jerry Vega	1986	99
179 0/8	23 0/8	23 0/8	21 4/8	6	5	Harney County	OR	Cameron Hanes	1991	99
179 0/8	22 6/8	23 0/8	20 4/8	5	5	Lincoln County	WY	Mike Barrett	1991	99
178 5/8	24 2/8	23 2/8	24 7/8	6	6	Rio Blanco County	CO	Rex Schmude	1968	104
178 4/8	24 6/8	25 0/8	23 1/8	5	5	Carter County	MT	R. C. Tucker	1958	105
178 4/8	24 0/8	23 6/8	18 2/8	5	5	Sandoval County	NM	Doug Aikin	1990	105
178 4/8	25 5/8	26 2/8	21 6/8	6	7	Boise County	ID	Thomas M. Szurgot	1990	105
178 3/8	28 3/8	27 3/8	28 3/8	5	5	Finney County	KS	Larry Ochs	1968	108
178 3/8	21 3/8	22 2/8	19 5/8	5	5	San Juan County	UT	Shane Barr	1992	108
178 3/8	27 4/8	27 3/8	26 5/8	5	5	Okanogan County	WA	Douglas Duane Kikendall	1992	108
178 0/8	23 4/8	23 7/8	23 4/8	5	6	Lake County	OR	Ronald C. Halpin	1966	111
178 0/8	24 4/8	23 6/8	24 6/8	5	5	Garfield County	CO	Larry Santek	1985	111
178 0/8	25 0/8	24 4/8	24 6/8	7	6	Lincoln County	MT	Jerry Brown	1986	111
177 7/8	23 2/8	23 7/8	23 2/8	4	4	Routt County	CO	Richard M. Hansen	1964	114
177 7/8	26 1/8	26 2/8	23 1/8	4	4	Gunnison County	CO	Glen Farnum	1978	114
177 7/8	23 6/8	23 0/8	19 3/8	6	6	Mesa County	CO	John D Wood	1984	114
177 7/8	24 3/8	26 4/8	23 1/8	6	5	Coconino County	AZ	James Miner	1987	114
177 7/8	26 1/8	25 3/8	26 7/8	5	5	Elbert County	CO	Robert Nelson	1990	114
177 6/8	27 2/8	26 0/8	32 2/8	6	7	McKinley County	NM	Eloy Salaz	1987	119
177 6/8	22 2/8	22 4/8	24 6/8	5	6	Sublette County	WY	Dana Patrick Furgason	1992	119
177 4/8	25 6/8	26 0/8	22 4/8	5	4	Fremont County	WY	Walter Millhollin	1960	121
177 4/8	23 0/8	22 5/8	22 2/8	5	5	Oneida County	ID	J. L. Shelton	1980	121
177 4/8	24 4/8	22 1/8	23 4/8	5	5	Oldman River	ALB	Kevin Wiebe	1991	121
177 3/8	25 5/8	26 4/8	20 7/8	6	6	Caribou County	ID	Jack Daniels	1990	124
177 2/8	22 6/8	23 6/8	28 6/8	6	6	Pima County	AZ	Sherwin Lipsitz	1977	125
177 2/8	21 5/8	23 2/8	20 6/8	6	5	Malheur County	OR	Bennie B. Simpson	1986	125
177 1/8	23 3/8	23 3/8	26 2/8	5	6	Logan County	KS	Thomas Standard	1967	127
177 1/8	23 7/8	24 4/8	22 0/8	4	6	Meagher County	MT	Mike Weitz	1981	127
177 1/8	23 4/8	23 7/8	22 1/8	6	5	La Plata County	CO	James N. Hinson	1987	127
177 1/8	23 1/8	23 1/8	22 7/8	5	5	Harney County	OR	Robert Reed	1991	127
177 1/8	25 2/8	26 1/8	25 1/8	5	5	Boulder County	CO	Greg Allen Nichols	1992	127
177 0/8	22 0/8	23 6/8	24 4/8	6	5	White Pine County	NV	Dr. Donald Wicher	1961	132
177 0/8	24 4/8	25 5/8	21 4/8	7	6	Garfield County	CO	Steve U'Selis	1967	132
176 6/8	26 3/8	25 1/8	26 0/8	4	5	Yuma County	CO	Mark Sievers	1985	134
176 6/8	27 4/8	26 6/8	22 4/8	5	5	Wasatch County	UT	Doug Strecker	1987	134
176 6/8	25 7/8	24 7/8	25 6/8	5	5	Humboldt County	NV	Robert G. Hopper	1990	134
176 6/8	24 6/8	24 2/8	24 0/8	4	4	Carbon County	WY	Donald A. Carpenter	1990	134
176 5/8	22 5/8	22 2/8	20 6/8	5	6	Lincoln County	WY	Bart DeCora	1989	138
176 5/8	28 0/8	27 6/8	29 7/8	6	6	Weld County	CO	Tim Bradley	1989	138
176 4/8	23 4/8	23 5/8	20 0/8	5	5	Ada County	ID	Edward Keeton	1983	140
176 4/8	21 5/8	21 7/8	19 0/8	6	7	Conejos County	CO	Rick Gabbard	1987	140
176 3/8	21 0/8	21 1/8	26 3/8	5	5	Torrance County	NM	Frank Johnson	1989	142
176 2/8	22 1/8	24 0/8	20 4/8	5	6	Lincoln County	NE	M. R. Buchtel	1959	143
176 2/8	24 1/8	24 3/8	23 2/8	5	5	Russell County	KS	Duane Mai	1982	143
176 2/8	21 4/8	23 1/8	21 5/8	5	6	Meade County	KS	Roger Davis	1986	143
176 1/8	24 3/8	24 3/8	23 1/8	7	6	Duchesne County	UT	M.H. 'Bill' Wilkinson, J	1964	146
176 0/8	23 6/8	23 7/8	21 2/8	6	5	San Juan County	UT	Charles Farmer	1964	147
176 0/8	22 3/8	21 5/8	18 6/8	5	5	Coconino County	AZ	Tom Dennis	1972	147
176 0/8	24 7/8	24 7/8	23 6/8	5	6	Cassia County	ID	Earl Peterson	1981	147
175 7/8	24 5/8	24 1/8	18 0/8	6	9	Presidio County	TX	Neal Bouldin	1987	150
175 7/8	20 6/8	20 0/8	19 5/8	5	5	Grand County	CO	Guy-Maurice Algier	1989	150
175 7/8	27 7/8	26 6/8	27 0/8	4	7	Cypress Hills	ALB	Russell Gregory Meidinger	1990	150
175 6/8	22 6/8	22 5/8	22 6/8	5	5	Uintah County	UT	Merlin L. Killpack	1957	153
175 6/8	24 4/8	24 4/8	25 4/8	6	6	Mesa County	CO	Joe Egner	1965	153
175 6/8	24 3/8	25 0/8	22 1/8	4	6	Larimer County	CO	Kevin Vinzant	1986	153
175 5/8	23 6/8	25 0/8	21 1/8	4	4	Grant County	OR	Larry Saunders	1985	156
175 5/8	23 4/8	25 3/8	24 7/8	5	5	San Miguel County	NM	Dick McClain	1989	156
175 4/8	24 6/8	24 7/8	21 7/8	6	9	Colfax County	NM	Max Crocker	1981	158
175 4/8	21 2/8	20 3/8	21 0/8	5	6	San Juan County	CO	Stan Overstreet	1989	158
175 4/8	25 5/8	23 0/8	21 0/8	5	5	Cheyenne County	CO	Ronald R. Smith	1991	158
175 3/8	21 5/8	23 1/8	19 5/8	6	7	Park County	CO	Marvin Clyncke	1981	161
175 3/8	24 4/8	24 0/8	23 1/8	5	5	Billings County	ND	Joe Kytoichuk	1983	161
175 2/8	24 1/8	24 4/8	24 4/8	7	6	Emery County	UT	Ron Myers	1958	163
175 2/8	24 6/8	25 3/8	23 6/8	6	7	Garfield County	CO	Robert Pitt	1978	163
175 1/8	24 6/8	27 1/8	27 5/8	5	5	Sawlog Creek	KS	Merle Schulte	1974	165
175 1/8	21 7/8	22 2/8	19 7/8	4	4	Lincoln County	NV	Fred B. Allen III	1975	165

SCORE	LENGTH OF MAIN BEAM		INSIDE SPREAD	NUMBER OF POINTS		AREA	STATE/ PROVINCE	HUNTER'S NAME	DATE	RANK
	R	L		R	L					
175 1/8	24 1/8	25 4/8	21 5/8	7	8	Delta County	CO	Michael Sturm	1977	165
175 1/8	21 4/8	22 7/8	21 6/8	6	6	Millard County	UT	Jason Woodland	1985	165
174 7/8	23 7/8	23 7/8	18 3/8	5	6	Delta County	CO	Paul Dickson	1969	169
174 7/8	22 5/8	21 7/8	23 0/8	5	5	Gallatin County	MT	Bob Savage	1970	169
174 7/8	21 5/8	22 1/8	23 7/8	5	5	Garfield County	CO	Norman L. Richerson	1978	169
174 7/8	25 5/8	23 0/8	28 2/8	5	5	Elbert County	CO	Robert D. Olivier	1981	169
174 6/8	26 2/8	26 0/8	26 2/8	5	5	Lake County	OR	Gene Lyons	1969	173
174 6/8	24 0/8	20 5/8	21 2/8	5	6	Garfield County	CO	Jewell Petz	1970	173
174 5/8	25 0/8	25 0/8	23 1/8	4	4	Moffat County	CO	Roland C. Gravenkemper	1961	175
174 5/8	23 6/8	22 6/8	19 4/8	6	6	Sevier County	UT	Kenneth L. Shirley	1968	175
174 5/8	22 7/8	23 1/8	20 5/8	7	5	Wichita County	KS	Stacy Hoeme	1990	175
174 4/8	26 0/8	23 5/8	26 4/8	6	5	Mesa County	CO	Douglas D. Watts	1976	178
174 4/8	24 3/8	24 1/8	22 6/8	4	5	Mesa County	CO	Jay Verzuh	1983	178
174 3/8	21 0/8	23 7/8	23 1/8	6	5	Pima County	AZ	Robert A. Edgar	1982	180
174 2/8	22 7/8	22 6/8	21 2/8	5	5	Natrona County	WY	Pat McAteer	1982	181
174 2/8	23 0/8	22 5/8	23 1/8	5	5	Billings County	ND	Mark Lothspeich	1984	181
174 2/8	24 7/8	24 6/8	21 0/8	5	6	Umatilla County	OR	Clifford W. Widel	1991	181
174 0/8	25 0/8	25 1/8	20 6/8	5	5	Ravalli County	MT	John Schulz	1976	184
173 7/8	25 3/8	25 2/8	26 0/8	4	4	Uintah County	UT	Hal Wallentine	1962	185
173 7/8	25 4/8	25 4/8	21 0/8	5	5	Garfield County	CO	Danny C. Lloyd	1969	185
173 7/8	24 2/8	24 1/8	22 6/8	7	6	Eagle County	CO	Edward L. Berlier	1970	185
173 7/8	25 0/8	24 5/8	23 5/8	7	7	Okotoks	ALB	Dave Demeter	1981	185
173 6/8	25 3/8	24 4/8	23 5/8	7	6	Sevier County	UT	Morris Stuart	1972	189
173 6/8	23 6/8	24 0/8	20 4/8	6	5	Boulder County	CO	Floyd Sullivan	1982	189
173 6/8	21 4/8	22 0/8	22 4/8	6	5	Humboldt County	NV	Joel C. Lenz	1984	189
173 6/8	25 4/8	20 3/8	27 4/8	5	6	Meadow Lake	BC	Chip Young	1987	189
173 6/8	24 6/8	22 5/8	18 6/8	5	5	Boise County	ID	Thomas M. Szurgot	1991	189
173 5/8	24 6/8	24 7/8	23 7/8	5	5	Morton County	ND	Pat Sullivan	1957	194
173 5/8	25 1/8	25 5/8	25 2/8	7	5	Pima County	AZ	Joe Nochta	1959	194
173 5/8	21 4/8	21 1/8	21 0/8	6	7	Chaffee County	CO	Lee Rowe	1966	194
173 5/8	23 3/8	23 7/8	24 5/8	5	5	San Juan County	UT	Robert G. Hester	1972	194
173 4/8	24 3/8	24 2/8	27 2/8	5	6	Garfield County	CO	Don Mayen	1966	198
173 4/8	22 1/8	22 1/8	20 4/8	6	7	Ada County	ID	David D. Howard	1971	198
173 4/8	23 5/8	24 4/8	21 0/8	4	6	Mesa County	CO	G. Fred Asbell	1974	198
173 4/8	21 5/8	20 4/8	21 2/8	5	5	Montrose County	CO	Chip Greene	1978	198
173 3/8	22 4/8	24 1/8	24 7/8	5	5	Coconino County	AZ	Jack Richards	1958	202
173 3/8	23 0/8	23 5/8	23 5/8	5	5	Sevier County	UT	Robert J. Shumway	1969	202
173 3/8	21 5/8	22 6/8	22 0/8	6	5	Caribou County	ID	Jim Walton	1983	202
173 2/8	22 6/8	23 1/8	22 6/8	6	6	Millard County	UT	George Kendall	1959	205
173 2/8	25 6/8	25 1/8	22 4/8	5	5	Dolores County	CO	Jack Acree	1969	205
173 2/8	24 0/8	24 0/8	21 4/8	5	7	Bernalillo County	NM	Rolland Hanna	1972	205
173 2/8	25 1/8	24 3/8	24 3/8	6	5	Carbon County	UT	Demar Guymon	1982	205
173 2/8	27 6/8	27 2/8	25 6/8	7	7	Norton County	KS	Mark S. Myers	1991	205
173 1/8	26 3/8	25 0/8	21 3/8	5	5	Coconino County	AZ	H. H. Harter	1961	210
173 1/8	23 3/8	24 1/8	20 5/8	5	5	Teton County	ID	Paul Beesley	1976	210
173 1/8	22 1/8	22 5/8	21 6/8	5	6	Bear Lake County	ID	Steven A. Dewey	1985	210
173 1/8	23 3/8	22 2/8	23 0/8	5	7	Deschutes County	OR	Jonathan Roy Manbeck	1987	210
173 0/8	23 4/8	24 0/8	24 1/8	5	5	Gray County	KS	Bob Barnes	1966	214
173 0/8	21 5/8	22 2/8	24 5/8	4	5	Mesa County	CO	Floyd Kendall	1966	214
173 0/8	26 6/8	26 5/8	23 5/8	6	6	Edmonton	ALB	Brian Berrecloth	1981	214
173 0/8	25 4/8	25 4/8	26 7/8	6	5	Carbon County	UT	Tom Riebe	1983	214
173 0/8	22 2/8	22 2/8	18 2/8	5	5	Caribou County	ID	Larry Jaeger	1985	214
173 0/8	24 3/8	22 4/8	22 2/8	5	5	Boise County	ID	Kenneth A. Hyde	1988	214
172 7/8	22 6/8	22 2/8	20 2/8	6	5	Boise County	ID	Marlin Tullis	1982	220
172 7/8	22 2/8	22 5/8	22 7/8	5	5	Cabri	SAS	Clarence R. Hughes	1989	220
172 7/8	22 5/8	23 3/8	18 7/8	6	5	Colfax County	NM	Joe Amador	1991	220
172 7/8	22 5/8	22 5/8	21 1/8	4	5	Cache County	UT	David Teuscher	1992	220
172 6/8	21 5/8	21 6/8	16 7/8	6	5	Bowman County	ND	Leroy Brandenburger	1967	224
172 6/8	28 7/8	26 3/8	28 7/8	6	6	Rio Arriba County	NM	Kerino H. Revel	1968	224
172 6/8	21 7/8	22 4/8	19 4/8	5	4	Ada County	ID	Ronald B. Jones	1971	224
172 6/8	23 4/8	24 0/8	20 7/8	7	5	San Juan County	UT	Harold Boyack	1975	224
172 6/8	22 3/8	23 0/8	20 6/8	4	5	Mabel Lake	BC	Mark Siegmueller	1984	224
172 6/8	23 1/8	22 5/8	22 0/8	4	4	Rio Blanco County	CO	Brad Murray	1985	224
172 6/8	23 3/8	23 1/8	20 4/8	5	5	Franklin County	ID	Lance Henderson	1992	224
172 5/8	23 6/8	24 2/8	22 3/8	5	5	Bernalillo County	NM	Noble Sinclair	1982	231
172 5/8	22 4/8	20 7/8	20 4/8	5	6	Lincoln County	WY	Mike Barrett	1990	231
172 4/8	24 3/8	22 7/8	24 3/8	6	5	Malheur County	OR	Carl R. Stone	1957	233
172 4/8	25 3/8	25 4/8	24 2/8	5	5	Owyhee County	ID	Don Rosenvall	1961	233
172 4/8	25 6/8	23 6/8	20 3/8	5	5	Chelan County	WA	Timothy E Pflugh	1984	233
172 4/8	25 4/8	25 7/8	22 2/8	6	6	Mesa County	CO	DeWayne Young	1986	233

MULE DEER (Typical Antlers)

SCORE	LENGTH OF R MAIN BEAM L		INSIDE SPREAD	NUMBER OF R POINTS L		AREA	STATE/ PROVINCE	HUNTER'S NAME	DATE	RANK
172 3/8	23 3/8	22 6/8	21 6/8	5	7	Garfield County	CO	Kenneth Rapp	1974	237
172 3/8	22 0/8	22 0/8	20 3/8	5	5	Ouray County	CO	Don Castrup	1975	237
172 3/8	25 3/8	25 4/8	23 0/8	6	6	Shasta County	CA	Russell Browning	1983	237
172 3/8	24 5/8	24 1/8	23 0/8	5	6	Norton County	KS	Greg J. McCall	1985	237
172 3/8	23 7/8	22 5/8	24 4/8	5	5	Montrose County	CO	Greg Blackburn	1986	237
172 2/8	24 4/8	25 3/8	21 0/8	6	7	Rock Creek	CO	Louis Prestridge	1961	242
172 2/8	26 0/8	26 0/8	25 6/8	5	5	Wasatch County	UT	Bill Dean	1965	242
172 2/8	21 4/8	22 3/8	19 2/8	5	5	Caribou County	ID	Bret Davis	1991	242
172 1/8	24 1/8	24 6/8	24 5/8	5	5	Rio Grande County	CO	Marvin Tompkins	1960	245
172 1/8	22 3/8	22 3/8	18 1/8	4	4	Lake County	OR	Ralph Hoover	1964	245
172 1/8	24 0/8	24 4/8	23 7/8	5	6	Sevier County	UT	Bob Covington	1965	245
172 1/8	21 1/8	22 2/8	20 7/8	5	5	Saguache County	CO	Rick Duggan	1984	245
172 1/8	20 3/8	20 6/8	20 6/8	5	6	Perkins County	SD	Travis Bies	1988	245
172 0/8	26 1/8	26 3/8	26 1/8	4	5	Baker County	OR	James D. Hanley	1960	250
172 0/8	25 6/8	26 0/8	21 4/8	4	5	Beechy	SAS	Terry Carruthers	1987	250
171 7/8	23 4/8	23 5/8	27 2/8	5	5	Uintah County	UT	Alvin Sisam	1966	252
171 7/8	26 4/8	24 5/8	24 5/8	4	5	Lancer	SAS	Del Erickson	1976	252
171 7/8	20 3/8	20 5/8	17 7/8	5	5	Larimer County	CO	Mike Kolano	1985	252
171 7/8	23 1/8	24 1/8	25 5/8	9	5	Scott County	KS	Mike Stoppel	1986	252
171 6/8	23 0/8	22 7/8	22 2/8	5	5	Carbon County	WY	Steve Parker	1974	256
171 6/8	22 7/8	21 6/8	23 3/8	8	8	Teton County	MT	James Dean	1977	256
171 6/8	24 7/8	25 4/8	21 6/8	5	6	Delta County	CO	Louis A. Brunett	1983	256
171 5/8	24 3/8	24 3/8	23 2/8	6	5	Harney County	OR	Chuck Warner	1977	259
171 5/8	23 5/8	24 0/8	19 1/8	4	5	Sweetwater County	WY	Keith Dana	1983	259
171 4/8	21 6/8	23 3/8	25 2/8	5	6	Uncompahgre N.F.	CO	Vito Benedetto	1976	261
171 4/8	24 4/8	24 3/8	21 2/8	5	5	Stutsman County	ND	Harold Hugelen	1977	261
171 4/8	23 0/8	22 6/8	22 3/8	6	5	Clark County	KS	Dan Fenton	1980	261
171 4/8	24 7/8	25 6/8	23 6/8	4	4	Baker County	OR	Mike Raney	1987	261
171 3/8	23 4/8	23 5/8	22 5/8	6	5	Ravalli County	MT	Joe Wandstrath	1980	265
171 3/8	24 5/8	25 5/8	26 5/8	5	5	Chaffee County	CO	Bruce Fish	1981	265
171 3/8	26 6/8	24 2/8	20 3/8	4	4	Lake County	OR	Michael Wright	1991	265
171 2/8	23 2/8	23 6/8	20 2/8	4	5	Summit County	UT	Kent Garfield	1959	268
171 2/8	24 0/8	23 7/8	19 2/8	5	5	Richland County	MT	Dennis Engle	1966	268
171 2/8	21 5/8	22 0/8	16 2/8	5	6	Routt County	CO	Joe Mucka	1975	268
171 1/8	28 0/8	26 4/8	22 4/8	8	7	Wasatch County	UT	Frank Snyder	1959	271
171 1/8	25 4/8	25 3/8	24 7/8	7	6	Millard County	UT	Shirley B. Pace	1962	271
171 1/8	23 3/8	23 2/8	22 7/8	5	5	Juab County	UT	Farren Anderson	1964	271
171 1/8	20 7/8	22 7/8	22 2/8	6	7	Mesa County	CO	Curtis Bateman	1983	271
171 1/8	22 7/8	23 2/8	21 5/8	5	5	Garden County	NE	Monte Shaul	1985	271
171 0/8	21 7/8	23 0/8	21 6/8	5	6	Meade County	KS	Keith Whitney	1986	276
170 7/8	21 1/8	22 7/8	19 3/8	4	4	Beaver County	UT	Richard L. Anderson	1960	277
170 7/8	22 7/8	21 5/8	24 4/8	5	5	Bernalillo County	NM	Dr. E. J. Bowser	1971	277
170 7/8	23 4/8	22 1/8	19 6/8	6	5	Uncompahgre N.F.	CO	Allen G. Hughes	1974	277
170 6/8	22 7/8	22 4/8	22 6/8	5	6	Chelan County	WA	Gerald Weiss	1967	280
170 6/8	25 2/8	24 5/8	25 0/8	5	5	Uintah County	UT	Eugene Damron	1974	280
170 5/8	24 7/8	25 6/8	19 7/8	5	6	Garfield County	CO	Robert H. Pitt	1971	282
170 4/8	23 2/8	23 0/8	22 0/8	5	5	Carbon County	WY	James E. Lawrence	1971	283
170 4/8	21 1/8	21 5/8	20 1/8	6	5	Humboldt County	NV	Vic Christison	1982	283
170 4/8	26 0/8	24 4/8	25 0/8	5	4	Torrance County	NM	Henry Montoya	1988	283
170 4/8	24 3/8	23 3/8	18 1/8	6	5	Camas County	ID	Bruce McStay	1988	283
170 3/8	20 7/8	19 4/8	21 4/8	5	5	Ada County	ID	Jim Spearman	1970	287
170 3/8	23 6/8	24 5/8	19 7/8	5	5	Chelan County	WA	Dave Johnson	1977	287
170 3/8	21 0/8	21 0/8	20 0/8	5	6	Harney County	OR	Chuck Warner	1979	287
170 3/8	23 4/8	23 3/8	19 6/8	6	6	Caribou County	ID	Gregg Welch	1988	287
170 3/8	23 2/8	23 2/8	21 6/8	5	6	Chelan County	WA	Wayne Pippin	1991	287
170 2/8	24 7/8	23 7/8	24 2/8	6	6	Slope County	ND	Jim Peters	1954	292
170 2/8	23 1/8	23 1/8	20 1/8	5	7	Fishlake National Forest	UT	Stan Rock	1961	292
170 2/8	23 0/8	23 3/8	20 1/8	7	5	Rio Arriba County	NM	Robert H. Keadle	1966	292
170 2/8	21 3/8	20 4/8	20 4/8	7	7	McKenzie County	ND	Don Davidson	1982	292
170 2/8	23 7/8	25 0/8	24 4/8	4	5	Colfax County	NM	Michael A. Sisneros	1991	292
170 1/8	23 3/8	24 0/8	19 7/8	5	5	Gray County	KS	Dick Masters	1968	297
170 1/8	22 7/8	22 7/8	20 3/8	5	5	Thomas County	KS	Gerald Paxton	1987	297
170 0/8	23 3/8	22 2/8	23 6/8	7	7	Pima County	AZ	James M. Fry	1975	299
170 0/8	22 4/8	23 0/8	20 6/8	4	5	Routt County	CO	Robert Syvertson, Jr.	1975	299
170 0/8	23 3/8	23 7/8	24 2/8	5	6	Uncompahgre N.F.	CO	Robert Meyler IV	1976	299
170 0/8	23 5/8	22 7/8	19 7/8	5	6	Grant County	OR	Timothy D. Palmore	1976	299
170 0/8	24 2/8	24 0/8	26 3/8	5	5	Saguache County	CO	Pat Schambow	1985	299
170 0/8	21 4/8	22 2/8	19 6/8	5	5	Norton County	KS	David Bainter	1988	299
169 7/8	23 3/8	22 7/8	24 3/8	4	5	Caribou County	ID	Chet Hopkins	1968	305
169 6/8	23 0/8	23 3/8	23 0/8	5	5	Garfield County	CO	C. W. Gilbreath	1967	306

SCORE	LENGTH OF MAIN BEAM		INSIDE SPREAD	NUMBER OF POINTS		AREA	STATE/ PROVINCE	HUNTER'S NAME	DATE	RANK
	R	L		R	L					
169 6/8	25 0/8	23 0/8	22 2/8	4	4	Platte County	WY	Jerry Bowen	1976	306
169 6/8	22 0/8	23 0/8	22 2/8	5	5	Elbert County	CO	Mike Amendt	1981	306
169 6/8	21 7/8	22 2/8	20 0/8	5	5	Garfield County	CO	Eddy Oliger	1986	306
169 6/8	22 3/8	22 3/8	20 4/8	5	6	Camas County	ID	Jim Walters	1988	306
169 5/8	24 3/8	24 3/8	22 0/8	5	7	Lincoln County	MT	Harold Leslie	1980	311
169 5/8	26 0/8	25 5/8	19 5/8	9	8	Garfield County	CO	Jay A. Keeler	1984	311
169 5/8	22 6/8	22 2/8	20 5/8	5	4	Eagle County	CO	Michael Dziekan	1988	311
169 4/8	23 0/8	23 3/8	26 7/8	5	5	Owyhee County	ID	Dwane Marler	1955	314
169 3/8	21 4/8	22 3/8	19 5/8	5	5	McKinley County	NM	Hayden Lambson	1979	315
169 3/8	22 5/8	22 2/8	26 2/8	5	5	Norton County	KS	Joseph E. Schroeder	1979	315
169 3/8	20 4/8	22 3/8	22 3/8	5	5	Elmore County	ID	Steve Bresnahan	1980	315
169 3/8	22 3/8	22 0/8	19 3/8	5	5	Box Elder County	UT	Bob Doutre	1981	315
169 2/8	22 3/8	21 6/8	23 4/8	6	5	Chelan County	WA	Larry Lockhart	1966	319
169 2/8	26 0/8	26 0/8	20 6/8	5	5	Umatilla County	OR	Dennis Hernley	1987	319
169 2/8	24 6/8	23 6/8	21 1/8	6	5	Pinal County	AZ	Robert Wakefield	1991	319
169 1/8	24 2/8	23 4/8	21 1/8	7	6	San Juan County	UT	Dean Wolf	1970	322
169 1/8	23 2/8	24 7/8	21 4/8	6	7	Elmore County	ID	Champ Church	1986	322
169 1/8	25 1/8	24 0/8	23 2/8	5	5	Dolores County	CO	Eugene Davenport	1990	322
169 0/8	22 0/8	21 5/8	20 0/8	5	4	Colfax County	NM	Gary Ginther	1973	325
169 0/8	23 5/8	24 6/8	22 6/8	5	5	Fremont County	CO	Bill W. Canterbury	1975	325
169 0/8	23 2/8	24 6/8	24 3/8	6	5	San Juan County	UT	Harold Boyack	1978	325
169 0/8	25 1/8	24 7/8	21 2/8	7	7	Bernalillo County	NM	John L. Padilla	1989	325
169 0/8	24 1/8	20 3/8	22 4/8	5	5	Elmore County	ID	David E. Sass	1991	325
168 7/8	21 1/8	21 1/8	24 2/8	5	5	Cache County	UT	Carl Roush	1979	330
168 7/8	21 6/8	24 3/8	22 7/8	5	6	Park County	CO	Jim Johnson	1980	330
168 7/8	21 3/8	22 3/8	21 5/8	5	5	Union County	OR	Jerry W. Simmons	1982	330
168 6/8	23 1/8	24 2/8	20 6/8	5	4	Baker County	OR	Joe Williamsen	1959	333
168 6/8	24 7/8	24 3/8	23 4/8	5	5	Little Belt Mountains	MT	James Ployhar	1969	333
168 6/8	21 5/8	21 5/8	17 6/8	6	5	Ravalli County	MT	Bob Brill	1977	333
168 6/8	20 5/8	19 0/8	19 2/8	5	6	Umatilla County	OR	Donald E. Durland	1983	333
168 6/8	22 4/8	23 0/8	17 4/8	6	5	Mesa County	CO	J.D. 'Butch' Shivers	1985	333
168 6/8	23 7/8	24 5/8	21 4/8	6	6	San Miguel County	CO	Jay Scott	1986	333
168 5/8	20 6/8	21 5/8	18 3/8	5	5	Gunnison County	CO	Edward Maxfield Vandersli	1991	339
168 4/8	24 6/8	24 7/8	21 6/8	5	5	Utah County	UT	Garland Bray	1970	340
168 4/8	23 4/8	22 4/8	23 7/8	5	5	Uncompahgre N.F.	CO	Paul R. Holmes	1974	340
168 4/8	22 2/8	21 6/8	22 5/8	4	4	Carbon County	WY	David Paskett	1990	340
168 3/8	23 5/8	23 3/8	17 5/8	5	5	Chelan County	WA	George Wells	1960	343
168 3/8	22 7/8	22 0/8	19 6/8	5	6	Mineral County	CO	Richard Kolish	1961	343
168 3/8	21 7/8	22 5/8	22 7/8	5	5	Weber County	UT	Dennis L. Shirley	1972	343
168 3/8	24 1/8	23 2/8	22 1/8	5	6	Eureka County	NV	Joel C. Lenz	1986	343
168 2/8	28 6/8	26 5/8	26 0/8	4	5	Uintah County	UT	S. K. Daniels	1908	347
168 2/8	25 0/8	24 0/8	21 7/8	5	5	Mesa County	CO	Jack Kenyon	1965	347
168 2/8	22 6/8	24 0/8	22 6/8	5	5	La Plata County	CO	Don Putterbaugh	1966	347
168 2/8	22 0/8	22 6/8	21 4/8	5	5	Mesa County	CO	Joseph Sverak	1968	347
168 2/8	24 1/8	22 1/8	21 4/8	4	4	Chaffee County	CO	Frank A. Morminello	1977	347
168 2/8	25 0/8	24 3/8	20 6/8	5	5	Humboldt County	NV	James A. Dallimore	1983	347
168 2/8	22 0/8	21 4/8	18 6/8	6	5	Caribou County	ID	Gene Keller	1985	347
168 2/8	25 3/8	24 2/8	25 0/8	6	5	Lincoln County	MT	Alan L. Davis	1992	347
168 1/8	21 4/8	21 5/8	19 7/8	5	5	Grand County	CO	Lenard Boughton	1968	355
168 1/8	21 3/8	22 2/8	19 7/8	6	6	McKenzie County	ND	Craig A. Ross	1983	355
168 1/8	24 3/8	25 5/8	25 4/8	6	4	Cochrane	ALB	Larry Collins	1990	355
168 0/8	25 3/8	24 3/8	23 0/8	4	6	Uncompahgre N.F.	CO	Dick Gulman	1976	358
168 0/8	23 0/8	22 7/8	24 2/8	5	4	Elko County	NV	James A. Algerio	1980	358
168 0/8	24 0/8	22 7/8	23 2/8	5	5	Jefferson County	CO	Robert Anderson	1980	358
167 7/8	24 3/8	24 0/8	27 2/8	6	6	Grand County	UT	Bob Paulson	1967	361
167 7/8	23 1/8	22 1/8	22 6/8	6	6	Routt County	CO	Edwin W. Foerster	1987	361
167 6/8	21 4/8	20 6/8	18 5/8	5	5	Wallowa County	OR	Leonard Brooks	1967	363
167 6/8	22 7/8	23 5/8	23 0/8	5	5	Boise County	ID	Ed Moser	1982	363
167 6/8	23 5/8	24 5/8	20 2/8	5	6	Okotoks	ALB	Grant Hill	1989	363
167 6/8	23 0/8	23 0/8	21 0/8	5	5	Jerome County	ID	Guy G. Fitzgerald	1992	363
167 5/8	21 2/8	22 1/8	26 0/8	5	5	Grand County	CO	Michael A. Contreras	1978	367
167 4/8	20 2/8	20 5/8	19 0/8	5	5	Cascade County	MT	Ron Johnson	1987	368
167 4/8	22 4/8	23 3/8	19 1/8	6	6	Pinal County	AZ	Sonny Nieto	1991	368
167 4/8	22 2/8	22 1/8	17 2/8	4	5	Abbey	SAS	Floyd Forster	1992	368
167 3/8	21 4/8	21 3/8	19 3/8	5	5	Owyhee County	ID	Eugene R. Mallard	1963	371
167 3/8	25 0/8	25 0/8	19 3/8	7	5	Klamath County	OR	V. Kenneth Murdock	1978	371
167 3/8	21 6/8	22 7/8	19 0/8	5	7	Mesa County	CO	Paul H. Dickson	1984	371
167 3/8	18 7/8	23 0/8	22 1/8	5	5	Baker County	OR	Kevin Kennedy	1987	371
167 3/8	22 5/8	23 7/8	25 3/8	5	5	Washoe County	NV	Ralph L. Albright	1988	371
167 3/8	23 7/8	24 1/8	20 7/8	5	5	Baker County	OR	Jeff McCrary	1991	371

SCORE	LENGTH OF MAIN BEAM R	L	INSIDE SPREAD	NUMBER OF POINTS R	L	AREA	STATE/ PROVINCE	HUNTER'S NAME	DATE	RANK
167 3/8	24 0/8	24 2/8	20 5/8	5	5	West Lake	BC	Bob Dunlop	1991	371
167 3/8	24 7/8	24 6/8	22 5/8	7	8	Gunnison County	CO	Duane Lyerly	1992	371
167 2/8	20 7/8	21 5/8	20 3/8	5	4	Lincoln County	WY	Ronell Skinner	1980	379
167 2/8	23 0/8	23 0/8	20 6/8	6	5	Mesa County	CO	Jim Bennett	1981	379
167 1/8	21 1/8	19 3/8	18 2/8	6	6	Anahim Lake	BC	Guy Antilla	1965	381
167 1/8	26 3/8	24 4/8	21 2/8	5	4	Humboldt County	NV	Jerry Stout	1965	381
167 1/8	24 1/8	24 2/8	23 7/8	6	7	Gunnison County	CO	Richard L. Geissler	1983	381
167 1/8	22 0/8	21 3/8	19 3/8	5	5	Converse County	WY	Barry J. Smith	1991	381
167 0/8	23 3/8	24 2/8	22 2/8	4	4	Eagle County	CO	Arvine Routh	1965	385
167 0/8	23 3/8	24 4/8	22 0/8	5	5	Mesa County	CO	Mike Gilbert	1973	385
167 0/8	23 2/8	23 1/8	22 1/8	7	8	Grand County	CO	Michael K. Ward	1973	385
167 0/8	21 2/8	19 7/8	18 4/8	5	5	Mesa County	CO	Glen Hitt	1975	385
167 0/8	23 5/8	22 5/8	20 4/8	5	6	Garfield County	CO	Randy Edwards	1987	385
167 0/8	23 4/8	23 2/8	19 6/8	4	5	Rio Arriba County	NM	Dennis A. Muirhead	1991	385
166 7/8	21 2/8	22 0/8	20 5/8	5	5	Uintah County	UT	Orson Stilson	1964	391
166 6/8	25 1/8	25 3/8	24 4/8	5	6	Uintah County	UT	Doug Walker	1967	392
166 6/8	24 3/8	23 4/8	23 4/8	5	4	Mesa County	CO	David E. Samuel	1974	392
166 6/8	23 4/8	23 0/8	20 2/8	5	5	Adams County	CO	John C. Schmidt	1974	392
166 5/8	22 6/8	23 0/8	20 1/8	5	5	Baker County	OR	Lloyd V. Christensen	1959	395
166 5/8	23 4/8	23 6/8	23 5/8	5	5	Montezuma County	CO	Marvin Reichenau	1983	395
166 5/8	22 0/8	22 1/8	19 7/8	5	5	Grant County	OR	Ray Kelton	1985	395
166 5/8	24 5/8	24 5/8	22 0/8	5	6	Milk River Ridge	ALB	Brian Carriere	1990	395
166 4/8	23 2/8	24 0/8	22 2/8	7	7	Owyhee County	ID	Bill Payne	1958	399
166 4/8	23 5/8	22 6/8	21 6/8	5	5	Owyhee County	ID	Blake Murphy	1961	399
166 4/8	20 3/8	20 5/8	16 6/8	5	5	Adams County	ID	Jack St. Germain	1986	399
166 4/8	23 6/8	23 3/8	20 0/8	5	4	Morrow County	OR	Phil Jackson	1992	399
166 3/8	21 7/8	22 5/8	21 0/8	6	7	Butte County	SD	L. G. Braun	1957	403
166 3/8	24 6/8	24 3/8	20 1/8	5	6	Lane County	KS	Dean Hamilton	1988	403
166 2/8	25 2/8	23 1/8	18 0/8	5	5	Mesa County	CO	Lloyd Kell	1967	405
166 2/8	21 3/8	22 2/8	23 6/8	5	5	Garfield County	CO	Jim Walters	1975	405
166 2/8	22 3/8	22 4/8	23 2/8	5	5	Scott County	KS	Mel Jamison	1986	405
166 1/8	21 4/8	22 1/8	18 1/8	5	5	Carbon County	WY	Duncan G. Weibel	1955	408
166 1/8	20 6/8	21 4/8	19 5/8	5	5	Ada County	ID	M. F. Smith	1968	408
166 1/8	20 4/8	22 4/8	21 3/8	5	5	Calgary	ALB	Dean Reed	1981	408
166 0/8	20 0/8	20 7/8	19 5/8	6	5	Lincoln County	NE	M. R. Buchtel	1958	411
166 0/8	19 7/8	21 1/8	17 6/8	5	5	Mohave County	AZ	Norman J. Brown	1966	411
166 0/8	24 4/8	23 0/8	21 6/8	4	4	Garfield County	CO	Robert G. Kuper	1966	411
166 0/8	24 6/8	24 4/8	26 0/8	5	5	Cassia County	ID	Jack B. Watts	1968	411
166 0/8	23 4/8	24 0/8	24 2/8	5	4	Lewis & Clark County	MT	Donald Davidson, Jr.	1980	411
166 0/8	22 2/8	23 1/8	17 6/8	6	6	Elbert County	CO	Billy Tillotson	1986	411
166 0/8	22 0/8	23 0/8	22 4/8	5	5	Maricopa County	AZ	Daniel Whitaker	1988	411
166 0/8	21 7/8	22 2/8	22 4/8	6	5	El Paso County	CO	Freeman Howard	1989	411
165 7/8	23 4/8	25 0/8	25 0/8	9	6	Owyhee County	ID	Thomas Eld	1964	419
165 7/8	23 6/8	25 6/8	20 3/8	5	5	Moffat County	CO	Albert A. Adams	1982	419
165 7/8	22 6/8	22 4/8	25 6/8	6	7	Gray County	KS	Allen D. Bailey	1985	419
165 7/8	25 3/8	25 1/8	20 5/8	5	6	Mesa County	CO	James C. Snortum	1991	419
165 6/8	24 0/8	23 2/8	19 2/8	6	6	Garfield County	CO	John Richard	1972	423
165 6/8	23 6/8	23 4/8	17 2/8	5	5	Grand County	CO	Burt Thompson	1983	423
165 6/8	23 0/8	21 5/8	16 6/8	4	5	Graham County	KS	Randy Wilson	1989	423
165 5/8	21 1/8	21 0/8	20 5/8	5	5	Utah County	UT	Frank Eicholt	1964	426
165 5/8	21 0/8	21 2/8	18 5/8	5	5	Zone 5	SAS	Ward Minifie	1985	426
165 5/8	21 7/8	21 0/8	23 3/8	5	5	McKinley County	NM	Richard W. Eustace, Jr.	1988	426
165 5/8	22 4/8	24 0/8	17 7/8	5	5	Rich County	UT	Colby Steffen Hagen	1992	426
165 4/8	23 1/8	23 6/8	24 1/8	6	5	Mesa County	CO	Bob Woodhouse	1978	430
165 4/8	22 4/8	23 4/8	19 0/8	5	5	San Miguel County	NM	Louis Baca	1985	430
165 4/8	21 6/8	22 6/8	25 7/8	5	5	Hodgeman County	KS	Charles Fuller	1985	430
165 4/8	24 1/8	24 7/8	19 3/8	7	6	Kane County	UT	Richard Jolley	1986	430
165 3/8	27 0/8	26 0/8	19 1/8	7	5	Mesa County	CO	Kent Stumpf	1973	434
165 3/8	24 4/8	25 0/8	18 3/8	7	7	Duchesne County	UT	Everett Burson	1984	434
165 3/8	23 2/8	21 2/8	20 0/8	5	6	Boise County	ID	Peter Cintorino	1985	434
165 2/8	26 5/8	27 0/8	25 2/8	5	5	Mesa County	CO	Ray Carpenter	1960	437
165 2/8	20 6/8	20 1/8	18 4/8	5	5	Clear Creek County	CO	John Marolt III	1967	437
165 1/8	20 5/8	22 3/8	20 2/8	5	6	Sevier County	UT	Severin Jensen	1959	439
165 1/8	23 2/8	24 0/8	27 3/8	6	6	Douglas County	CO	Dale Slade	1967	439
165 1/8	23 4/8	25 4/8	26 0/8	5	7	Mesa County	CO	George J. Hronkin III	1982	439
165 1/8	21 3/8	22 2/8	20 1/8	5	5	Valley County	ID	Charles "Chuck" Boatman	1985	439
165 1/8	25 6/8	24 2/8	24 3/8	6	6	Fremont County	WY	Jerry A. Bodar	1988	439
165 0/8	24 3/8	25 0/8	19 7/8	5	6	Rio Arriba County	NM	David L. Chandler	1967	444
165 0/8	23 4/8	22 6/8	23 5/8	5	6	Cochise County	AZ	Richard Dawe, Jr.	1976	444
165 0/8	22 2/8	22 1/8	22 0/8	5	5	Saguache County	CO	Michael Snodgrass	1977	444

MINIMUM SCORE 145

SCORE	LENGTH OF MAIN BEAM		INSIDE SPREAD	NUMBER OF POINTS		AREA	STATE/ PROVINCE	HUNTER'S NAME	DATE	RANK
	R	L		R	L					
165 0/8	26 4/8	25 2/8	25 0/8	4	5	Lake County	OR	Wayne Lamson, Jr.	1981	444
165 0/8	24 6/8	25 6/8	21 4/8	5	5	Los Alamos County	NM	Doug Aikin	1985	444
165 0/8	22 1/8	21 7/8	21 2/8	5	5	Sanders County	MT	Craig Phillips	1990	444
164 7/8	24 0/8	22 7/8	23 5/8	4	4	Mesa County	CO	Richard Rounds	1973	450
164 7/8	22 3/8	21 7/8	19 5/8	5	5	Routt County	CO	Paul Blotz	1974	450
164 7/8	24 3/8	23 0/8	25 5/8	5	5	Piute County	UT	Art Whitby	1992	450
164 6/8	22 4/8	21 3/8	18 2/8	5	5	Skyline Drive	UT	George Heath	1964	453
164 6/8	20 3/8	22 0/8	22 1/8	4	4	White Pine County	NV	Larry T. Gilbertson	1984	453
164 5/8	25 6/8	26 1/8	24 4/8	5	5	Fox Valley	SAS	Doug Findlay	1977	455
164 5/8	20 4/8	21 3/8	20 3/8	4	5	Grand County	UT	Don Dvoroznak	1979	455
164 5/8	22 2/8	23 2/8	19 4/8	5	6	Cassia County	ID	Richard Ponciano	1985	455
164 5/8	19 5/8	20 7/8	16 6/8	6	5	Mesa County	CO	Don Walsh	1986	455
164 5/8	23 6/8	24 2/8	21 0/8	6	5	Scott County	KS	Lynn Freese	1987	455
164 4/8	23 2/8	23 6/8	25 4/8	5	5	Calgary	ALB	David Lovo	1979	460
164 4/8	21 4/8	21 7/8	20 4/8	5	5	Fergus County	MT	Michael B. Bryson	1986	460
164 4/8	21 4/8	21 6/8	19 2/8	6	6	Lincoln County	WY	Mike Barrett	1989	460
164 4/8	21 5/8	22 2/8	22 3/8	6	6	Red Deer Lake	ALB	Larry Mandseth	1989	460
164 3/8	21 7/8	23 0/8	19 7/8	5	5	Siskiyou County	CA	Dale Gatlin	1959	464
164 3/8	24 6/8	23 4/8	24 6/8	8	8	Elko County	NV	Dick Woltering	1960	464
164 3/8	22 3/8	22 3/8	23 2/8	5	5	Sheridan County	KS	Kevin J. Ryan	1974	464
164 3/8	20 1/8	21 4/8	19 0/8	7	7	Conejos County	CO	Frank Holloway	1983	464
164 3/8	22 5/8	22 3/8	20 1/8	6	5	Routt County	CO	Richard L. Charles, Sr.	1990	464
164 3/8	23 6/8	22 4/8	19 5/8	5	5	Carbon County	WY	Dean P. Reed	1991	464
164 3/8	20 7/8	20 7/8	18 3/8	5	5	Lincoln County	WY	Mike Barrett	1992	464
164 2/8	23 2/8	24 0/8	19 4/8	7	9	Garfield County	CO	D. H. Nolting	1956	471
164 2/8	22 6/8	21 6/8	22 0/8	6	5	Routt County	CO	John Hale	1975	471
164 2/8	20 6/8	23 1/8	18 4/8	7	6	Dolores County	CO	Tommy C. Jeffcoat	1977	471
164 2/8	21 7/8	22 0/8	21 6/8	5	5	Greenlee County	AZ	Steve E. Allen	1980	471
164 2/8	24 4/8	24 3/8	23 7/8	6	6	Stafford County	KS	Rob Ginest	1982	471
164 2/8	22 0/8	20 4/8	18 4/8	4	4	Cassia County	ID	Bryan Sprauge	1984	471
164 2/8	26 6/8	24 1/8	25 7/8	5	4	San Juan County	NM	Ronnie H. Begay	1988	471
164 1/8	25 3/8	25 6/8	23 6/8	8	7	Owyhee County	ID	Merlie Hampton	1962	478
164 1/8	24 0/8	24 6/8	24 6/8	6	5	Summit County	CO	Russell F. Rider	1964	478
164 1/8	24 4/8	23 1/8	22 7/8	4	4	Garfield County	CO	Roy Hoff	1968	478
164 1/8	22 3/8	22 1/8	19 3/8	5	5	Columbia County	WA	Wayne Dickhaut	1983	478
164 1/8	23 4/8	23 1/8	20 7/8	5	5	Kananaskis	ALB	Don Warner	1992	478
164 0/8	19 4/8	20 1/8	19 6/8	5	5	Garfield County	CO	Dr. Lowell L. Eddy	1968	483
164 0/8	20 7/8	22 0/8	23 3/8	4	4	West Desert	UT	Myron Adams	1969	483
164 0/8	21 3/8	21 3/8	18 0/8	4	4	Ada County	ID	Richard C. Nichols	1971	483
164 0/8	24 6/8	25 3/8	23 7/8	7	6	White Pine County	NV	Robert Davie	1983	483
164 0/8	25 1/8	24 3/8	22 4/8	4	4	Yakima County	WA	Earl Prentice	1990	483
163 7/8	20 1/8	21 3/8	17 6/8	5	6	Frontier County	NE	Keene Hueftle	1961	488
163 7/8	19 0/8	20 6/8	18 1/8	5	5	Phillips County	KS	Phillip Pfortmiller	1986	488
163 7/8	24 1/8	25 7/8	27 3/8	5	5	McKinley County	NM	Dois Chesshir	1989	488
163 7/8	20 4/8	22 1/8	19 6/8	6	5	Maricopa County	AZ	Richard S. Jones	1990	488
163 7/8	23 0/8	20 3/8	17 7/8	5	5	Fergus County	MT	Paul L. Reese	1991	488
163 6/8	22 2/8	21 2/8	21 4/8	5	5	Pima County	AZ	Tom Bylina	1988	493
163 5/8	23 3/8	23 2/8	22 3/8	5	5	White Pine County	NV	Joe Marich	1978	494
163 5/8	19 0/8	19 0/8	17 7/8	5	5	Gallatin County	MT	Jim Diercks	1981	494
163 5/8	21 2/8	21 0/8	18 1/8	5	5	Mesa County	CO	Edwin L. Porter	1983	494
163 5/8	20 6/8	20 6/8	22 6/8	6	5	Bear Lake County	ID	Terry Davis	1984	494
163 4/8	23 1/8	23 2/8	20 4/8	5	5		UT	Darwin Crawford	1964	498
163 4/8	24 1/8	24 1/8	25 0/8	5	5	Lake County	OR	William P. Petredis	1972	498
163 4/8	24 4/8	24 0/8	22 2/8	9	5	Osborne County	KS	Gary Krier	1984	498
163 3/8	22 5/8	25 4/8	17 6/8	8	7	Coconino County	AZ	Jake Price	1963	501
163 3/8	21 6/8	22 1/8	17 5/8	5	5	Gunnison County	CO	Clark Gallup	1970	501
163 3/8	23 3/8	23 7/8	21 7/8	5	5	Val Marie	SAS	John Vinge	1992	501
163 2/8	22 6/8	22 6/8	23 4/8	5	5	Mesa County	CO	Larry D. Tillett	1972	504
163 2/8	21 5/8	20 1/8	19 7/8	6	6	Chaffee County	CO	J. Melvin Rose	1973	504
163 2/8	23 7/8	24 3/8	21 2/8	5	4	Coconino County	AZ	Edward R. Allen, Sr.	1974	504
163 2/8	20 6/8	21 2/8	22 0/8	5	5	Calgary	ALB	Richard P. King	1987	504
163 2/8	22 0/8	22 7/8	17 2/8	5	5	Kyle	SAS	Brian W. Johns	1991	504
163 2/8	23 0/8	23 6/8	21 2/8	5	5	Baker County	OR	T. Blaine McKnight	1992	504
163 1/8	20 0/8	22 6/8	19 5/8	4	4	Routt County	CO	Robert H. Blue	1983	510
163 1/8	21 6/8	21 6/8	20 7/8	4	4	McKenzie County	ND	Mike 'Myron' Rosemore	1986	510
163 0/8	24 2/8	23 4/8	24 2/8	5	7	La Plata County	CO	Bryan B. Owen	1964	512
163 0/8	23 3/8	25 3/8	20 6/8	5	5	Coconino County	AZ	Larry Hayden	1983	512
163 0/8	21 3/8	22 5/8	18 2/8	5	5	Teton County	WY	Al Nelson	1985	512
163 0/8	20 7/8	20 0/8	17 6/8	5	5	Mesa County	CO	Jim Hall	1987	512
163 0/8	22 3/8	23 0/8	21 6/8	5	5	Culberson County	TX	Kyle Johnson	1992	512

SCORE	LENGTH OF R MAIN BEAM L		INSIDE SPREAD	NUMBER OF R POINTS L		AREA	STATE/ PROVINCE	HUNTER'S NAME	DATE	RANK
162 7/8	23 6/8	23 7/8	24 1/8	5	4	Elko County	NV	Orrin M. Owens	1966	517
162 7/8	23 1/8	22 7/8	20 1/8	5	5	Billings County	ND	Allan R. Bottolfson	1981	517
162 7/8	23 5/8	21 6/8	20 5/8	5	5	Fremont County	CO	Jerry Tiemeyer	1981	517
162 7/8	24 0/8	23 6/8	23 5/8	5	5	Umatilla County	OR	Rick L. Evans	1985	517
162 6/8	21 1/8	23 4/8	23 2/8	5	5	Chelan County	WA	Les Eide	1954	521
162 6/8	23 5/8	24 2/8	18 5/8	5	6	Chelan County	WA	Brian Kayler	1984	521
162 6/8	22 1/8	23 1/8	22 2/8	5	5	Chelan County	WA	Rod Courter	1986	521
162 6/8	22 2/8	22 6/8	23 5/8	5	5	Weld County	CO	Dan Wacker	1988	521
162 5/8	19 6/8	20 1/8	22 0/8	5	5	Pima County	AZ	Jerry Clarno	1978	525
162 5/8	22 4/8	21 0/8	21 2/8	7	6	Washoe County	NV	Ed Fuller	1984	525
162 5/8	21 4/8	21 1/8	20 7/8	5	5	Las Animas County	CO	Chris J. Furia	1986	525
162 5/8	20 2/8	21 6/8	19 2/8	7	5	Ada County	ID	Ronald L. Cash	1990	525
162 5/8	22 4/8	23 3/8	19 1/8	6	5	Montrose County	CO	Thomas D. Thompson	1991	525
162 5/8	24 3/8	24 7/8	21 3/8	5	5	Sheridan County	WY	Butch West	1992	525
162 4/8	21 3/8	21 0/8	19 2/8	5	5	Emery County	UT	Kerry Ware	1964	531
162 4/8	24 5/8	25 7/8	27 6/8	5	8	Leader	SAS	Don Tourand	1982	531
162 4/8	21 0/8	21 7/8	17 2/8	5	5	Slope County	ND	Todd Seymonski	1983	531
162 4/8	21 2/8	20 7/8	23 0/8	5	5	Hooker County	NE	Will Boyer	1991	531
162 3/8	25 2/8	25 0/8	22 6/8	7	7	Bear Lake County	ID	Marriner Jensen	1957	535
162 3/8	25 6/8	26 3/8	27 5/8	4	5	Pima County	AZ	Steve Mikitish	1983	535
162 3/8	23 0/8	22 7/8	24 3/8	5	6	Mesa County	CO	Billy T. Edwards	1988	535
162 2/8	23 3/8	26 2/8	25 0/8	4	5	Owyhee County	ID	Ralph Collins	1960	538
162 2/8	20 7/8	20 2/8	22 3/8	6	5	Park County	WY	Jim Patterson	1968	538
162 2/8	22 5/8	23 0/8	17 0/8	5	5	Eureka County	NV	Gordon Diehl	1980	538
162 2/8	23 5/8	23 2/8	19 6/8	5	5	Lassen County	CA	Chuck Mazza	1984	538
162 2/8	23 4/8	23 5/8	21 4/8	5	5	Park County	CO	Randy W. Gorby, Jr.	1988	538
162 2/8	22 3/8	26 4/8	20 0/8	6	5	Bernalillo County	NM	William A. Brandon	1988	538
162 2/8	22 7/8	22 3/8	19 4/8	5	7	Camas County	ID	James C. O'Connor	1991	538
162 1/8	23 7/8	23 6/8	18 1/8	5	5	Fishlake National Forest	UT	R. E. Kerr	1957	545
162 1/8	23 2/8	22 5/8	22 1/8	5	5	Range Creek	UT	Frank Turner	1965	545
162 1/8	22 4/8	22 5/8	17 2/8	5	6	Mesa County	CO	Joel Prickett	1973	545
162 1/8	20 3/8	22 0/8	23 0/8	7	5	Mora County	NM	Michael J. Maes	1977	545
162 1/8	21 7/8	21 7/8	23 1/8	6	6	Dundy County	NE	Jim Lutz	1980	545
162 1/8	24 2/8	21 2/8	21 5/8	6	5	Logan County	KS	Mel Jamison	1985	545
162 0/8	22 3/8	23 1/8	21 2/8	5	5	Elko County	NV	Larry D Jones	1985	551
162 0/8	21 5/8	20 7/8	21 0/8	6	6	Rawlins County	KS	Ken Krien	1988	551
162 0/8	22 3/8	22 4/8	16 4/8	4	5	Lumby	BC	Owen Schoenberger	1990	551
161 7/8	21 4/8	21 7/8	20 3/8	4	5	Rio Blanco County	CO	Douglas Kenyon	1964	554
161 7/8	22 6/8	21 6/8	21 5/8	5	5	Sevier County	UT	Clark Richards	1967	554
161 7/8	23 0/8	22 1/8	20 0/8	5	5	Rio Blanco County	CO	Leonard Conley	1973	554
161 7/8	20 4/8	22 5/8	20 7/8	6	6	Beaver County	UT	Joe Cordonier	1975	554
161 7/8	21 1/8	20 3/8	18 5/8	5	5	Plumes County	CA	John Grochowski, Jr.	1976	554
161 7/8	24 3/8	24 1/8	20 7/8	5	4	Maricopa County	AZ	Paul N. Rambeau	1981	554
161 7/8	25 4/8	23 6/8	22 5/8	8	5	Catron County	NM	Richard D. Trapp	1986	554
161 6/8	21 3/8	21 3/8	21 6/8	5	5	Garfield County	CO	Warren Buss	1978	561
161 6/8	20 5/8	21 5/8	21 2/8	5	5	Elko County	NV	Gregory Higgins	1988	561
161 5/8	22 0/8	22 4/8	19 3/8	5	5	Lander County	NV	Paul Q. Lenz	1984	563
161 5/8	22 5/8	22 5/8	21 7/8	5	5	Rio Arriba County	NM	Craig A. Pilley	1987	563
161 5/8	23 5/8	22 3/8	21 6/8	5	6	Ford County	KS	Jeff Cuer	1988	563
161 5/8	23 5/8	22 5/8	22 6/8	6	5	Converse County	WY	Jeff Reynolds	1990	563
161 5/8	23 3/8	23 5/8	21 3/8	4	4	Boise County	ID	David Gallegos	1991	563
161 4/8	24 5/8	24 6/8	24 2/8	7	7	Salt Lake County	UT	Frank M. Davis	1957	568
161 4/8	24 4/8	24 2/8	23 6/8	4	3	Owyhee County	ID	William R. Vanderhoef	1958	568
161 4/8	22 5/8	23 5/8	19 2/8	5	5	Sheridan County	WY	Mike Barrett	1985	568
161 4/8	25 6/8	24 1/8	24 6/8	5	7	Apache County	AZ	Robert A. Wood	1987	568
161 4/8	21 6/8	20 2/8	18 4/8	5	6	Grant County	OR	Jeff McCrary	1990	568
161 4/8	21 4/8	22 0/8	21 2/8	5	5	Elbert County	CO	Patrick V. Mulhern, Jr.	1990	568
161 4/8	21 6/8	21 6/8	16 6/8	5	5	Lincoln County	WY	Delmar Bright	1992	568
161 3/8	22 5/8	21 7/8	19 1/8	5	5	Elko County	NV	Bert W. Fox	1961	575
161 3/8	23 2/8	21 6/8	22 3/8	4	4	Box Butte County	NE	Fred H. D. Krueger	1970	575
161 3/8	18 5/8	21 1/8	22 1/8	6	5	Cochrane	ALB	Colby Robison	1982	575
161 3/8	22 5/8	22 7/8	22 1/8	5	5	Rush County	KS	Clarence Tuzicka	1990	575
161 3/8	22 3/8	22 4/8	18 2/8	5	6	Stanislaus County	CA	Ron Crouch	1992	575
161 2/8	21 0/8	20 6/8	16 7/8	5	6	Ada County	ID	Ed Moser	1971	580
161 2/8	24 6/8	23 5/8	20 4/8	3	3	Mesa County	CO	Billy Ellis	1976	580
161 2/8	23 6/8	25 2/8	25 4/8	5	4	San Juan County	UT	Todd Hurst	1984	580
161 2/8	23 4/8	22 3/8	17 6/8	5	5	Big Horn County	MT	Mike Barrett	1984	580
161 2/8	23 7/8	23 0/8	22 4/8	5	5	Billings County	ND	Cally G Marsh	1989	580
161 1/8	25 0/8	24 0/8	25 0/8	5	5	Los Alamos County	NM	J. R. McDaniels	1960	585
161 1/8	20 5/8	20 4/8	15 5/8	5	5	Garfield County	CO	John Murray	1963	585

MULE DEER *(Typical Antlers)*

MINIMUM SCORE 145

(Continued)

SCORE	R LENGTH OF MAIN BEAM L		INSIDE SPREAD	NUMBER OF R POINTS L		AREA	STATE/ PROVINCE	HUNTER'S NAME	DATE	RANK
161 1/8	23 1/8	21 7/8	18 1/8	5	5	San Juan County	CO	Eddie Claypool	1984	585
161 1/8	24 6/8	25 6/8	20 3/8	5	4	Kittitas County	WA	Sam Grant	1988	585
161 0/8	23 0/8	23 4/8	19 2/8	4	5	Milk River	ALB	Archie Nesbitt	1992	589
160 7/8	24 0/8	23 5/8	22 3/8	4	5	Teton County	ID	Gary S. Paynter	1987	590
160 6/8	20 6/8	21 4/8	21 5/8	5	5	Colfax County	NM	Carl Osborne	1965	591
160 6/8	22 6/8	22 4/8	21 1/8	7	6	Chelan County	WA	Paul Cohoon	1967	591
160 6/8	21 3/8	22 2/8	26 7/8	6	6	San Juan County	UT	Dale Warren	1972	591
160 6/8	22 4/8	22 6/8	15 4/8	5	4	Washoe County	NV	Lawrence Heward	1974	591
160 6/8	20 5/8	20 3/8	19 4/8	5	5	Boise County	ID	Mike McCollum	1975	591
160 6/8	21 0/8	22 4/8	21 4/8	5	5	Grand County	CO	Terry J. Kramer	1978	591
160 6/8	21 7/8	23 2/8	19 2/8	6	5	Thomas County	KS	Darren Andrews	1986	591
160 6/8	22 2/8	21 1/8	19 6/8	6	7	Archuleta County	CO	James Daugherty	1987	591
160 6/8	24 6/8	25 0/8	28 2/8	5	7	Washoe County	NV	Tom Hauptman	1988	591
160 6/8	23 4/8	21 6/8	24 3/8	7	9	Cheyenne County	CO	Monte Baker	1990	591
160 5/8	20 5/8	20 5/8	19 7/8	4	4	Humboldt County	NV	Mike Toone	1961	601
160 5/8	22 3/8	22 1/8	24 7/8	5	5	San Juan County	UT	Russell Smith	1971	601
160 5/8	21 1/8	21 2/8	20 7/8	5	5	Routt County	CO	Mark Chapman	1975	601
160 5/8	21 1/8	21 6/8	17 7/8	4	4	Moffat County	CO	Glenn Pritchard	1985	601
160 5/8	23 5/8	23 3/8	21 5/8	5	5	Nevada County	CA	Richard L. Westervelt	1992	601
160 4/8	23 6/8	23 1/8	20 0/8	7	8	Elko County	NV	Robert Narrimore	1963	606
160 4/8	23 5/8	23 5/8	18 0/8	5	5	Lemhi County	ID	Robert J. Eckardt	1978	606
160 4/8	24 4/8	23 2/8	24 4/8	4	5	Coconino County	AZ	Bruce McIntyre	1979	606
160 4/8	23 0/8	22 2/8	23 6/8	5	5	Washoe County	NV	Robert L. Brooks, Jr.	1983	606
160 3/8	22 7/8	22 3/8	18 0/8	5	6	Tooele County	UT	Clair Adams	1958	610
160 3/8	22 4/8	22 4/8	18 2/8	6	6	Mesa County	CO	Ed Adkins	1974	610
160 3/8	20 6/8	22 1/8	20 1/8	4	4	Mesa County	CO	Ralph Ertz	1980	610
160 3/8	22 0/8	23 4/8	19 1/8	6	6	Jefferson County	CO	Steve Rehm	1984	610
160 3/8	24 4/8	22 2/8	22 0/8	6	6	Pima County	AZ	Ronald J. Hover	1987	610
160 3/8	23 3/8	23 5/8	20 3/8	5	5	Lake County	OR	Carl E. Garner	1991	610
160 2/8	19 2/8	21 2/8	19 0/8	5	5	Millard County	UT	Scott Chesley	1962	616
160 2/8	19 6/8	21 2/8	20 6/8	5	5	Lemhi County	ID	Kemper McMaster	1978	616
160 2/8	20 5/8	21 1/8	17 0/8	5	5	Mesa County	CO	Bill Dunbar	1984	616
160 2/8	25 6/8	24 6/8	23 3/8	6	6	Scott County	KS	Michael E. Woodard	1984	616
160 2/8	21 4/8	20 5/8	20 6/8	5	5	Gooding County	ID	Robert Dowen	1986	616
160 2/8	21 6/8	22 6/8	18 0/8	4	4	Sioux County	NE	Wayne Depperschmidt	1989	616
160 1/8	20 2/8	20 7/8	19 7/8	5	5	Meagher County	MT	Mickey Anderson, Jr.	1966	622
160 1/8	23 6/8	22 2/8	24 0/8	5	5	Moffat County	CO	Ron Hopkins	1970	622
160 1/8	22 7/8	22 7/8	23 3/8	5	5	Mesa County	CO	Gary J. Oden	1988	622
160 0/8	22 4/8	21 7/8	20 2/8	5	5	Chaffee County	CO	Paul J. Zeisler	1964	625
160 0/8	23 0/8	22 7/8	20 3/8	6	5	Gunnison County	CO	Wayne Depperschmidt	1973	625
160 0/8	21 4/8	21 7/8	19 2/8	5	5	Linn County	OR	Mary Cook	1980	625
160 0/8	23 3/8	24 2/8	20 2/8	5	5	Saguache County	CO	Russell Hull	1980	625
160 0/8	26 2/8	25 1/8	25 0/8	5	5	La Plata County	CO	Michael R. Hinson	1986	625
160 0/8	21 7/8	22 5/8	17 6/8	5	5	Cherry County	NE	Lloyd C. Smith	1990	625
159 7/8	24 2/8	25 0/8	19 4/8	5	6	Colfax County	NM	James Kelly	1957	631
159 7/8	20 7/8	21 6/8	21 6/8	5	5	Liberty County	MT	Kenneth Aaberge	1960	631
159 7/8	22 5/8	23 0/8	18 7/8	5	5	Sanders County	MT	Walt Borgmann	1968	631
159 7/8	23 1/8	21 3/8	17 3/8	5	5	Bernalillo County	NM	Lee Burnett	1972	631
159 7/8	25 4/8	22 4/8	21 0/8	6	6	Mesa County	CO	Ronald E. Stull	1974	631
159 7/8	21 5/8	22 3/8	20 1/8	5	5	Okotoks	ALB	Cam Cook	1990	631
159 6/8	23 4/8	22 7/8	22 3/8	7	7	Owyhee County	ID	Gilbert Martin	1960	637
159 6/8	22 2/8	21 4/8	19 4/8	5	5	Beaver County	UT	Joe Cordonier	1974	637
159 6/8	22 0/8	22 0/8	20 6/8	4	4	Kamloops	BC	Barry Anderson	1982	637
159 6/8	22 6/8	23 2/8	20 6/8	5	5	Labette County	KS	Steve Cooper	1986	637
159 6/8	21 3/8	22 0/8	22 0/8	5	4	Caribou County	ID	Paul Persano	1986	637
159 6/8	23 7/8	24 2/8	20 6/8	8	6	Norton County	KS	Eldon L. Myers	1991	637
159 5/8	22 7/8	22 5/8	25 3/8	5	5	Gove County	KS	Alan Kaiser	1986	643
159 5/8	24 5/8	23 6/8	20 1/8	7	6	Crook County	OR	Kent Gutches	1991	643
159 4/8	20 5/8	21 0/8	17 6/8	5	5	Franklin County	ID	Curtis Henderson	1992	645
159 3/8	21 1/8	20 4/8	16 5/8	4	4	Millard County	UT	Dean Todd	1956	646
159 3/8	22 4/8	22 7/8	18 4/8	5	5	Wasco County	OR	Bill Neary	1966	646
159 2/8	21 1/8	20 4/8	17 2/8	5	5	Garfield County	CO	Robert Pitt	1978	648
159 2/8	19 6/8	20 0/8	17 6/8	4	4	Crook County	WY	Mark L. Shumate	1986	648
159 1/8	22 6/8	21 6/8	20 5/8	5	7	Garfield County	CO	Jack Peters	1963	650
159 1/8	23 0/8	23 2/8	18 7/8	4	5	Garfield County	CO	Donald J. Walsh	1977	650
159 1/8	21 1/8	22 0/8	20 7/8	5	5	White Pine County	NV	Steve Wood	1978	650
159 1/8	25 6/8	26 2/8	27 5/8	5	7	Maricopa County	AZ	George Toot	1980	650
159 1/8	24 0/8	22 7/8	20 5/8	5	5	Clear Creek County	CO	Dave Skiff	1982	650
159 1/8	17 1/8	19 3/8	19 4/8	4	4	Jefferson County	CO	Calvin Farner	1986	650
159 0/8	22 3/8	21 2/8	25 2/8	5	6	Ada County	ID	Deloy Desaro	1973	656

196

SCORE	LENGTH OF MAIN BEAM		INSIDE SPREAD	NUMBER OF POINTS		AREA	STATE/ PROVINCE	HUNTER'S NAME	DATE	RANK
	R	L		R	L					
159 0/8	20 6/8	21 1/8	17 1/8	5	6	Montrose County	CO	David M. Gant	1977	656
159 0/8	21 3/8	22 7/8	22 2/8	6	5	San Juan County	CO	Dennis Atwater	1978	656
159 0/8	22 4/8	22 6/8	19 6/8	5	5	Lincoln County	MT	Christopher C. Crooks	1991	656
158 7/8	20 1/8	19 7/8	22 1/8	5	5	Sevier County	UT	Mike Otten	1973	660
158 7/8	21 2/8	22 6/8	21 7/8	5	5	Elmore County	ID	Peter J Cintorino	1981	660
158 7/8	20 1/8	19 4/8	21 4/8	5	6	Carbon County	WY	Daniel S. Christie	1982	660
158 7/8	22 7/8	22 2/8	17 0/8	5	5	Klamath County	OR	Harold McCraven	1986	660
158 7/8	21 7/8	22 0/8	17 5/8	5	5	Chase County	NE	John F. Burke	1987	660
158 7/8	24 6/8	26 3/8	24 0/8	5	5	Yavapai County	AZ	Wally Schwartz	1989	660
158 7/8	22 2/8	21 4/8	21 5/8	6	5	La Plata County	CO	Michael R. Hinson	1989	660
158 7/8	20 0/8	21 4/8	18 1/8	5	6	Logan County	KS	James Beougher	1989	660
158 6/8	21 3/8	22 3/8	22 0/8	5	5	Lake County	OR	Lyle Reeder	1954	668
158 6/8	21 6/8	20 7/8	17 0/8	6	4	Stacy	MT	Dewey Olsen	1960	668
158 6/8	22 3/8	23 3/8	20 4/8	4	4	Lassen County	CA	David Gallegos	1988	668
158 6/8	19 5/8	19 1/8	19 0/8	5	5	Campbell County	WY	Richard Hettinga	1990	668
158 6/8	21 5/8	20 7/8	21 2/8	5	5	Malheur County	OR	Steve C. Scott	1992	668
158 5/8	22 2/8	22 5/8	18 1/8	6	6	Weber County	UT	Bruce N. Moss	1974	673
158 5/8	22 1/8	22 3/8	18 5/8	6	5	Hodgeman County	KS	Ron Adams	1985	673
158 5/8	21 7/8	20 7/8	17 6/8	6	5	Morton County	KS	Kevin E. White	1987	673
158 4/8	23 3/8	23 6/8	22 6/8	4	4	Albany County	WY	Nelson W. Brower	1979	676
158 4/8	21 0/8	19 6/8	18 2/8	5	5	Greeley County	KS	Keith Foster	1981	676
158 4/8	20 0/8	20 3/8	15 4/8	5	5	Lane County	KS	Hurley T. Smith	1982	676
158 4/8	24 2/8	23 2/8	18 4/8	5	4	Garfield County	CO	Orvie E. Linsin	1989	676
158 4/8	19 5/8	18 5/8	18 4/8	6	6	Maricopa County	AZ	Lawrence Drake	1992	676
158 3/8	25 1/8	21 1/8	20 1/8	6	5	Sheridan County	NE	Gerald J. McKinney	1974	681
158 3/8	24 5/8	24 2/8	21 3/8	4	6	Ada County	ID	Robert E. Stauts	1979	681
158 2/8	23 4/8	19 3/8	21 4/8	6	4	Caribou County	ID	Gary L. Vaughn	1969	683
158 2/8	23 4/8	22 1/8	20 0/8	6	7	Gosper County	NE	Johnny Hemelstrand	1972	683
158 2/8	19 7/8	20 1/8	19 2/8	5	5	Las Animas County	CO	Byron E. Brown	1984	683
158 2/8	21 2/8	21 2/8	20 0/8	6	5	Butte County	ID	Gene Fitzgerald	1985	683
158 2/8	22 6/8	22 6/8	19 5/8	6	5	Pinal County	AZ	Mark Ovitt	1990	683
158 2/8	23 0/8	22 4/8	23 0/8	5	5	Billings County	ND	Mark Buehrer	1990	683
158 2/8	20 4/8	22 3/8	19 4/8	5	4	McKenzie County	ND	Terry Sivertson	1991	683
158 1/8	20 7/8	20 0/8	18 3/8	5	5		UT	Gordon Young	1963	690
158 1/8	21 0/8	22 3/8	24 0/8	6	6	Rio Blanco County	CO	Jerry R. Bowen	1970	690
158 1/8	20 6/8	20 3/8	17 7/8	5	4	Texas County	OK	J. Alva Hammond	1981	690
158 1/8	21 4/8	21 6/8	18 5/8	5	5	Boulder County	CO	Mike Miller	1987	690
158 1/8	21 5/8	21 7/8	21 3/8	5	5	Osborne County	KS	Blaine Parrott	1989	690
158 1/8	21 5/8	21 1/8	18 2/8	5	6	Converse County	WY	James Saunoris	1991	690
158 1/8	23 5/8	23 0/8	18 5/8	5	5	Moffat County	CO	Kieth Hardy	1991	690
158 1/8	22 6/8	24 4/8	28 0/8	8	5	Lane County	KS	Dean Hamilton	1991	690
158 0/8	21 4/8	21 0/8	21 4/8	7	7	Golden Valley County	ND	Bob Ross	1959	698
158 0/8	22 2/8	23 3/8	21 2/8	5	5	Owyhee County	ID	R. W. McIntire	1961	698
158 0/8	25 4/8	24 4/8	24 4/8	3	3	Garfield County	CO	Jimmy R. Speer	1970	698
158 0/8	21 7/8	22 6/8	19 2/8	5	5	Mesa County	CO	Matt Spohnhauer	1975	698
158 0/8	23 5/8	23 0/8	22 6/8	5	5	Rosebud County	MT	Irvin May	1990	698
157 7/8	23 6/8	24 0/8	21 3/8	4	5	Rio Arriba County	NM	Larry Wright	1972	703
157 7/8	20 2/8	22 2/8	22 5/8	5	6	Owyhee County	ID	Duane Zemliska	1985	703
157 7/8	21 6/8	22 0/8	21 4/8	5	6	Mesa County	CO	Jerol W. Vaughn	1985	703
157 7/8	20 7/8	21 2/8	19 2/8	6	7	Jackson County	CO	Vance E Phelps, II	1989	703
157 7/8	22 6/8	22 6/8	21 3/8	5	5	Culberson County	TX	Gary J. Oden	1989	703
157 7/8	19 7/8	19 6/8	18 3/8	5	5	Billings County	ND	Terry Buechler	1991	703
157 6/8	23 7/8	23 4/8	23 7/8	6	5	Owyhee County	ID	Roland Duram	1964	709
157 6/8	22 5/8	23 3/8	21 0/8	5	5	Mesa County	CO	Terry J. Gerber	1976	709
157 6/8	21 6/8	21 4/8	22 6/8	5	5	Elmore County	ID	Harold Lefler	1981	709
157 6/8	20 4/8	23 2/8	19 0/8	4	4	Archuleta County	CO	Bryan Rumbo	1989	709
157 6/8	19 0/8	19 3/8	19 3/8	6	5	Converse County	WY	Jerry Miller	1992	709
157 5/8	19 6/8	21 5/8	24 4/8	5	5	Owyhee County	ID	Fred Audette	1960	714
157 5/8	19 6/8	20 0/8	18 3/8	5	5	Montezuma County	CO	Marvin Reichenau	1973	714
157 5/8	24 1/8	23 4/8	21 7/8	5	5	Washoe County	NV	Donald J. Taysom	1984	714
157 5/8	23 6/8	24 1/8	20 3/8	9	6	Cheyenne County	KS	Chet Gardner	1984	714
157 5/8	23 0/8	22 3/8	20 5/8	4	4	McKinley County	NM	Frank Hausner	1991	714
157 4/8	23 1/8	23 2/8	23 2/8	5	6	Grand County	UT	Dean Caldwell	1960	719
157 4/8	22 2/8	22 4/8	19 4/8	5	5	Garfield County	CO	Bob Gulman	1966	719
157 4/8	18 5/8	19 2/8	16 0/8	4	4	Bernalillo County	NM	William R. Johnson	1969	719
157 4/8	22 1/8	20 2/8	21 0/8	5	6	Carter County	MT	Edward Susa	1983	719
157 4/8	22 3/8	23 5/8	20 6/8	5	5	Mesa County	CO	Paul H. Dickson	1986	719
157 4/8	21 4/8	21 0/8	19 2/8	5	5	Powder River County	MT	Mark L. Frank	1989	719
157 3/8	26 2/8	26 0/8	21 2/8	7	6	Sevier County	UT	Dale Gardner	1958	725
157 3/8	21 6/8	20 0/8	20 0/8	6	6	Routt County	CO	Bing Kemp	1966	725

SCORE	LENGTH OF MAIN BEAM		INSIDE SPREAD	NUMBER OF POINTS		AREA	STATE/ PROVINCE	HUNTER'S NAME	DATE	RANK
	R	L		R	L					
157 3/8	24 1/8	24 1/8	23 3/8	6	7	Montrose County	CO	James A. Davison	1984	725
157 3/8	17 4/8	19 0/8	16 3/8	5	5	Albany County	WY	Paul Ayotte	1985	725
157 3/8	21 0/8	21 0/8	20 5/8	5	5	Caribou County	ID	Gary Hunt	1986	725
157 3/8	22 1/8	22 7/8	17 7/8	6	5	Cypress	ALB	Mike Maloney	1991	725
157 2/8	22 5/8	21 4/8	20 6/8	6	6	McKenzie County	ND	Roy Mitten	1956	731
157 2/8	21 5/8	21 4/8	16 4/8	5	5	Bernalillo County	NM	Robert F. Knight	1970	731
157 2/8	24 4/8	24 2/8	20 1/8	6	5	Wheeler County	OR	Darrell J. Scheffer	1990	731
157 2/8	20 2/8	22 3/8	22 6/8	4	5	Bear Lake County	ID	Daved E. English	1991	731
157 1/8	22 0/8	23 4/8	23 3/8	6	4	Harney County	OR	Gary Soeth	1980	735
157 1/8	23 6/8	23 3/8	20 7/8	6	7	Boise County	ID	Gary Kinney	1981	735
157 1/8	21 4/8	21 6/8	20 5/8	5	5	Clear Creek County	CO	Janet Schreur	1987	735
157 1/8	21 5/8	21 1/8	19 0/8	5	7	Calgary	ALB	Stuart Sinclair-Smith	1987	735
157 1/8	23 0/8	20 7/8	21 6/8	5	6	Meade County	KS	Randy Blehm	1989	735
157 1/8	21 1/8	20 4/8	16 3/8	5	5	Boyd County	NE	Glenn T. Zink	1990	735
157 0/8	21 4/8	21 5/8	18 0/8	5	5	Mesa County	CO	Robert O. Bash	1976	741
157 0/8	22 6/8	21 4/8	16 0/8	5	5	Lassen County	CA	Tom McMurphy	1977	741
157 0/8	21 6/8	20 3/8	18 6/8	5	5	Lane County	KS	Dean Hamilton	1978	741
157 0/8	23 7/8	23 7/8	18 6/8	4	4	Clackamas County	OR	Thomas L. Carter	1984	741
157 0/8	21 4/8	21 1/8	23 3/8	5	6	Baker County	OR	Chuck Warner	1988	741
157 0/8	22 4/8	23 1/8	20 0/8	5	6	Pennington County	SD	Tim J. Hoeck	1990	741
156 7/8	24 3/8	24 0/8	23 4/8	4	4	Garfield County	CO	John Lamicq, Jr.	1966	747
156 7/8	21 2/8	20 6/8	18 3/8	5	5	Mesa County	CO	David H. Boland	1978	747
156 7/8	20 2/8	20 2/8	19 2/8	4	4	Rio Blanco County	CO	George David Epperson	1983	747
156 7/8	23 5/8	21 6/8	21 7/8	5	5	McKenzie County	ND	Steve Rehak	1985	747
156 7/8	21 4/8	20 2/8	15 7/8	5	5	Teller County	CO	Butch Smerkonich	1985	747
156 7/8	23 2/8	22 3/8	21 2/8	6	5	Chelan County	WA	Brian Kayler	1985	747
156 7/8	25 3/8	22 7/8	22 3/8	5	5	Laramie County	WY	Duane Christensen	1991	747
156 6/8	23 6/8	24 2/8	20 0/8	6	5	Uintah County	UT	Terry Peck	1964	754
156 6/8	22 5/8	22 6/8	19 4/8	5	5	Mesa County	CO	Ed Meyer	1967	754
156 6/8	21 6/8	22 6/8	23 4/8	6	6	Wallowa County	OR	Randy Hopp	1979	754
156 6/8	22 0/8	22 0/8	22 1/8	5	6	Routt County	CO	Moulton Larmay	1981	754
156 6/8	24 0/8	22 7/8	25 0/8	6	6	Lane County	KS	Dean Hamilton	1982	754
156 6/8	23 2/8	22 2/8	18 4/8	4	5	Kittitas County	WA	Rich Carnahan	1982	754
156 6/8	23 7/8	22 6/8	22 0/8	4	4	Lemhi County	ID	Glen Palmer	1988	754
156 6/8	20 5/8	20 6/8	19 2/8	5	5	Weld County	CO	Dale Elliott	1991	754
156 5/8	21 2/8	21 3/8	20 3/8	5	5	Slope County	ND	Vern R. Keim	1959	762
156 5/8	20 1/8	21 1/8	22 3/8	5	5	Rio Blanco County	CO	Jim Pickering	1966	762
156 5/8	20 0/8	21 6/8	18 6/8	6	6	Larimer County	CO	Leslie McKenzie	1970	762
156 5/8	21 7/8	21 0/8	19 3/8	7	6	Lower Arrow Lake	BC	Gerald Bond	1983	762
156 5/8	20 7/8	18 5/8	18 6/8	6	5	Caribou County	ID	Michael Aldrich	1984	762
156 4/8	21 7/8	22 1/8	22 0/8	5	4	Weston County	WY	Thomas L. A. Pucci	1956	767
156 4/8	20 0/8	20 0/8	19 2/8	5	5	Owyhee County	ID	Bill Leisi	1961	767
156 4/8	22 2/8	24 2/8	20 3/8	4	5	Summit County	UT	Richard Douglass	1964	767
156 4/8	23 1/8	21 4/8	20 4/8	4	4	Elko County	NV	Paul Dinan	1968	767
156 4/8	23 1/8	20 7/8	19 2/8	4	4	Chouteau County	MT	Michael R. Buesseler	1971	767
156 4/8	20 7/8	21 3/8	22 5/8	5	6	Gunnison County	CO	Jim Jarvis	1974	767
156 4/8	22 5/8	23 6/8	21 4/8	4	5	Campbell County	WY	James P. Smith	1983	767
156 4/8	20 1/8	20 6/8	18 4/8	5	5	Grant County	OR	Jeffrey A. Young	1986	767
156 4/8	22 2/8	22 7/8	17 6/8	4	5	Humboldt County	NV	Monte D. Fuller	1988	767
156 4/8	25 1/8	23 3/8	19 6/8	5	5	Boise County	ID	Kevin J.P. Stephenson	1988	767
156 3/8	21 6/8	22 6/8	25 0/8	5	6	Owyhee County	ID	Bill Kerr	1962	777
156 3/8	25 5/8	24 6/8	23 5/8	3	3	Mohave County	AZ	Bill Cross	1963	777
156 3/8	21 2/8	24 5/8	25 3/8	7	6	Lake County	OR	Orvil Winters	1965	777
156 3/8	24 5/8	24 2/8	23 4/8	5	7	Cottle County	TX	Mike Ramage	1991	777
156 2/8	21 5/8	20 6/8	20 0/8	5	5	Mesa County	CO	Donald Aaron	1971	781
156 2/8	20 5/8	20 2/8	19 2/8	5	5	Clark County	KS	Rod Lies	1976	781
156 2/8	22 6/8	21 2/8	21 2/8	5	5	Eureka County	NV	David Sharpe	1990	781
156 1/8	20 6/8	20 7/8	20 2/8	5	6	Millard County	UT	Jerry White	1962	784
156 1/8	25 1/8	25 6/8	18 5/8	5	5	Rio Arriba County	NM	Gary Isom	1985	784
156 0/8	21 4/8	21 0/8	18 2/8	5	5	Iron County	UT	Ken McKnight	1966	786
156 0/8	20 0/8	20 1/8	18 2/8	5	6	Chelan County	WA	Steve Gorr	1975	786
156 0/8	22 1/8	20 7/8	18 6/8	5	5	Powder River County	MT	Dan Brockman	1986	786
155 7/8	21 3/8	21 6/8	21 0/8	5	6	McKenzie County	ND	Mark E. Ferry	1981	789
155 7/8	22 5/8	23 1/8	22 3/8	5	5	Caribou County	ID	Randy J. Stephens	1988	789
155 6/8	24 1/8	24 1/8	22 0/8	3	4	Owyhee County	ID	Lynn Thomas	1960	791
155 6/8	22 2/8	21 3/8	18 4/8	4	5	Garfield County	CO	Henery Jaman	1966	791
155 6/8	21 7/8	21 4/8	20 0/8	5	6	White Pine County	NV	Roger A. Picchi	1986	791
155 6/8	22 0/8	21 1/8	19 0/8	6	6	Sheridan County	WY	Stan Chiras	1988	791
155 5/8	23 2/8	23 3/8	22 3/8	5	6	Chelan County	WA	R. F. Kelly	1960	795
155 5/8	20 7/8	20 4/8	21 6/8	5	5	Elko County	NV	Frank M. Davis	1967	795

SCORE	LENGTH OF MAIN BEAM		INSIDE SPREAD	NUMBER OF POINTS		AREA	STATE/ PROVINCE	HUNTER'S NAME	DATE	RANK
	R	L		R	L					
155 5/8	22 4/8	22 3/8	19 5/8	5	5	Dolores County	CO	Jay Jaburg	1975	795
155 5/8	24 0/8	25 6/8	22 0/8	7	5	Coconino County	AZ	Robert G. Arcieri	1977	795
155 5/8	21 0/8	20 5/8	18 1/8	4	4	Carbon County	WY	Robert K. Paulson	1979	795
155 5/8	21 0/8	20 4/8	18 7/8	5	5	Garfield County	CO	Joe Wiater	1982	795
155 5/8	21 4/8	20 4/8	17 7/8	5	5	Platte County	WY	James D. Wagner	1982	795
155 5/8	20 5/8	20 5/8	19 1/8	5	5	Carbon County	WY	Andy Lindahl	1984	795
155 5/8	19 5/8	19 7/8	20 4/8	5	4	Dunn County	ND	Todd Boechler	1989	795
155 4/8	22 2/8	23 6/8	23 2/8	5	4	Millard County	UT	Shirl Pace	1966	804
155 4/8	19 4/8	21 0/8	19 6/8	5	5	Wayne County	UT	Harold Boyack	1968	804
155 4/8	21 0/8	21 6/8	22 4/8	5	5	Lake County	OR	Wayne Lamson, Jr.	1980	804
155 4/8	21 6/8	20 4/8	21 0/8	5	5	Los Alamos County	NM	Doug Aikin	1987	804
155 4/8	22 7/8	21 4/8	17 4/8	5	6	Chelan County	WA	Danny Kohlman	1991	804
155 4/8	25 2/8	25 0/8	26 4/8	4	4	Walla Walla County	WA	Lance R. Rea	1992	804
153 3/8	22 4/8	22 2/8	25 2/8	5	6	Bow River	ALB	Michael D. Coupland	1986	810
153 3/8	21 1/8	20 5/8	19 7/8	5	5	Teller County	CO	James L. Anderson	1987	810
155 2/8	20 2/8	19 4/8	19 2/8	5	5	Owyhee County	ID	Ralph O. Collins	1957	812
155 2/8	23 6/8	24 2/8	22 4/8	6	5	Ada County	ID	Ronald K. White	1971	812
155 2/8	20 7/8	21 3/8	22 7/8	6	5	Uncompahgre N.F.	CO	Donald Click	1979	812
155 2/8	21 3/8	22 0/8	24 1/8	6	4	Box Elder County	UT	Richard Hess	1981	812
155 2/8	22 0/8	22 6/8	19 4/8	5	5	Lake County	OR	Chuck Warner	1981	812
155 2/8	21 7/8	22 1/8	17 6/8	5	5	Mesa County	CO	Rudy Wilkison	1984	812
155 2/8	19 1/8	20 6/8	18 5/8	6	5	Colfax County	NM	Dean K. Oatman	1985	812
155 2/8	21 0/8	22 4/8	19 6/8	5	5	Eagle County	CO	Tom Tietz	1985	812
155 2/8	23 5/8	24 0/8	24 7/8	5	4	Elbert County	CO	Billy Tillotson	1985	812
155 2/8	24 1/8	22 5/8	20 0/8	6	7	Hitchcock County	NE	Roger Lewis	1986	812
155 1/8	21 2/8	21 3/8	17 7/8	6	5	Sevier County	UT	Ray Shepard	1965	822
155 1/8	22 0/8	22 6/8	22 5/8	5	7	Lane County	KS	Dean Hamilton	1983	822
155 1/8	21 5/8	22 0/8	21 1/8	5	6	Custer County	NE	John Slack	1988	822
155 1/8	19 0/8	20 4/8	18 3/8	5	5	Powder River County	MT	Gene Smith	1991	822
155 0/8	23 2/8	21 4/8	22 0/8	5	4	Lake County	OR	Bill Chahon	1967	826
155 0/8	23 4/8	23 0/8	22 0/8	6	5	Broadwater County	MT	Larry P. Stevens	1968	826
155 0/8	19 7/8	22 4/8	17 6/8	4	4	Summit County	CO	Harley Smith	1976	826
155 0/8	22 6/8	23 0/8	21 2/8	6	6	Rio Blanco County	CO	Larry Streiff	1978	826
155 0/8	24 2/8	24 4/8	26 0/8	4	3	Mesa County	CO	Duane Beenblossom	1979	826
155 0/8	21 7/8	22 0/8	20 1/8	5	5	Mesa County	CO	Clarence Bowers, Jr.	1979	826
155 0/8	21 2/8	22 6/8	21 6/8	4	4	Slope County	ND	Bill Schwendinger	1982	826
155 0/8	20 5/8	19 3/8	18 4/8	5	5	Bernalillo County	NM	Doug Aikin	1983	826
155 0/8	21 2/8	21 6/8	21 4/8	5	5	Boise County	ID	Larry S. Zurgot	1985	826
155 0/8	22 6/8	23 2/8	18 6/8	5	5	Bernalillo County	NM	Joseph L. Moyer	1988	826
155 0/8	21 4/8	21 4/8	20 2/8	5	5	Sundre	ALB	Larry K. Nielsen	1989	826
154 7/8	22 3/8	23 4/8	23 3/8	5	5	Dolores County	CO	Oscar A. Harden	1957	837
154 7/8	19 4/8	21 2/8	19 2/8	5	6	Millard County	UT	Dale Moore	1961	837
154 7/8	21 6/8	21 7/8	16 7/8	4	4	Elko County	NV	Jim Cox	1974	837
154 7/8	21 5/8	22 3/8	18 3/8	5	6	Elko County	NV	John S. Chace, Jr.	1982	837
154 6/8	23 1/8	22 7/8	20 2/8	4	5	Montrose County	CO	Dave Reitz	1983	841
154 6/8	17 5/8	20 1/8	13 4/8	5	5	EL Paso County	CO	Michael Thompson	1984	841
154 6/8	20 3/8	20 4/8	22 4/8	5	5	Mesa County	CO	R. L. Harrison III	1985	841
154 5/8	20 3/8	21 7/8	21 7/8	5	5	Lincoln County	NV	Larry Gehre	1963	844
154 5/8	21 3/8	19 3/8	16 7/8	4	5	Garfield County	CO	Tommy Biffle	1975	844
154 5/8	23 6/8	23 2/8	20 0/8	5	8	San Juan County	UT	Bruce Gordon	1980	844
154 5/8	20 1/8	19 5/8	19 5/8	5	5	Lake County	OR	Dale A. Bolin	1983	844
154 5/8	19 6/8	21 1/8	18 7/8	5	5	Pennington County	SD	Scott Lindgren	1986	844
154 5/8	20 1/8	19 4/8	21 3/8	5	5	Crook County	WY	Calvin Farner	1986	844
154 5/8	22 3/8	21 3/8	19 3/8	5	6	Montrose County	CO	Eugene Roesler	1989	844
154 5/8	19 1/8	20 0/8	17 1/8	5	5	Pima County	AZ	Jeff Ferri	1990	844
154 4/8	22 3/8	22 5/8	21 0/8	6	6	Routt County	CO	Douglas J. Peterson	1965	852
154 4/8	22 5/8	24 0/8	18 1/8	6	6	Frontier County	NE	Mark Stencel	1986	852
154 3/8	21 7/8	23 1/8	20 5/8	4	5	Pawnee County	KS	Robert E. Lagree	1970	854
154 3/8	18 0/8	18 1/8	17 5/8	5	5	Yavapai County	AZ	James R. Reckas	1989	854
154 3/8	25 6/8	26 1/8	27 0/8	3	4	Elbert County	CO	Douglas Cringan	1991	854
154 2/8	21 7/8	21 5/8	17 4/8	8	8	Grant County	OR	Lloyd V. Christensen	1960	857
154 2/8	22 5/8	22 3/8	19 5/8	4	4	Mesa County	CO	Jimmy E. Ash	1966	857
154 2/8	22 2/8	21 2/8	21 0/8	7	8	Kirby	WY	Steve Gorr	1970	857
154 2/8	20 5/8	20 0/8	19 2/8	5	5	Moffat County	CO	Mary E. Nussberger	1978	857
154 2/8	21 2/8	23 7/8	22 4/8	5	5	Blaine County	ID	Dean Muchow	1979	857
154 2/8	21 2/8	21 5/8	18 6/8	5	5	Mesa County	CO	Carl Phillips	1980	857
154 2/8	23 4/8	23 0/8	19 1/8	5	6	Chelan County	WA	Daniel S Nelson	1984	857
154 1/8	18 3/8	16 6/8	16 1/8	5	7	Carbon County	UT	Lieb D. Miller	1959	864
154 1/8	21 4/8	21 4/8	20 4/8	4	4	Rio Grande County	CO	Kenneth G. McCombs	1969	864
154 1/8	20 3/8	21 0/8	16 0/8	5	6	Montrose County	CO	Arthur L. Pace	1974	864

SCORE	LENGTH OF MAIN BEAM		INSIDE SPREAD	NUMBER OF POINTS		AREA	STATE/ PROVINCE	HUNTER'S NAME	DATE	RANK
	R	L		R	L					
154 1/8	23 5/8	21 6/8	23 6/8	4	4	Montrose County	CO	Don Allen, Jr.	1979	864
154 1/8	22 6/8	22 5/8	22 5/8	5	4	Malheur County	OR	Jim Nielsen	1988	864
154 0/8	22 7/8	22 6/8	20 6/8	7	6	Coconino County	AZ	Stuart Diehl	1962	869
154 0/8	22 0/8	22 2/8	19 4/8	5	5	Mesa County	CO	Al Dawson	1964	869
154 0/8	24 6/8	24 4/8	29 0/8	5	4	Grant County	OR	Chuck Lynde	1972	869
154 0/8	25 2/8	24 4/8	21 2/8	5	4	Mesa County	CO	Dale Anderson	1973	869
154 0/8	20 4/8	21 4/8	19 3/8	6	5	Calgary	ALB	Manfred Grewe	1981	869
154 0/8	22 7/8	23 6/8	22 5/8	9	7	Lake County	OR	Charles F. Brown	1985	869
154 0/8	20 3/8	20 2/8	17 2/8	5	4	Converse County	WY	Lee Jernigan	1987	869
154 0/8	22 1/8	22 1/8	18 0/8	5	4	Elmore County	ID	Timothy J. Conrads	1988	869
154 0/8	18 5/8	18 5/8	16 4/8	5	4	Baker County	OR	John A. Eyers	1990	869
154 0/8	22 0/8	22 5/8	20 0/8	6	5	Sublette County	WY	Nelson J. Capestany	1991	869
154 0/8	21 3/8	22 3/8	19 0/8	5	5	Weld County	CO	Gary L. Clancy	1991	869
153 7/8	19 5/8	19 2/8	19 1/8	6	5	Meagher County	MT	Leroy Dukes	1972	880
153 7/8	22 6/8	21 7/8	16 6/8	6	6	Rio Blanco County	CO	Kevin Jackson	1973	880
153 7/8	22 4/8	19 6/8	17 7/8	5	5	Uintah County	UT	Matt Brooks	1974	880
153 7/8	23 3/8	22 4/8	23 1/8	6	6	Baker County	OR	Randy Jennings	1981	880
153 7/8	22 5/8	23 3/8	19 2/8	6	6	Pinal County	AZ	Jesse Pena	1988	880
153 7/8	20 5/8	20 0/8	19 3/8	5	5	Oneida County	ID	Dave Scott	1990	880
153 7/8	23 1/8	23 1/8	21 7/8	6	6	Billings County	ND	Steve Schaper	1990	880
153 6/8	23 0/8	21 7/8	18 0/8	5	5	Dawes County	NE	William W. Plooster	1958	887
153 5/8	22 0/8	22 4/8	20 7/8	4	4	Billings County	ND	Ed Bry, Jr.	1957	888
153 5/8	21 0/8	20 7/8	17 7/8	6	7	Moffat County	CO	Zenus E. Cozart	1962	888
153 5/8	21 4/8	21 4/8	18 7/8	5	6	Moffat County	CO	Hugh Cox	1971	888
153 5/8	22 3/8	22 7/8	23 4/8	5	5	Pinal County	AZ	James M. Fry	1974	888
153 5/8	22 6/8	23 1/8	24 0/8	5	5	Routt County	CO	Lee R. Hoxit	1978	888
153 4/8	22 5/8	21 7/8	22 4/8	5	5	San Juan County	UT	Roy D. Chesley	1963	893
153 4/8	23 0/8	23 0/8	17 4/8	6	5	Brown County	NE	Seth Fritzler	1965	893
153 4/8	20 1/8	22 1/8	20 2/8	6	5	Wasatch County	UT	Don Callister	1967	893
153 3/8	22 1/8	21 1/8	21 1/8	4	5	Garfield County	CO	John Nottingham	1974	896
153 3/8	19 6/8	21 1/8	22 5/8	5	5	Meagher County	MT	Chuck Adams	1979	896
153 3/8	22 0/8	23 1/8	21 2/8	5	6	Weld County	CO	Gary Thurow	1988	896
153 3/8	20 1/8	19 3/8	18 1/8	5	5	Carbon County	WY	Peter Schinke	1989	896
153 3/8	21 3/8	21 6/8	21 1/8	4	3	Rio Arriba County	NM	James Michael Bridges	1989	896
153 2/8	21 0/8	21 0/8	20 0/8	5	5	Custer County	MT	Gene T. Buck	1961	901
153 2/8	21 4/8	21 3/8	17 6/8	5	5	Garfield County	CO	Randy Gilmore	1982	901
153 2/8	21 2/8	20 3/8	20 0/8	6	6	Coconino County	AZ	Richard S Jones	1985	901
153 2/8	19 4/8	20 0/8	15 6/8	5	5	Gregory County	SD	Terry Marcukaitis	1985	901
153 2/8	20 1/8	20 6/8	14 6/8	6	5	Washoe County	NV	Ronald W. Lindquist	1986	901
153 2/8	20 3/8	22 3/8	20 0/8	5	5	Billings County	ND	Gary J. Peters	1987	901
153 1/8	22 0/8	22 3/8	24 0/8	5	4	Millard County	UT	Milton F. McQueary	1961	907
153 1/8	23 5/8	25 2/8	20 2/8	5	4	Rio Blanco County	CO	Thomas Nicholls	1967	907
153 1/8	22 0/8	21 5/8	21 5/8	5	4	Garfield County	CO	Lester Meredith	1974	907
153 1/8	21 5/8	22 3/8	22 3/8	5	5	Park County	WY	Jim Dinkins	1978	907
153 1/8	21 0/8	22 7/8	18 7/8	7	5	Converse County	WY	Ted Jaycox	1982	907
153 1/8	21 6/8	21 4/8	19 7/8	4	5	Chelan County	WA	Don McNees, Jr.	1983	907
153 1/8	19 5/8	19 7/8	19 1/8	5	5	Dolores County	CO	Mark Beeler	1992	907
153 0/8	21 1/8	22 1/8	23 2/8	5	6	Golden Valley County	MT	Tim Ford	1979	914
153 0/8	21 7/8	22 6/8	20 2/8	6	5	Valley County	ID	James J. Akenson	1988	914
153 0/8	22 0/8	21 6/8	19 0/8	5	6	Vertigris Lake	ALB	Keith Heppler	1989	914
153 0/8	21 5/8	24 0/8	21 6/8	5	5	Lake County	OR	Mike Benton	1990	914
153 0/8	17 6/8	20 0/8	20 2/8	6	5	Colfax County	NM	Justin L. Sanchez	1990	914
152 7/8	20 7/8	21 7/8	20 1/8	6	6	Gove County	KS	Alan D. Beougher	1970	919
152 7/8	20 4/8	21 7/8	15 3/8	4	4	White River N.F.	CO	Leonard Steiner	1978	919
152 7/8	22 1/8	23 0/8	21 3/8	5	6	Gila County	AZ	Steven Weekley	1985	919
152 6/8	21 6/8	21 0/8	21 6/8	6	5	Graham County	AZ	Herbert Tom	1981	922
152 6/8	22 0/8	21 4/8	22 0/8	5	4	Delta County	CO	Timothy L. McKay	1990	922
152 6/8	24 0/8	22 6/8	21 2/8	5	4	Converse County	WY	M. R. James	1991	922
152 6/8	19 5/8	19 1/8	18 0/8	4	4	Billings County	ND	William E. Lee	1991	922
152 5/8	21 3/8	21 5/8	20 3/8	4	4	Elko County	NV	Bill Freeman	1961	926
152 5/8	22 0/8	22 3/8	22 3/8	5	5	Fremont County	WY	Gene Farley	1964	926
152 5/8	23 3/8	23 4/8	19 4/8	7	5	Valley County	ID	James J. Akenson	1984	926
152 5/8	22 4/8	22 1/8	21 6/8	6	6	Mesa County	CO	Don Rogers	1986	926
152 5/8	19 5/8	16 4/8	22 6/8	5	4	Wichita County	KS	Jack D. Kuhlmann	1986	926
152 5/8	20 2/8	19 7/8	19 1/8	5	5	Graham County	KS	Danny G. Coday	1989	926
152 5/8	20 7/8	22 1/8	20 3/8	4	4	Humboldt County	NV	Rob Fletcher	1991	926
152 4/8	28 7/8	27 7/8	24 4/8	4	3	Montrose County	CO	John A. Wilk	1978	933
152 4/8	21 1/8	20 7/8	17 5/8	5	6	Madison County	MT	Tony Rebich	1982	933
152 4/8	21 6/8	21 7/8	16 6/8	5	5	Harney County	OR	Jim Hodson	1988	933
152 4/8	21 6/8	21 2/8	20 4/8	5	5	Harney County	OR	Michael J. Bradeen	1989	933

MULE DEER *(Typical Antlers)*

MINIMUM SCORE 145   *(Continued)*

SCORE	LENGTH OF MAIN BEAM R	LENGTH OF MAIN BEAM L	INSIDE SPREAD	NUMBER OF POINTS R	NUMBER OF POINTS L	AREA	STATE/ PROVINCE	HUNTER'S NAME	DATE	RANK
152 4/8	22 4/8	22 1/8	23 3/8	5	5	Calgary	ALB	Dave Browne	1991	933
152 3/8	20 6/8	20 7/8	20 2/8	5	6	Carbon County	UT	John C. Culpepper	1969	938
152 3/8	23 0/8	21 7/8	22 4/8	4	4	Montrose County	CO	Viron Barbay	1985	938
152 3/8	20 7/8	21 3/8	19 3/8	5	5	Cochise County	AZ	Stan Wacker	1989	938
152 2/8	21 0/8	21 0/8	19 0/8	5	6	Grand County	UT	Roger Smith	1962	941
152 2/8	19 3/8	20 4/8	20 4/8	5	5	Elko County	NV	Jack Konvalin	1963	941
152 2/8	26 0/8	26 0/8	22 0/8	4	4	Garfield County	CO	Jim Dougherty	1968	941
152 2/8	21 5/8	21 7/8	21 5/8	5	5	Millard County	UT	David G. Snyder	1968	941
152 2/8	21 0/8	21 0/8	24 6/8	6	6	Madison County	MT	Dave Bonczyk	1972	941
152 1/8	20 1/8	20 1/8	18 1/8	5	5	Cochise County	AZ	John Behrends	1969	946
152 1/8	23 4/8	22 5/8	23 6/8	6	6	Ross Lake	ALB	Darcy Barrett	1988	946
152 0/8	20 0/8	20 6/8	17 3/8	8	7	Garfield County	UT	Bob Mackinnon	1970	948
152 0/8	19 3/8	19 5/8	18 0/8	5	5	Bowman County	ND	Mark Loutzenhiser	1985	948
152 0/8	20 2/8	22 7/8	18 6/8	6	6	Elko County	NV	LeRoy McQueen	1986	948
151 7/8	22 0/8	22 2/8	20 0/8	6	8	Duchesne County	UT	Rowland S. Enomoto	1965	951
151 7/8	22 0/8	21 2/8	21 7/8	5	4	Chelan County	WA	L. James Bailey	1977	951
151 7/8	22 1/8	22 7/8	21 5/8	7	5	Pima County	AZ	Douglas L. Sweepe	1988	951
151 7/8	21 2/8	21 2/8	18 3/8	5	5	Bergen	ALB	Sandy Watt	1990	951
151 6/8	20 3/8	20 2/8	21 4/8	4	5	Garfield County	MT	Herman Hass	1961	955
151 6/8	18 7/8	21 7/8	21 7/8	6	6	Rio Blanco County	CO	Doug Kenyon	1967	955
151 6/8	17 5/8	15 4/8	14 4/8	5	5	Garfield County	CO	Roger Smith	1973	955
151 6/8	22 5/8	21 0/8	20 0/8	5	5	Mesa County	CO	Steve Fossen	1974	955
151 6/8	19 3/8	21 6/8	16 5/8	5	5	Grand County	CO	Mark Chapman	1978	955
151 6/8	20 3/8	20 4/8	15 7/8	7	7	Mesa County	CO	Jack O. Rothwell	1979	955
151 6/8	20 0/8	20 4/8	19 0/8	5	5	Lane County	KS	Dean Hamilton	1985	955
151 6/8	21 0/8	20 2/8	18 2/8	7	6	Carbon County	WY	Rene Suda	1990	955
151 5/8	21 5/8	20 5/8	20 5/8	5	5	Garfield County	UT	Dick Gulman	1968	963
151 5/8	20 2/8	18 7/8	18 1/8	6	6	Chaffee County	CO	Eugene K. Post	1971	963
151 5/8	20 5/8	20 5/8	18 1/8	5	5	Mesa County	CO	Richard E. Davis, Jr.	1977	963
151 5/8	19 4/8	20 3/8	16 3/8	6	5	Phillips County	KS	Michael L. Hoft	1985	963
151 5/8	20 0/8	20 1/8	20 2/8	5	5	Billings County	ND	Greg Obrigewitch	1987	963
151 5/8	22 4/8	22 2/8	21 1/8	5	5	Caribou County	ID	Roger Wright	1990	963
151 4/8	24 5/8	24 5/8	26 2/8	4	6	Bingham County	ID	Craig A. Young	1982	969
151 3/8	22 4/8	19 2/8	19 1/8	5	5	Dolores County	CO	Dennis Atwater	1979	970
151 3/8	22 0/8	21 5/8	21 7/8	5	5	Washoe County	NV	David J. Fujii	1981	970
151 3/8	19 0/8	20 5/8	21 4/8	5	5	Lane County	KS	Dean Hamilton	1986	970
151 3/8	21 0/8	22 0/8	18 3/8	4	6	Caribou County	ID	Randon Wright	1991	970
151 3/8	22 2/8	21 6/8	20 6/8	6	5	Sheridan County	WY	David L. Willis	1992	970
151 2/8	22 7/8	19 2/8	16 4/8	5	5	Chelan County	WA	G. H. Malinoski	1959	975
151 2/8	24 5/8	23 1/8	24 5/8	7	6	Bear Lake County	ID	Keith V. Hymos	1961	975
151 2/8	23 2/8	22 7/8	22 4/8	5	4	Chelan County	WA	Ron Carpenter	1973	975
151 2/8	20 6/8	22 6/8	22 0/8	7	5	Uncompahgre N.F.	CO	Clifford Patterson	1976	975
151 2/8	21 4/8	21 3/8	20 0/8	5	5	Phillips County	MT	Brian Roness	1984	975
151 2/8	21 0/8	20 6/8	17 0/8	7	5	Stanley County	SD	Dale DeBoer	1985	975
151 2/8	24 5/8	25 7/8	19 1/8	7	5	Dundy County	NE	Michael C. Dysh	1988	975
151 2/8	22 5/8	21 3/8	19 2/8	4	4	Black Diamond	ALB	Marc Nyrose	1989	975
151 2/8	22 4/8	21 0/8	22 6/8	5	5	County of 40 Mile	ALB	Tammy Glass	1992	975
151 1/8	21 4/8	22 2/8	20 2/8	6	7	Butte County	SD	John Kirk	1958	984
151 1/8	23 7/8	22 7/8	20 1/8	4	5	Mesa County	CO	Bill Martens	1984	984
151 1/8	20 3/8	20 6/8	16 7/8	5	5	McKenzie County	ND	Kurt T. Hovet	1988	984
151 1/8	19 0/8	19 2/8	13 7/8	5	5	Boise County	ID	Ken Dory	1989	984
151 1/8	20 6/8	21 1/8	19 3/8	7	6	Valmarie	SAS	Steve Von Hagen	1992	984
151 0/8	22 1/8	22 0/8	20 6/8	5	7	Chelan County	WA	Deryl E. Bland	1964	989
151 0/8	18 4/8	21 2/8	17 4/8	5	5	Moffat County	CO	Wayne Liskey	1966	989
151 0/8	22 0/8	19 1/8	23 2/8	5	4	Uncompahgre N.F.	CO	Roy Miller	1972	989
151 0/8	21 1/8	21 0/8	22 2/8	6	5	Rio Arriba County	NM	Howard Payne	1984	989
151 0/8	20 3/8	21 4/8	19 0/8	5	5	Platte County	WY	Jody Nordin	1984	989
151 0/8	19 0/8	18 4/8	19 4/8	5	5	Maricopa County	AZ	Dave Barnhart	1986	989
151 0/8	23 1/8	22 6/8	23 0/8	9	8	Wichita County	KS	Stacy C. Hoeme	1986	989
151 0/8	22 4/8	20 6/8	20 2/8	5	5	Coconino County	AZ	Randy Barnes	1986	989
151 0/8	25 1/8	24 7/8	23 1/8	4	6	Cochrane	ALB	Denny Williamson	1989	989
151 0/8	19 4/8	19 2/8	20 1/8	5	5	Abbey	SAS	Clarence Hughes	1990	989
151 0/8	20 6/8	20 4/8	21 6/8	6	5	Humboldt County	NV	Fred C. Church	1992	989
150 7/8	22 3/8	23 4/8	20 0/8	6	6	Hockberry Creek	KS	Dale Redmond	1967	1,000
150 7/8	22 5/8	19 3/8	25 3/8	5	4	San Juan County	UT	Ken Ciarelli	1968	1,000
150 7/8	22 6/8	22 6/8	20 1/8	6	6	Fremont County	CO	Dave Elliott	1976	1,000
150 7/8	20 4/8	20 2/8	19 1/8	5	5	Idaho County	ID	Gary Belvoir	1981	1,000
150 7/8	20 1/8	21 1/8	16 1/8	5	5	Coconino County	AZ	Les Shelton	1984	1,000
150 6/8	20 5/8	20 3/8	20 5/8	5	6	Washington County	UT	Jack Richards	1960	1,005
150 6/8	20 2/8	20 0/8	18 2/8	5	5	Bernalillo County	NM	Lee Braudt	1968	1,005

MULE DEER (Typical Antlers)

SCORE	LENGTH OF MAIN BEAM		INSIDE SPREAD	NUMBER OF POINTS		AREA	STATE/ PROVINCE	HUNTER'S NAME	DATE	RANK
	R	L		R	L					
150 6/8	21 6/8	22 1/8	22 4/8	4	5	Hamilton County	KS	Mike Gilbert	1976	1,005
150 6/8	22 5/8	21 2/8	23 2/8	5	6	Box Elder County	UT	Steven B. Perry	1980	1,005
150 6/8	21 2/8	20 6/8	18 4/8	5	5	Grant County	OR	Rodney Keenon	1982	1,005
150 6/8	22 4/8	22 6/8	19 0/8	5	4	County of Warner	ALB	Giuliano Coslovi	1987	1,005
150 6/8	25 7/8	23 2/8	25 0/8	4	5	Lassen County	CA	Rick Pollard	1992	1,005
150 5/8	24 2/8	24 7/8	19 6/8	6	5	Bernalillo County	NM	Alan Spitznagle	1982	1,012
150 5/8	22 3/8	22 4/8	16 1/8	5	5	Grant County	NM	Mark Garrison	1989	1,012
150 5/8	20 1/8	19 5/8	21 0/8	5	5	Boise County	ID	David R. Heck	1991	1,012
150 4/8	21 6/8	22 0/8	21 5/8	5	6	Pima County	AZ	Tony Don	1980	1,015
150 4/8	21 4/8	21 4/8	19 4/8	5	4	Garfield County	CO	Keith Backhaus	1981	1,015
150 4/8	22 0/8	21 6/8	22 5/8	5	5	Carbon County	UT	C. J. Coleman	1987	1,015
150 3/8	22 6/8	22 7/8	15 5/8	4	5	Summit County	UT	Clifton Rees	1962	1,018
150 3/8	19 6/8	20 3/8	19 7/8	4	5	Grand County	UT	Lowell W. Dobson	1968	1,018
150 3/8	21 0/8	21 0/8	15 7/8	5	5	Bernalillo County	NM	Michael M. Emery	1973	1,018
150 3/8	21 6/8	21 1/8	19 7/8	5	5	Washoe County	NV	Fred C. Church	1983	1,018
150 3/8	20 0/8	20 1/8	21 1/8	5	5	Lane County	KS	Dean Hamilton	1984	1,018
150 3/8	20 5/8	20 1/8	22 7/8	5	4	Cascade County	MT	Bennie J. Rossetto	1990	1,018
150 3/8	22 1/8	20 6/8	20 1/8	5	5	Boise County	ID	Russ Meyer	1991	1,018
150 3/8	19 7/8	19 4/8	23 7/8	4	4	Chouteau County	MT	Dwight P. Martin	1992	1,018
150 2/8	13 0/8	19 7/8	15 3/8	3	6	Boise County	ID	Ralph Hoobing	1964	1,026
150 2/8	21 3/8	22 1/8	23 7/8	4	4	Valley County	MT	Andy Hicks	1981	1,026
150 2/8	22 1/8	22 0/8	20 4/8	6	5	Maricopa County	AZ	Mike Ottenbacher	1987	1,026
150 2/8	22 1/8	22 0/8	15 6/8	5	5	Wasatch County	UT	Ronald Whaley	1987	1,026
150 2/8	22 2/8	22 4/8	22 0/8	4	5	Union County	OR	Brian J. Scott	1990	1,026
150 2/8	21 4/8	24 3/8	24 0/8	4	3	Bow River	ALB	Bob Gruszecki	1991	1,026
150 1/8	18 3/8	18 5/8	17 3/8	6	7	Garfield County	CO	J. B. Hogan	1961	1,032
150 1/8	24 7/8	26 2/8	24 0/8	5	5	Deschutes County	OR	Walter M. Graham	1963	1,032
150 1/8	22 3/8	22 2/8	18 3/8	5	5	Jackson County	CO	William B. Tutt	1964	1,032
150 1/8	22 6/8	22 7/8	22 3/8	4	4	Gove County	KS	Merton Ikenberry	1966	1,032
150 1/8	21 3/8	21 4/8	20 1/8	5	5	Washoe County	NV	Felton Hickman	1970	1,032
150 0/8	21 2/8	22 4/8	24 4/8	4	4	Eureka County	NV	B. Verlyn Ownes	1963	1,037
150 0/8	18 7/8	18 6/8	16 3/8	5	6	Garfield County	UT	Dick Gulman	1966	1,037
150 0/8	19 3/8	21 4/8	20 4/8	5	5	Elko County	NV	Dick Woltering	1968	1,037
150 0/8	20 0/8	20 1/8	18 1/8	6	6	Larimer County	Co	Tom Tietz	1979	1,037
150 0/8	22 4/8	21 7/8	18 4/8	5	4	White Pine County	NV	Scott Faiman	1987	1,037
150 0/8	24 2/8	23 2/8	20 4/8	6	4	Pima County	AZ	Rick Betten	1991	1,037
150 0/8	19 3/8	17 2/8	16 0/8	4	4	Weber County	UT	Robert G. Petersen	1992	1,037
149 7/8	21 2/8	23 0/8	20 5/8	4	4	Sevier County	UT	Milt McQueary	1964	1,044
149 7/8	20 1/8	20 1/8	17 3/8	5	5	Trego County	KS	Larry Pearson	1974	1,044
149 7/8	23 5/8	22 6/8	26 2/8	4	5	Pima County	AZ	Michael B. Cachero	1985	1,044
149 7/8	20 0/8	22 2/8	19 2/8	6	4	Platte County	WY	G. Fred Asbell	1988	1,044
149 7/8	21 0/8	20 7/8	19 7/8	4	5	Billings County	ND	Kevin Clyde	1989	1,044
149 7/8	21 4/8	21 5/8	19 5/8	5	4	McKenzie County	ND	Wade Leer	1990	1,044
149 7/8	20 4/8	22 0/8	18 3/8	5	5	Furnas County	NE	Walter S. Wright	1991	1,044
149 7/8	22 7/8	22 7/8	21 5/8	4	3	Campbell County	WY	Steve Boster	1991	1,044
149 6/8	21 3/8	21 1/8	19 6/8	4	4	Garfield County	CO	Skip Candahl	1966	1,052
149 6/8	26 5/8	27 5/8	25 0/8	7	4	Uncompahgre Plateau	CO	Jim Moan	1976	1,052
149 6/8	20 6/8	21 1/8	22 1/8	6	6	Mesa County	CO	Parker Leon	1984	1,052
149 6/8	21 1/8	21 6/8	19 5/8	5	5	Baker County	OR	Chuck Warner	1986	1,052
149 5/8	18 1/8	20 7/8	17 7/8	5	5	Rio Blanco County	CO	Joseph H. French	1972	1,056
149 5/8	21 2/8	20 2/8	19 1/8	6	8	Canmore	ALB	Karl Pachonik	1982	1,056
149 5/8	21 6/8	22 0/8	18 3/8	6	4	Boise County	ID	Tom Weston	1984	1,056
149 5/8	20 6/8	22 1/8	18 7/8	5	5	Nye County	NV	Ed Fuller	1986	1,056
149 5/8	22 3/8	21 4/8	22 5/8	5	5	Johnson County	WY	Edward H. Carmichael	1989	1,056
149 5/8	22 3/8	22 7/8	22 7/8	5	5	Garfield County	CO	John W. Borlang	1990	1,056
149 4/8	22 4/8	22 4/8	19 2/8	4	4	Colfax County	NM	Ed Foster	1966	1,062
149 4/8	22 2/8	22 4/8	22 4/8	4	5	Montrose County	CO	John A. Wilk	1977	1,062
149 4/8	21 1/8	20 5/8	20 0/8	6	5	Valencia County	NM	Frank Johnson	1985	1,062
149 4/8	21 4/8	20 7/8	23 0/8	5	5	Delta County	CO	Larry Tiner	1986	1,062
149 4/8	21 0/8	21 3/8	18 4/8	5	5	Valencia County	NM	Frank Johnson	1987	1,062
149 4/8	19 0/8	20 4/8	21 2/8	5	5	Meade County	KS	Randy Blehm	1988	1,062
149 3/8	22 4/8	21 6/8	17 1/8	4	4	Okanogan County	WA	Irl Stamps	1939	1,068
149 3/8	22 4/8	20 4/8	19 1/8	5	7	Baker County	OR	Chuck Brackin	1964	1,068
149 3/8	21 5/8	22 5/8	20 7/8	5	4	Mesa County	CO	John Smith	1964	1,068
149 3/8	23 0/8	24 0/8	22 4/8	4	4	White Pine County	NV	Milo W. Burt	1971	1,068
149 3/8	22 6/8	22 1/8	19 2/8	6	4	San Juan County	UT	Randy Radant	1984	1,068
149 3/8	20 7/8	21 6/8	20 6/8	6	5	Jackson County	OR	Greg Chakarun	1985	1,068
149 3/8	22 4/8	21 2/8	20 7/8	5	6	Coconino County	AZ	Duane R. Richardson	1987	1,068
149 3/8	21 2/8	21 7/8	17 7/8	5	5	Jackson County	OR	Jason Tarrant	1988	1,068
149 3/8	20 2/8	20 0/8	17 1/8	5	5	Slope County	ND	Todd Seymanski	1990	1,068

Score	Length of Main Beam R	L	Inside Spread	Number of Points R	L	Area	State/ Province	Hunter's Name	Date	Rank
149 3/8	22 3/8	22 5/8	20 1/8	6	5	Morrill County	NE	R. Matthew Bilby	1990	1,068
149 2/8	22 6/8	22 5/8	21 4/8	4	4	Lake County	CO	Thomas V. Sieverding	1972	1,078
149 2/8	25 5/8	25 2/8	25 0/8	6	4	Lincoln County	WY	Mike Barrett	1984	1,078
149 2/8	22 3/8	22 5/8	21 4/8	5	5	Garfield County	CO	James P. Speck	1984	1,078
149 2/8	19 5/8	19 2/8	17 2/8	5	5	San Juan County	NM	Michael R. Hinson	1987	1,078
149 2/8	19 4/8	20 4/8	19 0/8	5	5	Grant County	OR	Gary Kiepert	1990	1,078
149 1/8	24 4/8	24 0/8	18 1/8	6	5	Washoe County	NV	Cecil D. Martin	1987	1,083
149 0/8	24 0/8	22 5/8	22 4/8	4	4	Mesa County	CO	Tom Hentrick	1974	1,084
149 0/8	20 4/8	19 6/8	23 4/8	5	5	Lincoln County	WY	Vaughn Cross	1978	1,084
149 0/8	25 3/8	24 3/8	22 4/8	5	5	Beaver County	UT	William H. Chilvers	1987	1,084
148 7/8	19 4/8	19 6/8	20 2/8	5	6	Garfield County	CO	Charles E. Whaley	1974	1,087
148 7/8	22 3/8	23 5/8	20 3/8	6	4	Hodgeman County	KS	James Wiggins	1978	1,087
148 7/8	22 3/8	23 3/8	21 3/8	4	4	Crook County	OR	Vernon Simpson	1982	1,087
148 7/8	24 1/8	24 3/8	20 7/8	5	5	Gunnison County	CO	Mike Reedy	1992	1,087
148 6/8	20 7/8	20 6/8	13 2/8	5	4	Okanogan County	WA	Dennis N. Johnson	1971	1,091
148 6/8	21 3/8	20 5/8	15 7/8	5	7	Lane County	KS	Vernon L. McBee	1971	1,091
148 6/8	21 0/8	22 3/8	21 3/8	5	6	Umatilla County	OR	Loren R. Olsen	1981	1,091
148 6/8	19 4/8	20 7/8	19 4/8	5	5	Converse County	WY	Greg Popie	1982	1,091
148 6/8	22 6/8	23 4/8	19 6/8	5	4	Siskiyou County	CA	Jim Langley	1984	1,091
148 6/8	21 2/8	20 0/8	17 6/8	5	5	Sioux County	NE	Jeffrey Sales	1985	1,091
148 6/8	25 0/8	23 7/8	20 2/8	4	4	Garfield County	CO	Tom Urbenek	1988	1,091
148 6/8	21 2/8	21 1/8	20 6/8	5	4	Gove County	KS	Joel Beougher	1989	1,091
148 5/8	21 3/8	18 7/8	23 6/8	5	5	Park County	CO	Ed Zehner	1972	1,099
148 5/8	24 4/8	23 7/8	23 2/8	6	6	Chelan County	WA	Ted A. Kinsey	1983	1,099
148 5/8	22 0/8	22 0/8	21 1/8	5	5	Albany County	WY	Kevin Anderson	1988	1,099
148 5/8	22 5/8	22 5/8	18 7/8	4	5	Moffat County	CO	Larry Dean Bicknase	1992	1,099
148 5/8	20 5/8	21 0/8	15 5/8	5	5	Crook County	OR	Frank Sanders	1992	1,099
148 4/8	19 4/8	19 0/8	17 0/8	5	5	Boise County	ID	Floyd Audette	1964	1,104
148 4/8	21 7/8	19 7/8	19 2/8	7	6	Perkins County	SD	Dr. David W. Schrody	1979	1,104
148 4/8	21 7/8	22 4/8	20 4/8	5	5	Campbell County	WY	Carrol D. Wert	1979	1,104
148 4/8	22 2/8	22 6/8	20 4/8	5	5	Converse County	WY	James D. Miller	1980	1,104
148 4/8	22 5/8	21 2/8	24 0/8	6	9	Custer County	CO	Kurt Keskimaki	1981	1,104
148 4/8	22 0/8	21 7/8	19 6/8	5	4	San Juan County	UT	Bill Clink	1985	1,104
148 3/8	22 5/8	23 5/8	18 5/8	5	4	Huerfano County	CO	Loren Johnson	1966	1,110
148 3/8	21 1/8	20 4/8	21 5/8	5	5	Carbon County	WY	Rod Schmidt	1984	1,110
148 2/8	20 3/8	21 0/8	17 6/8	5	5	Fergus County	MT	Bob Wanner	1977	1,112
148 2/8	20 1/8	20 6/8	20 4/8	5	5	Billings County	ND	Thomas Treto	1982	1,112
148 2/8	21 0/8	23 1/8	21 1/8	4	5	Cochrane	ALB	David Richardson	1983	1,112
148 2/8	21 5/8	21 2/8	20 4/8	4	5	Chelan County	WA	Joe Lilley	1988	1,112
148 2/8	19 2/8	21 0/8	20 4/8	5	5	Cassia County	ID	Monte B. Carlson	1989	1,112
148 2/8	22 5/8	21 1/8	21 0/8	6	5	Pima County	AZ	Daniel C. Hicks	1991	1,112
148 1/8	20 4/8	21 7/8	22 7/8	9	4	Emery County	UT	Bob Jacobsen	1961	1,118
148 1/8	23 0/8	22 3/8	19 5/8	4	4	Pitkin County	CO	William F. Havel	1962	1,118
148 1/8	21 7/8	21 7/8	21 5/8	4	5	Lake County	OR	Richard G. Speer	1964	1,118
148 1/8	20 0/8	21 0/8	21 0/8	4	5	Ford County	KS	Aubrey Ballard	1966	1,118
148 1/8	20 7/8	20 1/8	18 5/8	5	4	Grand County	CO	Judd Cooney	1969	1,118
148 1/8	19 0/8	19 3/8	18 5/8	5	5	Carbon County	UT	Leonard Thompson	1973	1,118
148 1/8	20 3/8	21 5/8	21 2/8	6	5	Sheridan County	KS	Tom Reedy	1980	1,118
148 1/8	21 4/8	19 6/8	18 5/8	4	5	Mesa County	CO	Jay Verzuh	1982	1,118
148 1/8	21 4/8	22 1/8	19 3/8	5	4	Sheridan County	WY	Mike Barrett	1983	1,118
148 1/8	19 5/8	20 7/8	26 1/8	5	5	Grand County	CO	Guy Maurice Algier	1991	1,118
148 1/8	21 5/8	21 0/8	21 0/8	6	6	Michichi	ALB	Rodney Dyck	1991	1,118
148 1/8	20 4/8	20 1/8	21 2/8	7	7	Hettinger County	ND	Scott Wiseman	1991	1,118
148 1/8	23 6/8	23 0/8	18 0/8	6	6	Fraser River	BC	Rick Paquette	1991	1,118
148 1/8	20 5/8	21 0/8	17 5/8	7	7	Red Deer Lake	ALB	J. Linley Biblow	1991	1,118
148 0/8	21 7/8	21 4/8	21 1/8	6	6	White River N.F.	CO	Paul M. Ramsey	1959	1,132
148 0/8	20 5/8	20 7/8	16 6/8	6	6	Jones County	SD	Gene M. Hove	1990	1,132
147 7/8	22 3/8	24 0/8	23 3/8	3	4	Millard County	UT	Milton F. McQueary	1958	1,134
147 7/8	21 2/8	21 0/8	18 0/8	5	6	Deschutes County	OR	Joe Reynolds	1967	1,134
147 7/8	21 5/8	22 0/8	21 5/8	5	5	Johnson County	WY	Scott L. Koelzer	1978	1,134
147 7/8	23 3/8	23 7/8	24 0/8	5	4	Mesa County	CO	Garvin H. Gibbins	1984	1,134
147 7/8	23 7/8	22 7/8	20 7/8	5	4	Mesa County	CO	Richard Kunevicius	1985	1,134
147 7/8	22 2/8	21 0/8	21 5/8	5	4	Washoe County	NV	Cecil D. Martin	1986	1,134
147 7/8	22 2/8	21 0/8	21 5/8	5	4	Washoe County	NV	Cecil D. Martin	1986	1,134
147 6/8	20 0/8	20 2/8	20 2/8	5	4	Garfield County	CO	Steve Love	1972	1,141
147 6/8	19 4/8	21 0/8	21 0/8	5	5	Routt County	CO	John P. Hale	1974	1,141
147 6/8	20 5/8	21 6/8	15 6/8	7	5	Garfield County	CO	Edwin Hurt	1980	1,141
147 6/8	22 5/8	22 2/8	20 5/8	5	5	Boise County	ID	Matt March, Jr.	1983	1,141
147 6/8	17 6/8	22 0/8	20 0/8	4	4	Malheur County	OR	Steve Savage	1985	1,141
147 6/8	24 1/8	22 3/8	22 6/8	5	4	McKenzie County	ND	Bryan R. Stein	1988	1,141

Score	Length of Main Beam R	L	Inside Spread	Number of Points R	L	Area	State/ Province	Hunter's Name	Date	Rank
147 5/8	21 6/8	21 4/8	20 1/8	5	5	Sevier County	UT	Rowland Enomoto	1963	1,147
147 5/8	23 0/8	23 0/8	24 2/8	5	6	San Juan County	UT	Jack Howard	1966	1,147
147 5/8	19 1/8	17 0/8	21 0/8	6	5	Grant County	OR	Arthur Redinger	1972	1,147
147 5/8	21 1/8	18 7/8	17 5/8	5	4	Sevier County	UT	Robert W. Shilling	1974	1,147
147 5/8	25 2/8	24 2/8	22 1/8	7	5	Garfield County	CO	Terry Bridgman	1978	1,147
147 5/8	18 6/8	18 7/8	21 0/8	5	4	Elbert County	CO	Calvin Farner	1984	1,147
147 5/8	21 7/8	22 7/8	25 2/8	3	3	Butte County	SD	Glenn D Priebe	1984	1,147
147 4/8	22 1/8	22 2/8	19 4/8	5	5	Bernalillo County	NM	Larry W. Johnson	1969	1,154
147 4/8	21 2/8	22 1/8	19 0/8	5	5	Boulder County	CO	Jack Frank	1970	1,154
147 4/8	21 0/8	21 0/8	18 5/8	5	5	Garfield County	CO	Paul R. Shannon	1975	1,154
147 4/8	22 3/8	21 5/8	17 4/8	5	5	Maricopa County	AZ	Stephen C. Christensen	1976	1,154
147 4/8	20 1/8	20 5/8	19 6/8	5	5	Routt County	CO	Tom N. Garvin	1983	1,154
147 4/8	23 0/8	24 0/8	24 0/8	6	6	Sweetwater County	WY	Vic Dana	1983	1,154
147 4/8	24 2/8	22 2/8	20 2/8	4	5	Harney County	OR	Gary D. Nyden	1985	1,154
147 4/8	19 5/8	19 5/8	16 6/8	5	5	Coconino County	AZ	Steven H. Cook	1989	1,154
147 4/8	22 4/8	23 0/8	21 2/8	5	5	Converse County	WY	George A. Zanoni	1991	1,154
147 4/8	19 4/8	20 6/8	17 2/8	5	6	Converse County	WY	Harry Cerutti	1991	1,154
147 3/8	23 4/8	23 2/8	20 3/8	5	6	Cherry County	NE	Jack E. Joseph	1961	1,164
147 3/8	19 4/8	20 4/8	16 5/8	4	5	Latah County	ID	Chas. A. McDonald	1965	1,164
147 2/8	22 7/8	23 2/8	17 0/8	6	6	Cherry County	NE	Ken Hollpeter	1979	1,166
147 1/8	20 5/8	20 1/8	16 7/8	5	5	Uintah County	UT	Rolland Esterline	1967	1,167
147 1/8	19 6/8	23 6/8	17 0/8	6	5	Baker County	OR	Larry Garoutte	1970	1,167
147 0/8	20 3/8	20 7/8	20 2/8	5	5	Uintah County	UT	Merlin L. Killpack	1958	1,169
147 0/8	25 4/8	25 0/8	23 5/8	7	5	Grand County	UT	William W. Selby	1974	1,169
147 0/8	21 6/8	21 7/8	20 6/8	5	5	Dawson County	MT	Smucky Mann	1975	1,169
147 0/8	20 5/8	21 6/8	19 2/8	5	5	Laramie County	WY	Ronald J. Wedge	1978	1,169
147 0/8	20 4/8	20 4/8	17 2/8	5	5	Stanley County	SD	George Hipple	1982	1,169
147 0/8	21 6/8	21 3/8	18 2/8	5	5	Powder River County	MT	Max Miller	1990	1,169
147 0/8	22 6/8	22 3/8	20 2/8	6	6	Franklin County	ID	Dale Holpainen	1991	1,169
146 7/8	19 5/8	20 1/8	20 1/8	5	5	Grand County	UT	Norm Goodwin	1960	1,176
146 7/8	23 4/8	23 1/8	23 4/8	5	4	Emery County	UT	Bruce Ware	1961	1,176
146 7/8	19 2/8	20 0/8	18 5/8	5	5	Baker County	OR	James E. Hodson	1966	1,176
146 7/8	21 3/8	20 7/8	21 2/8	4	4	Carbon County	WY	John Swanson	1966	1,176
146 7/8	20 7/8	21 2/8	21 3/8	5	5	Meade County	SD	Kenneth McNenny	1967	1,176
146 7/8	21 2/8	21 4/8	18 7/8	5	5	Saguache County	CO	Skip Mulso	1974	1,176
146 7/8	21 0/8	20 2/8	18 3/8	4	4	Routt County	CO	Bob Stevens	1975	1,176
146 7/8	21 4/8	21 6/8	19 3/8	3	3	Clark County	ID	Robert Daniels	1978	1,176
146 7/8	20 3/8	21 5/8	20 3/8	6	5	Sheridan County	WY	David Shoop	1980	1,176
146 7/8	23 6/8	21 6/8	24 1/8	5	9	Pima County	AZ	Stacy Tompkinson	1984	1,176
146 7/8	19 7/8	20 4/8	17 3/8	5	5	Mesa County	CO	Gary L. Hoekman	1986	1,176
146 7/8	20 3/8	20 2/8	17 7/8	5	5	Orion	ALB	Kent Hillard	1990	1,176
146 7/8	22 0/8	23 1/8	26 7/8	6	5	Calgary	ALB	Archie Nesbitt	1991	1,176
146 6/8	19 6/8	20 3/8	15 7/8	4	4	Owyhee County	ID	Seneth Ward	1960	1,189
146 6/8	21 1/8	20 2/8	20 3/8	6	5	Mesa County	CO	Dennis Kelly	1981	1,189
146 6/8	20 4/8	19 7/8	19 0/8	6	7	Elbert County	CO	Donald Ace Morgan	1983	1,189
146 6/8	23 3/8	24 2/8	22 2/8	4	4	Pitkin County	CO	Bill Krenz	1983	1,189
146 6/8	18 7/8	20 1/8	19 6/8	5	4	Carbon County	WY	Rod Schmidt	1988	1,189
146 6/8	21 5/8	22 4/8	16 2/8	6	5	Meade County	KS	Mike Heinson	1989	1,189
146 6/8	21 6/8	21 0/8	22 5/8	6	5	Culberson County	TX	Curtis W. Mathis	1992	1,189
146 5/8	22 0/8	22 6/8	18 7/8	5	5	Chelan County	WA	Gerald King	1963	1,196
146 5/8	20 5/8	20 3/8	20 6/8	5	5	Johnson County	WY	Gary Olsen	1979	1,196
146 5/8	20 6/8	21 0/8	20 7/8	5	5	Uintah County	UT	Dave Lund	1987	1,196
146 5/8	21 2/8	22 2/8	15 7/8	4	5	Lemhi County	ID	Mike Muguira	1988	1,196
146 5/8	20 1/8	21 1/8	20 3/8	5	5	Sheridan County	WY	Mark Frank	1990	1,196
146 5/8	19 2/8	19 0/8	18 1/8	6	8	Wheatland County	MT	Jim Winjum	1992	1,196
146 4/8	23 3/8	23 0/8	21 0/8	4	5	Wayne County	UT	Harold Boyack	1968	1,202
146 4/8	20 0/8	20 7/8	19 4/8	5	4	Mesa County	CO	Kaye B. McCrory	1978	1,202
146 4/8	24 0/8	26 5/8	23 0/8	7	6	Eagle County	CO	Dave Mendoza	1983	1,202
146 4/8	22 4/8	22 3/8	20 4/8	5	5	Piute County	UT	Tim Sayer	1984	1,202
146 4/8	22 3/8	22 1/8	19 6/8	5	4	Rio Grande County	CO	Jerry Woodland	1984	1,202
146 4/8	21 0/8	23 2/8	22 4/8	5	5	Bowman County	ND	Dwight Eckart	1984	1,202
146 4/8	21 7/8	22 4/8	16 7/8	5	8	Cache County	UT	Robert Bronson	1985	1,202
146 4/8	21 4/8	21 2/8	18 0/8	5	5	Mesa County	CO	John Papenfuss	1988	1,202
146 4/8	18 6/8	19 2/8	19 3/8	5	5	Warner	ALB	Keith Heppler	1991	1,202
146 3/8	19 0/8	19 0/8	17 3/8	5	5	Mohave County	AZ	George Kili	1964	1,211
146 3/8	20 2/8	21 1/8	19 1/8	5	5	Grand County	UT	Bob Paulson	1967	1,211
146 3/8	21 0/8	21 2/8	19 5/8	5	5	Mesa County	CO	Curtis W. Dorroh	1979	1,211
146 3/8	22 1/8	22 2/8	22 5/8	7	6	Lane County	KS	Dean Hamilton	1980	1,211
146 3/8	19 2/8	21 2/8	19 3/8	4	4	Boulder County	CO	Al Miller	1983	1,211
146 3/8	20 4/8	21 3/8	19 5/8	5	6	San Miguel County	NM	Ricardo Roybal	1984	1,211

SCORE	LENGTH OF R MAIN BEAM L		INSIDE SPREAD	NUMBER OF R POINTS L		AREA	STATE/ PROVINCE	HUNTER'S NAME	DATE	RANK
146 3/8	21 1/8	19 4/8	21 4/8	5	5	Billings County	ND	Roy Boots	1985	1,211
146 3/8	24 7/8	24 6/8	24 3/8	4	4	Fall River County	SD	Michael A. Judas	1990	1,211
146 2/8	25 4/8	23 6/8	23 4/8	5	5	Las Animas County	CO	Tom Valamdro	1967	1,219
146 2/8	21 0/8	20 2/8	19 1/8	7	6	Gallatin County	MT	Scott Koelzer	1969	1,219
146 2/8	21 4/8	21 4/8	20 0/8	5	5	Powder River County	MT	Charles R. Maloney	1973	1,219
146 2/8	22 4/8	22 0/8	19 0/8	4	5	Powder River County	MT	Mike Barrett	1985	1,219
146 2/8	18 6/8	18 4/8	18 2/8	5	5	Cache County	UT	John A. Bogucki	1988	1,219
146 2/8	21 6/8	21 4/8	18 4/8	4	5	Sublette County	WY	Roger O. Wyant	1990	1,219
146 2/8	22 6/8	21 7/8	25 5/8	5	5	Hidalgo County	NM	Steven Tisdale	1992	1,219
146 1/8	20 6/8	19 0/8	15 7/8	5	5	Ada County	ID	Jim Wenzel	1971	1,226
146 1/8	20 6/8	22 2/8	22 1/8	5	5	Graham County	KS	Jim Kerbaugh	1989	1,226
146 1/8	20 1/8	19 2/8	17 3/8	5	5	Grand County	CO	Guy-Maurice Algier	1990	1,226
146 1/8	19 6/8	20 6/8	18 5/8	6	5	Morgan County	CO	Laszlo Nobi	1991	1,226
146 1/8	20 5/8	22 2/8	17 7/8	5	5	Otero County	NM	Roger Schoolcraft	1992	1,226
146 0/8	20 4/8	20 2/8	18 2/8	5	5	Elko County	NV	Howard Hill	1944	1,231
146 0/8	21 2/8	21 3/8	20 2/8	5	5	Mesa County	CO	William F. DeEsch	1966	1,231
146 0/8	18 6/8	19 7/8	17 0/8	5	5	Decatur County	KS	A. E. 'Butch' Whelchel	1977	1,231
146 0/8	19 6/8	19 2/8	20 6/8	5	5	Converse County	WY	David A. Widby	1990	1,231
146 0/8	22 0/8	19 2/8	23 3/8	5	5	Niobrara County	WY	John H. Williams	1991	1,231
145 7/8	21 1/8	20 4/8	20 5/8	5	6	Madera County	CA	Rodney York	1978	1,236
145 7/8	20 1/8	20 3/8	19 5/8	4	4	Chelan County	WA	Rick Morgan	1984	1,236
145 7/8	21 5/8	22 0/8	19 1/8	5	4	Billings County	ND	Tom Schills	1988	1,236
145 7/8	20 1/8	19 1/8	15 1/8	5	5	Carbon County	WY	Joseph Parziale	1992	1,236
145 6/8	17 0/8	18 3/8	16 0/8	5	5	Lake County	OR	George Rajnus	1961	1,240
145 6/8	22 2/8	24 3/8	21 4/8	5	3	Sevier County	UT	James R. Bell	1964	1,240
145 6/8	24 1/8	21 2/8	24 2/8	6	6	Chaffee County	CO	Gary Ginther	1973	1,240
145 6/8	22 3/8	22 0/8	20 2/8	5	5	Pecos County	TX	Butch Floyd	1975	1,240
145 6/8	20 6/8	22 0/8	21 0/8	6	5	Cheyenne County	KS	Kendall Helton	1988	1,240
145 6/8	22 5/8	24 2/8	17 3/8	6	5	Bernalillo County	NM	Alvin Chewiwi	1990	1,240
145 6/8	22 0/8	20 3/8	22 6/8	5	5	Wasco County	OR	Sean Corbin	1991	1,240
145 6/8	19 4/8	23 4/8	21 7/8	5	6	Estevan	SAS	Myron Duff	1992	1,240
145 5/8	21 0/8	20 4/8	17 5/8	4	4	Grant County	OR	Charlie Endicott	1979	1,248
145 5/8	22 5/8	21 2/8	21 7/8	4	5	Ellis County	KS	Mark A. Murphey	1983	1,248
145 5/8	22 0/8	22 5/8	20 3/8	7	6	Rich County	UT	Wade Steffenhagen	1992	1,248
145 4/8	20 5/8	18 4/8	19 4/8	6	6	Boulder County	CO	Bob Byerly	1967	1,251
145 4/8	19 6/8	14 2/8	18 4/8	7	4	Pima County	AZ	Peter C. Knagge	1976	1,251
145 4/8	21 5/8	21 6/8	19 6/8	5	5	Sioux County	NE	Steve Woitaszewski	1983	1,251
145 4/8	21 7/8	22 4/8	20 4/8	5	4	Converse County	WY	Frank N. Moore	1984	1,251
145 4/8	18 4/8	19 4/8	16 6/8	4	4	Platte County	WY	Dave Hiiva	1985	1,251
145 4/8	23 3/8	23 5/8	22 4/8	5	5	Lassen County	CA	Wayne Wood	1985	1,251
145 4/8	21 2/8	20 5/8	21 5/8	4	4	Jackson County	OR	Ron Schmelzer	1991	1,251
145 4/8	17 1/8	20 1/8	14 4/8	6	6	Sioux County	NE	Mike A. Ellingson	1992	1,251
145 3/8	27 2/8	26 5/8	26 2/8	5	4	Moffat County	CO	Scott Showalter	1971	1,259
145 3/8	21 1/8	20 4/8	19 7/8	4	4	Sioux County	NE	William A. Voor Vart	1978	1,259
145 3/8	21 6/8	22 0/8	21 7/8	4	4	Summit County	UT	Larry Dickerson	1985	1,259
145 2/8	24 0/8	24 4/8	19 6/8	4	4	Bernalillo County	NM	Robert Bulcock, Jr.	1969	1,262
145 2/8	20 1/8	20 2/8	16 2/8	5	5	Uncompahgre N.F.	CO	Larry Holak	1979	1,262
145 2/8	22 4/8	23 1/8	17 4/8	5	5	Mesa County	CO	Paul T Brown	1985	1,262
145 2/8	22 2/8	22 7/8	19 7/8	6	7	Norton County	KS	Gary Long	1987	1,262
145 2/8	21 4/8	21 4/8	18 2/8	5	5	Natrona County	WY	Larry Nelson	1989	1,262
145 1/8	23 0/8	23 3/8	22 7/8	5	4	Natrona County	WY	Bill Wade	1970	1,267
145 1/8	21 6/8	19 3/8	19 1/8	4	5	Eagle County	CO	Rick Duggan	1981	1,267
145 1/8	19 4/8	20 3/8	17 5/8	5	4	Coconino County	AZ	Dick Tone	1981	1,267
145 1/8	23 4/8	21 3/8	20 7/8	4	4	Summit County	CO	Mark Anderson	1982	1,267
145 1/8	18 5/8	19 4/8	17 5/8	5	5	Routt County	CO	Ronald P. Kelley, Sr.	1985	1,267
145 1/8	22 5/8	21 7/8	21 5/8	3	4	Baker County	OR	Arthur Marc Whisler	1986	1,267
145 1/8	22 2/8	22 3/8	17 7/8	4	4	Yakima County	WA	Robt. "Andy" Anderson	1986	1,267
145 1/8	21 3/8	20 6/8	19 1/8	4	5	Calgary	ALB	Jim Chapman	1991	1,267
145 0/8	22 1/8	21 6/8	17 6/8	5	5	El Paso County	CO	Thomas M. Farmer	1961	1,275
145 0/8	22 1/8	22 2/8	21 0/8	5	6	Trego County	KS	Don Howard	1966	1,275
145 0/8	22 1/8	22 4/8	21 2/8	5	5	Plumes County	CA	Wayne Ghidossi	1977	1,275
145 0/8	22 7/8	24 2/8	27 1/8	5	5	Cochise County	AZ	Joe F. Acosta	1986	1,275
145 0/8	20 5/8	20 4/8	19 4/8	4	5	Salt Lake County	UT	Lance Dalton	1989	1,275
145 0/8	19 7/8	19 7/8	17 4/8	5	5	Fremont County	WY	Gary Nyman	1990	1,275
145 0/8	22 2/8	20 7/8	19 2/8	6	5	Saguache County	CO	Mike Chatin	1991	1,275
145 0/8	17 4/8	19 0/8	19 6/8	5	5	Union County	OR	Russ Hultberg	1991	1,275
145 0/8	24 4/8	23 4/8	22 0/8	4	4	Vermilion	ALB	Graydon Bishop	1992	1,275

World Record Mule Deer (Non-Typical Antlers)
Score:274 7/8
Morgan County, Colorado - 1987
Hunter: Kenneth W. Plank

MULE DEER (Non-Typical Antlers)

Odocoileus hemionus
and certain related subspecies

SCORE	LENGTH OF MAIN BEAM R	L	INSIDE SPREAD	NUMBER OF POINTS R	L	AREA	STATE/ PROVINCE	HUNTER'S NAME	DATE	RANK
274 7/8	23 7/8	26 2/8	27 0/8	23	12	Morgan County	CO	Kenneth W. Plank	1987	1
274 4/8	28 6/8	29 0/8	21 1/8	12	12	Lincoln County	MT	Andrew Keim	1978	2
269 0/8	24 7/8	24 0/8	23 6/8	10	14	Lane County	KS	Dean Hamilton	1989	3
258 2/8	26 6/8	26 7/8	24 0/8	13	11	Mesa County	CO	David Glick	1976	4
246 6/8	25 1/8	27 4/8	24 6/8	12	11	Mesa County	CO	Dean Derby II	1976	5
236 1/8	25 5/8	25 2/8	18 3/8	10	11	Coconino County	AZ	Stanley L. McIntyre	1965	6
234 4/8	26 4/8	27 2/8	23 7/8	10	8	Juab County	UT	Dennis M. Hickman	1972	7
232 5/8	26 3/8	24 7/8	20 3/8	11	10	Rio Blanco County	CO	Harold Boyack	1979	8
232 3/8	23 2/8	21 2/8	23 0/8	12	14	Arapahoe County	CO	James P. Verney	1974	9
229 7/8	27 5/8	28 0/8	25 7/8	6	7	Lambs Canyon	UT	Lee Lindley	1942	10
226 5/8	24 0/8	23 6/8	22 4/8	12	8	Crook County	WY	Charles Lee Smith	1987	11
226 4/8	23 5/8	27 6/8	19 2/8	9	11	Iron County	UT	Neil "Bud" Rhodes	1959	12
226 2/8	19 1/8	22 1/8	19 5/8	12	11	Wichita County	KS	Stacy Hoeme	1992	13
225 4/8	23 4/8	23 2/8	22 0/8	10	13	Herd Unit 54	UT	John C. Balch	1965	14
225 2/8	24 2/8	24 2/8	23 1/8	12	7	Garfield County	CO	Dennis Quinn	1972	15
224 6/8	25 5/8	25 5/8	22 4/8	9	9	Ferry County	WA	Romie Hilderbrant	1963	16
224 1/8	25 7/8	24 6/8	24 2/8	10	9	Washakie County	WY	William T. Ivey	1987	17
224 0/8	25 6/8	23 6/8	25 6/8	8	12	Lake County	OR	Jeff Eggleston	1986	18
223 7/8	27 5/8	26 4/8	24 4/8	12	9	Uncompahgre Mtns.	CO	Steve Haynes	1972	19
222 6/8	21 0/8	22 4/8	21 2/8	13	8	Lane County	KS	Dean Hamilton	1990	20
222 4/8	24 6/8	23 7/8	25 3/8	9	8	Barber County	KS	Perry Smith	1990	21
222 3/8	27 1/8	27 4/8	22 5/8	11	11	DeWinton	ALB	Blaine Southgate	1991	22
222 1/8	23 2/8	23 7/8	19 4/8	8	7	San Juan County	UT	Louie Arko	1972	23
222 1/8	25 5/8	24 5/8	20 4/8	8	10	Montrose County	CO	LaVern Rucker	1975	23
221 1/8	26 4/8	26 1/8	22 6/8	11	11	Bernalillo County	NM	Timothy Dwyer	1985	25
220 6/8	20 4/8	18 4/8	19 0/8	15	12	Coconino County	AZ	Placido Alderette	1978	26
220 3/8	27 3/8	27 1/8	23 1/8	11	7	Sanpete County	UT	I. B. 'Blackie' Owen	1964	27
220 2/8	26 6/8	26 0/8	24 7/8	8	9	Uncompahgre Plateau	CO	Michael T. Schwitters	1971	28
219 5/8	21 2/8	23 1/8	26 0/8	9	8	Mesa County	CO	Roger Lewis	1980	29
218 1/8	22 0/8	24 1/8	16 5/8	9	8	Lincoln County	WY	Mike Barrett	1987	30
218 0/8	27 0/8	27 5/8	27 0/8	7	9	San Juan County	UT	Harold Boyack	1974	31
218 0/8	26 1/8	25 0/8	25 0/8	8	9	Garfield County	CO	Bob Hill	1979	31
217 6/8	25 6/8	26 4/8	23 6/8	8	10	Caribou County	ID	James C. Ashley	1977	33
217 2/8	23 5/8	23 7/8	21 0/8	14	7	Beaverhead County	MT	Bob L. Walker	1992	34
216 6/8	23 4/8	24 4/8	22 0/8	9	12	Garfield County	CO	Richard Lepak	1975	35
216 2/8	21 7/8	22 5/8	19 4/8	8	9	Mohave County	AZ	William Cross	1965	36
215 7/8	23 5/8	24 5/8	20 7/8	9	8	Clark County	KS	Dan Fenton	1988	37
215 5/8	21 3/8	23 0/8	16 6/8	7	10	Uintah County	UT	Jon E Bingham	1969	38
214 6/8	25 7/8	27 3/8	31 3/8	9	7	McKinley County	NM	R. Grant Clawson	1987	39
214 0/8	25 3/8	25 4/8	22 3/8	8	9	McCone County	MT	James F. Kosi	1974	40
213 0/8	22 2/8	23 3/8	18 7/8	10	9	Caribou County	ID	Bob McAteer	1966	41
212 6/8	23 4/8	23 3/8	24 4/8	8	8	Ness County	KS	Ralph Stum	1966	42
212 2/8	25 1/8	24 0/8	24 4/8	8	9	Sherman County	KS	Wayne Luckert	1987	43
212 0/8	21 0/8	20 5/8	19 5/8	10	9	Calgary	ALB	Bert Frelink	1985	44
211 1/8	23 5/8	24 4/8	20 6/8	7	7	Uintah County	UT	Vern Hatch	1962	45
210 4/8	24 3/8	25 0/8	27 5/8	7	8	Montrose County	CO	Thomas Gloden	1963	46
210 2/8	22 2/8	27 6/8	27 2/8	4	7	Mesa County	CO	Art Cook	1972	47
209 7/8	25 4/8	22 6/8	23 0/8	10	9	Caribou County	ID	Ray Kagel	1992	48
208 7/8	26 6/8	27 1/8	22 7/8	10	8	Duchesne County	UT	Smiley Arrowchis	1989	49
208 3/8	23 6/8	26 7/8	23 6/8	10	8	Adams County	ID	Donnie Lee Voss	1986	50
208 1/8	26 5/8	25 5/8	21 7/8	8	8	Grand County	UT	Charles Denver	1986	51
207 0/8	24 2/8	23 0/8	20 6/8	7	5	Elmore County	ID	Deloy Desaro	1972	52
206 7/8	22 2/8	24 1/8	22 1/8	7	9	Lemhi County	ID	A. LaVerne Hokanson	1967	53
205 3/8	24 2/8	24 0/8	22 0/8	8	8	Grand County	UT	C. B. 'John' Olsen	1958	54
205 1/8	22 7/8	20 7/8	20 6/8	7	8	Cabri	SAS	Gene Andreas	1987	55
204 4/8	26 2/8	22 6/8	17 5/8	7	9	Fishlake National Forest	UT	Dick Kerr	1955	56
204 3/8	23 6/8	25 3/8	18 1/8	8	8	Mesa County	CO	Don Zanow	1976	57
204 1/8	25 3/8	26 2/8	17 2/8	11	10	Umatilla County	OR	Dan Follett	1982	58
204 1/8	26 0/8	26 1/8	25 2/8	8	8	Routt County	CO	Dennis Rowley	1987	58
202 5/8	26 0/8	25 3/8	23 3/8	6	7	Garfield County	CO	A. H. Sandidge	1972	60
202 4/8	22 0/8	21 5/8	16 4/8	9	8	Sioux County	NE	Douglas Buckley	1982	61
202 3/8	21 7/8	21 5/8	20 3/8	7	9	Summit County	UT	Lynn C. Maxfield	1986	62
201 6/8	21 4/8	22 5/8	22 0/8	9	8	Caribou County	ID	Dennis Dockstader	1969	63
200 4/8	22 6/8	23 4/8	20 5/8	8	10	Cochrane	ALB	Dave Carles	1991	64
200 3/8	24 4/8	24 3/8	19 4/8	8	9	Farm Creek	UT	Tex Ross	1966	65
200 2/8	27 5/8	26 2/8	19 1/8	9	8	Montezuma County	CO	Bryon C. Neeley	1971	66
200 1/8	23 7/8	22 1/8	20 2/8	7	8	Pima County	AZ	Jim Johnson	1981	67
199 1/8	22 6/8	23 4/8	19 1/8	9	10	Mesa County	CO	James R. Boyles	1971	68
198 5/8	21 6/8	22 6/8	23 4/8	9	8	Franklin County	KS	John R. Coblentz	1966	69
198 5/8	24 1/8	23 3/8	19 2/8	5	11	Teller County	CO	Robert Runkles	1986	69

SCORE	LENGTH OF MAIN BEAM		INSIDE SPREAD	NUMBER OF POINTS		AREA	STATE/ PROVINCE	HUNTER'S NAME	DATE	RANK
	R	L		R	L					
198 0/8	21 5/8	22 0/8	19 0/8	8	9	Routt County	CO	Bruce F. Davison	1968	71
197 7/8	26 5/8	26 3/8	25 0/8	9	7	Lincoln County	MT	Gary Weber	1978	72
197 5/8	22 0/8	21 1/8	20 5/8	10	8	Elmore County	ID	Jerry G. Fetters	1970	73
197 4/8	24 6/8	24 4/8	25 5/8	9	7	Morton County	KS	Kevin White	1982	74
195 7/8	25 0/8	24 6/8	22 6/8	6	7	Lemhi County	ID	James Stuart	1982	75
195 6/8	21 2/8	22 6/8	19 3/8	9	9	Weld County	CO	Densel Bolin	1974	76
195 6/8	23 7/8	26 7/8	18 1/8	8	7	Sanders County	MT	Jerry V Finley	1989	76
195 4/8	25 2/8	23 2/8	22 3/8	9	14		CO	Douglas Kenyon	1964	78
195 0/8	23 4/8	22 3/8	18 7/8	7	10	County of Taber	ALB	Quincy Jensen	1990	79
194 7/8	23 0/8	22 7/8	19 7/8	6	7	Finney County	KS	Jay Sloan	1967	80
194 7/8	26 5/8	25 3/8	22 3/8	6	7	Duchesne County	UT	Frank Warburton	1969	80
193 7/8	23 4/8	24 0/8	22 1/8	9	7	Baker County	OR	B. G. Shurtleff	1980	82
193 7/8	22 4/8	23 5/8	23 2/8	8	5	Kearny County	KS	Robert J. Price	1985	82
193 7/8	27 3/8	26 3/8	27 2/8	12	10	Yakima County	WA	James R. Lucas	1990	82
193 6/8	22 5/8	22 6/8	20 0/8	9	9	Utah County	UT	Ivan B. Henderson, Jr.	1959	85
192 4/8	24 4/8	25 0/8	21 3/8	6	7	Caribou County	ID	Mack Tigert	1985	86
191 7/8	22 2/8	19 1/8	17 6/8	7	12	Bell Marsh Canyon	ID	Loren H. Dunn	1965	87
191 4/8	23 2/8	24 3/8	17 1/8	5	10	Garfield County	CO	J. D. Jones	1971	88
191 4/8	23 6/8	23 6/8	20 6/8	7	8	Grant County	OR	Joe Mengore	1981	88
191 1/8	23 1/8	24 3/8	22 0/8	7	9	Smith County	KS	Linton Haresnape	1981	90
191 0/8	23 6/8	21 2/8	16 2/8	8	9	Imperial County	CA	Michael S. Flynn	1986	91
190 6/8	23 5/8	22 4/8	21 3/8	6	7	Huerfano County	CO	Ron Johnson	1970	92
189 4/8	23 4/8	23 4/8	17 2/8	7	8	Johnson County	WY	Charles Jahnke	1979	93
189 3/8	26 2/8	25 4/8	16 7/8	11	16	Lincoln County	MT	Darryl L. Lyght	1992	94
189 1/8	20 1/8	22 2/8	19 3/8	6	8	Garfield County	CO	Robert C. McCardell	1974	95
189 0/8	25 1/8	24 6/8	25 2/8	12	11	Dawson County	MT	Monte Dassinger	1973	96
189 0/8	20 0/8	22 3/8	16 7/8	8	6	Garfield County	CO	Stephen Kennedy	1975	96
187 7/8	17 1/8	22 1/8	16 3/8	12	8	Grand County	UT	Lee Allred	1958	98
187 2/8	22 0/8	22 0/8	21 2/8	6	6	Eagle County	CO	Gary O. Glenn	1978	99
187 2/8	23 2/8	23 7/8	20 6/8	9	7	Ouray County	CO	Roger Wyant	1984	99
186 6/8	25 6/8	22 1/8	24 6/8	8	6	Dolores County	CO	Michael W. Forth	1978	101
186 5/8	23 0/8	23 6/8	22 6/8	8	9	Pin Horn Range	ALB	Giuliano Coslovi	1988	102
186 0/8	23 3/8	24 2/8	21 4/8	8	8	Chaffee County	CO	John D. Hambleton	1975	103
186 0/8	23 1/8	21 5/8	21 0/8	8	7	Ravalli County	MT	Ed Barrett	1983	103
185 7/8	22 7/8	22 3/8	18 0/8	11	8	Klamath County	OR	Charles A. Warner	1975	105
185 4/8	21 0/8	21 4/8	18 5/8	9	9	Hanna	ALB	Dale Drummond	1992	106
185 2/8	22 5/8	20 5/8	23 6/8	8	7	Scott County	KS	Richard B. Spencer	1986	107
184 2/8	20 5/8	21 5/8	19 3/8	8	6	Duchesne County	UT	Dean Reynolds	1961	108
183 3/8	25 5/8	25 1/8	25 0/8	6	7	Franklin County	ID	Doug Ransom	1985	109
182 5/8	19 5/8	19 5/8	16 3/8	7	7	Valley County	ID	Charles "Chuck" Boatman	1986	110
182 0/8	25 0/8	24 4/8	23 7/8	7	8	Kootenai County	ID	Rodney W. Willis	1977	111
181 5/8	27 0/8	24 3/8	23 4/8	7	9	Chelan County	WA	David M. Bartholemew	1967	112
181 4/8	27 5/8	26 3/8	27 4/8	5	7	Park County	CO	John Cliff	1967	113
180 7/8	22 5/8	23 3/8	21 0/8	6	6	Gray County	KS	James R. Sobba	1991	114
180 4/8	21 1/8	22 5/8	21 3/8	7	5	Utah County	UT	Frank Warburton	1972	115
178 5/8	25 3/8	24 6/8	31 0/8	6	7	San Juan County	UT	Guy Gates	1970	116
178 2/8	22 3/8	23 7/8	24 6/8	8	4	Calgary	ALB	Lindsey Paterson	1990	117
178 0/8	20 2/8	20 7/8	18 3/8	8	8	Las Animas County	CO	Michael A. Mattorano	1989	118
177 7/8	21 2/8	18 6/8	20 2/8	6	7	Garfield County	CO	Steve Byerly	1980	119
177 4/8	24 4/8	22 2/8	26 1/8	9	7	Rio Arriba County	NM	Michael D. Bruce	1986	120
177 3/8	21 1/8	22 4/8	23 3/8	9	8	Dawson County	MT	Gerald Polesky	1970	121
176 7/8	20 5/8	22 5/8	21 2/8	7	7	Rock Creek	CO	Adolph Kuhns	1961	122
176 6/8	25 1/8	22 4/8	27 0/8	6	5	Grant County	OR	Chuck Warner	1983	123
176 0/8	23 3/8	23 5/8	20 4/8	6	6	Scott County	KS	Vince Strickler	1975	124
176 0/8	22 1/8	23 0/8	17 4/8	7	7	Gove County	KS	Rick Kreuter	1991	124
175 7/8	19 4/8	20 7/8	18 6/8	6	6	Routt County	CO	Chuck Nemec	1974	126
175 3/8	20 6/8	24 2/8	29 0/8	9	9	Ness County	KS	Pete McBee	1969	127
175 3/8	24 2/8	23 2/8	17 3/8	7	8	Culberson County	TX	Gary Oden	1985	127
174 3/8	23 4/8	24 3/8	23 5/8	7	8	Dawson County	MT	Richard Harms	1972	129
174 2/8	23 6/8	23 1/8	22 0/8	9	10	Mesa County	CO	Art Cook	1958	130
174 1/8	25 7/8	24 5/8	18 7/8	7	5	Carbon County	UT	B. E. Epperson	1971	131
173 3/8	20 4/8	26 6/8	20 3/8	6	5	Morrow County	OR	Ray Kelton	1976	132
173 2/8	21 3/8	21 3/8	21 4/8	8	8	Elmore County	ID	Peter J. Cintorino	1980	133
173 1/8	19 7/8	22 1/8	17 1/8	8	7	Dawes County	NE	LaVerne J. Weber	1975	134
173 0/8	22 1/8	21 3/8	16 1/8	7	6	Culberson County	TX	Gary J. Oden	1988	135
172 7/8	25 6/8	26 4/8	29 0/8	6	6	Grant County	OR	Ray Kelton	1980	136
172 7/8	23 4/8	24 3/8	22 2/8	8	5	Slope County	ND	Todd Seymanski	1982	136
171 7/8	24 0/8	23 4/8	20 3/8	5	7	Campbell County	WY	Paul Vomela	1992	138
171 4/8	22 2/8	20 1/8	16 3/8	5	12	Mesa County	CO	Paul H. Dickson	1985	139
171 3/8	21 1/8	22 1/8	21 1/8	8	6	Meade County	KS	Richard A. Nordyke	1971	140

SCORE	LENGTH OF MAIN BEAM		INSIDE SPREAD	NUMBER OF POINTS		AREA	STATE/ PROVINCE	HUNTER'S NAME	DATE	RANK
	R	L		R	L					
170 7/8	18 4/8	20 0/8	17 1/8	6	6	Wallowa County	OR	Wayne van Zwoll	1977	141
170 6/8	23 6/8	24 1/8	21 2/8	7	7	Valley County	ID	John Pyle	1978	142
170 5/8	22 0/8	22 1/8	16 3/8	6	5	Lake County	OR	Bill Hendrick	1964	143
170 5/8	20 3/8	19 5/8	20 4/8	5	7	McCone County	MT	David Tofte	1985	143
170 0/8	19 5/8	17 5/8	19 5/8	7	5	Finney County	KS	Rod Lies	1968	145
169 4/8	23 4/8	22 4/8	18 5/8	7	8	Brewster County	TX	Roger Wintle	1986	146
169 0/8	25 2/8	25 4/8	21 0/8	6	7	Lassen County	CA	Wayne Wood	1984	147
166 5/8	20 3/8	20 1/8	20 2/8	7	7	Linn County	OR	Joe Mengore	1980	148
166 3/8	22 4/8	21 7/8	19 4/8	9	10	Grand County	CO	Jim Fitzgerald	1984	149
164 6/8	20 2/8	21 2/8	18 0/8	6	6	Meade County	KS	Kent Davis	1972	150

Mule Deer (Typical Velvet Antlers)
Score: 199 7/8
Garfield County, Utah - 1985
Hunter: Randal Peterson

MULE DEER *(Typical Velvet Antlers)*

MINIMUM SCORE 145

Odocoileus hemionus
and certain related subspecies

SCORE	LENGTH OF R MAIN BEAM L		INSIDE SPREAD	NUMBER OF R POINTS L		AREA	STATE/ PROVINCE	HUNTER'S NAME	DATE	RANK
199 7/8	26 6/8	26 1/8	23 7/8	6	5	Garfield County	UT	Randal Peterson	1985	1
198 3/8	25 4/8	24 2/8	23 5/8	6	5	Coconino County	AZ	Corky Richardson	1988	2
198 2/8	26 1/8	27 2/8	21 6/8	5	5	Garfield County	UT	Ed Burley	1989	3
196 5/8	26 6/8	25 7/8	25 7/8	5	5	Montrose County	CO	Dennis Garton	1970	4
190 7/8	25 3/8	25 1/8	24 5/8	5	6	Cibola County	NM	Max R. Gallegos	1991	5
190 3/8	20 7/8	22 5/8	21 7/8	6	5	Uinta County	WY	Joseph Gilmore	1978	6
190 0/8	25 4/8	26 7/8	23 0/8	5	5	Weber County	UT	Bruce Carlisle	1992	7
189 6/8	26 4/8	26 1/8	20 6/8	8	8	Coconino County	AZ	Mark Watkins	1990	8
189 2/8	26 6/8	24 6/8	27 6/8	5	5	Alamosa County	CO	Joseph Mazurek	1978	9
187 6/8	25 5/8	25 2/8	21 2/8	6	5	El Paso County	CO	Gene Johnson	1987	10
187 6/8	24 3/8	23 4/8	20 2/8	5	5	Rich County	UT	David Ellsworth	1991	10
187 4/8	26 3/8	25 1/8	22 6/8	5	5	San Juan County	UT	Jarod Yeager	1990	12
187 4/8	24 1/8	24 1/8	20 4/8	5	5	Yavapai County	AZ	John Yanez	1990	12
187 2/8	23 5/8	23 7/8	17 1/8	5	6	Coconino County	AZ	Noble E. Sinclair	1986	14
186 4/8	25 4/8	25 6/8	24 0/8	6	5	Grand County	UT	Perry Hansen	1982	15
186 4/8	22 6/8	22 2/8	20 0/8	5	5	Rich County	UT	Patrick Hogle	1992	15
186 3/8	25 6/8	24 2/8	22 0/8	5	6	Kane County	UT	Dwight Schuh	1990	17
185 5/8	25 5/8	23 5/8	26 6/8	5	5	Mesa County	CO	Tom Postel	1975	18
185 2/8	26 3/8	26 4/8	25 3/8	6	5	Kane County	UT	Greg L. Munther	1991	19
185 0/8	25 6/8	25 6/8	21 4/8	5	5	Clearwater County	ID	Don Larson	1987	20
184 2/8	24 1/8	21 4/8	24 3/8	7	5	Larimer County	CO	David M. Jackson	1991	21
184 0/8	26 1/8	25 1/8	24 2/8	5	5	San Juan County	CO	Robert C. Dawson	1978	22
183 6/8	25 7/8	25 5/8	29 1/8	6	5	Sanpete County	UT	Robert Rowley	1972	23
183 5/8	24 6/8	25 6/8	25 1/8	5	6	Delta County	CO	Michael Brannon Carver	1989	24
183 3/8	26 1/8	26 3/8	20 6/8	6	6	Albany County	WY	Darryl Cooper	1988	25
183 1/8	23 4/8	22 6/8	23 3/8	5	5	Coconino County	AZ	George Richardson	1990	26

SCORE	LENGTH OF MAIN BEAM		INSIDE SPREAD	NUMBER OF POINTS		AREA	STATE/ PROVINCE	HUNTER'S NAME	DATE	RANK
	R	L		R	L					
183 0/8	23 4/8	24 5/8	22 2/8	7	5	Coconino County	AZ	Ben Lara, Jr.	1990	27
182 7/8	27 2/8	25 3/8	25 1/8	5	5	Morgan County	UT	Larry Mathis	1990	28
182 7/8	26 0/8	25 3/8	22 2/8	7	7	Sandoval County	NM	Doug Aikin	1991	28
182 3/8	22 7/8	23 1/8	22 2/8	5	6	Washington County	UT	Wayne J. Wittwer	1990	30
182 2/8	27 7/8	26 7/8	22 4/8	5	5	San Juan County	CO	William Colley	1983	31
182 2/8	23 2/8	23 3/8	22 2/8	5	6	Humboldt County	NV	Roger Iveson	1984	31
182 0/8	24 2/8	23 7/8	22 2/8	5	5	Wayne County	UT	Thomas W. Powell	1990	33
181 4/8	25 2/8	25 0/8	25 7/8	6	5	Dolores County	CO	Hulen D. McEntire	1977	34
181 3/8	28 2/8	24 5/8	26 7/8	8	7	Sevier County	UT	Robert Cooper	1970	35
181 2/8	23 6/8	23 4/8	31 0/8	5	5	Mesa County	CO	George Morris	1974	36
181 2/8	26 2/8	26 1/8	23 0/8	5	5	Duchesne County	UT	Dennis Evans	1992	36
180 4/8	23 7/8	22 5/8	21 2/8	5	6	Fremont County	CO	John M. Adams, Jr.	1988	38
180 4/8	24 7/8	24 6/8	23 4/8	5	5	Lincoln County	WY	Kent Slovernick	1991	38
180 3/8	24 3/8	23 0/8	22 4/8	5	7	Caribou County	ID	Coby Tigert	1979	40
180 3/8	25 7/8	25 0/8	19 5/8	7	5	Garfield County	UT	Jed R. Ashworth	1992	40
180 2/8	25 2/8	24 5/8	23 2/8	6	7	San Juan County	UT	Stephan D. Zedney	1990	42
180 1/8	25 6/8	28 1/8	26 2/8	9	6	Sevier County	UT	Richard Rymer	1990	43
180 0/8	24 0/8	25 0/8	19 0/8	5	5	Valencia County	NM	Michael Crabb	1991	44
179 7/8	24 0/8	23 0/8	23 4/8	5	6	McKinley County	NM	Joe F. Chepin	1986	45
179 6/8	23 5/8	22 7/8	17 2/8	6	5	Washoe County	NV	Gregory G. Koehl	1984	46
179 4/8	26 1/8	25 5/8	23 0/8	5	5	San Juan County	UT	Tom M. Carter	1988	47
179 2/8	25 1/8	24 3/8	20 2/8	5	6	Coconino County	AZ	Andrew Stevens	1991	48
179 1/8	23 4/8	25 7/8	20 1/8	4	5	El Paso County	CO	Greg Walters	1987	49
178 7/8	25 0/8	24 2/8	18 7/8	5	5	Delta County	CO	Wright W. Allen, Sr.	1974	50
178 6/8	26 6/8	25 4/8	26 3/8	7	6	Washington County	UT	Wayne J. Wittwer	1989	51
178 6/8	25 2/8	25 4/8	21 0/8	5	5	Mesa County	CO	Burt Pitchford	1989	51
178 4/8	22 6/8	22 3/8	21 4/8	5	5	Lander County	NV	Don Cunningham	1990	53
178 4/8	23 2/8	23 2/8	23 2/8	5	5	San Juan County	UT	Gary A. Clum	1990	53
178 2/8	23 2/8	23 4/8	19 2/8	5	5	Larimer County	CO	Coy K. Glenn	1966	55
177 5/8	20 0/8	20 2/8	19 7/8	6	6	Box Elder County	UT	Gene Warr	1988	56
177 4/8	23 5/8	22 3/8	25 2/8	6	6	Wayne County	UT	Jay M. Ogden	1985	57
177 4/8	24 3/8	24 1/8	18 0/8	5	5	Coconino County	AZ	Joel Cullum	1989	57
177 4/8	23 0/8	22 7/8	19 6/8	5	5	Clear Creek County	CO	Scott George	1991	57
177 2/8	24 0/8	25 3/8	21 3/8	5	6	Valley County	ID	Paul Medel	1991	60
177 1/8	25 0/8	25 0/8	23 1/8	4	4	Carbon County	UT	Dee R. Smith	1985	61
177 0/8	25 6/8	25 6/8	23 6/8	4	5	Moffat County	CO	Joe Theaman	1990	62
176 6/8	23 7/8	23 5/8	25 2/8	6	6	High Prairie	ALB	Dave Dickson/Don Lind	1989	63
176 5/8	24 7/8	25 3/8	19 3/8	5	5	Sanpete County	UT	Kim D. Olsen	1978	64
176 5/8	23 6/8	23 5/8	23 1/8	5	6	Garfield County	UT	Vince Dimiceli	1982	64
176 4/8	23 4/8	24 3/8	17 0/8	5	5	White Pine County	NV	Fred C. Church	1987	66
176 3/8	25 3/8	24 2/8	19 5/8	5	5	Eagle County	CO	Mark Vogt	1987	67
176 1/8	25 1/8	26 1/8	25 1/8	6	5	Mesa County	CO	Gary R. Haske	1977	68
176 1/8	25 4/8	25 6/8	20 7/8	5	4	San Juan County	UT	Bill Krenz	1990	68
175 6/8	22 2/8	23 2/8	28 3/8	5	5	Delta County	CO	Roy G. Burton	1975	70
175 4/8	22 1/8	21 3/8	18 6/8	6	6	El Paso County	CO	Freeman Howard	1988	71
175 3/8	21 2/8	20 0/8	16 1/8	5	5	Routt County	CO	John P. Leick	1992	72
175 1/8	24 0/8	24 3/8	22 1/8	5	5	Mesa County	CO	Scott G. Poppy	1991	73
175 0/8	22 5/8	25 4/8	22 0/8	4	4	Churchill County	NV	David A. Coverston	1988	74
174 4/8	22 5/8	21 6/8	19 1/8	7	6	San Juan County	UT	David Larsen	1989	75
174 4/8	22 0/8	22 6/8	20 6/8	5	5	Pitkin County	CO	Marc C. McKinney	1991	75
174 3/8	24 2/8	24 1/8	23 3/8	5	5	Elko County	NV	Mike Tate	1987	77
174 2/8	21 6/8	22 1/8	19 2/8	5	5	Fremont County	WY	Dwight Sempert	1992	78
173 7/8	27 5/8	27 6/8	26 4/8	6	7	Grand County	UT	Dee R. Smith	1983	79
173 6/8	22 4/8	20 6/8	17 2/8	5	5	Carbon County	UT	Robert W. Scott	1987	80
173 4/8	20 4/8	21 6/8	18 4/8	5	5	Washington County	UT	Bob McGill	1992	81
173 3/8	26 0/8	24 4/8	22 5/8	5	5	Sandoval County	NM	Steve Alderete	1989	82
173 2/8	23 4/8	23 7/8	22 1/8	6	5	Routt County	CO	Lonny Vanatta	1991	83
173 1/8	24 2/8	25 7/8	21 5/8	6	6	Elko County	NV	Steven P. Adams	1986	84
172 7/8	25 1/8	23 6/8	26 1/8	7	7	Carbon County	UT	Robert L. Kampen	1991	85
172 6/8	22 4/8	22 7/8	22 0/8	5	5	Summit County	UT	Robert B. Jentzsch	1992	86
172 2/8	24 4/8	24 3/8	21 6/8	8	9	Mesa County	CO	Franklin E. Adams	1971	87
172 0/8	24 3/8	25 4/8	20 0/8	5	4	Garfield County	UT	Jim Hamberlin	1989	88
172 0/8	25 1/8	24 7/8	24 0/8	6	5	Lassen County	CA	Rick Pollard	1991	88
171 7/8	23 3/8	23 4/8	21 6/8	6	5	Campbell County	WY	Russell Guerndt	1992	90
171 6/8	22 6/8	23 5/8	17 1/8	5	5	Davis County	UT	David Miller	1987	91
171 6/8	22 6/8	22 4/8	23 0/8	4	4	Piute County	UT	Joe Hughes	1991	91
171 3/8	21 3/8	21 0/8	20 7/8	5	5	San Juan County	UT	Gary D. Whited	1985	93
171 3/8	22 4/8	21 7/8	22 3/8	5	5	San Juan County	UT	Don R. Logston	1991	93
171 3/8	24 3/8	20 5/8	23 5/8	5	6	Morgan County	UT	Tommy Land	1992	93
171 2/8	22 2/8	22 6/8	21 1/8	6	5	Montezuma County	CO	Don Miller	1990	96

SCORE	LENGTH OF MAIN BEAM		INSIDE SPREAD	NUMBER OF POINTS		AREA	STATE/ PROVINCE	HUNTER'S NAME	DATE	RANK
	R	L		R	L					
171 0/8	19 6/8	20 3/8	16 2/8	5	5	Emery County	UT	Kelly Farnsworth	1989	97
170 7/8	22 5/8	23 2/8	19 2/8	5	6	Humboldt County	NV	Michael J. Bradeen	1987	98
170 7/8	22 6/8	22 5/8	19 6/8	5	6	Mesa County	CO	Lee Ayres	1988	98
170 3/8	24 3/8	23 6/8	20 5/8	5	6	Delta County	CO	T. C. Gonyo	1975	100
169 7/8	23 0/8	23 1/8	20 5/8	5	5	Coconino County	AZ	DeeAnn Robinson	1989	101
169 5/8	26 4/8	25 5/8	21 5/8	5	5	Montrose County	CO	David P. Flanagan	1988	102
169 5/8	21 3/8	23 1/8	18 1/8	6	6	Fremont County	CO	J. V. Fernandez	1991	102
169 3/8	22 1/8	21 7/8	19 5/8	5	5	San Juan County	UT	Jim Phillips, Jr.	1988	104
169 2/8	25 6/8	25 1/8	21 6/8	5	4	Kane County	UT	Ryan C. Anderson	1990	105
169 2/8	21 6/8	21 6/8	19 2/8	5	5	Wayne County	UT	Verlyn Durfey	1992	105
169 1/8	22 2/8	22 7/8	19 7/8	5	5	White Pine County	NV	Gary Campbell	1988	107
169 1/8	23 6/8	23 5/8	19 3/8	5	4	Beaver County	UT	Gary Brown	1989	107
169 1/8	25 3/8	24 2/8	19 5/8	7	6	Duchesne County	UT	Lance Denver	1991	107
169 0/8	22 2/8	21 3/8	17 6/8	5	5	Mesa County	CO	C. E. Williams	1978	110
169 0/8	24 2/8	21 2/8	19 4/8	5	4	Custer County	CO	Tommy G. Flower	1988	110
169 0/8	21 1/8	21 7/8	22 5/8	6	6	Emery County	UT	Robert Lee Thompson	1989	110
169 0/8	23 5/8	25 1/8	21 4/8	5	5	Tooele County	UT	Steven Kirkham	1991	110
168 7/8	23 0/8	22 4/8	22 1/8	5	5	Wayne County	UT	Jay Clayson	1972	114
168 7/8	25 7/8	23 4/8	21 3/8	7	6	Coconino County	AZ	Sean Howard	1990	114
168 7/8	23 0/8	22 1/8	20 7/8	5	5	Three Hills	ALB	Doug Simpson	1990	114
168 6/8	23 6/8	24 4/8	24 6/8	5	5	Emery County	UT	Dale Richards	1990	117
168 6/8	23 1/8	23 1/8	18 5/8	5	6	Coconino County	AZ	Kasey Long	1991	117
168 5/8	24 0/8	24 4/8	21 1/8	4	5	Mesa County	CO	Bill Stonebraker	1978	119
168 5/8	23 4/8	23 3/8	18 5/8	5	5	Humboldt County	NV	Ken Mallory	1984	119
168 5/8	25 1/8	24 6/8	22 7/8	5	5	San Juan County	UT	Dave O'Bagy	1987	119
168 4/8	21 4/8	22 1/8	17 2/8	5	5	Humboldt County	NV	Fred C. Church	1988	122
168 4/8	24 4/8	20 7/8	26 1/8	5	5	Elko County	NV	David Caldwell	1989	122
168 4/8	22 2/8	22 7/8	20 2/8	4	4	Millard County	UT	Rodney Thompson	1990	122
168 4/8	21 6/8	22 2/8	18 6/8	5	5	Morgan County	UT	Jeffery J. Petersen	1992	122
168 2/8	22 5/8	22 2/8	18 4/8	5	5	Ravalli County	MT	Robin C. Bolles	1990	126
168 2/8	25 5/8	25 6/8	23 0/8	5	5	Deschutes County	OR	Rick Rogerson	1991	126
167 7/8	23 2/8	23 3/8	20 5/8	5	5	San Juan County	UT	Stephan D. Zedney	1986	128
167 7/8	25 2/8	25 0/8	22 5/8	5	5	San Juan County	UT	Todd Hurst	1990	128
167 6/8	22 2/8	22 1/8	19 6/8	4	4	White Pine County	NV	Mike McDougall	1989	130
167 4/8	18 4/8	22 7/8	20 5/8	6	5	San Juan County	UT	Kenneth G. Kirkham	1991	131
167 4/8	24 0/8	24 4/8	20 6/8	5	4	Coconino County	AZ	Michael L. Wolfe	1991	131
167 1/8	22 6/8	23 5/8	21 5/8	5	5	Carbon County	UT	John Lilygren	1986	133
167 1/8	22 4/8	24 5/8	23 5/8	5	5	Kane County	UT	Floyd Harward	1992	133
167 0/8	22 5/8	21 4/8	20 4/8	5	5	Sevier County	UT	Michael R. Labrum	1988	135
167 0/8	23 3/8	23 6/8	22 2/8	6	6	Caribou County	ID	Sid Huntsman	1989	135
167 0/8	25 3/8	25 3/8	22 4/8	5	5	Kane County	UT	Steve Bruggeman	1992	135
166 7/8	23 1/8	23 2/8	23 0/8	6	6	Converse County	WY	Jeff Reynolds	1991	138
166 3/8	24 3/8	21 1/8	16 1/8	5	4	Greenlee County	AZ	Larry R. Marin	1990	139
166 2/8	21 6/8	21 7/8	21 4/8	5	5	Montrose County	CO	Terry James	1989	140
166 2/8	22 4/8	22 0/8	19 6/8	4	4	Bernalillo County	NM	John Haley	1989	140
166 0/8	21 0/8	22 0/8	19 4/8	5	5	Grand County	UT	Larry R. Randall	1971	142
166 0/8	22 3/8	23 7/8	21 0/8	4	4	Mesa County	CO	James Paul Clover	1991	142
165 6/8	24 5/8	24 2/8	23 2/8	5	5	Humboldt County	NV	Gregg Welch	1987	144
165 6/8	22 4/8	23 5/8	14 2/8	5	4	Wallowa County	OR	Ron W. Schneider	1988	144
165 5/8	24 3/8	24 3/8	23 7/8	5	5	Garfield County	UT	Douglas Shelby	1991	146
165 5/8	22 1/8	21 6/8	20 0/8	8	7	Culberson County	TX	Sam Sowders	1991	146
165 4/8	22 7/8	24 0/8	24 0/8	5	5	Montrose County	CO	Richard Reddy	1988	148
165 4/8	24 1/8	24 3/8	21 4/8	7	6	Modoc County	CA	Anthony Moscarelli	1988	148
165 4/8	21 6/8	22 2/8	19 6/8	5	5	Garfield County	UT	Steven L. Christensen	1989	148
165 3/8	23 7/8	23 7/8	24 2/8	5	4	Saguache County	CO	Lloyd "Cart" Patterson	1990	151
165 3/8	25 0/8	25 5/8	25 1/8	6	5	Torrence County	NM	Butch Allen	1992	151
165 2/8	23 4/8	23 4/8	23 4/8	5	5	Garfield County	UT	Frank S. Hatch	1990	153
165 0/8	21 0/8	20 7/8	22 6/8	4	4	Emery County	UT	Max W. Lopan	1983	154
165 0/8	20 4/8	21 7/8	19 6/8	4	4	Rich County	UT	Don Keady	1992	154
164 6/8	18 4/8	20 3/8	16 2/8	5	5	Boulder County	CO	Daniel McCaffrey	1988	156
164 6/8	23 2/8	22 7/8	19 6/8	5	5	Beaver County	UT	Jack Smith	1989	156
164 4/8	23 0/8	22 7/8	22 5/8	5	6	Baker County	OR	Bruce Cockhill	1988	158
164 3/8	24 2/8	24 3/8	21 7/8	6	5	La Plata County	CO	Dave Gerhardt	1977	159
164 3/8	21 0/8	21 6/8	17 7/8	5	5	Mesa County	CO	Marvin Cochran	1988	159
164 3/8	24 3/8	25 1/8	26 5/8	5	5	San Juan County	UT	Todd Hurst	1989	159
164 2/8	23 0/8	23 0/8	24 6/8	5	5	Uintah County	UT	Terry Searle	1974	162
164 2/8	26 5/8	25 7/8	25 0/8	5	5	Kane County	UT	Harry W. Langston	1992	162
164 1/8	24 2/8	24 7/8	22 0/8	7	7	Box Elder County	UT	Pat Warr	1987	164
164 1/8	25 5/8	24 5/8	25 6/8	4	4	Humboldt County	NV	Tip Goldston	1988	164
164 1/8	24 1/8	23 2/8	22 5/8	5	5	Washington County	UT	John Gibson	1991	164

SCORE	LENGTH OF MAIN BEAM R	LENGTH OF MAIN BEAM L	INSIDE SPREAD	NUMBER OF POINTS R	NUMBER OF POINTS L	AREA	STATE/ PROVINCE	HUNTER'S NAME	DATE	RANK
164 0/8	22 4/8	23 2/8	21 0/8	6	6	San Juan County	UT	John Richardson	1987	167
164 0/8	23 1/8	22 6/8	22 6/8	5	5	Washoe County	NV	Rick Manion	1988	167
163 7/8	22 0/8	22 3/8	19 1/8	5	5	Valley County	ID	David L. Ekmark	1983	169
163 7/8	22 1/8	21 6/8	16 7/8	5	5	Sevier County	UT	Bruce Crane	1989	169
163 6/8	22 6/8	22 4/8	22 0/8	5	5	Kane County	UT	Kurt Wood	1991	171
163 5/8	21 3/8	22 3/8	21 1/8	5	5	Elko County	NV	Bill G. Davis, Sr.	1987	172
163 5/8	23 0/8	21 2/8	20 1/8	5	5	Huerfano County	CO	R. Kirk Ehren	1987	172
163 4/8	21 2/8	21 0/8	18 4/8	5	6	Rich County	UT	David D. Roberts	1990	174
163 3/8	22 3/8	22 6/8	22 3/8	5	5	Sevier County	UT	Paul H. Laver	1981	175
163 3/8	23 1/8	22 6/8	22 5/8	5	5	Washington County	UT	Ernie Hafen	1988	175
163 2/8	23 6/8	23 5/8	24 2/8	4	5	McKinley County	NM	Teddy Orr	1988	177
163 0/8	25 0/8	24 7/8	23 2/8	4	5	Morgan County	UT	Robert G. Petersen	1988	178
162 7/8	23 4/8	25 0/8	18 7/8	5	5	Elko County	NV	Ted Simpson	1989	179
162 6/8	21 4/8	21 6/8	21 0/8	5	6	Beaver County	UT	Gary Hoffer	1980	180
162 6/8	26 2/8	24 7/8	27 1/8	4	5	Iron County	UT	Neil Stratton	1990	180
162 5/8	22 4/8	23 2/8	19 3/8	5	5	Iron County	UT	Troy Truce Truman	1990	182
162 5/8	22 5/8	22 3/8	17 7/8	6	5	Weber County	UT	Craig P. Mitton	1992	182
162 4/8	22 0/8	22 3/8	19 2/8	5	7	Colfax County	NM	Mike Reid	1991	184
162 3/8	21 2/8	23 0/8	22 1/8	5	5	Garfield County	CO	Rod Van DeGraaf	1989	185
162 2/8	25 7/8	24 7/8	20 6/8	6	5	Bonner County	ID	Brian T. Farley	1980	186
162 1/8	21 4/8	22 2/8	21 5/8	5	5	Carbon County	UT	Don R. Logston	1989	187
162 1/8	22 0/8	23 0/8	21 7/8	5	5	Washington County	UT	Dana A. Truman	1989	187
162 1/8	22 1/8	21 4/8	19 7/8	5	6	Washoe County	NV	Mike Ellena	1991	187
162 1/8	22 5/8	22 1/8	22 6/8	5	5	Lassen County	CA	Steve Thurmon	1992	187
162 0/8	23 5/8	21 3/8	16 0/8	4	4	Cache County	UT	Valerie V. Parker	1989	191
162 0/8	22 4/8	22 7/8	22 2/8	5	5	Rich County	UT	Matthew Hogle	1992	191
161 5/8	23 2/8	21 6/8	23 1/8	4	5	Montrose County	CO	Dan Williams	1989	193
161 3/8	24 1/8	25 6/8	24 7/8	5	4	San Juan County	UT	Todd Hinkins	1985	194
161 2/8	25 0/8	23 2/8	25 0/8	5	6	Washoe County	NV	Dan Klebenow	1990	195
161 0/8	23 1/8	24 4/8	21 0/8	3	4	Albany County	WY	Nathan L. Andersohn	1987	196
161 0/8	27 3/8	26 1/8	21 6/8	5	5	Eureka County	NV	Gregg Welch	1990	196
160 6/8	20 7/8	22 4/8	18 4/8	5	5	Mesa County	CO	Gene Barcak	1980	198
160 6/8	26 7/8	26 6/8	23 1/8	7	5	Coconino County	AZ	Brian Hunter	1990	198
160 6/8	24 2/8	22 2/8	18 0/8	5	5	Humboldt County	NV	Robert Reed	1991	198
160 6/8	22 6/8	21 3/8	20 0/8	5	6	Coconino County	AZ	Mark Cole Brown	1991	198
160 4/8	21 2/8	20 6/8	21 7/8	5	5	Coconino County	AZ	James Ferris, Jr.	1989	202
160 4/8	22 0/8	22 0/8	20 6/8	5	5	Sevier County	UT	Jeffrey D. Barnes	1990	202
160 1/8	21 0/8	20 7/8	20 3/8	4	4	La Plata County	CO	Zack Morgan	1989	204
160 1/8	21 2/8	21 5/8	23 7/8	4	4	Sandoval County	NM	Alan Kernodle	1989	204
160 1/8	21 5/8	20 7/8	17 7/8	5	5	Duchesne County	UT	Lance Denver	1990	204
160 0/8	19 3/8	22 6/8	20 3/8	6	5	Park County	CO	John D. Hambleton	1974	207
160 0/8	22 0/8	22 2/8	23 7/8	5	5	Elko County	NV	Marty Eldridge	1991	207
160 0/8	19 1/8	20 6/8	16 6/8	5	5	Morgan County	UT	Cal Bambrough	1992	207
159 6/8	22 7/8	21 3/8	19 6/8	5	5	Huerfano County	CO	Tommy Mackey	1989	210
159 5/8	22 2/8	22 1/8	21 7/8	5	5	Pershing County	NV	Earl L. Malay	1990	211
159 4/8	26 1/8	24 4/8	25 2/8	4	5	San Juan County	UT	Larry Mathis	1985	212
159 4/8	22 4/8	22 5/8	21 4/8	5	5	Greenlee County	AZ	Jim Lusk	1988	212
159 3/8	23 7/8	23 1/8	25 2/8	5	5	Grand County	UT	Gordon Young	1990	214
159 2/8	22 4/8	21 4/8	22 4/8	5	5	Harding County	SD	Mike Barrett	1976	215
159 1/8	21 0/8	23 7/8	19 2/8	6	6	Coconino County	AZ	Cisco E. Folk	1988	216
159 1/8	21 7/8	22 0/8	19 3/8	6	6	Montrose County	CO	Carlos Burleson	1990	216
158 7/8	19 6/8	18 4/8	15 5/8	6	5	Sevier County	UT	Jade D. Shepard	1988	218
158 7/8	21 7/8	23 0/8	17 5/8	5	5	Dolores County	CO	Larry Edwards	1990	218
158 7/8	21 2/8	21 0/8	18 1/8	6	6	Yavapai County	AZ	Michael R. Vigueria	1990	218
158 7/8	23 3/8	23 2/8	24 2/8	4	4	Grand County	CO	Lehman Jaggers	1991	218
158 6/8	23 4/8	24 0/8	23 4/8	4	4	Elko County	NV	Ron McGuire	1987	222
158 5/8	20 7/8	22 5/8	16 3/8	5	5	Carbon County	UT	Ed Sitton	1991	223
158 4/8	22 7/8	20 7/8	18 6/8	5	5	Park County	CO	Marvin Clyncke	1978	224
158 3/8	23 6/8	23 4/8	20 3/8	4	3	Box Elder County	UT	Shawn Wadsworth	1990	225
158 3/8	22 1/8	21 6/8	24 2/8	5	5	Elko County	NV	Felton Hickman	1991	225
158 3/8	23 7/8	21 6/8	23 5/8	4	6	Elko County	NV	Kurt W. Carpenter	1991	225
158 3/8	21 7/8	22 4/8	21 1/8	4	4	Tooele County	UT	Michael L. Farr	1991	225
158 2/8	20 7/8	21 3/8	21 0/8	5	5	Otero County	NM	Brad A. King	1987	229
158 2/8	22 3/8	21 5/8	17 6/8	5	5	Weber County	UT	David A. Layton	1990	229
158 1/8	22 0/8	22 1/8	19 6/8	6	5	Mesa County	CO	Keith R. Hardy	1987	231
158 1/8	22 0/8	23 1/8	19 7/8	7	6	Elko County	NV	John Bell	1989	231
158 1/8	23 4/8	24 5/8	21 3/8	4	5	Cache County	UT	Mike Barrett	1992	231
158 0/8	23 7/8	22 5/8	23 0/8	7	6	San Juan County	UT	Troy M. Miller	1985	234
158 0/8	22 5/8	23 1/8	19 6/8	5	5	Humboldt County	NV	Gregg Welch	1989	234
157 5/8	21 3/8	22 0/8	19 1/8	5	5	Mesa County	CO	Dr. F. D. Elias	1986	236

SCORE	LENGTH OF MAIN BEAM		INSIDE SPREAD	NUMBER OF POINTS		AREA	STATE/ PROVINCE	HUNTER'S NAME	DATE	RANK
	R	L		R	L					
157 5/8	21 5/8	22 5/8	21 3/8	5	5	Box Elder County	UT	Gene Warr	1987	236
157 5/8	23 0/8	23 2/8	16 5/8	5	5	Montrose County	CO	Greg Blackburn	1989	236
157 5/8	20 7/8	22 0/8	17 6/8	6	6	Morgan County	UT	Hugh H. Hogle	1990	236
157 4/8	23 0/8	24 4/8	20 7/8	7	4	Uintah County	UT	Mark Smolen	1989	240
157 4/8	20 2/8	18 6/8	17 2/8	5	5	Garfield County	UT	Steve Sheehy	1991	240
157 4/8	23 3/8	23 2/8	18 5/8	6	6	Carbon County	UT	David A. Fox	1991	240
157 2/8	25 2/8	23 5/8	21 2/8	4	5	Dolores County	CO	Buddy MacFarlane	1984	243
157 2/8	20 6/8	20 1/8	19 0/8	5	5	Grand County	UT	Dave Scott	1989	243
157 2/8	22 2/8	21 4/8	23 3/8	4	4	Coconino County	AZ	John Toot	1990	243
157 1/8	23 2/8	22 5/8	20 0/8	7	6	Duchesne County	UT	Steven Partridge	1986	246
157 1/8	20 6/8	21 3/8	21 5/8	5	5	Montezuma County	CO	Carolyn Myers	1988	246
157 1/8	23 1/8	23 5/8	20 0/8	6	6	Humboldt County	NV	Ric Manion	1992	246
157 0/8	19 5/8	22 4/8	19 2/8	6	5	Garfield County	MT	Dean Rogge	1990	249
156 7/8	23 6/8	24 0/8	21 7/8	6	6	Delta County	CO	Lou Rollenhagen	1986	250
156 7/8	20 4/8	21 0/8	19 7/8	5	5	Coconino County	AZ	John Diedrich	1990	250
156 7/8	20 7/8	22 2/8	17 7/8	5	5	Carbon County	UT	Michael A. Baca	1991	250
156 6/8	23 0/8	23 1/8	21 0/8	5	5	Moffat County	CO	Glenn Pritchard	1975	253
156 6/8	21 4/8	21 1/8	15 7/8	6	5	Jackson County	CO	Brian McFarlane	1989	253
156 6/8	23 2/8	23 1/8	17 6/8	5	5	Elko County	NV	Rick Mason	1990	253
156 5/8	21 7/8	21 4/8	18 1/8	5	5	Summit County	UT	Max F. Park	1979	256
156 5/8	21 5/8	23 1/8	16 7/8	5	5	Tatlayoko Lake	BC	Glenn Dreger	1987	256
156 4/8	21 1/8	22 2/8	21 6/8	5	5	Converse County	WY	Bret Frye	1991	258
156 4/8	22 2/8	23 4/8	19 2/8	5	5	Elko County	NV	Terrill Riggs	1992	258
156 3/8	25 4/8	26 0/8	24 2/8	6	7	Kane County	UT	Jim Ryan	1990	260
156 3/8	26 6/8	25 0/8	21 3/8	4	4	Sevier County	UT	Jon Huff	1991	260
156 3/8	21 5/8	21 2/8	19 5/8	5	5	Nevada County	CA	David W. Rickert II	1992	260
156 0/8	20 7/8	19 3/8	16 6/8	5	5	Douglas County	CO	Reggie Spiegelberg	1990	263
155 7/8	21 5/8	22 2/8	19 1/8	5	5	San Juan County	UT	Roy Hampton	1987	264
155 6/8	20 2/8	21 1/8	17 4/8	5	5	Beaver County	UT	Gordon Tattersall	1990	265
155 5/8	21 0/8	21 4/8	19 1/8	5	5	Mesa County	CO	Roger Dale Burton II	1988	266
155 5/8	22 2/8	22 0/8	18 5/8	5	7	Catron County	NM	Owen Lockwood	1992	266
155 4/8	22 7/8	22 0/8	23 3/8	4	7	Mesa County	CO	Ronald L. Gullickson	1985	268
155 4/8	23 4/8	24 2/8	23 4/8	5	6	Washoe County	NV	T.C. McMillan	1987	268
155 4/8	21 1/8	22 5/8	19 6/8	5	4	La Plata County	CO	Terry Sanders	1987	268
155 4/8	21 6/8	20 7/8	18 4/8	5	5	Fremont County	CO	John Durham	1988	268
155 3/8	23 6/8	23 4/8	22 3/8	4	5	Elko County	NV	John Dits	1986	272
155 3/8	21 5/8	23 0/8	16 5/8	5	5	Catron County	NM	Kenneth Jay Jennings	1990	272
155 2/8	21 0/8	21 5/8	16 5/8	6	7	Coconino County	AZ	Ronnie P. Gifford	1986	274
155 2/8	23 5/8	24 3/8	17 6/8	4	5	Grant County	NM	Neddie B. Francisco	1991	274
155 0/8	22 0/8	21 4/8	21 0/8	6	5	Sevier County	UT	David R. Scott	1978	276
155 0/8	24 4/8	23 3/8	22 4/8	3	4	Washoe County	NV	Tom Hauptman	1988	276
154 6/8	24 4/8	22 4/8	18 2/8	5	5	Washoe County	NV	C. J. Coleman	1981	278
154 6/8	23 0/8	21 4/8	20 4/8	4	4	Rich County	UT	Earl Parker	1988	278
154 5/8	22 5/8	22 2/8	20 4/8	7	6	Coconino County	AZ	Larry Kindred	1990	280
154 5/8	19 2/8	20 1/8	17 7/8	7	5	Fergus County	MT	Richard Moeller	1991	280
154 5/8	23 7/8	21 1/8	22 7/8	5	5	Lassen County	CA	Robert Flores	1992	280
154 4/8	20 3/8	20 7/8	18 6/8	5	5	Elko County	NV	Doug Montrose	1987	283
154 3/8	22 6/8	23 5/8	18 7/8	5	5	El Paso County	CO	Dave Ondriezek	1987	284
154 3/8	24 0/8	22 4/8	23 1/8	5	5	San Juan County	UT	Philip E. Jones	1988	284
154 3/8	19 7/8	19 6/8	17 1/8	5	5	Elko County	NV	Randy Long	1990	284
154 1/8	21 2/8	21 3/8	19 5/8	5	5	Routt County	CO	Barry J. Smith	1976	287
154 1/8	25 4/8	24 6/8	25 5/8	5	6	San Juan County	UT	Jim Scott	1987	287
154 1/8	22 1/8	23 4/8	20 1/8	5	4	Washington County	UT	Troy Jolley	1990	287
154 0/8	20 6/8	20 0/8	22 7/8	4	4	Elko County	NV	Bill Krenz	1987	290
153 7/8	23 4/8	23 2/8	20 1/8	4	4	San Juan County	UT	Phillip C. Dalrymple	1990	291
153 6/8	22 4/8	22 6/8	20 6/8	4	4	Moffat County	CO	Dennis H. Slagle	1987	292
153 4/8	20 4/8	24 2/8	21 6/8	5	5	Dolores County	CO	Robert Myers	1984	293
153 4/8	24 2/8	25 3/8	21 2/8	5	4	Catron County	NM	Ignacio N. Chavez	1988	293
153 3/8	20 7/8	20 2/8	19 3/8	6	6	Mesa County	CO	Dennis C. Faulkenberry	1986	295
153 1/8	24 1/8	23 7/8	17 0/8	5	5	Carbon County	UT	Jared Gunter	1991	296
153 0/8	23 4/8	24 4/8	20 6/8	5	5	Morgan County	UT	Hugh H. Hogle	1991	297
152 6/8	22 2/8	20 6/8	19 6/8	4	4	Lake County	OR	Ronald Lindquist	1988	298
152 5/8	21 3/8	23 3/8	16 5/8	5	5	Mesa County	CO	Thomas M. Catlin	1983	299
152 4/8	22 0/8	21 7/8	20 0/8	5	5	Mesa County	CO	Jeff J Schaffner	1988	300
152 4/8	23 2/8	22 1/8	19 6/8	5	4	Carbon County	UT	Cathy Gunter	1991	300
152 4/8	20 7/8	20 4/8	17 6/8	5	5	Warner	ALB	Dale L. Halmrast	1991	300
152 3/8	25 3/8	23 6/8	23 2/8	5	5	Sanpete County	UT	Brad Gull	1989	303
152 2/8	19 5/8	20 2/8	19 7/8	6	6	San Juan County	UT	D. Bruce Whited	1985	304
152 0/8	21 4/8	21 3/8	20 0/8	5	5	Tooele County	UT	Les Blue	1985	305
152 0/8	23 1/8	24 0/8	25 5/8	4	5	Elko County	NV	Bill R. Davis	1987	305

MULE DEER (*Typical Velvet Antlers*)

Score	Length of Main Beam R	L	Inside Spread	Number of Points R	L	Area	State/ Province	Hunter's Name	Date	Rank
152 0/8	20 7/8	21 6/8	22 3/8	5	4	Catron County	NM	Bill Krenz	1989	305
152 0/8	21 0/8	22 4/8	23 3/8	5	4	San Juan County	UT	Don Merrell	1991	305
151 6/8	22 6/8	22 2/8	21 2/8	5	5	Lassen County	CA	Paul Bonnett	1989	309
151 6/8	23 5/8	22 5/8	19 3/8	5	5	Elko County	NV	Dave Justmann	1990	309
151 5/8	21 3/8	22 5/8	20 1/8	4	4	Harney County	OR	Steve Savage	1980	311
151 3/8	20 7/8	21 0/8	16 7/8	5	5	Saguache County	CO	Al Gurule	1987	312
151 3/8	23 0/8	23 0/8	19 2/8	5	6	Routt County	CO	Roy McCann	1990	312
151 3/8	20 5/8	21 0/8	19 1/8	5	5	Rich County	UT	Curt Pilcher	1992	312
151 2/8	20 4/8	20 6/8	21 4/8	5	6	Gallatin County	MT	Mark Heckel	1982	315
151 2/8	22 1/8	21 6/8	19 4/8	5	5	Wembley	ALB	Larry Scriba	1992	315
151 1/8	20 6/8	19 6/8	17 1/8	4	4	Mesa County	CO	Doug Walker	1988	317
151 1/8	18 2/8	18 6/8	17 2/8	6	5	Iron County	UT	Steven Joseph Sillitoe	1990	317
151 1/8	21 5/8	22 3/8	16 3/8	5	5	Carbon County	UT	Brad Timothy	1992	317
150 7/8	22 4/8	23 0/8	20 7/8	5	4	Carbon County	UT	Joseph Bongiovi	1988	320
150 7/8	23 2/8	23 3/8	20 5/8	5	4	San Juan County	UT	Joe P. Twitchell, Jr.	1990	320
150 6/8	22 2/8	20 0/8	21 4/8	5	5	Rio Blanco County	CO	Stanley Lauriski	1985	322
150 6/8	25 7/8	22 0/8	22 0/8	5	5	Carter County	MT	Jamie Byrne	1990	322
150 6/8	22 5/8	24 0/8	21 4/8	5	4	Garfield County	UT	Steve Benvegnu	1992	322
150 5/8	20 5/8	21 2/8	20 2/8	6	5	Coconino County	AZ	Clifford White	1984	325
150 5/8	19 7/8	19 5/8	17 1/8	4	5	Garfield County	UT	Mayben Crane	1990	325
150 2/8	24 7/8	26 0/8	24 2/8	5	4	Milk River	ALB	Giuliano Coslovi	1991	327
150 0/8	22 3/8	22 3/8	19 4/8	4	4	Shasta County	CA	Stacy Meyer	1989	328
149 7/8	18 5/8	19 2/8	15 1/8	5	5	Utah County	UT	Michael D. Lewis	1986	329
149 6/8	21 0/8	21 0/8	23 2/8	5	5	Sanpete County	UT	Gregg Larsen	1979	330
149 6/8	21 5/8	23 6/8	21 6/8	5	5	Klamath County	OR	Chuck Warner	1982	330
149 6/8	21 0/8	20 6/8	18 6/8	4	4	Wheeler County	OR	Pat Morton	1988	330
149 5/8	21 4/8	20 2/8	16 0/8	5	4	Grand County	UT	Jay Verzuh	1985	333
149 5/8	25 0/8	23 2/8	23 3/8	3	5	Rumsey	ALB	Steve Ouwerkerk	1991	333
149 4/8	20 2/8	19 7/8	22 2/8	5	5	Elko County	NV	Jerry Vega	1987	335
149 4/8	21 0/8	21 6/8	16 2/8	6	6	Sevier County	UT	Lynn Bryson	1988	335
149 3/8	21 1/8	20 0/8	23 0/8	5	5	Humboldt County	NV	Wayne Testolin	1991	337
149 2/8	21 6/8	22 2/8	28 1/8	3	3	Cibola County	NM	Benny Garcia	1987	338
149 2/8	21 7/8	21 4/8	18 2/8	5	5	White Pine County	NV	Danny Cracraft	1988	338
149 2/8	20 1/8	20 0/8	16 0/8	5	5	Saguache County	CO	Dirk Dieterich	1988	338
149 0/8	21 5/8	21 3/8	16 3/8	6	5	Lincoln County	WY	Jim Fowler	1991	341
148 7/8	20 2/8	20 3/8	20 1/8	5	6	McKenzie County	ND	DuWayne Larson	1990	342
148 5/8	21 3/8	21 6/8	19 1/8	5	5	Cache County	UT	Robert Bronson	1992	343
148 3/8	22 4/8	21 4/8	20 3/8	5	4	Iron County	UT	David Howard	1989	344
148 1/8	25 5/8	24 4/8	26 4/8	6	4	Washoe County	NV	Dave Schopper	1981	345
148 1/8	18 4/8	18 7/8	15 3/8	5	5	Carbon County	UT	Demar Guymon	1991	345
147 7/8	22 6/8	23 4/8	22 1/8	5	5	San Juan County	UT	Steve Stumbo	1990	347
147 6/8	23 2/8	23 7/8	20 0/8	3	3	Grand County	UT	Dennis Ingram	1986	348
147 2/8	22 5/8	23 0/8	18 4/8	5	6	Emery County	UT	Bob Jake Jacobsen	1975	349
147 2/8	23 5/8	23 7/8	21 4/8	4	4	McKenzie County	ND	Mike Robson	1990	349
147 0/8	23 6/8	22 7/8	26 6/8	4	5	Mesa County	CO	Jay Verzuh	1980	351
147 0/8	22 0/8	22 0/8	22 2/8	7	6	Kane County	UT	Tina Ryan	1990	351
146 7/8	22 4/8	24 4/8	19 1/8	5	4	Montezuma County	CO	William C. Shuster	1979	353
146 6/8	21 5/8	22 5/8	21 0/8	4	5	Delta County	CO	Robert Pollard, Jr.	1991	354
146 5/8	22 4/8	22 2/8	18 7/8	5	5	Moffat County	CO	Clint W. Powell	1988	355
146 4/8	24 2/8	23 2/8	20 6/8	5	6	Coconino County	AZ	Gregg Boudoures	1988	356
146 4/8	20 3/8	21 3/8	16 2/8	5	5	Carbon County	UT	Larry Schoenberger	1991	356
146 4/8	22 6/8	22 1/8	23 3/8	4	5	Churchill County	NV	Guy Fowler	1992	356
146 3/8	19 6/8	20 4/8	20 7/8	6	5	Mesa County	CO	Jay Verzuh	1981	359
146 3/8	20 5/8	20 6/8	17 3/8	4	4	Uintah County	UT	Kim D. Olsen	1985	359
146 1/8	22 6/8	23 1/8	18 0/8	5	6	Mesa County	CO	Terry Sears	1987	361
146 1/8	21 0/8	21 5/8	23 2/8	4	5	Coconino County	AZ	Rodolfo Montano	1991	361
145 7/8	20 0/8	20 6/8	16 1/8	4	5	Coconino County	AZ	Michael Magana	1988	363
145 5/8	20 5/8	19 3/8	18 3/8	6	5	San Juan County	UT	Ross Stokes	1989	364
145 5/8	19 4/8	20 0/8	16 7/8	4	4	Sheridan County	WY	Nelson Beane	1991	364
145 4/8	21 2/8	21 6/8	20 0/8	5	5	Grand County	UT	Joe Twitchell, Jr.	1986	366
145 3/8	22 1/8	22 3/8	21 0/8	6	6	Emery County	UT	Paul R. Brenneman	1985	367
145 1/8	22 5/8	21 4/8	20 7/8	5	5	Millard County	UT	David R. Scott	1964	368
145 1/8	19 0/8	20 2/8	18 5/8	4	5	Rich County	UT	Hugh H. Hogle	1989	368
145 1/8	21 6/8	22 0/8	20 5/8	5	5	San Juan County	UT	Kenneth F. Barton	1990	368

Mule Deer (Non-Typical Velvet Antlers)
Score: 233 5/8
Montrose County, Colorado - 1988
Hunter: Doug Aikin

MULE DEER (*Non-Typical Velvet Antlers*) *Odocoileus hemionus*
MINIMUM SCORE 160

and certain related subspecies

SCORE	LENGTH OF R MAIN BEAM L		INSIDE SPREAD	NUMBER OF R POINTS L		AREA	STATE/ PROVINCE	HUNTER'S NAME	DATE	RANK
233 5/8	29 5/8	27 4/8	26 7/8	7	9	Montrose County	CO	Doug Aikin	1988	1
228 6/8	25 2/8	27 2/8	19 3/8	12	8	Utah County	UT	Maurice T. Patterson	1971	2
227 3/8	26 4/8	26 5/8	20 7/8	8	7	White Pine County	NV	Tony Angelopoulos	1968	3
223 5/8	25 7/8	27 1/8	24 1/8	10	9	Jefferson County	CO	Daved English	1991	4
214 3/8	25 4/8	26 0/8	24 3/8	11	9	Caribou County	ID	Royce Brown	1984	5
214 3/8	22 1/8	21 3/8	21 7/8	12	9	Boise County	ID	Dan Higgs	1992	5
210 3/8	26 6/8	23 3/8	22 0/8	10	9	Mesa County	CO	Larry Stewart	1975	7
209 4/8	24 0/8	24 0/8	22 1/8	8	7	Kane County	UT	Marvin Thayn	1987	8
208 4/8	26 5/8	25 2/8	19 1/8	8	10	Box Elder County	UT	Peter D. Garcia III	1988	9
207 6/8	22 5/8	21 7/8	20 3/8	7	8	Sanpete County	UT	L. Boyd Brewer	1967	10
206 0/8	23 1/8	24 0/8	16 5/8	10	6	Sheridan County	WY	Stan Chiras	1989	11
204 7/8	24 5/8	24 4/8	21 2/8	10	6	Washoe County	NV	Michael Ellena	1992	12
203 3/8	23 0/8	25 1/8	25 4/8	13	8	Sheridan County	WY	Mike Barrett	1981	13
202 3/8	23 1/8	24 5/8	18 0/8	9	8	Eagle County	CO	Rudy Meyers	1974	14
202 3/8	21 3/8	22 4/8	20 0/8	8	8	Millard County	UT	Dennis Staley	1983	14
200 6/8	24 5/8	23 3/8	19 0/8	8	10	Duchesne County	UT	Randy Quick	1987	16
200 6/8	23 3/8	22 4/8	21 2/8	9	9	San Juan County	UT	Jeremy Harness	1991	16
197 4/8	22 2/8	22 5/8	23 1/8	9	8	Washoe County	NV	Thomas C. McMillan	1992	18
193 4/8	23 2/8	23 5/8	21 6/8	7	6	Saguache County	CO	Barry J. Smith	1987	19
193 1/8	23 3/8	23 2/8	19 7/8	8	7	Morgan County	UT	Dennis L. Shirley	1992	20
191 5/8	23 4/8	23 1/8	22 3/8	8	7	Pitkin County	CO	Glen L. Mahlum	1990	21
184 4/8	24 0/8	23 3/8	21 0/8	6	4	Lincoln County	NV	Rocky Chisholm	1988	22
183 2/8	24 0/8	22 7/8	23 0/8	10	7	Churchill County	NV	Gregg Tanner	1989	23
179 4/8	24 1/8	24 1/8	18 5/8	7	7	Baker County	OR	Chuck Warner	1989	24
177 6/8	25 7/8	25 5/8	22 1/8	8	6	Mesa County	CO	Thomas J. Hentrick	1972	25
175 6/8	24 6/8	26 6/8	20 1/8	4	9	Jackson County	CO	Rick Hatter	1986	26

216

World Record Whitetail Deer (Typical Antlers)
Score: 204 4/8
Peoria County, Illinois - 1965
Hunter: Melvin J. Johnson

WHITETAIL DEER *(Typical Antlers)*

Odocoileus virginianus
and certain related subspecies

MINIMUM SCORE 125

SCORE	LENGTH OF MAIN BEAM R	LENGTH OF MAIN BEAM L	INSIDE SPREAD	NUMBER OF POINTS R	NUMBER OF POINTS L	AREA	STATE/ PROVINCE	HUNTER'S NAME	DATE	RANK
204 4/8	27 5/8	26 6/8	23 5/8	7	6	Peoria County	IL	M. J. Johnson	1965	1
197 6/8	25 6/8	26 4/8	18 6/8	7	7	Monroe County	IA	Lloyd Goad	1962	2
197 6/8	29 1/8	30 2/8	20 4/8	6	5	Wright County	MN	Curt Van Lith	1986	2
197 1/8	30 0/8	27 7/8	29 0/8	6	7	Edmonton	ALB	Don McGarvey	1991	4
194 2/8	26 5/8	25 0/8	21 0/8	6	6	Jones County	IA	Robert L. Miller	1977	5
194 0/8	25 6/8	25 3/8	23 6/8	6	7	Logan County	CO	Stuart Clodfelder	1981	6
193 2/8	28 3/8	27 7/8	22 2/8	8	6	Jackson County	MI	Craig Calderone	1986	7
190 5/8	27 0/8	27 1/8	18 0/8	5	7	Warren County	IA	Richard Swim	1981	8
190 4/8	28 6/8	28 3/8	20 0/8	5	6	Parke County	IN	B. Dodd Porter	1985	9
189 1/8	27 3/8	28 6/8	20 1/8	8	7	Kearney County	NE	Robert Vrbsky	1978	10
188 1/8	28 6/8	27 3/8	22 2/8	8	8	Des Moines County	IA	Kevin Peterson	1989	11
186 1/8	25 3/8	24 0/8	16 7/8	6	8	Sumner County	KS	Greg Hill	1988	12
186 1/8	31 2/8	30 5/8	24 0/8	5	8	Morris County	KS	Craig Johnson	1991	12
185 1/8	25 7/8	26 6/8	20 3/8	9	7	Jackson County	IL	Mark Guetersloh	1990	14
183 2/8	29 1/8	28 3/8	20 4/8	5	6	Shawnee County	KS	Mark W. Young	1990	15
182 2/8	27 2/8	28 3/8	21 1/8	8	6	Jefferson County	KS	John Welborn	1982	16
182 0/8	26 5/8	28 6/8	22 1/8	6	7	Jefferson County	KS	Michael J. Rose	1982	17
181 7/8	28 6/8	27 0/8	21 6/8	5	7	Greenwood County	KS	Boyd Schneider	1984	18
181 7/8	26 6/8	26 5/8	21 7/8	7	6	Dakota County	MN	Eugene Lengsfeld	1985	18
181 7/8	25 3/8	27 3/8	21 3/8	5	5	Logan County	IL	Terry Lee Rich	1986	18
181 7/8	27 2/8	26 5/8	19 6/8	6	7	Jefferson County	OH	Brad L. Eibel	1988	18
181 6/8	26 1/8	26 4/8	17 6/8	5	5	Wabasha County	MN	Lee G. Partington	1971	22
181 6/8	27 5/8	27 7/8	21 4/8	5	5	Sussex County	DE	Donald Betts	1989	22
181 4/8	29 6/8	29 5/8	24 2/8	6	5	Keya Paha County	NE	Steve R. Pecsenye	1966	24
181 4/8	26 0/8	28 5/8	18 6/8	9	7	Fulton County	IL	Arnold Hegele	1968	24
181 4/8	26 5/8	26 7/8	24 4/8	5	6	North Norfolk	MAN	Lloyd Lintott	1986	24
180 5/8	26 6/8	26 4/8	20 5/8	5	5	Jefferson County	KS	Ron Artzer	1987	27
180 4/8	24 7/8	26 4/8	21 0/8	5	5	Henry County	IA	Jeff L. Weigert	1991	28
180 4/8	29 4/8	27 7/8	21 4/8	8	5	Ross County	OH	Gerald F. Hamm	1991	28
180 1/8	25 4/8	24 2/8	17 5/8	6	6	Winona County	MN	Kenneth W. Schreiber	1980	30
180 1/8	30 6/8	30 6/8	21 2/8	7	5	Mahoning County	OH	Robert A. Haney	1987	30
179 5/8	26 6/8	25 7/8	20 7/8	7	8	Lac qui Parle County	MN	Mary A. Barvels	1978	32
179 4/8	28 1/8	28 3/8	19 6/8	6	6	Clarke County	IA	Rodney D. Hommer	1990	33
179 3/8	26 2/8	26 5/8	17 3/8	5	5	Marshall County	SD	Phyllis Roehr	1976	34
179 1/8	28 1/8	27 7/8	24 6/8	5	6	Osage County	KS	Ralph Batchelor, Jr.	1985	35
179 0/8	25 7/8	25 7/8	22 1/8	6	6	Scotland County	MO	David Smith	1985	36
179 0/8	27 2/8	26 1/8	19 2/8	6	5	Wapello County	IA	Robert L. McDowell	1985	36
179 0/8	26 6/8	26 6/8	17 6/8	6	5	Edgar County	IL	Edward A. Inman	1985	36
179 0/8	27 3/8	27 7/8	19 3/8	7	7	Des Moines County	IA	Glen M. Thompson	1987	36
178 7/8	26 3/8	28 0/8	21 0/8	7	8	Washington County	IA	Ronald A. Murphy	1990	40
178 7/8	30 0/8	29 4/8	18 1/8	5	5	Whiteside County	IL	Bernard Higley, Jr.	1990	40
178 4/8	26 2/8	25 0/8	21 2/8	5	6	Meade County	KS	Tim Ross	1985	42
178 4/8	25 1/8	25 0/8	18 4/8	5	5	Fulton County	IL	Locie L. Murphy	1985	42
178 4/8	25 1/8	25 4/8	19 4/8	5	5	Firdale	MAN	Randy Bean	1988	42
178 3/8	25 6/8	26 4/8	21 2/8	7	8	McPherson County	KS	Larry Daniels	1967	45
178 0/8	27 5/8	27 3/8	21 4/8	5	5	Carroll County	IL	Art Heinze	1988	46
177 3/8	27 1/8	26 3/8	20 3/8	6	5	Greene County	IA	Roger V. Carlson	1973	47
177 3/8	28 3/8	28 1/8	18 6/8	6	6	Wayne County	OH	Gary E. Landry	1975	47
177 3/8	27 3/8	26 5/8	20 7/8	5	7	Jones County	IA	Ken Dausener	1984	47
177 3/8	25 2/8	25 1/8	16 4/8	8	6	Miami County	KS	Keith L. Groshong	1991	47
177 1/8	28 4/8	26 6/8	20 2/8	6	7	Washington County	IA	Ernie Aronson	1985	51
177 1/8	27 1/8	28 6/8	21 2/8	7	5	St. Croix County	WI	Phillip R. Hovde	1990	51
177 0/8	28 2/8	28 1/8	18 3/8	8	6	Baltimore County	MD	Richard B. Traband	1990	53
176 7/8	27 5/8	27 0/8	18 4/8	5	7	Will County	IL	David Davis	1990	54
176 6/8	25 2/8	25 0/8	23 4/8	6	6	Marshall County	KS	Ray A. Mosher	1966	55
176 6/8	26 4/8	25 6/8	20 2/8	6	6	Muscatine County	IA	Don McCullough	1980	55
176 6/8	27 4/8	26 0/8	22 7/8	7	5	McHenry County	IL	Gene Melby	1988	55
176 6/8	25 7/8	25 1/8	21 4/8	6	6	Kane County	IL	Mark DuLong	1991	55
176 4/8	25 7/8	25 3/8	21 4/8	10	10	Davis County	IA	Jeffrey A. Getz	1991	59
176 2/8	28 2/8	27 5/8	21 0/8	7	5	Houston County	MN	John Zahrte	1981	60
176 2/8	28 0/8	28 6/8	21 2/8	5	6	Kingman County	KS	Gerald Stroot	1981	60
176 1/8	25 1/8	26 1/8	21 0/8	7	5	Lewis County	KY	Alfred Simms	1985	62
176 1/8	28 3/8	27 4/8	25 1/8	7	7	Clay County	KS	Larry L. Thompson	1988	62
176 1/8	27 1/8	27 4/8	23 5/8	6	5	Johnson County	MO	James Stephens	1990	62
176 0/8	25 5/8	23 6/8	25 5/8	6	5	Clay County	KS	Rayford W. Willingham	1985	65
175 7/8	27 3/8	26 4/8	24 4/8	7	6	Kandiyohi County	MN	Eldon Hauser	1969	66
175 5/8	29 0/8	28 6/8	21 3/8	4	4	Burnett County	WI	Myles Keller	1977	67
175 5/8	25 4/8	25 2/8	22 2/8	7	7	Pratt County	KS	Gary Brehm	1984	67
175 5/8	26 0/8	25 6/8	22 2/8	5	6	Dickinson County	KS	Gary Stroda	1985	67
175 5/8	24 1/8	23 4/8	17 3/8	7	7	Woodbury County	IA	Paul Feddersen	1988	67

SCORE	LENGTH OF MAIN BEAM		INSIDE SPREAD	NUMBER OF POINTS		AREA	STATE/ PROVINCE	HUNTER'S NAME	DATE	RANK
	R	L		R	L					
175 5/8	25 5/8	25 6/8	19 3/8	7	7	Lucas County	IA	Dean Chandler	1991	67
175 4/8	26 0/8	25 4/8	17 7/8	9	5	Murray County	MN	Steven Wynia	1973	72
175 4/8	27 5/8	27 3/8	22 6/8	5	5	Jo Daviess County	IL	Richard McCartin	1991	72
175 3/8	25 7/8	26 5/8	19 7/8	5	5	Ottawa County	KS	Gary Gans	1985	74
175 2/8	28 5/8	27 2/8	23 5/8	6	6	Sangamon County	IL	Wm. Richard Olsen	1978	75
175 2/8	26 1/8	25 7/8	20 0/8	6	6	St. Mary Parish	LA	Shannon Presley	1981	75
175 1/8	24 4/8	24 4/8	21 5/8	5	6	Marion County	IA	Gordon Hayes	1973	77
175 1/8	26 3/8	28 0/8	21 3/8	7	9	Dodge County	MN	Bill Chase	1976	77
175 0/8	27 6/8	28 6/8	19 0/8	6	6	Lee County	IA	Stephen Douglas McKeehan,	1989	79
174 6/8	24 0/8	25 2/8	20 7/8	7	6	Randolph County	IL	Jack D. Carter	1988	80
174 5/8	25 1/8	25 7/8	18 7/8	5	5	Pickaway County	OH	Hunter R. Certain	1985	81
174 5/8	25 1/8	25 0/8	16 5/8	5	5	Livingston County	MI	Nicholas Scott Converse	1987	81
174 4/8	25 4/8	24 7/8	17 2/8	7	5	Toole County	MT	Dale Farnes	1979	83
174 4/8	25 6/8	25 6/8	19 6/8	5	5	Chariton County	MO	Roger D. Guilford	1988	83
174 3/8	25 5/8	24 3/8	18 3/8	5	5	Taylor County	KY	Barry Eastridge	1987	85
174 2/8	27 7/8	27 0/8	21 2/8	5	5	Ashland County	WI	Kelly McClaire	1986	86
174 2/8	24 2/8	24 6/8	18 2/8	5	5	Mower County	MN	Jason Blom	1987	86
174 2/8	25 5/8	25 5/8	18 6/8	6	6	Wabaunsee County	KS	Henry C. Boss II	1991	86
174 0/8	26 3/8	26 2/8	17 6/8	6	6	Harrison County	IA	Ricky G. Seydel	1989	89
173 7/8	24 0/8	24 2/8	19 1/8	5	5	Noble County	OK	Danny McCants	1968	90
173 6/8	26 6/8	27 1/8	19 7/8	7	5	Mercer County	IL	Floyd A. Clark	1961	91
173 6/8	26 1/8	25 0/8	21 5/8	6	5	Winneshiek County	IA	Herbert Amundson	1985	91
173 6/8	25 3/8	26 0/8	18 2/8	5	5	Crawford County	IA	Ed Willroth	1991	91
173 5/8	26 2/8	26 0/8	22 3/8	6	7	Muskingum County	OH	David R. Hatfield	1980	94
173 4/8	26 2/8	27 1/8	23 4/8	6	5	Lac qui Parle County	MN	Dale W. Shackelford	1981	95
173 4/8	25 7/8	27 0/8	23 0/8	5	5	McHenry County	IL	Gordon Sunderlage	1987	95
173 3/8	26 4/8	26 5/8	20 1/8	5	6	Warren County	IL	Larry C. Harding	1974	97
173 2/8	26 0/8	26 3/8	22 5/8	5	6	Miami County	KS	Dan R. Moore	1982	98
173 2/8	27 6/8	28 1/8	18 0/8	7	7	Monroe County	IN	Jake Wineinger	1990	98
173 1/8	28 0/8	28 2/8	21 5/8	7	7	Dunn County	WI	Jack K. Dodge	1987	100
173 0/8	25 6/8	25 5/8	19 4/8	5	5	White County	IN	Eric L. Mohler	1978	101
173 0/8	25 4/8	26 1/8	15 2/8	6	5	Russell County	KS	Michael J. Pasek	1990	101
172 7/8	27 6/8	27 1/8	18 5/8	5	6	Vermilion County	IL	Ed Gudgel	1988	103
172 7/8	27 2/8	27 7/8	19 7/8	5	5	Walworth County	WI	Robert Peterson	1988	103
172 6/8	26 7/8	27 6/8	19 4/8	5	5	Ripley County	IN	Steve A. Allen	1982	105
172 6/8	25 4/8	25 1/8	19 4/8	5	5	Sullivan County	TN	C. Alan Altizer	1984	105
172 6/8	26 6/8	25 5/8	16 4/8	5	5	Saline County	KS	Bruce Brown	1986	105
172 6/8	25 1/8	24 7/8	18 6/8	6	5	Fairfield County	OH	James Carmichael	1988	105
172 6/8	27 6/8	28 5/8	18 7/8	7	5	Pike County	IL	Jimmy Howard	1989	105
172 6/8	28 0/8	28 7/8	19 2/8	6	5	Moultrie County	IL	Joe Nelson	1991	105
172 5/8	26 7/8	27 1/8	18 7/8	5	5	Rosebud County	MT	Michael E Gayheart	1989	111
172 4/8	26 0/8	26 0/8	18 2/8	7	6	Lucas County	IA	Jim Barlow	1985	112
172 4/8	26 4/8	26 4/8	15 2/8	5	5	Scotland County	MO	Charlie L. Smith	1985	112
172 4/8	27 3/8	27 3/8	18 2/8	5	6	Shelby County	IL	Gene E. Thoele	1991	112
172 3/8	26 3/8	24 0/8	18 6/8	6	7	Clinton County	IL	James D. Rueter	1984	115
172 3/8	26 6/8	26 4/8	21 3/8	5	5	Marshall County	IA	Dale E. Smith	1988	115
172 3/8	27 0/8	26 7/8	19 1/8	5	5	Johnson County	KS	David Reed	1990	115
172 2/8	26 1/8	25 3/8	19 2/8	5	6	Iowa County	IA	Ardith Lockridge	1965	118
172 2/8	27 3/8	25 1/8	18 4/8	5	5	Clinton County	IA	Robert S. Stankee	1985	118
172 2/8	27 6/8	26 5/8	19 4/8	5	5	Butler County	PA	Ralph W. Stoltenberg, Jr.	1986	118
172 2/8	26 7/8	27 6/8	26 2/8	6	5	Saunders County	NE	John I. Kunert	1986	118
172 2/8	25 1/8	26 4/8	19 6/8	5	5	Clay County	KS	Scott Otto	1989	118
172 1/8	26 4/8	26 3/8	19 5/8	7	6	Rice County	MN	Mike Sannan	1989	123
172 1/8	27 6/8	26 6/8	17 7/8	7	7	Russell County	KS	James H. Skucius	1990	123
172 1/8	25 1/8	24 6/8	22 5/8	8	8	Lake County	IL	Mark J. Kramer	1990	123
172 0/8	24 6/8	24 2/8	18 6/8	5	5	Whiteside County	IL	Noel Feather	1977	126
172 0/8	27 0/8	26 6/8	21 2/8	5	5	Greene County	IN	Jason Anderson	1991	126
172 0/8	25 6/8	25 2/8	17 7/8	5	6	Nicollet County	MN	Bruce Kramer	1991	126
172 0/8	25 4/8	23 4/8	16 6/8	6	6	McMullen County	TX	Steve Best	1991	126
171 7/8	26 2/8	26 4/8	24 1/8	5	5	Scotland County	MO	David Smith	1984	130
171 7/8	28 5/8	28 0/8	20 7/8	8	7	Linn County	IA	Charles Bemer	1985	130
171 7/8	27 5/8	26 6/8	21 5/8	6	6	Lucas County	IA	Tim M. Whitlatch	1989	130
171 6/8	26 7/8	26 6/8	25 2/8	7	8	Richland County	ND	Todd Funfar	1982	133
171 6/8	28 1/8	27 1/8	17 6/8	7	6	Carroll County	OH	Randy S Mulheim	1983	133
171 6/8	24 6/8	23 4/8	20 6/8	5	5	Dunn County	WI	James W. Belmore	1991	133
171 6/8	28 0/8	28 0/8	20 6/8	7	8	Edmonton	ALB	Warren Witherspoon	1991	133
171 5/8	24 6/8	24 0/8	17 3/8	6	6	Calgary	ALB	Scott Simi	1979	137
171 5/8	25 3/8	25 2/8	20 3/8	8	6	Cowley County	KS	Michael L. Snyder	1985	137
171 5/8	26 3/8	25 5/8	19 3/8	5	5	Logan County	KY	Alan Scott	1987	137
171 4/8	24 3/8	23 2/8	16 6/8	6	6	Ellsworth County	KS	Jim Willems	1985	140

WHITETAIL DEER (*Typical Antlers*)

(*Continued*)

SCORE	LENGTH OF MAIN BEAM R	L	INSIDE SPREAD	NUMBER OF POINTS R	L	AREA	STATE/ PROVINCE	HUNTER'S NAME	DATE	RANK
171 3/8	22 4/8	23 7/8	24 7/8	6	6	Cass County	ND	Warren Buss	1966	141
171 3/8	23 7/8	24 5/8	18 7/8	5	5	Harrison County	IA	R. A. Cronk	1985	141
171 3/8	27 4/8	27 6/8	21 3/8	7	6	Washington County	IL	Robert Schneider	1985	141
171 3/8	27 3/8	26 5/8	26 0/8	8	8	Jefferson County	WI	Gary Moyer	1987	141
171 3/8	24 1/8	24 7/8	18 5/8	6	6	Sangamon County	IL	Michael R. Vincent	1991	141
171 2/8	25 1/8	23 2/8	20 6/8	5	6	Adams County	IA	Gary D. Maatsch	1990	146
171 1/8	26 3/8	26 4/8	20 5/8	5	5	Itasca County	MN	John Parmeter	1964	147
171 1/8	23 5/8	24 0/8	16 7/8	6	6	Piatt County	IL	Ronald E. Waugh	1971	147
171 1/8	24 3/8	23 2/8	17 4/8	8	7	Morton County	ND	Tony Schatz	1974	147
171 1/8	25 2/8	24 2/8	21 1/8	6	6	Tazewell County	IL	John P. Condis	1987	147
171 1/8	25 3/8	25 2/8	20 1/8	5	5	Clark County	OH	Lafayette Boggs III	1991	147
171 0/8	30 0/8	27 5/8	19 5/8	5	8	Belmont County	OH	Charles J. Wilson	1979	152
171 0/8	27 4/8	27 4/8	22 2/8	5	5	Parke County	IN	Fred Sills	1985	152
170 7/8	27 6/8	27 5/8	18 4/8	6	8	Republic County	KS	Carroll Couture	1986	154
170 7/8	27 4/8	28 4/8	21 4/8	7	8	Leavenworth County	KS	Jacob W. Dragieff	1987	154
170 7/8	25 6/8	25 7/8	22 1/8	6	6	Bureau County	IL	Steve W. Hayes	1990	154
170 6/8	26 1/8	25 3/8	17 4/8	5	5	Mitchell County	IA	Dan Block	1981	157
170 6/8	26 7/8	28 1/8	19 6/8	5	5	Racine County	WI	Anthony J Wozniak	1985	157
170 6/8	24 5/8	23 5/8	14 6/8	6	7	Jackson County	MI	Richard J. Galicki	1991	157
170 5/8	26 3/8	25 5/8	18 3/8	5	6	Vermilion County	IL	Mark Pittman	1980	160
170 5/8	23 6/8	23 4/8	16 5/8	6	6	Teton County	MT	James R. Dean	1983	160
170 5/8	26 1/8	26 2/8	18 5/8	7	5	Schuyler County	MO	Mike Meinhardt	1989	160
170 4/8	25 1/8	25 4/8	20 2/8	5	4	Des Moines County	IA	Bob Fudge	1966	163
170 4/8	25 3/8	24 7/8	20 0/8	6	6	Vilas County	WI	Rick R. Lax	1990	163
170 4/8	26 3/8	26 0/8	19 6/8	5	5	Rock Island County	IL	Joseph V. De Schepper	1991	163
170 4/8	29 0/8	29 3/8	19 1/8	6	5	Cerro Gordo County	IA	Chuck Harris	1991	163
170 4/8	24 6/8	24 5/8	18 0/8	7	7	Pawnee County	NE	Kenneth C. Mort	1991	163
170 3/8	28 5/8	28 2/8	21 6/8	6	4	Hall County	NE	Gust Bergman	1965	168
170 3/8	25 5/8	26 3/8	17 7/8	6	5	Decatur County	IA	Julian Toney	1982	168
170 3/8	27 0/8	26 1/8	20 3/8	5	5	Ogle County	IL	John E. Lawson	1985	168
170 3/8	27 3/8	28 4/8	18 5/8	7	6	Howard County	IA	Clarence Mincks	1991	168
170 2/8	27 1/8	27 2/8	21 0/8	4	4	Lee County	AL	George P. Mann	1980	172
170 2/8	25 4/8	26 1/8	19 1/8	5	6	Clayton County	IA	Myles Keller	1989	172
170 1/8	26 1/8	27 1/8	22 1/8	5	5	Edwards County	KS	Jay Schaller	1968	174
170 1/8	25 4/8	25 7/8	22 2/8	6	7	Winona County	MN	Roger Traxler	1980	174
170 1/8	25 6/8	25 2/8	21 3/8	5	5	Mower County	MN	Robert D. Plumb	1984	174
170 1/8	26 7/8	26 0/8	20 7/8	5	6	Harford County	MD	Ed Garrison	1987	174
170 1/8	26 0/8	26 4/8	18 1/8	7	6	Miami County	KS	Keith Groshong	1988	174
170 1/8	23 3/8	27 4/8	20 5/8	5	5	Racine County	WI	Michael H. Poeschel	1989	174
170 1/8	25 0/8	27 0/8	19 3/8	5	5	Winnebago County	IA	Matthew Modeland	1990	174
170 1/8	26 6/8	26 4/8	24 2/8	6	6	La Crosse County	WI	Scott R. Waura	1991	174
170 0/8	26 1/8	26 6/8	20 0/8	5	5	Scott County	KS	Monte L. Barker	1973	182
170 0/8	29 4/8	29 0/8	20 4/8	6	6	Puslinch Twp.	ONT	Richard Foss	1980	182
170 0/8	28 0/8	28 6/8	19 5/8	6	5	Jo Daviess County	IL	Bart Blocklinger	1982	182
170 0/8	25 1/8	24 7/8	19 1/8	8	8	Plymouth County	IA	David Erdmann	1987	182
170 0/8	25 1/8	25 5/8	19 6/8	5	5	Battle River	SAS	Gordon Stefanuk	1989	182
170 0/8	26 0/8	27 0/8	19 4/8	6	5	Jackson County	MI	Michael D. Fitzgerald	1990	182
170 0/8	25 4/8	23 4/8	21 0/8	5	5	Harvey County	KS	Dan Stahl	1991	182
169 6/8	26 0/8	27 3/8	20 6/8	4	4	Decatur County	IA	Bruce Jermyn	1979	189
169 6/8	29 6/8	29 2/8	27 0/8	6	6	Coffey County	KS	Jack McCullough	1984	189
169 5/8	24 0/8	23 4/8	22 1/8	6	7	Neosho County	KS	Jeff Friederich	1992	191
169 4/8	23 7/8	25 2/8	17 7/8	6	7	Charles Mix County	SD	Don Carda	1974	192
169 4/8	24 6/8	24 6/8	18 7/8	7	7	Hennepin County	MN	Mark Kirkwold	1989	192
169 4/8	23 6/8	24 6/8	17 2/8	6	6	Harvey County	KS	Ron Hershberger	1989	192
169 4/8	26 0/8	25 4/8	22 4/8	7	6	Rock Island County	IL	Leo Hoogerwerf	1990	192
169 4/8	24 6/8	24 6/8	19 2/8	5	5	Lafayette County	WI	E. Michael Kitral	1991	192
169 3/8	27 1/8	27 5/8	22 1/8	5	5	Hamilton County	OH	Christopher J. Ludwig	1990	197
169 2/8	26 1/8	27 2/8	21 6/8	6	6	Ashland County	OH	Darrell Huff	1985	198
169 1/8	28 6/8	28 2/8	19 3/8	6	5	La Salle County	IL	Dave Mrowicki	1985	199
169 0/8	25 6/8	26 0/8	18 0/8	7	5	Warren County	IA	Brad Vonk	1980	200
169 0/8	25 5/8	25 0/8	20 5/8	5	6	Marion County	KS	Max Williams	1985	200
169 0/8	27 2/8	26 7/8	22 2/8	5	5	Grant County	WI	Richard Hein	1986	200
168 7/8	24 3/8	24 4/8	20 7/8	5	5	Jackson County	IA	Al Weidenbacher	1984	203
168 7/8	27 4/8	27 0/8	19 0/8	5	6	Washington County	MN	Ronald Jacobson	1985	203
168 7/8	22 1/8	22 5/8	22 1/8	6	5	Jefferson County	IL	Rudy Moore	1987	203
168 6/8	27 7/8	27 0/8	16 6/8	7	7	Muskingum County	OH	Gerald Shepler	1988	206
168 5/8	26 2/8	26 0/8	18 5/8	5	6	Des Moines County	IA	Michael P. Anderson	1977	207
168 5/8	26 3/8	26 1/8	20 6/8	6	6	Mahoning County	OH	Jeff J Hartman	1984	207
168 5/8	25 0/8	24 5/8	17 1/8	7	7	Calhoun County	IL	Dennis A. Kendall	1985	207
168 5/8	25 7/8	25 7/8	22 1/8	5	5	Taylor County	WI	Bradley Cornell	1986	207

WHITETAIL DEER *(Typical Antlers)*

MINIMUM SCORE 125   *(Continued)*

Score	Length of R Main Beam L		Inside Spread	Number of R Points L		Area	State/ Province	Hunter's Name	Date	Rank
168 5/8	26 7/8	27 6/8	20 6/8	6	6	Hancock County	OH	Robert E. Ebert	1988	207
168 5/8	25 6/8	25 6/8	19 5/8	5	5	Winnebago County	IA	Jim Orthel	1990	207
168 5/8	26 0/8	26 1/8	18 3/8	8	7	Harrison County	KY	Sam Blackburn	1991	207
168 4/8	24 0/8	24 7/8	18 6/8	5	5	Lincoln County	KS	Gerald Huehl	1985	214
168 4/8	23 7/8	23 4/8	16 6/8	6	5	Grayson County	KY	John David Johnson	1989	214
168 3/8	25 1/8	26 1/8	19 5/8	5	5	Jefferson County	IL	Ben Howard	1988	216
168 3/8	25 0/8	24 6/8	19 3/8	5	5	Kingsbury County	SD	Donald B. Johnson	1989	216
168 2/8	27 0/8	26 5/8	19 2/8	5	7	Cowley County	KS	Larry G. Gann	1975	218
168 2/8	25 0/8	24 4/8	21 2/8	5	5	Macon County	IL	Larry D. Smith	1985	218
168 2/8	27 2/8	26 7/8	20 4/8	5	6	Lyon County	KS	John R. Clifton	1985	218
168 2/8	25 4/8	25 1/8	20 3/8	7	5	Mercer County	KY	Steve Baxter	1989	218
168 1/8	27 0/8	27 7/8	20 1/8	6	6	Blue Earth County	MN	Rich Detjen	1984	222
168 0/8	27 2/8	25 7/8	19 0/8	5	5	Vinton County	OH	Ronald E. Morgan	1978	223
168 0/8	26 0/8	25 6/8	19 1/8	10	5	Amherst County	VA	William Dixon Morgan	1980	223
168 0/8	25 4/8	23 7/8	15 6/8	7	7	De Witt County	IL	William R. Henson	1982	223
167 7/8	27 6/8	27 7/8	21 2/8	6	6	Brown County	OH	David Grayson	1976	226
167 7/8	26 0/8	25 5/8	20 3/8	5	6	Clay County	IL	Tom Corry	1985	226
167 6/8	26 4/8	26 2/8	19 6/8	5	5	Monona County	IA	Douglas M. Bonine	1985	228
167 6/8	27 2/8	27 1/8	21 2/8	5	5	Coffey County	KS	Edward L. Bess	1985	228
167 5/8	27 7/8	26 6/8	20 7/8	7	7	Chase County	KS	William E. Drummond	1984	230
167 5/8	23 6/8	23 1/8	15 0/8	7	7	Meigs County	OH	Rick Bolin	1987	230
167 5/8	24 0/8	24 1/8	17 7/8	5	5	Leavenworth County	KS	John W. Garrison	1990	230
167 5/8	22 4/8	23 0/8	18 7/8	6	5	Washita County	OK	Alan Cooper	1991	230
167 5/8	28 1/8	27 7/8	20 6/8	6	4	Macoupin County	IL	Justin Bonnell	1991	230
167 5/8	29 0/8	29 0/8	19 2/8	7	5	Fulton County	IL	Robert A. Hammerich	1991	230
167 4/8	22 4/8	23 1/8	18 4/8	5	5	Washington County	KS	Bill R. Mallean	1974	236
167 4/8	23 6/8	24 0/8	21 4/8	6	6	Coffey County	KS	Glen Stohs	1987	236
167 4/8	26 4/8	26 0/8	21 0/8	7	7	Sawyer County	WI	Gary R. Christman	1989	236
167 4/8	26 6/8	26 0/8	19 4/8	6	5	Winneshiek County	IA	Tom Gossman	1990	236
167 4/8	26 1/8	26 7/8	21 2/8	5	6	Pike County	IL	Timothy Fulmer	1990	236
167 3/8	25 1/8	25 0/8	20 5/8	5	7	Sauk County	WI	Daniel Kaczmar	1985	241
167 3/8	28 5/8	28 4/8	19 2/8	6	6	Sumner County	KS	Don Braddy	1986	241
167 3/8	28 6/8	26 1/8	20 1/8	5	6	Coshocton County	OH	Harold E. Frank	1989	241
167 3/8	24 6/8	24 2/8	19 3/8	5	5	Dawson County	MT	Jerry Fevold	1992	241
167 1/8	24 5/8	24 7/8	18 6/8	5	6	Chase County	KS	Ronald E. Rhodes	1985	245
167 1/8	22 5/8	22 6/8	25 2/8	5	7	Dodge County	MN	Myles Keller	1985	245
167 1/8	25 1/8	25 6/8	20 3/8	6	6	Reno County	KS	R. D. Loudenback	1987	245
167 1/8	23 4/8	24 0/8	18 5/8	6	5	McHenry County	IL	Charlie Rand	1989	245
167 0/8	28 0/8	27 6/8	19 0/8	6	5	Clay County	MN	Ryan Hines	1986	249
167 0/8	26 0/8	26 1/8	18 2/8	5	5	Montgomery County	IN	Joe W. Woodrow	1988	249
167 0/8	25 5/8	24 6/8	18 2/8	5	5	Montgomery County	TN	Larry Lee Murphy	1989	249
167 0/8	26 3/8	25 7/8	18 3/8	6	6	Fountain County	IN	Steve McQueen	1991	249
166 7/8	26 4/8	26 4/8	20 1/8	7	5	Saline County	NE	Scott Theis	1982	253
166 7/8	25 2/8	24 5/8	21 1/8	6	6	Geary County	KS	Dennis L. Gillam	1986	253
166 7/8	23 7/8	24 2/8	19 4/8	8	6	Lake County	MN	Mark Hal Tucker	1991	253
166 6/8	24 3/8	24 0/8	21 6/8	6	7	Lanigan	SAS	Bob Tempel	1985	256
166 6/8	27 3/8	26 6/8	17 6/8	5	5	Allegan County	MI	Larry Deater	1989	256
166 5/8	26 7/8	27 4/8	19 5/8	5	5	Lyon County	MN	Gene Gustafson	1982	258
166 5/8	25 2/8	25 0/8	17 5/8	6	7	Meade County	KS	Tim Ross	1987	258
166 5/8	26 4/8	25 0/8	17 2/8	6	8	Johnson County	IN	Joe F. Heath, Jr.	1989	258
166 5/8	25 0/8	25 2/8	21 3/8	8	6	Sarpy County	NE	Roy Symanietz	1990	258
166 4/8	27 6/8	28 4/8	21 4/8	5	7	Juniper	NBW	Ron Peterson	1989	262
166 4/8	26 0/8	26 6/8	19 0/8	5	4	Pierce County	WI	Garrett "Gary" L. Fleisha	1991	262
166 3/8	26 6/8	26 4/8	17 1/8	6	6	Clarke County	IA	Dwight E. Green	1965	264
166 3/8	26 3/8	26 0/8	18 2/8	8	5	Yankton County	SD	Roger Irwin	1985	264
166 3/8	25 2/8	25 1/8	17 6/8	9	7	Lake County	MN	Daniel H. Hall	1991	264
166 2/8	29 3/8	29 4/8	21 5/8	6	4	Monona County	IA	G. K. Tuttle	1967	267
166 2/8	27 4/8	27 1/8	20 2/8	9	6	Republic County	KS	Virgil Graham	1986	267
166 2/8	25 1/8	26 7/8	19 1/8	6	6	Monroe County	IA	Cliff VanZee	1987	267
166 2/8	26 2/8	27 2/8	19 2/8	7	7	Mower County	MN	Kerry Schroeder	1988	267
166 2/8	24 5/8	24 7/8	19 2/8	6	7	Cane County	IL	Roy Howard	1991	267
166 1/8	23 2/8	23 5/8	19 3/8	5	5	Morrison County	MN	Corey Loney	1963	272
166 1/8	27 0/8	27 1/8	18 0/8	5	6	Stearns County	MN	Bruce C. Meade	1978	272
166 1/8	25 6/8	25 2/8	21 2/8	5	4	Texas County	OK	Max Crocker	1986	272
166 1/8	25 4/8	25 0/8	19 5/8	4	5	Chase County	KS	Lee Ayers	1987	272
166 1/8	24 5/8	24 5/8	17 1/8	5	6	Bartholomew County	IN	Bryan D. Cook	1989	272
166 1/8	23 4/8	23 2/8	17 2/8	7	6	White County	IN	Kerry Dean Morton	1989	272
166 1/8	27 3/8	28 7/8	20 2/8	8	5	Wayne County	IL	Ronald Riley	1990	272
166 1/8	25 4/8	26 0/8	18 4/8	7	6	Ross County	OH	Keith W. Orr	1991	272
166 0/8	27 5/8	26 7/8	23 4/8	5	5	Clinton County	IA	Loy J. Brooker	1964	280

WHITETAIL DEER *(Typical Antlers)*

MINIMUM SCORE 125   *(Continued)*

Score	Length of Main Beam R	L	Inside Spread	Number of Points R	L	Area	State/ Province	Hunter's Name	Date	Rank
166 0/8	23 4/8	23 5/8	18 0/8	5	5	Bon Homme County	SD	Delbert Newman	1964	280
166 0/8	26 1/8	28 4/8	21 6/8	7	6	Shelby County	IL	Ernest D. Richardson	1977	280
166 0/8	26 6/8	24 2/8	22 7/8	6	6	Anoka County	MN	John A. Cardinal	1979	280
166 0/8	24 5/8	25 2/8	20 4/8	6	5	Tazewell County	IL	Jerry W. Kammerer	1981	280
166 0/8	24 4/8	25 5/8	19 2/8	5	5	Sedgwick County	KS	Louis Turner	1988	280
166 0/8	26 1/8	26 4/8	19 0/8	5	5	Martin County	IN	Terry L. McCrary	1988	280
165 7/8	23 4/8	23 4/8	16 3/8	5	5	Wapello County	IA	Richard L. Larsen	1976	287
165 7/8	25 4/8	26 1/8	17 5/8	7	6	Licking County	OH	Pat Walker	1978	287
165 7/8	27 2/8	27 0/8	19 5/8	5	5	Prowers County	CO	Edward Henson	1980	287
165 7/8	23 0/8	26 0/8	18 1/8	5	5	Vermilion County	IL	Dick Bayer	1987	287
165 7/8	26 2/8	25 6/8	20 0/8	7	5	Weld County	CO	Mark Houtchens	1991	287
165 6/8	27 0/8	26 1/8	19 0/8	7	6	Pottawattamie County	IA	Dan Bowen	1968	292
165 6/8	28 1/8	25 7/8	18 4/8	5	6	Darke County	OH	Dean Neff	1988	292
165 6/8	25 1/8	25 1/8	19 0/8	7	6	Morrison County	MN	Rodney Mysliwiec	1988	292
165 6/8	25 1/8	26 2/8	18 3/8	5	6	Ottawa County	KS	Patrick E. Helget	1988	292
165 4/8	25 6/8	25 1/8	21 0/8	5	5	Kent County	MD	Kent Price	1962	296
165 4/8	23 2/8	22 5/8	19 4/8	6	6	Peoria County	IL	Larry T Oppe	1984	296
165 4/8	29 1/8	28 3/8	18 1/8	7	8	Buffalo County	WI	Patrick Ryan	1985	296
165 4/8	27 6/8	27 5/8	21 0/8	6	5	Will County	IL	Donald R. Spence	1988	296
165 4/8	25 6/8	27 2/8	22 0/8	5	5	Cherry County	NE	Jack Joseph	1990	296
165 3/8	23 7/8	25 6/8	17 1/8	5	7	Owen County	KY	Joseph Caruso	1977	301
165 3/8	27 0/8	27 2/8	22 5/8	7	7	Grundy County	IL	Gary R. Kuriger	1978	301
165 3/8	26 2/8	26 0/8	20 0/8	5	8	Victoria	MAN	David Wiklund	1984	301
165 3/8	26 1/8	24 1/8	20 3/8	5	5	Guthrie County	IA	Scott C. Kemble	1989	301
165 3/8	25 2/8	26 0/8	17 7/8	5	6	Hancock County	IN	Gary Dusang	1991	301
165 3/8	25 6/8	24 7/8	16 5/8	6	7	Rock Island County	IL	Roman H. Atnip	1991	301
165 3/8	25 6/8	25 6/8	20 1/8	5	5	Baca County	CO	Eddie Claypool	1991	301
165 2/8	26 5/8	24 6/8	18 1/8	6	6	McPherson County	KS	Daniel Willems	1981	308
165 2/8	25 6/8	24 2/8	18 2/8	5	5	Clermont County	OH	Nick Lung	1985	308
165 2/8	25 6/8	25 6/8	21 5/8	5	6	Dubuque County	IA	Paul J. Kluesner	1988	308
165 2/8	26 0/8	25 1/8	19 3/8	6	6	Wapello County	IA	Robert L. McDowell	1988	308
165 2/8	25 0/8	24 7/8	18 6/8	7	7	Dunn County	WI	Lamoine Roatch	1989	308
165 2/8	24 4/8	25 2/8	19 0/8	6	6	Harvey County	KS	Bob Stroble	1989	308
165 1/8	25 3/8	25 5/8	21 7/8	5	5	Barry County	MI	Jim Birmingham	1977	314
165 1/8	24 0/8	24 2/8	20 1/8	6	6	Sawyer County	WI	Robert N. Dale	1980	314
165 1/8	22 1/8	18 1/8	21 7/8	6	6	Iowa County	IA	David Roberts	1980	314
165 1/8	25 4/8	25 7/8	22 4/8	9	7	Wilson County	KS	Dr. Steven G. Mitchell	1987	314
165 0/8	25 2/8	23 5/8	19 0/8	6	6	Stony Plain	ALB	Wayne C. Prier	1983	318
165 0/8	24 1/8	24 2/8	17 6/8	5	5	Doniphan County	KS	Richard Williams	1983	318
165 0/8	25 6/8	25 4/8	20 4/8	5	5	Jefferson County	KS	Emmet Copeland	1989	318
165 0/8	25 2/8	25 4/8	18 4/8	5	5	Montgomery County	IL	Steven L. Traylor	1989	318
165 0/8	27 2/8	28 1/8	19 6/8	5	5	Crawford County	IL	Charles E. Guyer	1990	318
165 0/8	25 1/8	25 3/8	19 4/8	5	5	Geary County	KS	Philip J. Palmer	1991	318
164 7/8	28 0/8	25 1/8	20 1/8	4	5	Kane County	IL	James A. Anderson	1980	324
164 7/8	25 4/8	26 2/8	19 3/8	5	5	Peoria County	IL	Joe R. McCord	1983	324
164 7/8	24 7/8	25 0/8	17 1/8	5	5	Elkhart County	IN	Joe Leszczynski	1984	324
164 7/8	25 0/8	25 4/8	19 3/8	6	6	Gray County	KS	Ralph W. Herron	1984	324
164 7/8	26 1/8	25 6/8	21 7/8	6	6	Madison County	MT	Gordan Sampson	1986	324
164 7/8	25 4/8	26 0/8	21 3/8	6	7	Coles County	IL	Ralph Garland	1988	324
164 7/8	26 5/8	27 3/8	18 7/8	6	5	Richland County	OH	Erwin Merkli	1988	324
164 7/8	27 5/8	27 6/8	23 1/8	7	7	Butler County	OH	Will McQueen	1989	324
164 6/8	28 1/8	26 5/8	20 7/8	8	5	Shelby County	OH	Jerry Atkinson	1975	332
164 6/8	26 4/8	28 2/8	22 2/8	5	6	Highland County	OH	Daniel L. Henges	1976	332
164 6/8	27 5/8	26 0/8	15 6/8	5	5	Sanilac County	MI	Michael J. Wines	1981	332
164 6/8	26 0/8	26 2/8	20 6/8	5	5	Macoupin County	IL	John E. Eldred	1985	332
164 6/8	26 5/8	26 5/8	26 4/8	8	5	Sullivan County	IN	John W. Hale	1988	332
164 6/8	23 6/8	22 3/8	20 2/8	5	5	La Salle County	IL	Randy Hooper	1988	332
164 6/8	24 5/8	24 5/8	17 0/8	5	5	Macon County	IL	Cal Heseman	1988	332
164 6/8	24 2/8	24 4/8	15 2/8	5	5	Emmet County	IA	Steven L. Reighard, Sr.	1990	332
164 5/8	25 2/8	23 5/8	18 5/8	8	6	Sumner County	KS	Archie A. Stralow	1967	340
164 5/8	25 7/8	25 7/8	19 3/8	6	6	Fayette County	IA	Jerry Brown	1989	340
164 5/8	26 5/8	25 4/8	20 4/8	6	6	Saginaw County	MI	William J. Twarog	1990	340
164 4/8	23 7/8	24 3/8	18 6/8	5	5	Morton County	ND	Butch Sammons	1985	343
164 4/8	27 5/8	27 0/8	19 3/8	5	6	Trempealeau County	WI	Keith Lynch	1985	343
164 4/8	23 5/8	23 5/8	20 7/8	6	6	Bond County	IL	Roger Munie	1987	343
164 4/8	26 6/8	26 4/8	18 6/8	7	6	Montgomery County	OH	Michael L. Mrusek	1990	343
164 4/8	26 7/8	26 6/8	17 0/8	5	5	Anoka County	MN	Paul Landberg	1991	343
164 3/8	25 4/8	25 4/8	19 6/8	8	7	Norman County	MN	Gilbert Guttormson	1953	348
164 3/8	21 4/8	21 6/8	16 5/8	6	6	Wibaux County	MT	Gerald Polesky	1959	348
164 3/8	28 4/8	28 0/8	20 4/8	7	8	Trigg County	KY	Charles Stahl	1965	348

SCORE	LENGTH OF MAIN BEAM R	LENGTH OF MAIN BEAM L	INSIDE SPREAD	NUMBER OF POINTS R	NUMBER OF POINTS L	AREA	STATE/ PROVINCE	HUNTER'S NAME	DATE	RANK
164 3/8	25 1/8	25 2/8	18 3/8	5	5	Cottonwood County	MN	Jim Hansen	1972	348
164 3/8	26 4/8	25 5/8	17 3/8	7	8	Madison County	MT	Jim Schilke	1978	348
164 3/8	25 6/8	25 4/8	20 1/8	5	7	Saginaw County	MI	Larry Steinley	1979	348
164 3/8	27 1/8	27 5/8	20 7/8	4	4	Hardin County	OH	Anthony A. Krummrey	1982	348
164 3/8	28 0/8	27 5/8	21 1/8	6	8	Fayette County	OH	Steven J. Guess	1984	348
164 3/8	26 7/8	27 0/8	20 7/8	4	4	Louisa County	IA	Roger Gipple	1984	348
164 3/8	26 6/8	27 7/8	21 3/8	5	6	Perth	ONT	Michael Burwell	1986	348
164 3/8	26 7/8	25 5/8	18 7/8	5	5	Colfax County	NE	Dennis Indra	1987	348
164 3/8	25 2/8	24 6/8	20 5/8	5	5	Rock Island County	IL	Mike Mitten	1989	348
164 3/8	26 2/8	26 2/8	15 7/8	5	5	Scotland County	MO	David Westmoreland	1991	348
164 3/8	29 5/8	26 5/8	17 7/8	5	4	Van Buren County	MI	Kenneth J. Gillan	1991	348
164 2/8	27 2/8	26 2/8	21 0/8	11	7	Grundy County	IL	Jerome M. Fris	1972	362
164 2/8	26 7/8	26 2/8	17 5/8	6	6	Buffalo County	WI	Mark Busch	1986	362
164 2/8	26 0/8	25 6/8	19 0/8	5	5	Morrison County	MN	Tim Steinhoff	1987	362
164 2/8	26 6/8	27 1/8	19 6/8	6	5	Pike County	IL	Roger Pepper	1987	362
164 2/8	25 1/8	24 2/8	17 0/8	5	5	Mason County	IL	Richard J. "Buck" Fuller	1988	362
164 2/8	23 6/8	22 3/8	22 0/8	8	9	Kendall County	IL	Christopher Kiernan	1989	362
164 2/8	22 0/8	22 5/8	17 4/8	6	6	Lake County	IL	Steven Tjader	1989	362
164 2/8	26 7/8	27 5/8	20 6/8	5	7	Clark County	IL	Cole Lee	1990	362
164 2/8	23 4/8	24 4/8	19 0/8	6	5	Guthrie County	IA	Joe Dowell	1991	362
164 1/8	26 5/8	26 3/8	18 2/8	6	5	Morrison County	MN	Lloyd Neuman	1971	371
164 1/8	26 2/8	26 4/8	22 5/8	5	5	Washington County	OH	Roger Pape	1980	371
164 1/8	24 6/8	24 5/8	16 5/8	5	6	Dundy County	NE	John Crump	1983	371
164 1/8	26 5/8	26 3/8	18 3/8	6	6	Otoe County	NE	Dale A. Hall	1989	371
164 0/8	24 3/8	25 0/8	16 6/8	5	5	Olmsted County	MN	Robert Meyer	1969	375
164 0/8	25 1/8	25 5/8	23 3/8	5	7	Morrison County	MN	Bruce Edberg	1977	375
164 0/8	28 0/8	26 4/8	22 6/8	5	5	Buffalo County	WI	Gerald Palmer	1986	375
164 0/8	25 5/8	26 5/8	19 6/8	6	5	Burnett County	WI	Gary A. Johnson	1989	375
163 7/8	26 3/8	26 4/8	19 3/8	9	10	Caldwell County	KY	Daniel R. Keith	1988	379
163 6/8	23 6/8	26 5/8	19 2/8	5	5	Fayette County	IA	Bob Nicolay	1981	380
163 6/8	23 5/8	25 4/8	19 4/8	7	8	Porter County	IN	Raymond T. Satterblom	1983	380
163 6/8	23 5/8	24 7/8	17 5/8	6	5	Graham County	KS	Russell Hull	1987	380
163 6/8	27 4/8	27 6/8	20 2/8	5	6	Clark County	IL	Gerald Shaffner	1991	380
163 5/8	25 6/8	25 4/8	21 6/8	5	5	Phillips County	KS	Bill Duncan	1969	384
163 5/8	26 5/8	26 1/8	21 3/8	6	6	Lawrence County	IL	Larry K. Karns	1975	384
163 5/8	25 5/8	25 1/8	19 3/8	5	5	Wright County	MN	Rick Heberling	1978	384
163 5/8	26 4/8	25 1/8	19 2/8	6	7	Fulton County	IL	Mike Reatherford	1982	384
163 5/8	25 1/8	25 4/8	19 4/8	6	8	Jackson County	MO	Chris Shotton	1985	384
163 5/8	25 4/8	26 2/8	19 0/8	6	7	Franklin County	IN	Roger Mullins	1987	384
163 5/8	23 4/8	23 1/8	19 3/8	5	6	Carver County	MN	Ryan Jopp	1991	384
163 4/8	25 4/8	25 5/8	18 0/8	5	7	Renville County	ND	Bobby Triplett	1958	391
163 4/8	23 4/8	23 0/8	17 6/8	5	5	Wright County	MN	Dale Guetzkow	1978	391
163 4/8	28 1/8	30 0/8	23 2/8	5	5	Lawrence County	OH	Berkley Pennington, Sr.	1981	391
163 4/8	24 7/8	23 6/8	21 6/8	8	6	Racine County	WI	Greg A. Hanson	1991	391
163 3/8	24 4/8	22 7/8	22 1/8	5	5	Linn County	IA	Delmar Phillips	1960	395
163 3/8	24 3/8	23 7/8	17 5/8	8	7	Morrison County	MN	Alvin A. Diemert	1973	395
163 3/8	26 4/8	26 2/8	20 5/8	5	5	Scott County	KY	Garry Hoffman	1982	395
163 3/8	26 1/8	26 7/8	15 3/8	6	7	Chase County	KS	John Moore	1983	395
163 3/8	24 4/8	25 0/8	19 0/8	8	8	Winnebago County	IL	Bradley S. Conrad	1984	395
163 3/8	27 2/8	26 1/8	19 1/8	5	5	Eaton County	MI	Dennis Orr	1987	395
163 2/8	28 2/8	27 3/8	23 7/8	6	6	Brown County	IL	Keith E. Meiser	1981	401
163 2/8	25 7/8	29 2/8	22 6/8	8	5	Drew County	AR	Larry Standley	1982	401
163 2/8	25 4/8	25 5/8	19 6/8	5	5	Mason County	KY	R. Kenton Ring	1982	401
163 2/8	26 1/8	24 6/8	16 3/8	5	7	Licking County	OH	Don Conrad	1985	401
163 2/8	24 1/8	24 4/8	21 2/8	5	5	Sumner County	KS	Kevin Disney	1985	401
163 2/8	26 4/8	27 2/8	21 5/8	7	5	Kiowa County	KS	Jesse Zook	1989	401
163 2/8	25 4/8	26 7/8	19 2/8	5	4	Crawford County	KS	Melinda S. Nutt	1991	401
163 2/8	24 2/8	24 3/8	20 4/8	5	5	Hennepin County	MN	Larry Watson	1991	401
163 2/8	27 1/8	28 3/8	20 4/8	5	5	Ross County	OH	Sam Detty	1992	401
163 1/8	24 2/8	26 0/8	16 4/8	7	7	Logan County	WV	Gilbert Sexton	1963	410
163 1/8	27 6/8	27 5/8	18 6/8	8	5	Knox County	OH	Robert L. Hammond	1983	410
163 1/8	25 3/8	25 0/8	20 0/8	6	6	Lake County	IL	Andrew Holst	1987	410
163 1/8	25 1/8	25 6/8	21 3/8	6	5	Logan County	OH	Jerrod Pooler	1988	410
163 1/8	22 5/8	24 3/8	18 7/8	5	7	Clayton County	IA	Daniel J. Brady	1988	410
163 1/8	25 6/8	25 2/8	18 5/8	5	5	Wright County	MN	Jerry Goodale	1990	410
163 1/8	24 6/8	26 4/8	18 0/8	6	6	Bayfield County	WI	Steve Polkoski	1992	410
163 0/8	24 0/8	24 6/8	20 0/8	5	5	Dickinson County	IA	Harold Ehrp	1959	417
163 0/8	25 2/8	25 0/8	15 1/8	6	6	Texas County	OK	Edward F. Bryan, Jr.	1976	417
163 0/8	26 3/8	25 3/8	22 0/8	7	8	Switzerland County	IN	Richard W. Keebler	1977	417
163 0/8	25 1/8	24 3/8	16 4/8	5	5	Ashland County	WI	Sid Kilger	1982	417

Score	Length of Main Beam R	Length of Main Beam L	Inside Spread	Number of Points R	Number of Points L	Area	State/ Province	Hunter's Name	Date	Rank
163 0/8	27 5/8	26 6/8	21 0/8	8	8	Gibson County	IN	Phil Scott	1986	417
163 0/8	25 6/8	24 2/8	20 0/8	5	6	Marshall County	KS	Tim Wanklyn	1986	417
163 0/8	24 6/8	24 0/8	19 2/8	6	6	Jefferson County	IN	Don Field	1987	417
163 0/8	27 4/8	27 2/8	19 3/8	6	8	Clarke County	IA	Gary Cobb	1988	417
163 0/8	24 4/8	24 1/8	20 4/8	5	6	Clermont County	OH	Larry W. Van	1990	417
162 7/8	29 0/8	30 4/8	19 0/8	6	8	Queen Annes County	MD	L. P. Stephens, Jr.	1962	426
162 7/8	24 6/8	24 6/8	22 4/8	6	7	Cowley County	KS	Kenneth Highfill	1968	426
162 7/8	26 6/8	26 7/8	19 5/8	5	5	Lee County	IA	Mike Bentler	1983	426
162 7/8	24 0/8	23 5/8	22 3/8	5	5	Perry County	IL	Kevin Tate	1989	426
162 7/8	25 0/8	25 0/8	18 5/8	5	5	Baltimore County	MD	Bruce Hoover	1991	426
162 7/8	26 7/8	27 3/8	18 6/8	5	6	Edmonton	ALB	Mark Daniel Stanley	1991	426
162 6/8	24 2/8	26 2/8	20 6/8	6	7	Rice County	MN	Ken Bakken	1957	432
162 6/8	26 2/8	26 2/8	19 4/8	5	6	Clayton County	IA	Dale Kartman	1984	432
162 6/8	24 1/8	24 7/8	17 4/8	5	5	Ozaukee County	WI	Joe Seaman	1989	432
162 5/8	26 2/8	24 0/8	20 7/8	8	7	Marshall County	KS	Gary W. Tobin	1966	435
162 5/8	26 4/8	27 5/8	20 3/8	4	4	Saunders County	NE	Robert Parkins	1967	435
162 5/8	26 6/8	26 6/8	21 5/8	5	7	Henry County	IL	Lewis E. Burson	1976	435
162 5/8	25 2/8	24 7/8	20 1/8	4	5	Lucas County	IA	Bill Brown	1979	435
162 5/8	25 2/8	25 3/8	15 7/8	5	8	Crawford County	KS	Fred Geier	1981	435
162 5/8	27 2/8	27 4/8	19 7/8	5	5	St. Charles County	MO	Roland Heiliger	1985	435
162 5/8	25 3/8	24 3/8	16 4/8	7	5	Buffalo County	WI	Paul Schultz	1986	435
162 5/8	25 4/8	25 3/8	16 3/8	7	6	Hubbard County	MN	Nick J. Thill, Jr.	1987	435
162 5/8	24 4/8	23 1/8	19 0/8	6	6	Pike County	IL	Leroy Leonard	1987	435
162 5/8	25 0/8	25 1/8	20 3/8	6	6	Cerro Gordo County	IA	R. C. Field	1989	435
162 5/8	26 3/8	26 7/8	17 7/8	5	7	Wyandot County	OH	David Weininger	1991	435
162 4/8	23 6/8	23 6/8	21 0/8	7	6	Branch County	MI	Randy Massey	1981	446
162 4/8	25 2/8	25 1/8	19 6/8	6	8	Louisa County	IA	Michael Bell	1983	446
162 4/8	25 4/8	27 0/8	18 6/8	5	5	Allegheny County	PA	Christopher T. Joyce	1985	446
162 4/8	26 0/8	26 4/8	22 0/8	5	5	Dundy County	NE	Bradley Wiese	1985	446
162 4/8	24 3/8	24 4/8	21 1/8	5	6	Stearns County	MN	Pat Gross	1986	446
162 4/8	23 1/8	24 1/8	18 0/8	5	6	Vermilion County	IL	Sandra Downing	1986	446
162 4/8	25 5/8	24 6/8	21 0/8	6	7	Will County	IL	Joseph R. Franco	1986	446
162 4/8	25 5/8	25 5/8	17 1/8	5	6	Anoka County	MN	Kim Van Tassel	1987	446
162 3/8	24 2/8	24 6/8	19 7/8	5	5	Barber County	KS	Glen Snell	1982	454
162 3/8	27 2/8	27 2/8	19 6/8	5	6	Lake County	IL	Donald M. Hewkin	1986	454
162 3/8	25 3/8	25 6/8	21 6/8	5	6	Menard County	IL	Mitchell Coffey	1987	454
162 3/8	23 4/8	23 4/8	20 5/8	5	5	Ogle County	IL	Jeffrey S. Burke	1989	454
162 3/8	24 7/8	24 4/8	14 7/8	5	5	Morrison County	MN	Edward J. Kastner	1989	454
162 3/8	27 7/8	28 0/8	19 4/8	8	7	Edmonton	ALB	Dale Spooner	1992	454
162 2/8	22 2/8	24 7/8	17 6/8	6	5	Kingsbury County	SD	Dale Peterson	1972	460
162 2/8	24 1/8	24 2/8	20 4/8	6	5	Le Sueur County	MN	Joe Rybus	1981	460
162 2/8	24 7/8	24 2/8	19 0/8	5	5	Marion County	KS	Leslie Lalouette	1983	460
162 2/8	25 3/8	24 7/8	17 6/8	5	5	Trego County	KS	Craig Doll	1985	460
162 2/8	24 0/8	23 4/8	16 6/8	5	5	Hendricks County	IN	Leon Smith	1986	460
162 2/8	26 2/8	25 7/8	16 4/8	8	6	Litchfield County	CT	Warren Hensel	1988	460
162 2/8	21 4/8	23 7/8	21 2/8	6	5	Miller County	MO	Steve Wyrick	1990	460
162 2/8	25 5/8	26 0/8	16 2/8	6	6	Will County	IL	Mike O'Connor	1991	460
162 2/8	25 1/8	23 7/8	19 6/8	6	6	Henry County	IA	Myles Keller	1991	460
162 1/8	23 6/8	24 7/8	17 6/8	6	6	Buffalo County	WI	Bruce Curtis	1983	469
162 1/8	23 4/8	24 2/8	20 4/8	6	5	Winnebago County	IL	Jeffrey A. Saxby	1984	469
162 1/8	25 2/8	26 0/8	16 4/8	8	6	Monroe County	IA	Larry Whitson	1985	469
162 1/8	27 5/8	24 7/8	18 1/8	6	7	Lafayette County	WI	Charles D. Potter	1986	469
162 1/8	25 6/8	26 4/8	21 4/8	7	7	Clinton County	OH	Mark A. Ross	1988	469
162 1/8	26 7/8	27 0/8	18 7/8	5	5	Adams County	IL	Randall Lummer	1990	469
162 0/8	25 0/8	27 1/8	20 4/8	8	6	Bond County	IL	Larry Nelson	1976	475
162 0/8	24 2/8	24 2/8	17 2/8	5	5	Wabash County	IL	Ron Hawf	1978	475
162 0/8	24 3/8	27 2/8	19 2/8	6	6	Edgar County	IL	John J. Dillon	1985	475
162 0/8	25 7/8	24 7/8	23 7/8	5	7	Marion County	KS	Don Bredemeier	1987	475
162 0/8	26 0/8	27 7/8	19 2/8	6	5	Mahoning County	OH	Mark A. Brooks	1988	475
162 0/8	28 0/8	28 6/8	19 0/8	6	5	Anoka County	MN	Dean Smith	1990	475
162 0/8	25 7/8	26 2/8	20 5/8	6	6	Tolland County	CT	Bruce Moore	1990	475
162 0/8	23 1/8	24 4/8	17 0/8	6	7	Richland County	ND	Tim Poehls	1992	475
161 7/8	23 4/8	25 4/8	18 3/8	5	5	Saunders County	NE	David Strimple	1961	483
161 7/8	24 2/8	24 1/8	20 7/8	5	5	Douglas County	NE	Noel Miller	1970	483
161 7/8	23 5/8	24 0/8	17 6/8	7	7	Fulton County	IL	Bob Neal	1981	483
161 7/8	26 0/8	27 2/8	20 7/8	5	5	Greene County	OH	Charles O. Hill	1982	483
161 7/8	25 3/8	26 0/8	20 6/8	7	7	Tuscarawas County	OH	Gary Stevens	1982	483
161 7/8	23 3/8	22 2/8	16 0/8	6	6	Brandon	MAN	Gary Kaluzniak	1985	483
161 7/8	26 5/8	25 6/8	18 3/8	6	5	Winona County	MN	Tim Rislow	1986	483
161 7/8	24 2/8	24 7/8	17 6/8	8	5	Jones County	IA	Paul Johnson	1986	483

| SCORE | LENGTH OF MAIN BEAM | | INSIDE SPREAD | NUMBER OF POINTS | | AREA | STATE/ PROVINCE | HUNTER'S NAME | DATE | RANK |
	R	L		R	L					
161 7/8	23 4/8	24 4/8	16 5/8	5	5	Marion County	MO	James Schaefer	1987	483
161 7/8	23 1/8	23 2/8	18 3/8	5	5	Jefferson County	WI	Adam Achilli	1988	483
161 7/8	21 5/8	24 4/8	17 5/8	7	6	Ontario County	NY	Adam T. Kupis	1989	483
161 7/8	27 0/8	27 7/8	18 0/8	9	6	Mahoning County	OH	Nicholas Young	1990	483
161 6/8	27 3/8	26 0/8	27 1/8	4	5	Lake County	IL	David Mitten	1987	495
161 6/8	22 6/8	23 6/8	17 6/8	5	6	Jo Daviess County	IL	Timothy T. Westemeier	1987	495
161 6/8	27 7/8	26 7/8	21 2/8	6	6	Pike County	IL	Brad Stamp	1988	495
161 6/8	26 2/8	24 0/8	19 0/8	6	5	Montgomery County	TN	Zane Mason	1991	495
161 5/8	23 3/8	23 1/8	14 5/8	6	6	Dunn County	WI	Leonard Hines	1970	499
161 5/8	22 6/8	22 5/8	18 6/8	5	6	Juneau County	WI	Harlan Steindl	1971	499
161 5/8	25 0/8	25 5/8	19 1/8	6	6	Jefferson County	IL	Rick Osborn	1982	499
161 5/8	22 5/8	24 3/8	17 7/8	5	5	Butler County	KS	Mike Turner	1982	499
161 5/8	26 3/8	24 4/8	16 4/8	5	6	Butler County	KS	Ronald Tilson	1983	499
161 5/8	27 2/8	27 4/8	18 1/8	7	8	Franklin County	KS	Dennis Ballweg	1987	499
161 5/8	25 4/8	24 2/8	19 1/8	5	5	Woodford County	IL	Lynn Roseman	1989	499
161 5/8	24 4/8	24 1/8	17 1/8	5	6	Forest County	WI	Daniel G. Van Hoosen	1990	499
161 4/8	26 1/8	26 1/8	19 2/8	5	4	Bond County	IL	Sam White	1974	507
161 4/8	26 0/8	25 6/8	17 4/8	8	6	Jackson Parish	LA	James K. Morgan	1977	507
161 4/8	25 2/8	27 0/8	20 2/8	5	5	Sumner County	KS	Phill Allton	1983	507
161 4/8	28 4/8	28 3/8	22 1/8	5	5	Jones County	IA	David A. Leuchs	1984	507
161 4/8	23 3/8	24 1/8	18 4/8	6	5	Cass County	NE	Ray Brock	1985	507
161 4/8	27 1/8	26 5/8	18 5/8	4	5	Crawford County	KS	Fred Geier	1988	507
161 4/8	26 1/8	26 6/8	16 7/8	5	6	Oconto County	WI	Jeffery J. Brabant	1989	507
161 4/8	25 0/8	25 1/8	18 7/8	6	7	Clinton County	IL	Tracy Hawes	1989	507
161 4/8	26 1/8	26 4/8	18 6/8	5	5	Dane County	WI	Greg Berndt	1990	507
161 4/8	24 6/8	25 3/8	19 6/8	5	5	Van Buren County	IA	Jim Francois	1990	507
161 4/8	25 2/8	25 5/8	18 0/8	6	6	Washburn County	WI	Larry Allen Blaylock	1991	507
161 3/8	25 0/8	23 6/8	16 6/8	8	7	Wyandotte County	KS	George F. Bigelow	1967	518
161 3/8	26 4/8	25 4/8	19 1/8	6	6	Sumner County	KS	Larry Wycoff	1980	518
161 3/8	29 1/8	27 2/8	23 4/8	7	8	Clark County	OH	Kenneth Preston	1982	518
161 3/8	27 2/8	25 4/8	22 3/8	4	6	Fayette County	IL	Bill Holman	1983	518
161 3/8	23 1/8	23 0/8	19 1/8	6	5	Auglaize County	OH	Lee Atha	1983	518
161 3/8	23 0/8	24 1/8	14 5/8	5	5	Butler County	KS	David R. Rogers	1985	518
161 3/8	27 7/8	27 1/8	19 3/8	4	4	Grant County	WI	Chris Nelson	1986	518
161 3/8	25 1/8	27 2/8	15 7/8	7	6	Anderson County	TN	John Johnson	1987	518
161 3/8	24 6/8	24 6/8	19 6/8	5	7	Lake County	IN	David R. Turbin	1988	518
161 3/8	26 4/8	25 1/8	19 0/8	6	6	Waukesha County	WI	Dirk Stolz	1989	518
161 3/8	25 1/8	25 3/8	19 1/8	5	5	McPherson County	KS	Daniel Willems	1990	518
161 2/8	24 2/8	24 0/8	20 0/8	5	5	Muskingum County	OH	Lee E Wilson	1984	529
161 2/8	23 3/8	24 7/8	18 7/8	6	5	Graham County	KS	Chris Jolly	1984	529
161 2/8	24 2/8	24 6/8	17 6/8	5	5	Sauk County	WI	Hank Loncki	1989	529
161 2/8	27 1/8	25 6/8	19 2/8	8	10	Cowley County	KS	Dwayne Graham	1990	529
161 1/8	26 0/8	27 1/8	18 6/8	6	5	Clark County	IN	Frank Mauk, Jr.	1966	533
161 1/8	24 2/8	25 1/8	16 7/8	5	5	Marinette County	WI	Dale J. Hanson	1985	533
161 1/8	24 3/8	25 4/8	21 5/8	5	5	Lake County	IL	John Schnider	1987	533
161 1/8	23 6/8	23 6/8	17 6/8	5	6	Polk County	IA	Jim Garton, Jr.	1989	533
161 1/8	24 2/8	24 5/8	18 5/8	5	5	Wayne County	IL	Will Sapia	1990	533
161 1/8	26 0/8	24 0/8	20 3/8	5	5	Butler County	OH	Dale Gross	1990	533
161 0/8	26 2/8	25 1/8	19 4/8	5	5	La Crosse County	WI	Ray Howell	1977	539
161 0/8	28 0/8	27 3/8	23 4/8	4	4	Jefferson County	IN	Donnie Ball	1984	539
161 0/8	27 7/8	26 4/8	21 3/8	6	5	Morris County	KS	Craig Johnson	1985	539
161 0/8	27 2/8	27 1/8	19 2/8	5	5	Orange County	NC	R. J. Hickman	1987	539
161 0/8	27 1/8	26 0/8	22 2/8	4	4	Lucas County	IA	Gary Goering	1987	539
161 0/8	24 1/8	23 4/8	18 5/8	7	6	Butler County	OH	Fred S Spurlin	1987	539
161 0/8	25 0/8	24 4/8	16 4/8	5	6	Fond du Lac County	WI	David E. Stubbe	1988	539
161 0/8	24 5/8	24 0/8	15 3/8	6	6	Lawrence County	IN	Dale Waldbieser	1988	539
161 0/8	22 5/8	24 1/8	19 2/8	5	5	Dakota County	MN	Dave Vomela	1988	539
161 0/8	26 0/8	25 4/8	16 0/8	6	5	Day County	SD	Jim Madsen	1990	539
161 0/8	26 3/8	27 4/8	21 4/8	4	4	McHenry County	IL	Richard A. Houge	1991	539
161 0/8	22 0/8	22 0/8	15 4/8	5	5	Marion County	IA	Dwight T. Robuck	1991	539
161 0/8	23 3/8	23 7/8	20 6/8	5	5	Peoria County	IL	Robert E. Grainger	1991	539
160 7/8	20 5/8	24 0/8	24 3/8	7	5	Frontier County	NE	Vernon Laverack	1959	552
160 7/8	25 5/8	27 3/8	21 4/8	5	6		IA	Everett Reid	1962	552
160 7/8	24 2/8	23 4/8	17 6/8	7	5	Smith County	KS	Ron Sturgeon	1965	552
160 7/8	22 6/8	23 1/8	21 1/8	5	5	Lincoln County	MN	Bernie Ahlberg	1974	552
160 7/8	25 5/8	25 1/8	16 7/8	5	5	Clark County	IL	Wes Romines	1977	552
160 7/8	24 2/8	23 5/8	19 3/8	5	5	Saline County	KS	Ray Peterman	1979	552
160 7/8	25 1/8	26 7/8	18 5/8	4	4	Pike County	IL	Richard Dewey	1981	552
160 7/8	24 5/8	23 4/8	15 3/8	5	6	Leavenworth County	KS	Albert Lyle Karl	1982	552
160 7/8	25 2/8	25 6/8	19 5/8	7	7	Rockingham County	VA	Jim Burtner	1989	552

WHITETAIL DEER (*Typical Antlers*)

Score	Length of R Main Beam L		Inside Spread	Number of R Points L		Area	State/ Province	Hunter's Name	Date	Rank
160 7/8	27 7/8	27 6/8	22 4/8	5	7	Clark County	OH	Ron McGuire	1989	552
160 7/8	28 1/8	28 6/8	21 5/8	4	4	Bond County	IL	James Coleman	1989	552
160 7/8	23 4/8	23 7/8	21 7/8	5	5	Sangamon County	IL	David C. Jostes	1990	552
160 7/8	25 2/8	24 1/8	17 1/8	5	5	Bulter County	OH	Norman R. Sampson	1991	552
160 7/8	25 6/8	25 0/8	17 3/8	6	7	Parkland County	ALB	Sam Halabi	1991	552
160 6/8	25 4/8	25 7/8	17 0/8	6	5	Sarpy County	NE	Lawrence A. Klabunde	1968	566
160 6/8	26 2/8	25 7/8	19 2/8	6	4	Fillmore County	MN	Doyle Tarrence	1974	566
160 6/8	26 2/8	27 0/8	21 5/8	5	6	Alleghany County	VA	Roger O. Wyant	1984	566
160 6/8	26 5/8	26 0/8	19 2/8	4	4	Lake County	IL	Charles R. Zradicka	1986	566
160 6/8	24 3/8	24 2/8	18 6/8	5	7	Muskegon County	MI	Dave Haack	1988	566
160 6/8	25 4/8	25 2/8	21 6/8	5	5	Bayfield County	WI	Jim Peters	1989	566
160 5/8	22 3/8	23 4/8	16 4/8	7	8	Lawrence County	IL	Bob Brian	1971	572
160 5/8	24 4/8	25 5/8	23 4/8	5	6	Murray County	MN	Paul Beech	1974	572
160 5/8	22 2/8	21 4/8	15 5/8	5	5	Montcalm County	MI	Rodney Snyder	1980	572
160 5/8	25 2/8	25 3/8	14 3/8	6	5	Hubbard County	MN	Myles Keller	1982	572
160 5/8	23 7/8	23 3/8	16 6/8	6	7	Morrison County	MN	Randy Johnson	1986	572
160 5/8	21 2/8	21 4/8	14 7/8	6	6	Kenedy County	TX	Cal Adger	1987	572
160 5/8	25 2/8	25 7/8	19 1/8	7	6	Waukesha County	WI	Dick Harris	1988	572
160 5/8	26 2/8	26 6/8	18 5/8	5	5	Van Buren County	IA	Noel E. Harlan	1988	572
160 5/8	27 3/8	24 4/8	18 5/8	5	5	Scott County	MN	Kris Huber	1988	572
160 5/8	26 2/8	24 6/8	19 5/8	5	6	Christian County	IL	Richard Krider	1988	572
160 5/8	25 1/8	25 6/8	16 6/8	5	6	Allamakee County	IA	Warren W. Woods	1991	572
160 4/8	26 6/8	25 4/8	20 7/8	7	7	Williams County	ND	John Bloom	1963	583
160 4/8	27 2/8	28 0/8	21 4/8	5	7	Lyon County	IA	Marvin H. Peterson	1970	583
160 4/8	23 1/8	22 4/8	19 0/8	6	7	Keith County	NE	Gil Wilkinson	1970	583
160 4/8	28 5/8	28 2/8	24 2/8	7	7	Fairfield County	OH	Robert A. Fletcher	1977	583
160 4/8	24 2/8	24 7/8	17 6/8	5	6	Dawson County	MT	Frank Legato	1978	583
160 4/8	26 0/8	26 2/8	19 2/8	5	5	Trempealeau County	WI	Duane Kupietz	1981	583
160 4/8	24 2/8	24 7/8	19 2/8	6	5	Waukesha County	WI	Donald T. Lurvey	1982	583
160 4/8	24 4/8	25 0/8	21 0/8	5	5	Daviess County	MO	Sam Boyd	1987	583
160 4/8	23 7/8	23 7/8	18 0/8	5	5	Jefferson County	OH	Robert E. Howell	1987	583
160 4/8	27 3/8	27 2/8	19 1/8	6	4	Wayne County	MO	Carl Roach	1988	583
160 4/8	26 2/8	26 7/8	18 6/8	5	5	Schuyler County	IL	Tom Grover	1991	583
160 4/8	25 6/8	23 7/8	17 1/8	5	7	Pike County	IL	Tim Fulmer	1991	583
160 4/8	25 7/8	24 7/8	19 6/8	4	5	Olmsted County	MN	Jim Hanson	1992	583
160 3/8	22 2/8	22 4/8	20 7/8	6	6	Sheridan County	NE	Wayne Krotz	1975	596
160 3/8	24 3/8	24 2/8	17 1/8	5	5	St. Charles County	MO	Dan Schulte	1976	596
160 3/8	23 6/8	24 7/8	20 1/8	7	6	Barber County	KS	Herbie M. Landwehr, Jr.	1980	596
160 3/8	27 5/8	26 0/8	19 7/8	4	4	Clark County	IL	Gerald Shaffner	1983	596
160 3/8	26 4/8	26 5/8	18 3/8	6	5	Hamilton County	IL	Clifford R. Schoolman	1984	596
160 3/8	23 4/8	25 2/8	19 1/8	6	6	Jefferson County	IL	Jerry Newell	1986	596
160 3/8	24 2/8	23 5/8	20 3/8	7	5	Saskatoon	SAS	Maurice Parent	1987	596
160 3/8	23 2/8	23 3/8	19 5/8	5	5	Rock County	WI	Ronald A. Vike, Jr.	1989	596
160 3/8	25 5/8	25 7/8	18 5/8	5	7	Clay County	MO	James Wollard	1991	596
160 3/8	24 6/8	25 6/8	19 6/8	5	6	Washita County	OK	Larry Snider	1991	596
160 2/8	25 6/8	26 3/8	19 2/8	5	5	Nance County	NE	Ralph I. Hansen	1963	606
160 2/8	25 7/8	26 0/8	21 4/8	4	4	Cherokee County	IA	Jerry L. Smith	1969	606
160 2/8	22 6/8	23 3/8	19 4/8	5	5	Valley County	MT	John 'Rosey' Roseland	1981	606
160 2/8	23 1/8	23 1/8	18 0/8	6	6	Mills County	IA	Dale R. Clayton	1983	606
160 2/8	24 5/8	24 6/8	18 1/8	6	6	Phelps County	NE	Bruce Nielsen	1984	606
160 2/8	24 4/8	24 5/8	18 0/8	5	5	La Salle County	IL	John Thomas	1987	606
160 2/8	25 2/8	25 6/8	25 1/8	7	6	Lake County	IL	Woody Scruggs	1987	606
160 2/8	27 0/8	26 4/8	17 5/8	5	6	Ashland County	WI	Steven Roginske	1988	606
160 2/8	24 0/8	25 7/8	19 0/8	5	5	Rusk County	WI	Shawn Harris	1991	606
160 2/8	26 0/8	26 5/8	22 6/8	6	5	Winnebago County	IL	Douglas R. Greensides	1991	606
160 1/8	25 7/8	26 2/8	18 5/8	5	6	Polk County	MN	Scott Gullickson	1985	616
160 1/8	25 3/8	25 6/8	17 3/8	6	6	Blue Earth County	MN	Darwin Arndt	1985	616
160 1/8	27 5/8	26 4/8	19 1/8	4	4	Ross County	OH	Randall W. Haines	1986	616
160 1/8	28 6/8	29 7/8	21 3/8	5	4	Lafayette County	WI	Jeff J. Kahle	1988	616
160 1/8	22 3/8	23 0/8	19 1/8	5	5	Clayton County	IA	Wayne M. Lau	1989	616
160 1/8	23 7/8	25 0/8	21 1/8	5	5	Washington County	MS	Odis Hill, Jr.	1990	616
160 1/8	25 3/8	26 6/8	18 4/8	7	10	Huntington County	IN	Troy Harris	1991	616
160 1/8	24 1/8	23 1/8	17 1/8	6	6	Fergus County	MT	John Fleharty	1992	616
160 0/8	24 6/8	24 5/8	21 3/8	6	6	Worth County	IA	Terry Lynch	1972	624
160 0/8	26 3/8	24 7/8	21 6/8	8	5	Winona County	MN	James Enderson	1973	624
160 0/8	23 0/8	22 3/8	20 0/8	5	5	Cooper County	MO	Nancy Smith	1984	624
160 0/8	25 4/8	26 0/8	18 2/8	4	5	Stephenson County	IL	Richard K. Kerr	1985	624
160 0/8	22 7/8	23 0/8	17 2/8	6	5	Morrill County	NE	Michael A. Brening	1985	624
160 0/8	25 2/8	25 4/8	25 2/8	5	5	Ellsworth County	KS	Dave Fisher	1986	624
160 0/8	24 6/8	23 4/8	16 5/8	5	8	Charles County	MD	William J. Kovach	1990	624

SCORE	LENGTH OF R MAIN BEAM L		INSIDE SPREAD	NUMBER OF R POINTS L		AREA	STATE/ PROVINCE	HUNTER'S NAME	DATE	RANK
160 0/8	23 5/8	25 1/8	20 4/8	5	5	Sawyer County	WI	Todd Carlson	1990	624
160 0/8	27 3/8	26 5/8	20 4/8	5	5	Clermont County	OH	John Fischer	1991	624
160 0/8	23 6/8	23 5/8	18 7/8	5	6	Becker County	MN	Kurt Holland	1992	624
159 7/8	22 7/8	22 5/8	18 2/8	5	6	Clark County	KS	William Rule	1983	634
159 7/8	24 4/8	25 4/8	20 1/8	6	5	Garden County	NE	Wynn Fontenot	1984	634
159 7/8	25 7/8	25 2/8	19 5/8	5	5	Brown County	NE	Lorne Allen	1988	634
159 7/8	22 1/8	22 2/8	18 2/8	6	7	Alberta Beach	ALB	Joe Hanson	1991	634
159 7/8	24 6/8	25 1/8	19 5/8	6	5	Will County	IL	Gene Hagberg	1991	634
159 7/8	24 4/8	23 4/8	17 5/8	5	6	Webster County	KS	Ronald G. Nicholson	1991	634
159 6/8	21 2/8	21 2/8	17 0/8	5	5	Vanderburgh County	IN	Floyd Jackson	1977	640
159 6/8	24 1/8	23 2/8	19 6/8	5	6	Sherburne County	MN	Allen Hugget	1981	640
159 6/8	26 7/8	25 6/8	17 6/8	6	6	Buffalo County	WI	Bill Peterson	1981	640
159 6/8	25 0/8	25 0/8	18 2/8	5	5	Miami County	KS	Tom Wiggin	1982	640
159 6/8	25 6/8	25 1/8	20 6/8	4	4	Washington County	MS	Steve Nichols	1986	640
159 6/8	24 6/8	24 7/8	19 5/8	6	5	Page County	IA	Dave Bayless	1986	640
159 6/8	24 5/8	23 6/8	18 4/8	5	6	Rock Island County	IL	Russ Courter	1988	640
159 6/8	26 7/8	27 2/8	17 2/8	4	5	Greenwood County	KS	John Porubski	1989	640
159 5/8	26 3/8	25 5/8	21 5/8	5	5	Des Moines County	IA	Richard Howard	1964	648
159 5/8	22 4/8	22 3/8	18 1/8	5	5	Pittsburg County	OK	John Baumann	1977	648
159 5/8	23 7/8	23 7/8	15 5/8	6	6	Reno County	KS	Richard A. Swisher	1978	648
159 5/8	24 6/8	23 1/8	18 1/8	5	5	Madison County	IL	Barry Ash	1980	648
159 5/8	24 5/8	26 1/8	18 5/8	6	5	Muskingum County	OH	Brent L. Taylor	1981	648
159 5/8	25 4/8	24 7/8	17 7/8	4	4	Ogle County	IL	Charles L. Martoglio	1982	648
159 5/8	24 6/8	24 6/8	20 7/8	6	5	Watonwan County	MN	Richard Enger	1983	648
159 5/8	26 2/8	26 2/8	23 6/8	6	6	Cochrane	ALB	Edward Defrancesco	1984	648
159 5/8	23 2/8	24 4/8	16 1/8	6	5	Hamilton County	IA	Stephen L. Cink	1987	648
159 5/8	23 3/8	23 6/8	15 7/8	6	7	Hennepin County	MN	John Earl Ford	1988	648
159 4/8	27 6/8	27 6/8	25 4/8	4	4	Blue Earth County	MN	Harold Tow	1963	658
159 4/8	22 6/8	21 5/8	17 5/8	6	5	Wabash County	IL	Tom J. McRaven	1967	658
159 4/8	24 5/8	24 6/8	21 2/8	5	5	Hocking County	OH	James Allen Downs	1980	658
159 4/8	22 5/8	22 6/8	18 0/8	5	4	Morris County	KS	Kenneth R. Bryant	1983	658
159 4/8	24 4/8	24 6/8	18 0/8	5	6	Dade County	MO	Charles A. Myers	1985	658
159 4/8	24 7/8	27 3/8	18 0/8	6	6	Scott County	IA	Albert Perreault	1985	658
159 4/8	26 0/8	25 2/8	19 0/8	5	4	Goodhue County	MN	Brad C. Nesseth	1986	658
159 4/8	24 4/8	25 1/8	18 4/8	5	5	Will County	IL	Larry Elumbaugh	1987	658
159 4/8	26 6/8	25 7/8	19 0/8	4	4	Linn County	IA	Jim Arp	1989	658
159 4/8	24 2/8	24 2/8	16 4/8	5	5	Buffalo County	WI	Ronald Brenner	1990	658
159 4/8	25 2/8	23 4/8	18 3/8	5	6	Foster County	ND	Bryon Hallwachs	1990	658
159 4/8	24 5/8	24 2/8	18 0/8	5	5	Pike County	IL	Kevin McCallister	1991	658
159 4/8	25 4/8	25 4/8	20 2/8	5	5	Randolph County	IN	Roy Patterson	1991	658
159 3/8	27 6/8	27 1/8	22 3/8	4	4	Pike County	OH	Ray C. Pritchett, Jr.	1977	671
159 3/8	25 5/8	25 4/8	18 5/8	4	4	Washington County	KS	Tony Mann	1985	671
159 3/8	24 6/8	23 6/8	18 3/8	6	6	Rock Island County	IL	Mike W. Greeno	1988	671
159 3/8	25 6/8	25 6/8	17 7/8	5	5	Pike County	IL	Phil McEuen	1988	671
159 3/8	28 0/8	26 2/8	21 3/8	5	5	Houston County	MN	Steve Bjerke	1989	671
159 3/8	26 0/8	26 0/8	19 1/8	8	5	Hillsdale County	MI	Dennis L. Burlew	1989	671
159 3/8	26 7/8	26 3/8	18 3/8	4	4	Washtenaw County	MI	Gregory Kuhn	1990	671
159 2/8	22 4/8	24 0/8	20 2/8	6	7	Hamlin County	SD	John R. Gregory	1975	678
159 2/8	25 0/8	25 1/8	18 0/8	5	5	Johnson County	AR	Kenn R. Young	1979	678
159 2/8	25 1/8	27 6/8	20 6/8	4	4	Yankton County	SD	Michael L. Tacke	1983	678
159 2/8	23 2/8	23 0/8	16 2/8	5	5	Anne Arundel County	MD	Jim Roy	1985	678
159 2/8	23 3/8	24 7/8	18 2/8	8	5	Madison County	IA	Tom Arpy	1987	678
159 2/8	24 1/8	24 3/8	18 0/8	5	6	Milwaukee County	WI	Terry R. Brandenburg	1989	678
159 1/8	23 7/8	23 0/8	20 1/8	6	6	Lucas County	OH	Martin Higley	1962	684
159 1/8	22 4/8	24 2/8	16 5/8	7	6	Clayton County	IA	Gary Troester	1978	684
159 1/8	26 2/8	25 6/8	17 4/8	6	6	Heard County	GA	Howard E. Taylor	1980	684
159 1/8	24 7/8	25 7/8	21 5/8	8	6	Saline County	KS	Raymond Peterman	1984	684
159 1/8	25 0/8	25 1/8	18 1/8	5	5	Winona County	MN	Vernon Zachariason	1986	684
159 1/8	25 1/8	23 5/8	19 7/8	5	5	Allamakee County	IA	Daniel R. Kennedy	1987	684
159 1/8	23 1/8	23 6/8	18 5/8	5	5	Livingston County	MI	Keith Joseph Daniels	1988	684
159 1/8	23 2/8	24 2/8	16 5/8	5	5	Vermilion County	IL	Horace E. Marsh	1990	684
159 1/8	27 2/8	27 5/8	19 2/8	7	5	Douglas County	KS	Paul Gordon	1991	684
159 0/8	25 7/8	26 1/8	17 6/8	5	5	Shelby County	IL	Gary E. Sievers	1971	693
159 0/8	22 6/8	22 6/8	18 4/8	5	5	Pulaski County	IN	William F. Bean	1977	693
159 0/8	23 3/8	23 7/8	18 3/8	7	7	Sarpy County	NE	Todd W. Steward	1985	693
159 0/8	26 0/8	25 6/8	20 0/8	5	5	Switzerland County	IN	Donald R. Barker	1986	693
159 0/8	24 0/8	24 2/8	16 6/8	5	5	Lawrence County	OH	Kevin Whitt	1986	693
159 0/8	25 6/8	25 2/8	14 4/8	5	5	Jackson County	MN	Ken Bute	1987	693
159 0/8	25 2/8	25 4/8	22 2/8	5	7	Pike County	IL	Steven R. Tice	1989	693
159 0/8	26 6/8	28 2/8	21 3/8	8	7	Clark County	IL	Ronald E. Pender	1989	693

SCORE	LENGTH OF MAIN BEAM		INSIDE SPREAD	NUMBER OF POINTS		AREA	STATE/ PROVINCE	HUNTER'S NAME	DATE	RANK
	R	L		R	L					
159 0/8	23 6/8	23 6/8	18 4/8	5	6	Adair County	OK	Dan Mallory	1990	693
158 7/8	24 7/8	22 4/8	20 3/8	5	6	Pope County	IL	Gary Thomas	1964	702
158 7/8	27 4/8	25 7/8	18 3/8	8	8	Blue Earth County	MN	Gordon F. Kopischke	1968	702
158 7/8	24 7/8	24 2/8	18 1/8	6	5	Owen County	IN	Steven Collins	1973	702
158 7/8	23 1/8	22 4/8	19 7/8	5	5	Sedgwick County	KS	Marion A. Crumm	1974	702
158 7/8	24 1/8	24 1/8	20 6/8	5	6	Putnam County	IL	David A. Heath	1975	702
158 7/8	27 2/8	26 7/8	19 4/8	7	8	Crawford County	OH	Charles Ellis	1977	702
158 7/8	24 4/8	24 1/8	17 7/8	5	5	Charles County	MD	Jim Wright	1986	702
158 7/8	25 2/8	25 2/8	20 3/8	6	7	Paulding County	OH	Karl A. Langham	1988	702
158 7/8	26 7/8	26 1/8	22 1/8	6	5	Henry County	MO	LaVern Rucker	1988	702
158 7/8	23 1/8	23 2/8	17 5/8	5	5	Pottawattamie County	IA	Mike L. Smith	1989	702
158 7/8	25 7/8	24 3/8	20 1/8	7	7	Marshall County	IA	Mark A. Hedum	1990	702
158 7/8	27 4/8	27 1/8	17 3/8	6	6	Chippewa County	WI	Dennis Johnson	1990	702
158 7/8	26 5/8	26 7/8	19 7/8	4	5	Westchester County	NY	Gregg Della Rocca	1991	702
158 6/8	22 5/8	22 7/8	15 6/8	7	7	Irion County	TX	John K. Watson	1977	715
158 6/8	26 5/8	26 5/8	18 6/8	6	6	Dodge County	MN	Mark A. Lenz	1986	715
158 6/8	25 0/8	25 4/8	19 2/8	5	6	Vernon County	WI	Dan Morrison	1988	715
158 6/8	25 1/8	24 0/8	20 2/8	5	5	Brooks County	TX	Billy Ellis III	1989	715
158 6/8	25 6/8	26 2/8	18 6/8	6	7	Howard County	IA	Mike Grube	1992	715
158 5/8	24 3/8	25 3/8	15 6/8	5	9	Marinette County	WI	Valerie P. Williams	1966	720
158 5/8	24 4/8	23 6/8	18 5/8	5	5	Shelby County	IL	Jim Helm	1977	720
158 5/8	25 5/8	26 1/8	18 1/8	4	4	Chariton County	MO	Brian Argetsinger	1986	720
158 5/8	22 7/8	23 3/8	17 1/8	5	5	Lee County	IA	Jeff Horsey	1989	720
158 5/8	23 4/8	23 1/8	20 1/8	7	7	Burlington County	NJ	Thomas A. Stevenson, Sr.	1989	720
158 5/8	26 5/8	27 6/8	19 1/8	5	5	Dane County	WI	Keith Matush	1990	720
158 4/8	23 5/8	22 3/8	20 0/8	5	6	Cedar	KS	Gordon Reneberg	1965	726
158 4/8	26 4/8	25 2/8	22 6/8	5	5	Des Moines County	IA	Michael P. Anderson	1978	726
158 4/8	23 7/8	24 1/8	16 7/8	6	6	Boone County	IA	Chris W. Doran	1984	726
158 4/8	25 3/8	25 0/8	17 0/8	9	6	Adair County	MO	Terry Clay	1987	726
158 4/8	27 4/8	26 4/8	19 2/8	5	5	Adams County	MS	John Harvey	1989	726
158 4/8	25 3/8	25 0/8	20 6/8	6	6	Douglas County	WI	John Lawler	1991	726
158 3/8	22 5/8	23 1/8	15 3/8	6	6	Texas County	OK	Edward F. Bryan, Jr.	1980	732
158 3/8	23 2/8	23 3/8	19 5/8	5	5	Jackson County	MI	Donald L. O'Dell	1984	732
158 3/8	27 5/8	28 6/8	23 4/8	8	4	Douglas County	WI	Gerald Berg	1988	732
158 3/8	24 2/8	24 6/8	20 1/8	5	5	La Porte County	IN	Scott Saliwanchik	1988	732
158 3/8	25 4/8	24 6/8	19 3/8	5	7	Logan County	IL	Douglas A. Hullinger	1989	732
158 3/8	26 5/8	26 6/8	20 3/8	7	7	Jo Daviess County	IL	Michael P. Pickel	1990	732
158 3/8	27 3/8	26 5/8	22 6/8	5	6	Euphrasia	ONT	Tom Perks	1990	732
158 3/8	25 3/8	26 0/8	16 4/8	7	7	Lake County	IL	James C. Carlson	1991	732
158 2/8	26 4/8	24 6/8	22 7/8	5	7	Lee County	IA	Gary Frost	1965	740
158 2/8	25 0/8	26 4/8	21 2/8	5	6	Barron County	WI	Gary Kohlmeyer	1989	740
158 1/8	25 2/8	25 4/8	16 5/8	5	4	Randolph County	IN	Ron J. Carlin	1973	742
158 1/8	22 4/8	22 5/8	17 6/8	6	5	Kossuth County	IA	Steve Rochleau	1981	742
158 1/8	25 1/8	24 2/8	21 5/8	5	4	King George County	VA	L. M. 'Ted' Williams	1981	742
158 1/8	25 2/8	25 4/8	17 7/8	6	6	Jackson County	IA	Jeff W. Ernst	1984	742
158 1/8	25 5/8	24 7/8	18 2/8	6	6	Brown County	OH	Michael W. Babcock	1985	742
158 1/8	26 4/8	26 4/8	18 1/8	6	6	Wyandot County	OH	Michael D Saam	1985	742
158 1/8	25 1/8	25 6/8	15 7/8	5	5	Columbiana County	OH	David S. Landsberger	1986	742
158 1/8	25 4/8	25 6/8	18 6/8	7	6	Rock Island County	IL	Donald G. Jones	1986	742
158 1/8	24 1/8	23 3/8	18 5/8	8	9	Racine County	WI	Joe Spang	1987	742
158 1/8	25 5/8	25 0/8	20 6/8	6	7	Allamakee County	IA	Joe Lieb	1988	742
158 1/8	26 1/8	27 0/8	20 5/8	4	4	Adams County	IL	Jim Vahle	1988	742
158 1/8	22 2/8	21 5/8	17 2/8	6	5	Berkeley County	WV	Robert W. Deeds	1990	742
158 1/8	23 4/8	26 4/8	20 1/8	5	5	Bullitt County	KY	Tim Williams	1991	742
158 0/8	24 0/8	23 5/8	18 6/8	6	6	Wayne County	IL	Bill Naney	1981	755
158 0/8	24 0/8	24 0/8	19 1/8	6	6	Lancaster County	NE	Martin Erickson	1983	755
158 0/8	26 5/8	26 1/8	19 6/8	4	5	Jackson County	OH	Jim Ridge	1986	755
158 0/8	24 2/8	23 6/8	19 2/8	5	5	Jackson County	IA	Terry Amling	1988	755
158 0/8	24 5/8	23 0/8	20 0/8	6	6	Houston County	MN	Michael Val Stevens	1989	755
158 0/8	24 6/8	24 5/8	20 6/8	5	6	Webster County	IA	Mike Jones	1989	755
158 0/8	24 1/8	24 7/8	17 6/8	5	7	Ogle County	IL	Art Heinze	1990	755
158 0/8	27 4/8	26 3/8	17 4/8	5	5	Van Buren County	IA	Gerald Palmer	1990	755
158 0/8	25 6/8	25 7/8	16 0/8	5	5	Bremer County	IA	Virgil Marlette	1991	755
157 7/8	23 0/8	25 0/8	19 5/8	5	5	Meeker County	MN	Russell T. Nelson	1974	764
157 7/8	28 5/8	28 6/8	25 7/8	4	4	Goodhue County	MN	John 'Jack' Cordes	1975	764
157 7/8	23 7/8	24 1/8	16 4/8	5	7	Harvey County	KS	P. Bruce Mosiman	1984	764
157 7/8	26 5/8	27 2/8	19 1/8	5	6	Boone County	MO	Robert Hagans	1986	764
157 7/8	27 2/8	25 6/8	17 2/8	6	7	Calhoun County	MI	Jeff Edward Titus	1986	764
157 7/8	21 2/8	22 6/8	16 5/8	5	7	Butler County	KS	Jim P. Smith	1987	764
157 7/8	24 2/8	24 2/8	19 7/8	5	5	Sedgwick County	KS	Jim Molitor	1988	764

SCORE	LENGTH OF R MAIN BEAM L		INSIDE SPREAD	NUMBER OF R POINTS L		AREA	STATE/ PROVINCE	HUNTER'S NAME	DATE	RANK
157 7/8	23 3/8	22 6/8	18 2/8	6	5	Boone County	IA	Jim Humberg	1988	764
157 7/8	24 0/8	23 7/8	14 6/8	5	7	Simpson County	KY	Mike Stovall	1990	764
157 6/8	23 7/8	24 2/8	15 4/8	5	5	Lyon County	MN	M. Dean Holm	1976	773
157 6/8	23 4/8	23 3/8	18 4/8	5	5	Phillips County	KS	Lavern A. Wheaton	1978	773
157 6/8	25 3/8	26 1/8	19 5/8	6	6	Des Moines County	IA	David Bollei	1979	773
157 6/8	24 7/8	25 2/8	21 4/8	4	6	Geauga County	OH	John A. Suszynski	1981	773
157 6/8	24 4/8	24 4/8	16 4/8	4	5	Oconto County	WI	Richard E. Liss	1983	773
157 6/8	23 3/8	23 6/8	17 1/8	6	6	Leavenworth County	KS	John Garrison	1983	773
157 6/8	23 6/8	23 6/8	17 5/8	8	6	Des Moines County	IA	Ken Thorndyke	1984	773
157 6/8	26 6/8	25 3/8	19 4/8	5	5	Genesee County	MI	Alfred L. Allen	1987	773
157 6/8	25 1/8	25 4/8	18 4/8	4	5	Martin County	IN	Terry Kirkman	1987	773
157 6/8	27 6/8	28 6/8	19 2/8	5	5	Shawnee County	KS	Steven E. Deever	1988	773
157 6/8	23 4/8	22 7/8	18 2/8	7	5	Yankton County	SD	Alan Peterson	1988	773
157 6/8	25 4/8	25 4/8	21 4/8	4	4	McLean County	IL	Jim Dicken	1991	773
157 6/8	23 0/8	25 4/8	21 2/8	4	4	Vermilion	ALB	Glenn Moir	1992	773
157 5/8	22 4/8	23 2/8	16 5/8	6	7	Marion County	KS	Ron Hershberger	1982	786
157 5/8	22 7/8	24 2/8	18 7/8	5	6	Fulton County	AR	Lynn Luther	1983	786
157 5/8	27 4/8	27 2/8	21 1/8	5	6	Saline County	KS	Richard Cockroft	1985	786
157 5/8	24 3/8	23 7/8	19 5/8	6	5	Bartholomew County	IN	Jean E. Sneed	1986	786
157 5/8	24 1/8	24 0/8	15 7/8	6	6	Atoka County	OK	Patrick C. Patton	1988	786
157 5/8	25 5/8	26 0/8	21 1/8	5	5	Morgan County	IL	Roger Smith	1989	786
157 5/8	26 0/8	26 1/8	21 3/8	5	6	Wayne County	MO	Rod Bowling	1989	786
157 5/8	24 4/8	25 3/8	22 2/8	4	7	McHenry County	IL	Dennis Huhn	1990	786
157 5/8	25 0/8	24 7/8	19 1/8	6	6	Wood County	WI	Michael L. Hewitt	1991	786
157 5/8	24 3/8	25 3/8	20 6/8	5	6	Du Page County	IL	Ron Knebel	1991	786
157 5/8	24 3/8	24 5/8	18 0/8	6	7	Washington County	IA	Chris Davies	1991	786
157 4/8	25 7/8	25 7/8	17 2/8	4	4	Marion County	IA	Charles H. Walter	1967	797
157 4/8	22 7/8	23 5/8	18 0/8	5	5	Kalamazoo County	MI	Guy Stutzman	1979	797
157 4/8	24 2/8	24 4/8	13 6/8	5	5	Webster County	IA	Larry K. Fossen	1980	797
157 4/8	23 1/8	22 4/8	20 4/8	4	6	Henry County	VA	Mike Weaver	1986	797
157 4/8	23 5/8	22 6/8	21 1/8	5	6	Jackson County	OH	Steven L. Roe	1987	797
157 4/8	23 5/8	23 4/8	19 2/8	5	5	Hardin County	IL	Larry Hall	1988	797
157 4/8	22 6/8	21 1/8	16 2/8	6	6	Grundy County	IL	Brian Bergmann	1988	797
157 4/8	24 7/8	24 3/8	18 4/8	4	5	Hennepin County	MN	Mike Hintzen	1990	797
157 4/8	21 3/8	27 3/8	21 4/8	5	5	Crawford County	IL	Steve Parker	1990	797
157 4/8	24 1/8	24 3/8	19 2/8	6	5	Sawyer County	WI	Gary Haus	1991	797
157 4/8	25 4/8	25 7/8	20 0/8	4	4	Lake County	IL	Russ Tallman	1992	797
157 3/8	23 0/8	23 2/8	22 7/8	5	5	Adams County	IL	John Musolino	1966	808
157 3/8	23 5/8	23 2/8	16 3/8	5	5	Harrison County	KY	Kevin Poe	1984	808
157 3/8	24 4/8	23 1/8	16 1/8	6	5	Yuma County	CO	Chuck Anderson, Sr.	1985	808
157 3/8	24 4/8	24 4/8	19 1/8	4	4	Vermilion County	IL	Russell A. Sill	1989	808
157 3/8	24 6/8	24 2/8	17 7/8	6	6	Price County	WI	Mike Case	1990	808
157 2/8	23 1/8	22 6/8	16 2/8	6	6	Johnson County	IL	Jim Casey	1963	813
157 2/8	22 3/8	23 2/8	16 4/8	5	5	Mountrail County	ND	Dean A. Rehak	1963	813
157 2/8	22 3/8	22 2/8	21 1/8	8	6	Cottonwood County	MN	Brian Grothe	1978	813
157 2/8	27 6/8	27 6/8	22 3/8	5	6	Jessamine County	KY	David Cartwright	1979	813
157 2/8	25 4/8	25 0/8	17 6/8	5	6	Argyle	MAN	Russ Snell	1982	813
157 2/8	26 2/8	28 0/8	20 4/8	8	5	Westchester County	NY	Ralph Finacchiaro	1983	813
157 2/8	25 5/8	26 2/8	17 0/8	5	5	Chickasaw County	IA	Theodore J. Steege IV	1987	813
157 2/8	25 2/8	25 0/8	20 4/8	5	5	Ashland County	OH	Bert P. Reynolds	1989	813
157 2/8	23 5/8	23 6/8	19 7/8	7	6	Elbert County	CO	Tom Kelley	1990	813
157 2/8	23 6/8	23 3/8	18 0/8	5	5	Houston County	MN	Rob Larson	1991	813
157 2/8	25 0/8	24 5/8	17 4/8	6	6	Chisago County	MN	Chris Peterson	1991	813
157 1/8	25 3/8	26 1/8	18 5/8	6	6	Puslinch Twp.	ONT	Jeff Sinclair	1977	824
157 1/8	25 4/8	24 4/8	23 3/8	6	5	Fairfax County	VA	Chris Jackson	1986	824
157 1/8	25 7/8	22 4/8	16 4/8	7	5	Eaton County	MI	Bryan Coburn	1990	824
157 1/8	23 5/8	22 4/8	18 5/8	5	5	McHenry County	IL	Rich Matras	1991	824
157 0/8	25 7/8	26 0/8	16 5/8	6	7	Watonwan County	MN	Dave Ellertson	1973	828
157 0/8	25 3/8	26 0/8	15 6/8	7	8	McKenzie County	ND	Donald Olson	1974	828
157 0/8	24 3/8	26 0/8	18 6/8	8	6	Ashland County	OH	William Kucic	1985	828
157 0/8	23 6/8	23 7/8	20 7/8	7	6	McLean County	IL	Daryle W. Tipsord	1985	828
157 0/8	24 5/8	23 4/8	17 5/8	5	6	Kiowa County	KS	Royce E. Frazier	1986	828
157 0/8	25 3/8	25 7/8	21 4/8	5	4	Blue Earth County	MN	Tom Lacina	1987	828
157 0/8	24 7/8	26 7/8	18 0/8	5	5	Roane County	TN	Larry T. Cook	1988	828
157 0/8	24 6/8	23 0/8	20 3/8	8	9	Lake County	IL	Mike Mitten	1988	828
157 0/8	23 6/8	23 4/8	18 2/8	6	7	Parke County	IN	Jeff Myers	1989	828
157 0/8	27 0/8	27 0/8	19 7/8	6	5	Clayton County	IA	Curt Ferguson	1989	828
157 0/8	25 6/8	26 1/8	19 4/8	7	6	Brown County	IL	Larry Grant	1992	828
156 7/8	28 7/8	26 6/8	19 7/8	5	5	Chippewa County	MN	Paul D. Lundgren	1969	839
156 7/8	25 2/8	24 5/8	19 7/8	6	5	Johnson County	KS	Jim Laybourne	1979	839

SCORE	LENGTH OF MAIN BEAM R / L		INSIDE SPREAD	NUMBER OF POINTS R / L		AREA	STATE/ PROVINCE	HUNTER'S NAME	DATE	RANK
156 7/8	25 6/8	25 4/8	19 7/8	6	5	Lake County	IL	Dennis P. Schor	1979	839
156 7/8	27 1/8	25 0/8	21 3/8	5	6	Clearwater County	MN	Dennis Engerbretson	1980	839
156 7/8	23 7/8	23 7/8	19 5/8	5	5	Cherokee County	IA	Dan Roberts	1982	839
156 7/8	24 0/8	23 7/8	18 0/8	6	6	Butler County	KS	William D. George	1986	839
156 7/8	23 6/8	24 4/8	19 6/8	5	6	Atoka County	OK	Kevin W. Guinn	1987	839
156 7/8	26 6/8	26 4/8	20 1/8	5	5	Eugenia	ONT	Ron Lusher	1987	839
156 7/8	25 1/8	24 1/8	20 2/8	6	5	Franklin County	IA	Ron Hansen	1990	839
156 7/8	24 5/8	23 4/8	19 1/8	6	5	Morrison County	MN	Stephan Felix	1992	839
156 6/8	27 1/8	26 5/8	20 5/8	5	5	Lincoln County	WV	Gary Smith	1970	849
156 6/8	24 1/8	24 0/8	16 6/8	5	5	Meigs County	OH	Brian Kelley	1982	849
156 6/8	26 7/8	26 4/8	20 0/8	6	5	Des Moines County	IA	Don Smith	1986	849
156 6/8	24 4/8	24 2/8	16 2/8	6	7	Clark County	IL	Gary Taylor	1986	849
156 6/8	24 4/8	24 4/8	20 2/8	5	4	Howard County	IA	Terry Larson	1987	849
156 6/8	25 4/8	24 6/8	19 2/8	5	5	Washington County	IL	Bruce Diedrich	1987	849
156 6/8	23 0/8	24 0/8	16 7/8	7	5	Walworth County	WI	Brian Strickler	1988	849
156 6/8	22 6/8	23 5/8	18 2/8	5	5	Miami County	OH	Gary L. Tipps	1988	849
156 6/8	26 4/8	26 5/8	18 4/8	6	5	Lapeer County	MI	Wayne Coulman	1990	849
156 5/8	26 1/8	25 2/8	20 2/8	6	6	Grant County	WI	Walter Edge	1957	858
156 5/8	24 6/8	26 3/8	19 5/8	5	4	Traverse County	MN	Roland L. Hausmann	1960	858
156 5/8	22 7/8	25 0/8	19 6/8	7	7	Des Moines County	IA	E. E. Smith	1965	858
156 5/8	23 7/8	24 1/8	18 7/8	7	7	Nicollet County	MN	Thomas J. Merkley	1967	858
156 5/8	27 3/8	26 2/8	21 5/8	5	5	Queen Annes County	MD	Charles Milford Squires	1969	858
156 5/8	24 7/8	24 3/8	21 1/8	6	5	Wabaunsee County	KS	Tom Willard	1983	858
156 5/8	22 0/8	22 2/8	16 1/8	6	8	Kossuth County	IA	Ron Burton	1985	858
156 5/8	24 3/8	24 3/8	19 3/8	5	5	Johnson County	IA	Larry Hermanstorfer	1987	858
156 5/8	22 6/8	23 3/8	20 7/8	5	5	Price County	WI	Larry Halvorson	1990	858
156 5/8	24 5/8	24 4/8	18 7/8	5	5	Eaton County	MI	Dudley Miller, Jr.	1990	858
156 4/8	26 4/8	25 7/8	22 5/8	4	5	Williamson County	IL	Roy Williams	1960	868
156 4/8	26 3/8	24 4/8	17 4/8	5	6	Forest County	WI	Daniel Radder	1968	868
156 4/8	24 1/8	23 3/8	15 0/8	6	5	Jones County	IA	Gary McCormick	1977	868
156 4/8	23 7/8	24 1/8	18 3/8	6	6	Graham County	KS	Russell Hull	1979	868
156 4/8	24 4/8	23 6/8	21 4/8	5	5	Waukesha County	WI	Steve Hoelz	1987	868
156 4/8	27 0/8	27 5/8	19 1/8	6	6	McLeod County	MN	Craig Hrkal	1988	868
156 4/8	24 3/8	21 0/8	19 4/8	5	5	Jackson County	OH	Michael L. Cornett	1988	868
156 4/8	25 4/8	25 5/8	17 6/8	7	7	Osage County	KS	Gerald Britschge	1988	868
156 4/8	22 0/8	24 0/8	19 3/8	6	8	Macoupin County	IL	Rick D. Tigo	1990	868
156 3/8	27 0/8	25 5/8	20 0/8	8	6	Hamilton County	KS	Mike Gilbert	1977	877
156 3/8	25 0/8	25 2/8	18 4/8	6	8	Russell County	KS	John W. Frost	1983	877
156 3/8	24 4/8	24 3/8	21 5/8	6	6	Mills County	IA	Douglas R. Roll	1986	877
156 3/8	25 4/8	25 2/8	16 7/8	6	5	Vernon County	WI	David Penchi	1987	877
156 3/8	22 1/8	23 4/8	17 1/8	6	7	Trempealeau County	WI	Ginger Molitor	1988	877
156 3/8	22 4/8	23 4/8	14 7/8	6	7	Polk County	WI	Jon Mattson	1989	877
156 3/8	25 0/8	24 5/8	20 5/8	5	4	Effingham County	IL	Tim Dillow	1989	877
156 3/8	24 4/8	24 2/8	19 7/8	5	7	Sioux County	IA	Owen Sandbulte	1991	877
156 3/8	27 4/8	26 4/8	21 4/8	6	6	Lawrence County	OH	Richard L. Carte	1991	877
156 2/8	26 1/8	26 4/8	21 0/8	6	6	Butler County	KS	Ralph R. Belt	1967	886
156 2/8	25 0/8	23 2/8	18 0/8	9	6	Palo Alto County	IA	Earl J. Gustafson	1972	886
156 2/8	23 3/8	23 6/8	16 6/8	5	5	Fulton County	IL	Sam Smith	1973	886
156 2/8	25 3/8	25 3/8	23 6/8	5	6	Winona County	MN	Daniel McIntire	1979	886
156 2/8	22 2/8	22 7/8	16 6/8	5	5	Garfield County	MT	Larry H. Hoyt	1982	886
156 2/8	25 2/8	26 2/8	18 6/8	6	5	Stevens County	WA	Tom Duffey	1983	886
156 2/8	25 5/8	26 1/8	19 0/8	4	5	Ogle County	IL	Gary D. Shaw	1984	886
156 2/8	25 1/8	26 0/8	19 4/8	5	5	Oakland County	MI	David B. Tater	1984	886
156 2/8	24 2/8	24 6/8	21 0/8	5	4	Cass County	IL	Dale Milstead	1985	886
156 2/8	26 2/8	27 0/8	20 0/8	5	5	Washington County	IA	Carl Stogdill	1986	886
156 2/8	24 5/8	24 3/8	20 6/8	8	5	Kankakee County	IL	Al Weissbohn	1988	886
156 2/8	26 4/8	26 1/8	16 0/8	4	4	Washburn County	WI	Cullan Hanacek	1989	886
156 2/8	27 0/8	26 6/8	22 2/8	5	7	Lafayette County	WI	Mike Sigafus	1989	886
156 2/8	25 1/8	25 0/8	20 6/8	5	5	La Salle County	TX	Dr. F. D. Elias	1990	886
156 2/8	25 5/8	24 5/8	18 6/8	6	5	Mitchell County	IA	Don Weber	1990	886
156 1/8	25 4/8	25 2/8	19 1/8	5	5	Crawford County	IL	Mickie D. Purcell	1972	901
156 1/8	24 3/8	23 7/8	19 7/8	5	5	Ravalli County	MT	Vernon L. Cooper	1977	901
156 1/8	25 4/8	25 6/8	19 1/8	5	5	Tompkins County	NY	Alan C. Boda	1981	901
156 1/8	22 6/8	23 2/8	17 7/8	5	5	Monroe County	OH	Wendell Newhouse	1982	901
156 1/8	24 3/8	25 0/8	19 7/8	7	8	Douglas County	NE	Oran L. Foxworthy	1984	901
156 1/8	25 5/8	24 6/8	22 1/8	4	4	Sumner County	KS	Ralph Shaver	1984	901
156 1/8	22 1/8	25 7/8	17 1/8	7	5	Cloud County	KS	Richard Bieker	1985	901
156 1/8	24 5/8	24 4/8	18 1/8	5	5	Prowers County	CO	Lynn Leonard	1988	901
156 1/8	24 5/8	26 0/8	17 5/8	7	5	Osage County	KS	Daniel Beavers	1989	901
156 1/8	25 3/8	26 3/8	21 4/8	6	6	Sarpy County	NE	Gregg E. Lind	1990	901

SCORE	LENGTH OF MAIN BEAM		INSIDE SPREAD	NUMBER OF POINTS		AREA	STATE/ PROVINCE	HUNTER'S NAME	DATE	RANK
	R	L		R	L					
156 1/8	25 4/8	27 0/8	19 4/8	6	6	Jackson County	IA	David Shepherd	1990	901
156 1/8	25 6/8	25 0/8	23 3/8	6	6	Hamilton County	OH	Dave Brackett	1990	901
156 1/8	27 6/8	28 1/8	20 1/8	7	5	Wayne County	IL	James Isles	1990	901
156 1/8	24 7/8	25 0/8	18 1/8	5	5	Jo Daviess County	IL	Brian Smith	1991	901
156 0/8	26 0/8	27 1/8	16 4/8	4	5	Bertie County	NC	Gordon Gardner	1975	915
156 0/8	23 4/8	23 7/8	19 6/8	5	5	Stark County	OH	Don Cerosky	1979	915
156 0/8	25 5/8	25 6/8	19 6/8	4	4	Louisa County	IA	Roger Gipple	1982	915
156 0/8	22 2/8	22 5/8	19 6/8	7	7	Perry County	IL	Terry Queen	1983	915
156 0/8	24 0/8	24 2/8	17 6/8	5	7	Owen County	IN	Michael A. Miller	1986	915
156 0/8	26 5/8	25 2/8	18 4/8	7	6	Licking County	OH	Robert R. Hutchison	1989	915
156 0/8	24 1/8	23 3/8	18 0/8	5	5	Alpena County	MI	Samuel Lee Freese	1989	915
156 0/8	23 1/8	22 7/8	18 2/8	5	5	Trempealeau County	WI	Dane Zielke	1989	915
156 0/8	22 7/8	24 5/8	16 7/8	6	7	Butler County	KS	Dave Cornish	1989	915
156 0/8	25 2/8	25 0/8	20 2/8	5	6	Carver County	MN	Brian Klingelhutz	1990	915
156 0/8	24 6/8	24 4/8	18 0/8	8	8	Oklahoma County	OK	Greg Boydston	1990	915
156 0/8	24 0/8	25 5/8	18 5/8	5	7	Warren County	IL	Brian P. Monroe	1990	915
156 0/8	25 3/8	25 2/8	19 0/8	4	5	Clearwater County	ID	Robert Willkas	1990	915
156 0/8	24 7/8	23 7/8	20 4/8	5	5	Macon County	IL	Charlie DeBose, Jr.	1991	915
156 0/8	23 3/8	24 4/8	18 2/8	5	5	Will County	IL	Larry G. Koerner	1991	915
155 7/8	24 7/8	24 4/8	19 7/8	5	5	Frontier County	NE	Charles Druse	1963	930
155 7/8	24 3/8	24 5/8	15 5/8	5	5	Harrison County	IA	Clarence N. Jackson, Jr.	1963	930
155 7/8	26 0/8	24 5/8	17 3/8	6	8	Neosho County	KS	Jeff Friederich	1983	930
155 7/8	25 4/8	25 1/8	16 7/8	5	5	Macon County	IL	Mike Nickell	1985	930
155 7/8	24 7/8	24 5/8	20 4/8	6	7	Becker County	MN	Paul Adams	1988	930
155 7/8	22 5/8	22 7/8	18 1/8	5	5	Bremer County	IA	John W. Breitbach	1989	930
155 7/8	26 7/8	26 5/8	23 1/8	5	5	Charles County	MD	Scott Bressler	1990	930
155 7/8	26 6/8	25 6/8	16 2/8	7	6	Anderson County	KS	Kurt A. Sayers	1990	930
155 7/8	22 1/8	23 5/8	21 5/8	6	5	Hardin County	IA	Tom Catlin	1990	930
155 7/8	22 1/8	20 6/8	21 5/8	5	5	Jackson County	WI	Calvin J. Haag	1991	930
155 6/8	25 1/8	24 4/8	18 4/8	4	5	Madison County	NE	Dick Gambill	1967	940
155 6/8	23 0/8	23 6/8	19 2/8	5	6	Monroe County	IA	John Vollmer	1982	940
155 6/8	24 0/8	23 6/8	16 7/8	5	6	Area 28	MAN	Gary Kaluzniak	1983	940
155 6/8	21 6/8	20 5/8	16 4/8	6	6	McHenry County	IL	Michael D. Patrick	1984	940
155 6/8	25 2/8	24 1/8	20 2/8	5	5	Lawrence County	MO	David T. Kail	1984	940
155 6/8	23 7/8	23 5/8	18 2/8	5	5	Morrison County	MN	Thomas Barron, Jr.	1987	940
155 6/8	24 5/8	24 6/8	16 2/8	5	6	Des Moines County	IA	Pat Stallman	1988	940
155 6/8	26 0/8	26 2/8	16 6/8	5	5	Allamakee County	IA	Dan Brimeyer	1988	940
155 6/8	23 4/8	23 1/8	18 4/8	5	5	Marion County	IA	Thomas L. Tucker	1988	940
155 6/8	22 2/8	22 2/8	16 0/8	5	6	Troup County	GA	James E. Hogan	1989	940
155 6/8	24 0/8	24 0/8	14 4/8	5	6	Shelby County	IL	Brian Herzog	1991	940
155 5/8	25 5/8	26 0/8	19 1/8	5	6	Rice County	KS	Gordon Leo Rayl	1967	951
155 5/8	22 5/8	23 0/8	18 5/8	5	5	Anne Arundel County	MD	Gene Hyatt	1976	951
155 5/8	25 2/8	23 7/8	17 1/8	5	5	Trempealeau County	WI	Greg Halpern	1982	951
155 5/8	25 7/8	25 3/8	20 5/8	4	4	Clayton County	IA	Gerald W. Kluesner	1986	951
155 5/8	24 5/8	23 3/8	18 7/8	5	5	Chase County	KS	Jerry Keller	1986	951
155 5/8	25 6/8	27 3/8	20 4/8	9	7	Perry County	IL	Jerry M. Smith	1987	951
155 5/8	26 6/8	28 0/8	18 5/8	5	5	Logan County	OH	Dan Jergens	1987	951
155 5/8	23 6/8	25 0/8	17 5/8	5	5	Pierce County	WI	Greg Koehler	1988	951
155 5/8	23 3/8	23 0/8	18 5/8	6	6	Kane County	IL	James A. Anderson	1989	951
155 5/8	23 6/8	23 7/8	15 2/8	6	5	Brown County	IN	Frank Cross	1989	951
155 5/8	25 1/8	24 1/8	18 3/8	4	4	Fairfield County	CT	Stephen M. Ruttkamp	1989	951
155 5/8	24 3/8	24 5/8	19 3/8	5	5	Morrison County	MN	James Anderson	1990	951
155 5/8	23 3/8	22 7/8	18 1/8	5	5	Kingman County	KS	Ed Laverentz	1991	951
155 5/8	25 1/8	24 7/8	15 7/8	5	5	Cook County	MN	Richard D. Nelson	1991	951
155 4/8	23 2/8	25 4/8	18 6/8	7	7	Westchester County	NY	Bernard J. Crescione	1960	965
155 4/8	25 5/8	25 5/8	16 4/8	5	5	Marion County	IA	Thomas L. Tucker	1967	965
155 4/8	26 2/8	25 4/8	22 3/8	5	6	Dubuque County	IA	Kurt Cable	1973	965
155 4/8	23 6/8	25 2/8	19 5/8	7	7	Flathead County	MT	Ralph Ertz	1977	965
155 4/8	22 3/8	22 3/8	18 1/8	5	6	Lucas County	IA	Lance Brauer	1980	965
155 4/8	23 2/8	23 6/8	16 6/8	5	5	Lyon County	KS	Ronald E. Rhodes	1981	965
155 4/8	27 0/8	26 2/8	20 0/8	4	4	Houston County	MN	Gary L. Maier	1985	965
155 4/8	23 4/8	24 0/8	20 0/8	5	5	Posey County	IN	Duane Daws	1985	965
155 4/8	24 1/8	24 0/8	19 4/8	5	5	Marinette County	WI	John Floriano	1985	965
155 4/8	25 1/8	24 6/8	18 0/8	5	6	Washburn County	WI	Wayne Dahlstrom	1986	965
155 4/8	25 7/8	26 3/8	22 0/8	7	6	Winnebago County	IL	Vaughn Zimmerman	1986	965
155 4/8	25 1/8	24 4/8	16 4/8	6	5	Jackson County	MO	Charles C. Shotton	1987	965
155 4/8	23 3/8	24 1/8	16 2/8	5	6	Hennepin County	MN	Delmer Bentz	1988	965
155 4/8	25 1/8	24 2/8	19 7/8	8	7	Meeker County	MN	Pete Roeser	1990	965
155 4/8	24 7/8	25 6/8	22 4/8	4	4	Morgan County	IL	Gerald L. Stone	1990	965
155 4/8	27 4/8	24 4/8	22 2/8	6	6	Rush County	IN	Daniel D. Drysdale	1991	965

SCORE	LENGTH OF MAIN BEAM R	L	INSIDE SPREAD	NUMBER OF POINTS R	L	AREA	STATE/ PROVINCE	HUNTER'S NAME	DATE	RANK
155 4/8	24 3/8	24 1/8	18 3/8	7	8	Jefferson County	OH	Michael W. Brown	1991	965
155 4/8	26 3/8	26 2/8	22 0/8	4	4	Montgomery County	OH	Kim Hammontree	1991	965
155 3/8	23 5/8	24 0/8	18 4/8	6	7	Finney County	KS	Wray Decker	1966	983
155 3/8	26 0/8	26 3/8	21 1/8	5	6	Chickasaw County	IA	William A. Harris	1978	983
155 3/8	23 3/8	24 2/8	16 0/8	6	5	Union County	OH	Jerry Faine	1982	983
155 3/8	26 2/8	25 5/8	19 6/8	6	4	Dodge County	MN	Jimmie Donald Hanna	1983	983
155 3/8	29 2/8	28 2/8	19 7/8	6	8	McDonough County	IL	Locie L. Murphy	1983	983
155 3/8	24 6/8	24 3/8	20 3/8	5	6	Codington County	SD	Mark Beutow	1983	983
155 3/8	24 4/8	24 5/8	21 3/8	5	5	Suffolk County	NY	John C. Wehrs	1984	983
155 3/8	21 4/8	22 0/8	15 5/8	5	6	McKenzie County	ND	Brent Smith	1985	983
155 3/8	23 7/8	23 6/8	16 5/8	5	5	Cherry County	NE	Gary Galloway	1985	983
155 3/8	25 4/8	25 6/8	20 3/8	7	5	Pulaski County	MO	Bruce Agee	1986	983
155 3/8	25 2/8	26 2/8	23 1/8	5	5	Sabine County	TX	Bobby Brundidge	1986	983
155 3/8	29 6/8	28 7/8	20 7/8	5	6	Highland County	OH	William E. Lee	1987	983
155 3/8	24 6/8	24 5/8	18 1/8	5	5	Vermilion County	IL	Gary L. Wilford	1988	983
155 3/8	26 3/8	25 4/8	20 0/8	4	5	Butler County	KS	Mike Demel	1990	983
155 3/8	22 6/8	23 0/8	15 0/8	5	8	Menard County	IL	Norman Horn	1991	983
155 3/8	24 0/8	24 1/8	16 5/8	5	5	Fillmore County	MN	Danny L. Cole	1991	983
155 2/8	22 0/8	21 6/8	17 4/8	6	5	Benton County	IA	Gene Pollock	1958	999
155 2/8	25 0/8	25 5/8	18 3/8	5	6	Floyd County	IA	Richard G. Long	1967	999
155 2/8	26 4/8	25 4/8	15 2/8	6	6	Scott County	VA	Hugh McConnell	1978	999
155 2/8	21 6/8	21 7/8	20 0/8	5	5	Des Moines County	IA	Brad Entsminger	1980	999
155 2/8	24 5/8	24 2/8	15 4/8	5	6	Knox County	OH	Robert Hammond	1980	999
155 2/8	23 7/8	24 3/8	17 1/8	5	6	Richland County	MT	Wynn Privratsky	1980	999
155 2/8	25 3/8	25 4/8	18 4/8	5	5	Licking County	OH	Richard E Pipes	1984	999
155 2/8	24 4/8	24 1/8	18 0/8	6	6	Lake County	MI	John Mudrovich	1984	999
155 2/8	27 0/8	25 4/8	21 6/8	4	5	Ogle County	IL	Vernon Rasmussen	1986	999
155 2/8	26 4/8	26 7/8	17 2/8	5	5	Holmes County	OH	Wanda L. Horwath	1988	999
155 2/8	27 0/8	26 0/8	18 6/8	5	5	Buffalo County	WI	Gary R. Stutz	1988	999
155 2/8	28 2/8	27 5/8	20 4/8	5	4	Parke County	IN	Charles Paxton	1989	999
155 2/8	23 7/8	25 2/8	18 0/8	6	5	Jefferson County	KS	Leon Lemons	1989	999
155 2/8	24 5/8	24 4/8	15 4/8	5	5	Burnett County	WI	William F. Hurley	1990	999
155 2/8	24 7/8	24 6/8	20 2/8	5	6	Appanoose County	IA	Steven P. Salmieri	1990	999
155 1/8	24 7/8	24 7/8	17 3/8	5	5	Roberts County	SD	Roland L. Hausmann	1959	1,014
155 1/8	25 2/8	24 7/8	19 3/8	6	6	Madison County	KY	Sonny Barker	1965	1,014
155 1/8	25 6/8	25 0/8	19 7/8	6	5	Morrison County	MN	Timothy L. Kampa	1984	1,014
155 1/8	24 7/8	25 7/8	19 7/8	5	5	Calhoun County	MI	Steve D. Munier	1985	1,014
155 1/8	29 0/8	26 6/8	22 0/8	5	4	Vermilion County	IL	Allen Walker	1986	1,014
155 1/8	25 7/8	25 4/8	17 3/8	5	5	Pawnee County	KS	Carol Moffatt	1986	1,014
155 1/8	24 4/8	24 7/8	16 7/8	5	5	Barron County	WI	Tom Lindquist	1987	1,014
155 1/8	25 4/8	26 7/8	19 7/8	6	5	Allegan County	MI	Craig S. Blank	1989	1,014
155 1/8	24 1/8	23 2/8	14 6/8	8	6	Chisago County	MN	James Lehman	1990	1,014
155 1/8	24 2/8	23 7/8	22 7/8	5	5	Clermont County	OH	Paul L. Voshell	1992	1,014
155 0/8	23 7/8	24 5/8	18 6/8	7	7	Pope County	MN	John Myhre	1982	1,024
155 0/8	24 6/8	24 1/8	22 7/8	6	7	Montgomery County	IL	Keith Pierce	1983	1,024
155 0/8	20 5/8	24 0/8	15 7/8	9	7	Lee County	IA	Ralph D. Zaehringer	1985	1,024
155 0/8	23 5/8	22 2/8	18 5/8	8	7	Clayton County	IA	Daniel L. Parker	1986	1,024
155 0/8	25 2/8	26 6/8	17 1/8	6	5	Barber County	KS	Robert Ricke	1987	1,024
155 0/8	24 7/8	24 6/8	16 4/8	6	5	Wayne County	MO	Steve Rueck	1988	1,024
155 0/8	25 3/8	25 1/8	18 6/8	7	8	Sawyer County	WI	Greg Peterson	1989	1,024
155 0/8	24 0/8	24 5/8	17 7/8	7	5	Jefferson County	WI	Scott Bolson	1989	1,024
155 0/8	27 1/8	26 2/8	21 2/8	5	7	St. Clair County	IL	Andy T. Contratto	1989	1,024
155 0/8	22 2/8	24 3/8	17 4/8	4	4	Wapello County	IA	Larry Johns	1990	1,024
155 0/8	23 6/8	23 1/8	18 4/8	6	6	Coffey County	KS	David W. Bess	1990	1,024
155 0/8	25 0/8	25 4/8	16 6/8	5	4	Marion County	KS	Ron Hershberger	1990	1,024
155 0/8	25 1/8	25 0/8	18 6/8	6	5	Polk County	MN	Steven Cornell	1990	1,024
155 0/8	25 7/8	25 4/8	18 0/8	5	5	Pope County	MN	Bradley D. Rosten	1991	1,024
155 0/8	27 4/8	27 3/8	23 6/8	5	6	Bent County	CO	Jay Waring	1991	1,024
154 7/8	26 7/8	25 7/8	18 2/8	5	5	Murray County	MN	Craig Cohrs	1968	1,039
154 7/8	26 5/8	25 6/8	17 6/8	7	8	Pendleton County	KY	Thomas P. Jones	1969	1,039
154 7/8	22 5/8	23 2/8	23 1/8	6	6	Auglaize County	OH	Gary L. Dues	1979	1,039
154 7/8	23 4/8	23 5/8	16 4/8	5	4	Kingsbury County	SD	Dan R. Limmer	1981	1,039
154 7/8	23 0/8	24 0/8	19 5/8	5	6	Hennepin County	MN	Harold Greseth	1983	1,039
154 7/8	23 4/8	23 7/8	16 4/8	10	6	Lincoln County	MN	Paul Erickson	1983	1,039
154 7/8	24 2/8	23 6/8	19 1/8	4	5	Blue Earth County	MN	Rory Deutchman	1984	1,039
154 7/8	24 1/8	24 5/8	19 5/8	6	5	Dane County	WI	Casey A. Blum	1986	1,039
154 7/8	25 3/8	24 5/8	23 5/8	5	5	Nelson County	KY	Tom Blincoe	1987	1,039
154 7/8	26 7/8	26 2/8	15 4/8	4	7	Mason County	IL	Mark Meyer	1988	1,039
154 7/8	24 4/8	25 7/8	18 4/8	7	6	Washtenaw County	MI	William G. Knight	1988	1,039
154 7/8	24 7/8	26 4/8	21 7/8	7	5	Morris County	NJ	Craig Werder	1989	1,039

SCORE	LENGTH OF R MAIN BEAM L		INSIDE SPREAD	NUMBER OF R POINTS L		AREA	STATE/ PROVINCE	HUNTER'S NAME	DATE	RANK
154 7/8	23 3/8	24 4/8	16 1/8	6	5	Traill County	ND	Paul Teegarden	1990	1,039
154 7/8	24 4/8	24 2/8	17 1/8	7	7	Brown County	WI	Michael J. Rasmussen	1990	1,039
154 7/8	24 4/8	24 6/8	21 5/8	5	4	Champaign County	IL	Robert A. Bryant	1990	1,039
154 7/8	25 5/8	25 0/8	19 7/8	5	5	Massac County	IL	Terry B. Lewis	1990	1,039
154 7/8	23 5/8	24 2/8	17 6/8	6	5	Dakota County	MN	Thomas Leach, Jr.	1991	1,039
154 7/8	23 0/8	23 3/8	20 5/8	6	6	Bureau County	IL	Gregory A. Bowers	1991	1,039
154 7/8	25 3/8	24 1/8	15 6/8	5	6	McLean County	IL	Daniel Rogers	1991	1,039
154 6/8	24 1/8	22 5/8	17 2/8	5	5	Minnehaha County	SD	Clifford Sudenga	1962	1,058
154 6/8	25 1/8	25 1/8	21 0/8	5	4	Cottonwood County	MN	Rodney Bailey	1975	1,058
154 6/8	24 7/8	25 6/8	20 0/8	5	5	Gray County	KS	Allen D. Bailey	1980	1,058
154 6/8	24 0/8	23 0/8	18 4/8	5	5	Van Buren County	MI	Rick Reese	1980	1,058
154 6/8	25 1/8	21 7/8	18 4/8	6	4	Mills County	IA	Doug Roll	1985	1,058
154 6/8	23 1/8	23 4/8	16 2/8	5	5	Wright County	MN	Rob Johnson	1987	1,058
154 6/8	24 5/8	24 4/8	18 3/8	6	5	Lincoln County	NE	Timothy M. Budin	1990	1,058
154 6/8	25 6/8	26 5/8	16 2/8	9	7	Pike County	IL	Stan Chamberlain	1990	1,058
154 6/8	24 2/8	24 7/8	18 2/8	8	6	Taylor County	WI	Barry Kappel	1991	1,058
154 6/8	24 0/8	24 4/8	17 3/8	7	5	Des Moines County	IA	Daniel W. Wegener	1991	1,058
154 6/8	25 0/8	25 5/8	20 4/8	5	5	Lewis County	KY	Alfred Lee Simms	1992	1,058
154 5/8	23 7/8	24 0/8	20 7/8	4	4	Buchanan County	IA	Frank Sanderson	1983	1,069
154 5/8	25 4/8	24 5/8	21 3/8	4	4	Anne Arundel County	MD	Jim Roy	1984	1,069
154 5/8	24 3/8	25 4/8	17 2/8	7	8	Miami County	KS	Gary Wurdack	1985	1,069
154 5/8	26 1/8	25 4/8	21 3/8	4	4	Dunnville	ONT	Randy Robins	1985	1,069
154 5/8	26 2/8	26 3/8	18 3/8	5	5	Kingman County	KS	Dan J. Jacobs	1985	1,069
154 5/8	25 3/8	26 0/8	19 2/8	5	5	Scott County	IA	Howard A. Goettsch	1987	1,069
154 5/8	25 6/8	25 6/8	19 3/8	5	5	Pierce County	WI	Greg Koehler	1987	1,069
154 5/8	21 5/8	22 6/8	21 1/8	5	5	Garfield County	WA	Lee Campbell	1990	1,069
154 5/8	25 3/8	23 0/8	22 6/8	8	6	McLean County	IL	Marvin RexRoat	1990	1,069
154 5/8	26 3/8	25 5/8	19 3/8	7	6	Gallia County	OH	Darres Craig	1990	1,069
154 5/8	23 6/8	24 5/8	16 2/8	7	5	Lincoln County	MO	Scott Hager	1991	1,069
154 5/8	24 4/8	24 7/8	17 5/8	5	5	Will County	IL	Rick Johns	1991	1,069
154 4/8	24 0/8	24 3/8	23 2/8	5	5	Allamakee County	IA	Dayton Jones	1968	1,081
154 4/8	23 6/8	24 5/8	18 6/8	5	5	Davis County	IA	Ronald L. Simmons	1970	1,081
154 4/8	22 6/8	22 6/8	16 6/8	6	5	Fillmore County	MN	James J. Johnston	1974	1,081
154 4/8	24 4/8	24 0/8	19 3/8	7	8	Waupaca County	WI	Gary L. Hintz	1978	1,081
154 4/8	25 3/8	24 1/8	18 0/8	5	5	Will County	IL	Fred Lukanc	1978	1,081
154 4/8	24 4/8	23 6/8	20 0/8	5	5	Phillips County	KS	Dennis Fredrickson	1983	1,081
154 4/8	24 3/8	25 4/8	20 6/8	5	7	Monona County	IA	Bob Reitan	1986	1,081
154 4/8	25 1/8	25 6/8	23 0/8	4	4	Washington County	MN	Kenneth Brandl	1987	1,081
154 4/8	23 4/8	23 5/8	18 4/8	6	7	Kent County	MD	Donald P. Travis	1987	1,081
154 4/8	25 0/8	25 7/8	21 0/8	6	6	Fairfax County	VA	Michael E. Bury	1989	1,081
154 4/8	26 1/8	25 0/8	22 6/8	6	6	Litchfield County	CT	Eugene J. Wrabel, Jr.	1990	1,081
154 4/8	26 4/8	25 4/8	16 7/8	5	4	Adams County	OH	David W. Gilbert	1990	1,081
154 4/8	22 7/8	22 5/8	20 4/8	5	5	Letellier	MAN	Todd Amenrud	1991	1,081
154 4/8	24 6/8	25 5/8	18 0/8	4	5	Jefferson County	WI	Mark Stinebrink	1991	1,081
154 3/8	23 4/8	24 3/8	18 5/8	7	7	Wythe County	VA	C. D. Tarter	1961	1,095
154 3/8	27 2/8	26 0/8	21 5/8	4	4	Martin County	IN	Bill Clark	1967	1,095
154 3/8	25 3/8	25 2/8	19 1/8	4	4	Jefferson County	IL	Kirby Laur	1981	1,095
154 3/8	23 1/8	24 0/8	21 1/8	5	5	Sherman County	KS	Keith A. Foster	1984	1,095
154 3/8	24 2/8	23 5/8	17 1/8	5	5	Polk County	WI	Doug Greene	1986	1,095
154 3/8	24 3/8	24 2/8	18 5/8	5	5	Darke County	OH	Roy W. Ditty	1986	1,095
154 3/8	23 5/8	22 2/8	17 7/8	5	5	Highland County	OH	Martin Bullock	1986	1,095
154 3/8	24 3/8	23 7/8	20 5/8	5	5	Jackson County	WI	Daryl Lanphere	1987	1,095
154 3/8	24 4/8	24 4/8	19 5/8	6	6	St. Clair County	MI	Randy Shaffer	1988	1,095
154 3/8	25 3/8	25 3/8	17 5/8	4	4	Clay County	IL	Mike Fry	1988	1,095
154 3/8	25 1/8	25 4/8	17 2/8	6	6	Ottawa County	KS	James Helget	1990	1,095
154 3/8	23 5/8	25 1/8	18 5/8	4	4	Weld County	CO	Larry Gann	1991	1,095
154 3/8	25 0/8	25 0/8	20 6/8	5	6	Logan County	WV	Jimmy Diamond	1991	1,095
154 2/8	25 4/8	27 0/8	16 6/8	6	6	Waupaca County	WI	Carl Schoenike	1948	1,108
154 2/8	25 1/8	25 7/8	17 6/8	5	6	Cloud County	KS	Jerrold L. Istas	1981	1,108
154 2/8	22 3/8	21 7/8	16 6/8	6	6	Clark County	MO	Myles Keller	1981	1,108
154 2/8	22 6/8	22 6/8	17 4/8	5	5	Burleigh County	ND	Tony Niemann	1984	1,108
154 2/8	24 6/8	25 1/8	17 0/8	5	5	Pendleton County	WV	Roger O. Wyant	1984	1,108
154 2/8	23 6/8	23 1/8	17 6/8	6	6	White County	IL	Bruce Masser	1984	1,108
154 2/8	24 6/8	23 1/8	18 0/8	8	7	Comanche County	KS	Tommie A. Berger	1985	1,108
154 2/8	24 3/8	23 7/8	18 3/8	5	6	Dane County	WI	Eric L. Hamele	1987	1,108
154 2/8	26 5/8	26 4/8	18 2/8	8	7	Coles County	IL	Rob King	1987	1,108
154 2/8	23 2/8	23 1/8	18 4/8	5	5	Millarville	ALB	Stuart Sinclair-Smith	1989	1,108
154 2/8	21 7/8	21 5/8	15 2/8	6	6	Fulton County	IL	Bruce A. Flynn	1989	1,108
154 2/8	23 6/8	23 0/8	19 2/8	6	5	Ashland County	WI	Joseph A. Schutte	1990	1,108
154 2/8	25 7/8	25 0/8	16 6/8	5	5	Washington County	MN	Lance Edward Vandeberg	1990	1,108

SCORE	LENGTH OF MAIN BEAM R	L	INSIDE SPREAD	NUMBER OF POINTS R	L	AREA	STATE/ PROVINCE	HUNTER'S NAME	DATE	RANK
154 2/8	24 0/8	24 7/8	20 7/8	5	6	Highland County	OH	David Doyle	1991	1,108
154 2/8	25 7/8	24 5/8	18 6/8	4	4	Anoka County	MN	Dan Kluth	1992	1,108
154 1/8	24 6/8	23 7/8	15 5/8	5	5	Brown County	IN	Glen E. Parton	1970	1,123
154 1/8	24 6/8	25 5/8	20 4/8	5	7	Noble County	OH	Donald J. Mace	1973	1,123
154 1/8	23 5/8	23 7/8	19 5/8	5	6	Stoddard County	MO	Gary Barton	1980	1,123
154 1/8	24 6/8	23 4/8	19 6/8	5	7	Shawano County	WI	John Popp	1980	1,123
154 1/8	23 0/8	23 1/8	18 7/8	6	7	Faribault County	MN	Carlton Eastvold, Jr.	1982	1,123
154 1/8	26 5/8	26 2/8	20 1/8	6	7	Nelson County	KY	Tom Bullock	1983	1,123
154 1/8	23 7/8	23 4/8	18 3/8	5	5	Merrick County	NE	Lauren N Erickson	1985	1,123
154 1/8	22 6/8	24 7/8	17 5/8	5	5	Miami County	IN	Charles Wecht	1986	1,123
154 1/8	28 0/8	27 1/8	25 1/8	4	4	Buffalo County	WI	Frank Frost	1987	1,123
154 1/8	22 5/8	21 2/8	19 5/8	5	5	Poinsett County	AR	Barry Deckelman	1988	1,123
154 1/8	26 4/8	26 1/8	17 5/8	6	7	Saline County	KS	Shane Roberts	1989	1,123
154 1/8	24 4/8	24 1/8	19 5/8	5	4	Phillips County	KS	Gary Fritzler	1990	1,123
154 1/8	24 0/8	24 0/8	16 1/8	5	5	Marion County	IA	Frank M. Hashman	1991	1,123
154 1/8	25 2/8	25 6/8	20 5/8	5	7	Harrison County	IA	Gerald D. Dickman	1991	1,123
154 0/8	26 2/8	26 1/8	17 6/8	5	5	Marshall County	KS	Tim Wanklyn	1976	1,137
154 0/8	26 5/8	26 5/8	19 1/8	4	5	Guthrie County	IA	Gordon Headlee	1977	1,137
154 0/8	27 0/8	26 7/8	19 2/8	6	6	Kosciusko County	IN	Charles L. Baker	1979	1,137
154 0/8	27 2/8	25 7/8	18 4/8	6	4	Knox County	IL	James C. Drake	1979	1,137
154 0/8	22 4/8	22 1/8	18 2/8	5	5	Price County	WI	Jim Sorensen	1982	1,137
154 0/8	24 4/8	24 5/8	17 4/8	5	5	Monroe County	MO	Dallas L. Miller	1985	1,137
154 0/8	24 6/8	24 3/8	15 4/8	5	5	Clay County	IN	Terry L. Dewey	1985	1,137
154 0/8	25 1/8	24 1/8	19 2/8	5	5	Kent County	MD	J. Richard Herr	1985	1,137
154 0/8	25 1/8	23 1/8	21 1/8	6	6	Tuscarawas County	OH	Stephen Hinkley	1986	1,137
154 0/8	27 1/8	27 2/8	17 4/8	5	5	Waukesha County	WI	Duane Turinske	1989	1,137
154 0/8	22 3/8	23 4/8	21 0/8	7	8	Jones County	GA	John Bragg	1990	1,137
154 0/8	25 0/8	25 7/8	20 4/8	5	4	Henry County	MO	Matt Hull	1991	1,137
153 7/8	22 6/8	22 2/8	17 5/8	5	5	McLean County	ND	Terry Cossette	1983	1,149
153 7/8	25 6/8	26 0/8	17 1/8	7	7	Black Hawk County	IA	Gary Schoeberl	1985	1,149
153 7/8	25 7/8	26 0/8	20 5/8	4	5	Bedford County	VA	Julian A. McFaden III	1986	1,149
153 7/8	24 2/8	24 6/8	18 7/8	5	5	Franklin County	IL	Dave Freeman	1987	1,149
153 7/8	24 4/8	25 4/8	19 7/8	6	6	Chase County	KS	Jerry Keller	1988	1,149
153 7/8	25 3/8	25 1/8	17 1/8	4	4	Stephenson County	IL	Richard Wickersham	1989	1,149
153 7/8	22 2/8	22 7/8	20 2/8	5	6	Cass County	ND	Dean Honrud	1991	1,149
153 6/8	22 1/8	22 7/8	17 0/8	5	5	Kent County	MD	S. Russell Edie	1966	1,156
153 6/8	24 5/8	25 1/8	18 2/8	6	5	Lee County	IL	George Nevins	1976	1,156
153 6/8	23 3/8	24 3/8	18 0/8	5	5	Lincoln County	SD	Mike Pederson	1979	1,156
153 6/8	24 1/8	23 7/8	16 0/8	5	5	Jasper County	MO	Steve Lewis	1983	1,156
153 6/8	24 5/8	23 6/8	18 0/8	5	5	Kenosha County	WI	John Schnider, Jr.	1984	1,156
153 6/8	25 1/8	24 7/8	18 4/8	5	5	Morrison County	MN	John Erdrich	1984	1,156
153 6/8	22 7/8	23 0/8	17 7/8	5	6	Crook County	WY	Steven Blair	1986	1,156
153 6/8	25 5/8	25 0/8	19 5/8	6	6	Adair County	MO	Roger Roberts	1986	1,156
153 6/8	23 2/8	23 6/8	20 6/8	6	6	Hennepin County	MN	Steve Clark	1987	1,156
153 6/8	24 2/8	23 2/8	22 4/8	5	5	Idaho County	ID	Ron Beitelspacher	1988	1,156
153 6/8	24 2/8	24 2/8	17 0/8	7	6	St. Croix County	WI	Steve Huppert	1988	1,156
153 6/8	24 0/8	23 2/8	23 2/8	4	4	Fulton County	IL	John Koster	1989	1,156
153 6/8	21 6/8	21 5/8	17 1/8	6	5	Lucas County	IA	Orval W. Bedell	1990	1,156
153 6/8	22 4/8	23 2/8	16 2/8	5	5	Winnebago County	IL	Mark P. Stock	1991	1,156
153 6/8	24 4/8	25 3/8	20 3/8	4	5	Priddis	ALB	Lorne D. Rinkel	1991	1,156
153 6/8	25 7/8	26 4/8	22 0/8	5	4	Baraga County	MI	David C. Sikorsky	1991	1,156
153 6/8	24 0/8	25 7/8	16 5/8	7	7	Atchison County	MO	Tom Nauman	1991	1,156
153 6/8	24 4/8	24 0/8	22 4/8	5	7	Suffolk County	NY	Richard Supinsky	1991	1,156
153 5/8	23 4/8	23 0/8	22 4/8	5	7	Harris	SAS	Garry Benson	1966	1,174
153 5/8	26 5/8	26 6/8	18 5/8	7	5	Hamilton County	IA	Harold Brown	1971	1,174
153 5/8	26 0/8	25 2/8	18 1/8	7	5	Halton Hills	ONT	Don Lewis	1978	1,174
153 5/8	23 4/8	24 0/8	18 7/8	5	5	Dorchester County	MD	David Logan White	1983	1,174
153 5/8	26 0/8	25 5/8	21 1/8	6	5	Will County	IL	John Madonis	1984	1,174
153 5/8	25 4/8	25 7/8	20 5/8	5	5	Stephenson County	IL	Clarence E. Hille, Jr.	1984	1,174
153 5/8	23 0/8	23 0/8	19 5/8	5	5	Sauk County	WI	Michael H. Smith	1986	1,174
153 5/8	24 0/8	24 4/8	19 6/8	5	6	Butler County	KS	Robert VanDeventer	1987	1,174
153 5/8	25 2/8	24 6/8	18 0/8	6	8	Lorain County	OH	Daniel T. Fortney	1988	1,174
153 5/8	25 0/8	25 0/8	17 5/8	5	5	Marathon County	WI	Paul Tuttle	1989	1,174
153 5/8	27 4/8	26 7/8	20 6/8	6	4	Allamakee County	IA	Raymond Boland	1989	1,174
153 5/8	25 7/8	24 7/8	17 5/8	5	6	Madison County	IA	Fred "Bud" Allen	1991	1,174
153 5/8	26 1/8	25 5/8	19 1/8	6	6	Boone County	IA	Dave Rimathe	1992	1,174
153 4/8	25 7/8	25 2/8	19 3/8	7	6	Jackson County	MN	Lyle Babcock	1973	1,187
153 4/8	25 1/8	23 6/8	22 0/8	6	5	Knox County	OH	John L. Yarman, Jr.	1975	1,187
153 4/8	23 5/8	24 1/8	20 6/8	6	5	Billings County	ND	David L. Torkelson	1976	1,187
153 4/8	26 2/8	26 0/8	23 2/8	6	6	Douglas County	KS	Richard D. Brown	1979	1,187

SCORE	LENGTH OF R MAIN BEAM L		INSIDE SPREAD	NUMBER OF R POINTS L		AREA	STATE/ PROVINCE	HUNTER'S NAME	DATE	RANK
153 4/8	25 5/8	25 7/8	23 4/8	6	5	Logan County	KY	Milton O. Gaddie	1979	1,187
153 4/8	24 4/8	24 2/8	16 2/8	5	6	Columbia County	FL	Robert Ballard	1980	1,187
153 4/8	22 5/8	22 4/8	14 6/8	5	5	Callaway County	MO	Marvin Giboney	1980	1,187
153 4/8	25 3/8	25 2/8	17 6/8	6	6	Morrison County	MN	Dennis Midas	1983	1,187
153 4/8	22 5/8	22 5/8	17 0/8	6	7	Licking County	OH	Jeff Fowls	1986	1,187
153 4/8	24 6/8	25 3/8	16 2/8	5	4	Trempealeau County	WI	David A. Stegemeyer	1987	1,187
153 4/8	24 6/8	24 1/8	19 0/8	5	5	Dubuque County	IA	Patrick J. McAndrew	1988	1,187
153 4/8	24 5/8	24 2/8	17 4/8	5	5	Ashland County	WI	Dennis A. Schmitt	1990	1,187
153 4/8	24 1/8	23 5/8	18 4/8	6	6	Montgomery County	MS	John M. Johnson	1991	1,187
153 4/8	23 5/8	24 1/8	17 2/8	5	7	Randolph County	MO	Harold Montgomery	1991	1,187
153 4/8	26 2/8	26 6/8	17 7/8	5	6	Knox County	IL	James Schmidt	1991	1,187
153 3/8	25 5/8	24 7/8	19 4/8	5	6	Grundy County	IL	Ed Vitko, Jr.	1972	1,202
153 3/8	21 2/8	22 3/8	19 0/8	7	6	Morrison County	MN	Robert R. Ganzer	1973	1,202
153 3/8	25 5/8	27 6/8	21 1/8	4	4	Knox County	IL	Bill Richards	1981	1,202
153 3/8	25 1/8	24 3/8	19 3/8	4	4	Webster County	WV	Charles P. Green	1982	1,202
153 3/8	22 7/8	22 7/8	20 6/8	7	7	Macoupin County	IL	Charles M. Woolfolk	1983	1,202
153 3/8	24 7/8	24 7/8	17 7/8	6	7	Calumet County	WI	Matt Fuchs	1986	1,202
153 3/8	24 2/8	26 1/8	18 6/8	6	6	McHenry County	IL	Lenny Vohasek	1987	1,202
153 3/8	28 4/8	27 6/8	21 3/8	4	4	Howard County	MD	Chris Apostolakos	1987	1,202
153 3/8	23 1/8	22 7/8	20 3/8	5	5	Morgan County	CO	Michael Paul Hansen	1988	1,202
153 3/8	25 2/8	24 6/8	17 5/8	5	5	Suffolk County	NY	Ronald W. Tybaert	1988	1,202
153 3/8	25 5/8	24 2/8	19 1/8	6	5	Greene County	MO	Don M. Andrews	1988	1,202
153 3/8	24 4/8	24 4/8	18 2/8	5	6	Webb County	TX	Gilberto Guajardo, Jr.	1989	1,202
153 3/8	24 4/8	25 4/8	20 4/8	5	6	Lake County	IL	Mark Nelsen	1990	1,202
153 3/8	25 4/8	25 3/8	20 3/8	5	5	Racine County	WI	Dave L. Krupp	1990	1,202
153 3/8	23 1/8	22 7/8	19 7/8	5	5	Westchester County	NY	Michael A. Chirico	1990	1,202
153 3/8	28 4/8	26 4/8	18 3/8	4	5	Bracken County	KY	George Clark	1990	1,202
153 2/8	24 4/8	24 3/8	24 4/8	5	6	Burt County	NE	Harold W. Hawkins	1966	1,218
153 2/8	26 0/8	26 7/8	20 6/8	6	6	Winnebago County	IA	Ronald Gordon	1972	1,218
153 2/8	22 5/8	22 3/8	20 4/8	5	5	Lincoln County	NE	Greg Wingfield	1978	1,218
153 2/8	21 6/8	21 7/8	15 0/8	5	5	Wood County	WI	James Wilke	1984	1,218
153 2/8	26 3/8	25 2/8	18 4/8	7	5	Butler County	KS	Larry Womack	1984	1,218
153 2/8	24 3/8	23 6/8	20 2/8	5	5	Jackson County	MN	Bill Vangsness	1985	1,218
153 2/8	22 1/8	23 3/8	17 1/8	9	8	Seminole County	OK	James V. Flowers III	1986	1,218
153 2/8	24 4/8	24 7/8	19 0/8	5	5	Frederick County	MD	Grayson Mercer, Jr.	1986	1,218
153 2/8	25 0/8	25 5/8	19 5/8	9	6	Morgan County	IL	Sam Alfand	1986	1,218
153 2/8	23 0/8	24 2/8	19 0/8	5	6	Wapello County	IA	Jim Smith	1987	1,218
153 2/8	23 4/8	24 7/8	17 0/8	7	5	Pulaski County	IN	Steve Knebel	1988	1,218
153 2/8	25 1/8	25 1/8	21 6/8	4	4	Stephenson County	IL	Robert J. Schiffman	1989	1,218
153 2/8	24 6/8	24 4/8	20 4/8	7	5	Edmonton	ALB	Dale Spooner	1991	1,218
153 1/8	25 2/8	25 0/8	18 5/8	4	5	Lincoln County	NE	Rich Birch	1965	1,231
153 1/8	25 6/8	25 1/8	19 1/8	6	5	Christian County	IL	Michael Miloncus	1983	1,231
153 1/8	25 6/8	25 1/8	17 1/8	7	6	Moody County	SD	Paul Schlobohm	1983	1,231
153 1/8	27 2/8	27 1/8	27 2/8	6	5	Lee County	IA	Ronald Elbe	1986	1,231
153 1/8	22 5/8	21 3/8	18 1/8	5	5	White County	AR	Harold Dwain Marlin	1987	1,231
153 1/8	20 4/8	21 6/8	18 5/8	5	5	St. Clair County	IL	Jim Fetters	1987	1,231
153 1/8	24 3/8	24 3/8	16 5/8	5	6	Lake County	IL	Steve Andrews	1988	1,231
153 1/8	22 6/8	23 1/8	17 3/8	7	8	Walworth County	WI	Charles Palmer	1990	1,231
153 1/8	25 4/8	25 2/8	19 3/8	5	5	Monroe County	NY	Dan Scorza	1990	1,231
153 0/8	25 0/8	25 2/8	17 4/8	5	5	Cambria County	PA	Andrew J. Getsy	1965	1,240
153 0/8	21 3/8	21 1/8	16 4/8	5	5	Burleigh County	ND	Jim Balzer	1977	1,240
153 0/8	24 7/8	25 1/8	16 3/8	5	6	Koochiching County	MN	Dr. Thomas Zbaracki	1980	1,240
153 0/8	23 2/8	23 6/8	16 0/8	5	5	Lawrence County	PA	Wayne Edwards	1981	1,240
153 0/8	23 5/8	23 6/8	15 7/8	6	6	Shelby County	IL	Bill D. Pesch	1983	1,240
153 0/8	23 7/8	24 3/8	18 4/8	5	5	Trumbull County	OH	Art Stanton	1985	1,240
153 0/8	25 3/8	25 2/8	19 4/8	4	5	Dane County	WI	Joe Eugster	1986	1,240
153 0/8	24 2/8	24 2/8	21 6/8	5	6	Lake County	IL	Roger A. Bacon	1987	1,240
153 0/8	24 0/8	25 4/8	23 1/8	5	5	Lake County	IL	Kris Laho	1987	1,240
153 0/8	26 1/8	26 3/8	22 2/8	5	4	Craig County	OK	Eddie Claypool	1988	1,240
153 0/8	26 0/8	26 3/8	18 4/8	5	4	Sangamon County	IL	Randy Black	1988	1,240
153 0/8	26 2/8	25 5/8	15 1/8	5	5	Saline County	NE	Don Kohout	1990	1,240
153 0/8	26 1/8	24 4/8	15 5/8	6	5	Kay County	OK	Guy L. LeMonnier, Jr.	1990	1,240
153 0/8	22 3/8	22 1/8	15 0/8	5	5	Henry County	IA	Paul Ginkens	1990	1,240
153 0/8	22 0/8	21 5/8	17 7/8	8	7	Washburn County	WI	Dennis Regenauer	1990	1,240
153 0/8	26 0/8	25 4/8	19 0/8	4	4	Vinton County	OH	Randy Boggs	1991	1,240
152 7/8	21 4/8	22 0/8	18 7/8	5	5	Polk County	WI	Wendle Johnson	1969	1,256
152 7/8	23 2/8	22 2/8	18 4/8	7	5	Morgan County	CO	Dr. Stuart Clodfelder	1974	1,256
152 7/8	22 1/8	23 0/8	17 0/8	6	5	Sullivan County	IN	Kenny Pirtle	1975	1,256
152 7/8	24 3/8	24 2/8	20 7/8	5	6	Missoula County	MT	Rick L. Stone	1981	1,256
152 7/8	23 2/8	23 4/8	19 1/8	6	5	Delaware County	PA	John A. Lashinsky	1984	1,256

WHITETAIL DEER (*Typical Antlers*)

SCORE	LENGTH OF MAIN BEAM R	L	INSIDE SPREAD	NUMBER OF POINTS R	L	AREA	STATE/ PROVINCE	HUNTER'S NAME	DATE	RANK
152 7/8	24 2/8	24 2/8	20 3/8	5	5	Washington County	WI	Lee A. Richard	1984	1,256
152 7/8	21 6/8	22 2/8	19 7/8	5	5	Henry County	IL	Willard "Woody" Moore	1986	1,256
152 7/8	25 1/8	26 1/8	16 7/8	5	5	Highland County	OH	Jeffrey A. Swerlein	1988	1,256
152 7/8	23 2/8	23 0/8	20 1/8	6	6	Wayne County	WV	Larry Sarver	1988	1,256
152 7/8	23 3/8	23 6/8	19 2/8	5	8	Guthrie County	IA	Leonard H. Mussell	1989	1,256
152 7/8	23 7/8	23 7/8	20 5/8	5	6	Olmsted County	MN	Chris A. Valli	1989	1,256
152 7/8	22 6/8	22 2/8	18 1/8	5	5	Sauk County	WI	Hank Lee	1989	1,256
152 7/8	22 2/8	22 3/8	16 2/8	5	6	Chisago County	MN	John R. Palmer	1989	1,256
152 7/8	24 3/8	24 4/8	17 1/8	4	4	Oconto County	WI	Gary DeBauch	1990	1,256
152 7/8	26 0/8	25 7/8	20 2/8	6	5	Strafford County	NH	William S. Carlsen	1990	1,256
152 7/8	23 3/8	21 0/8	17 5/8	6	6	McHenry County	IL	William D. Lilly	1990	1,256
152 7/8	23 1/8	23 6/8	21 6/8	6	5	Creek County	OK	Carmon G. Romine, Jr.	1991	1,256
152 6/8	25 6/8	25 1/8	21 2/8	4	5	Jefferson County	IN	Robert Schmidt	1959	1,273
152 6/8	24 6/8	23 2/8	17 7/8	7	7	Winona County	MN	Donald M. Bzoskie	1978	1,273
152 6/8	24 7/8	24 1/8	21 0/8	4	4	Randolph County	IL	Steven Wydeck	1979	1,273
152 6/8	25 2/8	24 3/8	18 4/8	5	5	Saginaw County	MI	Jack W. Bare	1981	1,273
152 6/8	23 3/8	23 0/8	20 0/8	5	5	Morrison County	MN	Floyd Foslien	1981	1,273
152 6/8	25 0/8	25 2/8	17 6/8	6	6	Holt County	MO	Frank Berkemeier	1984	1,273
152 6/8	22 6/8	22 2/8	14 2/8	6	5	Rogers County	OK	Byron Jasper	1984	1,273
152 6/8	27 0/8	27 2/8	16 4/8	4	5	Roane County	TN	Rod Brown	1986	1,273
152 6/8	25 4/8	26 2/8	18 2/8	5	5	Texas County	OK	Don Callaway	1986	1,273
152 6/8	23 2/8	23 6/8	18 2/8	5	6	Logan County	OH	Richard D. Fullerton	1988	1,273
152 6/8	26 3/8	28 3/8	22 3/8	4	5	Vermilion County	IL	John E. Fry	1989	1,273
152 6/8	26 1/8	25 5/8	17 0/8	6	5	Lawrence County	IL	Ron Wells	1989	1,273
152 6/8	22 3/8	21 4/8	17 4/8	6	5	Winnebago County	IL	Drake R. Branca	1990	1,273
152 6/8	25 0/8	24 0/8	18 0/8	5	6	Cass County	MI	Kim C. Deda	1991	1,273
152 6/8	24 4/8	24 7/8	20 3/8	6	7	Worcester County	MA	Peter J. Warakomski	1991	1,273
152 5/8	23 5/8	24 5/8	19 7/8	6	5	Ralls County	MO	Donald Curless	1959	1,288
152 5/8	23 2/8	23 0/8	17 2/8	5	6	Monroe County	MO	Carl T. Peak	1968	1,288
152 5/8	23 1/8	24 0/8	16 1/8	6	6	Roseau County	MN	Dave Hovda	1982	1,288
152 5/8	24 5/8	24 0/8	19 4/8	7	7	Delaware County	IA	Chet Goldsberry	1982	1,288
152 5/8	22 7/8	22 5/8	16 3/8	5	5	Lyon County	MN	Dwight A. Hemme	1984	1,288
152 5/8	25 2/8	22 2/8	17 1/8	5	5	Marathon County	WI	Marcell Wieloch	1986	1,288
152 5/8	22 6/8	24 2/8	17 7/8	7	6	Carver County	MN	Steve Polston	1986	1,288
152 5/8	26 0/8	25 0/8	20 5/8	4	4	Marion County	IA	Steven F. Donnelly, Jr.	1986	1,288
152 5/8	26 2/8	25 7/8	17 1/8	4	4	Forest County	WI	Greg Lenz	1988	1,288
152 5/8	23 0/8	21 2/8	17 3/8	5	5	Crawford County	IL	Steve Newkirk	1989	1,288
152 5/8	23 6/8	22 5/8	19 3/8	5	5	Winnebago County	IL	Tom Sanderson	1990	1,288
152 5/8	21 4/8	21 1/8	17 1/8	6	6	Hennepin County	MN	Dan Kittok	1990	1,288
152 5/8	26 4/8	26 1/8	23 1/8	6	7	Pike County	IL	Rick Conrad	1991	1,288
152 4/8	28 7/8	26 2/8	19 2/8	5	5	Somerset County	MD	Burgess Blevins	1974	1,301
152 4/8	24 3/8	24 0/8	19 2/8	5	5	Scott County	MN	Dean Jansen	1976	1,301
152 4/8	25 6/8	27 4/8	18 3/8	7	5	Westchester County	NY	Jack Dykstra	1986	1,301
152 4/8	21 5/8	21 3/8	18 6/8	5	5	Provost	ALB	Harvey McNalley	1987	1,301
152 4/8	24 5/8	25 5/8	20 4/8	7	7	Lake County	IL	Ted Bellefeuille	1987	1,301
152 4/8	23 6/8	24 6/8	17 6/8	5	5	Harris County	TX	John Hall	1987	1,301
152 4/8	23 0/8	22 7/8	19 0/8	6	6	Pike County	OH	Raymond McComas	1988	1,301
152 4/8	23 3/8	23 5/8	17 7/8	5	6	Lehigh County	PA	Steve C. Metzger	1989	1,301
152 4/8	26 1/8	27 4/8	21 6/8	5	5	Hocking County	OH	Chad Krahel	1990	1,301
152 4/8	25 6/8	25 5/8	20 3/8	5	6	St. Francois County	MO	Adam Ashby	1991	1,301
152 3/8	24 7/8	24 7/8	18 5/8	8	6	Pope County	IL	Dr. H. Neil Becker	1968	1,311
152 3/8	25 4/8	25 4/8	17 6/8	8	7	Jasper County	IA	Edward L. Stevens	1976	1,311
152 3/8	24 5/8	24 3/8	19 1/8	4	4	Guthrie County	IA	Barry Chalfant	1979	1,311
152 3/8	23 2/8	24 7/8	18 3/8	6	5	Schuyler County	IL	Stephen J. McCoy	1979	1,311
152 3/8	22 5/8	21 6/8	17 3/8	5	5	Butler County	KS	John Schwartz	1981	1,311
152 3/8	24 6/8	24 6/8	16 3/8	5	5	Oceana County	MI	J. C. Ingram	1982	1,311
152 3/8	24 7/8	25 3/8	19 7/8	4	4	Yorkton	SAS	Ron Vandermeulen	1983	1,311
152 3/8	24 0/8	24 4/8	19 5/8	5	5	Jewell County	KS	Rod Rose	1984	1,311
152 3/8	22 3/8	23 2/8	18 5/8	6	5	Kenosha County	WI	Howard Moore	1984	1,311
152 3/8	24 3/8	25 0/8	19 7/8	5	5	Logan County	IL	Charles E. Dumire	1984	1,311
152 3/8	25 0/8	24 3/8	17 2/8	5	8	Franklin County	KS	Joe Maloney	1985	1,311
152 3/8	23 0/8	22 5/8	17 7/8	5	6	Gasconade County	MO	John R Hawkins	1985	1,311
152 3/8	25 6/8	24 7/8	17 2/8	8	5	Washington County	KS	Stan Brustowicz	1985	1,311
152 3/8	26 6/8	29 1/8	21 1/8	6	5	Bullitt County	KY	Todd A. Edwards	1990	1,311
152 3/8	23 7/8	24 7/8	19 3/8	6	6	Pueblo County	CO	Steve Mayo	1990	1,311
152 3/8	26 1/8	25 2/8	18 5/8	5	7	Belmont County	OH	Chad Krahel	1991	1,311
152 3/8	22 4/8	21 5/8	17 7/8	5	5	Codington County	SD	Jerry Redlin	1991	1,311
152 2/8	24 6/8	24 4/8	18 4/8	5	5	Cowley County	KS	Michael L. Snyder	1978	1,328
152 2/8	28 4/8	27 4/8	20 2/8	4	4	Winona County	MN	Leonard Anglewitz	1978	1,328
152 2/8	24 5/8	24 4/8	20 2/8	6	7	Miami County	KS	Brian J. Hammond	1982	1,328

Score	Length of Main Beam R	L	Inside Spread	Number of Points R	L	Area	State/ Province	Hunter's Name	Date	Rank
152 2/8	24 2/8	23 5/8	17 4/8	6	4	Marshall County	KS	Dean C. Bookwalter	1982	1,328
152 2/8	22 2/8	21 7/8	19 5/8	5	7	Morrison County	MN	Willard L. Voight, Jr.	1984	1,328
152 2/8	24 3/8	23 4/8	16 6/8	6	5	Highland County	OH	James Stephens	1984	1,328
152 2/8	25 6/8	24 2/8	19 2/8	8	7	La Crosse County	WI	Kenne A. Happel	1985	1,328
152 2/8	25 3/8	25 3/8	21 6/8	5	5	Middlesex County	CT	Felix Nosewicz	1985	1,328
152 2/8	24 4/8	25 0/8	18 6/8	4	4	Marathon County	WI	Mark Schneider	1985	1,328
152 2/8	23 3/8	25 3/8	19 7/8	6	5	Columbia County	WI	Jeff A. Obrion	1986	1,328
152 2/8	26 4/8	25 7/8	19 1/8	7	5	Schuyler County	MO	Jim Pierceall	1990	1,328
152 2/8	24 4/8	24 1/8	15 2/8	5	6	Putnam County	OH	Pat Will	1990	1,328
152 2/8	24 4/8	24 1/8	17 6/8	5	5	Allamakee County	IA	Dennis L. Weber	1990	1,328
152 2/8	22 2/8	21 6/8	18 6/8	6	5	Spencer County	IN	Allen Kramer	1991	1,328
152 2/8	22 6/8	22 7/8	18 0/8	6	6	Winneshiek County	IA	David G. Baumler	1991	1,328
152 2/8	23 5/8	22 7/8	16 3/8	5	6	Rush County	KS	John Denk	1991	1,328
152 1/8	21 4/8	24 2/8	21 3/8	5	4	Owen County	IN	Edward L. Armstrong	1967	1,344
152 1/8	25 6/8	26 1/8	20 3/8	6	4	Watonwan County	MN	David Raney	1972	1,344
152 1/8	22 4/8	22 3/8	18 3/8	5	6	Ogle County	IL	Chuck Bowman	1974	1,344
152 1/8	25 1/8	25 3/8	17 1/8	6	6	Louisa County	IA	Duane O'Donnell	1979	1,344
152 1/8	24 1/8	24 5/8	19 3/8	5	5	Schuyler County	NY	Steve Herforth	1981	1,344
152 1/8	24 4/8	24 4/8	20 7/8	4	4	Iowa County	IA	Rick Ransom	1985	1,344
152 1/8	23 6/8	24 1/8	16 4/8	7	6	Pawnee County	KS	Karl E. Elmore	1987	1,344
152 1/8	24 7/8	22 7/8	18 1/8	5	6	Brooks County	TX	Jim L. McCrory	1988	1,344
152 1/8	24 2/8	24 0/8	17 1/8	6	5	Mercer County	ND	William F. Jensen	1989	1,344
152 1/8	23 1/8	23 2/8	19 5/8	5	6	Washington County	WI	Glenn E. Becker	1989	1,344
152 1/8	21 0/8	21 5/8	17 2/8	6	6	Pike County	IN	Keith M. Witte	1989	1,344
152 1/8	24 5/8	25 3/8	22 7/8	4	5	Monona County	IA	Rick Archer	1989	1,344
152 1/8	25 1/8	25 3/8	18 7/8	4	4	Scott County	IA	Gary Faley	1989	1,344
152 1/8	22 4/8	22 6/8	17 3/8	5	5	Powder River County	MT	Rich Driscoll	1990	1,344
152 1/8	24 4/8	24 0/8	17 3/8	4	4	Bond County	IL	James Grider	1990	1,344
152 1/8	24 3/8	24 0/8	20 7/8	4	5	Will County	IL	Robert L. Kamenjarin	1990	1,344
152 1/8	25 4/8	25 2/8	17 5/8	4	4	Kandiyohi County	MN	Elroy Thorson	1991	1,344
152 1/8	23 5/8	23 0/8	16 6/8	8	8	Clark County	MO	Duane Wilson	1991	1,344
152 1/8	22 4/8	23 7/8	16 1/8	4	4	Henry County	VA	Mike Weaver	1991	1,344
152 1/8	26 2/8	25 7/8	19 2/8	4	6	Franklin County	IL	Tom Haag	1991	1,344
152 1/8	23 7/8	23 6/8	20 5/8	5	5	Todd County	MN	Bruce Hudalla	1992	1,344
152 0/8	24 0/8	24 6/8	20 2/8	5	5	Finney County	KS	Howard Haug, Jr.	1973	1,365
152 0/8	23 0/8	23 0/8	16 0/8	5	5	Allen County	KY	Johnny Upton	1976	1,365
152 0/8	22 1/8	22 1/8	16 2/8	5	6	Marshall County	SD	Merle Funston	1982	1,365
152 0/8	26 6/8	26 3/8	17 6/8	5	4	Clay County	MN	Anthony Laddusaw	1985	1,365
152 0/8	24 6/8	25 6/8	17 6/8	7	6	Dakota County	MN	Tom Esslinger	1985	1,365
152 0/8	24 6/8	24 3/8	17 6/8	5	5	Itasca County	MN	Thomas A. Leedham	1985	1,365
152 0/8	22 7/8	23 1/8	17 0/8	5	5	Champaign County	IL	John W. Chumbley	1985	1,365
152 0/8	24 6/8	24 6/8	20 4/8	4	5	Winnebago County	IL	Ronald R. DeMus	1986	1,365
152 0/8	27 0/8	26 3/8	17 4/8	5	5	Lincoln County	MO	Donald E. Thompson, Jr.	1989	1,365
152 0/8	22 6/8	22 0/8	18 4/8	6	4	Cass County	NE	Mike Wright	1989	1,365
152 0/8	22 6/8	23 0/8	20 4/8	5	5	Iron County	WI	John A. Franke	1990	1,365
152 0/8	23 0/8	22 0/8	17 0/8	5	5	Yankton County	SD	Daryl Miller	1990	1,365
152 0/8	24 2/8	24 3/8	19 6/8	5	4	Logan County	IL	James Booth	1991	1,365
151 7/8	27 1/8	28 0/8	18 6/8	5	5	Morrison County	MN	Steve Smythe	1968	1,378
151 7/8	24 3/8	24 7/8	18 3/8	5	5	Davis County	IA	George C. Francis	1979	1,378
151 7/8	23 7/8	23 7/8	17 6/8	6	6	Tama County	IA	Kirk Lundberg	1980	1,378
151 7/8	26 1/8	25 6/8	18 0/8	5	7	Brown County	SD	Jan Hinrichs	1981	1,378
151 7/8	24 6/8	24 4/8	19 1/8	5	5	Will County	IL	Ike Rhodes	1984	1,378
151 7/8	24 6/8	25 4/8	18 1/8	6	6	McCook County	SD	James C. Perkins	1984	1,378
151 7/8	24 4/8	23 6/8	15 5/8	5	5	Grant County	WI	William Stetler	1985	1,378
151 7/8	25 1/8	24 5/8	16 7/8	7	6	Waukesha County	WI	Perry Scott Brummer	1986	1,378
151 7/8	24 1/8	22 3/8	17 2/8	6	5	Lewis County	MO	Sam Smith	1986	1,378
151 7/8	26 3/8	26 3/8	24 3/8	4	5	Peoria County	IL	Dick McKown	1986	1,378
151 7/8	23 7/8	23 4/8	19 7/8	5	5	Livingston County	MI	Charles D. Lemay	1987	1,378
151 7/8	21 6/8	21 5/8	17 3/8	6	6	Laurel County	KY	Jerry Hubbard	1987	1,378
151 7/8	25 3/8	24 5/8	17 0/8	5	8	Kingman County	KS	Terry Morisse	1988	1,378
151 7/8	25 4/8	25 5/8	22 7/8	6	5	Whitley County	IN	Frank J. Yaquinto	1990	1,378
151 7/8	22 1/8	22 2/8	16 1/8	5	6	Edmonton	ALB	Rick Bell	1991	1,378
151 6/8	22 1/8	23 2/8	15 4/8	6	5	Flathead County	MT	Jerry D. Almos	1970	1,393
151 6/8	25 4/8	24 7/8	21 0/8	8	6	Warren County	OH	Lundy Lewis	1981	1,393
151 6/8	25 0/8	24 7/8	17 4/8	5	5	Murray County	MN	Dennis Lunderborg	1982	1,393
151 6/8	25 7/8	22 1/8	20 1/8	5	9	Columbiana County	OH	Bill Lawrence	1983	1,393
151 6/8	23 7/8	24 0/8	21 4/8	4	4	Beaver County	OK	Max Crocker	1984	1,393
151 6/8	27 6/8	26 6/8	19 7/8	5	5	Champaign County	OH	Thomas R. Weaver	1984	1,393
151 6/8	24 2/8	24 0/8	21 5/8	5	6	Madison County	IA	Todd L. Fuson	1986	1,393
151 6/8	27 2/8	26 0/8	21 4/8	4	5	Greenwood County	KS	Jerry Ramshaw	1986	1,393

SCORE	LENGTH OF MAIN BEAM R	L	INSIDE SPREAD	NUMBER OF POINTS R	L	AREA	STATE/ PROVINCE	HUNTER'S NAME	DATE	RANK
151 6/8	23 5/8	23 4/8	16 3/8	6	7	Wabasha County	MN	Wayne Techaw, Jr.	1987	1,393
151 6/8	25 4/8	26 6/8	18 2/8	6	5	Ogle County	IL	Jim Hill	1987	1,393
151 6/8	24 1/8	23 4/8	20 4/8	4	4	Bond County	IL	Allen D. Ellsworth	1987	1,393
151 6/8	25 5/8	26 1/8	18 6/8	6	9	Pulaski County	IL	Garrett Wilson	1988	1,393
151 6/8	25 5/8	24 6/8	21 4/8	4	5	Christian County	IL	Lee Penn	1988	1,393
151 6/8	23 3/8	23 6/8	17 0/8	5	5	Greene County	IA	Glen Garnett	1990	1,393
151 6/8	25 4/8	24 3/8	16 1/8	7	5	Ross County	OH	Randy Johnson	1990	1,393
151 6/8	24 7/8	25 0/8	19 6/8	4	4	St. Clair County	MI	Lawrence S. Cowhy	1991	1,393
151 6/8	25 3/8	25 3/8	20 2/8	6	6	Bucks County	PA	Stephen Kollar	1992	1,393
151 5/8	26 2/8	24 7/8	20 6/8	6	6	Franklin County	KS	Kenneth Heinitz	1966	1,410
151 5/8	24 2/8	24 3/8	18 7/8	4	4	Douglas County	WI	Larry Allen Blaylock	1978	1,410
151 5/8	26 0/8	24 3/8	18 3/8	6	6	Reno County	KS	Dan Ropp	1981	1,410
151 5/8	26 6/8	26 1/8	17 3/8	4	4	Carter County	KY	Herbie Jackson	1982	1,410
151 5/8	25 6/8	25 4/8	21 5/8	6	7	Green County	WI	Alex Elkins	1982	1,410
151 5/8	26 6/8	26 5/8	17 5/8	4	4	Jackson County	OH	Jeffrey L. Walters	1984	1,410
151 5/8	24 7/8	25 2/8	20 7/8	5	5	Vermilion County	IL	Bill Fitton	1984	1,410
151 5/8	22 2/8	23 2/8	16 5/8	6	5	Fremont County	IA	Mike Laughlin	1989	1,410
151 5/8	25 7/8	25 3/8	21 7/8	4	4	Ringgold County	IA	Dale L. Clark	1989	1,410
151 5/8	25 1/8	25 3/8	20 3/8	5	5	St. Louis County	MO	Michael T. Horn	1989	1,410
151 5/8	23 4/8	22 2/8	20 1/8	5	5	Jefferson County	ID	Brent D. Barber	1990	1,410
151 5/8	24 5/8	24 4/8	20 4/8	6	6	Hunterdon County	NJ	Jack Baker	1990	1,410
151 5/8	26 0/8	24 2/8	16 0/8	6	5	Lee County	IA	Larry Galliart	1991	1,410
151 5/8	22 6/8	24 4/8	17 4/8	8	5	Wyandotte County	KS	Bruce McComb	1991	1,410
151 4/8	23 2/8	22 5/8	16 0/8	6	6	Gogebic County	MI	Fred Felbab	1959	1,424
151 4/8	23 2/8	22 7/8	16 2/8	5	5	Murray County	MN	Jim F. Wyffels	1968	1,424
151 4/8	21 1/8	21 7/8	18 6/8	6	5	Brown County	SD	Duane Trost	1973	1,424
151 4/8	24 2/8	24 3/8	19 4/8	5	5	Marshall County	IL	William J. McNutt	1979	1,424
151 4/8	23 6/8	22 5/8	17 3/8	6	5	Pittsburg County	OK	Harry Milican	1983	1,424
151 4/8	26 4/8	26 0/8	20 2/8	4	4	Mason County	IL	David C. Gillespie	1984	1,424
151 4/8	21 3/8	21 5/8	19 0/8	5	6	Lincoln County	MT	Glenn W. Gibson	1985	1,424
151 4/8	22 7/8	22 4/8	17 0/8	5	5	Buffalo County	WI	Gerald Palmer	1985	1,424
151 4/8	24 4/8	24 7/8	23 0/8	5	5	Riley County	KS	L. F. Howerton	1985	1,424
151 4/8	25 1/8	25 1/8	21 2/8	5	4	Pierce County	WI	Dave Clare	1985	1,424
151 4/8	26 3/8	25 0/8	18 2/8	5	5	Polk County	WI	Todd C. Swenson	1986	1,424
151 4/8	22 4/8	21 4/8	18 0/8	6	5	McLeod County	MN	Ed Homan	1986	1,424
151 4/8	21 5/8	23 0/8	17 6/8	8	6	Day County	SD	Sandy Heuer	1987	1,424
151 4/8	24 4/8	25 2/8	17 5/8	4	6	Morrison County	MN	Troy Brown	1988	1,424
151 4/8	26 7/8	27 2/8	19 0/8	4	4	Pierce County	WI	Victor Howe	1988	1,424
151 4/8	24 2/8	23 3/8	17 4/8	5	5	Sumner County	KS	Lynn Reed	1988	1,424
151 4/8	25 6/8	23 5/8	18 0/8	5	5	Fayette County	IA	Jim Smith	1989	1,424
151 4/8	24 7/8	25 0/8	19 6/8	5	5	Lewis County	MO	Blaine Emrick	1990	1,424
151 4/8	23 7/8	23 2/8	16 0/8	5	5	Otero County	CO	Ron Rockwell	1990	1,424
151 4/8	26 1/8	25 1/8	16 4/8	5	5	Tuscarawas County	OH	Karl Paulik	1991	1,424
151 4/8	22 1/8	21 3/8	17 2/8	5	5	Steuben County	IN	Barry Bowers	1991	1,424
151 3/8	26 3/8	25 4/8	15 6/8	6	7	Martin County	IN	Robert E. Sloan	1968	1,445
151 3/8	23 2/8	23 7/8	19 1/8	5	5	Amherst County	VA	Jerry Armes	1975	1,445
151 3/8	23 4/8	24 0/8	18 3/8	5	6	Morris County	NJ	Phil D'Ottavio	1980	1,445
151 3/8	23 4/8	23 1/8	17 7/8	5	5	Langlade County	WI	Larry Petts	1983	1,445
151 3/8	26 1/8	26 1/8	18 0/8	5	7	Clay County	MN	Randy Swanson	1984	1,445
151 3/8	26 2/8	26 4/8	17 7/8	5	5	Osage County	KS	Gene Beam	1984	1,445
151 3/8	22 3/8	22 4/8	18 5/8	5	5	Trempealeau County	WI	Michael Baer	1984	1,445
151 3/8	25 2/8	25 4/8	17 3/8	6	5	Sauk County	WI	Casey A. Blum	1985	1,445
151 3/8	25 5/8	25 0/8	17 7/8	5	6	Posey County	IN	Donald R. Koester	1986	1,445
151 3/8	22 0/8	22 6/8	15 7/8	7	6	Stearns County	MN	Chuck Thies	1987	1,445
151 3/8	26 3/8	26 3/8	20 3/8	4	4	Roberts County	SD	Myles Keller	1987	1,445
151 3/8	24 1/8	23 5/8	17 3/8	4	4	Eaton County	MI	John A. Lee	1988	1,445
151 3/8	21 4/8	22 5/8	18 7/8	6	5	Logan County	IL	Eldon R. Broster	1989	1,445
151 3/8	23 5/8	23 5/8	17 5/8	5	5	Prince Georges County	MD	Sam Lyon	1989	1,445
151 3/8	22 5/8	22 5/8	17 7/8	5	5	Clayton County	IA	Robert C. Ungs	1990	1,445
151 3/8	25 7/8	24 7/8	20 7/8	6	5	Knox County	OH	Stan Tyson	1990	1,445
151 3/8	23 0/8	23 4/8	19 0/8	7	5	Cook County	IL	Dean Assink	1990	1,445
151 3/8	26 3/8	25 0/8	18 5/8	5	5	Dakota County	MN	Jeff Kamrud	1991	1,445
151 2/3	25 5/8	25 6/8	17 2/8	4	4	Fillmore County	MN	David Carson	1967	1,463
151 2/8	24 1/8	23 4/8	14 1/8	7	5	Blue Earth County	MN	Rory Duetchman	1974	1,463
151 2/8	22 1/8	22 4/8	18 2/8	6	6	Clark County	SD	Dean L. Myers	1975	1,463
151 2/8	25 0/8	24 4/8	18 0/8	5	5	La Salle County	IL	John Sullivan	1977	1,463
151 2/8	25 3/8	24 6/8	18 6/8	4	5	Litchfield County	CT	Donald R. Groody	1982	1,463
151 2/8	23 4/8	24 4/8	17 6/8	7	6	Warrick County	IN	Thomas Scheucher	1982	1,463
151 2/8	26 2/8	25 3/8	18 0/8	5	5	Cowley County	KS	Michael L. Snyder	1984	1,463
151 2/8	22 4/8	22 3/8	13 7/8	6	5	Livingston County	IL	Tom Roe	1987	1,463

SCORE	LENGTH OF R MAIN BEAM L		INSIDE SPREAD	NUMBER OF R POINTS L		AREA	STATE/ PROVINCE	HUNTER'S NAME	DATE	RANK
151 2/8	24 7/8	21 4/8	16 4/8	5	5	Benton County	IA	Jeff L. Jacobi	1987	1,463
151 2/8	24 1/8	23 5/8	17 0/8	5	6	Clarke County	GA	Terry Pahl	1988	1,463
151 2/8	22 6/8	23 7/8	20 2/8	5	5	Iroquois County	IL	Eric Edwards	1988	1,463
151 2/8	24 5/8	24 3/8	20 5/8	5	4	Fulton County	GA	John Brooks	1989	1,463
151 2/8	24 4/8	25 4/8	19 0/8	5	8	Fulton County	IL	Don DeRenzy	1990	1,463
151 2/8	24 5/8	25 1/8	17 6/8	5	5	Will County	IL	Ty Orgas	1990	1,463
151 2/8	25 0/8	25 2/8	15 6/8	5	5	Burlington County	NJ	Elliston M. Jacobs	1991	1,463
151 1/8	22 3/8	23 4/8	18 4/8	7	5	Adair County	MO	Dr. Eddy Transano	1971	1,478
151 1/8	25 6/8	24 4/8	19 3/8	5	5	Lucas County	OH	Gail A. Rice	1978	1,478
151 1/8	22 6/8	22 6/8	17 4/8	7	6	Wood County	WI	Scott Arneson	1979	1,478
151 1/8	23 4/8	21 4/8	18 3/8	5	5	Minnehaha County	SD	Bradley D. Swier	1982	1,478
151 1/8	23 1/8	23 2/8	17 1/8	5	5	Barren County	KY	Steve England	1983	1,478
151 1/8	25 2/8	24 0/8	20 7/8	4	5	Franklin County	KS	Don Hrabe	1985	1,478
151 1/8	24 2/8	26 5/8	17 3/8	5	5	Bond County	IL	Gary Netzler	1987	1,478
151 1/8	24 5/8	23 4/8	17 7/8	5	5	Grant County	WI	Joe Devlin	1987	1,478
151 1/8	22 0/8	23 2/8	16 3/8	5	5	Jefferson County	MO	Steve North	1988	1,478
151 1/8	23 3/8	23 6/8	19 5/8	5	6	Okotoks	ALB	Dave Richardson	1989	1,478
151 1/8	22 2/8	21 0/8	17 1/8	5	5	Saline County	KS	James R. Weldy	1990	1,478
151 1/8	24 0/8	23 7/8	18 6/8	7	6	Stearns County	MN	Paul M. Froseth	1991	1,478
151 0/8	25 0/8	26 0/8	16 6/8	5	5	Warrick County	IN	Gerald G. Taylor	1970	1,490
151 0/8	23 6/8	24 5/8	19 6/8	5	5	Polk County	WI	Bryan Anderson	1976	1,490
151 0/8	30 1/8	29 0/8	20 2/8	7	5	Gray County	KS	Paul Meininger	1980	1,490
151 0/8	23 2/8	23 5/8	21 2/8	5	5	Grant County	WI	Doug J. Leibfried	1981	1,490
151 0/8	25 3/8	24 0/8	17 4/8	5	5	Columbia County	WI	Jeffrey M. Ballweg	1984	1,490
151 0/8	23 7/8	23 3/8	20 0/8	5	5	White County	IL	Eric D. Devore	1985	1,490
151 0/8	26 5/8	27 1/8	20 4/8	4	4	Appanoose County	IA	Steven P. Widmar	1986	1,490
151 0/8	26 7/8	24 5/8	18 0/8	5	4	Marshall County	IL	Bryan Blair	1987	1,490
151 0/8	24 4/8	24 6/8	18 2/8	5	5	Jefferson County	WI	Gary Goldbeck	1987	1,490
151 0/8	27 2/8	25 2/8	18 6/8	5	6	Northampton County	VA	Stanley I. Long	1988	1,490
151 0/8	26 0/8	25 4/8	19 0/8	6	6	Woodford County	IL	Stan Bocian	1988	1,490
151 0/8	25 6/8	23 6/8	21 2/8	5	5	Davis County	IA	Clayton Eakins	1990	1,490
151 0/8	23 3/8	24 4/8	19 6/8	5	5	Kosciusko County	IN	Ronald D. Newcomer	1990	1,490
151 0/8	24 5/8	25 0/8	18 4/8	6	6	Fayette County	IL	Kelly Tarter	1990	1,490
151 0/8	24 6/8	23 3/8	24 6/8	6	5	Kenedy County	TX	Carl Walker	1991	1,490
151 0/8	24 7/8	25 5/8	17 6/8	6	6	Jasper County	IL	David Staley	1991	1,490
150 7/8	23 2/8	22 2/8	18 1/8	5	5	Trempealeau County	WI	Phillip Lunde	1969	1,506
150 7/8	22 6/8	22 5/8	20 1/8	5	5	Harlan County	NE	Edwin Witte	1973	1,506
150 7/8	24 3/8	22 5/8	17 5/8	7	6	Lancaster County	PA	J. John Buhay	1980	1,506
150 7/8	26 0/8	26 0/8	21 1/8	5	5	Kent County	MI	Robert Ten Eyck	1980	1,506
150 7/8	23 4/8	26 6/8	20 1/8	8	5	Trempealeau County	WI	Tom Reedy	1984	1,506
150 7/8	22 5/8	23 1/8	18 3/8	6	6	Cumberland County	ME	David C. Smart	1984	1,506
150 7/8	23 2/8	22 7/8	17 6/8	6	6	Washington County	IA	David Greenlee	1986	1,506
150 7/8	23 0/8	22 2/8	20 5/8	6	6	Becker County	MN	Arnold F. Ostgarden	1987	1,506
150 7/8	24 0/8	23 6/8	20 3/8	6	7	Butler County	KS	Rodney Koehn	1987	1,506
150 7/8	24 4/8	23 2/8	20 5/8	5	5	Hopkins County	KY	Albert Hargis	1987	1,506
150 7/8	27 5/8	27 3/8	18 0/8	6	6	Menard County	IL	Darrell Holliday	1987	1,506
150 7/8	23 6/8	24 3/8	17 5/8	7	6	De Kalb County	IN	Eric L. Ditmars	1988	1,506
150 7/8	26 1/8	24 7/8	21 3/8	4	4	Black Hawk County	IA	Craig Cornelius	1989	1,506
150 7/8	28 6/8	27 4/8	19 4/8	5	6	Lawrence County	IL	Roger D. Wallace	1989	1,506
150 6/8	22 3/8	22 0/8	16 4/8	5	5	Redwood County	MN	Irvin Plotz	1975	1,520
150 6/8	22 2/8	21 7/8	19 0/8	5	6	Allegan County	MI	Lane Humphreys	1979	1,520
150 6/8	24 4/8	23 7/8	18 6/8	6	6	Columbia County	WI	Jerry Ulrich	1980	1,520
150 6/8	25 2/8	24 6/8	19 6/8	5	6	Jo Daviess County	IL	Michael Muehleip	1981	1,520
150 6/8	25 3/8	25 3/8	20 1/8	4	6	Winnebago County	IL	Fred L. Smith	1985	1,520
150 6/8	24 6/8	24 6/8	16 4/8	5	5	Wayne County	IL	Ginger Harvey	1986	1,520
150 6/8	22 5/8	23 3/8	19 2/8	6	5	Floyd County	IA	Mark Koenigsfeld	1986	1,520
150 6/8	24 6/8	24 5/8	27 1/8	5	5	Greenwood County	KS	Ray Penner	1986	1,520
150 6/8	21 2/8	21 4/8	21 6/8	5	5	Clearwater County	ID	Gordon Fout	1987	1,520
150 6/8	24 6/8	25 1/8	21 4/8	4	4	Boone County	IA	Dave Rimathe	1988	1,520
150 6/8	22 6/8	21 6/8	15 6/8	5	5	Hocking County	OH	James Earl Roberts, Jr.	1988	1,520
150 6/8	25 4/8	25 1/8	17 2/8	4	4	Suffolk County	NY	Ed Viola	1988	1,520
150 6/8	25 3/8	24 0/8	18 7/8	5	6	Webster County	IA	Darrell Promes	1990	1,520
150 6/8	24 1/8	24 0/8	16 6/8	4	4	Linn County	IA	David Hotz	1990	1,520
150 6/8	24 0/8	24 4/8	20 2/8	5	5	Price County	WI	Michael J. Lobner	1991	1,520
150 5/8	21 0/8	22 7/8	19 3/8	6	5	Madison County	NE	Darwin Heppner	1967	1,535
150 5/8	22 7/8	22 6/8	22 1/8	5	6	Eaton County	MI	Greg Hoefler	1982	1,535
150 5/8	22 7/8	22 5/8	18 5/8	5	5	Ashland County	OH	Lyle Bennett	1984	1,535
150 5/8	24 4/8	23 4/8	18 1/8	7	5	Pratt County	KS	Scott Haworth	1984	1,535
150 5/8	22 3/8	22 3/8	17 3/8	5	5	Chippewa County	WI	Tim Walters	1985	1,535
150 5/8	25 6/8	24 5/8	21 7/8	5	5	Randolph County	IL	Loren Eggemeyer	1987	1,535

SCORE	LENGTH OF MAIN BEAM R	LENGTH OF MAIN BEAM L	INSIDE SPREAD	NUMBER OF POINTS R	NUMBER OF POINTS L	AREA	STATE/ PROVINCE	HUNTER'S NAME	DATE	RANK
150 5/8	27 3/8	27 5/8	21 1/8	5	5	Adams County	IL	James A. Stupavsky	1988	1,535
150 5/8	26 2/8	26 1/8	18 5/8	5	5	Randolph County	AR	Joey White	1990	1,535
150 5/8	25 0/8	23 4/8	18 1/8	7	6	Randolph County	IL	Gary Vanpelt	1991	1,535
150 4/8	24 4/8	24 4/8	18 6/8	5	4	Scott County	IA	Howard A. Goettsch	1974	1,544
150 4/8	22 5/8	22 3/8	14 7/8	6	7	Wabasha County	MN	Lee Partington	1975	1,544
150 4/8	21 4/8	21 6/8	15 6/8	6	6	Dunn County	WI	Mary Nussberger	1976	1,544
150 4/8	24 7/8	24 7/8	17 6/8	5	5	Guernsey County	OH	Miltos Stefanitais	1979	1,544
150 4/8	23 6/8	23 4/8	19 0/8	5	5	Schuyler County	NY	Donald L. Lane	1980	1,544
150 4/8	22 1/8	22 0/8	20 4/8	5	5	Woodford County	IL	Roger Miller	1980	1,544
150 4/8	24 2/8	25 1/8	19 4/8	4	4	Monroe County	WI	Dirk Gillette	1981	1,544
150 4/8	26 3/8	25 0/8	18 4/8	5	4	Miami County	OH	Richard G. Williamson	1981	1,544
150 4/8	24 7/8	27 2/8	28 1/8	5	4	Greenwood County	KS	Ray Penner	1984	1,544
150 4/8	23 6/8	22 3/8	16 0/8	4	4	Osage County	KS	Bill Senne	1985	1,544
150 4/8	26 2/8	26 2/8	18 2/8	4	4	Pepin County	WI	Myles Keller	1985	1,544
150 4/8	23 4/8	23 2/8	17 1/8	5	7	Florence County	WI	Carolyn Lemanski	1986	1,544
150 4/8	26 0/8	26 1/8	20 3/8	7	6	Knox County	MO	Roger Gipple	1986	1,544
150 4/8	23 5/8	24 6/8	18 0/8	5	5	Gregory County	SD	Dan Swiler	1990	1,544
150 4/8	24 6/8	24 7/8	17 4/8	5	5	Stoddard County	MO	Ken Heuer	1990	1,544
150 4/8	23 1/8	22 5/8	17 2/8	5	5	Ravalli County	MT	Mark Moreland	1991	1,544
150 4/8	25 0/8	24 4/8	19 6/8	5	4	Prowers County	CO	Neal Heaton	1991	1,544
150 4/8	23 6/8	22 4/8	18 1/8	6	6	Comanche County	KS	Randall Eddy	1991	1,544
150 4/8	21 6/8	22 0/8	17 6/8	5	5	Saginaw County	MI	Jerry D. Pratt	1991	1,544
150 4/8	24 1/8	25 2/8	18 6/8	5	4	Claiborne County	MS	Tripp Stennett	1992	1,544
150 3/8	24 5/8	24 5/8	22 5/8	4	4	Oneida County	WI	Philip Hildebrand	1967	1,564
150 3/8	28 0/8	27 4/8	20 5/8	4	5	Jones County	GA	Sid Hester	1969	1,564
150 3/8	20 4/8	21 2/8	16 7/8	5	5	Langlade County	WI	Herbert Buettner	1970	1,564
150 3/8	23 3/8	23 5/8	18 3/8	6	7	Graham County	KS	Russell Hull	1977	1,564
150 3/8	24 0/8	23 4/8	15 4/8	5	6	Juneau County	WI	Anthony Wulin	1977	1,564
150 3/8	22 2/8	22 3/8	15 3/8	5	5	Souris River	MAN	Garry William Kaluzniak	1980	1,564
150 3/8	26 0/8	24 4/8	16 4/8	9	8	Oakland County	MI	Donald J. Fisher	1981	1,564
150 3/8	25 1/8	25 0/8	17 2/8	5	5	Jackson County	MO	Marvin Thomey	1983	1,564
150 3/8	23 1/8	22 3/8	16 4/8	5	6	Dakota County	MN	Dave Vomela	1985	1,564
150 3/8	23 1/8	23 5/8	19 5/8	7	7	Yuma County	CO	Richard King	1985	1,564
150 3/8	24 0/8	24 2/8	16 4/8	6	6	Benton County	IA	Okee Walker	1986	1,564
150 3/8	26 1/8	26 1/8	16 6/8	7	5	Jackson County	OH	Robert E. Thomas, Jr.	1987	1,564
150 3/8	24 2/8	23 2/8	18 5/8	4	5	Clark County	IL	Max M. LeCrone	1988	1,564
150 3/8	24 0/8	25 2/8	15 4/8	5	7	Clark County	OH	Rick Rounds	1988	1,564
150 3/8	23 4/8	24 0/8	16 7/8	5	7	Branch County	MI	James E. Marvin	1990	1,564
150 3/8	23 0/8	22 5/8	20 1/8	5	5	Mason County	IL	Jeff Heilman	1990	1,564
150 3/8	24 0/8	24 4/8	20 7/8	5	5	Suffolk County	NY	Bruce R. Dickerson	1990	1,564
150 3/8	25 3/8	25 6/8	19 1/8	5	5	Greene County	OH	Rodney Curtis Bailey	1990	1,564
150 2/8	23 5/8	23 3/8	17 2/8	6	6	Jackson County	WI	Roger Reinart	1972	1,582
150 2/8	26 0/8	24 2/8	19 0/8	4	5	Spink County	SD	Gerald A. Kettering	1978	1,582
150 2/8	23 3/8	23 5/8	14 0/8	5	5	Cottonwood County	MN	Leonard P. Thiner	1978	1,582
150 2/8	25 2/8	27 1/8	19 4/8	4	4	Fulton County	IL	William L. Beaird	1984	1,582
150 2/8	23 3/8	22 7/8	17 2/8	5	5	Marathon County	WI	Kevin Denzine	1985	1,582
150 2/8	25 1/8	25 2/8	16 7/8	7	5	Dodge County	WI	Fran Hallmeyer	1986	1,582
150 2/8	23 1/8	24 0/8	16 2/8	5	5	Price County	WI	Ben Grapa	1987	1,582
150 2/8	24 4/8	24 5/8	18 4/8	5	5	Wyoming	ONT	Pierre Parent	1987	1,582
150 2/8	24 4/8	25 3/8	17 1/8	7	5	Lawrence County	IL	James R. Griggs	1987	1,582
150 2/8	25 5/8	26 6/8	23 2/8	6	6	Meigs County	OH	Earl M. Johnson	1987	1,582
150 2/8	23 1/8	24 4/8	15 2/8	5	6	Crowley County	CO	Chuck Anderson, Sr.	1987	1,582
150 2/8	26 3/8	26 6/8	19 4/8	5	5	Howard County	MD	David Wilson	1988	1,582
150 2/8	24 0/8	23 7/8	20 3/8	4	7	Webster County	IA	Scott L. Powers	1988	1,582
150 2/8	22 4/8	23 1/8	18 1/8	6	7	Butler County	KS	Jack Evans	1988	1,582
150 2/8	25 3/8	24 1/8	19 2/8	4	4	Webster County	IA	Curtis Martens	1988	1,582
150 2/8	23 6/8	24 2/8	16 6/8	5	5	Cass County	MI	Donald Zehrung	1988	1,582
150 2/8	24 6/8	24 6/8	19 3/8	6	6	Lawrence County	OH	Scott Johnson	1989	1,582
150 2/8	24 1/8	24 0/8	17 1/8	6	8	Douglas County	WI	Steve Wittke	1990	1,582
150 2/8	21 4/8	21 5/8	15 2/8	5	5	Bremer County	IA	Rod Heidemann	1990	1,582
150 2/8	28 4/8	27 4/8	24 2/8	6	4	Napanee	ONT	Tim McCabe	1990	1,582
150 2/8	23 2/8	22 2/8	24 0/8	5	7	Kleberg County	TX	Wayne Peeples	1991	1,582
150 2/8	23 4/8	23 5/8	16 0/8	6	6	Sauk County	WI	Fred Hess	1991	1,582
150 1/8	23 5/8	23 0/8	16 7/8	5	6	Johnson County	IA	Jim Keefer	1969	1,604
150 1/8	22 5/8	23 7/8	16 1/8	5	5	Guthrie County	IA	Bill Barringen	1975	1,604
150 1/8	24 2/8	24 5/8	16 7/8	5	5	Freeborn County	MN	Robert Haney	1977	1,604
150 1/8	20 6/8	20 2/8	18 1/8	6	6	Spencer County	ND	Lyle Fritz	1978	1,604
150 1/8	26 0/8	26 2/8	19 0/8	4	5	Butler County	OH	Roger S. Trigg	1979	1,604
150 1/8	24 7/8	26 2/8	19 7/8	5	6	Anoka County	MN	Patricia Barry	1980	1,604
150 1/8	22 1/8	22 4/8	17 7/8	5	5	Dearborn County	IN	Mike Serio	1982	1,604

SCORE	LENGTH OF MAIN BEAM R	L	INSIDE SPREAD	NUMBER OF POINTS R	L	AREA	STATE/ PROVINCE	HUNTER'S NAME	DATE	RANK
150 1/8	22 7/8	22 5/8	17 1/8	5	4	Oldham County	KY	Phillip Burba	1985	1,604
150 1/8	23 4/8	24 2/8	17 3/8	4	5	Jefferson County	WI	Patrick Thiede	1985	1,604
150 1/8	24 4/8	24 3/8	20 1/8	7	8	Lake County	IL	James C. Carlson	1985	1,604
150 1/8	23 3/8	22 2/8	17 1/8	6	6	Guthrie County	IA	John D. Hambleton	1989	1,604
150 1/8	25 6/8	25 2/8	19 3/8	7	4	Leavenworth County	KS	Travis McGraw	1990	1,604
150 1/8	22 6/8	22 4/8	21 1/8	5	6	Louisa County	IA	Larry H. Thumann, Sr.	1990	1,604
150 0/8	25 3/8	24 3/8	15 6/8	5	6	Adams County	WI	Daniel Becker	1957	1,617
150 0/8	26 6/8	27 1/8	17 6/8	5	4	Benton County	IA	Robert L. Walker	1961	1,617
150 0/8	26 4/8	26 4/8	18 4/8	5	5	Shelby County	IA	Einar Leistad	1970	1,617
150 0/8	22 0/8	23 2/8	17 2/8	5	6	Ozaukee County	WI	Rand Krueger	1980	1,617
150 0/8	24 5/8	23 0/8	17 4/8	5	5	Kosciusko County	IN	Gil Reed	1981	1,617
150 0/8	22 3/8	22 4/8	17 1/8	6	6	Carroll County	AR	Larry Gasaway	1984	1,617
150 0/8	24 4/8	24 1/8	18 1/8	4	6	Penobscot County	ME	Kris T. Saunders	1985	1,617
150 0/8	21 0/8	21 4/8	15 7/8	4	5	Wabash County	IL	Paul Benham	1985	1,617
150 0/8	22 5/8	23 4/8	16 5/8	5	7	Tazewell County	IL	William H. Ray	1985	1,617
150 0/8	25 4/8	24 7/8	17 5/8	6	6	Livingston County	IL	James B. Smith	1985	1,617
150 0/8	23 7/8	23 3/8	20 0/8	5	5	White County	IL	Eric D. Devare	1985	1,617
150 0/8	23 6/8	24 2/8	17 0/8	5	5	Chase County	KS	Dan McClure	1985	1,617
150 0/8	22 2/8	21 4/8	16 4/8	5	6	Berkshire County	MA	Alan Ziegler	1986	1,617
150 0/8	25 1/8	25 3/8	20 0/8	4	4	Champaign County	OH	Douglas L. Hudson	1987	1,617
150 0/8	24 2/8	23 3/8	19 2/8	5	5	Ashtabula County	OH	Mike Morehouse	1988	1,617
150 0/8	25 6/8	26 2/8	18 4/8	5	5	Coles County	IL	Ron Osborne	1988	1,617
150 0/8	24 0/8	23 6/8	18 1/8	5	7	Lake County	IL	James D. Maricle	1989	1,617
150 0/8	22 3/8	22 5/8	15 0/8	6	6	Dane County	WI	Rick Krause	1990	1,617
150 0/8	23 5/8	23 0/8	18 2/8	5	5	Cedar County	IA	George R. Briggs	1990	1,617
150 0/8	24 4/8	25 2/8	20 2/8	6	5	Inglewood	ONT	Jack Leggo	1990	1,617
150 0/8	23 4/8	23 3/8	15 4/8	5	5	Allamakee County	IA	Rodney Smed	1991	1,617
150 0/8	24 6/8	24 4/8	19 0/8	4	4	Mercer County	NJ	Scott Lysenko	1991	1,617
150 0/8	25 6/8	26 2/8	20 0/8	4	4	Todd County	MN	Brad G. Lorentz	1991	1,617
150 0/8	24 6/8	25 7/8	20 6/8	6	6	Buffalo County	WI	John W. Zahrte	1991	1,617
150 0/8	26 0/8	26 2/8	17 2/8	4	4	Portage County	WI	Robert J. Karnowski	1992	1,617
150 0/8	24 6/8	24 4/8	16 6/8	5	5	Fremont County	IA	Dave Holt	1992	1,617
150 0/8	24 4/8	24 3/8	18 6/8	5	5	Brown County	IL	Kevin Weeks	1992	1,617
149 7/8	26 0/8	25 6/8	20 3/8	4	4	Pulaski County	VA	Ray S. Carter	1962	1,644
149 7/8	21 6/8	21 1/8	17 3/8	5	5	Adams County	IL	Lyndall W. Heyen	1967	1,644
149 7/8	24 6/8	24 1/8	20 1/8	6	6	Will County	IL	Jerry Yost	1978	1,644
149 7/8	23 5/8	23 5/8	17 1/8	5	5	Scott County	KY	Mike Northcut	1980	1,644
149 7/8	25 1/8	24 1/8	18 7/8	6	6	Dauphin County	PA	Larry D. Wiestling	1983	1,644
149 7/8	25 0/8	25 0/8	17 5/8	5	5	Pittsburg County	OK	Doug Larimer	1985	1,644
149 7/8	22 0/8	22 1/8	17 0/8	7	6	Cumberland County	NJ	Bob Eisele	1986	1,644
149 7/8	24 6/8	25 4/8	16 4/8	6	6	Madison County	IL	Frank W. Gavillet	1986	1,644
149 7/8	24 7/8	24 4/8	17 7/8	6	5	Allegheny County	PA	George M. Conway	1987	1,644
149 7/8	25 0/8	24 2/8	19 6/8	4	4	Nicollet County	MN	Neil Treml	1987	1,644
149 7/8	25 1/8	24 3/8	20 7/8	5	4	Meade County	KS	Keith Whitney	1987	1,644
149 7/8	23 0/8	23 5/8	17 3/8	6	5	Jackson County	MO	Ty Easley	1988	1,644
149 7/8	24 4/8	24 1/8	16 4/8	6	5	Arenac County	MI	Jim Gall	1989	1,644
149 7/8	23 3/8	23 2/8	18 4/8	5	6	Kenosha County	WI	Thomas C. Zeihen	1989	1,644
149 7/8	26 0/8	26 3/8	21 7/8	4	6	Dodge County	WI	Steve Moritz	1991	1,644
149 7/8	23 1/8	24 2/8	17 6/8	5	6	Graham County	KS	Jim Kerbaugh	1991	1,644
149 6/8	23 4/8	23 5/8	17 1/8	7	6	Gull Lake	SAS	Keith Roney	1978	1,660
149 6/8	23 6/8	24 7/8	21 6/8	4	4	Branch County	MI	Howard W. Loehr	1983	1,660
149 6/8	25 1/8	26 0/8	20 6/8	4	5	Piatt County	IL	Marvin R. Salmon	1983	1,660
149 6/8	25 0/8	24 5/8	17 4/8	5	5	La Salle County	IL	Gary Tabor	1984	1,660
149 6/8	26 1/8	25 7/8	21 5/8	6	6	Anderson County	TN	Daniel W. Chase	1985	1,660
149 6/8	25 6/8	23 3/8	18 1/8	6	6	Douglas County	KS	Samuel J. Tunget	1985	1,660
149 6/8	23 7/8	23 2/8	19 2/8	5	7	Hocking County	OH	John E Furderer	1987	1,660
149 6/8	25 6/8	24 7/8	19 4/8	6	7	Adams County	OH	Richard O. Ramsey	1990	1,660
149 6/8	23 4/8	23 7/8	20 4/8	6	5	Waukesha County	WI	Mike Scaff	1991	1,660
149 5/8	25 6/8	25 3/8	18 5/8	6	6	La Salle County	IL	Timothy L. Kakara	1975	1,669
149 5/8	25 4/8	25 2/8	20 1/8	6	5	Chase County	KS	John Moore	1981	1,669
149 5/8	24 5/8	25 2/8	20 1/8	5	7	Sheboygan County	WI	Leon Schultz	1983	1,669
149 5/8	24 4/8	23 5/8	20 1/8	5	5	Johnson County	NE	Brad Seitz	1984	1,669
149 5/8	22 4/8	23 1/8	16 5/8	6	5	York County	NE	Harold Bowman	1985	1,669
149 5/8	25 1/8	23 2/8	17 5/8	6	6	Livingston County	NY	John J. Valle	1985	1,669
149 5/8	22 7/8	23 3/8	21 1/8	5	5	Osage	SAS	Fred Paslawski	1986	1,669
149 5/8	25 1/8	25 0/8	16 7/8	5	4	McPherson County	KS	George E. Hoke	1986	1,669
149 5/8	27 3/8	28 6/8	20 3/8	5	6	Delaware County	IA	Robert J. Becker	1987	1,669
149 5/8	24 3/8	24 3/8	19 1/8	5	4	Kiowa County	KS	Karl L. Ballard	1987	1,669
149 5/8	26 4/8	26 1/8	20 7/8	4	4	Montgomery County	IL	Martin L. Leitschuh	1987	1,669
149 5/8	26 4/8	26 4/8	21 0/8	7	6	Jefferson County	IL	Terry Storey	1988	1,669

SCORE	LENGTH OF MAIN BEAM R	LENGTH OF MAIN BEAM L	INSIDE SPREAD	NUMBER OF POINTS R	NUMBER OF POINTS L	AREA	STATE/ PROVINCE	HUNTER'S NAME	DATE	RANK
149 5/8	23 4/8	24 3/8	18 6/8	6	6	Fayette County	IA	Mike Barker	1989	1,669
149 5/8	23 4/8	22 3/8	17 1/8	5	5	Ripley County	IN	Kevin D. Hall	1989	1,669
149 5/8	24 3/8	25 3/8	18 2/8	7	6	Carroll County	IL	Art Heinze	1989	1,669
149 5/8	24 4/8	24 2/8	19 4/8	6	5	Macon County	IL	Gary Wayne Scheland, Sr.	1990	1,669
149 5/8	26 2/8	27 3/8	19 4/8	5	4	Jo Daviess County	IL	Ronald J. Blauwkamp	1990	1,669
149 5/8	24 5/8	24 5/8	20 2/8	6	5	Barber County	KS	Jim F. Shadid	1991	1,669
149 5/8	24 4/8	24 7/8	15 5/8	6	6	Pottawatomie County	KS	Nathan Figge	1992	1,669
149 4/8	23 3/8	26 0/8	20 2/8	5	5	Woodbury County	IA	Don Gothier	1962	1,688
149 4/8	23 2/8	23 2/8	17 1/8	6	5	Newton County	IN	Gerald R. Metros	1973	1,688
149 4/8	22 5/8	22 3/8	17 4/8	7	5	Ogle County	IL	Jerome Bruns	1983	1,688
149 4/8	24 5/8	25 2/8	17 0/8	5	5	Sedgwick County	KS	Bob Shull	1984	1,688
149 4/8	25 3/8	25 0/8	21 4/8	4	4	Shawnee County	KS	Jim Dultmeier	1985	1,688
149 4/8	25 4/8	25 7/8	17 4/8	6	5	Dane County	WI	John Podebradsky	1986	1,688
149 4/8	23 5/8	24 5/8	22 0/8	5	5	Keokuk County	IA	Mike Krier	1986	1,688
149 4/8	22 6/8	22 3/8	16 7/8	6	5	Polk County	WI	Blaine Mortimer	1987	1,688
149 4/8	26 1/8	25 5/8	22 6/8	5	4	Lee County	IL	Rick Hornung	1988	1,688
149 4/8	23 1/8	21 6/8	19 6/8	5	7	Kossuth County	IA	Bruce K. Leeck	1989	1,688
149 4/8	28 2/8	25 2/8	19 0/8	5	6	Lancaster County	NE	Bog Spicha	1990	1,688
149 4/8	24 2/8	19 0/8	20 7/8	5	7	Buffalo County	WI	Matthew J. Gorniak	1990	1,688
149 4/8	25 0/8	24 4/8	18 4/8	6	5	Champaign County	IL	Bud Barnes	1991	1,688
149 4/8	24 2/8	23 6/8	18 6/8	5	4	Clayton County	IA	Joseph C. Hinderman	1991	1,688
149 3/8	26 6/8	25 4/8	22 1/8	4	4		NY	George Ferber	1957	1,702
149 3/8	23 4/8	23 3/8	15 7/8	5	5	Madison County	KY	Robert Young	1963	1,702
149 3/8	23 4/8	24 4/8	19 3/8	5	5	Newton County	IN	Philip Kozlowski	1968	1,702
149 3/8	23 7/8	23 2/8	15 7/8	5	5	Buffalo County	WI	Daniel J. Brunner	1969	1,702
149 3/8	24 1/8	24 2/8	19 3/8	5	5	Lawrence County	OH	Ronald E. Burnette	1971	1,702
149 3/8	23 7/8	23 4/8	17 5/8	5	5	Waushara County	WI	Ronald Anunson	1974	1,702
149 3/8	22 2/8	23 1/8	15 7/8	6	6	Lac qui Parle County	MN	Ron Patzer	1980	1,702
149 3/8	24 1/8	25 3/8	19 7/8	5	6	Perry County	IL	Vern Quillman	1981	1,702
149 3/8	24 2/8	23 3/8	19 3/8	6	7	Charles County	MD	Frank A. Rankin	1981	1,702
149 3/8	24 0/8	25 2/8	17 4/8	5	4	Washington County	OH	Charles E. Vaughan	1983	1,702
149 3/8	25 5/8	25 0/8	20 4/8	4	5	Noble County	OK	Bill Hughes	1984	1,702
149 3/8	22 5/8	22 6/8	15 5/8	5	5	Morgan County	CO	Stan Kingcade	1985	1,702
149 3/8	24 2/8	23 5/8	21 3/8	6	6	Iroquois County	IL	Dale W. Duits	1986	1,702
149 3/8	24 7/8	26 5/8	16 5/8	6	6	Athens County	OH	Ron Sallee	1986	1,702
149 3/8	21 7/8	23 4/8	18 7/8	6	6	Ozaukee County	WI	Mark Hoelz	1987	1,702
149 3/8	23 5/8	24 0/8	17 2/8	4	6	Sandusky County	OH	James Moll	1988	1,702
149 3/8	21 5/8	21 1/8	17 3/8	5	5	Morden	MAN	Allen K. Martens	1988	1,702
149 3/8	25 3/8	25 1/8	19 5/8	5	5	Muskingum County	OH	John W. Keefe	1988	1,702
149 3/8	23 1/8	22 5/8	18 7/8	4	5	Somerset County	NJ	Peter Paradise	1989	1,702
149 3/8	24 1/8	24 5/8	18 7/8	5	5	Buffalo County	WI	Randall Martin	1990	1,702
149 3/8	24 4/8	24 4/8	19 0/8	7	7	Johnson County	IA	Kevin Deets	1990	1,702
149 3/8	26 0/8	25 5/8	19 6/8	5	6	Monona County	IA	Richard Kelly	1990	1,702
149 3/8	27 0/8	25 4/8	21 1/8	5	4	Burt County	NE	Michael L. Johnson	1990	1,702
149 3/8	24 1/8	23 5/8	19 3/8	5	5	Stearns County	MN	Jeff Skinner	1991	1,702
149 3/8	24 6/8	26 2/8	20 7/8	6	6	McHenry County	IL	Brian Witte	1991	1,702
149 3/8	25 1/8	25 2/8	15 2/8	6	6	Owen County	KY	Robert C. Long, Jr.	1991	1,702
149 2/8	25 3/8	24 6/8	20 4/8	5	5	Westchester County	NY	Joseph H. Keeler	1957	1,728
149 2/8	22 0/8	22 1/8	16 6/8	5	5	Will County	IL	Daniel R. Altiery	1973	1,728
149 2/8	22 7/8	22 6/8	20 6/8	4	5	Auglaize County	OH	Fred Rostorfer	1980	1,728
149 2/8	23 3/8	23 4/8	15 3/8	5	7	Livingston County	MI	John Richmond	1981	1,728
149 2/8	23 4/8	22 6/8	18 6/8	6	6	Columbia County	WI	Gene R. Elsing	1981	1,728
149 2/8	24 0/8	22 1/8	17 4/8	5	5	Washtenaw County	MI	Fred Johnson	1984	1,728
149 2/8	27 4/8	26 6/8	20 2/8	7	7	Fulton County	IL	Locie L Murphy	1984	1,728
149 2/8	23 6/8	23 4/8	18 0/8	5	5	Jackson County	MO	Marvin Thomey	1984	1,728
149 2/8	23 4/8	23 2/8	19 4/8	6	5	Otter Tail County	MN	Kelly Shannon	1987	1,728
149 2/8	24 2/8	24 2/8	16 7/8	6	5	Warren County	KY	Jerry Sympson	1987	1,728
149 2/8	26 2/8	25 1/8	19 6/8	6	4	Tama County	IA	Travis Hansen	1988	1,728
149 2/8	23 1/8	23 7/8	17 0/8	5	4	Vinton County	OH	Brian D. Ehrhart	1989	1,728
149 2/8	21 6/8	19 7/8	15 6/8	5	5	Ashe County	NC	Marshall "Footsie" Eller	1991	1,728
149 1/8	25 4/8	25 0/8	17 0/8	5	7	Bon Homme County	SD	Terry Gretschman	1974	1,741
149 1/8	23 3/8	22 0/8	19 6/8	6	5	Coles County	IL	Bill Spaniol	1976	1,741
149 1/8	25 7/8	23 2/8	19 7/8	5	5	Clark County	IL	Gerald D. Shaffner	1984	1,741
149 1/8	24 0/8	24 6/8	19 4/8	6	6	Phillips County	KS	Bryan Henry	1984	1,741
149 1/8	22 3/8	24 2/8	17 2/8	6	5	Traill County	ND	Dale Grindeland	1986	1,741
149 1/8	26 1/8	27 3/8	19 5/8	7	7	Morrison County	MN	Jeff Moris	1987	1,741
149 1/8	25 6/8	24 7/8	16 3/8	5	4	Union County	KY	Joseph K. "Bo" Girten	1988	1,741
149 1/8	25 7/8	26 3/8	20 5/8	4	4	Washington County	MN	Scott Ralidak	1989	1,741
149 1/8	22 3/8	22 6/8	15 5/8	5	5	Stearns County	MN	Duane Gertken	1989	1,741
149 1/8	21 5/8	23 0/8	20 7/8	5	5	Peoria County	IL	Tom Missen	1989	1,741

SCORE	LENGTH OF MAIN BEAM		INSIDE SPREAD	NUMBER OF POINTS		AREA	STATE/ PROVINCE	HUNTER'S NAME	DATE	RANK
	R	L		R	L					
149 1/8	23 1/8	23 0/8	17 1/8	11	8	Clinton County	IL	Tracy Hawes	1990	1,741
149 1/8	24 2/8	25 4/8	16 3/8	7	7	Sarpy County	NE	Bernard J. Kubat, Jr.	1991	1,741
149 1/8	23 7/8	24 3/8	20 3/8	5	5	Iron County	WI	Kevin J. Genisot	1991	1,741
149 1/8	22 2/8	23 0/8	16 3/8	5	5	Neosho County	KS	Scotty Manbeck	1992	1,741
149 0/8	25 7/8	23 5/8	19 4/8	6	5	Mitchell County	IA	Elmer Krueger	1961	1,755
149 0/8	25 0/8	25 0/8	19 4/8	5	4	Black Hawk County	IA	Robert Riggle	1975	1,755
149 0/8	24 4/8	23 4/8	19 6/8	5	5	Marion County	KS	David C. Hett	1980	1,755
149 0/8	23 4/8	22 5/8	15 4/8	5	5	Pickaway County	OH	Weldon R. Snyder	1980	1,755
149 0/8	24 6/8	25 1/8	19 2/8	6	5	Warren County	IA	Grant Poindexter	1981	1,755
149 0/8	25 5/8	24 5/8	18 6/8	4	5	Kiowa County	KS	Dan Manwarren	1984	1,755
149 0/8	25 1/8	24 6/8	17 7/8	6	5	Calhoun County	MI	Larry C. Holcomb	1984	1,755
149 0/8	21 5/8	21 6/8	20 0/8	5	5	Atchison County	KS	Larry Bleier	1985	1,755
149 0/8	26 0/8	26 2/8	18 3/8	4	5	Morrison County	MN	Craig Krafthefer	1986	1,755
149 0/8	27 1/8	27 6/8	20 6/8	4	4	Dunn County	WI	Mark Sokup	1987	1,755
149 0/8	23 3/8	24 6/8	17 6/8	6	5	Marinette County	WI	Philip E. Bretl	1987	1,755
149 0/8	23 4/8	22 4/8	15 2/8	7	6	Kenosha County	WI	Alois Jeske, Sr.	1987	1,755
149 0/8	23 5/8	23 4/8	21 1/8	6	7	Washtenaw County	MI	Frank Schmidt, Jr.	1987	1,755
149 0/8	23 7/8	24 7/8	20 0/8	5	5	Clay County	IL	David Thompson	1987	1,755
149 0/8	23 0/8	22 7/8	17 4/8	5	6	Ozaukee County	WI	Jack Klotz	1988	1,755
149 0/8	24 1/8	24 4/8	19 1/8	6	7	San Augustine County	TX	Ed Gunter	1988	1,755
149 0/8	22 0/8	22 2/8	17 2/8	5	5	Kane County	IL	Bill Yoakum	1988	1,755
149 0/8	26 3/8	25 2/8	19 2/8	6	6	Dubuque County	IA	James A. Deckert	1990	1,755
149 0/8	23 3/8	22 6/8	18 6/8	5	5	Greene County	AR	Mike Croy	1990	1,755
149 0/8	23 0/8	22 4/8	17 7/8	6	6	Brown County	IN	Dale Snyder	1991	1,755
149 0/8	24 0/8	24 0/8	19 2/8	5	4	Schuyler County	IL	Bill Daugherty	1991	1,755
149 0/8	21 5/8	22 5/8	17 2/8	5	5	Du Page County	IL	Peter Schumacher	1991	1,755
149 0/8	25 3/8	25 0/8	19 0/8	5	5	Racine County	WI	Brek M. Zortman	1991	1,755
148 7/8	15 4/8	26 0/8	19 4/8	5	7	Lincoln County	WI	Ronald Pond	1961	1,778
148 7/8	24 6/8	24 0/8	18 7/8	4	5	Grant County	SD	Larry Turbak	1964	1,778
148 7/8	23 1/8	23 1/8	18 4/8	6	6	Knox County	OH	John E. Bumpus	1971	1,778
148 7/8	23 1/8	23 1/8	19 3/8	5	4	Clayton County	IA	Ralph Edward Livingston	1984	1,778
148 7/8	24 2/8	22 7/8	17 2/8	6	5	Clay County	KS	Larry Reed	1985	1,778
148 7/8	23 0/8	23 1/8	16 5/8	5	5	Erie County	NY	Martin Dollard	1986	1,778
148 7/8	24 3/8	22 7/8	20 3/8	6	6	Caledon Twp.	ONT	Jack Leggo	1988	1,778
148 7/8	24 4/8	26 2/8	18 5/8	4	4	Iroquois County	IL	Andrew C. McTaggart	1989	1,778
148 7/8	22 3/8	20 0/8	16 1/8	6	6	Lee County	IL	Marcus Nettz	1990	1,778
148 7/8	23 0/8	23 0/8	17 1/8	5	5	Fillmore County	MN	Brad Sutton	1990	1,778
148 7/8	24 6/8	25 0/8	21 1/8	5	5	Anoka County	MN	Bob Ross	1990	1,778
148 7/8	26 1/8	27 6/8	18 5/8	5	5	Heard County	GA	Jeffery T. Jackson	1990	1,778
148 7/8	22 0/8	22 7/8	18 5/8	5	5	Burleigh County	ND	Don Bieber	1991	1,778
148 7/8	24 1/8	24 6/8	19 7/8	6	6	Dane County	WI	Matthew A. Shimniok	1991	1,778
148 7/8	24 5/8	24 2/8	19 2/8	6	6	Stafford County	KS	Dan Schaad	1991	1,778
148 7/8	24 7/8	24 5/8	18 3/8	5	4	Cass County	MI	William L. Bethard, Jr.	1992	1,778
148 6/8	25 2/8	25 2/8	19 6/8	5	5	Iowa County	IA	Russ Sill	1967	1,794
148 6/8	23 0/8	23 0/8	18 4/8	5	5	Jefferson County	IN	Jim Coldiron	1969	1,794
148 6/8	21 3/8	21 1/8	19 1/8	6	6	Brown County	SD	Bill Franklin	1972	1,794
148 6/8	22 0/8	21 7/8	16 5/8	7	5	Schuylkill County	PA	Scott Bond	1979	1,794
148 6/8	24 2/8	23 4/8	22 6/8	6	7	Brookings County	SD	Larry Bohls	1982	1,794
148 6/8	24 1/8	23 6/8	17 2/8	5	5	Boone County	IA	Earl Taylor	1982	1,794
148 6/8	22 6/8	22 6/8	16 6/8	5	6	Reno County	KS	Davis J. Ediger	1982	1,794
148 6/8	22 6/8	22 3/8	15 2/8	5	4	Pierce County	ND	James Olson	1983	1,794
148 6/8	23 2/8	23 3/8	18 0/8	6	5	Kingsbury County	SD	Scott L. Laudenslager	1984	1,794
148 6/8	23 2/8	23 0/8	16 5/8	7	6	Jefferson County	WI	Steve Behm	1985	1,794
148 6/8	22 0/8	22 0/8	17 0/8	5	5	Monroe County	IN	Dene Snoddy	1986	1,794
148 6/8	23 1/8	25 3/8	18 7/8	6	5	Morgan County	IL	Steve North	1986	1,794
148 6/8	25 0/8	25 0/8	22 0/8	8	5	Jasper County	IA	William E. Webster	1987	1,794
148 6/8	25 0/8	23 4/8	17 5/8	5	6	Clermont County	OH	Timothy M. Singler	1988	1,794
148 6/8	24 0/8	23 0/8	17 0/8	5	5	Muscatine County	IA	Lyle Sindt	1988	1,794
148 6/8	25 1/8	25 0/8	18 6/8	5	5	Middlesex County	MA	Joe R. Shepard	1988	1,794
148 6/8	22 2/8	22 2/8	16 5/8	8	6	Edmonton	ALB	Dave Dickson	1990	1,794
148 6/8	23 1/8	23 3/8	16 6/8	5	5	Bon Homme County	SD	Leonard J. Magee	1990	1,794
148 6/8	24 6/8	25 2/8	24 3/8	5	5	Anne Arundel County	MD	Jim Roy	1990	1,794
148 6/8	23 4/8	23 5/8	18 2/8	5	5	Champaign County	IL	Terry Evans	1991	1,794
148 5/8	25 2/8	25 3/8	17 7/8	5	5	Newton County	IN	Larry Boezeman	1971	1,814
148 5/8	21 7/8	22 0/8	14 7/8	5	6	Pulaski County	MO	Ron Poston	1972	1,814
148 5/8	26 7/8	26 6/8	23 1/8	6	5	Coshocton County	OH	Charles H. Vlasek, Jr.	1979	1,814
148 5/8	23 0/8	22 6/8	22 1/8	5	5	Marion County	IA	Leonard Grimes	1981	1,814
148 5/8	23 1/8	24 5/8	18 6/8	5	5	Tuscola County	MI	Patrick C. Lewis	1983	1,814
148 5/8	25 6/8	25 6/8	19 6/8	6	5	Niobrara County	WY	Kenneth Fluck	1985	1,814
148 5/8	19 3/8	21 7/8	20 5/8	6	6	Dunn County	WI	Richard Urbaniak	1985	1,814

Score	Length of Main Beam R	Length of Main Beam L	Inside Spread	Number of Points R	Number of Points L	Area	State/ Province	Hunter's Name	Date	Rank
148 5/8	25 5/8	25 0/8	19 2/8	5	6	Piatt County	IL	David E. DeMoss	1985	1,814
148 5/8	22 1/8	24 1/8	20 5/8	5	5	Hancock County	WV	William Gary Rusinovich	1986	1,814
148 5/8	24 0/8	25 1/8	21 3/8	6	6	Houston County	MN	Bruce Norton	1987	1,814
148 5/8	23 3/8	23 5/8	17 7/8	5	5	Price County	WI	Dave A. Radosta	1987	1,814
148 5/8	26 4/8	25 7/8	18 5/8	4	5	Wabasha County	MN	Keith A. Ramthun	1988	1,814
148 5/8	20 3/8	21 3/8	16 7/8	5	5	Somerset County	PA	Brian Jones	1988	1,814
148 5/8	24 1/8	24 4/8	19 5/8	5	5	Sedgwick County	KS	Kent Lawson	1988	1,814
148 5/8	24 4/8	24 4/8	17 5/8	7	7	Chippewa County	MN	Gary Laughlin	1988	1,814
148 5/8	25 2/8	24 7/8	16 7/8	5	5	Crawford County	KS	Jim W. Heardt	1988	1,814
148 5/8	26 6/8	25 3/8	19 5/8	4	6	Hardin County	IL	Charles E. Spear	1989	1,814
148 5/8	23 1/8	24 2/8	19 5/8	4	5	Bureau County	IL	Gregory A. Bowers	1989	1,814
148 5/8	22 7/8	23 3/8	16 3/8	5	5	Rock County	WI	R. Wayne Douglas	1989	1,814
148 5/8	22 3/8	22 0/8	15 4/8	6	7	Licking County	OH	Randy Marcum	1990	1,814
148 5/8	23 2/8	23 1/8	18 5/8	5	5	Oneida County	WI	John L. Mueller	1990	1,814
148 5/8	23 4/8	22 6/8	18 5/8	5	7	Jackson County	MO	Donald Dutton	1991	1,814
148 5/8	20 7/8	21 3/8	19 1/8	6	8	Clinton County	OH	Vaughn Wright	1991	1,814
148 5/8	23 3/8	23 7/8	19 0/8	5	6	Warren County	IA	Mark Motsinger	1991	1,814
148 5/8	24 3/8	23 2/8	19 1/8	5	5	Hamilton County	IA	Steve Doering	1992	1,814
148 4/8	23 0/8	22 4/8	20 1/8	4	5	Murray County	MN	Mike Molitor	1968	1,839
148 4/8	20 7/8	21 4/8	16 6/8	5	5	Rock County	WI	Bruce Douglas	1978	1,839
148 4/8	26 0/8	22 0/8	18 0/8	5	5	Woodford County	IL	James M. Bill, Jr.	1982	1,839
148 4/8	24 2/8	24 5/8	21 5/8	5	5	Martin County	MN	Dean Roben	1982	1,839
148 4/8	25 1/8	24 4/8	16 6/8	5	5	Grant County	WI	William P Rodenkirch	1983	1,839
148 4/8	23 0/8	23 6/8	17 7/8	5	6	Pepin County	WI	Roger Anderson	1984	1,839
148 4/8	23 7/8	25 2/8	19 4/8	5	4	Jefferson County	OH	Larry C. Riggle	1984	1,839
148 4/8	25 5/8	24 2/8	18 4/8	5	5	Randolph County	IL	Conel H. Rogers, Jr.	1985	1,839
148 4/8	24 3/8	24 5/8	20 6/8	7	6	Meade County	KS	Randall J. VanDegrift	1985	1,839
148 4/8	22 2/8	22 2/8	19 6/8	5	5	Seward County	KS	Stuart G. Hazard III	1985	1,839
148 4/8	25 6/8	22 0/8	19 1/8	8	7	Kings County	NBW	Ken Kirkpatrick	1986	1,839
148 4/8	23 6/8	25 0/8	19 0/8	5	5	Edmonson County	KY	Marvin T. Pate	1987	1,839
148 4/8	26 2/8	26 1/8	18 6/8	6	6	Waukesha County	WI	Ron V. Schneider	1987	1,839
148 4/8	26 0/8	27 5/8	19 0/8	4	4	Orange County	NC	Todd McDonald	1988	1,839
148 4/8	21 6/8	21 4/8	17 6/8	5	5	Scott County	MN	Donald T. Turner	1989	1,839
148 4/8	22 1/8	23 1/8	15 2/8	5	6	Burleigh County	ND	Robert Matzke	1989	1,839
148 4/8	23 1/8	23 4/8	18 4/8	5	5	Woodford County	IL	Larry Messer	1989	1,839
148 4/8	24 3/8	24 2/8	16 4/8	6	5	Polk County	WI	Daniel Carlson	1989	1,839
148 4/8	22 5/8	22 7/8	17 2/8	5	5	Caldwell County	KY	Boyd Smith	1990	1,839
148 4/8	26 0/8	25 5/8	21 4/8	7	6	Cedar County	IA	Brian Barclay	1990	1,839
148 4/8	22 6/8	22 3/8	18 6/8	5	5	Oneida County	WI	Jeff Aulik	1990	1,839
148 4/8	25 2/8	26 0/8	16 7/8	5	5	Cumberland County	ME	Chester L. Brooks	1991	1,839
148 4/8	21 5/8	23 5/8	17 4/8	5	5	Warren County	IA	Dan Mork	1991	1,839
148 3/8	25 6/8	26 7/8	22 2/8	9	5	Scott County	MN	Bob Gregory	1967	1,862
148 3/8	23 5/8	23 7/8	17 5/8	5	5	Monroe County	NY	Robert J. Ranalletta	1976	1,862
148 3/8	23 0/8	23 4/8	18 0/8	6	7	Ballard County	KY	Gregory Joles	1978	1,862
148 3/8	22 5/8	22 1/8	17 5/8	6	6	Watonwan County	MN	Joe Graif	1981	1,862
148 3/8	23 5/8	23 7/8	24 1/8	6	5	Fairfield County	OH	Jim Jordan	1982	1,862
148 3/8	22 1/8	22 6/8	18 1/8	5	5	Morrison County	MN	Robert Redmann	1984	1,862
148 3/8	24 6/8	25 5/8	19 1/8	5	5	Baltimore County	MD	Donald Layne	1985	1,862
148 3/8	24 3/8	24 2/8	18 1/8	6	6	Phillips County	KS	Julius E. Schoenberger	1985	1,862
148 3/8	22 2/8	23 6/8	16 7/8	5	5	Ottawa County	KS	Wayne E. Smith	1985	1,862
148 3/8	22 0/8	21 7/8	17 5/8	7	7	Carter County	OK	Charles W. Chatham	1986	1,862
148 3/8	23 0/8	22 4/8	19 3/8	5	5	Macoupin County	IL	Don Snyder	1986	1,862
148 3/8	25 3/8	25 0/8	16 7/8	6	5	Noble County	IN	Daniel J. Bidwell	1987	1,862
148 3/8	24 5/8	24 2/8	22 0/8	5	4	Wright County	IA	Mark D. Slining	1987	1,862
148 3/8	23 2/8	23 0/8	20 1/8	5	6	Grant County	KY	Richard L. Koors	1988	1,862
148 3/8	23 4/8	23 4/8	19 3/8	5	6	Ionia County	MI	James E. Allen	1988	1,862
148 3/8	22 5/8	22 5/8	17 3/8	4	5	Morgan County	OH	Stacey Triplet	1989	1,862
148 3/8	22 5/8	24 4/8	18 3/8	5	5	Lewis & Clark County	MT	Sonny Templeton	1989	1,862
148 3/8	25 5/8	24 5/8	18 7/8	4	5	Stoddard County	MO	Clint Barnfield	1990	1,862
148 3/8	24 4/8	24 2/8	20 5/8	5	5	Boone County	IL	Wilmer V. Garlick	1990	1,862
148 3/8	27 0/8	23 6/8	18 3/8	4	4	Middlesex County	CT	Fredrick J. Massini	1990	1,862
148 3/8	26 1/8	25 6/8	19 1/8	4	6	Tama County	IA	Harold Cox	1990	1,862
148 3/8	27 3/8	27 5/8	18 5/8	5	4	Barton County	MO	Gregory W. Benander	1990	1,862
148 3/8	22 6/8	22 1/8	20 1/8	5	5	Kandiyohi County	MN	Bob Sampson	1991	1,862
148 2/8	22 3/8	21 6/8	16 2/8	5	5	Walworth County	SD	Irvin Guthmiller	1956	1,885
148 2/8	22 7/8	21 5/8	18 2/8	5	5	Harrison County	IA	James W. Glasscock	1968	1,885
148 2/8	25 1/8	24 1/8	15 4/8	5	5	Woodbury County	IA	Guy Hempey	1969	1,885
148 2/8	24 5/8	24 7/8	24 0/8	5	5	Jackson County	IL	Darrell Fritsche	1973	1,885
148 2/8	20 7/8	22 2/8	16 4/8	5	5	Pittsburg County	OK	Bill Hisle	1975	1,885
148 2/8	24 2/8	23 4/8	18 0/8	5	7	Latah County	ID	Don A. West	1976	1,885

WHITETAIL DEER (*Typical Antlers*)

MINIMUM SCORE 125

(Continued)

SCORE	LENGTH OF R MAIN BEAM L		INSIDE SPREAD	NUMBER OF R POINTS L		AREA	STATE/ PROVINCE	HUNTER'S NAME	DATE	RANK
148 2/8	26 5/8	24 3/8	19 7/8	6	8	Coshocton County	OH	Charles N. McDonald	1977	1,885
148 2/8	23 0/8	22 2/8	20 7/8	4	5	Sanford	MAN	Wayne Rodgers	1979	1,885
148 2/8	24 7/8	25 1/8	18 0/8	5	5	Winnebago County	IL	Fred Kelley	1981	1,885
148 2/8	24 6/8	23 3/8	16 5/8	4	6	Clark County	KS	Casey V. Rudd	1981	1,885
148 2/8	23 4/8	23 1/8	22 6/8	6	10	Marion County	IL	Paul Duncan	1982	1,885
148 2/8	27 3/8	27 0/8	20 7/8	5	6	Washington County	WI	Steve Karoses	1983	1,885
148 2/8	26 0/8	26 2/8	17 5/8	8	6	Adair County	MO	Tim Richardson	1983	1,885
148 2/8	23 0/8	23 6/8	17 0/8	5	5	Pierce County	WI	Mitchell C. Nelson	1984	1,885
148 2/8	21 2/8	21 6/8	18 4/8	5	5	Kenosha County	WI	Marty Daniels	1985	1,885
148 2/8	24 2/8	23 6/8	16 3/8	6	5	Polk County	IA	Robert E. Morterud	1987	1,885
148 2/8	23 0/8	24 1/8	21 4/8	6	5	Clay County	MN	James F. Thompson	1987	1,885
148 2/8	25 7/8	26 4/8	18 2/8	5	5	Cross County	AR	Rickey W. Proctor	1987	1,885
148 2/8	22 7/8	24 1/8	19 5/8	6	6	Allen County	KS	Curt Stahl	1988	1,885
148 2/8	24 7/8	25 7/8	19 6/8	4	4	Belmont County	OH	Chad Krahel	1989	1,885
148 2/8	26 0/8	26 4/8	19 4/8	6	6	Will County	IL	Dennis J. Lake	1990	1,885
148 2/8	23 5/8	23 0/8	20 4/8	5	7	Jersey County	IL	Judy Kovar	1990	1,885
148 2/8	23 2/8	23 3/8	17 0/8	7	5	Marshall County	OK	James B. Evans, Jr.	1990	1,885
148 2/8	26 0/8	26 3/8	18 3/8	4	5	Lake County	IL	Donald R. Powers	1990	1,885
148 2/8	25 3/8	23 3/8	19 6/8	6	8	Phillips County	KS	Charles Bockhorn	1991	1,885
148 2/8	23 4/8	23 7/8	19 0/8	5	5	Steuben County	NY	Mark S. O'Donal	1991	1,885
148 2/8	27 6/8	27 2/8	17 6/8	5	6	Howard County	MO	Bodie Beach	1991	1,885
148 2/8	22 5/8	22 0/8	17 4/8	5	5	Vermilion County	IL	Jeffery Parkerson	1991	1,885
148 2/8	25 0/8	24 4/8	18 0/8	5	5	Pike County	IL	Jerry Pennock	1991	1,885
148 2/8	24 3/8	25 0/8	16 7/8	9	8	Hennepin County	MN	Todd J. Zwak	1991	1,885
148 2/8	24 5/8	24 5/8	18 0/8	6	7	Dane County	WI	Alan Corlett	1991	1,885
148 1/8	24 2/8	24 2/8	20 5/8	4	4	Erie County	NY	William R. Helmich	1975	1,916
148 1/8	23 0/8	22 5/8	17 2/8	5	6	Wellington County	ONT	Barry Marshall	1975	1,916
148 1/8	27 3/8	27 5/8	21 6/8	6	6	Tazewell County	IL	David Huser	1980	1,916
148 1/8	24 2/8	22 5/8	19 3/8	5	5	Uvalde County	TX	Jim Jordan	1986	1,916
148 1/8	23 3/8	22 7/8	18 5/8	5	5	Calumet County	WI	Joseph R. Mader	1986	1,916
148 1/8	23 6/8	24 5/8	17 6/8	5	8	Cass County	ND	Rodney P. Mathison	1986	1,916
148 1/8	23 2/8	24 0/8	19 5/8	6	5	Brown County	WI	Andy Dobesh	1987	1,916
148 1/8	22 6/8	22 3/8	18 2/8	6	5	Hickory County	MO	David Langton	1987	1,916
148 1/8	23 7/8	23 6/8	20 3/8	5	5	Crow Wing County	MN	Bob Brown	1988	1,916
148 1/8	24 4/8	25 0/8	19 5/8	5	6	Pike County	IL	Ray Hatfield	1988	1,916
148 1/8	22 4/8	22 7/8	20 1/8	5	6	Sawyer County	WI	Brad B. Christensen	1989	1,916
148 1/8	25 2/8	25 5/8	18 2/8	5	6	Iron County	WI	D. J. Sullivan	1990	1,916
148 1/8	23 0/8	22 4/8	21 1/8	5	6	Burnett County	WI	Sheldon Wendorf	1990	1,916
148 1/8	25 0/8	24 5/8	20 5/8	4	5	McHenry County	IL	Dennis E. Straumann	1990	1,916
148 1/8	24 2/8	23 5/8	14 1/8	6	6	Whiteside County	IL	Abraham Wuebben	1991	1,916
148 1/8	25 3/8	25 0/8	17 7/8	8	6	Stoddard County	MO	Ken Heuer	1991	1,916
148 0/8	22 1/8	22 2/8	14 6/8	5	5	Stanley County	SD	Brad Taylor	1979	1,932
148 0/8	23 5/8	23 1/8	18 6/8	5	6	Uvalde County	TX	M.H. 'Bill' Wilkinson, J	1980	1,932
148 0/8	22 6/8	23 1/8	17 6/8	5	5	Green County	WI	E. Dussault	1983	1,932
148 0/8	25 2/8	25 2/8	18 3/8	5	5	Buffalo County	WI	Daniel Folkedahl	1984	1,932
148 0/8	24 6/8	25 5/8	23 6/8	4	5	Clay County	MN	Keith J Fischer	1984	1,932
148 0/8	24 3/8	25 0/8	18 3/8	6	8	McIntosh County	ND	Garnes Ruff	1985	1,932
148 0/8	22 4/8	22 0/8	15 3/8	5	6	Norman County	MN	Les Krogstad	1985	1,932
148 0/8	25 7/8	27 7/8	16 7/8	7	6	Madison County	NY	Lloyd Weigel	1985	1,932
148 0/8	20 0/8	23 1/8	22 4/8	6	5	Dorchester County	MD	Bob Reinert	1985	1,932
148 0/8	24 2/8	24 3/8	19 5/8	6	5	Kittson County	MN	Steve Lindberg	1986	1,932
148 0/8	24 1/8	24 4/8	15 6/8	5	6	Vernon County	WI	Harry J. Curtis	1986	1,932
148 0/8	27 3/8	28 1/8	19 0/8	5	5	Putnam County	IN	Kevin W. Jones	1986	1,932
148 0/8	22 1/8	22 6/8	21 0/8	5	5	Suffolk County	NY	Steven Schoen	1987	1,932
148 0/8	23 6/8	23 6/8	18 4/8	6	6	Bremer County	IA	LeRoy Matthias	1988	1,932
148 0/8	26 2/8	28 3/8	21 2/8	5	6	Jersey County	IL	Judy Kovar	1988	1,932
148 0/8	23 6/8	25 4/8	21 0/8	4	4	Marathon County	WI	Steven Marvin	1989	1,932
148 0/8	25 3/8	24 2/8	20 2/8	5	5	Shelby County	IL	David E. Varvil	1989	1,932
148 0/8	26 2/8	26 1/8	23 1/8	6	6	De Witt County	IL	Chris Dilks	1989	1,932
148 0/8	24 2/8	23 0/8	19 2/8	7	6	Allamakee County	IA	Tim Waid	1990	1,932
148 0/8	23 1/8	22 7/8	17 4/8	4	4	Boundary County	ID	Mike Hittle	1991	1,932
148 0/8	22 0/8	22 4/8	16 4/8	6	5	Deuel County	NE	Dirk Gosnell	1991	1,932
148 0/8	25 4/8	26 5/8	18 6/8	4	4	Vermilion County	IL	Darin Duitsman	1991	1,932
148 0/8	22 7/8	23 1/8	15 2/8	5	5	Chisago County	MN	Bill Barzydlo	1991	1,932
148 0/8	24 5/8	24 5/8	15 3/8	6	5	Clayton County	IA	Thomas Schremser	1991	1,932
148 0/8	24 1/8	23 5/8	16 6/8	7	6	Gallia County	OH	Gary Griffith	1991	1,932
148 0/8	25 1/8	23 2/8	16 4/8	5	5	Van Buren County	IA	Dan Brockman	1991	1,932
147 7/8	21 7/8	22 2/8	18 5/8	5	5	Green Lake County	WI	Al Hubbell	1974	1,958
147 7/8	25 6/8	24 7/8	21 7/8	4	4	Anne Arundel County	MD	James E. Roy	1977	1,958
147 7/8	22 2/8	22 3/8	18 5/8	5	5	Iron County	MI	David C. Tarsi	1978	1,958

SCORE	LENGTH OF MAIN BEAM R L		INSIDE SPREAD	NUMBER OF POINTS R L		AREA	STATE/ PROVINCE	HUNTER'S NAME	DATE	RANK
147 7/8	26 3/8	25 6/8	17 5/8	4	4	Lafayette County	WI	Kim D. Gruenberg	1979	1,958
147 7/8	20 6/8	21 6/8	18 4/8	6	6	Cass County	NE	David R. Kempnich	1981	1,958
147 7/8	27 0/8	26 0/8	23 2/8	4	6	Cowley County	KS	Virgil Dwayne Graham	1982	1,958
147 7/8	24 5/8	24 0/8	19 5/8	5	5	Guthrie County	IA	Vernie W. Grasty	1983	1,958
147 7/8	23 4/8	24 2/8	15 2/8	5	6	Harris County	TX	John Hall	1985	1,958
147 7/8	21 7/8	22 2/8	17 7/8	5	5	Butler County	OH	James Lynch	1985	1,958
147 7/8	21 2/8	21 1/8	19 6/8	6	5	Rice County	KS	David L. Boedeker	1986	1,958
147 7/8	23 6/8	23 3/8	18 2/8	6	6	Wabaunsee County	KS	Jim Hagan	1986	1,958
147 7/8	23 4/8	23 0/8	14 5/8	5	5	Langlade County	WI	Mark Helgeson	1986	1,958
147 7/8	23 4/8	23 4/8	20 3/8	5	5	Lake County	IL	David Mitten	1987	1,958
147 7/8	22 1/8	22 3/8	15 5/8	6	6	Scott County	IA	Gary W. Gilkison	1988	1,958
147 7/8	25 0/8	24 3/8	15 7/8	6	6	Chippewa County	WI	Joseph L. Couey	1989	1,958
147 7/8	22 1/8	22 6/8	17 1/8	5	5	Macon County	IL	Earl Nelson	1989	1,958
147 7/8	24 5/8	25 1/8	19 5/8	4	4	Eau Claire County	WI	Robert W. Hall	1990	1,958
147 7/8	26 0/8	25 5/8	23 3/8	4	4	Allamakee County	IA	Kevin Sweeney	1990	1,958
147 7/8	25 7/8	26 3/8	19 5/8	4	4	Lake County	IL	Allen G. Comstock	1990	1,958
147 7/8	23 3/8	23 1/8	16 7/8	5	6	Waukesha County	WI	Andrae D'Acquisto	1991	1,958
147 6/8	23 4/8	23 2/8	16 0/8	5	5	Morrison County	MN	John Zwickey	1955	1,978
147 6/8	23 5/8	24 3/8	16 6/8	6	7	Morrison County	MN	Allen E. Farmes	1957	1,978
147 6/8	25 3/8	24 5/8	19 7/8	6	5	Jo Daviess County	IL	Jerry Fritz	1971	1,978
147 6/8	24 1/8	25 6/8	19 0/8	5	5	Dickinson County	MI	Myles Keller	1976	1,978
147 6/8	24 6/8	23 0/8	17 6/8	6	6	Butler County	KY	O. D. Phelps	1977	1,978
147 6/8	24 0/8	24 2/8	17 2/8	6	5	Harlan County	NE	Ron Breitsprecher	1978	1,978
147 6/8	22 1/8	22 2/8	19 6/8	5	5	Union County	IL	Karen Mason	1980	1,978
147 6/8	22 3/8	22 1/8	17 4/8	4	4	Mercer County	ND	Steven J. Prock	1980	1,978
147 6/8	25 6/8	24 6/8	18 0/8	5	5	Jackson County	IA	Carl Severson	1982	1,978
147 6/8	23 2/8	23 1/8	18 0/8	5	5	Sumner County	KS	Danny S. Holden	1982	1,978
147 6/8	22 3/8	22 4/8	21 2/8	4	4	Kingsbury County	SD	Mack Butler	1984	1,978
147 6/8	22 5/8	23 2/8	19 2/8	5	6	Stafford County	KS	Larry E Bowser	1985	1,978
147 6/8	21 2/8	21 7/8	16 0/8	8	8	Macoupin County	IL	Leonard Koniak	1987	1,978
147 6/8	23 7/8	23 6/8	17 2/8	6	6	Crawford County	IL	Gary Bickers	1987	1,978
147 6/8	24 0/8	24 0/8	20 0/8	5	5	Iroquois County	IL	Gregory A. Hiser	1989	1,978
147 6/8	23 7/8	24 2/8	18 3/8	6	7	Monroe County	NY	Tim Bumbarger	1990	1,978
147 6/8	25 2/8	25 6/8	22 2/8	4	4	Delaware County	OH	Doug Fuller	1991	1,978
147 6/8	26 4/8	26 2/8	19 5/8	6	7	Clinton County	OH	Kevin L. Wilson	1991	1,978
147 6/8	22 1/8	21 6/8	18 4/8	8	7	Cedar County	IA	Paul Dykstra	1991	1,978
147 5/8	23 7/8	23 5/8	19 1/8	5	5	Fillmore County	MN	Dale Honsey	1951	1,997
147 5/8	24 2/8	26 0/8	20 2/8	6	6	Nicollet County	MN	Thomas J. Merkley	1970	1,997
147 5/8	22 7/8	23 2/8	18 1/8	4	4	Wilkin County	MN	Darrel G. Montieth	1978	1,997
147 5/8	23 5/8	23 4/8	18 3/8	4	5	Morrison County	MN	Leon Fuchs	1981	1,997
147 5/8	22 2/8	22 7/8	16 6/8	6	5	Merrimack County	NH	Jerry Smith	1982	1,997
147 5/8	24 7/8	25 3/8	19 5/8	5	6	Peoria County	IL	Joe Shryock, Jr.	1983	1,997
147 5/8	24 6/8	25 2/8	17 2/8	5	6	Koochiching County	MN	Terrance L. Jaeger	1983	1,997
147 5/8	23 5/8	22 7/8	18 3/8	5	5	De Witt County	IL	John H. Piatt	1983	1,997
147 5/8	25 3/8	24 7/8	17 7/8	5	5	Butler County	PA	David L. Travaglio	1986	1,997
147 5/8	26 0/8	25 3/8	18 3/8	5	6	Morgan County	OH	Ron Newsom	1986	1,997
147 5/8	25 0/8	24 3/8	21 4/8	5	5	Winona County	MN	Rodney Blake	1986	1,997
147 5/8	23 1/8	25 6/8	18 7/8	5	5	Rock County	WI	John G. Donstad	1986	1,997
147 5/8	24 3/8	24 3/8	18 3/8	6	5	Washington County	MN	Scott Moncur	1987	1,997
147 5/8	24 7/8	24 5/8	17 5/8	5	5	Shelby County	IL	Dennis J. Lynch	1987	1,997
147 5/8	23 2/8	25 2/8	16 1/8	5	6	Perry County	IL	Scott Rice	1987	1,997
147 5/8	27 0/8	26 6/8	21 3/8	4	5	Baltimore County	MD	Kevin Vogt	1990	1,997
147 5/8	24 2/8	24 5/8	15 3/8	5	5	Walton County	GA	Kenny Starnes	1991	1,997
147 5/8	23 2/8	23 5/8	20 6/8	4	5	Marion County	KS	Dennis N. Ballweg	1991	1,997
147 4/8	22 2/8	22 6/8	18 4/8	4	4	Shawano County	WI	John Schoenike	1960	2,015
147 4/8	23 7/8	23 2/8	16 4/8	7	5	Darke County	OH	Jim Duvall	1977	2,015
147 4/8	24 0/8	23 3/8	20 6/8	6	6	Fulton County	OH	Gary R. Bailey	1980	2,015
147 4/8	22 6/8	22 2/8	16 6/8	5	5	Burleigh County	ND	James A. Sauvageau	1980	2,015
147 4/8	25 3/8	25 6/8	19 0/8	4	5	Blue Earth County	MN	Aaron L. Urke	1981	2,015
147 4/8	23 7/8	23 7/8	16 5/8	7	5	Trempealeau County	WI	Donald Skaar	1982	2,015
147 4/8	21 0/8	20 5/8	17 6/8	5	5	Cloud County	KS	Jeff Gerard	1982	2,015
147 4/8	23 0/8	23 1/8	18 4/8	5	5	St. Charles County	MO	Harry L. Smith	1983	2,015
147 4/8	24 1/8	26 0/8	18 6/8	4	4	Prairie County	AR	Joe Moody	1984	2,015
147 4/8	25 0/8	25 1/8	19 4/8	5	5	Dane County	WI	John M. Welke, Jr.	1985	2,015
147 4/8	23 6/8	23 0/8	14 6/8	5	5	Leader	SAS	Clifton Schneider	1986	2,015
147 4/8	26 1/8	26 2/8	19 6/8	6	4	Lincoln County	MO	Terry F. Fry	1986	2,015
147 4/8	22 5/8	22 3/8	16 2/8	5	5	Henry County	MO	Cary Dennis	1987	2,015
147 4/8	25 6/8	25 0/8	20 7/8	5	7	Jackson County	MI	Scot E. Gazlay	1987	2,015
147 4/8	23 1/8	23 3/8	20 4/8	5	5	Pepin County	WI	Duane Peterson	1988	2,015
147 4/8	23 4/8	23 7/8	17 4/8	5	5	Sawyer County	WI	Mike Haegele	1988	2,015

SCORE	LENGTH OF MAIN BEAM R L		INSIDE SPREAD	NUMBER OF POINTS R L		AREA	STATE/ PROVINCE	HUNTER'S NAME	DATE	RANK
147 4/8	26 5/8	22 6/8	19 2/8	5	5	Jersey County	IL	Judy Kovar	1989	2,015
147 4/8	23 2/8	23 2/8	20 0/8	5	5	Dickens County	TX	Jim Eppler	1990	2,015
147 4/8	25 4/8	25 1/8	18 0/8	5	5	Pulaski County	GA	Chris Cornelius	1990	2,015
147 4/8	25 4/8	25 4/8	23 6/8	4	4	Wayne County	IA	Connie Pherigo	1990	2,015
147 4/8	24 0/8	22 7/8	18 3/8	4	6	Clinton County	OH	Robert L. Sargent	1990	2,015
147 4/8	25 2/8	24 7/8	17 2/8	5	5	Lawrence County	IN	Gary L. Brown	1991	2,015
147 4/8	25 3/8	25 5/8	17 2/8	5	5	Eau Claire County	WI	Wayne R. Brixen	1991	2,015
147 4/8	22 7/8	23 1/8	14 6/8	5	6	Dubuque County	IA	Curtis G. Steffen	1991	2,015
147 4/8	23 5/8	23 0/8	19 5/8	4	5	Henry County	IA	Troy Ailey	1991	2,015
147 3/8	22 4/8	22 4/8	17 7/8	5	6	Waushara County	WI	Mike Barth	1977	2,040
147 3/8	21 5/8	21 5/8	16 3/8	6	5	Lee County	IA	Mark Clemens	1978	2,040
147 3/8	28 1/8	28 1/8	19 7/8	5	4	Huntingdon County	PA	John A. Williams	1979	2,040
147 3/8	22 5/8	23 7/8	18 3/8	5	5	Guthrie County	IA	Steve Hunerdosse	1982	2,040
147 3/8	22 0/8	22 3/8	12 7/8	7	5	Jackson County	MO	Marvin Thomey	1984	2,040
147 3/8	21 1/8	20 2/8	15 7/8	6	6	Troup County	GA	Eddie D. Martin	1984	2,040
147 3/8	22 4/8	24 2/8	16 5/8	6	5	Union County	IL	Ronald L. Kosydor	1985	2,040
147 3/8	22 6/8	23 0/8	18 3/8	5	5	Lee County	IA	Glenn E. Wagner	1985	2,040
147 3/8	23 1/8	23 2/8	15 7/8	6	5	Buffalo County	WI	Bill R. Berg	1986	2,040
147 3/8	25 6/8	25 1/8	19 5/8	5	4	McHenry County	IL	William R. Bishop, Jr.	1988	2,040
147 3/8	23 1/8	22 3/8	19 5/8	5	5	Vermilion County	IL	Dr H. Neil Becker	1988	2,040
147 3/8	23 5/8	25 3/8	19 1/8	4	4	Ellsworth County	KS	Rick Kirkpatrick	1989	2,040
147 3/8	27 0/8	25 7/8	19 1/8	4	4	Shelby County	IL	Terry Jo Anderson	1989	2,040
147 3/8	23 3/8	24 0/8	17 7/8	6	5	Warren County	IL	Bryan E. DeJaynes	1989	2,040
147 3/8	23 7/8	22 6/8	18 0/8	5	6	Sussex County	VA	Frank Patterson	1989	2,040
147 3/8	22 7/8	21 4/8	16 3/8	5	5	Marathon County	WI	Mark J. Duerr	1989	2,040
147 3/8	23 0/8	22 4/8	18 2/8	7	5	Davis County	IA	Robert L. McDowell	1990	2,040
147 3/8	22 4/8	22 3/8	19 1/8	4	4	Webb County	TX	Alvin Levy	1991	2,040
147 2/8	23 2/8	25 1/8	20 4/8	9	8	Clay County	IA	Uriah M. Hostetler	1964	2,058
147 2/8	23 2/8	22 4/8	19 2/8	5	5	Madison County	IN	Pat Moreland	1969	2,058
147 2/8	23 1/8	23 1/8	15 6/8	5	5	Green Lake County	WI	Don Chier	1973	2,058
147 2/8	25 2/8	25 2/8	20 6/8	5	5	Fayette County	IA	Terry Cannady	1976	2,058
147 2/8	21 3/8	20 6/8	17 4/8	5	5	Iroquois County	IL	Scott L. Mohler	1979	2,058
147 2/8	25 7/8	24 3/8	25 4/8	4	4	Parke County	IN	Alan W. Brannan	1980	2,058
147 2/8	24 6/8	22 7/8	18 4/8	5	6	Waushara County	WI	Tim J. Terrell	1980	2,058
147 2/8	23 2/8	22 6/8	19 2/8	5	7	Pembina County	ND	Roger Furstenau	1983	2,058
147 2/8	24 7/8	25 0/8	18 7/8	7	8	Clay County	MN	John Randash	1984	2,058
147 2/8	21 5/8	21 6/8	18 2/8	6	5	Grant County	MN	Harold Forcier	1984	2,058
147 2/8	24 5/8	24 3/8	18 2/8	6	5	Jackson County	OH	Keith Kuhn	1984	2,058
147 2/8	25 1/8	25 6/8	23 2/8	4	4	Gage County	NE	Jerry Miller	1987	2,058
147 2/8	25 0/8	23 0/8	14 4/8	7	6	Blue Earth County	MN	Bruce Kramer	1987	2,058
147 2/8	20 2/8	21 5/8	20 6/8	5	5	Somerset County	NJ	Harold J. Tallett	1987	2,058
147 2/8	24 0/8	22 6/8	20 6/8	5	5	Monroe County	GA	Patrick Carter	1988	2,058
147 2/8	23 1/8	24 6/8	19 7/8	7	7	Vermilion County	IL	Robert G. Downing	1988	2,058
147 2/8	24 4/8	22 1/8	21 2/8	6	7	Meigs County	OH	Patrick D. Kearns	1988	2,058
147 2/8	25 0/8	25 5/8	23 6/8	4	5	Cook County	IL	Charles Gaidamavice	1989	2,058
147 2/8	23 0/8	22 6/8	16 0/8	6	5	Morgan County	CO	Dean Procunier	1990	2,058
147 2/8	22 5/8	23 4/8	17 7/8	5	6	Allamakee County	IA	Mark D. Christopherson	1991	2,058
147 2/8	29 1/8	28 5/8	22 0/8	4	4	Lawrence County	OH	Randy Boggs	1991	2,058
147 2/8	25 1/8	24 1/8	18 6/8	4	4	Flathead County	MT	John C. Bartlett	1992	2,058
147 2/8	23 3/8	21 1/8	21 0/8	5	5	Rock County	WI	Monica A. Freeman	1992	2,058
147 1/8	25 1/8	25 3/8	16 7/8	5	5	Delaware County	IA	Blair Berens	1963	2,081
147 1/8	24 7/8	24 4/8	18 4/8	7	7	Red Willow County	NE	Gary Ginther	1967	2,081
147 1/8	22 6/8	23 1/8	17 5/8	5	6	Iron County	WI	Dr. C. J. Rainaldo	1967	2,081
147 1/8	21 0/8	21 5/8	16 3/8	6	6	Vilas County	WI	Anthony J. Sahulcik, Jr.	1969	2,081
147 1/8	25 0/8	24 0/8	18 3/8	4	4	Dodge County	MN	Clark Gallup	1974	2,081
147 1/8	24 3/8	25 7/8	18 5/8	4	4	Coffey County	KS	Joyce Wilhite	1974	2,081
147 1/8	20 5/8	20 0/8	19 5/8	5	5	Redwood County	MN	Dennis Groebner	1975	2,081
147 1/8	22 1/8	22 1/8	19 3/8	5	5	Kiowa County	KS	Ralph A. Brown	1981	2,081
147 1/8	25 2/8	24 3/8	18 1/8	5	5	Hancock County	OH	Robert E. Ebert	1981	2,081
147 1/8	23 2/8	23 6/8	18 1/8	5	5	Teton County	MT	James R. Toms	1984	2,081
147 1/8	27 5/8	27 5/8	21 1/8	4	5	Highland County	OH	Larry K. Snoddy	1984	2,081
147 1/8	24 2/8	25 4/8	15 7/8	4	5	Wallace County	KS	Gerry Nix	1985	2,081
147 1/8	24 5/8	24 5/8	18 2/8	7	5	Burleigh County	ND	Chuck Welch	1986	2,081
147 1/8	24 1/8	24 5/8	15 3/8	6	5	Highland County	OH	Roger Dale Burton	1987	2,081
147 1/8	22 4/8	22 7/8	17 3/8	5	5	Vigo County	IN	Bob Miller	1987	2,081
147 1/8	23 6/8	23 5/8	19 6/8	6	8	Carroll County	IL	Edward Pannell	1987	2,081
147 1/8	24 2/8	23 1/8	17 0/8	5	4	Butler County	KS	Mike Schwelgert	1987	2,081
147 1/8	23 1/8	22 4/8	18 6/8	5	6	Phillips County	KS	Phillip Cromwell	1987	2,081
147 1/8	22 6/8	23 1/8	19 1/8	4	4	Hardin County	KY	Steve Crabtree	1987	2,081
147 1/8	23 3/8	24 0/8	19 5/8	5	4	Lake County	IL	Robert A. Turner	1989	2,081

SCORE	LENGTH OF MAIN BEAM R	L	INSIDE SPREAD	NUMBER OF POINTS R	L	AREA	STATE/ PROVINCE	HUNTER'S NAME	DATE	RANK
147 1/8	21 1/8	22 0/8	17 5/8	5	5	Codington County	SD	Bryan Monteith	1989	2,081
147 1/8	25 4/8	23 6/8	17 4/8	6	5	Worcester County	MA	Terry D. Atwater	1990	2,081
147 1/8	25 1/8	23 3/8	18 4/8	7	5	Goodhue County	MN	Scott Johnson	1990	2,081
147 1/8	24 4/8	24 0/8	18 1/8	5	5	Marinette County	WI	Robert J. Randerson	1990	2,081
147 1/8	22 2/8	22 0/8	17 1/8	5	5	Union County	PA	Matthew McGinnis	1991	2,081
147 1/8	24 1/8	25 3/8	23 3/8	5	5	Missoula County	MT	Matthew J. Stout	1992	2,081
147 0/8	23 6/8	24 0/8	20 3/8	6	5	Hancock County	IL	Ron Paul	1974	2,107
147 0/8	24 3/8	24 7/8	19 2/8	7	7	Dodge County	NE	Donald W. Robinson	1974	2,107
147 0/8	28 5/8	26 2/8	19 0/8	5	4	Fulton County	IL	Bernard Smith	1974	2,107
147 0/8	19 1/8	20 1/8	19 2/8	5	5	Platte County	WY	Robert V. Kiser	1978	2,107
147 0/8	25 4/8	24 1/8	21 2/8	6	7	Morrison County	MN	Gordon Bayerkohler	1979	2,107
147 0/8	23 5/8	23 5/8	20 0/8	5	5	Allamakee County	IA	Don Kieler	1979	2,107
147 0/8	26 4/8	26 2/8	16 0/8	5	7	Gage County	NE	Eldon C. Wellman	1981	2,107
147 0/8	24 4/8	23 7/8	18 6/8	4	5	Osborne County	KS	Mike Kidwell	1981	2,107
147 0/8	25 1/8	25 2/8	19 6/8	7	6	Charles County	MD	David G. Wilson	1981	2,107
147 0/8	22 3/8	22 2/8	18 4/8	5	5	Outagamie County	WI	Jim Vorland	1983	2,107
147 0/8	26 1/8	24 2/8	22 0/8	4	5	Dorchester County	MD	Michael F. Blair	1983	2,107
147 0/8	23 6/8	24 4/8	17 2/8	5	6	Lee County	IL	Donald E. Moore	1983	2,107
147 0/8	26 2/8	25 4/8	17 6/8	5	5	Vernon County	MO	Roger L. Hensley	1985	2,107
147 0/8	22 5/8	24 0/8	19 2/8	6	8	Cedar County	MO	David Barnard	1986	2,107
147 0/8	23 3/8	22 7/8	15 2/8	6	6	Bradley County	AR	Granville Pankey	1987	2,107
147 0/8	24 6/8	24 0/8	18 6/8	4	4	Wright County	MN	Dale Florek	1987	2,107
147 0/8	23 2/8	24 4/8	15 2/8	5	5	Washington County	MN	Richard Eisinger	1988	2,107
147 0/8	23 6/8	24 2/8	17 0/8	5	4	Livingston County	MI	Elmer DePlanche	1988	2,107
147 0/8	22 1/8	22 0/8	17 2/8	5	5	Winnebago County	IL	Timothy J. Stuebs	1988	2,107
147 0/8	24 6/8	24 6/8	18 0/8	8	7	Richland County	IL	Bill Taylor	1989	2,107
147 0/8	23 7/8	23 2/8	16 1/8	6	8	Jefferson County	OH	James Zink	1989	2,107
147 0/8	25 4/8	23 7/8	22 5/8	6	5	Woodford County	IL	Stan Bocian	1989	2,107
147 0/8	23 3/8	21 6/8	18 2/8	5	5	Warren County	IA	Larry Caldwell	1989	2,107
147 0/8	23 1/8	23 2/8	19 4/8	5	4	Boone County	IL	Michael A. Beasley	1989	2,107
147 0/8	22 7/8	24 3/8	16 2/8	5	5	Walsh County	ND	Dayton Larson	1990	2,107
147 0/8	25 2/8	25 6/8	17 6/8	5	5	Vermilion County	IL	Alexander Ramm	1990	2,107
147 0/8	22 3/8	23 1/8	18 6/8	6	5	Waupaca County	WI	Brian Shambeau	1991	2,107
147 0/8	24 7/8	24 5/8	18 1/8	6	6	Harrison County	OH	Robert M. Mensinger	1991	2,107
147 0/8	24 4/8	25 1/8	23 0/8	4	5	Ernestown	ONT	Detlef Udo Fischer	1991	2,107
146 7/8	24 0/8	24 3/8	22 1/8	5	7	Cass County	ND	Duane H. Olsen	1959	2,136
146 7/8	21 5/8	21 0/8	16 3/8	5	5	Buffalo County	NE	Dwight Bond	1970	2,136
146 7/8	24 2/8	24 2/8	15 5/8	4	4	Martin County	IN	Clarence McIntosh	1976	2,136
146 7/8	22 2/8	21 2/8	19 7/8	5	5	Waushara County	WI	Norman A. Moss	1976	2,136
146 7/8	21 1/8	20 7/8	22 4/8	5	5	Ogle County	IL	Art Heinze	1981	2,136
146 7/8	23 1/8	21 6/8	16 1/8	5	5	Day County	SD	Cary Gill	1982	2,136
146 7/8	22 6/8	21 6/8	16 1/8	5	5	Jasper County	IA	Mike Needham	1982	2,136
146 7/8	25 3/8	25 0/8	18 7/8	5	4	Powhatan County	VA	W. Scott Thorpe	1985	2,136
146 7/8	24 7/8	23 5/8	18 3/8	6	6	Jackson County	MI	Randy R. Peck	1986	2,136
146 7/8	24 4/8	23 5/8	18 6/8	6	6	Florence County	WI	Mark S. Becker	1987	2,136
146 7/8	22 1/8	23 1/8	18 5/8	6	5	Le Flore County	OK	Bill Brannon	1988	2,136
146 7/8	23 2/8	25 2/8	17 1/8	6	7	Houston County	MN	James Roth	1988	2,136
146 7/8	24 2/8	24 0/8	19 3/8	4	5	Calvert County	MD	David Herbert	1989	2,136
146 7/8	23 2/8	22 7/8	15 1/8	5	6	Mercer County	MO	David Gentry	1989	2,136
146 7/8	25 3/8	25 6/8	20 5/8	5	4	Queen Annes County	MD	Raymie J. Williams III	1990	2,136
146 7/8	23 5/8	20 0/8	18 3/8	6	5	Washington County	IL	Morris Lingle	1990	2,136
146 7/8	25 1/8	25 1/8	18 3/8	5	5	Berkshire County	MA	William Drumm	1990	2,136
146 7/8	21 6/8	21 6/8	16 5/8	5	5	Coke County	TX	Jack Mark Stone	1990	2,136
146 7/8	25 6/8	25 7/8	18 5/8	7	5	Keokuk County	IA	Roger Dekok	1991	2,136
146 7/8	22 5/8	22 0/8	17 1/8	6	5	Madison County	IL	Ronald Newby	1991	2,136
146 7/8	22 6/8	22 4/8	20 3/8	4	6	Fairfield County	OH	Kevin Blackstone	1991	2,136
146 7/8	23 4/8	24 4/8	17 1/8	5	6	Augusta Township	ONT	Henry P. Bouchard	1991	2,136
146 6/8	23 3/8	23 1/8	17 6/8	7	8	Roberts County	SD	Robert Hendren	1967	2,158
146 6/8	24 6/8	27 0/8	20 2/8	5	4	Neosho County	KS	Carl Walker	1968	2,158
146 6/8	26 1/8	25 3/8	18 1/8	4	5	Lee County	IA	Jim Bohenkamp	1970	2,158
146 6/8	25 6/8	25 5/8	18 0/8	5	5	Shelby County	IL	Gary E. Sievers	1972	2,158
146 6/8	21 5/8	21 5/8	18 3/8	6	7	Will County	IL	Richard Manegold	1976	2,158
146 6/8	23 0/8	25 6/8	16 3/8	6	5	Lafayette County	WI	Greg Penniston	1977	2,158
146 6/8	25 4/8	25 6/8	17 3/8	5	5	Tuscarawas County	OH	Tracy Sheaffer	1980	2,158
146 6/8	26 1/8	25 3/8	16 0/8	5	4	Waushara County	WI	James L. Reiff, Jr.	1981	2,158
146 6/8	24 7/8	25 0/8	18 6/8	5	6	Cedar County	IA	Mike Rummells	1982	2,158
146 6/8	25 2/8	24 3/8	18 0/8	5	5	Logan County	OH	David Katterheinrich	1984	2,158
146 6/8	21 6/8	22 5/8	22 4/8	5	5	Lincoln County	MO	Jerry Davis, Jr.	1987	2,158
146 6/8	26 6/8	25 6/8	24 4/8	5	5	Suffolk County	NY	Joe Barbato	1988	2,158
146 6/8	27 0/8	27 3/8	19 0/8	4	5	Noth Dumphries Twp.	ONT	Jeff Bendig	1988	2,158

Score	Length of R Main Beam L		Inside Spread	Number of R Points L		Area	State/ Province	Hunter's Name	Date	Rank
146 6/8	24 0/8	23 1/8	17 2/8	5	4	Howard County	IA	Terry Lee Larson	1988	2,158
146 6/8	21 4/8	22 1/8	16 3/8	6	6	Richland County	ND	Allen Perlenfein	1989	2,158
146 6/8	22 7/8	22 4/8	18 6/8	5	5	Powell County	MT	Dan D. Boy	1989	2,158
146 6/8	24 7/8	25 3/8	18 2/8	4	4	Montgomery County	TN	Julia C. Davidson	1989	2,158
146 6/8	23 2/8	23 1/8	19 4/8	5	5	Fergus County	MT	Stan Chiras	1989	2,158
146 6/8	20 2/8	20 4/8	15 1/8	6	5	Pulaski County	GA	Dan B. Clifton	1989	2,158
146 6/8	26 3/8	26 0/8	19 4/8	5	4	Rusk County	WI	Gordon Bohochik	1990	2,158
146 6/8	26 1/8	23 2/8	19 6/8	6	6	Vermilion County	IL	Jack Toms, Jr.	1990	2,158
146 6/8	26 0/8	20 2/8	23 1/8	6	6	Osborne County	KS	Cary L. Sommerla	1990	2,158
146 6/8	23 6/8	23 0/8	16 6/8	6	5	De Kalb County	MO	Dennis Collins	1991	2,158
146 5/8	22 5/8	22 5/8	18 7/8	4	3	Brown County	SD	Donald Grote	1963	2,181
146 5/8	23 2/8	24 1/8	17 3/8	5	6	Buckingham County	VA	Larry D. Baker	1974	2,181
146 5/8	25 2/8	25 6/8	18 7/8	4	5	Carroll County	IL	Art Heinze	1978	2,181
146 5/8	24 2/8	24 1/8	18 7/8	6	7	Des Moines County	IA	Larry R. Booth	1979	2,181
146 5/8	20 6/8	22 1/8	19 4/8	7	7	Clinton County	IN	Sheldon H. Stoops	1979	2,181
146 5/8	23 4/8	24 0/8	19 1/8	5	5	Morrison County	MN	Bart Brodt	1984	2,181
146 5/8	24 3/8	24 4/8	16 5/8	6	5	Cole County	MO	Norman P. Stucky	1984	2,181
146 5/8	24 3/8	24 3/8	16 2/8	8	8	Clark County	MO	Allen L. Courtney	1986	2,181
146 5/8	23 6/8	23 4/8	20 3/8	4	5	Kent County	MI	Benjamin V. Lapus, Jr.	1986	2,181
146 5/8	24 7/8	24 1/8	17 7/8	5	4	Hartford County	CT	Peter J.M. Kiendzoir	1986	2,181
146 5/8	22 4/8	22 0/8	16 1/8	5	6	Wabash County	IL	Robert E. Campbell	1987	2,181
146 5/8	24 7/8	25 5/8	20 4/8	5	7	Washington County	WI	Tony Snow	1988	2,181
146 5/8	21 7/8	21 2/8	15 5/8	5	5	Nueces County	TX	Wayne Peeples	1989	2,181
146 5/8	24 5/8	24 7/8	18 6/8	5	6	Crawford County	KS	Cary R. Rybnick	1989	2,181
146 5/8	24 7/8	24 4/8	19 6/8	6	7	Forest County	WI	Jim Sot	1990	2,181
146 5/8	22 7/8	23 1/8	17 7/8	5	5	Cecil County	MD	Steven D. Flanagan	1990	2,181
146 5/8	24 0/8	24 7/8	16 1/8	5	6	Macomb County	MI	Frank M. Malik, Jr.	1990	2,181
146 5/8	25 6/8	25 6/8	19 3/8	5	5	Polk County	IA	Steve Dilling	1990	2,181
146 5/8	21 3/8	21 4/8	16 3/8	4	4	Dodge County	MN	Myles Keller	1990	2,181
146 5/8	24 0/8	23 1/8	16 3/8	6	6	Giles County	TN	Jerry Case	1991	2,181
146 5/8	21 0/8	21 1/8	16 5/8	5	5	Shawnee County	KS	Dan McConnell	1991	2,181
146 4/8	22 0/8	22 1/8	17 4/8	5	5	Wood County	WI	George Davis	1967	2,202
146 4/8	24 4/8	24 0/8	15 0/8	5	5	Amherst County	VA	Garry B. Pruitt	1972	2,202
146 4/8	22 0/8	23 3/8	18 0/8	5	5	Vigo County	IN	Richard E. Smith	1973	2,202
146 4/8	25 0/8	24 7/8	18 6/8	5	5	Cayuga County	NY	John Andrews, Sr.	1974	2,202
146 4/8	24 2/8	25 2/8	17 6/8	6	5	Christian County	IL	Camron Fitzsimmons	1980	2,202
146 4/8	26 4/8	25 2/8	17 4/8	4	5	Polk County	MO	James Scott Hogan	1982	2,202
146 4/8	24 3/8	24 5/8	18 6/8	4	4	Greene County	IL	Daniel E. Kallal	1983	2,202
146 4/8	21 5/8	21 2/8	15 0/8	5	5	Forest County	WI	Eugene A. Pribek	1985	2,202
146 4/8	22 3/8	22 7/8	16 0/8	5	5	Ritchie County	WV	Tim Jividen	1985	2,202
146 4/8	24 0/8	23 6/8	16 2/8	4	4	Randolph County	IL	Edward J. Lannon	1985	2,202
146 4/8	23 0/8	22 5/8	13 4/8	6	6	Trempealeau County	WI	Greg J. Halama	1986	2,202
146 4/8	23 4/8	25 3/8	17 0/8	7	7	Washington County	WI	Eric Handeland	1986	2,202
146 4/8	26 2/8	26 4/8	18 2/8	5	5	Jackson County	AR	Doug C. Cockrill	1986	2,202
146 4/8	22 3/8	22 3/8	17 0/8	4	4	Dunn County	ND	Todd W. Boechler	1986	2,202
146 4/8	24 4/8	24 4/8	19 4/8	4	5	Pulaski County	KY	Bobbie Ryan	1986	2,202
146 4/8	23 3/8	24 1/8	17 4/8	5	5	Le Sueur County	MN	Joe Rybus	1987	2,202
146 4/8	24 6/8	23 4/8	19 4/8	5	5	Rock County	WI	Gary Hookstead	1987	2,202
146 4/8	23 3/8	23 2/8	17 7/8	6	5	Cottonwood County	MN	Steven L. Erickson	1987	2,202
146 4/8	25 0/8	24 1/8	19 2/8	5	5	Mercer County	NJ	Robert Pazdan	1988	2,202
146 4/8	23 1/8	23 4/8	16 6/8	5	5	Langlade County	WI	Dale G. Kemp	1988	2,202
146 4/8	22 0/8	21 5/8	17 3/8	6	5	Randolph County	IL	Dale Scherle	1988	2,202
146 4/8	24 2/8	23 1/8	19 0/8	5	5	Benton County	IA	Norm Madison	1988	2,202
146 4/8	23 0/8	23 4/8	19 0/8	5	4	Waukesha County	WI	Steven Hamme	1989	2,202
146 4/8	25 0/8	25 6/8	16 4/8	5	5	Nelson County	VA	Larry W. Toms	1989	2,202
146 4/8	23 0/8	23 4/8	16 0/8	5	5	Boone County	AR	Phillip Vanderpool	1990	2,202
146 4/8	27 6/8	25 6/8	18 2/8	5	6	Middlesex County	MA	Jared Apostolakes	1990	2,202
146 4/8	23 5/8	23 3/8	18 4/8	5	5	Okotoks	ALB	Randy Brown	1991	2,202
146 4/8	23 4/8	24 0/8	24 1/8	5	5	Randolph County	AR	Darrell Hagood	1992	2,202
146 3/8	23 5/8	23 1/8	27 1/8	5	5	De Kalb County	IN	Stanley Bremer	1969	2,230
146 3/8	24 6/8	24 5/8	15 3/8	5	5	Palo Alto County	IA	Kim E. Gustafson	1972	2,230
146 3/8	22 7/8	22 4/8	17 1/8	5	5	Shiawassee County	MI	David Asberry	1978	2,230
146 3/8	23 1/8	23 6/8	19 2/8	6	6	Chase County	KS	Jim Wilson	1980	2,230
146 3/8	23 5/8	23 5/8	20 1/8	5	5	Hamilton County	OH	Jerome R. Buschle, Jr.	1981	2,230
146 3/8	23 1/8	23 1/8	17 5/8	4	5	Cecil County	MD	John M. Martino	1981	2,230
146 3/8	23 5/8	23 1/8	16 1/8	5	6	Jo Daviess County	IL	David R. Kammerude	1983	2,230
146 3/8	22 5/8	22 1/8	16 7/8	6	6	Floyd County	IA	Mike Bull	1983	2,230
146 3/8	24 0/8	22 2/8	19 1/8	5	5	Perry County	IL	Richard Kuhnert	1984	2,230
146 3/8	24 6/8	25 7/8	20 7/8	5	5	Hamilton County	OH	Bob Miller	1985	2,230
146 3/8	21 0/8	22 0/8	16 1/8	5	5	Wilson County	KS	Kevin D. O'Neill	1986	2,230

Score	Length of Main Beam R	Length of Main Beam L	Inside Spread	Number of Points R	Number of Points L	Area	State/ Province	Hunter's Name	Date	Rank
146 3/8	22 1/8	22 1/8	16 5/8	5	5	Blue Earth County	MN	Paul Busse	1987	2,230
146 3/8	23 2/8	24 3/8	17 7/8	4	4	Montgomery County	IL	John Snoddy	1987	2,230
146 3/8	22 6/8	22 2/8	16 3/8	5	5	St. Francis County	AR	Johnny Smith	1989	2,230
146 3/8	24 0/8	24 0/8	20 3/8	4	4	Isanti County	MN	Kevin Caldwell	1990	2,230
146 3/8	24 0/8	23 2/8	17 3/8	6	5	Brown County	WI	Robert M. McLellan	1990	2,230
146 3/8	22 6/8	22 7/8	14 7/8	6	6	Polk County	WI	Barry Peterson	1991	2,230
146 3/8	25 4/8	25 0/8	15 4/8	7	6	Shelby County	MO	William P. McQuillen	1991	2,230
146 3/8	22 5/8	21 5/8	15 5/8	5	5	Hennepin County	MN	Greg Wermerskirchen	1991	2,230
146 3/8	22 4/8	23 4/8	17 5/8	5	5	McHenry County	IL	Donald E. Hoey	1991	2,230
146 2/8	24 3/8	24 1/8	18 2/8	5	5	Stearns County	MN	Mike Beuning	1945	2,250
146 2/8	26 5/8	25 6/8	20 6/8	5	5	Plymouth County	IA	Cash N. Howe	1974	2,250
146 2/8	24 6/8	24 1/8	18 2/8	5	5	Butler County	KS	David R. Rogers	1976	2,250
146 2/8	21 2/8	21 7/8	21 2/8	5	5	Clark County	KS	Danny R. Fenton	1977	2,250
146 2/8	22 7/8	23 5/8	16 5/8	6	6	Lafayette County	WI	Wayne Gassman	1977	2,250
146 2/8	24 4/8	24 6/8	15 6/8	4	4	Clark County	IL	Gerald Shaffner	1978	2,250
146 2/8	24 6/8	24 0/8	19 1/8	5	7	Berkeley County	SC	Hugh Gaskins	1980	2,250
146 2/8	25 1/8	24 2/8	20 2/8	6	4	Union County	OH	Charles Yoakum	1980	2,250
146 2/8	25 2/8	25 0/8	17 2/8	5	6	Graham County	KS	Russell Hull	1982	2,250
146 2/8	23 6/8	22 5/8	18 0/8	5	5	Brown County	OH	Ronald Akins	1982	2,250
146 2/8	24 4/8	24 3/8	19 4/8	5	4	Washington County	WI	J.J. Ziegler	1983	2,250
146 2/8	24 6/8	24 5/8	19 4/8	5	5	Lafayette County	WI	Roger Wand	1983	2,250
146 2/8	24 0/8	24 0/8	18 2/8	6	6	Dane County	WI	Roland G. Lettman	1983	2,250
146 2/8	26 7/8	26 3/8	16 5/8	7	6	Granville County	NC	Bradley Brann	1984	2,250
146 2/8	22 2/8	21 6/8	16 5/8	5	6	Parkland County	ALB	Michel Carigan	1984	2,250
146 2/8	26 1/8	25 0/8	18 6/8	5	5	St. Lawrence County	NY	Joseph W. Pudney	1985	2,250
146 2/8	25 0/8	22 7/8	14 4/8	4	4	Van Buren County	IA	Tom Weigand	1985	2,250
146 2/8	22 6/8	22 0/8	17 5/8	5	6	Dodge County	MN	David Lyke	1985	2,250
146 2/8	22 5/8	23 6/8	17 6/8	6	6	Ontonagon County	MI	Paul M. Kilpela	1986	2,250
146 2/8	24 3/8	24 5/8	19 1/8	5	6	Redwood County	MN	R. Tetrick/M. Tetrick	1986	2,250
146 2/8	24 1/8	25 6/8	20 6/8	6	5	Lake County	IL	Kenneth D. Staples	1986	2,250
146 2/8	25 5/8	25 0/8	17 6/8	6	4	Pike County	OH	John Ribic	1987	2,250
146 2/8	20 5/8	21 6/8	15 2/8	5	5	Jackson County	MI	Dale M. Leach	1987	2,250
146 2/8	24 0/8	22 7/8	19 6/8	4	4	Greenwood County	KS	Brian Deer	1987	2,250
146 2/8	21 4/8	22 2/8	18 2/8	6	6	Livingston County	IL	Tom Roe	1989	2,250
146 2/8	22 3/8	22 3/8	19 1/8	6	6	Fayette County	IA	Thomas D. Joyner, Jr.	1990	2,250
146 2/8	22 4/8	22 2/8	15 1/8	5	6	Sedgwick County	KS	Larry Buchholz	1991	2,250
146 2/8	25 0/8	24 3/8	18 4/8	9	7	Cowley County	KS	Larry J. McKean	1991	2,250
146 2/8	22 7/8	22 1/8	16 1/8	6	6	Morrison County	MN	Randy Loken	1991	2,250
146 1/8	23 5/8	24 5/8	17 7/8	6	5	Delaware County	IA	Douglas G. Dabroski	1975	2,279
146 1/8	25 2/8	25 6/8	21 2/8	6	8	Jefferson County	WI	Neil L. Lindemann	1977	2,279
146 1/8	24 1/8	25 0/8	18 3/8	5	5	Lamar County	GA	Joe A. Medcalf	1977	2,279
146 1/8	24 2/8	24 2/8	19 3/8	4	4	Chisago County	MN	Richard Brown	1980	2,279
146 1/8	25 2/8	23 3/8	18 2/8	6	5	Dickinson County	MI	Edward J. Henkel	1980	2,279
146 1/8	25 3/8	25 2/8	19 1/8	5	5	Darke County	OH	Larry Moore	1980	2,279
146 1/8	24 3/8	23 4/8	14 7/8	6	5	Chisago County	MN	Clancy Lindvall	1982	2,279
146 1/8	24 3/8	23 2/8	17 2/8	5	7	Waseca County	MN	Mark Williams	1982	2,279
146 1/8	23 4/8	21 5/8	16 1/8	5	5	Montcalm County	MI	David Tompsett	1985	2,279
146 1/8	25 5/8	25 7/8	20 0/8	5	4	Albert County	NBW	Mike Pugh	1986	2,279
146 1/8	23 4/8	23 4/8	15 1/8	6	6	Carlton County	MN	Rick Nelson	1986	2,279
146 1/8	23 1/8	23 0/8	14 5/8	5	5	Lucas County	IA	Bill Brown	1986	2,279
146 1/8	23 4/8	22 3/8	21 1/8	5	5	Huntington County	IN	R.D. Tessmer /R.S. Tessme	1988	2,279
146 1/8	24 4/8	24 2/8	18 5/8	5	4	Guernsey County	OH	Kerry Mora	1988	2,279
146 1/8	25 0/8	23 5/8	16 6/8	7	6	Coshocton County	OH	David M. Croft	1989	2,279
146 1/8	23 2/8	23 2/8	19 4/8	6	4	Gibson County	IN	Robert Bump	1990	2,279
146 1/8	25 0/8	24 0/8	22 3/8	5	6	Queen Annes County	MD	Ross F. Mills	1990	2,279
146 1/8	25 7/8	25 1/8	19 5/8	4	4	Medina County	OH	Chris Postle	1991	2,279
146 1/8	22 5/8	20 3/8	17 6/8	6	6	Oceana County	MI	Mark Rollenhagen	1991	2,279
146 1/8	21 7/8	21 5/8	15 5/8	5	5	Jo Daviess County	IL	Stan Godfrey	1992	2,279
146 0/8	22 1/8	22 2/8	19 2/8	6	6	Richland County	MT	James L. Kelly	1958	2,299
146 0/8	21 1/8	20 6/8	17 5/8	5	6	Cass County	IN	William D. Finks	1967	2,299
146 0/8	24 0/8	25 0/8	18 4/8	5	5	Will County	IL	Terry Marcukaitis	1971	2,299
146 0/8	25 0/8	24 0/8	22 0/8	5	5	Winona County	MN	Henry Scharmack,Jr.	1973	2,299
146 0/8	20 5/8	20 5/8	14 3/8	7	8	Murray County	MN	John Stenke	1973	2,299
146 0/8	24 1/8	24 4/8	16 0/8	6	6	Keith County	NE	Gerald Spurgin	1975	2,299
146 0/8	23 0/8	22 4/8	18 1/8	6	5	Calgary	ALB	Fred Walker	1981	2,299
146 0/8	21 6/8	21 5/8	16 2/8	5	5	Saline County	NE	Donald D. Matejka	1982	2,299
146 0/8	22 0/8	23 0/8	18 2/8	6	6	Kewaunee County	WI	Harold Blahnik	1982	2,299
146 0/8	21 5/8	22 1/8	18 2/8	5	5	Roberts County	SD	John Fridgen	1984	2,299
146 0/8	27 0/8	27 2/8	21 6/8	4	4	Morrison County	MN	John Sobaski	1985	2,299
146 0/8	23 4/8	22 6/8	19 4/8	5	5	Clayton County	IA	Joe Lieb	1986	2,299

Score	Length of Main Beam R	L	Inside Spread	Number of Points R	L	Area	State/Province	Hunter's Name	Date	Rank
146 0/8	24 4/8	24 4/8	19 7/8	6	6	Jo Daviess County	IL	William Stephanopoulos	1986	2,299
146 0/8	25 2/8	24 0/8	18 2/8	4	4	Saunders County	NE	Gary Frerichs	1988	2,299
146 0/8	25 0/8	23 2/8	21 2/8	5	6	Clay County	MN	Patrick Cox	1989	2,299
146 0/8	22 1/8	23 2/8	17 0/8	5	5	Allamakee County	IA	Casey A. Blum	1989	2,299
146 0/8	22 0/8	22 3/8	16 4/8	5	5	Robertson County	KY	Jim Whisman	1989	2,299
146 0/8	22 0/8	21 0/8	17 0/8	5	5	Heard County	GA	Ray Hand	1990	2,299
146 0/8	23 7/8	23 3/8	18 1/8	6	5	Fillmore County	MN	Dean C. Irish	1990	2,299
146 0/8	23 3/8	22 6/8	16 0/8	4	5	Westchester County	NY	Ronald Moore	1991	2,299
145 7/8	25 1/8	25 0/8	16 3/8	4	5	Wood County	WI	Laddimere Beranek	1959	2,319
145 7/8	25 4/8	24 4/8	19 1/8	4	5	Greeley County	NE	Bill W. Surface	1962	2,319
145 7/8	22 4/8	22 7/8	20 7/8	4	8	Lafayette County	WI	James Goetzke	1972	2,319
145 7/8	23 3/8	23 1/8	16 1/8	7	8	Polk County	MN	Willie Johnson/Tim Amuins	1981	2,319
145 7/8	21 4/8	22 0/8	15 2/8	5	6	Chase County	KS	John L. Moore	1982	2,319
145 7/8	22 6/8	24 4/8	18 7/8	6	5	Lewis & Clark County	MT	Royce Dake	1982	2,319
145 7/8	23 5/8	24 0/8	16 5/8	8	5	Manitowoc County	WI	Thomas L. Alfson	1983	2,319
145 7/8	22 4/8	22 3/8	20 1/8	5	5	Harvey County	KS	Gregory K. Dirksen	1983	2,319
145 7/8	25 1/8	25 2/8	19 1/8	5	5	Monroe County	NY	Pat M. Moore	1987	2,319
145 7/8	24 1/8	23 0/8	18 5/8	5	5	Kent County	MD	Steve J. Grabowski, Jr.	1987	2,319
145 7/8	25 2/8	27 2/8	17 4/8	5	6	Brown County	IL	Ron Hanna	1988	2,319
145 7/8	26 4/8	24 4/8	17 0/8	5	7	Republic County	KS	Gary Dahl	1988	2,319
145 7/8	22 7/8	23 1/8	15 0/8	8	5	Shawnee County	KS	Bradley D Porubsky	1989	2,319
145 7/8	23 5/8	23 7/8	18 7/8	6	6	Lake County	IL	Mike Serwa	1990	2,319
145 7/8	23 4/8	22 4/8	17 5/8	5	6	Republic County	KS	Jerry A. Thomas	1990	2,319
145 7/8	23 0/8	22 6/8	16 5/8	5	5	Arenac County	MI	Daryl Russell	1991	2,319
145 7/8	24 6/8	25 5/8	18 1/8	5	5	Aitkin County	MN	Daniel Picht	1991	2,319
145 7/8	22 2/8	22 3/8	18 4/8	7	7	Carroll County	IL	Paul Shipman	1991	2,319
145 7/8	24 0/8	24 0/8	19 3/8	5	6	Johnson County	IA	Bruce Charipar	1992	2,319
145 7/8	25 1/8	26 3/8	22 1/8	3	3	Steuben County	IN	Jim Loughran	1992	2,319
145 6/8	20 0/8	20 5/8	17 0/8	5	6	Okmulgee County	OK	Pat Giulioli	1973	2,339
145 6/8	21 5/8	22 4/8	17 0/8	5	5	Monroe County	WI	Bob Besch	1980	2,339
145 6/8	22 0/8	22 0/8	17 2/8	5	5	Millarville	ALB	Richard Freudenberg	1982	2,339
145 6/8	23 0/8	23 1/8	20 0/8	4	5	Aransas County	TX	Dr. Tip Coleman	1985	2,339
145 6/8	21 3/8	21 3/8	17 0/8	6	5	Clay County	MN	Darwin Cihak	1986	2,339
145 6/8	22 5/8	22 2/8	17 2/8	5	7	Jefferson County	WI	Randy Latsch	1986	2,339
145 6/8	23 1/8	22 2/8	15 2/8	6	6	Kenedy County	TX	George Cooper	1987	2,339
145 6/8	23 3/8	24 0/8	18 0/8	7	6	Van Buren County	IA	Don Kieler	1987	2,339
145 6/8	23 7/8	23 6/8	17 0/8	4	4	Polk County	WI	Andy Bollant	1988	2,339
145 6/8	21 4/8	21 7/8	15 2/8	5	5	Jefferson County	WI	Brad Hering	1989	2,339
145 6/8	23 3/8	24 1/8	17 6/8	5	7	St. Croix County	WI	David Saltness	1989	2,339
145 6/8	24 3/8	24 7/8	21 0/8	4	4	Cecil County	MD	Earl McSorley	1989	2,339
145 6/8	22 3/8	22 3/8	14 0/8	5	5	Iron County	WI	Scott Hultman	1989	2,339
145 6/8	22 3/8	23 5/8	18 4/8	5	5	Meade County	KY	Kevin Anderson	1989	2,339
145 6/8	23 4/8	23 4/8	18 2/8	5	6	Worcester County	MA	Mark Doucimo	1990	2,339
145 6/8	25 3/8	25 6/8	19 4/8	7	9	Florence County	WI	Steven C. Gevaert	1991	2,339
145 6/8	21 5/8	22 2/8	18 4/8	5	4	Mercer County	IL	Dennis Nelson	1991	2,339
145 6/8	23 4/8	24 0/8	17 0/8	6	5	Jasper County	IL	Elmer R. Luce, Jr.	1991	2,339
145 6/8	21 4/8	21 4/8	17 2/8	5	5	Plymouth County	IA	Cash N. Howe	1991	2,339
145 6/8	26 7/8	27 4/8	19 6/8	4	4	Middlesex County	MA	Joe R. Shepard	1991	2,339
145 5/8	25 1/8	24 4/8	19 7/8	6	5	Waseca County	MN	Robert Barrie	1971	2,359
145 5/8	23 7/8	24 0/8	21 2/8	4	6	Montgomery County	AL	Rett Kelly	1974	2,359
145 5/8	23 5/8	23 0/8	18 4/8	6	7	Stearns County	MN	Larry Schwarze	1979	2,359
145 5/8	23 0/8	23 6/8	17 3/8	5	5	Rich Valley	ALB	Eric Teege	1980	2,359
145 5/8	23 2/8	23 4/8	18 1/8	5	5	St. Croix County	WI	Keith Andrea	1981	2,359
145 5/8	24 0/8	24 4/8	18 5/8	6	5	Athens County	OH	Steve Wilkes	1983	2,359
145 5/8	26 1/8	25 7/8	18 2/8	5	5	Houston County	GA	Issac W. Horne	1985	2,359
145 5/8	22 2/8	22 7/8	15 5/8	6	6	Isanti County	MN	Tim Dugas	1985	2,359
145 5/8	24 1/8	23 4/8	19 2/8	5	6	Black Hawk County	IA	John L. Derifield	1985	2,359
145 5/8	26 2/8	25 1/8	20 6/8	5	7	Christian County	IL	Carl Tucker	1985	2,359
145 5/8	23 2/8	24 3/8	20 4/8	6	5	Coffey County	KS	James Bowman	1985	2,359
145 5/8	23 3/8	24 2/8	17 5/8	5	5	Isanti County	MN	Jon Anderson	1986	2,359
145 5/8	26 5/8	24 3/8	19 7/8	4	5	Johnson County	IL	Jack D. Lambert	1986	2,359
145 5/8	24 7/8	25 7/8	23 7/8	6	4	Lake County	IL	Robert Henry Torstenson	1986	2,359
145 5/8	24 1/8	22 5/8	18 7/8	4	4	Sawyer County	WI	Dan Sours	1989	2,359
145 5/8	22 6/8	21 6/8	19 7/8	6	6	Lake County	IL	William A. Murphy	1991	2,359
145 5/8	24 2/8	25 3/8	19 7/8	4	4	McHenry County	IL	Joe Roos	1991	2,359
145 4/8	23 3/8	24 0/8	17 2/8	6	7	Morton County	ND	Eddy Wallery	1959	2,376
145 4/8	25 5/8	24 4/8	19 0/8	4	5	Monroe County	WI	Larry Arentz	1977	2,376
145 4/8	23 2/8	22 0/8	18 2/8	7	6	Mower County	MN	Walter E. Bauer	1977	2,376
145 4/8	24 3/8	23 0/8	20 4/8	5	4	Marion County	IA	Donald Bennett	1977	2,376
145 4/8	22 1/8	21 6/8	17 2/8	5	5	Van Buren County	MI	Bob Zedeck	1979	2,376

251

SCORE	LENGTH OF MAIN BEAM		INSIDE SPREAD	NUMBER OF POINTS		AREA	STATE/ PROVINCE	HUNTER'S NAME	DATE	RANK
	R	L		R	L					
145 4/8	24 3/8	22 7/8	18 1/8	5	6	Lawrence County	AL	Richard McClanahan	1980	2,376
145 4/8	23 7/8	24 3/8	20 2/8	4	4	Kent County	MI	Peter Champnoise	1981	2,376
145 4/8	24 1/8	24 3/8	21 4/8	7	6	Hamilton County	OH	Jack Ranz	1982	2,376
145 4/8	24 0/8	24 1/8	18 7/8	5	4	Scott County	KY	Park Tackett	1984	2,376
145 4/8	23 0/8	24 0/8	19 4/8	4	5	Cass County	MI	Lee Davis	1985	2,376
145 4/8	24 0/8	22 6/8	18 0/8	6	6	Delaware County	OH	Ronald E. Murphy	1986	2,376
145 4/8	23 0/8	24 3/8	18 2/8	6	6	Trego County	KS	Morris Crisler	1986	2,376
145 4/8	24 0/8	25 1/8	21 3/8	6	6	Houston County	MN	Bruce Norton	1987	2,376
145 4/8	24 6/8	22 2/8	17 0/8	5	5	Jefferson County	MO	Steve North	1987	2,376
145 4/8	23 2/8	24 4/8	18 2/8	4	4	Adams County	IL	Gary Nebe	1987	2,376
145 4/8	23 6/8	23 7/8	18 4/8	4	4	Chester County	PA	Randy R. Caspersen	1988	2,376
145 4/8	24 4/8	24 6/8	17 2/8	4	4	Ravalli County	MT	Chris Landstrom	1988	2,376
145 4/8	23 5/8	23 3/8	17 0/8	7	6	Kankakee County	IL	Stanley Gawlinski	1990	2,376
145 4/8	22 3/8	22 4/8	17 4/8	5	5	Price County	WI	Phil Socwell	1990	2,376
145 4/8	23 4/8	23 4/8	19 0/8	5	6	Buffalo County	WI	Edward Brannen	1991	2,376
145 4/8	22 5/8	23 4/8	16 3/8	5	6	Appanoose County	IA	Steven P. Salmieri	1991	2,376
145 4/8	24 3/8	23 2/8	19 4/8	5	6	Baca County	CO	Kurt W. Keskimaki	1991	2,376
145 3/8	24 3/8	25 1/8	20 5/8	5	5	Lyon County	KS	Edward Bess	1967	2,398
145 3/8	22 4/8	22 5/8	18 1/8	5	5	Morrison County	MN	Gerald A. Young	1971	2,398
145 3/8	23 4/8	23 4/8	18 6/8	5	5	Kanawha County	WV	Luther McClure	1973	2,398
145 3/8	24 5/8	25 5/8	22 1/8	4	5	Will County	IL	Philip J. Gariboldi	1977	2,398
145 3/8	26 7/8	26 3/8	20 2/8	4	4	Jackson County	MI	Scot Gazlay	1977	2,398
145 3/8	22 7/8	23 0/8	19 1/8	4	5	Des Moines County	IA	John Jindrich	1979	2,398
145 3/8	22 6/8	21 3/8	17 4/8	6	6	Marshall County	SD	Tim Johnson	1980	2,398
145 3/8	23 7/8	23 7/8	17 5/8	4	4	Pike County	OH	William H. Koehler	1981	2,398
145 3/8	23 3/8	23 6/8	17 2/8	5	4	Jackson County	OH	Joe W. Wright	1982	2,398
145 3/8	23 4/8	22 2/8	18 1/8	5	4	Osage County	KS	Gary Hunsicker	1985	2,398
145 3/8	22 0/8	21 6/8	17 5/8	5	5	Otter Tail County	MN	Walter Rieckman	1986	2,398
145 3/8	23 0/8	23 4/8	17 1/8	6	5	Delaware County	OH	Mark Yarnell	1986	2,398
145 3/8	20 4/8	21 0/8	15 1/8	6	6	Bayfield County	WI	James Rohr	1986	2,398
145 3/8	24 3/8	24 4/8	18 7/8	4	4	Vilas County	WI	Bruce Jacobson	1987	2,398
145 3/8	24 6/8	24 6/8	17 4/8	5	6	Le Sueur County	MN	Donald Attenberger	1988	2,398
145 3/8	22 4/8	22 0/8	16 3/8	5	6	McHenry County	IL	Bill Gilstead	1988	2,398
145 3/8	25 4/8	24 0/8	19 2/8	5	4	Peoria County	IL	Donald R. Ragain	1988	2,398
145 3/8	21 5/8	22 5/8	18 1/8	5	5	Osborne County	KS	Craig E. Pottberg	1988	2,398
145 3/8	22 7/8	22 3/8	18 1/8	6	5	Tuscarawas County	OH	Emery Schlabach	1988	2,398
145 3/8	23 4/8	24 5/8	16 3/8	7	5	Montgomery County	MD	James C. Dalrymple, Jr.	1988	2,398
145 3/8	25 7/8	25 7/8	19 3/8	4	4	Langlade County	WI	David Nelson	1989	2,398
145 3/8	24 1/8	23 5/8	18 4/8	5	5	Scott County	KY	Darrell Sharp	1990	2,398
145 3/8	23 7/8	23 5/8	16 5/8	5	5	Jennings County	IN	Gregory Dean Tucker	1990	2,398
145 2/8	21 6/8	21 3/8	18 2/8	5	5	Des Moines County	IA	Gary Biles	1973	2,421
145 2/8	22 5/8	22 7/8	17 2/8	5	5	Yankton County	SD	Gordon Orton	1976	2,421
145 2/8	23 0/8	22 4/8	15 4/8	7	6	Douglas County	KS	Richard D. Brown	1978	2,421
145 2/8	23 3/8	23 0/8	16 2/8	5	5	Polk County	IA	Jim Young	1978	2,421
145 2/8	23 7/8	24 4/8	17 5/8	5	5	Livingston County	MI	Alan K. Newberry	1979	2,421
145 2/8	21 5/8	21 1/8	19 4/8	5	6	Clark County	AR	Thomas E. Taylor	1982	2,421
145 2/8	22 7/8	23 6/8	18 6/8	5	5	Madison County	IA	Stephen W. Kent	1982	2,421
145 2/8	26 2/8	25 7/8	22 1/8	6	6	Grant County	WI	Gary Wiest	1982	2,421
145 2/8	24 1/8	24 2/8	18 6/8	4	4	Vernon County	WI	David Penchi	1982	2,421
145 2/8	24 2/8	22 0/8	22 0/8	5	6	Stephenson County	IL	Dwight Pickard	1983	2,421
145 2/8	26 6/8	25 6/8	21 2/8	4	4	Mercer County	NJ	James E. McCloskey, Jr.	1984	2,421
145 2/8	22 6/8	21 0/8	16 4/8	5	5	Hennepin County	MN	Robert L. Halverson	1985	2,421
145 2/8	23 0/8	23 0/8	15 6/8	5	5	Holt County	NE	Thomas D. Lanz	1986	2,421
145 2/8	22 5/8	22 1/8	17 0/8	5	5	Cloud County	KS	Mark Copple	1986	2,421
145 2/8	24 6/8	23 5/8	18 6/8	4	4	Issaquena County	MS	Charles A. Peeples	1988	2,421
145 2/8	23 2/8	24 0/8	17 2/8	5	5	Peoria County	IL	Lenny Asbell	1988	2,421
145 2/8	25 6/8	25 3/8	19 2/8	5	6	Du Page County	IL	Gregg Weck	1988	2,421
145 2/8	23 1/8	23 6/8	16 3/8	6	4	Lawrence County	IL	Lary Caddell	1988	2,421
145 2/8	25 7/8	25 4/8	21 0/8	4	4	Daviess County	IN	John H. Kenworthy	1989	2,421
145 2/8	23 0/8	22 5/8	16 6/8	6	4	Delaware County	IA	Dean Dempster	1989	2,421
145 2/8	24 5/8	24 0/8	18 4/8	4	6	Clearwater County	ID	Michael L. McCabe	1990	2,421
145 2/8	24 0/8	24 2/8	17 4/8	4	4	Columbia County	PA	Robert Markle	1990	2,421
145 2/8	24 4/8	24 6/8	18 0/8	4	4	Rock Island County	IL	Tim Pressly	1990	2,421
145 2/8	23 4/8	23 4/8	20 5/8	5	5	Belmont County	OH	Aaron Wiley	1990	2,421
145 2/8	22 2/8	22 0/8	17 4/8	5	5	Davis County	IA	Roy Glosser	1990	2,421
145 2/8	21 1/8	21 7/8	18 0/8	5	5	Chester County	PA	Stephen Daniels Raeburn	1991	2,421
145 2/8	23 0/8	23 4/8	19 0/8	7	6	Webster County	IA	Steven W. Hiveley	1992	2,421
145 1/8	24 7/8	25 2/8	22 0/8	5	6	Grundy County	IL	Tony Muhich	1975	2,448
145 1/8	23 1/8	22 7/8	17 1/8	7	7	Dearborn County	IN	David Goodwin	1978	2,448
145 1/8	22 3/8	22 5/8	15 5/8	5	5	Kent County	MI	Virgil G. Baker, Jr.	1979	2,448

Score	Length of Main Beam R	L	Inside Spread	Number of Points R	L	Area	State/ Province	Hunter's Name	Date	Rank
145 1/8	23 6/8	23 2/8	18 5/8	5	6	Green County	WI	Dan Behring	1979	2,448
145 1/8	24 6/8	24 0/8	18 5/8	6	5	Leavenworth County	KS	Chris Calovich	1982	2,448
145 1/8	23 0/8	23 0/8	17 3/8	5	5	Berkshire County	MA	Richard Scorzafava	1984	2,448
145 1/8	21 7/8	21 6/8	17 1/8	5	5	Calgary	ALB	Dwayne Andrus	1986	2,448
145 1/8	22 6/8	23 0/8	20 5/8	6	6	Floyd County	VA	Jeffery Weddle	1987	2,448
145 1/8	23 6/8	23 6/8	21 1/8	4	4	Montgomery County	OH	Sam Dycus	1987	2,448
145 1/8	23 0/8	22 0/8	16 1/8	4	5	Warren County	OH	Jeffery W. Combs	1987	2,448
145 1/8	23 6/8	23 4/8	18 6/8	5	7	Livingston County	NY	Gary Hartford	1988	2,448
145 1/8	23 2/8	24 3/8	20 3/8	4	5	Stanton County	NE	Gary Frowick	1989	2,448
145 1/8	25 4/8	25 6/8	18 7/8	4	4	Monroe County	IA	Tom Starns	1989	2,448
145 1/8	25 3/8	24 0/8	19 7/8	4	5	Buffalo County	WI	Mark E. Fetting	1990	2,448
145 1/8	22 6/8	22 2/8	18 1/8	5	5	Jones County	IA	Ronald W. Post	1990	2,448
145 1/8	24 2/8	22 7/8	20 1/8	5	5	Carroll County	MD	Bill Roach	1990	2,448
145 1/8	23 5/8	23 5/8	20 7/8	4	5	Platte County	MO	Francisco Escobar	1991	2,448
145 1/8	22 2/8	21 7/8	16 5/8	5	5	Crawford County	IL	Charlie Guyer	1991	2,448
145 1/8	22 6/8	22 3/8	19 3/8	5	6	Weslock	ALB	Trevor Edwards	1992	2,448
145 0/8	22 5/8	21 2/8	14 2/8	6	6	Washington County	IA	Doron Whitlock	1966	2,467
145 0/8	24 0/8	24 5/8	20 0/8	4	4	Grant County	SD	Kevin Bronson	1973	2,467
145 0/8	24 0/8	22 2/8	15 2/8	6	6	Trigg County	KY	Donald Powell	1974	2,467
145 0/8	23 1/8	22 6/8	15 2/8	5	5	Mahaska County	IA	Randy Randall	1978	2,467
145 0/8	21 5/8	22 4/8	15 4/8	5	5	Jones County	IA	Jim H. Dougherty	1979	2,467
145 0/8	24 2/8	22 1/8	14 1/8	8	6	Ste Genevieve County	MO	Dr. Dennis Diaz	1980	2,467
145 0/8	23 6/8	24 2/8	19 6/8	5	5	Huntingdon County	PA	John A. Williams	1983	2,467
145 0/8	20 4/8	21 4/8	16 4/8	5	5	Polk County	MN	Grant Schultz	1984	2,467
145 0/8	23 0/8	23 4/8	19 1/8	9	5	St. Joseph County	IN	Monty Layne	1984	2,467
145 0/8	24 3/8	24 5/8	16 2/8	5	5	Peoria County	IL	Earl Evans	1985	2,467
145 0/8	23 3/8	24 4/8	18 2/8	4	4	Sumter County	AL	Denis Waldrop	1986	2,467
145 0/8	22 0/8	23 4/8	19 4/8	5	5	Champaign County	IL	David TenEyck	1986	2,467
145 0/8	22 4/8	22 3/8	17 6/8	6	6	Craighead County	AR	Rob Veach	1986	2,467
145 0/8	23 7/8	24 4/8	18 0/8	4	4	Bee County	TX	Gary Kraatz	1987	2,467
145 0/8	21 4/8	21 4/8	15 6/8	5	4	Traill County	ND	Chuck E. Spicer	1987	2,467
145 0/8	21 3/8	22 5/8	20 4/8	5	6	Bexar County	TX	Ben Wallace	1990	2,467
145 0/8	26 0/8	26 4/8	18 2/8	4	4	Milwaukee County	WI	Tony Snow	1990	2,467
145 0/8	24 5/8	23 2/8	16 6/8	5	5	Dougherty County	GA	Michael L. Layfield	1990	2,467
145 0/8	21 6/8	21 4/8	16 2/8	5	5	Washburn County	WI	Leonard L. Schneider	1991	2,467
145 0/8	22 0/8	21 6/8	14 2/8	5	5	Ohio County	IN	Richard English	1991	2,467
145 0/8	22 4/8	23 1/8	18 0/8	5	6	Polk County	WI	Vernon H. Simon	1992	2,467
144 7/8	23 0/8	23 4/8	19 7/8	6	6	Wyandotte County	KS	George F. Bigelow	1966	2,488
144 7/8	21 7/8	22 3/8	17 1/8	5	6	Sussex County	VA	Alvin D. Skinner	1972	2,488
144 7/8	25 1/8	25 0/8	18 3/8	5	6	Louisa County	IA	Harold E. Boysen	1978	2,488
144 7/8	25 7/8	25 4/8	21 7/8	4	5	Dallas County	IA	John M. Bascom	1979	2,488
144 7/8	20 2/8	20 1/8	15 2/8	6	5	Richland County	MT	Garth N. Kallevig	1980	2,488
144 7/8	25 7/8	25 4/8	19 3/8	4	4	Sumner County	KS	Dave Baldwin	1982	2,488
144 7/8	23 7/8	22 0/8	18 3/8	4	4	Cerro Gordo County	IA	Earl L. Goodman	1983	2,488
144 7/8	22 4/8	22 2/8	20 7/8	4	5	Perry County	IL	Greg Thompson	1985	2,488
144 7/8	22 3/8	22 1/8	17 5/8	5	5	Onondaga County	NY	Kim A. Schneider	1985	2,488
144 7/8	25 4/8	25 2/8	16 3/8	5	6	Mayes County	OK	John W. Madlock	1985	2,488
144 7/8	21 7/8	21 2/8	18 7/8	6	5	Texas County	OK	Max Crocker	1985	2,488
144 7/8	21 2/8	21 1/8	18 7/8	5	5	Osborne County	KS	Gary L. Ozias	1985	2,488
144 7/8	25 7/8	25 6/8	18 7/8	7	7	Washburn County	WI	William "Mike" Johnson	1987	2,488
144 7/8	22 4/8	21 4/8	16 6/8	6	5	Lake County	IL	Carl H. Spaeth	1987	2,488
144 7/8	24 6/8	24 4/8	16 2/8	5	6	Dearborn County	IN	Jerry O. Kent	1988	2,488
144 7/8	22 4/8	23 4/8	19 5/8	5	4	Buffalo County	WI	Gary Dorn	1988	2,488
144 7/8	26 4/8	26 0/8	15 7/8	6	5	Chambers County	AL	Craig Reynolds	1988	2,488
144 7/8	22 6/8	22 7/8	17 5/8	5	5	Kossuth County	IA	Robert Barslou	1989	2,488
144 7/8	23 3/8	24 1/8	16 5/8	4	5	Mower County	MN	Robert Frost	1989	2,488
144 7/8	21 5/8	21 0/8	15 7/8	5	6	Kleberg County	TX	Wayne Peeples	1990	2,488
144 7/8	26 4/8	25 1/8	20 7/8	5	5	Berrien County	MI	Larry McLaughlin	1990	2,488
144 7/8	23 4/8	23 6/8	18 1/8	4	5	Worcester County	MD	David Johnson	1990	2,488
144 7/8	22 7/8	22 5/8	16 6/8	5	6	Pike County	IL	James Kerr	1990	2,488
144 7/8	24 4/8	23 0/8	21 1/8	4	5	Mills County	IA	John Bantz	1990	2,488
144 7/8	25 3/8	25 6/8	18 1/8	5	4	Ardrossan	ALB	Terry Alan Myroniuk	1991	2,488
144 6/8	19 6/8	20 0/8	15 2/8	6	7	Powell County	MT	Danny Moore	1974	2,513
144 6/8	21 7/8	22 1/8	17 4/8	6	7	Christian County	IL	Scott M. Cassidy	1983	2,513
144 6/8	25 2/8	24 6/8	19 2/8	4	5	Delaware County	PA	James Taylor	1984	2,513
144 6/8	21 0/8	21 4/8	17 0/8	5	5	Sumner County	KS	Jeffrey L. Nash	1984	2,513
144 6/8	23 4/8	23 0/8	16 2/8	5	4	Powell County	MT	Sonny Templeton	1986	2,513
144 6/8	25 7/8	25 4/8	19 0/8	4	4	Lake County	IL	Carl H. Spaeth	1986	2,513
144 6/8	24 1/8	25 4/8	18 0/8	4	5	Hancock County	MS	Alan J. Guess	1987	2,513
144 6/8	26 4/8	25 2/8	21 4/8	5	4	Lincoln County	ME	Darryl Flagg	1988	2,513

SCORE	LENGTH OF MAIN BEAM R	LENGTH OF MAIN BEAM L	INSIDE SPREAD	NUMBER OF POINTS R	NUMBER OF POINTS L	AREA	STATE/ PROVINCE	HUNTER'S NAME	DATE	RANK
144 6/8	24 5/8	23 3/8	18 0/8	5	5	Bent County	CO	Kurt W. Keskimaki	1988	2,513
144 6/8	24 7/8	24 6/8	20 4/8	6	4	Clayton County	IA	Jim Kerns	1989	2,513
144 6/8	23 0/8	22 2/8	18 6/8	5	5	Fairfield County	OH	John W. Todhunter, Jr.	1989	2,513
144 6/8	26 0/8	25 7/8	14 3/8	6	5	Tazewell County	IL	Kevin Eggen	1989	2,513
144 6/8	23 7/8	23 7/8	15 6/8	4	5	Lee County	IA	Mark Webb	1989	2,513
144 6/8	22 3/8	21 0/8	16 4/8	5	5	Irion County	TX	William Jay Wilson	1989	2,513
144 6/8	24 3/8	23 6/8	16 6/8	6	5	Portage County	WI	Mike Kurzinski	1990	2,513
144 6/8	21 0/8	21 4/8	17 4/8	5	5	Middlesex	ONT	Kim Slobojin	1990	2,513
144 6/8	24 6/8	24 3/8	20 6/8	4	4	La Salle County	IL	Bart Pals	1991	2,513
144 6/8	25 7/8	26 2/8	18 2/8	5	5	Door County	WI	Larry Page	1991	2,513
144 6/8	22 3/8	22 1/8	18 6/8	5	4	County of St. Hyacinthe	QUE	Guy Turcotte	1991	2,513
144 6/8	24 1/8	23 5/8	19 2/8	5	5	Livingston County	IL	Tom Roe	1991	2,513
144 5/8	24 0/8	24 4/8	21 3/8	4	4	Spink County	SD	Jerald Shantz	1959	2,533
144 5/8	23 6/8	23 6/8	19 7/8	4	4	Geauga County	OH	Rudy Grecar	1970	2,533
144 5/8	24 7/8	26 3/8	21 7/8	5	6	Valley County	MT	Leith Wimmer	1971	2,533
144 5/8	22 2/8	22 7/8	17 7/8	5	6	Vermillion County	IN	Robert McClara	1972	2,533
144 5/8	23 6/8	24 2/8	16 5/8	5	5	Will County	IL	Joseph Wyer	1978	2,533
144 5/8	23 2/8	23 6/8	18 3/8	5	5	Huntingdon County	PA	John A. Williams	1980	2,533
144 5/8	24 4/8	22 7/8	16 3/8	5	5	Douglas County	WI	Oren Hanson	1982	2,533
144 5/8	22 2/8	21 2/8	18 1/8	4	5	Oconto County	WI	David Nelsen	1982	2,533
144 5/8	24 2/8	23 4/8	15 1/8	5	6	Traill County	ND	Arlin Ingebretson	1983	2,533
144 5/8	23 0/8	22 1/8	14 5/8	5	5	Price County	WI	Peter Koenig	1983	2,533
144 5/8	22 5/8	21 5/8	16 3/8	6	6	Stanley County	SD	Randy Kleinschmidt	1985	2,533
144 5/8	24 5/8	25 0/8	19 3/8	4	4	Calvert County	MD	Tom Hosselrode	1986	2,533
144 5/8	24 2/8	25 1/8	16 5/8	4	4	Washburn County	WI	Tom Elliot	1987	2,533
144 5/8	28 1/8	25 6/8	20 1/8	5	5	Howard County	MD	David Wilson	1988	2,533
144 5/8	22 2/8	22 3/8	15 1/8	6	6	Cherokee County	KS	David B. Price	1988	2,533
144 5/8	22 7/8	22 4/8	15 5/8	6	5	Pike County	IL	Jim Murphy	1988	2,533
144 5/8	23 0/8	23 6/8	17 5/8	5	5	Ramsey County	MN	Rick Westberg	1989	2,533
144 5/8	25 3/8	24 0/8	20 7/8	6	5	Lenawee County	MI	Melvin D. Hoffman	1989	2,533
144 5/8	22 7/8	23 1/8	19 3/8	6	7	Hopkins County	KY	Tracy Daves	1989	2,533
144 5/8	24 6/8	23 5/8	16 7/8	5	5	Prowers County	CO	Daniel Kavalunas	1989	2,533
144 5/8	22 7/8	25 0/8	20 5/8	5	6	Jasper County	IA	Brian Vander Velden	1989	2,533
144 5/8	25 3/8	26 0/8	22 1/8	5	5	Jo Daviess County	IL	Scott R. Jackson	1989	2,533
144 5/8	25 7/8	24 5/8	21 5/8	4	5	Chase County	KS	Rod Koehn	1989	2,533
144 5/8	26 0/8	26 3/8	20 1/8	4	4	Fayette County	IL	Dean Harrison	1990	2,533
144 5/8	23 0/8	23 3/8	20 5/8	4	4	Kankakee County	IL	Jim Wetmore	1991	2,533
144 5/8	27 6/8	27 1/8	22 3/8	5	4	Sauk County	WI	Mark A. Parrott	1991	2,533
144 4/8	22 6/8	22 6/8	16 3/8	5	7	Hall County	NE	Verne Skow	1958	2,559
144 4/8	23 2/8	23 6/8	16 3/8	5	6	Day County	SD	John E. Sigdestad	1963	2,559
144 4/8	25 3/8	26 1/8	16 4/8	5	4	Montgomery County	MD	Victor Ezerski	1975	2,559
144 4/8	23 0/8	24 5/8	14 5/8	6	8	Scott County	MN	Charlie Abeln	1977	2,559
144 4/8	23 1/8	22 2/8	17 2/8	5	5	Winnebago County	IA	Ronald Gorden	1977	2,559
144 4/8	23 2/8	22 5/8	18 4/8	5	6	Greene County	OH	Don F. Necina	1981	2,559
144 4/8	26 2/8	26 1/8	18 3/8	5	6	Jo Daviess County	IL	Kenneth Pluym	1985	2,559
144 4/8	25 6/8	26 4/8	19 7/8	7	7	Madison County	NY	John Loveday	1985	2,559
144 4/8	21 7/8	22 0/8	17 0/8	5	5	Morrison County	MN	Will Carlson	1986	2,559
144 4/8	25 1/8	24 5/8	19 2/8	4	4	Montgomery County	OH	Anthony W. Miller	1986	2,559
144 4/8	21 6/8	22 2/8	15 5/8	7	7	Peoria County	IL	Kevin Walsh	1986	2,559
144 4/8	22 3/8	23 3/8	16 4/8	5	5	Lincoln County	MO	Denton C. Raymond	1988	2,559
144 4/8	22 4/8	22 2/8	15 1/8	6	5	Howard County	IA	John R. Koschmeder	1988	2,559
144 4/8	24 7/8	24 5/8	22 6/8	5	4	Ravalli County	MT	Tom Storm	1988	2,559
144 4/8	25 1/8	24 0/8	21 0/8	5	6	Westchester County	NY	Frank Reindl	1988	2,559
144 4/8	22 2/8	23 0/8	18 6/8	5	5	Allegheny County	PA	John H. Matthews	1989	2,559
144 4/8	24 3/8	23 2/8	21 3/8	5	7	Jefferson County	WI	Mark A. Meyer	1989	2,559
144 4/8	23 7/8	24 3/8	21 2/8	6	6	Vermilion County	IL	Robert G. Downing	1989	2,559
144 4/8	24 4/8	24 5/8	22 6/8	4	4	Appanoose County	IA	Frank Delouis	1990	2,559
144 4/8	23 0/8	23 1/8	18 6/8	4	4	Lewis & Clark County	MT	Sonny Templeton	1990	2,559
144 4/8	25 4/8	25 1/8	20 1/8	6	6	Clark County	OH	Randy McConnaughey	1990	2,559
144 4/8	26 4/8	26 2/8	20 2/8	5	4	Colchester Township	ONT	Leo Potvin	1990	2,559
144 4/8	25 2/8	25 0/8	19 4/8	7	5	Pottawattamie County	IA	Mark E. Raney	1991	2,559
144 4/8	24 3/8	23 5/8	19 6/8	5	5	Iowa County	WI	Troy K. Koelzer	1991	2,559
143 3/8	23 7/8	23 5/8	17 2/8	6	7	Rock County	NE	Dick Mauch	1963	2,583
143 3/8	23 7/8	24 5/8	19 5/8	6	4	Delaware County	OH	Jack R. Hecker	1975	2,583
143 3/8	23 6/8	23 6/8	16 4/8	4	5	Columbia County	WI	Ronald Bordson	1976	2,583
143 3/8	22 5/8	23 7/8	16 5/8	5	6	Sawyer County	WI	Dave Phillips	1981	2,583
143 3/8	22 4/8	23 5/8	16 6/8	6	5	Murray County	MN	John Laundre	1981	2,583
143 3/8	23 1/8	22 7/8	17 7/8	6	6	Kingman County	KS	Scott Helmke	1982	2,583
143 3/8	23 0/8	23 6/8	19 7/8	5	6	Clayton County	IA	Kenneth Clayton	1982	2,583
143 3/8	22 6/8	22 4/8	18 7/8	6	5	Columbia County	WI	Jerry Ulrich	1984	2,583

SCORE	LENGTH OF MAIN BEAM		INSIDE SPREAD	NUMBER OF POINTS		AREA	STATE/ PROVINCE	HUNTER'S NAME	DATE	RANK
	R	L		R	L					
144 3/8	24 1/8	24 4/8	19 5/8	5	6	Morrison County	MN	Rick Hayner	1984	2,583
144 3/8	21 6/8	22 1/8	18 3/8	5	5	Ripley County	IN	Dick Gambrel	1984	2,583
144 3/8	23 7/8	24 1/8	17 1/8	4	5	Anderson County	TN	Johnny Wayne Jobe	1985	2,583
144 3/8	21 1/8	21 5/8	19 7/8	6	5	Sussex County	NJ	Frank Tropona	1987	2,583
144 3/8	26 4/8	25 6/8	19 4/8	6	6	Decatur County	IA	Julian Toney	1987	2,583
144 3/8	23 5/8	23 1/8	15 3/8	5	6	Blue Earth County	MN	John Chatleain	1987	2,583
144 3/8	25 7/8	24 6/8	17 7/8	4	4	Lambton County	ONT	Robert B. Kennedy	1988	2,583
144 3/8	22 3/8	22 0/8	20 7/8	6	5	Anoka County	MN	Greg Seymour	1990	2,583
144 3/8	23 1/8	22 2/8	15 6/8	7	6	Beausejour	MAN	Dave DeLeeuw	1991	2,583
144 3/8	22 5/8	22 2/8	16 2/8	5	8	Norman County	MN	Joel Gwin	1991	2,583
144 3/8	23 1/8	24 0/8	19 1/8	5	6	Goodhue County	MN	John "Jack" Cordes	1991	2,583
144 3/8	22 2/8	22 7/8	15 7/8	5	6	Rockdale County	GA	Jim Conway	1991	2,583
144 3/8	25 4/8	25 0/8	19 5/8	5	6	Madison County	AR	Gary R. Catron	1991	2,583
144 2/8	25 7/8	26 2/8	23 0/8	4	4	Bucks County	PA	Robert Weaver	1923	2,604
144 2/8	21 5/8	21 4/8	17 2/8	5	5	Miner County	SD	William Hueners	1965	2,604
144 2/8	21 7/8	21 7/8	14 2/8	5	5	Brown County	SD	Harold Larson	1966	2,604
144 2/8	20 6/8	20 7/8	15 4/8	5	5	Juneau County	WI	Gordon Stittleburg	1966	2,604
144 2/8	22 4/8	23 4/8	17 6/8	5	5	Steele County	MN	Maynard Bauer	1977	2,604
144 2/8	24 2/8	22 6/8	19 6/8	5	5	Miami County	OH	Dale Stull	1980	2,604
144 2/8	22 7/8	23 2/8	17 0/8	5	5	Coffey County	KS	Marc Chester	1983	2,604
144 2/8	20 3/8	20 1/8	15 4/8	5	6	Brown County	KS	Ken Spencer	1983	2,604
144 2/8	25 1/8	24 2/8	20 6/8	5	4	Hamilton County	IL	Paul Sebby	1984	2,604
144 2/8	24 0/8	24 3/8	19 3/8	7	6	Fairfield County	OH	Merle D. Strope	1986	2,604
144 2/8	21 5/8	20 6/8	20 4/8	5	6	Lake County	IL	Mike Mitten	1986	2,604
144 2/8	24 5/8	23 6/8	16 5/8	5	6	Clay County	IL	William Brummer	1988	2,604
144 2/8	23 6/8	23 0/8	16 4/8	6	6	Christian County	IL	David Loyd	1988	2,604
144 2/8	29 0/8	28 2/8	19 1/8	5	5	Charles County	MD	Mel Wolfe	1989	2,604
144 2/8	22 4/8	22 6/8	14 0/8	5	5	Kenosha County	WI	John R. Griffin	1991	2,604
144 2/8	24 6/8	24 7/8	21 4/8	6	5	Beltrami County	MN	Scott LaCoursiere	1992	2,604
144 1/8	21 3/8	21 2/8	17 2/8	5	7	Marshall County	KS	Jack Thornton	1965	2,620
144 1/8	25 0/8	24 0/8	17 7/8	5	4	Union County	IL	Pat Mitchell	1974	2,620
144 1/8	21 6/8	22 1/8	17 5/8	5	5	Jackson County	IL	Dave Yearian	1979	2,620
144 1/8	25 0/8	25 7/8	16 0/8	4	5	Vinton County	OH	Randy Fee	1981	2,620
144 1/8	23 7/8	23 1/8	19 1/8	4	4	Defiance County	OH	Alan Stark	1981	2,620
144 1/8	21 1/8	21 0/8	17 1/8	5	5	Maverick County	TX	Dean Oatman	1982	2,620
144 1/8	22 3/8	21 6/8	14 7/8	7	7	Calumet County	WI	Myron E. Jochmann	1982	2,620
144 1/8	26 3/8	26 0/8	20 3/8	3	4	Charles County	MD	Fred Dolinger	1982	2,620
144 1/8	21 1/8	21 6/8	17 0/8	7	7	Pittsburg County	OK	Brett Jones	1984	2,620
144 1/8	23 1/8	22 7/8	19 4/8	5	4	Des Moines County	IA	Ray Waschkat	1985	2,620
144 1/8	22 6/8	22 4/8	17 1/8	5	5	Woodbury County	IA	Ritch A. Stolpe	1985	2,620
144 1/8	24 7/8	24 3/8	20 3/8	4	4	Berkeley County	SC	Hugh Gaskins	1986	2,620
144 1/8	25 3/8	25 1/8	19 5/8	5	4	Shawnee County	KS	Steve Deever	1986	2,620
144 1/8	20 7/8	20 2/8	16 2/8	6	5	Hampshire County	MA	Larry Davis	1986	2,620
144 1/8	22 2/8	23 2/8	17 2/8	6	7	Hughes County	OK	Randy Fletcher	1987	2,620
144 1/8	21 6/8	22 1/8	17 0/8	5	6	Pepin County	WI	Joe Weiss	1987	2,620
144 1/8	24 4/8	22 0/8	17 3/8	6	6	Benton County	MO	Curtis A. Powell	1988	2,620
144 1/8	23 1/8	23 7/8	19 3/8	5	5	Montgomery County	IL	Mark Everett	1988	2,620
144 1/8	21 7/8	22 2/8	17 5/8	5	6	Kenedy County	TX	Pink Atkins	1988	2,620
144 1/8	26 2/8	26 0/8	16 6/8	4	5	Surry County	VA	William Allen Rickmond	1989	2,620
144 1/8	22 1/8	23 4/8	19 7/8	5	5	Marinette County	WI	Chuck Gerbenskey	1989	2,620
144 1/8	25 3/8	24 4/8	19 3/8	5	4	Hennepin County	MN	Ken Fluck	1989	2,620
144 1/8	23 4/8	23 7/8	16 1/8	7	7	Blue Earth County	MN	Terry R. Wehr	1989	2,620
144 1/8	23 1/8	22 7/8	13 3/8	5	5	Hood County	TX	Mike Searles	1990	2,620
144 1/8	25 0/8	24 1/8	20 7/8	4	4	Ferry County	WA	Don Ohman, Jr.	1990	2,620
144 1/8	24 1/8	23 7/8	17 1/8	6	5	Benton County	MO	Kelly Collins	1990	2,620
144 1/8	22 7/8	23 1/8	15 1/8	6	6	Cedar County	IA	Ron Peterson	1991	2,620
144 1/8	24 0/8	24 2/8	16 6/8	6	6	Hopkins County	KY	Randy Slinger	1991	2,620
144 1/8	21 6/8	22 2/8	14 5/8	5	5	Hendricks County	IN	Chester D. Aiduks	1991	2,620
144 1/8	25 1/8	25 5/8	16 5/8	4	4	Iron County	WI	Daniel J. Van Oss	1991	2,620
144 1/8	25 4/8	26 3/8	17 4/8	6	5	Scotland County	MO	Jim Johnson	1991	2,620
144 1/8	25 6/8	25 6/8	19 7/8	6	5	Leduc	ALB	Floyd Brunes	1992	2,620
144 1/8	22 7/8	19 2/8	21 5/8	5	5	Marquette County	WI	Dennis P. Gohlke	1992	2,620
144 0/8	21 4/8	22 0/8	16 6/8	5	5	Adams County	IL	Gerald Morton	1963	2,653
144 0/8	22 4/8	23 0/8	18 6/8	5	5	Fayette County	IA	Kenneth Durnin	1971	2,653
144 0/8	24 4/8	23 5/8	17 6/8	5	4	Wayne County	WV	Eddie Mullins	1976	2,653
144 0/8	23 4/8	24 0/8	17 2/8	5	5	Hocking County	OH	Greg Bonecutter, Sr.	1979	2,653
144 0/8	23 2/8	23 3/8	18 4/8	5	5	Lee County	AL	George P. Mann	1979	2,653
144 0/8	24 2/8	24 4/8	18 4/8	5	4	Murray County	MN	Alan Metz	1979	2,653
144 0/8	23 5/8	24 4/8	18 6/8	4	4	Juneau County	WI	Kelly Urban	1980	2,653
144 0/8	25 6/8	25 6/8	17 5/8	4	5	Jackson County	OH	Thomas Hart	1981	2,653

SCORE	LENGTH OF MAIN BEAM		INSIDE SPREAD	NUMBER OF POINTS		AREA	STATE/ PROVINCE	HUNTER'S NAME	DATE	RANK
	R	L		R	L					
144 0/8	22 4/8	22 3/8	18 2/8	5	5	Logan County	OH	Mark A. Payne	1981	2,653
144 0/8	22 0/8	22 1/8	21 7/8	7	8	Hennepin County	MN	Clarence D. Huls	1984	2,653
144 0/8	23 5/8	23 6/8	19 2/8	6	4	Franklin County	KS	J. R. Oshel	1985	2,653
144 0/8	23 6/8	24 2/8	18 4/8	5	6	Monmouth County	NJ	Cliff Underwood	1985	2,653
144 0/8	23 7/8	23 2/8	19 0/8	5	5	Lewis & Clark County	MT	Sonny Templeton	1985	2,653
144 0/8	23 7/8	23 0/8	18 0/8	5	5	Hubbard County	MN	Tim Leeseberg	1985	2,653
144 0/8	25 7/8	24 7/8	17 6/8	4	4	Union County	SD	Derrall Minor	1987	2,653
144 0/8	22 4/8	22 0/8	17 3/8	5	7	Mercer County	ND	Chris S. Hadland	1988	2,653
144 0/8	24 0/8	23 6/8	18 4/8	4	5	Lycoming County	PA	Peter Salamone	1988	2,653
144 0/8	22 4/8	24 7/8	17 2/8	5	5	Kane County	IL	Kurt J. Bird	1988	2,653
144 0/8	22 4/8	23 6/8	16 6/8	4	4	Starke County	IN	Daniel H. Chaney	1989	2,653
144 0/8	23 4/8	23 6/8	17 4/8	5	5	Du Page County	IL	Richard Maish	1989	2,653
144 0/8	25 6/8	26 2/8	16 0/8	6	6	Kankakee County	IL	Al Weissbohn	1989	2,653
144 0/8	24 7/8	24 6/8	17 2/8	4	5	Yellow Medicine County	MN	Brent Hassel	1990	2,653
144 0/8	22 5/8	22 5/8	16 7/8	7	6	Stark County	ND	Howard Sharpe	1990	2,653
144 0/8	24 1/8	25 0/8	18 6/8	5	4	Fulton County	OH	Mike Krasny	1990	2,653
144 0/8	24 5/8	24 0/8	19 0/8	4	5	Wapello County	IA	Dave D. Young	1990	2,653
144 0/8	26 4/8	25 2/8	17 1/8	6	5	Stokes County	NC	Phillip D. Ring	1991	2,653
144 0/8	24 5/8	24 6/8	18 0/8	5	5	McHenry County	IL	Ray Kraeplin	1991	2,653
144 0/8	22 4/8	22 4/8	15 0/8	5	5	Patrick County	VA	Ricky D. Boyd	1991	2,653
143 7/8	21 5/8	22 2/8	15 7/8	5	5	Oktibbeha County	MS	Frank Cascio, Jr.	1978	2,681
143 7/8	22 5/8	21 6/8	14 7/8	6	5	Traverse County	MN	Gary Anderson	1980	2,681
143 7/8	23 1/8	23 0/8	19 1/8	4	5	White County	IN	Richard Zaring	1980	2,681
143 7/8	27 3/8	26 2/8	19 0/8	5	6	Erie County	NY	Mark A. Bennett	1981	2,681
143 7/8	22 1/8	23 1/8	17 3/8	5	5	Taylor County	WI	Tony Kliscz	1981	2,681
143 7/8	28 6/8	26 3/8	21 1/8	4	5	Ross County	OH	Jack F. Hatton	1982	2,681
143 7/8	24 1/8	23 0/8	17 7/8	6	5	Morrill County	NE	Gerry Hrasky	1983	2,681
143 7/8	20 4/8	20 3/8	15 3/8	5	5	Macon County	AL	George P. Mann	1984	2,681
143 7/8	24 3/8	23 2/8	19 1/8	7	7	Allegheny County	PA	Richard J. Kudranski	1985	2,681
143 7/8	23 4/8	23 5/8	17 5/8	5	5	Ashland County	WI	Neal Turney	1987	2,681
143 7/8	26 0/8	26 3/8	21 4/8	7	7	Clinton County	MI	Louie Mrazek	1987	2,681
143 7/8	25 5/8	24 2/8	15 7/8	4	4	St. Croix County	WI	Robert K. Weaver	1987	2,681
143 7/8	21 2/8	21 6/8	15 5/8	5	5	Allamakee County	IA	Gary P. Cole	1987	2,681
143 7/8	23 6/8	23 5/8	21 5/8	5	5	La Salle County	IL	Gary Tabor	1987	2,681
143 7/8	21 4/8	22 4/8	18 3/8	5	5	Iroquois County	IL	Jerry Putnam	1987	2,681
143 7/8	23 4/8	24 5/8	17 4/8	5	8	Camden County	MO	John Cartwright	1989	2,681
143 7/8	22 7/8	22 5/8	18 3/8	6	6	Monroe County	WI	Chuck Underberg	1989	2,681
143 7/8	22 6/8	22 2/8	16 3/8	5	5	Hamilton County	IN	Scott Griffin	1990	2,681
143 7/8	23 5/8	22 0/8	17 7/8	5	5	Olmsted County	MN	Steven Laudon	1990	2,681
143 7/8	27 4/8	26 6/8	21 1/8	5	4	Bartholomew County	IN	James W. Smith	1990	2,681
143 7/8	26 2/8	24 6/8	17 5/8	6	4	Winnebago County	IL	Mark P. Stock	1990	2,681
143 7/8	24 3/8	24 5/8	16 3/8	5	5	Custer County	NE	Dan Dowse	1991	2,681
143 7/8	25 6/8	25 4/8	22 5/8	4	4	Calhoun County	MI	Greg H. St. John	1991	2,681
143 7/8	24 0/8	24 2/8	17 7/8	4	4	Porter County	IN	James Frahm	1991	2,681
143 7/8	24 5/8	23 4/8	17 2/8	6	7	DeKalb County	IL	Jim Zielinski	1992	2,681
143 6/8	22 3/8	21 0/8	18 6/8	6	10	Ionia County	MI	Bob Jones	1966	2,706
143 6/8	23 7/8	23 4/8	19 0/8	4	5	Iron County	WI	Lee C. Dix	1968	2,706
143 6/8	21 1/8	21 1/8	17 2/8	7	6	McHenry County	ND	William J. Berg	1978	2,706
143 6/8	20 7/8	21 2/8	15 2/8	6	5	Sabine County	TX	Max L. Turner	1982	2,706
143 6/8	23 0/8	21 3/8	17 4/8	5	5	Oneida County	WI	Pat Abraham	1983	2,706
143 6/8	24 6/8	26 1/8	24 1/8	4	6	Isanti County	MN	Donald Vandermey	1985	2,706
143 6/8	24 4/8	25 2/8	21 2/8	6	4	Shawnee County	KS	Kevin Hogan	1985	2,706
143 6/8	23 3/8	23 2/8	18 6/8	5	5	Ottawa County	OK	Ed Hammons	1986	2,706
143 6/8	24 7/8	25 4/8	19 2/8	5	5	Belmont County	OH	Tony Abranovic, Jr.	1986	2,706
143 6/8	23 1/8	23 1/8	17 0/8	5	5	Jackson County	OH	Randy Moore	1986	2,706
143 6/8	22 2/8	23 2/8	15 4/8	5	6	Platte County	NE	Brad Marler	1987	2,706
143 6/8	25 0/8	24 5/8	18 6/8	5	8	Washington County	MN	Scott Gerry	1987	2,706
143 6/8	25 0/8	24 4/8	18 2/8	7	7	Butler County	KS	Claude Allen	1987	2,706
143 6/8	27 0/8	27 3/8	23 3/8	5	5	Fairfax County	VA	Larry C. Sherertz	1987	2,706
143 6/8	24 5/8	23 6/8	18 0/8	6	6	Chester County	PA	Steve Thais	1987	2,706
143 6/8	22 7/8	24 7/8	18 2/8	4	5	Cloud County	KS	Gerald Dockins	1991	2,706
143 6/8	23 7/8	23 2/8	21 5/8	5	5	Clay County	MN	Bill Lunden	1992	2,706
143 6/8	24 4/8	23 7/8	18 1/8	6	5	Kleberg County	TX	Tom Winn	1992	2,706
143 5/8	22 5/8	23 4/8	17 4/8	6	4	Washington County	MN	Keith Christensen	1975	2,724
143 5/8	23 5/8	23 5/8	17 3/8	5	6	Neosha County	KS	Hugh B. Woolard	1976	2,724
143 5/8	23 2/8	23 5/8	15 7/8	5	6	Polk County	WI	Ron Simmons	1977	2,724
143 5/8	23 3/8	22 4/8	18 6/8	6	8	Houston County	MN	Arden M. Schock	1980	2,724
143 5/8	25 0/8	24 7/8	17 5/8	5	4	Miami County	OH	Philip C. Gudorf	1982	2,724
143 5/8	24 5/8	24 5/8	19 5/8	4	4	Vinton County	OH	Robert Irwin Bazell	1982	2,724
143 5/8	23 7/8	22 7/8	19 7/8	5	5	Randolph County	WV	Charles Byrd	1982	2,724

SCORE	LENGTH OF R MAIN BEAM L		INSIDE SPREAD	NUMBER OF R POINTS L		AREA	STATE/ PROVINCE	HUNTER'S NAME	DATE	RANK
143 5/8	23 6/8	23 4/8	15 3/8	5	5	Union County	OR	Kim Tameris	1983	2,724
143 5/8	23 7/8	23 5/8	18 3/8	6	5	Blue Earth County	MN	LeRoy Urban	1983	2,724
143 5/8	22 1/8	22 7/8	20 1/8	5	5	Carroll County	IL	Art Heinze	1984	2,724
143 5/8	20 1/8	20 6/8	16 4/8	6	6	Pine County	MN	Mike Stauty	1984	2,724
143 5/8	25 1/8	23 6/8	16 3/8	7	8	Fayette County	IA	Roger DeKok	1985	2,724
143 5/8	23 4/8	24 4/8	20 1/8	4	4	Pike County	IL	Rick L. Rodhouse	1986	2,724
143 5/8	23 4/8	23 7/8	18 3/8	6	5	Bremer County	IA	Tom Markussen	1986	2,724
143 5/8	23 4/8	22 2/8	17 1/8	5	6	Itasca County	MN	Tom Meyer	1987	2,724
143 5/8	22 4/8	23 6/8	17 1/8	5	5	Dane County	WI	Tom Isaac	1987	2,724
143 5/8	24 5/8	25 1/8	17 2/8	6	6	Van Buren County	IA	Jim Francois	1988	2,724
143 5/8	23 0/8	23 0/8	19 7/8	4	5	Mahaska County	IA	David Walker, Sr.	1988	2,724
143 5/8	22 3/8	22 0/8	18 5/8	6	5	Mingo County	WV	Jerry W. Sammons	1988	2,724
143 5/8	23 4/8	23 5/8	17 3/8	5	5	Tompkins	SAS	Clarence R Hughes	1989	2,724
143 5/8	21 6/8	21 4/8	17 1/8	4	4	Reno County	KS	Robert Williams	1989	2,724
143 5/8	22 5/8	22 3/8	15 3/8	5	5	Isanti County	MN	Greg Seymour	1989	2,724
143 5/8	24 2/8	24 2/8	17 2/8	5	6	Grand Traverse County	MI	Bill Alpers	1990	2,724
143 5/8	23 5/8	24 2/8	19 7/8	5	5	Wright County	MN	Nick Daleiden	1991	2,724
143 5/8	22 3/8	22 3/8	20 3/8	4	4	Harrison County	OH	Brent Heavilin	1991	2,724
143 5/8	21 0/8	21 1/8	19 6/8	6	6	Monroe County	OH	Darby A. Bender, Jr.	1991	2,724
143 5/8	19 4/8	19 6/8	17 3/8	5	5	Tazewell County	IL	Jim Plemmons	1991	2,724
143 5/8	25 0/8	24 4/8	17 5/8	6	5	St. Croix County	WI	Tom Jensen	1992	2,724
143 4/8	23 7/8	23 0/8	20 0/8	5	7	Traverse County	MN	Roland L. Hausmann	1958	2,752
143 4/8	22 5/8	22 7/8	21 4/8	6	6	Ellis County	KS	Lee Couture	1969	2,752
143 4/8	24 3/8	25 0/8	17 2/8	5	5	Miami County	KS	Fred Supulver	1969	2,752
143 4/8	23 0/8	22 4/8	16 6/8	5	6	Sheboygan County	WI	Gary Mueller	1971	2,752
143 4/8	23 4/8	22 1/8	18 4/8	5	5	Saginaw County	MI	Dorm Haskins	1978	2,752
143 4/8	23 5/8	22 7/8	19 2/8	4	5	Belmont County	OH	Fred Holub	1980	2,752
143 4/8	23 4/8	24 0/8	17 2/8	6	5	Cherokee County	KS	Brett Thomas	1981	2,752
143 4/8	24 5/8	23 3/8	17 0/8	5	5	St. Clair County	MI	Art Brown	1981	2,752
143 4/8	24 2/8	24 4/8	17 6/8	5	6	Pike County	OH	Billy Ray Jenkins	1981	2,752
143 4/8	24 0/8	23 5/8	17 6/8	4	4	Finney County	KS	Wilferd Nichols	1981	2,752
143 4/8	23 6/8	23 1/8	18 2/8	7	5	Winona County	MN	Jim Keim	1982	2,752
143 4/8	23 6/8	23 1/8	18 6/8	4	4	Stafford County	KS	Larry Hoffman	1982	2,752
143 4/8	22 4/8	22 5/8	18 4/8	6	5	Huntingdon County	PA	John A. Williams	1984	2,752
143 4/8	24 4/8	23 7/8	17 6/8	5	5	Otter Tail County	MN	Ross R Grothe	1984	2,752
143 4/8	25 5/8	25 6/8	17 2/8	7	6	Sheboygan County	WI	Randy Mavis	1985	2,752
143 4/8	24 6/8	24 7/8	21 0/8	4	5	Logan County	IL	Mark E. Humbert	1985	2,752
143 4/8	23 3/8	25 4/8	19 0/8	6	4	Clayton County	IA	Paul 'Buck' Farni, Jr.	1986	2,752
143 4/8	24 6/8	24 4/8	18 2/8	5	5	Henderson County	IL	Steve Fausel	1986	2,752
143 4/8	23 1/8	23 5/8	18 0/8	5	5	Lafayette County	WI	James D. Beau	1987	2,752
143 4/8	21 1/8	22 6/8	18 6/8	5	5	Blue Earth County	MN	Larry Tapper	1987	2,752
143 4/8	26 2/8	27 2/8	18 4/8	4	4	Anoka County	MN	Dean Leshovsky	1988	2,752
143 4/8	23 3/8	23 2/8	17 4/8	5	4	La Salle County	IL	Gene Brandolino	1988	2,752
143 4/8	22 4/8	22 7/8	16 3/8	7	7	Clay County	IA	Charles Norgaard	1988	2,752
143 4/8	22 6/8	22 6/8	16 0/8	5	5	Lewis County	WV	Clyde Moses	1988	2,752
143 4/8	24 4/8	24 3/8	19 2/8	5	5	Westchester County	NY	George R. Newman	1988	2,752
143 4/8	24 2/8	22 5/8	18 2/8	5	5	Greene County	IL	Leonard R. Walters	1988	2,752
143 4/8	22 6/8	22 3/8	19 0/8	6	5	Elk County	KS	Lance McIntosh	1988	2,752
143 4/8	24 2/8	23 3/8	17 5/8	6	5	Pottawatomie County	OK	Jerry Braziel	1988	2,752
143 4/8	21 6/8	22 6/8	20 4/8	4	5	Baltimore County	MD	William F. Smeltzer	1989	2,752
143 4/8	24 5/8	26 0/8	19 6/8	5	5	Winnebago County	IL	Andy L. Ballinger	1989	2,752
143 4/8	23 5/8	24 0/8	20 2/8	6	5	Andrew County	MO	Bill Wolf, Jr.	1990	2,752
143 4/8	21 3/8	22 3/8	16 2/8	5	6	Will County	IL	James Kamenjarin	1991	2,752
143 4/8	23 6/8	23 3/8	17 2/8	4	4	Pike County	MO	Henry F. Benson, Jr.	1991	2,752
143 4/8	25 1/8	23 6/8	19 0/8	6	6	Rusk County	WI	Ron Welch	1991	2,752
143 4/8	22 4/8	22 4/8	15 0/8	6	6	Madison County	IA	Scott Creger	1991	2,752
143 4/8	21 6/8	21 5/8	19 2/8	5	6	Houghton County	MI	Randy Hinton	1992	2,752
143 3/8	25 0/8	23 6/8	16 3/8	6	5	Otter Tail County	MN	J. P. Maurins	1956	2,788
143 3/8	23 0/8	23 1/8	15 7/8	5	5	Comanche County	OK	Kenneth D. Cook	1971	2,788
143 3/8	22 2/8	22 0/8	17 2/8	7	7	Morrison County	MN	Glen Marklowitz	1972	2,788
143 3/8	22 3/8	22 4/8	20 1/8	4	6	Allamakee County	IA	Jim Schmidt	1974	2,788
143 3/8	24 1/8	25 2/8	17 1/8	5	5	Cass County	MN	Richard J. Schabert	1977	2,788
143 3/8	27 0/8	26 0/8	20 1/8	4	4	Charles County	MD	John Allen Williams	1980	2,788
143 3/8	24 1/8	24 0/8	15 5/8	4	5	Saginaw County	MI	Paul Mickey	1981	2,788
143 3/8	22 0/8	23 4/8	19 0/8	8	8	Pike County	IL	Steve Carlen	1982	2,788
143 3/8	24 1/8	23 7/8	17 5/8	5	5	Green County	WI	B. Duane Byrne	1984	2,788
143 3/8	23 6/8	24 3/8	18 1/8	4	4	Ogle County	IL	Dr. Juanito E. Delfinado	1984	2,788
143 3/8	25 3/8	24 7/8	19 1/8	4	4	Norman County	MN	Bryan Mickelson	1985	2,788
143 3/8	22 7/8	24 2/8	17 7/8	4	4	Walworth County	WI	Gary Jordan	1985	2,788
143 3/8	18 6/8	21 0/8	16 3/8	5	5	Slope County	ND	Jack Lefor	1985	2,788

SCORE	LENGTH OF R MAIN BEAM L		INSIDE SPREAD	NUMBER OF R POINTS L		AREA	STATE/ PROVINCE	HUNTER'S NAME	DATE	RANK
143 3/8	24 0/8	23 6/8	22 2/8	5	6	Pennington County	MN	John A. Monroe	1986	2,788
143 3/8	22 6/8	22 2/8	20 6/8	6	4	Clayton County	IA	Francis Winter	1986	2,788
143 3/8	23 0/8	23 6/8	20 1/8	5	5	Green County	WI	Ernie V. Hutchinson	1986	2,788
143 3/8	22 1/8	22 2/8	15 7/8	5	6	Adams County	WI	Danny C. Winchester	1988	2,788
143 3/8	23 2/8	22 3/8	19 1/8	5	6	Du Page County	IL	Joseph Keim	1988	2,788
143 3/8	24 6/8	25 0/8	17 3/8	7	5	Pierce County	WI	Daniel D. Kern	1988	2,788
143 3/8	22 0/8	22 5/8	18 3/8	5	5	Greene County	IL	Mark Petersen	1988	2,788
143 3/8	21 3/8	22 3/8	17 1/8	5	7	Dodge County	WI	Jim Bauer	1989	2,788
143 3/8	22 5/8	22 1/8	18 1/8	5	5	Burlington County	NJ	Raymond Woodruff	1989	2,788
143 3/8	24 4/8	25 0/8	19 3/8	4	4	Mills County	IA	John Bantz	1989	2,788
143 3/8	23 6/8	23 5/8	20 1/8	5	4	Lake County	IL	John Roscop	1989	2,788
143 3/8	25 4/8	27 4/8	19 5/8	4	4	Montgomery County	PA	Charlie Haydt	1990	2,788
143 3/8	23 4/8	24 4/8	17 4/8	4	5	Gibson County	IN	Steve Feller	1990	2,788
143 3/8	25 2/8	25 1/8	20 5/8	4	6	Caledon Township	ONT	Carl Whittier	1990	2,788
143 3/8	24 5/8	24 3/8	16 7/8	4	4	Morris County	NJ	Geoffrey Stewart	1991	2,788
143 3/8	22 7/8	23 4/8	19 5/8	4	5	Adams County	WI	Michael E. Rykiel	1991	2,788
143 3/8	21 7/8	20 6/8	15 7/8	5	5	Burleigh County	ND	Ron Geffre	1991	2,788
143 2/8	25 0/8	24 0/8	16 6/8	5	6	Phillips County	AR	Stanley Zellner	1964	2,818
143 2/8	25 0/8	23 7/8	19 4/8	5	5	Geauga County	OH	Rudy Grecar	1971	2,818
143 2/8	26 0/8	25 0/8	17 4/8	8	7	Comanche County	OK	Lloyd Payne III	1976	2,818
143 2/8	25 2/8	26 1/8	18 4/8	4	4	Monroe County	IN	Mike Webb	1977	2,818
143 2/8	22 0/8	23 1/8	16 0/8	5	5	Fond du Lac County	WI	Jim Rickmeyer	1979	2,818
143 2/8	25 4/8	25 0/8	19 2/8	5	5	Price County	WI	Todd R. Sorensen	1981	2,818
143 2/8	24 6/8	25 0/8	18 4/8	5	5	Marion County	TN	Larry Gravitt	1981	2,818
143 2/8	21 7/8	21 6/8	18 4/8	5	5	Jefferson County	MT	Bob Peterson	1983	2,818
143 2/8	24 2/8	24 6/8	16 2/8	5	6	Green County	WI	Wellington W. Wert	1983	2,818
143 2/8	24 3/8	24 3/8	20 0/8	4	4	Edgar County	IL	Benton B. Caldwell	1983	2,818
143 2/8	23 2/8	23 3/8	13 4/8	5	5	Hardin County	IA	Rick McDowell	1983	2,818
143 2/8	24 5/8	23 4/8	19 0/8	5	4	Fairfield County	OH	Gary Lockwood	1984	2,818
143 2/8	23 2/8	22 4/8	18 7/8	5	6	Winona County	MN	Bill Clink	1984	2,818
143 2/8	24 3/8	24 6/8	15 6/8	6	6	Cooper County	MO	Vaughn Sell	1985	2,818
143 2/8	26 0/8	25 6/8	21 4/8	5	4	Montgomery County	MD	Bobby Ray Waters	1985	2,818
143 2/8	23 4/8	23 3/8	16 6/8	5	5	Warren County	IA	Lanny Caligiuri	1985	2,818
143 2/8	22 3/8	22 4/8	19 0/8	5	5	Washington County	MN	Ronald H. Krienke	1986	2,818
143 2/8	24 3/8	24 2/8	20 6/8	4	4	Greene County	AR	Danny J. Walker	1986	2,818
143 2/8	23 5/8	25 1/8	16 4/8	4	4	Sumner County	KS	Robert E. Daley	1986	2,818
143 2/8	23 1/8	23 5/8	18 6/8	6	5	Union County	SD	Larry Minter	1987	2,818
143 2/8	26 6/8	25 0/8	18 6/8	5	6	Spokane County	WA	Paul Fisher	1988	2,818
143 2/8	23 3/8	23 2/8	15 4/8	6	6	Butler County	OH	Robert G. Banks, Jr.	1988	2,818
143 2/8	23 1/8	22 5/8	16 6/8	6	5	Jackson County	MI	John R. Ahrens	1988	2,818
143 2/8	23 0/8	23 2/8	17 0/8	5	5	Lawrence County	KY	Michael Hatfield	1988	2,818
143 2/8	24 0/8	24 1/8	21 0/8	5	4	Hamilton County	OH	George Robert Freudiger	1988	2,818
143 2/8	21 7/8	22 2/8	17 2/8	5	5	Hancock County	IL	David Lee Sanderson	1988	2,818
143 2/8	24 2/8	25 2/8	21 4/8	5	4	Hamilton County	OH	John L. Cox	1989	2,818
143 2/8	24 4/8	23 4/8	22 2/8	4	4	Montcalm County	MI	Rickey P. Allen	1989	2,818
143 2/8	21 4/8	21 4/8	16 5/8	6	6	Defiance County	OH	Stanley Knittle	1989	2,818
143 2/8	22 5/8	22 4/8	18 0/8	5	4	Goodhue County	MN	Michael Schmidt	1990	2,818
143 2/8	22 4/8	21 2/8	17 0/8	6	5	Norton County	KS	Larry R. Hillman	1990	2,818
143 2/8	23 0/8	23 1/8	17 6/8	5	5	Greene County	OH	Richard McClelland	1990	2,818
143 2/8	26 5/8	26 6/8	19 6/8	6	6	Will County	IL	Chad Elumbaugh	1990	2,818
143 2/8	23 6/8	22 6/8	14 0/8	6	5	Licking County	OH	Thomas E. Lott	1991	2,818
143 2/8	21 1/8	22 0/8	16 4/8	5	5	Kleberg County	TX	Johnnie R. Walters	1991	2,818
143 2/8	22 5/8	23 4/8	17 3/8	8	7	Richland County	WI	Ronald S. Pulcine	1991	2,818
143 2/8	22 1/8	24 3/8	17 7/8	6	5	Iowa County	IA	Thomas Dvorak	1991	2,818
143 1/8	23 0/8	23 2/8	17 1/8	5	4	Graham County	KS	Russell Hull	1965	2,855
143 1/8	21 7/8	23 2/8	21 5/8	5	5	Linn County	IA	Tom Postel	1979	2,855
143 1/8	21 2/8	22 7/8	18 3/8	6	7	Lincoln County	MN	David J. Rouge	1981	2,855
143 1/8	22 6/8	22 1/8	18 6/8	6	5	Barry County	MI	Jay W. Gaston	1981	2,855
143 1/8	21 6/8	21 2/8	19 5/8	6	6	Holmes County	OH	Dale R. Kaufman	1983	2,855
143 1/8	22 5/8	22 4/8	19 5/8	5	5	Missoula County	MT	Greg Munther	1983	2,855
143 1/8	20 6/8	20 3/8	18 7/8	6	6	Olmsted County	MN	Brian Veloske	1984	2,855
143 1/8	24 6/8	25 4/8	17 7/8	6	7	Riley County	KS	Kenneth W. Lynch	1985	2,855
143 1/8	22 2/8	22 1/8	15 7/8	5	5	Washburn County	WI	Michael Elliot	1986	2,855
143 1/8	23 0/8	23 2/8	20 0/8	7	5	Iowa County	WI	Brad Burbach	1986	2,855
143 1/8	25 0/8	22 2/8	20 1/8	6	5	Crawford County	WI	John Becwar	1987	2,855
143 1/8	24 1/8	23 2/8	19 2/8	6	5	Cherry County	NE	Gary Galloway	1987	2,855
143 1/8	24 0/8	23 2/8	17 3/8	7	5	Shawnee County	KS	William A. Konrade	1987	2,855
143 1/8	24 1/8	22 2/8	22 5/8	4	4	Montcalm County	MI	A. Gene Higginson	1987	2,855
143 1/8	24 3/8	24 2/8	20 3/8	5	5	Clayton County	IA	Albert A. Weidenbacher	1987	2,855
143 1/8	23 6/8	24 6/8	21 1/8	4	4	Le Sueur County	MN	Randall Mathwig	1988	2,855

SCORE	LENGTH OF MAIN BEAM		INSIDE SPREAD	NUMBER OF POINTS		AREA	STATE/ PROVINCE	HUNTER'S NAME	DATE	RANK
	R	L		R	L					
143 1/8	23 0/8	21 7/8	14 7/8	5	5	Ripley County	IN	Van R. Craft	1988	2,855
143 1/8	24 7/8	24 6/8	19 7/8	5	4	Fairfax County	VA	Kevin R. Lake	1989	2,855
143 1/8	22 7/8	23 5/8	17 5/8	5	4	Piatt County	IL	David M. James	1991	2,855
143 1/8	25 5/8	25 7/8	19 3/8	7	6	Schuyler County	IL	John Johnston	1991	2,855
143 1/8	22 0/8	22 4/8	18 5/8	5	5	Crawford County	IL	Charlie Guyer	1991	2,855
143 1/8	22 5/8	22 2/8	16 0/8	6	6	Vilas County	WI	Frank E. Caroselli	1991	2,855
143 1/8	24 1/8	21 2/8	17 0/8	5	6	Lafayette County	WI	Todd Hanson	1991	2,855
143 1/8	22 4/8	23 0/8	19 5/8	5	5	Carter County	MT	Keith L. Folk	1992	2,855
143 0/8	23 5/8	22 0/8	19 4/8	5	5	Wright County	IA	Ronald Gorden	1958	2,879
143 0/8	24 0/8	24 5/8	20 5/8	5	5	Pope County	IL	Bob E. Sims	1964	2,879
143 0/8	25 4/8	21 0/8	14 6/8	5	6	Ottawa County	KS	Scotty Baugh	1967	2,879
143 0/8	22 7/8	21 7/8	16 2/8	5	5	Edwards County	KS	Gerald L. Schaller	1972	2,879
143 0/8	20 2/8	19 6/8	15 4/8	5	5	Madison County	IA	Larry L. Cavanaugh	1979	2,879
143 0/8	24 3/8	24 4/8	18 1/8	6	5	Black Hawk County	IA	Richard Minahan	1980	2,879
143 0/8	24 3/8	25 0/8	18 2/8	4	4	Sawyer County	WI	Steve Olson	1981	2,879
143 0/8	22 6/8	22 0/8	19 2/8	5	6	Henry County	VA	Mike Weaver	1981	2,879
143 0/8	20 5/8	20 5/8	15 4/8	5	5	Seward County	KS	Lynn Leonard	1983	2,879
143 0/8	22 1/8	23 0/8	17 4/8	5	6	Montgomery County	PA	Robert J. Bochnak	1983	2,879
143 0/8	24 6/8	23 1/8	22 0/8	6	5	Kankakee County	IL	Rick Renzi	1983	2,879
143 0/8	21 0/8	21 4/8	17 6/8	6	7	Des Moines County	IA	Tom Delaney	1985	2,879
143 0/8	23 2/8	23 5/8	19 5/8	5	4	La Salle County	IL	LeRoy W. Buckley, Jr.	1986	2,879
143 0/8	23 5/8	24 6/8	17 4/8	5	5	Alfalfa County	OK	David W. Dowell	1986	2,879
143 0/8	23 1/8	23 4/8	17 0/8	5	6	Sauk County	WI	Richard L. Kirkland	1987	2,879
143 0/8	20 3/8	21 1/8	18 2/8	6	5	Columbia County	WI	Howard H. Hill	1987	2,879
143 0/8	22 3/8	21 3/8	18 0/8	6	5	Missoula County	MT	Jon Cusker	1987	2,879
143 0/8	23 5/8	23 3/8	17 2/8	5	5	Fairfax County	VA	Harry R. Husch, Jr.	1988	2,879
143 0/8	22 6/8	24 0/8	18 0/8	5	5	Marathon County	WI	Mark Timken	1988	2,879
143 0/8	22 7/8	23 4/8	18 4/8	4	5	Bayfield County	WI	Wayne Zirn	1988	2,879
143 0/8	22 5/8	21 4/8	18 2/8	6	6	Licking County	OH	Stoney May	1988	2,879
143 0/8	24 4/8	25 0/8	17 2/8	5	5	Beltrami County	MN	Ross Campbell	1988	2,879
143 0/8	22 6/8	23 5/8	20 4/8	5	5	Montgomery County	MD	Richard H. Stabler	1989	2,879
143 0/8	23 1/8	24 1/8	17 4/8	4	4	Allen County	IN	Randy McIntosh	1989	2,879
143 0/8	23 6/8	22 2/8	17 2/8	6	6	Lee County	IA	Russell (Rusty) Robbins	1990	2,879
143 0/8	25 2/8	23 4/8	17 6/8	5	5	Christian County	KY	Gary Holbrook	1990	2,879
143 0/8	23 1/8	23 7/8	17 4/8	5	5	Watauga County	NC	Chris Carlton	1991	2,879
143 0/8	24 7/8	23 1/8	16 4/8	5	5	Dodge County	MN	Myles Keller	1991	2,879
143 0/8	24 6/8	24 3/8	17 0/8	5	5	Lincoln County	MO	Hugh Steavenson	1991	2,879
143 0/8	23 1/8	24 5/8	19 4/8	4	4	Jefferson County	OH	Joseph Daniel Nemitt	1991	2,879
143 0/8	23 1/8	23 2/8	19 0/8	5	5	Lafayette County	WI	Bradley D. Phillips	1991	2,879
142 7/8	20 4/8	20 6/8	16 3/8	5	5	Brown County	SD	Wayne Miller	1971	2,910
142 7/8	21 3/8	21 7/8	16 1/8	6	5	Becker County	MN	Kurt Lepping	1972	2,910
142 7/8	21 1/8	22 4/8	16 1/8	5	5	Jackson County	WI	Clark Gallup	1972	2,910
142 7/8	24 1/8	24 2/8	20 1/8	4	5	Douglas County	NE	Walter Ruff, Jr.	1973	2,910
142 7/8	26 2/8	25 6/8	22 7/8	4	4	Carroll County	IL	Donald Lauer	1978	2,910
142 7/8	21 0/8	23 5/8	19 6/8	6	5	Teton County	MT	Richard C. Semrad	1979	2,910
142 7/8	22 2/8	21 5/8	13 7/8	4	4	St. Louis County	MN	Dan Tanner	1979	2,910
142 7/8	22 7/8	23 0/8	17 1/8	5	6	Redwood County	MN	Kenneth A. Gilb	1980	2,910
142 7/8	22 0/8	23 2/8	18 1/8	4	5	Warren County	IA	Charly Stills	1980	2,910
142 7/8	25 2/8	25 2/8	18 3/8	5	6	Freeborn County	MN	Kermit Askland	1982	2,910
142 7/8	21 2/8	21 2/8	16 7/8	5	5	Richland County	MT	Dave McGough	1983	2,910
142 7/8	21 0/8	20 4/8	18 0/8	5	6	Jefferson County	NE	Bob Funke	1983	2,910
142 7/8	22 3/8	23 1/8	17 7/8	5	4	Shelby County	IL	David Russell	1983	2,910
142 7/8	23 6/8	23 1/8	16 3/8	5	5	Webster County	IA	Edward E. Ulicki	1984	2,910
142 7/8	24 4/8	25 5/8	21 1/8	4	4	Will County	IL	Terry Marcukaitis	1984	2,910
142 7/8	24 4/8	24 5/8	20 1/8	5	5	Marshall County	KS	Steve Johnson	1984	2,910
142 7/8	24 5/8	24 6/8	20 3/8	6	4	Lafayette County	WI	Larry Rose	1985	2,910
142 7/8	25 0/8	26 1/8	15 5/8	4	5	Clark County	IN	Steve Bower	1986	2,910
142 7/8	25 5/8	26 6/8	19 2/8	6	5	Florence County	WI	Dale T. Nixon	1988	2,910
142 7/8	22 3/8	24 1/8	19 2/8	7	9	Murray County	OK	Charles R. Sanford	1988	2,910
142 7/8	24 0/8	24 0/8	17 7/8	6	6	Cass County	MI	Randall Smith	1988	2,910
142 7/8	23 4/8	23 2/8	15 1/8	4	4	Atascosa County	TX	Gene Lasseter	1989	2,910
142 7/8	23 6/8	23 2/8	20 1/8	4	5	Jo Daviess County	IL	James F. Delaney	1989	2,910
142 7/8	23 1/8	24 3/8	17 3/8	5	6	Hardin County	OH	Mark Preston	1989	2,910
142 7/8	26 7/8	24 3/8	21 2/8	7	5	White County	IL	Peter P. Fiala	1990	2,910
142 7/8	22 3/8	22 4/8	16 5/8	5	5	Cedar County	NE	Cathy M. Tramp	1990	2,910
142 7/8	23 6/8	24 5/8	18 1/8	5	4	Crawford County	KS	Shawn Pipkin	1991	2,910
142 7/8	25 2/8	24 5/8	20 3/8	5	5	Holmes County	OH	Charles Larue	1991	2,910
142 7/8	24 1/8	23 1/8	17 5/8	8	5	Adams County	IL	Steve Cornwell	1991	2,910
142 7/8	24 3/8	24 3/8	18 2/8	7	6	Green County	WI	Steve J. Gobeli	1992	2,910
142 7/8	24 4/8	25 4/8	18 1/8	5	5	Zavala County	TX	Joseph D. Krout, III	1992	2,910

SCORE	LENGTH OF R MAIN BEAM L		INSIDE SPREAD	NUMBER OF R POINTS L		AREA	STATE/ PROVINCE	HUNTER'S NAME	DATE	RANK
142 6/8	23 5/8	23 0/8	19 5/8	4	5	Green Lake County	WI	Mark Novitske	1969	2,941
142 6/8	22 2/8	21 7/8	18 7/8	6	6	Douglas County	MN	David Koenen	1973	2,941
142 6/8	25 3/8	25 4/8	16 6/8	4	4	Darke County	OH	Wayne Goubeaux	1974	2,941
142 6/8	25 6/8	25 7/8	16 6/8	4	4	Prairie County	AR	John W. Hogue	1978	2,941
142 6/8	21 3/8	21 3/8	18 6/8	5	6	Empress	ALB	Alan R. Francis	1980	2,941
142 6/8	22 4/8	21 1/8	19 4/8	4	4	De Kalb County	MO	Mark Garr	1982	2,941
142 6/8	23 6/8	24 0/8	19 5/8	6	5	Jefferson County	WI	Jed Kottwitz	1983	2,941
142 6/8	24 2/8	23 7/8	19 2/8	6	5	Madison County	AL	Rocky Drake	1983	2,941
142 6/8	22 3/8	23 1/8	17 6/8	5	4	Clay County	KS	Larry Reed	1984	2,941
142 6/8	21 7/8	22 5/8	15 4/8	5	6	Lycoming County	PA	Kelly J. Cooper	1985	2,941
142 6/8	14 4/8	22 0/8	17 4/8	6	6	Waukesha County	WI	John Riehle	1985	2,941
142 6/8	22 0/8	22 1/8	17 2/8	5	5	Hamilton County	KS	Scott Showalter	1985	2,941
142 6/8	22 1/8	21 6/8	16 0/8	5	6	Cherokee County	TX	John Hall	1986	2,941
142 6/8	22 3/8	22 4/8	18 2/8	7	7	Lincoln County	MT	David R. Erickson	1987	2,941
142 6/8	23 5/8	23 3/8	15 4/8	6	6	Clayton County	IA	Scott W. Miller	1988	2,941
142 6/8	24 6/8	26 1/8	24 4/8	5	5	Oneida County	WI	Joseph Kwaterski	1988	2,941
142 6/8	20 5/8	21 0/8	16 4/8	6	5	Dodge County	NE	Mike Diers	1988	2,941
142 6/8	21 5/8	22 5/8	19 0/8	5	5	Woodford County	IL	Sid Schertz	1988	2,941
142 6/8	20 0/8	21 0/8	18 1/8	5	6	New Castle County	DE	Earl McSorley	1988	2,941
142 6/8	24 3/8	23 5/8	16 6/8	4	4	Saunders County	NE	Richard Cherovsky	1989	2,941
142 6/8	22 3/8	22 5/8	15 0/8	8	7	Cherokee County	OK	Monte Reid	1989	2,941
142 6/8	22 1/8	22 7/8	18 4/8	7	7	Price County	WI	Tom G. Verkilen	1989	2,941
142 6/8	23 5/8	23 5/8	16 6/8	5	5	Hancock County	IL	William T. Kirby	1989	2,941
142 6/8	21 3/8	22 0/8	20 6/8	7	9	Linn County	IA	Craig Cutts	1989	2,941
142 6/8	23 0/8	24 1/8	15 0/8	6	5	Tom Green County	TX	Ronnie Parsons	1990	2,941
142 6/8	23 2/8	24 3/8	15 4/8	5	5	Allegheny County	PA	David C. Williams	1990	2,941
142 6/8	24 1/8	23 6/8	16 2/8	5	5	Eau Claire County	WI	Riley Allen Fletschock	1990	2,941
142 6/8	23 1/8	23 2/8	18 6/8	6	5	Warren County	OH	Bruce Woods	1991	2,941
142 6/8	23 3/8	23 5/8	20 4/8	5	5	Outagamie County	WI	Joe P. DeBruin	1991	2,941
142 6/8	23 6/8	23 0/8	18 0/8	4	6	McLean County	IL	Eric B. Hill	1991	2,941
142 6/8	21 4/8	22 1/8	16 7/8	6	8	Ravalli County	MT	Melvin Harold Monson	1992	2,941
142 6/8	24 3/8	24 7/8	19 6/8	4	5	Saunders County	NE	William D. Meyers	1992	2,941
142 6/8	22 6/8	22 4/8	16 0/8	5	5	McCulloch County	TX	Cecil Carder	1992	2,941
142 5/8	24 2/8	22 7/8	15 5/8	5	5	Fleming County	KY	Dewey Miller	1976	2,974
142 5/8	22 2/8	22 3/8	18 5/8	5	5	Richland County	OH	Joey A. Garcia	1980	2,974
142 5/8	22 0/8	22 2/8	16 7/8	5	5	Chase County	KS	Lanny Deering	1981	2,974
142 5/8	25 6/8	25 4/8	16 4/8	4	6	Darke County	OH	Norbert D. Schlecty	1981	2,974
142 5/8	22 5/8	22 2/8	18 1/8	6	6	Waukesha County	WI	Mike Edlebeck	1982	2,974
142 5/8	24 7/8	24 1/8	18 1/8	5	5	Dane County	WI	Dean Stolen	1982	2,974
142 5/8	24 0/8	24 2/8	20 3/8	5	5	Cochrane	ALB	Kenneth Bills	1982	2,974
142 5/8	21 4/8	22 3/8	15 7/8	7	5	Pepin County	WI	James D. Williams	1984	2,974
142 5/8	22 6/8	22 5/8	20 3/8	5	4	Berkshire County	MA	Richard Scorzafava	1985	2,974
142 5/8	23 6/8	23 0/8	16 7/8	6	7	Stafford County	KS	Larry Hamby	1986	2,974
142 5/8	24 0/8	24 0/8	20 0/8	6	5	Page County	IA	Chris Barton	1987	2,974
142 5/8	22 5/8	23 6/8	16 3/8	6	8	Kossuth County	IA	Roger M. Batt	1987	2,974
142 5/8	25 1/8	24 1/8	18 5/8	4	4	Westchester County	NY	Kenneth Martin	1987	2,974
142 5/8	21 5/8	22 0/8	15 1/8	5	5	Will County	IL	Thomas J. Suggs	1987	2,974
142 5/8	22 3/8	23 0/8	17 0/8	7	6	Fairfield County	OH	Dean J. Kiourtsis	1988	2,974
142 5/8	23 1/8	20 4/8	18 7/8	5	5	Kalamazoo County	MI	Vern Kuipers	1988	2,974
142 5/8	25 4/8	25 3/8	17 7/8	4	4	Jackson County	IL	Dan Young	1988	2,974
142 5/8	25 3/8	24 5/8	19 1/8	5	5	Chickasaw County	IA	T. J. Colburn	1989	2,974
142 5/8	26 6/8	26 4/8	20 5/8	4	3	Scotland County	MO	John Emerson	1989	2,974
142 5/8	23 1/8	23 4/8	18 5/8	4	4	Parkland County	ALB	Sam Halabi	1990	2,974
142 5/8	26 7/8	26 2/8	17 6/8	8	7	Martin County	KY	James W. Howard	1990	2,974
142 5/8	22 0/8	23 0/8	16 0/8	6	5	Buffalo County	WI	Eric Matheson	1990	2,974
142 5/8	22 6/8	22 4/8	16 7/8	6	7	Will County	IL	Joseph E. Voltolina	1990	2,974
142 5/8	24 0/8	22 5/8	18 7/8	5	6	St. Joesph County	IN	Mike Ritter	1991	2,974
142 5/8	23 3/8	23 1/8	18 0/8	6	5	Vilas County	WI	Phil Dreger	1991	2,974
142 5/8	23 5/8	24 5/8	18 0/8	6	5	Mission Creek	BC	Colin L. Fazan	1991	2,974
142 5/8	26 3/8	26 1/8	18 7/8	5	5	Louisa County	IA	Jeff Sindt	1991	2,974
142 4/8	22 5/8	22 4/8	19 0/8	5	5	Newton County	IN	Jim Manes	1963	3,001
142 4/8	23 3/8	23 4/8	18 4/8	4	5	Winnebago County	IA	Duane Peterson	1966	3,001
142 4/8	22 0/8	21 1/8	14 6/8	6	6	Dunn County	WI	John J. Logan	1970	3,001
142 4/8	24 7/8	24 0/8	19 6/8	4	4	Ballard County	KY	Archie Jacobs	1977	3,001
142 4/8	24 7/8	24 3/8	19 3/8	6	5	Jackson County	IL	Mark A. Bollman	1979	3,001
142 4/8	23 3/8	22 6/8	17 0/8	5	5	Musselshell County	MT	Larry W. Ostermiller	1979	3,001
142 4/8	21 0/8	21 5/8	18 4/8	6	5	Jo Daviess County	IL	Kelly John Arnold	1981	3,001
142 4/8	24 2/8	24 3/8	20 6/8	5	5	Robertson County	KY	Glen Arnold	1981	3,001
142 4/8	23 5/8	24 1/8	15 6/8	5	5	Treasure County	MT	Scott Brockway	1981	3,001
142 4/8	21 0/8	20 6/8	16 3/8	5	6	Winona County	MN	Ron J. Parks	1981	3,001

SCORE	LENGTH OF MAIN BEAM		INSIDE SPREAD	NUMBER OF POINTS		AREA	STATE/ PROVINCE	HUNTER'S NAME	DATE	RANK
	R	L		R	L					
142 4/8	22 5/8	23 2/8	20 1/8	5	6	Murray County	MN	David Swanson	1983	3,001
142 4/8	22 0/8	22 2/8	14 6/8	5	5	McKenzie County	ND	David Tofte	1983	3,001
142 4/8	23 7/8	23 6/8	18 2/8	4	4	Bon Homme County	SD	Leon Somsen	1984	3,001
142 4/8	20 4/8	20 4/8	16 0/8	5	5	McLean County	ND	Curt Radke	1985	3,001
142 4/8	22 6/8	24 4/8	19 3/8	4	5	Lyon County	KS	Frank Mowdey	1986	3,001
142 4/8	24 7/8	25 0/8	19 3/8	5	5	Vilas County	WI	David Jablonski	1987	3,001
142 4/8	24 2/8	23 5/8	19 2/8	4	5	Jo Daviess County	IL	Brian Spillane	1988	3,001
142 4/8	20 4/8	20 3/8	16 6/8	5	5	Camrose	ALB	Dave Gerber	1988	3,001
142 4/8	25 4/8	25 6/8	17 5/8	5	5	Gallia County	OH	Alan Runyon	1988	3,001
142 4/8	23 0/8	24 6/8	18 3/8	6	6	Kingman County	KS	Ed Laverentz	1988	3,001
142 4/8	25 0/8	25 2/8	18 5/8	6	7	Bowman County	ND	Stan Chiras	1988	3,001
142 4/8	24 0/8	24 2/8	20 4/8	5	7	Shawnee County	KS	Randy Hildreth	1989	3,001
142 4/8	22 5/8	23 1/8	17 0/8	4	4	Crawford County	IL	Jim Sexton	1989	3,001
142 4/8	22 4/8	21 4/8	17 0/8	4	6	Dakota County	MN	Joseph Butler	1989	3,001
142 4/8	21 1/8	20 5/8	14 5/8	5	6	Hardin County	KY	Eugene Cotton	1990	3,001
142 4/8	23 7/8	23 0/8	17 4/8	5	5	Vilas County	WI	Dick Mutsch	1990	3,001
142 4/8	22 0/8	21 6/8	17 5/8	6	6	Adams County	WI	Mark Hoffman	1990	3,001
142 4/8	22 6/8	23 7/8	18 0/8	4	4	De Kalb County	GA	Michael Flowers	1990	3,001
142 4/8	24 3/8	24 5/8	18 6/8	5	5	Lincoln County	MO	Greg Grooms	1990	3,001
142 4/8	21 2/8	22 6/8	16 6/8	6	5	Wilkin County	MN	Brad Buth	1991	3,001
142 4/8	25 0/8	26 0/8	20 6/8	4	5	Charlevoix County	MI	Thomas B. Bacon	1991	3,001
142 4/8	21 0/8	21 4/8	17 5/8	5	5	Shawnee County	KS	Daniel L. Amspacker	1991	3,001
142 4/8	21 0/8	21 1/8	16 6/8	5	5	McHenry County	IL	Richard Tudor	1992	3,001
142 3/8	25 4/8	24 3/8	20 7/8	4	5	Mercer County	NJ	John K. Deveney	1975	3,034
142 3/8	21 5/8	21 5/8	15 1/8	5	5	Wapello County	IA	Larry Terrell	1977	3,034
142 3/8	23 4/8	22 4/8	18 1/8	5	5	Jersey County	IL	Jerry Cover	1979	3,034
142 3/8	22 0/8	21 6/8	16 7/8	5	4	Henry County	VA	Mike Weaver	1980	3,034
142 3/8	21 1/8	24 4/8	20 4/8	6	6	St. Charles County	MO	Edward J. Davidson	1980	3,034
142 3/8	22 5/8	22 0/8	18 1/8	5	5	Washtenaw County	MI	Philip John Maly	1983	3,034
142 3/8	21 4/8	22 5/8	17 5/8	6	7	Barton County	KS	Craig Doll	1984	3,034
142 3/8	20 6/8	21 0/8	17 5/8	5	5	Hardin County	TX	Mike Allen	1985	3,034
142 3/8	24 2/8	26 5/8	16 1/8	4	4	Wright County	MN	Donald J. Emons	1985	3,034
142 3/8	20 0/8	19 5/8	19 3/8	5	5	Shelby County	MO	Willard Otto	1985	3,034
142 3/8	24 6/8	23 5/8	19 1/8	4	4	Bremer County	IA	Dave Sullivan	1986	3,034
142 3/8	22 2/8	22 4/8	16 1/8	7	5	Wilson County	KS	Keith Jabben	1986	3,034
142 3/8	25 5/8	26 4/8	19 7/8	4	4	Benton County	IA	Ted Walton	1986	3,034
142 3/8	23 2/8	24 5/8	17 1/8	5	6	Muhlenberg County	KY	Kent Rhoads	1987	3,034
142 3/8	24 3/8	24 6/8	17 3/8	4	4	Kent County	MI	Frank J. Tusch	1987	3,034
142 3/8	22 6/8	25 2/8	15 6/8	5	6	Cumberland County	KY	Michael Groce	1987	3,034
142 3/8	20 4/8	20 3/8	17 0/8	6	6	Kenedy County	TX	Cal Adger	1988	3,034
142 3/8	22 4/8	22 4/8	17 3/8	5	5	St. Charles County	MO	Marty Marler	1988	3,034
142 3/8	23 0/8	24 2/8	16 5/8	5	6	Iron County	WI	Robert Peltonen	1988	3,034
142 3/8	23 2/8	23 2/8	17 2/8	8	6	Peoria County	IL	Larry Oppe	1988	3,034
142 3/8	22 6/8	24 6/8	18 2/8	6	6	Fairfield County	CT	Mitchell R. Ziemba	1988	3,034
142 3/8	23 3/8	23 2/8	16 1/8	4	4	Meade County	SD	Frank E. Virchow	1989	3,034
142 3/8	21 6/8	21 5/8	16 3/8	8	6	Osage County	KS	Mike VandeVord	1989	3,034
142 3/8	24 4/8	25 1/8	18 3/8	5	5	Knox County	IL	Brad Wunder	1990	3,034
142 3/8	22 5/8	23 2/8	16 3/8	5	5	Henderson County	TN	Pat Davis	1990	3,034
142 3/8	21 4/8	22 3/8	19 1/8	4	5	Monona County	IA	Patrick Salmen	1990	3,034
142 3/8	23 2/8	23 5/8	13 2/8	7	9	Allegheny County	PA	Paul W. Zoller	1991	3,034
142 3/8	24 5/8	24 4/8	16 6/8	7	7	De Witt County	IL	Jack Bray	1991	3,034
142 3/8	25 5/8	25 5/8	19 7/8	4	4	Hampshire County	MA	Eric Jalque	1991	3,034
142 3/8	22 4/8	22 7/8	16 7/8	4	5	Comal County	TX	Jim Butcher	1991	3,034
142 2/8	23 3/8	24 0/8	20 0/8	4	5	McLean County	ND	Robert Loftin	1959	3,064
142 2/8	23 2/8	22 6/8	17 6/8	5	6	Grant County	WI	Bob Woods	1962	3,064
142 2/8	21 1/8	22 2/8	18 1/8	6	4	Morrison County	MN	Dale Nieters	1971	3,064
142 2/8	21 2/8	21 1/8	17 1/8	6	5	Sabine County	TX	Norman D. Davis	1972	3,064
142 2/8	27 3/8	28 5/8	19 6/8	4	5	Harrison County	OH	Joe Cola	1976	3,064
142 2/8	24 3/8	23 7/8	19 6/8	4	4	Gallatin County	KY	Thomas W. Roberts	1976	3,064
142 2/8	24 1/8	24 1/8	17 0/8	6	5	Le Sueur County	MN	Gene Solyntjes	1976	3,064
142 2/8	22 4/8	23 6/8	19 0/8	7	5	Jones County	IA	Donald Bohlken	1978	3,064
142 2/8	21 7/8	21 0/8	17 0/8	6	6	Dodge County	MN	Myles Keller	1980	3,064
142 2/8	21 1/8	20 3/8	18 2/8	5	5	Edgar County	IL	Rory Steidl	1983	3,064
142 2/8	24 7/8	24 3/8	21 4/8	5	5	Jackson County	MI	Russell P. Blair	1983	3,064
142 2/8	22 7/8	24 5/8	18 0/8	5	5	Buffalo County	WI	Patrick Myers	1985	3,064
142 2/8	23 5/8	26 1/8	18 3/8	5	6	Eau Claire County	WI	Kenneth A. Sweeny	1985	3,064
142 2/8	21 4/8	22 0/8	18 4/8	5	5	Lake County	IL	Robert K. Lapacek	1986	3,064
142 2/8	24 0/8	25 0/8	17 2/8	6	4	Licking County	OH	Robert H. Wise	1987	3,064
142 2/8	22 6/8	23 3/8	16 1/8	7	6	Roberts County	SD	Myles Keller	1988	3,064
142 2/8	22 2/8	22 4/8	16 4/8	5	5	Cherokee County	IA	Brad Husman	1988	3,064

Score	Length of Main Beam R	Length of Main Beam L	Inside Spread	Number of Points R	Number of Points L	Area	State/ Province	Hunter's Name	Date	Rank
142 2/8	20 7/8	20 7/8	15 4/8	5	5	Miller County	MO	John Patterson	1989	3,064
142 2/8	25 7/8	24 6/8	19 2/8	4	5	Dunn County	WI	Michael E. Suckow	1989	3,064
142 2/8	25 3/8	26 5/8	18 3/8	5	5	Hamilton County	IA	Larry Haren	1989	3,064
142 2/8	25 0/8	23 3/8	17 4/8	6	4	Leavenworth County	KS	Jacob W. Dragieff	1989	3,064
142 2/8	24 4/8	25 1/8	19 2/8	5	5	Madison County	OH	Timothy A. Chenoweth	1990	3,064
142 2/8	22 3/8	23 4/8	16 4/8	5	5	Wetzel County	WV	Paul Pichardo	1990	3,064
142 2/8	23 5/8	24 1/8	16 4/8	4	4	Ashland County	WI	Lawrence D. Wollock	1990	3,064
142 2/8	25 2/8	25 6/8	22 6/8	5	5	Burlington County	NJ	Frank R. Buckman	1990	3,064
142 2/8	25 2/8	25 2/8	19 6/8	4	4	Clayton County	IA	Richard A. Preston	1990	3,064
142 2/8	25 5/8	26 3/8	21 2/8	4	4	Livingston County	IL	Tom Roe	1991	3,064
142 2/8	21 0/8	22 1/8	16 4/8	5	5	Cross County	AR	Wilburn Holt	1992	3,064
142 1/8	23 1/8	22 7/8	18 6/8	5	5	Huron County	OH	Thomas Sheldon	1956	3,092
142 1/8	23 6/8	23 1/8	15 3/8	6	6	Morgan County	GA	Jerry Wall	1966	3,092
142 1/8	25 1/8	25 2/8	20 3/8	6	6	Faribault County	MN	Timothy Anderson	1970	3,092
142 1/8	24 2/8	25 7/8	22 1/8	5	4	Pope County	AR	Danny L. Mathis	1971	3,092
142 1/8	24 2/8	24 0/8	18 3/8	6	5	Buffalo County	WI	Myles Keller	1973	3,092
142 1/8	23 7/8	23 7/8	17 5/8	5	5	Port Perry	ONT	Ken Steele	1979	3,092
142 1/8	23 4/8	23 4/8	16 7/8	4	4	Ripley County	IN	Dick Gambrel	1981	3,092
142 1/8	22 7/8	22 2/8	16 3/8	5	5	McPherson County	KS	James Willems	1981	3,092
142 1/8	22 1/8	21 6/8	14 5/8	5	5	Charles County	MD	John L. Penny	1982	3,092
142 1/8	20 1/8	20 5/8	13 7/8	5	5	Juneau County	WI	Dennis Dreischmeier	1982	3,092
142 1/8	24 6/8	25 3/8	18 1/8	4	4	Lawrence County	OH	Carl G. Coburn	1982	3,092
142 1/8	26 0/8	25 0/8	22 1/8	6	6	Medina County	OH	Bruce Hamilton	1983	3,092
142 1/8	21 2/8	21 4/8	16 5/8	6	6	Washington County	MD	David M. Kumsher	1985	3,092
142 1/8	25 0/8	24 2/8	18 3/8	6	7	Ohio County	IN	Ernest Frady	1985	3,092
142 1/8	20 2/8	20 7/8	17 0/8	6	5	Trego County	KS	William R. Whitworth	1985	3,092
142 1/8	25 0/8	24 6/8	17 7/8	4	4	Logan County	CO	Kent Sump	1985	3,092
142 1/8	24 4/8	25 2/8	19 1/8	4	5	Waushara County	WI	Lester W. Lant, Jr.	1986	3,092
142 1/8	23 3/8	22 3/8	18 5/8	4	5	Somerset County	NJ	John Maddaluna	1986	3,092
142 1/8	22 3/8	22 1/8	17 5/8	5	5	Pope County	AR	Todd Fountain	1987	3,092
142 1/8	24 0/8	24 3/8	16 2/8	5	6	Winnebago County	IA	Jerry Reynolds	1987	3,092
142 1/8	25 0/8	24 5/8	19 1/8	5	6	Rock County	WI	Gary Schiefelbein	1987	3,092
142 1/8	24 6/8	25 4/8	19 5/8	5	5	Jackson County	KS	Dayton R. Wright	1987	3,092
142 1/8	26 3/8	26 1/8	19 1/8	4	4	Charles County	MD	Douglas M. Garcia	1988	3,092
142 1/8	21 6/8	22 2/8	17 5/8	5	5	Noble County	IN	Frank M. McDonald	1989	3,092
142 1/8	25 7/8	25 5/8	22 7/8	7	6	Dubuque County	IA	Ken Treanor	1989	3,092
142 1/8	22 1/8	23 0/8	17 5/8	7	5	Saline County	MO	Jerry Underwood	1989	3,092
142 1/8	23 3/8	24 5/8	16 4/8	5	6	Logan County	IL	Donald D. Stiner	1989	3,092
142 1/8	23 2/8	23 6/8	17 7/8	5	5	Langlade County	WI	Robert A. Winkler	1990	3,092
142 1/8	25 3/8	24 5/8	20 7/8	4	4	Renville County	MN	Tom Neubauer	1990	3,092
142 1/8	25 4/8	23 3/8	17 1/8	4	4	Crawford County	IL	Steve L. Hobbs	1990	3,092
142 1/8	19 3/8	19 6/8	18 7/8	5	5	Weld County	CO	Dave Culter	1990	3,092
142 1/8	22 3/8	21 7/8	18 3/8	5	5	Winneshiek County	IA	Lonnie Tiedt	1990	3,092
142 1/8	24 0/8	22 6/8	17 3/8	5	6	Bucks County	PA	Michael J. Mullin	1991	3,092
142 1/8	21 1/8	21 5/8	18 7/8	5	5	Kendall County	IL	John D. Rogers II	1991	3,092
142 1/8	24 4/8	24 1/8	16 7/8	5	5	Lawrence County	OH	Jerry L. Scythes	1991	3,092
142 1/8	23 0/8	22 3/8	16 7/8	5	5	Chariton County	MO	Dennis Meyers	1991	3,092
142 1/8	22 0/8	22 0/8	17 3/8	6	5	Crawford County	IL	Jim Liffick	1991	3,092
142 0/8	22 4/8	23 0/8	17 2/8	6	5	Logan County	IL	Irwin L. Miller	1976	3,129
142 0/8	24 1/8	24 1/8	17 6/8	5	6	Winona County	MN	Clayton Bentson	1977	3,129
142 0/8	24 0/8	23 7/8	15 5/8	5	6	Bayfield County	WI	James J. Messerschmidt	1979	3,129
142 0/8	24 5/8	24 4/8	18 6/8	4	4	Woodford County	IL	Byron L. Davenport	1980	3,129
142 0/8	20 7/8	19 5/8	18 2/8	5	5	Shelby County	IL	Richard W. Neumann	1982	3,129
142 0/8	23 4/8	21 6/8	19 6/8	5	7	Union County	IL	Randy Cronk	1983	3,129
142 0/8	27 0/8	27 0/8	20 0/8	4	4	Ravalli County	MT	Harry Potton	1983	3,129
142 0/8	22 2/8	22 5/8	18 5/8	5	7	Will County	IL	Joseph R. Pergram	1983	3,129
142 0/8	21 5/8	20 5/8	17 6/8	5	5	Dubuque County	IA	Joe Lieb	1984	3,129
142 0/8	23 1/8	23 3/8	16 6/8	5	5	Dane County	WI	Joseph A. Radecki	1984	3,129
142 0/8	20 6/8	20 6/8	17 0/8	5	5	Shawnee County	KS	Eldon Johnson	1985	3,129
142 0/8	24 5/8	24 4/8	15 2/8	5	5	Morrison County	MN	Stan Spychalla	1986	3,129
142 0/8	22 6/8	23 2/8	16 0/8	5	5	Fergus County	MT	Mike Sweeney	1986	3,129
142 0/8	21 3/8	21 0/8	15 6/8	5	5	Burnett County	WI	Doug Anderson	1987	3,129
142 0/8	21 6/8	23 3/8	16 4/8	5	5	La Salle County	IL	William Weygand	1988	3,129
142 0/8	22 0/8	22 5/8	16 4/8	5	5	Buffalo County	WI	Jeff Wendorf	1988	3,129
142 0/8	23 0/8	22 7/8	16 6/8	5	5	Creek County	OK	Larry V Fears	1988	3,129
142 0/8	25 0/8	24 2/8	16 4/8	4	5	St. Croix County	WI	Keith Andrea	1990	3,129
142 0/8	24 4/8	24 6/8	18 1/8	5	5	Suffolk County	NY	John Jeff Pfeifer	1990	3,129
142 0/8	21 0/8	20 6/8	18 0/8	5	5	Cooper County	MO	Fred Storozyszyn	1990	3,129
142 0/8	24 5/8	23 4/8	20 0/8	6	5	Henderson County	KY	Lawrence F. Smithhart	1991	3,129
142 0/8	22 1/8	21 7/8	17 2/8	6	5	Poweshiek County	IA	Kevin Kudart	1991	3,129

WHITETAIL DEER *(Typical Antlers)*

(Continued)

SCORE	LENGTH OF MAIN BEAM R	L	INSIDE SPREAD	NUMBER OF POINTS R	L	AREA	STATE/ PROVINCE	HUNTER'S NAME	DATE	RANK
142 0/8	24 2/8	24 3/8	17 0/8	7	6	Cook County	MN	Bruce Zimpel	1991	3,129
142 0/8	22 6/8	21 3/8	19 2/8	5	5	Sharkey County	MS	Kirby Deer, Jr.	1992	3,129
141 7/8	24 2/8	24 5/8	23 3/8	4	6	Jackson County	IA	Thomas L. Berkley	1959	3,153
141 7/8	23 0/8	22 0/8	20 1/8	5	4	Pottawattamie County	IA	Gary A. Green	1968	3,153
141 7/8	21 0/8	19 6/8	15 7/8	5	5	Lincoln County	SD	Kai R. Anderson	1972	3,153
141 7/8	23 6/8	22 1/8	17 1/8	5	5	Stony Plain	ALB	Barry A. Olsen	1979	3,153
141 7/8	26 0/8	26 2/8	20 5/8	4	4	Hocking County	OH	Paul T. Sater	1979	3,153
141 7/8	23 7/8	23 3/8	17 3/8	5	5	Pine County	MN	Jack Pichotta	1980	3,153
141 7/8	25 5/8	26 2/8	18 3/8	4	4	Shelby County	OH	Kenneth E. Huffman	1982	3,153
141 7/8	26 2/8	26 3/8	21 0/8	5	6	Coshocton County	OH	Mike Stumph	1983	3,153
141 7/8	21 2/8	20 6/8	18 3/8	5	5	Dunn County	WI	Bruce Olson	1983	3,153
141 7/8	25 1/8	24 7/8	20 5/8	5	5	Kent County	ONT	John McGuigan	1984	3,153
141 7/8	25 7/8	24 4/8	19 5/8	4	4	Muskingum County	OH	Rick A. Goodin	1984	3,153
141 7/8	23 6/8	23 6/8	17 3/8	4	5	Camden County	MO	Steve West	1985	3,153
141 7/8	24 7/8	24 4/8	16 1/8	5	5	Anderson County	SC	J. Alan Wilson, Jr.	1985	3,153
141 7/8	25 3/8	24 6/8	20 0/8	5	5	Seneca County	NY	Dominic D'Amico	1985	3,153
141 7/8	22 6/8	21 1/8	18 3/8	5	5	Richland County	WI	Jerry L. Gander	1986	3,153
141 7/8	24 1/8	23 3/8	14 3/8	5	4	Waushara County	WI	Douglas F. Kornel	1987	3,153
141 7/8	24 6/8	25 2/8	21 3/8	5	8	Carroll County	IL	Art Heinze	1987	3,153
141 7/8	23 5/8	22 2/8	19 6/8	5	4	Kane County	IL	Carl S. Diesel	1987	3,153
141 7/8	20 6/8	21 7/8	17 5/8	6	6	Hunterdon County	NJ	Bob Petner	1987	3,153
141 7/8	23 6/8	25 0/8	22 5/8	4	5	Suffolk County	NY	Dennis Marinuzzi	1987	3,153
141 7/8	23 7/8	23 5/8	15 7/8	5	5	Kane County	IL	Bruce R. Cummins	1988	3,153
141 7/8	19 7/8	19 2/8	15 6/8	5	6	Burleigh County	ND	Gordon Smith	1988	3,153
141 7/8	21 4/8	21 4/8	18 7/8	5	5	Kittson County	MN	James B Frederick	1989	3,153
141 7/8	23 0/8	23 7/8	17 2/8	5	6	Calhoun County	MI	Edward A. Conkell	1989	3,153
141 7/8	24 2/8	24 6/8	22 3/8	4	4	Somerset County	NJ	Bob Santiago	1990	3,153
141 7/8	21 7/8	22 1/8	17 3/8	5	5	Schuyler County	IL	John Johnston	1990	3,153
141 7/8	23 3/8	24 1/8	22 3/8	4	5	Crawford County	WI	Ivan Heisz	1991	3,153
141 7/8	24 4/8	25 1/8	19 3/8	5	6	Allegheny County	PA	Michael Barberich	1991	3,153
141 7/8	24 2/8	23 6/8	18 7/8	4	5	Massac County	IL	David T. Harris	1991	3,153
141 7/8	24 0/8	24 0/8	18 5/8	4	4	Webster County	IA	Edward E. Ulicki	1991	3,153
141 7/8	26 1/8	26 1/8	18 1/8	4	4	Marion County	OH	Sam M. Derugen	1991	3,153
141 6/8	24 3/8	24 2/8	20 0/8	4	4	Morrison County	MN	Rodney W. Olson	1958	3,184
141 6/8	21 6/8	22 3/8	15 2/8	5	5	Eau Claire County	WI	Gordy Robinson	1962	3,184
141 6/8	23 6/8	23 7/8	17 4/8	5	4	Dodge County	MN	Cy Champa	1969	3,184
141 6/8	23 6/8	24 4/8	24 0/8	4	4	Newton County	IN	Denny Raper	1980	3,184
141 6/8	26 2/8	25 2/8	22 6/8	4	4	Johnson County	NE	Ronald G. Filip	1981	3,184
141 6/8	20 5/8	22 6/8	17 2/8	5	5	Alpena County	MI	Michael E. Kaiser	1981	3,184
141 6/8	24 7/8	24 2/8	20 2/8	4	4	Todd County	MN	Ted Pilgrim	1981	3,184
141 6/8	24 4/8	23 2/8	17 2/8	5	6	Pittsburg County	OK	Richard H. Gill	1984	3,184
141 6/8	21 4/8	21 4/8	17 2/8	5	7	Hughes County	SD	Kent D. Keenlyne	1984	3,184
141 6/8	21 4/8	21 2/8	16 1/8	5	6	Lyon County	MN	Randy S Van Overbeke	1985	3,184
141 6/8	24 1/8	24 3/8	19 2/8	5	5	Strathcona	ALB	Jack Kempf	1985	3,184
141 6/8	20 6/8	21 2/8	16 4/8	5	5	Jefferson County	WI	Mike Leslie	1986	3,184
141 6/8	21 7/8	22 1/8	16 2/8	6	5	Audrain County	MO	Darrell Miller	1986	3,184
141 6/8	25 5/8	25 7/8	18 5/8	7	5	Meigs County	OH	James J. Vitale, Jr.	1987	3,184
141 6/8	23 1/8	23 7/8	17 1/8	6	6	Mower County	MN	Jeffrey L. Boucher	1987	3,184
141 6/8	25 2/8	25 1/8	18 2/8	4	4	Chisago County	MN	Patrick Smith	1988	3,184
141 6/8	23 1/8	23 5/8	19 4/8	5	6	Lee County	IL	Tim Robinson	1988	3,184
141 6/8	22 7/8	21 1/8	18 0/8	5	5	Highland County	OH	Roger O. Wyant	1988	3,184
141 6/8	25 0/8	25 0/8	16 5/8	4	5	York	ONT	Dave Barnacal	1989	3,184
141 6/8	22 3/8	22 3/8	15 4/8	5	5	Caldwell County	MO	Michael C. Burr	1989	3,184
141 6/8	23 1/8	23 1/8	17 2/8	4	4	Brazos County	TX	John Dury	1990	3,184
141 6/8	22 2/8	22 6/8	16 0/8	5	5	Clay County	MO	John Godfrey	1991	3,184
141 6/8	22 6/8	23 0/8	19 2/8	5	5	Columbia County	WI	Richard A. Prescott	1991	3,184
141 6/8	21 7/8	21 5/8	17 0/8	5	5	New Castle County	DE	Earl McSorley	1991	3,184
141 6/8	23 5/8	22 3/8	17 0/8	4	4	Mercer County	IL	Charles L. Winston	1991	3,184
141 6/8	21 2/8	22 0/8	16 0/8	6	6	Buffalo County	WI	James K. Kraft	1992	3,184
141 6/8	24 1/8	25 5/8	20 1/8	6	8	Berrien County	MI	David Kennedy	1992	3,184
141 5/8	24 0/8	24 3/8	21 6/8	6	3	Allegan County	MI	Stan Skorch	1967	3,211
141 5/8	23 3/8	23 5/8	19 5/8	4	5	Crawford County	IL	Jim Earleywine	1978	3,211
141 5/8	21 7/8	23 0/8	19 7/8	4	5	Shelby County	IL	Ed Ikemire	1979	3,211
141 5/8	24 5/8	24 6/8	17 2/8	5	6	Gallia County	OH	Buck Blankenship	1981	3,211
141 5/8	24 7/8	23 7/8	20 1/8	5	4	Roane County	TN	Thomas K. Grause	1981	3,211
141 5/8	25 2/8	26 0/8	18 1/8	4	4	Highland County	OH	Douglas Ambroza	1982	3,211
141 5/8	23 3/8	22 3/8	19 2/8	5	6	Missoula County	MT	Bob Jacobsen	1982	3,211
141 5/8	25 5/8	26 0/8	18 3/8	5	4	Dane County	WI	Don Magnuson	1983	3,211
141 5/8	22 2/8	23 2/8	18 1/8	5	5	Grant County	WI	Randy Dressler	1984	3,211
141 5/8	22 0/8	22 1/8	17 1/8	5	5	Yellow Medicine County	MN	Harold Greseth	1985	3,211

SCORE	LENGTH OF MAIN BEAM		INSIDE SPREAD	NUMBER OF POINTS		AREA	STATE/ PROVINCE	HUNTER'S NAME	DATE	RANK
	R	L		R	L					
141 5/8	21 7/8	22 4/8	15 5/8	4	4	Sedgwick County	KS	Vince Albert	1986	3,211
141 5/8	22 4/8	22 4/8	17 1/8	6	7	Slope County	ND	Dick Cheatley	1987	3,211
141 5/8	22 3/8	22 4/8	16 3/8	5	5	Fillmore County	MN	Jim Vagts	1987	3,211
141 5/8	23 2/8	22 3/8	17 1/8	5	5	Ozaukee County	WI	Michael Karrels	1988	3,211
141 5/8	23 5/8	26 2/8	19 0/8	7	7	Rock County	WI	Dale Snyder	1988	3,211
141 5/8	22 3/8	23 2/8	18 1/8	5	5	Wagoner County	OK	Terry Moody	1988	3,211
141 5/8	22 7/8	22 6/8	17 1/8	4	4	Strathcona	ALB	Ryk Visscher	1989	3,211
141 5/8	24 4/8	23 2/8	17 3/8	7	7	Butler County	KS	Mike Demel	1989	3,211
141 5/8	23 4/8	23 7/8	15 4/8	7	8	Sawyer County	WI	Dan Pleoger	1990	3,211
141 5/8	22 7/8	22 6/8	18 5/8	6	4	Washington County	MN	Rodney P. Bailey	1990	3,211
141 5/8	23 4/8	23 6/8	16 6/8	6	5	Wyandot County	OH	Richard V. Ebert	1990	3,211
141 5/8	22 6/8	22 0/8	21 1/8	5	5	Boone County	IL	Anthony T. Smith	1990	3,211
141 5/8	25 1/8	26 1/8	18 0/8	5	6	Vermilion County	IL	Lonnie D. Massengale	1991	3,211
141 5/8	22 3/8	23 0/8	19 6/8	5	6	Athens County	OH	Michael A. Rex	1991	3,211
141 4/8	21 1/8	21 4/8	19 6/8	5	5	Hyde County	SD	Gordon Sampson	1974	3,235
141 4/8	22 3/8	22 3/8	17 4/8	5	5	Richland County	OH	Walter A. Bartashus	1976	3,235
141 4/8	23 3/8	22 7/8	17 3/8	5	7	Trigg County	KY	Wayne R. Brooks	1978	3,235
141 4/8	23 6/8	24 4/8	19 0/8	5	5	Jackson County	IA	Thomas E. Maas	1979	3,235
141 4/8	22 2/8	22 1/8	16 0/8	5	4	Stephenson County	IL	John Miller	1983	3,235
141 4/8	20 6/8	20 7/8	17 0/8	5	5	Cowley County	KS	George B. Smith	1983	3,235
141 4/8	22 2/8	22 2/8	20 0/8	6	5	Pepin County	WI	Brian Berger	1984	3,235
141 4/8	24 0/8	24 4/8	15 2/8	5	5	Jackson County	IA	Todd Simmons	1984	3,235
141 4/8	25 4/8	21 0/8	21 0/8	10	9	Wyandotte County	KS	Robert A. Bentz	1984	3,235
141 4/8	27 4/8	25 3/8	20 4/8	6	5	McNairy County	TN	Arlus Ray Burney	1985	3,235
141 4/8	22 2/8	22 7/8	17 3/8	7	6	Osborne County	KS	Craig Pottberg	1986	3,235
141 4/8	25 5/8	25 6/8	16 4/8	7	6	Knox County	IN	Keith Richard Bosecker	1988	3,235
141 4/8	22 4/8	22 7/8	17 4/8	5	6	Texas County	OK	Max Crocker	1988	3,235
141 4/8	21 7/8	20 6/8	13 2/8	5	6	Langlade County	WI	Mike Sheldon	1988	3,235
141 4/8	21 5/8	22 1/8	17 2/8	5	5	Westchester County	NY	Rayot A. DiFate	1988	3,235
141 4/8	24 7/8	24 0/8	20 2/8	5	5	Shawano County	WI	Jeffrey J. Gipp	1988	3,235
141 4/8	21 3/8	21 0/8	15 0/8	5	6	McHenry County	IL	James Coley	1989	3,235
141 4/8	26 5/8	26 6/8	21 0/8	5	4	Warren County	OH	Russell L. Wiessinger	1989	3,235
141 4/8	23 0/8	22 6/8	17 6/8	4	4	Sullivan County	IN	David Ridge	1989	3,235
141 4/8	21 6/8	21 4/8	18 4/8	5	5	Monona County	IA	Pat Boyle	1989	3,235
141 4/8	23 6/8	23 0/8	18 0/8	4	4	Knox County	OH	Gregg A. Melfe	1989	3,235
141 4/8	21 5/8	21 7/8	13 6/8	5	7	Powell County	MT	Julian Proctor	1990	3,235
141 4/8	22 2/8	21 4/8	16 6/8	6	5	La Porte County	IN	Wayne Wood	1990	3,235
141 4/8	22 1/8	22 3/8	18 6/8	5	4	Jo Daviess County	IL	David W. Seas	1990	3,235
141 4/8	23 4/8	23 4/8	19 6/8	4	6	McHenry County	IL	Russ Tallman	1990	3,235
141 4/8	25 6/8	24 7/8	18 4/8	4	4	Oconto County	WI	John Pashek	1990	3,235
141 4/8	22 7/8	22 5/8	15 2/8	5	5	Waupaca County	WI	Jeff Behrens	1991	3,235
141 4/8	20 7/8	22 3/8	14 6/8	5	5	Loudoun County	VA	Roger Lane Pearce	1991	3,235
141 4/8	22 2/8	22 6/8	22 0/8	5	5	Hocking County	OH	Ernie Glason, Jr.	1991	3,235
141 4/8	23 3/8	22 7/8	15 4/8	6	6	Loudown County	VA	Stephen L. George	1991	3,235
141 4/8	22 1/8	20 4/8	18 2/8	5	5	Anderson County	KS	Robert G. Coplen	1991	3,235
141 3/8	23 3/8	22 4/8	17 1/8	7	6	Hughes County	SD	Ross Krull	1969	3,266
141 3/8	24 5/8	26 3/8	16 3/8	5	6	Vilas County	WI	Dennis W. Essers	1976	3,266
141 3/8	24 6/8	24 5/8	18 2/8	6	10	Seneca County	OH	Bruce R. Stover	1980	3,266
141 3/8	24 0/8	23 1/8	19 7/8	5	5	Mitchell County	KS	Charlie Stevens	1981	3,266
141 3/8	23 5/8	23 3/8	17 4/8	7	5	Warren County	VA	Ronnie Wines	1981	3,266
141 3/8	22 3/8	21 5/8	15 1/8	5	5	Eau Claire County	WI	Terry R. Zich	1982	3,266
141 3/8	24 7/8	24 0/8	16 7/8	5	4	Burleigh County	ND	Andrew M. Schneider	1982	3,266
141 3/8	24 6/8	24 6/8	19 2/8	5	7	Putnam County	WV	James H. Myers	1983	3,266
141 3/8	25 1/8	25 0/8	19 7/8	5	4	Fayette County	IL	Mike Kistler	1983	3,266
141 3/8	22 2/8	22 1/8	18 5/8	4	5	Clermont County	OH	Harold A. Thompson, Jr.	1983	3,266
141 3/8	27 7/8	26 2/8	18 5/8	7	5	Boone County	IA	Dan A. Dillavou	1984	3,266
141 3/8	23 5/8	23 4/8	18 5/8	5	5	Dakota County	MN	Brad Bieber	1984	3,266
141 3/8	21 2/8	23 0/8	19 5/8	6	9	Louisa County	IA	Jay Schmelzer	1985	3,266
141 3/8	23 5/8	23 2/8	15 2/8	6	5	Kay County	OK	Guy LeMonnier	1985	3,266
141 3/8	25 5/8	25 3/8	19 5/8	4	5	Jackson County	MN	Merlin Jurgens	1985	3,266
141 3/8	18 6/8	23 1/8	15 5/8	5	5	Lake County	IL	Robert H. Fugett	1985	3,266
141 3/8	21 7/8	23 0/8	16 2/8	5	7	Jackson County	IA	David Schrody	1985	3,266
141 3/8	24 5/8	22 7/8	17 5/8	5	5	Howard Twp.	ONT	Wm. K. Jamieson	1985	3,266
141 3/8	22 6/8	23 1/8	19 3/8	5	5	Greene County	OH	Daniel J. Gereg	1987	3,266
141 3/8	23 5/8	23 1/8	16 1/8	5	5	Langlade County	WI	Bernhardt Behlke	1987	3,266
141 3/8	26 1/8	26 1/8	18 5/8	5	5	Fairfield County	OH	Thomas Moore	1988	3,266
141 3/8	23 6/8	22 3/8	18 2/8	5	6	Douglas County	WI	Perry Cunningham	1988	3,266
141 3/8	23 1/8	22 3/8	16 3/8	5	4	Licking County	OH	Ron Lohrman, Sr.	1988	3,266
141 3/8	19 7/8	21 4/8	15 3/8	4	5	Wapello County	IA	Stephen A. Cullinan	1989	3,266
141 3/8	25 3/8	25 6/8	18 3/8	5	5	Racine County	WI	Mark Wilcox	1989	3,266

SCORE	LENGTH OF R MAIN BEAM L		INSIDE SPREAD	NUMBER OF R POINTS L		AREA	STATE/ PROVINCE	HUNTER'S NAME	DATE	RANK
141 3/8	25 4/8	26 4/8	18 7/8	5	4	Grant County	WI	Clifford T. Bailey	1990	3,266
141 3/8	23 1/8	23 0/8	17 0/8	7	6	Douglas County	WI	William James Back	1991	3,266
141 3/8	21 3/8	21 2/8	15 5/8	5	5	Jackson County	MO	Wendell Hood	1991	3,266
141 3/8	20 3/8	20 3/8	15 7/8	5	5	St. Joseph County	IN	Michael L. Ritter	1992	3,266
141 2/8	24 4/8	23 1/8	16 6/8	5	5	Lee County	IA	Terry E. Woodworth	1973	3,295
141 2/8	22 5/8	23 1/8	22 2/8	4	5	Bon Homme County	SD	Jeff Miedema	1978	3,295
141 2/8	25 7/8	25 7/8	20 4/8	5	4	Douglas County	KS	Russell Stevens	1978	3,295
141 2/8	23 3/8	23 2/8	17 2/8	5	5	Cottonwood County	MN	Robert K. Vincent	1978	3,295
141 2/8	24 2/8	23 4/8	20 2/8	4	5	DeKalb County	IL	Bob Broos	1980	3,295
141 2/8	21 6/8	20 2/8	16 0/8	7	6	Grant County	WI	Thomas A. Franseen	1982	3,295
141 2/8	22 4/8	22 4/8	20 3/8	5	6	Allamakee County	IA	Glen A. Jones	1983	3,295
141 2/8	24 4/8	25 7/8	20 6/8	6	5	Powell County	MT	Steve Pocha	1984	3,295
141 2/8	21 6/8	20 5/8	19 2/8	6	5	Green County	WI	Randall A. Schupbach	1984	3,295
141 2/8	24 4/8	23 2/8	21 0/8	4	6	Fayette County	IL	Charlie Gelsinger, Jr.	1985	3,295
141 2/8	26 1/8	26 1/8	18 4/8	5	4	Lawrence County	OH	Don Nickles	1985	3,295
141 2/8	24 5/8	24 3/8	20 2/8	5	6	Pike County	OH	Harry R. Fite	1985	3,295
141 2/8	23 3/8	23 3/8	16 2/8	4	4	Kandiyohi County	MN	Jeffrey L. Danielson	1986	3,295
141 2/8	23 7/8	23 1/8	15 6/8	4	4	Green County	WI	Michael J. Beckwith	1986	3,295
141 2/8	21 4/8	20 7/8	19 6/8	5	5	Mercer County	OH	Rick Kaud, Sr.	1986	3,295
141 2/8	23 0/8	23 0/8	19 5/8	5	6	Portage County	WI	Philip P. Kalata	1987	3,295
141 2/8	21 1/8	21 5/8	19 6/8	5	6	Weld County	CO	Dale A. Elliott	1988	3,295
141 2/8	22 3/8	22 1/8	18 0/8	6	6	Price County	WI	Gerald Kozey	1988	3,295
141 2/8	22 7/8	23 3/8	18 4/8	5	5	La Salle County	TX	Dr. F. D. Elias	1989	3,295
141 2/8	23 0/8	23 1/8	16 2/8	5	5	Brown County	WI	David J. Schauer	1989	3,295
141 2/8	24 2/8	23 7/8	17 5/8	6	6	Berrien County	MI	Michael Holy	1989	3,295
141 2/8	20 0/8	21 4/8	16 4/8	5	5	Osborne County	KS	Craig E. Pottberg	1989	3,295
141 2/8	24 3/8	25 4/8	17 4/8	6	7	Hennepin County	MN	Rob't Nash	1990	3,295
141 2/8	23 4/8	23 6/8	20 3/8	6	6	Calgary	ALB	David R. Coupland	1990	3,295
141 2/8	24 2/8	25 4/8	21 7/8	5	5	Monroe County	NY	Dane R. Edwards	1990	3,295
141 2/8	22 5/8	22 3/8	18 0/8	5	5	Walworth County	WI	Ernie Meinen	1990	3,295
141 2/8	22 1/8	22 1/8	17 0/8	10	9	Delaware County	IA	Jeffrey J. Tobin	1991	3,295
141 2/8	23 5/8	22 3/8	18 0/8	5	5	Walworth County	WI	Robert R. Friend	1991	3,295
141 2/8	24 2/8	22 7/8	18 2/8	8	6	Holt County	MO	Collis Bosworth	1991	3,295
141 1/8	26 2/8	27 6/8	19 0/8	4	5	Dodge County	NE	Gary Trost	1961	3,324
141 1/8	22 0/8	24 2/8	18 1/8	4	6	Shelby County	IL	Ron Ragan	1979	3,324
141 1/8	21 5/8	22 2/8	17 5/8	5	6	Talbot County	MD	Gary W. Sommers	1979	3,324
141 1/8	25 0/8	25 0/8	17 2/8	6	6	Jefferson County	OH	William J. Fedor	1981	3,324
141 1/8	24 2/8	24 6/8	17 1/8	5	4	Tuscaloosa County	AL	Bobby Hemphill	1981	3,324
141 1/8	24 0/8	23 1/8	23 3/8	5	5	Pittsburg County	OK	Dave Jilge	1981	3,324
141 1/8	22 1/8	22 7/8	19 0/8	6	5	Des Moines County	IA	David R. Bessine	1982	3,324
141 1/8	23 7/8	22 1/8	17 7/8	5	5	Stanley County	SD	Jim P. Hallock	1983	3,324
141 1/8	22 5/8	21 7/8	15 4/8	8	7	Boone County	MO	Craig S Gemming	1984	3,324
141 1/8	27 1/8	26 6/8	18 0/8	4	5	Boone County	MO	Dale Robb	1984	3,324
141 1/8	22 4/8	22 2/8	21 0/8	6	6	Wabaunsee County	KS	Charles Bisnette	1985	3,324
141 1/8	24 3/8	24 2/8	19 1/8	4	5	Kit Carson County	CO	Kenneth Assmus	1986	3,324
141 1/8	22 4/8	23 2/8	15 6/8	7	6	Texas County	OK	Max Crocker	1986	3,324
141 1/8	23 3/8	21 1/8	18 4/8	5	6	Jefferson County	IN	Dan Oliver	1986	3,324
141 1/8	24 1/8	23 3/8	17 5/8	5	5	Oneida County	WI	Rollie H. Bessett	1986	3,324
141 1/8	22 3/8	22 4/8	16 7/8	5	6	Harvey County	KS	Mark M. Jones	1987	3,324
141 1/8	22 5/8	21 7/8	17 5/8	4	4	Jasper County	MO	Roger Lindsey	1988	3,324
141 1/8	21 6/8	22 6/8	17 1/8	5	5	Buffalo County	WI	Bruce B. Pronschinske	1988	3,324
141 1/8	22 2/8	23 1/8	18 5/8	5	5	Madison County	IL	Roger Downer	1988	3,324
141 1/8	20 7/8	21 3/8	19 1/8	5	5	Indiana County	PA	David W. Magiera	1990	3,324
141 1/8	22 4/8	22 4/8	15 5/8	5	5	Kandiyohi County	MN	David Rannestad	1991	3,324
141 1/8	24 0/8	23 7/8	21 1/8	5	5	Allamakee County	IA	Cody Hawkins	1991	3,324
141 1/8	23 5/8	23 0/8	20 1/8	5	5	Anne Arundel County	MD	J. J. Fegan	1991	3,324
141 1/8	24 7/8	24 2/8	17 3/8	4	5	McHenry County	IL	Ernie Meinen	1991	3,324
141 0/8	22 2/8	21 7/8	16 0/8	4	4	Hand County	SD	Robert Werdel	1963	3,348
141 0/8	21 5/8	22 0/8	16 0/8	4	4	Nobles County	MN	Rod McNab	1974	3,348
141 0/8	24 2/8	24 4/8	18 0/8	5	4	Vermilion County	IL	Larry Mollet	1974	3,348
141 0/8	24 2/8	24 1/8	18 3/8	4	5	Ohio County	IN	Mike Meyer	1979	3,348
141 0/8	22 4/8	22 4/8	16 2/8	5	5	Marion County	IA	Steven F. Donnelly, Jr.	1982	3,348
141 0/8	22 5/8	23 1/8	15 4/8	6	5	Marion County	WV	Samuel E. Clingan	1983	3,348
141 0/8	21 2/8	22 0/8	17 1/8	6	5	Floyd County	IA	Dennis Grauerholz	1983	3,348
141 0/8	24 3/8	23 5/8	18 1/8	5	4	Pine County	MN	Dave Hartl	1984	3,348
141 0/8	23 4/8	23 3/8	21 2/8	5	5	Flathead County	MT	Wes Plummer	1984	3,348
141 0/8	23 4/8	23 4/8	19 4/8	5	6	Douglas County	KS	Russell Stevens	1984	3,348
141 0/8	24 3/8	24 1/8	17 2/8	4	4	Pottawatomie County	KS	Loyd C. Flowers, Sr.	1984	3,348
141 0/8	24 5/8	23 7/8	17 4/8	5	4	Chatham County	NC	James T. Noonan III	1984	3,348
141 0/8	22 3/8	21 5/8	18 6/8	4	4	Cass County	NE	Roger E. Buck	1985	3,348

SCORE	LENGTH OF MAIN BEAM R	L	INSIDE SPREAD	NUMBER OF POINTS R	L	AREA	STATE/ PROVINCE	HUNTER'S NAME	DATE	RANK
141 0/8	25 1/8	25 1/8	20 6/8	4	4	Prince Georges County	MD	Robert O. Turner II	1985	3,348
141 0/8	21 4/8	17 2/8	17 0/8	5	6	Guernsey County	OH	Todd E. Feichter	1986	3,348
141 0/8	25 0/8	24 5/8	17 6/8	5	5	Waterloo	ONT	John Wyszynski	1986	3,348
141 0/8	25 0/8	24 2/8	19 2/8	4	4	Williams County	OH	Timothy L. Garber	1987	3,348
141 0/8	23 1/8	23 6/8	18 4/8	5	4	Forest County	WI	Robert DuFek	1987	3,348
141 0/8	24 1/8	25 4/8	19 1/8	6	6	Westchester County	NY	Wayne Alan Simko	1987	3,348
141 0/8	24 5/8	23 3/8	22 0/8	5	5	Warren County	IL	Jim M. Bratkovic	1988	3,348
141 0/8	23 6/8	24 3/8	18 5/8	5	5	Wayne County	IL	Paul Fearn	1988	3,348
141 0/8	21 3/8	21 4/8	15 4/8	6	5	Livingston County	IL	Michael G. Keesee	1989	3,348
141 0/8	24 7/8	24 7/8	18 0/8	5	4	Riley County	KS	Robert L. Gardner	1989	3,348
141 0/8	21 4/8	22 2/8	15 0/8	6	6	Thorsby	ALB	John Trout, Jr.	1989	3,348
141 0/8	23 0/8	23 0/8	17 2/8	4	4	Burleigh County	ND	Jim Domaskin	1989	3,348
141 0/8	25 4/8	25 2/8	16 0/8	4	4	Anderdon Twp.	ONT	Leo Potvin	1989	3,348
141 0/8	26 6/8	26 2/8	19 0/8	5	5	La Salle County	TX	Dr. F. D. Elias	1990	3,348
141 0/8	23 6/8	23 3/8	20 5/8	5	5	Mercer County	NJ	Frank Prato	1990	3,348
141 0/8	23 2/8	22 7/8	17 0/8	5	5	Guthrie County	IA	John D. Hambleton	1990	3,348
141 0/8	22 2/8	22 4/8	15 2/8	5	5	Franklin County	IA	Arlynn Ahrens	1990	3,348
141 0/8	23 0/8	24 1/8	17 0/8	5	6	Weld County	CO	Chuck Brewer	1990	3,348
141 0/8	23 4/8	22 5/8	17 0/8	5	6	Gallia County	OH	Bobby Clenney	1991	3,348
141 0/8	22 7/8	23 3/8	17 3/8	5	5	Woodson County	KS	Joe Chippeaux	1991	3,348
141 0/8	29 4/8	29 0/8	19 0/8	4	4	Richardson County	NE	Perry Oates	1991	3,348
141 0/8	23 4/8	21 6/8	17 2/8	4	4	Ontario County	NY	Neil R. Ross	1991	3,348
141 0/8	21 6/8	20 2/8	15 0/8	5	5	McHenry County	IL	William D. Weiss	1991	3,348
141 0/8	25 3/8	25 1/8	18 4/8	5	5	Warren County	OH	W. H. "Billy" Brock III	1991	3,348
141 0/8	22 1/8	21 0/8	15 2/8	6	6	Wood Mtn.	SAS	A. Jeff Best	1992	3,348
141 0/8	24 1/8	22 3/8	15 7/8	4	5	Brown County	IL	Charles R. Figge	1992	3,348
140 7/8	21 7/8	21 1/8	16 7/8	5	6	Hughes County	SD	Gerald Snyder	1962	3,387
140 7/8	24 5/8	24 5/8	17 1/8	4	4	Ripley County	IN	Melvin M. Weddell	1968	3,387
140 7/8	24 7/8	24 6/8	17 5/8	5	5	Jackson County	OH	Bob McGuire	1975	3,387
140 7/8	21 1/8	21 4/8	16 2/8	5	7	Guthrie County	IA	Dennis Rote	1977	3,387
140 7/8	21 7/8	21 6/8	14 3/8	5	6	Dunn County	WI	Douglas G. Clements	1981	3,387
140 7/8	22 0/8	21 7/8	19 7/8	6	5	St. Louis County	MO	Jack Repp	1982	3,387
140 7/8	21 7/8	23 1/8	17 3/8	4	4	Scott County	KS	Lynn Freese	1983	3,387
140 7/8	25 2/8	25 5/8	16 3/8	4	5	Morrison County	MN	Bob Woodhouse	1984	3,387
140 7/8	20 2/8	21 5/8	16 1/8	5	5	Saunders County	NE	David L Prochaska	1984	3,387
140 7/8	22 7/8	23 2/8	16 2/8	5	6	Sauk County	WI	Brad J. Luce	1984	3,387
140 7/8	22 3/8	22 3/8	16 7/8	5	5	Monroe County	WI	John W. Zahrte	1984	3,387
140 7/8	21 1/8	19 7/8	16 3/8	6	6	Claiborne County	MS	John Robert Moon	1985	3,387
140 7/8	26 5/8	26 2/8	12 3/8	5	6	Jefferson County	KY	William J. Paul III	1986	3,387
140 7/8	21 7/8	20 4/8	17 5/8	5	5	Macoupin County	IL	Richard E. Carter	1986	3,387
140 7/8	23 4/8	24 2/8	21 0/8	6	6	McHenry County	IL	John Totemeier	1986	3,387
140 7/8	22 5/8	23 2/8	19 1/8	4	4	Kleberg County	TX	William M. Wheless III	1986	3,387
140 7/8	21 4/8	21 1/8	17 3/8	5	4	Des Moines County	IA	Ronald L. Mott	1987	3,387
140 7/8	22 1/8	21 5/8	19 1/8	5	5	Lake County	IL	Robert Tropple	1987	3,387
140 7/8	23 2/8	21 5/8	18 5/8	5	4	Stearns County	MN	Mike Beuning	1988	3,387
140 7/8	24 7/8	24 3/8	18 3/8	5	6	Harrison County	IA	Marvin Purcell	1988	3,387
140 7/8	23 5/8	23 3/8	17 1/8	4	5	Houston County	MN	Ronald Ehlers	1989	3,387
140 7/8	23 6/8	23 1/8	21 7/8	4	4	Winnebago County	WI	Tom Otto	1989	3,387
140 7/8	23 1/8	20 7/8	19 1/8	5	5	Waupaca County	WI	Dan Bauman	1989	3,387
140 7/8	22 2/8	23 1/8	17 1/8	4	5	Allegheny County	PA	James E. Lambert	1989	3,387
140 7/8	22 2/8	22 2/8	21 7/8	5	4	Walworth County	WI	Dale Sjoerdsma	1989	3,387
140 7/8	22 1/8	23 0/8	17 1/8	5	6	Wright County	MN	Ronald Dircks	1989	3,387
140 7/8	25 4/8	25 2/8	19 3/8	4	4	Clark County	IL	Mark Johnson	1989	3,387
140 7/8	23 0/8	22 2/8	15 5/8	4	5	Maverick County	TX	F. H. Becker III	1990	3,387
140 7/8	25 2/8	25 2/8	14 7/8	8	7	Kossuth County	IA	Michael J. Miller	1991	3,387
140 7/8	24 5/8	24 3/8	18 6/8	6	5	Oklahoma County	OK	Tim Reid	1991	3,387
140 7/8	24 7/8	26 7/8	20 1/8	4	4	Butler County	OH	Kenny Butler	1991	3,387
140 7/8	22 3/8	23 4/8	20 3/8	5	6	Waukesha County	WI	Dan Infalt	1992	3,387
140 6/8	24 2/8	24 6/8	19 5/8	5	6	Blue Earth County	MN	Earl D. Kopischke	1967	3,419
140 6/8	24 0/8	23 3/8	20 0/8	4	4	Cottonwood County	MN	Kerry Ella	1973	3,419
140 6/8	22 6/8	23 3/8	18 0/8	5	5	Morrison County	MN	Galen Miller	1973	3,419
140 6/8	21 4/8	22 1/8	18 0/8	7	5	Weld County	CO	Roger Bechler	1974	3,419
140 6/8	23 6/8	24 2/8	19 6/8	6	5	Grant County	MN	Ronald W. Johnson	1974	3,419
140 6/8	24 2/8	24 6/8	16 4/8	5	5	Brant Twp.	ONT	Kent Callen	1979	3,419
140 6/8	21 5/8	21 1/8	18 4/8	5	5	Kossuth County	IA	Larry M. Johnson	1979	3,419
140 6/8	21 5/8	22 2/8	18 2/8	6	6	Redwood County	MN	Todd Gilb	1981	3,419
140 6/8	20 0/8	19 2/8	16 7/8	6	9	Gregory County	SD	Leroy Lamp	1983	3,419
140 6/8	23 0/8	24 2/8	18 0/8	6	7	Putnam County	IN	E. Duyane Tucker	1984	3,419
140 6/8	23 0/8	23 5/8	18 0/8	4	4	Vinton County	OH	Randy Boggs	1984	3,419
140 6/8	23 6/8	24 1/8	18 3/8	5	6	Hancock County	WV	Daniel Salatino	1985	3,419

SCORE	LENGTH OF MAIN BEAM R L		INSIDE SPREAD	NUMBER OF POINTS R L		AREA	STATE/ PROVINCE	HUNTER'S NAME	DATE	RANK
140 6/8	21 1/8	21 1/8	17 2/8	5	5	Hamlin County	SD	Ronald Schoffelman	1985	3,419
140 6/8	26 0/8	25 1/8	20 6/8	5	4	Lake County	IL	Carl H. Spaeth	1985	3,419
140 6/8	24 6/8	25 1/8	19 2/8	5	5	Dearborn County	IN	John B. Gosney	1986	3,419
140 6/8	22 6/8	22 7/8	16 4/8	6	5	Adams County	WI	Richardo L. Garza	1986	3,419
140 6/8	25 2/8	25 2/8	22 1/8	4	5	Carroll County	IL	Art Heinze	1986	3,419
140 6/8	24 7/8	23 3/8	18 2/8	5	4	Morgan County	CO	Gary Stampka	1986	3,419
140 6/8	24 6/8	24 6/8	18 2/8	6	5	Anoka County	MN	Byron Thomas	1986	3,419
140 6/8	23 0/8	23 3/8	18 6/8	4	4	Roberts County	SD	Myles Keller	1986	3,419
140 6/8	21 4/8	21 7/8	18 0/8	5	6	Morris County	NJ	Frank DeFilippis, Jr.	1987	3,419
140 6/8	25 2/8	24 7/8	21 2/8	4	5	Fairfield County	CT	Robert Bain	1987	3,419
140 6/8	20 7/8	21 5/8	15 5/8	5	6	Lyon County	MN	Charles Obler	1987	3,419
140 6/8	22 6/8	23 5/8	17 6/8	5	6	Jersey County	IL	Judy Kovar	1987	3,419
140 6/8	23 5/8	24 0/8	19 2/8	6	5	Ohio County	WV	Mike Pompeo	1987	3,419
140 6/8	25 6/8	24 7/8	21 3/8	4	5	Coles County	IL	Brad Sloat	1987	3,419
140 6/8	21 5/8	22 7/8	18 0/8	5	5	Monroe County	KY	Darrell Butler	1988	3,419
140 6/8	23 3/8	21 6/8	21 4/8	5	6	Du Page County	IL	Ronald Knebel	1989	3,419
140 6/8	22 7/8	23 1/8	15 7/8	5	5	Dane County	WI	Dennis L. Stiklestad	1989	3,419
140 6/8	22 2/8	21 7/8	17 4/8	6	5	Hennepin County	MN	Thomas Michael Knox	1989	3,419
140 6/8	21 7/8	20 4/8	17 6/8	4	4	Las Animas County	CO	Patrick E. Powell	1989	3,419
140 6/8	24 0/8	24 2/8	18 6/8	4	4	Union County	IL	Robert DuBois	1990	3,419
140 6/8	22 3/8	23 2/8	20 0/8	5	4	Scott County	KS	Brett Eisenhour	1990	3,419
140 6/8	20 0/8	21 1/8	16 0/8	5	5	Creek County	OK	Don Peterson	1990	3,419
140 6/8	22 6/8	23 1/8	22 7/8	5	4	Dodge County	WI	Larry Unertl	1990	3,419
140 6/8	24 3/8	24 7/8	17 5/8	6	5	Carter County	OK	Bob Boone	1991	3,419
140 6/8	25 2/8	25 4/8	17 2/8	8	5	Lawrence County	OH	Eddie Ray Belville, Jr.	1992	3,419
140 5/8	20 7/8	21 0/8	14 2/8	5	5	Dodge County	WI	Donald D. Voss	1960	3,456
140 5/8	22 7/8	23 1/8	17 4/8	6	5	Fremont County	IA	Scott Morris	1972	3,456
140 5/8	25 0/8	26 0/8	19 4/8	6	5	Edgar County	IL	Richard Griffin	1973	3,456
140 5/8	25 5/8	25 0/8	19 2/8	5	5	Lewis County	WV	David A. Hill	1978	3,456
140 5/8	23 5/8	23 1/8	15 6/8	7	6	Morrison County	MN	Joan Morris	1979	3,456
140 5/8	23 4/8	23 3/8	19 4/8	6	6	Sargent County	ND	Richard Williams	1980	3,456
140 5/8	23 6/8	23 6/8	20 1/8	4	4	Hardin County	IA	Bill Stonebraker	1981	3,456
140 5/8	22 4/8	22 6/8	17 1/8	6	6	Kandiyohi County	MN	Mike Hannemann	1982	3,456
140 5/8	22 0/8	23 7/8	20 4/8	5	4	Christian County	IL	Richard E. Davis	1983	3,456
140 5/8	23 6/8	25 0/8	13 5/8	5	5	Surry County	VA	David W. Huffman	1983	3,456
140 5/8	21 2/8	21 6/8	17 5/8	5	6	Jefferson County	IA	Victor Stickels	1983	3,456
140 5/8	22 0/8	22 4/8	17 3/8	4	5	Oconto County	WI	Ron Thompson	1986	3,456
140 5/8	22 3/8	22 4/8	16 5/8	4	4	Marion County	IL	Ivan W. Barnett	1986	3,456
140 5/8	26 2/8	25 7/8	18 7/8	4	4	Roberts County	SD	Kevin Saxton	1986	3,456
140 5/8	24 4/8	24 2/8	17 4/8	5	6	Waushara County	WI	Mark D. Miller	1987	3,456
140 5/8	22 0/8	21 4/8	20 7/8	5	5	Burnett County	WI	Michael D. Roberts	1987	3,456
140 5/8	22 1/8	21 7/8	19 1/8	4	5	Macoupin County	IL	Don Koniak	1988	3,456
140 5/8	27 1/8	27 4/8	20 6/8	8	8	Franklin County	OH	Lloyd E Evans	1988	3,456
140 5/8	22 3/8	22 4/8	19 7/8	5	5	Llano County	TX	Larry Rodolph	1989	3,456
140 5/8	23 6/8	24 0/8	18 1/8	5	5	Buchanan County	IA	Larry Chesmore	1989	3,456
140 5/8	22 5/8	21 7/8	18 3/8	5	4	Washington County	MN	Kenneth Brandl	1989	3,456
140 5/8	20 4/8	20 4/8	15 1/8	4	4	Montgomery County	IN	John Foster	1989	3,456
140 5/8	22 2/8	22 4/8	19 7/8	4	5	Keya Paha County	NE	Terry Marcukaitis	1989	3,456
140 5/8	23 4/8	25 1/8	17 0/8	5	5	Zavala County	TX	Dan Lansford	1990	3,456
140 5/8	20 3/8	20 3/8	16 3/8	5	5	Waupaca County	WI	Chester Cychosz	1990	3,456
140 5/8	24 3/8	24 2/8	20 1/8	5	6	Fulton County	IL	Mark Watkins	1990	3,456
140 5/8	23 3/8	23 7/8	17 1/8	5	4	Vernon County	WI	Louis Larry Franks	1991	3,456
140 5/8	22 1/8	21 6/8	18 1/8	5	6	Laurens County	SC	Galen F. Shinkle	1991	3,456
140 5/8	27 6/8	26 4/8	17 6/8	6	6	Jo Daviess County	IL	Jim Horneck	1991	3,456
140 5/8	21 6/8	22 1/8	17 5/8	4	4	Grovedale	ALB	Brent Watson	1991	3,456
140 5/8	22 7/8	23 1/8	16 6/8	6	6	Harrison County	IA	Marvin Purcell	1991	3,456
140 5/8	22 0/8	22 2/8	17 3/8	5	5	Arkansas County	AR	Johnnie Wages	1991	3,456
140 5/8	26 1/8	26 2/8	19 6/8	6	7	Suffolk County	NY	Chester Berry, Jr.	1991	3,456
140 5/8	25 0/8	26 0/8	18 4/8	5	6	E. Carroll Parish	LA	Dr. Trellis G. Green	1992	3,456
140 5/8	24 5/8	24 7/8	17 1/8	4	4	Randolph County	NC	Dr. Raymond E. Pifer	1992	3,456
140 4/8	24 5/8	22 7/8	18 2/8	7	6	Guthrie County	IA	Dale Kromrie	1964	3,491
140 4/8	21 1/8	21 1/8	15 5/8	5	5	Dickinson County	MI	Bernard Schmidt	1964	3,491
140 4/8	22 4/8	22 4/8	17 2/8	6	6	Pendleton County	KY	Gerald Bezold	1971	3,491
140 4/8	24 2/8	24 1/8	20 2/8	5	5	Fairfax County	VA	Daniel C. Holtz	1971	3,491
140 4/8	25 4/8	24 7/8	17 0/8	6	5	Berks County	PA	John R. Intelisano	1975	3,491
140 4/8	20 0/8	20 0/8	16 2/8	5	5	Osage County	KS	Mike Vandevord	1977	3,491
140 4/8	23 3/8	23 7/8	20 2/8	5	5	Clayton County	IA	Dave White	1977	3,491
140 4/8	26 1/8	24 5/8	17 5/8	7	5	Calhoun County	MI	Roger L. Sims	1979	3,491
140 4/8	22 2/8	22 1/8	18 4/8	5	5	Bradley County	AR	Barnard Smith	1979	3,491
140 4/8	25 0/8	23 5/8	19 0/8	5	4	Marquette County	WI	Ed Shields	1980	3,491

SCORE	LENGTH OF MAIN BEAM		INSIDE SPREAD	NUMBER OF POINTS		AREA	STATE/ PROVINCE	HUNTER'S NAME	DATE	RANK
	R	L		R	L					
140 4/8	23 6/8	24 3/8	18 6/8	5	7	Marion County	KS	Max Williams	1980	3,491
140 4/8	21 7/8	22 0/8	17 7/8	6	5	Berkeley County	SC	Hugh Gaskins	1981	3,491
140 4/8	21 6/8	22 0/8	16 6/8	5	5	Hempstead County	AR	Dan Moore	1982	3,491
140 4/8	24 1/8	23 4/8	17 6/8	6	6	Oconto County	WI	Richard L. Roth	1982	3,491
140 4/8	24 3/8	24 6/8	19 0/8	5	4	Logan County	IL	William Edwards	1983	3,491
140 4/8	22 2/8	22 3/8	17 4/8	5	5	Jackson County	KY	David A. Cornett	1984	3,491
140 4/8	24 2/8	24 0/8	16 6/8	4	4	Waukesha County	WI	Paul B. Kressin	1984	3,491
140 4/8	23 3/8	22 5/8	15 6/8	4	5	Pike County	IL	Joseph M. Cerny	1984	3,491
140 4/8	22 3/8	21 5/8	17 6/8	5	5	Harford County	MD	Hank Voigt	1984	3,491
140 4/8	22 4/8	22 0/8	16 2/8	5	5	McPherson County	KS	Jon Crouse	1986	3,491
140 4/8	24 3/8	24 2/8	17 4/8	5	4	Morrison County	MN	Brian Busch	1986	3,491
140 4/8	25 6/8	26 1/8	19 5/8	4	6	Monroe County	MO	Rick Schwieter	1987	3,491
140 4/8	24 2/8	24 6/8	17 5/8	6	6	Greenup County	KY	Bill Fraley	1987	3,491
140 4/8	22 0/8	21 7/8	16 3/8	6	6	Iron County	MI	Gary Schnicke	1988	3,491
140 4/8	22 1/8	21 7/8	15 4/8	6	5	Jefferson County	WI	Ernie Turpin	1988	3,491
140 4/8	25 0/8	23 7/8	17 1/8	6	6	Greene County	IL	Michael E. Newingham	1988	3,491
140 4/8	23 4/8	23 5/8	17 2/8	7	5	Mitchell County	IA	Kevin West	1989	3,491
140 4/8	23 3/8	22 1/8	17 4/8	4	4	Washington County	MS	Bob Bruss	1989	3,491
140 4/8	21 6/8	22 2/8	16 2/8	5	5	Washtenaw County	MI	Donald Clarke	1989	3,491
140 4/8	25 0/8	24 5/8	17 6/8	5	5	Logan County	KY	Mike K. Kirby	1989	3,491
140 4/8	22 1/8	23 0/8	20 5/8	4	6	Caldwell County	KY	Mickey Mason	1989	3,491
140 4/8	23 5/8	22 4/8	23 4/8	6	7	Coffey County	KS	Russell W. Terry	1989	3,491
140 4/8	24 0/8	22 5/8	18 4/8	5	5	Jackson County	OK	Bill Akins	1989	3,491
140 4/8	22 3/8	22 1/8	14 5/8	5	6	Washington County	KS	Bob Funke	1990	3,491
140 4/8	23 5/8	23 6/8	17 2/8	5	5	Carlton County	MN	Scott Fredrickson	1990	3,491
140 4/8	25 4/8	23 6/8	17 4/8	5	5	Dane County	WI	Greg McGraw	1990	3,491
140 4/8	24 0/8	24 2/8	16 4/8	4	4	Hardin County	KY	John Standafer	1990	3,491
140 4/8	23 0/8	23 0/8	16 6/8	4	4	Jasper County	IA	Ed Stevens	1990	3,491
140 4/8	25 0/8	23 3/8	19 6/8	4	5	McHenry County	IL	David A. Bauman	1990	3,491
140 4/8	26 3/8	25 7/8	22 5/8	4	6	Lake County	IL	Kenneth J. Pratt	1990	3,491
140 4/8	24 2/8	25 4/8	21 4/8	4	5	La Salle County	TX	Francis D. Elias	1991	3,491
140 4/8	23 1/8	21 2/8	19 2/8	5	5	Chariton County	MO	Ben Gibson	1991	3,491
140 4/8	25 6/8	25 2/8	18 4/8	5	4	Carroll County	OH	Martin Vincent Joliat	1991	3,491
140 4/8	23 0/8	22 1/8	16 0/8	5	5	Allamakee County	IA	Todd Zeuske	1991	3,491
140 4/8	21 5/8	22 5/8	17 6/8	4	4	Vermilion County	IL	Timothy T. Welker	1991	3,491
140 3/8	23 5/8	23 6/8	16 4/8	6	7	Guthrie County	IA	Leland Purviance	1964	3,536
140 3/8	27 0/8	26 1/8	19 5/8	0	0	Pulaski County	VA	Harold M. Peters	1965	3,536
140 3/8	22 6/8	23 5/8	19 0/8	5	4	Morrison County	MN	Gary D. Wells	1972	3,536
140 3/8	23 7/8	23 6/8	19 4/8	7	4	Goodhue County	MN	Dwight Dankers	1975	3,536
140 3/8	20 5/8	22 0/8	20 1/8	5	5	Rusk County	WI	Mark A. Rufledt	1977	3,536
140 3/8	21 3/8	21 4/8	15 1/8	5	5	Essex County	NY	Donald Frazier	1979	3,536
140 3/8	21 4/8	22 2/8	17 5/8	5	5	Washington County	NE	John Christopher	1981	3,536
140 3/8	23 6/8	23 0/8	20 3/8	5	4	Aitkin County	MN	Lloyd Boelter	1981	3,536
140 3/8	27 0/8	27 0/8	21 2/8	5	5	Hardin County	OH	Devere Sams	1984	3,536
140 3/8	24 0/8	24 0/8	19 2/8	5	4	Union County	IL	Steve Wilhite	1984	3,536
140 3/8	21 6/8	22 1/8	17 6/8	5	5	Chester County	PA	Jess A. Hassinger	1986	3,536
140 3/8	20 1/8	20 2/8	15 1/8	5	5	Pennington County	SD	Glenn DelaBarre	1989	3,536
140 3/8	23 0/8	22 7/8	19 1/8	4	5	McHenry County	IL	Donald Kerns	1989	3,536
140 3/8	21 4/8	21 3/8	15 7/8	5	5	Logan County	KY	Russell Johnson	1989	3,536
140 3/8	22 6/8	23 5/8	17 7/8	4	4	Meeker County	MN	Lee Peterson	1989	3,536
140 3/8	22 4/8	24 4/8	14 4/8	6	4	Ripley County	IN	Kevin D. Hall	1990	3,536
140 3/8	25 2/8	25 4/8	19 1/8	4	5	Fairfax County	VA	Mark A. Palmer	1990	3,536
140 3/8	22 3/8	24 0/8	16 7/8	4	4	Fulton County	IL	Ronald R. Bahnsen	1990	3,536
140 3/8	21 6/8	22 6/8	16 3/8	5	5	Jo Daviess County	IL	Jack T. Wolf	1990	3,536
140 3/8	25 3/8	23 7/8	17 7/8	5	4	Chippewa County	WI	Allen Larson	1990	3,536
140 3/8	25 2/8	25 3/8	19 5/8	5	4	Jo Daviess County	IL	Thomas J. Smith	1990	3,536
140 3/8	24 2/8	24 4/8	17 7/8	5	6	Kenosha County	WI	Robin L. Schuirmann	1991	3,536
140 3/8	23 1/8	23 6/8	18 6/8	6	8	Sawyer County	WI	Christopher J. Radtke	1991	3,536
140 3/8	22 4/8	22 0/8	16 5/8	5	5	Fairfield County	CT	Robert P. McCarty	1991	3,536
140 2/8	20 5/8	21 5/8	25 0/8	6	6	Harrison County	IA	Larry Vaughn	1961	3,560
140 2/8	23 7/8	23 1/8	18 4/8	4	4	Redwood County	MN	Irvin Plotz	1967	3,560
140 2/8	25 1/8	25 2/8	16 2/8	8	9	Big Stone County	MN	Peter Behlen	1972	3,560
140 2/8	20 4/8	20 7/8	19 4/8	5	5	Morrison County	MN	Gary Sutherland	1973	3,560
140 2/8	21 2/8	20 4/8	18 0/8	5	5	Walworth County	WI	Michael Stang	1975	3,560
140 2/8	22 2/8	21 6/8	12 4/8	5	5	Platte County	MO	Edward D. Johnson	1977	3,560
140 2/8	24 5/8	24 2/8	21 4/8	4	4	Buffalo County	WI	Brent Bauer	1978	3,560
140 2/8	23 1/8	23 1/8	18 2/8	5	4	Cochrane	ALB	Warren McInenly	1980	3,560
140 2/8	23 5/8	23 2/8	17 6/8	6	5	Dunn County	WI	Terry W. Stallman	1981	3,560
140 2/8	22 6/8	23 7/8	17 2/8	4	5	Tazewell County	IL	Jim Plemmons	1982	3,560
140 2/8	21 2/8	20 6/8	16 2/8	7	8	Jackson County	WI	Gary L. Barneson	1985	3,560

SCORE	LENGTH OF MAIN BEAM		INSIDE SPREAD	NUMBER OF POINTS		AREA	STATE/ PROVINCE	HUNTER'S NAME	DATE	RANK
	R	L		R	L					
140 2/8	24 1/8	24 6/8	17 4/8	5	4	Pike County	OH	Edwin H. Lynch	1985	3,560
140 2/8	21 7/8	22 5/8	16 6/8	5	4	Morrison County	MN	Jeffrey J. Moris	1985	3,560
140 2/8	23 1/8	22 3/8	15 6/8	4	4	Saline County	KS	Barry Miller	1985	3,560
140 2/8	26 3/8	27 2/8	21 2/8	4	3	Highland County	OH	Floyd Wagers, Jr.	1985	3,560
140 2/8	23 7/8	27 1/8	15 4/8	6	5	Butler County	KS	Mark Scott	1985	3,560
140 2/8	24 7/8	24 7/8	22 1/8	5	5	Dodge County	WI	Ron Tiedt	1986	3,560
140 2/8	23 4/8	23 0/8	18 4/8	5	4	Logan County	KY	Terry Baldwin	1987	3,560
140 2/8	23 0/8	23 2/8	20 2/8	4	5	Dubois County	IN	Glen J. Uebelhor	1987	3,560
140 2/8	23 1/8	23 2/8	15 6/8	8	8	Johnson County	IA	Shawn Smith	1988	3,560
140 2/8	23 5/8	24 4/8	21 4/8	4	5	Greenup County	KY	Dale Brown	1988	3,560
140 2/8	22 4/8	22 2/8	16 7/8	8	5	Kandiyohi County	MN	Gene Retka	1988	3,560
140 2/8	24 7/8	25 0/8	17 6/8	4	4	New Castle County	DE	Mike Smith	1988	3,560
140 2/8	21 5/8	21 5/8	21 0/8	5	5	Buffalo County	WI	David Baum	1988	3,560
140 2/8	24 0/8	24 2/8	17 2/8	6	7	Kit Carson County	CO	Dave Holt	1988	3,560
140 2/8	23 6/8	25 0/8	19 4/8	5	6	Baltimore County	MD	Wayne R. McElwain	1988	3,560
140 2/8	24 4/8	26 0/8	18 5/8	4	5	Pike County	OH	Stephen C. Miller	1988	3,560
140 2/8	22 0/8	22 7/8	18 6/8	5	5	Buffalo County	WI	David Stuhr	1989	3,560
140 2/8	21 0/8	22 2/8	15 2/8	4	5	Thurston County	NE	Scott R. Urbanec	1989	3,560
140 2/8	20 6/8	20 3/8	17 2/8	5	5	Tama County	IA	Loren W. Knoop	1989	3,560
140 2/8	23 7/8	24 2/8	18 3/8	6	5	Isanti County	MN	Craig Dugas	1989	3,560
140 2/8	25 2/8	26 0/8	17 0/8	4	4	Bennington County	VT	William Werner	1990	3,560
140 2/8	24 4/8	24 6/8	17 6/8	5	4	Jackson County	IL	Jim Rickhoff	1990	3,560
140 2/8	22 5/8	22 6/8	22 6/8	5	5	Lawrence County	PA	Kevin James Barber	1990	3,560
140 2/8	23 7/8	23 1/8	19 4/8	4	5	Monroe County	NY	Tony Casciani	1990	3,560
140 2/8	24 0/8	23 1/8	16 2/8	4	5	McHenry County	IL	Tom Pigott	1990	3,560
140 2/8	25 7/8	25 4/8	20 0/8	4	5	Ralls County	MO	Mike Hardy	1990	3,560
140 2/8	25 5/8	24 4/8	19 4/8	5	5	Highland County	OH	James Landrum	1991	3,560
140 2/8	23 5/8	23 4/8	18 2/8	4	4	Douglas County	MO	Charlie Johnston	1991	3,560
140 2/8	20 6/8	21 2/8	16 0/8	5	5	Richland County	MT	Sam McCorkel, Jr.	1992	3,560
140 1/8	23 5/8	22 1/8	16 5/8	6	7	Morrison County	MN	Bernie Nieters	1971	3,600
140 1/8	24 5/8	24 2/8	18 6/8	5	5	Freeborn County	MN	Kent Dugstad	1973	3,600
140 1/8	20 5/8	21 3/8	16 7/8	5	5	Jennings County	IN	Fred Hodson	1973	3,600
140 1/8	22 4/8	23 2/8	17 1/8	6	5	Douglas County	NE	Carl Martin	1973	3,600
140 1/8	22 1/8	21 2/8	16 1/8	5	4	Hitchcock County	NE	Roger Stewart	1976	3,600
140 1/8	23 4/8	23 6/8	18 3/8	4	4	Coweta County	GA	Doug Miller	1979	3,600
140 1/8	24 4/8	24 4/8	19 1/8	6	5	Champaign County	OH	Dave Anders	1980	3,600
140 1/8	25 2/8	24 2/8	19 0/8	6	5	McPherson County	KS	Daniel R. Koehn	1981	3,600
140 1/8	22 7/8	23 1/8	20 1/8	5	5	Hillsdale County	MI	William C. Mittlestat	1982	3,600
140 1/8	22 0/8	21 7/8	16 1/8	6	6	Nez Perce County	ID	Mark Deyo	1982	3,600
140 1/8	22 0/8	21 6/8	17 1/8	6	7	Barron County	WI	Dave Peterson	1983	3,600
140 1/8	23 1/8	22 1/8	15 3/8	4	4	Dane County	WI	Scott J. Maloney	1985	3,600
140 1/8	23 7/8	24 0/8	15 1/8	7	6	Henry County	VA	Keith M. Braddock	1986	3,600
140 1/8	21 0/8	21 5/8	15 7/8	6	5	Vilas County	WI	Dan Tuchscherer	1986	3,600
140 1/8	26 2/8	26 3/8	21 1/8	5	6	Douglas County	WI	Vince Holcombe	1987	3,600
140 1/8	21 2/8	21 0/8	13 4/8	6	8	Grey	MAN	Russell Lelliott	1988	3,600
140 1/8	24 5/8	22 4/8	15 3/8	7	5	Goshen County	WY	Danny R. Sterkel	1988	3,600
140 1/8	22 5/8	23 1/8	21 1/8	5	4	Hand County	SD	William J. Bushong	1989	3,600
140 1/8	23 3/8	23 7/8	17 7/8	5	5	Ashland County	WI	Steve Wartgow	1989	3,600
140 1/8	24 6/8	23 4/8	20 5/8	5	5	Erie County	NY	Paul Schroeder	1989	3,600
140 1/8	21 3/8	21 0/8	18 1/8	5	5	Wyandotte County	KS	Robert D. Hall	1990	3,600
140 1/8	22 5/8	22 3/8	15 7/8	5	5	Stoddard County	MO	John M. Wright	1990	3,600
140 1/8	21 0/8	22 7/8	17 1/8	5	6	Henry County	MO	Lavern Rucker	1990	3,600
140 1/8	24 0/8	24 0/8	19 7/8	4	5	Livingston County	IL	Robert Maurer	1990	3,600
140 1/8	26 0/8	25 0/8	18 7/8	4	4	Westchester County	NY	Charles P. Wiseman	1990	3,600
140 1/8	22 1/8	21 5/8	17 7/8	5	5	Hamilton County	OH	Neal Ramsey	1991	3,600
140 1/8	23 1/8	23 0/8	17 5/8	5	5	Peoria County	IL	Kenneth M. Taylor	1991	3,600
140 1/8	21 1/8	21 4/8	17 5/8	5	6	Kay County	OK	Kirk Peace	1991	3,600
140 1/8	23 3/8	24 4/8	18 5/8	5	5	Pike County	IL	Kenneth E. Carter	1991	3,600
140 1/8	21 3/8	21 7/8	15 5/8	5	5	Barry County	MI	Arthur J. Hayward, Jr.	1991	3,600
140 1/8	21 4/8	21 7/8	17 0/8	5	5	Marion County	IA	Chris Pendroy	1991	3,600
140 1/8	24 3/8	23 5/8	16 5/8	5	5	Marshall County	IA	Dale Smith	1991	3,600
140 1/8	22 0/8	20 7/8	15 1/8	5	5	Burnett County	WI	Michael Wynn	1991	3,600
140 1/8	22 2/8	21 6/8	17 5/8	7	6	Kit Carson County	CO	Dave Holt	1991	3,600
140 1/8	23 0/8	22 5/8	16 0/8	5	6	Kleberg County	TX	Chad Clark	1991	3,600
140 0/8	25 3/8	24 7/8	20 0/8	4	4	Houghton County	MI	Dr. V. R. Graber	1957	3,635
140 0/8	27 7/8	27 6/8	19 0/8	6	5	Ford County	KS	Melvin Miller	1973	3,635
140 0/8	23 1/8	22 0/8	19 2/8	6	6	Winona County	MN	Robert Fratzke	1974	3,635
140 0/8	22 0/8	22 1/8	15 5/8	8	6	Ottawa County	KS	Edward L. Wright	1974	3,635
140 0/8	23 3/8	22 3/8	15 0/8	5	5	Jackson County	MO	Marvin Thomey	1977	3,635
140 0/8	23 5/8	22 6/8	15 6/8	4	4	Rock County	WI	Bob Boden	1979	3,635

SCORE	LENGTH OF MAIN BEAM R	LENGTH OF MAIN BEAM L	INSIDE SPREAD	NUMBER OF POINTS R	NUMBER OF POINTS L	AREA	STATE/ PROVINCE	HUNTER'S NAME	DATE	RANK
140 0/8	22 6/8	22 3/8	17 4/8	5	5	Macoupin County	IL	Terry Jenkins	1979	3,635
140 0/8	22 1/8	21 7/8	16 0/8	5	5	Brown County	SD	Todd T. Tunby	1980	3,635
140 0/8	22 3/8	22 7/8	16 4/8	5	5	Clay County	MN	Joe Lahlum	1981	3,635
140 0/8	20 6/8	21 2/8	16 2/8	5	5	Burleigh County	ND	Doran D. Alfstad	1982	3,635
140 0/8	23 3/8	21 7/8	19 2/8	5	5	Lucas County	IA	Bill Brown	1983	3,635
140 0/8	22 4/8	22 4/8	17 0/8	4	4	Washington County	KS	Stanley Brustowicz	1983	3,635
140 0/8	21 3/8	21 7/8	14 4/8	5	5	Hill County	MT	Steve Gorr	1984	3,635
140 0/8	25 3/8	26 2/8	20 6/8	5	5	Adams County	OH	Harry Tudor, Jr.	1984	3,635
140 0/8	21 5/8	21 7/8	16 4/8	5	5	Lake County	IL	Steve M. Andrews	1985	3,635
140 0/8	24 6/8	25 2/8	17 2/8	5	4	Pratt County	KS	Shawn M. James	1985	3,635
140 0/8	23 6/8	23 1/8	20 0/8	5	7	Brown County	MN	Hap Raabe	1986	3,635
140 0/8	20 2/8	21 6/8	14 6/8	5	5	Waupaca County	WI	Brian D. Korb	1986	3,635
140 0/8	27 4/8	23 1/8	20 0/8	5	5	Jackson County	OH	Dennis Crabtree	1986	3,635
140 0/8	22 7/8	22 4/8	18 2/8	5	4	Wabasha County	MN	Dan Rettmann	1986	3,635
140 0/8	24 7/8	22 2/8	18 4/8	5	6	Floyd County	IA	Scott Ginther	1987	3,635
140 0/8	25 0/8	24 6/8	20 0/8	3	3	Mahoning County	OH	Ronald K. Osborne	1987	3,635
140 0/8	22 4/8	23 1/8	19 0/8	4	4	Oceana County	MI	Robin Howard	1988	3,635
140 0/8	23 1/8	23 3/8	16 0/8	4	4	Monroe County	WI	Denis D. Haugrud	1988	3,635
140 0/8	22 5/8	22 0/8	16 2/8	5	6	Clearwater County	ID	Bob Carlson	1988	3,635
140 0/8	20 4/8	22 1/8	19 0/8	5	5	Nemaha County	NE	Keith Williams	1988	3,635
140 0/8	20 6/8	20 6/8	18 0/8	5	5	Washington County	MN	Douglas Wilson	1989	3,635
140 0/8	24 7/8	25 1/8	20 2/8	5	4	Jennings County	IN	Billy Neal	1989	3,635
140 0/8	22 0/8	22 7/8	17 2/8	5	5	Highland County	OH	Martin H. Bullock	1989	3,635
140 0/8	23 7/8	23 6/8	16 1/8	6	6	Blue Earth County	MN	Dave Lobb	1989	3,635
140 0/8	24 5/8	24 5/8	20 2/8	6	6	Flathead River	BC	John P. Shannon	1990	3,635
140 0/8	25 1/8	24 7/8	18 6/8	6	5	Butler County	KS	Tim Ridder	1990	3,635
140 0/8	22 7/8	23 5/8	18 6/8	4	4	Todd County	MN	Steven R. Maack	1990	3,635
140 0/8	22 2/8	22 5/8	15 6/8	5	5	Ashland County	WI	David A. Stacey	1991	3,635
140 0/8	23 7/8	25 4/8	17 7/8	5	6	Lawrence County	IN	Arter Thompson	1991	3,635
140 0/8	22 2/8	23 0/8	17 0/8	6	5	Vinton County	OH	Tom Dishong, Jr.	1991	3,635
140 0/8	23 6/8	23 2/8	15 2/8	5	5	Franklin County	MO	William O. Schatz, Jr.	1991	3,635
140 0/8	23 7/8	23 4/8	17 0/8	4	5	Will County	IL	Richard L. Andre	1991	3,635
140 0/8	24 7/8	25 0/8	21 2/8	6	5	Monroe County	NY	Warren C. Bloom	1991	3,635
139 7/8	22 6/8	23 3/8	16 3/8	5	5	Martin County	IN	Warren Trinkle	1968	3,674
139 7/8	24 2/8	23 1/8	18 2/8	6	7	Jackson County	MI	Alfred A. Brenner	1973	3,674
139 7/8	23 0/8	23 4/8	18 0/8	8	5	St. Charles County	MO	Jerry D. Dale	1975	3,674
139 7/8	24 3/8	23 0/8	19 3/8	5	6	Woodford County	IL	Byron L. Davenport	1977	3,674
139 7/8	22 3/8	22 7/8	16 2/8	6	6	Lee County	IL	Charles L. Osborne	1977	3,674
139 7/8	23 6/8	22 0/8	14 0/8	5	6	Lyon County	KY	Denny Eubanks	1978	3,674
139 7/8	24 6/8	22 1/8	21 5/8	4	4	Perry County	IL	Dennis Vancil	1981	3,674
139 7/8	21 4/8	21 1/8	17 5/8	5	5	Roberts County	SD	Brian Sand	1983	3,674
139 7/8	23 1/8	23 6/8	18 5/8	4	4	Pike County	IL	Frank Dolbeare	1984	3,674
139 7/8	22 7/8	23 3/8	17 5/8	5	5	Walworth County	WI	James Kurth	1986	3,674
139 7/8	23 4/8	24 7/8	18 7/8	4	4	Cowley County	KS	Steve Owen	1986	3,674
139 7/8	23 4/8	23 5/8	16 7/8	4	4	La Crosse County	WI	Rodney P. Schroeder	1987	3,674
139 7/8	23 1/8	24 5/8	18 3/8	5	4	Taylor County	WI	Diamond Dean	1988	3,674
139 7/8	22 6/8	22 0/8	18 7/8	4	4	Walworth County	WI	Eli Nieuwenhuis	1988	3,674
139 7/8	22 7/8	22 5/8	19 5/8	4	4	Prince Georges County	MD	Kevin Ball	1988	3,674
139 7/8	21 7/8	23 0/8	19 7/8	4	4	Washington County	MS	Richard Matthews	1989	3,674
139 7/8	24 6/8	25 1/8	19 7/8	5	5	Knox County	IL	Don Owen	1990	3,674
139 7/8	26 1/8	25 5/8	19 3/8	5	5	Waldo County	ME	Paul C. Hatch, Jr.	1990	3,674
139 7/8	23 5/8	23 2/8	16 3/8	5	5	Heard County	GA	Dennis Ray Graham	1990	3,674
139 7/8	23 1/8	24 0/8	13 1/8	4	5	Price County	WI	Kyle Graf	1991	3,674
139 7/8	22 5/8	22 6/8	16 3/8	5	5	Manitowoc County	WI	Alan M. Rodewald	1991	3,674
139 7/8	22 6/8	21 0/8	17 2/8	6	5	Putnam County	OH	Jeffrey L. Kosch	1991	3,674
139 7/8	22 0/8	22 2/8	17 6/8	6	7	Lafayette County	WI	Mark E. Piper	1991	3,674
139 7/8	21 5/8	22 3/8	16 0/8	6	6	Jerauld County	SD	Curtis L. Meylor	1992	3,674
139 7/8	24 3/8	24 5/8	18 1/8	5	5	Jersey County	IL	John Grounds	1992	3,674
139 6/8	22 5/8	23 2/8	20 6/8	5	5	Barton County	KS	Charles Batman	1968	3,699
139 6/8	20 1/8	21 2/8	15 0/8	5	6	Macoupin County	IL	Mike Pirok	1978	3,699
139 6/8	23 4/8	23 0/8	20 4/8	5	5	Morgan County	OH	Marion Reed	1978	3,699
139 6/8	23 1/8	23 0/8	16 3/8	5	7	Ozaukee County	WI	Steven J. Baumann	1980	3,699
139 6/8	21 6/8	20 6/8	16 4/8	5	5	Clark County	AR	David McLemore	1980	3,699
139 6/8	28 0/8	27 4/8	21 3/8	3	5	Buffalo County	WI	Dean Sankey	1981	3,699
139 6/8	21 4/8	20 4/8	15 2/8	5	5	Idaho County	ID	Jim Sherman	1981	3,699
139 6/8	22 7/8	22 6/8	16 6/8	8	6	Pierce County	WI	Lee Langer	1982	3,699
139 6/8	24 1/8	22 4/8	16 6/8	5	5	Union County	IL	Leon Lane	1983	3,699
139 6/8	21 4/8	20 0/8	17 0/8	5	5	McLean County	IL	Willie Martin	1983	3,699
139 6/8	25 3/8	25 6/8	22 5/8	5	4	Reno County	KS	Wayne Finch	1983	3,699
139 6/8	22 5/8	22 3/8	19 0/8	4	4	Richland County	IL	Billy Joe Hicks	1983	3,699

SCORE	LENGTH OF MAIN BEAM R	L	INSIDE SPREAD	NUMBER OF POINTS R	L	AREA	STATE/ PROVINCE	HUNTER'S NAME	DATE	RANK
139 6/8	23 2/8	23 5/8	19 0/8	4	4	Wabasha County	MN	Myles Keller	1983	3,699
139 6/8	22 6/8	22 4/8	16 1/8	6	6	Columbia County	WI	Steve Deminsky	1985	3,699
139 6/8	20 0/8	20 5/8	18 2/8	5	5	Campbell County	TN	Harold D. Tackett	1985	3,699
139 6/8	23 1/8	23 5/8	16 4/8	4	4	Kankakee County	IL	Dan Loyd	1986	3,699
139 6/8	24 4/8	25 6/8	20 0/8	5	5	Montgomery County	TN	Jim Asbury	1986	3,699
139 6/8	24 1/8	22 6/8	20 2/8	4	5	Harford County	MD	Mike Garrett	1987	3,699
139 6/8	26 2/8	25 3/8	17 7/8	5	5	Dane County	WI	Jeffrey P. Schultz	1987	3,699
139 6/8	25 2/8	23 6/8	19 2/8	4	4	Knox County	MO	Roger Gipple	1987	3,699
139 6/8	22 6/8	23 2/8	16 0/8	5	5	Iron County	MI	Dennis Schnicke	1988	3,699
139 6/8	25 1/8	25 4/8	15 6/8	4	4	Barber County	KS	Mark Asplund	1988	3,699
139 6/8	22 6/8	23 3/8	17 6/8	5	5	Dane County	WI	Donald K. Isaacson	1988	3,699
139 6/8	20 5/8	19 4/8	16 2/8	5	5	Webster County	IA	Terry D. Parker	1989	3,699
139 6/8	21 4/8	22 4/8	17 0/8	6	4	Southampton County	VA	John W. Alligood	1989	3,699
139 6/8	22 0/8	20 5/8	16 6/8	8	7	Washington County	OH	Brad Biehl	1989	3,699
139 6/8	24 0/8	22 7/8	17 3/8	6	5	Harrison County	IN	Paul Barker	1990	3,699
139 6/8	22 5/8	23 0/8	18 2/8	4	4	Logan County	WV	Jerry Sammons	1990	3,699
139 6/8	25 0/8	25 5/8	17 4/8	5	4	Chester County	PA	Blake S. Gibson	1990	3,699
139 6/8	23 4/8	23 4/8	16 5/8	6	5	Dodge County	WI	Randy Firari	1990	3,699
139 6/8	25 3/8	25 1/8	17 4/8	4	4	Montgomery County	AL	Nathan Lester	1990	3,699
139 6/8	21 0/8	21 6/8	16 0/8	5	5	Livingston County	MI	Thomas P. James	1991	3,699
139 6/8	24 1/8	24 1/8	17 0/8	5	4	Effingham County	IL	James Dirks	1991	3,699
139 5/8	22 0/8	22 3/8	18 6/8	6	6	Johnson County	IN	Howard VanSweringer	1961	3,732
139 5/8	24 4/8	24 6/8	19 1/8	5	4	Custer County	NE	Paul Ekberg	1974	3,732
139 5/8	27 3/8	28 1/8	20 0/8	4	7	Nicollet County	MN	Steve Suess	1976	3,732
139 5/8	22 2/8	23 3/8	18 5/8	5	5	Custer County	MT	Dale Drilling	1980	3,732
139 5/8	26 7/8	25 1/8	21 7/8	5	6	Westchester County	NY	Michael Iuzzolino	1980	3,732
139 5/8	23 2/8	22 3/8	16 5/8	5	5	La Salle County	IL	Jack Tabor	1983	3,732
139 5/8	22 4/8	22 2/8	16 5/8	4	5	Dickinson County	IA	Eldon L. Kraninger	1983	3,732
139 5/8	21 5/8	23 3/8	17 1/8	5	5	Dawson County	MT	Martin P. Weiske	1985	3,732
139 5/8	21 3/8	19 0/8	19 7/8	5	7	Ottawa County	MI	Thomas A. Dennis	1986	3,732
139 5/8	23 3/8	22 5/8	19 1/8	5	5	Fairfield County	CT	James A. McFadden, Sr.	1988	3,732
139 5/8	21 4/8	21 7/8	15 1/8	5	5	Clark County	IL	Gerald Shaffner	1988	3,732
139 5/8	24 2/8	23 3/8	19 0/8	4	5	Union County	IL	Jerry Koerkenmeier	1988	3,732
139 5/8	24 1/8	23 3/8	18 5/8	5	4	Suffolk County	NY	Carlos Squires	1988	3,732
139 5/8	21 5/8	21 0/8	14 0/8	5	6	Burleigh County	ND	Marcus Vogel	1989	3,732
139 5/8	24 1/8	23 4/8	18 1/8	4	5	Sabine County	TX	William Allen Duvall, Jr.	1989	3,732
139 5/8	21 2/8	22 6/8	18 5/8	5	5	St. Croix County	WI	Roger Ruelin	1989	3,732
139 5/8	26 1/8	25 7/8	19 7/8	3	5	Lac qui Parle County	MN	Mark Graham	1989	3,732
139 5/8	21 6/8	21 3/8	16 7/8	5	6	Blue Earth County	MN	Jim Wakefield	1989	3,732
139 5/8	23 5/8	22 4/8	17 7/8	4	4	Clay County	MO	Jeff Utz	1989	3,732
139 5/8	20 1/8	19 6/8	15 4/8	7	6	Lincoln County	WA	Monty K. Thomas	1991	3,732
139 5/8	22 4/8	18 6/8	15 7/8	5	7	Dane County	WI	Paul O. Jorstad	1991	3,732
139 5/8	25 3/8	24 0/8	18 1/8	4	4	Franklin County	IL	Ronald Jackson	1991	3,732
139 5/8	22 1/8	21 5/8	17 5/8	6	6	Coleman County	TX	J. Paul Ellis	1991	3,732
139 4/8	23 5/8	23 0/8	20 0/8	5	4	Hart County	KY	Robert L. Galloway	1967	3,755
139 4/8	20 1/8	19 3/8	17 4/8	5	5	Clinton County	MI	Richard H. Wilt	1968	3,755
139 4/8	22 4/8	23 4/8	19 0/8	5	5	Fillmore County	MN	Orvis J. Dahl	1971	3,755
139 4/8	25 5/8	27 1/8	20 2/8	4	5	Jack County	TX	Ray Brewster	1975	3,755
139 4/8	22 2/8	23 2/8	17 5/8	5	4	Marshall County	KS	Tim Wanklyn	1978	3,755
139 4/8	22 0/8	21 5/8	16 4/8	6	7	Dane County	WI	Mike Schoenbeck	1981	3,755
139 4/8	21 6/8	22 0/8	17 4/8	5	5	Idaho County	ID	Dwight Schuh	1981	3,755
139 4/8	23 5/8	23 2/8	20 3/8	6	6	Rock County	WI	Dennis L. Meyer	1981	3,755
139 4/8	23 4/8	22 0/8	18 0/8	5	5	Licking County	OH	Richard E Pipes	1983	3,755
139 4/8	22 0/8	21 3/8	17 4/8	6	6	Jackson County	IN	Michael D. Clark	1984	3,755
139 4/8	21 0/8	21 0/8	16 6/8	4	4	Marion County	IA	Tim Pottorff	1985	3,755
139 4/8	23 1/8	23 4/8	17 4/8	5	5	Kittson County	MN	Stephen P. Skjold	1986	3,755
139 4/8	24 3/8	25 2/8	18 6/8	4	4	Jackson County	IL	David P. Beer	1986	3,755
139 4/8	24 0/8	23 1/8	21 0/8	6	4	Trego County	KS	Brian Miller	1986	3,755
139 4/8	23 2/8	24 4/8	16 7/8	5	7	Jersey County	IL	Herman Kovar	1986	3,755
139 4/8	22 4/8	21 5/8	15 6/8	5	5	Kenedy County	TX	Harold R. Arve, Jr.	1987	3,755
139 4/8	22 7/8	22 6/8	17 2/8	5	5	Waushara County	WI	Russell Marks	1987	3,755
139 4/8	25 4/8	26 2/8	18 1/8	6	7	Morrison County	MN	Martin Husnik	1987	3,755
139 4/8	24 6/8	24 4/8	18 4/8	6	5	Dukes County	MA	Louis Ashley	1987	3,755
139 4/8	24 3/8	23 4/8	17 0/8	5	5	Lowndes County	MS	Tim Graber	1987	3,755
139 4/8	22 7/8	22 2/8	19 2/8	5	5	Rooks County	KS	Michael Jirak	1987	3,755
139 4/8	22 5/8	22 7/8	18 4/8	5	5	Claiborne County	MS	Bill Cassell	1988	3,755
139 4/8	21 0/8	21 5/8	14 0/8	5	5	Jackson County	WI	Aaron Dow	1988	3,755
139 4/8	25 5/8	26 3/8	17 0/8	6	6	Atlantic County	NJ	Bob Eisele	1988	3,755
139 4/8	24 5/8	25 3/8	20 0/8	6	6	Dubuque County	IA	Thomas Schwendinger	1988	3,755
139 4/8	24 7/8	24 4/8	18 2/8	4	5	Butler County	PA	David Penn	1990	3,755

SCORE	LENGTH OF MAIN BEAM R	L	INSIDE SPREAD	NUMBER OF POINTS R	L	AREA	STATE/ PROVINCE	HUNTER'S NAME	DATE	RANK
139 4/8	24 1/8	25 0/8	17 2/8	5	7	Washington County	WI	Fred Geidel	1990	3,755
139 4/8	20 3/8	20 0/8	15 4/8	5	5	Florence County	WI	James W. Ernst	1991	3,755
139 4/8	22 6/8	23 2/8	19 4/8	5	5	Douglas County	WI	Dr. Michael R. Lawler	1991	3,755
139 4/8	19 4/8	22 1/8	17 2/8	5	5	Gogebic County	MI	Robert L. Peterson	1991	3,755
139 4/8	22 4/8	22 1/8	15 6/8	5	5	Berkshire County	MA	Jerry A. Shampang	1991	3,755
139 4/8	21 4/8	22 1/8	16 6/8	4	5	Whiteside County	IL	Trent McKenna	1991	3,755
139 4/8	21 5/8	22 7/8	14 6/8	6	5	Christian County	KY	Bruce Pyle	1992	3,755
139 3/8	24 0/8	27 0/8	18 2/8	5	5	Fulton County	IL	Raymond Rumler	1968	3,788
139 3/8	21 1/8	21 6/8	17 1/8	5	5	Outagamie County	WI	Thomas L. Haber	1975	3,788
139 3/8	21 1/8	21 1/8	16 3/8	6	6	Kalamazoo County	MI	Walter Myers	1977	3,788
139 3/8	24 7/8	22 5/8	16 3/8	5	6	Cumberland County	NJ	Winfield Cassaboon	1978	3,788
139 3/8	23 0/8	22 2/8	17 5/8	5	4	Des Moines County	IA	Ronald L. Cover	1978	3,788
139 3/8	23 0/8	21 2/8	14 7/8	5	5	Chatham County	NC	James Noonan III	1981	3,788
139 3/8	22 3/8	21 6/8	16 1/8	6	6	Jackson County	TN	Michael Mitchell	1983	3,788
139 3/8	20 1/8	20 3/8	15 5/8	6	6	Dodge County	WI	Lester C. Neuman	1985	3,788
139 3/8	23 0/8	21 7/8	17 7/8	5	6	Jefferson County	KS	Robert Ulmer	1985	3,788
139 3/8	24 1/8	23 4/8	17 7/8	5	5	Clayton County	IA	Ralph Livingston	1985	3,788
139 3/8	21 0/8	21 0/8	15 3/8	5	5	Morrison County	MN	Timothy Droher	1986	3,788
139 3/8	25 0/8	24 4/8	20 0/8	5	5	Lake County	IL	Kris A. Laho	1986	3,788
139 3/8	23 5/8	23 5/8	16 3/8	4	4	Ogle County	IL	Leo Pastuska, Jr.	1986	3,788
139 3/8	23 2/8	23 6/8	19 5/8	5	5	Rock County	WI	Ricky W. Peil	1986	3,788
139 3/8	23 6/8	23 5/8	16 7/8	6	5	Morgan County	OH	Jerry Beale	1986	3,788
139 3/8	23 5/8	23 2/8	17 7/8	5	5	McLeod County	MN	Don Ranzau	1986	3,788
139 3/8	20 4/8	22 0/8	17 3/8	5	5	Medina County	TX	Jimmy Glass	1987	3,788
139 3/8	22 4/8	23 0/8	14 3/8	5	5	Darke County	OH	Bruce Knick	1987	3,788
139 3/8	21 1/8	21 2/8	15 4/8	7	6	Adams County	WI	John W. Faber	1988	3,788
139 3/8	22 0/8	22 3/8	15 1/8	5	5	Oconto County	WI	Gary L. Christensen	1988	3,788
139 3/8	24 4/8	24 2/8	18 4/8	5	4	Westchester County	NY	Morgan Seymour, Jr.	1988	3,788
139 3/8	21 2/8	22 1/8	16 2/8	7	5	Winnebago County	IL	Larry D. Stangl	1988	3,788
139 3/8	21 7/8	21 4/8	17 3/8	7	5	Columbia County	WI	Jerome Benisch	1989	3,788
139 3/8	21 2/8	21 2/8	17 1/8	6	5	Allen County	IN	Randy McCombs	1989	3,788
139 3/8	23 5/8	24 2/8	17 5/8	4	4	Wilkenson County	MS	Bruce Saale	1990	3,788
139 3/8	22 5/8	21 0/8	18 5/8	5	5	St. Joseph County	IN	Eric Erickson	1990	3,788
139 3/8	23 2/8	23 2/8	15 1/8	4	4	Boone County	AR	Phillip Vanderpool	1991	3,788
139 3/8	24 3/8	23 1/8	19 5/8	5	6	Waukesha County	WI	Michael T. McCann	1991	3,788
139 3/8	24 5/8	25 2/8	19 7/8	4	5	Jefferson County	IL	Lloyd Sweetin	1991	3,788
139 3/8	23 0/8	22 1/8	16 2/8	6	7	Carroll County	MO	Stanley L. Cooksey	1991	3,788
139 3/8	24 4/8	23 1/8	19 5/8	4	5	Saton	QUE	Guy-Maurice Algier	1992	3,788
139 2/8	21 6/8	22 6/8	16 4/8	6	6	Shelby County	IL	David McSchooler	1968	3,819
139 2/8	20 2/8	20 7/8	15 2/8	5	5	Burleigh County	ND	Burnell F. Paul	1971	3,819
139 2/8	22 1/8	23 2/8	17 2/8	5	5	Buffalo County	WI	Leonard Anglewitz	1972	3,819
139 2/8	24 2/8	23 4/8	17 6/8	4	4	McPherson County	KS	Glenn Waggoner	1977	3,819
139 2/8	23 1/8	23 1/8	18 2/8	4	4	Bayfield County	WI	Thomas E. Smith	1979	3,819
139 2/8	22 3/8	23 6/8	15 6/8	4	5	O'Brien County	IA	Ted Bruning	1980	3,819
139 2/8	21 3/8	21 6/8	17 1/8	6	5	Dodge County	NE	Dave Hain	1981	3,819
139 2/8	22 3/8	22 3/8	22 2/8	4	5	Whiteside County	IL	B. J. Higley	1981	3,819
139 2/8	24 6/8	23 7/8	17 2/8	5	6	Greenwood County	KS	Ed Tarver	1981	3,819
139 2/8	22 7/8	24 3/8	18 4/8	4	4	Richland County	WI	Dennis Kaderavek	1985	3,819
139 2/8	21 6/8	22 1/8	18 0/8	6	6	St. Charles County	MO	John Yacup	1985	3,819
139 2/8	23 5/8	25 0/8	14 6/8	6	5	Camden County	MO	Dewayne Holloway	1986	3,819
139 2/8	23 3/8	22 7/8	19 0/8	6	4	Saline County	KS	Hal Morris	1986	3,819
139 2/8	23 2/8	22 4/8	20 2/8	4	4	Delaware County	OH	David Orndorf	1986	3,819
139 2/8	24 3/8	23 6/8	17 6/8	5	4	Hennepin County	MN	Gary Gregg	1986	3,819
139 2/8	21 3/8	21 5/8	15 0/8	5	5	Dallas County	IA	Dave Rimathe	1987	3,819
139 2/8	25 2/8	23 6/8	19 6/8	5	4	Kenosha County	WI	William J. Raboine	1987	3,819
139 2/8	22 5/8	22 5/8	18 6/8	4	4	Hennepin County	MN	Paul H. Schutte	1987	3,819
139 2/8	21 1/8	22 0/8	22 3/8	4	4	Marion County	KS	Bret Lindsey	1988	3,819
139 2/8	20 5/8	21 4/8	17 6/8	5	5	Pepin County	WI	Ben Manor	1989	3,819
139 2/8	21 4/8	22 6/8	17 2/8	5	5	Atascosa County	TX	Joe Braun	1989	3,819
139 2/8	25 7/8	25 6/8	22 2/8	4	4	Kershaw County	SC	Wayne R. Gainey	1989	3,819
139 2/8	22 5/8	23 0/8	19 4/8	6	7	Livingston County	IL	Richard Halko	1990	3,819
139 2/8	18 1/8	20 7/8	14 2/8	6	6	Schuyler County	NY	Michael C. Voorheis	1990	3,819
139 2/8	21 2/8	20 5/8	15 7/8	5	6	Blue Earth County	MN	Darwin D. Arndt	1990	3,819
139 2/8	24 0/8	24 0/8	15 0/8	6	7	Montgomery County	AL	William R. "Bill" Henders	1991	3,819
139 1/8	24 0/8	24 0/8	20 7/8	4	4	Pottawattamie County	IA	James R. Kirlin	1968	3,845
139 1/8	21 0/8	20 5/8	17 7/8	6	5	Calumet County	WI	Leo A. Broeckel	1969	3,845
139 1/8	20 3/8	21 7/8	18 1/8	5	6	Kalamazoo County	MI	Dr. Ronald L. Mahan	1975	3,845
139 1/8	23 2/8	22 4/8	19 7/8	5	5	Johnson County	IL	Billy J. Hillebrand	1977	3,845
139 1/8	23 1/8	20 0/8	16 3/8	5	5	Switzerland County	IN	James T. Brent	1979	3,845
139 1/8	22 2/8	22 4/8	20 1/8	5	5	Milton	ONT	Ernest Groh	1979	3,845

SCORE	LENGTH OF R MAIN BEAM L		INSIDE SPREAD	NUMBER OF R POINTS L		AREA	STATE/ PROVINCE	HUNTER'S NAME	DATE	RANK
139 1/8	23 0/8	22 6/8	18 2/8	5	5	Montgomery County	PA	Joseph Maddock	1980	3,845
139 1/8	22 4/8	20 1/8	17 3/8	7	5	Green County	WI	Ora Howard	1980	3,845
139 1/8	21 4/8	21 3/8	16 4/8	6	5	Finney County	KS	Rodney Stapleton	1980	3,845
139 1/8	19 4/8	20 1/8	14 2/8	6	5	Shelby County	MO	Jamie McWilliams	1981	3,845
139 1/8	23 6/8	23 3/8	19 1/8	5	5	Boone County	IN	James L. Schenck	1981	3,845
139 1/8	22 4/8	23 2/8	18 7/8	5	5	Franklin County	MO	Tom Mitchell	1982	3,845
139 1/8	25 1/8	25 4/8	17 7/8	5	5	Tazewell County	IL	Scott A. Knight	1983	3,845
139 1/8	23 0/8	23 3/8	18 2/8	6	4	Douglas County	WI	Paul Ashley	1984	3,845
139 1/8	22 4/8	22 2/8	19 3/8	5	5	Ogle County	IL	Earl B. Thomas, Jr.	1984	3,845
139 1/8	23 4/8	24 7/8	18 1/8	4	5	McLean County	KY	Earl R. Smith	1985	3,845
139 1/8	22 4/8	22 2/8	16 4/8	6	5	Montgomery County	MD	Steve Hoffman	1985	3,845
139 1/8	22 1/8	23 5/8	18 7/8	4	4	Brown County	KS	Pat Bauman	1985	3,845
139 1/8	21 5/8	22 5/8	16 7/8	6	4	Preble County	OH	Jerrol L. Meredith	1985	3,845
139 1/8	19 5/8	23 6/8	17 1/8	5	5	Dakota County	NE	Michael W. McKenna	1986	3,845
139 1/8	20 7/8	20 5/8	14 1/8	5	5	Goodhue County	MN	Deick Bridley	1986	3,845
139 1/8	24 1/8	24 6/8	19 5/8	4	5	Clay County	MN	Terry Leach	1986	3,845
139 1/8	24 4/8	23 6/8	19 4/8	4	5	Webb County	TX	Mike Palmer	1986	3,845
139 1/8	25 5/8	24 7/8	20 3/8	4	5	Pike County	IL	Steve North	1987	3,845
139 1/8	25 7/8	24 2/8	19 5/8	5	6	Plymouth County	IA	Ed Fowler	1987	3,845
139 1/8	21 1/8	21 6/8	16 0/8	7	5	Linn County	IA	Jeff Vanourney	1989	3,845
139 1/8	23 5/8	23 2/8	17 3/8	5	5	Jackson County	WI	Gary Barneson	1989	3,845
139 1/8	25 3/8	23 2/8	19 5/8	6	6	McHenry County	IL	Dennis E. Straumann	1989	3,845
139 1/8	25 0/8	24 2/8	19 4/8	5	6	Hamilton County	OH	Matthew J. Smith	1990	3,845
139 1/8	24 2/8	23 4/8	20 3/8	6	5	Macoupin County	IL	Daniel Brown	1991	3,845
139 1/8	22 2/8	22 3/8	16 0/8	9	6	Oglethorpe County	GA	Vernon Segars	1991	3,845
139 0/8	23 2/8	23 5/8	18 5/8	5	4	Warren County	IA	Grant A. Poindexter	1964	3,876
139 0/8	21 6/8	20 4/8	19 0/8	7	5	Butler County	KS	John Holzrechtes	1967	3,876
139 0/8	25 0/8	25 2/8	19 2/8	4	4	Mower County	MN	Ronald Grothe	1971	3,876
139 0/8	20 4/8	20 1/8	16 0/8	5	5	Fillmore County	MN	Richard Fryar	1972	3,876
139 0/8	24 2/8	24 5/8	15 7/8	7	6	Lewis County	WV	James Cogar	1976	3,876
139 0/8	21 3/8	21 0/8	14 2/8	5	5	Phillips County	MT	Bill Beede	1980	3,876
139 0/8	22 3/8	23 1/8	18 6/8	5	5	Grundy County	IL	Ronald A. Thompson	1980	3,876
139 0/8	25 4/8	25 5/8	19 4/8	5	5	Shelby County	OH	Richard A. Havenar	1981	3,876
139 0/8	18 7/8	23 2/8	17 4/8	6	5	Martin County	IN	Jan J. Armour	1981	3,876
139 0/8	22 1/8	20 7/8	16 2/8	8	8	Moultrie County	IL	Jim Dallefeld	1981	3,876
139 0/8	22 2/8	22 1/8	15 2/8	6	5	Linn County	MO	Robert L. 'Bob' Schultz	1981	3,876
139 0/8	23 0/8	22 0/8	16 2/8	5	5	Cass County	MI	Allen Welburn	1981	3,876
139 0/8	24 2/8	25 1/8	18 2/8	5	6	Dawson County	NE	Randy Wilson	1982	3,876
139 0/8	25 1/8	25 7/8	21 1/8	4	5	Morrison County	MN	Pat Mckenzie	1982	3,876
139 0/8	20 4/8	23 4/8	18 0/8	5	5	Lake County	IL	Gary S. Rogers	1982	3,876
139 0/8	23 4/8	22 5/8	22 4/8	6	4	Clark County	IN	Noble E. McCutcheon	1985	3,876
139 0/8	23 2/8	22 4/8	16 2/8	4	4	Morrison County	MN	Doug Schmode	1985	3,876
139 0/8	21 4/8	22 1/8	17 6/8	4	4	Racine County	WI	Mark Nelsen	1985	3,876
139 0/8	22 7/8	23 1/8	17 0/8	5	6	Monroe County	NY	David Smith	1985	3,876
139 0/8	22 4/8	24 0/8	17 2/8	5	5	Adams County	IN	Rick A. Goldner	1985	3,876
139 0/8	25 4/8	25 4/8	17 6/8	4	4	Baltimore County	MD	Danny Stivers	1985	3,876
139 0/8	21 2/8	23 2/8	16 4/8	5	4	Morgan County	OH	Lynn A. Weingart	1985	3,876
139 0/8	28 3/8	27 0/8	21 2/8	6	6	Ashtabula County	OH	Brian G. Dingle	1986	3,876
139 0/8	21 5/8	21 3/8	19 4/8	4	5	Clay County	IL	William Brummer	1987	3,876
139 0/8	24 4/8	24 6/8	19 7/8	5	5	Minnehaha County	SD	Jeffrey W. Satter	1987	3,876
139 0/8	24 2/8	23 3/8	18 4/8	6	4	Fairfield County	CT	Stephen M. Ruttkamp	1988	3,876
139 0/8	23 1/8	22 3/8	16 6/8	6	5	Ottawa County	KS	Rod Ponton	1988	3,876
139 0/8	24 4/8	24 6/8	18 7/8	5	6	Greenwood County	KS	Rod Dankert	1988	3,876
139 0/8	22 6/8	23 4/8	18 4/8	4	4	Jackson County	IL	Tim Cobin	1988	3,876
139 0/8	22 4/8	23 6/8	16 4/8	5	5	Renfrew	ONT	Glen McCutcheon	1989	3,876
139 0/8	22 4/8	23 1/8	17 1/8	7	5	Lake County	IL	Daniel Frey	1990	3,876
139 0/8	23 3/8	22 7/8	19 2/8	4	4	Calumet County	WI	Jeff Morgen	1990	3,876
139 0/8	20 7/8	20 4/8	14 6/8	5	5	Sawyer County	WI	John W. Olson	1990	3,876
139 0/8	21 4/8	21 3/8	15 4/8	5	5	Wilson County	KS	Sterling Bruce Collins	1990	3,876
139 0/8	24 2/8	26 2/8	18 0/8	4	4	Caroline County	MD	Jay Downes, Jr.	1991	3,876
139 0/8	21 5/8	20 5/8	16 4/8	5	5	Winnebago County	IL	Dennis Frichtl	1991	3,876
139 0/8	24 5/8	24 2/8	18 5/8	6	5	Marshall County	WV	Jerry Smith	1991	3,876
138 7/8	22 5/8	21 4/8	16 1/8	5	6	Sullivan County	IN	Mike Burch	1976	3,913
138 7/8	24 4/8	23 0/8	18 6/8	6	7	Cedar County	IA	Tom Foley	1978	3,913
138 7/8	22 5/8	24 1/8	19 3/8	4	6	Williams County	OH	Gary Bowles	1978	3,913
138 7/8	24 1/8	26 1/8	17 3/8	5	4	Delaware County	IA	Tom Wilhelm	1978	3,913
138 7/8	23 0/8	23 0/8	15 1/8	5	4	Hamilton County	OH	Donald R. Buehler	1980	3,913
138 7/8	27 6/8	25 4/8	21 2/8	6	4	Cowley County	KS	Maloy Rollins	1981	3,913
138 7/8	23 5/8	24 1/8	17 1/8	5	4	Clark County	SD	Jerry Comes	1982	3,913
138 7/8	23 1/8	26 3/8	19 1/8	6	4	Crawford County	MO	Bill Kaltenbach	1985	3,913

SCORE	LENGTH OF MAIN BEAM R	LENGTH OF MAIN BEAM L	INSIDE SPREAD	NUMBER OF POINTS R	NUMBER OF POINTS L	AREA	STATE/ PROVINCE	HUNTER'S NAME	DATE	RANK
138 7/8	21 5/8	19 2/8	18 1/8	5	5	Jackson County	KS	Jimmy Braden	1985	3,913
138 7/8	20 3/8	20 7/8	18 1/8	5	6	Trigg County	KY	Ronnie Fox	1986	3,913
138 7/8	23 5/8	22 6/8	17 0/8	5	4	Sarpy County	NE	Richard L. Chandler	1986	3,913
138 7/8	22 6/8	22 4/8	19 1/8	4	4	Barber County	KS	Bob A. Christensen	1986	3,913
138 7/8	23 4/8	22 6/8	18 5/8	4	4	Charles County	MD	Florentino B. Garcia, Jr.	1986	3,913
138 7/8	22 5/8	22 6/8	17 6/8	5	5	Harlan County	NE	Bill Blincow	1987	3,913
138 7/8	23 3/8	23 5/8	14 7/8	5	5	Price County	WI	Howard Briske	1987	3,913
138 7/8	23 1/8	22 5/8	20 1/8	6	5	Seneca County	OH	Larry Farson	1987	3,913
138 7/8	25 0/8	25 0/8	17 7/8	5	4	Freeborn County	MN	Robert S. Mullenbach	1987	3,913
138 7/8	20 0/8	21 4/8	16 7/8	5	5	McMullen County	TX	Kevin Hilbig	1987	3,913
138 7/8	24 7/8	24 5/8	18 7/8	4	5	Onondaga County	NY	Paul A. Douglass	1988	3,913
138 7/8	21 7/8	23 1/8	17 5/8	5	5	Fayette County	IA	Scott Golberg	1988	3,913
138 7/8	23 6/8	23 7/8	20 5/8	5	4	Cecil County	MD	Daniel K. Shivery	1988	3,913
138 7/8	22 3/8	20 6/8	18 7/8	7	6	Henderson County	KY	Aubrey C. Hazelwood	1989	3,913
138 7/8	24 0/8	25 0/8	17 3/8	6	5	Woodson County	KS	Jerry Ramshaw	1989	3,913
138 7/8	23 5/8	23 3/8	23 1/8	4	4	Hillsdale County	MI	John Stadler	1989	3,913
138 7/8	22 0/8	22 4/8	19 3/8	5	5	Garrett County	MD	Donald C. Hade, Jr.	1990	3,913
138 7/8	23 2/8	23 6/8	18 3/8	5	4	Juneau County	WI	David Magnussen	1990	3,913
138 7/8	24 1/8	24 1/8	17 7/8	4	5	Vigo County	IN	Tom Mundy	1990	3,913
138 7/8	22 3/8	22 5/8	19 0/8	7	6	Oswego County	NY	Rodney G. Wallace	1990	3,913
138 7/8	22 1/8	21 0/8	16 1/8	5	6	Lee County	IL	Timothy W. Broos	1990	3,913
138 7/8	24 1/8	23 3/8	18 1/8	4	5	Racine County	WI	John S. Burrows	1990	3,913
138 7/8	19 6/8	20 3/8	19 3/8	5	7	Marinette County	WI	Douglas A. Nelson	1990	3,913
138 7/8	23 5/8	22 3/8	17 7/8	5	5	Kent County	MD	Bruce F. Bartenfelder	1990	3,913
138 7/8	24 1/8	22 6/8	19 5/8	4	4	Anderson County	TN	Alan Brown	1991	3,913
138 7/8	22 6/8	23 1/8	18 5/8	5	5	Winona County	MN	Lonnie W. Virnig	1991	3,913
138 7/8	24 1/8	22 1/8	16 7/8	4	4	Crawford County	IL	Cecil Brassfield	1991	3,913
138 7/8	24 0/8	24 4/8	16 7/8	4	4	Green County	IL	Todd McGill	1992	3,913
138 6/8	25 0/8	23 7/8	20 4/8	4	4	Phillips County	AR	Everett Foley	1968	3,949
138 6/8	22 0/8	20 7/8	20 3/8	6	5	Leavenworth County	KS	Michael Pearce	1977	3,949
138 6/8	21 5/8	21 5/8	15 2/8	5	5	Putnam County	GA	Tim S. Doxsey	1978	3,949
138 6/8	23 0/8	22 5/8	18 0/8	5	5	Des Moines County	IA	Dennis R. Morgan	1978	3,949
138 6/8	23 5/8	23 4/8	18 6/8	4	4	St. Joseph County	MI	Jack R. Menges	1979	3,949
138 6/8	26 6/8	26 5/8	17 5/8	5	5	Crawford County	IL	James R. Griggs	1980	3,949
138 6/8	24 3/8	24 1/8	17 6/8	6	4	Latah County	ID	Dolan McLean	1980	3,949
138 6/8	23 4/8	23 4/8	18 4/8	5	4	Chase County	KS	Jerry D. Keller	1982	3,949
138 6/8	25 1/8	24 2/8	18 5/8	5	3	Calgary	ALB	Keith Riddell	1983	3,949
138 6/8	23 0/8	22 7/8	17 2/8	5	6	Dane County	WI	Walter S. Jankowski	1985	3,949
138 6/8	22 3/8	23 3/8	18 2/8	5	5	Jefferson County	MT	Jeff Nathan	1986	3,949
138 6/8	21 3/8	20 6/8	17 2/8	4	4	Scott County	KS	Travess Funk	1986	3,949
138 6/8	23 1/8	23 1/8	21 4/8	4	4	Wyandotte County	KS	Dave Crockett	1986	3,949
138 6/8	20 1/8	20 1/8	18 3/8	7	6	Mercer County	MO	David N. Clark	1987	3,949
138 6/8	21 6/8	22 0/8	17 0/8	6	5	Elkhart County	IN	Jeffrey B. Isnogle	1987	3,949
138 6/8	23 5/8	22 2/8	20 2/8	5	5	Christian County	KY	Dwight Good	1987	3,949
138 6/8	21 4/8	22 3/8	19 3/8	4	5	Waukesha County	WI	Steve J. Cull	1987	3,949
138 6/8	22 7/8	23 2/8	19 2/8	4	4	Macoupin County	IL	Ernie Gagnor	1987	3,949
138 6/8	22 5/8	21 7/8	16 2/8	5	5	Menominee County	MI	Craig S. Haglund	1988	3,949
138 6/8	23 4/8	23 2/8	20 6/8	5	4	Winnebago County	IL	James R. Petersen	1988	3,949
138 6/8	24 4/8	23 1/8	16 0/8	5	4	Hardin County	OH	Ray Davis	1988	3,949
138 6/8	26 4/8	27 2/8	18 0/8	4	4	Jo Daviess County	IL	Pat Schambow	1990	3,949
138 6/8	23 0/8	23 2/8	18 4/8	4	5	Jasper County	IL	Elmer R. Luce, Jr.	1990	3,949
138 6/8	23 6/8	24 2/8	19 2/8	5	6	Jasper County	IL	David Roepke	1990	3,949
138 6/8	20 4/8	21 6/8	18 0/8	6	6	Shawano County	WI	Bradley D. Resch	1991	3,949
138 6/8	25 6/8	25 1/8	15 3/8	3	6	Vernon County	WI	Roger Ferries	1991	3,949
138 6/8	23 4/8	24 2/8	16 6/8	4	4	Champaign County	OH	Kenny Pond	1991	3,949
138 6/8	23 6/8	23 1/8	20 6/8	4	5	Vilas County	WI	Jeff Reeves	1991	3,949
138 5/8	23 1/8	21 3/8	16 3/8	5	5	Washington County	KS	Stan Brustowicz	1923	3,977
138 5/8	24 6/8	23 3/8	17 3/8	5	5	Vilas County	WI	B. C. Roemer	1963	3,977
138 5/8	21 0/8	21 3/8	16 7/8	5	5	Martin County	IN	Tom Vieke	1967	3,977
138 5/8	24 0/8	24 3/8	17 3/8	4	6	Logan County	IL	Lee Miller	1971	3,977
138 5/8	23 0/8	23 4/8	16 2/8	4	5	Hennepin County	MN	Thomas F. Rose	1973	3,977
138 5/8	24 0/8	24 0/8	17 7/8	4	4	Chippewa County	WI	Patrick Kohls	1980	3,977
138 5/8	25 7/8	24 3/8	19 5/8	4	4	Auglaize County	OH	Bob Moser	1980	3,977
138 5/8	23 2/8	23 5/8	16 5/8	5	5	Colquitt County	GA	David A. Carmichael	1981	3,977
138 5/8	22 3/8	21 7/8	20 6/8	4	5	Greenwood County	KS	Gary Hughes	1985	3,977
138 5/8	25 3/8	24 5/8	18 0/8	6	6	Pickaway County	OH	John Walker	1986	3,977
138 5/8	25 1/8	24 3/8	19 0/8	6	5	Allen County	KY	Mark Lambert	1986	3,977
138 5/8	24 1/8	21 4/8	18 2/8	7	6	Wabasha County	MN	George Thomforde	1987	3,977
138 5/8	21 4/8	21 7/8	18 3/8	5	8	Sandridge	MAN	Bruce Huewan	1987	3,977
138 5/8	24 5/8	24 4/8	22 1/8	6	6	La Salle County	IL	Bill Goodin	1987	3,977

SCORE	LENGTH OF MAIN BEAM R	L	INSIDE SPREAD	NUMBER OF POINTS R	L	AREA	STATE/ PROVINCE	HUNTER'S NAME	DATE	RANK
138 5/8	22 2/8	21 3/8	16 3/8	5	5	Maries County	MO	Wade Hicks, Jr.	1987	3,977
138 5/8	26 4/8	25 6/8	20 5/8	4	4	Ashtabula County	OH	Bob Wodzisz	1988	3,977
138 5/8	22 6/8	24 2/8	17 2/8	5	6	Kiowa County	KS	Karl Ballard	1988	3,977
138 5/8	20 5/8	20 4/8	13 3/8	5	5	Lincoln County	SD	Duane Larson	1988	3,977
138 5/8	23 0/8	23 1/8	16 3/8	5	5	Bremer County	IA	Jon Wolter	1988	3,977
138 5/8	26 0/8	25 6/8	17 7/8	5	4	McHenry County	IL	Tim Henn	1989	3,977
138 5/8	24 6/8	26 1/8	14 1/8	6	6	Texas County	MO	Victor Ray Wood	1989	3,977
138 5/8	22 5/8	22 4/8	17 7/8	4	5	Jasper County	IA	Russell Allspach	1989	3,977
138 5/8	24 3/8	22 7/8	16 2/8	4	5	Hancock County	IL	Marte McKee	1989	3,977
138 5/8	23 1/8	23 2/8	15 5/8	4	4	Buffalo County	WI	Donald R. Fox	1990	3,977
138 5/8	25 7/8	25 5/8	19 5/8	4	4	Richland County	OH	Chris Wilcox	1990	3,977
138 5/8	25 4/8	24 4/8	17 7/8	5	4	Fairfield County	CT	Warren C. Hensel	1990	3,977
138 5/8	21 7/8	21 3/8	14 7/8	5	5	Douglas County	MN	Milton Brede	1991	3,977
138 5/8	24 1/8	24 3/8	18 5/8	5	4	Columbia County	WI	Robert A. Schmitt	1991	3,977
138 5/8	22 5/8	22 5/8	16 1/8	5	5	Cherry County	NE	Lloyd C. Smith	1991	3,977
138 5/8	22 7/8	24 4/8	19 5/8	6	4	Grundy County	IL	Lindell Dorrough	1991	3,977
138 5/8	24 3/8	24 3/8	17 3/8	5	4	Jackson County	IN	Jeff Montgomery	1991	3,977
138 5/8	24 5/8	24 2/8	17 7/8	4	5	Woodbury County	IA	David A. Rodman	1992	3,977
138 5/8	25 0/8	24 7/8	14 5/8	4	5	Hancock County	OH	Robert E. Ebert	1992	3,977
138 4/8	24 4/8	25 4/8	18 1/8	5	7	Emmet County	IA	Dr. Jerald T. Waite	1966	4,010
138 4/8	21 4/8	21 3/8	18 4/8	5	6	Mackinac County	MI	Terry Konle	1977	4,010
138 4/8	20 4/8	20 0/8	19 0/8	5	6	Jefferson County	WI	Edwin C. Wollin	1978	4,010
138 4/8	24 4/8	25 2/8	18 6/8	6	4	Pulaski County	KY	Eddie Howard	1979	4,010
138 4/8	24 0/8	23 7/8	21 0/8	4	4	Reno County	KS	Carl L. Gaston	1981	4,010
138 4/8	24 1/8	24 0/8	21 6/8	10	6	Lake County	IN	Horace Weaver	1981	4,010
138 4/8	24 4/8	23 4/8	19 0/8	5	5	Darke County	OH	Jim H. Duvall	1982	4,010
138 4/8	22 2/8	23 0/8	16 4/8	6	6	Hennepin County	MN	Raymen Peterson	1982	4,010
138 4/8	22 7/8	23 7/8	21 6/8	5	4	Jones County	IA	Hugh Shaw	1984	4,010
138 4/8	21 2/8	21 7/8	15 0/8	5	5	Des Moines County	IA	Brad Entsminger	1984	4,010
138 4/8	27 0/8	26 1/8	18 0/8	4	4	Anson County	NC	John Harris	1985	4,010
138 4/8	22 7/8	23 5/8	18 1/8	5	7	Greene County	IN	John W. Burks	1985	4,010
138 4/8	21 1/8	22 0/8	18 4/8	4	4	Adair County	OK	Fred Storozyszyn	1986	4,010
138 4/8	22 1/8	22 1/8	15 4/8	5	5	Sauk County	WI	Dale L. Luther	1986	4,010
138 4/8	26 0/8	25 0/8	19 6/8	6	6	Hancock County	OH	LeEdwin C. Smith	1986	4,010
138 4/8	22 6/8	22 2/8	15 6/8	5	5	Tompkins County	NY	John A. Nichol	1987	4,010
138 4/8	19 3/8	21 4/8	18 7/8	5	6	Gray County	KS	Carl D. Christensen	1987	4,010
138 4/8	23 6/8	25 3/8	19 2/8	5	4	Lee County	AL	George P. Mann	1987	4,010
138 4/8	21 6/8	22 5/8	17 0/8	6	5	Jennings County	IN	Kevin D. Hall	1988	4,010
138 4/8	20 7/8	20 6/8	17 5/8	6	5	Genesee County	NY	Brian E. Wardell	1988	4,010
138 4/8	24 3/8	24 2/8	17 0/8	5	6	Pike County	IL	Dallas L. Miller	1988	4,010
138 4/8	24 6/8	23 5/8	16 6/8	4	4	Pike County	OH	Todd Frazier	1988	4,010
138 4/8	24 0/8	22 6/8	17 2/8	6	5	Page County	IA	Chris Barton	1988	4,010
138 4/8	23 0/8	21 7/8	19 1/8	5	6	Blue Earth County	MN	Rick Thompson	1989	4,010
138 4/8	23 1/8	23 1/8	21 0/8	4	4	Worcester County	MA	Dana Hanna	1989	4,010
138 4/8	23 1/8	23 2/8	19 2/8	7	5	Fairfax County	VA	Michael P. Hayes, Jr.	1989	4,010
138 4/8	24 2/8	25 0/8	16 2/8	6	5	Day County	SD	Joe George	1990	4,010
138 4/8	24 6/8	25 6/8	18 1/8	5	5	Jasper County	IL	James Meinhart	1990	4,010
138 4/8	23 3/8	22 6/8	19 4/8	6	5	Des Moines County	IA	John Bruckert	1990	4,010
138 4/8	22 6/8	23 2/8	15 2/8	4	4	Claiborne County	MS	Hubert Kleinpeter	1991	4,010
138 4/8	22 1/8	22 1/8	17 0/8	4	5	Wood County	WI	Joel Binder	1991	4,010
138 4/8	24 0/8	24 2/8	19 6/8	4	4	Sebastian County	AR	Donald L. Kendrick	1991	4,010
138 3/8	20 1/8	20 2/8	18 3/8	6	6	Marshall County	SD	Robert Peterson	1962	4,042
138 3/8	22 4/8	20 3/8	16 7/8	6	5	Adams County	IL	David DeMoss	1967	4,042
138 3/8	22 0/8	21 3/8	16 5/8	5	5	Chase County	KS	Larry Krom	1971	4,042
138 3/8	22 1/8	22 7/8	16 7/8	4	4	O'Brien County	IA	Chuck Pemble	1973	4,042
138 3/8	20 4/8	21 4/8	17 6/8	5	6	Ferry County	WA	Robert Lantiegne	1980	4,042
138 3/8	21 4/8	21 5/8	19 1/8	7	5	Screven County	GA	John Frankhouser	1982	4,042
138 3/8	22 3/8	22 2/8	17 7/8	4	4	Republic County	KS	Carroll W. Couture	1982	4,042
138 3/8	22 4/8	22 1/8	16 5/8	6	5	Wilcox County	GA	George L. Haynie	1983	4,042
138 3/8	22 4/8	21 5/8	19 5/8	6	5	St. Clair County	MO	LaVern Rucker	1983	4,042
138 3/8	25 2/8	25 5/8	16 2/8	5	5	Vernon County	WI	Stan Getter	1984	4,042
138 3/8	24 4/8	23 2/8	17 7/8	5	5	Allen County	IN	Robert M. Wallin	1984	4,042
138 3/8	21 6/8	22 5/8	16 3/8	5	6	Marquette County	WI	David M. Borzick	1985	4,042
138 3/8	22 6/8	22 7/8	17 7/8	5	5	Clark County	WI	James F. Baker	1985	4,042
138 3/8	23 2/8	23 3/8	16 7/8	6	5	Fayette County	IA	Brad Volker	1986	4,042
138 3/8	23 4/8	26 5/8	18 5/8	4	5	McHenry County	IL	Edward Koenig	1986	4,042
138 3/8	24 0/8	23 4/8	17 5/8	4	4	Barton County	KS	Dan Byers	1986	4,042
138 3/8	22 6/8	22 1/8	17 3/8	4	4	Marshall County	KS	Frank Cornelison	1986	4,042
138 3/8	24 4/8	25 0/8	16 7/8	4	4	Fillmore County	MN	Neil Fishbaugher	1986	4,042
138 3/8	22 0/8	21 3/8	15 5/8	5	5	Ontario County	NY	Harry F. Voss	1987	4,042

Score	Length of Main Beam R	L	Inside Spread	Number of Points R	L	Area	State/ Province	Hunter's Name	Date	Rank
138 3/8	22 7/8	22 0/8	19 7/8	5	5	Weld County	CO	Roger Bechler	1987	4,042
138 3/8	19 4/8	20 7/8	14 1/8	6	6	Crook County	WY	Glen R. Shrewsbury	1988	4,042
138 3/8	22 5/8	24 1/8	15 4/8	7	8	Cerro Gordo County	IA	Danny D. Ruiter	1988	4,042
138 3/8	22 0/8	22 5/8	20 7/8	4	5	Champaign County	IL	Rich Schrock	1988	4,042
138 3/8	21 7/8	22 7/8	14 6/8	4	6	Monona County	IA	Duane R. Miller	1988	4,042
138 3/8	25 3/8	25 1/8	16 5/8	4	7	Crawford County	IL	Robert Loveall	1988	4,042
138 3/8	24 0/8	24 0/8	16 7/8	5	5	Bremer County	IA	Tom Bluhm	1988	4,042
138 3/8	22 5/8	22 4/8	15 3/8	5	5	Saunders County	NE	Randy Banghart	1988	4,042
138 3/8	22 4/8	22 4/8	16 7/8	5	5	Dodge County	WI	Ben Beine	1989	4,042
138 3/8	22 3/8	23 5/8	18 3/8	5	5	Polk County	WI	Terry A. Sveback	1989	4,042
138 3/8	21 6/8	22 2/8	15 3/8	5	5	Nueces County	TX	Tom Winn	1989	4,042
138 3/8	23 2/8	25 0/8	20 0/8	6	6	Lake County	IL	James R. Swan	1989	4,042
138 3/8	24 0/8	24 4/8	22 5/8	5	5	Meigs County	OH	Jeff Russell	1990	4,042
138 3/8	26 1/8	25 1/8	18 6/8	4	6	Pope County	IL	Gordon Beal	1990	4,042
138 3/8	22 6/8	22 3/8	16 1/8	4	5	Minnehaha County	SD	Arnie Sudenga	1991	4,042
138 3/8	24 4/8	24 5/8	17 1/8	4	4	Nicholas County	WV	David A. Moore	1991	4,042
138 3/8	24 0/8	23 5/8	19 3/8	4	5	Winnebago County	WI	Daniel R. Platta	1991	4,042
138 2/8	20 6/8	20 6/8	17 0/8	5	5	Kent County	MD	Paul W. Broadhurst	1962	4,078
138 2/8	20 4/8	20 2/8	13 6/8	5	5	Adams County	IL	Russ Griffin	1970	4,078
138 2/8	23 3/8	21 3/8	18 4/8	5	5	Ripley County	IN	Pat Wolf	1971	4,078
138 2/8	23 3/8	22 0/8	16 4/8	5	4	Des Moines County	IA	Cory Dalton	1973	4,078
138 2/8	23 5/8	22 1/8	20 2/8	5	6	Crawford County	WI	Jim Ferebee	1976	4,078
138 2/8	21 2/8	21 2/8	16 3/8	5	7	Edmonton	ALB	Wilf Hunter	1978	4,078
138 2/8	23 4/8	23 2/8	17 2/8	5	5	Huron Twp.	ONT	Jim McAuley	1980	4,078
138 2/8	21 4/8	23 0/8	16 2/8	5	5	La Salle County	IL	Leonard Cochran	1981	4,078
138 2/8	21 6/8	22 4/8	17 4/8	5	6	Johnson County	AR	Jeff Adams	1981	4,078
138 2/8	25 2/8	25 1/8	19 7/8	4	5	Preble County	OH	William J. Hahn	1981	4,078
138 2/8	24 3/8	24 3/8	18 6/8	4	4	Cass County	IA	Reggie Schuler	1982	4,078
138 2/8	22 7/8	23 2/8	17 6/8	4	4	Clark County	OH	David Parrott	1983	4,078
138 2/8	24 7/8	26 0/8	16 0/8	7	6	Morgan County	GA	Rod Ayers	1983	4,078
138 2/8	22 4/8	23 3/8	20 4/8	4	5	Lenawee County	MI	Kevin S. Zalecki	1983	4,078
138 2/8	22 3/8	22 2/8	17 4/8	5	5	Washburn County	WI	Russell Worman	1983	4,078
138 2/8	22 1/8	22 5/8	17 4/8	5	5	Chippewa County	WI	Ty Sweeney	1984	4,078
138 2/8	24 6/8	25 4/8	18 4/8	5	4	Berks County	PA	Joseph W. Ruppe	1984	4,078
138 2/8	23 1/8	23 0/8	17 4/8	4	5	Waushara County	WI	Michael A. Hale	1984	4,078
138 2/8	23 4/8	23 6/8	16 6/8	5	5	Houston County	MN	Richard Crabtree	1985	4,078
138 2/8	22 6/8	21 7/8	17 2/8	5	5	Cass County	MO	Rusty Murry	1985	4,078
138 2/8	22 4/8	23 1/8	16 2/8	4	4	Morgan County	CO	Rodney Washburn	1985	4,078
138 2/8	22 5/8	22 1/8	18 2/8	6	6	Tazewell County	IL	Gary D. Stamm	1985	4,078
138 2/8	21 3/8	20 7/8	15 6/8	6	6	Hubbard County	MN	Jerry Lemke	1986	4,078
138 2/8	22 1/8	22 2/8	21 0/8	5	5	Will County	IL	William A. Spreitzer	1986	4,078
138 2/8	22 6/8	21 0/8	16 3/8	6	7	Brown County	IN	Roger D. Eads	1986	4,078
138 2/8	24 2/8	23 3/8	14 6/8	6	6	McLean County	IL	Roger D. List	1986	4,078
138 2/8	24 1/8	26 1/8	22 4/8	7	7	Jo Daviess County	IL	Mike Traub	1987	4,078
138 2/8	21 3/8	22 6/8	17 0/8	4	4	Oneida County	WI	Steve Graceffa	1988	4,078
138 2/8	24 5/8	23 4/8	16 5/8	5	6	Southampton County	VA	Alan Kee	1988	4,078
138 2/8	21 7/8	22 7/8	16 5/8	7	6	Plymouth County	IA	Jason J. Dannenberg	1988	4,078
138 2/8	24 0/8	23 1/8	20 2/8	5	6	Peoria County	IL	Henry Kirkham	1988	4,078
138 2/8	21 6/8	23 1/8	18 5/8	6	5	Warren County	IA	Bruce Hupke	1988	4,078
138 2/8	25 7/8	26 6/8	19 6/8	5	4	Howard County	MD	Dave Wilson	1989	4,078
138 2/8	23 6/8	24 1/8	15 6/8	5	5	Mingo County	WV	Shelia Sammons	1989	4,078
138 2/8	23 5/8	23 0/8	18 2/8	4	4	Pearl Lake	MAN	Michael N. Hust	1989	4,078
138 2/8	22 3/8	22 6/8	16 0/8	5	5	Jackson County	MI	James E. Plumb	1989	4,078
138 2/8	21 1/8	21 0/8	17 2/8	5	5	Bayfield County	WI	Frank A. Goodwin, Jr.	1989	4,078
138 2/8	23 3/8	23 0/8	18 6/8	5	5	Cape Girardeau County	MO	Timothy E. Bender	1989	4,078
138 2/8	22 6/8	23 1/8	16 6/8	4	5	Mercer County	MO	Henry Houk	1989	4,078
138 2/8	22 2/8	23 5/8	16 3/8	5	6	Polk County	WI	Warren P. Prellwitz	1990	4,078
138 2/8	25 2/8	23 3/8	17 3/8	6	6	Fairfield County	OH	Larry Sharp	1990	4,078
138 2/8	25 7/8	24 5/8	21 2/8	5	5	Marathon County	WI	Gary Heckendorf	1990	4,078
138 2/8	23 3/8	22 0/8	18 2/8	4	4	Belmont County	OH	Jerry Smith	1991	4,078
138 2/8	26 0/8	26 7/8	19 4/8	5	5	Allen County	OH	Gregory J. McMillen	1991	4,078
138 2/8	22 0/8	22 0/8	16 4/8	5	5	Cook County	MN	Dennis Gary Schlienz	1991	4,078
138 2/8	26 2/8	24 2/8	16 5/8	6	7	Parker County	TX	Ralph C. Wiggins, Jr.	1991	4,078
138 1/8	25 4/8	24 0/8	17 2/8	4	5	Cottonwood County	MN	Rodney Ella	1971	4,124
138 1/8	23 1/8	22 5/8	19 7/8	5	5	Pocahontas County	WV	Jim Manley II	1971	4,124
138 1/8	23 0/8	22 4/8	18 3/8	4	4	Anoka County	MN	Johnny E. Boatner	1978	4,124
138 1/8	22 1/8	21 0/8	19 3/8	5	5	Kalamazoo County	MI	Dale Gray	1978	4,124
138 1/8	22 5/8	24 6/8	20 1/8	6	7	Goodhue County	MN	Victor LoPresto	1979	4,124
138 1/8	24 0/8	25 4/8	17 3/8	4	5	Grand Traverse County	MI	Roger Kirby	1980	4,124
138 1/8	22 4/8	22 5/8	17 1/8	5	5	Huron County	OH	Larry Smith	1980	4,124

SCORE	LENGTH OF MAIN BEAM		INSIDE SPREAD	NUMBER OF POINTS		AREA	STATE/ PROVINCE	HUNTER'S NAME	DATE	RANK
	R	L		R	L					
138 1/8	23 4/8	23 3/8	18 4/8	6	5	Bond County	IL	Donald E. Cruse, Jr.	1981	4,124
138 1/8	23 4/8	23 2/8	16 3/8	4	5	Jackson County	MO	Marvin Thomey	1982	4,124
138 1/8	20 6/8	20 6/8	18 0/8	5	6	San Augustine County	TX	Billy E. Corley	1982	4,124
138 1/8	22 5/8	24 3/8	15 7/8	5	5	Price County	WI	Allen F. Feltz	1983	4,124
138 1/8	23 6/8	23 1/8	19 7/8	4	4	Allegan County	MI	Tim Leslie	1983	4,124
138 1/8	24 1/8	23 3/8	17 1/8	5	5	Jersey County	IL	Herman W. Kovar	1983	4,124
138 1/8	22 0/8	21 7/8	17 7/8	5	6	Franklin County	IN	Pearl Houston	1986	4,124
138 1/8	22 4/8	21 4/8	15 5/8	5	5	Greene County	MO	Jackie Davis	1986	4,124
138 1/8	22 5/8	22 3/8	17 3/8	4	5	Allamakee County	IA	Dan Brimeyer	1987	4,124
138 1/8	22 3/8	22 3/8	17 5/8	8	5	Jackson County	WI	Todd D. Reichert	1988	4,124
138 1/8	21 1/8	19 2/8	15 7/8	5	5	Dane County	WI	Mark Overland	1988	4,124
138 1/8	22 0/8	20 7/8	15 5/8	8	6	Nelson County	ND	Douglas Magnus	1989	4,124
138 1/8	21 1/8	21 6/8	18 5/8	5	5	Knox County	IL	C. F. Peterson	1989	4,124
138 1/8	23 7/8	23 0/8	19 5/8	5	5	Morris County	NJ	David Bright	1989	4,124
138 1/8	22 2/8	22 2/8	16 5/8	5	5	Oneida County	WI	Trygve Solberg	1989	4,124
138 1/8	19 1/8	21 7/8	20 5/8	5	5	Butler County	KS	Ron Shipman	1989	4,124
138 1/8	24 1/8	23 7/8	18 5/8	4	4	Webster County	IA	Tim Bacon	1990	4,124
138 1/8	20 3/8	20 2/8	15 7/8	6	7	Grant County	WI	Glen A. Klais	1990	4,124
138 1/8	21 4/8	21 3/8	19 3/8	5	6	Pike County	IL	William W. Singer	1990	4,124
138 1/8	21 6/8	22 2/8	19 5/8	5	5	Canadian County	OK	Keith Darrow	1990	4,124
138 1/8	23 1/8	22 6/8	21 1/8	6	6	Lucas County	IA	Bruce Elrod	1991	4,124
138 1/8	24 1/8	23 6/8	21 7/8	4	4	Pike County	IL	Wayne B. Puterbaugh	1991	4,124
138 1/8	24 0/8	23 0/8	18 5/8	4	4	Issaquena County	MS	Albert Tucker Hossley	1992	4,124
138 0/8	24 1/8	23 7/8	19 1/8	8	6	Frederick County	MD	Donald R. Shipley	1962	4,154
138 0/8	22 2/8	22 3/8	18 4/8	4	4	Dane County	WI	Ernest Kalar	1966	4,154
138 0/8	21 3/8	21 7/8	19 4/8	5	6	Washburn County	WI	John C. Gehlen	1971	4,154
138 0/8	21 4/8	21 6/8	13 0/8	5	5	Taylor County	KY	James Hedgespeth	1978	4,154
138 0/8	23 0/8	23 4/8	14 0/8	5	5	Jefferson County	WI	Dennis Roberts	1980	4,154
138 0/8	22 6/8	23 6/8	20 4/8	4	5	Traverse County	MN	Danny Hormann	1981	4,154
138 0/8	23 1/8	23 7/8	18 4/8	5	5	Langlade County	WI	Mike Plzak	1982	4,154
138 0/8	20 3/8	21 6/8	15 5/8	5	7	Payne County	OK	David Ray Beene	1983	4,154
138 0/8	22 6/8	22 5/8	16 6/8	5	5	Tyler County	WV	John S McMulley	1984	4,154
138 0/8	23 6/8	23 1/8	17 2/8	5	5	Lake County	IL	John R. Love	1984	4,154
138 0/8	22 1/8	21 2/8	14 4/8	5	5	De Kalb County	MO	Daniel E. Terry	1985	4,154
138 0/8	23 1/8	23 3/8	15 4/8	5	5	Marquette County	WI	Dennis J. Buchholz	1986	4,154
138 0/8	22 7/8	23 5/8	19 0/8	5	4	Waukesha County	WI	Steve Pease	1986	4,154
138 0/8	22 3/8	22 4/8	16 4/8	5	4	Waukesha County	WI	Edward P. Papp, Jr.	1986	4,154
138 0/8	24 4/8	26 2/8	16 2/8	7	7	Iroquois County	IL	Terry Doehring	1986	4,154
138 0/8	22 3/8	22 4/8	16 6/8	4	4	Harrison County	OH	Andy Staneart	1986	4,154
138 0/8	22 3/8	21 2/8	17 4/8	5	5	Vermilion County	IL	Carl Cornwell	1986	4,154
138 0/8	23 4/8	23 4/8	14 1/8	6	6	Price County	WI	Brent M. Zierer	1986	4,154
138 0/8	22 4/8	18 4/8	20 0/8	6	6	Rock County	NE	Doug Otte	1987	4,154
138 0/8	23 3/8	23 4/8	19 0/8	5	5	Outagamie County	WI	Bill Sullivan	1987	4,154
138 0/8	24 7/8	26 1/8	20 0/8	5	7	Washington County	MN	Rodney P. Bailey	1987	4,154
138 0/8	21 1/8	20 7/8	15 4/8	5	5	Marshall County	MN	Leland J. Bratlie	1987	4,154
138 0/8	23 4/8	23 1/8	15 4/8	4	4	Linn County	MO	Earl Jones	1987	4,154
138 0/8	23 0/8	21 2/8	15 5/8	5	6	Shelby County	IL	Charlie V. DeBose, Jr.	1987	4,154
138 0/8	25 1/8	25 0/8	17 6/8	6	6	Scott County	MN	Jay M. Scherer	1988	4,154
138 0/8	22 6/8	23 2/8	18 4/8	5	5	Wright County	IA	Jack Jenkins	1988	4,154
138 0/8	23 0/8	23 1/8	21 6/8	5	4	Sioux County	NE	Dan Coffee	1988	4,154
138 0/8	25 0/8	25 0/8	18 4/8	4	5	Highland County	OH	Chris Dopel	1988	4,154
138 0/8	20 1/8	20 5/8	15 6/8	4	5	Todd County	MN	David Puetz	1989	4,154
138 0/8	25 5/8	26 5/8	21 0/8	4	4	Jefferson County	OH	Mike Sauer	1989	4,154
138 0/8	22 6/8	23 2/8	16 4/8	5	5	Meeker County	MN	Susan Barrick-Smith	1990	4,154
138 0/8	23 4/8	23 3/8	16 2/8	5	5	Tazewell County	IL	David A. Cufaude	1990	4,154
138 0/8	24 5/8	23 2/8	16 6/8	5	5	Geary County	KS	Ilija P. Milovanovic	1990	4,154
138 0/8	22 6/8	21 6/8	16 0/8	6	6	Kingman County	KS	Terry Morisse	1991	4,154
138 0/8	23 7/8	24 3/8	18 2/8	5	5	Morgan County	IL	Steve Barfield	1991	4,154
138 0/8	22 0/8	22 0/8	14 0/8	5	5	Polk County	WI	Kevin Thaemert	1992	4,154
138 0/8	20 7/8	21 6/8	18 7/8	5	6	Powell County	MT	Grant Richards	1992	4,154
137 7/8	22 3/8	22 7/8	21 1/8	6	8	Williams County	ND	Ray Hoveskeland	1959	4,191
137 7/8	21 0/8	21 2/8	17 1/8	4	4	Platte County	NE	Lee Rupp	1968	4,191
137 7/8	21 5/8	21 3/8	16 3/8	5	5	Roseau County	MN	Terry Wilson	1977	4,191
137 7/8	23 0/8	23 4/8	17 5/8	5	5	Chippewa County	MN	Layton Albrecht	1978	4,191
137 7/8	21 6/8	22 2/8	19 0/8	5	4	Kay County	OK	Guy L. LeMonnier, Jr.	1979	4,191
137 7/8	21 7/8	22 4/8	19 0/8	6	6	Labette County	KS	Rick R. Williamson	1986	4,191
137 7/8	23 3/8	23 2/8	19 0/8	5	5	Prince William County	VA	Franklin A. Siwik	1986	4,191
137 7/8	24 2/8	24 0/8	14 7/8	5	6	Waseca County	MN	Paul Hauck	1986	4,191
137 7/8	23 0/8	21 2/8	18 3/8	4	4	Williamson County	IL	Charles Zeigler	1986	4,191
137 7/8	22 3/8	21 7/8	22 2/8	5	7	Rock Island County	IL	Steve Holmgren	1986	4,191

SCORE	LENGTH OF MAIN BEAM R	LENGTH OF MAIN BEAM L	INSIDE SPREAD	NUMBER OF POINTS R	NUMBER OF POINTS L	AREA	STATE/ PROVINCE	HUNTER'S NAME	DATE	RANK
137 7/8	23 4/8	23 5/8	17 2/8	6	6	Jo Daviess County	IL	Richard Geyer	1987	4,191
137 7/8	22 4/8	22 7/8	15 3/8	4	4	Osborne County	KS	Byron G. Siemiller	1987	4,191
137 7/8	24 0/8	24 1/8	19 7/8	5	6	Sangamon County	IL	Mike Capranica	1988	4,191
137 7/8	25 1/8	24 6/8	20 1/8	4	5	Orange County	NY	Scott Fairchild	1988	4,191
137 7/8	25 1/8	25 4/8	18 1/8	5	4	Hampden County	MA	Richard Bissaillon	1988	4,191
137 7/8	24 2/8	24 1/8	19 7/8	4	4	McLean County	IL	Larry Messer	1988	4,191
137 7/8	21 6/8	21 0/8	20 5/8	6	5	Beltrami County	MN	Matt Stone	1989	4,191
137 7/8	22 6/8	24 4/8	17 2/8	7	6	Brooks County	TX	Jim L. McCrory	1989	4,191
137 7/8	21 7/8	23 1/8	16 7/8	4	6	Morris County	KS	Jeff L. Newbury	1989	4,191
137 7/8	23 1/8	23 4/8	21 1/8	4	5	Morris County	NJ	Tom LaMantia	1989	4,191
137 7/8	24 1/8	23 6/8	17 4/8	6	6	Anoka County	MN	Bruce Krinkie	1990	4,191
137 7/8	23 1/8	23 7/8	16 4/8	4	6	Holmes County	OH	Ronald S. Kline	1990	4,191
137 7/8	21 3/8	21 3/8	16 7/8	5	5	Ravalli County	MT	Charles Dooner	1990	4,191
137 7/8	23 1/8	24 0/8	15 5/8	4	4	Pike County	OH	Larry Cornett	1991	4,191
137 7/8	22 5/8	23 5/8	20 5/8	6	6	McHenry County	IL	Thomas A. Berthold	1991	4,191
137 7/8	22 7/8	23 1/8	15 5/8	4	4	Creek County	OK	Pat Murphy	1991	4,191
137 7/8	24 6/8	26 2/8	19 0/8	6	4	Prince Georges County	MD	Rob Clark	1991	4,191
137 7/8	22 5/8	23 5/8	16 0/8	5	6	Washington County	IA	Brent J. Graber	1991	4,191
137 6/8	24 5/8	23 7/8	19 2/8	4	5	Adams County	IL	William D. Force	1970	4,219
137 6/8	22 1/8	20 1/8	18 1/8	6	5	Watonwan County	MN	Thomas E. Isley	1972	4,219
137 6/8	20 7/8	21 1/8	16 4/8	5	5	Polk County	IA	John Dykes	1973	4,219
137 6/8	22 7/8	23 6/8	18 4/8	4	5	Roscommon County	MI	James J. Osentoski	1978	4,219
137 6/8	21 2/8	21 2/8	18 2/8	5	5	Goodhue County	MN	Tom Nesseth	1979	4,219
137 6/8	23 6/8	23 0/8	16 1/8	5	5	Middlesex County	CT	James Matulis	1980	4,219
137 6/8	22 0/8	22 6/8	17 6/8	5	5	Walkworth	ONT	Ken McGarrity	1982	4,219
137 6/8	20 4/8	21 5/8	26 2/8	4	6	Suffolk County	NY	Glenn L. Neuschwender	1982	4,219
137 6/8	21 2/8	21 7/8	19 6/8	5	5	Cowley County	KS	Michael R. Bowlin	1983	4,219
137 6/8	23 6/8	24 5/8	20 3/8	6	6	McHenry County	IL	Al Stroh	1983	4,219
137 6/8	21 7/8	22 6/8	16 4/8	5	5	Pine County	MN	Pat Riley	1984	4,219
137 6/8	23 1/8	23 2/8	16 2/8	4	4	Vernon County	WI	Gary Holcombe	1984	4,219
137 6/8	20 7/8	21 4/8	18 4/8	5	5	Crawford County	IL	Todd McDaniel	1985	4,219
137 6/8	22 4/8	21 7/8	17 0/8	5	5	Jefferson County	NE	Bob Funke	1985	4,219
137 6/8	25 1/8	26 1/8	16 7/8	5	4	Cumberland County	NS	P. Jeff Comeau	1985	4,219
137 6/8	23 7/8	23 3/8	17 6/8	5	4	Grand Forks County	ND	Dan M. Finnie	1986	4,219
137 6/8	23 5/8	22 4/8	19 6/8	5	4	Sauk County	WI	Kevin Pavelka	1986	4,219
137 6/8	19 0/8	20 4/8	14 4/8	5	5	Buffalo County	WI	John Kerhin	1986	4,219
137 6/8	20 7/8	19 6/8	17 2/8	5	5	Fulton County	IN	Bart Dauenhauer	1986	4,219
137 6/8	20 6/8	19 4/8	15 0/8	5	6	Russell County	KS	Terry W. Maier	1986	4,219
137 6/8	23 3/8	22 4/8	18 0/8	5	5	Morgan County	IL	Michael Cors	1987	4,219
137 6/8	24 1/8	23 0/8	20 3/8	6	5	Willow Creek	ALB	Randy Biegler	1988	4,219
137 6/8	23 2/8	23 6/8	19 4/8	6	5	Jo Daviess County	IL	John A. Basten	1988	4,219
137 6/8	23 2/8	23 2/8	21 2/8	5	5	Shawano County	WI	Don Armstrong	1989	4,219
137 6/8	23 0/8	23 1/8	17 6/8	4	4	Day County	SD	Jim Cooper	1989	4,219
137 6/8	22 1/8	21 1/8	15 7/8	8	6	Reno County	KS	Greig Sims	1989	4,219
137 6/8	22 6/8	22 6/8	17 4/8	4	5	Washington County	MN	John Bailey	1989	4,219
137 6/8	21 0/8	20 6/8	14 0/8	5	5	Kenedy County	TX	Romulo Rangel, Jr.	1990	4,219
137 6/8	23 5/8	24 6/8	21 0/8	4	5	Mahaska County	IA	James E. Roe	1990	4,219
137 6/8	21 1/8	21 5/8	16 4/8	5	4	Des Moines County	IA	Mike Carter	1990	4,219
137 6/8	22 7/8	23 0/8	19 6/8	4	4	St. Croix County	WI	Phil Hovde	1991	4,219
137 6/8	24 5/8	23 2/8	17 6/8	5	4	Vermilion County	IL	Michael Olson	1991	4,219
137 6/8	21 4/8	21 6/8	16 0/8	5	5	Davis County	IA	Gary Biles	1991	4,219
137 5/8	20 4/8	19 7/8	15 5/8	5	5	Clark County	SD	Delmar Tobey	1959	4,252
137 5/8	26 4/8	26 4/8	14 7/8	4	4	Rock County	NE	William Tutt	1963	4,252
137 5/8	20 4/8	20 4/8	17 1/8	4	4	Custer County	MT	Dale Drilling	1976	4,252
137 5/8	23 3/8	24 1/8	21 5/8	4	4	Hardin County	KY	Thomas R. Abner	1979	4,252
137 5/8	21 6/8	22 6/8	16 5/8	5	5	Pittsburg County	OK	John Badger	1979	4,252
137 5/8	21 1/8	21 1/8	14 5/8	5	6	Hamilton County	OH	Jack McConnell	1979	4,252
137 5/8	23 3/8	22 5/8	15 5/8	4	4	Cloud County	KS	Don Watowa	1982	4,252
137 5/8	17 7/8	20 5/8	15 7/8	5	6	Waukesha County	WI	Tom Millane	1982	4,252
137 5/8	23 1/8	23 0/8	20 5/8	4	4	Prince Georges County	MD	Dave Williams	1982	4,252
137 5/8	22 5/8	22 2/8	15 3/8	5	5	Chippewa County	MN	Douglas Mittag	1983	4,252
137 5/8	24 5/8	24 0/8	16 5/8	6	5	Suffolk County	VA	Mark T. Smith	1984	4,252
137 5/8	20 3/8	20 0/8	16 7/8	5	5	Parke County	IN	Leonard Outcalt	1986	4,252
137 5/8	22 6/8	23 1/8	18 7/8	5	5	Rogers County	OK	Jimmy Wilson	1986	4,252
137 5/8	22 3/8	22 1/8	17 6/8	7	7	Fayette County	OH	Jeff Sheridan	1986	4,252
137 5/8	22 7/8	23 2/8	15 3/8	5	5	St. Croix County	WI	Doug Severude	1987	4,252
137 5/8	23 3/8	22 6/8	19 7/8	5	5	Schoolcraft County	MI	Dennis W. Kleeman	1987	4,252
137 5/8	21 5/8	20 6/8	18 1/8	4	4	Clarke County	IA	Doyle Curnes	1988	4,252
137 5/8	21 7/8	21 6/8	14 7/8	5	5	Hardin County	IA	Terry Portz	1988	4,252
137 5/8	21 7/8	20 7/8	15 1/8	5	5	Sheboygan County	WI	Wayne Ustby	1988	4,252

SCORE	LENGTH OF R MAIN BEAM L		INSIDE SPREAD	NUMBER OF R POINTS L		AREA	STATE/ PROVINCE	HUNTER'S NAME	DATE	RANK
137 5/8	23 1/8	23 3/8	15 4/8	7	7	Shawnee County	KS	Mark Broxterman	1988	4,252
137 5/8	24 6/8	23 5/8	15 6/8	6	4	Washington County	IL	Paul Graves, Jr.	1988	4,252
137 5/8	21 5/8	22 2/8	17 1/8	5	4	Hancock County	MS	Clifford E. Chauvin	1989	4,252
137 5/8	21 1/8	22 5/8	17 7/8	5	5	Switzerland County	IN	Rick Ritz	1989	4,252
137 5/8	24 1/8	23 3/8	15 2/8	5	5	Calhoun County	MI	Steven F. Collier	1989	4,252
137 5/8	20 1/8	21 3/8	15 0/8	6	5	Woodbury County	IA	John W. Beeson	1989	4,252
137 5/8	23 7/8	24 6/8	18 3/8	5	4	Fairfield County	CT	Gary W. Liljengren	1990	4,252
137 5/8	22 2/8	21 2/8	15 7/8	5	5	La Salle County	IL	Dirk Foltynewicz	1990	4,252
137 5/8	24 5/8	25 0/8	22 1/8	4	4	Caroline County	MD	J. Eric Wise	1991	4,252
137 5/8	22 1/8	21 3/8	19 3/8	5	5	Peoria County	IL	David Emken	1991	4,252
137 5/8	22 6/8	22 7/8	16 7/8	5	5	Miami County	KS	David L. Scott	1991	4,252
137 5/8	22 2/8	23 0/8	15 7/8	5	5	Missoula County	MT	Tom Kiesel	1992	4,252
137 5/8	20 3/8	21 6/8	17 7/8	5	5	Harding County	SD	Kim Smith	1992	4,252
137 4/8	23 4/8	23 6/8	18 2/8	5	4	Rice County	MN	Robert W. Berg	1965	4,284
137 4/8	23 6/8	22 0/8	21 4/8	5	5	Spink County	SD	Ray McIntyre	1967	4,284
137 4/8	25 4/8	24 0/8	18 6/8	4	4	Berrien County	MI	Lawrence C. Ford	1981	4,284
137 4/8	21 5/8	20 7/8	14 2/8	5	6	Pope County	MN	Roger Tollefson	1982	4,284
137 4/8	22 6/8	22 6/8	18 2/8	4	4	Newaygo County	MI	David Davis	1982	4,284
137 4/8	23 3/8	23 0/8	16 4/8	4	5	Vernon County	WI	Jerry Willer	1983	4,284
137 4/8	21 2/8	20 3/8	15 4/8	6	5	Pierson	MAN	Brad Minshull	1984	4,284
137 4/8	23 5/8	23 1/8	18 6/8	5	5	Nelson County	KY	James H. Stiles	1984	4,284
137 4/8	21 2/8	20 4/8	19 0/8	5	5	Sauk County	WI	Jimmie S Gluth	1984	4,284
137 4/8	22 5/8	20 4/8	16 4/8	5	5	Albany County	NY	James O'Connor	1984	4,284
137 4/8	22 3/8	22 7/8	16 6/8	5	5	Rogers County	OK	Ernie Merydith	1986	4,284
137 4/8	23 3/8	20 0/8	22 0/8	7	7	Union County	IL	Louis Biggs	1986	4,284
137 4/8	22 2/8	21 4/8	17 0/8	5	5	Crittenden County	KY	Karl W. Brantley	1986	4,284
137 4/8	22 3/8	22 0/8	19 6/8	4	4	Chilton County	AL	James White	1986	4,284
137 4/8	24 7/8	23 7/8	18 3/8	5	6	Waukesha County	WI	Max Mollgaard	1987	4,284
137 4/8	24 0/8	23 2/8	17 0/8	5	5	Forest County	WI	Ron H. Vander Kelen	1987	4,284
137 4/8	23 3/8	22 5/8	17 2/8	5	5	Garrett County	MD	Albert Schrock	1987	4,284
137 4/8	21 0/8	21 2/8	16 0/8	6	6	St. Joseph County	IN	Michael L. Ritter	1988	4,284
137 4/8	23 3/8	23 3/8	15 0/8	4	4	Racine County	WI	Robert Zortman	1988	4,284
137 4/8	21 4/8	21 5/8	19 0/8	5	5	Brooks County	TX	J. Dale Hale	1988	4,284
137 4/8	22 7/8	24 4/8	17 4/8	5	4	Forest County	WI	Duwayne C. Schneider	1988	4,284
137 4/8	25 4/8	24 7/8	17 6/8	4	4	Webster County	IA	Gary Forkner	1988	4,284
137 4/8	22 2/8	21 6/8	16 4/8	5	6	Sauk County	WI	Ronald VanSwol	1988	4,284
137 4/8	21 6/8	23 7/8	19 7/8	5	4	Stearns County	MN	Mike Poss	1989	4,284
137 4/8	21 1/8	21 3/8	15 0/8	6	5	Dubuque County	IA	Jim Hedley	1989	4,284
137 4/8	24 3/8	24 4/8	17 0/8	4	4	Choctaw County	MS	Charles B. Box	1990	4,284
137 4/8	22 7/8	24 2/8	14 3/8	6	8	St. Croix County	WI	Robert H. Olson	1990	4,284
137 4/8	24 1/8	24 1/8	18 4/8	4	4	Waushara County	WI	Jeffry J. Paulus	1990	4,284
137 4/8	25 0/8	24 4/8	19 2/8	5	5	Lunenburg County	VA	Thomas M. Hicks, Jr.	1990	4,284
137 4/8	22 2/8	23 0/8	18 4/8	5	5	Waukesha County	WI	Kevin Anderson	1990	4,284
137 4/8	22 0/8	22 5/8	18 0/8	5	5	Beltrami County	MN	Arnold Christanson	1990	4,284
137 4/8	22 0/8	21 5/8	15 6/8	5	5	Adams County	WI	Gary L. Ackerman	1990	4,284
137 4/8	23 7/8	22 7/8	17 5/8	7	8	Baca County	CO	Eddie Claypool	1990	4,284
137 4/8	23 3/8	23 7/8	18 3/8	6	5	Ogle County	IL	Lyle Bonnell	1990	4,284
137 4/8	25 1/8	26 1/8	23 3/8	5	5	Washtenaw County	MI	Brenda J. Brown	1991	4,284
137 4/8	21 1/8	21 4/8	17 2/8	5	5	Bureau County	IL	Mark E. Michael	1991	4,284
137 4/8	22 1/8	21 7/8	17 7/8	5	6	Brown County	IL	Kevin Weeks	1991	4,284
137 4/8	24 4/8	22 5/8	14 5/8	5	5	Washington County	KS	Stan Brustowicz	1991	4,284
137 4/8	21 7/8	21 4/8	17 3/8	4	5	Berks County	PA	Paul S. Strunk, Jr.	1992	4,284
137 3/8	22 0/8	21 4/8	19 7/8	5	4	Comanche County	OK	Edward J. Baumlin, Jr.	1960	4,323
137 3/8	20 6/8	20 2/8	12 6/8	5	10	Kootenai County	ID	John Ruthuen	1961	4,323
137 3/8	23 5/8	23 3/8	16 6/8	4	5	Allegan County	MI	Clayton Foster	1964	4,323
137 3/8	25 6/8	23 1/8	15 7/8	4	4	Madison County	IN	Lee Middleton	1966	4,323
137 3/8	25 1/8	24 4/8	20 7/8	4	4	Trempealeau County	WI	Randall J. Van Vleet	1966	4,323
137 3/8	20 2/8	19 7/8	16 5/8	5	5	Stone County	MO	Charles A. Myers	1974	4,323
137 3/8	22 3/8	22 3/8	19 1/8	4	4	Guthrie County	IA	John D. Hambleton	1974	4,323
137 3/8	23 2/8	20 2/8	17 0/8	5	6	Wood County	OH	Othon E. Katakis	1980	4,323
137 3/8	22 2/8	23 3/8	19 7/8	4	5	Dane County	WI	Donald W. Pache	1980	4,323
137 3/8	20 7/8	21 2/8	15 4/8	6	5	Jo Daviess County	IL	Herb Imbus	1981	4,323
137 3/8	21 4/8	20 6/8	15 3/8	5	5	St. Croix County	WI	Daniel A. Score	1982	4,323
137 3/8	23 4/8	23 2/8	15 5/8	4	5	Kootenai County	ID	David R. Oliver	1983	4,323
137 3/8	23 1/8	25 2/8	20 3/8	4	5	Meeker County	MN	Thomas Wylie	1983	4,323
137 3/8	22 5/8	22 5/8	16 6/8	6	4	Marion County	IL	Joseph B. Smith III	1983	4,323
137 3/8	21 0/8	19 7/8	15 7/8	5	5	Henry County	VA	Mike Weaver	1985	4,323
137 3/8	23 6/8	23 5/8	17 7/8	4	4	Green County	WI	Steve Bergemann	1986	4,323
137 3/8	23 6/8	20 7/8	19 7/8	5	5	Stephenson County	IL	Jeff S. Olsen	1986	4,323
137 3/8	23 7/8	23 6/8	16 4/8	5	6	Vinton County	OH	Daniel E. Kaiser	1986	4,323

Score	Length of Main Beam R	L	Inside Spread	Number of Points R	L	Area	State/ Province	Hunter's Name	Date	Rank
137 3/8	24 5/8	23 6/8	21 3/8	4	4	Monroe County	PA	Terry R. Schneck	1987	4,323
137 3/8	25 5/8	24 3/8	17 3/8	5	5	Clay County	IL	Gary D. Cornell	1988	4,323
137 3/8	24 6/8	25 2/8	17 3/8	6	7	Pulaski County	KY	Bobbie Ryan	1988	4,323
137 3/8	21 5/8	21 2/8	14 1/8	6	6	Waushara County	WI	Chad Kropp	1989	4,323
137 3/8	25 3/8	25 3/8	19 7/8	4	5	Dane County	WI	James S. Obrecht	1989	4,323
137 3/8	24 6/8	20 7/8	17 2/8	5	7	Yankton County	SD	Gary Sejnohn	1989	4,323
137 3/8	24 1/8	23 5/8	19 7/8	4	4	Lancaster County	PA	J. John Buhay	1990	4,323
137 3/8	23 6/8	23 6/8	16 1/8	4	4	Delaware County	IA	Robert Becker	1990	4,323
137 3/8	20 2/8	20 1/8	17 3/8	6	5	Athens County	OH	Bruce Hann	1990	4,323
137 3/8	24 1/8	24 7/8	18 3/8	4	4	Jefferson County	WI	Rodney A. Sheldon	1990	4,323
137 3/8	23 2/8	23 3/8	19 5/8	7	7	Suffolk County	NY	Richard Berger	1990	4,323
137 3/8	19 5/8	20 3/8	17 1/8	5	5	Oconto County	WI	Keith M. Goodwill	1990	4,323
137 3/8	21 7/8	22 0/8	16 3/8	6	5	Henry County	MO	W. Chapman Spangler	1991	4,323
137 3/8	23 6/8	23 2/8	16 7/8	4	5	McKenzie County	ND	James Raymond Legdre	1991	4,323
137 3/8	23 2/8	23 7/8	17 6/8	6	4	Hardin County	KY	John Standafer	1991	4,323
137 3/8	23 4/8	22 7/8	17 5/8	4	4	Calhoun County	MI	Peter R. Grevers	1992	4,323
137 2/8	23 2/8	24 7/8	18 5/8	8	5	Phelps County	NE	Dick Cepel	1959	4,357
137 2/8	21 1/8	20 0/8	17 4/8	6	5	Brown County	SD	Richard Felch	1966	4,357
137 2/8	23 1/8	24 1/8	16 4/8	5	5	Marion County	IA	David Hedgecock	1973	4,357
137 2/8	22 7/8	23 2/8	17 2/8	5	4	Murray County	MN	Dale Florek	1976	4,357
137 2/8	21 4/8	21 1/8	17 2/8	7	7	Laramie River	WY	Mark A. Brant	1976	4,357
137 2/8	23 2/8	23 6/8	17 4/8	5	5	Brown County	OH	Howard Ayers	1977	4,357
137 2/8	22 4/8	22 6/8	19 0/8	5	5	Sanders County	MT	Dyrk Eddie	1980	4,357
137 2/8	25 0/8	24 4/8	16 6/8	4	4	Putnam County	TN	Doyle B. Wilmoth	1980	4,357
137 2/8	20 6/8	20 7/8	15 2/8	5	5	Rock County	WI	Ronald S. Pulcine	1981	4,357
137 2/8	21 4/8	22 5/8	16 6/8	5	5	Teton County	MT	William McRae	1982	4,357
137 2/8	21 7/8	18 5/8	16 4/8	7	6	St. Charles County	MO	Donald L. Hauser	1982	4,357
137 2/8	21 6/8	21 4/8	17 6/8	7	5	Linn County	IA	Dennis W. Frye	1983	4,357
137 2/8	23 6/8	23 5/8	20 0/8	4	4	Jo Daviess County	IL	Kenneth Scharfenorth	1983	4,357
137 2/8	23 1/8	22 4/8	16 2/8	4	5	Hughes County	SD	Alvin Truax	1983	4,357
137 2/8	22 1/8	20 2/8	17 2/8	5	5	Delaware County	OH	David Orndorf	1983	4,357
137 2/8	24 1/8	24 2/8	17 0/8	5	4	Arkansas County	AR	Sam Snowden	1984	4,357
137 2/8	22 1/8	21 7/8	18 0/8	4	4	Belmont County	OH	Walter Kapiskovsky	1984	4,357
137 2/8	22 0/8	21 4/8	17 0/8	5	5	Rock County	WI	Ronald S. Pulcine	1984	4,357
137 2/8	25 4/8	25 1/8	18 6/8	5	5	Sauk County	WI	Daniel A. Mundth	1985	4,357
137 2/8	22 4/8	23 0/8	17 4/8	5	4	Jewell County	KS	Mahlon McDill	1985	4,357
137 2/8	23 0/8	23 5/8	19 0/8	4	5	Outagamie County	WI	Greg D. Haese	1986	4,357
137 2/8	23 7/8	23 6/8	20 6/8	4	4	St. Joseph County	MI	Eric Roberts	1986	4,357
137 2/8	22 4/8	22 0/8	17 4/8	6	4	Benson County	ND	Clarence Toso, Jr.	1986	4,357
137 2/8	22 1/8	21 1/8	17 4/8	5	6	Allen County	KS	John C. Cleaver	1986	4,357
137 2/8	23 1/8	22 6/8	16 3/8	7	5	Jo Daviess County	IL	Thomas J. Smith	1986	4,357
137 2/8	22 4/8	22 0/8	16 0/8	5	5	Vermilion County	IL	David Downing	1986	4,357
137 2/8	23 4/8	23 5/8	18 2/8	6	6	Jefferson County	IN	George E Yazel	1988	4,357
137 2/8	21 3/8	21 6/8	15 7/8	7	6	Iron County	WI	Steve Innes	1988	4,357
137 2/8	21 5/8	20 4/8	16 0/8	5	5	Wright County	MN	Gregory T. Krieger	1988	4,357
137 2/8	23 1/8	22 0/8	17 0/8	4	4	Dakota County	NE	Michael W. McKenna	1988	4,357
137 2/8	24 5/8	24 4/8	24 5/8	5	4	Lehigh County	PA	Scott J. Schrader	1989	4,357
137 2/8	21 3/8	21 6/8	19 4/8	5	6	Huntingdon County	PA	Carl Zimmerman	1989	4,357
137 2/8	25 4/8	24 4/8	16 6/8	5	4	Hot Springs County	AR	Johnny L. Fryar	1989	4,357
137 2/8	21 2/8	20 5/8	16 2/8	4	4	Champaign County	IL	Bud Barnes	1989	4,357
137 2/8	23 7/8	24 0/8	18 1/8	6	6	Hamilton County	IA	Arlin Dickinson	1989	4,357
137 2/8	22 5/8	22 6/8	18 6/8	5	4	Kingman County	KS	Dan Jacobs	1989	4,357
137 2/8	22 3/8	22 7/8	15 7/8	5	4	Kidder County	ND	Steven L. Weisenburger	1990	4,357
137 2/8	23 0/8	23 3/8	16 4/8	5	4	Pepin County	WI	Leonard Schneider	1990	4,357
137 2/8	22 3/8	22 3/8	18 2/8	5	5	Buffalo County	WI	Steve Rucinski	1990	4,357
137 2/8	22 3/8	21 6/8	17 1/8	7	7	Jo Daviess County	IL	Steve Cole	1990	4,357
137 2/8	22 6/8	22 2/8	18 0/8	6	5	Wright County	IA	Jeff Nelson	1990	4,357
137 2/8	23 6/8	23 1/8	16 1/8	5	5	Marquette County	MI	John Carl Clark	1990	4,357
137 2/8	20 6/8	21 4/8	17 2/8	5	5	Somerset County	PA	Sheldon Barron	1991	4,357
137 2/8	23 3/8	22 1/8	21 2/8	6	6	Madison County	IA	Kent McMillen	1991	4,357
137 2/8	21 1/8	23 0/8	18 2/8	6	5	Jasper County	IL	Jack Houser	1991	4,357
137 2/8	23 0/8	21 6/8	18 6/8	5	5	Hillsborough County	NH	Bruce A. Thibodeau	1991	4,357
137 1/8	26 5/8	24 7/8	18 5/8	4	4	Bartholomew County	IN	Jimmy Middleton	1963	4,403
137 1/8	22 4/8	21 4/8	19 7/8	5	5	Rock County	MN	Orville Hamm	1976	4,403
137 1/8	26 6/8	24 2/8	17 3/8	4	5	Muskingum County	OH	William H. Archer	1976	4,403
137 1/8	25 2/8	24 2/8	19 7/8	5	5	Newton County	IN	James Manes	1976	4,403
137 1/8	22 6/8	22 4/8	16 1/8	5	5	Itasca County	MN	Donald Kenneth Kress	1977	4,403
137 1/8	21 0/8	21 5/8	16 1/8	6	5	Tompkins County	NY	Carlo Troise	1978	4,403
137 1/8	23 7/8	23 3/8	18 0/8	6	5	Grant County	WI	Lloyd J. Hach	1982	4,403
137 1/8	21 6/8	20 0/8	18 2/8	6	6	Fairfield County	OH	Paul R. Baker	1982	4,403

WHITETAIL DEER *(Typical Antlers)*

(Continued)

SCORE	LENGTH OF R MAIN BEAM L		INSIDE SPREAD	NUMBER OF R POINTS L		AREA	STATE/ PROVINCE	HUNTER'S NAME	DATE	RANK
137 1/8	24 0/8	23 4/8	18 7/8	5	4	Hardin County	IA	Tom Herold	1982	4,403
137 1/8	26 4/8	24 1/8	22 1/8	4	4	Christian County	IL	Daniel Hinds	1983	4,403
137 1/8	21 7/8	22 1/8	14 7/8	4	5	Rhea County	TN	Leland H. Rothwell, Sr.	1983	4,403
137 1/8	22 5/8	22 7/8	18 7/8	4	4	Carroll County	IL	Gary R. Schneider	1983	4,403
137 1/8	24 3/8	23 7/8	17 5/8	5	4	Allamakee County	IA	Craig Riechmann	1983	4,403
137 1/8	20 7/8	20 5/8	16 3/8	5	6	Jasper County	IA	Kevin Lynn Patterson	1984	4,403
137 1/8	21 3/8	22 1/8	17 7/8	4	4	Union County	IL	Kevin G. Bach	1985	4,403
137 1/8	20 6/8	21 7/8	14 7/8	6	5	Rock Island County	IL	Dr. Tom Brozovich	1987	4,403
137 1/8	22 1/8	23 0/8	18 1/8	5	4	Warren County	IA	Dale Smith	1987	4,403
137 1/8	23 2/8	22 7/8	16 3/8	4	4	Muskegon County	MI	Dan Thompson	1987	4,403
137 1/8	21 3/8	21 0/8	15 6/8	6	5	La Salle County	IL	Fran Klaas	1987	4,403
137 1/8	22 0/8	22 0/8	17 5/8	5	5	Putnam County	IN	Steve Buckallew	1987	4,403
137 1/8	22 5/8	23 3/8	15 2/8	4	5	Langlade County	WI	Jerry Aulik	1988	4,403
137 1/8	21 2/8	21 3/8	16 3/8	5	5	Columbia County	WI	Daniel L. Kaehne	1988	4,403
137 1/8	22 7/8	22 7/8	13 2/8	7	5	Pittsburg County	OK	Jeff Beach	1988	4,403
137 1/8	20 0/8	20 3/8	17 5/8	5	6	Ogle County	IL	Russell Robak	1988	4,403
137 1/8	24 0/8	23 7/8	17 0/8	7	4	Southampton County	VA	Jerry Vick	1988	4,403
137 1/8	20 3/8	19 6/8	18 1/8	5	5	Barron County	WI	Albert Fox	1989	4,403
137 1/8	21 6/8	22 1/8	20 7/8	5	5	Lake County	IN	James C. Gates	1989	4,403
137 1/8	26 0/8	24 4/8	19 5/8	4	4	Queen Annes County	MD	Mervin Lee Beiler	1989	4,403
137 1/8	24 6/8	26 6/8	21 6/8	6	6	Washington County	MN	Robert Wild	1989	4,403
137 1/8	25 1/8	24 6/8	18 1/8	6	6	Baltimore County	MD	Rick Thompson	1990	4,403
137 1/8	21 6/8	24 0/8	15 6/8	4	5	Woodbury County	IA	Mike McBride	1990	4,403
137 1/8	20 7/8	21 1/8	15 7/8	5	6	Saline County	IL	John Choate	1990	4,403
137 1/8	24 2/8	25 6/8	15 6/8	5	5	Harford County	MD	Mark McGovern	1991	4,403
137 1/8	22 2/8	22 3/8	16 3/8	5	6	Buffalo County	WI	Mike Chelf	1991	4,403
137 1/8	23 6/8	23 3/8	18 5/8	5	4	Clayton County	IA	Eugene Arndt	1991	4,403
137 1/8	21 5/8	22 4/8	18 7/8	8	7	Sac County	IA	Lee C. Green	1991	4,403
137 0/8	26 0/8	24 0/8	19 6/8	5	4	Hughes County	SD	Gerald Snyder	1963	4,439
137 0/8	22 0/8	22 3/8	20 4/8	4	5	Berks County	PA	Frank 'Rit' Heller	1971	4,439
137 0/8	21 4/8	22 3/8	18 2/8	4	7	Black Hawk County	IA	Bob Wood	1971	4,439
137 0/8	23 5/8	23 6/8	22 4/8	4	4	Freeborn County	MN	Brian Johnson	1978	4,439
137 0/8	24 5/8	25 7/8	20 2/8	5	4	Iroquois County	IL	Terry D. McDaniel	1978	4,439
137 0/8	22 1/8	22 3/8	17 0/8	5	4	Custer County	MT	Jim Walters	1978	4,439
137 0/8	21 5/8	22 2/8	14 6/8	4	4	Blue Earth County	MN	Stanley Defries	1980	4,439
137 0/8	22 2/8	23 1/8	15 5/8	5	6	Drew County	AR	Herman S. Fleming	1980	4,439
137 0/8	23 3/8	22 7/8	16 4/8	4	4	Walworth County	WI	Robert Mereness	1980	4,439
137 0/8	21 5/8	21 6/8	16 6/8	5	5	Scott County	KY	Milton Lee Pribble	1980	4,439
137 0/8	26 3/8	25 7/8	20 4/8	3	3	Cumberland County	ME	Richard L. Cote	1981	4,439
137 0/8	21 5/8	20 3/8	17 2/8	5	5	Randolph County	MO	Ronald Chirillo	1982	4,439
137 0/8	20 0/8	20 3/8	17 0/8	5	5	Douglas County	WI	Carl Ellison	1983	4,439
137 0/8	24 0/8	23 3/8	18 0/8	5	5	Crawford County	WI	Ken Fernette	1984	4,439
137 0/8	21 7/8	22 1/8	17 3/8	5	7	La Crosse County	WI	Steve Puent	1984	4,439
137 0/8	22 3/8	24 1/8	15 0/8	4	5	Green County	WI	William H. Holt	1986	4,439
137 0/8	22 3/8	20 7/8	17 6/8	5	5	Litchfield County	CT	John C. Murphy, Sr.	1986	4,439
137 0/8	23 1/8	24 7/8	12 4/8	6	7	Shawano County	WI	William E. Stoltenberg	1986	4,439
137 0/8	22 4/8	23 1/8	17 6/8	4	5	Pierce County	WI	Jim Klein	1986	4,439
137 0/8	21 5/8	22 1/8	18 2/8	4	4	Sauk County	WI	Randy Neises	1986	4,439
137 0/8	22 2/8	22 2/8	15 7/8	6	6	Reno County	KS	John R. Richardson	1986	4,439
137 0/8	21 3/8	23 2/8	15 6/8	5	5	Bucks County	PA	Harold E. Smith	1987	4,439
137 0/8	20 1/8	20 4/8	14 6/8	5	5	Kosciusko County	IN	Dave Shively	1987	4,439
137 0/8	22 7/8	22 6/8	18 6/8	4	4	Fillmore County	MN	John W. Zahrte	1987	4,439
137 0/8	24 5/8	24 1/8	19 0/8	4	4	Hancock County	IN	Kent L. Fisk	1987	4,439
137 0/8	22 0/8	22 1/8	17 4/8	5	5	Wyoming County	WV	Lloyd Whitt	1987	4,439
137 0/8	22 6/8	21 4/8	19 4/8	5	4	Medina County	TX	Mike Palmer	1988	4,439
137 0/8	23 0/8	23 3/8	16 4/8	5	7	Macon County	MO	Harlan DeBoer	1988	4,439
137 0/8	26 6/8	26 0/8	17 6/8	5	4	Nelson County	VA	Larry W. Toms	1988	4,439
137 0/8	24 0/8	23 6/8	17 0/8	4	5	Wabasha County	MN	Dale Hoffman	1989	4,439
137 0/8	23 6/8	23 2/8	19 0/8	5	5	Somerset County	NJ	Anthony Beceiro	1989	4,439
137 0/8	26 1/8	24 2/8	18 0/8	5	4	Baltimore County	MD	Richard B. Traband	1989	4,439
137 0/8	24 0/8	23 4/8	16 4/8	4	4	Cass County	NE	Tommy M. Brown	1990	4,439
137 0/8	22 7/8	24 0/8	17 4/8	5	5	Bedford County	VA	Rocky Lee Williams	1990	4,439
137 0/8	20 3/8	20 5/8	15 3/8	6	5	Price County	WI	Rubert Retzlaff	1991	4,439
137 0/8	22 6/8	23 3/8	16 4/8	6	5	Plymouth County	IA	Jason J. Dannenberg	1991	4,439
137 0/8	21 4/8	24 3/8	18 4/8	6	5	Knox County	KY	Tony Morris	1991	4,439
137 0/8	23 4/8	23 4/8	20 2/8	4	5	Dunn County	WI	Scott Stuart	1991	4,439
137 0/8	22 5/8	23 4/8	18 4/8	4	4	Fayette County	IL	Jon Washburn	1991	4,439
137 0/8	22 0/8	23 2/8	19 0/8	6	5	Meigs County	OH	Mike Whitley	1991	4,439
137 0/8	23 0/8	23 7/8	19 6/8	4	4	Allegheny County	PA	Paul W. Zoller	1992	4,439
136 7/8	20 2/8	19 1/8	15 2/8	8	7	Ashland County	WI	Jim McGarvey	1965	4,480

WHITETAIL DEER *(Typical Antlers)*

MINIMUM SCORE 125

(Continued)

SCORE	LENGTH OF MAIN BEAM R	L	INSIDE SPREAD	NUMBER OF POINTS R	L	AREA	STATE/ PROVINCE	HUNTER'S NAME	DATE	RANK
136 7/8	23 5/8	23 6/8	18 1/8	4	5	Jefferson County	IN	James Coldiron	1972	4,480
136 7/8	22 3/8	22 6/8	17 0/8	6	5	Sullivan County	IN	John Chesterfield	1977	4,480
136 7/8	21 2/8	21 4/8	18 7/8	5	5	Fulton County	IL	Jeffrey L. Keefauver	1979	4,480
136 7/8	23 2/8	23 7/8	20 1/8	5	4	Muskingum County	OH	Larry Shoop	1979	4,480
136 7/8	23 5/8	24 0/8	19 3/8	5	5	Montgomery County	IN	Derrick Kidd	1980	4,480
136 7/8	24 6/8	23 7/8	21 1/8	4	4	Union County	IL	Carl E. Cronk	1983	4,480
136 7/8	20 7/8	19 5/8	15 3/8	5	5	Ozaukee County	WI	Scott T. Frank	1983	4,480
136 7/8	19 7/8	20 1/8	17 5/8	5	5	Kingsbury County	SD	Joe Jensen	1983	4,480
136 7/8	22 5/8	22 2/8	16 4/8	9	6	Washington County	KS	Randy Wilson	1983	4,480
136 7/8	22 3/8	22 2/8	18 3/8	4	5	Montgomery County	PA	Robert Pyne	1985	4,480
136 7/8	22 4/8	21 4/8	17 7/8	5	5	Woodson County	KS	Jerry Ramshaw	1985	4,480
136 7/8	25 1/8	25 1/8	17 6/8	6	5	Coshocton County	OH	Keith Duncan	1985	4,480
136 7/8	23 6/8	24 0/8	16 2/8	7	7	Door County	WI	Daniel W. Herrbold	1986	4,480
136 7/8	24 5/8	24 6/8	21 7/8	4	4	Pike County	MO	Robert Frank	1986	4,480
136 7/8	22 3/8	22 3/8	20 1/8	4	4	Iron County	MI	Gene Luttrull	1986	4,480
136 7/8	23 3/8	24 0/8	21 7/8	5	5	Somerset County	NJ	Dave Cutting	1987	4,480
136 7/8	21 0/8	21 1/8	15 1/8	7	5	Green Lake County	WI	Michael D. Price	1987	4,480
136 7/8	19 2/8	18 2/8	15 7/8	5	5	Jefferson County	KS	Steve Gomel	1987	4,480
136 7/8	21 2/8	20 6/8	16 4/8	6	6	Jo Daviess County	IL	Thomas J. Smith	1987	4,480
136 7/8	23 6/8	23 4/8	16 5/8	4	5	McCreary County	KY	Eddie Howard	1988	4,480
136 7/8	21 1/8	20 1/8	21 1/8	5	5	Monona County	IA	Dennis Rush	1988	4,480
136 7/8	23 7/8	23 7/8	16 1/8	5	5	Adams County	OH	J. Dale Gaffin	1988	4,480
136 7/8	24 1/8	25 1/8	21 1/8	5	4	Alleghany County	NC	Todd Evans	1989	4,480
136 7/8	23 7/8	23 2/8	17 3/8	5	5	New Haven County	CT	Thomas C Ravizza	1989	4,480
136 7/8	22 5/8	23 0/8	15 3/8	5	5	Lawrence County	KY	Alfred Adkins	1989	4,480
136 7/8	21 6/8	22 0/8	16 5/8	5	5	Dunn County	WI	Mark Gardow	1989	4,480
136 7/8	21 6/8	21 3/8	19 1/8	4	4	Madison County	IL	Leroy Shea	1990	4,480
136 7/8	22 3/8	23 1/8	17 3/8	5	5	Sawyer County	WI	David Jacobson	1991	4,480
136 7/8	23 5/8	24 4/8	18 3/8	5	5	Trempealeau County	WI	Todd Nelson	1991	4,480
136 7/8	25 2/8	23 7/8	20 5/8	5	4	Montgomery County	MD	Roger D. Stewart	1992	4,480
136 7/8	22 7/8	23 0/8	19 5/8	5	5	Marathon County	WI	Paul D. Waliczek	1992	4,480
136 6/8	23 2/8	22 4/8	15 4/8	4	5	Ogle County	IL	Edwin Fitzgerald	1963	4,512
136 6/8	22 0/8	20 6/8	16 5/8	5	6	Hamlin County	SD	James Larson	1963	4,512
136 6/8	23 5/8	24 2/8	17 4/8	4	4	Mower County	MN	Robert Meyer	1965	4,512
136 6/8	21 4/8	20 6/8	18 2/8	5	6	Watonwan County	MN	Gary G. Miest	1969	4,512
136 6/8	22 1/8	20 6/8	17 4/8	5	5	Lake County	SD	Dennis DeBoer	1974	4,512
136 6/8	23 3/8	24 5/8	21 1/8	5	5	Whiteside County	IL	Art Heinze	1975	4,512
136 6/8	22 4/8	21 2/8	20 5/8	4	5	Queen Annes County	MD	Norman C. Herdegen	1977	4,512
136 6/8	27 4/8	24 0/8	18 4/8	6	6	Livingston County	MI	Peter Bolen	1979	4,512
136 6/8	22 4/8	23 5/8	17 0/8	6	5	Coahoma County	MS	David Holcomb	1979	4,512
136 6/8	22 0/8	20 6/8	16 0/8	5	4	Houston County	MN	Howard Lampert	1979	4,512
136 6/8	21 7/8	22 3/8	17 2/8	4	4	Waukesha County	WI	Jeff Dickenson	1984	4,512
136 6/8	22 0/8	22 3/8	17 6/8	5	5	Chippewa County	MI	James R. Dreves	1985	4,512
136 6/8	23 2/8	23 3/8	17 0/8	4	4	Sequoyah County	OK	Kyle Holt	1986	4,512
136 6/8	24 2/8	24 3/8	15 5/8	5	4	Dane County	WI	Jack Schulenberg	1986	4,512
136 6/8	22 3/8	23 2/8	17 0/8	5	5	Des Moines County	IA	Thomas E. Knoll	1986	4,512
136 6/8	19 3/8	21 3/8	14 2/8	5	5	Coffey County	KS	Dennis DeForest	1986	4,512
136 6/8	23 5/8	23 5/8	16 4/8	4	4	Anoka County	MN	Anthony J. Emmerich	1987	4,512
136 6/8	29 6/8	28 2/8	18 6/8	8	8	Perry County	IL	Danny Dauksch	1987	4,512
136 6/8	22 0/8	21 3/8	16 6/8	5	5	Athens County	OH	Alan W. Shafer	1987	4,512
136 6/8	19 0/8	21 4/8	15 2/8	5	5	Rock Island County	IL	Mikel D. Angel	1987	4,512
136 6/8	21 2/8	20 6/8	15 0/8	5	5	Grant County	SD	Russel L. Christensen	1987	4,512
136 6/8	23 5/8	22 7/8	19 7/8	4	5	Fayette County	IA	Paul C. Crawford	1987	4,512
136 6/8	22 6/8	22 2/8	19 2/8	6	6	Sangamon County	IL	Steve Tice	1987	4,512
136 6/8	22 6/8	23 1/8	16 6/8	5	5	Buffalo County	WI	Rodney Peterson	1988	4,512
136 6/8	22 5/8	23 1/8	17 6/8	4	5	Bayfield County	WI	Steven Schillinger	1988	4,512
136 6/8	22 2/8	22 7/8	17 4/8	6	7	Clark County	WI	Larry Davel	1988	4,512
136 6/8	27 3/8	25 3/8	20 4/8	4	4	Knox County	IL	Rod Combs	1988	4,512
136 6/8	22 5/8	22 3/8	14 6/8	5	4	Putnam County	IL	Jerome Sampson	1988	4,512
136 6/8	21 7/8	22 4/8	20 0/8	4	4	Kiowa County	KS	Karl Ballard	1988	4,512
136 6/8	21 3/8	21 0/8	20 6/8	4	4	Langlade County	WI	John Woltman	1989	4,512
136 6/8	21 3/8	19 7/8	15 4/8	6	5	Polk County	IA	Richard Roberts	1990	4,512
136 6/8	23 1/8	23 2/8	17 6/8	4	4	Hillsdale County	MI	Fred Abbas	1990	4,512
136 6/8	22 5/8	21 2/8	14 6/8	6	7	Waupaca County	WI	Charles Edminster	1990	4,512
136 6/8	23 4/8	23 4/8	19 2/8	4	4	Du Page County	IL	Richard B. Maish	1990	4,512
136 6/8	24 0/8	25 0/8	16 0/8	4	5	Macon County	GA	Ricky L. Gibbs	1991	4,512
136 6/8	22 7/8	22 5/8	18 2/8	5	5	Dodge County	MN	James Kuasnicka	1991	4,512
136 6/8	21 3/8	20 6/8	17 0/8	6	6	Spruce Grove	ALB	Lawrence Huot	1991	4,512
136 6/8	23 3/8	23 1/8	16 2/8	4	7	Oakland County	MI	Walter Poplawski	1991	4,512
136 6/8	23 1/8	23 1/8	19 6/8	6	6	Van Buren County	IA	Bill Grahlherr	1991	4,512

MINIMUM SCORE 125

(Continued)

SCORE	LENGTH OF MAIN BEAM		INSIDE SPREAD	NUMBER OF POINTS		AREA	STATE/ PROVINCE	HUNTER'S NAME	DATE	RANK
	R	L		R	L					
136 6/8	24 4/8	23 2/8	18 6/8	5	4	Jefferson County	NE	Norman Tedrow	1991	4,512
136 6/8	19 6/8	19 6/8	15 4/8	5	4	Uvalde County	TX	Wyatt Birkner	1992	4,512
136 5/8	24 6/8	24 6/8	18 5/8	4	4	Braxton County	WV	John M. Friend	1965	4,553
136 5/8	23 4/8	22 5/8	16 5/8	4	4	Marathon County	WI	Leroy Kazmierczak	1966	4,553
136 5/8	20 0/8	22 0/8	18 6/8	5	5	Perry County	IL	Robert P. Berry	1980	4,553
136 5/8	21 4/8	20 6/8	14 7/8	5	5	Huron County	MI	John F. Deroche	1981	4,553
136 5/8	22 1/8	22 0/8	16 3/8	5	5	Phillips County	AR	Larry Scott	1981	4,553
136 5/8	23 1/8	22 0/8	16 1/8	4	4	Crawford County	IL	Brentley D. Smith	1981	4,553
136 5/8	21 3/8	20 7/8	17 3/8	5	5	Jackson County	AL	Rocky Drake	1982	4,553
136 5/8	25 2/8	26 1/8	22 2/8	8	4	Champaign County	IL	Carl Park	1982	4,553
136 5/8	21 6/8	21 4/8	16 7/8	5	5	Jackson County	IA	Gregory L. Schulte	1982	4,553
136 5/8	23 5/8	23 1/8	20 1/8	4	4	Ripley County	IN	Steve A. Allen	1983	4,553
136 5/8	21 1/8	22 0/8	14 6/8	6	6	Oneida County	WI	Jeff Aulik	1983	4,553
136 5/8	22 0/8	22 2/8	18 1/8	5	5	Montgomery County	PA	Glenn Kuklick	1983	4,553
136 5/8	22 1/8	22 1/8	18 7/8	4	4	Cowley County	KS	Don Smith	1984	4,553
136 5/8	20 4/8	20 4/8	16 1/8	5	5	Pierce County	WI	Lester Clare	1985	4,553
136 5/8	21 4/8	21 1/8	18 7/8	5	4	Pine County	MN	Ron Ekstrand	1986	4,553
136 5/8	21 6/8	20 6/8	17 2/8	6	7	Hillsdale County	MI	Kim Cinglie	1986	4,553
136 5/8	22 3/8	22 3/8	16 3/8	4	4	Anoka County	MN	Jarrod Fondie	1986	4,553
136 5/8	22 1/8	21 3/8	14 7/8	5	4	Meagher County	MT	William R. Asevica	1987	4,553
136 5/8	21 4/8	21 3/8	16 7/8	5	7	La Salle County	IL	Kevin R. Mallie	1987	4,553
136 5/8	24 2/8	23 4/8	18 4/8	5	5	Washington County	WI	Jack Brugger	1988	4,553
136 5/8	24 5/8	23 6/8	20 3/8	5	4	Effingham County	IL	Tony Hille	1988	4,553
136 5/8	21 6/8	21 7/8	15 3/8	4	4	Sedgwick County	KS	Gary Voth	1988	4,553
136 5/8	21 1/8	21 6/8	16 3/8	5	4	Huntington County	IN	Rusty Egolf	1988	4,553
136 5/8	23 6/8	24 7/8	17 5/8	4	4	Montgomery County	IL	Floyd Dennis Scheifer	1989	4,553
136 5/8	23 0/8	23 3/8	18 7/8	5	5	McCurtain County	OK	Jody Metcalf	1989	4,553
136 5/8	23 4/8	23 3/8	19 7/8	4	5	Fairfax County	VA	James E. Chabreck	1989	4,553
136 5/8	25 7/8	20 7/8	19 3/8	5	5	Effingham County	IL	Terry Westendorf	1989	4,553
136 5/8	22 4/8	22 2/8	18 1/8	5	5	Wabaunsee County	KS	Michael J. Rose	1989	4,553
136 5/8	23 1/8	23 0/8	17 7/8	4	4	Trinity County	TX	Blake Carlton Muirhead	1990	4,553
136 5/8	23 2/8	23 0/8	15 2/8	4	5	Williams County	ND	Corey Moen	1990	4,553
136 5/8	23 5/8	24 4/8	18 4/8	5	5	Stoddard County	MO	Ken Heuer	1990	4,553
136 5/8	24 5/8	22 7/8	20 5/8	5	5	Westchester County	NY	Gary Mammana	1990	4,553
136 5/8	23 3/8	23 3/8	15 0/8	6	6	Pike County	IL	Gary Wombles	1990	4,553
136 5/8	24 6/8	25 3/8	17 6/8	6	5	Marinette County	WI	Scott Dyer	1990	4,553
136 5/8	24 5/8	24 7/8	23 3/8	5	4	Washington County	MS	Frank H. Dallas	1991	4,553
136 5/8	21 3/8	22 6/8	14 2/8	6	5	Morgan County	GA	Scott Baldwin	1991	4,553
136 5/8	21 2/8	21 4/8	16 1/8	5	5	Price County	WI	Ronald Spatz	1991	4,553
136 5/8	21 7/8	23 2/8	20 7/8	5	5	Frio County	TX	Marc Knight	1991	4,553
136 5/8	23 1/8	22 3/8	21 1/8	5	5	E. Carroll Parish	LA	Alan T. Howard	1991	4,553
136 4/8	25 3/8	24 4/8	20 4/8	4	4	Roberts County	SD	Byron Siegel	1963	4,592
136 4/8	24 6/8	23 6/8	21 6/8	4	4	Jo Daviess County	IL	Todd Muehleip	1975	4,592
136 4/8	27 4/8	26 2/8	17 3/8	6	6	Wake County	NC	Robert E. Butler	1977	4,592
136 4/8	23 1/8	22 3/8	17 0/8	5	5	Brevard County	FL	Mike Field	1979	4,592
136 4/8	22 0/8	23 7/8	18 4/8	5	5	Clark County	IL	Gerald Shaffner	1980	4,592
136 4/8	21 7/8	22 1/8	17 2/8	5	5	Coweta County	GA	Bobby Edwards	1981	4,592
136 4/8	22 4/8	22 4/8	18 2/8	5	5	Richardson County	NE	Don J. Wickham	1981	4,592
136 4/8	24 0/8	24 0/8	18 3/8	6	7	Hancock County	IN	Paul E. Williams	1982	4,592
136 4/8	21 6/8	22 3/8	18 4/8	4	4	Oneida County	WI	Dennis Steinberger	1983	4,592
136 4/8	23 2/8	22 6/8	16 4/8	5	5	Cottonwood County	MN	Leonard P. Thiner	1983	4,592
136 4/8	22 0/8	22 0/8	17 6/8	6	5	Livingston County	MI	Thomas E. Shay	1984	4,592
136 4/8	22 5/8	22 4/8	16 4/8	5	5	Wyoming County	NY	Ray Minnick	1985	4,592
136 4/8	22 3/8	21 7/8	14 4/8	5	5	Clayton County	IA	Betty Jane Jungk	1985	4,592
136 4/8	21 7/8	22 7/8	17 2/8	4	4	Washington County	TN	Bobby Davis	1985	4,592
136 4/8	21 6/8	21 2/8	17 0/8	5	5	Marshall County	IA	Ed Albee	1985	4,592
136 4/8	23 3/8	23 2/8	17 2/8	4	5	Larue County	KY	Steve Crabtree	1986	4,592
136 4/8	23 0/8	22 5/8	19 0/8	4	4	Plymouth County	IA	Gary G. Bentley	1986	4,592
136 4/8	20 7/8	21 0/8	16 2/8	5	5	Buffalo County	WI	Peter Sehrbrock	1987	4,592
136 4/8	21 2/8	21 1/8	18 0/8	8	5	Montcalm County	MI	Byron J. Burton	1988	4,592
136 4/8	20 0/8	21 4/8	12 0/8	4	5	Wayne County	MO	Jeff Daves	1988	4,592
136 4/8	21 5/8	22 2/8	13 6/8	5	6	Vermillion County	IN	Lewis Peery	1988	4,592
136 4/8	22 3/8	21 2/8	16 6/8	4	4	Macon County	MO	Robert Brundage	1988	4,592
136 4/8	22 6/8	22 6/8	15 0/8	5	6	Adams County	OH	Joseph D. Gaffin	1988	4,592
136 4/8	22 3/8	22 6/8	20 0/8	5	5	Madison Parish	LA	Carl Childress	1988	4,592
136 4/8	24 6/8	25 5/8	16 4/8	4	4	Callaway County	MO	Bryan K. Coursey	1989	4,592
136 4/8	22 2/8	19 7/8	16 1/8	6	5	Kalamazoo County	MI	Michael E. McNaughton	1989	4,592
136 4/8	23 3/8	20 5/8	15 0/8	4	6	Waushara County	WI	Terry Flesch	1989	4,592
136 4/8	22 0/8	21 6/8	18 2/8	5	5	Cullman County	AL	James Trakel	1989	4,592
136 4/8	22 6/8	21 3/8	21 0/8	4	4	Harlan County	NE	Robert Elias	1989	4,592

SCORE	LENGTH OF MAIN BEAM R	LENGTH OF MAIN BEAM L	INSIDE SPREAD	NUMBER OF POINTS R	NUMBER OF POINTS L	AREA	STATE/ PROVINCE	HUNTER'S NAME	DATE	RANK
136 4/8	25 4/8	25 0/8	18 6/8	4	6	Rockingham County	VA	Roger O. Wyant	1989	4,592
136 4/8	23 3/8	22 6/8	19 3/8	5	6	Beltrami County	MN	Denise Wiebolt	1989	4,592
136 4/8	21 5/8	22 1/8	18 5/8	7	7	Clark County	WI	David W. Calkins	1990	4,592
136 4/8	21 4/8	22 0/8	15 4/8	5	5	Vernon County	MO	Jerry M. Worley	1990	4,592
136 4/8	25 0/8	24 7/8	17 0/8	4	4	Saline County	IL	Ronald Phelps	1990	4,592
136 4/8	21 3/8	23 1/8	18 2/8	5	4	Buffalo County	WI	Lynn R. Moeller	1990	4,592
136 4/8	22 6/8	23 6/8	16 1/8	4	5	Madison Parish	LA	Martin B. Harthcock III	1990	4,592
136 4/8	24 4/8	24 2/8	19 1/8	6	7	Union County	NC	Westley Keller	1990	4,592
136 4/8	22 7/8	22 6/8	19 2/8	5	5	Delta County	MI	Eugene Percy Robinson	1991	4,592
136 4/8	21 3/8	21 5/8	17 6/8	4	4	Henry County	IL	Gary Felske	1991	4,592
136 3/8	23 5/8	24 2/8	17 6/8	4	5	Pope County	IL	Murray Schuchardt	1973	4,631
136 3/8	23 6/8	23 6/8	18 5/8	5	7	Pope County	MN	Ernie Janish	1976	4,631
136 3/8	24 4/8	24 3/8	18 5/8	5	5	Delaware County	OH	Ron E. Murphy	1979	4,631
136 3/8	22 7/8	22 1/8	16 3/8	4	5	Des Moines County	IA	John Thompson	1982	4,631
136 3/8	21 1/8	21 1/8	15 1/8	5	5	Iron County	WI	John W. Schulz	1983	4,631
136 3/8	22 2/8	22 2/8	18 1/8	4	4	Clay County	MO	Kent Robb Waters	1983	4,631
136 3/8	22 0/8	22 4/8	18 7/8	4	4	Webster County	KY	John Wayne Elkins	1983	4,631
136 3/8	25 0/8	24 3/8	18 1/8	5	4	Jackson County	MI	Johnny Lee Fry	1984	4,631
136 3/8	25 0/8	25 6/8	21 3/8	4	4	McPherson County	KS	Dan Koons	1985	4,631
136 3/8	22 4/8	20 7/8	15 6/8	6	5	Sedgwick County	KS	Gary Voth	1986	4,631
136 3/8	24 7/8	24 2/8	17 3/8	4	4	Antrim County	MI	Clifford L. Tulpa	1987	4,631
136 3/8	21 7/8	20 2/8	14 7/8	6	7	Rowan County	KY	Danny Mabry	1987	4,631
136 3/8	20 7/8	21 1/8	16 3/8	7	5	Clearwater County	MN	Christopher Kuam	1987	4,631
136 3/8	21 7/8	22 4/8	17 5/8	7	7	Wabaunsee County	KS	Charles Bisnette	1987	4,631
136 3/8	24 4/8	22 3/8	18 3/8	5	5	Waukesha County	WI	Dirk Stolz	1988	4,631
136 3/8	23 1/8	22 4/8	17 3/8	5	4	Vermilion County	IL	David E. Demoss	1988	4,631
136 3/8	20 0/8	19 7/8	15 1/8	5	5	Noxubee County	MS	Wayne Stewart, Jr.	1989	4,631
136 3/8	22 2/8	22 0/8	18 3/8	5	5	Washtenaw County	MI	Michael R. Sheats	1989	4,631
136 3/8	23 4/8	23 3/8	15 3/8	5	5	Linn County	KS	Loren J. Sayers	1989	4,631
136 3/8	21 3/8	22 2/8	16 5/8	5	5	Faribault County	MN	Randy Boettcher	1989	4,631
136 3/8	22 6/8	22 0/8	17 3/8	4	4	Walworth County	WI	Jim Janz	1989	4,631
136 3/8	24 7/8	23 2/8	19 4/8	4	5	Litchfield County	CT	Michael S. Camarota	1990	4,631
136 3/8	21 5/8	22 1/8	17 1/8	5	5	Mower County	MN	Gary Landherr	1990	4,631
136 3/8	21 6/8	21 5/8	15 7/8	5	5	Bayfield County	WI	Glenn Sotona	1990	4,631
136 3/8	20 3/8	21 7/8	19 7/8	5	5	Madison County	IL	Steve Bell	1990	4,631
136 3/8	21 7/8	21 3/8	16 3/8	7	5	Shelby County	MO	Dwaine Totten	1990	4,631
136 3/8	22 3/8	22 0/8	17 5/8	5	4	Price County	WI	Kenneth L. Cork	1990	4,631
136 3/8	25 5/8	24 2/8	19 5/8	4	4	Tensas Parish	LA	James D. Vinson	1990	4,631
136 3/8	21 6/8	22 4/8	16 5/8	6	6	Sarpy County	NE	Gary W. Dillon	1990	4,631
136 3/8	19 3/8	19 6/8	15 1/8	5	5	Richland County	MT	Michael Barbula	1991	4,631
136 3/8	22 0/8	22 2/8	15 3/8	5	5	Sawyer County	WI	Randy Patko	1991	4,631
136 3/8	19 5/8	19 1/8	19 4/8	5	8	Panola County	TX	Robert David Fulgium	1991	4,631
136 3/8	21 6/8	22 1/8	19 7/8	5	5	Saginaw County	MI	Bill Holden	1991	4,631
136 3/8	23 5/8	25 0/8	18 4/8	6	8	Richland County	OH	Lon Greer	1991	4,631
136 3/8	23 6/8	22 7/8	18 1/8	4	4	Waukesha County	WI	Craig Markham	1991	4,631
136 3/8	23 2/8	23 0/8	16 0/8	5	4	Jackson County	OH	Les Barto	1991	4,631
136 3/8	22 0/8	21 4/8	21 5/8	5	5	Trempealeau County	WI	Bobby E. Lince	1991	4,631
136 3/8	25 1/8	25 1/8	19 0/8	4	5	McHenry County	IL	Dan Englund	1991	4,631
136 3/8	20 7/8	22 4/8	18 3/8	5	5	Webster County	IA	Tim Michehl	1991	4,631
136 3/8	23 1/8	24 3/8	17 7/8	5	5	Crow Wing County	MN	Kevin Smedbron	1991	4,631
136 2/8	21 2/8	21 2/8	17 0/8	5	5	Sheridan County	ND	Robert Conklin	1967	4,671
136 2/8	22 0/8	22 4/8	17 4/8	5	4	Taylor County	WI	Roger Williams	1968	4,671
136 2/8	22 3/8	22 0/8	14 2/8	4	5	Lucas County	IA	Cynthia Squibb	1973	4,671
136 2/8	21 1/8	20 6/8	16 4/8	5	5	Mercer County	NJ	John K. Deveney	1977	4,671
136 2/8	21 7/8	21 7/8	14 0/8	5	6	Jefferson County	IA	Scott Dillon	1980	4,671
136 2/8	21 4/8	22 0/8	15 3/8	4	7	Cass County	MI	Clark A. Baugher	1981	4,671
136 2/8	22 4/8	22 6/8	18 0/8	4	5	Nelson County	KY	Mark Gies	1982	4,671
136 2/8	21 6/8	21 6/8	16 5/8	6	5	McKenzie County	ND	David Tofte	1982	4,671
136 2/8	23 0/8	23 2/8	16 4/8	5	5	Loudoun County	VA	Larry Clayton Sherertz	1983	4,671
136 2/8	22 2/8	23 2/8	18 2/8	4	5	Fairfax County	VA	Frederick Alf, Jr.	1983	4,671
136 2/8	22 3/8	22 7/8	16 6/8	5	6	Fairfield County	CT	Paul Fitzgerald	1984	4,671
136 2/8	22 7/8	22 4/8	18 5/8	5	5	Crawford County	KS	Don Garritson	1984	4,671
136 2/8	22 1/8	22 3/8	15 0/8	6	5	Isabella County	MI	Donald E. Carlson	1985	4,671
136 2/8	21 0/8	23 0/8	20 0/8	6	5	Howard County	NE	Dwayne Berggren	1985	4,671
136 2/8	24 5/8	24 4/8	17 2/8	6	6	Gray County	KS	Melvin L. Weber	1985	4,671
136 2/8	22 0/8	22 2/8	18 4/8	5	5	Otter Tail County	MN	Lyle Tabbut	1986	4,671
136 2/8	22 7/8	22 4/8	19 7/8	7	6	Columbia County	WI	Troy M. McReath	1986	4,671
136 2/8	21 4/8	21 1/8	16 3/8	7	6	Goodhue County	MN	Terry Krahn	1987	4,671
136 2/8	26 2/8	24 6/8	16 4/8	5	4	Peoria County	IL	Robert Hammerich	1987	4,671
136 2/8	23 6/8	22 6/8	20 6/8	5	4	Vinton County	OH	Greg Bonecutter, Sr.	1988	4,671

SCORE	LENGTH OF MAIN BEAM		INSIDE SPREAD	NUMBER OF POINTS		AREA	STATE/ PROVINCE	HUNTER'S NAME	DATE	RANK
	R	L		R	L					
136 2/8	22 3/8	22 3/8	18 6/8	4	4	Dakota County	MN	Michael Kennedy, Jr.	1989	4,671
136 2/8	23 2/8	23 4/8	20 2/8	4	4	Livingston County	IL	Alan E. Gray	1989	4,671
136 2/8	20 5/8	20 1/8	17 0/8	5	5	Livingston County	IL	Michael Horning	1989	4,671
136 2/8	24 1/8	23 7/8	16 3/8	5	5	Vigo County	IN	Mike Mundy	1989	4,671
136 2/8	23 3/8	23 4/8	20 2/8	4	5	St. Joseph County	IN	Bruce E. Thompson	1989	4,671
136 2/8	22 7/8	21 3/8	18 6/8	5	5	Oneida County	WI	Russell Ostermann	1989	4,671
136 2/8	23 1/8	22 6/8	21 6/8	4	4	Wayne County	IL	Pee Wee Hall	1989	4,671
136 2/8	23 6/8	23 2/8	16 2/8	5	4	Johnson County	MO	Roy A. Simpson	1989	4,671
136 2/8	23 2/8	24 0/8	18 0/8	4	4	Baltimore County	MD	Bruce D. Hoover	1989	4,671
136 2/8	23 3/8	22 6/8	16 0/8	5	4	Evans County	GA	Michael H. Clark, Sr.	1990	4,671
136 2/8	20 2/8	20 3/8	16 2/8	5	5	Bond County	IL	Len Hall	1990	4,671
136 2/8	22 3/8	22 5/8	18 0/8	5	5	Morrison County	MN	Jeff Schwartz	1990	4,671
136 2/8	22 7/8	22 7/8	18 6/8	5	6	Winnebago County	IL	Richard Van Wambeke	1990	4,671
136 2/8	23 6/8	24 3/8	19 2/8	4	4	Ballard County	KY	Scott Allen Drummond	1990	4,671
136 2/8	21 4/8	22 4/8	18 6/8	4	4	Meigs County	OH	Ronnie Plemmons, Jr.	1991	4,671
136 1/8	21 5/8	21 2/8	18 0/8	5	4	Spink County	SD	Louis Smith	1963	4,706
136 1/8	23 3/8	23 4/8	19 7/8	6	6	Litchfield County	CT	Eugene Clini, Jr.	1970	4,706
136 1/8	21 1/8	23 2/8	19 1/8	5	5	Morrison County	MN	Raymond G. Fair	1981	4,706
136 1/8	21 7/8	23 6/8	18 5/8	5	5	Mason County	WV	Darrell C. Hoffman	1982	4,706
136 1/8	23 2/8	23 5/8	19 1/8	5	5	Jefferson County	IL	Kevin Lisenby	1982	4,706
136 1/8	22 2/8	21 6/8	17 3/8	5	4	El Paso County	CO	Michael Thompson	1983	4,706
136 1/8	21 4/8	22 1/8	17 3/8	4	4	Fillmore County	MN	Glenn Hisey	1983	4,706
136 1/8	20 5/8	21 1/8	15 0/8	8	6	Atchison County	MO	Orville L. Chaslain	1983	4,706
136 1/8	23 3/8	23 3/8	18 1/8	5	6	Franklin County	OH	Richard J. Ferguson	1983	4,706
136 1/8	24 7/8	23 5/8	19 7/8	4	5	Wayne County	IA	Gary Purvis	1983	4,706
136 1/8	26 1/8	24 7/8	21 3/8	4	4	Claiborne Parish	LA	Joe M. Tuggle	1985	4,706
136 1/8	24 4/8	22 4/8	16 7/8	4	4	Washington County	IA	Marc Phelps	1985	4,706
136 1/8	20 0/8	21 1/8	17 1/8	5	5	Dickinson County	KS	Donald L. Ackerman	1985	4,706
136 1/8	20 1/8	20 1/8	18 5/8	5	5	Lincoln County	MT	Michael F. Shepard	1985	4,706
136 1/8	21 3/8	21 5/8	15 3/8	5	6	Adams County	WI	Brad A. Bauer	1986	4,706
136 1/8	21 3/8	21 0/8	15 7/8	5	5	Duval County	TX	Peggy Barcak	1986	4,706
136 1/8	22 6/8	23 3/8	23 6/8	5	5	Oneida County	WI	Donald Strum	1986	4,706
136 1/8	24 2/8	23 5/8	17 7/8	5	5	Idaho County	ID	Art Christensen	1986	4,706
136 1/8	20 0/8	21 0/8	16 3/8	5	5	Petroleum County	MT	Todd Vogl	1987	4,706
136 1/8	18 4/8	18 2/8	15 7/8	6	6	Morrison County	MN	Matt Goethel	1987	4,706
136 1/8	20 0/8	19 7/8	14 3/8	6	6	Fairfax County	VA	Brian K. McCormick	1987	4,706
136 1/8	23 3/8	23 7/8	18 5/8	4	4	Dane County	WI	Scott Dahlk	1987	4,706
136 1/8	22 7/8	22 3/8	18 5/8	5	5	Bucks County	PA	Neil D. Adams	1988	4,706
136 1/8	26 0/8	24 6/8	20 4/8	6	6	Dane County	WI	Clyde J. Carpenter	1988	4,706
136 1/8	21 7/8	22 0/8	19 7/8	5	5	Vermilion County	IL	Floyd Lee Walton	1988	4,706
136 1/8	22 0/8	23 0/8	18 5/8	4	4	Meade County	KS	Mike Heinson	1988	4,706
136 1/8	24 4/8	23 1/8	19 5/8	4	6	Henry County	VA	Mike Weaver	1989	4,706
136 1/8	23 2/8	22 5/8	20 1/8	5	4	Osgoode Township	ONT	Andy Girard	1989	4,706
136 1/8	21 1/8	21 7/8	17 1/8	5	5	Brooke County	WV	Brian Johnston	1990	4,706
136 1/8	21 0/8	21 4/8	16 1/8	7	6	St. Louis County	MO	Donald Meissner	1990	4,706
136 1/8	21 7/8	21 4/8	16 5/8	6	6	Sussex County	NJ	Greg Coughlin	1991	4,706
136 1/8	20 4/8	21 4/8	16 3/8	5	5	La Salle County	TX	Dennis Faulkenberry	1991	4,706
136 1/8	23 0/8	23 5/8	19 1/8	4	4	Logan County	WV	Richard Breton	1991	4,706
136 1/8	24 4/8	25 2/8	19 1/8	4	4	Will County	IL	Richard T. Ginnetti	1991	4,706
136 1/8	24 3/8	23 7/8	17 1/8	4	4	Giles County	VA	Scotty Dean Perdue	1991	4,706
136 1/8	18 7/8	19 2/8	18 0/8	7	7	Green Lake County	WI	Michael "Mickey" Becker	1991	4,706
136 1/8	23 4/8	23 4/8	18 5/8	5	5	Dubuque County	IA	Mike Strader	1991	4,706
136 1/8	24 0/8	23 7/8	16 1/8	5	4	Jackson County	IA	Aaron Lincoln	1991	4,706
136 1/8	21 4/8	22 1/8	18 1/8	4	5	Taylor County	WI	Mark A. Deml	1991	4,706
136 0/8	19 6/8	19 5/8	19 4/8	4	4	Jackson County	IL	Henry Mika	1962	4,745
136 0/8	23 2/8	23 4/8	17 2/8	5	5	Brookings County	SD	Douglas Tschetter	1964	4,745
136 0/8	23 6/8	23 0/8	18 0/8	4	4	Hamilton County	IN	Sondra K. Scifres	1975	4,745
136 0/8	23 3/8	23 2/8	18 2/8	4	4	Greene County	IN	Guy Aldrich	1977	4,745
136 0/8	22 2/8	22 2/8	18 0/8	5	5	Morris County	NJ	Len Cardinale	1980	4,745
136 0/8	22 7/8	23 3/8	19 4/8	4	4	Delaware County	IA	David Becker	1981	4,745
136 0/8	23 3/8	23 1/8	18 4/8	5	5	Houston County	MN	Roger Giese	1981	4,745
136 0/8	20 1/8	20 6/8	16 6/8	5	5	Ottawa County	KS	Rodney Ponton	1981	4,745
136 0/8	21 3/8	21 5/8	16 4/8	5	5	Juneau County	WI	Terry Taft	1981	4,745
136 0/8	22 1/8	23 5/8	17 2/8	5	5	Berkeley County	SC	Hugh Gaskins	1982	4,745
136 0/8	22 5/8	22 0/8	18 0/8	5	5	Red Willow County	NE	Dudley Jackson	1983	4,745
136 0/8	23 4/8	21 4/8	18 6/8	4	4	Hancock County	IL	Tim Lee	1983	4,745
136 0/8	24 0/8	23 5/8	17 1/8	7	5	Cherokee County	KS	Darren Collins	1983	4,745
136 0/8	21 5/8	21 1/8	18 0/8	5	5	Johnson County	IA	Danny Stegall	1983	4,745
136 0/8	23 2/8	22 5/8	18 4/8	4	4	Clark County	KS	William Rule	1984	4,745
136 0/8	22 4/8	21 6/8	17 4/8	5	5	Wayne County	NY	Eugene Vincent	1984	4,745

SCORE	LENGTH OF MAIN BEAM R L		INSIDE SPREAD	NUMBER OF POINTS R L		AREA	STATE/ PROVINCE	HUNTER'S NAME	DATE	RANK
136 0/8	21 5/8	20 5/8	17 2/8	6	5	Flathead County	MT	Carter Jensen	1985	4,745
136 0/8	21 3/8	21 6/8	16 4/8	6	5	Winona County	MN	George McIntire	1985	4,745
136 0/8	23 3/8	23 6/8	13 6/8	6	5	Fayette County	OH	Ronnie L. Jenkins	1985	4,745
136 0/8	22 0/8	23 0/8	19 0/8	5	5	Jackson County	MI	William D. Burgess	1985	4,745
136 0/8	21 3/8	20 2/8	15 1/8	6	5	Jefferson County	MT	Mike Davis	1986	4,745
136 0/8	20 4/8	20 3/8	14 2/8	6	5	Clinton County	IA	Tom Wing	1986	4,745
136 0/8	23 1/8	22 5/8	17 0/8	5	5	Cortland County	NY	Ted W. Renninger	1986	4,745
136 0/8	23 0/8	23 0/8	16 4/8	5	5	Pike County	IN	Chris Schmitt	1986	4,745
136 0/8	22 7/8	23 4/8	17 6/8	5	5	Litchfield County	CT	Henry B. Church	1986	4,745
136 0/8	24 0/8	24 6/8	15 6/8	4	5	Hancock County	OH	Steven E. Smith	1987	4,745
136 0/8	20 3/8	19 4/8	18 3/8	6	6	Ogle County	IL	Jeffrey S. Burke	1987	4,745
136 0/8	25 1/8	25 4/8	21 0/8	4	4	Green County	WI	Will Pick	1987	4,745
136 0/8	22 7/8	22 5/8	21 1/8	5	6	Dane County	WI	Deane H. Brabender	1988	4,745
136 0/8	23 3/8	22 3/8	17 2/8	4	4	Meigs County	OH	Earl M. Johnson	1988	4,745
136 0/8	22 5/8	21 5/8	18 4/8	7	5	Dane County	WI	John Podebradsky	1989	4,745
136 0/8	21 1/8	21 4/8	16 6/8	4	4	La Salle County	IL	J. R. Price	1989	4,745
136 0/8	21 5/8	21 7/8	15 4/8	5	5	Otoe County	NE	Michael E. Rush	1989	4,745
136 0/8	24 0/8	25 0/8	17 4/8	5	4	Steuben County	IN	William A. Regadanz	1990	4,745
136 0/8	24 4/8	24 6/8	16 1/8	5	5	Buffalo County	WI	Daniel Motszko	1990	4,745
136 0/8	24 6/8	25 1/8	18 2/8	4	4	Pottawattamie County	IA	David M. Flenker	1990	4,745
136 0/8	25 4/8	25 0/8	21 2/8	5	4	Penobscot County	ME	Benjamin C. Brown	1991	4,745
136 0/8	24 5/8	25 0/8	19 3/8	5	6	Todd County	KY	Darrell Monroe	1991	4,745
136 0/8	19 5/8	21 3/8	16 2/8	6	8	Clay County	MN	Joe Lahlum	1991	4,745
136 0/8	20 4/8	22 0/8	17 6/8	6	5	Bayfield County	WI	Jeffrey R. Krawczyk	1991	4,745
136 0/8	24 5/8	24 7/8	14 4/8	4	4	Racine County	WI	Steve Holterman	1991	4,745
136 0/8	23 5/8	23 1/8	15 6/8	4	5	Muskegon County	MI	John Hansen	1991	4,745
136 0/8	21 2/8	22 3/8	18 0/8	7	6	Ontonagon County	MI	Lawrence Nuyen	1991	4,745
135 7/8	23 6/8	22 2/8	16 7/8	6	8	Adams County	IL	Joe Johnson	1967	4,788
135 7/8	24 6/8	21 6/8	20 1/8	4	5	Westchester County	NY	Colin M. Pierson	1967	4,788
135 7/8	22 5/8	22 3/8	15 3/8	4	5	Brown County	IN	Junior R. Hutchings	1974	4,788
135 7/8	21 4/8	21 6/8	16 3/8	5	5	Sumner County	KS	Len Sanders	1980	4,788
135 7/8	24 6/8	24 3/8	15 5/8	5	5	Elgin	ONT	Mike Rusnak	1982	4,788
135 7/8	24 0/8	25 0/8	23 4/8	6	5	Suffolk County	NY	Richard W. Geminski	1982	4,788
135 7/8	24 1/8	23 0/8	21 1/8	4	4	Vermilion County	IL	Frank Palmer	1983	4,788
135 7/8	19 7/8	20 0/8	15 7/8	5	5	Renville County	MN	Daniel J. Scharba	1983	4,788
135 7/8	20 2/8	20 6/8	16 3/8	5	5	Duval County	TX	John Clinton Manges	1984	4,788
135 7/8	23 1/8	23 0/8	19 5/8	5	6	Monroe County	OH	Mark A. Landefeld	1984	4,788
135 7/8	22 4/8	22 2/8	18 3/8	4	4	Sauk County	WI	Dan Bauer	1985	4,788
135 7/8	21 5/8	21 5/8	14 6/8	8	8	Bibb County	GA	Robbie Whalen	1986	4,788
135 7/8	23 2/8	23 2/8	18 7/8	5	4	Burke County	GA	O. Jack Barrett, Jr.	1986	4,788
135 7/8	21 0/8	21 3/8	17 5/8	5	5	Greene County	OH	Charles W. Shoemaker	1986	4,788
135 7/8	25 5/8	26 5/8	18 7/8	3	3	Effingham County	IL	Don Thoele	1987	4,788
135 7/8	22 3/8	22 6/8	20 5/8	5	5	La Salle County	TX	Dr. F. D. Elias	1987	4,788
135 7/8	20 3/8	20 4/8	15 1/8	5	5	Greene County	IN	Jan J. Armour	1987	4,788
135 7/8	21 5/8	24 1/8	17 3/8	8	6	La Salle County	IL	Winston Parkinson	1987	4,788
135 7/8	21 0/8	22 2/8	16 7/8	4	4	Henry County	VA	Mike Weaver	1987	4,788
135 7/8	23 6/8	22 7/8	20 7/8	6	7	Jasper County	MO	Bob Lambeth	1987	4,788
135 7/8	18 4/8	20 0/8	19 6/8	7	5	Calgary	ALB	Dwight Liliedahl	1987	4,788
135 7/8	22 3/8	22 0/8	16 5/8	5	5	Sheboygan County	WI	Earl J. Halbach	1988	4,788
135 7/8	21 0/8	21 1/8	16 7/8	4	5	Todd County	MN	Don Wienhold	1988	4,788
135 7/8	22 4/8	23 0/8	17 4/8	5	7	Stillwater County	MT	William A. Hever, Jr.	1988	4,788
135 7/8	22 6/8	22 2/8	17 7/8	5	5	Meigs County	OH	Mike Reynolds	1989	4,788
135 7/8	21 5/8	22 2/8	15 5/8	5	5	Cumberland County	IL	Gary D. Hanley	1989	4,788
135 7/8	21 5/8	21 7/8	17 5/8	4	4	Dane County	WI	Ed Emberson	1989	4,788
135 7/8	21 7/8	22 0/8	20 1/8	6	7	Marshall County	OK	Joel A. Trammell	1989	4,788
135 7/8	22 4/8	23 2/8	19 5/8	4	4	Sagadahoc County	ME	Robert Harper	1990	4,788
135 7/8	22 4/8	23 2/8	16 7/8	4	4	Cortland County	NY	Charles Streeter	1990	4,788
135 7/8	21 3/8	21 2/8	15 7/8	5	5	Kenosha County	WI	Jeffery A. Kloet	1990	4,788
135 7/8	24 3/8	22 6/8	17 7/8	4	4	Shawano County	WI	Brett A. Olson	1990	4,788
135 7/8	21 3/8	22 6/8	18 5/8	4	5	Shelby County	IL	Mel J. Johnson	1990	4,788
135 7/8	22 5/8	22 7/8	18 7/8	4	4	Marathon County	WI	Terry Nikolai	1991	4,788
135 7/8	22 1/8	20 6/8	13 7/8	5	5	Waukesha County	WI	Richard Anderson	1991	4,788
135 7/8	20 6/8	21 1/8	16 1/8	5	5	Lorain County	OH	Clyde E. Strader	1991	4,788
135 7/8	22 1/8	22 0/8	19 1/8	5	4	Winnebago County	IL	James R. Peterson	1991	4,788
135 7/8	23 1/8	21 5/8	15 0/8	6	6	Sauk County	WI	Russell T. Reimer	1991	4,788
135 7/8	23 4/8	22 4/8	21 5/8	5	5	Whiteside County	IL	Art Heinze	1991	4,788
135 6/8	24 4/8	22 7/8	19 2/8	5	5	Winnebago County	IL	Edward Fuller	1963	4,827
135 6/8	22 6/8	23 2/8	20 6/8	4	4	Shawano County	WI	Darryl Erdman	1968	4,827
135 6/8	25 5/8	24 4/8	19 7/8	6	4	Knox County	IL	Fred E. Miller	1968	4,827
135 6/8	22 3/8	22 5/8	15 2/8	6	7	Dodge County	MN	Bradley Blanchard	1973	4,827

SCORE	LENGTH OF MAIN BEAM R	L	INSIDE SPREAD	NUMBER OF POINTS R	L	AREA	STATE/ PROVINCE	HUNTER'S NAME	DATE	RANK
135 6/8	24 0/8	24 0/8	20 2/8	5	5	Parke County	IN	Charles Loomis	1978	4,827
135 6/8	23 0/8	24 1/8	16 0/8	4	4	Pine County	MN	Paul L. Videen	1979	4,827
135 6/8	20 7/8	22 7/8	15 0/8	6	6	Fayette County	GA	Tom Mann, Jr.	1980	4,827
135 6/8	20 2/8	20 2/8	16 0/8	5	5	Fulton County	IN	James L. Kerr	1981	4,827
135 6/8	22 0/8	23 0/8	15 2/8	5	6	Ozark County	MO	Bruce Webb	1981	4,827
135 6/8	20 3/8	21 0/8	15 2/8	5	5	Dubuque County	IA	Harry Bries	1982	4,827
135 6/8	22 5/8	21 1/8	15 6/8	5	5	Saline County	KS	Kenneth D. Sterling	1982	4,827
135 6/8	23 0/8	22 0/8	18 0/8	5	5	Shawano County	WI	Ron Vander Kelen	1982	4,827
135 6/8	22 1/8	22 5/8	16 6/8	5	5	Tompkins County	NY	Michael R. Deschamps	1982	4,827
135 6/8	21 4/8	21 6/8	14 2/8	4	4	Watonwan County	MN	Brad Nielsen	1984	4,827
135 6/8	21 1/8	21 2/8	15 3/8	7	6	Pope County	IL	Roy L. Arnold	1984	4,827
135 6/8	21 5/8	22 4/8	16 4/8	5	4	Oldham County	KY	Garnett B. Morgan, Jr.	1985	4,827
135 6/8	23 4/8	23 2/8	19 4/8	6	6	Allamakee County	IA	Mark E. Walleser	1985	4,827
135 6/8	25 1/8	26 3/8	19 4/8	4	4	Clarion County	PA	Gary D. Miller	1986	4,827
135 6/8	22 2/8	21 5/8	16 0/8	4	4	Crawford County	WI	James Yatzeck	1986	4,827
135 6/8	22 3/8	22 4/8	17 6/8	5	5	Jackson County	MI	Garland Paul Ring	1988	4,827
135 6/8	19 5/8	19 2/8	15 4/8	5	5	Waukesha County	WI	Brian Tweeden	1988	4,827
135 6/8	21 0/8	21 7/8	17 6/8	4	5	Madison County	IA	Chuck Jordan	1988	4,827
135 6/8	21 6/8	21 4/8	16 2/8	6	7	Shelby County	MO	Jim Belt	1989	4,827
135 6/8	23 0/8	23 2/8	21 2/8	5	5	Will County	IL	Terry Adams	1989	4,827
135 6/8	20 7/8	21 1/8	16 4/8	5	5	Kankakee County	IL	Paul Karwoski	1989	4,827
135 6/8	25 5/8	25 4/8	19 6/8	5	5	Washington County	MD	Larry Stouffer	1989	4,827
135 6/8	23 3/8	23 2/8	16 6/8	5	4	Rockingham County	NH	Dana Standley	1990	4,827
135 6/8	23 4/8	24 6/8	15 4/8	4	5	Dakota County	MN	Mike Nowack	1990	4,827
135 6/8	24 4/8	23 5/8	19 7/8	6	6	Hart County	KY	Larry Baldwin	1990	4,827
135 6/8	25 1/8	24 6/8	17 2/8	4	4	Jackson County	OH	Keith Kauk	1990	4,827
135 6/8	23 7/8	22 6/8	18 0/8	5	5	Marshall County	IN	Michael A. Splix	1990	4,827
135 6/8	20 1/8	20 5/8	16 0/8	5	5	La Salle County	IL	John Liles	1990	4,827
135 6/8	22 5/8	21 7/8	15 6/8	4	4	Douglas County	NE	Jeff Christoffersen	1991	4,827
135 6/8	21 5/8	21 2/8	14 4/8	5	4	Buffalo County	WI	Curt Rotering	1991	4,827
135 6/8	20 5/8	19 7/8	16 4/8	5	6	Washburn County	WI	Mike Barrett	1991	4,827
135 6/8	22 2/8	21 2/8	16 2/8	5	6	Clay County	IN	Ted Froderman	1991	4,827
135 6/8	20 4/8	20 5/8	12 4/8	6	6	Hamilton County	OH	Kim S. Brockhoff	1991	4,827
135 6/8	23 2/8	22 6/8	18 0/8	5	5	Hampshire County	MA	Steve Drumm	1991	4,827
135 6/8	24 3/8	25 4/8	20 0/8	8	6	Mahaska County	IA	Kelly Gordon	1991	4,827
135 6/8	23 6/8	23 4/8	16 2/8	4	5	Stokes County	NC	Jonathan Lee Brewer	1992	4,827
135 5/8	22 1/8	23 6/8	19 1/8	6	4	Montgomery County	IN	Derrick W. Kidd	1932	4,867
135 5/8	21 4/8	20 0/8	16 1/8	5	5	Sheboygan County	WI	Earl Uhl	1960	4,867
135 5/8	22 7/8	21 6/8	21 1/8	4	4	Union County	KY	Randy Joe Duncan	1965	4,867
135 5/8	22 1/8	22 1/8	19 3/8	5	5	Ringgold County	IA	William K. Seitz	1973	4,867
135 5/8	23 4/8	23 2/8	14 7/8	4	4	Jasper County	IN	Gary L. Hepler	1980	4,867
135 5/8	23 7/8	22 6/8	14 3/8	5	5	Allegheny County	PA	John Camillo	1980	4,867
135 5/8	23 5/8	21 2/8	17 5/8	4	5	Winona County	MN	Hank Scharmach	1981	4,867
135 5/8	22 6/8	22 0/8	18 3/8	4	4	Dodge County	MN	Robert Rhodes, Jr.	1982	4,867
135 5/8	21 4/8	21 4/8	16 5/8	5	5	Adams County	IN	Randy Johnson	1983	4,867
135 5/8	22 4/8	23 2/8	14 0/8	4	7	Anderson County	KS	Steve Spangler	1983	4,867
135 5/8	22 6/8	23 7/8	20 5/8	4	4	Jones County	IA	Donald Stuefen	1984	4,867
135 5/8	24 2/8	23 2/8	17 3/8	4	4	Buffalo County	WI	Edward Brannen	1984	4,867
135 5/8	21 3/8	22 2/8	19 7/8	4	4	Tama County	IA	Clyde Bearden	1985	4,867
135 5/8	23 7/8	25 4/8	21 5/8	4	4	Charles Mix County	SD	Frank Mingo	1985	4,867
135 5/8	22 1/8	22 2/8	17 7/8	4	4	Price County	WI	Leonard J. Stein	1985	4,867
135 5/8	19 7/8	20 1/8	15 7/8	7	6	Morrison County	MN	Kevin Hagstron	1986	4,867
135 5/8	23 0/8	24 2/8	16 3/8	5	5	Delaware County	PA	Earl McSorley	1986	4,867
135 5/8	22 2/8	22 2/8	15 7/8	4	5	Texas County	OK	Max Crocker	1986	4,867
135 5/8	19 6/8	19 3/8	15 7/8	5	4	Brown County	KS	Robert L. Hodge	1986	4,867
135 5/8	23 2/8	23 4/8	16 5/8	4	4	Price County	WI	Bill Fischer	1987	4,867
135 5/8	19 5/8	19 0/8	13 4/8	6	6	Pope County	IL	John F. Perso	1987	4,867
135 5/8	21 6/8	21 2/8	17 1/8	5	5	Madison County	IL	Jon Schmalz	1987	4,867
135 5/8	22 6/8	23 0/8	19 0/8	6	4	Crawford County	WI	Robert McCann	1987	4,867
135 5/8	23 0/8	22 1/8	18 5/8	5	6	Wabash County	IN	Tim Roberts	1987	4,867
135 5/8	23 0/8	22 2/8	21 7/8	4	5	Suffolk County	NY	Bret Jayne	1987	4,867
135 5/8	23 3/8	23 3/8	17 5/8	6	5	Cass County	IN	Roger Whitehead	1988	4,867
135 5/8	22 6/8	22 6/8	18 5/8	5	4	Steuben County	NY	John E. Steen, Sr.	1988	4,867
135 5/8	21 2/8	21 6/8	14 7/8	5	5	Kalamazoo County	MI	Mike Ovens	1988	4,867
135 5/8	22 3/8	22 2/8	19 1/8	4	4	Phillips County	KS	Monty Mai	1988	4,867
135 5/8	24 3/8	24 1/8	17 1/8	4	4	Guernsey County	OH	Thomas J. Hentrick	1989	4,867
135 5/8	22 1/8	23 1/8	20 7/8	5	5	Sharkey County	MS	Terry Murrell	1990	4,867
135 5/8	23 2/8	22 6/8	17 7/8	6	5	Ozaukee County	WI	Raymond Schultz	1990	4,867
135 5/8	21 4/8	21 4/8	16 6/8	6	6	Winona County	MN	Dan Pettersen	1990	4,867
135 5/8	23 2/8	23 4/8	17 3/8	4	4	Richland County	IL	Terry L. Mehl	1990	4,867

SCORE	LENGTH OF MAIN BEAM R	LENGTH OF MAIN BEAM L	INSIDE SPREAD	NUMBER OF POINTS R	NUMBER OF POINTS L	AREA	STATE/ PROVINCE	HUNTER'S NAME	DATE	RANK
135 5/8	23 1/8	24 0/8	16 5/8	4	5	Forest County	WI	Elmer H. Van Gheem	1991	4,867
135 5/8	23 1/8	23 0/8	18 5/8	4	4	Coshocton County	OH	Gene Mathias	1991	4,867
135 5/8	23 0/8	22 6/8	16 7/8	4	4	Vermilion County	IL	Bob Gravely	1991	4,867
135 5/8	23 3/8	23 2/8	16 5/8	5	5	Dearborn County	IN	Tom Koch	1991	4,867
135 5/8	20 5/8	20 2/8	16 1/8	5	5	Spokane County	WA	Ronald J. Olmstead	1991	4,867
135 5/8	24 5/8	23 6/8	15 3/8	5	4	Kleberg County	TX	Dr. Terry W. Brandt	1991	4,867
135 4/8	21 0/8	23 0/8	18 6/8	6	5	Mitchell County	IA	Arthur Cepeda	1962	4,907
135 4/8	23 4/8	23 4/8	18 6/8	4	4	Dodge County	WI	Daniel J. Rozek	1966	4,907
135 4/8	21 6/8	21 4/8	19 4/8	5	5	Mower County	MN	Arthur McKenzie	1972	4,907
135 4/8	21 3/8	23 0/8	18 0/8	5	5	Ripley County	IN	G. Fred Asbell	1973	4,907
135 4/8	20 5/8	20 5/8	13 2/8	5	5	Dickinson County	MI	Dave Bath	1973	4,907
135 4/8	23 0/8	23 6/8	18 0/8	5	5	Lyon County	KY	Kenneth McKay	1973	4,907
135 4/8	21 7/8	21 6/8	18 0/8	5	5	Mower County	MN	Clark Gallup	1975	4,907
135 4/8	22 7/8	22 6/8	19 0/8	6	5	Pittsburg County	OK	Bill Nelson	1977	4,907
135 4/8	23 4/8	23 2/8	17 3/8	5	4	Lincoln County	SD	Merle A. Henry	1980	4,907
135 4/8	21 3/8	22 2/8	16 6/8	5	4	Lincoln County	SD	Eldon D. Hagen	1981	4,907
135 4/8	19 0/8	19 0/8	14 3/8	6	8	Lee County	IA	Glenn E. Wagner	1981	4,907
135 4/8	22 5/8	22 1/8	14 6/8	5	5	Richland County	WI	Terry Yanske	1982	4,907
135 4/8	24 3/8	25 7/8	18 4/8	5	4	Freeborn County	MN	Richard Rippentrap	1982	4,907
135 4/8	25 2/8	23 3/8	19 3/8	5	6	Mercer County	IL	David McCaw	1983	4,907
135 4/8	22 0/8	22 4/8	14 3/8	7	6	Adams County	WI	David A. Schmitt	1984	4,907
135 4/8	25 0/8	20 5/8	18 0/8	5	6	Tazewell County	IL	Darrell A Lee	1984	4,907
135 4/8	23 1/8	22 5/8	17 4/8	5	5	Muskegon County	MI	R. Lawrence Meyers	1985	4,907
135 4/8	22 5/8	22 5/8	19 0/8	4	6	Meeker County	MN	Dan Winter	1986	4,907
135 4/8	23 0/8	23 1/8	16 2/8	5	5	Dane County	WI	Dave H. Klaas	1986	4,907
135 4/8	22 1/8	22 4/8	17 5/8	5	6	Breckinridge County	KY	Steve Drake	1986	4,907
135 4/8	21 4/8	23 1/8	18 2/8	5	6	Wright County	MN	Ed Rudenburg	1987	4,907
135 4/8	24 6/8	24 7/8	18 2/8	4	4	Pope County	MN	David A. Thompson	1987	4,907
135 4/8	24 2/8	23 6/8	17 4/8	4	4	Pulaski County	IL	Keith Wilson	1988	4,907
135 4/8	22 0/8	21 4/8	15 4/8	5	8	Jefferson County	IN	Roman C.E. Lawson	1988	4,907
135 4/8	22 7/8	23 3/8	15 6/8	4	4	Leavenworth County	KS	Richard L. Jackson	1988	4,907
135 4/8	23 1/8	23 2/8	18 0/8	4	4	Dunn County	WI	Joseph Gessner	1989	4,907
135 4/8	22 1/8	21 5/8	16 0/8	5	5	Dallas County	IA	Duane Albrecht	1989	4,907
135 4/8	22 3/8	24 1/8	17 5/8	4	6	Fayette County	IL	Jeff Fulk	1989	4,907
135 4/8	24 4/8	25 4/8	19 0/8	5	5	Suffolk County	NY	John Kowalski	1989	4,907
135 4/8	22 1/8	23 6/8	17 6/8	4	4	Buffalo County	WI	Robyn Lowenhagen	1990	4,907
135 4/8	21 5/8	21 7/8	18 3/8	6	5	Washington County	KS	Andy T. Bruna	1990	4,907
135 4/8	22 4/8	22 1/8	17 2/8	5	5	Waushara County	WI	Lewis J. Lewis	1990	4,907
135 4/8	21 4/8	21 3/8	16 2/8	5	6	Woodbury County	IA	Terry Guffy	1990	4,907
135 4/8	22 0/8	22 2/8	18 4/8	6	6	Wayne County	IA	Andy Merritt	1990	4,907
135 4/8	21 7/8	22 1/8	18 6/8	4	4	Boone County	IA	Bill Wiebe	1990	4,907
135 4/8	21 1/8	20 7/8	16 2/8	5	5	Jim Wells County	TX	Gary G. McKinny	1990	4,907
135 4/8	20 5/8	19 4/8	15 0/8	5	5	Columbia County	WA	Lyle C. Laughery	1991	4,907
135 4/8	21 4/8	20 5/8	16 6/8	5	5	Dodge County	MN	Mark Symes	1991	4,907
135 4/8	23 3/8	23 0/8	18 4/8	5	9	Madison County	IA	David Falke	1991	4,907
135 4/8	20 6/8	21 2/8	15 6/8	5	5	Walworth County	WI	Chuck Palmer	1991	4,907
135 4/8	21 7/8	21 2/8	17 2/8	5	5	McMullen County	TX	Jerry B. Bogle	1991	4,907
135 4/8	22 3/8	22 2/8	19 0/8	5	5	Ferry County	WA	David D. Gillespie	1991	4,907
135 4/8	23 6/8	23 2/8	19 4/8	5	5	La Salle County	TX	Howard Scott Reynolds	1991	4,907
135 3/8	22 0/8	22 2/8	17 1/8	5	5	Columbia County	WI	Chester Sroka	1936	4,950
135 3/8	23 2/8	23 0/8	21 0/8	6	6	Sully County	SD	R. L. Marso	1965	4,950
135 3/8	21 6/8	23 2/8	19 1/8	4	5	Brown County	SD	Arnie Goldade	1974	4,950
135 3/8	22 6/8	22 6/8	16 5/8	4	4	Iowa County	WI	Jerry Statz	1977	4,950
135 3/8	21 0/8	21 0/8	14 7/8	4	4	Richland County	MT	Dan Sturgis	1977	4,950
135 3/8	23 7/8	23 0/8	17 5/8	4	4	Iowa County	WI	Paul Klingelhoets	1978	4,950
135 3/8	22 3/8	21 5/8	15 5/8	5	5	Clark County	IN	Robert W. Thompson	1979	4,950
135 3/8	23 5/8	24 6/8	16 1/8	5	5	Burnett County	WI	Gene Hill	1980	4,950
135 3/8	22 7/8	23 0/8	19 1/8	4	4	Washington County	MN	Rodney P. Bailey	1981	4,950
135 3/8	24 1/8	24 1/8	19 7/8	4	4	Warren County	NJ	Bill L. Raub	1982	4,950
135 3/8	22 6/8	22 4/8	16 3/8	5	5	Dodge County	WI	George Warden	1983	4,950
135 3/8	20 7/8	21 3/8	16 3/8	5	5	Olmsted County	MN	Robert J. Constantine, Jr	1983	4,950
135 3/8	21 2/8	21 1/8	16 1/8	5	5	Latah County	ID	Jim Frazier	1983	4,950
135 3/8	21 7/8	21 4/8	18 2/8	5	4	Champaign County	IL	Gary Ray Varner	1984	4,950
135 3/8	23 3/8	23 3/8	21 1/8	4	5	Ottawa County	MI	Ed Diemer	1984	4,950
135 3/8	21 7/8	21 3/8	15 3/8	5	5	Strathcona	ALB	Ryk Visscher	1985	4,950
135 3/8	22 5/8	22 5/8	18 3/8	4	4	Jones County	IA	William Janssen	1986	4,950
135 3/8	24 0/8	23 3/8	20 5/8	4	4	Harford County	MD	Eugene Sinar	1987	4,950
135 3/8	24 0/8	22 3/8	22 7/8	4	4	Geauga County	OH	Chris A. Waldron	1988	4,950
135 3/8	21 6/8	22 3/8	16 7/8	5	5	Trempealeau County	WI	Glen L. Mahlum	1989	4,950
135 3/8	20 4/8	20 1/8	14 1/8	6	5	Dane County	WI	Edward M. Cleven	1989	4,950

288

SCORE	LENGTH OF MAIN BEAM R	LENGTH OF MAIN BEAM L	INSIDE SPREAD	NUMBER OF POINTS R	NUMBER OF POINTS L	AREA	STATE/ PROVINCE	HUNTER'S NAME	DATE	RANK
135 3/8	23 1/8	21 4/8	19 7/8	4	5	Keokuk County	IA	Mike Krier	1989	4,950
135 3/8	23 4/8	23 2/8	20 5/8	4	5	Jo Daviess County	IL	Richard P. Geyer	1990	4,950
135 3/8	22 5/8	22 5/8	17 4/8	6	5	Scott County	MN	Terry Regnier	1990	4,950
135 3/8	23 5/8	23 6/8	19 7/8	4	4	Fairfax County	VA	James E. Chabreck	1990	4,950
135 3/8	22 2/8	22 5/8	18 5/8	5	5	Webster County	KY	E. Bert Combs	1991	4,950
135 3/8	23 3/8	23 4/8	19 7/8	3	4	Kane County	IL	Earl Sirchia	1991	4,950
135 3/8	22 2/8	24 0/8	17 4/8	5	4	Lapeer County	MI	Robert Fiore	1991	4,950
135 3/8	21 3/8	21 3/8	15 7/8	6	7	Sullivan County	IN	Steve Eastham	1991	4,950
135 3/8	21 6/8	20 6/8	16 4/8	6	6	Mower County	MN	Pat Johnson	1991	4,950
135 3/8	20 5/8	21 5/8	17 7/8	5	5	Dane County	WI	John Podebradsky	1991	4,950
135 3/8	23 0/8	21 3/8	18 5/8	5	5	Lincoln County	MN	David Rouge	1991	4,950
135 3/8	22 2/8	23 0/8	17 3/8	5	5	Champaign County	IL	Greg Burr	1991	4,950
135 3/8	20 3/8	21 1/8	15 1/8	6	5	Parker County	TX	John L. Chapman	1991	4,950
135 3/8	23 3/8	22 4/8	16 7/8	5	5	Clearwater County	ID	Len Young	1992	4,950
135 2/8	25 0/8	24 0/8	18 2/8	5	4	Lucas County	IA	Everett Parsons	1964	4,985
135 2/8	21 3/8	22 7/8	16 0/8	5	8	Brown County	SD	Jack Eagleson	1966	4,985
135 2/8	23 0/8	23 2/8	20 2/8	4	4	Cedar County	IA	Fred Wesselink	1971	4,985
135 2/8	20 6/8	21 2/8	18 0/8	5	5	Johnson County	IN	Thomas J. Brown	1978	4,985
135 2/8	17 4/8	16 5/8	13 1/8	7	7	Marshall County	IA	Mike Thomas	1978	4,985
135 2/8	24 0/8	23 2/8	17 4/8	5	6	Winona County	MN	Jim Keim	1979	4,985
135 2/8	22 2/8	21 0/8	15 4/8	4	4	Wood County	WI	Gordon Steidl	1982	4,985
135 2/8	21 5/8	22 5/8	16 6/8	5	6	Juneau County	WI	Steven Hysell	1983	4,985
135 2/8	21 3/8	22 0/8	17 6/8	4	4	Hocking County	OH	Rex Wollett	1983	4,985
135 2/8	22 0/8	21 6/8	16 0/8	5	5	Green Lake County	WI	Arwin Moldenhauer	1984	4,985
135 2/8	22 0/8	21 7/8	17 6/8	4	4	Reno County	KS	Gary D. Walker	1985	4,985
135 2/8	23 4/8	23 7/8	14 6/8	4	4	Lincoln County	WI	Ken Rasmussen	1986	4,985
135 2/8	23 7/8	24 1/8	18 2/8	4	5	Clinton County	IA	Larry A. Lind	1986	4,985
135 2/8	20 3/8	21 6/8	17 1/8	5	5	Beaver County	PA	Ted Kramer	1987	4,985
135 2/8	20 4/8	21 2/8	13 6/8	5	5	Waupaca County	WI	Eugene K. Nuernberger	1987	4,985
135 2/8	21 0/8	21 2/8	17 5/8	6	10	Sedgewick County	CO	Dennis Myer	1987	4,985
135 2/8	23 4/8	23 0/8	21 4/8	4	5	Winneshiek County	IA	Sam Sexton	1987	4,985
135 2/8	25 1/8	25 1/8	17 5/8	5	6	Texas County	OK	Max Crocker	1987	4,985
135 2/8	22 0/8	22 0/8	16 0/8	4	4	Poweshiek County	IA	Robert Rotherham	1988	4,985
135 2/8	25 1/8	25 3/8	16 6/8	7	5	Forest County	WI	Ron H. Vander Kelen	1988	4,985
135 2/8	20 0/8	20 0/8	15 5/8	6	7	Jasper County	IA	Don Morris, Jr.	1988	4,985
135 2/8	21 1/8	20 2/8	15 6/8	5	6	Somerset County	PA	Lynn A. Henry	1989	4,985
135 2/8	22 3/8	22 1/8	15 6/8	8	7	Orange County	IN	Harold L. Lamb	1989	4,985
135 2/8	20 0/8	19 7/8	14 0/8	5	5	Mercer County	NJ	Glenn R. Kuklick	1990	4,985
135 2/8	22 0/8	21 5/8	15 6/8	5	5	Waushara County	WI	Richard J. Tokarski	1990	4,985
135 2/8	23 5/8	24 1/8	18 4/8	5	5	Vernon County	WI	Ron J. Zeihen	1990	4,985
135 2/8	22 6/8	22 4/8	17 6/8	5	5	Morris County	NJ	Theodore Cameron	1990	4,985
135 2/8	22 1/8	22 4/8	13 6/8	5	6	Osage County	OK	George Bennett	1990	4,985
135 2/8	23 1/8	23 2/8	16 4/8	4	4	Clarke County	IA	Jeff Jorgensen	1990	4,985
135 2/8	21 7/8	22 3/8	14 4/8	5	5	Sutton County	TX	Greg Howard	1991	4,985
135 2/8	22 5/8	23 6/8	16 2/8	5	5	Clay County	IL	Jay Lee Newby	1991	4,985
135 2/8	23 4/8	23 7/8	21 4/8	6	6	Waukesha County	WI	Bob Loepfe	1991	4,985
135 2/8	23 4/8	23 4/8	20 2/8	5	5	Will County	IL	Jim DeSmidt	1991	4,985
135 2/8	23 4/8	23 7/8	16 0/8	5	5	Marshall County	KS	Tim Wanklyn	1991	4,985
135 1/8	21 0/8	20 4/8	17 3/8	5	5	Westchester County	NY	Francis E. Hill	1958	5,019
135 1/8	21 6/8	21 3/8	19 7/8	6	5	Brookings County	SD	Ray Buckley	1961	5,019
135 1/8	21 5/8	21 5/8	17 7/8	4	4	Clark County	SD	Jack D. Chesmore	1971	5,019
135 1/8	21 5/8	21 6/8	18 0/8	5	6	Edmonson County	KY	Steve England	1974	5,019
135 1/8	21 7/8	22 0/8	16 3/8	4	4	Greene County	IN	Jan J. Armour	1976	5,019
135 1/8	22 2/8	22 7/8	17 3/8	4	5	Nodaway County	MO	Larry Davison	1982	5,019
135 1/8	23 4/8	22 7/8	18 3/8	5	4	Hamilton County	OH	Jerome Buschle, Jr.	1983	5,019
135 1/8	19 4/8	20 1/8	16 1/8	5	4	McLean County	IL	Robert P. Ryburn	1984	5,019
135 1/8	22 3/8	21 4/8	16 5/8	5	5	Missoula County	MT	Monty Moravec	1985	5,019
135 1/8	20 1/8	19 0/8	15 4/8	6	6	Dawes County	NE	Allen Mintken	1985	5,019
135 1/8	23 4/8	22 0/8	19 3/8	5	5	Eaton County	MI	Dr. Daniel C. Gulick	1985	5,019
135 1/8	23 1/8	23 6/8	18 3/8	6	5	Iowa County	WI	Joe Esser	1985	5,019
135 1/8	22 0/8	22 6/8	17 3/8	5	5	Maries County	MO	Darrel C. Littrell	1986	5,019
135 1/8	24 4/8	23 4/8	17 7/8	4	4	Arkansas County	AR	Wade D. Sweetin	1987	5,019
135 1/8	22 3/8	22 2/8	15 7/8	4	4	Lee County	IL	James R. Bonnell	1987	5,019
135 1/8	20 5/8	20 2/8	17 0/8	7	6	Buena Vista County	IA	Dale F. Kraft	1988	5,019
135 1/8	23 6/8	24 2/8	17 3/8	5	4	Juneau County	WI	Bennie L. Voigt	1988	5,019
135 1/8	23 0/8	22 5/8	16 2/8	4	5	Knox County	IL	Richard Carr	1988	5,019
135 1/8	24 7/8	24 1/8	16 1/8	5	5	Marshall County	KS	Jon Gunn	1988	5,019
135 1/8	22 0/8	22 4/8	20 2/8	6	5	Johnson County	IA	Dallas Eakes	1988	5,019
135 1/8	24 2/8	24 2/8	19 7/8	4	5	McHenry County	IL	Richard Martin	1988	5,019
135 1/8	23 1/8	21 7/8	17 5/8	7	5	Freeborn County	MN	Marvin Thompson	1989	5,019

WHITETAIL DEER *(Typical Antlers)*

(Continued)

SCORE	LENGTH OF MAIN BEAM R	L	INSIDE SPREAD	NUMBER OF POINTS R	L	AREA	STATE/ PROVINCE	HUNTER'S NAME	DATE	RANK
135 1/8	24 3/8	24 3/8	19 5/8	4	4	Menard County	IL	George E. Hypke	1989	5,019
135 1/8	21 2/8	21 3/8	15 3/8	6	5	Columbia County	WI	Robert J. Lenz	1989	5,019
135 1/8	21 2/8	22 0/8	16 7/8	5	5	Jo Daviess County	IL	Raymond H. Bradt	1989	5,019
135 1/8	21 3/8	21 2/8	18 0/8	8	7	Brooks County	TX	Bear Brewer	1990	5,019
135 1/8	23 4/8	22 6/8	16 1/8	5	5	Floyd County	VA	Jeffery Dale Weddle	1990	5,019
135 1/8	23 5/8	23 0/8	16 7/8	4	4	Oldham County	KY	Edwynn Burckle	1990	5,019
135 1/8	23 4/8	22 7/8	17 5/8	5	5	Starke County	IN	Morris Teague	1990	5,019
135 1/8	22 7/8	22 6/8	15 1/8	5	5	Marinette County	WI	James R. Vickman	1990	5,019
135 1/8	24 4/8	24 2/8	20 6/8	7	9	Athens County	OH	Ron M. Hawk	1990	5,019
135 1/8	23 0/8	23 0/8	20 1/8	5	5	Emmet County	IA	Richard D. Berry	1990	5,019
135 1/8	23 1/8	22 6/8	18 1/8	5	5	Olmsted County	MN	Skip Danewick	1991	5,019
135 1/8	23 5/8	24 4/8	18 1/8	4	4	Gogebic County	MI	Eugene A. Pribek	1991	5,019
135 1/8	21 4/8	21 4/8	16 3/8	4	4	Adams County	WI	Ronald R. Manz	1991	5,019
135 1/8	25 6/8	25 0/8	18 1/8	4	4	Upson County	GA	Tony Chapman	1991	5,019
135 1/8	20 1/8	21 6/8	15 5/8	5	5	Lafayette County	WI	Roger W. Davis	1991	5,019
135 1/8	21 0/8	20 0/8	16 7/8	5	5	Jackson County	IN	Paul Vice	1991	5,019
135 0/8	22 0/8	20 6/8	17 0/8	4	4	Grant County	MN	Stanley D. Miles	1963	5,057
135 0/8	20 1/8	20 2/8	15 4/8	5	5	Dodge County	MN	Clark Gallup	1973	5,057
135 0/8	22 6/8	17 7/8	15 6/8	6	6	Butler County	KS	Phil Hamilton	1974	5,057
135 0/8	20 7/8	19 2/8	17 3/8	8	7	Peoria County	IL	Harry L. Stalter	1975	5,057
135 0/8	24 4/8	24 3/8	14 0/8	5	4	Buffalo County	WI	Steve Segerstrom	1978	5,057
135 0/8	20 5/8	20 7/8	18 0/8	6	6	Morrison County	MN	Larry Hochmayr	1979	5,057
135 0/8	22 0/8	22 4/8	17 0/8	5	5	Noble County	OK	Glen Elliott	1981	5,057
135 0/8	25 7/8	26 6/8	22 4/8	7	6	Pickaway County	OH	Mouse Bailey	1982	5,057
135 0/8	24 2/8	24 2/8	20 6/8	8	6	Whiteside County	IL	Art Heinze	1983	5,057
135 0/8	23 4/8	24 0/8	17 4/8	5	4	Jackson County	MN	Kerry Ella	1984	5,057
135 0/8	22 3/8	22 1/8	19 4/8	5	5	Linn County	IA	David Padget	1985	5,057
135 0/8	23 6/8	23 6/8	17 0/8	4	5	Bayfield County	WI	Charles Wallisch	1985	5,057
135 0/8	21 2/8	22 5/8	20 2/8	6	5	Union County	IL	Robert Gordon	1985	5,057
135 0/8	22 2/8	22 1/8	17 4/8	5	5	Cherry County	NE	J. Philip Fuchs	1986	5,057
135 0/8	27 0/8	25 2/8	20 6/8	7	5	Waukesha County	WI	Jean Keller	1986	5,057
135 0/8	22 0/8	24 1/8	14 2/8	8	6	Putnam County	MO	William A. Knight	1986	5,057
135 0/8	22 3/8	22 1/8	16 4/8	5	6	Will County	IL	Ken Ericksen	1987	5,057
135 0/8	21 4/8	21 5/8	16 1/8	7	7	Waupaca County	WI	Jim Fauske	1988	5,057
135 0/8	23 4/8	21 4/8	15 4/8	5	6	Columbia County	WI	Stephen Schwarz	1988	5,057
135 0/8	21 0/8	20 3/8	15 2/8	5	5	Dixon County	NE	Tim Nelson	1988	5,057
135 0/8	22 0/8	22 0/8	14 4/8	4	5	Douglas County	WI	Gordon L. Retka	1988	5,057
135 0/8	22 1/8	20 7/8	18 0/8	5	5	Furnas County	NE	Robert Elias	1988	5,057
135 0/8	24 7/8	25 2/8	18 0/8	4	4	Douglas County	NE	Norman Armstrong	1988	5,057
135 0/8	23 0/8	21 0/8	18 0/8	6	5	Warren County	IL	Scott Johnson	1989	5,057
135 0/8	20 7/8	21 6/8	15 6/8	5	5	Indiana County	PA	Bernard E. Lazor	1990	5,057
135 0/8	20 3/8	20 2/8	16 0/8	5	5	Atascosa County	TX	Steven W. Self	1990	5,057
135 0/8	22 2/8	21 6/8	18 4/8	5	4	Guthrie County	IA	Dean Jackson	1990	5,057
135 0/8	22 0/8	22 2/8	16 2/8	5	5	Brooks County	TX	John W. Fullilove	1990	5,057
135 0/8	24 2/8	23 2/8	20 2/8	4	4	Champaign County	IL	Charles Flora	1990	5,057
135 0/8	21 3/8	22 7/8	15 7/8	4	6	Clinton County	IA	George D. Aurand	1990	5,057
135 0/8	24 0/8	23 6/8	20 2/8	4	4	Powell County	MT	Cary Gee	1990	5,057
135 0/8	24 0/8	24 2/8	15 4/8	4	5	Warren County	IA	Jim Baker	1991	5,057
135 0/8	24 3/8	24 0/8	15 6/8	5	4	Grenada County	MS	Larry G. West	1991	5,057
135 0/8	22 2/8	21 7/8	17 0/8	5	5	Berkshire County	MA	Steve McCartney	1991	5,057
135 0/8	22 2/8	22 0/8	17 4/8	4	4	Clark County	IL	Thomas E. Rothrock	1991	5,057
135 0/8	23 0/8	24 3/8	19 4/8	6	5	Crow Wing County	MN	Danny G. O'Neil	1992	5,057
135 0/8	18 7/8	19 3/8	14 4/8	6	6	Kay County	OK	Greggory D. Frederick	1992	5,057
134 7/8	20 1/8	21 4/8	16 3/8	5	5	Spokane County	WA	Harold Bratlie	1960	5,094
134 7/8	20 6/8	20 6/8	16 7/8	4	4	Lawrence County	SD	Oliver Lewis	1960	5,094
134 7/8	20 4/8	21 0/8	17 2/8	6	6	Cherokee County	OK	Addison Harrison	1965	5,094
134 7/8	20 7/8	21 6/8	17 7/8	5	5	Morrison County	MN	Thomas Ackerman	1971	5,094
134 7/8	24 5/8	24 1/8	21 3/8	7	6	Washington County	OH	Lyle W. Townson, Sr.	1974	5,094
134 7/8	19 3/8	20 3/8	14 0/8	7	5	Ottawa County	KS	Michael D. Patterson	1975	5,094
134 7/8	21 7/8	20 7/8	21 3/8	4	4	Mercer County	NJ	Jim Vandermark	1978	5,094
134 7/8	22 6/8	23 5/8	17 3/8	6	5	Dawson County	NE	Randy Wilson	1978	5,094
134 7/8	22 1/8	21 0/8	16 1/8	4	4	Morrison County	MN	James G. Hurrle	1980	5,094
134 7/8	21 0/8	21 2/8	16 5/8	5	5	Jackson County	MO	Marvin Thomey	1981	5,094
134 7/8	22 0/8	22 3/8	18 4/8	5	4	St. Marys County	MD	Samuel H. Wilson, Jr.	1981	5,094
134 7/8	24 4/8	23 4/8	20 4/8	4	5	St. Charles County	MO	T. J. Sorenson	1983	5,094
134 7/8	21 3/8	21 1/8	14 5/8	4	4	Polk County	WI	Larry Nicholas	1983	5,094
134 7/8	25 3/8	27 4/8	20 1/8	4	4	Morrow County	OH	Tony Burns	1983	5,094
134 7/8	24 1/8	22 0/8	16 7/8	5	6	Alcona County	MI	Galen M. Vernon	1983	5,094
134 7/8	24 3/8	24 4/8	17 1/8	5	5	Itasca County	MN	Karen L. Spotts	1984	5,094
134 7/8	22 1/8	19 5/8	17 1/8	4	4	Cass County	ND	David Skjei	1984	5,094

Score	Length of Main Beam R	L	Inside Spread	Number of Points R	L	Area	State/ Province	Hunter's Name	Date	Rank
134 7/8	21 4/8	20 6/8	17 7/8	5	5	Bayham Twp.	ONT	Max Ward	1984	5,094
134 7/8	21 5/8	22 5/8	18 5/8	5	5	Owen County	KY	James B Bevins	1985	5,094
134 7/8	22 6/8	22 7/8	17 7/8	4	4	Washington County	PA	Thomas W. Eiler	1986	5,094
134 7/8	21 4/8	22 6/8	15 6/8	4	5	Morrow County	OH	Jerry West	1986	5,094
134 7/8	21 2/8	20 6/8	16 5/8	5	5	Kit Carson County	CO	Dave Holt	1986	5,094
134 7/8	23 2/8	23 3/8	19 1/8	4	5	Clinton County	IA	John Sander	1986	5,094
134 7/8	23 0/8	23 0/8	18 3/8	4	4	Howard County	MD	Ron Thomas	1986	5,094
134 7/8	25 4/8	26 5/8	16 6/8	5	5	Anderson County	TN	Robert Allen Hendren	1987	5,094
134 7/8	22 4/8	22 5/8	16 7/8	6	6	Dodge County	WI	Roger Steger	1987	5,094
134 7/8	24 1/8	24 1/8	15 5/8	4	5	Dane County	WI	Dennis W. Brown	1987	5,094
134 7/8	20 4/8	21 0/8	11 3/8	5	5	Johnson County	KS	William A. Logue	1987	5,094
134 7/8	21 2/8	21 6/8	14 7/8	7	6	Texas County	OK	David Pennington	1988	5,094
134 7/8	22 3/8	22 5/8	20 3/8	5	6	Mower County	MN	Jeffrey L. Boucher	1988	5,094
134 7/8	24 4/8	24 3/8	19 5/8	4	4	Pope County	IL	Ed Hoke	1988	5,094
134 7/8	21 6/8	22 3/8	16 5/8	4	4	Morgan County	IL	John Conklin	1988	5,094
134 7/8	24 3/8	24 7/8	21 7/8	4	4	Suffolk County	NY	Richard Jensen	1988	5,094
134 7/8	23 3/8	23 1/8	18 4/8	5	6	Dawes County	NE	Stan Chiras	1988	5,094
134 7/8	21 0/8	21 5/8	16 3/8	5	5	Burnett County	WI	Ron Stellrecht	1989	5,094
134 7/8	24 5/8	24 1/8	17 1/8	4	4	Fayette County	PA	Spurgeon Kent	1989	5,094
134 7/8	21 6/8	20 6/8	13 7/8	5	6	Dane County	WI	Dave Dilley	1989	5,094
134 7/8	24 4/8	24 3/8	19 1/8	4	4	Cumberland County	NS	Richard Russell	1989	5,094
134 7/8	20 3/8	21 2/8	18 7/8	5	5	Bond County	IL	Steve Gower	1989	5,094
134 7/8	21 5/8	20 0/8	16 5/8	5	5	Morton County	ND	Art Dunn	1990	5,094
134 7/8	22 4/8	22 3/8	15 1/8	4	5	Steuben County	IN	Scott Feller	1990	5,094
134 7/8	22 5/8	22 3/8	17 7/8	5	5	Buffalo County	WI	Bob Kriesel	1990	5,094
134 7/8	21 6/8	22 5/8	19 3/8	5	5	Berks County	PA	Randall L. Schoenly	1990	5,094
134 7/8	22 2/8	22 1/8	14 1/8	5	5	Pike County	IL	Jimmy F. Howard	1990	5,094
134 7/8	20 7/8	21 0/8	15 2/8	5	6	Douglas County	WI	Mark J. Bergren	1990	5,094
134 7/8	24 4/8	23 7/8	15 7/8	4	4	Woolwrich	ONT	Peter Hartley	1990	5,094
134 7/8	22 5/8	22 3/8	19 3/8	4	5	Woodford County	IL	Steve M. Crisp	1990	5,094
134 7/8	22 6/8	22 1/8	18 1/8	4	4	Iron County	WI	William T. Scheels	1990	5,094
134 7/8	21 6/8	22 0/8	16 1/8	5	5	Langlade County	WI	Gerald McGee	1991	5,094
134 7/8	19 3/8	19 3/8	16 3/8	5	5	Lincoln County	SD	Dave Krier	1991	5,094
134 7/8	23 7/8	22 5/8	18 2/8	5	6	Sumner County	KS	Lynn Reed	1991	5,094
134 7/8	22 4/8	22 0/8	17 3/8	5	4	Holmes County	MS	Clarence C. Steelman	1991	5,094
134 7/8	22 3/8	21 2/8	18 3/8	4	4	Sangamon County	IL	David C. Jostes	1991	5,094
134 7/8	25 1/8	23 3/8	17 3/8	4	4	Licking County	OH	Dave Novotny	1991	5,094
134 6/8	25 2/8	24 7/8	15 6/8	4	4	Newton County	IN	Charles Oliver, Sr.	1967	5,148
134 6/8	20 0/8	20 0/8	16 5/8	5	6	Hughes County	SD	Dean Gretschmann	1970	5,148
134 6/8	20 7/8	20 6/8	17 2/8	5	5	St. Charles County	MO	James Ronquest	1979	5,148
134 6/8	20 3/8	20 5/8	16 4/8	5	5	Ionia County	MI	Barry Jackson	1980	5,148
134 6/8	22 6/8	22 1/8	15 4/8	8	5	Johnson County	KS	Richard J. Seidel	1980	5,148
134 6/8	21 1/8	20 3/8	15 4/8	5	6	Goodhue County	MN	Dennis Wille	1981	5,148
134 6/8	24 3/8	24 3/8	19 6/8	4	4	Vinton County	OH	Patrick D. Kearns	1982	5,148
134 6/8	24 4/8	24 1/8	20 2/8	4	4	Johnson County	NE	Michael G. Remund	1982	5,148
134 6/8	24 0/8	22 7/8	18 2/8	4	5	Dane County	WI	Daniel J. Gartner	1983	5,148
134 6/8	26 0/8	26 3/8	13 5/8	7	5	De Kalb County	MO	J. W. Martin	1984	5,148
134 6/8	25 6/8	25 7/8	17 3/8	6	4	Killam	ALB	Tim Colwell	1985	5,148
134 6/8	23 6/8	24 7/8	19 6/8	5	4	Summit County	OH	Dave Cvelbar	1985	5,148
134 6/8	21 5/8	22 2/8	14 0/8	5	5	Waukesha County	WI	John Fonslow	1985	5,148
134 6/8	23 0/8	23 0/8	19 2/8	6	6	Guernsey County	OH	Marty L. Matthews	1986	5,148
134 6/8	21 5/8	22 6/8	15 6/8	5	5	Republic County	KS	Paul Hill	1986	5,148
134 6/8	24 0/8	25 1/8	15 6/8	4	4	Anoka County	MN	Don Strozyk	1986	5,148
134 6/8	20 4/8	20 7/8	18 1/8	6	5	Rock Island County	IL	Alan L. Black	1986	5,148
134 6/8	19 5/8	21 6/8	14 6/8	5	5	Nemaha County	NE	Lonnie Wing	1987	5,148
134 6/8	20 7/8	21 1/8	15 0/8	5	5	Jefferson County	WI	Mark Beaudoin	1987	5,148
134 6/8	22 5/8	23 4/8	21 4/8	5	5	Washington County	MS	Bobby R. Woods	1987	5,148
134 6/8	24 2/8	23 5/8	15 7/8	5	4	Shelby County	IL	Michael E. Vest	1987	5,148
134 6/8	22 4/8	21 3/8	18 7/8	8	7	Kenedy County	TX	Miguel Mireles	1987	5,148
134 6/8	21 1/8	22 1/8	17 0/8	6	6	Adams County	WI	Dale Mueller	1988	5,148
134 6/8	20 1/8	20 2/8	16 6/8	5	5	Jackson County	OH	Earl Ireland	1988	5,148
134 6/8	27 1/8	25 1/8	21 0/8	3	4	Spotsylvania County	VA	Michael Richards	1988	5,148
134 6/8	22 5/8	22 3/8	19 4/8	5	5	Jefferson County	WI	Dean Evenson	1989	5,148
134 6/8	21 0/8	21 2/8	18 2/8	4	4	St. Clair County	MO	Ray Lochridge	1989	5,148
134 6/8	22 7/8	23 1/8	16 2/8	4	4	Warren County	IA	Michael T. Olson	1989	5,148
134 6/8	23 3/8	22 5/8	17 4/8	5	4	Washington County	WI	Ken Zimmer	1989	5,148
134 6/8	22 2/8	22 1/8	18 6/8	5	5	Madison County	IL	Kirby Knackstedt	1989	5,148
134 6/8	22 0/8	22 2/8	16 2/8	5	5	Athens County	OH	Mark A. Cross	1989	5,148
134 6/8	22 3/8	22 6/8	17 0/8	5	5	Phillips County	KS	Julius E. Schoenberger	1989	5,148
134 6/8	22 5/8	22 1/8	17 6/8	5	5	Westmoreland County	PA	Mark Martini	1990	5,148

SCORE	LENGTH OF R MAIN BEAM L		INSIDE SPREAD	NUMBER OF R POINTS L		AREA	STATE/ PROVINCE	HUNTER'S NAME	DATE	RANK
134 6/8	22 7/8	23 4/8	17 4/8	5	5	Forest County	WI	Daniel J. Brezinski	1990	5,148
134 6/8	21 4/8	21 2/8	15 0/8	4	4	Racine County	WI	Ronald H. Coates	1990	5,148
134 6/8	21 7/8	23 0/8	16 2/8	4	5	Des Moines County	IA	Dave Bailey	1990	5,148
134 6/8	21 4/8	22 6/8	15 2/8	4	5	Mercer County	IL	Neil Hamerlinck	1990	5,148
134 6/8	21 2/8	22 2/8	16 0/8	5	4	Cass County	ND	Tim Poehls	1991	5,148
134 6/8	21 6/8	21 5/8	16 2/8	5	5	La Salle County	IL	Micheal Underhill	1991	5,148
134 6/8	24 0/8	23 2/8	15 4/8	6	6	Laurens County	GA	Timothy S. Knight	1991	5,148
134 6/8	21 7/8	23 0/8	17 2/8	6	4	McLean County	IL	David Grizzle	1991	5,148
134 6/8	21 6/8	21 6/8	15 2/8	5	5	Jackson County	IL	Tim Cobin	1991	5,148
134 6/8	22 2/8	23 4/8	21 0/8	5	4	Lake County	IL	Lee C. Papendorf	1991	5,148
134 6/8	23 1/8	22 6/8	17 2/8	5	5	Lincoln County	NE	Dave Hinton	1992	5,148
134 5/8	20 6/8	22 4/8	18 7/8	7	6	Floyd County	IA	James K. Harris	1972	5,192
134 5/8	22 7/8	23 0/8	17 5/8	5	5	Brown County	WI	Michael J. Goza	1976	5,192
134 5/8	21 4/8	22 2/8	17 1/8	5	6	Republic County	KS	Don R. Dejmal	1978	5,192
134 5/8	24 1/8	24 3/8	18 1/8	5	4	Jasper County	IL	William Dowland	1979	5,192
134 5/8	22 2/8	22 0/8	16 2/8	7	6	Randolph County	WV	Robert E. Nace	1979	5,192
134 5/8	24 5/8	24 7/8	18 3/8	4	5	Dodge County	WI	Ken Bialoszynski	1980	5,192
134 5/8	22 1/8	22 2/8	17 3/8	4	4	Vinton County	OH	Paul Ingram	1980	5,192
134 5/8	22 2/8	21 5/8	19 6/8	5	5	Fulton County	IL	Cliff C. Conover	1982	5,192
134 5/8	23 0/8	22 3/8	18 0/8	6	6	Clark County	KS	William A. Rule	1982	5,192
134 5/8	24 0/8	24 4/8	15 5/8	4	5	Marion County	TN	Paul E. Worley	1983	5,192
134 5/8	23 0/8	22 2/8	17 2/8	7	8	Morrison County	MN	Harold 'Nook' Blank	1983	5,192
134 5/8	22 0/8	22 4/8	14 5/8	5	5	Bedford County	VA	Robert Sutton	1983	5,192
134 5/8	21 7/8	21 5/8	17 5/8	5	5	Russell County	AL	Jesse Waldrop	1983	5,192
134 5/8	22 7/8	23 4/8	14 1/8	4	5	Brooke County	WV	Myron Rees	1983	5,192
134 5/8	21 2/8	22 2/8	17 3/8	6	5	Pulaski County	KY	Glen Whitis, Jr.	1985	5,192
134 5/8	19 4/8	19 0/8	18 0/8	5	6	Brown County	KS	Ray Kirk	1985	5,192
134 5/8	25 7/8	23 6/8	19 1/8	6	5	Fairfield County	CT	Milan G. Bull	1985	5,192
134 5/8	20 7/8	21 5/8	15 2/8	5	6	Bremer County	IA	Tom Bluhm	1986	5,192
134 5/8	19 2/8	19 3/8	15 3/8	5	5	Ford County	KS	Brent Whitaker	1986	5,192
134 5/8	23 7/8	24 5/8	20 4/8	5	4	Meigs County	OH	Randie Lawson	1987	5,192
134 5/8	21 1/8	21 1/8	17 3/8	5	5	Sauk County	WI	Gregory D. Wilson	1987	5,192
134 5/8	23 1/8	21 4/8	16 7/8	4	4	Morrison County	MN	Mike Gulbrandson	1988	5,192
134 5/8	22 1/8	23 1/8	15 3/8	5	5	Knox County	IL	David Emken	1988	5,192
134 5/8	22 5/8	22 4/8	15 4/8	4	6	Dane County	WI	Aaron Halverson	1988	5,192
134 5/8	22 4/8	21 2/8	20 1/8	4	5	Athens County	OH	John P. Lavelle	1988	5,192
134 5/8	24 1/8	24 0/8	17 2/8	6	7	Douglas County	MN	James Dykema	1988	5,192
134 5/8	25 3/8	25 6/8	17 1/8	4	5	Stokes County	NC	Harold Teague	1989	5,192
134 5/8	22 2/8	22 0/8	18 3/8	4	4	Tunica County	MS	Beau Gregory	1989	5,192
134 5/8	20 2/8	20 0/8	16 3/8	5	5	Stephenson County	IL	Dwight Peterson	1990	5,192
134 5/8	20 6/8	21 5/8	16 5/8	6	5	Hancock County	WV	Terry A. Markle	1990	5,192
134 5/8	22 5/8	22 4/8	16 7/8	4	5	Racine County	WI	Michael Habrat	1990	5,192
134 5/8	24 0/8	23 7/8	16 5/8	5	5	Orange County	IN	Jan J. Armour	1990	5,192
134 5/8	24 0/8	23 7/8	19 7/8	6	5	Allamakee County	IA	Don Heim	1990	5,192
134 5/8	23 3/8	23 6/8	17 1/8	4	5	Delaware County	IA	N. Sperfslage	1990	5,192
134 5/8	21 0/8	20 6/8	16 1/8	5	5	Kenosha County	WI	Stephen Scheibl	1990	5,192
134 5/8	24 4/8	21 4/8	19 5/8	6	6	Sussex County	DE	Randall Johnson	1990	5,192
134 5/8	18 0/8	18 4/8	13 1/8	5	5	Kandiyohi County	MN	Jerry Johnson	1991	5,192
134 5/8	22 0/8	22 2/8	18 1/8	5	4	Kit Carson County	CO	Stephen Kotz	1991	5,192
134 5/8	23 3/8	23 4/8	18 5/8	6	5	Washington County	MN	Joe Ugro III	1991	5,192
134 5/8	22 7/8	21 7/8	17 5/8	5	4	Morrison County	MN	Scott R. Kiekow	1992	5,192
134 4/8	23 5/8	21 1/8	17 2/8	4	4	Faribault County	MN	Sherwood F. Krosch	1969	5,232
134 4/8	19 0/8	20 4/8	20 5/8	5	5	Morrison County	MN	Harold A. Walsh	1971	5,232
134 4/8	19 7/8	19 5/8	17 6/8	5	5	Ripley County	IN	Robert Pitt	1974	5,232
134 4/8	22 2/8	21 2/8	18 6/8	5	5	Des Moines County	IA	Ron Cover	1975	5,232
134 4/8	23 1/8	23 1/8	18 2/8	4	4	Carroll County	OH	Thomas E. Geibel	1978	5,232
134 4/8	25 0/8	24 0/8	15 6/8	4	4	Dane County	WI	Douglas E. Seals	1980	5,232
134 4/8	22 3/8	20 7/8	17 6/8	5	5	Carroll County	MD	Thomas Creech	1980	5,232
134 4/8	20 7/8	20 2/8	17 6/8	5	5	Lincoln County	MT	Sonny Templeton	1980	5,232
134 4/8	21 6/8	21 4/8	15 2/8	4	5	Vernon County	MO	Roger Hensley	1981	5,232
134 4/8	21 2/8	24 4/8	21 2/8	5	4	Wagoner County	OK	Harold Clay	1982	5,232
134 4/8	24 3/8	24 2/8	16 5/8	5	5	Yell County	AR	Gary Worm	1983	5,232
134 4/8	19 2/8	23 4/8	17 6/8	5	5	Somerset County	MD	Clint Kelbel	1983	5,232
134 4/8	22 6/8	23 0/8	16 6/8	4	5	Chippewa County	WI	Larry Paulsen	1984	5,232
134 4/8	21 2/8	24 2/8	22 0/8	4	4	Morris County	NJ	David Paddock	1984	5,232
134 4/8	22 7/8	23 5/8	15 6/8	5	5	Morgan County	OH	Dean Spears	1984	5,232
134 4/8	21 1/8	21 1/8	17 6/8	4	4	Monroe County	WV	Clarence J Burns	1984	5,232
134 4/8	19 4/8	19 6/8	16 4/8	6	5	Kingsbury County	SD	Reginald E. Faber, Jr.	1984	5,232
134 4/8	24 2/8	22 5/8	15 7/8	6	6	Hickman County	TN	Stanley Hunt	1985	5,232
134 4/8	23 1/8	24 2/8	18 0/8	5	4	Marshall County	MN	Bruce Becklund	1985	5,232

Score	Length of Main Beam R	L	Inside Spread	Number of Points R	L	Area	State/ Province	Hunter's Name	Date	Rank
134 4/8	24 0/8	23 1/8	17 2/8	5	6	Clay County	IL	Myron Woomer	1985	5,232
134 4/8	21 3/8	19 7/8	18 0/8	5	5	McCulloch County	TX	Richard R. Curry	1986	5,232
134 4/8	22 0/8	22 3/8	14 2/8	5	5	Buffalo County	WI	Douglas Henderson	1986	5,232
134 4/8	25 3/8	24 6/8	20 1/8	5	5	Coffey County	KS	Glen Neilson	1986	5,232
134 4/8	24 5/8	23 7/8	16 6/8	4	4	Delta County	MI	Ronald E. Quick	1986	5,232
134 4/8	24 5/8	25 0/8	18 2/8	4	4	Morrison County	MN	Scott Bruber	1987	5,232
134 4/8	21 6/8	21 1/8	15 6/8	4	5	Preble County	OH	Robert B. Lickliter	1987	5,232
134 4/8	22 7/8	23 2/8	14 6/8	5	5	Claiborne County	TN	Glen Montgomery	1987	5,232
134 4/8	20 0/8	20 1/8	17 2/8	5	4	Lee County	IL	Gordon Gableman	1987	5,232
134 4/8	21 0/8	21 0/8	16 2/8	5	5	Lambton County	ONT	J. Barry Lugsdin	1987	5,232
134 4/8	24 6/8	22 6/8	19 3/8	7	6	Suffolk County	NY	John W. Wobst	1987	5,232
134 4/8	21 0/8	18 1/8	17 0/8	6	6	Charles County	MD	Scott Cutter	1987	5,232
134 4/8	20 4/8	20 7/8	14 5/8	5	6	Bosque County	TX	Charles E. Rushing	1987	5,232
134 4/8	20 0/8	21 5/8	16 2/8	5	5	Clark County	IL	Thomas E. Rothrock	1988	5,232
134 4/8	22 2/8	21 4/8	17 0/8	5	5	Door County	WI	Daniel W. Herrbold	1988	5,232
134 4/8	24 6/8	19 2/8	19 2/8	4	5	Winnebago County	IA	Tom Brakke	1988	5,232
134 4/8	20 4/8	20 5/8	14 0/8	6	6	Atascosa County	TX	Russell Janek	1989	5,232
134 4/8	23 5/8	23 3/8	18 0/8	4	4	Taylor County	WI	Paul A. Biederman	1989	5,232
134 4/8	24 5/8	24 3/8	16 0/8	5	5	Price County	WI	David Kelnhofer	1989	5,232
134 4/8	22 4/8	21 1/8	16 2/8	6	6	Grant County	WI	Ronald D. Olson	1989	5,232
134 4/8	22 4/8	22 7/8	17 0/8	5	5	Roberts County	SD	Ronnie Bucklin	1989	5,232
134 4/8	22 4/8	23 3/8	17 0/8	4	5	Traill County	ND	Michael Toomey	1990	5,232
134 4/8	24 4/8	23 5/8	20 2/8	4	4	Montgomery County	PA	Joseph A. Rizzo	1990	5,232
134 4/8	21 5/8	21 2/8	15 4/8	5	5	Goliad County	TX	Roy M. Goodwin	1990	5,232
134 4/8	22 6/8	22 3/8	13 6/8	5	5	Jefferson County	OH	James C. Riggle	1990	5,232
134 4/8	22 1/8	22 2/8	18 0/8	5	5	Beltrami County	MN	Irving Strom	1990	5,232
134 4/8	20 6/8	20 7/8	14 4/8	6	6	Hitchcock County	NE	William Elfland	1990	5,232
134 4/8	25 2/8	25 5/8	16 6/8	5	7	Clay County	MO	Joe Zuber	1990	5,232
134 4/8	21 1/8	21 0/8	18 4/8	5	5	Calhoun County	MI	John Eldridge	1991	5,232
134 4/8	22 7/8	23 7/8	14 0/8	5	5	Douglas County	WI	John L. Schnell	1991	5,232
134 4/8	20 2/8	22 3/8	11 6/8	5	5	Hillsdale County	MI	Jim Thiel	1991	5,232
134 4/8	22 6/8	21 2/8	13 6/8	6	6	Lee County	IA	Glenn E. Wagner	1991	5,232
134 4/8	23 6/8	23 6/8	17 1/8	5	5	Live Oak County	TX	Beau Walker	1991	5,232
134 3/8	23 4/8	22 1/8	17 1/8	4	5	Arkansas County	AR	Louis Rush	1959	5,284
134 3/8	20 5/8	20 5/8	17 3/8	5	5	Rice County	MN	Gary Roemhildt	1965	5,284
134 3/8	21 6/8	21 3/8	15 4/8	4	5	Cecil County	MD	Bernard Langhorne	1972	5,284
134 3/8	20 5/8	20 4/8	17 1/8	5	5	Powell County	MT	Paul E. Tadlock	1972	5,284
134 3/8	22 1/8	23 4/8	18 5/8	4	4	Tompkins County	NY	H. R. Swansbrough, Jr.	1977	5,284
134 3/8	24 2/8	24 1/8	22 6/8	5	5	Nicollet County	MN	John Seifert	1978	5,284
134 3/8	21 4/8	21 2/8	16 6/8	5	8	Phelps County	NE	Kirk Stroup	1981	5,284
134 3/8	20 6/8	20 0/8	15 1/8	5	5	Cumberland County	NJ	Bob Eisele	1981	5,284
134 3/8	22 7/8	22 0/8	17 6/8	5	4	Pike County	IL	Dan Wombles	1981	5,284
134 3/8	21 6/8	21 2/8	15 7/8	5	5	Pope County	AR	Danny Bennett	1981	5,284
134 3/8	23 4/8	23 7/8	18 5/8	6	3	Morrison County	MN	Arnie Borchert	1982	5,284
134 3/8	22 1/8	22 3/8	18 1/8	4	4	Texas County	OK	Curtis Clayton	1982	5,284
134 3/8	22 3/8	21 2/8	19 2/8	6	5	Chippewa County	MI	Joe Johnston	1983	5,284
134 3/8	23 4/8	22 4/8	18 5/8	4	4	Kingman County	KS	Ken Marsh	1984	5,284
134 3/8	22 7/8	22 3/8	14 4/8	6	5	Dawson County	MT	Alan H. Winkel	1984	5,284
134 3/8	25 2/8	25 3/8	18 3/8	4	4	Scioto County	OH	Ed Asbury	1984	5,284
134 3/8	24 5/8	24 7/8	16 0/8	5	6	Morrison County	MN	Gary Thomas	1985	5,284
134 3/8	21 2/8	22 1/8	18 0/8	7	6	Vermilion County	IL	Ken Gabehart	1986	5,284
134 3/8	24 2/8	24 7/8	16 0/8	5	5	Breckinridge County	KY	James R. Parks	1987	5,284
134 3/8	23 6/8	23 4/8	19 1/8	5	4	Montgomery County	AL	Foy H. Tatum	1987	5,284
134 3/8	22 2/8	22 3/8	16 1/8	4	4	Barbour County	AL	Harold Reynolds	1987	5,284
134 3/8	22 1/8	23 6/8	15 5/8	6	5	Kendall County	IL	Dean V. Ashton	1988	5,284
134 3/8	21 7/8	22 6/8	17 5/8	5	5	Pickaway County	OH	Tim Ritchie	1988	5,284
134 3/8	19 6/8	20 4/8	15 3/8	6	6	Florence County	WI	Chris H. Larson	1988	5,284
134 3/8	24 5/8	24 4/8	17 1/8	5	4	Washburn County	WI	Todd M. Skille	1988	5,284
134 3/8	22 1/8	22 5/8	16 4/8	4	6	Albert County	NBW	John Carty	1989	5,284
134 3/8	22 3/8	22 3/8	17 5/8	5	5	Kenosha County	WI	James D. Maricle	1989	5,284
134 3/8	25 4/8	25 3/8	20 5/8	5	5	Malden Twp.	ONT	Ed Faucher	1989	5,284
134 3/8	21 5/8	21 7/8	14 5/8	5	5	Panola County	TX	Twanda Paul Rozelle II	1990	5,284
134 3/8	23 7/8	23 6/8	17 5/8	7	7	Crawford County	IL	Michael W. Elliott II	1990	5,284
134 3/8	23 6/8	24 0/8	16 5/8	4	4	Rock County	WI	Erik Hanson	1990	5,284
134 3/8	21 7/8	22 0/8	19 1/8	4	4	Knox County	IL	Michael J. McCall	1990	5,284
134 3/8	24 1/8	22 6/8	21 1/8	7	6	Linn County	IA	William Kula	1990	5,284
134 3/8	21 5/8	21 1/8	15 7/8	6	5	Brown County	IL	John Knight	1991	5,284
134 3/8	21 2/8	21 4/8	15 3/8	5	5	Kenedy County	TX	John W. Wallace	1992	5,284
134 2/8	21 0/8	21 2/8	16 4/8	5	5	Benton County	IA	Larry Walker	1961	5,319
134 2/8	22 2/8	21 4/8	16 0/8	5	5	Derby	IN	Jack E. Hungate	1963	5,319

SCORE	LENGTH OF R MAIN BEAM L		INSIDE SPREAD	NUMBER OF R POINTS L		AREA	STATE/ PROVINCE	HUNTER'S NAME	DATE	RANK
134 2/8	21 4/8	22 7/8	18 0/8	4	4	Barton County	KS	Nicholas J. Gray	1973	5,319
134 2/8	24 2/8	23 4/8	20 4/8	5	5	McLean County	IL	Norman Price, Jr.	1973	5,319
134 2/8	23 4/8	22 1/8	21 0/8	5	7	Du Page County	IL	William M. Voight	1973	5,319
134 2/8	22 5/8	23 2/8	16 2/8	5	4	Burnett County	WI	Severin A. Wanous	1976	5,319
134 2/8	24 0/8	24 4/8	17 2/8	5	5	Fond du Lac County	WI	Doug Bilgo	1978	5,319
134 2/8	21 4/8	21 0/8	15 4/8	4	5	Morrison County	MN	Rodney Forbrook	1979	5,319
134 2/8	22 0/8	22 0/8	18 2/8	4	5	Spink County	SD	Douglas Price	1980	5,319
134 2/8	20 4/8	21 4/8	17 4/8	5	5	Muskingum County	OH	Allen R. Smith	1980	5,319
134 2/8	25 0/8	25 1/8	20 4/8	8	6	Osborne County	KS	Robert Grabast	1981	5,319
134 2/8	22 7/8	23 4/8	16 4/8	4	4	Reno County	KS	Monte Long	1982	5,319
134 2/8	23 4/8	23 3/8	17 6/8	5	5	Johnson County	IA	Ken Sovers	1983	5,319
134 2/8	22 7/8	23 4/8	21 1/8	6	6	McLean County	ND	Rich Radke	1984	5,319
134 2/8	22 4/8	23 1/8	18 0/8	4	4	Sheboygan County	WI	Randy Kolpin	1984	5,319
134 2/8	20 5/8	20 0/8	18 4/8	5	5	Dodge County	MN	Chad A. Lenz	1984	5,319
134 2/8	22 4/8	22 3/8	17 6/8	5	5	Monroe County	WI	Steve Heintz	1985	5,319
134 2/8	22 7/8	21 7/8	18 2/8	4	5	Columbia County	WI	Brian P. Schepp	1985	5,319
134 2/8	22 7/8	22 1/8	15 4/8	4	4	Edwards County	TX	Steve Payne	1985	5,319
134 2/8	25 5/8	26 0/8	19 0/8	3	4	Barren County	KY	Wesley Bales	1985	5,319
134 2/8	24 1/8	22 4/8	16 2/8	4	5	Will County	IL	Hugh M. MacCracken	1986	5,319
134 2/8	23 4/8	24 3/8	14 6/8	4	4	St. Clair County	MI	Gerald Conrad	1986	5,319
134 2/8	22 0/8	21 7/8	16 4/8	5	5	Marinette County	WI	Gerald Valley, Jr.	1986	5,319
134 2/8	22 0/8	23 3/8	18 2/8	5	4	Kay County	OK	Jim Sheets	1986	5,319
134 2/8	23 3/8	21 6/8	17 2/8	5	5	Herkimer County	NY	Stanley D. Pomichter	1986	5,319
134 2/8	21 5/8	21 5/8	16 6/8	5	5	Flathead County	MT	Larry Hadley	1986	5,319
134 2/8	26 7/8	26 3/8	20 0/8	6	9	Crawford County	IL	Charlie Guyer	1987	5,319
134 2/8	21 5/8	21 1/8	16 6/8	5	5	Waukesha County	WI	Frank Turck, Jr.	1987	5,319
134 2/8	21 6/8	24 2/8	19 0/8	5	4	Westchester County	NY	Michael Wallace	1987	5,319
134 2/8	22 4/8	20 5/8	15 4/8	5	5	Hamilton County	OH	Ken Pfierman	1988	5,319
134 2/8	21 3/8	21 1/8	17 1/8	7	5	Chippewa County	WI	Rich Varsho	1988	5,319
134 2/8	26 5/8	26 4/8	21 2/8	3	3	Poinsett County	AR	Gary Flemon	1988	5,319
134 2/8	24 0/8	23 6/8	16 6/8	4	4	Kane County	IL	Tony Litts	1988	5,319
134 2/8	23 0/8	22 5/8	19 6/8	5	8	Oakland County	MI	Timothy Rock	1989	5,319
134 2/8	21 2/8	21 1/8	16 0/8	5	5	Logan County	KY	T. J. Faenza	1989	5,319
134 2/8	19 7/8	19 6/8	16 0/8	6	6	Greene County	IA	Glen Garnett	1989	5,319
134 2/8	21 3/8	22 3/8	16 6/8	6	5	Morrison County	MN	Dave Vomela	1989	5,319
134 2/8	20 3/8	20 3/8	16 6/8	5	4	Outagamie County	WI	Daryl Van Geffen	1989	5,319
134 2/8	23 1/8	22 1/8	19 2/8	4	4	Wabasha County	MN	Keith A. Ramthun	1990	5,319
134 2/8	19 4/8	20 2/8	16 4/8	5	5	Butler County	IA	Kent Karsjens	1990	5,319
134 2/8	22 6/8	23 5/8	16 6/8	6	8	Racine County	WI	Michael H. Poeschel	1990	5,319
134 2/8	19 5/8	20 6/8	16 2/8	4	4	Massac County	IL	Chris Sielbeck	1991	5,319
134 2/8	24 2/8	25 2/8	20 2/8	5	5	Genesee County	MI	Ned A. Gibson	1991	5,319
134 2/8	23 4/8	24 0/8	17 2/8	5	5	Athens County	OH	John P. Tolerton	1991	5,319
134 2/8	24 6/8	25 1/8	18 2/8	4	6	Montgomery County	IN	Chad Smith	1991	5,319
134 2/8	23 7/8	23 4/8	19 0/8	7	7	Monroe County	NY	Daniel C. Willard	1991	5,319
134 2/8	24 5/8	26 7/8	23 4/8	6	5	Knox County	KY	Dink Garland	1991	5,319
134 2/8	23 1/8	24 3/8	19 0/8	5	5	Waukesha County	WI	Dirk Stolz	1991	5,319
134 1/8	23 2/8	23 3/8	20 1/8	5	5	Brown County	IN	Jason Thompson	1966	5,367
134 1/8	21 2/8	22 6/8	18 2/8	7	5	Vanderburgh County	IN	William H. Davis	1967	5,367
134 1/8	24 7/8	25 4/8	21 3/8	6	5	Morrison County	MN	Vincent Pajak	1973	5,367
134 1/8	24 3/8	23 6/8	20 2/8	4	5	Hopkins County	KY	James R. Williams	1978	5,367
134 1/8	19 6/8	19 7/8	16 2/8	7	7	Benton County	TN	Robert Blackstock	1978	5,367
134 1/8	24 6/8	22 7/8	17 3/8	5	5	Jones County	IA	Harold Erger	1979	5,367
134 1/8	22 4/8	22 7/8	16 3/8	4	4	Allen County	IN	Martin C. Yager	1979	5,367
134 1/8	23 0/8	21 0/8	16 3/8	4	4	Jackson County	MO	Marvin Thomey	1980	5,367
134 1/8	23 4/8	22 2/8	19 1/8	5	5	Allamakee County	IA	Brian Carlson	1981	5,367
134 1/8	21 1/8	19 4/8	17 3/8	5	5	Genesee County	MI	Richard J. Parkhurst	1982	5,367
134 1/8	19 6/8	18 3/8	16 1/8	6	5	Washington County	WI	Christopher J. Dequardo	1982	5,367
134 1/8	22 2/8	22 0/8	17 4/8	6	7	Wabaunsee County	KS	Gary Hunsicker	1983	5,367
134 1/8	23 0/8	22 3/8	18 1/8	5	5	Westmoreland County	PA	Joseph Ringling	1985	5,367
134 1/8	22 3/8	17 3/8	15 3/8	8	5	Crawford County	WI	Randall Nash	1985	5,367
134 1/8	23 0/8	21 6/8	19 3/8	4	4	Perry County	IN	Junis S. Ingle	1985	5,367
134 1/8	24 0/8	23 0/8	18 5/8	5	6	Frederick County	MD	Melvin R. Keith, Jr.	1986	5,367
134 1/8	21 6/8	21 0/8	15 3/8	5	5	Clinton County	MI	Jeffery A. Tolliver	1986	5,367
134 1/8	23 3/8	24 0/8	19 3/8	4	4	Poinsett County	AR	Jeff Vaughn	1986	5,367
134 1/8	25 4/8	26 2/8	19 3/8	4	4	Holmes County	OH	Richard A. Hawkins	1987	5,367
134 1/8	23 4/8	24 6/8	19 5/8	5	6	Pierce County	WI	Patrick McKenzie	1987	5,367
134 1/8	20 1/8	22 3/8	15 1/8	5	5	Buffalo County	WI	Marlin Mueller	1988	5,367
134 1/8	23 6/8	23 6/8	20 1/8	4	6	Madison County	IA	Glenn D. Vondra	1988	5,367
134 1/8	23 1/8	23 4/8	17 3/8	5	5	Dodge County	MN	Robert Oldefendt	1989	5,367
134 1/8	23 2/8	23 3/8	18 5/8	4	4	Arkansas County	AR	Chuck Wallace	1989	5,367

SCORE	LENGTH OF R MAIN BEAM L		INSIDE SPREAD	NUMBER OF R POINTS L		AREA	STATE/ PROVINCE	HUNTER'S NAME	DATE	RANK
134 1/8	22 0/8	22 0/8	16 0/8	7	5	Brooks County	TX	Mark Culver	1989	5,367
134 1/8	21 2/8	21 4/8	17 1/8	5	5	Broadwater County	MT	Barry Howard	1989	5,367
134 1/8	22 5/8	22 1/8	18 3/8	4	4	Sullivan County	IN	Ron Medley	1989	5,367
134 1/8	22 7/8	22 7/8	15 7/8	5	4	Hillsdale County	MI	John T. Glassburn	1989	5,367
134 1/8	20 0/8	20 0/8	15 5/8	5	5	Rock County	MN	David Paquette	1989	5,367
134 1/8	20 0/8	19 0/8	17 1/8	5	5	Pierce County	WI	Jeremy Shutz	1990	5,367
134 1/8	20 4/8	22 0/8	16 7/8	5	5	Parkland County	ALB	Christopher R. Green	1990	5,367
134 1/8	22 1/8	22 5/8	18 1/8	4	4	Meade County	KY	William H. Biddle	1991	5,367
134 1/8	22 3/8	23 2/8	18 7/8	5	5	Lehigh County	PA	Ron Wentz, Jr.	1991	5,367
134 1/8	22 2/8	23 6/8	18 0/8	4	5	Watonwan County	MN	David G. Raney	1991	5,367
134 1/8	24 0/8	23 7/8	15 1/8	6	8	Linn County	KS	Gary Robertson	1991	5,367
134 1/8	21 2/8	21 3/8	12 6/8	8	7	Parker County	TX	Dustin Meaders	1991	5,367
134 1/8	23 2/8	23 6/8	18 3/8	4	4	Berkshire County	MA	Joseph Shaheen	1991	5,367
134 1/8	22 4/8	22 4/8	15 5/8	5	6	Franklin County	KS	Teryl Hrabe	1991	5,367
134 1/8	19 4/8	19 6/8	17 0/8	8	5	Kerr County	TX	Stephen W. Dean	1992	5,367
134 1/8	21 6/8	19 2/8	17 3/8	5	5	Weyburn	SAS	Scott Brady	1992	5,367
134 0/8	23 7/8	23 7/8	19 0/8	4	5	Grundy County	IL	Henry F. Blaha	1977	5,407
134 0/8	23 1/8	22 6/8	15 6/8	7	6	Calhoun County	MI	James D. Warner	1979	5,407
134 0/8	23 4/8	24 1/8	17 6/8	6	5	St. Joseph County	MI	Randy A. Gordon	1981	5,407
134 0/8	23 6/8	22 7/8	20 4/8	5	6	Coshocton County	OH	William Randles	1981	5,407
134 0/8	23 6/8	25 2/8	17 6/8	4	4	Lawrence County	OH	Robert D. Wilson	1981	5,407
134 0/8	21 6/8	20 5/8	18 0/8	6	6	Nicollet County	MN	Karsten Severns	1982	5,407
134 0/8	22 2/8	21 7/8	20 0/8	5	4	Eau Claire County	WI	Donald E. Moss	1983	5,407
134 0/8	21 2/8	21 2/8	15 3/8	5	7	Reno County	KS	Norbert Bechtel	1983	5,407
134 0/8	22 2/8	21 6/8	17 0/8	4	5	Miami County	KS	Jackie Bethel	1984	5,407
134 0/8	25 0/8	24 4/8	17 3/8	4	5	Fayette County	OH	Don M. Curtin	1984	5,407
134 0/8	19 5/8	20 2/8	16 6/8	6	6	Stephenson County	IL	Greg Deutsch	1984	5,407
134 0/8	23 3/8	24 0/8	18 6/8	4	4	Crawford County	IL	Robert Loveall	1985	5,407
134 0/8	22 1/8	22 0/8	17 4/8	4	4	Waukesha County	WI	James J. Mislang	1985	5,407
134 0/8	22 5/8	23 0/8	17 0/8	4	4	Washtenaw County	MI	James E. Bauer	1986	5,407
134 0/8	24 0/8	23 6/8	19 6/8	4	4	Jones County	MS	Samuel Husser	1986	5,407
134 0/8	20 0/8	20 4/8	13 4/8	5	5	Kenedy County	TX	David Almaraz	1986	5,407
134 0/8	21 4/8	22 6/8	16 0/8	5	5	Dane County	WI	Gordy M. Brings	1986	5,407
134 0/8	20 5/8	21 2/8	15 0/8	4	4	Morton County	ND	Doug Schlosser	1986	5,407
134 0/8	21 2/8	19 5/8	17 4/8	5	6	Shawnee County	KS	Tom Crites	1987	5,407
134 0/8	19 6/8	19 6/8	15 2/8	6	6	Butler County	KS	Mike Demel	1987	5,407
134 0/8	22 3/8	23 0/8	17 6/8	8	7	Seward County	NE	Pat Bogenreif	1988	5,407
134 0/8	22 3/8	21 4/8	17 2/8	5	4	Trempealeau County	WI	LaVerne Dettinger	1988	5,407
134 0/8	24 4/8	24 1/8	17 6/8	6	5	Racine County	WI	Willie Montieth	1988	5,407
134 0/8	19 6/8	19 3/8	16 0/8	5	5	Saline County	MO	John F. Bacon	1988	5,407
134 0/8	20 1/8	20 0/8	15 6/8	5	6	Lake County	IL	John Roscop	1988	5,407
134 0/8	24 0/8	23 3/8	16 0/8	4	4	Mercer County	NJ	Wayne Kalinowski	1989	5,407
134 0/8	22 7/8	22 6/8	15 0/8	5	5	Fayette County	IL	Mike Cauble	1989	5,407
134 0/8	18 7/8	18 1/8	16 4/8	5	5	McHenry County	IL	William D. Weiss	1989	5,407
134 0/8	24 2/8	23 3/8	18 0/8	5	5	Wellington County	ONT	Jan Koszler	1989	5,407
134 0/8	22 7/8	22 7/8	18 6/8	6	5	Steuben County	NY	Paul Rowan	1989	5,407
134 0/8	22 7/8	22 7/8	17 5/8	6	7	Frederick County	MD	Harry T. Lackey, Jr.	1990	5,407
134 0/8	22 3/8	22 1/8	17 6/8	5	5	Labette County	KS	Kevin Frogley	1990	5,407
134 0/8	22 3/8	23 1/8	21 2/8	4	4	Randolph County	IN	Don Fields	1990	5,407
134 0/8	23 4/8	23 1/8	16 5/8	6	6	Lawrence County	OH	Gerald W. Kouns	1990	5,407
134 0/8	21 3/8	23 1/8	16 6/8	6	6	Waupaca County	WI	Rod T. Gullixon	1990	5,407
134 0/8	23 7/8	23 4/8	19 1/8	6	10	Beltrami County	MN	Harold A. Borchers	1990	5,407
134 0/8	22 3/8	21 2/8	17 4/8	4	4	Harvey County	KS	Rick Dodd	1990	5,407
134 0/8	23 7/8	23 3/8	16 4/8	6	5	Peoria County	IL	Don Harper	1991	5,407
134 0/8	23 1/8	24 0/8	16 0/8	4	5	Becker County	MN	Perry L. Bertek	1991	5,407
134 0/8	22 2/8	22 0/8	18 0/8	5	5	Madison County	NY	Llyod L. Weigel	1991	5,407
134 0/8	24 4/8	24 5/8	18 6/8	5	5	Sedgwick County	CO	John Graham	1991	5,407
134 0/8	24 0/8	23 1/8	16 6/8	5	5	Osage County	OK	Johnny Lamb	1991	5,407
133 7/8	22 7/8	23 0/8	20 5/8	6	7	Dodge County	MN	Myles Keller	1976	5,449
133 7/8	19 5/8	20 2/8	15 6/8	5	6	Newton County	IN	Howard Severs	1976	5,449
133 7/8	24 4/8	24 1/8	19 1/8	4	5	Barnstable County	MA	Randy Fisher	1977	5,449
133 7/8	23 5/8	22 1/8	18 1/8	4	4	Calhoun County	MI	Douglas Tasker	1978	5,449
133 7/8	20 2/8	20 2/8	16 7/8	5	4	Wabaunsee County	KS	Charles L. Bisnette	1979	5,449
133 7/8	22 1/8	21 7/8	21 1/8	4	4	Kalamazoo County	MI	Louis G. Sari	1979	5,449
133 7/8	19 7/8	20 2/8	16 5/8	6	7	Cortland County	NY	John S. Cutler	1982	5,449
133 7/8	20 4/8	19 6/8	14 5/8	5	6	Hennepin County	MN	Robert Boynton	1982	5,449
133 7/8	23 1/8	23 3/8	16 1/8	5	4	Knox County	IL	Dave Emken	1982	5,449
133 7/8	19 6/8	20 2/8	17 1/8	5	5	Wood County	WI	David J. Rademan	1983	5,449
133 7/8	20 4/8	20 1/8	17 6/8	6	5	Darke County	OH	Richard D. Baird	1983	5,449
133 7/8	22 3/8	22 1/8	18 5/8	4	5	Washington County	KS	Bill R. Mallean	1983	5,449

SCORE	LENGTH OF MAIN BEAM		INSIDE SPREAD	NUMBER OF POINTS		AREA	STATE/ PROVINCE	HUNTER'S NAME	DATE	RANK
	R	L		R	L					
133 7/8	20 2/8	19 3/8	15 6/8	5	6	Brookings County	SD	William Gibbons	1983	5,449
133 7/8	24 6/8	25 5/8	18 3/8	4	4	Guernsey County	OH	Don Cady	1984	5,449
133 7/8	22 3/8	22 0/8	16 6/8	5	5	Brown County	IN	Ronald L. Gish	1984	5,449
133 7/8	22 1/8	21 4/8	19 5/8	5	5	Morrow County	OH	Mark D. Mann	1984	5,449
133 7/8	22 7/8	24 4/8	17 1/8	4	4	Jefferson County	WI	Gilbert Krueger	1985	5,449
133 7/8	23 7/8	24 6/8	21 3/8	5	5	Iroquois County	IL	Ray Savoie	1985	5,449
133 7/8	21 1/8	20 5/8	18 5/8	5	4	Stephenson County	IL	Steven Sager	1985	5,449
133 7/8	22 3/8	23 3/8	23 3/8	5	5	Green County	WI	Jeffrey D. Miller	1985	5,449
133 7/8	22 7/8	23 3/8	17 4/8	5	4	Hardin County	KY	Phillip Crady	1985	5,449
133 7/8	22 0/8	22 0/8	17 0/8	6	5	Barron County	WI	David Jansen	1986	5,449
133 7/8	23 3/8	23 1/8	16 5/8	5	5	Oconto County	WI	Daniel Bodart	1986	5,449
133 7/8	20 4/8	20 4/8	18 5/8	4	5	Clay County	MN	Craig Enervold	1987	5,449
133 7/8	21 7/8	21 3/8	15 3/8	4	5	Arenac County	MI	Kenneth C. Bender	1987	5,449
133 7/8	23 4/8	23 6/8	17 1/8	4	4	Rogers County	OK	Ernest Ross	1987	5,449
133 7/8	20 5/8	23 0/8	15 5/8	5	4	Boone County	MO	Tim Grace	1987	5,449
133 7/8	22 1/8	20 2/8	17 0/8	5	7	Adams County	IL	George Kimbrell	1987	5,449
133 7/8	21 2/8	22 1/8	13 5/8	5	5	Osage County	OK	Lonny Bearden	1987	5,449
133 7/8	24 4/8	24 5/8	17 3/8	4	4	Logan County	OH	Alan Regier	1987	5,449
133 7/8	20 6/8	19 7/8	15 3/8	5	6	Miami County	KS	Dan Williams	1988	5,449
133 7/8	25 1/8	23 5/8	16 3/8	5	5	Chisago County	MN	Emil Folsom	1988	5,449
133 7/8	23 2/8	21 3/8	17 3/8	5	6	Bates County	MO	Mark J. Coster	1988	5,449
133 7/8	22 2/8	22 5/8	15 7/8	5	5	Polk County	MN	Darrell Ramsey	1989	5,449
133 7/8	23 2/8	23 4/8	18 3/8	4	4	Washington County	MN	Tim Kabrick	1989	5,449
133 7/8	23 0/8	22 4/8	16 7/8	4	4	Kalamazoo County	MI	Daniel Maurer	1989	5,449
133 7/8	22 4/8	22 2/8	15 0/8	6	6	Kenedy County	TX	Ron Serwa	1989	5,449
133 7/8	23 1/8	23 4/8	19 1/8	4	4	Livingston County	NY	David H. Kosowski	1989	5,449
133 7/8	24 0/8	22 7/8	18 5/8	4	4	Chippewa County	WI	Wayne Krejci	1989	5,449
133 7/8	20 1/8	20 5/8	15 7/8	6	5	Osage County	OK	Terry Mills	1989	5,449
133 7/8	23 1/8	23 1/8	19 3/8	4	4	Sawyer County	WI	Gary Haus	1990	5,449
133 7/8	20 4/8	21 6/8	18 1/8	5	5	Onondaga County	NY	Ron Daniels	1990	5,449
133 7/8	21 5/8	21 5/8	18 2/8	6	6	La Salle County	IL	Richard E. Bolden	1990	5,449
133 7/8	24 1/8	24 3/8	16 5/8	4	5	Lake County	IN	Bernie Pawlasek	1990	5,449
133 7/8	22 6/8	22 4/8	19 2/8	5	6	Salem County	NJ	Mark D. Olson	1990	5,449
133 7/8	26 5/8	26 4/8	21 7/8	5	7	Lake County	IL	Tom Kough	1990	5,449
133 7/8	21 2/8	22 0/8	16 2/8	5	6	Troup County	GA	Chris L. Wright	1991	5,449
133 7/8	24 4/8	24 2/8	19 5/8	5	4	Allegheny County	PA	Thomas W. Eiler	1991	5,449
133 7/8	22 0/8	22 4/8	17 3/8	5	5	Westchester County	NY	Steve Cristantiello	1991	5,449
133 7/8	22 4/8	22 7/8	17 7/8	5	6	Morrison County	MN	Joe Poirier	1991	5,449
133 7/8	22 4/8	23 6/8	17 5/8	6	5	Goodhue County	MN	Bill Prigge	1992	5,449
133 6/8	22 6/8	24 7/8	17 2/8	5	4	Tama County	IA	Chad Sivertsen	1971	5,500
133 6/8	19 6/8	20 1/8	15 2/8	5	5	Stanley County	SD	Rick Ray	1972	5,500
133 6/8	24 2/8	25 2/8	19 7/8	4	6	McPherson County	KS	Mike Chambers	1975	5,500
133 6/8	22 5/8	21 5/8	17 4/8	4	4	St. Marys County	MD	Marvin T. Breeden	1979	5,500
133 6/8	19 5/8	21 5/8	15 6/8	5	5	Harrison County	WV	John Lowther	1982	5,500
133 6/8	22 4/8	22 4/8	17 1/8	6	5	Shawnee County	KS	Frank J. Delci, Jr.	1984	5,500
133 6/8	24 2/8	22 7/8	17 4/8	4	4	Rock County	WI	Gary Johnson	1985	5,500
133 6/8	23 0/8	23 6/8	18 6/8	4	5	Bon Homme County	SD	David B. Cull	1985	5,500
133 6/8	21 6/8	22 0/8	16 0/8	5	4	Oakland County	MI	Joseph Q. Quin	1986	5,500
133 6/8	22 0/8	21 2/8	15 6/8	6	7	Madison County	KY	Duff Wolfinbarger	1986	5,500
133 6/8	22 7/8	22 6/8	19 4/8	6	6	Canmore	ALB	Kenneth Baker	1986	5,500
133 6/8	22 5/8	22 6/8	17 2/8	5	5	Pottawatomie County	KS	Dennis Wilson	1986	5,500
133 6/8	23 0/8	22 6/8	18 2/8	6	4	Dodge County	WI	Steven H. Ohlemiller	1987	5,500
133 6/8	20 6/8	20 5/8	17 5/8	6	5	Delaware County	IA	John Dillon	1987	5,500
133 6/8	20 5/8	19 7/8	17 6/8	5	4	Jefferson County	IL	Terry Kash	1987	5,500
133 6/8	27 1/8	24 7/8	18 2/8	4	3	Clark County	IL	Gerald Shaffner	1987	5,500
133 6/8	22 4/8	23 1/8	14 3/8	6	5	Scott County	IL	Jack Wallis, Jr.	1988	5,500
133 6/8	24 0/8	22 5/8	18 5/8	4	5	Monroe County	NY	David E. Lang	1988	5,500
133 6/8	22 2/8	22 2/8	15 0/8	7	7	Okfuskee County	OK	Jake Crutchfield	1988	5,500
133 6/8	24 3/8	23 1/8	17 3/8	4	6	Story County	IA	Jon E. Von Feldt	1988	5,500
133 6/8	23 0/8	25 0/8	20 4/8	6	4	Jackson County	IN	Jack L. Young	1988	5,500
133 6/8	23 0/8	25 2/8	18 0/8	4	4	Dallas County	IA	Dan Pickell	1989	5,500
133 6/8	22 6/8	22 6/8	16 4/8	4	4	Albany County	NY	Louis Coluccio	1989	5,500
133 6/8	22 1/8	21 4/8	16 2/8	5	5	Sheboygan County	WI	Mark "Kissy" Kissinger	1989	5,500
133 6/8	24 6/8	24 1/8	18 7/8	5	5	Jo Daviess County	IL	Monte J. White	1990	5,500
133 6/8	22 0/8	22 0/8	16 0/8	5	5	Pepin County	WI	Donald W. Stewart	1990	5,500
133 6/8	24 1/8	23 4/8	20 6/8	4	5	Champaign County	IL	Bud Barnes	1990	5,500
133 6/8	20 2/8	21 3/8	16 4/8	5	5	Furnas County	NE	Kevin J. Bergstrom	1990	5,500
133 6/8	25 1/8	25 1/8	19 0/8	4	4	Irwin County	GA	J. Tony Coleman	1991	5,500
133 6/8	23 1/8	22 2/8	14 0/8	4	5	Jackson County	MO	George Fischer	1991	5,500
133 6/8	22 4/8	23 1/8	17 2/8	5	5	Tom Green County	TX	Ronnie Parsons	1991	5,500

SCORE	LENGTH OF MAIN BEAM R	LENGTH OF MAIN BEAM L	INSIDE SPREAD	NUMBER OF POINTS R	NUMBER OF POINTS L	AREA	STATE/ PROVINCE	HUNTER'S NAME	DATE	RANK
133 6/8	21 1/8	21 5/8	19 6/8	4	4	Harford County	MD	Thomas Paulachok	1991	5,500
133 6/8	22 2/8	23 0/8	17 2/8	4	4	Wabash County	IN	Herbert Jr. Hall	1991	5,500
133 6/8	21 6/8	21 3/8	18 0/8	5	5	Oconto County	WI	Patrick J. Gauthier	1991	5,500
133 6/8	21 4/8	20 1/8	16 2/8	5	5	Clay County	MN	Max Fuxa	1991	5,500
133 6/8	21 1/8	21 1/8	17 3/8	6	6	Waukesha County	WI	Scott H. Van Lare	1991	5,500
133 6/8	25 6/8	26 2/8	16 6/8	8	7	Lake County	IL	Carl Pavlin	1991	5,500
133 6/8	21 7/8	20 4/8	19 2/8	5	5	La Porte County	IN	Ted J. Saliwanchik	1991	5,500
133 6/8	23 2/8	24 0/8	21 2/8	4	5	Effingham County	IL	Tony Hille	1991	5,500
133 6/8	24 3/8	24 6/8	18 4/8	4	5	Madison County	IL	Dennis Collman	1991	5,500
133 6/8	22 3/8	21 6/8	19 0/8	4	4	Shannon County	MO	Norman Yarber	1991	5,500
133 6/8	20 7/8	21 1/8	17 6/8	5	5	Humboldt County	IA	Jerry Lee	1991	5,500
133 6/8	26 4/8	23 7/8	21 6/8	6	6	Fairfax County	VA	Jeffrey S. Dambaugh	1991	5,500
133 6/8	23 2/8	23 6/8	16 2/8	6	5	Crockett County	TX	James Batchelor	1992	5,500
133 5/8	23 3/8	23 2/8	17 1/8	4	4	Tripp County	SD	Larry Diehm	1965	5,544
133 5/8	19 6/8	19 4/8	16 5/8	5	5	Brookings County	SD	Rodney Foster	1967	5,544
133 5/8	26 6/8	25 7/8	19 3/8	3	4	Blue Earth County	MN	Dean Como	1973	5,544
133 5/8	22 6/8	22 7/8	15 3/8	5	5	Murray County	MN	David D. Swanson	1979	5,544
133 5/8	24 0/8	23 7/8	16 7/8	4	4	Trempealeau County	WI	Robert J. Skroch	1979	5,544
133 5/8	21 6/8	21 7/8	17 2/8	5	6	Washington County	MN	Leonard Ellingson	1979	5,544
133 5/8	21 6/8	22 2/8	17 3/8	4	4	Republic County	KS	Curtis Klima	1979	5,544
133 5/8	21 0/8	21 4/8	16 7/8	4	4	Norton County	KS	Robbie L. Madden	1980	5,544
133 5/8	24 1/8	24 7/8	19 5/8	4	4	Shelby County	IL	Walter Lash	1981	5,544
133 5/8	24 2/8	23 0/8	17 6/8	4	5	Lincoln County	SD	Robert Souter	1981	5,544
133 5/8	20 5/8	21 5/8	17 1/8	5	5	Sanders County	MT	Justin Hoy	1981	5,544
133 5/8	22 4/8	25 6/8	17 7/8	4	5	Dickinson County	IA	Rod M. Sheldon	1981	5,544
133 5/8	21 4/8	21 2/8	17 3/8	5	5	Buffalo County	WI	Tom Pehler	1983	5,544
133 5/8	22 5/8	22 2/8	16 5/8	5	6	Pittsburg County	OK	William A. Willis	1983	5,544
133 5/8	22 6/8	24 4/8	19 1/8	5	4	Strathcona	ALB	David Rose	1983	5,544
133 5/8	23 2/8	23 6/8	17 4/8	5	4	Winona County	MN	Dean K. Reidt	1984	5,544
133 5/8	23 3/8	24 1/8	19 7/8	5	4	St. Joseph County	MI	Timothy A. Balk	1984	5,544
133 5/8	21 4/8	23 1/8	17 5/8	5	5	Buffalo County	WI	Paul M Baures	1985	5,544
133 5/8	22 4/8	22 2/8	19 3/8	4	4	Dodge County	WI	Jim Gregory	1985	5,544
133 5/8	23 5/8	23 6/8	19 1/8	7	4	Rock County	MN	Al Kuehl	1985	5,544
133 5/8	20 7/8	21 1/8	17 2/8	5	4	Jefferson County	MT	Wayne Andersen	1986	5,544
133 5/8	22 2/8	22 3/8	18 7/8	4	4	Kanabec County	MN	Jim Kilpatrick	1986	5,544
133 5/8	21 5/8	22 1/8	17 1/8	5	5	Flathead County	MT	George Charles	1986	5,544
133 5/8	22 5/8	23 6/8	20 7/8	4	4	Holmes County	OH	William Boley, Jr.	1987	5,544
133 5/8	27 2/8	25 4/8	17 2/8	5	5	Campbell County	KY	Jim Young	1987	5,544
133 5/8	22 4/8	23 0/8	16 5/8	4	4	Dodge County	MN	John Fondell	1987	5,544
133 5/8	21 7/8	22 1/8	17 3/8	5	4	Sheboygan County	WI	Glenn Luedtke	1987	5,544
133 5/8	22 0/8	22 4/8	17 2/8	6	6	Linn County	IA	Mike Halsor	1987	5,544
133 5/8	24 4/8	24 4/8	17 5/8	4	4	Juneau County	WI	Karl Coyer	1987	5,544
133 5/8	22 0/8	22 3/8	18 5/8	4	4	Rock County	WI	Timothy Fett	1988	5,544
133 5/8	21 6/8	21 2/8	16 4/8	6	5	Green Lake	SAS	Pink Atkins	1988	5,544
133 5/8	24 1/8	24 3/8	18 3/8	5	5	Allamakee County	IA	James M. Vogel	1988	5,544
133 5/8	23 7/8	24 7/8	20 3/8	4	4	Sussex County	DE	Myles Bennett	1988	5,544
133 5/8	23 5/8	24 2/8	17 3/8	6	4	Pike County	IL	Randy Long	1989	5,544
133 5/8	24 0/8	24 0/8	18 7/8	4	4	Crawford County	IL	Charlie Guyer	1990	5,544
133 5/8	22 3/8	22 0/8	20 6/8	8	4	Page County	IA	Chris Barton	1990	5,544
133 5/8	22 1/8	23 0/8	20 0/8	6	8	McHenry County	IL	Richard G. Hickey	1991	5,544
133 5/8	25 2/8	25 0/8	20 1/8	5	8	Grant County	WI	Charles P. Fralick	1991	5,544
133 5/8	24 3/8	23 7/8	18 7/8	5	5	Steuben County	NY	Cy R. Mowery	1991	5,544
133 5/8	19 5/8	20 3/8	14 7/8	5	5	Cass County	MI	Stanley Eugene Andersen	1991	5,544
133 5/8	24 0/8	26 0/8	21 7/8	3	5	Stearns County	MN	Steve Nelson	1991	5,544
133 5/8	22 5/8	22 2/8	17 3/8	5	5	Madison County	IL	Randall L. Perkins	1991	5,544
133 5/8	20 2/8	21 3/8	15 7/8	5	5	Kenedy County	TX	Ben B. Wallace	1991	5,544
133 5/8	23 1/8	21 3/8	17 5/8	5	5	Pierce County	WI	Alan Hines	1992	5,544
133 5/8	19 3/8	20 3/8	15 0/8	5	5	Blue Earth County	MN	Darwin D. Arndt	1992	5,544
133 4/8	22 2/8	22 0/8	17 2/8	5	5	Burleigh County	ND	Lyle F. Fischer	1956	5,589
133 4/8	23 5/8	23 1/8	19 5/8	4	4	Washington County	NE	John Johnson	1958	5,589
133 4/8	22 7/8	23 2/8	16 5/8	5	4	Hocking County	OH	Ted Schultz	1974	5,589
133 4/8	19 5/8	19 3/8	15 0/8	5	5	Sargent County	ND	Frank Pfeifer	1975	5,589
133 4/8	24 0/8	23 2/8	19 2/8	5	5	Charlotte County	VA	George A. Orme, Sr.	1976	5,589
133 4/8	22 3/8	22 6/8	17 0/8	4	4	Edmonton	ALB	Wilf Hunter	1978	5,589
133 4/8	20 3/8	21 5/8	16 0/8	4	5	Stanley County	SD	Patrick Hoing	1979	5,589
133 4/8	21 0/8	21 0/8	18 6/8	4	4	Jefferson County	WI	Larry Pohlman	1979	5,589
133 4/8	24 7/8	23 5/8	19 1/8	6	8	Pittsburg County	OK	Dwayne Durant	1981	5,589
133 4/8	23 7/8	24 6/8	18 6/8	4	4	Green Lake County	WI	Dan Walker	1982	5,589
133 4/8	21 1/8	20 7/8	16 5/8	5	7	Waupaca County	WI	Randy Hillskotter	1982	5,589
133 4/8	20 7/8	19 5/8	16 4/8	4	5	Portage County	WI	Tom Doyle	1983	5,589

SCORE	LENGTH OF MAIN BEAM R / L		INSIDE SPREAD	NUMBER OF POINTS R / L		AREA	STATE/ PROVINCE	HUNTER'S NAME	DATE	RANK
133 4/8	25 5/8	24 2/8	19 2/8	5	4	Black Hawk County	IA	Jim Lee	1983	5,589
133 4/8	21 4/8	23 1/8	14 1/8	6	5	Door County	WI	Bill J. Peissig	1984	5,589
133 4/8	23 5/8	21 7/8	16 1/8	5	5	Roane County	TN	Ronald C. Cassell	1985	5,589
133 4/8	23 3/8	23 6/8	18 3/8	6	5	St. Croix County	WI	Tod Sturgul	1985	5,589
133 4/8	21 4/8	20 4/8	16 4/8	6	6	Marshall County	KS	Brian McNulty	1985	5,589
133 4/8	22 5/8	23 4/8	14 6/8	5	5	Dodge County	MN	Jimmie Hanna	1985	5,589
133 4/8	23 3/8	22 2/8	20 2/8	4	4	Morris County	NJ	Gary Schmitz	1986	5,589
133 4/8	21 4/8	20 7/8	16 5/8	6	5	Flathead County	MT	Dr. Bennie J. Rossetto	1987	5,589
133 4/8	22 2/8	22 2/8	17 0/8	6	5	Dawson County	NE	Randy Ray Wilson	1988	5,589
133 4/8	24 4/8	23 6/8	17 4/8	4	5	Gull Lake	SAS	Robert D. Nye	1988	5,589
133 4/8	22 4/8	22 3/8	21 0/8	5	5	Bradford County	PA	Gary Dewey	1988	5,589
133 4/8	25 4/8	20 4/8	19 2/8	5	5	La Salle County	IL	Tom Sampson	1988	5,589
133 4/8	21 2/8	21 1/8	16 0/8	5	5	Kenosha County	WI	Gerald L. Johnson	1988	5,589
133 4/8	23 4/8	23 1/8	20 6/8	5	4	Polk County	WI	Gordon Bibeau	1988	5,589
133 4/8	23 6/8	23 5/8	16 4/8	6	6	Butler County	KY	Donald K. Russ	1989	5,589
133 4/8	21 7/8	21 6/8	16 4/8	5	5	Texas County	MO	Randy Nickels	1989	5,589
133 4/8	21 7/8	21 4/8	17 6/8	7	7	Tompkins County	NY	James S. Smiley, Sr.	1989	5,589
133 4/8	22 0/8	22 0/8	16 4/8	4	5	Wayne County	MO	Donald P. Roper	1989	5,589
133 4/8	20 4/8	20 4/8	16 0/8	5	6	Waukesha County	WI	John A. Gilles	1989	5,589
133 4/8	23 6/8	23 3/8	19 2/8	5	6	Anne Arundel County	MD	Charles J. Pate, Sr.	1990	5,589
133 4/8	20 2/8	20 2/8	14 4/8	5	5	Ozark County	MO	Lane Crisp	1990	5,589
133 4/8	20 0/8	20 7/8	19 6/8	5	5	Florence County	WI	Scott R. Wilson	1990	5,589
133 4/8	23 2/8	23 4/8	18 6/8	4	4	DeKalb County	IL	Larry Scultz	1990	5,589
133 4/8	22 4/8	21 0/8	17 2/8	4	4	St. Landry Parish	LA	Charles R. Mistric	1991	5,589
133 4/8	21 6/8	21 4/8	15 3/8	5	6	Sheridan County	WY	Jeanette Neisess	1991	5,589
133 4/8	25 2/8	23 6/8	16 3/8	6	4	Clarke County	AL	D. Lee Guyton, Jr.	1991	5,589
133 4/8	23 1/8	23 6/8	16 4/8	5	4	Dubuque County	IA	Brian J. Krier	1991	5,589
133 4/8	21 1/8	20 7/8	19 0/8	4	4	Hillsdale County	MI	Ronald D. Truitt, Jr.	1991	5,589
133 3/8	21 0/8	21 2/8	19 6/8	5	4	Watonwan County	MN	Issac Davis	1962	5,629
133 3/8	24 7/8	24 1/8	23 1/8	6	6	Morrison County	MN	Frank Salisbury	1963	5,629
133 3/8	22 6/8	24 0/8	18 0/8	5	5	Dickinson County	IA	Keith F. Ellis	1973	5,629
133 3/8	21 0/8	21 3/8	17 1/8	6	6	Juneau County	WI	James M. Carriveau	1977	5,629
133 3/8	20 2/8	20 0/8	12 3/8	5	5	Pittsburg County	OK	Richard Gill	1977	5,629
133 3/8	19 4/8	20 0/8	15 1/8	5	5	Arkansas County	AR	Dennis Chapman	1980	5,629
133 3/8	22 0/8	22 1/8	16 1/8	4	7	Stearns County	MN	Kevin Sabrowsky	1981	5,629
133 3/8	21 7/8	21 2/8	17 3/8	5	4	Columbia County	WI	Dennis Riggs	1983	5,629
133 3/8	23 5/8	22 3/8	16 7/8	4	4	McHenry County	IL	Randy Lehr	1984	5,629
133 3/8	21 3/8	20 7/8	16 5/8	6	4	Perry County	MO	Dale Korando	1985	5,629
133 3/8	21 6/8	21 6/8	17 5/8	5	5	Winona County	MN	Jim Reidt	1986	5,629
133 3/8	22 4/8	21 4/8	17 3/8	4	4	Fillmore County	MN	Gary Zahn	1986	5,629
133 3/8	22 0/8	21 4/8	17 0/8	7	5	Becker County	MN	David Dahring	1986	5,629
133 3/8	25 0/8	23 2/8	19 1/8	5	5	Jackson County	OH	Robert E. Thomas, Jr.	1986	5,629
133 3/8	22 4/8	22 2/8	15 7/8	6	4	Scott County	MN	Paul Welin	1987	5,629
133 3/8	24 3/8	22 6/8	16 3/8	4	4	Bandera County	TX	Richard M. Young, Jr.	1987	5,629
133 3/8	23 3/8	23 3/8	17 6/8	5	5	Pickaway County	OH	James McElhatton	1987	5,629
133 3/8	22 0/8	22 1/8	16 7/8	5	5	Winona County	MN	Arden M. Schock	1988	5,629
133 3/8	23 0/8	22 5/8	17 4/8	5	4	Rock County	WI	Jerry E. Shear	1988	5,629
133 3/8	21 5/8	20 6/8	18 3/8	4	5	Dodge County	MN	Clinton Wicks	1988	5,629
133 3/8	19 4/8	19 4/8	17 3/8	5	5	Harrison County	KY	Kevin Poe	1989	5,629
133 3/8	22 0/8	22 6/8	15 3/8	4	5	La Crosse County	WI	Tim Candahl	1989	5,629
133 3/8	20 2/8	20 4/8	16 5/8	5	5	Lucas County	IA	Bill Brown	1989	5,629
133 3/8	25 6/8	27 4/8	20 0/8	6	5	Hamilton County	TN	Robert L. Moon, Jr.	1989	5,629
133 3/8	23 1/8	22 5/8	20 0/8	4	6	Fulton County	IL	William T. Trainor, Jr.	1989	5,629
133 3/8	21 4/8	21 4/8	15 5/8	5	5	Columbia County	WA	Al Campbell	1990	5,629
133 3/8	22 4/8	22 0/8	16 6/8	5	6	Waukesha County	WI	Jim Schaefer	1990	5,629
133 3/8	23 5/8	21 4/8	16 5/8	5	4	Black Hawk County	IA	Jim Hinke	1990	5,629
133 3/8	20 0/8	20 2/8	18 3/8	5	5	Lincoln County	WI	David Van De Weerd	1990	5,629
133 3/8	21 2/8	20 0/8	16 4/8	5	7	La Porte County	IN	Bill Patton	1991	5,629
133 3/8	22 2/8	22 6/8	20 6/8	6	6	Clinton County	IA	Kenneth Hartmann	1991	5,629
133 3/8	22 5/8	22 2/8	18 7/8	4	4	Webster County	IA	Darle Myers	1991	5,629
133 3/8	21 6/8	21 4/8	14 5/8	4	4	Cedar County	NE	David (Bruce) Cull	1992	5,629
133 3/8	21 3/8	21 3/8	16 1/8	5	6	Washington County	MN	Rich Urbaniak	1992	5,629
133 3/8	22 3/8	22 0/8	15 1/8	6	6	Adams County	WI	Todd D. Stammen	1992	5,629
133 2/8	18 4/8	18 6/8	14 7/8	5	6	Mitchell County	IA	Omar A. Toye	1958	5,664
133 2/8	23 6/8	22 5/8	18 2/8	8	8	Olmsted County	MN	Roger E. Enderson	1961	5,664
133 2/8	24 2/8	23 6/8	18 5/8	4	4	Pittsburg County	OK	Fred Parkison	1968	5,664
133 2/8	21 1/8	20 7/8	18 2/8	5	5	Wabasha County	MN	Myles Keller	1977	5,664
133 2/8	22 1/8	22 5/8	16 0/8	8	7	Lafayette County	WI	Dave Carey	1979	5,664
133 2/8	19 0/8	19 1/8	16 4/8	5	5	Waushara County	WI	Kenneth A. Wollermann	1979	5,664
133 2/8	21 2/8	22 1/8	13 1/8	5	7	Portage County	WI	Alan Carter	1981	5,664

SCORE	LENGTH OF MAIN BEAM		INSIDE SPREAD	NUMBER OF POINTS		AREA	STATE/ PROVINCE	HUNTER'S NAME	DATE	RANK
	R	L		R	L					
133 2/8	20 2/8	20 3/8	15 0/8	5	5	St. Louis County	MN	Greg Opland	1981	5,664
133 2/8	24 7/8	24 6/8	20 2/8	4	3	Davis County	IA	Richard Squire	1981	5,664
133 2/8	20 4/8	20 4/8	20 0/8	4	5	Noble County	OH	Elroy Kuhner	1982	5,664
133 2/8	24 1/8	23 2/8	17 0/8	6	7	Kingsbury County	SD	Stanley A. Rauch	1982	5,664
133 2/8	23 7/8	24 0/8	18 4/8	4	5	Shelby County	IL	Charles Martin, Jr.	1983	5,664
133 2/8	22 7/8	22 5/8	18 1/8	5	6	Harper County	KS	Steven R. Lowe	1983	5,664
133 2/8	23 4/8	25 4/8	19 1/8	6	6	Ford County	KS	Melvin Habiger	1983	5,664
133 2/8	23 3/8	23 2/8	20 6/8	4	4	Union County	IL	Brad Harris	1984	5,664
133 2/8	20 0/8	20 5/8	14 2/8	5	5	Madison County	AL	Tony Robinson	1985	5,664
133 2/8	22 4/8	22 2/8	19 5/8	5	6	Whiteside County	IL	Art Heinze	1985	5,664
133 2/8	22 7/8	24 0/8	16 6/8	6	7	Jersey County	IL	David F. Woolsey	1986	5,664
133 2/8	21 6/8	22 2/8	18 6/8	4	4	Forest County	WI	Rick H. Pendl	1988	5,664
133 2/8	24 6/8	23 3/8	19 3/8	8	6	Fulton County	IL	Patrick Cebuhar	1988	5,664
133 2/8	22 3/8	22 6/8	18 2/8	4	4	Hancock County	IL	William T. Kirby	1988	5,664
133 2/8	22 5/8	24 6/8	20 2/8	4	4	Pulaski County	GA	David Pounds	1988	5,664
133 2/8	22 5/8	22 6/8	16 2/8	5	4	Polk County	WI	Barry Wickstrom	1988	5,664
133 2/8	22 5/8	23 2/8	17 4/8	4	4	Keya Paha County	NE	Wesley Hitchcock	1989	5,664
133 2/8	21 3/8	21 6/8	15 0/8	5	5	Marinette County	WI	James L. Lesperance	1989	5,664
133 2/8	23 0/8	19 2/8	18 6/8	5	5	Adams County	IA	Dennis Haley	1989	5,664
133 2/8	24 4/8	23 6/8	18 0/8	5	5	Montgomery County	IL	Roy Alvin Burris	1989	5,664
133 2/8	21 5/8	23 3/8	19 0/8	4	5	Waukesha County	WI	Ralph Zalewski	1989	5,664
133 2/8	19 0/8	20 0/8	15 4/8	6	5	Brown County	SD	Bradley K. Larson	1989	5,664
133 2/8	22 3/8	23 3/8	20 0/8	4	5	Jefferson County	WI	Robert Green	1989	5,664
133 2/8	21 4/8	21 3/8	18 2/8	5	5	Rice County	KS	Hughlene Gillespie	1990	5,664
133 2/8	21 4/8	20 1/8	16 2/8	5	5	Pike County	IL	Chris Johnson	1990	5,664
133 2/8	24 4/8	22 4/8	15 4/8	5	5	Albany County	NY	Michael Rudolph	1990	5,664
133 2/8	23 2/8	22 2/8	16 4/8	5	7	Howard County	IA	Scott Runde	1990	5,664
133 2/8	23 7/8	23 5/8	14 1/8	5	5	Otoe County	NE	Larry Starner	1990	5,664
133 2/8	21 5/8	20 7/8	15 2/8	5	5	Dane County	WI	Steve Grabandt	1991	5,664
133 2/8	22 2/8	22 0/8	20 2/8	5	5	Warren County	GA	Ralph Owen	1991	5,664
133 2/8	24 5/8	24 4/8	19 1/8	7	5	Wagoner County	OK	Jon Brewer	1991	5,664
133 2/8	23 0/8	23 2/8	17 6/8	5	5	Winneshiek County	IA	Martin Andera	1991	5,664
133 2/8	24 0/8	23 4/8	18 4/8	5	6	Pike County	IL	Dale Carter	1991	5,664
133 2/8	23 6/8	22 6/8	16 4/8	6	5	Montgomery County	IA	Dick Paul	1991	5,664
133 2/8	21 2/8	21 7/8	15 6/8	6	6	Jo Daviess County	IL	Lynn Busch	1991	5,664
133 1/8	22 2/8	21 5/8	16 1/8	4	4	Roberts County	SD	Roland L. Hausmann	1964	5,706
133 1/8	24 5/8	23 7/8	20 1/8	4	4	Perry County	IL	Ron Lay	1974	5,706
133 1/8	20 5/8	20 5/8	17 2/8	6	6	Cowley County	KS	Dr. Phil L. Bradley	1975	5,706
133 1/8	23 2/8	25 2/8	16 3/8	5	5	Scott County	MN	George R. Arimond	1976	5,706
133 1/8	26 0/8	26 3/8	19 6/8	5	5	Litchfield County	CT	Phillip M. Demetri	1976	5,706
133 1/8	20 1/8	20 7/8	16 1/8	5	5	Monroe County	IN	Jeffrey S. Finley	1977	5,706
133 1/8	22 2/8	22 6/8	17 1/8	5	5	Jefferson County	WI	Dennis E. Dabel	1978	5,706
133 1/8	21 6/8	22 6/8	16 5/8	5	6	Hocking County	OH	Ted Schultz	1978	5,706
133 1/8	22 3/8	21 6/8	18 7/8	5	5	Muskingum County	OH	Randy Whitehair	1978	5,706
133 1/8	23 5/8	23 7/8	16 1/8	4	4	Pike County	MO	Jim Holdenried	1979	5,706
133 1/8	23 5/8	23 0/8	15 7/8	4	5	Sauk County	WI	Keith Peetz	1980	5,706
133 1/8	20 4/8	21 6/8	16 1/8	4	4	Bullitt County	KY	Dwight Hughes	1981	5,706
133 1/8	21 3/8	21 5/8	17 1/8	6	6	Marion County	IL	Paul Duncan	1981	5,706
133 1/8	23 6/8	22 6/8	17 7/8	4	5	Morgan County	OH	Milan W. Boone	1981	5,706
133 1/8	21 3/8	20 5/8	15 3/8	5	5	Calvert County	MD	Al Sullivan	1982	5,706
133 1/8	22 2/8	22 4/8	17 7/8	4	4	Oakland County	MI	Gordon E. Bowser	1982	5,706
133 1/8	21 7/8	24 3/8	22 3/8	4	4	Geary County	KS	Mark Junghans	1982	5,706
133 1/8	22 4/8	25 4/8	21 1/8	4	5	Green County	WI	James K. Campbell	1984	5,706
133 1/8	22 7/8	24 0/8	17 4/8	7	4	Phillips County	KS	Michael Hoft	1984	5,706
133 1/8	21 6/8	23 6/8	18 1/8	5	6	Cascade County	MT	Tom Storm	1984	5,706
133 1/8	21 4/8	21 3/8	16 5/8	5	5	Leavenworth County	KS	John Garrison	1985	5,706
133 1/8	20 0/8	19 4/8	18 0/8	5	7	Clinton County	MI	Mark G. Rademacher	1986	5,706
133 1/8	23 1/8	23 2/8	18 3/8	4	5	Charlevoix County	MI	Norbert Scharenbroch	1986	5,706
133 1/8	24 3/8	24 3/8	19 1/8	5	5	Crawford County	KS	Fred Geier	1986	5,706
133 1/8	20 1/8	19 0/8	15 7/8	5	6	Douglas County	WI	Wallace K. Campbell	1986	5,706
133 1/8	21 3/8	23 4/8	17 3/8	4	4	Kenosha County	WI	Alan Weis	1986	5,706
133 1/8	25 1/8	24 2/8	18 3/8	5	5	Westchester County	NY	Anthony J. Capodicci	1986	5,706
133 1/8	21 1/8	20 3/8	13 7/8	5	5	Dallas County	MO	Thomas N. Crunkleton	1987	5,706
133 1/8	22 6/8	23 1/8	18 1/8	4	4	Hubbard County	MN	James Willet	1988	5,706
133 1/8	21 6/8	21 4/8	20 1/8	6	6	Chippewa County	WI	Daniel J. Sweeney	1988	5,706
133 1/8	25 2/8	24 5/8	16 7/8	5	5	Houston County	MN	Richard Gulbranson	1988	5,706
133 1/8	20 5/8	22 5/8	16 3/8	5	6	Woodbury County	IA	Tony Flesjer	1988	5,706
133 1/8	24 0/8	24 4/8	15 5/8	5	5	Carroll County	MD	Merl T. Brilhart	1988	5,706
133 1/8	22 3/8	21 7/8	19 1/8	5	4	Wellington County	ONT	R. Brian Oates	1989	5,706
133 1/8	22 0/8	22 4/8	21 1/8	4	4	Reno County	KS	Edward Laverentz	1989	5,706

SCORE	LENGTH OF MAIN BEAM		INSIDE SPREAD	NUMBER OF POINTS		AREA	STATE/ PROVINCE	HUNTER'S NAME	DATE	RANK
	R	L		R	L					
133 1/8	22 5/8	23 1/8	19 3/8	4	5	Marshall County	IL	Richard L. Johnson	1989	5,706
133 1/8	24 6/8	24 2/8	19 7/8	10	6	Jackson County	IL	Mark Guetersloh	1990	5,706
133 1/8	19 2/8	18 4/8	17 7/8	5	6	Crawford County	KS	Bryan E. Messmer	1990	5,706
133 1/8	26 2/8	25 4/8	15 0/8	7	5	Northampton County	PA	Paul H. Beahn, Jr.	1990	5,706
133 1/8	23 0/8	22 4/8	17 3/8	4	4	Kent County	MI	Robert Groenke	1990	5,706
133 1/8	23 4/8	24 6/8	17 1/8	4	4	Pierce County	WI	Larry Hoyer	1990	5,706
133 1/8	21 3/8	22 1/8	16 1/8	5	5	Wayne County	MO	Donald Roper	1990	5,706
133 1/8	23 6/8	24 1/8	14 3/8	5	6	Price County	WI	Kevin W. Shibilski	1990	5,706
133 1/8	21 1/8	21 7/8	16 7/8	5	5	Clinton County	MI	Dan Bertalan	1990	5,706
133 1/8	22 1/8	22 4/8	18 1/8	5	5	Dodge County	WI	Jeff Pankow	1990	5,706
133 1/8	22 5/8	23 1/8	18 5/8	4	4	Medina County	OH	Tom Walker	1990	5,706
133 1/8	26 5/8	24 0/8	20 1/8	3	3	Anoka County	MN	William Lewno	1990	5,706
133 1/8	21 2/8	21 4/8	15 3/8	5	5	Des Moines County	IA	Kirk D. Wilson	1990	5,706
133 1/8	25 3/8	25 1/8	15 5/8	4	4	White County	AR	Kirk D. King	1990	5,706
133 1/8	20 2/8	19 7/8	15 1/8	5	5	Crawford County	PA	Gary L. Galford	1991	5,706
133 1/8	23 6/8	22 4/8	17 3/8	4	4	Ripley County	IN	Michael D. Meisberger	1991	5,706
133 1/8	20 3/8	20 1/8	16 1/8	5	5	Rock Creek	BC	Ken A. Davidson	1991	5,706
133 1/8	23 0/8	22 4/8	20 3/8	5	5	Kingston	ONT	Randy J. Carlberg	1991	5,706
133 1/8	22 5/8	21 7/8	13 5/8	5	5	Bayfield County	WI	Terrence L. Peters	1991	5,706
133 1/8	22 5/8	20 7/8	16 3/8	5	5	Sumner County	KS	Stan Jones	1991	5,706
133 1/8	21 3/8	21 1/8	16 4/8	5	6	Florence County	WI	James Majewski	1992	5,706
133 1/8	23 1/8	21 5/8	16 4/8	5	4	Stonyplain	ALB	Dave Paplawski	1992	5,706
133 0/8	22 2/8	21 3/8	16 4/8	4	4	Luce County	MI	Rondell Bisbee	1953	5,763
133 0/8	24 0/8	24 1/8	17 6/8	4	4	Dunn County	WI	George Woodington	1969	5,763
133 0/8	19 0/8	19 3/8	16 6/8	5	5	Kingsbury County	SD	Arnold Aulner	1970	5,763
133 0/8	20 7/8	21 0/8	17 4/8	5	5	Litchfield County	CT	Dan Ferrara, Jr.	1976	5,763
133 0/8	21 0/8	20 7/8	17 4/8	5	5	Somerset County	NJ	Dennis Bailey	1977	5,763
133 0/8	22 2/8	21 0/8	18 6/8	4	5	Jackson County	MI	Randy Childs	1977	5,763
133 0/8	23 5/8	22 1/8	17 4/8	5	6	Macon County	IL	Frank B. Graham	1977	5,763
133 0/8	23 3/8	23 1/8	19 4/8	5	7	Dawson County	MT	Bryant Shurtliff	1977	5,763
133 0/8	24 5/8	24 2/8	19 2/8	5	6	Huntingdon County	PA	John A. Williams	1978	5,763
133 0/8	23 2/8	22 6/8	18 4/8	4	4	Dane County	WI	Dean Cooper	1981	5,763
133 0/8	22 2/8	21 7/8	16 4/8	4	5	Geary County	KS	Mike Ehlebracht	1981	5,763
133 0/8	20 6/8	20 2/8	16 6/8	6	5	Burleigh County	ND	Donald Magstadt	1981	5,763
133 0/8	21 1/8	21 3/8	15 4/8	5	5	Montgomery County	MS	Harold L. Tutor	1981	5,763
133 0/8	22 7/8	22 6/8	15 6/8	4	5	Polk County	IA	Jeff Greider	1982	5,763
133 0/8	22 2/8	22 6/8	16 4/8	4	4	Jefferson County	OH	Edward D. Whitmore	1983	5,763
133 0/8	24 4/8	24 0/8	18 7/8	6	4	Pepin County	WI	Gerald Berg	1984	5,763
133 0/8	22 4/8	22 0/8	19 4/8	5	4	Middlesex County	ONT	Anna Burket	1985	5,763
133 0/8	24 0/8	23 0/8	18 7/8	5	6	Prince George County	VA	William Robert McCabe III	1986	5,763
133 0/8	22 7/8	23 0/8	16 6/8	4	4	Vermilion County	IL	Michael Lange	1986	5,763
133 0/8	27 2/8	28 3/8	16 1/8	6	6	Lawrence County	IL	Hugh Sexton	1986	5,763
133 0/8	22 6/8	22 3/8	15 6/8	5	5	Norman County	MN	Dick Stegeman	1987	5,763
133 0/8	23 5/8	23 7/8	20 6/8	4	4	Union County	KY	Dennis Helms	1987	5,763
133 0/8	24 0/8	24 1/8	18 0/8	5	4	Cass County	NE	Roger Buck	1987	5,763
133 0/8	23 4/8	22 2/8	18 0/8	4	4	Boone County	MO	Tommy Foster	1988	5,763
133 0/8	25 5/8	26 4/8	17 4/8	4	5	McHenry County	IL	William Adams	1988	5,763
133 0/8	22 3/8	22 4/8	17 0/8	5	6	Hampden County	MA	David Cox	1988	5,763
133 0/8	22 1/8	20 7/8	15 0/8	5	6	Geary County	KS	James L. Ullmer	1988	5,763
133 0/8	20 5/8	21 1/8	16 0/8	5	5	Prairie County	AR	Clay Bowie	1988	5,763
133 0/8	22 7/8	22 0/8	15 1/8	6	5	Lapeer County	MI	Thomas J. Baker	1989	5,763
133 0/8	22 0/8	22 6/8	18 6/8	5	5	Coles County	IL	Dave Miller	1989	5,763
133 0/8	24 0/8	23 4/8	15 1/8	6	6	Brooks County	TX	George W. Gallaspy	1990	5,763
133 0/8	22 3/8	23 1/8	17 6/8	5	5	Goliad County	TX	Roy M. Goodwin	1990	5,763
133 0/8	24 5/8	24 6/8	14 5/8	7	6	Scott County	KY	Gayle Humphrey	1990	5,763
133 0/8	23 1/8	23 2/8	15 7/8	4	6	Chickasaw County	IA	Robert F. Marion	1990	5,763
133 0/8	22 3/8	21 5/8	17 4/8	7	6	Greene County	MO	Clifford Kelley	1990	5,763
133 0/8	22 4/8	21 5/8	16 4/8	4	5	Rocky Mtn. House	ALB	Brian Sztym	1991	5,763
133 0/8	19 6/8	19 5/8	15 0/8	6	6	Alpena County	MI	David N. Robinette	1991	5,763
133 0/8	22 0/8	21 2/8	17 2/8	5	5	Rusk County	WI	Thomas Anders	1991	5,763
133 0/8	25 6/8	24 6/8	17 0/8	5	5	Darke County	OH	Rocky W. Stahl	1991	5,763
133 0/8	24 0/8	25 4/8	18 6/8	4	4	Jefferson County	WI	John E. Thurow	1992	5,763
132 7/8	21 0/8	21 0/8	15 3/8	5	7	Jefferson County	IN	Jerome Sexton	1962	5,803
132 7/8	20 0/8	18 6/8	15 5/8	5	6	Wilson County	KS	Warren Townsend	1970	5,803
132 7/8	24 4/8	20 6/8	20 2/8	7	7	Pine County	MN	Bob Sandwick	1973	5,803
132 7/8	20 0/8	20 6/8	14 6/8	5	6	Waushara County	WI	Gary Gundrum	1977	5,803
132 7/8	21 3/8	22 0/8	18 1/8	5	5	St. Croix County	WI	Randy St. Ores	1978	5,803
132 7/8	20 4/8	21 3/8	16 1/8	5	6	Wagoner County	OK	Sonny Charboneau	1978	5,803
132 7/8	20 3/8	21 0/8	14 5/8	5	5	Gallia County	OH	Gail C. Snyder	1980	5,803
132 7/8	21 2/8	21 4/8	16 3/8	6	6	Martin County	MN	James Zanke	1982	5,803

SCORE	LENGTH OF MAIN BEAM R	L	INSIDE SPREAD	NUMBER OF POINTS R	L	AREA	STATE/ PROVINCE	HUNTER'S NAME	DATE	RANK
132 7/8	20 7/8	21 2/8	14 7/8	5	5	Warren County	MS	Ray Bufkin	1983	5,803
132 7/8	21 4/8	21 3/8	14 7/8	5	5	Anoka County	MN	John Cardinal	1983	5,803
132 7/8	21 2/8	22 6/8	17 5/8	4	4	Riley County	KS	Mike Huff	1983	5,803
132 7/8	23 4/8	23 2/8	17 3/8	5	5	Cherokee County	KS	Samuel F. Lancaster	1983	5,803
132 7/8	21 4/8	21 4/8	17 4/8	6	6	Sawyer County	WI	Ronald Lee Fischer	1983	5,803
132 7/8	24 3/8	22 6/8	14 1/8	5	4	Butler County	KS	David R. Rogers	1984	5,803
132 7/8	19 4/8	21 0/8	18 0/8	7	6	Alexander County	IL	Daniel Boyd	1985	5,803
132 7/8	20 2/8	20 3/8	17 7/8	5	6	Cowley County	KS	David M. Ross	1985	5,803
132 7/8	19 2/8	19 6/8	17 1/8	5	5	Mitchell County	KS	Connie Galliher	1986	5,803
132 7/8	18 1/8	21 4/8	19 7/8	5	4	Mason County	WV	Keith Donahue	1986	5,803
132 7/8	23 4/8	22 4/8	15 4/8	5	4	Greene County	MO	Jacob Estep	1986	5,803
132 7/8	20 2/8	21 4/8	15 7/8	5	5	Clearwater County	ID	Mark Neer	1986	5,803
132 7/8	23 0/8	24 2/8	18 5/8	4	4	Charles County	MD	Ralph L. Purcell, Jr.	1987	5,803
132 7/8	24 1/8	21 3/8	16 3/8	4	4	Gage County	NE	Gene Tupa	1987	5,803
132 7/8	23 0/8	23 3/8	18 6/8	6	7	Sauk County	WI	Richard J. Osgood	1987	5,803
132 7/8	24 0/8	24 0/8	16 5/8	7	6	Butler County	KS	Denny Zimmerman	1988	5,803
132 7/8	21 7/8	22 6/8	17 5/8	4	5	Trempealeau County	WI	Dave Mikrut	1988	5,803
132 7/8	19 6/8	22 1/8	16 1/8	8	6	Henry County	VA	Mike Weaver	1988	5,803
132 7/8	20 6/8	21 0/8	17 7/8	4	4	Washtenaw County	MI	Chris Ehnis	1989	5,803
132 7/8	23 6/8	23 0/8	15 6/8	5	7	Jefferson County	WI	Peter Newcomb	1989	5,803
132 7/8	21 0/8	21 3/8	17 7/8	5	5	Fond du Lac County	WI	Steven J. Bethel	1989	5,803
132 7/8	22 1/8	21 7/8	14 2/8	5	6	Donalda	ALB	Garfield Vikse	1989	5,803
132 7/8	22 3/8	21 5/8	16 2/8	5	5	Jefferson County	MT	Sean S. Walp	1990	5,803
132 7/8	23 0/8	22 7/8	19 3/8	5	4	Livingston County	MI	Jean M. Musolf	1990	5,803
132 7/8	23 3/8	22 7/8	18 7/8	4	4	Latah County	ID	Roger A. Rea	1990	5,803
132 7/8	21 3/8	22 2/8	17 1/8	5	5	Burnett County	WI	Mikel Duncan	1991	5,803
132 7/8	20 3/8	20 5/8	14 3/8	4	4	Jackson County	IA	Nick Fondell	1991	5,803
132 7/8	23 5/8	24 3/8	20 2/8	4	6	Pendleton County	KY	Randy Sipple	1991	5,803
132 7/8	23 7/8	23 4/8	17 1/8	5	5	Pushmataha County	OK	Jason B. Manous	1991	5,803
132 7/8	26 2/8	27 5/8	19 1/8	6	6	De Soto County	MS	Chris Sanders	1991	5,803
132 7/8	22 2/8	21 2/8	19 4/8	6	5	Marshall County	IL	Mike Rinehart	1991	5,803
132 7/8	22 0/8	22 7/8	18 3/8	4	4	Williamson County	IL	Tony Kreke	1991	5,803
132 7/8	21 6/8	20 7/8	12 6/8	4	5	Jefferson County	IN	Doug Ross	1991	5,803
132 7/8	22 7/8	23 0/8	20 0/8	4	5	Suffolk County	NY	James Matuszewski	1991	5,803
132 6/8	23 0/8	23 4/8	20 0/8	4	4	Summit County	OH	Dana C. Feather	1960	5,845
132 6/8	21 0/8	20 1/8	16 4/8	5	5	Worcester County	MD	Clifford A. Denney	1972	5,845
132 6/8	22 3/8	23 0/8	14 6/8	5	5	Jackson County	OH	Robert C. McGuire	1976	5,845
132 6/8	19 7/8	22 7/8	17 4/8	6	6	Union County	IL	Fred W. Achilles	1978	5,845
132 6/8	22 0/8	22 0/8	19 4/8	5	4	Waterloo County	ONT	Jim Scoggins	1979	5,845
132 6/8	22 2/8	22 0/8	14 6/8	4	5	Lancaster County	PA	Albert A. Swider	1980	5,845
132 6/8	21 2/8	23 1/8	20 6/8	7	6	Loup County	NE	Syl Glos	1981	5,845
132 6/8	21 3/8	21 1/8	17 4/8	4	4	Clinton County	IA	Kent Hoffmann	1982	5,845
132 6/8	19 6/8	20 2/8	16 0/8	5	5	Butler County	KS	Mark Scott	1983	5,845
132 6/8	21 7/8	22 4/8	17 0/8	4	4	Dawes County	NE	Darrell A. Bendel	1984	5,845
132 6/8	24 7/8	23 6/8	17 4/8	4	7	Carroll County	MO	Joe D. Earnest	1984	5,845
132 6/8	20 2/8	22 2/8	19 2/8	5	4	Buffalo County	WI	Michael L Gates	1984	5,845
132 6/8	20 7/8	20 7/8	18 0/8	5	5	Cherry County	NE	Russell Burge	1984	5,845
132 6/8	23 4/8	23 1/8	16 4/8	4	4	Sawyer County	WI	Dave Phillips	1984	5,845
132 6/8	21 7/8	21 6/8	16 6/8	5	5	Linn County	IA	Jon Klein	1985	5,845
132 6/8	19 7/8	19 1/8	16 2/8	5	5	Mason County	TX	Thomas Joseph Hicks	1986	5,845
132 6/8	19 1/8	19 7/8	17 2/8	5	5	Oneida County	WI	Trygve Solberg	1986	5,845
132 6/8	19 5/8	20 2/8	17 0/8	5	5	Marshall County	WV	Dave Gibson	1986	5,845
132 6/8	23 4/8	24 2/8	16 4/8	4	4	Green County	WI	Mike Stone	1986	5,845
132 6/8	23 6/8	23 0/8	17 2/8	4	5	Vinton County	OH	Charles Barker, Jr.	1986	5,845
132 6/8	25 6/8	25 2/8	19 6/8	3	4	Troup County	GA	Kirby Fidler	1986	5,845
132 6/8	23 3/8	23 5/8	16 4/8	5	5	Pearl River County	MS	Chris Upton	1987	5,845
132 6/8	23 0/8	22 5/8	18 6/8	5	4	Peoria County	IL	Paul L. Gilles	1987	5,845
132 6/8	24 1/8	23 0/8	18 2/8	6	6	Stark County	OH	Robert L Knerr	1987	5,845
132 6/8	23 1/8	22 7/8	17 4/8	4	4	Isle of Wight County	VA	Robert Emory Caldwell	1988	5,845
132 6/8	22 3/8	23 5/8	17 0/8	4	5	Otsego County	MI	Keith Earl Crandall	1988	5,845
132 6/8	22 0/8	21 0/8	18 4/8	4	4	Choctaw County	OK	Mark Holbrook	1988	5,845
132 6/8	23 3/8	24 5/8	17 2/8	5	4	Baltimore County	MD	Robert W. Brooks	1989	5,845
132 6/8	22 2/8	24 1/8	18 4/8	6	5	Jackson County	OH	Francis Keith Tomlinson	1989	5,845
132 6/8	25 2/8	26 2/8	20 0/8	7	7	Rock County	WI	Jerry Shear	1989	5,845
132 6/8	22 6/8	23 0/8	16 1/8	4	6	Forest County	WI	Norman C. Schmelling	1990	5,845
132 6/8	20 2/8	20 1/8	16 2/8	5	5	Columbia County	WI	Mark L. Preuss	1990	5,845
132 6/8	23 2/8	24 3/8	20 0/8	5	4	Clinton County	OH	Cliff Doyle	1990	5,845
132 6/8	21 5/8	22 0/8	18 0/8	4	4	Waupaca County	WI	Howard R. Becker	1990	5,845
132 6/8	23 6/8	24 6/8	16 5/8	7	7	Butler County	KS	Robert Van Deventer	1990	5,845
132 6/8	25 0/8	25 5/8	19 3/8	5	6	Albemarle County	VA	Larry Wayne Roberts	1990	5,845

SCORE	LENGTH OF MAIN BEAM		INSIDE SPREAD	NUMBER OF POINTS		AREA	STATE/ PROVINCE	HUNTER'S NAME	DATE	RANK
	R	L		R	L					
132 6/8	20 6/8	23 3/8	16 6/8	5	6	Suffolk County	NY	Paul E. Jansen	1990	5,845
132 6/8	21 3/8	21 1/8	17 6/8	5	5	Jones County	IA	John Kertels	1990	5,845
132 6/8	20 7/8	20 4/8	17 0/8	5	5	Olmsted County	MN	Steven Tebay	1991	5,845
132 6/8	22 7/8	23 6/8	16 4/8	5	5	Cherokee County	KS	Danny Langerot, Jr.	1991	5,845
132 6/8	23 2/8	23 1/8	22 6/8	4	4	Hampden County	MA	Ian McLean	1991	5,845
132 6/8	19 6/8	20 4/8	16 4/8	5	5	Wood County	WV	Ron Schultz	1991	5,845
132 6/8	23 0/8	22 1/8	16 6/8	4	4	La Salle County	TX	Dennis Faulkenberry	1992	5,845
132 5/8	23 3/8	24 4/8	21 5/8	4	6	Tazewell County	IL	Don Lounsberry	1964	5,888
132 5/8	21 1/8	21 0/8	16 3/8	5	5	Irion County	TX	James E. Fox III	1977	5,888
132 5/8	24 2/8	23 0/8	19 2/8	6	6	Juneau County	WI	Michael Sigler	1978	5,888
132 5/8	23 1/8	22 5/8	18 5/8	4	5	Monmouth County	NJ	William Rusznak	1979	5,888
132 5/8	23 2/8	22 6/8	23 7/8	4	5	Burnett County	WI	James Larrabee	1980	5,888
132 5/8	19 4/8	20 0/8	16 1/8	6	6	Brookings County	SD	Timothy Modde	1981	5,888
132 5/8	23 4/8	24 1/8	18 1/8	4	4	Clearwater County	ID	Bob Proctor	1981	5,888
132 5/8	22 3/8	22 7/8	17 5/8	5	5	Furnas County	NE	Doug Huxoll	1982	5,888
132 5/8	20 4/8	20 0/8	16 1/8	5	5	W. Baton Rouge Parrish	LA	Jim Thibodeaux	1984	5,888
132 5/8	21 5/8	21 2/8	17 1/8	5	5	Genesee County	MI	Jack Iman	1984	5,888
132 5/8	19 7/8	20 4/8	16 1/8	5	6	Morrison County	MN	John A. Pennoyer	1985	5,888
132 5/8	20 5/8	21 3/8	18 2/8	6	7	Buffalo County	WI	Glen Axness	1985	5,888
132 5/8	21 3/8	20 5/8	16 6/8	6	5	Goodhue County	MN	John 'Jack' Cordes	1985	5,888
132 5/8	20 4/8	20 2/8	15 7/8	5	4	Iowa County	WI	Bill Snelgrove	1985	5,888
132 5/8	20 0/8	19 6/8	14 7/8	5	5	Goshen County	WY	Doug Starks	1986	5,888
132 5/8	19 6/8	20 6/8	14 7/8	6	6	Pittsburg County	OK	Ron Pennington	1986	5,888
132 5/8	21 2/8	21 2/8	15 1/8	5	5	Lewis & Clark County	MT	Sonny Templeton	1986	5,888
132 5/8	22 3/8	23 2/8	17 1/8	5	6	Meigs County	OH	William Charles Brewer	1986	5,888
132 5/8	21 7/8	22 4/8	15 7/8	5	5	Steele County	MN	Kyle N. Wolfe	1987	5,888
132 5/8	20 0/8	21 7/8	18 5/8	6	7	Montgomery County	IN	James Gates	1987	5,888
132 5/8	22 4/8	22 0/8	16 7/8	4	4	St. Clair County	MI	Jerry E. Korneffel	1987	5,888
132 5/8	21 5/8	21 3/8	19 1/8	4	4	Clinton County	IA	Gary G. Olson	1987	5,888
132 5/8	22 4/8	22 4/8	17 7/8	5	4	Saline County	KS	Doug Perrill	1987	5,888
132 5/8	20 0/8	20 0/8	15 3/8	6	5	Atascosa County	TX	Mike Palmer	1987	5,888
132 5/8	21 5/8	21 0/8	15 1/8	5	5	Sawyer County	WI	Rick Misfeldt	1989	5,888
132 5/8	21 5/8	20 2/8	17 3/8	4	4	Isanti County	MN	Mitch Reiners	1989	5,888
132 5/8	23 5/8	22 3/8	19 5/8	4	5	Trempealeau County	WI	Larry Tiedemann	1989	5,888
132 5/8	20 2/8	20 0/8	15 5/8	5	4	Montgomery County	IL	Joseph E. Carrilier	1989	5,888
132 5/8	22 1/8	21 1/8	16 7/8	4	4	Leelanau County	MI	William Ver Snyder	1990	5,888
132 5/8	22 0/8	24 4/8	17 3/8	5	5	Delaware County	OH	Brent Forman	1990	5,888
132 5/8	24 1/8	24 2/8	20 1/8	6	4	Randolph County	IL	Scott Giovanetti	1990	5,888
132 5/8	22 3/8	22 1/8	18 5/8	6	4	Eau Claire County	WI	Jason Meyer	1991	5,888
132 5/8	24 2/8	22 6/8	17 5/8	5	5	Wyandotte County	KS	Tim K. Fowler	1991	5,888
132 5/8	19 5/8	21 5/8	17 4/8	5	6	Washburn County	WI	Jeff Tomesh	1991	5,888
132 4/8	23 4/8	23 0/8	16 3/8	6	5	Jackson County	WI	Howard Knockel	1957	5,922
132 4/8	25 4/8	26 0/8	21 0/8	4	4	Valley County	MT	Clare F. Mates	1961	5,922
132 4/8	21 5/8	21 7/8	15 6/8	4	4	Iowa County	IA	Mel Berstler	1965	5,922
132 4/8	21 6/8	21 6/8	16 0/8	5	5	Cowley County	KS	William L. Walker	1965	5,922
132 4/8	23 2/8	24 2/8	18 0/8	5	6	Morrison County	MN	Jerry James	1971	5,922
132 4/8	25 1/8	24 5/8	16 6/8	5	6	Sarpy County	NE	William R. Dengate	1972	5,922
132 4/8	24 6/8	23 7/8	18 3/8	5	5	Carbon County	PA	Frank Jackson	1972	5,922
132 4/8	23 2/8	23 1/8	15 2/8	5	5	Giles County	VA	Donald Lee Francis	1979	5,922
132 4/8	21 7/8	21 4/8	16 2/8	6	6	Tioga County	NY	Floyd Bowman, Jr.	1981	5,922
132 4/8	23 2/8	22 0/8	17 6/8	4	5	Medicine Hat	ALB	Warren McInenly	1981	5,922
132 4/8	26 0/8	26 6/8	16 6/8	6	6	Lake County	IL	Gary S. Rogers	1981	5,922
132 4/8	23 0/8	25 0/8	14 0/8	4	4	Lamar County	GA	David Brown	1982	5,922
132 4/8	19 3/8	18 5/8	16 2/8	5	5	Tuscola County	MI	Stanley N. Visniski	1982	5,922
132 4/8	20 0/8	20 3/8	17 4/8	4	4	Lyon County	MN	Bruce Londgren	1983	5,922
132 4/8	20 6/8	21 1/8	14 2/8	4	4	Live Oak County	TX	Rick Hayley	1983	5,922
132 4/8	22 3/8	22 2/8	17 0/8	4	4	Washington County	MD	Ronald D. Shank	1985	5,922
132 4/8	20 7/8	21 1/8	14 0/8	5	5	Iowa County	WI	Don Caron	1985	5,922
132 4/8	21 5/8	22 4/8	16 2/8	5	5	Washington County	WI	James O. Werner	1985	5,922
132 4/8	22 1/8	21 6/8	16 6/8	5	6	Columbia County	WI	Wayne Woodstock	1985	5,922
132 4/8	22 7/8	22 1/8	15 2/8	4	5	La Crosse County	WI	Tom Blank	1986	5,922
132 4/8	21 1/8	20 7/8	19 2/8	4	4	Oconto County	WI	Duane Neumann	1986	5,922
132 4/8	22 3/8	22 4/8	16 4/8	5	4	Peoria County	IL	Dan Beaird	1986	5,922
132 4/8	22 0/8	22 2/8	17 7/8	7	8	Muscatine County	IA	Daryle Finley	1986	5,922
132 4/8	21 0/8	20 2/8	13 0/8	5	5	Atascosa County	TX	Joe Hernandez	1987	5,922
132 4/8	22 2/8	22 5/8	15 2/8	5	5	Eaton County	MI	Steven W. Kellogg	1987	5,922
132 4/8	21 5/8	22 0/8	17 0/8	4	4	Dodge County	WI	Joseph G. Tubbs	1987	5,922
132 4/8	22 1/8	22 7/8	15 7/8	4	5	Wyoming County	WV	Michael Prichard	1987	5,922
132 4/8	21 3/8	20 6/8	18 6/8	5	4	Delaware County	IA	Anthony Bass	1987	5,922
132 4/8	23 2/8	23 6/8	17 3/8	6	6	Morris County	NJ	John P. Sibilski	1987	5,922

SCORE	LENGTH OF MAIN BEAM R	L	INSIDE SPREAD	NUMBER OF POINTS R	L	AREA	STATE/ PROVINCE	HUNTER'S NAME	DATE	RANK
132 4/8	20 7/8	20 2/8	17 2/8	5	5	Todd County	KY	David D. Haley	1988	5,922
132 4/8	22 6/8	23 0/8	18 0/8	4	4	Franklin County	OH	Tom Vernon	1988	5,922
132 4/8	22 6/8	21 1/8	16 4/8	6	5	Rockingham County	NC	Tim Myers	1988	5,922
132 4/8	19 4/8	20 0/8	17 2/8	5	5	Randolph County	IN	Don Fields	1988	5,922
132 4/8	21 1/8	20 2/8	15 4/8	4	4	Cass County	MI	Sylvester Ignowski	1988	5,922
132 4/8	18 5/8	18 7/8	15 0/8	5	5	Morton County	ND	Todd Schaedler	1988	5,922
132 4/8	22 0/8	22 2/8	17 0/8	5	4	Meagher County	MT	D. Mitch Kottas	1988	5,922
132 4/8	21 3/8	21 6/8	20 3/8	7	6	Will County	IL	Robert L. Bowermaster	1989	5,922
132 4/8	24 3/8	24 0/8	19 0/8	4	4	Sarpy County	NE	Michael S. Goodlander	1989	5,922
132 4/8	22 0/8	22 3/8	18 2/8	5	6	Lake County	IL	Mark M. Fugett	1989	5,922
132 4/8	23 6/8	24 5/8	15 4/8	5	5	Lincoln County	NE	Steve Stumbo	1989	5,922
132 4/8	24 6/8	23 0/8	20 4/8	4	3	Comanche County	KS	David Birmingham	1989	5,922
132 4/8	21 7/8	24 2/8	16 4/8	4	5	Bond County	IL	William A. Rench	1989	5,922
132 4/8	20 3/8	20 3/8	17 4/8	5	5	Stevens County	MN	Gary Joos	1989	5,922
132 4/8	21 2/8	21 3/8	16 0/8	5	5	Rusk County	WI	Edward H. Cichacki III	1990	5,922
132 4/8	20 7/8	21 1/8	17 0/8	5	5	Hardin County	IA	Dan Zoske	1990	5,922
132 4/8	20 2/8	21 0/8	15 0/8	5	5	Appanoose County	IA	Scott Rolffs	1990	5,922
132 4/8	24 5/8	25 1/8	20 0/8	5	4	Coles County	IL	Bret Patrick	1990	5,922
132 4/8	23 4/8	23 0/8	19 7/8	6	5	Grundy County	IL	Jay Truty	1990	5,922
132 4/8	21 4/8	23 0/8	15 6/8	6	6	Kleberg County	TX	Jarred W. Peeples	1990	5,922
132 4/8	23 7/8	24 4/8	17 0/8	4	4	Newton County	AR	Alex Billings	1991	5,922
132 4/8	18 3/8	18 1/8	13 4/8	6	5	Coke County	TX	Stanley Mayfield	1991	5,922
132 4/8	22 5/8	22 1/8	17 2/8	4	4	Walworth County	WI	Christopher Klein	1991	5,922
132 4/8	20 5/8	21 7/8	17 0/8	5	6	Jefferson County	IL	Matt Farabee	1991	5,922
132 4/8	22 1/8	21 6/8	16 2/8	5	4	Montgomery County	IN	Derrick W. Kidd	1991	5,922
132 4/8	23 1/8	23 4/8	17 2/8	4	5	Hancock County	OH	Steve Shilling	1991	5,922
132 4/8	22 2/8	23 4/8	18 4/8	5	5	Fillmore County	MN	Steve W. Utley	1991	5,922
132 4/8	22 4/8	22 1/8	18 2/8	4	4	Lee County	IL	Steve Cecchetti	1991	5,922
132 3/8	20 5/8	20 6/8	14 3/8	4	4	Buffalo County	NE	Al Dawson	1961	5,979
132 3/8	21 2/8	21 0/8	14 5/8	4	4	St. Joseph County	IN	Harry Ramsbey, Jr.	1963	5,979
132 3/8	22 0/8	21 2/8	17 4/8	4	4	Morrison County	MN	Jay J. Jost	1968	5,979
132 3/8	21 6/8	22 6/8	18 7/8	5	6	Spink County	SD	Roger Michels	1968	5,979
132 3/8	22 6/8	21 7/8	15 3/8	4	4	Shawano County	WI	Gene M. Waite	1971	5,979
132 3/8	22 7/8	22 2/8	17 5/8	4	4	Sarpy County	NE	Doug Bowen	1974	5,979
132 3/8	25 4/8	24 3/8	19 3/8	7	7	Davis County	IA	Tommy Thompson	1975	5,979
132 3/8	22 6/8	24 1/8	15 7/8	5	4	Dunn County	WI	Loyd Donnelly	1980	5,979
132 3/8	22 0/8	21 7/8	15 5/8	5	4	Pine County	MN	Galen Miller	1982	5,979
132 3/8	25 3/8	25 1/8	19 2/8	8	5	Fulton County	IL	Ray Brown	1982	5,979
132 3/8	21 6/8	21 2/8	17 5/8	5	5	Kane County	IL	Gordon Sunderlage	1982	5,979
132 3/8	21 7/8	22 0/8	16 1/8	4	4	Greenwood County	SC	Warren Johnson	1985	5,979
132 3/8	21 4/8	21 2/8	13 6/8	5	5	Otter Tail County	MN	Kelly Shannon	1985	5,979
132 3/8	22 4/8	22 4/8	18 6/8	5	4	Kent County	MD	Michael A. Snyder	1985	5,979
132 3/8	21 6/8	22 2/8	14 5/8	4	4	Greene County	AL	Mike Wood	1986	5,979
132 3/8	20 4/8	19 5/8	14 3/8	5	5	Okmulgee County	OK	Howard D. Massie	1987	5,979
132 3/8	25 0/8	25 0/8	20 3/8	4	4	Allamakee County	IA	Jon Wolter	1987	5,979
132 3/8	21 6/8	21 4/8	19 4/8	5	6	Meigs County	OH	Steve Price	1987	5,979
132 3/8	20 3/8	20 6/8	17 0/8	5	7	Tripp County	SD	Byron E. Foreman	1988	5,979
132 3/8	20 4/8	19 7/8	14 1/8	5	5	Roberts County	SD	Ronald Backman	1988	5,979
132 3/8	24 1/8	24 4/8	17 5/8	3	4	Shawnee County	KS	Stuart Hazard	1988	5,979
132 3/8	22 4/8	23 3/8	15 3/8	5	5	Elmore County	AL	Rett Kelly	1988	5,979
132 3/8	23 2/8	21 4/8	18 3/8	4	8	Kane County	IL	John K. Zawaski	1989	5,979
132 3/8	22 4/8	21 5/8	14 7/8	6	5	Delta County	MI	William E. Heitman	1989	5,979
132 3/8	21 1/8	21 1/8	17 4/8	8	8	Creek County	OK	Joe Morgan	1989	5,979
132 3/8	21 2/8	21 1/8	16 5/8	4	4	Sangamon County	IL	Larry Skinner	1989	5,979
132 3/8	20 7/8	22 0/8	15 6/8	5	4	Marinette County	WI	Joseph J. Nushart	1990	5,979
132 3/8	21 5/8	21 6/8	15 1/8	4	4	Linn County	IA	John Aarni	1990	5,979
132 3/8	24 2/8	23 3/8	19 2/8	7	7	Baltimore County	MD	Shawn King	1990	5,979
132 3/8	19 2/8	18 7/8	18 1/8	5	5	Waukesha County	WI	Craig Pagenkopf	1990	5,979
132 3/8	23 3/8	23 7/8	18 2/8	9	6	Allamakee County	IA	Rodney Blake	1990	5,979
132 3/8	24 3/8	23 2/8	18 0/8	4	7	Wood County	OH	Othan E. Katakis	1990	5,979
132 3/8	24 6/8	23 7/8	19 3/8	4	4	Madison County	MS	Stanley Coring	1990	5,979
132 3/8	24 6/8	24 0/8	16 5/8	3	5	De Witt County	IL	Thomas Wilson	1991	5,979
132 3/8	20 7/8	20 6/8	16 3/8	5	5	Patrick County	VA	David Mabe	1991	5,979
132 3/8	25 4/8	26 3/8	25 5/8	3	3	Fairfax County	VA	Jeffrey A. Bieniek	1992	5,979
132 2/8	22 1/8	21 7/8	16 6/8	5	4	Waupaca County	WI	Al Wiltzius	1949	6,015
132 2/8	21 7/8	23 2/8	16 6/8	5	8	Cherokee County	IA	Darrell Magnussen	1962	6,015
132 2/8	22 0/8	22 4/8	19 2/8	4	4	Bullitt County	KY	Dell Pack	1962	6,015
132 2/8	21 4/8	23 5/8	20 4/8	4	5	Roberts County	SD	Clayton Forrette	1967	6,015
132 2/8	24 6/8	25 2/8	23 4/8	3	3	Stoddard County	MO	Ted Denkins	1971	6,015
132 2/8	21 3/8	21 7/8	16 4/8	4	4	Westmoreland County	PA	Robert C. Kichner	1971	6,015

Score	Length of Main Beam R	L	Inside Spread	Number of Points R	L	Area	State/ Province	Hunter's Name	Date	Rank
132 2/8	24 3/8	23 6/8	17 4/8	4	4	Talbot County	MD	Walter Krom	1976	6,015
132 2/8	23 2/8	21 6/8	16 5/8	5	6	Clinton County	IL	James D. Rueter	1980	6,015
132 2/8	21 0/8	20 6/8	17 6/8	5	6	Perry County	IL	Bob Clark	1981	6,015
132 2/8	24 1/8	23 1/8	18 0/8	7	5	Brown County	SD	Jack Ness	1981	6,015
132 2/8	21 7/8	21 4/8	19 6/8	4	4	Vernon County	WI	Robert S. Navrestad	1982	6,015
132 2/8	21 5/8	22 5/8	16 1/8	6	5	Adams County	WI	David J. Niesen	1982	6,015
132 2/8	22 1/8	21 6/8	19 2/8	4	4	Carroll County	IL	Jeffrey Mathew	1983	6,015
132 2/8	23 6/8	22 0/8	15 1/8	4	5	Polk County	TX	James K. Hignett	1984	6,015
132 2/8	22 6/8	23 4/8	17 1/8	4	5	Phillips County	KS	Rick Chapin	1984	6,015
132 2/8	21 7/8	22 5/8	18 2/8	5	4	Montgomery County	PA	Ted Sherk	1985	6,015
132 2/8	21 2/8	21 5/8	15 4/8	5	5	Pepin County	WI	Bruce Hayden	1986	6,015
132 2/8	22 5/8	22 3/8	16 6/8	4	4	Champaign County	OH	Gene Watson	1986	6,015
132 2/8	21 6/8	22 4/8	16 4/8	6	7	Waushara County	WI	Lee D. Faust	1986	6,015
132 2/8	22 1/8	20 6/8	15 6/8	5	5	Waukesha County	WI	Dick Carlson	1986	6,015
132 2/8	23 4/8	22 4/8	18 0/8	4	5	Washington County	WI	Tony Snow	1986	6,015
132 2/8	23 1/8	23 2/8	16 7/8	6	4	Jackson County	WV	Charles E. Osborne, Jr.	1986	6,015
132 2/8	21 3/8	22 2/8	15 2/8	5	5	Troup County	GA	Tommy Roberts	1986	6,015
132 2/8	23 1/8	22 2/8	17 2/8	5	5	Otsego County	MI	Tom J. Holmes	1987	6,015
132 2/8	19 6/8	20 1/8	14 2/8	6	5	Pulaski County	KY	Casper Carroll Gibson	1987	6,015
132 2/8	22 4/8	21 4/8	18 1/8	4	5	Montgomery County	IL	Michael L. McCoy	1988	6,015
132 2/8	21 7/8	22 3/8	17 2/8	6	5	Vilas County	WI	Dan Vernetti	1988	6,015
132 2/8	21 3/8	22 3/8	13 7/8	7	5	Pawnee County	OK	Mark D. Riddle	1988	6,015
132 2/8	22 1/8	22 5/8	16 7/8	5	4	Tomahawk	ALB	David Cox	1989	6,015
132 2/8	20 6/8	22 1/8	17 2/8	5	5	Wilcox County	AL	Joe Headley	1989	6,015
132 2/8	23 7/8	24 7/8	17 2/8	6	7	Fulton County	OH	Mike Krasny	1989	6,015
132 2/8	24 2/8	24 1/8	17 0/8	4	4	Branch County	MI	Byron L. Harper	1989	6,015
132 2/8	21 4/8	20 6/8	15 4/8	4	5	Turner County	SD	Monte J. Waltner	1989	6,015
132 2/8	23 7/8	23 3/8	19 4/8	4	4	Jo Daviess County	IL	David J. Gerber	1989	6,015
132 2/8	22 5/8	24 0/8	21 0/8	4	5	Adolphustown	ONT	Mike Burriss	1989	6,015
132 2/8	22 0/8	21 6/8	16 0/8	5	5	Kenedy County	TX	B. J. McCord	1989	6,015
132 2/8	20 1/8	21 1/8	17 6/8	5	5	Rice County	MN	Richard Bohlmann	1990	6,015
132 2/8	22 6/8	22 7/8	18 3/8	5	5	Onondaga County	NY	James A. Terranova	1990	6,015
132 2/8	22 2/8	22 2/8	16 6/8	5	6	Le Sueur County	MN	Randy Mathwig	1990	6,015
132 2/8	21 2/8	20 5/8	15 4/8	5	5	Lowndes County	AL	Rett Kelly	1990	6,015
132 2/8	23 4/8	23 2/8	19 2/8	5	6	Stoddard County	MO	Lawson Metcalf	1990	6,015
132 2/8	19 0/8	19 1/8	16 2/8	6	5	Gregory County	SD	Daniel J. Roskos, Jr.	1991	6,015
132 2/8	21 2/8	19 5/8	15 4/8	5	4	Sauk County	WI	Dale Peat	1991	6,015
132 2/8	23 6/8	23 2/8	19 6/8	4	4	Hunterdon County	NJ	Joseph Guerino	1991	6,015
132 2/8	24 6/8	24 1/8	17 0/8	5	5	Buffalo County	WI	Daniel H. Folkedahl	1991	6,015
132 2/8	21 5/8	20 5/8	16 0/8	5	5	Parke County	IN	Philip A. Prock	1991	6,015
132 2/8	22 7/8	24 1/8	18 6/8	5	4	Rush County	KS	George J. Seuser III	1991	6,015
132 2/8	19 5/8	20 4/8	17 0/8	5	5	Jasper County	IA	Craig Hoskins	1991	6,015
132 1/8	18 1/8	19 7/8	18 3/8	5	5	Buffalo County	NE	Bill Orsborn	1962	6,063
132 1/8	20 3/8	20 0/8	17 1/8	5	5	Rice County	KS	Robert Lagree	1967	6,063
132 1/8	20 2/8	20 0/8	16 1/8	5	5	Kerr County	TX	Randolph Coleman	1972	6,063
132 1/8	22 4/8	24 1/8	16 3/8	4	5	Jasper County	IA	Paul Casper	1972	6,063
132 1/8	21 6/8	22 0/8	15 3/8	5	5	Pittsburg County	OK	Joe Admire	1975	6,063
132 1/8	21 5/8	21 5/8	17 7/8	5	6	Freeborn County	MN	Jerry Christenson	1977	6,063
132 1/8	20 5/8	20 2/8	16 5/8	6	5	Olmsted County	MN	Jerry V. Finley	1981	6,063
132 1/8	22 1/8	21 4/8	16 0/8	5	4	Black Hawk County	IA	Larry Graham	1981	6,063
132 1/8	19 6/8	20 0/8	16 4/8	6	5	Pepin County	WI	Terry A. G. Moline	1981	6,063
132 1/8	21 0/8	21 1/8	13 3/8	4	4	Cowley County	KS	Bill E. Wilson	1981	6,063
132 1/8	21 5/8	21 5/8	16 7/8	4	4	Mills County	TX	Tony Thomas	1982	6,063
132 1/8	22 0/8	20 7/8	15 5/8	5	5	Eau Claire County	WI	Thomas R. Budik	1982	6,063
132 1/8	24 1/8	24 1/8	18 7/8	4	4	Dunn County	WI	Richard O'Mara	1983	6,063
132 1/8	22 2/8	22 7/8	15 5/8	4	5	Walworth County	WI	Gifford Hisel	1984	6,063
132 1/8	22 5/8	24 4/8	17 7/8	4	5	McLean County	KY	Earl Smith	1985	6,063
132 1/8	23 3/8	23 4/8	19 0/8	5	4	Carroll County	MD	Herbert Eyler	1985	6,063
132 1/8	24 1/8	23 7/8	20 1/8	4	4	Chautauqua County	NY	Greg Buckley	1986	6,063
132 1/8	19 0/8	20 2/8	19 5/8	6	6	Morgan County	IL	Terry Joe Day	1987	6,063
132 1/8	22 6/8	22 6/8	17 1/8	4	4	Crawford County	PA	David H. Ingalls	1987	6,063
132 1/8	21 5/8	22 1/8	16 7/8	4	4	Waupaca County	WI	Pete Kallas	1987	6,063
132 1/8	22 1/8	22 2/8	16 3/8	4	4	Harvey County	KS	Dan Wilkerson	1987	6,063
132 1/8	20 1/8	20 7/8	14 3/8	5	5	Buffalo County	WI	David J. Gard	1987	6,063
132 1/8	25 0/8	23 4/8	20 3/8	4	4	Jackson County	IL	Tim Cobin	1987	6,063
132 1/8	22 5/8	21 5/8	19 1/8	4	5	Montgomery County	KS	John Battitori	1987	6,063
132 1/8	21 3/8	21 3/8	18 3/8	4	5	Portage County	WI	Bob Kitowski	1988	6,063
132 1/8	22 1/8	21 0/8	13 5/8	5	6	Barry County	MI	Brian Elliston	1988	6,063
132 1/8	23 2/8	21 2/8	16 3/8	5	4	Meigs County	OH	Jack Satterfield, Jr.	1988	6,063
132 1/8	22 5/8	22 1/8	23 2/8	4	4	Carroll County	MD	Dean Richardson	1988	6,063

SCORE	LENGTH OF MAIN BEAM R	LENGTH OF MAIN BEAM L	INSIDE SPREAD	NUMBER OF POINTS R	NUMBER OF POINTS L	AREA	STATE/ PROVINCE	HUNTER'S NAME	DATE	RANK
132 1/8	22 7/8	23 0/8	20 5/8	4	4	St. Landry Parish	LA	Brent Fontenot	1989	6,063
132 1/8	24 2/8	23 6/8	17 2/8	5	6	Chatham County	NC	Tom McIntosh	1989	6,063
132 1/8	21 6/8	22 2/8	16 0/8	6	6	McHenry County	IL	Jim Neuses	1989	6,063
132 1/8	23 4/8	22 4/8	18 1/8	6	7	Kenosha County	WI	Myron L Hayes	1989	6,063
132 1/8	23 2/8	22 4/8	17 5/8	5	4	Woodbury County	IA	Michael W. McKenna	1989	6,063
132 1/8	21 0/8	23 0/8	18 5/8	4	4	Stokes County	NC	Roy R. Bullins	1989	6,063
132 1/8	23 6/8	21 4/8	14 1/8	5	5	Jefferson County	WI	Jeffrey Schemm	1989	6,063
132 1/8	22 1/8	22 4/8	16 3/8	4	4	Kankakee County	IL	Terry Marcukaitis	1989	6,063
132 1/8	24 1/8	24 0/8	17 7/8	6	6	McKenzie County	ND	Mark Stewart	1990	6,063
132 1/8	23 4/8	24 1/8	18 1/8	4	4	Forest County	WI	Steven C. Gevaert	1990	6,063
132 1/8	22 4/8	20 3/8	15 2/8	6	5	Norman County	MN	Rick Sorensen	1990	6,063
132 1/8	21 5/8	21 3/8	15 1/8	5	5	Dunn County	WI	Peter Moss	1990	6,063
132 1/8	20 0/8	21 6/8	19 1/8	6	5	Shannon County	MO	Bill Ipock	1990	6,063
132 1/8	25 3/8	21 6/8	19 5/8	4	4	De Witt County	IL	Kent Sharp	1990	6,063
132 1/8	23 4/8	23 1/8	16 7/8	4	4	Stoddard County	MO	Eddie McDowell	1990	6,063
132 1/8	23 0/8	24 2/8	18 5/8	4	4	Hennepin County	MN	Rick Simonson	1990	6,063
132 1/8	24 3/8	23 7/8	21 1/8	4	4	Lake County	IL	Curtis Adams	1990	6,063
132 1/8	22 4/8	22 7/8	20 1/8	4	4	Washington County	MS	Bobby R. Woods	1991	6,063
132 1/8	22 2/8	22 0/8	17 6/8	4	5	Dakota County	MN	Patrick Henderson	1991	6,063
132 1/8	23 1/8	24 0/8	17 3/8	5	5	Oklahoma County	OK	Darrell Edwin Fesler	1991	6,063
132 0/8	21 4/8	21 2/8	18 2/8	4	4	Juneau County	WI	Arthur Witz	1966	6,111
132 0/8	22 5/8	22 2/8	18 6/8	5	5	Iowa County	IA	Larry King	1967	6,111
132 0/8	21 6/8	22 4/8	17 0/8	4	4	Harlan County	NE	Edward H. Backes	1969	6,111
132 0/8	20 0/8	20 5/8	14 6/8	4	4	Pittsburg County	OK	Fred Parkison	1969	6,111
132 0/8	21 4/8	21 1/8	16 4/8	6	5	Dunn County	WI	John R. Bilderback	1970	6,111
132 0/8	20 2/8	20 7/8	13 7/8	6	5	Burleigh County	ND	Scott Lang	1976	6,111
132 0/8	23 4/8	23 5/8	16 6/8	5	4	Wabasha County	MN	Myles Keller	1978	6,111
132 0/8	21 6/8	22 1/8	15 3/8	5	5	Monroe County	NY	Tyler D. Smith	1978	6,111
132 0/8	23 4/8	22 0/8	15 3/8	5	6	Portage County	WI	Michael K. Nuernberger	1979	6,111
132 0/8	20 6/8	21 3/8	18 5/8	5	5	Cambridge	ONT	Fred Law	1979	6,111
132 0/8	20 2/8	20 6/8	16 2/8	5	6	Pope County	MN	Wayne Charles	1980	6,111
132 0/8	21 4/8	21 1/8	15 6/8	5	4	Redwood County	MN	June E. Gilb	1980	6,111
132 0/8	20 0/8	21 6/8	14 0/8	5	5	Polk County	IA	Glenn D. Vondra	1980	6,111
132 0/8	22 4/8	22 4/8	17 2/8	5	4	Guernsey County	OH	Darwin D. Jirles	1981	6,111
132 0/8	21 6/8	21 5/8	16 1/8	6	5	Coweta County	GA	C. M. Edwards, Jr.	1982	6,111
132 0/8	22 6/8	23 4/8	17 2/8	4	4	Pierce County	WI	Mark Schafhauser	1982	6,111
132 0/8	21 6/8	22 0/8	20 4/8	4	4	Lee County	IA	Randy Waschkat	1983	6,111
132 0/8	23 6/8	22 7/8	17 0/8	5	5	Dubuque County	IA	Richard P. Munz	1983	6,111
132 0/8	21 4/8	20 1/8	15 4/8	5	5	Shelby County	IL	Joe Thompson	1984	6,111
132 0/8	21 6/8	21 2/8	18 0/8	5	5	Buffalo County	WI	Robert L. Kampen	1984	6,111
132 0/8	21 6/8	22 3/8	20 6/8	5	5	Buffalo County	WI	Rex Secrist	1984	6,111
132 0/8	21 5/8	22 4/8	17 0/8	4	4	Winnebago County	IL	Glenn A. Johnson	1984	6,111
132 0/8	21 1/8	20 1/8	15 0/8	5	6	Marinette County	WI	John Katers	1985	6,111
132 0/8	23 4/8	24 4/8	17 2/8	4	5	Scott County	IA	Bob Hankins	1985	6,111
132 0/8	22 6/8	22 0/8	14 3/8	5	4	Humphreys County	TN	Tom Hutson	1986	6,111
132 0/8	22 2/8	22 1/8	16 6/8	4	5	Suffolk County	NY	Frederick Donarummo	1986	6,111
132 0/8	23 1/8	23 0/8	18 2/8	4	4	Edgar County	IL	Russell Guthrie	1987	6,111
132 0/8	20 5/8	21 4/8	14 0/8	5	5	Kenedy County	TX	Harold R. Arve, Jr.	1987	6,111
132 0/8	24 0/8	22 1/8	16 6/8	4	4	Door County	WI	Neil Groeschel	1987	6,111
132 0/8	23 5/8	24 0/8	18 2/8	4	4	De Kalb County	IN	Danny Lynn Helbert	1987	6,111
132 0/8	22 7/8	20 4/8	20 0/8	6	7	Morton County	ND	John Finck	1987	6,111
132 0/8	23 4/8	23 4/8	18 2/8	4	4	Guernsey County	OH	Dick Bayer	1987	6,111
132 0/8	21 1/8	21 6/8	17 2/8	8	8	Powder River County	MT	Mark L. Frank	1988	6,111
132 0/8	21 5/8	21 2/8	17 1/8	5	6	Rock County	WI	Dudley D. Rhoades	1988	6,111
132 0/8	22 4/8	21 1/8	15 4/8	5	6	Olmsted County	MN	Gary Kowalewski	1988	6,111
132 0/8	20 7/8	21 4/8	15 4/8	5	5	Hancock County	OH	Jill A. Smith	1988	6,111
132 0/8	21 0/8	21 1/8	16 2/8	4	4	Marquette County	WI	John Steckling	1988	6,111
132 0/8	20 3/8	20 3/8	15 0/8	5	5	Buffalo County	WI	Jeff Binger	1989	6,111
132 0/8	23 0/8	25 2/8	16 2/8	6	5	Newton County	AR	David Tomlinson	1989	6,111
132 0/8	21 3/8	22 4/8	17 6/8	5	4	Lafayette County	WI	Gregory S. Kuehne	1989	6,111
132 0/8	22 2/8	23 4/8	19 2/8	4	4	Berrien County	MI	Robert F. Svoboda, Jr.	1989	6,111
132 0/8	23 0/8	22 4/8	19 5/8	6	5	Mecklenburg County	VA	John W. McAden	1989	6,111
132 0/8	20 4/8	20 7/8	19 2/8	5	6	Winnebago County	IL	Derek Boeger	1989	6,111
132 0/8	21 2/8	21 5/8	16 4/8	5	5	Fayette County	IL	Richard L. Perry	1989	6,111
132 0/8	23 5/8	23 1/8	16 6/8	5	5	Brown County	OH	Mike Doyle	1989	6,111
132 0/8	20 1/8	20 7/8	17 6/8	4	4	Rockdale County	GA	Ricky L. Crumbley	1990	6,111
132 0/8	21 0/8	20 3/8	15 7/8	5	5	Mercer County	IL	Brad Peterson	1990	6,111
132 0/8	19 6/8	20 1/8	16 6/8	6	5	Clayton County	IA	Dan J. Nicks	1990	6,111
132 0/8	19 5/8	19 1/8	18 6/8	5	5	Douglas County	MN	Matt Perdue	1990	6,111
132 0/8	23 6/8	25 0/8	18 6/8	6	8	Twiggs County	GA	Stephen Cline Roberts, Jr	1991	6,111

SCORE	LENGTH OF R MAIN BEAM L		INSIDE SPREAD	NUMBER OF R POINTS L		AREA	STATE/ PROVINCE	HUNTER'S NAME	DATE	RANK
132 0/8	22 2/8	22 0/8	16 0/8	6	5	Madison County	MT	Michael Mitale	1991	6,111
132 0/8	22 6/8	23 4/8	19 2/8	4	4	McHenry County	IL	Richard Tudor	1991	6,111
132 0/8	21 2/8	20 2/8	15 4/8	5	5	Jackson County	MI	Larry Kettinger	1991	6,111
132 0/8	23 4/8	23 4/8	17 6/8	7	5	Worcester County	MA	Peter R. Couillard	1991	6,111
132 0/8	20 6/8	20 5/8	17 6/8	5	5	Meeker County	MN	Chuck Schultz	1991	6,111
131 7/8	22 0/8	22 7/8	22 2/8	6	4	Goodhue County	MN	James Jarvis	1964	6,166
131 7/8	22 0/8	23 1/8	15 1/8	4	5	Trempealeau County	WI	Clark Gallup	1967	6,166
131 7/8	21 1/8	22 1/8	17 5/8	4	4	Brown County	SD	Barry Smith	1967	6,166
131 7/8	20 3/8	20 6/8	14 6/8	6	6	Adams County	IL	David E. DeMoss	1970	6,166
131 7/8	22 2/8	21 1/8	20 5/8	4	5	Rock County	WI	Richard W. Pieterek	1972	6,166
131 7/8	21 3/8	20 4/8	15 7/8	6	5	Fulton County	AR	Larry Luther	1977	6,166
131 7/8	21 0/8	20 3/8	16 7/8	4	4	Washington County	KS	Bill R. Mallean	1977	6,166
131 7/8	21 3/8	21 2/8	19 7/8	5	4	Washtenaw County	MI	Philip J. Maly	1980	6,166
131 7/8	23 5/8	25 3/8	19 1/8	4	4	Logan County	OH	Thomas R. Weaver	1980	6,166
131 7/8	21 7/8	21 6/8	15 5/8	4	4	Russell County	KS	Joe Schulte	1982	6,166
131 7/8	22 3/8	23 4/8	16 1/8	5	5	Saline County	MO	Ed Coates	1983	6,166
131 7/8	21 3/8	21 5/8	17 1/8	4	4	Will County	IL	Mike Sheehan	1984	6,166
131 7/8	21 7/8	20 6/8	17 1/8	4	4	Lincoln County	KS	Robert Chitty	1985	6,166
131 7/8	22 3/8	20 6/8	16 1/8	5	5	Putnam County	OH	Randy Schroeder	1985	6,166
131 7/8	22 3/8	22 6/8	17 5/8	4	4	Douglas County	WI	Edward Flood	1985	6,166
131 7/8	19 6/8	20 5/8	15 1/8	5	5	Knox County	OH	Tom Bowman	1985	6,166
131 7/8	24 1/8	25 4/8	20 3/8	4	4	Westchester County	NY	Roger Jensen	1985	6,166
131 7/8	22 1/8	23 2/8	15 3/8	4	4	Garden County	NE	Reggie Spiegelberg	1985	6,166
131 7/8	21 3/8	21 2/8	25 2/8	5	4	Pratt County	KS	C. J. Eifert	1985	6,166
131 7/8	21 4/8	21 4/8	17 7/8	6	5	Morrison County	MN	Bruce A. Carlson	1986	6,166
131 7/8	21 2/8	20 6/8	16 5/8	6	5	Ripley County	IN	Clinton C. Miller	1986	6,166
131 7/8	23 1/8	22 6/8	15 5/8	4	4	Vernon County	WI	Dave Sarnowski	1986	6,166
131 7/8	22 1/8	22 2/8	16 7/8	7	5	Pittsburg County	OK	Charles Rake	1986	6,166
131 7/8	21 2/8	21 6/8	14 3/8	5	6	Johnson County	IN	Dan Craig	1987	6,166
131 7/8	20 1/8	22 0/8	19 1/8	4	5	Clark County	WI	John Schultz	1987	6,166
131 7/8	24 0/8	24 3/8	20 4/8	6	7	Harrison County	KY	Kendall Techau	1987	6,166
131 7/8	20 1/8	20 4/8	17 5/8	6	5	Shelby County	MO	Gregory R. Troyer	1988	6,166
131 7/8	21 6/8	21 4/8	16 5/8	5	5	Buffalo County	WI	Bernard Becker	1988	6,166
131 7/8	21 1/8	21 7/8	17 3/8	4	5	Boone County	IL	Joseph C. Ware	1988	6,166
131 7/8	19 4/8	19 6/8	16 1/8	6	5	Hand County	SD	Terry Boomsma	1988	6,166
131 7/8	20 6/8	20 4/8	18 1/8	5	4	Buffalo County	WI	Roger Comero	1989	6,166
131 7/8	20 6/8	22 4/8	15 7/8	5	5	Crittenden County	KY	Mickey Tinsley	1989	6,166
131 7/8	24 2/8	25 1/8	19 3/8	4	5	Highland County	OH	Jeffrey A. Swerlein	1989	6,166
131 7/8	23 7/8	24 0/8	17 4/8	6	5	Morrison County	MN	Michael J. Crandall	1989	6,166
131 7/8	20 5/8	19 3/8	17 4/8	7	5	Ramsey County	ND	Wayne Carlson	1989	6,166
131 7/8	20 5/8	22 3/8	16 3/8	4	5	Callaway County	MO	Ken Morse	1989	6,166
131 7/8	22 5/8	22 5/8	15 3/8	7	7	Cumberland County	IL	Jerome Light	1989	6,166
131 7/8	21 5/8	20 7/8	18 1/8	5	5	Ogle County	IL	Ted Hysell	1989	6,166
131 7/8	21 0/8	20 0/8	16 3/8	5	5	Hennepin County	MN	Craig M. Johnson	1989	6,166
131 7/8	25 6/8	24 4/8	20 1/8	5	4	Shelby County	TN	Jim Baker	1990	6,166
131 7/8	20 3/8	21 0/8	16 5/8	5	6	Chariton County	MO	Donald W. Abeln	1990	6,166
131 7/8	20 5/8	21 4/8	18 5/8	6	5	Iron County	MO	Robert Eaves	1990	6,166
131 7/8	20 7/8	21 2/8	17 1/8	4	5	Allen County	OH	Mark A. Halker	1990	6,166
131 7/8	20 0/8	21 4/8	18 0/8	5	7	Hamilton County	IA	Larry Haren	1990	6,166
131 7/8	22 6/8	22 7/8	22 1/8	4	4	Bureau County	IL	Raymond Schindel	1990	6,166
131 7/8	23 2/8	22 2/8	20 1/8	5	4	Worcester County	MD	Mike Hill	1990	6,166
131 7/8	23 3/8	23 2/8	16 6/8	5	7	Anoka County	MN	Pat Ellias	1991	6,166
131 7/8	21 5/8	22 4/8	20 1/8	5	5	Starke County	IN	Scott Vieting	1991	6,166
131 7/8	20 5/8	20 4/8	15 5/8	5	5	Decatur County	IA	Ronald E. Tennant	1991	6,166
131 7/8	24 3/8	22 6/8	18 3/8	4	4	Winnebago County	IL	Jeff S. Olsen	1991	6,166
131 7/8	21 6/8	21 5/8	16 7/8	5	5	Wayne County	IL	Peewee Hall	1991	6,166
131 6/8	19 0/8	18 6/8	13 6/8	6	6	Norton County	KS	Harold Fisher	1966	6,217
131 6/8	22 3/8	22 1/8	17 2/8	4	5	Tuscarawas County	OH	Del Karnuth	1976	6,217
131 6/8	22 2/8	21 0/8	18 0/8	5	6	Kalamazoo County	MI	Richard Hettinga	1978	6,217
131 6/8	23 2/8	22 3/8	17 6/8	4	4	Randolph County	IL	Kevin Lucht	1981	6,217
131 6/8	20 1/8	19 2/8	15 6/8	5	5	Marquette County	WI	Steven McReath	1981	6,217
131 6/8	21 4/8	21 1/8	18 6/8	4	4	Hunterdon County	NJ	Chris Jensen	1982	6,217
131 6/8	24 1/8	23 7/8	17 4/8	6	6	Brookings County	SD	Joseph M. Creager	1983	6,217
131 6/8	21 3/8	22 7/8	18 0/8	4	5	Walworth County	WI	Mike Jacobs	1983	6,217
131 6/8	19 3/8	21 0/8	18 0/8	10	8	Roscommon County	MI	David Lacey	1984	6,217
131 6/8	23 4/8	24 2/8	16 6/8	4	4	Saline County	NE	C. Michael Morrow	1984	6,217
131 6/8	24 0/8	24 1/8	17 6/8	4	5	Sawyer County	WI	Bob Swenson	1985	6,217
131 6/8	23 1/8	22 0/8	17 0/8	5	5	Trempealeau County	WI	John McKeeth	1987	6,217
131 6/8	22 7/8	23 2/8	14 0/8	5	5	Jackson County	MI	William H. Leslie III	1987	6,217
131 6/8	22 2/8	21 6/8	16 4/8	5	5	Walworth County	WI	Jeff Schmalfeldt	1987	6,217

Score	Length of Main Beam R	L	Inside Spread	Number of Points R	L	Area	State/Province	Hunter's Name	Date	Rank
131 6/8	23 6/8	24 0/8	17 0/8	4	4	Eau Claire County	WI	Doug A. Larson	1987	6,217
131 6/8	21 5/8	22 3/8	16 4/8	4	4	St. Croix County	WI	Mark Crandall	1987	6,217
131 6/8	22 4/8	21 3/8	17 0/8	4	4	McLean County	IL	Tilfred Eades	1987	6,217
131 6/8	22 2/8	22 1/8	19 6/8	5	5	Caroline County	MD	Garland L. Turner	1987	6,217
131 6/8	23 7/8	24 5/8	19 6/8	4	4	Pittsburg County	OK	Todd Tobey	1988	6,217
131 6/8	25 4/8	25 0/8	20 0/8	7	5	Bayfield County	WI	Paul M. Halverson	1988	6,217
131 6/8	22 7/8	22 7/8	19 2/8	4	4	Jackson County	OH	Terry S. Speakman	1988	6,217
131 6/8	18 0/8	18 0/8	14 0/8	5	5	Waukesha County	WI	Bob Koepp	1988	6,217
131 6/8	24 0/8	23 3/8	15 2/8	5	5	Randolph County	IL	Danny T. Wahl	1988	6,217
131 6/8	23 1/8	22 3/8	17 0/8	5	6	Winneshiek County	IA	Duane C. Baumler	1989	6,217
131 6/8	21 2/8	22 2/8	17 0/8	4	4	Spedden	ALB	Darryl Kublik	1989	6,217
131 6/8	18 7/8	19 4/8	17 0/8	5	5	Williams County	ND	Richard Liesener	1989	6,217
131 6/8	21 0/8	21 0/8	16 0/8	4	4	Marathon County	WI	Bruce Stieber	1989	6,217
131 6/8	21 7/8	23 7/8	17 4/8	4	4	Wyandotte County	KS	Earl A. Cooksey	1989	6,217
131 6/8	22 7/8	23 5/8	17 4/8	5	5	Desha County	AR	Greg Sharp	1989	6,217
131 6/8	22 5/8	21 0/8	18 4/8	5	5	Saginaw County	MI	Bill H. Schack	1989	6,217
131 6/8	23 1/8	23 3/8	17 0/8	4	4	Floyd County	IA	Joel Gray	1990	6,217
131 6/8	22 2/8	23 0/8	16 5/8	4	5	Vernon County	WI	Mike Slivinski	1990	6,217
131 6/8	23 2/8	22 6/8	18 2/8	4	4	Hardin County	IL	Charles E. Spear	1990	6,217
131 6/8	20 1/8	21 3/8	14 6/8	5	6	Greene County	IN	James Tyree	1990	6,217
131 6/8	22 5/8	22 7/8	15 2/8	4	4	Seneca County	NY	Kenneth E. Briggs	1990	6,217
131 6/8	24 5/8	24 0/8	16 2/8	4	4	Albany County	NY	Mark Cintula	1990	6,217
131 6/8	24 6/8	24 1/8	18 6/8	4	4	McMullen County	TX	Guy Allcorn	1991	6,217
131 6/8	25 0/8	24 0/8	17 2/8	8	7	McPherson County	KS	Hal G. Krehbiel	1991	6,217
131 6/8	19 4/8	18 6/8	17 4/8	5	5	Woodward County	OK	Phil Lanier	1991	6,217
131 6/8	21 4/8	22 5/8	17 6/8	4	4	Parke County	IN	Wayne Loomis	1991	6,217
131 6/8	21 2/8	23 2/8	13 4/8	4	4	Pottawatomie County	KS	Larry Carroll	1991	6,217
131 6/8	20 7/8	23 1/8	18 0/8	4	4	Isle of Wight County	VA	Raymond W. West	1991	6,217
131 5/8	21 4/8	22 1/8	18 5/8	4	4	Forest County	WI	Max Wisnefske	1950	6,259
131 5/8	19 7/8	19 7/8	12 3/8	5	5	Jefferson County	IN	Ted Taylor	1959	6,259
131 5/8	23 4/8	22 5/8	14 1/8	4	5	Otter Tail County	MN	Gordon Swenson	1964	6,259
131 5/8	22 4/8	21 6/8	16 1/8	5	5	Hale County	AL	Bo Bonds	1976	6,259
131 5/8	23 4/8	25 0/8	18 4/8	5	5	Carroll County	OH	Charles B. Platt	1977	6,259
131 5/8	21 7/8	22 2/8	16 3/8	5	5	Washington County	WI	Steven L. Hoelz	1980	6,259
131 5/8	23 4/8	24 0/8	19 3/8	5	5	Marquette County	WI	Bryan Anderson	1982	6,259
131 5/8	23 7/8	22 4/8	16 7/8	6	7	Allen County	KS	Larry Robertson	1983	6,259
131 5/8	23 1/8	21 7/8	18 2/8	5	6	Kandiyohi County	MN	Mike Dallman	1983	6,259
131 5/8	19 5/8	20 2/8	17 3/8	5	5	Jefferson County	WI	Donald L. Zubke	1983	6,259
131 5/8	22 0/8	20 5/8	18 7/8	4	4	Gratiot County	MI	Robert Allen Mallory	1984	6,259
131 5/8	22 4/8	22 5/8	14 5/8	5	5	Fond du Lac County	WI	Daryl Zacharias	1985	6,259
131 5/8	20 4/8	19 2/8	15 1/8	5	7	Miller County	MO	John Ash	1985	6,259
131 5/8	24 3/8	23 3/8	20 0/8	5	8	Lake County	IL	Robert Norman Tropple	1985	6,259
131 5/8	25 1/8	25 2/8	16 7/8	4	4	Chatham County	NC	Jimmy Womble	1986	6,259
131 5/8	23 2/8	23 3/8	16 1/8	4	4	Manistee County	MI	Jerry L. Fink	1986	6,259
131 5/8	24 4/8	23 2/8	20 5/8	5	4	Morris County	NJ	Glenn Hullings	1986	6,259
131 5/8	20 5/8	20 4/8	15 7/8	4	5	Todd County	MN	Jim Friedrichs	1987	6,259
131 5/8	25 4/8	24 2/8	17 1/8	6	5	Woodbury County	IA	Lester J. Zahnley	1987	6,259
131 5/8	25 3/8	24 4/8	19 3/8	4	4	Preble County	OH	Stephen L. Parker	1987	6,259
131 5/8	23 0/8	23 0/8	17 3/8	6	7	Sawyer County	WI	Ron Miller	1987	6,259
131 5/8	20 4/8	21 4/8	17 1/8	5	9	Sheboygan County	WI	Keith D. Darling	1987	6,259
131 5/8	23 3/8	23 3/8	19 5/8	5	6	Pepin County	WI	Michael Schmidt	1988	6,259
131 5/8	20 5/8	21 1/8	14 5/8	5	6	Clay County	MN	Philip Reiling	1988	6,259
131 5/8	19 5/8	21 0/8	16 5/8	5	5	Cavalier County	ND	William Wightman	1988	6,259
131 5/8	22 6/8	23 2/8	18 0/8	5	5	Sherburne County	MN	Bill Cashman	1989	6,259
131 5/8	21 6/8	22 4/8	15 5/8	6	6	Fort Bend County	TX	Pat Byrne	1989	6,259
131 5/8	21 3/8	22 4/8	18 2/8	7	5	Pulaski County	IL	Bill Spaulding	1990	6,259
131 5/8	21 2/8	20 0/8	17 1/8	5	5	Hancock County	OH	Tom Phillips	1990	6,259
131 5/8	23 4/8	23 0/8	17 1/8	4	6	Suffolk County	NY	Leland Winslow	1990	6,259
131 5/8	23 3/8	21 4/8	17 0/8	5	4	Montgomery County	IN	John Donald	1991	6,259
131 5/8	21 1/8	20 4/8	18 2/8	6	7	Washburn County	WI	Steven J. Genson	1991	6,259
131 5/8	21 3/8	21 6/8	18 1/8	4	4	Forest County	WI	Flint Gilbert	1991	6,259
131 5/8	23 7/8	24 7/8	19 1/8	5	6	Jo Daviess County	IL	Ron Mann	1991	6,259
131 5/8	22 3/8	23 5/8	17 5/8	5	5	Buffalo County	WI	Jim Wondzell	1991	6,259
131 5/8	22 2/8	22 3/8	17 7/8	4	4	Henry County	VA	Mike Weaver	1991	6,259
131 5/8	21 3/8	21 0/8	16 3/8	5	6	Fremont County	IA	Dave Holt	1991	6,259
131 5/8	22 1/8	21 5/8	16 7/8	4	4	Henry County	IA	Todd Wibben	1991	6,259
131 5/8	23 0/8	23 5/8	19 0/8	6	5	Walworth County	WI	Allen Lehman	1991	6,259
131 5/8	23 5/8	23 1/8	16 5/8	5	5	Columbia County	WI	Bruce R. Walker	1992	6,259
131 4/8	20 4/8	20 1/8	17 2/8	5	5	Benton County	IA	Wayne Keefer	1956	6,299
131 4/8	21 2/8	21 7/8	16 2/8	5	5	Johnson County	IN	James E. Thompson	1962	6,299

SCORE	LENGTH OF MAIN BEAM		INSIDE SPREAD	NUMBER OF POINTS		AREA	STATE/ PROVINCE	HUNTER'S NAME	DATE	RANK
	R	L		R	L					
131 4/8	20 2/8	22 1/8	14 2/8	5	5	Price County	WI	Frank W. Taylor	1964	6,299
131 4/8	21 3/8	21 2/8	16 0/8	7	5	Roberts County	SD	Martin Carlson	1966	6,299
131 4/8	23 1/8	21 5/8	17 4/8	5	4	Calvert County	MD	William L. Neal	1970	6,299
131 4/8	20 7/8	22 5/8	18 3/8	5	5	Allamakee County	IA	Dayton Jones	1971	6,299
131 4/8	19 2/8	19 2/8	15 2/8	5	5	Sheboygan County	WI	Donald P. Feidmann	1974	6,299
131 4/8	23 3/8	23 4/8	16 4/8	4	4	Clinton County	IA	Gary Olson	1975	6,299
131 4/8	21 2/8	21 5/8	15 0/8	5	5	Newton County	IN	Ronnie Styck	1976	6,299
131 4/8	22 3/8	22 1/8	19 6/8	5	5	Fairfax County	VA	Dickie R. Powell	1979	6,299
131 4/8	21 2/8	21 5/8	15 0/8	5	5	Ward County	ND	Richard Huber	1980	6,299
131 4/8	24 2/8	22 6/8	16 6/8	4	4	Shelby County	OH	Wayne L. Goubeaux	1981	6,299
131 4/8	21 7/8	21 6/8	15 6/8	4	5	Christian County	IL	Dale W. Simmons	1982	6,299
131 4/8	21 6/8	21 1/8	16 6/8	5	4	Clay County	KS	Doug Adams	1982	6,299
131 4/8	21 6/8	21 0/8	15 2/8	5	5	Dawson County	MT	James C. Slaska	1984	6,299
131 4/8	23 3/8	23 6/8	19 5/8	7	5	Calhoun County	MI	Samuel E. Farrington	1984	6,299
131 4/8	20 2/8	21 5/8	17 6/8	4	6	Clay County	MN	Don Pake	1984	6,299
131 4/8	21 3/8	21 3/8	20 6/8	4	4	Montgomery County	IN	John R Clark	1984	6,299
131 4/8	24 4/8	24 5/8	15 6/8	5	4	McNairy County	TN	Howard Russom	1984	6,299
131 4/8	21 4/8	23 1/8	19 0/8	6	5	Yuma County	CO	Greg Mekelburg	1985	6,299
131 4/8	22 6/8	21 4/8	14 6/8	5	5	Morrill County	NE	Kurt Gaertner	1985	6,299
131 4/8	22 3/8	22 5/8	17 6/8	4	5	Grant County	WI	Gary R. Bald	1985	6,299
131 4/8	20 5/8	20 1/8	15 4/8	5	5	Webster County	IA	Randy Bennett	1985	6,299
131 4/8	22 4/8	22 6/8	17 2/8	4	4	Dakota County	MN	Steve Dahnke	1986	6,299
131 4/8	21 4/8	23 0/8	18 4/8	4	4	Strathcona	ALB	John Visscher	1986	6,299
131 4/8	23 0/8	23 0/8	16 4/8	4	4	Edmunds County	SD	Jerry Leair	1986	6,299
131 4/8	23 0/8	25 2/8	14 0/8	5	5	Jackson County	WV	Michael B. Sankoff	1987	6,299
131 4/8	21 3/8	21 4/8	18 6/8	4	4	Knox County	IL	Bill T. Alton, Jr.	1987	6,299
131 4/8	26 6/8	26 3/8	18 4/8	4	5	Greenwood County	KS	Scott Moore	1987	6,299
131 4/8	22 7/8	22 4/8	23 6/8	5	5	Union County	IL	Steve Wilhite	1987	6,299
131 4/8	20 4/8	20 6/8	17 0/8	5	5	Lake County	IL	John F. Nobilio	1988	6,299
131 4/8	21 3/8	20 6/8	18 2/8	5	5	Lake County	IL	Carl Spaeth	1988	6,299
131 4/8	26 4/8	25 0/8	20 0/8	5	4	Douglas County	WI	Jim Webb	1988	6,299
131 4/8	23 5/8	24 2/8	19 1/8	5	7	Macoupin County	IL	Donald D. Snow, Sr.	1988	6,299
131 4/8	22 6/8	23 1/8	17 0/8	4	4	Newton County	TX	Mike Perdue	1989	6,299
131 4/8	22 0/8	23 4/8	20 2/8	4	4	Houston County	MN	Tony Rostad	1989	6,299
131 4/8	21 1/8	21 5/8	16 4/8	5	5	Buffalo County	WI	Mark Fetting	1989	6,299
131 4/8	22 2/8	23 1/8	17 4/8	4	5	Lapeer County	MI	Larry Rae Faught	1989	6,299
131 4/8	25 0/8	25 0/8	19 0/8	5	4	Hillsborough County	NH	Robert Dupuis	1990	6,299
131 4/8	23 3/8	23 2/8	17 4/8	4	4	Becker County	MN	Duane Hendrickson	1990	6,299
131 4/8	21 4/8	21 2/8	15 6/8	4	5	Sawyer County	WI	Roger A. Niewiadomski	1990	6,299
131 4/8	20 2/8	23 0/8	17 2/8	6	5	Fairfield County	CT	Robert Padovani	1990	6,299
131 4/8	21 6/8	22 1/8	18 0/8	5	5	Dodge County	WI	Michael Vande Slunt	1990	6,299
131 4/8	22 4/8	22 0/8	16 6/8	5	6	Logan County	CO	Terry Weimer	1990	6,299
131 4/8	21 6/8	21 7/8	17 0/8	5	5	Morrison County	MN	Bob Deiley	1990	6,299
131 4/8	22 6/8	23 2/8	17 4/8	5	4	Suffolk County	NY	Richard Jensen	1990	6,299
131 4/8	21 2/8	20 7/8	18 5/8	5	7	Fillmore County	MN	David L. Carson	1991	6,299
131 4/8	22 0/8	22 4/8	19 0/8	4	5	Onondaga County	NY	Richard J. Canestrare	1991	6,299
131 4/8	22 0/8	21 6/8	15 7/8	5	4	Stevens County	WA	Steve Mitchell	1992	6,299
131 3/8	22 2/8	22 6/8	18 7/8	5	5	Beltrami County	MN	Charles R. Bowman	1961	6,348
131 3/8	21 7/8	21 6/8	17 7/8	4	4	Waushara County	WI	Reginald Vergin	1967	6,348
131 3/8	21 0/8	20 4/8	16 5/8	5	6	Delaware County	OH	Bobby Clenney	1975	6,348
131 3/8	21 3/8	21 4/8	18 3/8	4	5	Pope County	AR	Tom Quinton	1976	6,348
131 3/8	23 0/8	23 3/8	16 7/8	4	4	Trigg County	KY	Bruce E. Hollkamp	1978	6,348
131 3/8	22 2/8	20 5/8	13 6/8	5	5	Burleigh County	ND	Robert Baker	1980	6,348
131 3/8	21 7/8	21 1/8	15 4/8	5	5	Guernsey County	OH	Jim Conrad	1980	6,348
131 3/8	23 1/8	23 1/8	19 7/8	4	5	Morrison County	MN	Tim Deadrick	1981	6,348
131 3/8	21 1/8	21 1/8	17 1/8	5	5	Crawford County	WI	Michael G. O'Dair	1983	6,348
131 3/8	22 7/8	24 1/8	19 3/8	4	4	Dubuque County	IA	Michael W. Moore	1983	6,348
131 3/8	22 3/8	22 1/8	18 1/8	5	5	Marquette County	WI	Roger L. Abraham	1984	6,348
131 3/8	22 2/8	22 4/8	19 1/8	4	4	Roane County	TN	Doan Boling	1986	6,348
131 3/8	21 2/8	20 7/8	18 1/8	5	5	Racine County	WI	Steven Holterman	1986	6,348
131 3/8	21 4/8	22 4/8	17 1/8	4	4	Jefferson County	WI	Robert L. Cummings	1986	6,348
131 3/8	23 2/8	23 0/8	17 7/8	4	4	Jo Daviess County	IL	Bill Randecker	1986	6,348
131 3/8	21 5/8	22 1/8	17 7/8	5	5	Clark County	WI	Norbert Allan Lewis	1987	6,348
131 3/8	22 1/8	22 1/8	18 3/8	5	5	Dallas County	IA	William Chaplin	1987	6,348
131 3/8	22 1/8	22 2/8	16 3/8	5	5	Polk County	WI	Daniel Carlson	1987	6,348
131 3/8	22 5/8	24 3/8	17 4/8	6	6	Dane County	WI	Rollen "Bud" Fries	1987	6,348
131 3/8	23 5/8	24 4/8	16 5/8	5	4	Columbia County	WI	Mark L. Preuss	1987	6,348
131 3/8	20 4/8	21 5/8	15 1/8	5	6	Iron County	MI	Bernard Ohmer	1987	6,348
131 3/8	24 1/8	24 6/8	21 7/8	6	4	Door County	WI	Bruce H. Hartman	1987	6,348
131 3/8	22 0/8	23 1/8	15 2/8	7	7	Linn County	IA	John Dunham	1987	6,348

SCORE	LENGTH OF R MAIN BEAM L		INSIDE SPREAD	NUMBER OF R POINTS L		AREA	STATE/ PROVINCE	HUNTER'S NAME	DATE	RANK
131 3/8	21 4/8	21 4/8	17 3/8	5	5	Lancaster County	PA	Henry O. Fromm	1988	6,348
131 3/8	21 0/8	21 6/8	18 3/8	6	5	Cass County	ND	John Baird	1988	6,348
131 3/8	20 3/8	20 0/8	16 5/8	6	7	Sherburne County	MN	Bryan J. Wieber	1988	6,348
131 3/8	21 2/8	20 1/8	15 7/8	5	6	Buffalo County	WI	John W. Zahrte	1988	6,348
131 3/8	23 3/8	23 1/8	17 1/8	5	5	Schuyler County	NY	Tim G. Carlton	1988	6,348
131 3/8	19 7/8	20 5/8	16 5/8	5	5	Francis	SAS	Ken Paslawski	1989	6,348
131 3/8	23 3/8	23 1/8	17 5/8	8	5	Colfax County	NE	Neil Chaudler	1989	6,348
131 3/8	23 0/8	23 0/8	17 5/8	4	4	Vermilion County	IL	Michael J. Howie	1989	6,348
131 3/8	22 7/8	22 5/8	21 1/8	4	4	Winneshiek County	IA	John Mullen	1989	6,348
131 3/8	21 6/8	22 2/8	19 1/8	4	5	Oakland County	MI	Gerald J. Pennington	1989	6,348
131 3/8	22 6/8	23 3/8	14 7/8	5	6	Hocking County	OH	Jim Bowman	1989	6,348
131 3/8	21 3/8	20 6/8	18 3/8	5	5	Champaign County	OH	E. Jeffrey Horne	1989	6,348
131 3/8	19 0/8	19 3/8	17 7/8	6	5	Warren County	KY	Tony Shoemake	1989	6,348
131 3/8	22 0/8	22 0/8	17 1/8	5	5	Lincoln County	SD	Chris A. Benson	1990	6,348
131 3/8	21 6/8	21 6/8	16 5/8	5	5	Carroll County	IL	Greg McGinnis	1990	6,348
131 3/8	21 0/8	20 4/8	16 3/8	5	5	Kemper County	MS	David L. Black	1990	6,348
131 3/8	20 2/8	20 2/8	18 3/8	4	5	Wayne County	MI	William Benedict	1990	6,348
131 3/8	22 2/8	23 4/8	18 0/8	5	5	Vernon County	MO	Mike Goucher	1990	6,348
131 3/8	23 3/8	22 7/8	18 3/8	5	5	Mills County	IA	Dave Messner	1990	6,348
131 3/8	20 6/8	22 2/8	16 1/8	4	4	Door County	WI	Wayne Lautenbach	1990	6,348
131 3/8	21 5/8	21 5/8	18 1/8	4	4	Huron County	OH	Michael Scheel	1990	6,348
131 3/8	22 0/8	21 4/8	17 1/8	5	4	St. Joseph County	IN	Rodney Reeder	1991	6,348
131 3/8	23 5/8	23 1/8	16 3/8	4	4	Claibourne County	MS	James R. House	1991	6,348
131 3/8	19 2/8	22 0/8	16 5/8	6	6	Cuming County	NE	Ricky Heller	1992	6,348
131 2/8	19 2/8	19 4/8	17 0/8	5	5	Shawnee County	KS	Guy C. Michael	1968	6,395
131 2/8	20 3/8	19 4/8	14 6/8	5	5	Ripley County	IN	Robert Pitt	1969	6,395
131 2/8	24 5/8	22 5/8	16 0/8	4	5	Waushara County	WI	Randy Marks	1975	6,395
131 2/8	20 5/8	22 0/8	17 4/8	5	5	Scott County	KY	Jerry Peavler	1975	6,395
131 2/8	20 6/8	22 0/8	16 0/8	4	5	Clearwater County	ID	Edward L. Russell	1978	6,395
131 2/8	25 0/8	26 3/8	17 6/8	3	4	Scioto County	OH	Charles E. Stambaugh	1979	6,395
131 2/8	21 6/8	21 6/8	18 6/8	4	5	Claiborne County	MS	Mike Parker	1980	6,395
131 2/8	19 7/8	22 4/8	16 3/8	4	4	Osage County	MO	Rocky Pointer	1980	6,395
131 2/8	24 3/8	24 2/8	20 2/8	5	4	Boyle County	KY	Randy Webb	1980	6,395
131 2/8	22 0/8	22 0/8	17 2/8	4	5	Des Moines County	IA	Chuck Hawkins	1981	6,395
131 2/8	22 6/8	22 6/8	17 6/8	5	6	Carter County	MT	Jamie Byrne	1981	6,395
131 2/8	21 5/8	21 6/8	18 2/8	4	4	Scott County	IA	Robert D. Hankins	1983	6,395
131 2/8	22 0/8	22 1/8	19 0/8	4	5	Barren County	KY	Tony Deckard	1983	6,395
131 2/8	21 3/8	23 1/8	14 0/8	5	5	Edmonson County	KY	Joe Shereliff	1984	6,395
131 2/8	23 4/8	24 4/8	16 5/8	6	5	Allegany County	NY	Lawrence L Davis	1984	6,395
131 2/8	21 7/8	21 1/8	18 0/8	4	4	Ogle County	IL	Jerome F. Bruns	1984	6,395
131 2/8	21 6/8	21 2/8	14 0/8	6	5	Randolph County	IN	Ronald L. Arnold	1985	6,395
131 2/8	22 1/8	22 1/8	18 3/8	6	5	La Crosse County	WI	Don C. Polivoda	1986	6,395
131 2/8	23 6/8	24 4/8	20 6/8	9	7	Pittsburg County	OK	Neil Keyes	1986	6,395
131 2/8	22 6/8	22 3/8	17 2/8	4	4	Jo Daviess County	IL	Dave Martinek	1986	6,395
131 2/8	21 6/8	22 0/8	16 0/8	4	5	Greene County	IA	Darrel Mischke	1986	6,395
131 2/8	22 7/8	22 7/8	17 4/8	4	4	Westchester County	NY	Jim Cordeira	1986	6,395
131 2/8	22 5/8	23 6/8	15 6/8	6	5	Menard County	TX	Paul Garvin Beeson	1987	6,395
131 2/8	22 0/8	22 0/8	16 2/8	4	4	Washington County	MS	Bobby R. Woods	1987	6,395
131 2/8	20 0/8	22 2/8	21 4/8	3	3	Crawford County	IL	Billy Waddell	1987	6,395
131 2/8	23 3/8	21 1/8	16 4/8	4	4	McMullen County	TX	Pete Swenson	1987	6,395
131 2/8	21 4/8	21 0/8	17 2/8	4	4	Butler County	PA	James F. Govan	1988	6,395
131 2/8	21 6/8	22 0/8	18 0/8	4	4	Walworth County	WI	Dan Peters	1988	6,395
131 2/8	22 7/8	22 0/8	18 0/8	4	4	Washington County	MS	Bobby R. Woods	1988	6,395
131 2/8	23 7/8	22 4/8	17 6/8	6	5	Waukesha County	WI	Robert Bowe	1989	6,395
131 2/8	23 0/8	22 5/8	17 2/8	6	5	Charles County	MD	Scott Cutter	1989	6,395
131 2/8	23 6/8	24 1/8	20 4/8	4	4	Hampden County	MA	Michael P. Foote	1989	6,395
131 2/8	24 5/8	25 0/8	17 0/8	5	5	Vilas County	WI	Joseph Herzog	1990	6,395
131 2/8	22 3/8	21 6/8	16 4/8	4	4	Baraga County	MI	Fred W. Mikels	1990	6,395
131 2/8	22 3/8	22 5/8	16 6/8	5	5	Walworth County	WI	Russell Van Beek	1990	6,395
131 2/8	23 4/8	23 2/8	17 2/8	4	4	Livingston County	MI	Thomas R. Dorsey II	1990	6,395
131 2/8	22 3/8	22 4/8	18 4/8	5	5	Adams County	WI	Gerry L. Riddle	1990	6,395
131 2/8	22 4/8	23 0/8	14 6/8	5	5	Forest County	WI	Donald R. Welhouse	1990	6,395
131 2/8	20 6/8	20 6/8	14 7/8	5	6	Woodford County	IL	Ronald A. DeFreitas	1990	6,395
131 2/8	19 1/8	20 1/8	17 2/8	5	5	Columbia County	WI	Bradd W. Price	1991	6,395
131 2/8	22 1/8	21 7/8	15 6/8	5	5	Forest County	WI	Thomas J. Wolf	1991	6,395
131 2/8	21 2/8	21 5/8	16 4/8	4	5	Williamson County	IL	Dale Reamy	1991	6,395
131 2/8	20 7/8	21 2/8	15 6/8	5	5	Langlade County	WI	Jerry Aulik	1991	6,395
131 2/8	21 6/8	20 6/8	16 4/8	5	5	New Castle County	DE	Dave Christian	1992	6,395
131 2/8	22 5/8	21 6/8	16 2/8	6	5	Dixon County	NE	Lane L. Ostendorf	1992	6,395
131 1/8	22 2/8	22 1/8	20 1/8	4	5	Lafayette County	WI	Bob Wand	1971	6,440

SCORE	LENGTH OF MAIN BEAM R	L	INSIDE SPREAD	NUMBER OF POINTS R	L	AREA	STATE/ PROVINCE	HUNTER'S NAME	DATE	RANK
131 1/8	25 2/8	25 6/8	18 7/8	4	5	Columbiana County	OH	Bill Henrich	1976	6,440
131 1/8	20 6/8	21 5/8	19 3/8	7	6	Neosho County	KS	Robert E. Willis	1979	6,440
131 1/8	23 1/8	21 7/8	19 1/8	4	4	Harford County	MD	Ronald D. Anderson	1980	6,440
131 1/8	22 7/8	22 7/8	17 7/8	4	5	Adams County	WI	Rich Varsho	1982	6,440
131 1/8	22 7/8	22 6/8	17 7/8	5	4	Jefferson County	WI	Scott Mill	1982	6,440
131 1/8	21 6/8	21 0/8	15 7/8	5	5	Frederick County	VA	Steven E Shoemaker	1983	6,440
131 1/8	22 2/8	22 4/8	17 1/8	4	4	Sedgwick County	KS	Delbert Antle	1983	6,440
131 1/8	24 7/8	23 7/8	18 3/8	5	6	Wright County	MN	John W. Horstman	1984	6,440
131 1/8	22 3/8	20 4/8	18 3/8	5	4	Washington County	KS	Bob Funke	1984	6,440
131 1/8	22 6/8	23 4/8	20 5/8	4	4	Suffolk County	NY	Conrad Grimm	1984	6,440
131 1/8	21 4/8	21 5/8	16 7/8	5	4	Buffalo	ALB	Russell Thornberry	1985	6,440
131 1/8	25 0/8	24 0/8	17 3/8	4	5	Saline County	KS	David Keith Grittman	1985	6,440
131 1/8	23 2/8	23 3/8	20 0/8	4	5	Morris County	NJ	Donald Howering	1985	6,440
131 1/8	21 5/8	22 4/8	15 3/8	4	5	Outagamie County	WI	Dion R Heinemeyer	1985	6,440
131 1/8	24 1/8	23 4/8	18 3/8	4	4	Latah County	ID	Howard Holmes	1985	6,440
131 1/8	22 5/8	21 0/8	20 1/8	5	5	Brown County	SD	Mark Janco	1986	6,440
131 1/8	22 5/8	21 5/8	19 4/8	5	6	Washington County	NE	H. Dan Thompson	1987	6,440
131 1/8	21 5/8	22 0/8	17 3/8	5	6	Chickasaw County	IA	David J. Kerkove	1987	6,440
131 1/8	21 5/8	21 0/8	18 3/8	4	4	Schuyler County	IL	Steve McCoy	1987	6,440
131 1/8	23 0/8	21 7/8	15 3/8	4	4	Tazewell County	IL	Robert J. Pratt	1987	6,440
131 1/8	23 2/8	22 5/8	15 3/8	6	4	Yell County	AR	Jackie Teel	1987	6,440
131 1/8	20 5/8	20 4/8	16 7/8	4	5	Bladen County	NC	Mike Wingenfeld	1988	6,440
131 1/8	19 3/8	19 6/8	15 7/8	5	5	Grand Traverse County	MI	Diane C. McPhall	1988	6,440
131 1/8	20 1/8	21 4/8	16 7/8	6	5	Oneida County	WI	Dennis Brock	1988	6,440
131 1/8	24 6/8	25 4/8	20 3/8	5	5	Morris County	NJ	Andy Zukowski	1988	6,440
131 1/8	23 7/8	23 3/8	20 1/8	5	4	Oakland County	MI	Mark DeGroat	1988	6,440
131 1/8	23 0/8	22 6/8	18 1/8	4	4	Ashland County	WI	Gary R. Jones	1988	6,440
131 1/8	21 0/8	21 2/8	16 3/8	5	5	Waukesha County	WI	Steven Schroeder	1988	6,440
131 1/8	24 4/8	24 0/8	16 7/8	5	6	Wapello County	IA	Doug Johnson	1989	6,440
131 1/8	23 0/8	22 6/8	16 5/8	5	4	Clinton County	IA	Stan Schmidt	1989	6,440
131 1/8	21 2/8	20 6/8	18 5/8	5	5	Lake County	IL	Ted Hysell	1990	6,440
131 1/8	18 6/8	19 4/8	13 5/8	5	5	Cape Girardeau County	MO	Randy Windeknecht	1990	6,440
131 1/8	21 1/8	20 3/8	15 3/8	5	5	Jasper County	IA	Gary D. Hobbs, Jr.	1990	6,440
131 1/8	23 1/8	22 0/8	17 3/8	4	4	Bay County	MI	Jim Barcia	1990	6,440
131 1/8	21 6/8	21 0/8	16 5/8	5	5	Branch County	MI	Robin M. Hutchison	1990	6,440
131 1/8	23 4/8	22 6/8	19 6/8	7	5	Franklin County	IA	Craig Eckhardt	1990	6,440
131 1/8	22 2/8	23 0/8	15 1/8	6	6	Jackson County	OH	James C. Ridge	1990	6,440
131 1/8	22 4/8	22 4/8	16 3/8	4	4	Clay County	MN	David Peckskamp	1990	6,440
131 1/8	20 3/8	20 7/8	17 3/8	5	5	Portage County	WI	Randy D. Niewiadomski	1991	6,440
131 1/8	22 3/8	21 6/8	15 1/8	4	4	Webb County	TX	Steve Leal	1991	6,440
131 1/8	23 3/8	22 7/8	16 5/8	4	4	Pike County	OH	Keith Howard	1991	6,440
131 1/8	21 2/8	21 5/8	18 7/8	5	5	Duval County	TX	Willie Esparza	1991	6,440
131 0/8	21 3/8	21 5/8	16 6/8	5	5	Flathead County	MT	Jack Whitney	1959	6,483
131 0/8	23 5/8	23 5/8	17 0/8	4	5	Scott County	IA	Ron Anderson	1966	6,483
131 0/8	21 7/8	22 0/8	14 6/8	4	4	Louisa County	IA	Larry King	1968	6,483
131 0/8	19 5/8	20 3/8	18 0/8	5	5	Sheboygan County	WI	Steve Rortvedt	1974	6,483
131 0/8	22 0/8	23 5/8	16 0/8	6	6	Union County	OH	Bill Steele	1974	6,483
131 0/8	21 7/8	21 4/8	16 2/8	4	5	Benton County	IA	Robert Kerkman	1975	6,483
131 0/8	21 3/8	21 0/8	17 0/8	5	5	Litchfield County	CT	Elmer L. Perry, Jr.	1978	6,483
131 0/8	23 6/8	23 1/8	18 2/8	5	4	Butler County	PA	John E. Fry	1979	6,483
131 0/8	19 7/8	20 3/8	15 5/8	5	6	Richland County	MT	Verne L. Cashman	1980	6,483
131 0/8	20 7/8	20 3/8	15 4/8	4	5	Watonwan County	MN	George Nasman	1980	6,483
131 0/8	20 3/8	19 5/8	16 0/8	5	5	Burleigh County	ND	Jerry Schmitcke	1980	6,483
131 0/8	19 0/8	20 5/8	16 6/8	5	5	Manitowoc County	WI	Roger B. Schroeder	1981	6,483
131 0/8	22 6/8	22 0/8	17 0/8	5	5	Dane County	WI	Jeff Bauer	1981	6,483
131 0/8	22 3/8	22 4/8	17 6/8	4	4	Fulton County	PA	John A. Williams	1981	6,483
131 0/8	19 1/8	19 1/8	14 4/8	4	4	Codington County	SD	Gerald J. Comes	1981	6,483
131 0/8	22 6/8	22 5/8	18 2/8	5	5	Grundy County	IL	Michael Marchio	1981	6,483
131 0/8	18 4/8	19 3/8	17 4/8	5	5	Berkeley County	SC	Hugh Gaskins	1982	6,483
131 0/8	22 3/8	22 3/8	20 6/8	5	5	Menominee County	MI	Theodore R. Olsen	1982	6,483
131 0/8	20 0/8	20 4/8	15 4/8	5	5	Hamilton County	IN	Larry E. Eversole	1982	6,483
131 0/8	18 3/8	17 1/8	14 4/8	6	6	Will County	IL	Richard D. Tenute	1982	6,483
131 0/8	23 6/8	21 6/8	18 0/8	4	4	Shelby County	MO	Rodney Gander	1984	6,483
131 0/8	20 6/8	21 5/8	19 0/8	5	5	Crawford County	MO	Ray Morris	1984	6,483
131 0/8	23 4/8	22 0/8	18 0/8	4	4	Ottawa County	MI	Steve Lamberts	1985	6,483
131 0/8	21 3/8	21 2/8	15 0/8	5	6	Buffalo County	WI	Gary K. Robinson	1985	6,483
131 0/8	23 1/8	23 5/8	17 0/8	5	5	Chase County	KS	Jerry Keller	1985	6,483
131 0/8	21 3/8	21 0/8	19 0/8	5	5	Dodge County	WI	Mike O'Brien	1986	6,483
131 0/8	22 1/8	22 5/8	18 4/8	4	4	Henderson County	KY	Edward Wayne Wallace	1986	6,483
131 0/8	21 6/8	21 5/8	15 6/8	5	4	Lehigh County	PA	Daniel R. Bachman	1987	6,483

SCORE	LENGTH OF R MAIN BEAM L		INSIDE SPREAD	NUMBER OF R POINTS L		AREA	STATE/ PROVINCE	HUNTER'S NAME	DATE	RANK
131 0/8	24 4/8	23 5/8	19 0/8	4	4	Gloucester County	NJ	Ken Klodnicki	1987	6,483
131 0/8	21 4/8	22 3/8	16 4/8	5	5	Chemung County	NY	Chuck L. Reynolds	1988	6,483
131 0/8	24 1/8	23 7/8	17 2/8	5	6	Ross County	OH	Tony L. Wheaton	1988	6,483
131 0/8	19 6/8	19 3/8	16 0/8	5	5	Saline County	MO	John F. Bacon	1988	6,483
131 0/8	21 2/8	20 4/8	14 6/8	5	4	Cavalier County	ND	James Sondeland	1988	6,483
131 0/8	18 3/8	18 6/8	15 0/8	5	5	Winnebago County	IL	Robert W. Shallenberger,	1989	6,483
131 0/8	21 6/8	22 1/8	18 4/8	5	6	Fayette County	WV	Michael D. King	1989	6,483
131 0/8	21 3/8	20 4/8	15 2/8	4	4	Kane County	IL	John Kloeckner	1989	6,483
131 0/8	22 4/8	25 6/8	18 6/8	7	7	Logan County	OH	David L. Katterheinrich	1989	6,483
131 0/8	22 5/8	23 7/8	17 6/8	4	5	Chautauqua County	KS	Nels Hoadley	1989	6,483
131 0/8	23 0/8	21 2/8	16 4/8	4	4	Beltrami County	MN	Rick Mikesh	1990	6,483
131 0/8	22 4/8	23 6/8	15 4/8	7	7	Monroe County	IL	Kevin Alexander	1990	6,483
131 0/8	22 0/8	21 1/8	18 2/8	4	4	Franklin County	IA	Nancy L. Kramer	1990	6,483
131 0/8	22 0/8	23 2/8	15 3/8	5	6	Russell County	AL	Dr. Daniel Morgan	1990	6,483
131 0/8	22 6/8	22 6/8	18 0/8	5	4	Washington County	WI	Jeffrey Lutz	1990	6,483
131 0/8	20 1/8	19 6/8	14 0/8	5	5	Lee County	IL	David L. Munch	1990	6,483
131 0/8	21 3/8	20 7/8	17 6/8	5	6	Putnam County	IL	Richard Kingsley	1990	6,483
131 0/8	22 0/8	22 3/8	17 1/8	5	5	Meade County	SD	Ray Glover	1990	6,483
131 0/8	19 7/8	20 1/8	15 4/8	5	5	Athens County	OH	John Edman	1991	6,483
131 0/8	20 5/8	21 0/8	16 4/8	5	4	Crawford County	IA	Steve Reetz	1991	6,483
131 0/8	22 1/8	19 5/8	18 2/8	4	5	Chippewa County	WI	John Baker	1991	6,483
130 7/8	22 3/8	23 0/8	14 1/8	4	5	Sarpy County	NE	Ronald Beranek	1966	6,532
130 7/8	21 6/8	23 1/8	15 4/8	6	5	Trempealeau County	WI	David Cater	1968	6,532
130 7/8	23 2/8	24 1/8	15 6/8	4	5	Clayton County	IA	Bryan Sears	1969	6,532
130 7/8	21 4/8	21 4/8	17 1/8	6	5	Trempealeau County	WI	Myles Keller	1975	6,532
130 7/8	20 0/8	19 0/8	17 0/8	6	5	Bedford County	VA	Bill Hurley	1977	6,532
130 7/8	23 6/8	24 4/8	16 3/8	5	4	Sangamon County	IL	Keith Stigleman	1979	6,532
130 7/8	24 6/8	24 4/8	17 5/8	5	5	Coshocton County	OH	Gary L. Fischer	1979	6,532
130 7/8	22 3/8	22 6/8	15 7/8	5	5	Mercer County	NJ	William P. Krueger	1979	6,532
130 7/8	22 2/8	21 5/8	16 5/8	5	4	Chickasaw County	IA	James Harris	1980	6,532
130 7/8	24 5/8	24 4/8	18 1/8	4	4	Saginaw County	MI	Tom Perrin	1980	6,532
130 7/8	23 1/8	22 5/8	16 5/8	5	4	Waukesha County	WI	Mark Heffner	1981	6,532
130 7/8	23 2/8	25 2/8	19 7/8	5	5	Licking County	OH	Thomas Hughes	1981	6,532
130 7/8	20 5/8	21 4/8	15 5/8	5	5	Fillmore County	MN	Dr. Eugene T. Altiere	1983	6,532
130 7/8	19 5/8	20 0/8	14 5/8	5	5	Camden County	MO	Mike Hutton	1983	6,532
130 7/8	22 3/8	22 6/8	21 2/8	7	7	Muscatine County	IA	Charles D. Linder	1984	6,532
130 7/8	22 3/8	23 0/8	16 5/8	5	4	Vermilion County	IL	Robert G. Downing	1985	6,532
130 7/8	22 6/8	22 3/8	15 7/8	4	5	Dodge County	WI	Franklin Koch	1986	6,532
130 7/8	20 7/8	21 0/8	15 5/8	4	4	Columbia County	WI	Michael J. Goza	1987	6,532
130 7/8	20 2/8	19 1/8	17 3/8	5	6	Clay County	MN	Kyle Bauman	1987	6,532
130 7/8	20 2/8	19 7/8	17 3/8	6	5	Flathead County	MT	Michael Arneson	1987	6,532
130 7/8	19 0/8	20 0/8	20 3/8	5	5	Butler County	KS	Charles A. Genter, Jr.	1987	6,532
130 7/8	22 6/8	22 4/8	20 3/8	4	4	Calhoun County	MI	Mary L. Aldrich	1987	6,532
130 7/8	23 6/8	24 0/8	20 3/8	5	5	Pike County	IL	Conel H. Rogers, Jr.	1987	6,532
130 7/8	19 6/8	20 4/8	15 3/8	6	7	Brown County	SD	Joseph J. Rieger	1987	6,532
130 7/8	24 2/8	23 2/8	19 7/8	3	4	Columbia County	WI	Norbert Wipperfurth	1988	6,532
130 7/8	22 1/8	22 1/8	17 3/8	5	5	Richland County	IL	Tony Harmon	1988	6,532
130 7/8	22 6/8	22 3/8	17 1/8	6	7	Berks County	PA	Vincent P Essig	1989	6,532
130 7/8	20 6/8	20 1/8	13 7/8	6	5	Sumner County	TN	Darrell C. Hamlett	1989	6,532
130 7/8	21 1/8	21 2/8	13 5/8	4	4	Jackson County	IL	Gerald L. Loepker	1989	6,532
130 7/8	22 1/8	22 5/8	18 5/8	6	4	Lake County	IL	Steven Derkson	1989	6,532
130 7/8	19 3/8	20 1/8	14 5/8	5	5	Ohio County	WV	Gene Petri	1990	6,532
130 7/8	24 6/8	23 1/8	14 4/8	5	6	Polk County	IA	Mitch Hosler	1990	6,532
130 7/8	21 7/8	22 7/8	16 1/8	5	5	Sutton County	TX	Monty Shropshire	1990	6,532
130 7/8	21 6/8	21 6/8	15 3/8	4	5	Waupaca County	WI	Dan Herson	1991	6,532
130 7/8	21 4/8	21 5/8	17 5/8	4	4	Ottertail County	MN	Joseph G. Reeve, DDS	1991	6,532
130 7/8	20 5/8	21 2/8	20 1/8	4	4	St. Georges de	QUE	Antonio Incollingo	1992	6,532
130 6/8	23 2/8	21 1/8	14 2/8	5	4	Dewey County	SD	Bill Dunn	1969	6,568
130 6/8	20 1/8	20 4/8	15 0/8	7	5	Rock County	WI	Mark Butzler	1978	6,568
130 6/8	22 1/8	21 7/8	17 6/8	4	5	Alfalfa County	OK	Hal Utsler	1980	6,568
130 6/8	21 0/8	21 0/8	16 0/8	5	4	Calhoun County	MI	Harold Vander Horst	1980	6,568
130 6/8	23 4/8	21 7/8	19 6/8	5	4	Washington County	MN	Joe Kohler	1981	6,568
130 6/8	22 7/8	22 3/8	18 4/8	4	4	Sullivan County	IN	Ron L. Buchanan	1982	6,568
130 6/8	22 1/8	23 0/8	19 4/8	4	4	Hayes County	NE	Randy Griffiths	1983	6,568
130 6/8	22 5/8	23 7/8	17 4/8	4	5	Shawano County	WI	Patrick G. Shulze	1984	6,568
130 6/8	21 4/8	21 7/8	17 0/8	4	5	Clarion County	PA	Gary Alan Bullers	1984	6,568
130 6/8	21 6/8	22 0/8	17 6/8	5	4	Stephenson County	IL	Eric Zimmerman	1984	6,568
130 6/8	23 4/8	23 4/8	14 6/8	4	4	Owen County	IN	Lanse C. Hale	1985	6,568
130 6/8	23 6/8	23 4/8	16 6/8	4	4	Jefferson County	WI	Ernie Turpin	1985	6,568
130 6/8	20 1/8	20 1/8	14 4/8	5	5	Ravalli County	MT	Terry See	1985	6,568

SCORE	LENGTH OF MAIN BEAM		INSIDE SPREAD	NUMBER OF POINTS		AREA	STATE/ PROVINCE	HUNTER'S NAME	DATE	RANK
	R	L		R	L					
130 6/8	24 0/8	23 4/8	19 0/8	6	5	Burleigh County	ND	Todd Hecker	1986	6,568
130 6/8	22 7/8	22 7/8	18 2/8	4	4	Lincoln County	WI	Dick Yaeger	1986	6,568
130 6/8	21 0/8	20 6/8	18 2/8	5	5	Shawnee County	KS	Ed Stadler	1986	6,568
130 6/8	20 6/8	21 5/8	16 6/8	5	5	Lake County	IL	Donald W. Hansen, Jr.	1986	6,568
130 6/8	21 2/8	23 5/8	16 5/8	6	4	Vermilion County	IL	Kenneth Gabehart	1987	6,568
130 6/8	20 2/8	22 0/8	16 6/8	4	4	Fairfield County	OH	Gary Lockwood	1987	6,568
130 6/8	20 4/8	19 6/8	15 2/8	5	6	Clayton County	IA	Arlan E. Kickbush	1987	6,568
130 6/8	22 7/8	22 0/8	18 1/8	5	6	Bent County	CO	J. Keith Chastain	1987	6,568
130 6/8	22 3/8	22 3/8	15 6/8	4	4	Houston County	MN	Todd Grissman	1988	6,568
130 6/8	21 2/8	19 5/8	16 2/8	5	5	Jones County	IA	Brian A. Jacque	1988	6,568
130 6/8	21 3/8	21 4/8	16 6/8	5	6	Fairfield County	OH	Mark McCafferty	1988	6,568
130 6/8	24 4/8	24 0/8	18 2/8	4	4	Price County	WI	William Leonard	1989	6,568
130 6/8	19 4/8	19 0/8	16 3/8	5	7	Coryell County	TX	Andy Cloud	1989	6,568
130 6/8	24 7/8	24 0/8	21 0/8	3	3	Emmet County	IA	Mike G. Cornwell	1989	6,568
130 6/8	22 7/8	23 4/8	16 0/8	6	6	Essex County	NJ	Michael Nigro	1989	6,568
130 6/8	21 3/8	20 7/8	15 4/8	4	4	Ramsey County	ND	Dale Risinger	1989	6,568
130 6/8	20 4/8	19 4/8	15 4/8	5	5	Lee County	IA	Glenn Wagner	1989	6,568
130 6/8	22 3/8	20 7/8	15 6/8	4	4	Clinton County	OH	Kevin Lee Wilson	1989	6,568
130 6/8	24 1/8	22 5/8	17 4/8	3	4	Loudoun County	VA	Kenneth M. Fleming	1989	6,568
130 6/8	23 6/8	23 3/8	17 2/8	5	5	La Porte County	IN	Charles L. Allen	1989	6,568
130 6/8	24 4/8	23 7/8	19 3/8	7	7	Phelps County	MO	Derek Carroll	1990	6,568
130 6/8	23 0/8	22 5/8	17 6/8	5	7	Jefferson County	OH	Ron McFarland	1990	6,568
130 6/8	23 3/8	22 1/8	17 7/8	7	7	Buffalo County	WI	Bill Peterson	1990	6,568
130 6/8	24 4/8	23 4/8	16 2/8	4	6	Jefferson County	OH	Lawrence Roush	1990	6,568
130 6/8	21 1/8	22 1/8	15 4/8	5	5	Scott County	KY	Michael R. Duncan	1990	6,568
130 6/8	22 3/8	21 5/8	16 4/8	5	4	Dooly County	GA	Curtis Kitchens, Jr.	1990	6,568
130 6/8	26 1/8	24 2/8	19 0/8	5	6	Dearborn County	IN	David R. "Skeeter" McKain	1990	6,568
130 6/8	25 0/8	24 3/8	19 0/8	4	5	Lake County	IL	James D. Maricle II	1991	6,568
130 6/8	21 0/8	20 7/8	18 4/8	5	5	Copiah County	MS	Chris C. Toney	1991	6,568
130 6/8	21 6/8	22 4/8	15 0/8	4	6	Gasconade County	MO	Mark Witte	1991	6,568
130 6/8	20 5/8	20 7/8	14 0/8	5	5	Trempealeau County	WI	Ed Vallee	1991	6,568
130 6/8	21 6/8	22 0/8	15 2/8	4	4	Switzerland County	IN	Joe Ruffin	1991	6,568
130 6/8	22 0/8	22 0/8	18 0/8	5	4	Missoula County	MT	Monty Moravec	1991	6,568
130 5/8	23 4/8	21 4/8	18 1/8	4	5	Roberts County	SD	Franic W. Sherer, Jr.	1965	6,614
130 5/8	21 5/8	21 3/8	16 3/8	4	4	Tuscola County	MI	Gary A. Bower	1974	6,614
130 5/8	20 7/8	21 4/8	14 5/8	5	6	Marquette County	WI	Tom Murphy	1974	6,614
130 5/8	20 6/8	20 3/8	18 1/8	5	4	Fairfield County	CT	Mark Hensel	1979	6,614
130 5/8	25 3/8	25 2/8	18 2/8	6	7	Lucas County	OH	Patrick Miller	1979	6,614
130 5/8	19 4/8	19 4/8	17 6/8	5	6	Throckmorton County	TX	Steve Fikes	1980	6,614
130 5/8	20 4/8	21 0/8	15 1/8	5	5	Montgomery County	AL	Rett Kelly	1980	6,614
130 5/8	21 4/8	22 0/8	17 2/8	4	6	Knox County	IL	Fred Miller	1981	6,614
130 5/8	21 7/8	21 5/8	18 1/8	4	4	Darlingford	MAN	Robert Hunt	1982	6,614
130 5/8	24 2/8	24 3/8	18 7/8	4	4	Orange County	NY	David Babcock	1983	6,614
130 5/8	23 4/8	23 0/8	18 5/8	4	4	Chisago County	MN	James Swing	1983	6,614
130 5/8	21 4/8	21 7/8	16 3/8	4	4	Graham County	KS	Russell Hull	1983	6,614
130 5/8	22 2/8	21 5/8	15 5/8	5	5	Frontier County	NE	Steve Cole	1984	6,614
130 5/8	22 1/8	23 1/8	18 6/8	4	5	Sarpy County	NE	Don L. Harnish	1984	6,614
130 5/8	23 0/8	22 2/8	16 1/8	4	4	Westchester County	NY	Richard Manchur	1984	6,614
130 5/8	20 0/8	20 4/8	19 2/8	4	5	Sussex County	DE	Allen Rogers	1986	6,614
130 5/8	22 0/8	22 2/8	18 3/8	4	4	Putnam County	NY	Alan Rossignol	1986	6,614
130 5/8	23 3/8	23 6/8	22 0/8	6	7	Lake County	IL	John Schnider, Jr.	1986	6,614
130 5/8	22 2/8	22 6/8	16 5/8	5	4	Rock County	WI	Greg Curl	1986	6,614
130 5/8	24 3/8	22 6/8	16 7/8	6	5	Copiah County	MS	Victor A. Youngblood	1988	6,614
130 5/8	22 1/8	21 1/8	16 7/8	5	5	Wood County	WI	Dale Kleifgen	1988	6,614
130 5/8	21 7/8	21 5/8	19 5/8	5	6	Caldwell County	KY	Boyd Smith	1988	6,614
130 5/8	21 7/8	21 4/8	14 5/8	6	5	Jackson County	WI	Ronald Aide	1988	6,614
130 5/8	22 2/8	23 5/8	18 1/8	4	4	Crawford County	IL	William David Johnson	1988	6,614
130 5/8	22 4/8	22 6/8	16 2/8	4	7	Becker County	MN	Gordon Retka	1989	6,614
130 5/8	21 0/8	20 1/8	14 5/8	4	5	Tama County	IA	Monte Read	1989	6,614
130 5/8	22 5/8	23 0/8	18 5/8	6	4	Price County	WI	Jerry J. Bedor	1989	6,614
130 5/8	21 6/8	21 2/8	18 0/8	4	5	Erie County	OH	Mark Costilow	1989	6,614
130 5/8	21 7/8	22 3/8	14 1/8	4	4	Walker County	TX	Jimmy Glass	1989	6,614
130 5/8	21 0/8	22 5/8	17 3/8	6	5	Bayfield County	WI	Jim Johnson	1989	6,614
130 5/8	23 2/8	24 1/8	18 5/8	4	4	Westchester County	NY	Gary Mammana	1989	6,614
130 5/8	23 0/8	23 5/8	16 6/8	5	4	Florence County	WI	John "Muzzy" Isajiw	1990	6,614
130 5/8	20 0/8	20 0/8	16 3/8	5	5	Wicomico County	MD	James J. Samis	1990	6,614
130 5/8	22 0/8	23 4/8	18 2/8	5	6	Leflore County	MS	Pittman Edwards	1990	6,614
130 5/8	22 1/8	23 4/8	18 3/8	4	5	Logan County	AR	T. L. Weir	1990	6,614
130 5/8	21 4/8	20 3/8	14 3/8	4	4	Ottoe County	NE	Raymond Bliss	1990	6,614
130 5/8	24 7/8	23 7/8	20 1/8	4	4	Delaware County	IA	Travis P. Heyer	1990	6,614

SCORE	LENGTH OF R MAIN BEAM L		INSIDE SPREAD	NUMBER OF R POINTS L		AREA	STATE/ PROVINCE	HUNTER'S NAME	DATE	RANK
130 5/8	22 5/8	22 4/8	16 3/8	4	5	Yankton County	SD	Tom Sonichsen	1990	6,614
130 5/8	26 4/8	21 5/8	21 1/8	4	4	Mercer County	MO	Robert Trefz, Jr.	1990	6,614
130 5/8	21 6/8	22 2/8	19 0/8	6	4	Potter County	PA	Francis J. Simmitt	1991	6,614
130 5/8	21 7/8	22 1/8	17 7/8	4	4	Greene County	PA	Dominick Barbetta	1991	6,614
130 5/8	23 0/8	22 6/8	15 3/8	4	4	Vigo County	IN	Joseph Spurgeon	1991	6,614
130 5/8	20 7/8	21 0/8	14 5/8	5	5	Marathon County	WI	Floyd D. Matteson	1991	6,614
130 5/8	20 1/8	20 5/8	14 7/8	5	5	Adair County	MO	Kelvin Koger	1991	6,614
130 5/8	20 6/8	22 3/8	15 1/8	5	5	Florence County	WI	Dan T. Leahy	1991	6,614
130 5/8	22 3/8	22 1/8	16 1/8	4	5	Wabaunsee County	KS	Kevin Townsend	1991	6,614
130 4/8	21 2/8	21 3/8	17 0/8	5	5	Allegan County	MI	Jack Yaeger	1942	6,660
130 4/8	21 0/8	20 4/8	18 2/8	5	5	Putnam County	WV	Dan Lloyd	1966	6,660
130 4/8	23 4/8	22 7/8	19 2/8	5	5	Berrien County	MI	Thomas L. Bommersbach	1978	6,660
130 4/8	23 3/8	21 1/8	17 6/8	5	5	Marquette County	WI	Gary J. Craig	1978	6,660
130 4/8	23 2/8	23 1/8	16 0/8	4	4	Harvey County	KS	Bob Stroble	1979	6,660
130 4/8	20 5/8	20 6/8	15 0/8	5	5	Louisa County	IA	Roger Gipple	1979	6,660
130 4/8	23 5/8	22 0/8	13 4/8	5	4	Cleveland County	OK	Tom Quinton	1979	6,660
130 4/8	23 5/8	22 7/8	18 2/8	6	5	Pittsburg County	OK	Bill Starry	1981	6,660
130 4/8	21 0/8	20 4/8	15 6/8	5	5	Clay County	NE	Rick Sadd	1981	6,660
130 4/8	21 5/8	22 2/8	14 6/8	5	5	Rusk County	TX	Dr. David Norman	1982	6,660
130 4/8	22 3/8	22 1/8	16 0/8	4	5	Riley County	KS	Dennis Peterson	1982	6,660
130 4/8	21 7/8	21 7/8	18 2/8	6	6	Knox County	OH	Mark E. Bretz	1983	6,660
130 4/8	22 4/8	22 2/8	17 0/8	4	4	Russell County	AL	Owen Veasey	1983	6,660
130 4/8	22 0/8	20 7/8	14 6/8	5	5	Wood County	WV	William G. Smith	1983	6,660
130 4/8	22 7/8	22 5/8	19 6/8	4	4	Hawkins County	TN	Johnny Ford	1985	6,660
130 4/8	22 6/8	22 7/8	17 2/8	4	4	Butler County	IA	Dave Bright	1985	6,660
130 4/8	23 5/8	23 3/8	18 0/8	4	4	Ionia County	MI	David L. Cooper	1986	6,660
130 4/8	21 2/8	21 0/8	17 1/8	6	5	Eaton County	MI	Westley J. Whitinger	1986	6,660
130 4/8	22 6/8	22 3/8	18 0/8	5	5	Passaic County	NJ	John G. Tucker	1987	6,660
130 4/8	21 2/8	21 6/8	18 0/8	8	6	Allen County	IN	Curtis P. Butler	1987	6,660
130 4/8	19 6/8	20 6/8	15 5/8	8	5	McHenry County	IL	Martin A. Pingel	1987	6,660
130 4/8	21 7/8	21 5/8	16 4/8	4	4	Okanogan County	WA	D. Kirk Sapp	1987	6,660
130 4/8	18 1/8	19 7/8	16 2/8	5	5	Bandera County	TX	Wayne Wilson	1988	6,660
130 4/8	22 4/8	23 5/8	13 7/8	5	5	Carroll County	OH	John M. Shockey	1988	6,660
130 4/8	22 2/8	22 6/8	18 4/8	4	4	Westchester County	NY	John Frevele	1988	6,660
130 4/8	21 0/8	21 2/8	16 2/8	4	4	Hocking County	OH	Martin R. Lohn	1988	6,660
130 4/8	21 6/8	21 0/8	15 7/8	4	5	Osage County	OK	Joe Admire	1988	6,660
130 4/8	22 5/8	21 4/8	16 6/8	4	4	Trempealeau County	WI	Richard J. Baures	1988	6,660
130 4/8	23 1/8	24 5/8	16 5/8	4	5	Kent County	MD	Ralph I Miller II	1989	6,660
130 4/8	22 4/8	23 5/8	19 4/8	5	5	Washington County	OH	Steven R. Davis	1989	6,660
130 4/8	21 7/8	22 5/8	17 6/8	4	4	Kent County	MI	Alan Ray Swendrowski	1989	6,660
130 4/8	22 0/8	21 4/8	14 5/8	12	8	Washington County	WI	Dave Klermund	1990	6,660
130 4/8	23 0/8	25 1/8	17 6/8	5	5	Crawford County	IL	Terry Sorgenfrey	1990	6,660
130 4/8	23 2/8	22 3/8	16 5/8	5	4	Rock County	MN	Al Kuehl	1990	6,660
130 4/8	21 0/8	20 7/8	18 7/8	6	6	Hughes County	OK	Tom Cartwright	1990	6,660
130 4/8	22 1/8	23 2/8	17 2/8	4	5	Logan County	WV	Kenneth Wilson	1990	6,660
130 4/8	23 5/8	22 2/8	18 1/8	5	6	Putnam County	IN	Gary Carmack	1990	6,660
130 4/8	20 6/8	22 3/8	16 0/8	6	6	Shawnee County	KS	Steve McPeek	1990	6,660
130 4/8	24 1/8	24 2/8	17 3/8	5	4	Westchester County	NY	Jerry Decarlo	1990	6,660
130 4/8	25 4/8	25 1/8	18 6/8	4	4	Madison County	IA	John Garrison	1990	6,660
130 4/8	23 6/8	23 0/8	17 4/8	4	4	Dunn County	WI	Dave Lieffort	1990	6,660
130 4/8	20 1/8	20 2/8	17 2/8	4	4	E. Feliciana Parish	LA	C. A. "Rick" Vallet	1990	6,660
130 4/8	23 2/8	23 7/8	21 4/8	4	5	Ramsey County	MN	Louie Peltier	1990	6,660
130 4/8	22 2/8	22 5/8	20 4/8	5	5	Dent County	MO	Jim Lewis	1990	6,660
130 4/8	20 7/8	19 6/8	16 4/8	7	6	Green County	WI	Tod A. Bean	1991	6,660
130 4/8	23 4/8	23 2/8	17 4/8	5	5	Alcona County	MI	Jim Thompson	1991	6,660
130 4/8	19 3/8	20 1/8	14 6/8	5	5	Pierce County	WI	Gary Seidling	1991	6,660
130 4/8	25 3/8	25 0/8	18 0/8	4	6	Woodford County	IL	Donald T. Bishop	1991	6,660
130 4/8	22 0/8	21 6/8	19 2/8	6	7	Missoula County	MT	Jim Bradford	1991	6,660
130 4/8	20 4/8	20 7/8	13 5/8	6	7	Chittick Lake	SAS	Clarence Bowers, Jr.	1991	6,660
130 4/8	23 3/8	25 0/8	16 6/8	4	4	Westchester County	NY	Thomas Iezzi	1991	6,660
130 3/8	21 2/8	20 6/8	14 1/8	5	5	Jefferson Prov. Grnds.	IN	Larry R. Smith	1966	6,711
130 3/8	18 6/8	17 3/8	15 4/8	5	6	Douglas County	NE	John Prentis	1978	6,711
130 3/8	20 1/8	20 4/8	15 3/8	6	5	Otter Tail County	MN	Dick Schmidt	1978	6,711
130 3/8	23 6/8	23 1/8	17 7/8	7	6	Adams County	IL	David Shupe	1981	6,711
130 3/8	20 2/8	20 4/8	17 7/8	5	5	Monroe County	WI	Tony P. Snow	1982	6,711
130 3/8	21 1/8	21 5/8	16 5/8	5	5	Polk County	WI	Russell Lee Johnson	1982	6,711
130 3/8	23 4/8	22 4/8	17 1/8	4	5	Garfield County	MT	Mitch Kottas	1983	6,711
130 3/8	21 5/8	21 1/8	13 5/8	5	6	Lawrence County	MO	Jim Botts	1983	6,711
130 3/8	21 2/8	21 7/8	16 7/8	4	4	Morrison County	MN	Arne Mickelberg	1983	6,711
130 3/8	22 0/8	22 0/8	18 3/8	9	8	Brown County	KS	Gerry Hertzel	1983	6,711

SCORE	LENGTH OF MAIN BEAM R	L	INSIDE SPREAD	NUMBER OF POINTS R	L	AREA	STATE/ PROVINCE	HUNTER'S NAME	DATE	RANK
130 3/8	21 3/8	22 0/8	17 3/8	5	5	Ellsworth County	KS	Jeff Dohrman	1983	6,711
130 3/8	19 6/8	19 3/8	14 3/8	5	5	Buffalo County	WI	Roger Harm	1984	6,711
130 3/8	21 4/8	22 0/8	17 1/8	5	4	Allegheny County	PA	Richard J. Blauser	1984	6,711
130 3/8	22 5/8	22 2/8	15 1/8	5	5	Becker County	MN	David Schiller	1985	6,711
130 3/8	25 1/8	23 0/8	21 0/8	4	5	Buffalo County	WI	Jeff Joslin	1985	6,711
130 3/8	24 2/8	24 0/8	20 5/8	5	4	Middlesex County	CT	James Boczar	1985	6,711
130 3/8	21 7/8	21 6/8	16 5/8	4	4	Coles County	IL	John Gossett	1986	6,711
130 3/8	23 2/8	23 1/8	15 5/8	4	4	Sussex County	NJ	Andy Chappell	1986	6,711
130 3/8	21 2/8	22 0/8	16 3/8	5	5	Goodhue County	MN	Paul Hauck	1987	6,711
130 3/8	21 4/8	22 6/8	20 2/8	7	5	Van Buren County	MI	Al Rybarski	1987	6,711
130 3/8	20 6/8	20 7/8	15 2/8	5	6	Crawford County	WI	Robert Hamann	1987	6,711
130 3/8	19 1/8	19 6/8	13 2/8	6	5	Buffalo County	WI	Jeff R. Owen	1987	6,711
130 3/8	22 3/8	22 1/8	15 4/8	6	5	Racine County	WI	Steve Holterman	1988	6,711
130 3/8	21 7/8	22 0/8	17 7/8	6	5	McHenry County	IL	Richard Sabat	1988	6,711
130 3/8	20 1/8	20 2/8	17 7/8	5	5	Brown County	SD	John Wanous	1988	6,711
130 3/8	21 7/8	23 4/8	19 5/8	5	5	Franklin County	KS	William A. Ferris	1988	6,711
130 3/8	22 2/8	22 2/8	15 1/8	4	5	Springbank Creek	ALB	David R Coupland	1989	6,711
130 3/8	20 3/8	21 5/8	15 3/8	5	5	Cherry County	NE	Randy D. Loken	1989	6,711
130 3/8	22 1/8	22 1/8	16 1/8	4	4	Mercer County	MO	Norman Folkerts	1989	6,711
130 3/8	23 0/8	22 0/8	16 5/8	5	4	Champaign County	IL	Kenny During	1989	6,711
130 3/8	25 3/8	24 1/8	18 1/8	4	4	Issaquena County	MS	Bobby R. Woods	1989	6,711
130 3/8	23 2/8	23 0/8	12 5/8	4	4	Coosa County	AL	Harry W. Strength	1989	6,711
130 3/8	22 4/8	23 2/8	22 7/8	6	4	Calgary	ALB	Richard Belbin	1990	6,711
130 3/8	21 0/8	21 1/8	14 5/8	6	6	Clay County	NE	Lonnie Goble	1990	6,711
130 3/8	23 6/8	25 1/8	16 2/8	4	5	Greene County	OH	Mike Walsh	1990	6,711
130 3/8	21 7/8	21 4/8	17 7/8	6	5	Wagoner County	OK	David M. Harris	1990	6,711
130 3/8	19 6/8	20 0/8	16 0/8	5	4	Dukes County	MA	David J. Medeiros	1990	6,711
130 3/8	24 6/8	24 2/8	20 7/8	4	4	Union County	IL	Eric P. Emmons	1990	6,711
130 3/8	23 4/8	22 7/8	18 3/8	4	5	Brooks County	TX	Larry Barton	1990	6,711
130 3/8	20 7/8	20 1/8	15 5/8	5	5	Chariton County	MO	Ben W. Gibson	1990	6,711
130 3/8	20 7/8	21 7/8	17 4/8	6	6	Belmont County	OH	Larry Michael	1991	6,711
130 3/8	22 3/8	22 0/8	16 1/8	4	5	St. Croix County	WI	Bruce Hatch	1991	6,711
130 3/8	24 6/8	24 6/8	16 2/8	6	4	Douglas County	NE	Brad Lewis	1991	6,711
130 3/8	23 7/8	24 0/8	19 4/8	4	5	King William County	VA	Marcel Joseph Lalik	1991	6,711
130 3/8	22 2/8	23 0/8	19 7/8	4	5	La Salle County	TX	Peter C. Swenson	1991	6,711
130 3/8	21 5/8	21 4/8	15 3/8	5	4	Steuben County	NY	Steven E. Dobles	1992	6,711
130 2/8	20 3/8	20 6/8	16 2/8	4	4	Yankton County	SD	Jack Begley	1959	6,757
130 2/8	26 7/8	26 3/8	17 3/8	8	6	Blue Earth County	MN	Ron Herz	1966	6,757
130 2/8	21 4/8	22 5/8	17 4/8	5	5	Montgomery County	AL	Charles D. Robinson	1976	6,757
130 2/8	16 0/8	20 3/8	18 6/8	6	6	Carroll County	IL	Arthur Heinze	1977	6,757
130 2/8	20 4/8	21 3/8	17 4/8	5	5	Pine County	MN	Ron Larsen	1978	6,757
130 2/8	21 5/8	21 7/8	15 0/8	6	5	Johnson County	IN	Ronnie L. Fiesbeck	1979	6,757
130 2/8	23 3/8	24 0/8	17 0/8	5	4	Washburn County	WI	William "Mike" Johnson	1980	6,757
130 2/8	20 3/8	20 7/8	13 4/8	4	5	Stanley County	SD	Richard Ray	1980	6,757
130 2/8	21 5/8	21 6/8	17 6/8	4	4	Saginaw County	MI	Charles R. Harper	1980	6,757
130 2/8	21 3/8	20 7/8	20 0/8	5	5	Allegheny County	PA	Thomas Fitz	1981	6,757
130 2/8	21 1/8	21 5/8	14 4/8	6	6	Dane County	WI	Thomas B. Gannon	1982	6,757
130 2/8	22 0/8	21 2/8	19 5/8	7	5	St. Louis County	MO	Jack Repp	1982	6,757
130 2/8	22 0/8	21 0/8	20 2/8	5	6	Jefferson County	KS	Wayne Wenger	1983	6,757
130 2/8	22 1/8	23 1/8	20 2/8	4	5	Cheyenne County	NE	Marvin Clyncke	1983	6,757
130 2/8	21 1/8	21 6/8	16 0/8	4	4	Dodge County	WI	Steve Muche	1984	6,757
130 2/8	21 6/8	21 7/8	18 6/8	5	4	Jackson County	MI	Bruce A. Andrews	1984	6,757
130 2/8	21 7/8	21 2/8	16 4/8	5	6	Baltimore County	MD	Jay Holstein	1984	6,757
130 2/8	20 6/8	20 7/8	14 4/8	5	5	Clay County	MN	Randy Blankenship	1985	6,757
130 2/8	20 7/8	20 4/8	16 2/8	5	4	Shawnee County	KS	Randy Hildreth	1985	6,757
130 2/8	22 5/8	23 2/8	16 0/8	5	5	Licking County	OH	Glenn Dale Anderson	1986	6,757
130 2/8	23 3/8	23 0/8	14 7/8	5	7	St. Croix County	WI	Mike Cain	1986	6,757
130 2/8	22 2/8	22 4/8	22 6/8	5	4	Lincoln County	OK	Ronnie J. Wolfe	1986	6,757
130 2/8	20 1/8	20 5/8	16 2/8	5	4	Clay County	IA	Gene A. Hall	1987	6,757
130 2/8	20 4/8	19 6/8	14 0/8	5	5	Wright County	MN	Brett Jarmuzek	1987	6,757
130 2/8	25 2/8	26 2/8	15 1/8	7	4	Saline County	MO	Mike Beach	1988	6,757
130 2/8	23 0/8	22 4/8	16 0/8	4	4	Sussex County	VA	Barry N. Hogge	1988	6,757
130 2/8	23 0/8	23 2/8	19 4/8	4	5	Fayette County	IA	Hugh Wright	1988	6,757
130 2/8	24 1/8	24 0/8	18 4/8	4	4	Forest County	WI	Jeff L. Steede	1988	6,757
130 2/8	24 0/8	23 7/8	18 0/8	4	5	Columbia County	WI	Dennis L. Simonson	1988	6,757
130 2/8	24 1/8	23 4/8	16 0/8	6	5	Berkshire County	MA	Dale Martin	1988	6,757
130 2/8	22 4/8	22 7/8	18 0/8	4	4	Hardin County	KY	Donald J. Vittitow, Jr.	1988	6,757
130 2/8	21 1/8	21 4/8	17 2/8	4	4	Lake County	IL	Carl Spaeth	1988	6,757
130 2/8	20 4/8	19 3/8	15 0/8	5	5	Osage County	OK	Dean Gratias	1989	6,757
130 2/8	20 4/8	20 2/8	13 6/8	4	4	Winneshiek County	IA	Kurt W. Stuebs	1989	6,757

SCORE	LENGTH OF R MAIN BEAM L		INSIDE SPREAD	NUMBER OF R POINTS L		AREA	STATE/ PROVINCE	HUNTER'S NAME	DATE	RANK
130 2/8	21 5/8	22 1/8	18 6/8	5	5	Warren County	OH	Sam Y. Perone	1989	6,757
130 2/8	25 2/8	23 5/8	21 2/8	4	5	Jasper County	IL	Todd Hewing	1989	6,757
130 2/8	19 4/8	19 4/8	14 6/8	5	5	Menard County	IL	Dennis P. McCormick	1989	6,757
130 2/8	20 3/8	20 4/8	13 6/8	5	4	Traill County	ND	Tim Pederson	1990	6,757
130 2/8	21 7/8	22 6/8	17 0/8	4	4	Genesee County	MI	Billie R. Nash, Jr.	1991	6,757
130 2/8	20 5/8	21 4/8	14 2/8	6	6	Leflore County	MS	Brian Neely	1991	6,757
130 2/8	23 1/8	22 1/8	16 3/8	7	5	Jefferson County	OH	Kennith Mullins, Sr.	1991	6,757
130 2/8	23 0/8	22 1/8	17 2/8	5	5	New Haven County	CT	Gene J. Bialek	1991	6,757
130 2/8	20 6/8	21 4/8	17 4/8	5	5	Barry County	MI	Steve G. Norris	1991	6,757
130 2/8	22 2/8	22 4/8	14 0/8	5	5	Oconto County	WI	Dennis R. Ullman	1991	6,757
130 2/8	20 5/8	22 3/8	18 0/8	4	5	Devon	ALB	Mike Mitchell	1991	6,757
130 2/8	22 2/8	22 1/8	15 5/8	5	6	Atascosa County	TX	R. G. Stein	1991	6,757
130 2/8	21 3/8	19 5/8	14 4/8	5	5	Todd County	KY	Larry Ross	1992	6,757
130 1/8	24 4/8	25 7/8	19 7/8	4	3	Waupaca County	WI	John Schoenike	1952	6,804
130 1/8	22 5/8	21 6/8	16 7/8	5	5	Oneida County	WI	Fred Felbab	1964	6,804
130 1/8	22 6/8	24 4/8	17 4/8	6	5	Morrison County	MN	Stephen L. Marklund	1964	6,804
130 1/8	21 4/8	21 4/8	20 1/8	4	4	Garden County	NE	Larry Pierce	1976	6,804
130 1/8	20 4/8	21 4/8	13 7/8	5	5	Plymouth County	IA	Cash N. Howe	1978	6,804
130 1/8	25 2/8	25 4/8	16 0/8	5	5	Edwards County	KS	Matthew W. Schartz	1979	6,804
130 1/8	19 4/8	19 3/8	15 3/8	5	5	Warren County	MO	David A. Wilson	1980	6,804
130 1/8	23 0/8	21 7/8	17 7/8	4	4	Vernon County	WI	Michael R. Gregory	1981	6,804
130 1/8	20 4/8	20 3/8	16 3/8	4	4	Tazewell County	IL	Gary Joe Smith	1982	6,804
130 1/8	21 1/8	21 0/8	16 7/8	4	5	Perry County	OH	Michael W. Wintgens	1982	6,804
130 1/8	19 3/8	20 6/8	17 5/8	5	4	Muscatine County	IA	Brian Nebergall	1983	6,804
130 1/8	23 4/8	21 6/8	15 6/8	6	5	Clay County	MN	Joe Lahlum	1983	6,804
130 1/8	22 6/8	24 6/8	15 5/8	5	5	Door County	WI	Philip K. Riddle	1984	6,804
130 1/8	22 5/8	24 4/8	21 3/8	4	4	Hamilton County	IL	Richard Phelps	1984	6,804
130 1/8	22 5/8	22 5/8	19 1/8	4	5	Powell County	MT	Danny Moore	1984	6,804
130 1/8	23 1/8	22 3/8	18 5/8	4	4	Hardin County	OH	John B. Britton	1985	6,804
130 1/8	23 7/8	23 4/8	17 6/8	5	6	Montgomery County	MD	Donald Stancil Waters, Jr	1985	6,804
130 1/8	23 0/8	22 6/8	16 3/8	4	5	Anderson County	TN	Harold D. Tackett	1985	6,804
130 1/8	24 4/8	23 0/8	16 1/8	5	4	Calhoun County	MI	David K. McWhorter	1985	6,804
130 1/8	24 2/8	23 2/8	20 1/8	4	4	Pepin County	WI	Michael J. Schmidt	1985	6,804
130 1/8	24 5/8	23 4/8	18 6/8	4	5	Dane County	WI	Thomas J. Sheahan	1986	6,804
130 1/8	21 7/8	21 1/8	17 4/8	5	6	Polk County	TX	O. H. Campbell, Jr.	1987	6,804
130 1/8	20 6/8	20 5/8	16 5/8	5	5	Price County	WI	Simon Britts	1987	6,804
130 1/8	21 0/8	21 3/8	15 7/8	5	5	Mason County	WV	Ed Jefferson	1987	6,804
130 1/8	22 0/8	21 5/8	16 3/8	4	4	Holmes County	OH	Myron A. Hershberger	1987	6,804
130 1/8	18 2/8	19 4/8	16 1/8	5	5	Fayette County	PA	Scott Murray	1988	6,804
130 1/8	23 6/8	23 3/8	18 1/8	4	4	Gloucester County	NJ	William D. Latham, Jr.	1988	6,804
130 1/8	20 5/8	20 4/8	17 1/8	4	5	Price County	WI	Ralph Trzinski	1988	6,804
130 1/8	20 1/8	20 2/8	15 3/8	5	5	Clay County	MN	Brian Winter	1988	6,804
130 1/8	21 7/8	22 7/8	18 3/8	6	5	Hughes County	OK	Tom L. Cartwright	1989	6,804
130 1/8	23 1/8	22 4/8	18 1/8	5	4	Chariton County	MO	David L. Williams	1989	6,804
130 1/8	21 6/8	20 7/8	17 7/8	5	5	Kanawha County	WV	William H. Baldwin	1989	6,804
130 1/8	24 1/8	22 6/8	15 5/8	5	5	Brown County	MN	Gary Braun	1989	6,804
130 1/8	23 5/8	23 3/8	16 2/8	4	5	McMullen County	TX	W. Walker Lowry, Jr.	1989	6,804
130 1/8	20 4/8	20 4/8	17 5/8	4	4	Eau Claire County	WI	Steve Julson	1989	6,804
130 1/8	23 0/8	24 5/8	17 6/8	5	7	McDonough County	IL	Roger Wayne Jackson	1989	6,804
130 1/8	22 7/8	22 5/8	20 4/8	6	4	Albany County	NY	Skip Reilly	1989	6,804
130 1/8	23 4/8	22 3/8	18 6/8	6	5	Athens County	OH	Ron Tank, Jr.	1989	6,804
130 1/8	23 0/8	22 7/8	16 5/8	6	6	Bremer County	IA	Henry J. Rodrique	1989	6,804
130 1/8	22 2/8	23 2/8	15 1/8	5	5	Baldwin County	GA	Randy W. Wilson	1990	6,804
130 1/8	23 5/8	22 7/8	15 5/8	5	5	Morrison County	MN	Richard Jeska	1990	6,804
130 1/8	22 6/8	22 1/8	18 7/8	4	4	Dallas County	IA	John Flies	1990	6,804
130 1/8	21 1/8	20 6/8	18 3/8	5	5	Dodge County	WI	Randy Grulke	1990	6,804
130 1/8	22 3/8	21 2/8	16 2/8	4	6	Dane County	WI	John Schulz	1991	6,804
130 1/8	22 1/8	21 7/8	14 7/8	5	5	Webster County	MO	Link Stevens	1991	6,804
130 1/8	22 6/8	24 5/8	17 7/8	4	5	Macon County	IL	Dave Meyer	1991	6,804
130 1/8	23 1/8	21 4/8	15 3/8	6	6	Moultrie County	IL	Bruce Hill	1991	6,804
130 1/8	21 0/8	21 4/8	15 7/8	5	5	Grand Traverse County	MI	Bill Alpers	1991	6,804
130 1/8	21 1/8	19 3/8	19 1/8	5	5	Fillmore County	MN	Kevin Joyce	1992	6,804
130 0/8	23 4/8	23 5/8	19 0/8	4	4	Wicomico County	MD	Donald J. Brown	1956	6,853
130 0/8	21 0/8	19 3/8	17 4/8	5	4	Roberts County	SD	Byron Siegel	1962	6,853
130 0/8	22 2/8	22 5/8	18 6/8	4	5	Berrien County	MI	Leon L. Williams	1965	6,853
130 0/8	20 2/8	20 6/8	15 0/8	5	5	Bucks County	PA	Don Fitting	1967	6,853
130 0/8	21 3/8	21 4/8	19 0/8	5	5	Vanderburgh County	IN	Scott E. Webster	1973	6,853
130 0/8	24 3/8	25 0/8	18 6/8	6	5	Pope County	AR	Douglas M. Atchley	1975	6,853
130 0/8	20 2/8	21 0/8	14 6/8	5	5	Stanly County	NC	Steve Efird	1978	6,853
130 0/8	22 4/8	22 2/8	19 0/8	4	4	Licking County	OH	James E. Sorg	1978	6,853

SCORE	LENGTH OF MAIN BEAM		INSIDE SPREAD	NUMBER OF POINTS		AREA	STATE/ PROVINCE	HUNTER'S NAME	DATE	RANK
	R	L		R	L					
130 0/8	22 0/8	21 4/8	17 0/8	4	4	Will County	IL	Terry Marcukaitis	1979	6,853
130 0/8	23 2/8	24 2/8	18 0/8	4	4	Onondaga County	NY	Jack Sipfle	1980	6,853
130 0/8	21 7/8	21 2/8	16 1/8	6	6	Polk County	WI	Paul Petersen	1981	6,853
130 0/8	23 0/8	24 2/8	19 6/8	4	4	Westchester County	NY	Richard T. Burke	1982	6,853
130 0/8	23 4/8	23 3/8	15 4/8	5	5	McDonough County	IL	John E. Whalon	1982	6,853
130 0/8	24 1/8	23 6/8	13 6/8	5	4	Scott County	VA	Charles William Moore	1983	6,853
130 0/8	20 5/8	21 0/8	15 4/8	5	6	Fond du Lac County	WI	Tom Dickmann	1983	6,853
130 0/8	20 0/8	21 4/8	18 0/8	5	5	Kenosha County	WI	Ted Hysell	1983	6,853
130 0/8	25 1/8	25 2/8	17 6/8	6	7	Ottawa County	KS	Rod Ponton	1983	6,853
130 0/8	20 3/8	18 7/8	17 4/8	6	5	Perkins County	SD	H. Melvin Dutton	1983	6,853
130 0/8	22 7/8	21 6/8	18 0/8	6	7	Sauk County	WI	Duane Olson	1984	6,853
130 0/8	21 0/8	21 1/8	17 4/8	4	4	Rock County	WI	DaLee E. Applebee	1984	6,853
130 0/8	21 3/8	21 5/8	17 0/8	4	4	Marinette County	WI	Tom Hirte	1984	6,853
130 0/8	21 1/8	20 5/8	15 4/8	5	5	Shawnee County	KS	Roxie Kelly	1984	6,853
130 0/8	22 2/8	24 1/8	19 0/8	4	4	Orange County	NY	Richard F Kaufmann	1985	6,853
130 0/8	23 0/8	23 3/8	17 4/8	5	5	Minnehaha County	SD	Rick Rang	1985	6,853
130 0/8	19 2/8	21 7/8	16 0/8	4	5	Sarpy County	NE	Randy Stitt	1986	6,853
130 0/8	21 5/8	21 4/8	20 0/8	4	4	Roberts County	SD	Jeffery A. Nelson	1986	6,853
130 0/8	22 3/8	23 4/8	16 1/8	6	6	Charlevoix County	MI	Richard K. Arnold	1987	6,853
130 0/8	19 0/8	19 4/8	14 4/8	6	5	Clay County	MN	Phillip Reiling	1987	6,853
130 0/8	22 1/8	23 0/8	17 0/8	5	4	Dane County	WI	Gerald Westphal	1988	6,853
130 0/8	22 6/8	22 0/8	14 4/8	5	4	Pike County	OH	Larry Cornett	1988	6,853
130 0/8	20 5/8	20 2/8	15 6/8	5	5	Benzie County	MI	David Acha	1989	6,853
130 0/8	22 6/8	22 3/8	20 6/8	4	5	Wayne County	NY	Dallas Sumner	1989	6,853
130 0/8	22 0/8	23 2/8	19 0/8	4	4	Queensville	ONT	Paul Vaicunas	1989	6,853
130 0/8	21 6/8	21 2/8	16 2/8	6	6	Hampshire County	MA	Stephen E. Drumm	1989	6,853
130 0/8	21 5/8	21 3/8	17 6/8	4	4	Crawford County	IL	Bill Waddell	1989	6,853
130 0/8	19 7/8	20 0/8	16 2/8	5	5	Iron County	WI	Perry V. Elsemore	1990	6,853
130 0/8	22 2/8	22 5/8	18 6/8	5	4	Will County	IL	Scott A. Siuda	1990	6,853
130 0/8	21 2/8	21 1/8	17 0/8	5	4	Douglas County	WI	Ron Roen	1990	6,853
130 0/8	24 5/8	23 4/8	18 4/8	4	5	Custer County	NE	Rick Thaden	1991	6,853
130 0/8	20 5/8	21 4/8	17 4/8	5	5	Isanti County	MN	Rick Bryant	1991	6,853
130 0/8	19 2/8	19 5/8	15 4/8	5	5	Meeker County	MN	Lee R. Peterson	1991	6,853
130 0/8	21 2/8	21 5/8	21 0/8	4	4	Saline County	MO	David L. Hedgpeth	1991	6,853
130 0/8	23 0/8	22 6/8	17 2/8	4	4	Jasper County	IL	Jim Hunsaker	1991	6,853
130 0/8	26 2/8	27 0/8	18 0/8	4	5	Logan County	CO	Pete Lauer	1991	6,853
130 0/8	22 7/8	22 0/8	17 2/8	4	4	Muskegon County	MI	Dwayne Levandowski	1991	6,853
130 0/8	21 5/8	21 3/8	19 4/8	5	5	La Salle County	TX	Michael Corley	1991	6,853
129 7/8	23 6/8	21 6/8	18 0/8	5	5	Winnebago County	IL	Leo M. Ruefer, Jr.	1958	6,899
129 7/8	21 7/8	22 0/8	16 5/8	4	4	Monroe County	WI	Jeff Skrade	1962	6,899
129 7/8	23 3/8	23 2/8	16 5/8	5	6	Allegan County	MI	Clayton Foster	1964	6,899
129 7/8	23 0/8	21 7/8	15 1/8	5	5	Jefferson County	KS	Delmar Tucking, Jr.	1966	6,899
129 7/8	22 3/8	22 6/8	20 7/8	4	4	Ashland County	WI	William Sutton	1968	6,899
129 7/8	19 7/8	19 3/8	20 2/8	5	5	Vilas County	WI	Art Heinze	1970	6,899
129 7/8	19 2/8	19 5/8	15 3/8	5	5	Columbia County	WI	Jay Rosendick	1970	6,899
129 7/8	22 4/8	21 7/8	17 1/8	4	4	Ogle County	IL	Henry E. Zimmerman	1970	6,899
129 7/8	20 3/8	20 6/8	15 5/8	6	5	Cottonwood County	MN	Gene Gustafson	1977	6,899
129 7/8	21 5/8	22 2/8	17 1/8	5	5	Sauk County	WI	Clair E. Keylock	1977	6,899
129 7/8	21 6/8	22 4/8	20 5/8	4	4	Tioga County	NY	Arthur Schumacher	1977	6,899
129 7/8	19 7/8	20 4/8	16 5/8	5	5	Adair County	IA	Wallace R. Waddell	1980	6,899
129 7/8	22 0/8	21 5/8	17 3/8	4	4	Hardin County	IA	Randall Martinson	1980	6,899
129 7/8	24 6/8	24 6/8	17 3/8	5	5	Oneida County	WI	Tom Knudsen	1981	6,899
129 7/8	20 6/8	21 1/8	18 7/8	6	6	Kingman County	KS	Kevin Wasson	1981	6,899
129 7/8	22 5/8	22 4/8	17 2/8	6	5	Berkeley County	SC	Hugh Gaskins	1983	6,899
129 7/8	20 5/8	20 7/8	16 1/8	4	5	Calumet County	WI	Bill Mertens	1983	6,899
129 7/8	21 5/8	21 2/8	15 7/8	5	5	Waupaca County	WI	William Millard	1984	6,899
129 7/8	21 2/8	22 7/8	17 1/8	4	4	Rock County	WI	Richard A. Viken	1984	6,899
129 7/8	20 6/8	20 4/8	14 7/8	4	5	Butler County	KS	Clifford Rogers	1984	6,899
129 7/8	20 6/8	21 1/8	14 5/8	6	5	De Kalb County	IN	Jay Vance	1987	6,899
129 7/8	21 4/8	21 3/8	17 1/8	6	6	Pepin County	WI	Shaughn Laehn	1987	6,899
129 7/8	22 4/8	23 0/8	17 1/8	5	5	Loudoun County	VA	Larry Bassett	1987	6,899
129 7/8	19 7/8	20 1/8	17 5/8	6	5	Washington County	MO	Jim Emily	1987	6,899
129 7/8	20 6/8	21 6/8	16 5/8	5	4	Walsh County	ND	Terry L. Lund	1988	6,899
129 7/8	25 6/8	25 4/8	15 5/8	4	5	Lamar County	GA	Joel Vaughn, Jr.	1989	6,899
129 7/8	20 1/8	20 3/8	17 1/8	5	5	Ravalli County	MT	Carol Karen Miller	1989	6,899
129 7/8	22 4/8	22 7/8	18 4/8	5	5	Winona County	MN	Douglas Kerska	1989	6,899
129 7/8	21 4/8	21 4/8	17 4/8	5	6	Allegheny County	PA	Rich Pavicic	1989	6,899
129 7/8	22 4/8	23 5/8	20 1/8	5	5	Franklin County	MA	John D. O'Brien, Jr.	1989	6,899
129 7/8	23 3/8	23 2/8	19 5/8	6	6	Burnett County	WI	Kent Bassett	1990	6,899
129 7/8	24 0/8	22 5/8	17 1/8	5	5	Camden County	MO	Scott Whitlock	1990	6,899

Score	Length of Main Beam R	Length of Main Beam L	Inside Spread	Number of Points R	Number of Points L	Area	State/ Province	Hunter's Name	Date	Rank
129 7/8	22 2/8	22 3/8	14 5/8	5	5	Waldo County	ME	Joseph L. Hall	1990	6,899
129 7/8	22 2/8	21 4/8	16 7/8	4	5	Chippewa County	WI	Jon D. Schroeder	1991	6,899
129 7/8	22 1/8	22 7/8	14 7/8	6	6	Scott County	MN	Lyle E. Krueger	1991	6,899
129 7/8	21 2/8	20 0/8	13 5/8	5	5	Douglas County	WI	Darren Lee	1991	6,899
129 7/8	22 0/8	21 1/8	14 5/8	5	4	Forest County	WI	Brent M. Kadubek	1991	6,899
129 7/8	21 0/8	21 6/8	15 4/8	6	5	Henry County	VA	Mike Weaver	1991	6,899
129 7/8	23 0/8	21 3/8	14 3/8	8	8	Cherokee County	OK	Norman Gale Culver	1991	6,899
129 7/8	21 5/8	21 0/8	16 1/8	5	6	Kanabec County	MN	Dale M. Anderson	1992	6,899
129 6/8	19 5/8	20 7/8	16 2/8	5	6	Adams County	IL	Mel Powell	1964	6,939
129 6/8	20 2/8	18 0/8	17 2/8	5	5	Johnson County	WY	Jim Bartz	1969	6,939
129 6/8	22 5/8	22 2/8	20 2/8	7	5	Morrison County	MN	Robert E. Nordstrom	1973	6,939
129 6/8	22 2/8	21 0/8	17 0/8	5	4	Lee County	IA	Jim Bohenkamp	1974	6,939
129 6/8	21 4/8	22 0/8	20 0/8	4	5	Washtenaw County	MI	Richard A. Hollo	1980	6,939
129 6/8	21 1/8	22 7/8	17 4/8	6	5	Prince Georges County	MD	Russell A. Nichols	1980	6,939
129 6/8	23 6/8	23 2/8	16 4/8	4	4	Lawrence County	OH	Ronald E. Clark	1981	6,939
129 6/8	24 2/8	23 0/8	15 7/8	6	5	Lawrence County	OH	Randy Gilmore	1982	6,939
129 6/8	22 1/8	22 1/8	15 6/8	4	4	Gallia County	OH	Jack Satterfield, Jr.	1982	6,939
129 6/8	22 5/8	23 1/8	16 6/8	4	4	Jo Daviess County	IL	Tom Smith	1982	6,939
129 6/8	20 5/8	22 2/8	19 0/8	4	4	Juneau County	WI	Larry Southworth	1983	6,939
129 6/8	21 4/8	22 1/8	15 4/8	5	5	Calhoun County	MI	Dick Coon	1983	6,939
129 6/8	18 6/8	18 5/8	21 2/8	7	5	Lake County	MI	James H. Wichman	1984	6,939
129 6/8	22 1/8	22 0/8	20 2/8	4	4	Will County	IL	Richard 'Rick' Gagle	1984	6,939
129 6/8	22 3/8	22 0/8	15 2/8	5	5	Morrison County	MN	Richard W. Gamache	1984	6,939
129 6/8	22 1/8	21 1/8	17 2/8	5	5	Hunterdon County	NJ	Thaddeus A. Tykarsky III	1984	6,939
129 6/8	23 1/8	23 0/8	16 4/8	7	4	Grant County	WI	Jim Johnson	1985	6,939
129 6/8	20 2/8	20 5/8	14 4/8	5	5	White County	AR	Robbie Snowden	1986	6,939
129 6/8	24 7/8	23 0/8	16 6/8	5	5	Jefferson County	WI	David Springer, Jr.	1986	6,939
129 6/8	23 4/8	23 1/8	15 4/8	4	4	Scott County	KY	Michael R. Duncan	1986	6,939
129 6/8	22 5/8	23 0/8	19 2/8	5	5	Mercer County	NJ	Frank Prato	1986	6,939
129 6/8	22 0/8	21 6/8	17 0/8	4	4	Racine County	WI	Denis Sommers	1987	6,939
129 6/8	21 5/8	20 5/8	21 4/8	4	5	Calhoun County	MI	John P. Walters	1987	6,939
129 6/8	20 6/8	19 5/8	15 5/8	5	6	Kane County	IL	Thomas E. Prosser	1987	6,939
129 6/8	23 3/8	23 1/8	19 0/8	4	4	Wicomico County	MD	H. Noel Dykes, Jr.	1987	6,939
129 6/8	21 2/8	21 3/8	17 6/8	4	4	St. Charles County	MO	Larry Doe	1988	6,939
129 6/8	23 7/8	22 5/8	19 0/8	4	4	Howard County	MD	Leon Lantz II	1988	6,939
129 6/8	24 7/8	22 5/8	16 1/8	6	7	Ellsworth County	KS	Steven Siemsen	1988	6,939
129 6/8	20 4/8	20 6/8	17 0/8	5	4	Vermilion County	IL	Alan E. Cessna	1988	6,939
129 6/8	22 2/8	22 1/8	14 2/8	7	5	Taylor County	WI	Glen Ogle	1989	6,939
129 6/8	22 7/8	21 4/8	15 6/8	5	5	Kalamazoo County	MI	Mark Van Dalen	1989	6,939
129 6/8	23 1/8	22 2/8	19 4/8	5	5	Allegany County	MD	Gary Loar	1990	6,939
129 6/8	22 7/8	22 7/8	19 0/8	5	5	Tompkins County	NY	David E. Barnes	1990	6,939
129 6/8	21 3/8	20 6/8	17 0/8	5	5	Wayne County	NY	Rick Fox	1990	6,939
129 6/8	22 6/8	22 4/8	16 0/8	4	4	Douglas County	WI	Gary W. Holcombe	1990	6,939
129 6/8	24 0/8	22 1/8	14 2/8	4	4	Monona County	IA	Dennis Rush	1990	6,939
129 6/8	21 6/8	22 4/8	17 6/8	5	5	Powell County	MT	Roberta R. Culp	1990	6,939
129 6/8	22 7/8	25 2/8	20 1/8	4	5	Hardin County	KY	Donald V. Hitow, Jr.	1991	6,939
129 6/8	21 6/8	21 2/8	17 6/8	4	5	Crawford County	MO	Monty R. Cooper	1991	6,939
129 6/8	21 0/8	20 2/8	16 0/8	5	5	Camden County	MO	Ronald J. Paskon	1991	6,939
129 6/8	20 5/8	21 1/8	18 3/8	5	6	Morgan County	IN	Joe Ferran	1991	6,939
129 6/8	21 7/8	23 3/8	18 0/8	4	4	Kent County	MD	Lewin S. Blackiston III	1991	6,939
129 6/8	21 3/8	20 4/8	18 6/8	4	4	Goliad County	TX	Gil Baumgarten	1991	6,939
129 6/8	20 5/8	21 1/8	15 4/8	6	5	Warren County	MS	Billy Bryant	1991	6,939
129 6/8	20 5/8	21 1/8	18 1/8	5	5	Henry County	VA	Mike Weaver	1991	6,939
129 6/8	22 3/8	23 6/8	18 0/8	5	4	Cookstown	ONT	Dan Hutchinson	1992	6,939
129 5/8	23 2/8	24 0/8	17 6/8	4	4	Taylor County	WV	Jimmie R. Auvil	1959	6,985
129 5/8	22 5/8	22 1/8	20 1/8	5	5	Cowley County	KS	Charles O'Daniel	1966	6,985
129 5/8	21 6/8	21 2/8	18 5/8	5	4	Waushara County	WI	Roger D. Johnson	1979	6,985
129 5/8	22 4/8	23 5/8	17 3/8	6	5	Ontario County	NY	Richard Rockefeller	1979	6,985
129 5/8	20 7/8	20 4/8	17 1/8	4	4	Fillmore County	MN	Robert Meyer	1981	6,985
129 5/8	23 0/8	23 2/8	19 5/8	4	5	Ontario County	NY	Ronald Molinari	1981	6,985
129 5/8	22 4/8	22 3/8	18 6/8	4	5	Lucas County	OH	James L. Davies	1982	6,985
129 5/8	20 6/8	19 2/8	13 7/8	5	5	Traill County	ND	Willis Mueller	1982	6,985
129 5/8	21 0/8	20 2/8	18 7/8	6	5	Scott County	KY	Ronnie Jacobs	1983	6,985
129 5/8	23 2/8	23 4/8	21 5/8	5	4	Dorchester County	MD	Thomas R. Pohuski	1984	6,985
129 5/8	23 4/8	23 4/8	15 1/8	4	4	Washington County	MN	Patrick F. Dolan	1984	6,985
129 5/8	24 4/8	26 0/8	16 5/8	4	4	Livingston County	NY	Christopher D. Walp	1985	6,985
129 5/8	20 6/8	21 4/8	19 0/8	6	6	Williams County	OH	Steven Reader	1985	6,985
129 5/8	22 6/8	20 3/8	17 6/8	4	6	Madison County	IL	Mark A. Thompson	1985	6,985
129 5/8	20 1/8	21 4/8	19 1/8	4	4	Henderson County	KY	Ken McKay	1986	6,985
129 5/8	22 3/8	21 5/8	17 1/8	5	4	Pike County	MO	Ray Hatfield	1986	6,985

SCORE	LENGTH OF MAIN BEAM R	LENGTH OF MAIN BEAM L	INSIDE SPREAD	NUMBER OF POINTS R	NUMBER OF POINTS L	AREA	STATE/ PROVINCE	HUNTER'S NAME	DATE	RANK
129 5/8	23 0/8	22 3/8	19 1/8	4	4	Montgomery County	IN	Douglas P. Kellerman	1986	6,985
129 5/8	22 4/8	23 1/8	18 7/8	5	5	Mineral County	WV	Brad K. Gentzler	1986	6,985
129 5/8	21 6/8	22 0/8	16 3/8	5	4	Somerset County	NJ	Steven Niedzielski	1986	6,985
129 5/8	22 7/8	23 6/8	18 5/8	4	4	Somerset County	NJ	Steven J. Niedzielski	1987	6,985
129 5/8	23 1/8	23 0/8	18 3/8	5	5	Forest County	WI	Mark Schad	1987	6,985
129 5/8	21 3/8	21 1/8	15 7/8	5	4	Franklin Municipality	MAN	James Sondeland	1988	6,985
129 5/8	19 4/8	21 2/8	17 5/8	4	4	Schuyler County	IL	Charles W. Trone, Jr.	1988	6,985
129 5/8	18 3/8	16 4/8	17 5/8	5	5	Custer County	NE	James J. Spanel	1989	6,985
129 5/8	21 7/8	22 0/8	16 6/8	6	4	Northampton County	VA	Jeffre L. Jones	1989	6,985
129 5/8	23 1/8	22 4/8	16 7/8	5	5	Dane County	WI	Robert Bischel	1989	6,985
129 5/8	21 1/8	21 1/8	17 1/8	5	5	Dane County	WI	Paul T. Ovadal	1989	6,985
129 5/8	21 6/8	21 3/8	16 1/8	4	5	Kossuth County	IA	Kevin Peterson	1989	6,985
129 5/8	21 6/8	21 2/8	15 6/8	5	6	Callaway County	MO	Gene Nelson	1989	6,985
129 5/8	22 7/8	23 4/8	17 7/8	5	5	Duval County	TX	Shirley Oatman	1990	6,985
129 5/8	21 1/8	19 7/8	15 4/8	5	6	Graham County	KS	Gary Long	1990	6,985
129 5/8	23 5/8	22 4/8	18 7/8	4	5	Prince William County	VA	Christopher Nichol	1990	6,985
129 5/8	21 1/8	20 5/8	17 2/8	7	5	St. Croix County	WI	Jerry Yaritz	1990	6,985
129 5/8	19 6/8	19 5/8	16 7/8	4	4	York County	NE	Marlin Seeman	1990	6,985
129 5/8	26 4/8	25 7/8	19 2/8	4	5	Union County	KY	Robert W. Ervin	1990	6,985
129 5/8	20 2/8	21 5/8	17 3/8	6	5	Dane County	WI	Randy Ree	1990	6,985
129 5/8	22 7/8	22 2/8	19 7/8	6	4	Champaign County	OH	Tim Pond	1990	6,985
129 5/8	20 0/8	19 0/8	16 5/8	5	5	Houston County	TN	Bobby Bryant	1991	6,985
129 5/8	22 2/8	21 7/8	17 5/8	5	5	Lawrence County	IN	Arter Thompson II	1991	6,985
129 5/8	22 6/8	22 0/8	15 6/8	5	6	Perry County	AR	Allen Lovell	1991	6,985
129 5/8	21 5/8	21 4/8	16 1/8	5	6	Sauk County	WI	Gregory W. Stebler	1991	6,985
129 5/8	24 4/8	23 5/8	16 7/8	5	6	Washtenaw County	MI	Carl T. Ticknor	1991	6,985
129 5/8	19 6/8	21 1/8	14 7/8	5	5	Edmonson County	KY	Marvin Pate	1992	6,985
129 4/8	21 5/8	20 2/8	15 4/8	5	5	Sarpy County	NE	Russ Calloway	1962	7,028
129 4/8	22 4/8	21 7/8	17 6/8	5	5	Monroe County	GA	Robert S. Carey	1973	7,028
129 4/8	23 1/8	23 3/8	19 2/8	4	3	Green County	WI	Jerry Amundson	1976	7,028
129 4/8	23 4/8	22 0/8	15 4/8	5	5	Newton County	IN	Howard Culbertson	1976	7,028
129 4/8	20 2/8	20 4/8	16 5/8	5	5	Elk County	PA	Charles F. Eckl	1977	7,028
129 4/8	21 6/8	21 6/8	22 0/8	4	5	Puslinch Twp.	ONT	Larry Knarr	1980	7,028
129 4/8	22 2/8	22 1/8	16 4/8	4	5	Chippewa County	WI	John M. Hanzlik	1981	7,028
129 4/8	23 7/8	23 2/8	16 5/8	5	4	Lindsay	ONT	Ken Steele	1983	7,028
129 4/8	22 6/8	22 2/8	16 0/8	4	5	La Salle County	IL	Steve Wagner	1984	7,028
129 4/8	19 1/8	19 6/8	16 5/8	5	5	Juneau County	WI	Dean Tompkins	1984	7,028
129 4/8	21 7/8	22 1/8	16 0/8	5	5	La Salle County	IL	John Liles	1984	7,028
129 4/8	19 0/8	18 7/8	15 0/8	5	5	Marion County	TX	Woody L. Harmon	1985	7,028
129 4/8	22 6/8	23 7/8	18 2/8	5	5	Sherburne County	MN	Marvin Vogelgesang	1985	7,028
129 4/8	19 1/8	19 5/8	15 2/8	4	4	Pike County	IL	Lloyd Bateman	1985	7,028
129 4/8	19 6/8	21 5/8	14 2/8	5	5	Johnson County	MO	Scott Simmons	1986	7,028
129 4/8	23 5/8	23 2/8	19 0/8	4	5	Sheboygan County	WI	Paul Beimborn	1986	7,028
129 4/8	20 0/8	20 1/8	17 0/8	5	5	Dodge County	MN	Jay F. Deones	1986	7,028
129 4/8	21 1/8	21 4/8	16 2/8	5	5	Columbia County	WI	Mark Toso	1986	7,028
129 4/8	21 7/8	21 3/8	18 2/8	7	6	Lewis & Clark County	MT	Jim Ryan	1986	7,028
129 4/8	24 0/8	22 5/8	17 6/8	5	6	Fulton County	OH	Lonnie D. Blosser	1987	7,028
129 4/8	22 4/8	22 0/8	17 0/8	5	4	Randolph County	WV	Jesse Ramsey	1987	7,028
129 4/8	21 7/8	21 1/8	16 6/8	4	4	Walworth County	WI	David A. Bennett	1987	7,028
129 4/8	24 3/8	25 1/8	18 2/8	4	4	Greene County	OH	William T. Ashmore III	1987	7,028
129 4/8	21 1/8	21 3/8	17 4/8	4	4	Buffalo County	WI	Glen R. Axness	1987	7,028
129 4/8	23 2/8	23 5/8	15 2/8	5	6	Madison County	IL	Dennis Collman	1988	7,028
129 4/8	19 5/8	20 2/8	13 1/8	6	6	Lewis & Clark County	MT	Steven Leigh Jones	1988	7,028
129 4/8	20 0/8	19 6/8	14 4/8	5	5	Patrick County	VA	Mike Mitchell	1988	7,028
129 4/8	22 5/8	22 7/8	18 7/8	4	9	Cooke County	TX	David James Hoedebeck	1988	7,028
129 4/8	22 2/8	21 7/8	16 4/8	4	4	Lucas County	IA	Bill Brown	1988	7,028
129 4/8	22 5/8	23 1/8	21 0/8	5	6	Forest County	WI	Terry A. Kickbusch	1988	7,028
129 4/8	24 0/8	21 6/8	17 5/8	4	5	St. Croix County	WI	Randall Offner	1988	7,028
129 4/8	20 6/8	21 1/8	19 7/8	6	5	Parkland County	ALB	Sam Halabi	1988	7,028
129 4/8	22 6/8	23 6/8	16 4/8	5	5	Rock County	WI	Raymond Klug	1989	7,028
129 4/8	22 0/8	22 0/8	17 6/8	5	5	Jo Daviess County	IL	Mike Schubert	1989	7,028
129 4/8	20 2/8	20 0/8	14 6/8	5	5	Sedgwick County	KS	Louis Turner	1989	7,028
129 4/8	24 0/8	23 3/8	15 7/8	4	5	Suffolk County	VA	Scott W. Liebold	1989	7,028
129 4/8	20 4/8	20 6/8	15 1/8	7	6	Franklin County	NE	Troy Patterson	1990	7,028
129 4/8	22 6/8	22 4/8	17 1/8	5	4	Weld County	CO	Doug Kayl	1990	7,028
129 4/8	22 7/8	23 0/8	17 6/8	4	4	Oneida County	WI	Tim Johnson	1990	7,028
129 4/8	22 3/8	23 4/8	15 4/8	6	6	Sullivan County	NH	Larry Dufresne	1991	7,028
129 4/8	21 4/8	21 6/8	16 6/8	4	4	Caswell County	NC	David E. Lancaster	1991	7,028
129 4/8	20 4/8	21 0/8	15 4/8	4	6	Coshocton County	OH	Gary Lynn Fischer	1991	7,028
129 4/8	22 3/8	22 7/8	17 0/8	4	5	Grant County	SD	Scott R. Miller	1991	7,028

WHITETAIL DEER *(Typical Antlers)*

MINIMUM SCORE 125 *(Continued)*

Score	Length of Main Beam R	L	Inside Spread	Number of Points R	L	Area	State/ Province	Hunter's Name	Date	Rank
129 4/8	21 4/8	20 3/8	19 4/8	5	5	Iron County	WI	D. J. Sullivan	1991	7,028
129 4/8	22 5/8	21 0/8	18 0/8	5	5	Monroe County	IL	Randy Rettinghouse	1991	7,028
129 4/8	21 4/8	22 2/8	15 4/8	5	5	Emanuel County	GA	James L. Brown, Jr.	1992	7,028
129 4/8	24 1/8	24 1/8	20 4/8	4	4	Cheshire County	NH	Gregory G. Bath	1992	7,028
129 3/8	23 4/8	22 1/8	20 3/8	4	5	Bayfield County	WI	Kenneth R. Sweeny	1965	7,075
129 3/8	23 2/8	22 5/8	19 0/8	4	5	Carroll County	IL	Noel Feather	1965	7,075
129 3/8	25 1/8	24 0/8	21 5/8	4	3	Des Moines County	IA	Jerry Snyder	1978	7,075
129 3/8	22 3/8	22 0/8	13 7/8	4	4	Waukesha County	WI	Gary S. Luedtke	1982	7,075
129 3/8	20 7/8	21 1/8	14 5/8	5	5	Monroe County	WI	Paul Moser	1983	7,075
129 3/8	20 6/8	20 7/8	20 2/8	7	9	White County	IN	Mark Mohler	1983	7,075
129 3/8	21 3/8	21 4/8	14 7/8	5	5	Carroll County	MD	Herbert Eyler	1984	7,075
129 3/8	20 4/8	20 4/8	15 4/8	6	5	Waupaca County	WI	Rick Lohff	1985	7,075
129 3/8	22 2/8	22 0/8	17 2/8	6	4	Door County	WI	Randy Berndt	1985	7,075
129 3/8	21 3/8	20 3/8	16 5/8	5	5	Albany County	NY	Frank Frederick	1986	7,075
129 3/8	21 5/8	21 3/8	16 1/8	4	4	Hunterdon County	NJ	John DeStefano	1986	7,075
129 3/8	20 4/8	20 3/8	16 7/8	4	4	Shawnee County	KS	Randy Hildreth	1986	7,075
129 3/8	19 6/8	21 2/8	15 1/8	4	5	Jersey County	IL	Howard Shaw	1987	7,075
129 3/8	21 0/8	21 0/8	15 3/8	6	5	Putnam County	MO	John Pherigo	1987	7,075
129 3/8	23 6/8	22 1/8	18 5/8	4	4	Baltimore County	MD	Bruce D. Hoover	1987	7,075
129 3/8	22 4/8	22 3/8	18 1/8	4	4	Montgomery County	IL	Mark Laurent	1987	7,075
129 3/8	21 7/8	22 2/8	16 0/8	4	5	Grant County	SD	Steven Karels	1988	7,075
129 3/8	20 1/8	21 0/8	16 5/8	5	5	Eaton County	MI	Randall W. Jecks	1988	7,075
129 3/8	22 0/8	21 7/8	20 3/8	4	5	McHenry County	IL	Gary Noe	1988	7,075
129 3/8	21 6/8	20 7/8	16 5/8	5	5	Missoula County	MT	Jeff Traska	1988	7,075
129 3/8	23 3/8	22 6/8	19 5/8	5	5	Buffalo County	WI	Dennis Palmer	1988	7,075
129 3/8	20 6/8	21 7/8	18 7/8	5	5	Sundre	NBW	Andrew Cariello, Jr.	1989	7,075
129 3/8	22 4/8	22 7/8	19 1/8	4	5	Fountain County	IN	Kenny Corey	1989	7,075
129 3/8	22 3/8	22 2/8	15 5/8	4	5	Waupaca County	WI	Kevin W. Hoffman	1989	7,075
129 3/8	20 6/8	20 6/8	13 5/8	5	5	Worth County	IA	Larry B. Porter	1989	7,075
129 3/8	20 4/8	21 7/8	15 5/8	5	5	Effingham County	IL	Dave Pontious	1989	7,075
129 3/8	24 7/8	23 0/8	17 1/8	7	5	Ionia County	MI	William D. Yoder	1989	7,075
129 3/8	23 2/8	22 5/8	16 7/8	5	4	Brown County	WI	Jeffrey G. Blake	1989	7,075
129 3/8	20 6/8	20 0/8	14 3/8	5	5	Rowan County	KY	Danny Mabry	1990	7,075
129 3/8	21 2/8	19 6/8	17 3/8	5	5	Morgan County	MO	David A. Haake	1990	7,075
129 3/8	22 7/8	20 4/8	18 3/8	4	5	Du Page County	IL	James J. Malek, Jr.	1990	7,075
129 3/8	26 4/8	25 4/8	18 5/8	3	3	Jefferson County	MO	Barry Geatley	1990	7,075
129 3/8	21 2/8	22 4/8	17 2/8	6	5	Tom Green County	TX	Jack Bains	1991	7,075
129 3/8	24 1/8	23 0/8	15 0/8	5	5	Ozark County	MO	Richard Eakins	1991	7,075
129 3/8	20 6/8	21 0/8	12 7/8	5	5	Passaic County	NJ	Dennis Sterzel	1991	7,075
129 3/8	23 0/8	24 1/8	15 5/8	4	5	Baltimore County	MD	Paul A. Waters	1991	7,075
129 3/8	22 0/8	22 4/8	15 3/8	5	5	Strathcona	ALB	Sheldon Fiske	1992	7,075
129 2/8	19 2/8	20 1/8	16 5/8	7	6	Columbia County	WA	Al Farrell	1956	7,112
129 2/8	23 2/8	24 0/8	17 4/8	4	4	Juneau County	WI	Robert E. Schober	1977	7,112
129 2/8	21 7/8	21 4/8	16 2/8	5	5	Kendall County	IL	Fred W. Achilles	1979	7,112
129 2/8	20 3/8	20 4/8	17 4/8	5	5	Canmore	ALB	J. C. Mackid	1982	7,112
129 2/8	22 0/8	22 5/8	16 2/8	5	5	Muskingum County	OH	Dr. Jim Emerson	1982	7,112
129 2/8	20 6/8	21 6/8	17 2/8	4	4	Buffalo County	NE	Dan Johnson	1983	7,112
129 2/8	20 0/8	19 6/8	15 0/8	5	5	Portage County	WI	Jay W. Torkilsen	1984	7,112
129 2/8	19 4/8	19 2/8	14 4/8	5	5	Walsh	ALB	Reg Brooks	1984	7,112
129 2/8	24 1/8	23 0/8	15 0/8	5	4	Jasper County	IL	Guy Douglas Page	1984	7,112
129 2/8	20 7/8	21 3/8	18 6/8	5	5	Ross County	OH	Steven E Bower	1984	7,112
129 2/8	20 4/8	21 0/8	13 6/8	5	6	Pierce County	WI	William Kearns	1984	7,112
129 2/8	22 2/8	22 2/8	18 4/8	4	4	Calhoun County	MI	Jerry L. Teller	1984	7,112
129 2/8	21 6/8	22 1/8	16 6/8	4	4	Des Moines County	IA	Ray Waschkat	1984	7,112
129 2/8	20 1/8	19 7/8	18 4/8	5	5	Hillsdale County	MI	Garry Witfoth	1984	7,112
129 2/8	24 4/8	23 1/8	20 4/8	5	6	Columbiana County	OH	Robert Souders	1985	7,112
129 2/8	23 3/8	23 0/8	17 6/8	4	4	Hocking County	OH	Donald Webb	1985	7,112
129 2/8	20 5/8	21 7/8	16 0/8	4	4	Anderson County	KS	Jerry Howarter	1985	7,112
129 2/8	23 0/8	23 2/8	18 0/8	5	5	Waukesha County	WI	Gary Buck	1986	7,112
129 2/8	22 3/8	22 1/8	18 6/8	4	5	Lake County	IL	Eugene L. Miller	1987	7,112
129 2/8	20 5/8	20 5/8	15 4/8	5	5	Somerset County	NJ	Barry C. Ott	1987	7,112
129 2/8	22 6/8	20 2/8	18 4/8	4	4	Perry County	IL	Thomas R. Wilkens	1987	7,112
129 2/8	19 4/8	19 6/8	15 4/8	5	5	Custer County	SD	Stan Chiras	1988	7,112
129 2/8	23 3/8	23 1/8	16 1/8	4	5	Cedar County	MO	Ralph Burns	1988	7,112
129 2/8	21 6/8	21 5/8	15 0/8	5	5	Olmsted County	MN	Jim Leqve	1988	7,112
129 2/8	19 4/8	20 2/8	14 7/8	6	6	Kingfisher County	OK	Bruce Boyd	1988	7,112
129 2/8	18 7/8	19 4/8	18 0/8	6	5	Callahan County	TX	William B. Brown, Jr.	1989	7,112
129 2/8	22 5/8	22 5/8	17 4/8	4	4	La Salle County	IL	Jack Tabor	1989	7,112
129 2/8	22 2/8	23 1/8	17 4/8	5	5	Grant County	WI	Bob Bloom	1989	7,112
129 2/8	21 0/8	21 0/8	18 0/8	5	5	Sawyer County	WI	Michael Sawyer	1989	7,112

319

| SCORE | LENGTH OF MAIN BEAM | | INSIDE SPREAD | NUMBER OF POINTS | | AREA | STATE/ PROVINCE | HUNTER'S NAME | DATE | RANK |
	R	L		R	L					
129 2/8	22 1/8	22 1/8	18 4/8	4	5	Kane County	IL	Charles E. Allen	1989	7,112
129 2/8	21 4/8	21 3/8	21 0/8	4	5	Calhoun County	MI	Douglas L. Rial	1989	7,112
129 2/8	20 0/8	22 0/8	16 2/8	5	4	Waukesha County	WI	Todd Meyers	1990	7,112
129 2/8	23 0/8	23 1/8	16 4/8	5	5	Price County	WI	Jerry J. Bedor	1990	7,112
129 2/8	22 2/8	22 7/8	17 2/8	4	4	Jackson County	IL	Richard Beckman	1990	7,112
129 2/8	22 0/8	21 6/8	16 6/8	4	4	Chautaqua County	KS	Bill Wilmeth	1990	7,112
129 2/8	19 7/8	20 1/8	14 6/8	4	5	Stony Plain	ALB	James W. Thomson	1990	7,112
129 2/8	20 5/8	20 2/8	17 2/8	5	5	Creek County	OK	Bill Morgan	1990	7,112
129 2/8	22 6/8	21 1/8	19 0/8	6	6	Richland County	ND	Andy Boyer	1991	7,112
129 2/8	19 2/8	19 5/8	13 0/8	5	5	Door County	WI	Steven R. Pluff	1991	7,112
129 2/8	19 6/8	19 5/8	14 6/8	5	5	Iron County	MI	Ted Sammond	1991	7,112
129 2/8	21 4/8	21 7/8	16 6/8	6	5	Suffolk County	VA	Waverly E. White	1991	7,112
129 2/8	24 7/8	22 3/8	16 6/8	5	7	Kanabec County	MN	Roger A. Eggert	1991	7,112
129 1/8	22 4/8	21 4/8	17 5/8	5	5	Lee County	IA	Jim Bohenkamp	1973	7,154
129 1/8	20 6/8	21 6/8	16 5/8	5	5	Burnett County	WI	James G. Hurrle	1974	7,154
129 1/8	22 2/8	22 1/8	16 5/8	5	8	Wabasha County	MN	Richard H. McKnight	1975	7,154
129 1/8	22 0/8	22 4/8	15 5/8	6	6	Holt County	NE	Greg Wetthaufer	1980	7,154
129 1/8	22 2/8	22 1/8	17 7/8	5	5	Greene County	MS	Russell Herring	1980	7,154
129 1/8	22 1/8	22 0/8	15 7/8	4	4	Hancock County	OH	Kenneth E. Hornick	1980	7,154
129 1/8	19 2/8	20 0/8	15 3/8	5	5	Sheboygan County	WI	John Steinbruecker	1980	7,154
129 1/8	25 1/8	24 1/8	20 5/8	6	4	Houston County	MN	Gary Maier	1981	7,154
129 1/8	19 6/8	19 7/8	14 7/8	5	5	Clark County	SD	Bill Soyland	1981	7,154
129 1/8	21 5/8	21 7/8	17 1/8	4	5	Schuyler County	NY	Scott D. Bond	1982	7,154
129 1/8	21 6/8	21 0/8	17 5/8	4	4	Hughes County	SD	Alvin Truax	1984	7,154
129 1/8	19 5/8	19 4/8	14 7/8	5	5	Marathon County	WI	Richard J. Tokarski	1985	7,154
129 1/8	24 0/8	24 3/8	17 3/8	4	4	Jackson County	MI	Mark D. Bacon	1985	7,154
129 1/8	21 0/8	21 6/8	16 6/8	6	6	Walsh County	ND	Tobin L. Welch	1986	7,154
129 1/8	21 0/8	20 6/8	17 3/8	5	5	Wexford County	MI	Mike Goodrich	1986	7,154
129 1/8	22 1/8	22 4/8	17 5/8	6	5	Clark County	MO	Dennis Fish	1986	7,154
129 1/8	21 0/8	21 4/8	17 6/8	6	5	Bexar County	TX	Leonard E. Barbus	1986	7,154
129 1/8	20 2/8	19 5/8	14 7/8	5	5	Warren County	NJ	Theodore Barchowski, Jr.	1987	7,154
129 1/8	22 1/8	22 1/8	16 3/8	4	4	Ozaukee County	WI	Doug Hartwig	1987	7,154
129 1/8	24 6/8	25 0/8	16 5/8	6	5	Wayne County	MS	Robert Hall	1987	7,154
129 1/8	22 6/8	21 2/8	15 1/8	6	5	Anderson County	TN	Mack Hicks	1987	7,154
129 1/8	20 6/8	20 4/8	16 7/8	5	5	Shawano County	WI	Frank J. Kugel	1987	7,154
129 1/8	22 0/8	22 0/8	14 7/8	5	5	Des Moines County	IA	Kevin M. Peterson	1987	7,154
129 1/8	26 6/8	26 1/8	19 2/8	5	5	Gage County	NE	Russell Klein	1988	7,154
129 1/8	24 1/8	22 5/8	17 1/8	5	6	Columbia County	WI	Alva D. Fuller	1988	7,154
129 1/8	22 1/8	22 2/8	15 3/8	5	5	Litchfield County	CT	Paul Mirabelle	1988	7,154
129 1/8	22 4/8	22 5/8	19 3/8	5	4	McHenry County	IL	David A. Bennett	1988	7,154
129 1/8	21 0/8	21 6/8	16 1/8	5	6	Madison County	IA	Fred "Bud" Allen	1989	7,154
129 1/8	24 2/8	23 6/8	18 6/8	6	5	Ashland County	WI	Bill Plizka	1989	7,154
129 1/8	24 0/8	23 1/8	15 3/8	4	4	Ingham County	MI	Ted Harrison	1989	7,154
129 1/8	19 7/8	20 2/8	17 5/8	5	5	Barry County	MI	Kenneth W. Blauvelt	1989	7,154
129 1/8	20 1/8	20 2/8	16 2/8	6	7	Ohio County	WV	Gene Petri	1989	7,154
129 1/8	22 5/8	23 5/8	19 1/8	4	5	Westchester County	NY	Douglas Greenwich	1989	7,154
129 1/8	20 1/8	20 1/8	16 1/8	5	4	Morton County	ND	Leslie Ciavarella	1989	7,154
129 1/8	24 1/8	24 0/8	19 5/8	4	5	Allegheny County	PA	Lonnie R. Bowser	1990	7,154
129 1/8	23 5/8	22 6/8	17 7/8	4	5	Peoria County	IL	Frank R. Barnhart	1990	7,154
129 1/8	20 5/8	22 0/8	17 5/8	4	5	Menominee County	MI	Steve G. Drabick	1990	7,154
129 1/8	20 5/8	20 7/8	17 1/8	4	4	Warren County	NJ	Timothy Matthews	1990	7,154
129 1/8	22 2/8	22 3/8	18 6/8	4	5	Suffolk County	NY	Neal Heaton	1990	7,154
129 1/8	21 2/8	20 3/8	15 7/8	4	4	Cass County	NE	Steve Rueck	1991	7,154
129 1/8	22 6/8	22 4/8	15 7/8	4	5	Defiance County	OH	Don Willitzer	1991	7,154
129 1/8	21 6/8	21 5/8	18 3/8	5	4	Shawnee County	KS	Eldon Johnson	1991	7,154
129 1/8	21 4/8	21 1/8	17 7/8	4	4	Oakland County	MI	Perry S. Russo	1992	7,154
129 0/8	22 6/8	22 5/8	17 5/8	5	5	Adams County	IL	Roger W. Seehafer	1964	7,197
129 0/8	21 4/8	21 3/8	17 4/8	5	5	Monmouth County	NJ	Joseph N. Lazar	1967	7,197
129 0/8	23 4/8	24 0/8	19 6/8	5	4	Shawano County	WI	Merton Giessel	1970	7,197
129 0/8	19 6/8	20 6/8	19 0/8	4	4	Oneida County	WI	Gary Bohlman	1970	7,197
129 0/8	23 7/8	24 3/8	17 4/8	5	5	Erie County	OH	William G. Hlavin	1973	7,197
129 0/8	20 3/8	20 2/8	13 7/8	5	6	Ottawa County	KS	Martin Nunn	1976	7,197
129 0/8	20 6/8	21 2/8	15 5/8	6	6	Columbia County	WI	Greg Jacobson	1978	7,197
129 0/8	22 1/8	22 6/8	17 4/8	4	5	Mower County	MN	Jim Keim	1978	7,197
129 0/8	22 2/8	23 4/8	19 4/8	5	4	Trempealeau County	WI	Brian Skroch	1978	7,197
129 0/8	20 2/8	20 2/8	15 4/8	5	5	Washington County	WI	Francis N. Vande Boom	1978	7,197
129 0/8	20 3/8	20 4/8	19 0/8	4	4	Washington County	MS	Dan Hensley	1979	7,197
129 0/8	23 2/8	22 5/8	20 4/8	7	6	Carroll County	OH	Chuck Caldwell	1981	7,197
129 0/8	20 4/8	20 1/8	15 6/8	5	5	Columbia County	WI	Brent J. Nowak	1982	7,197
129 0/8	21 0/8	21 4/8	16 0/8	4	4	Wabaunsee County	KS	Tom Willard	1982	7,197

SCORE	LENGTH OF MAIN BEAM		INSIDE SPREAD	NUMBER OF POINTS		AREA	STATE/ PROVINCE	HUNTER'S NAME	DATE	RANK
	R	L		R	L					
129 0/8	21 1/8	21 0/8	17 6/8	4	4	Grant County	WI	Wayne J. Droessler	1985	7,197
129 0/8	22 1/8	22 1/8	16 2/8	5	4	Cass County	ND	Ellery Kundert	1985	7,197
129 0/8	21 7/8	22 2/8	15 4/8	4	5	Iowa County	WI	Tim Palzkill	1985	7,197
129 0/8	22 2/8	22 7/8	17 2/8	4	4	Woodford County	IL	Bill Salsman	1985	7,197
129 0/8	21 2/8	21 3/8	16 2/8	6	6	Bremer County	IA	Martin Culpepper	1985	7,197
129 0/8	21 4/8	21 4/8	16 2/8	4	5	Pike County	MO	Richard Dewey	1985	7,197
129 0/8	20 0/8	20 4/8	16 5/8	6	6	Fond du Lac County	WI	Jeffrey D. Flitter	1986	7,197
129 0/8	22 1/8	22 2/8	16 4/8	5	5	Vernon County	WI	Bruce A. Gardner	1986	7,197
129 0/8	21 5/8	21 5/8	19 4/8	5	4	Suffolk County	NY	Joe Buscemi	1986	7,197
129 0/8	20 3/8	20 1/8	14 6/8	5	5	Morgan County	GA	Scot Rucker	1987	7,197
129 0/8	21 4/8	21 4/8	17 6/8	5	4	McHenry County	IL	David C. Novak	1987	7,197
129 0/8	22 3/8	21 1/8	16 6/8	5	5	Eau Claire County	WI	Anthony W. Olson	1988	7,197
129 0/8	21 0/8	22 0/8	16 2/8	6	7	Codington County	SD	Peter C. DeVille	1988	7,197
129 0/8	21 0/8	21 6/8	14 3/8	5	6	Tuscola County	MI	Dean Alan Broecker	1988	7,197
129 0/8	20 6/8	21 7/8	16 0/8	5	6	Daviess County	IN	Dennis R. Eger	1988	7,197
129 0/8	22 5/8	21 4/8	19 7/8	4	5	Jackson County	IL	Tim Cobin	1988	7,197
129 0/8	24 2/8	24 1/8	14 6/8	4	4	Wright County	MO	Buster Miller	1988	7,197
129 0/8	19 4/8	19 4/8	13 2/8	5	5	Wagoner County	OK	Lowell Due	1988	7,197
129 0/8	22 2/8	21 6/8	20 4/8	5	5	Llano County	TX	Bart J. Gillan III	1989	7,197
129 0/8	21 5/8	22 2/8	18 5/8	5	5	Douglas County	WI	Bruce Johnson	1989	7,197
129 0/8	20 6/8	20 7/8	16 4/8	5	5	Douglas County	MO	Matt Hensley	1989	7,197
129 0/8	21 4/8	21 4/8	17 2/8	4	4	Meigs County	OH	Jack Satterfield, Jr.	1989	7,197
129 0/8	22 1/8	21 1/8	14 0/8	5	4	Stearns County	MN	Paul Heinen	1990	7,197
129 0/8	21 2/8	21 4/8	17 0/8	4	5	Eels Lake	ONT	Ron McGarrity	1990	7,197
129 0/8	21 7/8	21 7/8	16 0/8	5	5	Allamakee County	IA	Paul "Buck" Farni, Jr.	1990	7,197
129 0/8	20 7/8	19 5/8	16 0/8	5	5	Jackson County	WV	Glenn Lacy	1990	7,197
129 0/8	23 5/8	22 7/8	18 0/8	5	6	E. Carroll Parish	LA	Mike Jones	1990	7,197
129 0/8	23 1/8	21 2/8	16 0/8	6	6	Montgomery County	TN	Adrien Boudin	1990	7,197
129 0/8	24 4/8	25 0/8	20 5/8	6	6	Edgar County	IL	Clark Piper	1990	7,197
129 0/8	24 4/8	23 3/8	17 4/8	5	5	Clinton County	OH	Brad Howard	1991	7,197
129 0/8	22 2/8	22 6/8	17 6/8	5	4	Bosque County	TX	Thomas Buxton	1991	7,197
129 0/8	21 4/8	21 6/8	16 2/8	4	4	Greene County	MO	Norm Nothnagel	1991	7,197
129 0/8	21 7/8	21 4/8	16 7/8	8	6	Crawford County	MO	Mike B. Jackson	1991	7,197
129 0/8	22 1/8	22 2/8	19 4/8	5	5	Price County	WI	Michael R. Lepak	1991	7,197
129 0/8	22 4/8	22 4/8	15 6/8	4	5	Kane County	IL	John Hoffman	1991	7,197
129 0/8	22 0/8	22 4/8	18 2/8	5	4	Westchester County	NY	Richard Semenza	1991	7,197
128 7/8	19 1/8	20 6/8	13 7/8	5	5	Martin County	IN	J. Steve Albertson	1969	7,247
128 7/8	22 4/8	21 1/8	16 3/8	5	5	Grant County	WI	Kevin Freymiller	1975	7,247
128 7/8	22 6/8	22 3/8	15 2/8	5	5	Taylor County	WI	Eugene L. Racibowski	1976	7,247
128 7/8	21 0/8	20 1/8	18 1/8	5	4	Clark County	WI	Clarence J. Biddle	1977	7,247
128 7/8	23 3/8	23 1/8	15 4/8	5	4	Lake County	MN	Michael Seeber	1980	7,247
128 7/8	22 0/8	23 0/8	15 5/8	5	4	Erie County	NY	David J. Wetzler, Sr.	1980	7,247
128 7/8	24 1/8	25 3/8	21 6/8	7	6	Gentry County	MO	Bruce Shisler	1982	7,247
128 7/8	20 4/8	20 4/8	16 5/8	4	4	Blue Earth County	MN	Dean Como	1982	7,247
128 7/8	19 7/8	20 4/8	16 3/8	5	6	Richland County	MT	Dan Sturgis	1985	7,247
128 7/8	20 0/8	21 2/8	15 1/8	7	6	Washtenaw County	MI	Gerald Opsahl, Sr.	1985	7,247
128 7/8	22 7/8	23 3/8	19 6/8	5	6	Gallia County	OH	James E. Harris I	1986	7,247
128 7/8	22 2/8	22 3/8	17 7/8	5	4	Dubuque County	IA	Jeff Vogel	1986	7,247
128 7/8	22 0/8	21 4/8	19 1/8	4	4	Ramsey County	ND	Larry Kuntz	1986	7,247
128 7/8	21 1/8	22 2/8	18 3/8	4	5	Colfax County	NE	Dan Steiner	1987	7,247
128 7/8	20 6/8	21 1/8	17 7/8	5	7	Powell County	MT	Mark A. Balavender	1987	7,247
128 7/8	24 1/8	23 4/8	18 5/8	4	4	Union County	SC	Ronald Moon	1988	7,247
128 7/8	21 6/8	21 5/8	18 1/8	4	4	Morrison County	MN	David R. Wall	1988	7,247
128 7/8	21 6/8	22 1/8	19 3/8	4	4	Burnett County	WI	Michael D. Roberts	1988	7,247
128 7/8	22 0/8	22 6/8	16 5/8	4	4	McDowell County	WV	Ted Blankenship	1988	7,247
128 7/8	22 5/8	23 3/8	16 7/8	5	4	Franklin County	KS	Benjamin W. Braden	1989	7,247
128 7/8	20 5/8	21 0/8	17 7/8	4	4	Chisago County	MN	Michael R. Langin	1989	7,247
128 7/8	21 6/8	22 2/8	16 7/8	4	4	Ramsey County	ND	Charles McGarvey	1989	7,247
128 7/8	22 1/8	20 6/8	15 1/8	4	4	Trego County	KS	Fred Hunsicker	1989	7,247
128 7/8	23 7/8	23 1/8	16 0/8	5	5	Pike County	IL	Frank Dolbeare	1989	7,247
128 7/8	22 4/8	22 0/8	16 5/8	5	5	Delaware County	IA	Jeffrey J. Tobin	1990	7,247
128 7/8	20 0/8	21 1/8	20 1/8	5	5	Polk County	MN	Bart Ott	1991	7,247
128 7/8	23 7/8	22 3/8	17 5/8	6	5	Anoka County	MN	Greg Walter	1991	7,247
128 7/8	21 3/8	20 4/8	15 1/8	4	4	Cass County	IL	Mike Cox	1991	7,247
128 7/8	20 4/8	21 1/8	15 5/8	5	5	Boone County	IL	Jay Allen Ervin	1991	7,247
128 7/8	20 2/8	20 2/8	17 5/8	5	5	Iroquois County	IL	Steven K. Scharlach	1991	7,247
128 7/8	21 1/8	20 5/8	15 1/8	5	5	Livingston County	MI	Gerald Patrick Schleicher	1991	7,247
128 7/8	23 7/8	23 1/8	17 3/8	4	4	Grafton County	NH	Ronald W. Carpenter	1991	7,247
128 6/8	23 0/8	25 2/8	16 4/8	4	4	Buffalo County	NE	Bill Orsborn	1963	7,279
128 6/8	21 1/8	20 2/8	18 6/8	4	4	Johnson County	IA	Claire Doyle	1971	7,279

WHITETAIL DEER *(Typical Antlers)*

Score	Length of Main Beam R	L	Inside Spread	Number of Points R	L	Area	State/Province	Hunter's Name	Date	Rank
128 6/8	23 2/8	22 5/8	15 3/8	4	6	Lake County	IN	Bruce R. Prue	1977	7,279
128 6/8	19 4/8	20 0/8	18 2/8	6	5	Seward County	NE	Ronald G. Filip	1978	7,279
128 6/8	20 6/8	21 2/8	17 0/8	5	5	Brown County	SD	Jerome J. Lingor	1978	7,279
128 6/8	20 1/8	20 1/8	17 2/8	5	5	Adams County	OH	Larry David Adams	1981	7,279
128 6/8	25 5/8	25 6/8	18 1/8	5	6	Blount County	TN	David Dotson	1981	7,279
128 6/8	21 6/8	22 2/8	17 0/8	5	4	Riley County	KS	Dwayne Roepke	1981	7,279
128 6/8	22 0/8	22 2/8	16 6/8	4	4	Pierce County	WI	Joe Sukowatey	1981	7,279
128 6/8	23 3/8	23 6/8	17 6/8	4	5	Houston County	MN	James P. Finn	1982	7,279
128 6/8	21 4/8	21 4/8	17 0/8	5	5	Shelby County	IL	Larry E. Gibson	1982	7,279
128 6/8	22 6/8	21 0/8	17 4/8	5	5	Sangamon County	IL	James L. Aebel	1983	7,279
128 6/8	24 0/8	23 7/8	18 6/8	8	5	Buffalo County	WI	Michael Zastrow	1984	7,279
128 6/8	23 3/8	24 3/8	19 6/8	4	4	Dodge County	WI	Dale A. Hawkinson	1984	7,279
128 6/8	19 6/8	20 3/8	17 0/8	5	5	Robertson County	TN	Terry Louis Carter	1985	7,279
128 6/8	22 1/8	20 3/8	19 0/8	5	6	Beaver County	PA	Mark Tallon	1985	7,279
128 6/8	18 4/8	20 5/8	17 0/8	4	4	Pittsburg County	OK	Edward P. Martin III	1985	7,279
128 6/8	24 1/8	25 5/8	18 1/8	5	4	Buffalo County	WI	Ed Brannen	1985	7,279
128 6/8	20 7/8	20 5/8	17 4/8	5	4	Adams County	WI	John Balaine	1986	7,279
128 6/8	20 7/8	19 6/8	16 2/8	5	5	Winona County	MN	John R. Micheel	1986	7,279
128 6/8	20 5/8	20 4/8	16 1/8	6	4	Stony Plain	ALB	Stan Chiras	1986	7,279
128 6/8	22 2/8	22 4/8	18 4/8	5	4	Hubbard County	MN	Pascal Perrin	1987	7,279
128 6/8	22 0/8	21 5/8	17 6/8	4	4	Newton County	MO	Brad Harris	1987	7,279
128 6/8	22 4/8	23 4/8	16 1/8	4	6	Logan County	IL	Gary W. Conrady	1987	7,279
128 6/8	22 5/8	23 5/8	16 6/8	4	4	Ripley County	IN	Terry G. Moore	1988	7,279
128 6/8	17 6/8	22 5/8	16 3/8	7	7	Williams County	OH	Charles Murray	1988	7,279
128 6/8	23 4/8	23 7/8	16 6/8	5	6	Anne Arundel County	MD	Mark D. Sanders	1988	7,279
128 6/8	20 5/8	24 4/8	20 6/8	4	4	Mercer County	NJ	Scott Lysenko	1988	7,279
128 6/8	19 4/8	18 7/8	15 0/8	5	5	Lynn County	TX	Al Kowalski	1988	7,279
128 6/8	22 3/8	23 2/8	17 6/8	4	4	Geary County	KS	Michael P. Boyer	1988	7,279
128 6/8	20 5/8	21 6/8	14 4/8	4	4	Iroquois County	IL	Warren Cary	1989	7,279
128 6/8	24 0/8	21 4/8	16 4/8	4	4	Medina County	TX	James Blocker, Jr.	1989	7,279
128 6/8	22 3/8	22 3/8	19 2/8	4	4	Stephenson County	IL	Jim Hastings	1989	7,279
128 6/8	21 3/8	21 1/8	17 6/8	4	4	Portage County	WI	Theodore Johnson	1989	7,279
128 6/8	26 5/8	25 4/8	21 4/8	3	5	St. Croix County	WI	Steve C. Ashley	1989	7,279
128 6/8	20 4/8	21 2/8	14 4/8	4	5	Barry County	MO	Robert Prisk	1989	7,279
128 6/8	24 2/8	24 2/8	19 0/8	4	4	Hampshire County	MA	John Higgins	1989	7,279
128 6/8	20 0/8	19 7/8	17 4/8	4	4	Cottonwood County	MN	Dennis Highby	1989	7,279
128 6/8	20 5/8	20 6/8	16 0/8	5	5	Juneau County	WI	Kurt R. Bassuener	1990	7,279
128 6/8	21 0/8	21 7/8	18 2/8	6	6	Brown County	IL	Jerry D. Dale	1990	7,279
128 6/8	22 2/8	23 0/8	18 0/8	4	4	Harvey County	KS	Danny Stahl	1990	7,279
128 6/8	19 4/8	19 5/8	15 6/8	5	6	Lincoln County	SD	Michael A. Deckert	1990	7,279
128 6/8	21 7/8	20 5/8	17 6/8	4	5	Peel	ONT	Carmen G. Bumbaca	1991	7,279
128 6/8	21 0/8	20 3/8	16 0/8	5	5	Hayes County	NE	William E. Wuerthele	1991	7,279
128 6/8	20 7/8	20 4/8	15 6/8	5	5	Freeborn County	MN	Darrell Loew	1991	7,279
128 6/8	19 2/8	21 4/8	18 3/8	6	5	Warren County	IA	Tom Steil	1992	7,279
128 5/8	20 6/8	20 2/8	14 7/8	5	5	Mille Lacs County	MN	Milton J. Mattson	1952	7,325
128 5/8	14 7/8	26 2/8	20 5/8	5	5	Ford County	KS	Rod Lies	1966	7,325
128 5/8	18 1/8	18 5/8	15 3/8	5	5	Harford County	MD	Joseph Egner	1969	7,325
128 5/8	20 4/8	20 4/8	18 0/8	6	6	Lawrence County	SD	Ronald Hazledine	1969	7,325
128 5/8	21 6/8	22 0/8	17 5/8	4	4	Mercer County	IL	Kenneth E. Yeater	1971	7,325
128 5/8	21 3/8	21 0/8	18 5/8	5	5	Delaware County	IA	Jim L. Mahan	1974	7,325
128 5/8	22 2/8	22 4/8	15 7/8	5	5	Fond du Lac County	WI	Kevin Clark	1975	7,325
128 5/8	21 3/8	21 3/8	17 6/8	5	6	Whiteside County	IL	Art Heinze	1976	7,325
128 5/8	23 0/8	23 3/8	17 2/8	8	5	Kendall County	IL	David Martinek	1978	7,325
128 5/8	20 4/8	20 1/8	15 1/8	5	5	Ontario County	NY	William Danno	1980	7,325
128 5/8	21 0/8	20 7/8	14 5/8	5	5	Ionia County	MI	Ronald A. Denney	1980	7,325
128 5/8	23 4/8	24 0/8	19 0/8	6	6	Jackson County	WI	John D. Card	1981	7,325
128 5/8	22 2/8	21 5/8	16 7/8	5	5	Franklin County	MO	Lance Tyree	1982	7,325
128 5/8	21 5/8	23 0/8	17 1/8	8	6	Cedar County	NE	Charles Benertz	1982	7,325
128 5/8	22 6/8	23 4/8	19 6/8	5	6	Carroll County	IL	Art Heinze	1982	7,325
128 5/8	19 1/8	19 3/8	15 7/8	5	5	Juneau County	WI	Steve Baker	1982	7,325
128 5/8	20 1/8	20 2/8	17 1/8	5	5	Wetzel County	WV	Paul Pichardo	1983	7,325
128 5/8	22 1/8	21 4/8	17 7/8	4	4	Pike County	PA	Joseph V. Caccamo, Jr.	1984	7,325
128 5/8	21 6/8	22 7/8	16 3/8	5	4	Richland County	OH	Tod O. Duffner	1984	7,325
128 5/8	20 2/8	20 2/8	18 5/8	5	5	Kanabec County	MN	Milo L. Carlson	1985	7,325
128 5/8	22 1/8	22 1/8	14 5/8	5	5	Kenosha County	WI	Mike Mitten	1985	7,325
128 5/8	20 3/8	20 3/8	16 5/8	5	5	Iowa County	WI	Ralph J. Blum	1985	7,325
128 5/8	20 2/8	20 5/8	17 5/8	5	5	Kane County	IL	Roger Eberly	1985	7,325
128 5/8	22 5/8	22 5/8	19 0/8	6	4	Green County	WI	Michael G. Martin	1985	7,325
128 5/8	21 3/8	21 4/8	18 1/8	4	4	Suffolk County	NY	Richard Kent	1985	7,325
128 5/8	23 5/8	24 6/8	18 7/8	6	4	Kandiyohi County	MN	Timothy G. Caven	1986	7,325

SCORE	LENGTH OF MAIN BEAM		INSIDE SPREAD	NUMBER OF POINTS		AREA	STATE/ PROVINCE	HUNTER'S NAME	DATE	RANK
	R	L		R	L					
128 5/8	19 4/8	19 7/8	14 7/8	5	5	Juneau County	WI	Scott Prucha	1986	7,325
128 5/8	22 0/8	21 6/8	15 5/8	4	5	Grant County	WI	Dean Lease	1986	7,325
128 5/8	21 3/8	22 0/8	18 1/8	4	4	Jackson County	OH	Terry S. Speakman	1986	7,325
128 5/8	18 7/8	19 1/8	15 4/8	6	5	Benton County	IA	Corby Miller	1986	7,325
128 5/8	22 0/8	21 7/8	17 3/8	5	5	Morris County	NJ	Larry Cacchio	1987	7,325
128 5/8	20 7/8	21 5/8	15 1/8	4	4	Jackson County	MN	Gary E. Anderson	1987	7,325
128 5/8	21 2/8	22 0/8	16 0/8	5	5	Iron County	MI	Ted Sammond	1988	7,325
128 5/8	22 4/8	21 0/8	14 7/8	5	4	Dickinson County	IA	Jeff Hiveley	1988	7,325
128 5/8	20 7/8	20 6/8	15 5/8	4	5	Anoka County	MN	Greg Seymour	1988	7,325
128 5/8	21 1/8	21 0/8	17 1/8	5	5	McHenry County	IL	John F. Schorsch,Jr.	1988	7,325
128 5/8	20 2/8	19 1/8	14 1/8	4	7	Hall County	NE	Steve Cool	1989	7,325
128 5/8	21 1/8	21 0/8	16 5/8	5	5	Ashland County	WI	Maggie Falkenstein	1989	7,325
128 5/8	20 3/8	19 6/8	17 5/8	5	5	Chester County	PA	Robert L. Stephens, Jr.	1989	7,325
128 5/8	17 3/8	19 6/8	16 1/8	5	5	Clark County	WI	Richard Reddy	1989	7,325
128 5/8	20 2/8	21 3/8	18 6/8	5	5	Clark County	MO	Gary Twigg	1989	7,325
128 5/8	20 5/8	21 2/8	17 5/8	4	5	Washington County	IL	Edward Kurwicki	1990	7,325
128 5/8	20 3/8	21 1/8	15 5/8	5	5	Dodge County	WI	Rich Kluge	1990	7,325
128 5/8	20 5/8	20 3/8	18 3/8	5	5	Oakland County	MI	Keith Phillips	1990	7,325
128 5/8	23 1/8	22 2/8	17 7/8	6	5	Waukesha County	WI	Robert Rajnicek	1990	7,325
128 5/8	23 7/8	22 0/8	17 7/8	5	5	Van Buren County	IA	John "Rosey" Roseland	1990	7,325
128 5/8	25 6/8	25 5/8	17 2/8	7	7	Goodhue County	MN	Bob Friedrick	1991	7,325
128 5/8	22 6/8	22 2/8	16 7/8	4	4	Jefferson County	WI	Steve Hein	1991	7,325
128 5/8	24 2/8	24 0/8	17 1/8	4	4	Oconto County	WI	Mitchell Meunier	1991	7,325
128 5/8	22 0/8	21 0/8	15 7/8	5	5	Waukesha County	WI	Steve Hoelz	1991	7,325
128 5/8	21 4/8	21 4/8	11 5/8	5	6	Warren County	IA	Erv Wagner	1991	7,325
128 5/8	22 3/8	22 7/8	15 5/8	5	4	Iroquois County	IL	Chad McGinnis	1991	7,325
128 4/8	25 0/8	23 7/8	17 0/8	4	4	Mozart	AR	Alfred Hirt	1959	7,377
128 4/8	20 4/8	21 0/8	17 7/8	7	5	Clay County	NE	Rollan Johnson	1961	7,377
128 4/8	21 1/8	21 2/8	15 0/8	5	4	Marion County	IA	Thomas Tucker	1968	7,377
128 4/8	20 0/8	21 2/8	16 7/8	6	7	McLeod County	MN	Merlin Eggersgluess	1971	7,377
128 4/8	21 6/8	22 3/8	16 6/8	5	5	Jones County	IA	Tom Postel	1971	7,377
128 4/8	22 3/8	23 2/8	17 5/8	5	6	Wright County	MN	Elwood Rokala	1971	7,377
128 4/8	22 6/8	23 0/8	23 7/8	4	4	Broad River	SC	John V. Orr	1973	7,377
128 4/8	20 1/8	20 2/8	15 2/8	5	5	Delaware County	OH	Denton O. Baumbarger	1973	7,377
128 4/8	25 4/8	23 0/8	15 1/8	5	6	Wapello County	IA	Rick Grooms	1974	7,377
128 4/8	23 1/8	22 0/8	19 0/8	4	6	Henry County	MO	LaVern Rucker	1974	7,377
128 4/8	19 5/8	20 3/8	15 4/8	5	5	Ozaukee County	WI	Ronald Mayer	1975	7,377
128 4/8	22 0/8	20 4/8	18 2/8	4	4	Rosebud County	MT	Bob Brill	1976	7,377
128 4/8	19 2/8	19 5/8	15 0/8	5	5	Park County	MT	John Christiansen	1983	7,377
128 4/8	21 0/8	20 6/8	17 4/8	5	5	Kankakee County	IL	Wayne Webber	1983	7,377
128 4/8	22 6/8	22 4/8	14 6/8	6	7	Mississippi County	AR	Davy J. Shaw	1983	7,377
128 4/8	23 0/8	22 5/8	19 6/8	4	4	Delaware County	PA	Mark Gentry	1984	7,377
128 4/8	21 7/8	19 6/8	17 3/8	7	4	Griggs County	ND	Blaine Larson	1984	7,377
128 4/8	20 2/8	21 2/8	16 6/8	5	5	Grant County	WI	Jeffery Redfearn	1985	7,377
128 4/8	21 5/8	21 4/8	16 0/8	5	5	Kane County	IL	Jeff Stephens	1985	7,377
128 4/8	22 7/8	21 5/8	20 4/8	4	5	Platte County	WY	Jayde Allbright	1986	7,377
128 4/8	20 2/8	20 5/8	16 6/8	5	4	Sumner County	KS	Larry J. Pacey	1986	7,377
128 4/8	18 6/8	20 3/8	16 2/8	4	4	Plymouth County	IA	Donald F. Pankowski	1986	7,377
128 4/8	20 7/8	20 4/8	16 2/8	5	5	La Crosse County	WI	Gary Thomas Severson	1986	7,377
128 4/8	19 0/8	19 1/8	13 4/8	5	5	Eddy County	ND	Tim Finley	1987	7,377
128 4/8	21 4/8	21 0/8	14 6/8	5	5	Edmonson County	KY	Marvin Pate	1987	7,377
128 4/8	18 5/8	20 0/8	15 2/8	5	5	Porter County	IN	Thomas David Katona	1987	7,377
128 4/8	24 0/8	23 6/8	14 2/8	4	4	Jackson County	IN	Jeff Montgomery	1987	7,377
128 4/8	22 0/8	23 2/8	17 6/8	4	5	Somerset County	NJ	Brian Todaro	1987	7,377
128 4/8	23 4/8	22 6/8	17 0/8	5	4	Lawrence County	IL	Mike Forsythe	1987	7,377
128 4/8	20 5/8	20 5/8	16 4/8	5	5	Stearns County	MN	Roy Saari	1987	7,377
128 4/8	22 5/8	20 2/8	16 4/8	4	4	Boone County	IL	Ottie W. Rowe	1988	7,377
128 4/8	21 0/8	22 3/8	18 4/8	5	5	Indiana County	PA	Leonard Maday, Jr.	1988	7,377
128 4/8	20 3/8	20 1/8	16 4/8	6	5	Langlade County	WI	Scott A. McCann	1988	7,377
128 4/8	21 0/8	21 1/8	17 4/8	5	5	St. Joseph County	IN	Steve Sokol	1988	7,377
128 4/8	21 4/8	21 5/8	15 4/8	5	4	Oconto County	WI	Steven L. DeBauche	1988	7,377
128 4/8	23 1/8	23 2/8	18 0/8	5	5	Will County	IL	Henry John Christianson	1989	7,377
128 4/8	25 4/8	24 0/8	20 2/8	5	5	Jefferson County	OH	Jim Still	1989	7,377
128 4/8	21 0/8	21 0/8	19 0/8	5	5	Morgan County	OH	David G. Ferguson	1989	7,377
128 4/8	22 6/8	22 2/8	18 4/8	4	4	Wayne County	OH	Keith R. Dotterer	1990	7,377
128 4/8	23 3/8	23 5/8	21 0/8	5	4	Somerset County	NJ	Stephen Kotz	1990	7,377
128 4/8	21 2/8	21 3/8	15 4/8	4	4	Nacogdoches County	TX	Stephen Shinn	1990	7,377
128 4/8	24 3/8	24 0/8	19 6/8	4	5	Carroll County	MO	Charles Lichte III	1990	7,377
128 4/8	24 0/8	23 5/8	19 7/8	5	6	Cecil County	MD	James P. White II	1990	7,377
128 4/8	21 1/8	21 2/8	19 6/8	5	4	Wayne County	OH	Ronald Elliott	1990	7,377

SCORE	LENGTH OF R MAIN BEAM L		INSIDE SPREAD	NUMBER OF R POINTS L		AREA	STATE/ PROVINCE	HUNTER'S NAME	DATE	RANK
128 4/8	22 2/8	24 1/8	17 4/8	4	5	Cochrane	ALB	Robin Ryan	1990	7,377
128 4/8	20 4/8	19 4/8	14 6/8	5	5	Atchison County	MO	Steve McManaman	1990	7,377
128 4/8	21 7/8	21 6/8	17 4/8	4	4	Sussex County	NJ	Michael Badami	1991	7,377
128 4/8	23 3/8	23 5/8	17 4/8	5	5	Pierce County	WI	Dan Beyer	1991	7,377
128 4/8	22 7/8	23 4/8	18 3/8	6	6	Ottertail County	MN	Marlin "Doc" Peach	1991	7,377
128 4/8	19 2/8	20 1/8	14 2/8	5	4	Johnson County	IA	Scott Ogden	1991	7,377
128 3/8	23 3/8	23 0/8	20 3/8	4	5	Williamson County	IL	Don Walker	1959	7,427
128 3/8	23 4/8	23 2/8	17 3/8	6	7	Poncil	MT	Bob Samson	1962	7,427
128 3/8	19 1/8	19 6/8	15 2/8	6	4	Douglas County	NE	Cecil Smith	1962	7,427
128 3/8	20 6/8	20 5/8	14 1/8	5	4	Morrison County	MN	Ronald Thole	1964	7,427
128 3/8	19 6/8	19 7/8	16 7/8	6	5	Columbia County	WI	David D. Luetkens	1965	7,427
128 3/8	22 1/8	20 0/8	20 7/8	4	4	Brown County	SD	T. Michael Dunn	1966	7,427
128 3/8	21 0/8	22 1/8	18 5/8	5	5	Bartholomew County	IN	Harold Frye	1966	7,427
128 3/8	22 0/8	21 6/8	14 5/8	5	4	Allegany County	NY	Joseph Famiglietti	1972	7,427
128 3/8	23 4/8	23 3/8	19 5/8	4	4	Union County	IL	Randy Edmonds	1974	7,427
128 3/8	22 0/8	21 7/8	17 7/8	4	4	Switzerland County	IN	Samuel M. Durham	1979	7,427
128 3/8	20 4/8	22 1/8	15 1/8	5	5	Highland County	OH	Dean Herschede	1980	7,427
128 3/8	21 7/8	22 4/8	18 5/8	5	6	Menominee County	MI	James Saunoris	1980	7,427
128 3/8	21 4/8	21 2/8	16 5/8	5	5	Cameron County	TX	Jerry Spencer	1980	7,427
128 3/8	24 3/8	23 1/8	20 3/8	4	3	Tazewell County	IL	Jimmy C. Plemmons	1981	7,427
128 3/8	20 0/8	19 6/8	16 1/8	4	5	Henry County	KY	Donald Cornett	1982	7,427
128 3/8	22 5/8	22 1/8	16 1/8	6	5	Clark County	OH	Rick Rust	1983	7,427
128 3/8	23 6/8	23 3/8	20 1/8	4	4	Muskingum County	OH	Mike Spring	1983	7,427
128 3/8	20 7/8	21 3/8	17 1/8	5	4	Rock County	WI	Henry W. Holdorf, Jr.	1983	7,427
128 3/8	22 2/8	22 6/8	14 7/8	6	6	Clay County	SD	Marlowe Rames	1983	7,427
128 3/8	21 1/8	20 5/8	15 3/8	6	6	Anoka County	MN	John Cardinal	1984	7,427
128 3/8	23 7/8	22 5/8	20 1/8	4	4	Sheridan County	KS	Tom E. Bowman	1985	7,427
128 3/8	19 6/8	20 5/8	19 5/8	6	6	Kit Carson County	CO	Dave Holt	1985	7,427
128 3/8	20 6/8	20 7/8	17 0/8	6	4	Yuma County	CO	Bill Grammer	1986	7,427
128 3/8	23 1/8	23 1/8	17 5/8	5	4	Lawrence County	OH	Robert E. Burcham	1986	7,427
128 3/8	20 4/8	20 5/8	15 3/8	5	5	McLean County	ND	Lynn Wentz	1987	7,427
128 3/8	23 1/8	24 1/8	16 4/8	5	5	Dunn County	WI	Charles Storing	1987	7,427
128 3/8	21 7/8	22 0/8	15 7/8	5	5	Calumet County	WI	Ronald Campbell	1987	7,427
128 3/8	23 3/8	22 0/8	16 7/8	6	5	Forest County	WI	Darrow Bedor	1987	7,427
128 3/8	20 4/8	20 7/8	15 3/8	5	6	Lincoln County	NE	David J. Hinton	1987	7,427
128 3/8	23 3/8	23 5/8	17 7/8	5	4	Nevo Leon	MEX	Paul H. Dickson	1988	7,427
128 3/8	20 2/8	20 2/8	17 5/8	5	7	Clay County	SD	Craig W. Myron	1988	7,427
128 3/8	22 5/8	22 4/8	17 5/8	4	4	Dane County	WI	Gene R. Herman	1988	7,427
128 3/8	24 5/8	24 6/8	19 3/8	4	4	Montgomery County	PA	Joseph D. Maddock	1988	7,427
128 3/8	20 1/8	20 2/8	16 1/8	4	5	Polk County	NE	Jim Czapla	1989	7,427
128 3/8	21 3/8	21 5/8	18 5/8	4	5	Warren County	OH	Dennis R. Gosney	1989	7,427
128 3/8	22 6/8	23 6/8	17 5/8	4	5	Monroe County	IA	Chris Keyes	1989	7,427
128 3/8	21 0/8	21 4/8	14 7/8	6	5	Tom Green County	TX	Mike Hegefeld	1989	7,427
128 3/8	23 1/8	23 6/8	17 4/8	5	4	Montgomery County	IN	Stacy A. Hightower	1990	7,427
128 3/8	23 5/8	24 4/8	18 5/8	4	5	Vermillion County	IN	Brent Summerville	1990	7,427
128 3/8	24 5/8	22 2/8	17 1/8	4	4	Wayne County	NY	John W. Stringer	1990	7,427
128 3/8	21 6/8	21 1/8	18 3/8	4	4	Morris County	NJ	Michael F. De Pompe	1990	7,427
128 3/8	22 1/8	22 1/8	19 7/8	4	4	Hardin County	KY	Woody Noe	1990	7,427
128 3/8	21 6/8	21 1/8	17 5/8	6	5	Jackson County	IA	Joseph H. Krier	1990	7,427
128 3/8	21 7/8	21 4/8	17 3/8	4	4	Warren County	IL	Tom Toops	1990	7,427
128 3/8	22 6/8	23 7/8	19 5/8	5	5	Warren County	OH	Danny J. Dykes	1990	7,427
128 3/8	21 6/8	22 4/8	15 3/8	4	5	La Salle County	TX	Dicky Newberry	1991	7,427
128 3/8	22 6/8	22 7/8	15 3/8	4	5	Eaton County	MI	Jeffrey J. Jolley	1991	7,427
128 3/8	22 2/8	20 6/8	15 3/8	4	5	Hickory County	MO	Billy Adams	1991	7,427
128 3/8	23 0/8	23 1/8	16 1/8	4	5	Ripley County	IN	Brian K. Hamer	1991	7,427
128 3/8	20 3/8	20 4/8	16 1/8	4	4	Glenboro	MAN	Robert R. Blain	1991	7,427
128 3/8	22 3/8	23 0/8	17 3/8	4	4	Vinton County	OH	Brian D. Ehrhart	1991	7,427
128 3/8	22 2/8	22 1/8	14 1/8	5	5	Douglas County	WI	Richard S. Gondik, Jr.	1991	7,427
128 3/8	22 5/8	22 0/8	17 7/8	6	5	Buffalo County	WI	Bryan A. Tamke	1991	7,427
128 3/8	21 1/8	21 0/8	13 7/8	5	5	Winneshiek County	IA	Joel Goodman	1991	7,427
128 3/8	24 2/8	23 5/8	18 5/8	5	6	Polk County	MN	James A. Strom	1991	7,427
128 3/8	22 0/8	20 6/8	15 0/8	5	5	Pike County	IL	Jim Pierceall	1991	7,427
128 2/8	22 1/8	21 1/8	15 6/8	5	5	Franklin County	KS	Gary Hunsicker	1966	7,483
128 2/8	20 5/8	21 3/8	14 4/8	5	5	Waupaca County	WI	Dennis Arndt	1967	7,483
128 2/8	23 0/8	22 5/8	19 1/8	5	5	Lackawanna County	PA	Gary E. Schreck	1971	7,483
128 2/8	19 3/8	20 0/8	18 4/8	5	5	Pittsburg County	OK	Pack Giacomo	1972	7,483
128 2/8	22 2/8	22 3/8	17 0/8	4	4	Cherokee County	OK	Eddie Goss	1973	7,483
128 2/8	20 5/8	21 4/8	17 0/8	5	5	Buffalo County	NE	Lynn Bombeck	1974	7,483
128 2/8	23 1/8	22 7/8	20 3/8	4	5	Jefferson County	OH	Michael W. Brown	1976	7,483
128 2/8	21 0/8	21 3/8	17 2/8	4	5	Spokane County	WA	Michael A. Shane	1977	7,483

SCORE	LENGTH OF MAIN BEAM		INSIDE SPREAD	NUMBER OF POINTS		AREA	STATE/ PROVINCE	HUNTER'S NAME	DATE	RANK
	R	L		R	L					
128 2/8	21 1/8	21 4/8	17 0/8	5	5	Green Lake County	WI	Albert G. Slife	1979	7,483
128 2/8	19 0/8	19 0/8	14 4/8	5	5	Walworth County	SD	Ronald Arbach	1980	7,483
128 2/8	19 0/8	19 1/8	14 4/8	5	5	Travis County	TX	Russell Schmidt	1982	7,483
128 2/8	20 4/8	19 6/8	17 6/8	6	5	Floyd County	IA	Johnny Nelson	1982	7,483
128 2/8	19 4/8	18 4/8	17 4/8	5	6	Dallas County	IA	Mike Inman	1982	7,483
128 2/8	21 7/8	22 4/8	16 6/8	4	4	Todd County	KY	Terry R. Baldwin	1983	7,483
128 2/8	22 5/8	22 3/8	17 4/8	3	5	Brown County	KS	Chuck McNally	1983	7,483
128 2/8	22 5/8	22 6/8	16 3/8	6	7	Juneau County	WI	Steve Hysell	1984	7,483
128 2/8	20 3/8	21 4/8	17 6/8	4	4	Nelson County	ND	Darren Asperheim	1985	7,483
128 2/8	22 1/8	22 0/8	17 2/8	6	6	Bleckley County	GA	Wallace Mullis	1985	7,483
128 2/8	20 4/8	20 0/8	16 4/8	5	5	Grant County	WI	Robert Govier	1985	7,483
128 2/8	21 2/8	19 6/8	17 6/8	4	4	Pottawatomie County	OK	Tom Larman	1986	7,483
128 2/8	21 7/8	21 1/8	16 6/8	4	4	Waupaca County	WI	John Harris	1987	7,483
128 2/8	21 7/8	22 4/8	19 1/8	5	6	Washington County	KS	Ronald Montague	1987	7,483
128 2/8	21 0/8	21 0/8	17 4/8	5	5	Jasper County	IA	Gordon L. Johnson	1987	7,483
128 2/8	23 2/8	23 3/8	20 4/8	4	5	Missoula County	MT	Greg L. Munther	1987	7,483
128 2/8	21 2/8	21 6/8	15 0/8	5	6	Haskell County	OK	Jerry C. Sturdy	1987	7,483
128 2/8	21 7/8	22 7/8	19 4/8	5	5	Graves County	KY	Robert Eubanks	1988	7,483
128 2/8	19 2/8	19 5/8	16 4/8	5	6	Lafayette County	WI	Robert Wedige	1988	7,483
128 2/8	21 4/8	21 1/8	16 6/8	4	4	Henry County	VA	Mike Weaver	1988	7,483
128 2/8	22 4/8	23 0/8	16 0/8	4	4	Oconto County	WI	David L. Follett	1988	7,483
128 2/8	22 6/8	23 0/8	21 0/8	4	5	Washtenaw County	MI	Donald L. Cox	1988	7,483
128 2/8	20 1/8	20 6/8	14 2/8	5	5	Dearborn County	IN	David R. "Skeeter" McKain	1989	7,483
128 2/8	21 2/8	21 7/8	14 1/8	6	7	Kay County	OK	Dean Gratias	1989	7,483
128 2/8	22 2/8	22 1/8	16 2/8	6	5	Montgomery County	IL	Rick L. Rork	1989	7,483
128 2/8	22 7/8	22 0/8	19 6/8	5	6	Yellow Medicine County	MN	Butch West	1989	7,483
128 2/8	22 2/8	21 7/8	17 1/8	4	7	Price County	WI	John D. Haydock	1989	7,483
128 2/8	20 0/8	19 6/8	14 2/8	4	4	Ogle County	IL	Daniel M. Pierce	1989	7,483
128 2/8	24 1/8	23 3/8	16 6/8	4	4	Monroe County	NY	Wayne Meritt	1989	7,483
128 2/8	21 7/8	21 5/8	16 0/8	5	5	Buffalo County	WI	David W. Stuhr	1990	7,483
128 2/8	24 4/8	24 2/8	17 2/8	9	5	Ashland County	OH	Randy Beavers	1990	7,483
128 2/8	22 4/8	23 0/8	16 4/8	4	5	Erie County	NY	Michael R. Nowaczyk	1990	7,483
128 2/8	21 4/8	21 0/8	19 0/8	4	4	Langlade County	WI	Thomas Schuette	1990	7,483
128 2/8	23 1/8	24 0/8	16 6/8	4	4	Hardin County	OH	Kelly Jackson	1990	7,483
128 2/8	23 6/8	23 6/8	15 2/8	4	4	Chatham County	NC	Ricky Canoy	1991	7,483
128 2/8	20 0/8	20 5/8	15 5/8	7	6	Washington County	PA	Jason H. Snyder	1991	7,483
128 2/8	21 4/8	21 5/8	17 6/8	4	4	Jennings County	IN	Daniel E. Ramey	1991	7,483
128 2/8	24 6/8	25 1/8	17 5/8	4	6	Somerset County	NJ	Steven J. Niedzielski	1991	7,483
128 2/8	22 1/8	21 6/8	17 3/8	6	5	Parke County	IN	Philip A. Prock	1991	7,483
128 2/8	25 5/8	26 2/8	16 2/8	6	4	Allamakee County	IA	Joe Lieb	1991	7,483
128 2/8	23 4/8	23 1/8	19 6/8	6	4	Boone County	IL	Wilmer V. Garlick	1991	7,483
128 2/8	22 2/8	22 1/8	16 2/8	5	5	Jo Daviess County	IL	Steve Cole	1992	7,483
128 1/8	20 1/8	21 0/8	17 5/8	5	5	Dorchester County	MD	Powell D. Cook	1964	7,533
128 1/8	21 6/8	21 0/8	19 0/8	4	5	Adams County	IL	Clarence Grandt	1972	7,533
128 1/8	20 6/8	19 7/8	14 7/8	5	5	Ripley County	IN	Sam M. Durham	1978	7,533
128 1/8	21 1/8	22 2/8	17 0/8	5	4	Lafayette County	WI	W. Grinnell/G. Grinnell	1978	7,533
128 1/8	22 6/8	24 0/8	15 1/8	4	4	Chilton County	AL	Dennis Burnett	1980	7,533
128 1/8	19 5/8	20 5/8	19 5/8	5	5	Sheboygan County	WI	Mark Kissinger	1980	7,533
128 1/8	21 4/8	23 3/8	20 3/8	5	4	Hastings	ONT	Ken McGarrity	1980	7,533
128 1/8	22 7/8	22 0/8	19 5/8	5	6	Kingman County	KS	Mark Renollet	1980	7,533
128 1/8	20 7/8	19 6/8	18 3/8	4	4	Jefferson County	IL	David R. Darnell	1981	7,533
128 1/8	22 7/8	21 7/8	20 1/8	4	4	Carter County	MO	Bill Howe	1981	7,533
128 1/8	22 1/8	20 0/8	17 0/8	5	6	Lake County	IL	Donald Schram	1981	7,533
128 1/8	21 4/8	22 0/8	17 4/8	4	5	Elgin	ONT	Peter Hartmann	1982	7,533
128 1/8	21 4/8	21 2/8	16 3/8	6	7	Winnebago County	IL	Robert W. Shallenberger,	1982	7,533
128 1/8	21 1/8	21 5/8	16 3/8	4	4	Calhoun County	MI	Clarence Bowers, Jr.	1982	7,533
128 1/8	22 1/8	22 1/8	18 3/8	5	5	Marquette County	WI	Newell Easley	1984	7,533
128 1/8	22 6/8	19 0/8	16 6/8	5	7	Rock County	WI	Rodger Veneman	1984	7,533
128 1/8	22 6/8	23 3/8	17 1/8	5	4	Brown County	SD	Ron Rockwell	1984	7,533
128 1/8	20 0/8	20 1/8	16 3/8	5	5	Mower County	MN	John S. Adams	1985	7,533
128 1/8	21 5/8	21 2/8	18 5/8	4	4	Washington County	MS	Bobby Ray Woods	1985	7,533
128 1/8	23 1/8	22 7/8	16 1/8	5	4	Peoria County	IL	Dan P. Hollingsworth	1985	7,533
128 1/8	21 7/8	21 4/8	15 4/8	6	6	Dallas County	MO	Jay Strain	1985	7,533
128 1/8	22 4/8	22 3/8	18 5/8	5	5	Barry County	MI	Ron Rolfe	1985	7,533
128 1/8	23 0/8	22 6/8	16 1/8	4	4	Ripley County	IN	Thomas R. Martin	1986	7,533
128 1/8	22 4/8	22 2/8	16 3/8	5	5	Winona County	MN	Terry F. Banitt	1986	7,533
128 1/8	20 5/8	22 7/8	16 7/8	5	5	Effingham County	IL	Randy Hall	1987	7,533
128 1/8	22 2/8	21 5/8	18 5/8	5	6	St. Charles County	MO	Michael Vogt	1987	7,533
128 1/8	20 1/8	21 6/8	15 0/8	5	6	Gibson County	IN	Dean Monroe Deal	1987	7,533
128 1/8	22 0/8	22 4/8	18 2/8	4	6	Marquette County	MI	Loyal Norkett	1987	7,533

SCORE	LENGTH OF MAIN BEAM R	LENGTH OF MAIN BEAM L	INSIDE SPREAD	NUMBER OF POINTS R	NUMBER OF POINTS L	AREA	STATE/ PROVINCE	HUNTER'S NAME	DATE	RANK
128 1/8	23 4/8	22 3/8	19 1/8	4	4	Monroe County	NY	Paul H. Beicke	1987	7,533
128 1/8	23 6/8	23 1/8	16 7/8	4	4	Jackson County	OH	Bob "Smokey" Lotts	1987	7,533
128 1/8	20 2/8	20 6/8	18 4/8	5	4	Crook County	WY	Wendell W. Koontz	1988	7,533
128 1/8	21 0/8	22 4/8	18 6/8	6	5	New Castle County	DE	Joseph J. Subolefsky	1988	7,533
128 1/8	21 1/8	20 2/8	16 5/8	4	5	Cheyenne County	KS	Kahle Helton	1988	7,533
128 1/8	23 0/8	22 1/8	17 7/8	5	4	Langlade County	WI	Bob Antoinewicz	1988	7,533
128 1/8	20 6/8	20 5/8	12 5/8	5	4	Adair County	MO	Joe Ed McCray	1988	7,533
128 1/8	20 4/8	20 4/8	15 4/8	6	5	Fergus County	MT	John "Rosey" Roseland	1988	7,533
128 1/8	20 1/8	20 3/8	16 5/8	5	5	Suffolk County	NY	Doug Brady	1988	7,533
128 1/8	21 6/8	21 7/8	17 1/8	5	6	Jones County	GA	Billy Ussery	1989	7,533
128 1/8	21 1/8	20 6/8	17 0/8	6	6	Winnebago County	IL	Richard C. McCormick	1989	7,533
128 1/8	20 5/8	20 4/8	14 5/8	5	5	Clinton County	IL	Glen F. Zurliene	1989	7,533
128 1/8	24 6/8	24 7/8	20 1/8	3	4	Hampden County	MA	Dick Scorzafava	1989	7,533
128 1/8	23 2/8	22 7/8	16 3/8	4	4	Page County	IA	Chris Barton	1989	7,533
128 1/8	20 6/8	22 0/8	14 6/8	4	6	Washburn County	WI	Andy Sirek	1990	7,533
128 1/8	20 2/8	21 0/8	13 7/8	5	5	Hancock County	OH	Steve Shilling	1990	7,533
128 1/8	21 7/8	22 5/8	17 5/8	4	4	Washburn County	WI	Ken Morse	1990	7,533
128 1/8	21 1/8	20 0/8	16 1/8	5	5	Marshall County	IL	Scott Sager	1990	7,533
128 1/8	24 2/8	23 7/8	15 3/8	4	4	Fairfield County	CT	Kerry Simard	1990	7,533
128 1/8	22 3/8	22 6/8	17 0/8	6	6	Macon County	IL	Jeff Slunder	1990	7,533
128 1/8	21 2/8	18 4/8	16 3/8	5	5	Queen Annes County	MD	Tim D. Rand	1991	7,533
128 1/8	19 5/8	19 5/8	14 7/8	5	5	Oakland County	MI	Kerry K. Kammer	1991	7,533
128 1/8	22 1/8	22 0/8	15 0/8	5	6	Greene County	PA	Ronald Virgili, Jr.	1991	7,533
128 1/8	23 1/8	22 3/8	17 1/8	4	4	Goliad County	TX	Edmond H. Fadal, Jr.	1991	7,533
128 1/8	22 2/8	23 0/8	18 3/8	4	4	Burleigh County	ND	Jason Sjol	1991	7,533
128 1/8	22 6/8	23 1/8	17 1/8	5	4	Hamilton County	IA	Arlin Dickinson	1991	7,533
128 1/8	21 7/8	22 4/8	20 6/8	6	7	Knox County	OH	Jeffrey R. Kerr	1991	7,533
128 1/8	21 0/8	21 0/8	14 3/8	5	5	Poweshiek County	IA	Ed Stevens	1991	7,533
128 1/8	23 0/8	23 1/8	16 7/8	4	5	Walworth County	WI	Gergory G. Henan	1991	7,533
128 1/8	19 2/8	19 2/8	16 0/8	5	5	Hardin County	IA	Wayne Dewey	1991	7,533
128 1/8	21 0/8	20 3/8	14 1/8	5	5	Price County	WI	Ken Cork	1991	7,533
128 1/8	22 6/8	22 6/8	18 1/8	4	4	Greene County	OH	Douglas A. Skrlac	1992	7,533
128 0/8	18 7/8	18 1/8	17 4/8	5	5	McLean County	ND	Bennie R. Maytum	1960	7,593
128 0/8	22 7/8	23 0/8	19 0/8	6	8	Sibley County	MN	Darwin Grack	1972	7,593
128 0/8	22 1/8	22 6/8	17 4/8	5	5	Pine County	MN	Larry Hochmayr	1973	7,593
128 0/8	22 3/8	21 2/8	17 0/8	4	4	Macon County	MO	Joe E. McCray	1973	7,593
128 0/8	23 2/8	23 0/8	18 2/8	5	5	Jasper County	IA	Paul Casper	1974	7,593
128 0/8	19 3/8	19 1/8	15 2/8	5	4	Clearwater County	MN	Warren Nelson	1975	7,593
128 0/8	21 5/8	20 5/8	16 0/8	4	4	Otter Tail County	MN	Scott M. Dirks	1978	7,593
128 0/8	19 6/8	21 0/8	15 5/8	5	6	Winona County	MN	Martin Szekeresh, Jr.	1978	7,593
128 0/8	18 7/8	17 6/8	15 2/8	5	6	Carroll County	IL	Art Heinze	1979	7,593
128 0/8	22 7/8	22 6/8	19 4/8	5	4	Manitowoc County	WI	Steve E. Nelson	1979	7,593
128 0/8	21 4/8	21 1/8	16 6/8	5	5	Harris County	GA	David M. Gallops	1980	7,593
128 0/8	20 1/8	19 5/8	18 6/8	4	4	Cumberland County	NJ	John J. Newton III	1980	7,593
128 0/8	21 5/8	21 7/8	17 6/8	4	5	Butler County	KS	Darrell Wolf	1980	7,593
128 0/8	21 1/8	21 6/8	18 0/8	6	8	Allegheny County	PA	Albert Polovich, Jr.	1981	7,593
128 0/8	21 2/8	21 1/8	16 4/8	5	6	La Salle County	IL	Richard Schupp	1983	7,593
128 0/8	20 6/8	20 0/8	18 6/8	5	5	St. Charles County	MO	Joseph L. Vincent	1983	7,593
128 0/8	22 1/8	22 0/8	15 2/8	5	5	Montgomery County	OH	Gary W. Roberson	1984	7,593
128 0/8	22 6/8	22 5/8	17 6/8	4	4	Effingham County	IL	Rick J. Hartke	1985	7,593
128 0/8	20 2/8	20 1/8	15 4/8	7	6	Pittsburg County	OK	Everett Laney	1985	7,593
128 0/8	21 2/8	21 4/8	16 4/8	5	4	Clark County	OH	Ronald Lockhart	1985	7,593
128 0/8	21 7/8	21 0/8	17 7/8	6	5	Rock County	WI	Jerry D. Amundson	1985	7,593
128 0/8	21 7/8	22 0/8	19 6/8	4	4	Licking County	OH	Randy D. Ricketts	1985	7,593
128 0/8	21 4/8	21 6/8	16 0/8	4	4	Louisa County	IA	Roger Gipple	1985	7,593
128 0/8	19 2/8	20 5/8	17 2/8	5	5	Green County	WI	David R. Covert	1986	7,593
128 0/8	21 0/8	21 4/8	15 2/8	5	5	Switzerland County	IN	James Holsapple	1986	7,593
128 0/8	20 1/8	19 3/8	16 6/8	4	4	Jefferson County	IL	Brian Scruggs	1986	7,593
128 0/8	21 5/8	22 0/8	18 0/8	4	4	Clark County	IL	Gerald Shaffner	1986	7,593
128 0/8	22 0/8	22 2/8	18 6/8	4	4	Washington County	MN	John Berglund	1987	7,593
128 0/8	22 7/8	22 1/8	16 0/8	4	4	Jo Daviess County	IL	Robert J. Chamberlain	1987	7,593
128 0/8	21 0/8	21 0/8	15 4/8	6	5	Dakota County	MN	Rick Nelson, Sr.	1987	7,593
128 0/8	22 2/8	22 1/8	15 0/8	4	5	Buffalo County	WI	Randy Moy	1987	7,593
128 0/8	23 7/8	23 3/8	20 4/8	4	4	Sawyer County	WI	Eric Carlson	1988	7,593
128 0/8	19 6/8	19 4/8	16 4/8	4	4	Dubuque County	IA	Dwayne A. Murphy	1988	7,593
128 0/8	21 5/8	22 4/8	18 6/8	4	4	Oregon County	MO	Clifford Hayes	1988	7,593
128 0/8	22 6/8	22 0/8	16 4/8	4	4	Berkeley County	WV	Kenneth F. Moore	1988	7,593
128 0/8	22 3/8	22 6/8	21 5/8	5	4	Orleans County	NY	Warren L. Lewis	1988	7,593
128 0/8	20 6/8	22 7/8	18 2/8	4	5	Woodford County	IL	Dave Stine	1989	7,593
128 0/8	18 4/8	18 6/8	15 6/8	5	5	Throckmorton County	TX	Bruce Holt	1989	7,593

SCORE	LENGTH OF MAIN BEAM R	L	INSIDE SPREAD	NUMBER OF POINTS R	L	AREA	STATE/ PROVINCE	HUNTER'S NAME	DATE	RANK
128 0/8	23 0/8	23 7/8	18 4/8	4	4	Baltimore County	MD	Mark Steven Petrucci	1989	7,593
128 0/8	20 2/8	21 1/8	17 6/8	6	5	Pepin County	WI	Richard Crabtree	1989	7,593
128 0/8	19 7/8	19 3/8	15 2/8	5	5	Hennepin County	MN	Dan Fellows	1989	7,593
128 0/8	22 3/8	22 3/8	18 6/8	4	5	Wayne County	OH	Tom P. Dotterer	1990	7,593
128 0/8	24 2/8	25 0/8	18 0/8	5	5	Licking County	OH	Les Carver	1990	7,593
128 0/8	21 0/8	21 4/8	17 4/8	5	4	Columbia County	WI	Richard Schreiber	1990	7,593
128 0/8	21 4/8	22 4/8	15 6/8	4	4	Isle of Wight County	VA	Arthur Ray Phillips	1990	7,593
128 0/8	23 1/8	22 7/8	15 4/8	5	5	E. Carroll Parish	LA	Trip Hadad	1990	7,593
128 0/8	22 4/8	22 6/8	18 2/8	4	4	Frio County	TX	Terry Chambers	1991	7,593
128 0/8	20 2/8	20 1/8	13 4/8	5	6	Kleberg County	TX	Bradley Peltier	1991	7,593
127 7/8	21 4/8	20 0/8	18 1/8	4	4	Monroe County	IN	Jerry L. Swafford	1968	7,641
127 7/8	21 5/8	21 2/8	15 5/8	6	6	Henderson County	IL	Randy Moore	1971	7,641
127 7/8	21 4/8	21 1/8	18 1/8	4	4	Fairfield County	OH	James Munyon	1971	7,641
127 7/8	19 2/8	20 3/8	15 7/8	6	5	Jones County	IA	Larry Stewart	1972	7,641
127 7/8	20 3/8	20 2/8	18 5/8	4	4	Dawes County	NE	Roger Adamson	1975	7,641
127 7/8	23 5/8	24 5/8	16 7/8	5	6	Burleigh County	ND	Kevin Hertz	1980	7,641
127 7/8	22 7/8	23 1/8	17 1/8	5	5	Scott County	MN	Jim Manuel	1980	7,641
127 7/8	18 2/8	18 1/8	15 6/8	6	6	St. Croix County	WI	Larry Williamson	1981	7,641
127 7/8	22 1/8	22 0/8	18 1/8	6	5	Boyle County	KY	Carroll Williams	1981	7,641
127 7/8	21 7/8	20 4/8	17 7/8	5	5	Robertson County	TN	Walter C. Kirby	1983	7,641
127 7/8	21 1/8	21 4/8	16 7/8	4	4	Reno County	KS	Todd Murray	1983	7,641
127 7/8	20 4/8	21 0/8	15 3/8	5	5	Delta County	MI	Donald M. Seeley	1984	7,641
127 7/8	21 0/8	20 7/8	14 6/8	5	5	Genesee County	MI	Bob Bouck	1985	7,641
127 7/8	22 4/8	23 5/8	21 4/8	5	6	Lake County	IL	Edward H. Bellmore	1985	7,641
127 7/8	22 0/8	22 0/8	18 1/8	6	8	Nez Perce County	ID	Brad Johnson	1985	7,641
127 7/8	21 7/8	22 4/8	19 1/8	4	6	Marquette County	WI	James C. Lakin	1986	7,641
127 7/8	21 5/8	20 6/8	16 2/8	6	6	Clark County	IL	Tomas E. Rothrock	1986	7,641
127 7/8	23 1/8	22 6/8	18 1/8	5	4	Kane County	IL	Dennis Busto	1986	7,641
127 7/8	24 4/8	23 3/8	15 5/8	4	5	Green County	WI	Paul Ovadal	1987	7,641
127 7/8	19 7/8	20 1/8	20 3/8	5	5	Pontotoc County	OK	Joe David Abbott	1987	7,641
127 7/8	19 7/8	20 1/8	17 2/8	6	6	Portage County	WI	Gerald Pavelski	1987	7,641
127 7/8	20 4/8	21 2/8	17 0/8	6	6	Towner County	ND	Mike Haberstroh	1987	7,641
127 7/8	22 5/8	23 4/8	19 5/8	4	5	Saline County	NE	Larry E. Andelt	1987	7,641
127 7/8	21 4/8	20 1/8	15 3/8	6	8	Kenedy County	TX	Steven W. Vaughn	1988	7,641
127 7/8	23 3/8	22 5/8	16 4/8	6	4	Juneau County	WI	Merle D. Jensen	1988	7,641
127 7/8	23 1/8	23 1/8	19 0/8	5	4	Sawyer County	WI	Pat Stone	1988	7,641
127 7/8	21 0/8	20 4/8	13 1/8	5	5	Trumbull County	OH	Mark J. Drotar	1988	7,641
127 7/8	25 6/8	26 5/8	19 5/8	4	3	Fayette County	OH	Millard B. Stone, Jr.	1988	7,641
127 7/8	22 0/8	21 7/8	14 2/8	6	4	Putnam County	MO	Carl Robbins	1988	7,641
127 7/8	21 6/8	23 1/8	19 2/8	5	5	Mercer County	NJ	Keith Gadsby	1989	7,641
127 7/8	20 3/8	20 6/8	18 1/8	5	5	Crook County	WY	Steven F. Rogers	1989	7,641
127 7/8	23 6/8	23 2/8	16 1/8	4	4	Keokuk County	IA	Terry L. Bringman	1989	7,641
127 7/8	21 1/8	21 5/8	17 7/8	5	5	Genesee County	MI	Darrell S. King	1989	7,641
127 7/8	21 3/8	22 0/8	19 3/8	5	5	Woodford County	KY	James Humphrey	1989	7,641
127 7/8	20 6/8	21 3/8	19 7/8	5	4	Polk County	WI	Brian Estes	1989	7,641
127 7/8	22 4/8	23 2/8	15 6/8	5	6	Osage County	OK	Lester James Dibble	1989	7,641
127 7/8	21 5/8	20 6/8	18 2/8	5	8	Vermilion County	IL	David DeMoss	1989	7,641
127 7/8	21 7/8	21 5/8	17 1/8	5	5	Muskingum County	OH	Terry Romain	1989	7,641
127 7/8	22 5/8	22 2/8	17 7/8	4	4	Grundy County	IL	Rick Marks	1990	7,641
127 7/8	22 1/8	22 4/8	14 1/8	4	5	Buffalo County	WI	Fred Neitzel	1990	7,641
127 7/8	23 2/8	24 1/8	20 7/8	5	4	Putnam County	WV	Kevin Davis	1990	7,641
127 7/8	21 0/8	21 6/8	19 1/8	4	4	Henry County	VA	Mike Weaver	1990	7,641
127 7/8	22 7/8	23 0/8	19 7/8	5	4	Worth County	IA	Larry B. Porter	1990	7,641
127 7/8	24 2/8	26 0/8	19 2/8	4	5	Lincoln County	MO	Mark Peasel	1990	7,641
127 7/8	19 5/8	20 4/8	14 5/8	5	5	Athens County	OH	Curtis D. Rutter	1990	7,641
127 7/8	20 7/8	21 3/8	18 0/8	5	6	Douglas County	WI	Steve Hedrington	1990	7,641
127 7/8	21 2/8	22 5/8	16 5/8	5	5	Fayette County	OH	George Massie	1990	7,641
127 7/8	24 2/8	23 2/8	19 7/8	4	5	Iowa County	IA	Rodney Smith	1990	7,641
127 7/8	19 0/8	22 2/8	15 3/8	4	5	Suffolk County	NY	William R. Simmons III	1990	7,641
127 7/8	22 0/8	22 0/8	17 6/8	4	5	Slope County	ND	William H. Guile	1990	7,641
127 7/8	24 4/8	23 5/8	19 5/8	5	5	Willacy County	TX	Al Kowalski	1990	7,641
127 7/8	21 0/8	22 2/8	15 7/8	4	5	McHenry County	IL	Edward C. Schultz	1990	7,641
127 7/8	22 2/8	21 3/8	19 1/8	5	5	Jasper County	MO	Frankie Reynolds	1990	7,641
127 7/8	22 1/8	22 0/8	16 3/8	5	4	Travis County	TX	Raymond G. McRae	1991	7,641
127 7/8	22 5/8	20 6/8	15 1/8	4	4	Newton County	MO	Craig Koelling	1991	7,641
127 7/8	23 0/8	24 2/8	16 5/8	4	5	Franklin County	MA	David M. Lauder	1991	7,641
127 7/8	21 6/8	23 1/8	15 4/8	6	5	Adams County	IL	Timothy Walmsley	1991	7,641
127 7/8	22 5/8	23 5/8	17 5/8	5	5	Onieda County	WI	Dan J. Blenker	1991	7,641
127 7/8	22 4/8	23 1/8	18 1/8	5	4	McHenry County	IL	Jeff Lunk	1991	7,641
127 6/8	21 3/8	22 2/8	16 2/8	4	4	Rice County	MN	David Knutson	1969	7,700

SCORE	LENGTH OF MAIN BEAM R	L	INSIDE SPREAD	NUMBER OF POINTS R	L	AREA	STATE/ PROVINCE	HUNTER'S NAME	DATE	RANK
127 6/8	24 4/8	23 6/8	18 3/8	6	5	Muskingum County	OH	Charles F. Fineran	1974	7,700
127 6/8	20 0/8	19 3/8	17 0/8	4	4	Tucker County	WV	Larry A. Williams	1975	7,700
127 6/8	20 2/8	21 2/8	16 0/8	6	5	Rice County	MN	James Caron	1979	7,700
127 6/8	21 6/8	21 5/8	15 6/8	4	4	Ward County	ND	Larry Ziech	1979	7,700
127 6/8	23 2/8	23 6/8	18 1/8	5	5	Sumner County	KS	Mark Disney	1980	7,700
127 6/8	20 6/8	21 0/8	16 4/8	5	5	Marion County	KY	Hugh Glasscock	1980	7,700
127 6/8	21 7/8	21 7/8	17 6/8	5	5	Waupaca County	WI	Bryon Gyldenvand	1981	7,700
127 6/8	23 6/8	22 2/8	17 4/8	4	4	Hardin County	IA	Richard Pugh	1981	7,700
127 6/8	24 7/8	24 5/8	19 0/8	5	5	Clark County	SD	Jan Buri	1982	7,700
127 6/8	20 0/8	20 4/8	18 2/8	4	4	Yell County	AR	Keith L. Chronister	1982	7,700
127 6/8	24 2/8	23 1/8	20 0/8	4	4	Blue Earth County	MN	Bruce Barrie	1983	7,700
127 6/8	23 4/8	24 4/8	20 4/8	4	4	Waukesha County	WI	Max Mollgaard	1983	7,700
127 6/8	20 4/8	20 5/8	18 0/8	5	4	Monongalia County	WV	Marshall Ridenour	1984	7,700
127 6/8	22 1/8	21 6/8	16 6/8	4	4	Rogers County	OK	Tom Woosley	1984	7,700
127 6/8	22 1/8	21 5/8	17 0/8	4	5	St. Albert	ALB	Gary Kieser	1984	7,700
127 6/8	23 6/8	22 1/8	17 2/8	5	4	Darke County	OH	Bruce Knick	1985	7,700
127 6/8	20 4/8	20 6/8	15 4/8	4	5	Buffalo County	WI	David J. Gard	1985	7,700
127 6/8	23 6/8	23 1/8	20 4/8	3	3	Kearney County	NE	Larry Kuskie	1986	7,700
127 6/8	23 2/8	22 2/8	17 2/8	4	5	Trego County	KS	Brian Batman	1986	7,700
127 6/8	24 3/8	23 6/8	16 2/8	5	4	Guernsey County	OH	William E. Lee	1986	7,700
127 6/8	20 1/8	20 6/8	13 4/8	5	5	Carroll County	IL	William Lilly	1986	7,700
127 6/8	24 3/8	24 0/8	18 1/8	5	5	St. Clair County	MO	Tim Donnelly	1987	7,700
127 6/8	23 7/8	24 0/8	16 6/8	4	4	Bent County	CO	Kurt W. Keskimaki	1987	7,700
127 6/8	23 4/8	23 1/8	17 0/8	6	5	Rockingham County	NH	George Denoncour	1988	7,700
127 6/8	20 2/8	20 5/8	18 0/8	5	6	Brooks County	TX	J. Dale Hale	1988	7,700
127 6/8	22 4/8	22 2/8	23 3/8	5	5	Green County	WI	Dan Cupp	1988	7,700
127 6/8	20 4/8	21 1/8	17 0/8	4	4	Lyon County	KS	Joe Buchtel	1988	7,700
127 6/8	22 7/8	22 6/8	18 6/8	4	4	Cedar County	IA	David Fleener	1988	7,700
127 6/8	22 4/8	22 4/8	16 6/8	4	4	Erie County	OH	Jeff Mallory	1988	7,700
127 6/8	20 6/8	19 7/8	18 6/8	5	4	Martin County	MN	Troy Kakeldey	1988	7,700
127 6/8	22 1/8	22 0/8	17 4/8	4	5	White County	AR	Freddy King, Jr.	1988	7,700
127 6/8	20 2/8	19 6/8	16 0/8	5	5	Teton County	MT	Brad Stewart	1989	7,700
127 6/8	23 2/8	23 1/8	17 1/8	6	4	Ingham County	MI	Michael A. Barnes	1989	7,700
127 6/8	22 5/8	21 4/8	14 6/8	5	4	Clarke County	GA	Walter P. Wood	1989	7,700
127 6/8	19 4/8	19 7/8	19 1/8	6	6	Bureau County	IL	Ronald Franklin	1989	7,700
127 6/8	24 7/8	24 6/8	17 3/8	6	6	Sullivan County	NH	Maurice Flinn	1989	7,700
127 6/8	20 6/8	21 2/8	17 2/8	5	6	Brooks County	TX	Thomas L. "Tag" Reed IV	1989	7,700
127 6/8	18 0/8	17 6/8	13 6/8	5	5	Allegan County	MI	Brian M. Nichols	1989	7,700
127 6/8	20 6/8	21 4/8	18 0/8	6	6	Reno County	KS	Monte Long	1989	7,700
127 6/8	19 7/8	19 6/8	16 0/8	5	5	Whitman County	WA	Pat McFadden	1990	7,700
127 6/8	20 2/8	20 5/8	16 0/8	5	5	Winston County	MS	Carl Mangrum, Jr.	1990	7,700
127 6/8	23 0/8	22 0/8	17 0/8	4	5	McKenzie County	ND	Steve Rehak	1990	7,700
127 6/8	21 5/8	21 5/8	17 6/8	5	4	Seneca County	OH	Michael E. Halbeisen	1990	7,700
127 6/8	19 7/8	20 1/8	15 0/8	5	6	Sheboygan County	WI	Troy Klein	1990	7,700
127 6/8	21 5/8	23 3/8	14 6/8	5	4	Waukesha County	WI	Ronald J. Mayer	1990	7,700
127 6/8	18 7/8	19 7/8	16 0/8	5	5	Harris County	GA	Gorman S. Riley	1990	7,700
127 6/8	22 0/8	21 6/8	17 4/8	4	4	Walworth County	WI	Michael Pautz	1990	7,700
127 6/8	23 6/8	22 5/8	17 4/8	5	5	Putnam County	OH	Ben Warnimont	1990	7,700
127 6/8	24 1/8	23 5/8	21 2/8	5	4	Desha County	AR	Allan Goodwin	1990	7,700
127 6/8	20 3/8	19 4/8	15 6/8	5	5	Dane County	WI	Stephen J. Field	1991	7,700
127 6/8	21 0/8	21 2/8	17 0/8	5	4	Iron County	MI	Erick Friestrom	1991	7,700
127 6/8	22 4/8	22 1/8	21 4/8	4	6	Tulsa County	OK	Terry Buckner	1991	7,700
127 6/8	21 7/8	22 6/8	19 0/8	5	5	Marathon County	WI	Neil Daul	1991	7,700
127 6/8	21 1/8	22 0/8	17 0/8	4	4	Palo Alto County	IA	Roger V. Faulstick	1991	7,700
127 6/8	22 1/8	20 7/8	16 6/8	5	6	Oconto County	WI	Patrick J. Gauthier	1992	7,700
127 6/8	20 7/8	22 0/8	18 6/8	5	5	San Patricio County	TX	Audie W. Stephens	1992	7,700
127 5/8	21 4/8	22 1/8	17 3/8	5	5	Monroe County	MO	C. R. Jackson	1962	7,757
127 5/8	22 3/8	22 3/8	16 5/8	6	5	Vilas County	WI	Carl R. Strauss	1968	7,757
127 5/8	21 2/8	21 0/8	18 3/8	5	5	Warren County	NJ	Jerry W. Kauffman	1972	7,757
127 5/8	22 0/8	22 6/8	14 7/8	4	4	Winnebago County	IA	Kenneth R. Coe, Jr.	1973	7,757
127 5/8	24 4/8	24 5/8	19 0/8	4	5	Wayne County	OH	Ronald Stine	1975	7,757
127 5/8	21 5/8	22 1/8	14 4/8	6	6	Sauk County	WI	Walter S. Jankowski	1976	7,757
127 5/8	21 0/8	21 3/8	16 5/8	4	4	Dickson County	TN	Andy Jackson	1976	7,757
127 5/8	23 2/8	22 4/8	16 1/8	5	5	Tuscarawas County	OH	Jon Scheetz	1976	7,757
127 5/8	21 6/8	21 6/8	20 1/8	5	5	Rock County	WI	Jeffrey L. Kersten	1979	7,757
127 5/8	20 6/8	21 4/8	15 7/8	5	5	Clark County	WI	James Kleinschmidt	1979	7,757
127 5/8	21 7/8	22 4/8	18 5/8	5	5	Tuscarawas County	OH	John H. Raber	1981	7,757
127 5/8	19 6/8	19 4/8	17 7/8	5	5	Scott County	KY	Michael A. Fry	1982	7,757
127 5/8	24 2/8	25 1/8	14 5/8	4	4	Franklin County	KS	David R. Poore	1982	7,757
127 5/8	21 2/8	20 5/8	16 5/8	5	5	Polk County	WI	Tim Bump	1983	7,757

SCORE	LENGTH OF R MAIN BEAM L		INSIDE SPREAD	NUMBER OF R POINTS L		AREA	STATE/ PROVINCE	HUNTER'S NAME	DATE	RANK
127 5/8	22 5/8	23 3/8	17 7/8	4	4	Roane County	TN	William A. 'Bill' Simms	1985	7,757
127 5/8	21 3/8	23 5/8	14 5/8	5	5	Anoka County	MN	Robert G. Ross	1985	7,757
127 5/8	23 7/8	24 4/8	16 7/8	5	5	Licking County	OH	Michael Stumph	1985	7,757
127 5/8	21 2/8	20 7/8	16 7/8	7	8	Christian County	IL	Jeffrey S. Burdick	1985	7,757
127 5/8	21 0/8	21 2/8	20 1/8	5	5	Meigs County	OH	Eric A. Harris	1985	7,757
127 5/8	24 2/8	23 4/8	17 3/8	4	4	Kandiyohi County	MN	Mark Harder	1986	7,757
127 5/8	19 1/8	19 2/8	14 3/8	5	5	Newton County	MO	William V. Patterson	1986	7,757
127 5/8	24 2/8	23 5/8	15 6/8	5	7	Marshall County	IL	Howard P. Olson	1986	7,757
127 5/8	22 7/8	24 3/8	17 1/8	4	4	Pike County	OH	John Ribic	1986	7,757
127 5/8	21 6/8	21 6/8	15 6/8	6	4	Cavalier County	ND	Dayton H. Larson	1987	7,757
127 5/8	19 5/8	19 5/8	17 1/8	5	5	De Kalb County	MO	J. W. Martin	1987	7,757
127 5/8	20 1/8	19 6/8	16 1/8	5	5	Dodge County	WI	Joel F. Weber	1987	7,757
127 5/8	20 6/8	20 2/8	18 5/8	5	5	Price County	WI	David Baratka	1988	7,757
127 5/8	22 0/8	22 2/8	18 5/8	5	5	Ozaukee County	WI	William J. Ferguson	1988	7,757
127 5/8	23 5/8	23 1/8	16 1/8	5	4	Portage County	WI	Ronald S. Rosera	1989	7,757
127 5/8	21 6/8	22 3/8	16 7/8	5	4	Dane County	WI	Larry Sperry	1989	7,757
127 5/8	19 2/8	20 3/8	17 1/8	4	4	Cass County	MI	Richard N. Ayers	1989	7,757
127 5/8	21 0/8	22 0/8	16 4/8	6	5	Washington County	KS	Toby Bruna	1989	7,757
127 5/8	20 5/8	22 4/8	18 7/8	5	6	Fillmore County	MN	Duane C. Baumler	1990	7,757
127 5/8	23 6/8	21 7/8	16 7/8	4	4	Sheboygan County	WI	Jim Ziegler, Jr.	1990	7,757
127 5/8	21 2/8	20 3/8	15 3/8	5	5	Macon County	MO	Roger Rector	1990	7,757
127 5/8	20 4/8	20 0/8	18 1/8	5	5	Plymouth County	IA	Bob D. Schlesser	1990	7,757
127 5/8	21 7/8	21 7/8	17 1/8	5	5	Sheboygan County	WI	James Drake	1990	7,757
127 5/8	20 0/8	21 1/8	15 1/8	5	5	Lee County	IA	James D. Bohnenkamp	1990	7,757
127 5/8	20 0/8	19 4/8	15 5/8	5	5	Woodford County	KY	Tony Bobbitt	1991	7,757
127 5/8	22 3/8	22 3/8	15 5/8	5	5	Mason County	WV	Keith Reynolds	1991	7,757
127 5/8	20 2/8	22 1/8	14 5/8	5	4	Crawford County	IL	Dennis Sturgis, Jr.	1991	7,757
127 5/8	23 3/8	23 4/8	17 5/8	5	4	Montgomery County	MD	James C. Dalrymple, Jr.	1991	7,757
127 5/8	19 2/8	20 3/8	17 1/8	5	5	Sheboygan County	WI	George W. Klein	1991	7,757
127 5/8	23 2/8	23 2/8	19 5/8	4	4	Wabasha County	MN	Lee G. Partington	1992	7,757
127 5/8	21 2/8	24 4/8	18 7/8	5	4	Columbia County	PA	Randy Yasenchak	1992	7,757
127 5/8	22 4/8	22 3/8	17 1/8	5	4	Milwaukee County	WI	Steven B. Schroeder	1992	7,757
127 4/8	20 5/8	20 5/8	16 2/8	5	5	Boone County	MO	Roger Soukup	1978	7,803
127 4/8	20 3/8	20 6/8	16 6/8	5	5	Wapello County	IA	Arnold E. Vest	1978	7,803
127 4/8	23 5/8	22 5/8	17 2/8	6	5	Muskingum County	OH	Mike Harris	1980	7,803
127 4/8	21 4/8	21 5/8	17 1/8	4	7	Trego County	KS	Ron Bain	1981	7,803
127 4/8	21 5/8	22 6/8	18 5/8	7	5	Des Moines County	IA	Jim Edwards	1982	7,803
127 4/8	19 4/8	18 5/8	16 4/8	5	5	Allen County	KS	Ivan Cooper	1983	7,803
127 4/8	21 3/8	22 4/8	17 0/8	4	4	Lake County	IL	Mike Mitten	1983	7,803
127 4/8	23 0/8	23 2/8	19 2/8	4	4	Van Buren County	MI	Ken Probst	1983	7,803
127 4/8	21 1/8	20 7/8	15 0/8	5	4	Nodaway County	MO	Jeff Davison	1983	7,803
127 4/8	19 6/8	20 0/8	16 6/8	5	5	Cherokee County	KS	Larry Thomas	1983	7,803
127 4/8	22 4/8	22 5/8	20 3/8	5	4	Nacogdoches County	TX	Harvy Hamby	1984	7,803
127 4/8	20 2/8	20 5/8	14 4/8	5	6	Crawford County	WI	Emil H. Loether, Jr.	1984	7,803
127 4/8	23 6/8	23 5/8	18 0/8	4	4	Lee County	IA	David D. Zaehringer	1984	7,803
127 4/8	21 1/8	19 7/8	17 0/8	4	4	Henderson County	KY	Wesley Campbell	1985	7,803
127 4/8	23 5/8	23 3/8	19 4/8	4	4	Somerset County	NJ	Steve Kotz	1985	7,803
127 4/8	22 2/8	21 5/8	15 2/8	6	6	Lake County	IL	David Mitten	1986	7,803
127 4/8	23 2/8	23 3/8	17 2/8	5	4	Waukesha County	WI	Ron Hill	1986	7,803
127 4/8	21 0/8	21 0/8	15 4/8	5	5	Buffalo County	WI	Richard J. Conrad	1986	7,803
127 4/8	23 1/8	24 4/8	23 0/8	4	6	Athens County	OH	Keith E. Moody	1986	7,803
127 4/8	21 4/8	21 6/8	18 4/8	4	4	Delaware County	IA	John Dillon	1986	7,803
127 4/8	21 3/8	21 7/8	16 4/8	5	5	Dimmit County	TX	Brett Crawford	1987	7,803
127 4/8	22 2/8	21 6/8	15 0/8	5	4	Pittsburg County	OK	David L. Scott	1987	7,803
127 4/8	20 1/8	19 3/8	16 4/8	5	6	Cooper County	MO	Joe Stenger	1988	7,803
127 4/8	22 3/8	22 3/8	18 2/8	4	5	Somerset County	NJ	James C. Kelly	1988	7,803
127 4/8	20 6/8	23 2/8	20 4/8	4	5	Putnam County	MO	Floyd Innis	1988	7,803
127 4/8	20 2/8	20 7/8	14 2/8	5	5	Johnson County	IN	Frank Cross	1988	7,803
127 4/8	23 3/8	23 3/8	16 4/8	4	4	Lake County	IL	Gene NeSmith	1988	7,803
127 4/8	21 0/8	20 2/8	13 0/8	4	6	Nelson County	KY	Cliff Buzick	1988	7,803
127 4/8	20 0/8	21 1/8	15 0/8	5	5	Osage County	OK	Paul Robinson	1989	7,803
127 4/8	23 6/8	23 7/8	20 0/8	3	4	Fillmore County	MN	Duane C. Baumler	1989	7,803
127 4/8	19 3/8	19 2/8	14 0/8	5	5	Amite County	MS	Bob Miller	1989	7,803
127 4/8	23 3/8	23 7/8	23 0/8	4	4	Muhlenberg County	KY	Scott Harper	1989	7,803
127 4/8	21 6/8	21 4/8	17 0/8	4	5	Cayuga County	NY	Donald W. Dennis	1989	7,803
127 4/8	21 6/8	21 4/8	15 4/8	4	4	Waushara County	WI	Andrew D. Sobieski	1989	7,803
127 4/8	22 4/8	22 6/8	18 0/8	4	4	La Salle County	IL	Bill Yessa	1989	7,803
127 4/8	22 0/8	20 6/8	18 2/8	4	5	Dodge County	MN	Steve Hughes	1989	7,803
127 4/8	20 3/8	20 4/8	15 6/8	5	5	Oneida County	WI	George Nowak	1989	7,803
127 4/8	20 5/8	21 2/8	14 5/8	6	4	Jefferson County	MT	George A. Vinal	1990	7,803

WHITETAIL DEER *(Typical Antlers)*

SCORE	LENGTH OF MAIN BEAM R	LENGTH OF MAIN BEAM L	INSIDE SPREAD	NUMBER OF POINTS R	NUMBER OF POINTS L	AREA	STATE/ PROVINCE	HUNTER'S NAME	DATE	RANK
127 4/8	22 2/8	22 6/8	17 0/8	4	4	Cass County	MI	Daniel R. Horak	1990	7,803
127 4/8	22 1/8	20 1/8	14 4/8	6	8	Henry County	MO	Marvin Ferguson	1990	7,803
127 4/8	21 1/8	20 0/8	16 2/8	4	4	Houston County	TX	Jerry Pruitt, Jr.	1990	7,803
127 4/8	22 1/8	21 1/8	13 1/8	5	5	Genesee County	NY	Mike L. Martin	1990	7,803
127 4/8	20 2/8	20 0/8	12 4/8	6	7	Calumet County	WI	Tom Brink	1990	7,803
127 4/8	24 1/8	14 5/8	18 4/8	5	4	Vernon County	MO	Greg Harris	1990	7,803
127 4/8	21 0/8	21 0/8	15 3/8	6	6	Washburn County	WI	Scott McFarren	1990	7,803
127 4/8	21 6/8	20 6/8	13 4/8	4	5	Genesee County	MI	Mark Joseph O'Brien	1991	7,803
127 4/8	19 7/8	19 7/8	17 4/8	5	5	Magrath	ALB	Cam Cook	1991	7,803
127 4/8	20 6/8	21 6/8	15 4/8	4	4	Livingston County	MI	James D. Duke	1991	7,803
127 4/8	20 4/8	21 0/8	18 0/8	5	5	Freeborn County	MN	Marvin Thompson	1991	7,803
127 4/8	22 4/8	22 0/8	18 0/8	4	4	Ste. Genevieve County	MO	Alvin Donze, Jr.	1991	7,803
127 4/8	19 2/8	19 1/8	12 6/8	5	5	Switzerland County	IN	Dennis Hardesty	1991	7,803
127 4/8	20 6/8	20 6/8	15 3/8	5	6	Ravalli County	MT	Ned Coorough	1991	7,803
127 4/8	20 2/8	20 2/8	15 4/8	4	6	Forest County	WI	Ron Matzdorf	1991	7,803
127 3/8	22 0/8	22 1/8	17 3/8	4	4	Lee County	IA	Lewallen Foster	1972	7,856
127 3/8	19 5/8	19 7/8	17 1/8	6	5	Scott County	KY	John Farris	1977	7,856
127 3/8	20 1/8	20 4/8	16 7/8	4	5	Suffolk County	NY	William R. Quarltere	1979	7,856
127 3/8	21 6/8	21 1/8	15 6/8	5	6	Waupaca County	WI	Daniel E. Yaeger	1979	7,856
127 3/8	21 6/8	22 0/8	22 0/8	5	5	Cortland County	NY	John B. Andrews	1980	7,856
127 3/8	22 3/8	22 1/8	17 1/8	5	5	Washington County	KS	Bob Funke	1981	7,856
127 3/8	20 5/8	21 7/8	17 1/8	8	7	Sauk County	WI	Roger D. Vondrasek	1981	7,856
127 3/8	21 1/8	20 3/8	15 5/8	6	6	Miami County	KS	Tom Wiggin	1982	7,856
127 3/8	20 3/8	20 2/8	17 3/8	4	4	Neosho County	KS	John R. Blackburn	1983	7,856
127 3/8	23 6/8	23 0/8	18 1/8	4	4	Reno County	KS	Greig Sims	1983	7,856
127 3/8	20 0/8	20 0/8	17 7/8	5	5	Waldo County	ME	Debbie A. Small	1984	7,856
127 3/8	21 3/8	22 6/8	13 7/8	5	5	Columbia County	WI	Richard J. Sutter	1985	7,856
127 3/8	20 5/8	21 3/8	18 7/8	4	4	Outagamie County	WI	Robert Randerson	1985	7,856
127 3/8	22 2/8	23 0/8	15 7/8	4	4	La Salle County	IL	Rich Castelli	1986	7,856
127 3/8	18 7/8	18 6/8	17 2/8	5	6	Wallowa County	OR	Ken Purnell	1987	7,856
127 3/8	20 4/8	20 7/8	22 3/8	4	4	Carroll County	OH	John M Shockey	1987	7,856
127 3/8	21 3/8	22 2/8	17 2/8	5	6	Sauk County	WI	Mike Jensen	1987	7,856
127 3/8	20 2/8	22 0/8	16 3/8	4	4	Will County	IL	Mike Kluska	1987	7,856
127 3/8	23 4/8	23 1/8	18 1/8	4	4	Chippewa County	MI	Gary E. Messer	1987	7,856
127 3/8	22 5/8	22 2/8	16 5/8	4	4	Woodbury County	IA	Terry Lee Hansen	1988	7,856
127 3/8	22 3/8	20 4/8	17 1/8	7	5	Sauk County	WI	Garry D. Bunz	1988	7,856
127 3/8	22 7/8	22 7/8	15 7/8	5	4	Lawrence County	OH	Mike Dickess	1988	7,856
127 3/8	20 6/8	21 3/8	15 3/8	6	5	Chisago County	MN	Daniel Carlson	1988	7,856
127 3/8	21 2/8	20 0/8	18 1/8	4	4	Clay County	IA	Steve Stoermer	1988	7,856
127 3/8	20 1/8	20 4/8	15 1/8	4	4	Somerset County	MD	Donald H. Ennis	1988	7,856
127 3/8	21 1/8	21 2/8	17 4/8	7	5	McLean County	IL	Barbara Eades	1988	7,856
127 3/8	20 0/8	20 0/8	15 1/8	5	5	Forest County	WI	Chuck W. Wruck	1989	7,856
127 3/8	23 7/8	23 2/8	17 5/8	4	4	Buffalo County	WI	Greg Lorenz	1989	7,856
127 3/8	22 1/8	22 3/8	16 5/8	4	4	Kingman County	KS	Terry Morisse	1989	7,856
127 3/8	20 2/8	20 0/8	14 5/8	5	5	Brown County	WI	Don Maurer	1989	7,856
127 3/8	23 1/8	23 0/8	17 3/8	7	5	Clinton County	MI	Mark J. Morgan	1989	7,856
127 3/8	21 0/8	21 0/8	16 1/8	5	5	Chippewa County	WI	Steve R. Rank	1989	7,856
127 3/8	21 6/8	20 2/8	18 1/8	4	4	Caroline County	MD	Eric Wise	1989	7,856
127 3/8	21 2/8	20 4/8	17 6/8	5	5	Marathon County	WI	Barry Gertschen	1990	7,856
127 3/8	19 7/8	20 5/8	19 7/8	5	5	Ogle County	IL	Brent Rutherford	1990	7,856
127 3/8	22 6/8	22 1/8	18 5/8	4	4	Perry County	IL	Scott Rice	1990	7,856
127 3/8	23 4/8	24 1/8	19 3/8	5	4	Lee County	IL	Gordon Gableman	1990	7,856
127 3/8	21 7/8	22 0/8	18 4/8	4	6	Tulsa County	OK	Carl Chisom	1990	7,856
127 3/8	20 6/8	23 0/8	20 5/8	4	5	Berks County	PA	Richard S. Steiger	1991	7,856
127 3/8	22 2/8	22 6/8	16 5/8	4	5	Rusk County	WI	Roger Schumacher	1991	7,856
127 3/8	22 6/8	24 0/8	17 7/8	4	4	Talbot County	MD	Mark E. Laustsen	1991	7,856
127 3/8	22 5/8	20 1/8	17 2/8	5	7	Andrew County	MO	Dan A. McLaughlin	1991	7,856
127 2/8	22 2/8	23 1/8	16 2/8	5	5	Madison County	AR	Johnny Darris	1964	7,898
127 2/8	23 5/8	23 7/8	16 4/8	4	3	Lawrence County	IL	Steven R. Tice	1967	7,898
127 2/8	22 0/8	21 3/8	17 2/8	4	5	Champaign County	IL	Pete Shepley	1972	7,898
127 2/8	20 1/8	20 2/8	16 0/8	5	5	Ontario County	NY	Robert G. Achter	1973	7,898
127 2/8	19 2/8	19 0/8	15 2/8	5	5	Blue Earth County	MN	Stanley R. Defries	1973	7,898
127 2/8	21 7/8	22 3/8	17 2/8	4	4	Latah County	ID	Mike VonLindern	1978	7,898
127 2/8	21 7/8	21 2/8	15 6/8	5	4	Jefferson County	IN	Robert Pitt	1978	7,898
127 2/8	23 6/8	22 4/8	20 2/8	4	4	Bayfield County	WI	Mark Milford	1980	7,898
127 2/8	22 4/8	21 6/8	16 4/8	4	5	Oconto County	WI	Don Fullerton	1982	7,898
127 2/8	23 3/8	21 3/8	20 3/8	5	5	Hunterdon County	NJ	Wayne Lisehora	1982	7,898
127 2/8	22 1/8	21 3/8	17 4/8	4	4	Stanley County	SD	Brad Taylor	1983	7,898
127 2/8	22 2/8	22 1/8	17 4/8	5	5	Sauk County	WI	James Byrnes	1983	7,898
127 2/8	23 1/8	24 0/8	19 4/8	6	9	Morrison County	MN	Ken Arnzen	1984	7,898

Score	Length of Main Beam R	Length of Main Beam L	Inside Spread	Number of Points R	Number of Points L	Area	State/ Province	Hunter's Name	Date	Rank
127 2/8	22 0/8	21 5/8	16 7/8	7	5	Christian County	IL	James Eck	1984	7,898
127 2/8	20 2/8	20 0/8	20 3/8	4	4	Towner County	ND	Trent Halberstroh	1984	7,898
127 2/8	22 6/8	23 2/8	14 6/8	4	4	Grant County	OK	Ronnie B Smart	1985	7,898
127 2/8	21 0/8	19 6/8	13 6/8	5	4	Marshall County	KS	Ray Aslin	1985	7,898
127 2/8	23 2/8	20 5/8	16 6/8	5	4	Clay County	KS	Jan Kissinger	1985	7,898
127 2/8	22 3/8	21 7/8	16 3/8	6	5	Powell County	MT	Sonny Templeton	1985	7,898
127 2/8	22 1/8	22 0/8	16 4/8	4	4	Dane County	WI	Perry R. Peterson	1986	7,898
127 2/8	20 5/8	20 6/8	13 6/8	4	4	McLean County	ND	Eugene Radke	1986	7,898
127 2/8	20 6/8	20 3/8	14 2/8	4	4	Keya Paha County	NE	Keith Nordeen	1986	7,898
127 2/8	24 0/8	23 4/8	16 4/8	5	5	Bertie County	NC	Roy Copeland	1986	7,898
127 2/8	19 0/8	16 4/8	17 4/8	5	5	Buffalo County	WI	Peter J. Mancl	1986	7,898
127 2/8	21 3/8	21 0/8	16 2/8	4	4	Pierce County	WI	Danny White	1986	7,898
127 2/8	20 5/8	22 2/8	15 6/8	5	4	Calgary	ALB	Eric Soderberg	1986	7,898
127 2/8	20 6/8	20 6/8	15 2/8	5	4	Piatt County	IL	Eileen De Moss	1986	7,898
127 2/8	18 1/8	18 5/8	15 6/8	5	5	Botetourt County	VA	Charles E. Speck	1987	7,898
127 2/8	21 7/8	22 2/8	18 4/8	4	5	Peoria County	IL	Roger Arends	1987	7,898
127 2/8	21 2/8	21 3/8	16 6/8	4	4	Kent County	MI	Steve VanDerLaan	1987	7,898
127 2/8	22 3/8	21 4/8	18 0/8	4	5	Llano County	TX	Mark Warren	1988	7,898
127 2/8	20 2/8	20 5/8	15 0/8	4	4	Oklahoma County	OK	Bill F. Noble	1988	7,898
127 2/8	20 3/8	22 2/8	16 7/8	7	6	Cerro Gordo County	IA	Vern Schnoebelen	1988	7,898
127 2/8	23 0/8	21 6/8	18 6/8	6	4	Wayne County	NY	Jason S. Haas	1988	7,898
127 2/8	21 2/8	21 3/8	16 1/8	6	4	Cass County	MI	Michael L. Ritter	1988	7,898
127 2/8	21 1/8	21 0/8	17 4/8	4	4	Kane County	IL	Chuck Grant	1988	7,898
127 2/8	20 6/8	21 3/8	14 4/8	5	5	Otoe County	NE	Rick Lee Sedersten	1988	7,898
127 2/8	21 2/8	21 2/8	16 4/8	5	4	Barber County	KS	Bob Christensen	1988	7,898
127 2/8	18 6/8	18 7/8	17 2/8	6	6	Will County	IL	Tom S. Spence	1989	7,898
127 2/8	22 5/8	22 7/8	18 4/8	4	4	Jackson County	WI	Dave Arentz	1989	7,898
127 2/8	20 0/8	19 7/8	14 2/8	5	5	McPherson County	KS	Jimmy Dean Beard	1989	7,898
127 2/8	21 2/8	22 0/8	20 0/8	4	4	Prince Georges County	MD	Russell A. Nichols	1989	7,898
127 2/8	20 6/8	20 4/8	15 2/8	5	4	Butler County	KS	Dean Roedel, Jr.	1989	7,898
127 2/8	24 0/8	23 4/8	16 1/8	5	5	Henry County	KY	Kenneth R. Fante	1990	7,898
127 2/8	23 2/8	23 0/8	16 6/8	4	4	Clayton County	GA	Rodney Chris Bishop	1990	7,898
127 2/8	23 7/8	23 2/8	19 2/8	4	4	Trimble County	KY	Bill Drane	1990	7,898
127 2/8	19 7/8	19 1/8	12 4/8	6	5	Jefferson County	KS	Brian Artzer	1990	7,898
127 2/8	21 5/8	21 5/8	16 0/8	5	5	Trempealeau County	WI	Rusty Severson	1990	7,898
127 2/8	19 7/8	20 2/8	15 0/8	5	4	Wayne County	NY	Allan C. Tyo	1990	7,898
127 2/8	21 2/8	21 6/8	17 6/8	5	6	Athens County	OH	James S. Shipley	1990	7,898
127 2/8	23 0/8	22 5/8	19 0/8	4	5	Ellis County	OK	Bill Parry	1991	7,898
127 2/8	22 1/8	22 7/8	17 4/8	4	4	Wentworth	ONT	Kevin Parchem	1991	7,898
127 2/8	20 4/8	19 7/8	16 6/8	5	5	Washington County	PA	Bill B. Carden	1991	7,898
127 2/8	23 2/8	22 5/8	14 4/8	4	4	Highland County	OH	Martin Bullock	1991	7,898
127 2/8	20 3/8	21 3/8	14 6/8	5	7	Burleigh County	ND	Garett Strandemo	1991	7,898
127 2/8	21 6/8	21 6/8	20 6/8	4	4	Logan County	IL	Steve Schilling	1991	7,898
127 2/8	22 6/8	23 0/8	23 0/8	5	4	Walworth County	WI	Jesse Adams, Jr.	1991	7,898
127 2/8	21 3/8	21 6/8	16 2/8	4	4	Roscommon County	MI	Donald V. Hine	1992	7,898
127 2/8	25 0/8	26 0/8	20 6/8	4	4	Peoria County	IL	Larry E. Pollack	1992	7,898
127 2/8	20 4/8	20 5/8	14 2/8	5	5	Webster County	KY	Robert George	1992	7,898
127 1/8	19 5/8	20 5/8	15 1/8	4	4	Oneida County	WI	Fred Felbab	1961	7,958
127 1/8	21 0/8	20 4/8	18 3/8	6	5	Marion County	IA	Donald C. Clark	1970	7,958
127 1/8	18 0/8	20 5/8	15 5/8	5	4	Des Moines County	IA	Roy Veach	1970	7,958
127 1/8	23 0/8	23 0/8	16 7/8	4	4	Union County	IA	Richard Siddens	1971	7,958
127 1/8	22 7/8	21 6/8	16 5/8	5	5	Gratiot County	MI	Kim Hagerman	1979	7,958
127 1/8	20 6/8	21 4/8	16 5/8	4	4	Keith County	NE	Tom Tietz	1981	7,958
127 1/8	21 6/8	23 3/8	18 7/8	4	4	Massac County	IL	John Shelby	1981	7,958
127 1/8	19 4/8	20 2/8	16 3/8	5	6	Bon Homme County	SD	John P. Freidel	1982	7,958
127 1/8	20 3/8	19 1/8	16 5/8	5	5	Jefferson County	IL	Ed Knaus	1983	7,958
127 1/8	20 2/8	21 3/8	18 5/8	5	5	Leavenworth County	KS	Albert Lyle Karl	1983	7,958
127 1/8	21 3/8	21 4/8	17 0/8	5	5	Bullock County	AL	James D Sims	1984	7,958
127 1/8	21 6/8	21 7/8	15 3/8	5	5	Madison County	NY	Louis A Colasanti	1984	7,958
127 1/8	23 4/8	21 5/8	18 3/8	5	5	Wyandotte County	KS	Spencer G. Ishmael	1984	7,958
127 1/8	19 6/8	21 2/8	14 0/8	5	6	Scott County	MN	Ron Stier	1984	7,958
127 1/8	22 1/8	20 7/8	18 5/8	5	5	Somerset County	NJ	Joe Cotone	1985	7,958
127 1/8	23 1/8	24 1/8	19 0/8	8	6	Ogle County	IL	Bifford J. Wyatt	1985	7,958
127 1/8	22 6/8	23 4/8	16 3/8	5	4	Scott County	IA	Ronald L. Mott	1985	7,958
127 1/8	20 2/8	20 0/8	16 1/8	4	5	Cowley County	KS	Jack L. Dennett, Jr.	1986	7,958
127 1/8	23 0/8	22 5/8	18 4/8	6	5	Yuma County	CO	Tony Seahorn	1986	7,958
127 1/8	19 4/8	20 0/8	15 5/8	4	4	Forest County	WI	Ron Van Straten	1987	7,958
127 1/8	21 2/8	20 7/8	15 6/8	4	5	Licking County	OH	Michael J Boucher	1987	7,958
127 1/8	20 2/8	20 6/8	16 1/8	6	6	Huntington County	IN	Dennis I. Cottam	1987	7,958
127 1/8	23 1/8	24 2/8	20 0/8	5	4	Edgar County	IL	M. Mark Davis	1987	7,958

SCORE	LENGTH OF MAIN BEAM		INSIDE SPREAD	NUMBER OF POINTS		AREA	STATE/ PROVINCE	HUNTER'S NAME	DATE	RANK
	R	L		R	L					
127 1/8	20 1/8	20 2/8	18 1/8	4	4	Lake County	IL	Dave Pederson	1987	7,958
127 1/8	20 5/8	19 7/8	16 6/8	6	5	Fulton County	IL	Jay D. Van Voorhis	1987	7,958
127 1/8	20 6/8	20 6/8	17 5/8	4	4	Franklin County	MA	Richard Scorzafava	1987	7,958
127 1/8	22 1/8	22 6/8	15 5/8	5	6	Angelina County	TX	Ben Bartlett	1987	7,958
127 1/8	21 7/8	22 4/8	16 1/8	4	4	Lake County	IL	Woody Scruggs	1988	7,958
127 1/8	21 6/8	20 6/8	17 3/8	4	4	Jo Daviess County	IL	Lewis Heidenreich	1988	7,958
127 1/8	21 5/8	21 6/8	18 3/8	4	4	Sussex County	DE	Rick Mazol	1989	7,958
127 1/8	22 3/8	22 3/8	20 5/8	4	4	Wyoming County	NY	Greg Hoffmeister	1989	7,958
127 1/8	22 2/8	21 5/8	17 2/8	5	4	Harlan County	NE	Paul Ekberg	1989	7,958
127 1/8	21 0/8	21 2/8	15 3/8	4	4	Washburn County	WI	Kevin P. Tripp	1990	7,958
127 1/8	20 7/8	21 4/8	18 0/8	5	6	Pike County	IL	Gary L. Goldasich	1990	7,958
127 1/8	21 7/8	21 7/8	15 3/8	4	5	Jasper County	TX	Kevin W. Walker, Sr.	1990	7,958
127 1/8	20 1/8	21 0/8	16 1/8	5	5	St. Joseph County	MI	Jeffery Daniel Stephens	1990	7,958
127 1/8	21 7/8	23 2/8	18 0/8	5	6	Ashtabula County	OH	Paul Drotar	1990	7,958
127 1/8	18 5/8	18 6/8	11 7/8	5	5	Marathon County	WI	Tom R. Pankratz	1991	7,958
127 1/8	24 0/8	23 6/8	19 3/8	4	5	Edwards County	IL	Tim Brake	1991	7,958
127 1/8	24 1/8	23 7/8	18 0/8	5	4	Mercer County	NJ	Dennis Graber	1991	7,958
127 0/8	26 1/8	26 3/8	17 6/8	5	5	Boone County	KY	Steve Toles	1976	7,998
127 0/8	20 3/8	20 3/8	15 6/8	6	6	Sauk County	WI	Adrian Julson	1979	7,998
127 0/8	23 5/8	23 3/8	19 0/8	5	4	Licking County	OH	Curtis W. Price	1979	7,998
127 0/8	20 0/8	20 7/8	18 2/8	5	5	Harris County	TX	Daniel Barnes	1980	7,998
127 0/8	22 4/8	21 4/8	15 4/8	5	6	Tuscarawas County	OH	David Pappas	1980	7,998
127 0/8	22 2/8	22 2/8	14 2/8	8	6	Kittson County	MN	John S. Ritter	1981	7,998
127 0/8	19 5/8	18 4/8	18 4/8	5	5	Graham County	KS	Russell Hull	1981	7,998
127 0/8	20 7/8	21 4/8	18 4/8	4	4	Miller County	MO	Gary Haupt	1982	7,998
127 0/8	21 1/8	20 3/8	14 6/8	5	5	Coahoma County	MS	Charles L. Campassi	1983	7,998
127 0/8	21 6/8	20 3/8	17 2/8	4	5	Dane County	WI	Charles F. Hilgendorf	1983	7,998
127 0/8	22 6/8	22 6/8	17 2/8	5	5	Spokane County	WA	William J. Lantiegne	1983	7,998
127 0/8	22 2/8	22 4/8	15 6/8	5	5	Sauk County	WI	Richard A. Galston	1984	7,998
127 0/8	23 1/8	23 1/8	17 6/8	4	5	Litchfield County	CT	Michael Cristillo	1984	7,998
127 0/8	19 6/8	18 3/8	16 6/8	5	5	Wayne County	NE	Mike Lutt	1984	7,998
127 0/8	19 6/8	19 3/8	16 4/8	5	5	Door County	WI	Wayne Lautenbach	1985	7,998
127 0/8	20 0/8	19 4/8	15 0/8	5	5	Audrain County	MO	Marty Bertels	1985	7,998
127 0/8	21 5/8	21 1/8	17 0/8	5	4	Powell County	MT	Sonny Templeton	1985	7,998
127 0/8	19 6/8	20 3/8	16 0/8	4	4	Dickinson County	KS	Bradley Wayne Whisler	1985	7,998
127 0/8	21 0/8	23 6/8	18 4/8	5	5	Lafayette County	WI	Jerod Ray	1985	7,998
127 0/8	19 1/8	20 4/8	15 6/8	4	4	Franklin County	OH	Craig A. Bonham	1985	7,998
127 0/8	23 7/8	24 3/8	16 0/8	4	5	Montgomery County	AL	David Barrow	1986	7,998
127 0/8	21 4/8	22 3/8	15 6/8	4	4	Marquette County	MI	Everett W. Shaw	1986	7,998
127 0/8	20 5/8	20 1/8	14 6/8	5	5	Big Stone County	MN	Pete Karels	1986	7,998
127 0/8	19 6/8	20 2/8	15 2/8	5	5	Portage County	WI	Brian Klesmith	1986	7,998
127 0/8	23 2/8	22 3/8	16 0/8	5	6	Ray County	MO	Kenneth Coats	1987	7,998
127 0/8	22 7/8	22 3/8	16 4/8	4	4	Dubuque County	IA	Kevin R. Schmitt	1987	7,998
127 0/8	22 3/8	22 2/8	15 2/8	4	4	Hitchcock County	NE	Dave Holt	1987	7,998
127 0/8	22 2/8	21 6/8	17 0/8	5	5	McNairy County	TN	Paul Steward	1988	7,998
127 0/8	21 3/8	20 5/8	15 6/8	5	5	Pulaski County	KY	Harold Allen	1988	7,998
127 0/8	22 3/8	22 7/8	17 6/8	6	5	Greene County	IL	Gerald Isringhausen	1988	7,998
127 0/8	19 7/8	19 1/8	16 0/8	6	5	Nicollet County	MN	Ronny Cordes	1989	7,998
127 0/8	22 1/8	21 6/8	17 6/8	5	5	Atascosa County	TX	Mike Palmer	1989	7,998
127 0/8	17 2/8	17 5/8	15 4/8	5	5	Bexar County	TX	John W. Wallace	1989	7,998
127 0/8	23 0/8	22 6/8	22 5/8	6	6	Will County	IL	Russell Robak	1989	7,998
127 0/8	22 5/8	22 2/8	18 0/8	4	4	Burleigh County	ND	Bill Helphrey	1989	7,998
127 0/8	20 5/8	20 4/8	19 0/8	5	5	De Witt County	IL	Sylvan Purcell	1989	7,998
127 0/8	21 6/8	21 3/8	16 6/8	4	4	New Castle County	DE	Joseph J. Subolesky	1990	7,998
127 0/8	22 2/8	21 0/8	17 3/8	6	4	Lawrence County	IL	Jeff Jones	1990	7,998
127 0/8	21 1/8	20 0/8	17 0/8	4	4	Portage County	WI	Jeffrey D. Carter	1990	7,998
127 0/8	23 0/8	22 2/8	13 6/8	5	6	Pawnee County	KS	Bob Faris	1990	7,998
127 0/8	21 4/8	21 5/8	16 4/8	5	4	McHenry County	IL	Matt N. Dieter	1991	7,998
127 0/8	22 0/8	21 7/8	15 1/8	7	5	St. Croix County	WI	Randal Ramberg	1991	7,998
127 0/8	20 1/8	20 2/8	14 6/8	5	5	Buffalo County	WI	Brian R. Potter	1991	7,998
127 0/8	22 6/8	22 0/8	18 4/8	5	5	Morris County	NJ	Andrew Murnock, Sr.	1991	7,998
127 0/8	23 1/8	23 6/8	16 7/8	5	4	Murray County	OK	Bobby Pope	1991	7,998
127 0/8	21 5/8	21 5/8	15 6/8	6	5	Yates County	NY	Mark R. Urban	1991	7,998
126 7/8	22 5/8	22 6/8	17 4/8	5	4	Dade County	MO	Paul Watson	1970	8,044
126 7/8	21 7/8	21 0/8	14 4/8	5	4	Calhoun County	MI	Tom A. Longnecker	1976	8,044
126 7/8	20 0/8	20 4/8	18 3/8	5	5	Muscatine County	IA	Ronald W. Crain	1978	8,044
126 7/8	22 4/8	22 0/8	17 3/8	6	6	Waukesha County	WI	Daniel J. Hanrahan	1978	8,044
126 7/8	21 3/8	21 2/8	16 7/8	6	5	Pine County	MN	Randy Krone	1979	8,044
126 7/8	25 5/8	24 6/8	20 3/8	4	4	Washington County	WI	Brent Grensavitch	1980	8,044
126 7/8	20 0/8	23 3/8	16 3/8	5	5	Tazewell County	IL	Kenneth Hoback	1981	8,044

Score	Length of Main Beam R	Length of Main Beam L	Inside Spread	Number of Points R	Number of Points L	Area	State/Province	Hunter's Name	Date	Rank
126 7/8	21 4/8	21 4/8	17 7/8	5	6	Huron County	MI	Greg Talaski	1981	8,044
126 7/8	22 7/8	22 2/8	17 3/8	4	4	Brown County	MN	Robert Hertling	1982	8,044
126 7/8	22 3/8	22 7/8	16 5/8	4	5	Ogle County	IL	Jerry Taylor	1982	8,044
126 7/8	21 5/8	22 2/8	17 3/8	4	5	Vinton County	OH	Mitchell Barnett	1982	8,044
126 7/8	22 4/8	23 2/8	18 7/8	4	4	Lake County	IL	Carl H. Spaeth	1983	8,044
126 7/8	24 4/8	22 6/8	15 5/8	4	5	Walworth County	WI	Ray Radtke	1984	8,044
126 7/8	20 5/8	20 4/8	15 7/8	5	4	Brown County	SD	Jack Ness	1984	8,044
126 7/8	17 7/8	18 3/8	14 5/8	5	5	Howard County	IN	James E Taylor	1984	8,044
126 7/8	24 0/8	23 1/8	17 7/8	4	4	Isanti County	MN	Gary Lamecker	1985	8,044
126 7/8	22 0/8	22 5/8	15 1/8	5	5	De Kalb County	GA	William C. Abernethy	1985	8,044
126 7/8	22 3/8	22 1/8	17 1/8	5	4	Price County	WI	Jeff Kluever	1985	8,044
126 7/8	21 7/8	21 4/8	15 5/8	4	5	Polk County	WI	Steve Hischer	1986	8,044
126 7/8	20 4/8	20 5/8	18 7/8	4	4	Buffalo County	WI	Lee Scharr	1986	8,044
126 7/8	21 6/8	21 4/8	17 3/8	5	5	Racine County	WI	Patrick Blaskowski	1986	8,044
126 7/8	21 5/8	22 4/8	15 5/8	4	4	Parke County	IN	Charles R. Smith, Jr.	1986	8,044
126 7/8	20 4/8	21 1/8	16 2/8	5	4	Marion County	KY	Tommy Fowler, Jr.	1987	8,044
126 7/8	21 1/8	21 4/8	15 2/8	5	4	Tom Green County	TX	Ronnie Parsons	1987	8,044
126 7/8	21 3/8	20 7/8	18 3/8	4	4	Van Buren County	IA	Steven J. Lepic	1987	8,044
126 7/8	19 7/8	20 7/8	15 5/8	6	6	Jasper County	GA	Chris Atkinson	1988	8,044
126 7/8	22 3/8	22 2/8	16 5/8	6	5	Washington County	WI	Mark Grissman	1988	8,044
126 7/8	21 4/8	25 5/8	18 3/8	4	4	Monmouth County	NJ	Greg Szulecki	1988	8,044
126 7/8	22 3/8	20 6/8	16 0/8	4	5	Suffolk County	NY	Peter G. Behnen	1988	8,044
126 7/8	22 6/8	22 4/8	17 6/8	6	6	Ross County	OH	Al Kowalski	1989	8,044
126 7/8	21 0/8	20 6/8	14 1/8	5	5	Iron County	MI	Arvid A. Ames	1989	8,044
126 7/8	22 2/8	22 3/8	19 7/8	4	7	Llano County	TX	Carl Walker	1989	8,044
126 7/8	22 5/8	22 1/8	14 5/8	5	5	Morrison County	MN	Mark L. Meyer	1989	8,044
126 7/8	19 2/8	20 4/8	13 4/8	5	6	Clarke County	IA	David Meyers	1989	8,044
126 7/8	21 6/8	21 4/8	14 7/8	4	5	Westchester County	NY	Michael Fedor	1989	8,044
126 7/8	21 4/8	21 1/8	17 1/8	4	5	Butler County	KS	Tracey Chamberline	1989	8,044
126 7/8	20 0/8	19 7/8	14 3/8	6	5	Webster County	IA	Chad Foster	1989	8,044
126 7/8	21 1/8	20 4/8	18 7/8	6	5	Greene County	AR	Danny Sellers	1989	8,044
126 7/8	20 7/8	21 3/8	17 4/8	5	5	Kandiyohi County	MN	Howard Parker	1990	8,044
126 7/8	21 7/8	21 7/8	17 5/8	4	5	Buffalo County	WI	Brook A. Baumann	1990	8,044
126 7/8	24 4/8	24 1/8	22 4/8	5	4	Missoula County	MT	Michael L. Simpson	1990	8,044
126 7/8	21 5/8	19 6/8	14 5/8	5	5	Tom Green County	TX	Ronnie Parsons	1991	8,044
126 7/8	20 4/8	20 7/8	16 3/8	4	4	Wayne County	IL	Wade Loupe	1991	8,044
126 7/8	25 0/8	24 0/8	19 4/8	3	6	Eau Claire County	WI	Riley Fletschock	1991	8,044
126 7/8	20 6/8	20 2/8	15 7/8	5	5	Lapeer County	MI	John E. Wencley	1991	8,044
126 7/8	22 6/8	20 2/8	17 1/8	8	7	Grant County	MN	Carlos Gust	1991	8,044
126 7/8	19 7/8	20 1/8	16 1/8	7	7	Clayton County	IA	Dean Engelken	1991	8,044
126 7/8	21 0/8	20 2/8	19 2/8	5	6	Webster County	IA	Tim Bacon	1991	8,044
126 7/8	21 7/8	22 1/8	16 1/8	4	4	Burleigh County	ND	Don Ressler	1991	8,044
126 6/8	22 5/8	22 0/8	17 2/8	6	4	Winneshiek County	IA	Nick Bowlus	1952	8,093
126 6/8	20 0/8	19 5/8	13 4/8	5	6	Pine County	MN	Marvin W. Brown	1968	8,093
126 6/8	18 1/8	18 2/8	15 6/8	5	5	Todd County	MN	Paul Jenc	1973	8,093
126 6/8	22 0/8	20 7/8	17 4/8	5	5	Fulton County	IN	John W. Baker	1974	8,093
126 6/8	21 6/8	24 1/8	17 2/8	4	4	Calhoun County	MI	James Birmingham	1976	8,093
126 6/8	20 7/8	21 1/8	15 2/8	5	5	Montgomery County	KS	Mike Nixon	1976	8,093
126 6/8	21 0/8	21 0/8	16 2/8	5	4	Woodford County	IL	Rickie D. Snell	1976	8,093
126 6/8	23 0/8	22 5/8	18 4/8	4	4	Grant County	WV	Carl Muth	1977	8,093
126 6/8	21 5/8	21 6/8	16 0/8	4	4	Webster County	IA	Robert B. Seger II	1979	8,093
126 6/8	21 7/8	23 1/8	16 6/8	4	4	Whiteside County	IL	Art Heinze	1980	8,093
126 6/8	22 1/8	22 1/8	17 0/8	4	5	Jasper County	IN	Gary Shaw	1980	8,093
126 6/8	25 0/8	24 0/8	19 2/8	4	4	Auglaize County	OH	Lee Atha	1981	8,093
126 6/8	22 2/8	22 5/8	18 6/8	4	4	Genesee County	MI	Bob Bouck	1983	8,093
126 6/8	20 0/8	22 0/8	14 6/8	5	5	Licking County	OH	Dana E. Kevelder	1983	8,093
126 6/8	20 2/8	20 6/8	16 0/8	5	5	Lee County	IA	Dan Wilcox	1983	8,093
126 6/8	24 2/8	22 7/8	17 6/8	6	6	Douglas County	NE	Jim Walter	1985	8,093
126 6/8	20 4/8	21 4/8	17 6/8	4	4	Crawford County	WI	Calvin Hendrick	1985	8,093
126 6/8	21 4/8	20 4/8	15 7/8	7	5	Bollinger County	MO	Rodney C. Bowling	1985	8,093
126 6/8	21 5/8	21 6/8	16 2/8	4	5	Osage County	MO	Michael Dinger	1986	8,093
126 6/8	25 3/8	24 2/8	17 6/8	4	4	Dunn County	WI	Daryl Iverson	1986	8,093
126 6/8	22 2/8	22 6/8	18 6/8	4	5	Union County	IL	Sam Shafer	1986	8,093
126 6/8	25 1/8	23 1/8	18 2/8	4	4	Defiance County	OH	William Riley	1986	8,093
126 6/8	25 1/8	23 1/8	18 2/8	4	4	Defiance County	OH	William Riley	1986	8,093
126 6/8	23 2/8	23 4/8	20 4/8	4	3	Jo Daviess County	IL	Jerry Smith	1986	8,093
126 6/8	23 7/8	23 6/8	15 7/8	5	6	Williamson County	IL	Wallace Mick	1986	8,093
126 6/8	19 7/8	18 2/8	18 6/8	5	5	Madison County	IA	Marc A. Headington	1987	8,093
126 6/8	19 3/8	19 4/8	15 0/8	5	5	Waupaca County	WI	William J. Peterson	1987	8,093
126 6/8	21 1/8	20 3/8	15 4/8	6	6	Lincoln County	WI	Keene Robl	1987	8,093

SCORE	LENGTH OF MAIN BEAM		INSIDE SPREAD	NUMBER OF POINTS		AREA	STATE/ PROVINCE	HUNTER'S NAME	DATE	RANK
	R	L		R	L					
126 6/8	23 0/8	22 0/8	14 4/8	4	5	Knox County	IN	Michael E. Hartigan	1988	8,093
126 6/8	21 1/8	21 1/8	15 6/8	5	5	Carroll County	OH	Dean Stebner	1988	8,093
126 6/8	23 3/8	24 0/8	18 4/8	5	4	La Crosse County	WI	Gerard Passe	1988	8,093
126 6/8	20 7/8	20 3/8	17 2/8	5	5	Louisa County	IA	Roger Gipple	1988	8,093
126 6/8	23 7/8	23 2/8	16 0/8	5	5	Boone County	MO	David J. Westmoreland	1988	8,093
126 6/8	21 3/8	21 3/8	17 0/8	5	5	Warren County	IA	Richard Roberts	1989	8,093
126 6/8	22 4/8	21 2/8	15 2/8	5	5	Vigo County	IN	Tom Mundy	1989	8,093
126 6/8	22 3/8	22 0/8	16 2/8	5	5	Warrick County	IN	Dale Rash	1989	8,093
126 6/8	20 4/8	20 5/8	17 4/8	4	5	Traill County	ND	James Strand	1990	8,093
126 6/8	19 5/8	20 6/8	13 6/8	5	5	Arenac County	MI	Anthony D. Windt	1990	8,093
126 6/8	21 6/8	21 5/8	15 0/8	5	5	Wayne County	MI	Paul Nash	1990	8,093
126 6/8	20 1/8	20 6/8	15 2/8	5	5	Flathead County	MT	Dennis Brieske	1990	8,093
126 6/8	19 2/8	20 5/8	16 2/8	6	5	Dane County	WI	Mike Crisman	1990	8,093
126 6/8	23 6/8	24 0/8	15 4/8	5	4	Pierce County	WI	Erik Jensen	1990	8,093
126 6/8	25 1/8	24 6/8	17 3/8	5	3	Clark County	IL	Jim Baker	1990	8,093
126 6/8	22 3/8	23 3/8	17 6/8	4	5	Franklin County	MA	Timothy J. Wendell	1990	8,093
126 6/8	21 1/8	21 4/8	17 2/8	5	6	Chase County	KS	Larry Walker, Jr.	1991	8,093
126 6/8	21 5/8	22 6/8	14 4/8	5	5	Ashe County	NC	Roger L. Richardson	1991	8,093
126 6/8	22 1/8	21 5/8	18 1/8	5	4	Tippecanoe County	IN	L. Paul Lewis	1991	8,093
126 6/8	22 0/8	22 2/8	18 2/8	5	5	Meade County	KS	Terry Cordes	1991	8,093
126 6/8	21 7/8	21 2/8	17 6/8	4	4	Price County	WI	Jerry J. Bedor	1991	8,093
126 6/8	22 2/8	22 4/8	18 4/8	4	4	Warren County	MS	Bob Lane	1991	8,093
126 6/8	18 6/8	18 7/8	14 6/8	5	5	Richland County	ND	Rob Punton	1992	8,093
126 5/8	22 4/8	22 0/8	21 5/8	4	4	Pine County	MN	Buck Doran	1945	8,144
126 5/8	22 5/8	23 0/8	19 0/8	5	5	Roberts County	SD	Roland L. Hausmann	1961	8,144
126 5/8	21 5/8	21 3/8	19 3/8	4	4	Johnson County	IN	Roger E. Harvey	1975	8,144
126 5/8	23 4/8	25 0/8	19 7/8	6	6	Wellington County	ONT	James A. Reid	1976	8,144
126 5/8	21 4/8	21 6/8	17 2/8	7	7	Jackson County	MI	Gary A. Dawson	1980	8,144
126 5/8	21 0/8	19 7/8	16 5/8	4	4	Greene County	AL	Alvin Pearson	1980	8,144
126 5/8	19 7/8	19 3/8	14 1/8	5	4	Owen County	IN	Bill G. Tanner	1980	8,144
126 5/8	23 6/8	24 7/8	17 3/8	5	4	Jackson County	MN	Kerry Ella	1981	8,144
126 5/8	19 5/8	20 4/8	16 3/8	5	5	Waupaca County	WI	Mark Jahr	1981	8,144
126 5/8	20 7/8	22 6/8	16 1/8	4	4	Jefferson County	ID	Roger W. Atwood	1982	8,144
126 5/8	18 2/8	18 2/8	12 7/8	6	5	Johnson County	WY	Jerry N. Blossom	1983	8,144
126 5/8	21 2/8	21 7/8	14 3/8	4	4	Boone County	IA	Tim Marshall	1983	8,144
126 5/8	21 5/8	21 3/8	16 6/8	6	6	Lake County	IL	Mark Fugett	1984	8,144
126 5/8	23 0/8	22 7/8	15 3/8	5	5	Bedford County	VA	Russell A. Barton	1985	8,144
126 5/8	22 3/8	21 0/8	16 1/8	5	6	Jefferson County	KS	Brian Artzer	1986	8,144
126 5/8	22 2/8	22 4/8	18 5/8	5	4	Grand Traverse County	MI	Daniel D. Morrison	1986	8,144
126 5/8	21 7/8	23 0/8	17 5/8	4	4	Lafayette County	WI	Mike Traub	1986	8,144
126 5/8	21 4/8	21 2/8	15 5/8	5	5	Switzerland County	IN	Edwin L. McDaniel	1986	8,144
126 5/8	21 2/8	20 7/8	19 5/8	5	4	Roberts County	SD	Paul Sand	1986	8,144
126 5/8	22 1/8	22 2/8	18 5/8	4	4	Warren County	NJ	Dennis Stankovitz	1987	8,144
126 5/8	19 6/8	19 6/8	16 3/8	5	5	Uvalde County	TX	William E. Legg	1987	8,144
126 5/8	19 4/8	19 6/8	16 0/8	6	5	Jefferson County	NE	Kevin Wagner	1988	8,144
126 5/8	22 2/8	21 6/8	18 2/8	7	4	Columbia County	WI	Robert L. Lex	1988	8,144
126 5/8	22 0/8	22 5/8	17 4/8	6	6	Marshall County	IN	Richard Flory	1988	8,144
126 5/8	19 3/8	20 3/8	14 5/8	5	5	Grant County	OK	Jim Sheets	1988	8,144
126 5/8	23 1/8	22 6/8	18 4/8	4	6	Crawford County	IL	Bill Waddell	1988	8,144
126 5/8	22 2/8	21 1/8	15 1/8	4	4	Forest County	WI	Ralph L. Horsens	1989	8,144
126 5/8	18 5/8	19 1/8	17 3/8	7	6	Thomas County	NE	Dan Neal	1989	8,144
126 5/8	20 0/8	20 0/8	14 1/8	5	5	Russell County	AL	James Vernon Adcock	1989	8,144
126 5/8	21 6/8	21 2/8	16 6/8	5	5	Jackson County	WV	Joseph H. Bigley	1989	8,144
126 5/8	20 5/8	21 0/8	14 5/8	4	4	Eau Claire County	WI	Robert Nelson	1989	8,144
126 5/8	23 4/8	22 6/8	16 5/8	4	8	Warren County	IA	Lanny Caligiuri	1989	8,144
126 5/8	19 3/8	18 3/8	15 5/8	5	5	Grand Forks County	ND	Kirke Henry	1990	8,144
126 5/8	21 4/8	21 7/8	16 5/8	4	4	Dukes County	MA	Paul C. Jackson, Sr.	1990	8,144
126 5/8	21 5/8	21 0/8	16 1/8	4	5	Carroll County	IL	John L. Ashby	1990	8,144
126 5/8	20 5/8	20 3/8	14 3/8	4	5	Pender County	NC	Randy Carroll	1991	8,144
126 5/8	19 2/8	19 2/8	14 3/8	5	5	Nemaha County	KS	D. Jay Hartter	1991	8,144
126 5/8	20 4/8	19 3/8	16 7/8	5	5	Walworth County	WI	Mark Luther	1991	8,144
126 5/8	23 2/8	24 4/8	20 7/8	6	4	Fayette County	IL	DeWayne E. Maples	1991	8,144
126 5/8	21 4/8	21 6/8	16 2/8	6	6	Dodge County	WI	Brian Zubke	1991	8,144
126 4/8	20 4/8	21 2/8	18 6/8	5	5	Warren County	PA	Fred Massa	1967	8,184
126 4/8	21 2/8	21 3/8	15 2/8	4	4	Chester County	PA	Joseph R. Yannelli	1967	8,184
126 4/8	19 7/8	19 6/8	16 4/8	5	5	Owen County	IN	G. Fred Asbell	1971	8,184
126 4/8	22 4/8	21 6/8	17 4/8	4	4	Waupaca County	WI	Arlin Kersten, Jr.	1971	8,184
126 4/8	22 1/8	22 0/8	18 2/8	5	4	Cayuga County	NY	John Pardee	1971	8,184
126 4/8	21 2/8	21 3/8	12 4/8	4	4	Bayfield County	WI	Del Zwiefelhofer	1972	8,184
126 4/8	24 6/8	25 0/8	17 0/8	5	4	Portage County	OH	Burt Thompson, Jr.	1976	8,184

SCORE	LENGTH OF MAIN BEAM R	L	INSIDE SPREAD	NUMBER OF POINTS R	L	AREA	STATE/ PROVINCE	HUNTER'S NAME	DATE	RANK
126 4/8	23 4/8	24 2/8	17 6/8	4	4	Westchester County	NY	Richard T. Burke	1977	8,184
126 4/8	22 3/8	20 7/8	15 6/8	4	4	Phillips County	KS	Orville D. Blubaugh	1977	8,184
126 4/8	21 1/8	21 5/8	17 6/8	4	4	Macon County	MO	Bruce Hamel	1979	8,184
126 4/8	20 4/8	20 3/8	16 2/8	5	5	Harford County	MD	Donald P. Conley	1980	8,184
126 4/8	21 6/8	22 3/8	18 4/8	4	4	Cameron County	TX	Louis Skrobarczyk, Jr.	1981	8,184
126 4/8	21 7/8	21 0/8	16 0/8	4	5	Edmonton	ALB	Al Schulz	1981	8,184
126 4/8	20 4/8	19 6/8	13 2/8	5	5	Olmsted County	MN	Tom Lofgren	1983	8,184
126 4/8	20 6/8	21 1/8	15 2/8	4	4	Dane County	WI	Victor H. Mittelstaedt	1983	8,184
126 4/8	19 4/8	21 4/8	20 4/8	5	5	Schuyler County	NY	Richard Murphy	1983	8,184
126 4/8	21 0/8	21 3/8	15 6/8	5	5	Kent County	MD	Raymond A. Boley	1984	8,184
126 4/8	21 6/8	21 6/8	15 4/8	5	5	Somerset County	NJ	Ronald L. Taylor, Sr.	1985	8,184
126 4/8	20 0/8	20 3/8	17 4/8	5	4	Marshall County	IN	Gene E. Smith	1985	8,184
126 4/8	20 1/8	20 1/8	17 2/8	6	5	Hancock County	WV	Mark G. Konchar	1985	8,184
126 4/8	23 4/8	21 2/8	17 5/8	6	5	Menard County	IL	Donald Alwerdt	1985	8,184
126 4/8	21 6/8	21 0/8	17 6/8	5	6	Muskingum County	OH	Allen Randal Smith	1985	8,184
126 4/8	19 6/8	20 2/8	13 6/8	5	5	Dallas County	IA	Glenn D. Vondra	1985	8,184
126 4/8	22 1/8	21 1/8	17 4/8	6	6	Ionia County	MI	Todd E. Peacock	1986	8,184
126 4/8	20 5/8	21 1/8	17 4/8	7	6	Ozaukee County	WI	Jack T. Klotz	1986	8,184
126 4/8	21 3/8	21 4/8	17 2/8	6	4	Ford County	KS	James A. Konda	1986	8,184
126 4/8	21 0/8	20 3/8	16 0/8	5	5	Marinette County	WI	Paul Becker	1986	8,184
126 4/8	24 2/8	21 7/8	17 0/8	6	5	Ohio County	WV	Robert B. Ewing	1986	8,184
126 4/8	25 7/8	26 7/8	18 7/8	5	5	Hamilton County	IA	Larry Haren	1987	8,184
126 4/8	20 0/8	19 7/8	16 0/8	4	4	Allegan County	MI	Mark A. Dykstra	1988	8,184
126 4/8	21 7/8	23 0/8	18 0/8	4	5	Cayuga County	NY	John E. Ryan, Jr.	1988	8,184
126 4/8	20 4/8	20 0/8	17 6/8	4	4	Henderson County	KY	Edward Wayne Wallace	1988	8,184
126 4/8	22 6/8	22 7/8	18 2/8	4	5	Union County	KY	Chad Robison	1988	8,184
126 4/8	21 4/8	21 7/8	16 6/8	6	4	Saginaw County	MI	Dave L. Tanney	1988	8,184
126 4/8	23 7/8	22 6/8	18 0/8	4	5	Douglas County	NE	Dave Simon	1988	8,184
126 4/8	20 1/8	21 2/8	17 4/8	5	4	Bucks County	PA	Jerome F. Robideau	1989	8,184
126 4/8	20 3/8	20 4/8	17 0/8	4	5	Dane County	WI	Gerald Westphal	1989	8,184
126 4/8	20 3/8	19 6/8	15 4/8	5	5	Maries County	MO	Tracy L. Crider	1989	8,184
126 4/8	22 3/8	22 6/8	15 0/8	6	4	Marinette County	WI	Mike R. Collette	1989	8,184
126 4/8	21 2/8	21 2/8	12 0/8	5	5	Boone County	KY	Stan Clore	1989	8,184
126 4/8	22 2/8	20 7/8	16 2/8	5	5	Price County	WI	Wayne J. Steiner	1989	8,184
126 4/8	19 4/8	18 7/8	18 2/8	4	5	Benton County	MO	Rex M. Suiter	1989	8,184
126 4/8	19 7/8	20 7/8	17 4/8	5	5	Boone County	IA	Chris Doran	1989	8,184
126 4/8	21 4/8	21 2/8	17 0/8	5	4	Northampton County	PA	David Lichtenwalner	1990	8,184
126 4/8	23 2/8	24 0/8	14 6/8	5	6	Saline County	NE	Roger D. Hanneman	1990	8,184
126 4/8	17 0/8	22 0/8	20 6/8	4	4	Kalamazoo County	MI	Larry A. Bussema	1990	8,184
126 4/8	20 0/8	18 5/8	15 4/8	5	5	Cass County	MO	David Johnson	1990	8,184
126 4/8	22 7/8	22 1/8	16 4/8	4	5	St. Croix County	WI	Mike Mattis	1990	8,184
126 4/8	20 4/8	21 4/8	15 1/8	4	5	Saline County	KS	Philip D. Baltazor	1990	8,184
126 4/8	23 5/8	22 4/8	16 2/8	4	3	Washington County	IA	Brent J. Graber	1990	8,184
126 4/8	21 1/8	22 2/8	19 6/8	4	4	Kleberg County	TX	Jarred W. Peeples	1991	8,184
126 4/8	21 1/8	22 5/8	16 0/8	4	4	Callaway County	MO	Dennis Crane	1991	8,184
126 4/8	23 3/8	21 5/8	17 2/8	5	4	Missoula County	MT	Tim Hunt	1991	8,184
126 4/8	20 5/8	21 0/8	18 2/8	5	5	Harris County	TX	Daniel K. Barnes	1991	8,184
126 4/8	22 5/8	22 3/8	15 2/8	5	5	Lincoln County	WI	Jerry W. Badeau	1991	8,184
126 4/8	22 4/8	22 2/8	15 6/8	4	4	Waukesha County	WI	Bruce L. Leben	1992	8,184
126 3/8	23 1/8	23 3/8	17 5/8	4	4	Sussex County	NJ	Jim Ott	1972	8,240
126 3/8	21 5/8	20 2/8	17 0/8	5	6	Gallatin County	KY	Robert L. Hegge, Jr.	1973	8,240
126 3/8	22 4/8	22 4/8	16 3/8	5	5	Eau Claire County	WI	Steven P. Gilbertson	1977	8,240
126 3/8	21 0/8	21 5/8	17 7/8	7	6	Clark County	KS	William Rule	1978	8,240
126 3/8	25 3/8	25 0/8	18 4/8	5	5	Morris County	NJ	Kurt Carlson	1982	8,240
126 3/8	23 3/8	22 4/8	15 3/8	4	4	Cayuga County	NY	John Pardee	1982	8,240
126 3/8	20 0/8	20 5/8	14 1/8	5	5	Shoshone County	ID	Richard J. O'Grady	1983	8,240
126 3/8	22 4/8	23 4/8	16 5/8	5	5	Sheboygan County	WI	Ronald Cook	1983	8,240
126 3/8	19 3/8	19 4/8	15 5/8	4	4	Polk County	WI	Allen Lunde	1984	8,240
126 3/8	22 3/8	21 4/8	18 2/8	6	6	Rock County	WI	John Van Altena	1984	8,240
126 3/8	21 2/8	21 1/8	14 6/8	6	6	Washington County	KS	Stan Brustowicz	1984	8,240
126 3/8	21 4/8	20 0/8	16 7/8	5	5	Dodge County	WI	Carl Schuett	1985	8,240
126 3/8	21 7/8	20 4/8	16 3/8	4	4	Waukesha County	WI	Dale J. Henderson	1985	8,240
126 3/8	20 2/8	18 2/8	16 1/8	4	5	Gregory County	SD	Dennis Lengkeek	1986	8,240
126 3/8	21 7/8	22 3/8	16 4/8	5	5	Brooke County	WV	Don Weekley	1986	8,240
126 3/8	21 1/8	21 3/8	17 4/8	8	5	Stephenson County	IL	Donald Miller	1986	8,240
126 3/8	19 7/8	20 4/8	15 5/8	4	4	Dodge County	GA	C. W. Wright	1987	8,240
126 3/8	22 7/8	23 4/8	18 7/8	4	4	Bay County	MI	Andrew F. Zawacki	1987	8,240
126 3/8	24 6/8	24 3/8	20 4/8	8	6	Reno County	KS	Bob Williams	1987	8,240
126 3/8	24 0/8	22 4/8	18 0/8	6	6	Union County	IL	Sam Shafer	1987	8,240
126 3/8	21 3/8	21 5/8	20 7/8	6	5	Washington County	MN	David L. Hart	1988	8,240

335

SCORE	LENGTH OF MAIN BEAM R	LENGTH OF MAIN BEAM L	INSIDE SPREAD	NUMBER OF POINTS R	NUMBER OF POINTS L	AREA	STATE/ PROVINCE	HUNTER'S NAME	DATE	RANK
126 3/8	22 0/8	22 2/8	17 1/8	5	5	Hardin County	TN	Tom Oaks	1988	8,240
126 3/8	21 1/8	19 7/8	14 6/8	5	4	Pike County	IL	Emmett D. Carter	1988	8,240
126 3/8	22 2/8	22 3/8	16 5/8	5	5	Blue Earth County	MN	Dave Schultz	1988	8,240
126 3/8	23 1/8	21 4/8	18 7/8	4	4	Chase County	KS	Lee Ayres	1988	8,240
126 3/8	24 4/8	23 6/8	19 3/8	3	3	Perry County	IL	Terrence E. Dierkes	1988	8,240
126 3/8	22 2/8	22 1/8	16 7/8	6	6	Kenedy County	TX	Romulo Rangel, Jr.	1989	8,240
126 3/8	22 6/8	22 1/8	15 7/8	4	4	Webster County	IA	Curtis Martens	1989	8,240
126 3/8	23 0/8	22 4/8	17 7/8	4	5	Linn County	IA	Jim Maxson	1989	8,240
126 3/8	20 4/8	19 4/8	18 7/8	4	5	Washington County	MS	Bobby R. Woods	1990	8,240
126 3/8	19 2/8	21 0/8	19 1/8	5	5	Price County	WI	Timothy Welch	1990	8,240
126 3/8	20 7/8	21 1/8	14 7/8	6	5	Chippewa County	WI	Mark Nelson	1990	8,240
126 3/8	23 2/8	21 7/8	17 0/8	6	7	Dodge County	MN	Ed Pitzenberger	1990	8,240
126 3/8	20 1/8	20 7/8	15 2/8	6	5	Goodhue County	MN	John "Jack" Cordes	1990	8,240
126 3/8	23 3/8	22 2/8	18 0/8	5	4	Montgomery County	MD	Frank H. Wilmot	1990	8,240
126 3/8	21 3/8	22 1/8	16 7/8	5	6	Malahide Township	ONT	Tim Rochette	1991	8,240
126 3/8	20 0/8	20 3/8	16 1/8	5	5	Logan County	OK	Eric D. Wynn	1991	8,240
126 3/8	22 1/8	20 6/8	14 5/8	4	5	Butler County	KS	Gary Talkington	1991	8,240
126 3/8	21 5/8	21 6/8	16 1/8	4	4	Lake County	IN	Thomas A. Cope	1991	8,240
126 3/8	21 6/8	19 5/8	16 5/8	5	5	Polk County	WI	Gene Hill	1991	8,240
126 3/8	21 6/8	22 1/8	16 3/8	5	5	Burleigh County	ND	Eric L. Martel	1991	8,240
126 3/8	20 7/8	21 4/8	17 7/8	6	6	York County	PA	Roy T. Weaver	1992	8,240
126 2/8	22 7/8	22 0/8	17 2/8	5	5	Lee County	IL	Edmund R. Braun	1959	8,282
126 2/8	22 0/8	20 6/8	17 6/8	4	4	Johnson County	IA	Paul F. Spicer	1963	8,282
126 2/8	20 0/8	19 3/8	16 0/8	4	4	Harding County	SD	Gerald Swayze	1965	8,282
126 2/8	21 3/8	21 4/8	15 4/8	4	4	Morrison County	MN	Frank Hogan	1967	8,282
126 2/8	20 6/8	20 2/8	15 6/8	5	5	Adams County	IL	Adrian K. Smith	1967	8,282
126 2/8	21 4/8	21 4/8	16 2/8	4	4	Ford County	KS	Bob Stephenson	1967	8,282
126 2/8	20 1/8	20 7/8	14 4/8	5	5	Platte County	NE	Keith Bruhn	1968	8,282
126 2/8	23 7/8	23 5/8	17 3/8	5	4	Marathon County	WI	Dan Niehaus	1968	8,282
126 2/8	24 1/8	23 7/8	14 6/8	4	4	Winneshiek County	IA	Marc Headington	1971	8,282
126 2/8	21 0/8	20 7/8	16 0/8	5	5	Carroll County	IL	Art Heinze	1972	8,282
126 2/8	22 1/8	21 5/8	16 0/8	5	5	Dade County	MO	Charles A. Myers	1975	8,282
126 2/8	20 0/8	20 0/8	14 6/8	5	5	Washington County	OH	Joe D. Schofield	1977	8,282
126 2/8	20 7/8	21 4/8	16 0/8	5	5	Dodge County	WI	Keith Peterson	1977	8,282
126 2/8	18 0/8	18 5/8	15 0/8	5	5	Wood County	WI	David Kievet	1978	8,282
126 2/8	20 6/8	20 5/8	13 5/8	6	6	Stevens County	WA	David B. Muffly	1978	8,282
126 2/8	21 4/8	21 7/8	17 2/8	5	5	Waupaca County	WI	Daniel E. Yaeger	1978	8,282
126 2/8	22 2/8	22 4/8	16 4/8	4	3	Franklin County	OH	Steven H. Byerly	1979	8,282
126 2/8	20 0/8	20 3/8	16 2/8	4	4	Greenwood County	SC	E. Dale Carwile	1980	8,282
126 2/8	22 5/8	21 6/8	17 2/8	6	5	Livingston County	MO	Myles Keller	1980	8,282
126 2/8	24 0/8	24 4/8	19 0/8	4	4	Autauga County	AL	George Poston, Jr.	1981	8,282
126 2/8	21 5/8	22 4/8	16 4/8	9	4	Jefferson County	NE	Bob Funke	1981	8,282
126 2/8	21 5/8	20 7/8	20 2/8	4	5	Lyon County	MN	Wayne Kumm	1981	8,282
126 2/8	22 2/8	22 2/8	17 2/8	4	6	Kearny County	KS	David Meyers	1981	8,282
126 2/8	21 2/8	21 2/8	15 2/8	4	5	Meigs County	OH	Charles H. Murray	1982	8,282
126 2/8	22 1/8	22 2/8	15 4/8	5	5	Live Oak County	TX	Rick Hayley	1983	8,282
126 2/8	23 1/8	23 0/8	20 3/8	6	6	Marquette County	WI	Stewart McReath	1983	8,282
126 2/8	22 2/8	21 2/8	17 2/8	5	5	Venango County	PA	Jeffrey S. Morrison	1983	8,282
126 2/8	22 6/8	22 5/8	13 4/8	5	6	Preble County	OH	Roger D. Dolph	1983	8,282
126 2/8	21 0/8	21 1/8	17 4/8	4	4	Lake County	IL	Henry J. Schwarz	1983	8,282
126 2/8	19 2/8	20 5/8	17 6/8	6	5	Clay County	MN	Steve Steinhoff	1983	8,282
126 2/8	22 6/8	22 1/8	14 4/8	4	5	Dane County	WI	Dennis L. Stiklestad	1983	8,282
126 2/8	19 6/8	19 6/8	13 4/8	6	6	Montcalm County	MI	Steve A. Alexander	1984	8,282
126 2/8	21 0/8	20 0/8	12 6/8	5	5	Augusta County	VA	Nicholas C. Taylor	1984	8,282
126 2/8	19 0/8	20 0/8	18 0/8	5	5	Athens County	OH	Craig Littler	1984	8,282
126 2/8	20 3/8	19 6/8	14 4/8	5	5	McKenzie County	ND	Tim Finley	1985	8,282
126 2/8	18 4/8	19 6/8	15 2/8	4	4	Pulaski County	IN	Tony Bean	1985	8,282
126 2/8	22 2/8	21 2/8	17 2/8	4	5	Pittsburg County	OK	Jim Stith	1985	8,282
126 2/8	22 0/8	22 4/8	15 4/8	5	6	Boone County	MO	Tommy Foster	1985	8,282
126 2/8	20 2/8	20 0/8	15 2/8	5	5	Meeker County	MN	Brent Swanson	1986	8,282
126 2/8	24 0/8	23 5/8	17 4/8	9	5	Sullivan County	TN	Austin Morrison	1986	8,282
126 2/8	21 4/8	20 1/8	16 6/8	5	5	Pushmataha County	OK	Jan R. Coleman	1987	8,282
126 2/8	23 0/8	22 5/8	15 4/8	5	5	Darke County	OH	Matt Arnold	1987	8,282
126 2/8	19 7/8	20 4/8	18 5/8	6	7	Ogle County	IL	Gary Shaw	1987	8,282
126 2/8	23 6/8	23 3/8	16 5/8	4	6	Iroquois County	IL	Bill Price	1987	8,282
126 2/8	24 0/8	24 2/8	16 1/8	6	4	Kent County	MD	Tony M. Panaro	1988	8,282
126 2/8	20 4/8	21 1/8	18 4/8	4	5	Dunn County	WI	George Woodington	1988	8,282
126 2/8	23 1/8	23 4/8	17 4/8	4	6	Buffalo County	WI	Gunner J. Hagen	1988	8,282
126 2/8	20 4/8	20 2/8	18 0/8	4	4	Le Sueur County	MN	Randy Mathwig	1989	8,282
126 2/8	21 6/8	21 4/8	15 6/8	4	4	Passaic County	NJ	Michael Stabile	1989	8,282

SCORE	LENGTH OF MAIN BEAM R	L	INSIDE SPREAD	NUMBER OF POINTS R	L	AREA	STATE/ PROVINCE	HUNTER'S NAME	DATE	RANK
126 2/8	20 0/8	20 0/8	13 6/8	4	4	Codington County	SD	Tim Chandler	1989	8,282
126 2/8	22 3/8	22 0/8	17 0/8	5	5	Wood County	WI	Paul S. Esser	1989	8,282
126 2/8	21 0/8	20 4/8	17 2/8	4	4	Guernsey County	OH	Edward E. Vasko	1989	8,282
126 2/8	22 1/8	23 0/8	18 4/8	7	6	Butler County	KS	Larry Yarbrough	1989	8,282
126 2/8	22 6/8	23 4/8	15 2/8	4	4	Clark County	IL	Charles E. Guyer	1989	8,282
126 2/8	23 7/8	17 2/8	15 4/8	4	4	Woodford County	IL	Lyle E. Stine	1989	8,282
126 2/8	19 7/8	21 3/8	17 0/8	5	4	Macomb County	MI	Barry Martin	1990	8,282
126 2/8	21 3/8	21 6/8	17 6/8	4	4	Guernsey County	OH	Daniel L. Kerns	1990	8,282
126 2/8	21 5/8	22 1/8	16 4/8	4	4	Allegheny County	PA	Jared Roscart	1991	8,282
126 2/8	22 2/8	22 2/8	17 6/8	4	4	Ashland County	WI	Ryan S. Mesko	1991	8,282
126 2/8	22 2/8	22 4/8	18 6/8	4	4	Marathon County	WI	Randy L. Feltz	1991	8,282
126 2/8	21 0/8	21 2/8	16 2/8	5	5	Creek County	OK	Shane Murphy	1991	8,282
126 2/8	21 0/8	22 7/8	18 0/8	5	5	Kleberg County	TX	Dr. Terry W. Brandt	1991	8,282
126 1/8	25 2/8	24 5/8	18 5/8	4	4	York County	PA	Gregory E. Smith	1969	8,344
126 1/8	22 1/8	21 7/8	16 5/8	5	4	Monmouth County	NJ	Charles C. Lasala	1970	8,344
126 1/8	20 4/8	18 6/8	18 1/8	4	4	Pope County	IL	Murray Schuhart	1972	8,344
126 1/8	21 4/8	21 4/8	16 3/8	4	5	Lincoln County	SD	Stephen K. Sona	1975	8,344
126 1/8	21 3/8	20 5/8	14 4/8	5	4	Oconto County	WI	Rick Moudry	1977	8,344
126 1/8	22 0/8	21 1/8	17 1/8	5	5	Gladwin County	MI	Dave Longstreth	1980	8,344
126 1/8	18 1/8	18 7/8	15 3/8	5	5	Brown County	SD	Charles Fulker	1980	8,344
126 1/8	23 4/8	22 3/8	16 6/8	6	5	Rice County	MN	Jeff Purdie	1981	8,344
126 1/8	21 4/8	21 5/8	17 1/8	5	5	Richland County	WI	David P. Berns	1982	8,344
126 1/8	20 2/8	20 2/8	15 7/8	4	4	Pulaski County	KY	Johnny Farmer	1983	8,344
126 1/8	22 1/8	21 5/8	18 7/8	4	4	Lamoure County	ND	Rodney W. Peterson	1985	8,344
126 1/8	23 2/8	21 5/8	15 7/8	4	4	Iowa County	WI	Jamie Gottschall	1986	8,344
126 1/8	23 5/8	23 4/8	16 7/8	4	6	Waukesha County	WI	Bob Blunck	1986	8,344
126 1/8	19 7/8	19 3/8	13 7/8	5	5	Mobile County	AL	Scott Jordon	1987	8,344
126 1/8	20 0/8	20 1/8	16 2/8	6	6	Pittsburg County	OK	Wanda Larimer	1987	8,344
126 1/8	23 6/8	22 6/8	19 4/8	6	7	Dane County	WI	Dale H. Anderson	1987	8,344
126 1/8	22 5/8	21 6/8	15 7/8	4	4	Highland County	OH	Dan Sowders	1987	8,344
126 1/8	22 4/8	20 0/8	16 0/8	5	6	Hocking County	OH	Greg Sutton	1987	8,344
126 1/8	21 2/8	21 5/8	15 5/8	4	4	New Castle County	DE	Joseph J. Subolefsky	1988	8,344
126 1/8	20 2/8	19 4/8	13 1/8	5	6	Adams County	WI	Jim Haslow	1988	8,344
126 1/8	22 7/8	23 6/8	17 2/8	4	7	Monmouth County	NJ	Bob Sacher	1988	8,344
126 1/8	21 7/8	23 1/8	18 3/8	4	5	Calhoun County	MI	Ron Allen	1989	8,344
126 1/8	20 7/8	20 2/8	16 7/8	5	5	Jefferson County	IN	Rodney W. Stratton	1989	8,344
126 1/8	24 1/8	23 6/8	19 1/8	7	6	Lake County	IN	Doyle Niemeyer	1989	8,344
126 1/8	20 3/8	20 4/8	14 3/8	6	5	Ralls County	MO	Larry David	1989	8,344
126 1/8	19 6/8	19 5/8	15 7/8	5	5	Llano County	TX	Kip Reagor	1989	8,344
126 1/8	22 4/8	22 0/8	16 1/8	6	7	Putnam County	OH	Isidore Schnipke	1989	8,344
126 1/8	23 2/8	23 2/8	18 7/8	4	3	Bollinger County	MO	Jesse Whittley, Jr.	1989	8,344
126 1/8	21 1/8	21 5/8	16 3/8	4	4	Knox County	MO	Mike Siebeneck	1990	8,344
126 1/8	21 0/8	19 2/8	16 1/8	5	5	La Salle County	TX	Dennis C. Faulkenberry	1990	8,344
126 1/8	21 2/8	21 7/8	16 7/8	4	4	Marathon County	WI	Randy Feltz	1990	8,344
126 1/8	20 1/8	20 6/8	15 3/8	6	6	Somerset County	NJ	Robert Staudt, Jr.	1990	8,344
126 1/8	19 7/8	20 5/8	20 6/8	4	5	Macon County	AL	George P. Mann	1990	8,344
126 1/8	20 5/8	20 6/8	19 5/8	5	5	Craig County	OK	Eddie Claypool	1990	8,344
126 1/8	21 2/8	21 3/8	17 3/8	4	4	Dunn County	WI	Paul C. Becker	1991	8,344
126 1/8	21 3/8	22 5/8	16 7/8	4	4	Monongalia County	WV	Dave McLaughlin	1991	8,344
126 1/8	20 7/8	22 2/8	17 1/8	5	5	Granville County	NC	Ricky Lewis Keller	1991	8,344
126 1/8	20 3/8	21 6/8	17 3/8	5	5	St. Clair County	IL	Gregory F. Elceser	1991	8,344
126 1/8	21 3/8	21 3/8	16 3/8	4	4	Tuscaloosa County	AL	Larry E. Lee	1991	8,344
126 1/8	23 5/8	24 4/8	21 3/8	4	5	Rock County	WI	Robert J. Coleman	1992	8,344
126 0/8	20 3/8	20 3/8	14 0/8	4	4	Cherry County	NE	Dean Bergman	1975	8,384
126 0/8	22 1/8	20 4/8	16 2/8	5	4	McMinn County	TN	Wesley B. Snyder	1975	8,384
126 0/8	18 4/8	17 5/8	13 6/8	5	5	Delaware County	NY	Alan Beyer	1976	8,384
126 0/8	20 4/8	21 6/8	17 0/8	4	4	Dunn County	WI	Richard Paul	1977	8,384
126 0/8	20 2/8	18 6/8	15 0/8	4	4	Polk County	IA	Ervin Wagner	1978	8,384
126 0/8	20 0/8	20 3/8	16 0/8	5	5	Oneida County	WI	Gerald Bonfigt	1980	8,384
126 0/8	18 3/8	18 4/8	15 4/8	5	5	Bexar County	TX	James R. Carter	1980	8,384
126 0/8	20 4/8	20 4/8	15 4/8	4	5	Iron County	MI	Bill Paiter, Sr.	1980	8,384
126 0/8	20 0/8	20 4/8	13 6/8	4	4	Kandiyohi County	MN	Dwayne B. Power	1980	8,384
126 0/8	22 1/8	22 6/8	19 0/8	4	4	Westchester County	NY	Thomas Ippolito	1981	8,384
126 0/8	19 5/8	19 7/8	15 4/8	4	4	Des Moines County	IA	Doris Hawkins	1981	8,384
126 0/8	19 4/8	18 1/8	14 3/8	5	6	Calhoun County	MI	Jerry L. Boggess, Jr.	1981	8,384
126 0/8	22 2/8	23 2/8	16 2/8	5	5	Washington County	OH	James D. Boyce	1981	8,384
126 0/8	21 4/8	19 6/8	16 4/8	4	4	Reno County	KS	Otto Henning	1982	8,384
126 0/8	20 4/8	21 0/8	15 4/8	5	6	Cayuga County	NY	Arthur Quadrini	1982	8,384
126 0/8	20 4/8	21 5/8	19 5/8	4	6	Burleigh County	ND	Scott Fairman	1982	8,384
126 0/8	20 0/8	20 2/8	18 6/8	4	5	Jo Daviess County	IL	Jerry Smith	1982	8,384

SCORE	LENGTH OF MAIN BEAM		INSIDE SPREAD	NUMBER OF POINTS		AREA	STATE/ PROVINCE	HUNTER'S NAME	DATE	RANK
	R	L		R	L					
126 0/8	20 7/8	21 3/8	16 6/8	4	6	Brookings County	SD	Michael Kjellsen	1982	8,384
126 0/8	20 2/8	19 3/8	13 7/8	6	6	Buffalo County	NE	Richard D. Lange	1983	8,384
126 0/8	19 4/8	20 0/8	16 2/8	5	4	Watonwan County	MN	Rory Jensen	1983	8,384
126 0/8	20 0/8	20 0/8	13 2/8	5	5	Jefferson County	IN	Dwight Webb	1983	8,384
126 0/8	21 0/8	20 4/8	15 2/8	5	5	Dallas County	IA	John S. Winslow	1983	8,384
126 0/8	20 6/8	20 6/8	16 4/8	4	4	Dawson County	NE	Randy Wilson	1983	8,384
126 0/8	21 5/8	21 6/8	16 6/8	4	4	St. Louis County	MO	Huston Martin	1983	8,384
126 0/8	22 4/8	20 7/8	15 6/8	5	4	Iowa County	WI	Mark E. Bennett	1984	8,384
126 0/8	20 1/8	20 2/8	14 4/8	5	6	Des Moines County	IA	Duane R. Mabry	1984	8,384
126 0/8	24 3/8	23 4/8	16 0/8	3	4	Bissett Creek	BC	Mark Siegmueller	1984	8,384
126 0/8	22 2/8	22 7/8	19 4/8	4	4	Mackinac County	MI	Kirk A. Radtke	1984	8,384
126 0/8	20 0/8	20 3/8	16 0/8	6	6	Pittsburg County	OK	Rocky Williams	1985	8,384
126 0/8	20 2/8	19 7/8	16 6/8	5	5	Monroe County	NY	Gregrey Madison	1985	8,384
126 0/8	21 5/8	22 4/8	16 6/8	5	4	Stearns County	MN	Rick Kantor	1985	8,384
126 0/8	19 3/8	19 1/8	13 5/8	6	5	Sauk County	WI	Arend Harms	1985	8,384
126 0/8	22 4/8	22 4/8	17 1/8	4	5	Westchester County	NY	Louis J. Miceli III	1985	8,384
126 0/8	23 3/8	22 3/8	16 0/8	5	5	Outagamie County	WI	Chad Buss	1986	8,384
126 0/8	22 1/8	21 4/8	17 2/8	5	5	Polk County	WI	Dan Johnson	1986	8,384
126 0/8	24 0/8	24 4/8	16 2/8	6	4	Van Buren County	IA	Don Kieler	1986	8,384
126 0/8	21 6/8	21 6/8	18 2/8	6	6	Douglas County	NE	Bryce Lambley	1987	8,384
126 0/8	22 4/8	21 5/8	17 2/8	4	4	Isanti County	MN	John Armstrong	1987	8,384
126 0/8	22 6/8	22 5/8	15 4/8	4	4	Tuscaloosa County	AL	Elbert J. Buckelew	1987	8,384
126 0/8	22 3/8	20 0/8	15 7/8	4	6	Marshall County	IN	David Wagoner	1988	8,384
126 0/8	21 2/8	20 6/8	16 2/8	4	4	Sussex County	NJ	Alex Wiecek	1988	8,384
126 0/8	20 0/8	20 4/8	17 0/8	4	5	Newton County	IN	James Gates	1988	8,384
126 0/8	20 4/8	20 4/8	16 2/8	4	5	Hubbard County	MN	Kelly Craft	1988	8,384
126 0/8	20 3/8	20 3/8	16 6/8	5	5	Mille Lacs County	MN	Daniel Newcombe	1988	8,384
126 0/8	22 5/8	20 6/8	16 6/8	4	5	Edgar County	IL	Jerry R. David	1988	8,384
126 0/8	22 5/8	22 5/8	16 2/8	4	5	Jackson County	MO	Steve Gowen	1988	8,384
126 0/8	23 6/8	24 1/8	19 5/8	5	5	New Haven County	CT	Lawrence St.John	1989	8,384
126 0/8	22 3/8	21 7/8	20 7/8	6	5	Hunterdon County	NJ	Gary W. Dudbridge	1989	8,384
126 0/8	21 3/8	21 6/8	18 2/8	4	4	Missoula County	MT	Myron Holland	1989	8,384
126 0/8	19 3/8	20 1/8	14 2/8	4	4	Fox Valley	SAS	Richard G. Paice	1990	8,384
126 0/8	22 4/8	22 5/8	17 2/8	4	4	Henrico County	VA	Robert A. Brooke	1990	8,384
126 0/8	20 0/8	20 5/8	18 4/8	5	5	Scott County	IA	Richard D. Bergert	1990	8,384
126 0/8	20 7/8	20 6/8	15 0/8	4	4	Russell County	KS	Mark J. Ferrero	1990	8,384
126 0/8	25 6/8	24 0/8	20 4/8	5	5	Westchester County	NY	Ralph Maietta	1990	8,384
126 0/8	21 3/8	21 7/8	19 1/8	6	7	Milwaukee County	WI	Tony Snow	1991	8,384
126 0/8	16 1/8	17 6/8	17 7/8	5	5	Haskell County	OK	James Woods	1991	8,384
126 0/8	22 6/8	22 6/8	18 5/8	6	4	Iron County	WI	Perry V. Elsemore	1991	8,384
126 0/8	22 1/8	23 1/8	18 4/8	4	5	St. Joseph County	IN	Shane Hansen	1991	8,384
126 0/8	22 6/8	21 4/8	16 4/8	4	4	Monroe County	MO	Coy C. Dollens	1991	8,384
125 7/8	20 0/8	20 0/8	14 5/8	5	5	Oconto County	WI	Chuck Matyska	1972	8,443
125 7/8	22 4/8	23 0/8	15 1/8	4	4	Fayette County	IL	Edward G. Myers	1975	8,443
125 7/8	20 6/8	22 7/8	15 5/8	5	5	Butler County	PA	John Schmiedlin	1976	8,443
125 7/8	20 2/8	20 2/8	15 1/8	5	5	Waupaca County	WI	Thomas E. Labisch	1976	8,443
125 7/8	20 0/8	20 2/8	16 2/8	5	6	Greene County	IN	Jim Cunningham	1977	8,443
125 7/8	21 5/8	22 0/8	15 1/8	4	4	Douglas County	MN	Dan Zinda	1977	8,443
125 7/8	24 0/8	22 4/8	14 5/8	7	6	Jones County	GA	William R. Shaw	1979	8,443
125 7/8	23 4/8	22 5/8	15 7/8	5	4	Boone County	IA	Max Brower	1980	8,443
125 7/8	22 2/8	21 7/8	20 1/8	6	4	Ionia County	MI	David Seidelman	1980	8,443
125 7/8	20 4/8	20 7/8	15 1/8	4	4	Lewis & Clark County	MT	Tom Storm	1981	8,443
125 7/8	21 7/8	21 7/8	16 1/8	5	5	Dakota County	MN	John M. Lippka	1982	8,443
125 7/8	21 0/8	21 0/8	16 3/8	5	4	Lake County	IL	Russell F. Orr	1982	8,443
125 7/8	23 0/8	21 7/8	15 5/8	4	4	Sauk County	WI	Dan Cupp	1982	8,443
125 7/8	20 7/8	20 7/8	17 7/8	4	4	Marion County	IL	Lavon Doremire, Sr.	1983	8,443
125 7/8	21 7/8	22 2/8	18 4/8	4	5	Westchester County	NY	John Cucinella	1983	8,443
125 7/8	20 2/8	20 0/8	15 1/8	5	6	Ferry County	WA	Robert McIntosh	1983	8,443
125 7/8	20 4/8	21 1/8	17 1/8	5	5	Des Moines County	IA	Mark Sivill	1984	8,443
125 7/8	19 4/8	18 7/8	14 7/8	5	5	Dodge County	WI	James G. Schoebeck	1984	8,443
125 7/8	22 4/8	23 6/8	18 0/8	4	5	Sumner County	KS	Warren C. Townsend	1985	8,443
125 7/8	20 1/8	19 2/8	15 3/8	5	5	Green County	WI	David R. Covert	1985	8,443
125 7/8	20 4/8	18 4/8	15 5/8	5	5	Johnson County	WY	Jimmy Womble	1986	8,443
125 7/8	22 1/8	22 1/8	18 1/8	4	4	Middlesex County	NJ	William J. Matuchek	1987	8,443
125 7/8	19 6/8	18 6/8	15 7/8	5	4	Pope County	MN	Dennis Linde	1987	8,443
125 7/8	21 7/8	21 7/8	20 4/8	4	5	Isabella County	MI	Roger L. Roberson	1988	8,443
125 7/8	20 5/8	21 5/8	17 1/8	4	4	Hutchinson County	SD	Terry Waltner	1988	8,443
125 7/8	22 7/8	22 1/8	15 4/8	5	6	St. Croix County	WI	Jack Rasmussen	1989	8,443
125 7/8	19 1/8	19 1/8	16 3/8	5	5	Morris County	NJ	Tony Salernitano	1989	8,443
125 7/8	21 5/8	22 0/8	16 5/8	5	5	Rockingham County	NH	Mark A. George	1989	8,443

Score	Length of Main Beam R	Length of Main Beam L	Inside Spread	Number of Points R	Number of Points L	Area	State/Province	Hunter's Name	Date	Rank
125 7/8	20 2/8	20 4/8	17 5/8	5	5	Ohio County	WV	Matt Farabee	1989	8,443
125 7/8	20 7/8	20 5/8	17 3/8	4	4	St. Charles County	MO	Terry Schulte	1989	8,443
125 7/8	21 6/8	20 7/8	19 1/8	5	5	Todd County	KY	Donald Wayne Bryant	1989	8,443
125 7/8	18 5/8	19 1/8	14 5/8	5	5	Luzerne County	PA	Dennis Beck	1990	8,443
125 7/8	21 1/8	20 3/8	17 3/8	5	5	Shelby County	KY	Kenneth E. Ferrell	1990	8,443
125 7/8	20 4/8	19 4/8	17 0/8	5	4	Cherry County	NE	Ken Colburn	1990	8,443
125 7/8	23 3/8	22 7/8	17 7/8	4	4	Kettle River	BC	Ken Davidson	1990	8,443
125 7/8	19 5/8	19 6/8	18 1/8	5	4	Crook County	WY	Susan Syvertson	1991	8,443
125 7/8	23 1/8	20 6/8	17 1/8	4	4	Chisago County	MN	Dave Condon	1991	8,443
125 7/8	20 5/8	21 2/8	16 1/8	4	4	St. Croix County	WI	Dennis J. Armbruster	1991	8,443
125 7/8	22 1/8	22 2/8	16 3/8	4	4	Jefferson County	OH	Genevieve K. Rogers	1991	8,443
125 7/8	21 4/8	22 1/8	20 5/8	4	4	Wabash County	IL	Mike Beesley	1991	8,443
125 7/8	23 2/8	18 6/8	15 5/8	6	4	Hamilton County	IA	Larry Haren	1991	8,443
125 7/8	22 0/8	22 5/8	16 7/8	4	5	Lake County	IL	John Roscop	1992	8,443
125 6/8	23 0/8	23 4/8	19 2/8	4	4	Bath County	VA	W. C. Bedall, Jr.	1958	8,485
125 6/8	19 5/8	19 3/8	16 2/8	5	5	Wood County	WI	Dennis Palmer	1967	8,485
125 6/8	21 4/8	21 5/8	18 6/8	4	5	Martin County	MN	Robert Barnett	1970	8,485
125 6/8	20 0/8	21 6/8	20 1/8	6	4	Palo Alto County	IA	Earl J. Gustafson	1971	8,485
125 6/8	22 0/8	22 4/8	16 4/8	4	4	Muskingum County	OH	Jim L. Lewis	1976	8,485
125 6/8	20 6/8	20 5/8	14 0/8	5	5	Buffalo County	WI	Rudy Klink	1981	8,485
125 6/8	20 4/8	20 2/8	17 0/8	5	5	Douglas County	MN	Jerry D. Kuhlman	1981	8,485
125 6/8	19 4/8	20 4/8	18 0/8	5	5	Miami County	KS	Gary L. Robertson	1982	8,485
125 6/8	20 2/8	21 2/8	18 2/8	4	5	Sauk County	WI	Hank Lee	1982	8,485
125 6/8	22 6/8	22 2/8	15 4/8	4	4	Sedgwick County	KS	Jim Nicholson	1983	8,485
125 6/8	21 1/8	21 2/8	17 5/8	6	6	Licking County	OH	Roy L Wilson, Jr.	1984	8,485
125 6/8	21 3/8	21 5/8	15 2/8	5	5	Montgomery County	KS	Grady Jabben	1985	8,485
125 6/8	19 7/8	22 0/8	19 2/8	5	6	Cedar County	MO	Terry Myers	1985	8,485
125 6/8	21 5/8	21 5/8	14 4/8	5	4	Vernon County	WI	Thomas Erie	1985	8,485
125 6/8	20 2/8	20 4/8	15 2/8	4	4	Branch County	MI	Douglas L. Curey	1985	8,485
125 6/8	18 1/8	18 1/8	14 2/8	5	5	Cerro Gordo County	IA	Eric Coe	1985	8,485
125 6/8	21 6/8	22 0/8	17 4/8	4	4	Buffalo County	WI	Richard A. Viken	1985	8,485
125 6/8	22 2/8	21 4/8	16 4/8	4	4	Green County	WI	Evan Steinhorst	1986	8,485
125 6/8	21 1/8	22 0/8	17 2/8	4	4	Mason County	WV	John C. Cochran	1986	8,485
125 6/8	25 2/8	25 3/8	21 0/8	4	4	Westchester County	NY	Carl Ranieri	1986	8,485
125 6/8	22 0/8	21 7/8	19 4/8	5	4	Jackson County	OH	Mike Parrish	1986	8,485
125 6/8	20 4/8	19 6/8	16 6/8	5	5	Coahoma County	MS	Allen Rauch	1987	8,485
125 6/8	22 1/8	20 6/8	17 2/8	4	5	Grundy County	IL	Ernest J. Brown	1987	8,485
125 6/8	20 2/8	21 0/8	17 6/8	4	5	St. Charles County	MO	Dennis Orf	1987	8,485
125 6/8	23 4/8	25 3/8	20 2/8	4	4	Henry County	IA	Carolyn Prottsman	1987	8,485
125 6/8	19 1/8	21 1/8	16 6/8	5	5	Parke County	IN	Phillip E. Walker	1988	8,485
125 6/8	22 1/8	21 3/8	17 2/8	7	6	Marquette County	WI	Russell N. Reetz	1988	8,485
125 6/8	21 5/8	20 2/8	18 0/8	4	4	Boone County	MO	David Westmoreland	1988	8,485
125 6/8	20 0/8	19 7/8	14 2/8	4	4	Morgan County	IL	Dennis Heitz	1988	8,485
125 6/8	21 6/8	21 3/8	17 6/8	4	4	Rutherford County	TN	Randall Richardson	1989	8,485
125 6/8	23 6/8	24 3/8	15 5/8	6	5	Hillsdale County	MI	Bert Wilson	1989	8,485
125 6/8	20 7/8	22 7/8	18 6/8	5	4	Lake County	IL	Robert H. Fugett	1989	8,485
125 6/8	20 4/8	20 6/8	14 4/8	5	4	Kane County	IL	Alan S. Runde	1989	8,485
125 6/8	22 3/8	19 2/8	20 2/8	4	4	Winnebago County	WI	Donald Werner	1989	8,485
125 6/8	21 7/8	21 6/8	16 0/8	4	4	Creek County	OK	James L. Fowler	1989	8,485
125 6/8	21 5/8	21 1/8	18 2/8	5	4	Mower County	MN	Joseph Landherr	1989	8,485
125 6/8	19 0/8	18 6/8	18 0/8	5	4	Greenlake	SAS	Pink Atkins	1989	8,485
125 6/8	22 4/8	21 3/8	20 6/8	5	4	Jefferson County	MS	George L. Pink II	1990	8,485
125 6/8	21 6/8	22 3/8	16 6/8	5	5	Wayne County	IL	Peewee Hall	1990	8,485
125 6/8	21 5/8	22 1/8	18 0/8	4	4	Jackson County	OH	Gary Turner	1990	8,485
125 6/8	22 2/8	22 6/8	20 0/8	4	4	Edgar County	IL	Russell O. Weir	1990	8,485
125 6/8	21 3/8	22 0/8	16 6/8	4	5	Morrison County	MN	Mike Hiltner	1990	8,485
125 6/8	23 0/8	22 1/8	18 2/8	4	5	Sawyer County	WI	Nick V. Loshuk	1991	8,485
125 6/8	21 1/8	22 1/8	15 6/8	5	5	Onieda County	WI	Mike Novak	1991	8,485
125 6/8	20 2/8	20 0/8	16 2/8	5	5	Reagan County	TX	James E. Borron	1991	8,485
125 6/8	20 2/8	19 7/8	17 0/8	5	5	Morrison County	MN	James Bittner	1991	8,485
125 6/8	19 7/8	19 0/8	16 0/8	5	5	Washington County	MN	Wayne Edgerton	1991	8,485
125 6/8	21 3/8	20 5/8	18 1/8	6	4	Iron County	WI	Mark D. Levra	1991	8,485
125 6/8	21 6/8	21 4/8	18 0/8	4	5	Dane County	WI	Mark Hirssig	1991	8,485
125 6/8	18 0/8	18 0/8	16 6/8	5	5	Appanoose County	IA	Scott Rolffs	1991	8,485
125 5/8	21 4/8	21 3/8	18 3/8	4	4	Brown County	SD	Leo J. Weber	1965	8,535
125 5/8	21 5/8	21 4/8	17 5/8	4	4	Lyman County	SD	Dennis Lien	1966	8,535
125 5/8	19 2/8	19 3/8	16 3/8	5	5	Sauk County	WI	Andre J. Jestafie	1968	8,535
125 5/8	22 1/8	25 0/8	20 1/8	5	6	Meade County	KS	Kent Davis	1971	8,535
125 5/8	19 7/8	18 7/8	15 5/8	5	5	Jo Daviess County	IL	Tom Spraetz	1976	8,535
125 5/8	21 5/8	21 4/8	16 5/8	5	5	Kent County	MD	Harry A. Weishaar	1977	8,535

MINIMUM SCORE 125   (Continued)

Score	Length of Main Beam R	Length of Main Beam L	Inside Spread	Number of Points R	Number of Points L	Area	State/Province	Hunter's Name	Date	Rank
125 5/8	24 6/8	24 2/8	15 5/8	4	4	Fairfield County	SC	Danny Duncan	1978	8,535
125 5/8	22 6/8	22 6/8	14 0/8	6	6	Ripley County	IN	Richard Gambrel	1979	8,535
125 5/8	22 4/8	22 0/8	17 5/8	4	4	Keokuk County	IA	Roger E. Claypool	1980	8,535
125 5/8	23 1/8	23 7/8	14 7/8	5	5	Alpena County	MI	Cameron Cogsdill	1981	8,535
125 5/8	21 1/8	21 2/8	17 5/8	4	4	Green Lake County	WI	Raymond E. Golomski	1981	8,535
125 5/8	19 7/8	19 3/8	16 1/8	6	6	Jackson County	MN	Rodney Borer	1982	8,535
125 5/8	21 2/8	21 1/8	18 7/8	4	4	Clermont County	OH	Claud F. Combs	1982	8,535
125 5/8	19 3/8	18 5/8	14 3/8	5	6	Washington County	OH	Ronald G. Boone	1982	8,535
125 5/8	23 3/8	22 7/8	15 3/8	5	5	Vernon County	MO	Roger L. Hensley	1982	8,535
125 5/8	21 0/8	20 7/8	16 1/8	4	4	Ozaukee County	WI	Thomas G. Bloomingdale	1983	8,535
125 5/8	21 5/8	21 1/8	17 3/8	4	4	Will County	IL	Angelo L. Chirban	1983	8,535
125 5/8	21 6/8	21 6/8	17 5/8	4	4	Cherokee County	OK	Jon C. Rogers	1983	8,535
125 5/8	20 2/8	20 2/8	14 3/8	5	5	Oliver County	ND	Al Zeller	1984	8,535
125 5/8	22 6/8	22 3/8	19 3/8	4	5	Lycoming County	PA	Gary A Pennycoff	1985	8,535
125 5/8	22 0/8	22 1/8	15 3/8	4	4	Polk County	WI	Jon Leisch	1986	8,535
125 5/8	24 7/8	23 7/8	21 4/8	5	5	Jackson County	IL	Charles Barwick	1986	8,535
125 5/8	21 4/8	21 6/8	17 5/8	4	4	McDowell County	WV	Jerry Carroll	1986	8,535
125 5/8	18 4/8	19 4/8	14 7/8	7	5	Uvalde County	TX	Mark Ezell	1987	8,535
125 5/8	20 6/8	20 5/8	14 3/8	5	5	Menominee County	MI	Robert Brittson	1987	8,535
125 5/8	24 1/8	22 5/8	14 7/8	5	4	Bradford County	PA	Kyle Dewey	1987	8,535
125 5/8	20 0/8	20 2/8	18 1/8	5	5	Trigg County	KY	Ricky Boatright	1987	8,535
125 5/8	21 6/8	21 3/8	16 7/8	5	7	Knox County	IL	Bill Crowden	1987	8,535
125 5/8	21 1/8	21 5/8	17 5/8	5	4	Frontier County	NE	Steven P. Salmieri	1987	8,535
125 5/8	22 7/8	21 7/8	17 1/8	4	4	Starke County	IN	Paul W. Arndt	1987	8,535
125 5/8	21 3/8	20 3/8	17 1/8	5	5	Lawrence County	MO	David L. Lundy	1988	8,535
125 5/8	20 5/8	20 4/8	17 5/8	5	4	Jefferson County	WI	Bob Chaveriat	1988	8,535
125 5/8	22 3/8	21 6/8	19 4/8	6	4	Faribault County	MN	Bob Prange	1988	8,535
125 5/8	20 4/8	22 0/8	17 0/8	6	6	Logan County	IL	Gary W. Conrady	1988	8,535
125 5/8	23 2/8	23 2/8	18 1/8	5	6	Jefferson County	OH	Kevin Sokolowski	1988	8,535
125 5/8	21 3/8	22 3/8	16 7/8	4	4	Richland County	IL	Billy Joe Hicks	1988	8,535
125 5/8	19 6/8	20 2/8	14 5/8	5	5	Woodbury County	IA	Todd Carr	1988	8,535
125 5/8	19 0/8	18 6/8	15 5/8	5	5	Prairie County	AR	Scotty Burch	1988	8,535
125 5/8	23 2/8	23 0/8	18 3/8	4	5	Lyon County	KS	Gary Atchison	1988	8,535
125 5/8	21 2/8	21 5/8	19 1/8	5	5	Jefferson County	OH	William Gary Rusinovich	1989	8,535
125 5/8	23 2/8	22 5/8	18 5/8	5	4	La Salle County	IL	John Thomas	1989	8,535
125 5/8	24 1/8	25 0/8	18 3/8	3	3	Calhoun County	MI	Ron Allen	1989	8,535
125 5/8	21 0/8	21 3/8	17 7/8	7	6	Pittsylvania County	VA	Robbie Lee Bryant	1989	8,535
125 5/8	21 3/8	22 2/8	17 5/8	5	4	Wayne County	MO	Don Reynolds	1989	8,535
125 5/8	19 4/8	19 0/8	15 7/8	5	5	Uvalde County	TX	Mark Ezell	1989	8,535
125 5/8	22 2/8	21 6/8	14 3/8	4	4	Heard County	GA	Robert M. Foran	1990	8,535
125 5/8	21 2/8	20 3/8	16 3/8	4	4	Perry County	IN	Thomas L. Goeppner	1990	8,535
125 5/8	20 4/8	20 6/8	17 3/8	5	5	Bent County	CO	Chris Anderson	1990	8,535
125 5/8	19 5/8	20 5/8	15 5/8	5	5	Arenac County	MI	Patrick D. York	1990	8,535
125 5/8	23 1/8	23 1/8	17 5/8	4	5	Morris County	NJ	Russ Davidson	1990	8,535
125 5/8	21 6/8	21 5/8	18 3/8	4	4	Whiteside County	IL	Art Heinze	1990	8,535
125 5/8	23 1/8	22 1/8	17 3/8	4	6	Ballard County	KY	Albert Hargis	1991	8,535
125 5/8	22 6/8	22 7/8	18 1/8	5	4	Jenkins County	GA	Frank J. Nelson, Jr.	1991	8,535
125 5/8	21 5/8	20 5/8	21 5/8	5	4	Mercer County	NJ	Richard Deveney	1991	8,535
125 5/8	24 3/8	24 2/8	17 1/8	3	5	Schoharie County	NY	Chris Aernecke	1991	8,535
125 5/8	22 4/8	21 1/8	16 1/8	5	6	Whiteside County	IL	Clint Walker	1991	8,535
125 5/8	22 1/8	22 1/8	16 7/8	4	4	Oswego County	NY	Ellis B. Barber	1991	8,535
125 4/8	24 7/8	21 6/8	17 2/8	4	4	Marion County	IA	Thomas Tucker	1962	8,592
125 4/8	20 4/8	20 7/8	19 0/8	4	4	Clark County	MO	Allen L. Courtney	1971	8,592
125 4/8	20 2/8	21 3/8	16 6/8	5	5	Otter Tail County	MN	Terry Tamke	1971	8,592
125 4/8	20 7/8	21 0/8	16 0/8	4	5	Meeker County	MN	Chuck Schultz	1978	8,592
125 4/8	22 6/8	22 7/8	15 1/8	4	5	Williams County	OH	Norman J. Spindler	1979	8,592
125 4/8	19 7/8	20 1/8	15 2/8	4	5	Rice County	KS	Daniel G. Willems	1979	8,592
125 4/8	20 1/8	20 2/8	17 1/8	5	4	Bearspaw Dam	ALB	David R. Coupland	1979	8,592
125 4/8	21 4/8	21 6/8	14 2/8	5	4	Worcester County	MA	David M. Peters	1980	8,592
125 4/8	23 0/8	24 1/8	17 4/8	5	4	Murray County	MN	Kerry Ella	1981	8,592
125 4/8	20 5/8	20 3/8	17 4/8	5	5	Union County	KY	Brad Tucker	1982	8,592
125 4/8	21 3/8	21 5/8	12 6/8	5	5	Oktibbeha County	MS	Stennis Jones	1983	8,592
125 4/8	21 7/8	22 5/8	14 2/8	4	4	Knox County	OH	Tom Kayser	1984	8,592
125 4/8	20 3/8	19 3/8	14 0/8	6	5	Trempealeau County	WI	Chris Fechner	1985	8,592
125 4/8	21 1/8	21 2/8	15 6/8	4	4	Vernon County	WI	Michael Lang	1985	8,592
125 4/8	21 4/8	22 6/8	15 6/8	4	4	Greene County	AR	Danny J. Walker	1985	8,592
125 4/8	16 4/8	22 0/8	16 4/8	5	4	Monona County	IA	Larry Couron	1985	8,592
125 4/8	21 7/8	21 7/8	19 4/8	5	4	Warren County	IL	Bob Rawlings	1985	8,592
125 4/8	21 4/8	22 0/8	16 6/8	4	4	Buffalo County	WI	Brian P. Bork	1986	8,592
125 4/8	22 5/8	21 5/8	18 4/8	4	4	Delaware County	OH	William D. Merdeath	1986	8,592

340

WHITETAIL DEER (*Typical Antlers*)

MINIMUM SCORE 125

(*Continued*)

SCORE	R LENGTH OF MAIN BEAM L		INSIDE SPREAD	NUMBER OF R POINTS L		AREA	STATE/ PROVINCE	HUNTER'S NAME	DATE	RANK
125 4/8	18 6/8	19 6/8	16 4/8	5	4	Des Moines County	IA	Randy R. Mack	1986	8,592
125 4/8	24 4/8	17 4/8	17 2/8	4	5	Gibson County	IN	Darvin Hulfachor	1986	8,592
125 4/8	21 4/8	20 4/8	17 3/8	7	7	Lawrence County	MS	Robert L. George	1987	8,592
125 4/8	21 2/8	22 1/8	17 2/8	4	5	Iron County	MI	John Ohmer	1987	8,592
125 4/8	21 4/8	21 3/8	18 0/8	4	4	Washtenaw County	MI	Charles E. Benedict	1987	8,592
125 4/8	23 2/8	23 0/8	20 2/8	4	4	Washtenaw County	MI	Robert Lee Smith, Jr.	1987	8,592
125 4/8	19 1/8	19 3/8	14 1/8	5	5	Crook County	WY	Scotty Powell	1988	8,592
125 4/8	23 1/8	23 6/8	18 0/8	4	6	Monroe County	WI	Lesley Strunk	1988	8,592
125 4/8	21 1/8	20 2/8	14 0/8	4	4	Jasper County	IA	James L. Seieroe	1988	8,592
125 4/8	20 1/8	20 4/8	15 2/8	4	4	Weld County	CO	Doug Kayl	1988	8,592
125 4/8	22 2/8	21 5/8	15 7/8	9	6	Carver County	MN	Paul Welin	1988	8,592
125 4/8	22 3/8	22 6/8	17 6/8	5	5	McKenzie County	ND	Kelly Evanson	1988	8,592
125 4/8	22 4/8	22 1/8	19 4/8	4	5	Sauk County	WI	Michael J. McGann	1989	8,592
125 4/8	24 6/8	24 7/8	17 4/8	5	4	Montgomery County	PA	Martin R. Graner	1989	8,592
125 4/8	19 6/8	20 3/8	16 5/8	5	5	Carbon County	PA	Salvatore Sorace	1989	8,592
125 4/8	19 5/8	19 6/8	13 7/8	4	6	Cedar County	NE	Kevin Schmidt	1989	8,592
125 4/8	19 0/8	19 3/8	15 0/8	5	5	Brown County	IL	Barry Rich	1989	8,592
125 4/8	21 4/8	23 0/8	15 2/8	5	4	Lake County	IL	Lynn Anderson	1989	8,592
125 4/8	21 2/8	22 1/8	17 1/8	6	4	Monmouth County	NJ	Matthew McGowan	1989	8,592
125 4/8	24 3/8	24 1/8	15 4/8	4	4	Washington County	RI	Kenneth W. Gordon	1989	8,592
125 4/8	21 2/8	21 3/8	16 2/8	5	5	Webb County	TX	Cliff Barnett	1990	8,592
125 4/8	22 4/8	22 3/8	16 6/8	4	4	Atascosa County	TX	Marc Knight	1990	8,592
125 4/8	23 0/8	23 2/8	15 4/8	4	4	Ste. Genevieve County	MO	Thomas Layton	1990	8,592
125 4/8	21 4/8	21 0/8	15 4/8	6	5	Sanford	MAN	Martin Lavoie	1990	8,592
125 4/8	22 5/8	21 7/8	21 0/8	4	4	Powell County	MT	Daniel K. Kuehn	1991	8,592
125 4/8	19 5/8	19 5/8	14 6/8	5	5	Meagher County	MT	D. Mitch Kottas	1991	8,592
125 4/8	21 7/8	21 3/8	18 4/8	5	5	La Salle County	TX	Gary Pitts	1991	8,592
125 4/8	22 1/8	22 0/8	19 6/8	4	4	Crawford County	PA	Bob Dunton	1991	8,592
125 4/8	23 4/8	22 5/8	17 2/8	4	4	Ross County	OH	Mark E. Rickey	1991	8,592
125 3/8	20 5/8	21 4/8	16 5/8	5	4	Stephenson County	IL	Vaughn Zimmerman	1969	8,640
125 3/8	24 0/8	24 6/8	17 3/8	4	5	Wabasha County	MN	David Mohler	1971	8,640
125 3/8	20 7/8	20 3/8	15 3/8	4	4	Newport News County	VA	Dr. Glenn A. Parker	1972	8,640
125 3/8	21 7/8	22 6/8	16 3/8	4	5	Warren County	IA	Michael Woolman	1974	8,640
125 3/8	22 6/8	23 4/8	18 4/8	7	6	Pawnee County	KS	Don Jensen	1977	8,640
125 3/8	19 2/8	19 7/8	14 1/8	5	5	Jasper County	IN	Frank Benka	1978	8,640
125 3/8	22 2/8	23 6/8	16 3/8	4	4	Louisa County	IA	Lee Cassabaum	1979	8,640
125 3/8	22 0/8	22 2/8	15 5/8	4	4	Saginaw County	MI	James L. Bassett	1980	8,640
125 3/8	20 5/8	21 7/8	18 1/8	4	4	Neosho County	KS	Damie Coomes	1982	8,640
125 3/8	20 1/8	20 1/8	14 7/8	5	5	Dorchester County	MD	Jim Roy	1983	8,640
125 3/8	20 4/8	20 1/8	17 7/8	4	5	Hardin County	IA	Bill Stonebraker	1983	8,640
125 3/8	19 4/8	20 1/8	15 7/8	5	5	Watson	SAS	Wayne Dickson	1983	8,640
125 3/8	20 7/8	20 1/8	15 5/8	5	5	Suffolk County	NY	Anthony Bernard	1983	8,640
125 3/8	21 3/8	21 2/8	18 1/8	4	4	Oconto County	WI	Bob Richardson, Jr.	1984	8,640
125 3/8	22 4/8	22 0/8	18 5/8	5	5	Scott County	MN	Bruce Kramer	1984	8,640
125 3/8	18 7/8	18 4/8	15 3/8	5	5	Wellington County	ONT	Fred Law	1984	8,640
125 3/8	21 4/8	20 6/8	15 7/8	5	5	Cheboygan County	MI	Steven Schrauben	1984	8,640
125 3/8	22 1/8	21 5/8	18 1/8	4	4	Washington County	WI	Gordon Bell	1985	8,640
125 3/8	22 6/8	21 5/8	14 3/8	4	4	Somerset County	ME	Alfred Corson	1985	8,640
125 3/8	22 0/8	22 3/8	18 0/8	4	6	Morrison County	MN	Mike Mitten	1985	8,640
125 3/8	18 6/8	18 7/8	16 3/8	5	5	Ramsey County	ND	Charles McGarvey	1985	8,640
125 3/8	21 4/8	22 4/8	16 3/8	4	5	Iowa County	WI	Don Schuld	1985	8,640
125 3/8	23 1/8	21 5/8	13 6/8	5	4	St. Charles County	MO	Edgar Ralph Welch	1985	8,640
125 3/8	21 2/8	23 1/8	20 5/8	5	5	Augusta County	VA	Mark D. Huffman	1986	8,640
125 3/8	24 3/8	22 4/8	18 3/8	5	5	Caroline County	MD	Eric Wise	1986	8,640
125 3/8	20 5/8	21 6/8	18 5/8	4	4	Sawyer County	WI	Mike Fawley	1987	8,640
125 3/8	21 1/8	20 3/8	15 3/8	5	5	Waukesha County	WI	Daniel Buchta	1987	8,640
125 3/8	20 1/8	20 1/8	15 1/8	4	4	Fayette County	IL	Terry Jackson	1987	8,640
125 3/8	24 4/8	22 5/8	20 3/8	5	4	Vermilion County	IL	Allen Walker	1987	8,640
125 3/8	19 7/8	20 3/8	14 7/8	4	4	Campbell County	TN	Truman E. Wilson	1987	8,640
125 3/8	21 3/8	21 5/8	16 7/8	4	5	Carroll County	MD	Dana P. Calhoun	1987	8,640
125 3/8	20 0/8	20 2/8	15 7/8	5	5	Muskingum County	OH	G. Vernon Sowers	1987	8,640
125 3/8	20 2/8	20 7/8	18 3/8	6	5	Dorchester County	MD	Mark Alan Gadow	1987	8,640
125 3/8	21 7/8	22 0/8	17 6/8	6	5	Polk County	WI	Mark Gustafson	1988	8,640
125 3/8	19 0/8	18 7/8	15 5/8	5	5	Jefferson County	KS	Mike Campbell	1988	8,640
125 3/8	23 5/8	23 2/8	18 3/8	4	4	Buffalo County	WI	Randy A. Harms	1988	8,640
125 3/8	20 7/8	20 7/8	17 1/8	5	5	Dunn County	WI	Leroy Leftwich	1988	8,640
125 3/8	21 4/8	20 7/8	16 3/8	5	5	Kewaunee County	WI	David D. Zima	1988	8,640
125 3/8	20 5/8	21 4/8	12 3/8	5	5	Coles County	IL	Robert A. Bryant	1988	8,640
125 3/8	22 1/8	22 2/8	16 1/8	4	4	St. Croix County	WI	Glenn D. Khalar	1988	8,640
125 3/8	20 4/8	19 6/8	13 7/8	5	5	Chippewa County	WI	Jon Oemig	1989	8,640

Score	Length of Main Beam R	Length of Main Beam L	Inside Spread	Number of Points R	Number of Points L	Area	State/ Province	Hunter's Name	Date	Rank
125 3/8	20 6/8	21 4/8	17 2/8	6	4	Douglas County	WI	David P. Lindelof	1989	8,640
125 3/8	21 2/8	21 0/8	17 3/8	5	5	Logan County	IL	Eldon R. Broster	1989	8,640
125 3/8	21 2/8	24 7/8	18 5/8	4	4	Cross County	AR	Chris Vanaman	1989	8,640
125 3/8	21 6/8	21 4/8	16 1/8	5	5	Wood County	WI	Steve Peterson	1990	8,640
125 3/8	21 3/8	21 3/8	16 1/8	5	5	Richland County	WI	Dean A. Jewell	1990	8,640
125 3/8	19 2/8	18 7/8	17 2/8	5	6	Osage County	OK	Terry Brady	1990	8,640
125 3/8	19 6/8	20 0/8	13 7/8	6	6	Orange County	NY	Ben Risley	1990	8,640
125 3/8	23 3/8	23 4/8	18 3/8	4	4	Delaware County	PA	Jay P. Kelly	1990	8,640
125 3/8	21 3/8	22 2/8	14 6/8	5	5	Flathead County	MT	Gordon L. Lewis	1991	8,640
125 3/8	21 1/8	21 1/8	17 1/8	5	5	Swift County	MN	Jan Rangens	1991	8,640
125 3/8	22 2/8	21 1/8	16 1/8	5	4	Hall County	GA	Tim Butler	1991	8,640
125 3/8	20 4/8	20 4/8	16 3/8	4	5	Polk County	MN	Greg Ranz	1991	8,640
125 3/8	20 1/8	20 2/8	14 3/8	5	5	Bartow County	GA	Christopher C. King	1991	8,640
125 3/8	21 2/8	21 0/8	15 3/8	4	4	Marion County	KS	Galen Chizek	1991	8,640
125 3/8	22 6/8	23 3/8	15 7/8	6	4	Vigo County	IN	Billy Wright	1991	8,640
125 3/8	22 7/8	22 3/8	19 1/8	4	3	Lawrence County	IN	Larry Deaton	1991	8,640
125 3/8	19 6/8	19 7/8	16 1/8	5	5	Van Buren County	MI	Martin L. Price	1991	8,640
125 3/8	18 6/8	18 1/8	13 5/8	5	6	Sawyer County	WI	James C. Snortum	1991	8,640
125 3/8	23 5/8	24 4/8	16 1/8	7	6	Sullivan County	MO	Darren Stephenson	1991	8,640
125 3/8	20 0/8	20 4/8	13 1/8	5	5	Perry County	OH	Gary J. Boley	1991	8,640
125 3/8	23 6/8	22 4/8	16 3/8	6	4	St. Clair County	MI	Kurt M. Zurawski	1991	8,640
125 3/8	20 6/8	20 4/8	15 3/8	5	5	Warren County	IA	Dan Thomlinson	1991	8,640
125 3/8	20 5/8	20 6/8	17 7/8	4	4	Marathon County	WI	Larry A. Karlmann	1992	8,640
125 2/8	19 3/8	20 0/8	15 0/8	4	4	Missaukee County	MI	Dr. B. P. Garris	1966	8,704
125 2/8	26 5/8	25 2/8	22 2/8	4	3	Fulton County	IL	Arnold C. Hegele	1967	8,704
125 2/8	20 6/8	20 7/8	15 6/8	4	4	Sussex County	NJ	Tom Barber	1973	8,704
125 2/8	22 6/8	22 2/8	17 2/8	4	3	Washington County	IA	Danny B. Jirsa	1974	8,704
125 2/8	21 5/8	21 4/8	17 6/8	5	4	Columbia County	WI	Gary Cahoon	1977	8,704
125 2/8	22 2/8	24 7/8	17 6/8	4	4	Guernsey County	OH	Butch Todd	1977	8,704
125 2/8	21 7/8	21 7/8	16 2/8	4	4	Jackson County	MI	Bernard Stachowicz	1979	8,704
125 2/8	23 2/8	24 6/8	19 2/8	4	4	Baltimore County	MD	Robert E. Arndt	1980	8,704
125 2/8	22 3/8	21 6/8	18 6/8	5	6	Goodhue County	MN	John 'Jack' Cordes	1981	8,704
125 2/8	18 6/8	18 1/8	13 6/8	5	5	Boone County	MO	Jeff Jennings	1981	8,704
125 2/8	21 6/8	22 4/8	15 0/8	4	4	Shawano County	WI	David J. Gard	1983	8,704
125 2/8	20 6/8	21 4/8	15 2/8	5	5	Calvert County	MD	Gary Fillmann	1983	8,704
125 2/8	20 0/8	21 0/8	17 6/8	6	5	Cherokee County	KS	Sam F. Lancaster	1984	8,704
125 2/8	19 3/8	19 0/8	14 0/8	4	4	Kiowa County	KS	Susan Manwarren	1984	8,704
125 2/8	24 1/8	23 4/8	17 4/8	4	4	Blue Earth County	MN	Ray Smothers	1985	8,704
125 2/8	21 0/8	21 4/8	19 4/8	8	8	Des Moines County	IA	Rod Waschkat	1985	8,704
125 2/8	24 0/8	23 0/8	17 0/8	4	5	Harford County	MD	Warren J. Barth	1986	8,704
125 2/8	21 1/8	21 1/8	16 3/8	6	5	Mingo County	WV	Danny Thompson	1986	8,704
125 2/8	22 2/8	22 6/8	18 5/8	6	6	Suffolk County	NY	Lee James Garrant	1986	8,704
125 2/8	21 5/8	20 6/8	17 4/8	4	4	Butler County	KS	Ray Manfull	1986	8,704
125 2/8	24 0/8	23 2/8	20 7/8	5	4	Suffolk County	NY	Steve Schoen	1986	8,704
125 2/8	21 6/8	21 3/8	19 0/8	4	4	Dubuque County	IA	Andy Chase	1986	8,704
125 2/8	21 5/8	20 5/8	19 7/8	5	6	Buffalo County	WI	Wayne Olson	1986	8,704
125 2/8	20 1/8	21 2/8	18 2/8	5	5	Sabine County	TX	Russell C. Lantier	1986	8,704
125 2/8	21 5/8	21 3/8	14 6/8	4	4	Otoe County	NE	Richard R. Pope	1987	8,704
125 2/8	21 1/8	21 0/8	18 6/8	4	4	Morris County	NJ	Gene Rurka	1987	8,704
125 2/8	22 0/8	23 0/8	17 0/8	4	4	Adams County	WI	Randall Ebbe	1987	8,704
125 2/8	20 6/8	21 3/8	16 4/8	5	5	La Grange County	IN	David Sauders	1987	8,704
125 2/8	22 3/8	21 5/8	17 6/8	4	4	Cayuga County	NY	Brian Fenner	1987	8,704
125 2/8	22 1/8	22 4/8	18 6/8	4	4	Langlade County	WI	Andrae D'Acquisto	1987	8,704
125 2/8	21 1/8	20 7/8	16 6/8	4	4	Litchfield County	CT	John Swiklas	1987	8,704
125 2/8	21 3/8	20 2/8	16 2/8	5	5	Washington County	PA	Victor J. Columbus	1988	8,704
125 2/8	20 4/8	21 0/8	15 0/8	5	5	Dunn County	WI	Mike J. Kurschner	1988	8,704
125 2/8	20 6/8	20 2/8	16 6/8	5	5	Kent County	MD	Randy L. Heim	1988	8,704
125 2/8	24 2/8	24 4/8	17 5/8	6	5	Dane County	WI	Todd P. Schultz	1988	8,704
125 2/8	22 0/8	22 6/8	16 6/8	4	5	Jackson County	IN	Jeffrey J. Hurd	1988	8,704
125 2/8	19 7/8	19 2/8	19 2/8	4	4	Washington County	MS	Bobby R. Woods	1989	8,704
125 2/8	23 6/8	23 5/8	12 4/8	4	5	Sequatchie County	TN	Robert L. Moon, Jr.	1989	8,704
125 2/8	20 5/8	21 4/8	14 6/8	6	5	Hardin County	KY	Jimmie Williams	1989	8,704
125 2/8	21 5/8	20 5/8	18 0/8	4	4	Sussex County	DE	Jeff Minor	1989	8,704
125 2/8	21 7/8	22 7/8	14 2/8	8	5	Greene County	AR	Andy Vangilder	1989	8,704
125 2/8	21 3/8	21 1/8	16 6/8	4	4	Johnson County	IA	Jim Bohnenkamp	1989	8,704
125 2/8	21 6/8	22 6/8	13 4/8	5	5	Wilcox County	AL	Billy Perryman	1989	8,704
125 2/8	18 4/8	19 7/8	13 4/8	6	6	Duval County	TX	Dean Oatman	1989	8,704
125 2/8	22 3/8	21 2/8	17 0/8	4	4	Washington County	WI	Mark Reinert	1990	8,704
125 2/8	18 5/8	18 4/8	15 6/8	5	5	Big Stone County	MN	Steven Butzke	1990	8,704
125 2/8	20 0/8	20 3/8	17 5/8	7	5	Waupaca County	WI	Dan Herson	1990	8,704

SCORE	LENGTH OF R MAIN BEAM L		INSIDE SPREAD	NUMBER OF R POINTS L		AREA	STATE/ PROVINCE	HUNTER'S NAME	DATE	RANK
125 2/8	23 0/8	23 0/8	18 0/8	4	4	Bucks County	PA	Chuck Metz	1990	8,704
125 2/8	22 1/8	22 2/8	17 6/8	4	6	Antrim County	MI	Mike Losee	1990	8,704
125 2/8	20 7/8	20 5/8	16 4/8	5	5	Pike County	OH	Robert Irwin Bazell	1990	8,704
125 2/8	23 4/8	24 5/8	17 0/8	4	4	Isle of Wight County	VA	Mark W. Trybe	1990	8,704
125 2/8	20 1/8	20 7/8	15 4/8	5	5	Osage County	OK	Jeff Fitts	1990	8,704
125 2/8	24 7/8	23 2/8	19 2/8	4	4	Fremont County	IA	John W. Nebel	1990	8,704
125 2/8	21 3/8	21 1/8	19 2/8	4	4	Will County	IL	Robert L. Kamenjarin	1990	8,704
125 2/8	22 1/8	21 7/8	14 2/8	5	6	Atascosa County	TX	Mike Palmer	1990	8,704
125 2/8	22 2/8	21 6/8	15 5/8	6	5	Delaware County	OH	Dave Ware	1990	8,704
125 2/8	20 5/8	20 2/8	12 4/8	6	6	St. Marys County	MD	Dale K. Hubbartt	1991	8,704
125 2/8	19 0/8	18 6/8	14 6/8	7	6	Clarion County	PA	V. Craig Hagan	1991	8,704
125 2/8	21 5/8	21 4/8	16 4/8	4	4	Burnett County	WI	Larry M. Looman	1991	8,704
125 1/8	19 1/8	19 7/8	14 7/8	5	5	Ozaukee County	WI	Don Schwerin	1966	8,763
125 1/8	20 7/8	20 6/8	15 3/8	4	4	Graham County	KS	Russell Hull	1975	8,763
125 1/8	22 3/8	23 5/8	20 0/8	5	5	Vermilion County	IL	Mel Mueller	1976	8,763
125 1/8	18 3/8	19 0/8	15 1/8	5	5	Ogle County	IL	Gary Shaw	1979	8,763
125 1/8	21 1/8	20 7/8	13 5/8	5	5	Muskogee County	OK	Don Anderson	1979	8,763
125 1/8	22 3/8	22 5/8	18 7/8	4	5	Cortland County	NY	Ted W. Renninger	1981	8,763
125 1/8	19 4/8	19 4/8	18 5/8	6	5	Manitowoc County	WI	Peter J. Ording	1982	8,763
125 1/8	20 0/8	21 0/8	14 1/8	6	5	Adair County	MO	Terry Findling	1982	8,763
125 1/8	21 7/8	22 0/8	17 5/8	5	4	Morrison County	MN	Gordie Rieber	1982	8,763
125 1/8	19 7/8	20 1/8	18 6/8	6	7	Des Moines County	IA	David R. Bessine	1983	8,763
125 1/8	20 7/8	20 0/8	17 1/8	5	5	Brown County	SD	Jim C. Hill	1983	8,763
125 1/8	22 1/8	22 3/8	18 3/8	5	7	Codington County	SD	Brad Bach	1983	8,763
125 1/8	22 3/8	22 1/8	17 5/8	4	4	Hillsdale County	MI	Andy Keefe	1983	8,763
125 1/8	19 3/8	19 6/8	17 1/8	5	5	Waupaca County	WI	Peter J. Burton	1984	8,763
125 1/8	20 2/8	21 2/8	16 3/8	4	4	De Witt County	IL	Thomas E. Wilson	1984	8,763
125 1/8	18 6/8	19 6/8	15 0/8	5	6	Valley County	MT	Leith S Wimmer	1984	8,763
125 1/8	20 1/8	21 0/8	16 1/8	5	5	Lapeer County	MI	Daniel Kavalunas	1984	8,763
125 1/8	21 1/8	21 4/8	16 7/8	4	5	Forest County	WI	Joseph P. Weber	1984	8,763
125 1/8	22 4/8	23 0/8	19 3/8	4	5	Winnebago County	IL	Richard Amundson	1985	8,763
125 1/8	21 3/8	20 7/8	16 3/8	4	4	Clayton County	IA	Duane F. Kennicker	1985	8,763
125 1/8	21 0/8	21 3/8	19 3/8	5	5	Washington County	WI	Judy Staedler	1986	8,763
125 1/8	22 4/8	21 3/8	16 3/8	4	4	Westmoreland County	PA	Robert L. Waddell	1986	8,763
125 1/8	20 4/8	20 5/8	14 7/8	5	4	Clinton County	MI	Dan Bertalan	1986	8,763
125 1/8	19 2/8	19 5/8	14 7/8	5	5	Dakota County	MN	Arthur Ellsworth	1987	8,763
125 1/8	22 4/8	23 0/8	17 3/8	4	5	Webb County	TX	Frank Ramirez	1987	8,763
125 1/8	23 1/8	23 7/8	16 7/8	5	5	Coweta County	GA	Jerry M. Kirby, Jr.	1987	8,763
125 1/8	21 7/8	21 1/8	18 7/8	5	5	Mason County	WV	George A. Kearns	1987	8,763
125 1/8	18 3/8	18 2/8	14 7/8	5	5	Linn County	MO	Roy A. Simpson	1987	8,763
125 1/8	22 6/8	22 2/8	16 7/8	4	4	Waushara County	WI	Rodney L. Hering	1988	8,763
125 1/8	20 0/8	20 1/8	15 3/8	5	5	Iron County	MI	Steven P. Sendek	1988	8,763
125 1/8	22 4/8	22 7/8	17 2/8	5	6	Morgan County	MO	Steve Rollins	1988	8,763
125 1/8	22 7/8	21 2/8	16 1/8	4	6	Coffey County	KS	Glen Neilson	1988	8,763
125 1/8	20 4/8	20 3/8	16 7/8	5	7	Strathcona	ALB	Corey Rasmussen	1988	8,763
125 1/8	21 2/8	21 3/8	20 1/8	4	4	Muskegon County	MI	Arthur Langlois	1989	8,763
125 1/8	20 1/8	20 0/8	18 3/8	5	4	Burleigh County	ND	Mark Froelich	1989	8,763
125 1/8	20 3/8	20 7/8	16 7/8	4	4	Sangamon County	IL	Steve Tice	1989	8,763
125 1/8	21 6/8	22 2/8	15 5/8	4	4	Wheeler County	GA	Terry Fountain	1989	8,763
125 1/8	22 4/8	21 0/8	17 3/8	4	4	Spencer County	IN	Russ Meyer	1989	8,763
125 1/8	23 3/8	23 3/8	16 1/8	4	4	Morgan County	MO	Steve Rollins	1989	8,763
125 1/8	21 1/8	21 2/8	16 5/8	4	4	Sanilac County	MI	Randolph J. Hempton	1989	8,763
125 1/8	23 6/8	21 3/8	17 7/8	4	4	Jackson County	MO	Ernie Bigler	1990	8,763
125 1/8	23 0/8	22 3/8	16 3/8	5	4	Sullivan County	IN	John D. Thomas	1990	8,763
125 1/8	22 5/8	22 2/8	17 3/8	4	5	Oneida County	WI	Michael Schreiner	1990	8,763
125 1/8	21 1/8	21 4/8	16 1/8	4	4	Hand County	SD	Bob Templeton	1990	8,763
125 1/8	23 1/8	22 7/8	16 5/8	4	5	Pierce County	WI	Ron Zaudke	1990	8,763
125 1/8	21 7/8	23 0/8	14 7/8	5	5	Plymouth County	IA	Bill Conlon	1990	8,763
125 1/8	19 1/8	19 1/8	15 3/8	5	5	Allamakee County	IA	Robert L. Kampen	1990	8,763
125 1/8	21 3/8	20 7/8	17 7/8	4	4	Licking County	OH	Robert H. Wise	1990	8,763
125 1/8	21 5/8	20 6/8	16 5/8	4	6	Fillmore County	MN	Wayne Volkart	1991	8,763
125 1/8	23 0/8	22 7/8	17 0/8	4	5	Jackson County	IA	Warren F. Amling	1991	8,763
125 1/8	19 3/8	18 7/8	15 5/8	6	5	Wright County	IA	Scott Smith	1991	8,763
125 1/8	20 2/8	20 1/8	17 1/8	5	5	Carver County	MN	Anthony Noor	1991	8,763
125 1/8	20 7/8	20 3/8	16 1/8	4	4	Carroll County	IL	Paul Shipman	1991	8,763
125 1/8	20 4/8	19 6/8	15 3/8	5	5	Bates County	MO	Tony A. Davis	1991	8,763
125 1/8	18 5/8	19 1/8	15 6/8	7	5	Spruce Grove	ALB	James Thomson	1991	8,763
125 1/8	25 1/8	23 7/8	19 7/8	4	4	Wake County	NC	Robert Thomas Hodge	1992	8,763
125 0/8	20 6/8	20 6/8	16 6/8	5	5	Sheboygan County	WI	Earl Uhl	1962	8,819
125 0/8	22 4/8	23 0/8	15 4/8	5	5	Hughes County	SD	Robert A. Clough	1967	8,819

SCORE	LENGTH OF MAIN BEAM		INSIDE SPREAD	NUMBER OF POINTS		AREA	STATE/ PROVINCE	HUNTER'S NAME	DATE	RANK
	R	L		R	L					
125 0/8	20 5/8	20 5/8	17 2/8	4	4	Livingston County	NY	Robert A. Carone	1969	8,819
125 0/8	22 0/8	22 0/8	17 4/8	6	6	Dodge County	WI	Charles E. Songstad	1970	8,819
125 0/8	24 2/8	24 4/8	17 5/8	8	4	Pope County	AR	Tom Quinton	1977	8,819
125 0/8	20 5/8	20 6/8	18 2/8	4	4	Freeborn County	MN	Jerry Christenson	1980	8,819
125 0/8	23 0/8	21 6/8	17 0/8	4	4	Switzerland County	IN	Barry Scott	1981	8,819
125 0/8	19 1/8	20 0/8	16 6/8	5	5	Indiana County	PA	Stephen C. Shesko	1981	8,819
125 0/8	21 3/8	20 4/8	16 0/8	5	5	Ontario County	NY	Jim Wicks	1982	8,819
125 0/8	23 0/8	22 7/8	16 2/8	5	4	Yates County	NY	Ed O`Dell	1982	8,819
125 0/8	21 6/8	21 7/8	15 2/8	4	5	Somerset County	NJ	Thomas Takacs	1982	8,819
125 0/8	20 4/8	21 0/8	16 2/8	5	5	Bexar County	TX	John E. West	1982	8,819
125 0/8	23 0/8	23 3/8	21 4/8	4	4	Seneca County	NY	Richard Williamson	1982	8,819
125 0/8	19 6/8	19 4/8	15 2/8	7	6	Richland County	MT	Bill Cundiff	1984	8,819
125 0/8	20 5/8	20 0/8	17 6/8	4	4	Alfalfa County	OK	Paul E. Keck	1984	8,819
125 0/8	20 0/8	20 0/8	17 4/8	4	4	Sauk County	WI	Robert E. McKenna	1984	8,819
125 0/8	22 2/8	21 2/8	17 0/8	4	4	Price County	WI	Dennis W. Steinberger	1984	8,819
125 0/8	17 7/8	19 1/8	14 6/8	6	5	Dane County	WI	Keith Peterson	1984	8,819
125 0/8	20 2/8	21 2/8	19 6/8	5	4	Kane County	IL	Tom Cousland	1984	8,819
125 0/8	21 4/8	21 4/8	15 4/8	5	5	Crow Wing County	MN	Richard Stokke	1985	8,819
125 0/8	22 5/8	22 7/8	18 4/8	7	4	Burleigh County	ND	Dave Feist	1985	8,819
125 0/8	19 4/8	21 1/8	18 0/8	4	5	Orange County	NY	Richard Powles	1985	8,819
125 0/8	21 0/8	21 4/8	14 6/8	5	5	Monroe County	WI	Jeffery S. Oler	1985	8,819
125 0/8	21 4/8	20 5/8	13 6/8	5	5	Roane County	WV	Richard Prine	1986	8,819
125 0/8	22 1/8	22 1/8	17 0/8	5	4	Tama County	IA	Dick Baker	1986	8,819
125 0/8	21 6/8	22 0/8	15 7/8	5	5	Westchester County	NY	Robert Frees	1986	8,819
125 0/8	22 5/8	22 6/8	15 6/8	4	4	St. Clair County	MO	Rickey D. Adams	1987	8,819
125 0/8	21 2/8	21 3/8	16 4/8	5	4	Oneida County	WI	John P. Butler	1987	8,819
125 0/8	20 0/8	20 4/8	14 0/8	4	4	Winona County	MN	John W. Zahrte	1988	8,819
125 0/8	18 2/8	18 6/8	16 6/8	4	4	Norman County	MN	Cordell Willison	1988	8,819
125 0/8	21 1/8	21 1/8	17 4/8	4	4	Licking County	OH	Randy D. Ricketts	1988	8,819
125 0/8	21 0/8	21 1/8	18 2/8	4	4	Pecos County	TX	Joe Christman	1989	8,819
125 0/8	21 4/8	21 3/8	18 4/8	4	4	Susquehanna County	PA	Norris Cobb	1989	8,819
125 0/8	24 3/8	23 2/8	21 1/8	5	4	Jackson County	IA	Larry Nemmers	1989	8,819
125 0/8	21 3/8	21 4/8	16 2/8	4	4	Powell County	MT	Therman Madeira	1989	8,819
125 0/8	19 0/8	19 1/8	13 6/8	5	6	Sebastian County	AR	Frank Theising	1989	8,819
125 0/8	24 3/8	19 7/8	16 1/8	6	6	Racine County	WI	Brad M. Antoniak	1989	8,819
125 0/8	22 1/8	22 1/8	18 2/8	4	4	Dodge County	WI	Timothy J. Minnema	1990	8,819
125 0/8	22 5/8	21 4/8	15 3/8	5	5	Manitowoc County	WI	Kevin A. Young	1990	8,819
125 0/8	23 2/8	23 5/8	22 2/8	3	4	Ogle County	IL	Mark E. Guffey	1990	8,819
125 0/8	20 6/8	21 7/8	19 2/8	5	4	Caroline County	MD	Eric Wise	1990	8,819
125 0/8	23 2/8	24 3/8	17 4/8	4	5	Ducthess County	NY	Tom Pampalone	1990	8,819
125 0/8	19 0/8	20 7/8	17 6/8	4	4	Richland County	WI	Terry L. Laufenberg	1990	8,819
125 0/8	18 3/8	18 4/8	16 2/8	4	4	Natrona County	WY	Dave McCoy	1991	8,819
125 0/8	20 7/8	20 5/8	17 2/8	5	5	Burnett County	WI	John Lindstrom	1991	8,819
125 0/8	21 0/8	21 0/8	15 6/8	5	5	Adair County	MO	Tony L. Jones	1991	8,819
125 0/8	20 5/8	19 6/8	16 4/8	5	5	Portage County	WI	Pete J. Klismith	1991	8,819
125 0/8	19 0/8	19 2/8	14 6/8	4	5	Morgan County	IL	John Conklin	1991	8,819
125 0/8	22 7/8	22 4/8	20 3/8	5	5	Ferry County	WA	Allen Payne	1991	8,819
125 0/8	21 1/8	20 4/8	16 4/8	5	5	Windham County	CT	Myron Wojnilo	1991	8,819
125 0/8	20 6/8	21 7/8	17 3/8	5	6	Brown County	IL	Robert Cunningham	1992	8,819

World Record Whitetail Deer (Non-Typical Antlers)
Score: 279 7/8
Shelton, Nebraska - 1962
Hunter: Del Austin

SCORE	LENGTH OF MAIN BEAM R	L	INSIDE SPREAD	NUMBER OF POINTS R	L	AREA	STATE/ PROVINCE	HUNTER'S NAME	DATE	RANK
279 7/8	27 7/8	28 1/8	21 3/8	21	18	Hall County	NE	Del Austin	1962	1
257 0/8	27 1/8	25 7/8	18 6/8	12	11	Reno County	KS	Kenneth B. Fowler	1988	2
249 6/8	28 0/8	27 7/8	20 2/8	8	10	Greenwood County	KS	Clifford Pickell	1968	3
245 5/8	29 4/8	29 3/8	20 3/8	16	15	Vermilion County	IL	Robert E. Chestnut	1981	4
245 4/8	28 5/8	28 4/8	19 1/8	18	12	Chase County	KS	Douglas A. Siebert	1988	5
241 2/8	25 4/8	26 3/8	18 2/8	19	20	Cochrane	ALB	Dean Dwernuchuk	1984	6
238 6/8	22 6/8	22 2/8	18 3/8	18	15	Mahoning County	OH	Ronald K. Osborne	1986	7
237 5/8	22 4/8	25 4/8	16 5/8	13	12	Wilson County	KS	Gilbert Boss	1986	8
233 7/8	28 4/8	27 1/8	22 0/8	17	16	Greenwood County	KS	Randy Young	1989	9
232 7/8	26 0/8	25 3/8	20 6/8	12	10	Kiowa County	KS	Royce E. Frazier	1987	10
231 5/8	28 1/8	26 5/8	19 2/8	11	11	Dane County	WI	Dennis Shanks	1979	11
231 4/8	26 0/8	25 6/8	18 3/8	11	10	Iroquois County	IL	Sam G. Townsend	1986	12
231 0/8	25 2/8	26 2/8	22 4/8	16	12	Phillips County	KS	Virgil Henry	1987	13
230 6/8	26 1/8	27 6/8	19 5/8	11	11	Peoria County	IL	Tophil L. Simon	1984	14
229 7/8	25 2/8	25 6/8	19 1/8	12	15	Yuma County	CO	David "Jake" Powell	1986	15
227 6/8	25 5/8	25 4/8	20 6/8	13	20	Fulton County	IL	Richard Keener	1977	16
225 1/8	29 4/8	28 4/8	23 1/8	9	12	Walworth County	WI	F. Dan Dinelli	1992	17
224 3/8	28 5/8	27 1/8	23 0/8	9	10	Stevens County	WA	J. C. Baker	1987	18
224 0/8	23 1/8	21 6/8	17 3/8	13	14	La Salle County	IL	Ronald R. Lahman, Sr.	1989	19
222 7/8	27 5/8	28 1/8	18 6/8	9	7	Coles County	IL	Kim L. Boes	1989	20
222 1/8	26 5/8	25 6/8	17 5/8	15	12	Hancock County	IA	J. M. Monson	1977	21
222 0/8	26 2/8	25 7/8	20 6/8	8	8	Marion County	KS	Claude Allen	1989	22
220 7/8	26 1/8	25 1/8	25 2/8	9	11	Gove County	KS	Mike Shull	1986	23
220 6/8	24 6/8	25 2/8	17 6/8	18	16	Rock Island County	IL	John L. Angel	1979	24
220 3/8	25 3/8	24 5/8	18 3/8	13	9	Riley County	KS	Melvin D. Padgett	1989	25
219 3/8	28 1/8	27 5/8	20 5/8	12	17	Webster County	IA	David Propst	1987	26
219 0/8	27 3/8	27 0/8	17 6/8	8	11	Morrison County	MN	Michael R. Langin	1992	27
218 1/8	26 2/8	25 6/8	17 3/8	10	9	Clay County	IA	Blaine R. Salzkorn	1970	28
217 0/8	28 7/8	28 3/8	21 6/8	9	8	Carroll County	IL	Noel Feather	1982	29
215 6/8	27 4/8	28 7/8	18 6/8	11	14	Meeker County	MN	Steve Turck	1982	30
215 5/8	24 2/8	27 0/8	22 2/8	11	7	Wayne County	IA	Chris Hackney	1983	31
214 4/8	20 5/8	20 6/8	15 7/8	16	15	Parker County	TX	George C. Courtney	1991	32
214 2/8	23 7/8	26 6/8	15 6/8	13	9	Lyons County	KS	Gary Dall, Jr.	1992	33
212 5/8	23 5/8	25 5/8	20 1/8	8	7	Allamakee County	IA	George A. Smith	1991	34
212 4/8	23 4/8	23 3/8	19 1/8	11	9	Martin County	IN	David D. Foote	1988	35
210 7/8	23 1/8	23 2/8	18 6/8	9	9	Teton County	MT	Todd Jensen	1986	36
210 6/8	25 5/8	24 5/8	19 4/8	9	8	Marion County	KS	Bruce Schroeder	1985	37
210 5/8	25 7/8	27 1/8	20 3/8	7	7	Waukesha County	WI	Gerald J. Roethle, Jr.	1991	38
210 3/8	27 2/8	28 4/8	19 1/8	12	6	Lac qui Parle County	MN	Steven J. Karels	1974	39
209 7/8	30 0/8	30 0/8	22 3/8	10	12	Richardson County	NE	Albert W. Montgomery	1989	40
209 6/8	25 4/8	25 0/8	19 5/8	14	18	Pulaski County	KY	Alan Sidwell	1988	41
209 2/8	26 5/8	27 6/8	21 4/8	10	10	McPherson County	KS	Lonnie Ensminger	1968	42
208 5/8	26 2/8	26 4/8	22 3/8	9	9	Buffalo County	NE	Carl Clements	1985	43
207 7/8	28 3/8	27 5/8	19 0/8	8	10	Otter Tail County	MN	Patrick Millard	1986	44
207 0/8	27 7/8	28 1/8	17 7/8	9	11	Noble County	IN	Joesph A. Fulford	1987	45
206 7/8	27 2/8	24 3/8	20 6/8	8	8	Smoky River	ALB	Kirby Smith	1991	46
206 0/8	22 3/8	24 1/8	17 4/8	9	11	Saunders County	NE	Nordean E. Bade	1964	47
205 6/8	25 7/8	25 4/8	21 3/8	14	9	Cottonwood County	MN	Larry Gravely	1975	48
205 4/8	27 0/8	26 7/8	24 6/8	7	9	Seward County	KS	Lynn Leonard	1988	49
205 3/8	25 1/8	24 0/8	15 0/8	8	12	Beltrami County	MN	Matt Stone	1990	50
204 1/8	26 5/8	26 2/8	22 0/8	7	9	Dubuque County	IA	Joe Rettenmeier	1987	51
203 7/8	25 7/8	25 1/8	20 2/8	11	9	Union County	OR	Joe Mengore	1982	52
203 5/8	25 1/8	25 1/8	17 5/8	9	11	Warren County	IA	Ted Miller	1986	53
203 4/8	26 6/8	27 6/8	17 0/8	7	13	Dodge County	MN	Lawrence Sowieja	1955	54
203 3/8	24 3/8	24 5/8	20 5/8	10	9	Adams County	IL	Elroy Little	1981	55
203 3/8	24 3/8	25 3/8	20 4/8	12	10	Lehigh County	PA	Craig E. Krisher	1988	55
203 0/8	25 0/8	25 4/8	19 3/8	12	10	Geauga County	OH	Rudy Grecar	1969	57
202 2/8	23 3/8	25 6/8	19 6/8	12	9	Clay County	SD	Patrick Hudson	1969	58
202 0/8	29 0/8	27 1/8	22 6/8	9	8	Clark County	KS	Dennis Rule	1982	59
201 5/8	24 2/8	24 6/8	16 6/8	15	9	Kane County	IL	Keith Kampert	1991	60
201 4/8	23 3/8	22 6/8	25 5/8	10	10	Rock Island County	IL	Jeff Maier	1989	61
201 2/8	23 7/8	24 5/8	20 0/8	13	8	Stearns County	MN	Richard D. Berens	1991	62
201 1/8	28 0/8	27 2/8	20 6/8	8	10	Carroll County	IL	Mel Landwehr	1991	63
200 7/8	25 3/8	25 1/8	20 0/8	10	12	Morgan County	KY	Greg Powers	1989	64
200 7/8	28 2/8	28 1/8	18 7/8	6	9	Washington County	KS	Ronald Montague	1990	64
200 5/8	25 1/8	27 0/8	18 7/8	7	7	Clayton County	IA	Dorrance Arnold	1977	66
199 6/8	28 3/8	28 4/8	18 2/8	8	16	Jackson County	MO	Jack Hollingsworth	1989	67
199 3/8	24 3/8	23 4/8	22 2/8	12	11	Atchison County	KS	Kirby A. Clifton	1973	68
199 3/8	24 3/8	23 1/8	17 6/8	8	8	Comanche County	KS	Phillip L. Kirkland	1981	68
198 7/8	27 0/8	26 7/8	17 7/8	11	13	Logan County	KY	Oscar Howard	1989	70

SCORE	LENGTH OF R MAIN BEAM L		INSIDE SPREAD	NUMBER OF R POINTS L		AREA	STATE/ PROVINCE	HUNTER'S NAME	DATE	RANK
198 6/8	22 5/8	24 5/8	15 0/8	11	11	Peoria County	IL	Roger Woodcock	1989	71
198 5/8	26 2/8	25 0/8	22 6/8	5	5	Douglas County	NE	Ivan Masher	1961	72
198 5/8	27 2/8	29 5/8	19 4/8	6	9	Montgomery County	IL	Earl W. Law, Jr.	1989	72
198 3/8	24 3/8	24 3/8	20 7/8	10	10	Lyon County	MN	Edward Matthys	1966	74
198 3/8	27 2/8	26 6/8	18 6/8	10	7	Reno County	KS	Greig Sims	1987	74
198 3/8	23 6/8	23 3/8	19 7/8	9	7	Pottawattamie County	IA	Rodney P. Stahlnecker	1991	74
198 2/8	27 5/8	27 2/8	19 5/8	7	9	Fulton County	IL	Mike Massingale	1991	77
198 1/8	27 0/8	26 3/8	20 2/8	10	7	Hocking County	OH	Hugh Cox	1964	78
197 6/8	23 6/8	22 4/8	17 4/8	8	11	Pratt County	KS	Mike Patton	1987	79
197 4/8	25 0/8	23 7/8	22 2/8	7	7	Johnson County	IA	Dennis R. Ballard	1971	80
197 4/8	25 3/8	26 3/8	16 7/8	6	8	Lyon County	KS	John R. Clifton	1984	80
197 3/8	27 3/8	26 3/8	20 4/8	8	9	Faribault County	MN	Randy Lee Sandt	1982	82
197 2/8	27 3/8	27 6/8	19 1/8	9	10	Nemaha County	KS	D. Jay Hartter	1990	83
197 1/8	26 4/8	24 2/8	18 5/8	9	12	Linn County	IA	Marsha Fairbanks	1974	84
197 1/8	26 1/8	26 3/8	17 3/8	8	7	Jackson County	MO	Jim Martin	1984	84
197 1/8	16 4/8	18 3/8	18 0/8	10	10	Bullock County	AL	Ronnie Everett	1990	84
197 0/8	26 1/8	26 4/8	21 5/8	8	9	Marshall County	IL	Larry Rowe	1975	87
196 7/8	30 1/8	26 5/8	21 0/8	9	7	Lake County	IL	Kory Lang	1991	88
196 6/8	24 5/8	25 1/8	23 6/8	6	8	Lawrence County	IN	John E. Johnson	1987	89
196 1/8	27 5/8	26 2/8	20 2/8	7	8	Edgar County	IL	Jerry R. David	1988	90
195 6/8	27 1/8	26 6/8	21 5/8	7	6	Dubuque County	IA	Jim H. Dougherty	1985	91
195 5/8	28 6/8	28 2/8	20 2/8	9	10	Martin County	MN	Ben Johnson	1973	92
195 5/8	24 1/8	24 2/8	19 0/8	9	7	Waushara County	WI	Randy Chamberlain	1984	92
195 4/8	27 2/8	28 1/8	18 2/8	9	7	Putnam County	IN	Chris M. Tanner	1982	94
195 4/8	25 2/8	26 2/8	19 7/8	6	7	Crawford County	IA	Larry Sparks	1985	94
195 4/8	21 4/8	23 4/8	15 2/8	11	8	Jessamine County	KY	Tony W. Drury	1991	94
195 0/8	26 6/8	25 0/8	16 3/8	9	13	Juneau County	WI	Maurice Sterba	1955	97
194 7/8	27 7/8	26 1/8	19 0/8	11	10	Warren County	MO	Dennis Jones	1982	98
194 5/8	26 3/8	24 7/8	20 7/8	7	8	Guernsey County	OH	Dick Bayer	1985	99
194 5/8	26 2/8	24 0/8	23 7/8	6	7	Lake County	IL	Paul H. Woit	1991	99
194 4/8	28 1/8	26 2/8	18 4/8	8	7	Miami County	KS	Alfred E. Smith	1990	101
194 4/8	26 7/8	27 0/8	24 2/8	9	8	Polk County	IA	Paul Beesley	1990	101
194 2/8	27 1/8	26 0/8	23 5/8	9	6	Pike County	MO	William E. Knowles	1980	103
193 7/8	25 1/8	27 2/8	18 0/8	11	11	Blaine County	MT	Gene Wensel	1981	104
193 7/8	27 6/8	26 3/8	21 1/8	9	9	Eau Claire County	WI	Greg Miller	1990	104
193 6/8	29 6/8	28 0/8	20 2/8	9	9	Lake County	IN	Walter Sobczak	1979	106
193 3/8	24 3/8	25 3/8	19 3/8	16	9	Roanoke County	VA	Randy Brookshier	1983	107
193 0/8	27 4/8	27 1/8	19 7/8	8	7	Lake County	IL	Steven Derkson	1989	108
192 6/8	27 0/8	27 7/8	21 7/8	8	6	Washington County	KS	Jim Snyder	1986	109
192 6/8	27 3/8	26 2/8	17 7/8	9	7	Vermilion County	IL	Ed Gudgel	1988	109
192 5/8	25 0/8	27 0/8	22 1/8	6	8	Republic County	KS	Don Dejmal	1983	111
192 4/8	21 4/8	20 5/8	15 4/8	11	10	Redwood County	MN	Mark A. Steinle	1973	112
192 1/8	24 3/8	21 1/8	17 3/8	11	10	Gray County	KS	Randall Koehn	1985	113
192 1/8	28 2/8	27 0/8	19 5/8	10	9	Brown County	OH	Paul R. Durbin	1992	113
192 0/8	26 2/8	25 6/8	25 6/8	7	10	Day County	SD	Doug Rumpca	1985	115
191 7/8	21 3/8	21 4/8	15 4/8	9	9	Du Page County	IL	Pete Heliotis	1986	116
191 6/8	23 2/8	20 7/8	16 5/8	6	15	Murray County	MN	Delbert Peck	1956	117
191 6/8	28 5/8	28 6/8	16 4/8	7	6	Preble County	OH	Claude Adkins	1989	117
191 3/8	22 1/8	22 5/8	20 1/8	9	9	St. Joseph County	IN	Daniel T. Karaszewski	1979	119
191 2/8	25 7/8	25 0/8	22 3/8	8	9	Westchester County	NY	Nick Rigano	1987	120
191 2/8	27 2/8	27 1/8	18 5/8	7	9	Pike County	IL	Timothy M. Fulmer	1991	120
191 1/8	26 2/8	26 2/8	21 0/8	7	6	Crawford County	OH	Michael B. Hoffman	1988	122
191 0/8	23 5/8	24 1/8	20 6/8	13	11	Pope County	MN	Ron Johnson	1985	123
190 7/8	25 0/8	18 4/8	15 1/8	11	13	Douglas County	KS	Leon J. Bidinger	1983	124
190 5/8	23 5/8	22 3/8	21 1/8	13	11	Lee County	IA	Tim Digman	1981	125
190 4/8	29 2/8	28 0/8	18 6/8	8	8	Licking County	OH	John McGee	1982	126
190 3/8	25 4/8	24 1/8	16 5/8	9	9	Saginaw County	MI	Robert T. Morey	1975	127
190 2/8	20 0/8	23 4/8	19 7/8	8	9	Isanti County	MN	Johnny J. Williams	1982	128
190 2/8	27 5/8	29 0/8	20 2/8	12	8	Montgomery County	PA	David S. Krempasky	1985	128
190 0/8	24 3/8	24 6/8	18 0/8	8	8	Douglas County	KS	Dan Norris	1977	130
190 0/8	24 4/8	25 2/8	19 1/8	7	8	McHenry County	IL	Edward Schultz	1984	130
189 7/8	26 1/8	26 3/8	24 3/8	7	7	Logan County	OH	Larry Pooler	1989	132
189 6/8	24 4/8	23 0/8	16 3/8	9	7	Chisago County	MN	Reinhold L. Lind	1956	133
189 5/8	21 1/8	22 4/8	15 5/8	14	10	Stearns County	MN	Nathan Batzel	1991	134
189 2/8	21 4/8	23 1/8	21 3/8	10	8	Clayton County	IA	Jim Monat	1981	135
189 2/8	23 1/8	23 0/8	20 0/8	6	7	Buffalo County	WI	Roger Comero	1987	135
189 1/8	21 5/8	24 2/8	17 3/8	13	7	Graham County	KS	Don Berry	1970	137
189 1/8	23 5/8	25 0/8	19 4/8	8	6	McDowell County	WV	Lonnie Wolfe	1991	137
189 0/8	22 4/8	21 7/8	22 4/8	10	9	Scott County	MN	Chris Rivers	1987	139
188 7/8	27 4/8	28 1/8	18 3/8	11	9	Marinette County	WI	James Spielvogel	1981	140

Score	Length of Main Beam R	Length of Main Beam L	Inside Spread	Number of Points R	Number of Points L	Area	State/Province	Hunter's Name	Date	Rank
188 6/8	23 5/8	22 6/8	19 1/8	8	10	Adair County	MO	David C. Reid	1991	141
188 5/8	27 3/8	27 0/8	18 6/8	7	5	Ross County	OH	Dan Seymour	1987	142
188 3/8	24 0/8	24 4/8	18 4/8	9	7	Benton County	IA	Lyle Miller	1977	143
188 3/8	26 0/8	26 7/8	19 0/8	6	9	Rock County	WI	Steven J. Shull	1988	143
188 1/8	26 5/8	26 0/8	19 4/8	7	10	Barnes County	ND	William Cruff	1961	145
188 1/8	26 3/8	26 0/8	19 5/8	10	7	Dane County	WI	Bill Needham	1983	145
188 0/8	23 2/8	22 3/8	17 3/8	8	8	La Salle County	IL	Gary Tabor	1983	147
188 0/8	24 5/8	25 5/8	16 2/8	8	11	Buffalo County	WI	Russell G. Goldsmith	1991	147
187 7/8	24 4/8	24 7/8	20 3/8	8	8	Shiawassee County	MI	Joseph S. Lunkas	1978	149
187 6/8	22 7/8	25 0/8	19 1/8	7	7	Hitchcock County	NE	Tom Chance	1986	150
187 6/8	23 1/8	24 0/8	16 7/8	10	7	Bent County	CO	Chris Malden	1991	150
187 5/8	27 6/8	25 2/8	18 0/8	8	6	Monroe County	IA	Cecil Dicks	1961	152
187 5/8	26 0/8	26 0/8	17 4/8	11	9	Washburn County	WI	Russell Worman	1988	152
187 3/8	23 2/8	23 1/8	17 1/8	11	10	Vernon County	WI	Darrell A. Bendel	1986	154
187 2/8	25 3/8	23 6/8	21 0/8	7	9	Morrill County	NE	Glenn Schmidt	1975	155
187 2/8	27 1/8	26 1/8	16 6/8	7	7	Waupaca County	WI	Timothy J. Dercks	1991	155
186 6/8	24 2/8	25 1/8	19 3/8	9	10	Traverse County	MN	Roland L. Hausmann	1964	157
186 6/8	24 6/8	23 6/8	18 3/8	10	10	Mackinac County	MI	Steve Gorsuch	1989	157
186 5/8	25 3/8	25 0/8	20 7/8	7	9	Scotland County	MO	Charles Lee Smith	1984	159
186 2/8	23 1/8	22 5/8	18 6/8	9	9	Otter Tail County	MN	D. F. Vraspir	1959	160
186 1/8	25 3/8	26 2/8	18 0/8	8	9	Lake County	IL	Alan F. Benson	1990	161
186 1/8	23 0/8	24 4/8	17 7/8	8	9	Lyon County	KS	Edward Bess	1991	161
185 7/8	24 7/8	22 2/8	18 0/8	6	10	Jones County	GA	Wallace Reeves, Jr.	1973	163
185 6/8	26 1/8	26 0/8	25 0/8	7	6	Christian County	IL	Donald D. Stiner	1990	164
185 5/8	27 0/8	25 3/8	18 6/8	11	12	Anderson County	KS	Wayne Hanna	1991	165
185 4/8	29 2/8	28 0/8	22 1/8	8	8	Pickaway County	OH	Jerry R. Forson	1979	166
185 3/8	27 6/8	27 4/8	23 5/8	8	8	Allamakee County	IA	LeRoy B. Spiker	1968	167
185 3/8	27 3/8	26 7/8	20 7/8	6	6	Rice County	MN	Wayne Jahnke	1975	167
185 2/8	26 1/8	25 0/8	16 6/8	9	8	Sedgwick County	KS	Alfred Weaver	1965	169
185 1/8	27 3/8	26 7/8	18 0/8	9	9	Lewis County	KY	Jeremie Lee Bretz	1992	170
184 7/8	25 0/8	25 4/8	25 2/8	7	9	Monona County	IA	Patrick Salmen	1989	171
184 6/8	30 4/8	28 0/8	22 2/8	8	7	Scioto County	OH	Ryan Darnell	1990	172
184 5/8	26 1/8	24 7/8	20 4/8	10	11	Vinton County	OH	Dan Davis	1985	173
184 3/8	22 7/8	22 6/8	17 6/8	8	11	Texas County	OK	William E. Miller	1983	174
184 3/8	23 2/8	23 3/8	21 5/8	10	8	Black Hawk County	IA	Paul Hughson	1985	174
184 1/8	25 1/8	26 3/8	21 3/8	7	6	St. Charles County	MO	Larry D. Stelzer	1962	176
184 1/8	24 3/8	26 5/8	19 1/8	8	9	Waushara County	WI	Dwight A. Olson	1979	176
183 6/8	25 3/8	25 4/8	18 2/8	7	10	Lake County	MN	Christopher Harristhal	1990	178
183 5/8	25 1/8	25 0/8	17 7/8	10	10	Lincoln County	SD	Mervin Sterk	1985	179
183 3/8	24 3/8	25 2/8	19 0/8	11	10	Morrison County	MN	Ralph Hakel	1974	180
183 3/8	24 4/8	25 5/8	16 5/8	8	9	Fillmore County	MN	Michael M. Gehrking	1985	180
183 2/8	27 3/8	24 5/8	21 7/8	6	9	Holt County	NE	Lyle Ruff	1967	182
183 2/8	28 4/8	26 6/8	16 4/8	10	9	Christian County	MO	Roger J. Newell	1984	182
183 2/8	27 4/8	26 4/8	20 7/8	7	7	Riley County	KS	Larry Larson	1985	182
183 2/8	24 0/8	25 3/8	20 3/8	10	8	Washburn County	WI	Jerry J. Genson	1989	182
182 7/8	24 2/8	25 5/8	19 2/8	9	7	Arkansas County	AR	Tommy Horton	1972	186
182 7/8	24 3/8	25 2/8	18 0/8	11	5	Olmsted County	MN	Dan Matheson	1973	186
182 4/8	19 5/8	26 7/8	17 2/8	11	11	Will County	IL	Richard Heintz	1971	188
182 4/8	25 7/8	25 5/8	19 0/8	9	9	Macoupin County	IL	John Tevini	1991	188
182 3/8	29 3/8	27 7/8	20 5/8	6	8	Goodhue County	MN	Jim Danielson	1984	190
182 3/8	25 5/8	25 5/8	19 5/8	6	8	Warren County	IN	Gregory S. Zak	1990	190
182 2/8	27 2/8	26 2/8	18 1/8	11	7	Pike County	IL	Dennis Kendall	1990	192
182 1/8	22 4/8	22 4/8	17 1/8	10	9	Brown County	KS	Bill Butrick	1985	193
182 0/8	24 3/8	24 5/8	17 1/8	6	7	Albemarle County	VA	Richard A. Shifflett	1989	194
181 7/8	24 4/8	24 4/8	18 6/8	7	10	Marion County	IA	Roger DeMoss	1990	195
181 6/8	23 2/8	22 6/8	20 1/8	8	7	Adams County	IL	Festal McCarty	1967	196
181 6/8	25 4/8	25 0/8	18 1/8	7	11	Kiowa County	KS	Royce E. Frazier	1985	196
181 5/8	21 3/8	23 5/8	19 7/8	9	6	Bureau County	IL	Louis J. Guerrini	1990	198
181 5/8	25 5/8	26 7/8	18 6/8	9	8	Pike County	IL	Steven R. Tice	1991	198
181 4/8	26 1/8	26 0/8	21 0/8	10	9	Morrison County	MN	Peter De Chaine	1984	200
181 4/8	25 6/8	26 0/8	19 7/8	9	8	Wyoming County	WV	Bobby Smith	1985	200
181 4/8	20 6/8	23 0/8	19 1/8	8	14	Edgar County	IL	Dennis Gosnell	1991	200
181 3/8	28 0/8	28 0/8	20 5/8	11	6	Hardin County	IA	Howard Nelson	1963	203
181 3/8	26 2/8	24 3/8	16 6/8	9	8	Sawyer County	WI	Bill "Red" Gilbert	1989	203
181 2/8	22 1/8	24 5/8	19 0/8	12	8	Desha County	AR	John T. Greer	1962	205
181 2/8	26 1/8	25 4/8	25 0/8	12	9	Darke County	OH	Dean P. Neff	1979	205
181 2/8	24 5/8	22 3/8	20 6/8	9	7	Clark County	IA	Larry Bear	1991	205
181 1/8	24 1/8	24 1/8	17 6/8	9	6	Coles County	IL	Gerald L. Davis	1973	208
181 0/8	24 6/8	25 4/8	19 6/8	11	8	Knox County	OH	Don Quick	1984	209
181 0/8	23 7/8	23 5/8	19 1/8	12	9	Pittsburg County	OK	Harold Jones	1986	209

SCORE	LENGTH OF R MAIN BEAM L		INSIDE SPREAD	NUMBER OF R POINTS L		AREA	STATE/ PROVINCE	HUNTER'S NAME	DATE	RANK
181 0/8	23 4/8	24 1/8	17 2/8	8	9	Clark County	IL	Harold A. Funk	1991	209
180 6/8	22 3/8	24 1/8	17 3/8	8	7	Pope County	AR	Johnny Reed	1983	212
180 5/8	28 5/8	28 6/8	24 5/8	7	7	Preble County	OH	James R. Whittaker	1978	213
180 5/8	27 5/8	26 3/8	21 1/8	9	6	Linn County	IA	Craig Shepard	1980	213
180 4/8	23 0/8	23 0/8	16 3/8	7	8	Teton County	MT	James Dean	1981	215
180 4/8	26 7/8	27 3/8	21 1/8	7	6	Buffalo County	WI	John L. Smith	1988	215
180 4/8	24 7/8	25 4/8	21 2/8	8	6	Butler County	KS	John Parsons	1989	215
180 4/8	23 6/8	24 2/8	15 2/8	10	7	Osage County	OK	James H. Farmer	1991	215
180 4/8	24 6/8	24 7/8	19 1/8	8	7	Jewel County	KS	Bruce Meyer	1991	215
180 4/8	25 7/8	26 1/8	17 6/8	10	8	Price County	WI	John Michalski	1991	215
180 1/8	24 2/8	23 4/8	18 5/8	10	8	Winnebago County	IA	Jim Orthel	1983	221
179 6/8	24 4/8	24 2/8	21 0/8	7	8	Creek County	OK	Marion Lewis	1975	222
179 6/8	24 7/8	25 7/8	22 0/8	6	7	Hamilton County	OH	Lawrence Ashbrook	1981	222
179 5/8	24 4/8	25 6/8	19 5/8	9	11	Fillmore County	MN	Wayne Pfremmer	1972	224
179 5/8	29 4/8	25 7/8	20 1/8	5	8	Dane County	WI	Kip Kalscheur	1989	224
179 2/8	25 4/8	23 4/8	23 0/8	12	7	Marion County	IA	Roger DeMoss	1982	226
179 2/8	24 7/8	25 7/8	21 5/8	8	7	Chippewa County	WI	Kip Knez	1986	226
179 1/8	26 0/8	26 3/8	20 1/8	6	8	Will County	IL	Michael Suggs	1990	228
178 6/8	21 2/8	25 3/8	20 5/8	9	8	Lincoln County	SD	H. L. Tuggle	1975	229
178 6/8	22 2/8	23 1/8	13 4/8	10	9	Madison County	IL	Michael B. Fenton	1984	229
178 5/8	24 5/8	25 3/8	16 0/8	8	7	Clay County	IN	Jim Tracy	1989	231
178 5/8	24 4/8	23 6/8	17 6/8	6	9	Ozaukee County	WI	Robert A. Wallock	1989	231
178 5/8	25 0/8	26 3/8	17 3/8	10	9	Ozaukee County	WI	Gerald Berres	1991	231
178 4/8	22 1/8	23 6/8	17 0/8	12	11	Keokuk County	IA	Ron Turner	1983	234
178 4/8	26 2/8	25 2/8	18 2/8	8	6	St. Croix County	WI	James Walsh	1988	234
178 3/8	23 3/8	22 7/8	19 6/8	8	8	Traverse County	MN	Roland L. Hausmann	1953	236
178 3/8	25 1/8	24 4/8	19 6/8	8	10	Mineral County	MT	Gene Wensel	1981	236
178 3/8	22 6/8	24 7/8	17 0/8	11	10	Finney County	KS	Randy Miller	1984	236
178 1/8	24 7/8	25 4/8	19 0/8	11	9	Montgomery County	OH	Jack B. Odum	1990	239
178 0/8	24 1/8	25 4/8	19 0/8	8	6	Jefferson County	WI	Mike Leslie	1988	240
178 0/8	24 7/8	25 3/8	14 0/8	9	8	Kenedy County	TX	Miguel Mireles	1991	240
177 7/8	28 2/8	27 0/8	18 3/8	6	6	Ross County	OH	Robert L. Elliott	1981	242
177 7/8	26 5/8	25 2/8	18 2/8	8	7	Pottawatomie County	KS	Loyd C. Flowers	1983	242
177 6/8	21 4/8	22 2/8	18 1/8	10	9	Pope County	MN	Roger Tollefson	1977	244
177 6/8	23 0/8	21 2/8	16 0/8	6	13	Delaware County	OH	Ronald Eugene Murphy	1983	244
177 4/8	23 4/8	22 6/8	18 1/8	7	8	Flathead County	MT	Jerry Karsky	1972	246
177 3/8	25 2/8	22 7/8	16 1/8	15	19	Pike County	IL	Daniel Doran	1992	247
177 1/8	23 0/8	22 6/8	18 6/8	7	12	Pope County	MN	Doyle Anderson	1988	248
177 0/8	25 2/8	25 6/8	18 6/8	7	9	Rock County	WI	Kirk C. Douglas	1987	249
177 0/8	24 3/8	22 6/8	17 6/8	7	9	Boone County	IA	Robert J. Van Roekel	1989	249
177 0/8	24 0/8	24 3/8	16 0/8	7	7	Olmsted County	MN	Leo Kuisle	1991	249
176 6/8	28 4/8	28 2/8	19 4/8	8	9	Dodge County	WI	Erwin C. Koehler	1957	252
176 5/8	22 2/8	21 3/8	16 4/8	10	7	Day County	SD	Lonnie L. Heuer	1987	253
176 5/8	24 1/8	24 0/8	19 4/8	8	8	Polk County	WI	Jesse Tonn	1991	253
176 3/8	24 6/8	25 4/8	20 3/8	8	8	Greene County	OH	Leroy M. Thompson	1982	255
176 1/8	22 0/8	23 3/8	21 4/8	7	6	Brandon	MAN	Larry J. Pollock	1980	256
175 7/8	27 4/8	28 1/8	23 3/8	8	7	Guernsey County	OH	Jack L. Milligan	1971	257
175 7/8	24 3/8	25 1/8	17 4/8	9	8	Freeborn County	MN	Douglas Swank	1979	257
175 4/8	22 4/8	22 7/8	19 2/8	10	10	Woodbury County	IA	Everett Gothier	1962	259
175 4/8	28 4/8	27 5/8	20 6/8	7	7	Belmont County	OH	Dan Clutter	1985	259
175 3/8	24 5/8	23 7/8	20 1/8	8	7	Grant County	MN	Lee Offerdahl	1972	261
175 3/8	26 2/8	25 3/8	14 4/8	8	11	Buffalo County	WI	Timothy L. Brommer	1984	261
175 3/8	23 4/8	24 3/8	19 6/8	7	9	Salem County	NJ	Richard Wendt	1985	261
175 2/8	26 1/8	26 0/8	17 1/8	9	7	McHenry County	IL	Richard G. Hickey	1988	264
175 1/8	26 4/8	25 1/8	20 0/8	6	7	Dubuque County	IA	Gregory Klein	1983	265
175 1/8	24 4/8	23 3/8	17 2/8	9	10	Cherokee County	KS	Darren Collins	1988	265
175 1/8	25 7/8	25 2/8	18 3/8	6	8	Franklin County	KS	Dennis N. Ballweg	1988	265
175 1/8	24 6/8	24 5/8	18 6/8	7	9	Wayne County	MO	Jesse Whittley, Jr.	1988	265
175 1/8	25 6/8	26 5/8	19 0/8	6	6	Chase County	KS	Greg Windler	1988	265
174 7/8	26 6/8	25 3/8	19 7/8	9	9	Waseca County	MN	Robert Barrie	1974	270
174 7/8	25 5/8	27 3/8	19 2/8	10	6	Des Moines County	IA	Tom Lappe	1985	270
174 4/8	24 0/8	25 4/8	22 5/8	5	6	Otter Tail County	MN	Don Oelschlager	1976	272
174 4/8	22 1/8	22 3/8	16 4/8	8	8	Benson County	ND	Curtis A. Ehnert	1977	272
174 4/8	21 1/8	21 0/8	17 2/8	8	9	Brown County	IL	Angela Vogel	1988	272
174 3/8	26 0/8	25 7/8	18 2/8	9	7	Vinton County	OH	Jack McConnell	1982	275
174 3/8	28 4/8	28 3/8	22 2/8	6	8	Winnebago County	IL	Dave Fisher	1986	275
174 2/8	26 6/8	25 1/8	19 7/8	9	6	Clay County	IA	Darrell Magnussen	1962	277
174 1/8	26 1/8	25 7/8	26 2/8	7	8	Charles County	MD	Robert H. Jones, Sr.	1971	278
174 0/8	26 0/8	27 6/8	26 6/8	7	6	Delaware County	OH	Michael H. Seamster	1983	279
173 6/8	25 4/8	25 2/8	22 0/8	8	9	Spink County	SD	Milton Haag	1959	280

WHITETAIL DEER *(Non-Typical Antlers)*

(Continued)

Score	Length of Main Beam R	L	Inside Spread	Number of Points R	L	Area	State/ Province	Hunter's Name	Date	Rank
173 6/8	19 3/8	19 5/8	17 1/8	9	9	Douglas County	MN	John Duberowski	1980	280
173 5/8	25 4/8	24 3/8	18 1/8	7	6	Gray County	KS	Allen D. Bailey	1982	282
173 5/8	22 7/8	23 2/8	18 4/8	8	6	Pepin County	WI	Don Linse	1988	282
173 5/8	23 1/8	22 3/8	17 2/8	11	7	St. Louis County	MO	Michael M. Branson	1989	282
173 5/8	29 1/8	28 4/8	17 4/8	11	9	Chippewa County	WI	George A. Olson	1991	282
173 4/8	24 7/8	25 5/8	21 6/8	6	6	Barton County	KS	Norman Kimber	1967	286
173 4/8	22 4/8	23 7/8	14 1/8	6	8	Trumbull County	OH	Peter Bradley	1969	286
173 4/8	26 1/8	21 7/8	16 7/8	7	10	Renville County	MN	Larry Godejahn	1973	286
173 3/8	26 4/8	26 2/8	19 5/8	8	7	Pike County	IL	Ronnie Bauer	1988	289
173 0/8	22 4/8	21 5/8	16 6/8	7	8	Lincoln County	KS	Scott Kingery	1988	290
172 7/8	24 0/8	21 4/8	14 4/8	10	10	McIntosh County	OK	Clark Utley	1976	291
172 7/8	23 6/8	24 1/8	16 7/8	9	9	Morrison County	MN	Harlan Grams	1988	291
172 7/8	22 5/8	23 7/8	19 3/8	8	8	Sedgwick County	KS	Cary Renner	1989	291
172 6/8	22 2/8	22 6/8	16 2/8	9	11	Washburn County	WI	Clint Atkinson	1986	294
172 5/8	24 2/8	25 2/8	17 6/8	11	7	Trumbull County	OH	Dick Keagy	1989	295
172 4/8	18 0/8	25 2/8	19 0/8	14	7	Marshall County	MN	James C. Pederson	1992	296
172 3/8	23 6/8	23 0/8	18 4/8	7	8	Mississippi County	AR	Dennis Perkins	1990	297
172 3/8	23 2/8	24 5/8	18 6/8	9	5	Chariton County	MO	Dennis W. Meyers	1991	297
172 2/8	24 5/8	23 6/8	15 4/8	9	10	Calhoun County	MI	Roger W. Hanselman	1989	299
172 2/8	22 3/8	23 5/8	18 2/8	7	7	Cadogan	ALB	Howard Schreiber	1991	299
172 1/8	22 6/8	23 2/8	24 7/8	8	7	Green County	WI	Dean Dilly	1974	301
172 0/8	24 4/8	25 4/8	17 4/8	7	7	Warren County	IA	Dennis R. Jacobe	1988	302
171 7/8	22 4/8	22 3/8	19 6/8	11	9	Will County	IL	James Giese	1987	303
171 6/8	22 3/8	21 5/8	20 5/8	8	9	Dubuque County	IA	Dick Theis	1975	304
171 6/8	26 0/8	26 7/8	19 6/8	9	7	Vermilion County	IL	Gene Maier	1984	304
171 6/8	23 7/8	18 3/8	18 0/8	7	10	Leavenworth County	KS	Albert Lyle Karl	1987	304
171 6/8	23 0/8	23 5/8	15 6/8	7	7	Montgomery County	TN	Dennis Morris	1991	304
171 5/8	22 7/8	24 1/8	16 4/8	7	7	Wapello County	IA	Rex Jones	1983	308
171 5/8	26 1/8	21 4/8	24 0/8	6	8	Iroquois County	IL	Frank Snow	1987	308
171 4/8	24 5/8	24 5/8	19 1/8	7	7	Butler County	KS	Jeff Stevens	1982	310
171 3/8	20 4/8	23 7/8	19 4/8	8	10	Logan County	OK	Billy Wayne McBride	1989	311
171 3/8	24 1/8	21 7/8	19 5/8	6	8	Kane County	IL	Matthew Peterson	1991	311
171 2/8	27 0/8	27 0/8	18 5/8	4	5	Van Buren County	MI	David Anderson	1979	313
171 2/8	23 5/8	24 7/8	14 4/8	6	6	Scotts Bluff County	NE	Doug Hauser	1984	313
171 1/8	23 4/8	24 0/8	20 2/8	8	6	Jackson County	MI	Shawn R. Surque	1985	315
171 1/8	25 4/8	25 4/8	18 6/8	6	8	Birds Hill	MAN	Daniel Kowalchuk	1991	315
171 0/8	24 0/8	24 4/8	18 1/8	7	7	Dodge County	WI	Dallas Johnson	1955	317
171 0/8	26 3/8	22 6/8	22 4/8	4	10	Lee County	IA	Gary Frost	1967	317
170 7/8	24 5/8	25 2/8	15 3/8	6	6	Redwood County	MN	Todd G. Gilb	1982	319
170 7/8	21 6/8	23 2/8	14 6/8	10	12	Kleberg County	TX	Bradley Peltier	1989	319
170 6/8	24 3/8	23 6/8	17 2/8	9	8	Nobles County	MN	David Janssen	1973	321
170 6/8	23 7/8	23 6/8	18 2/8	6	12	Washtenaw County	MI	Dennis D. Clarke	1989	321
170 6/8	22 0/8	20 7/8	14 5/8	9	7	Anoka County	MN	Wayne Nicholson	1991	321
170 5/8	18 1/8	26 2/8	21 7/8	10	6	Oklahoma County	OK	Tim R. Reid	1990	324
170 4/8	26 3/8	26 1/8	20 5/8	7	7	Tazewell County	IL	Bret Hamilton	1982	325
170 3/8	24 1/8	22 7/8	21 1/8	6	8	Fairfield County	OH	Brian Morrison	1987	326
170 3/8	24 1/8	22 7/8	21 1/8	6	8	Fairfield County	OH	Brian Morrison	1987	326
170 2/8	24 7/8	25 5/8	17 6/8	11	9	Callaway County	MO	Larry Murphy	1988	328
170 1/8	24 1/8	22 3/8	17 6/8	7	9	Lyon County	KS	Russell Reed	1986	329
170 1/8	22 6/8	23 0/8	17 2/8	9	8	Cowley County	KS	Aaron Chaplin	1990	329
170 0/8	25 1/8	21 6/8	19 5/8	9	12	Van Buren County	IA	Gary W. Schutt	1987	331
169 6/8	24 4/8	25 1/8	17 7/8	6	6	Carter County	KY	Timothy Carter	1974	332
169 5/8	26 5/8	27 6/8	22 0/8	7	7	Dodge County	MN	Lawrence Sowieja	1973	333
169 5/8	22 7/8	20 4/8	20 0/8	7	8	Pike County	MO	Marlin E. Foree	1988	333
169 4/8	25 5/8	24 2/8	23 0/8	6	8	Branch County	MI	Roy D. Grigsby	1988	335
169 4/8	25 2/8	25 4/8	21 0/8	6	7	Price County	WI	James E. Johnson	1990	335
169 3/8	25 6/8	25 0/8	18 6/8	8	6	Emmet County	IA	Paul Love	1992	337
169 2/8	23 4/8	23 7/8	18 5/8	6	8	Rice County	MN	Vernon J. Kleve	1972	338
169 2/8	25 4/8	26 4/8	19 4/8	7	8	Schuyler County	IL	Robert J. Logsdon	1981	338
169 2/8	23 2/8	23 6/8	17 4/8	7	8	Washington County	WI	Tony Snow	1991	338
169 0/8	23 5/8	22 6/8	22 6/8	11	9	Suffolk County	NY	John Bennett	1991	341
168 7/8	22 4/8	21 6/8	19 4/8	7	8	Meeker County	MN	Ralph Hakel	1964	342
168 7/8	25 5/8	23 5/8	19 7/8	6	8	Otoe County	NE	Roberto Z. Duran	1990	342
168 6/8	24 1/8	25 1/8	20 3/8	9	8	Olmsted County	MN	Jeff Meyer	1974	344
168 5/8	21 0/8	19 4/8	13 7/8	7	7	Lyon County	KS	Russell Reed	1984	345
168 5/8	23 6/8	23 6/8	17 5/8	7	10	Waukesha County	WI	Jeff Stanton	1991	345
168 4/8	24 5/8	23 5/8	16 1/8	5	7	Stearns County	MN	Robert Opatz	1987	347
168 4/8	24 4/8	24 4/8	18 1/8	7	6	Fulton County	IN	Dennis L. Kamp	1988	347
168 4/8	19 7/8	21 1/8	13 0/8	8	6	Pend Oreille County	WA	Aaron Coleman	1991	347
168 3/8	23 1/8	22 7/8	18 7/8	6	8	Jefferson County	IN	Michael Abston	1987	350

Score	Length of Main Beam R	L	Inside Spread	Number of Points R	L	Area	State/ Province	Hunter's Name	Date	Rank
168 2/8	20 6/8	19 7/8	23 1/8	7	8	Washington County	OH	Mike Ferrell	1982	351
168 1/8	22 3/8	23 0/8	18 3/8	6	7	Ozaukee County	WI	Joe Spata	1991	352
168 0/8	21 3/8	21 2/8	15 6/8	7	9	Martin County	MN	Charles Sutphin	1974	353
167 7/8	22 2/8	22 2/8	19 7/8	6	8	Cypress River	MAN	Harvey Gagne	1987	354
167 7/8	27 6/8	26 1/8	18 2/8	5	6	Greenwood County	KS	Danny Linnebur	1991	354
167 6/8	24 3/8	24 3/8	19 7/8	9	7	Scott County	IA	Gordon Vrana	1967	356
167 6/8	21 7/8	23 3/8	14 5/8	8	8	Barton County	KS	Lance Hockett	1990	356
167 4/8	24 1/8	23 6/8	16 0/8	9	10	Iroquois County	IL	Al Weissbohn	1986	358
167 2/8	24 0/8	24 3/8	17 1/8	7	6	Sauk County	WI	Charles Davenport	1969	359
167 1/8	23 1/8	22 0/8	21 6/8	7	9	Floyd County	IA	Patrick E. Barrett	1990	360
167 0/8	22 2/8	22 1/8	18 3/8	8	5	Wright County	IA	Robert Filbrandt	1974	361
167 0/8	24 7/8	24 0/8	19 0/8	7	9	Pawnee County	NE	Ed Baburek	1987	361
166 7/8	25 3/8	25 6/8	18 2/8	6	6	Hubbard County	MN	Jack Smythe	1973	363
166 6/8	25 1/8	24 5/8	17 7/8	7	7	Kenedy County	TX	Steve Ray Dollar	1990	364
166 5/8	28 3/8	26 6/8	15 1/8	8	9	Shelby County	IA	Billy Custer	1968	365
166 5/8	22 7/8	21 7/8	20 5/8	7	7	Wabaunsee County	KS	Charles Bisnette	1991	365
166 4/8	22 0/8	23 3/8	14 5/8	9	5	Midland County	MI	Michael D. Pretzer	1987	367
166 3/8	24 5/8	24 5/8	16 2/8	6	6	Brown County	SD	Frank Bauer	1974	368
166 3/8	21 6/8	20 3/8	17 3/8	7	7	Okotoks	ALB	Darren Dale	1980	368
166 2/8	23 3/8	23 2/8	18 0/8	7	9	Linn County	IA	Guy D. Williams, Jr.	1986	370
166 2/8	27 0/8	25 3/8	21 3/8	6	10	Cecil County	MD	John E. Kostic	1991	370
166 0/8	23 0/8	27 0/8	20 1/8	8	7	Ross County	OH	Randy Johnson	1981	372
166 0/8	21 5/8	20 2/8	15 3/8	8	8	Pope County	AR	Donald Alan Barnett	1983	372
166 0/8	24 4/8	22 5/8	18 1/8	7	8	Talbot County	MD	Ritchy Eason	1987	372
165 7/8	24 2/8	22 2/8	17 3/8	6	6	Arkansas County	AR	Bruce Wiggins	1959	375
165 7/8	21 1/8	25 6/8	19 3/8	8	8	Gallatin County	KY	John C. Vetter	1977	375
165 7/8	23 0/8	22 7/8	19 4/8	6	6	Brown County	IL	Angela Vogel	1983	375
165 7/8	20 3/8	21 6/8	14 5/8	8	9	Sedgwick County	KS	Gary Raney	1988	375
165 5/8	25 0/8	24 5/8	20 4/8	11	8	Washington County	MS	James Goss, Jr.	1987	379
165 4/8	23 5/8	22 2/8	16 2/8	5	8	Boundary County	ID	Gary Stueve	1991	380
165 2/8	20 3/8	21 0/8	15 2/8	8	10	Lee County	IA	Gary Frost	1991	381
165 1/8	21 1/8	23 4/8	17 0/8	7	8	Creek County	OK	Gary Roberson	1991	382
165 0/8	24 3/8	24 3/8	19 0/8	9	9	Columbia County	WI	Daniel L. Golz	1987	383
165 0/8	22 3/8	22 1/8	15 0/8	7	8	Wabaunsee County	KS	Ron Phillips	1991	383
164 7/8	20 1/8	22 4/8	16 4/8	7	6	Murray County	MN	Lanny Engler	1975	385
164 7/8	23 2/8	23 7/8	17 2/8	9	8	Beltrami County	MN	Kelly O'Brien	1986	385
164 7/8	20 1/8	20 4/8	19 3/8	6	9	Bentley	ALB	Gary Bruns	1990	385
164 7/8	22 3/8	22 2/8	17 2/8	9	9	Plymouth County	IA	Dale E. Brock	1990	385
164 6/8	18 0/8	20 4/8	16 1/8	9	9	Chippewa County	MN	Steven P. Ellingson	1975	389
164 6/8	21 4/8	20 3/8	17 4/8	7	10	Will County	IL	Gene R. Francisco	1988	389
164 6/8	18 3/8	22 4/8	18 3/8	12	8	Piatt County	IL	Boomer Dolbert	1990	389
164 2/8	22 1/8	23 4/8	14 2/8	10	6	Rush County	KS	Shawn McHaley	1988	392
164 2/8	26 2/8	25 5/8	19 7/8	4	7	Lawrence County	OH	Pete G. McCloud	1990	392
164 1/8	23 5/8	22 1/8	18 5/8	9	8	Winona County	MN	Charles W. Benson	1974	394
164 1/8	20 6/8	22 3/8	16 3/8	7	9	Meeker County	MN	Mike Rollinger	1989	394
164 0/8	20 6/8	21 7/8	15 0/8	7	7	Guthrie County	IA	Dick Rote	1980	396
164 0/8	22 0/8	22 3/8	17 6/8	6	6	Lake County	IL	Ted Hysell	1990	396
164 0/8	23 6/8	23 4/8	16 0/8	7	6	Randolph County	IL	Scott Oathout	1991	396
163 7/8	27 1/8	25 1/8	20 5/8	6	6	Dickinson County	IA	Eldon L. Kraninger	1969	399
163 6/8	22 0/8	20 6/8	18 7/8	8	7	Kenedy County	TX	Miguel Mireles	1987	400
163 5/8	23 4/8	20 7/8	17 6/8	7	8	Pepin County	WI	Mike J. Breitung	1988	401
163 4/8	25 1/8	25 1/8	18 1/8	6	5	Hancock County	ME	Daniel D. Hardy	1990	402
163 3/8	21 2/8	23 5/8	15 5/8	9	5	Wapello County	IA	Rick Grooms	1990	403
163 1/8	21 6/8	22 0/8	16 7/8	7	7	Cherry County	NE	Walter Cady	1975	404
163 1/8	20 5/8	20 2/8	17 1/8	7	7	Burke County	GA	John A. "Andy" Tisdale	1989	404
163 0/8	20 6/8	21 1/8	17 0/8	10	11	Caddo County	OK	Donald Boling	1975	406
162 7/8	20 5/8	20 4/8	17 3/8	7	8	Walsh County	ND	Randy Schuster	1985	407
162 6/8	23 4/8	24 3/8	22 4/8	9	7	Webb County	TX	James Richter, Jr.	1977	408
162 6/8	23 2/8	22 4/8	11 3/8	7	6	Franklin County	OH	Randy Kelley	1991	408
162 5/8	25 2/8	24 1/8	19 1/8	7	5	Burnett County	WI	Scott L. Treague	1989	410
162 5/8	22 1/8	22 1/8	18 7/8	7	8	Columbia County	PA	Paul Weisser, Jr.	1989	410
162 5/8	25 0/8	22 7/8	16 3/8	6	9	Iroquois County	IL	James Albricht	1991	410
162 4/8	25 7/8	26 5/8	18 3/8	6	9	Houston County	MN	Russell Craig Kruse	1991	413
162 4/8	24 2/8	25 5/8	15 5/8	7	5	Jasper County	MO	Douglas H. Roberts	1991	413
162 2/8	24 6/8	25 0/8	20 7/8	6	7	Elma	MAN	Wendell Schatkowsky	1990	415
162 1/8	25 4/8	23 6/8	18 2/8	7	11	Jackson County	IA	Larry R. Zirkelbach	1990	416
162 0/8	23 4/8	24 6/8	16 6/8	8	8	Coshocton County	OH	Richard Morgan	1987	417
161 7/8	24 7/8	25 5/8	22 0/8	7	9	Cascade County	MT	Kits Smith	1980	418
161 7/8	24 4/8	28 4/8	17 3/8	6	11	Warren County	IA	Bob R. Branchcomb	1988	418
161 4/8	22 3/8	23 4/8	15 4/8	9	9	Butler County	KS	Dave Rogers	1989	420

SCORE	LENGTH OF MAIN BEAM		INSIDE SPREAD	NUMBER OF POINTS		AREA	STATE/ PROVINCE	HUNTER'S NAME	DATE	RANK
	R	L		R	L					
161 2/8	25 2/8	28 4/8	20 1/8	5	9	Des Moines County	IA	Whitey Johnson	1987	421
161 1/8	22 2/8	24 4/8	17 3/8	9	8	Marshall County	MN	Richard Hoff	1983	422
161 0/8	24 4/8	23 3/8	17 6/8	5	8	Johnson County	NE	Stan Pfingsten	1988	423
160 7/8	22 6/8	23 4/8	19 4/8	7	6	Saginaw County	MI	Marty Massa	1986	424
160 7/8	23 5/8	26 7/8	17 3/8	8	8	Roane County	TN	Rodney Maynard	1986	424
160 6/8	20 4/8	21 4/8	18 4/8	7	5	Bremer County	IA	Steven Sims	1983	426
160 6/8	25 4/8	23 4/8	17 0/8	8	8	Columbiana County	OH	David Tice	1987	426
160 5/8	19 6/8	21 6/8	17 0/8	11	9	Adams County	IL	Ray Gedaminski	1967	428
160 5/8	22 2/8	23 4/8	18 4/8	5	9	Rice County	KS	Carl Gillespie	1990	428
160 4/8	22 1/8	24 7/8	21 6/8	8	10	McDonough County	IL	David S. Irwin	1987	430
160 3/8	23 1/8	23 1/8	16 1/8	8	13	Winnebago County	WI	John M. Duchatschek	1980	431
160 3/8	22 0/8	23 5/8	16 7/8	7	7	Jackson County	MO	Wendell Hood	1991	431
160 2/8	23 1/8	23 1/8	15 3/8	6	7	Lawrence County	IL	Mike Deckard	1978	433
160 2/8	21 3/8	21 3/8	15 7/8	7	6	Scott County	IA	Jeffrey R. Coonts	1989	433
160 0/8	27 4/8	26 6/8	18 0/8	7	6	Gallatin County	KY	William J. Epeards	1980	435
160 0/8	19 0/8	20 2/8	17 2/8	7	9	Rockingham County	NC	Michael R. Chrismon	1987	435
159 7/8	22 1/8	24 4/8	19 2/8	9	8	Edmonton	ALB	Brian Bruce	1981	437
159 7/8	23 2/8	24 1/8	18 2/8	5	6	Huron County	OH	Donald W. Howard	1984	437
159 7/8	21 4/8	20 2/8	16 2/8	6	6	Huron County	OH	John R. Gockstetter	1984	437
159 6/8	21 6/8	26 5/8	15 6/8	10	7	Greene County	AR	Randy Ladd	1985	440
159 4/8	20 7/8	20 5/8	15 4/8	6	8	McPherson County	KS	Kenneth L. Vogts	1979	441
159 3/8	25 2/8	25 3/8	16 1/8	10	6	Vernon County	WI	Daniel F. Malin	1986	442
159 3/8	22 6/8	22 2/8	18 5/8	7	8	Brown County	IL	Angela Vogel	1987	442
159 1/8	21 5/8	21 6/8	13 3/8	8	10	Scott County	KY	Vic Morrison	1972	444
159 0/8	24 0/8	24 4/8	17 3/8	7	5	Lake County	IL	Robert H. Fugett	1976	445
159 0/8	22 5/8	21 5/8	21 1/8	6	8	Sullivan County	IN	Steve Hobbs	1980	445
158 7/8	27 1/8	25 1/8	22 7/8	5	6	Buffalo County	WI	Ted Bauer	1984	447
158 7/8	25 4/8	25 1/8	15 4/8	7	7	Washtenaw County	MI	Larry R. Lange	1984	447
158 7/8	25 5/8	25 3/8	16 5/8	7	7	Monroe County	IL	Wayne Doerr	1987	447
158 6/8	23 2/8	21 2/8	17 7/8	7	7	Jo Daviess County	IL	Gerald J. Dupasquier	1987	450
158 5/8	21 2/8	21 1/8	14 5/8	6	7	Sullivan County	IN	John P. Hale	1986	451
158 4/8	22 6/8	24 1/8	19 4/8	7	4	Winona County	MN	Randy SuPalla	1985	452
158 3/8	24 7/8	24 0/8	16 2/8	8	6	Morrison County	MN	Duane Rodine	1987	453
158 2/8	23 0/8	23 1/8	21 0/8	7	6	La Salle County	IL	John Thomas	1988	454
158 1/8	19 2/8	21 0/8	17 1/8	6	8	Jackson County	MI	Kim H. Whittman	1982	455
157 7/8	22 6/8	23 2/8	16 7/8	10	8	Dane County	WI	Donald W. Pache	1982	456
157 6/8	23 7/8	22 7/8	17 4/8	7	7	Lincoln County	SD	Mac Butler	1987	457
157 5/8	25 3/8	25 1/8	17 5/8	8	8	Black Hawk County	IA	Darrell Zacharias	1976	458
157 2/8	22 4/8	19 6/8	22 4/8	6	6	Crawford County	IA	Scott Pelino	1990	459
157 2/8	23 4/8	25 3/8	19 1/8	8	7	Montgomery County	IL	Charles O. Herman III	1991	459
157 1/8	23 1/8	22 7/8	16 4/8	8	6	Rock County	WI	Daniel T. Steinke	1982	461
156 6/8	26 7/8	24 7/8	18 4/8	9	7	Prince Georges County	MD	Anthony C. Malpasso	1979	462
156 6/8	22 1/8	22 2/8	18 1/8	8	9	Jackson County	MO	Daniel L. Johnson	1986	462
156 4/8	24 6/8	23 3/8	20 2/8	7	9	Winnebago County	IL	Jim Dorney	1975	464
156 4/8	21 2/8	22 0/8	18 1/8	7	6	Monroe County	NY	David Stymus	1991	464
156 3/8	18 2/8	20 1/8	16 1/8	8	6	Boulder County	CO	Guy-Maurice Algier	1988	466
156 2/8	23 2/8	20 0/8	16 4/8	8	5	Holt County	NE	Darrell Clyde	1963	467
156 2/8	21 5/8	22 4/8	17 2/8	7	5	Meriwether County	GA	William Clark Brown	1990	467
156 1/8	24 4/8	27 7/8	23 3/8	8	9	Cottonwood County	MN	Joe Earl	1959	469
156 1/8	24 5/8	25 5/8	20 3/8	5	5	Lake County	IL	Mike Mitten	1984	469
156 1/8	23 4/8	23 0/8	20 6/8	6	7	Walworth County	WI	Al Lehman	1988	469
156 0/8	25 3/8	24 0/8	15 7/8	8	6	Stewart County	TN	Ronald M. Widner	1974	472
156 0/8	21 0/8	22 0/8	18 5/8	7	7	Lake County	SD	Lonnie Iverson	1987	472
155 6/8	23 2/8	23 7/8	20 2/8	6	6	Sedgwick County	KS	Keith Jopp	1987	474
155 4/8	25 1/8	25 1/8	16 3/8	9	9	Pottawatomie County	KS	Richard L. Ruetti	1970	475
155 4/8	23 0/8	21 0/8	19 4/8	6	8	Douglas County	MN	Al Ratajesak	1986	475
155 4/8	21 5/8	23 0/8	17 3/8	6	6	Fayette County	IA	James E. Smith	1991	475
155 3/8	21 2/8	21 3/8	16 5/8	12	8	Winona County	MN	John W. Zahrte	1974	478
155 3/8	24 2/8	23 6/8	17 6/8	7	8	Morton County	ND	Dennis Simenson	1981	478
155 3/8	22 0/8	22 4/8	15 2/8	6	6	Vigo County	IN	Lowell Leturgez	1991	478
155 0/8	24 4/8	23 7/8	17 2/8	8	5	McCreary County	KY	Eddie Howard	1985	481
154 7/8	19 4/8	20 0/8	15 4/8	6	10	Calhoun County	MI	Norman E. Nuding	1982	482
154 6/8	24 5/8	17 1/8	16 6/8	8	10	Marshall County	IN	Sennett Dietl	1965	483
154 4/8	21 4/8	20 0/8	15 3/8	7	7	Marinette County	WI	LeRoy Olson	1974	484
154 3/8	20 6/8	22 5/8	17 2/8	7	7	Morrow County	OH	Nancy Shade	1982	485
154 1/8	20 2/8	20 7/8	13 3/8	11	11	Butler County	KY	Dolores G. Renfrow	1988	486
153 7/8	21 1/8	21 2/8	11 4/8	12	8	Bayfield County	WI	Claude B. Butler	1954	487
153 7/8	24 3/8	23 4/8	15 6/8	7	6	Branch County	MI	Keith Ackerman	1973	487
153 7/8	20 5/8	20 1/8	13 7/8	7	7	Wabasha County	MN	Robert W. Mann	1991	487
153 6/8	22 6/8	22 0/8	17 0/8	8	8	Custer County	SD	Bennie Spring	1961	490

Score	Length of Main Beam R	Length of Main Beam L	Inside Spread	Number of Points R	Number of Points L	Area	State/ Province	Hunter's Name	Date	Rank
153 3/8	22 7/8	22 2/8	20 5/8	6	6	Blue Earth County	MN	Maynard L. Nelson	1968	491
153 3/8	22 5/8	21 6/8	14 0/8	9	10	Juneau County	WI	Jeffery J. Scott	1991	491
153 2/8	20 2/8	19 5/8	16 2/8	7	6	Orleans County	NY	Randy Piedmonte	1987	493
153 1/8	23 0/8	21 6/8	18 5/8	5	8	Richland County	ND	Lamarr Van Dame	1992	494
153 0/8	23 0/8	23 6/8	19 1/8	5	5	Ripley County	IN	Robert H. Pitt	1970	495
153 0/8	20 4/8	19 7/8	13 2/8	6	12	Lee County	AL	Leonard Hochstedler	1975	495
153 0/8	19 7/8	20 0/8	16 0/8	7	6	Lake County	IL	Steve E. Menter	1990	495
152 5/8	22 4/8	20 3/8	17 4/8	5	6	Mercer County	IL	Kenneth E. Yeater	1990	498
152 3/8	24 2/8	21 4/8	20 0/8	8	5	Allegan County	MI	Elwood Snell	1947	499
152 2/8	20 4/8	23 4/8	22 5/8	5	7	Clay County	KS	Robert D. Ridley	1987	500
152 2/8	21 7/8	21 6/8	15 1/8	6	7	Sauk County	WI	Jane Nelson	1989	500
152 2/8	20 6/8	20 1/8	14 4/8	7	8	Westmoreland County	PA	Louis Dodaro	1991	500
151 6/8	23 1/8	23 0/8	14 1/8	8	8	Van Buren County	MI	Rex S. Millard	1986	503
151 6/8	23 5/8	23 4/8	17 2/8	6	6	Florence County	WI	Carole M. Englebert	1986	503
151 5/8	17 0/8	20 5/8	18 0/8	8	10	McIntosh County	ND	Craig Lambrecht	1980	505
151 5/8	19 7/8	18 1/8	14 7/8	5	9	Hunterdon County	NJ	Jeff Anderson	1982	505
151 5/8	24 1/8	23 7/8	19 0/8	4	7	Barry County	MI	Donald G. Cordray	1989	505
151 3/8	21 4/8	24 7/8	21 0/8	9	5	Scott County	KY	Johnny Mulberry	1982	508
151 3/8	25 0/8	23 3/8	19 7/8	5	6	Coshocton County	OH	William Randles	1983	508
151 2/8	26 6/8	25 4/8	17 4/8	8	6	Anoka County	MN	Mike Hiltner	1988	510
150 7/8	21 1/8	19 1/8	17 1/8	7	9	Cumberland County	NJ	Bob Eisele	1980	511
150 5/8	19 4/8	23 6/8	17 2/8	8	5	Berkshire County	MA	Chris Lawson	1988	512
150 4/8	25 1/8	23 7/8	15 0/8	8	7	Jackson County	IL	Carl D. Todd	1982	513
150 4/8	24 3/8	21 5/8	22 2/8	6	6	Suffolk County	NY	John Bennett	1990	513
150 3/8	22 3/8	22 1/8	16 0/8	8	7	Harnett County	NC	Neil Vernon Wilson	1989	515
150 2/8	20 2/8	20 2/8	13 5/8	6	8	Cottonwood County	MN	Matthew Michael Peacock	1989	516

World Record Roosevelt *"Olympic"* **Elk**
Score: 367 3/8
Tillamook County, Oregon - 1985
Hunter: Dale Baumgartner/Ken Sisco

ROOSEVELT *"OLYMPIC"* ELK

MINIMUM SCORE 210

Cervus elaphus roosevelti

Score	Length of Main Beam R	L	Inside Spread	Number of Points R	L	Area	State/ Province	Hunter's Name	Date	Rank
367 3/8	43 5/8	45 6/8	40 0/8	7	8	Tillamook County	OR	D. Baumgartner / K. Sisco	1985	1
353 3/8	51 6/8	53 1/8	38 2/8	7	7	Columbia County	OR	Ken R. Adamson	1985	2
343 6/8	54 7/8	56 0/8	39 5/8	7	7	Curry County	OR	Kendal Smith	1986	3
343 2/8	48 4/8	49 5/8	38 6/8	8	7	Lewis County	WA	Keith Heldreth	1988	4
324 4/8	45 3/8	44 6/8	44 6/8	7	7	Jefferson County	WA	Larry Haddock	1988	5
318 6/8	45 7/8	44 5/8	37 0/8	6	6	Jefferson County	WA	David J. Miller	1986	6
312 4/8	52 1/8	49 5/8	36 2/8	6	6	Coos County	OR	Robert Dean Dunson	1982	7
309 1/8	47 3/8	40 6/8	40 7/8	7	7	Jefferson County	WA	Walter L. Campbell	1987	8
309 0/8	47 2/8	48 2/8	38 6/8	7	6	Douglas County	OR	Bert Petit	1984	9
308 1/8	48 4/8	48 4/8	42 3/8	6	7	Coos County	OR	Dean Dunson	1986	10
306 6/8	50 2/8	50 4/8	38 6/8	6	6	Polk County	OR	James Wallen	1980	11
306 1/8	49 2/8	45 4/8	40 4/8	7	6	Jefferson County	WA	Monte Dahlstrom	1987	12
301 0/8	45 0/8	47 3/8	37 1/8	8	8	Washington County	OR	Jon King	1987	13
298 7/8	46 3/8	46 5/8	41 6/8	6	6	Jefferson County	WA	Wayne McReynolds	1990	14
298 6/8	48 3/8	49 3/8	33 6/8	5	6	Lane County	OR	Joe Waite	1981	15
298 0/8	44 3/8	46 7/8	38 6/8	8	8	Washington County	OR	Ron Adamson	1992	16
297 3/8	41 5/8	41 1/8	38 1/8	6	6	Jefferson County	WA	Doug Smith	1989	17
297 2/8	46 0/8	45 7/8	42 7/8	6	6	Clallam County	WA	Arnold LaGambina	1988	18
296 6/8	40 3/8	41 2/8	39 3/8	6	7	Clatsop County	OR	Edwin J. Thompson	1987	19
296 6/8	43 0/8	43 5/8	41 4/8	6	6	Jefferson County	WA	Kurt Goesch	1989	19
296 4/8	46 6/8	47 0/8	41 3/8	7	7	Pacific County	WA	Jess Martin, Jr.	1971	21
295 0/8	45 6/8	45 4/8	39 0/8	8	7	Columbia County	OR	Smokey Crews	1987	22
294 7/8	46 7/8	49 0/8	41 6/8	6	6	Jefferson County	WA	Bob Rosie	1990	23
293 6/8	50 3/8	47 5/8	37 6/8	5	6	Jefferson County	WA	Ronald E. Ihrig	1984	24
292 1/8	42 3/8	44 0/8	40 0/8	6	6	Lane County	OR	Thomas A. Whitaker	1988	25
291 4/8	41 0/8	43 1/8	33 5/8	6	7	Pacific County	WA	Dan Free	1983	26
291 2/8	41 1/8	42 1/8	41 4/8	6	6	Clallam County	WA	Russ Spaulding	1985	27
291 1/8	42 3/8	44 1/8	40 0/8	6	7	Curry County	OR	James Atherton	1985	28
289 2/8	44 7/8	44 7/8	32 4/8	6	5	Pacific County	WA	Dan Free	1980	29
285 1/8	47 3/8	48 1/8	37 1/8	6	6	Clackamas County	OR	Randy W. Kubitz	1986	30
284 0/8	42 1/8	43 3/8	40 1/8	8	7	Jefferson County	WA	Daniel J. Siegner	1991	31
283 5/8	47 4/8	48 0/8	40 7/8	6	6	Jefferson County	WA	Robert J. Rosie	1990	32
283 3/8	46 0/8	42 7/8	29 7/8	6	5	Skamania County	WA	Jerry L. Carter	1973	33
283 3/8	46 0/8	47 1/8	30 5/8	6	6	Polk County	OR	Terry Smith	1991	33
283 3/8	43 0/8	41 7/8	44 0/8	6	6	Jefferson County	WA	Paul Szumlanski	1991	33
283 2/8	45 3/8	45 3/8	34 4/8	6	6	Pacific County	WA	Jerry Webster	1979	36
283 2/8	43 4/8	41 1/8	38 6/8	6	7	Clallam County	WA	Wayne Haag	1982	36
282 5/8	42 6/8	45 2/8	38 6/8	6	6	Jefferson County	WA	Gary M. Douthit	1986	38
282 4/8	44 6/8	44 1/8	38 7/8	7	6	Afognak Island	AK	Edward L. Russell	1980	39
282 0/8	45 0/8	43 6/8	42 0/8	6	6	Jefferson County	WA	Dave Robertson	1970	40
282 0/8	45 2/8	44 7/8	35 6/8	7	7	Jefferson County	WA	Michael C. Giardino	1992	40
281 0/8	41 6/8	40 7/8	34 4/8	6	6	Jefferson County	WA	Talmadge Dobbs	1989	42
280 6/8	45 6/8	44 1/8	38 1/8	6	6	Jefferson County	WA	Donald N. Morey	1978	43
280 4/8	43 2/8	43 0/8	33 0/8	6	6	Lane County	OR	Jeff Sindt	1982	44
280 2/8	42 0/8	43 0/8	39 2/8	6	5	Jefferson County	WA	Wayne McReynolds	1984	45
279 7/8	47 4/8	47 2/8	37 2/8	5	6	Grays Harbor County	WA	G. A. "Toby" Hart	1986	46
276 6/8	40 4/8	40 1/8	39 7/8	6	6	Clallam County	WA	Clyde E. Graham	1985	47
275 5/8	48 4/8	45 1/8	38 3/8	5	6	Jefferson County	WA	Jerry Childs	1991	48
275 3/8	37 0/8	37 4/8	36 1/8	7	7	Tillamook County	OR	Alan Richardson	1980	49
275 2/8	41 2/8	38 3/8	36 0/8	7	8	Jefferson County	WA	Jon E. Nelson	1986	50
274 6/8	42 3/8	44 0/8	39 4/8	5	5	Columbia County	OR	Steve Cox	1989	51
273 7/8	42 4/8	42 4/8	32 5/8	7	7	Jefferson County	WA	Dave Dasher	1989	52
273 4/8	44 6/8	45 1/8	38 3/8	6	6	Pacific County	WA	Glen Watland	1980	53
273 0/8	44 2/8	44 0/8	35 0/8	5	5	Jefferson County	WA	Ken Chamberlin	1987	54
272 5/8	46 4/8	45 1/8	36 1/8	5	5	Jefferson County	WA	Bryan Mittge	1986	55
272 1/8	39 4/8	40 6/8	33 5/8	5	5	Wahkiakum County	WA	Russ Poppe	1982	56
271 3/8	44 3/8	44 3/8	38 0/8	6	5	Grays Harbor County	WA	Scott Bergen	1985	57
271 1/8	46 0/8	45 3/8	33 3/8	6	6	Afognak Island	AK	David Harper	1970	58
270 3/8	38 2/8	39 5/8	36 4/8	8	6	Clatsop County	OR	James L. Friesz	1981	59
270 2/8	44 6/8	44 1/8	44 4/8	4	5	Grays Harbor County	WA	Bill Brown	1959	60
270 0/8	41 1/8	42 1/8	36 0/8	5	5	Clallam County	WA	Arne Swanson	1990	61
269 4/8	39 3/8	40 6/8	39 0/8	5	5	Clallam County	WA	George McDonald	1985	62
269 2/8	45 6/8	45 0/8	33 1/8	6	6	Jefferson County	WA	Ray Capp	1987	63
269 1/8	40 5/8	41 5/8	35 3/8	6	6	Clatsop County	OR	David M. Jones	1982	64
268 7/8	40 5/8	41 1/8	34 1/8	5	7	Coos County	OR	Thomas E. Tipton	1986	65
268 2/8	43 7/8	43 7/8	41 0/8	5	5	Grays Harbor County	WA	Terry Plato	1984	66
268 1/8	38 0/8	39 2/8	37 3/8	6	6	Clatsop County	OR	Ed Beisley	1967	67
267 3/8	37 0/8	36 3/8	34 3/8	6	6	Clatsop County	OR	Douglas W. Hamilton	1982	68
267 2/8	43 3/8	42 4/8	40 2/8	5	5	Jefferson County	WA	Dave Mirka	1987	69
266 5/8	37 3/8	38 1/8	35 5/8	5	5	Clallam County	WA	George McDonald	1989	70

MINIMUM SCORE 210

Score	Length of Main Beam R	Length of Main Beam L	Inside Spread	Number of Points R	Number of Points L	Area	State/ Province	Hunter's Name	Date	Rank
266 3/8	46 3/8	41 6/8	45 0/8	5	6	Grays Harbor County	WA	Mark R. Nieznalski	1984	71
265 4/8	39 7/8	40 0/8	35 6/8	5	6	Clallam County	WA	George McDonald	1990	72
265 3/8	39 3/8	37 4/8	44 5/8	5	5	Clallam County	WA	Ray Capp	1989	73
263 5/8	42 5/8	42 1/8	34 4/8	6	6	Lincoln County	OR	Malcam Moberly	1988	74
263 3/8	41 2/8	42 6/8	29 1/8	6	6	Lane County	OR	Max Lee	1980	75
262 7/8	40 1/8	40 0/8	34 0/8	6	6	Coos County	OR	Larry Frost	1985	76
262 2/8	45 4/8	45 5/8	28 6/8	6	6	Douglas County	OR	Dennis Olson	1984	77
262 0/8	39 6/8	40 2/8	41 0/8	5	5	Coos County	OR	Tom Tipton	1991	78
261 6/8	43 0/8	43 3/8	38 3/8	6	6	Jefferson County	WA	Robert C. Allan	1988	79
261 5/8	40 7/8	41 2/8	38 7/8	5	5	Jefferson County	WA	Mark J. Tupper	1986	80
261 5/8	40 0/8	40 2/8	36 3/8	6	6	Clatsop County	OR	William H. Stevens	1991	80
260 5/8	41 2/8	40 0/8	37 4/8	6	7	Jefferson County	WA	Gaillard R. Graham	1990	82
260 4/8	41 4/8	41 1/8	34 4/8	6	5	Douglas County	OR	J. B. Hollander	1984	83
260 3/8	45 0/8	44 2/8	35 1/8	6	5	Benton County	OR	Timothy Pearson	1989	84
260 0/8	40 1/8	38 6/8	38 7/8	6	6	Columbia County	OR	Smokey Crews	1988	85
259 6/8	43 1/8	42 1/8	37 6/8	6	6	Columbia County	OR	Don Malloy	1988	86
259 2/8	42 3/8	42 4/8	37 0/8	5	5	Coos County	OR	James M. Speelman	1974	87
259 1/8	42 1/8	40 2/8	34 2/8	6	6	Clallam County	WA	Frank LaGambina	1980	88
258 5/8	40 3/8	38 4/8	32 6/8	7	7	Columbia County	OR	Larry W. Fox	1987	89
257 1/8	40 4/8	40 0/8	43 1/8	6	6	Columbia County	OR	Randy Jennings	1985	90
253 7/8	45 2/8	43 5/8	29 5/8	5	7	Yamhill County	OR	Jerry S. Bailey	1986	91
253 4/8	39 3/8	39 2/8	28 6/8	7	7	Coos County	OR	Craig Matson	1980	92
253 1/8	43 1/8	42 0/8	33 6/8	5	6	Pacific County	WA	Bill Egner	1977	93
253 0/8	35 1/8	36 4/8	36 1/8	6	5	Clatsop County	OR	John C. Bernards	1985	94
252 7/8	40 7/8	42 1/8	31 3/8	6	6	Pacific County	WA	John Wall	1979	95
251 5/8	41 4/8	36 2/8	40 6/8	6	6	Jefferson County	WA	Sanford Windle	1972	96
251 2/8	39 1/8	40 4/8	33 2/8	6	6	Jefferson County	WA	Bill Pudell	1982	97
249 5/8	43 2/8	44 6/8	30 3/8	6	6	Tillamook County	OR	Steve Pieren	1982	98
249 4/8	45 3/8	45 7/8	32 6/8	6	6	Polk County	OR	Kevin Dean Zook	1992	99
249 3/8	41 1/8	39 3/8	32 4/8	6	6	Clatsop County	OR	Charles Lee Smith	1990	100
248 4/8	40 0/8	39 3/8	43 1/8	5	5	Jefferson County	WA	Chris Krueger	1987	101
248 4/8	41 7/8	43 4/8	32 2/8	7	5	Jefferson County	WA	Mike Sturman	1991	101
248 3/8	39 1/8	40 2/8	35 3/8	5	5	Jefferson County	WA	Larry Haddock	1987	103
248 2/8	42 6/8	43 0/8	40 2/8	5	5	Jefferson County	WA	Robert J. Rosie	1992	104
247 6/8	34 4/8	36 6/8	37 1/8	5	5	Grays Harbor County	WA	Wayne McReynolds	1981	105
247 6/8	45 2/8	44 2/8	38 7/8	6	5	Coos County	OR	Mark E. Cox	1990	105
247 0/8	39 6/8	38 4/8	39 6/8	5	5	Olympic Peninsula	WA	Lloyd Beebe	1951	107
246 6/8	39 5/8	37 3/8	34 0/8	6	6	Jefferson County	WA	Eugene Wells	1960	108
245 1/8	38 3/8	37 5/8	34 7/8	7	5	Columbia County	OR	Leroy E. Lewis	1989	109
244 4/8	36 5/8	36 2/8	35 7/8	7	7	Clallam County	WA	Arnold La Gambina	1989	110
243 6/8	43 4/8	41 4/8	33 0/8	5	5	Clallam County	WA	Glenn St. Charles	1952	111
243 0/8	45 0/8	44 0/8	40 2/8	5	5	Jefferson County	WA	James M. Stark	1977	112
241 6/8	39 7/8	39 1/8	34 6/8	6	5	Clatsop County	OR	David Lawrence	1982	113
241 6/8	39 7/8	38 2/8	39 4/8	5	5	Clallam County	WA	Arnold LaGambina	1986	113
241 5/8	37 1/8	37 1/8	36 1/8	5	5	Washington County	OR	Douglas Rick Clark	1991	115
241 2/8	36 0/8	36 2/8	27 3/8	6	7	Clatsop County	OR	Robert G. Mucken	1989	116
238 6/8	36 5/8	37 6/8	38 0/8	5	6	Grays Harbor County	WA	Richard Mazzei	1984	117
238 6/8	40 3/8	39 3/8	32 4/8	6	6	Lincoln County	OR	Warren Lynch	1986	117
238 5/8	40 3/8	40 0/8	38 3/8	5	5	Benton County	OR	Donald E. Zuhlke	1989	119
238 2/8	46 2/8	45 1/8	39 6/8	5	4	Pacific County	WA	John R. Martin	1978	120
238 2/8	39 4/8	37 3/8	37 0/8	5	5	Grays Harbor County	WA	Jack McDougall	1986	120
238 0/8	39 7/8	40 4/8	34 2/8	5	5	Jefferson County	WA	Larry Jensen	1985	122
237 2/8	32 4/8	33 1/8	36 2/8	6	6	Clatsop County	OR	Robert J. Wilkie	1984	123
236 6/8	39 0/8	37 3/8	31 3/8	6	6	Jefferson County	WA	Mathew Hayvaz	1984	124
235 7/8	37 1/8	37 0/8	35 4/8	6	6	Polk County	OR	Joseph K. Saboe	1990	125
235 2/8	38 0/8	39 1/8	34 0/8	5	5	Tillamook County	OR	Smokey Crews	1983	126
235 2/8	37 4/8	38 5/8	33 7/8	5	6	Clallam County	WA	Daniel Siegner	1986	126
235 0/8	39 1/8	39 2/8	31 2/8	6	5	Josephine County	OR	Joel Robertson	1982	128
234 2/8	39 5/8	38 4/8	33 6/8	5	5	Clallam County	WA	Dean R. Swerin	1985	129
233 4/8	40 2/8	40 6/8	28 6/8	5	5	Grays Harbor County	WA	John J. Durst	1987	130
233 4/8	36 1/8	37 4/8	33 0/8	6	6	Tillamook County	OR	Joe Hulburt	1992	130
233 1/8	41 4/8	40 3/8	30 0/8	5	6	Curry County	OR	Kendal Smith	1982	132
233 0/8	35 6/8	37 1/8	28 0/8	5	5	Pacific County	WA	Parry Bagley	1991	133
231 7/8	35 5/8	37 4/8	32 3/8	5	5	Clallam County	WA	Frank LaGambina	1979	134
231 3/8	35 3/8	33 5/8	30 6/8	6	6	Washington County	OR	Gregory D. Lueptow	1990	135
231 1/8	37 3/8	38 0/8	29 7/8	5	5	Yamhill County	OR	Curtis C. Altman	1983	136
231 0/8	34 2/8	34 6/8	40 0/8	5	6	Clatsop County	OR	Ronald Ray Noel	1989	137
230 6/8	35 2/8	34 4/8	32 2/8	5	5	Clallam County	WA	Wayne Haag	1980	138
230 2/8	38 5/8	36 4/8	38 0/8	5	5	Coos County	OR	Thomas Tipton	1984	139
229 0/8	44 3/8	44 3/8	35 6/8	5	4	Clallam County	WA	Pete J. Germeau	1982	140

ROOSEVELT "OLYMPIC" ELK

(Continued)

SCORE	LENGTH OF MAIN BEAM R	L	INSIDE SPREAD	NUMBER OF POINTS R	L	AREA	STATE/ PROVINCE	HUNTER'S NAME	DATE	RANK
228 1/8	36 7/8	34 7/8	34 1/8	5	5	Columbia County	OR	Mitch Elliott	1987	141
228 0/8	36 2/8	36 0/8	32 1/8	6	6	Curry County	OR	Ken French	1988	142
227 5/8	40 3/8	38 1/8	34 2/8	6	7	Clatsop County	OR	Ray C Nelson	1985	143
227 5/8	41 3/8	38 6/8	34 5/8	5	4	Clallam County	WA	Arnold LaGambina	1987	143
227 2/8	37 5/8	40 4/8	29 4/8	5	6	Benton County	OR	Felix Alan Lafond	1986	145
227 1/8	36 2/8	31 0/8	29 5/8	5	7	Clatsop County	OR	Randy Jennings	1980	146
227 1/8	42 1/8	40 6/8	28 3/8	6	5	Clatsop County	OR	David Braem	1982	146
227 0/8	38 1/8	36 3/8	35 1/8	6	6	Lincoln County	OR	Richard Smith	1989	148
227 0/8	37 4/8	37 4/8	30 5/8	5	6	Clatsup County	OR	Roy R. Stevens	1992	148
225 4/8	37 0/8	35 6/8	35 2/8	5	5	Jefferson County	WA	Rodger Squirrel	1984	150
225 3/8	33 0/8	32 7/8	33 3/8	6	7	Polk County	OR	Gary Freuler	1988	151
224 6/8	36 6/8	38 7/8	30 4/8	5	5	Jefferson County	WA	Francis W. Robinson, Jr.	1965	152
224 2/8	35 7/8	34 6/8	27 0/8	5	6	Polk County	OR	Rand Sether	1984	153
224 0/8	32 1/8	30 7/8	31 0/8	6	7	Douglas County	OR	Whitley Stephenson	1990	154
223 3/8	36 5/8	35 7/8	32 7/8	5	5	Tillamook County	OR	Smokey Crews	1985	155
222 4/8	33 6/8	34 5/8	34 0/8	5	5	Tillamook County	OR	Ben R. Cook	1990	156
222 1/8	40 3/8	36 5/8	31 3/8	5	5	Jefferson County	WA	Ron Stoller	1991	157
221 1/8	39 0/8	38 7/8	29 3/8	5	5	Lane County	OR	Bruce Evans	1989	158
221 0/8	38 1/8	38 4/8	31 4/8	5	5	Pacific County	WA	Tim Schneider	1988	159
219 5/8	33 0/8	32 3/8	28 2/8	6	7	Clatsop County	OR	Tim Streight	1984	160
218 7/8	38 5/8	40 4/8	35 1/8	5	5	Jefferson County	WA	Harold Wellan	1985	161
218 3/8	36 1/8	35 2/8	35 1/8	5	5	Lane County	OR	Cameron Hanes	1992	162
217 7/8	38 1/8	39 3/8	28 1/8	5	5	Pacific County	WA	Clyde Kennedy	1975	163
217 2/8	35 7/8	34 1/8	28 2/8	6	6	Clatsop County	OR	Kurt Klaffke	1986	164
216 6/8	34 0/8	32 5/8	34 3/8	5	5	Clallam County	WA	Arnold LaGambina	1983	165
216 6/8	34 2/8	33 7/8	31 2/8	5	5	Lane County	OR	John H. Buss	1988	165
216 6/8	35 5/8	35 4/8	32 0/8	5	5	Pacific County	WA	Brent Hatch	1990	165
212 2/8	36 1/8	32 4/8	35 6/8	5	5	Pacific County	WA	Doug Schnebly	1991	168
212 0/8	36 6/8	36 4/8	33 0/8	5	5	Grays Harbor County	WA	Dan Boeholt	1985	169
212 0/8	38 5/8	40 7/8	39 6/8	5	4	Clallam County	WA	Chris Krueger	1990	169
211 0/8	33 6/8	31 0/8	32 0/8	6	6	Coos County	OR	Gary Wallace	1981	171

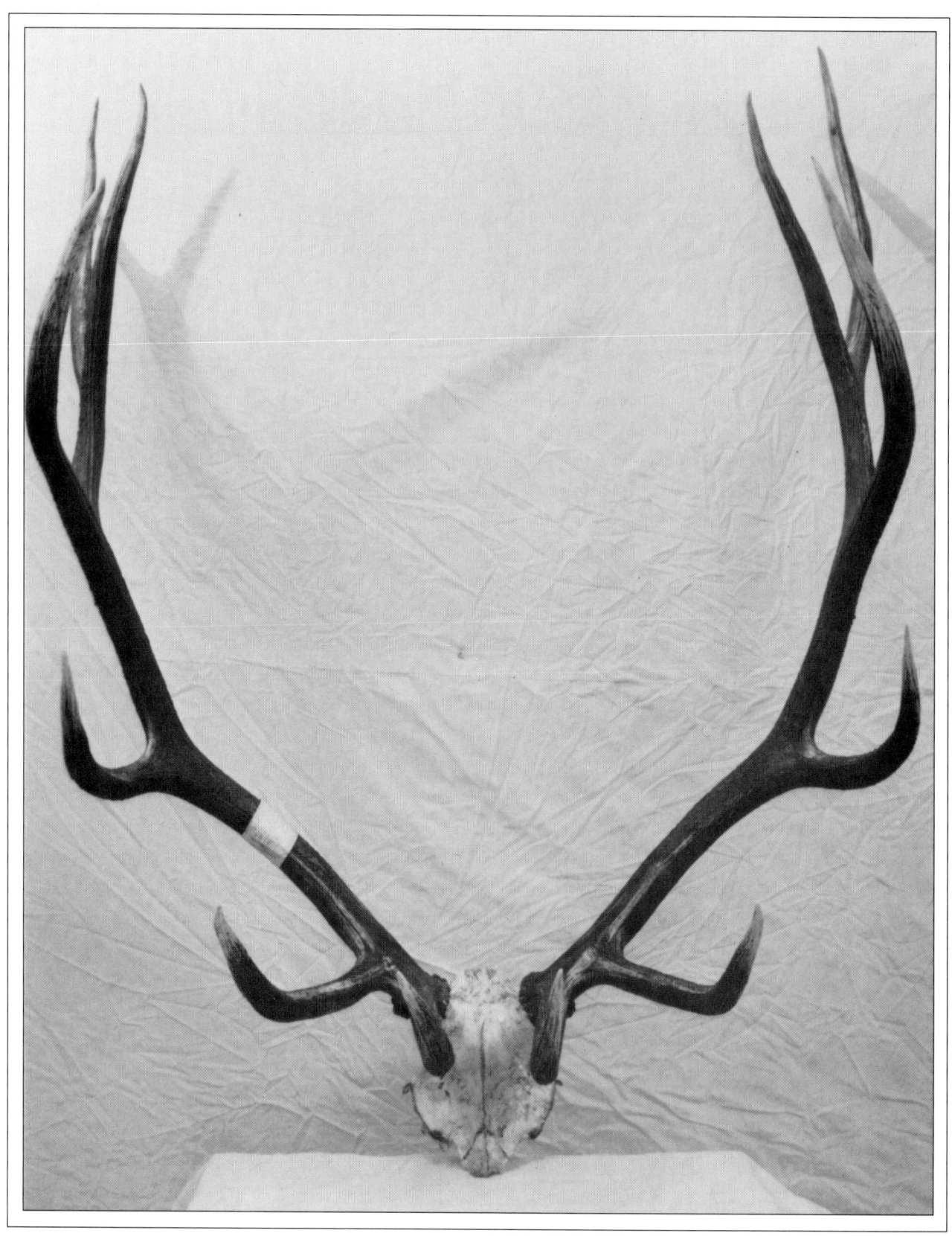

World Record Yellowstone *"American"* Elk (Typical Antlers)
Score: 404 0/8
Coconino County, Arizona - 1992
Hunter: William Wright

YELLOWSTONE "AMERICAN" ELK (Typical Antlers)

Cervus elaphus nelsoni and certain related subspecies

SCORE	LENGTH OF MAIN BEAM		INSIDE SPREAD	NUMBER OF POINTS		AREA	STATE/ PROVINCE	HUNTER'S NAME	DATE	RANK
	R	L		R	L					
404 0/8	56 4/8	57 1/8	44 0/8	7	7	Coconino County	AZ	William Wright	1992	1
393 1/8	61 5/8	63 0/8	43 7/8	7	9	Montrose County	CO	Wayne Bradley	1986	2
390 7/8	55 3/8	55 1/8	36 5/8	6	6	Duck Mtns.	MAN	Melvin J. Podaima	1991	3
390 7/8	57 5/8	60 2/8	42 7/8	9	8	Grant County	NM	David L. Morgan	1992	3
389 2/8	63 6/8	63 0/8	42 1/8	7	7	Coconino County	AZ	Jay Elmer	1980	5
386 5/8	53 5/8	53 6/8	41 2/8	8	7	Madison County	MT	Allan Mintken	1986	6
386 0/8	61 2/8	59 6/8	37 2/8	8	8	Coconino County	AZ	Randy Elmer	1988	7
384 6/8	55 2/8	53 4/8	44 2/8	6	7	Coconino County	AZ	Jay Elmer	1979	8
384 4/8	53 4/8	54 6/8	45 4/8	7	7	Meagher County	MT	David Snyder	1981	9
384 1/8	57 6/8	62 6/8	47 7/8	6	7	Coconino County	AZ	Mike Taylor	1985	10
383 3/8	65 0/8	61 7/8	48 5/8	6	6	Catron County	NM	Rudy O. Duran	1988	11
382 2/8	60 0/8	60 0/8	47 2/8	6	6	Coconino County	AZ	Don R. Newton, Jr.	1985	12
380 6/8	56 7/8	55 5/8	48 0/8	6	7	Socorro County	NM	Michael S. Weldon	1992	13
380 3/8	53 4/8	53 2/8	51 7/8	7	7	Rich County	UT	Fahy S. Robinson, Jr.	1988	14
380 3/8	56 3/8	58 0/8	44 1/8	7	6	Catron County	NM	Don Parks, Jr.	1988	14
380 2/8	56 2/8	54 1/8	45 0/8	7	6	Coconino County	AZ	Doug Kittredge	1975	16
379 6/8	57 7/8	56 5/8	47 6/8	6	6	Coconino County	AZ	Gregory K. Scott	1986	17
379 3/8	53 4/8	56 0/8	42 7/8	7	8	Coconino County	AZ	Jeff Elmer	1984	18
378 6/8	57 4/8	57 7/8	39 0/8	9	8	Shoshone County	ID	Steven W. Mullin	1981	19
377 0/8	59 2/8	57 1/8	39 4/8	6	6	Coconino County	AZ	Jack Frazier	1981	20
377 0/8	56 1/8	51 1/8	40 3/8	7	8	Coconino County	AZ	Larry Thomas	1985	20
376 6/8	47 2/8	50 3/8	39 2/8	6	7	Adams County	ID	Jack D. Sheppard	1966	22
376 3/8	60 1/8	59 1/8	40 3/8	6	7	Catron County	NM	Wayne K. Curtis	1986	23
375 2/8	56 0/8	55 0/8	38 0/8	6	6	Converse County	WY	Don Stewart	1981	24
375 1/8	53 5/8	55 7/8	46 7/8	6	6	Jackson County	CO	Vincent Kvidera	1976	25
375 0/8	52 3/8	53 7/8	39 1/8	6	7	Sierra County	NM	Jim Wagner	1986	26
375 0/8	55 6/8	53 1/8	41 2/8	6	6	Catron County	NM	Ed Sautier	1991	26
374 3/8	53 5/8	53 7/8	41 1/8	6	6	Grant County	NM	Jesse O. Ogas	1990	28
373 1/8	57 5/8	57 6/8	41 5/8	6	6	Crook County	OR	Jeffrey E. Hale	1988	29
373 1/8	49 1/8	48 4/8	41 7/8	7	6	Albany County	WY	Wes Walton	1990	29
372 3/8	50 7/8	49 1/8	39 7/8	6	6	Minitonas	MAN	Brian Brownlie	1989	31
372 0/8	52 2/8	52 2/8	44 0/8	7	6	Lincoln County	MT	Jerry Regh	1986	32
371 7/8	52 3/8	53 0/8	46 5/8	6	6	Mineral County	MT	Scott J. Stern	1983	33
371 7/8	59 3/8	57 2/8	42 7/8	6	6	Coconino County	AZ	George Flournoy	1986	33
371 2/8	55 1/8	53 7/8	42 2/8	6	6	Skamania County	WA	Kevin Schmid	1990	35
370 7/8	56 0/8	58 0/8	42 5/8	6	6	Coconino County	AZ	Mike Moulton	1987	36
370 5/8	49 5/8	49 5/8	38 1/8	6	6	Spruce Woods	MAN	Peter Sawatzky	1992	37
370 3/8	56 3/8	56 3/8	42 3/8	6	6	Sheridan County	WY	Ron Johnson	1991	38
370 3/8	60 7/8	59 0/8	43 5/8	7	7	Coconino County	AZ	Michael S. Weldon	1992	38
370 1/8	51 5/8	50 7/8	41 5/8	6	6	Petroleum County	MT	G. L. 'Buck' Damone	1985	40
369 6/8	54 6/8	53 0/8	47 6/8	6	6	Greenlee County	AZ	Clifford White	1986	41
369 5/8	59 7/8	58 6/8	44 7/8	6	6	Coconino County	AZ	Jeff Schorey	1992	42
369 4/8	53 2/8	51 2/8	39 4/8	7	7	Bonner County	ID	Steve Noort	1986	43
369 4/8	53 0/8	53 0/8	42 4/8	6	7	Catron County	NM	Frank A. Hayes	1986	43
369 2/8	51 0/8	55 4/8	48 4/8	6	6	Madison County	MT	Jeff Engler	1977	45
369 0/8	57 2/8	56 4/8	38 2/8	7	6	Coconino County	AZ	Tom Hinson	1987	46
368 6/8	52 1/8	51 0/8	39 6/8	6	6	Coconino County	AZ	John V. Beaufeaux	1990	47
368 2/8	53 0/8	53 1/8	40 2/8	7	7	Kittitas County	WA	Robert Carl Sater	1987	48
368 0/8	52 7/8	52 3/8	44 4/8	6	6	Grant County	OR	Greg E. Willmore	1988	49
367 3/8	47 7/8	49 3/8	45 1/8	8	7	Larimer County	CO	H. Troxell/B. Alexander	1970	50
367 3/8	54 1/8	51 7/8	43 2/8	8	8	Gila County	AZ	Patrick Kirby	1992	50
367 2/8	55 4/8	57 7/8	46 0/8	6	6	Lemhi County	ID	Ben Fahnholz	1982	52
367 2/8	55 4/8	54 3/8	42 4/8	6	6	Rio Arriba County	NM	David O. Conrad	1990	52
366 7/8	53 2/8	52 1/8	40 4/8	7	7	Mineral County	MT	Gerry Lamarre	1977	54
366 5/8	53 0/8	53 2/8	45 3/8	7	7	Shoshone County	ID	D. A. Johnson	1962	55
366 5/8	46 1/8	47 1/8	35 6/8	6	7	Phillips County	MT	Ronnie Molstad	1983	55
366 5/8	50 4/8	52 4/8	45 5/8	6	6	Valencia County	NM	Dean Dunaway	1991	55
366 4/8	49 7/8	55 1/8	39 6/8	6	6	Duck Mtns.	MAN	Brian W. Brownlie	1992	58
366 3/8	52 5/8	50 7/8	41 7/8	6	6	Fergus County	MT	J. Douglas Krings	1980	59
366 3/8	55 5/8	57 6/8	40 5/8	6	6	Catron County	NM	J. W. Young	1990	59
366 1/8	52 3/8	51 0/8	43 7/8	6	6	Berland River	ALB	Brad Sidebottom	1986	61
365 1/8	51 4/8	51 2/8	38 5/8	7	7	Sandoval County	NM	John C. McClendon	1985	62
365 0/8	60 6/8	61 4/8	50 2/8	7	7	Fergus County	MT	John Jeide	1983	63
364 6/8	50 3/8	46 2/8	39 2/8	6	6	Grant County	OR	William C. Sanowski	1976	64
364 3/8	57 2/8	51 6/8	37 3/8	8	7	Kootenai County	ID	Curtis Yanzick	1990	65
364 1/8	54 4/8	56 5/8	46 3/8	6	6	Catron County	NM	Lee Hetrick	1991	66
364 0/8	52 7/8	52 7/8	40 4/8	6	7	Catron County	NM	Paul J. Butler	1988	67
363 7/8	50 5/8	47 0/8	41 4/8	7	8	Converse County	WY	David P. Lindman	1986	68
363 5/8	56 3/8	54 7/8	43 1/8	6	6	Graham County	AZ	Steve M. Titla	1988	69
362 2/8	50 2/8	49 4/8	46 2/8	7	7	Jackson County	CO	Alfred H. O'Brien	1972	70

Score	Length of Main Beam R	L	Inside Spread	Number of Points R	L	Area	State/ Province	Hunter's Name	Date	Rank
361 4/8	51 5/8	54 0/8	48 0/8	6	6	Fergus County	MT	D. Mitch Kottas	1992	71
361 3/8	54 3/8	51 0/8	47 3/8	6	6	Coconino County	AZ	Dean Dunaway	1990	72
361 2/8	58 4/8	56 4/8	37 0/8	6	6	Coconino County	AZ	Tom Phelps	1986	73
361 0/8	54 0/8	55 0/8	44 4/8	6	6	Coconino County	AZ	Laura Wuertz	1986	74
361 0/8	51 7/8	49 2/8	34 6/8	7	6	Gila County	AZ	Dick Gephard	1990	74
360 7/8	54 7/8	56 1/8	41 7/8	7	6	Lemhi County	ID	Tony Latham	1983	76
360 6/8	51 1/8	49 7/8	37 0/8	6	6	Petroleum County	MT	Kerby A. Durbin	1987	77
360 4/8	61 7/8	57 3/8	43 5/8	8	7	White Pine County	NV	Thomas Enewold	1990	78
360 4/8	54 2/8	54 4/8	42 6/8	8	7	Catron County	NM	Blaine Underwood	1991	78
360 3/8	57 5/8	53 2/8	48 7/8	7	6	Socorro County	NM	James A. Trujillo	1987	80
359 5/8	50 4/8	52 0/8	47 1/8	6	6	Pierce County	WA	Doug Nearhood	1985	81
359 3/8	48 1/8	49 2/8	48 1/8	6	6	Mesa County	CO	David W. Christopherson	1978	82
359 2/8	51 0/8	52 5/8	42 0/8	6	9	Coconino County	AZ	Robert Cecrle	1972	83
359 2/8	58 2/8	56 7/8	42 0/8	6	6	Coconino County	AZ	Jim David	1974	83
359 2/8	56 3/8	53 7/8	40 0/8	7	6	Greenlee County	AZ	N. Richard McMullan	1992	83
359 1/8	49 0/8	52 4/8	36 0/8	7	6	Coconino County	AZ	Frank J. Mayorga	1987	86
359 0/8	56 4/8	57 2/8	36 4/8	6	6	Coconino County	AZ	Michael J. Proulx	1986	87
358 7/8	55 5/8	54 5/8	40 7/8	6	6	Coconino County	AZ	Gary Bills	1986	88
358 6/8	51 7/8	55 0/8	47 6/8	6	6	Sheridan County	WY	Mike Barrett	1986	89
358 5/8	53 0/8	49 7/8	38 3/8	6	6	Cibola County	NM	Moises Perea	1980	90
358 3/8	52 3/8	52 5/8	39 5/8	6	6	Sanders County	MT	Eugene Roesler	1986	91
358 3/8	55 6/8	55 6/8	31 5/8	6	6	Catron County	NM	Steve D. Lozano	1992	91
358 2/8	54 1/8	51 4/8	47 0/8	6	6	Crook County	OR	Oliver Weger	1983	93
358 1/8	56 2/8	60 2/8	42 7/8	6	6	Catron County	NM	Robert E. Duke	1991	94
357 7/8	54 2/8	54 6/8	45 1/8	7	7	Coconino County	AZ	Mark Clammer	1987	95
357 7/8	54 6/8	57 1/8	45 5/8	6	6	Albany County	WY	Richard L. Andre	1990	95
357 7/8	54 0/8	53 3/8	42 7/8	6	6	Catron County	NM	Mike Moore	1990	95
357 7/8	54 1/8	50 7/8	37 7/8	6	6	Sierra County	NM	David Swisher	1992	95
357 6/8	50 2/8	50 6/8	40 4/8	6	6	Park County	CO	Donald R. Looper	1975	99
357 6/8	53 4/8	56 3/8	46 4/8	6	6	Apache County	AZ	John B. Bowman	1991	99
357 4/8	52 5/8	55 0/8	37 6/8	7	6	Fergus County	MT	Michael B. Hedrick	1981	101
357 3/8	56 2/8	49 2/8	37 1/8	6	6	Meagher County	MT	David G. Snyder	1978	102
357 3/8	50 4/8	50 4/8	34 5/8	6	6	Swan River	MAN	Kelly Shykitka	1986	102
357 3/8	55 6/8	54 0/8	37 7/8	6	6	Moffat County	CO	Kurt W. Keskimaki	1987	102
357 3/8	55 0/8	53 7/8	41 5/8	7	6	Missoula County	MT	Andrew J. Kelly	1990	102
357 0/8	54 2/8	56 0/8	41 0/8	6	6	Caribou County	ID	Howard E. Johnson	1968	106
357 0/8	56 5/8	56 7/8	46 6/8	6	6	Gila County	AZ	David L. Crockett	1973	106
357 0/8	53 5/8	53 6/8	43 2/8	6	7	Strawberry Lake	CO	Frank Fraser	1977	106
356 7/8	54 1/8	53 6/8	53 7/8	6	7	Park County	MT	Charles Alkire	1964	109
356 7/8	49 6/8	51 0/8	46 3/8	7	6	Flathead County	MT	Terry Krogstad	1984	109
356 6/8	51 0/8	50 2/8	41 2/8	6	6	Grant County	OR	James M. Carter	1988	111
356 4/8	57 3/8	53 1/8	46 4/8	6	6	Catron County	NM	Bill Elmer	1986	112
356 4/8	54 5/8	56 0/8	40 2/8	6	6	Coconino County	AZ	Blaine "Bub" Mathews	1990	112
356 3/8	52 4/8	48 6/8	36 1/8	6	7	Fergus County	MT	Leonard L. Weeks	1984	114
356 1/8	54 3/8	53 0/8	39 3/8	6	8	Catron County	NM	Edward Eskew	1990	115
356 0/8	52 1/8	50 1/8	36 4/8	7	6	Linn County	OR	David E. Renoud	1983	116
356 0/8	61 2/8	60 2/8	51 0/8	6	6	Coconino County	AZ	Kent G. Frei	1990	116
355 5/8	49 7/8	46 7/8	41 0/8	8	8	Catron County	NM	Doug Aikin	1987	118
355 4/8	54 7/8	56 5/8	42 6/8	6	6	Beaverhead County	MT	Robert B. McKay	1973	119
355 4/8	52 4/8	50 5/8	45 4/8	6	6	Catron County	NM	Phil Kirkland	1991	119
355 2/8	52 1/8	51 5/8	35 2/8	6	6	Otero County	NM	Jimmy King	1989	121
355 0/8	50 1/8	50 1/8	38 0/8	6	6	Shoshone County	ID	Vern Clary/Ed Oliver	1978	122
354 7/8	51 4/8	51 0/8	41 6/8	6	7	Greenlee County	AZ	David Dickson	1986	123
354 7/8	56 3/8	56 4/8	43 5/8	6	6	Coconino County	AZ	Noel Harris	1991	123
354 6/8	54 0/8	53 7/8	36 6/8	6	6	Valley County	MT	Kenneth R. Johnson	1986	125
354 6/8	56 5/8	56 4/8	44 3/8	7	8	Custer County	ID	Wayne VanVechten	1987	125
354 5/8	55 6/8	56 6/8	37 7/8	6	6	Catron County	NM	Duane "Corky" Richardson	1991	127
354 4/8	49 1/8	50 4/8	38 6/8	6	6	Coconino County	AZ	Ron Scherer	1980	128
354 3/8	56 0/8	55 3/8	39 1/8	6	7	Converse County	WY	Edward Coy	1972	129
354 3/8	53 2/8	58 3/8	46 1/8	6	6	Coconino County	AZ	James M. Frey	1980	129
354 3/8	52 5/8	52 7/8	45 1/8	6	6	Valley County	MT	Gregg Pauley	1985	129
354 3/8	51 3/8	53 1/8	39 7/8	6	6	Lincoln County	MT	Keith Krumbeck	1986	129
354 2/8	48 0/8	44 2/8	50 4/8	6	6	Morgan County	UT	Dennis Shirley	1987	133
354 0/8	60 4/8	61 2/8	34 4/8	7	6	Coconino County	AZ	Jack Cahill	1982	134
354 0/8	53 0/8	51 1/8	41 0/8	6	6	Duck Mtns.	MAN	Bob Ginther	1992	134
353 6/8	53 5/8	50 2/8	44 2/8	6	6	Coconino County	AZ	Rodney Robinson	1987	136
353 6/8	53 4/8	55 5/8	44 2/8	7	6	Catron County	NM	C. H. Anderson	1992	136
353 5/8	50 5/8	51 0/8	40 5/8	6	6	Sheridan County	WY	Ron Johnson	1990	138
353 4/8	54 3/8	54 3/8	43 0/8	6	6	Flathead County	MT	Cory Lamb	1989	139
353 1/8	59 6/8	60 4/8	40 1/8	7	6	Coconino County	AZ	Richard S. Jones	1991	140

SCORE	LENGTH OF MAIN BEAM		INSIDE SPREAD	NUMBER OF POINTS		AREA	STATE/ PROVINCE	HUNTER'S NAME	DATE	RANK
	R	L		R	L					
353 1/8	48 0/8	50 2/8	41 1/8	6	8	Converse County	WY	Glen Mark Gates	1991	140
353 0/8	50 4/8	49 6/8	43 2/8	6	6	Coconino County	AZ	Richard M. Larsen	1980	142
353 0/8	47 2/8	46 1/8	38 0/8	6	7	Grant County	OR	Kenneth Mills	1983	142
352 7/8	54 4/8	53 4/8	42 0/8	6	7	Teton County	MT	Jack Howard	1972	144
352 7/8	51 6/8	52 1/8	41 7/8	6	6	Sandoval County	NM	John W. Rose	1981	144
352 5/8	50 1/8	50 0/8	37 5/8	6	6	Woody Ridge	AZ	Oscar Dale Porter	1982	146
352 4/8	54 2/8	52 1/8	37 2/8	6	6	Coconino County	AZ	John F. Gurasich	1988	147
352 1/8	53 2/8	53 1/8	36 3/8	6	6	Petroleum County	MT	Gorm Scarpholt	1987	148
352 0/8	51 4/8	53 0/8	38 5/8	6	7	Coconino County	AZ	Bill Elmer	1981	149
352 0/8	51 3/8	51 2/8	43 6/8	6	6	Powell County	MT	Philip L. Karper	1987	149
352 0/8	49 4/8	51 0/8	44 3/8	8	7	Catron County	NM	Tom Hoffman	1991	149
351 7/8	50 6/8	50 2/8	40 4/8	7	6	Crook County	OR	Curtis Demaris	1983	152
351 7/8	46 4/8	46 4/8	39 5/8	7	7	Park County	MT	Randy F. Petrich	1991	152
351 4/8	51 7/8	51 2/8	39 4/8	7	7	Coconino County	AZ	Marvin L. Slaughter	1979	154
351 4/8	50 6/8	49 7/8	40 0/8	6	6	Grant County	OR	Curtis Demaris	1980	154
351 4/8	56 5/8	56 0/8	46 4/8	6	6	Coconino County	AZ	John F. Gurasich	1986	154
351 4/8	43 7/8	45 3/8	40 0/8	6	6	Lincoln County	NM	Terry Arnim	1986	154
351 3/8	49 6/8	54 2/8	48 2/8	8	7	Grant County	OR	Bob Lindsay	1981	158
351 3/8	50 3/8	50 4/8	39 1/8	6	6	Millarville	ALB	Barry Pocha	1991	158
351 3/8	53 6/8	55 0/8	40 3/8	6	6	Greenlee County	AZ	Dennis Jensen	1991	158
351 2/8	55 6/8	53 5/8	41 6/8	6	6	Coconino County	AZ	Jay Elmer	1977	161
351 2/8	51 5/8	50 3/8	34 0/8	7	7	Missoula County	MT	James P. Loughran	1986	161
351 1/8	54 0/8	52 3/8	40 3/8	6	6	Lincoln County	NM	Frank Scott	1989	163
351 0/8	54 6/8	51 3/8	36 0/8	6	6	Greenlee County	AZ	Jim Coleman	1987	164
351 0/8	51 7/8	51 6/8	38 2/8	6	6	Canmore	ALB	Gunter Lemke	1987	164
350 6/8	53 5/8	53 0/8	40 2/8	6	6	Sheridan County	WY	Kurt M. Baughman	1980	166
350 5/8	49 7/8	49 5/8	40 6/8	7	6	Catron County	NM	Cary Cuba	1987	167
350 5/8	53 4/8	52 6/8	39 3/8	6	6	Catron County	NM	Billy R. Leach	1992	167
350 3/8	48 7/8	48 5/8	41 7/8	8	7	Fergus County	MT	G. L. 'Buck' Damone	1981	169
350 2/8	51 6/8	48 7/8	40 2/8	6	6	Routt County	CO	Mark L. Houslet	1977	170
350 2/8	53 4/8	53 1/8	41 2/8	6	6	Sandoval County	NM	Jose Montalvo	1981	170
350 1/8	50 2/8	52 5/8	37 7/8	6	6	Cibola County	NM	Ted Shinn	1987	172
350 1/8	54 7/8	52 5/8	44 7/8	6	7	Summit County	CO	Jeffrey J. Granowsky	1987	172
350 0/8	53 1/8	51 5/8	38 6/8	6	6	Sandoval County	NM	Tom David	1984	174
350 0/8	51 6/8	50 2/8	33 6/8	6	6	Catron County	NM	Philip G. McClelland	1988	174
350 0/8	51 6/8	53 6/8	41 4/8	6	6	Catron County	NM	Eddie Claypool	1990	174
349 7/8	50 1/8	51 1/8	48 5/8	6	6	Crook County	OR	Dale Shiery	1984	177
349 7/8	43 6/8	46 0/8	38 1/8	6	6	Catron County	NM	Kenny T. Rhodes	1991	177
349 6/8	53 0/8	52 6/8	41 6/8	6	6	Wheeler County	OR	Dale Shiery	1983	179
349 5/8	46 0/8	44 4/8	37 1/8	6	6	Huerfano County	CO	Richard L. Doman	1972	180
349 5/8	51 4/8	52 2/8	40 4/8	8	7	Coconino County	AZ	Cindi J. Richardson	1991	180
349 5/8	50 5/8	49 7/8	33 7/8	6	7	Taos County	NM	Michael R. Deschamps	1992	180
349 3/8	52 2/8	51 7/8	36 7/8	6	6	Fergus County	MT	Charles R. Bowman	1966	183
349 3/8	50 4/8	45 6/8	46 1/8	6	6	Park County	CO	Gary Jones	1984	183
349 3/8	53 3/8	54 6/8	43 1/8	6	6	Apache County	AZ	David Sullivan	1986	183
349 2/8	50 6/8	51 0/8	39 4/8	7	6	Clackamas County	OR	Paul Smith	1984	186
349 1/8	56 4/8	60 2/8	45 3/8	6	7	Coconino County	AZ	Alan R. Miller	1975	187
349 1/8	59 4/8	58 6/8	45 5/8	6	6	San Miguel County	NM	James L. Maves	1991	187
349 0/8	51 1/8	47 6/8	39 2/8	6	6	Los Alamos County	NM	Chuck Adams	1982	189
348 6/8	50 1/8	50 2/8	37 0/8	6	6	Phillips County	MT	Ron Bachmeier	1990	190
348 6/8	48 1/8	50 4/8	48 5/8	7	6	Mora County	NM	George P. Mann	1990	190
348 5/8	52 2/8	53 5/8	46 3/8	6	6	Caribou County	ID	Kenneth P. Kelley	1991	192
348 4/8	55 0/8	55 0/8	43 6/8	6	6	Coconino County	AZ	Bob Jensen	1981	193
348 4/8	45 3/8	44 6/8	41 6/8	6	6	Bonneville County	ID	Ronald L. Mueller	1982	193
348 3/8	50 0/8	51 7/8	34 4/8	7	7	Pierce County	WA	John Lyday	1984	195
348 2/8	30 7/8	47 3/8	34 4/8	6	7	Rio Blanco County	CO	Clark Gallup	1976	196
348 2/8	50 0/8	50 4/8	41 6/8	6	7	Carbon County	UT	Rick G. Huempfner	1989	196
348 2/8	47 7/8	48 2/8	39 2/8	6	6	Sanders County	MT	Glen Haas	1991	196
348 0/8	53 4/8	53 6/8	43 6/8	6	6	Sheridan County	WY	Mark S. Hutchins	1992	199
347 7/8	49 2/8	47 2/8	36 5/8	6	6	Swan River	MAN	Carl Robblee	1988	200
347 6/8	51 4/8	47 6/8	38 0/8	6	6	Valley County	MT	Greg Zahn	1981	201
347 6/8	49 6/8	52 1/8	38 6/8	6	6	Phillips County	MT	Craig Hall	1986	201
347 5/8	54 4/8	54 1/8	41 3/8	6	6	Coconino County	AZ	Allen L. King II	1992	203
347 4/8	50 2/8	49 5/8	45 6/8	7	6	Fremont County	ID	Bob Baird	1961	204
347 4/8	48 2/8	48 5/8	38 0/8	6	6	Fergus County	MT	Mark DeBoo	1988	204
347 1/8	54 1/8	53 2/8	37 3/8	6	6	Clackamas County	OR	Bill Lancaster	1986	206
347 0/8	49 1/8	51 2/8	36 0/8	7	8	Apache County	AZ	Jesus T. Guerena	1988	207
346 7/8	54 1/8	51 4/8	35 5/8	7	7	Lake County	MT	Scott Ganz	1984	208
346 7/8	50 7/8	51 7/8	37 5/8	6	6	Mora County	NM	James L. Romero	1987	208
346 6/8	44 2/8	45 4/8	41 0/8	6	6	Bighorn Mountain	WY	John Yeager	1980	210

SCORE	LENGTH OF MAIN BEAM		INSIDE SPREAD	NUMBER OF POINTS		AREA	STATE/ PROVINCE	HUNTER'S NAME	DATE	RANK
	R	L		R	L					
346 5/8	52 6/8	53 6/8	44 5/8	7	6	San Miguel County	NM	Frank C. Sciorilli	1977	211
346 4/8	51 4/8	51 1/8	42 5/8	7	6	Coconino County	AZ	Brett Kendall	1990	212
346 1/8	50 7/8	50 0/8	40 7/8	7	8	White Pine County	NV	James R. Puryear	1988	213
346 1/8	56 2/8	51 3/8	39 5/8	7	6	Catron County	NM	Teddy Orr	1992	213
345 7/8	52 5/8	52 0/8	41 5/8	7	6	Blaine County	ID	Danny F. Watson	1977	215
345 7/8	47 6/8	47 4/8	36 1/8	6	7	White Pine County	NV	Gregg Tanner	1989	215
345 7/8	59 1/8	57 4/8	35 5/8	6	6	Catron County	NM	A. E. McCaskill	1991	215
345 7/8	52 6/8	52 2/8	42 3/8	6	6	Phillips County	MT	Michael J. McFate	1992	215
345 6/8	54 0/8	55 6/8	40 0/8	6	6	Graham County	AZ	Steve M. Titla	1987	219
345 4/8	52 1/8	52 3/8	37 4/8	7	7	Ravalli County	MT	Howard Nichols	1983	220
345 1/8	49 2/8	51 7/8	43 7/8	6	6	Catron County	NM	Ron Adam	1987	221
345 0/8	52 3/8	55 0/8	37 4/8	6	7	Archuleta County	CO	Val M. Koeberlein	1989	222
344 6/8	53 6/8	55 0/8	41 0/8	8	7	Coconino County	AZ	Les Shelton	1979	223
344 6/8	50 7/8	49 3/8	38 6/8	7	7	Coconino County	AZ	Mark R. Harvey	1986	223
344 6/8	53 4/8	52 7/8	34 0/8	7	7	King County	WA	Robin F. Buck	1989	223
344 3/8	52 0/8	52 6/8	45 1/8	6	6	Lincoln County	MT	Lance Sink	1984	226
344 3/8	50 0/8	49 7/8	36 3/8	7	7	Petroleum County	MT	Dennis R. Thompson	1985	226
344 2/8	49 0/8	48 4/8	38 4/8	6	6	Ravalli County	MT	Steven Welty	1987	228
344 0/8	49 7/8	52 7/8	41 4/8	6	7	Catron County	NM	Wayne Ludington	1985	229
343 7/8	49 0/8	49 4/8	42 3/8	6	6	Union County	OR	Craig Gorham	1983	230
343 6/8	45 6/8	46 2/8	45 2/8	6	6	Catron County	NM	Russell Gash	1990	231
343 5/8	52 4/8	55 3/8	38 7/8	6	7	Coconino County	AZ	J. R. Wilhelmy	1976	232
343 4/8	49 2/8	46 6/8	49 5/8	6	6	Grand County	CO	Leon Lambert	1981	233
343 4/8	49 2/8	47 0/8	37 6/8	6	6	Lemhi County	ID	Roger Brockhoff	1985	233
343 4/8	51 4/8	52 1/8	38 4/8	6	7	Socorro County	NM	Richard Dewey	1986	233
343 2/8	52 2/8	51 2/8	40 0/8	6	6	Idaho County	ID	Mike Schlegel	1978	236
342 7/8	54 3/8	54 3/8	42 2/8	8	8	Grand County	CO	G. Fred Asbell	1980	237
342 7/8	56 3/8	56 1/8	43 0/8	7	6	Catron County	NM	Bill Elmer	1991	237
342 6/8	48 6/8	49 4/8	46 0/8	5	6	Catron County	NM	Carlton Armstrong	1990	239
342 6/8	51 4/8	52 6/8	41 4/8	6	6	Catron County	NM	Glenn W. Isler	1992	239
342 5/8	48 4/8	46 6/8	38 3/8	6	6	Routt County	CO	Brad Jones	1987	241
342 5/8	53 2/8	49 4/8	36 1/8	6	6	Coconino County	AZ	Victor Lee	1991	241
342 4/8	55 4/8	55 0/8	42 0/8	6	6	Morgan County	UT	Hugh H. Hogle	1990	243
342 2/8	49 7/8	49 2/8	37 2/8	6	6	Grant County	NM	Larry M. Sellers	1985	244
342 2/8	49 2/8	48 6/8	35 1/8	6	7	Uintah County	UT	Charles "Smiley" Denver	1988	244
342 2/8	49 6/8	48 4/8	35 6/8	8	7	Coconino County	AZ	Gary Steinmann	1991	244
342 2/8	56 6/8	56 4/8	35 4/8	7	7	Catron County	NM	David H. Boland	1992	244
342 1/8	52 3/8	52 4/8	45 1/8	6	6	Routt County	CO	Jerry A. Krueger	1981	248
342 1/8	53 7/8	50 4/8	34 7/8	6	7	Jackson County	OR	J. T. Tepper	1986	248
342 0/8	58 6/8	59 0/8	46 6/8	6	6	Cibola County	NM	Dois R. Chesshir	1986	250
341 6/8	54 7/8	53 1/8	44 2/8	6	6	Greenlee County	AZ	Pete Shepley	1983	251
341 6/8	55 3/8	53 3/8	45 6/8	6	6	Garfield County	CO	Gary Frauenkron	1983	251
341 6/8	55 3/8	55 0/8	33 5/8	7	6	Catron County	NM	Mike Hillis	1988	251
341 6/8	51 4/8	50 1/8	38 3/8	7	6	Grant County	NM	Dick Stoll	1989	251
341 5/8	54 4/8	56 2/8	44 3/8	6	6	Socorro County	NM	Ross Johnson	1982	255
341 5/8	54 1/8	52 2/8	45 1/8	6	6	Garfield County	MT	Darryl Turner	1985	255
341 5/8	47 0/8	47 2/8	39 3/8	6	6	Clackamas County	OR	Paul Smith	1987	255
341 5/8	48 7/8	46 5/8	33 7/8	6	6	Navajo County	AZ	Leon W. Smith	1989	255
341 4/8	45 6/8	47 5/8	37 4/8	6	6	Las Animas County	CO	Douglas F. Murray	1974	259
341 4/8	53 4/8	54 6/8	36 6/8	6	6	Pitkin County	CO	Nelson Harrington	1977	259
341 4/8	50 5/8	48 5/8	39 4/8	6	6	Adams County	ID	Emery Meeks	1982	259
341 4/8	52 3/8	51 7/8	46 0/8	7	7	Routt County	CO	Todd Bandemer	1991	259
341 3/8	47 7/8	48 1/8	44 5/8	6	6	Chaffee County	CO	Tom E. Bowman	1979	263
341 3/8	54 0/8	52 3/8	37 7/8	9	7	Missoula County	MT	Ted Miller	1984	263
341 3/8	54 1/8	51 6/8	42 3/8	6	6	McKinley County	NM	Glenn W. Isler	1988	263
341 3/8	49 7/8	50 4/8	46 2/8	7	7	Canmore	ALB	Lee Oshust	1989	263
341 3/8	55 6/8	53 4/8	35 3/8	7	7	Klickitat County	WA	Bill "Razz" Philley, Jr.	1991	263
341 2/8	53 0/8	54 6/8	44 6/8	6	7	Coconino County	AZ	Dean Dunaway	1991	268
341 0/8	54 2/8	54 1/8	40 6/8	6	6	Catron County	NM	Ronnie Coburn	1986	269
341 0/8	53 0/8	53 0/8	42 6/8	6	6	Custer County	ID	John R. Sample	1986	269
340 7/8	48 1/8	47 4/8	37 5/8	6	6	Carbon County	WY	Roger Swensen	1977	271
340 7/8	56 3/8	56 4/8	39 5/8	7	7	Yakima County	WA	Randy Kaech	1986	271
340 6/8	56 6/8	59 5/8	33 6/8	6	6	Coconino County	AZ	Earnest E. Milton	1976	273
340 6/8	54 0/8	51 7/8	41 2/8	7	6	Petroleum County	MT	John 'Rosey' Roseland	1983	273
340 6/8	46 0/8	46 4/8	40 2/8	6	6	Granite County	MT	Tom Adams	1991	273
340 5/8	47 3/8	48 6/8	33 1/8	6	6	Nordegg	ALB	Thaddaus Fenske	1978	276
340 5/8	54 5/8	53 2/8	39 1/8	6	6	Coconino County	AZ	Gregory S. Wood	1990	276
340 5/8	52 4/8	54 6/8	41 3/8	6	6	Sierra County	NM	Dr. Hamid Massiha	1991	276
340 5/8	54 2/8	53 7/8	40 7/8	6	7	Coconino County	AZ	Paul Hicks	1991	276
340 4/8	51 5/8	49 1/8	41 2/8	6	6	Sanders County	MT	Walt Borgmann	1983	280

362

SCORE	LENGTH OF MAIN BEAM		INSIDE SPREAD	NUMBER OF POINTS		AREA	STATE/ PROVINCE	HUNTER'S NAME	DATE	RANK
	R	L		R	L					
340 4/8	51 0/8	52 4/8	42 0/8	6	7	Catron County	NM	Brice McWethy	1985	280
340 4/8	50 6/8	50 5/8	39 2/8	6	7	Sierra County	NM	Tony L. Jones	1988	280
340 3/8	51 0/8	51 1/8	38 1/8	6	6	Crook County	OR	Curtis Edwards	1989	283
340 2/8	53 3/8	54 2/8	40 4/8	6	6	Missoula County	MT	David M. Anderson	1978	284
340 2/8	50 4/8	51 3/8	36 7/8	7	6	Socorro County	NM	Randy B. Furr	1983	284
340 2/8	54 4/8	56 4/8	43 2/8	6	7	Catron County	NM	John Fehrenbacher	1986	284
340 1/8	52 2/8	52 6/8	46 7/8	6	6	Coconino County	AZ	Richard H. Wetnight	1984	287
340 0/8	49 2/8	50 7/8	37 4/8	7	7	Flathead County	MT	Henry Herman	1984	288
339 7/8	52 6/8	53 3/8	38 1/8	6	6	Yavapai County	AZ	Gene Barcak	1991	289
339 6/8	47 7/8	46 7/8	41 4/8	6	6	Lewis & Clark County	MT	Doug J. Powell	1983	290
339 6/8	51 4/8	51 4/8	46 4/8	6	6	Otero County	NM	Bonnie A. Allen	1987	290
339 5/8	51 6/8	53 5/8	47 1/8	6	6	Coconino County	AZ	Bruce D. Ludeke	1977	292
339 5/8	45 2/8	43 3/8	44 7/8	6	7	Bighorn Mountains	WY	Edward F. Hanlon	1979	292
339 4/8	49 0/8	48 7/8	38 0/8	7	7	Grant County	OR	Dan Dorn	1986	294
339 4/8	51 3/8	50 5/8	39 2/8	6	6	Mineral County	MT	Tom Porter	1986	294
339 4/8	51 0/8	51 2/8	38 0/8	6	7	Colfax County	NM	Christopher Green	1990	294
339 3/8	48 4/8	49 5/8	42 1/8	6	6	Cibola County	NM	Delbert Mariano	1980	297
339 3/8	47 4/8	44 7/8	43 6/8	6	7	Petroleum County	MT	Steven A. Barstow	1989	297
339 2/8	51 7/8	51 0/8	40 6/8	7	6	Fremont County	ID	Gary Skoy	1981	299
339 1/8	50 5/8	49 5/8	42 6/8	6	7	Coconino County	AZ	Stretch Penberthy	1987	300
339 1/8	56 0/8	52 7/8	39 3/8	6	6	Sublette County	WY	Tony Burchett	1988	300
339 1/8	52 2/8	52 2/8	42 1/8	6	8	Grant County	OR	Brad Miller	1988	300
339 1/8	47 5/8	46 3/8	40 3/8	9	8	Catron County	NM	Danny V. Bennett	1990	300
339 1/8	44 1/8	44 4/8	34 1/8	7	7	Bonner County	ID	H. Dale Stone	1990	300
338 6/8	45 6/8	45 6/8	43 0/8	6	7	Greenlee County	AZ	Jed Dahar	1989	305
338 6/8	47 4/8	45 6/8	44 0/8	7	6	Beaverhead County	MT	Gene Loder	1991	305
338 5/8	50 4/8	53 4/8	42 1/8	6	6	Rio Arriba County	NM	Lee Braudt	1983	307
338 5/8	49 2/8	48 4/8	36 5/8	6	6	Lincoln County	WY	Doug Jenkins	1986	307
338 3/8	55 5/8	54 0/8	36 7/8	6	6	Sheridan County	WY	Mike Barrett	1981	309
338 2/8	48 1/8	52 2/8	38 3/8	7	7	Garfield County	MT	Richard R. Chamberlin	1989	310
338 2/8	47 7/8	47 4/8	36 2/8	7	6	Catron County	NM	Nick Arnett	1990	310
338 2/8	49 0/8	51 0/8	39 6/8	7	7	Deer Lodge County	MT	Stephen Herrera	1990	310
338 1/8	50 4/8	50 5/8	37 1/8	7	7	Lincoln County	NM	Kurt Hollis	1987	313
338 0/8	47 4/8	46 6/8	45 5/8	7	6	Caribou County	ID	Jim L. Fowler	1987	314
338 0/8	53 5/8	54 7/8	41 6/8	6	7	Catron County	NM	James Baumgardner	1990	314
338 0/8	51 4/8	52 5/8	41 0/8	6	6	Coconino County	AZ	Mike Leach	1991	314
337 6/8	45 0/8	46 0/8	37 4/8	6	7	Boulder County	CO	Roger Schuett	1977	317
337 6/8	55 2/8	55 2/8	45 6/8	5	5	Socorro County	NM	Wesley Henderson	1986	317
337 6/8	51 1/8	50 3/8	38 4/8	7	6	Coconino County	AZ	Robert Dishmon	1991	317
337 6/8	47 6/8	49 0/8	42 0/8	7	6	Washakie County	WY	Roger Peabody	1991	317
337 6/8	48 2/8	47 4/8	43 2/8	6	6	Otero County	NM	Allen Dalton	1991	317
337 5/8	49 1/8	49 6/8	39 1/8	6	6	Granite County	MT	George E. Wood	1978	322
337 5/8	52 1/8	52 6/8	37 3/8	6	6	Missoula County	MT	Mel Nyman, Jr.	1983	322
337 5/8	49 3/8	51 4/8	36 1/8	6	6	Coconino County	AZ	Danny Eloy Martinez	1985	322
337 4/8	52 3/8	54 5/8	41 4/8	7	6	Coconino County	AZ	Alan Blanchard	1972	325
337 4/8	63 6/8	62 3/8	42 0/8	6	6	Coconino County	AZ	Gregory B. Minton	1992	325
337 3/8	53 0/8	49 2/8	42 1/8	6	5	Mesa County	CO	Mike Flores	1970	327
337 2/8	50 4/8	53 3/8	44 4/8	6	6	Coconino County	AZ	Henry L. Roberts	1990	328
337 1/8	51 3/8	50 0/8	37 1/8	6	6	Catron County	NM	Larry Evanson	1992	329
337 0/8	52 4/8	51 4/8	38 2/8	6	6	Socorro County	NM	Ron White	1976	330
337 0/8	57 6/8	57 6/8	36 2/8	7	7	Lewis County	WA	Terry I LaFrance	1984	330
337 0/8	49 2/8	49 4/8	39 4/8	6	6	Idaho County	ID	Roger O. Wyant	1987	330
336 7/8	49 3/8	48 0/8	43 1/8	7	7	Apache County	AZ	Eric Penrod	1982	333
336 6/8	50 7/8	51 3/8	34 6/8	6	7	Uintah County	UT	Everett Burson	1981	334
336 6/8	53 5/8	53 3/8	39 4/8	6	6	Taos County	NM	Jeff Lampe	1992	334
336 4/8	56 2/8	55 6/8	36 6/8	6	7	Coconino County	AZ	David M. Geiger	1990	336
336 4/8	50 7/8	50 1/8	41 4/8	7	6	Meagher County	MT	George O. Johnson	1991	336
336 4/8	51 2/8	48 7/8	43 7/8	7	6	Big Horn County	WY	Lance Crawford	1992	336
336 3/8	47 7/8	48 2/8	34 1/8	6	6	Meagher County	MT	Ronald K. Granneman	1973	339
336 3/8	56 0/8	54 5/8	41 3/8	6	6	Custer County	ID	Gregg Welch	1984	339
336 2/8	52 4/8	50 6/8	33 2/8	6	6	Lewis & Clark County	MT	Ronald K. Granneman	1979	341
336 1/8	54 6/8	52 1/8	40 2/8	7	6	Catron County	NM	R. Grant Clawson	1986	342
336 1/8	48 0/8	48 2/8	34 6/8	7	7	Fergus County	MT	Randall L. Zeman	1991	342
336 0/8	50 0/8	50 1/8	42 4/8	6	6	Granite County	MT	Tom Storm	1982	344
336 0/8	50 3/8	50 6/8	40 4/8	5	7	White Pine County	NV	Don Snodgrass	1989	344
335 6/8	53 4/8	53 1/8	37 6/8	7	8	Phillips County	MT	John 'Rosey' Roseland	1977	346
335 6/8	51 2/8	53 6/8	39 2/8	6	6	Shoshone County	ID	Ernest W. Clanton	1983	346
335 6/8	51 3/8	51 6/8	40 0/8	8	7	Fergus County	MT	Larry L. Schweitzer	1985	346
335 6/8	49 1/8	50 0/8	41 6/8	6	6	Spray Lakes	ALB	Danny Moore	1987	346
335 6/8	53 2/8	53 0/8	51 4/8	6	6	Catron County	NM	Scot P. McClelland	1988	346

SCORE	LENGTH OF MAIN BEAM R	LENGTH OF MAIN BEAM L	INSIDE SPREAD	NUMBER OF POINTS R	NUMBER OF POINTS L	AREA	STATE/ PROVINCE	HUNTER'S NAME	DATE	RANK
335 6/8	51 2/8	49 4/8	41 4/8	7	6	Coconino County	AZ	James Whitaker	1989	346
335 6/8	53 4/8	52 3/8	41 2/8	6	7	Powell County	MT	Theodore J. Poper	1991	346
335 5/8	52 6/8	50 7/8	43 3/8	6	6	Catron County	NM	Barrett L. Lemmon	1991	353
335 4/8	47 4/8	48 6/8	49 0/8	6	6	Clearwater County	ID	Robert J. Kreisher	1958	354
335 4/8	52 0/8	52 6/8	45 4/8	7	7	Skamania County	WA	Ted Jaycox	1985	354
335 1/8	46 4/8	46 2/8	38 1/8	6	6	Camas County	ID	Derek Trent	1991	356
335 1/8	51 6/8	50 7/8	40 3/8	6	6	Coconino County	AZ	David J. Martin	1992	356
335 1/8	50 6/8	51 5/8	40 3/8	6	6	Phillips County	MT	Tom S. Crabill	1992	356
335 0/8	50 7/8	50 5/8	40 0/8	6	6	Caribou County	ID	Charles Humphreys	1977	359
335 0/8	53 3/8	52 0/8	39 4/8	6	6	Sanders County	MT	Gil Gilbertson	1984	359
335 0/8	50 6/8	49 1/8	34 2/8	8	7	Petroleum County	MT	Craig Wagner	1992	359
334 6/8	51 4/8	51 7/8	44 6/8	6	6	Summit County	CO	Michael Beckwith	1976	362
334 6/8	52 0/8	52 2/8	43 0/8	6	6	Custer County	ID	Hal J. Dillashaw	1991	362
334 6/8	54 3/8	52 4/8	36 0/8	6	7	White Pine County	NV	Gene A. Jones	1992	362
334 5/8	50 0/8	49 5/8	34 1/8	7	7	Garfield County	CO	Darren Mack	1989	365
334 4/8	49 7/8	48 5/8	46 4/8	6	6	Gunnison County	CO	Roy M. Goodwin	1988	366
334 3/8	53 3/8	52 5/8	38 5/8	6	6	Coconino County	AZ	Stephen Jon McGaughey	1988	367
334 2/8	52 5/8	49 0/8	38 4/8	6	6	Sweetwater County	WY	Lawrence Branson	1984	368
334 2/8	47 7/8	46 4/8	44 0/8	6	6	Albany County	WY	Thomas Bradach	1988	368
334 2/8	50 3/8	49 7/8	32 6/8	6	6	White Pine County	NV	Richard A. Hanson	1992	368
334 1/8	48 3/8	51 0/8	39 5/8	6	6	Madison County	MT	John Aalto	1979	371
334 1/8	46 2/8	49 2/8	43 5/8	6	6	Boulder County	CO	Billy E. Corley	1991	371
334 0/8	45 5/8	47 6/8	41 2/8	7	6	Boulder County	CO	Gus Roe	1984	373
333 7/8	51 6/8	49 0/8	34 6/8	7	7	Fergus County	MT	Edwin Evans	1983	374
333 6/8	49 4/8	49 4/8	45 0/8	6	6	Baker County	OR	Russell B. Jones	1946	375
333 6/8	53 4/8	52 2/8	44 2/8	7	6	Sheridan County	WY	Chuck McKenzie	1976	375
333 4/8	47 2/8	47 0/8	35 0/8	6	6	Waterton Park	ALB	Barry Linklater	1987	377
333 4/8	49 1/8	48 0/8	39 6/8	7	7	Canmore	ALB	Jordon Ohrn	1988	377
333 3/8	45 6/8	47 4/8	39 7/8	6	6	Catron County	NM	Gary A Littauer	1984	379
333 3/8	46 0/8	46 0/8	34 3/8	7	6	Union County	OR	Mark Simmons	1985	379
333 3/8	54 7/8	55 3/8	43 2/8	6	7	Canmore	ALB	Brian Francis	1986	379
333 2/8	47 0/8	48 4/8	39 4/8	6	6	Jefferson County	CO	Jerry Gruenberg	1988	382
333 2/8	52 6/8	54 0/8	38 0/8	7	6	Teton County	WY	Jerry W. Lashuay	1988	382
333 2/8	47 1/8	46 5/8	41 4/8	6	6	Carbon County	UT	Tom Paluso	1989	382
333 2/8	50 0/8	50 2/8	37 6/8	6	6	Catron County	NM	Bill Powell	1991	382
333 1/8	41 3/8	46 2/8	41 3/8	6	6	Grand County	CO	Dennis Wehling	1981	386
332 7/8	48 4/8	49 3/8	41 3/8	7	7	Grant County	OR	Neil Hinton	1985	387
332 7/8	52 1/8	49 6/8	36 1/8	6	6	Phillips County	MT	Todd A. Erickson	1989	387
332 7/8	51 3/8	53 7/8	40 1/8	6	6	Catron County	NM	Marvin H. Walter	1992	387
332 7/8	48 1/8	47 3/8	41 7/8	7	7	Valley County	ID	Tracy Hunt	1992	387
332 6/8	53 7/8	51 6/8	43 2/8	6	6	Albany County	WY	Pat McAteer	1981	391
332 6/8	52 0/8	49 2/8	37 0/8	6	6	Catron County	NM	John Howard	1984	391
332 6/8	51 1/8	51 7/8	32 0/8	7	6	King County	WA	Curtis H. Fowler	1987	391
332 6/8	51 6/8	50 4/8	40 4/8	6	6	Carbon County	UT	Dan Summers	1989	391
332 4/8	54 4/8	53 2/8	41 6/8	7	7	Apache County	AZ	Steve Schaufer	1989	395
332 4/8	47 2/8	47 0/8	45 1/8	6	7	Coconino County	AZ	Gregory B. Minton	1991	395
332 3/8	54 4/8	52 0/8	33 7/8	7	6	Apache County	AZ	Charles G. Dawe	1986	397
332 3/8	49 4/8	49 4/8	42 7/8	6	6	Coconino County	AZ	Jerry Vogel	1990	397
332 1/8	53 4/8	54 6/8	36 7/8	6	6	Coconino County	AZ	James R. Moore	1980	399
332 0/8	49 2/8	50 5/8	38 2/8	7	7	Caribou County	ID	Joseph M. Hulse	1967	400
332 0/8	52 0/8	51 6/8	42 0/8	7	6	Clearwater County	ID	Don West	1983	400
332 0/8	51 3/8	50 6/8	37 2/8	6	6	Custer County	ID	Delos G. Robinson	1987	400
332 0/8	49 5/8	49 0/8	37 0/8	6	6	Catron County	NM	Christopher Green	1990	400
332 0/8	47 1/8	46 1/8	38 4/8	6	6	Clearwater County	ID	Richard L. Sandusky	1990	400
332 0/8	52 3/8	51 0/8	56 1/8	6	7	Coconino County	AZ	Andrew L. Grannan	1991	400
332 0/8	50 3/8	49 6/8	37 2/8	6	6	Grant County	OR	Robert Reed	1992	400
331 7/8	53 3/8	50 4/8	36 7/8	6	7	Los Alamos County	NM	Robert Barrie	1986	407
331 7/8	50 0/8	50 5/8	41 3/8	6	6	Catron County	NM	Thomas Blaeser	1991	407
331 6/8	48 0/8	49 6/8	45 7/8	7	6	Canmore	ALB	Ken Madsen	1985	409
331 6/8	48 0/8	50 4/8	37 2/8	6	6	Catron County	NM	Randall S. Madding	1988	409
331 5/8	51 3/8	48 6/8	43 7/8	6	6	Sublette County	WY	Rod Knight	1983	411
331 5/8	49 0/8	47 4/8	41 5/8	6	6	Fremont County	ID	Rick Harris	1986	411
331 5/8	48 0/8	46 5/8	35 1/8	6	7	Flathead County	MT	David L. Thompson	1991	411
331 4/8	47 1/8	48 5/8	40 6/8	6	6	Shoshone County	ID	John C. Dawson II	1990	414
331 4/8	53 0/8	54 7/8	42 6/8	7	6	Coconino County	AZ	Mike Norman Oliver	1990	414
331 4/8	54 0/8	53 5/8	39 4/8	6	6	Boulder County	CO	Ron Readmond	1991	414
331 4/8	51 2/8	49 3/8	38 4/8	7	8	Coconino County	AZ	Kevin Forsman	1992	414
331 1/8	48 3/8	48 1/8	38 3/8	6	6	Sheridan County	WY	Mike Barrett	1984	418
331 0/8	51 5/8	52 5/8	45 2/8	7	6	Sublette County	WY	Clair Adams	1987	419
330 7/8	53 5/8	50 4/8	39 5/8	6	6	Coconino County	AZ	Jeff W. Elmer	1985	420

SCORE	LENGTH OF MAIN BEAM R L		INSIDE SPREAD	NUMBER OF POINTS R L		AREA	STATE/ PROVINCE	HUNTER'S NAME	DATE	RANK
330 7/8	50 2/8	50 0/8	41 1/8	6	6	Catron County	NM	J. D. Mills	1988	420
330 7/8	52 1/8	51 6/8	38 7/8	7	7	Coconino County	AZ	Douglas W. Koepsel	1992	420
330 4/8	44 6/8	46 4/8	38 1/8	6	6	Latah County	ID	John K. Pell	1964	423
330 4/8	54 7/8	54 3/8	34 0/8	7	6	Shoshone County	ID	Kelly Thompson	1986	423
330 4/8	55 3/8	55 4/8	38 0/8	6	6	Coconino County	AZ	Larry Moore	1991	423
330 3/8	50 6/8	49 1/8	38 5/8	6	6	Madison County	MT	Tom Koelzer	1975	426
330 3/8	53 6/8	52 1/8	39 5/8	8	10	Coconino County	AZ	James L. Ludrigson	1985	426
330 3/8	48 6/8	48 5/8	38 7/8	6	6	Grant County	NM	Jack W. Hooper	1989	426
330 3/8	53 1/8	53 4/8	42 5/8	7	8	Fergus County	MT	John Fleharty	1992	426
330 1/8	50 1/8	50 0/8	42 7/8	6	6	Grant County	OR	James M. Carter	1986	430
330 0/8	53 2/8	53 5/8	45 0/8	6	6	Socorro County	NM	Ron White	1977	431
330 0/8	48 7/8	49 0/8	37 0/8	7	7	Sanders County	MT	Steve Larson	1981	431
330 0/8	52 7/8	50 4/8	33 4/8	6	6	Petroleum County	MT	John Fleharty	1985	431
330 0/8	46 7/8	49 7/8	43 6/8	6	6	Albany County	WY	Paul Ayotte	1985	431
329 7/8	46 1/8	45 1/8	36 7/8	6	6	Eagle County	CO	Jeffrey A. Duckworth	1981	435
329 7/8	51 4/8	48 6/8	39 3/8	6	6	Powell County	MT	Marlon J. Clapham	1986	435
329 7/8	47 2/8	49 2/8	34 3/8	6	6	Crook County	OR	Terry Luther	1991	435
329 7/8	50 3/8	49 1/8	37 5/8	7	7	Catron County	NM	Donald M. Graves	1991	435
329 7/8	47 4/8	46 5/8	33 1/8	6	6	Phillips County	MT	Rick Miller	1992	435
329 6/8	49 1/8	49 0/8	37 4/8	6	6	Rio Blanco County	CO	Myles Keller	1974	440
329 6/8	48 1/8	47 6/8	38 0/8	6	6	Coconino County	AZ	Mike Moulton	1983	440
329 6/8	53 0/8	51 0/8	34 4/8	6	6	Phillips County	MT	Gregg Pauley	1987	440
329 6/8	44 0/8	47 0/8	36 6/8	6	6	Catron County	NM	Eddie Claypool	1991	440
329 6/8	57 2/8	58 0/8	50 0/8	6	6	Cibola County	NM	Johnny M. Perea	1991	440
329 5/8	42 1/8	44 7/8	34 2/8	6	7	Adams County	ID	Curtis Lemon	1978	445
329 5/8	54 6/8	52 7/8	40 5/8	6	7	Silver Bow County	MT	William E. Bullock	1981	445
329 4/8	47 4/8	47 3/8	43 2/8	6	6	Custer County	ID	Gary Kimball	1979	447
329 4/8	48 2/8	48 4/8	35 2/8	6	6	Catron County	NM	Donald W. Duewall	1982	447
329 4/8	49 2/8	51 4/8	45 0/8	6	8	Phillips County	MT	Dennis R. King	1989	447
329 3/8	55 4/8	51 1/8	37 2/8	7	6	Catron County	NM	James Scarbrough	1986	450
329 3/8	50 0/8	49 7/8	39 1/8	6	6	Gallatin County	MT	Mark Hanshue	1987	450
329 3/8	52 7/8	53 1/8	37 2/8	6	7	Lincoln County	NM	Henry Vega	1988	450
329 2/8	52 3/8	52 4/8	44 4/8	6	6	Valley County	ID	B. C. Cunningham	1969	453
329 2/8	50 1/8	52 4/8	35 6/8	6	6	Valley County	MT	Thomas L. Solem	1981	453
329 2/8	48 6/8	51 1/8	38 2/8	7	6	Bonneville County	ID	Paul H. Laver	1981	453
329 2/8	50 0/8	53 2/8	38 2/8	7	6	Sanders County	MT	Glenn Nerby	1991	453
329 1/8	47 7/8	49 4/8	40 1/8	6	6	Adams County	ID	Curt Lemmons	1965	457
329 1/8	51 5/8	53 7/8	44 3/8	7	7	Moffat County	CO	Glenn W. Pritchard	1972	457
329 1/8	44 6/8	44 2/8	37 0/8	6	6	Rio Blanco County	CO	Harold Boyack	1976	457
329 1/8	45 4/8	46 1/8	39 7/8	6	6	Mineral County	MT	Gary A. Hudson	1988	457
329 0/8	56 0/8	54 3/8	40 2/8	8	6	Yakima County	WA	Jerry Harris	1963	461
329 0/8	48 1/8	48 1/8	38 6/8	6	7	Sanders County	MT	Fred Mensik	1983	461
328 6/8	48 5/8	49 0/8	43 6/8	6	6	Crook County	OR	Gary Kiepert	1983	463
328 5/8	52 7/8	54 0/8	34 3/8	7	7	Catron County	NM	George F. Corriher	1991	464
328 4/8	50 1/8	47 6/8	39 0/8	6	6	Sanders County	MT	Kenneth B. Neubauer	1983	465
328 2/8	48 4/8	49 4/8	40 4/8	6	7	Crook County	OR	Scott Reed	1984	466
328 2/8	52 3/8	50 6/8	43 4/8	6	7	Adams County	ID	Ted Cutler/Craig Keyser	1985	466
328 2/8	52 0/8	52 6/8	37 2/8	6	6	Coconino County	AZ	Richard D. Tone	1989	466
328 1/8	44 7/8	44 3/8	41 3/8	6	6	Lewis County	WA	Larry F. Smith	1986	469
328 1/8	45 6/8	47 6/8	37 1/8	6	7	Albany County	WY	Brian L. Biel	1986	469
328 0/8	54 1/8	51 3/8	40 0/8	6	7	Coconino County	AZ	James L. Hyde	1977	471
328 0/8	44 2/8	44 3/8	39 6/8	6	6	Larimer County	CO	J. G. Hamblet, Jr.	1979	471
328 0/8	50 6/8	52 0/8	39 6/8	6	7	Coconino County	AZ	Clay Stazenski	1991	471
327 7/8	48 1/8	46 2/8	46 3/8	6	6	Lewis & Clark County	MT	Darrell J. Archey	1984	474
327 7/8	48 0/8	48 4/8	43 5/8	5	6	Cochrane	ALB	Rod Newsham	1986	474
327 6/8	51 6/8	53 1/8	36 2/8	6	6	Coconino County	AZ	Jim Parker	1989	476
327 6/8	50 7/8	52 6/8	40 0/8	6	6	Mesa County	CO	Brian Karsten	1991	476
327 5/8	48 5/8	49 4/8	38 3/8	6	6	Lincoln County	WY	Kirby Booth	1990	478
327 4/8	48 4/8	46 6/8	43 6/8	6	6	Beaverhead County	MT	Dave Knudsen	1974	479
327 4/8	49 4/8	47 4/8	40 4/8	6	6	Lewis & Clark County	MT	Richard J. Kornick	1980	479
327 4/8	49 6/8	48 0/8	39 0/8	6	6	Beaverhead County	MT	Roy F. Bach	1984	479
327 4/8	49 5/8	48 5/8	37 6/8	6	6	Yakima County	WA	Jim Rathbun	1989	479
327 3/8	47 4/8	47 0/8	34 3/8	7	7	Coconino County	AZ	Richard D. Tone	1991	483
327 1/8	50 3/8	48 2/8	43 3/8	6	6	Park County	MT	Dale Alt	1968	484
327 0/8	50 6/8	51 7/8	40 4/8	6	6	Clearwater County	ID	C. Randall Byers	1976	485
327 0/8	48 0/8	48 2/8	39 6/8	6	6	Catron County	NM	David Chavez	1981	485
327 0/8	50 0/8	50 2/8	36 0/8	6	7	Rossburn	MAN	Glen J. White	1986	485
327 0/8	48 7/8	47 0/8	37 4/8	7	6	Sandoval County	NM	Freddie Barber	1989	485
327 0/8	44 7/8	44 1/8	33 2/8	6	6	Meagher County	MT	Robert L. Crafts	1991	485
326 7/8	48 6/8	47 4/8	38 1/8	6	6	Custer County	CO	Rohn L. Garnhart	1990	490

Score	Length of Main Beam R	L	Inside Spread	Number of Points R	L	Area	State/ Province	Hunter's Name	Date	Rank
326 6/8	48 5/8	50 3/8	43 0/8	7	6	Bighorn Mountains	WY	Rick Mitchell	1981	491
326 6/8	50 4/8	47 4/8	48 2/8	6	7	Larimer County	CO	Tom Duncan	1983	491
326 6/8	46 6/8	46 4/8	39 4/8	6	6	Colfax County	NM	John L. Chapman	1984	491
326 6/8	52 1/8	51 5/8	35 6/8	6	6	Rio Arriba County	NM	Vincent R. Vicenti	1989	491
326 5/8	52 1/8	53 5/8	42 1/8	6	7	Coconino County	AZ	Larry Glasson	1975	495
326 5/8	48 3/8	50 3/8	40 7/8	6	6	Clackamas County	OR	William E. Lancaster	1987	495
326 5/8	47 2/8	47 3/8	39 1/8	6	6	Wallowa County	OR	Dusty Powers	1988	495
326 4/8	51 5/8	51 0/8	37 6/8	6	6	King County	WA	Leonard L Stolen	1984	498
326 4/8	53 1/8	52 1/8	36 0/8	6	6	Coconino County	AZ	John Coffman	1990	498
326 3/8	51 3/8	51 1/8	47 1/8	5	6	Socorro County	NM	Billy R. Spears	1976	500
326 3/8	55 0/8	55 4/8	39 3/8	6	6	Flathead County	MT	Phil Von Bargen	1976	500
326 2/8	48 3/8	53 3/8	38 0/8	7	7	Carbon County	UT	Scott Wilkins	1989	502
326 1/8	44 6/8	46 6/8	35 5/8	6	6	Lemhi County	ID	Ray Torrey	1967	503
326 1/8	54 2/8	54 5/8	37 5/8	6	6	Grand County	CO	Paul Adams	1977	503
326 0/8	51 1/8	50 6/8	46 2/8	7	6	Boulder County	CO	Duke Prentup	1977	505
326 0/8	51 4/8	51 3/8	38 4/8	6	6	Beaverhead County	MT	Scott P. Swan	1978	505
326 0/8	49 3/8	47 4/8	36 4/8	6	6	Catron County	NM	Randall Cooley	1984	505
326 0/8	53 1/8	49 2/8	39 6/8	6	6	Socorro County	NM	Ray Hatfield	1984	505
325 7/8	50 7/8	47 1/8	35 4/8	7	7	Idaho County	ID	Robert C. Mitchell	1978	509
325 7/8	45 3/8	45 1/8	34 5/8	6	6	Canmore	ALB	Douglas A. Parker	1984	509
325 6/8	49 1/8	51 5/8	43 6/8	6	6	Beaverhead County	MT	Bob Helming	1980	511
325 6/8	46 7/8	46 5/8	40 0/8	6	6	Marion County	OR	Ron Bergeron	1983	511
325 5/8	43 6/8	45 0/8	39 1/8	7	7	Beaverhead County	MT	Danny Moore	1983	513
325 5/8	51 2/8	52 3/8	41 5/8	6	6	Wheeler County	OR	Robert V. Martin	1986	513
325 4/8	49 6/8	50 3/8	40 4/8	6	6	Montrose County	CO	Carol Cassidy	1973	515
325 4/8	48 1/8	51 2/8	38 0/8	6	6	Catron County	NM	Steve Van Zile	1991	515
325 3/8	47 3/8	45 2/8	33 3/8	7	6	Benewah County	ID	Tim Chandler	1984	517
325 3/8	51 0/8	51 4/8	40 3/8	6	7	Coconino County	AZ	Les Shelton	1989	517
325 3/8	50 2/8	51 5/8	40 7/8	6	6	Coconino County	AZ	Gary D. Bills	1991	517
325 2/8	49 0/8	49 0/8	36 6/8	6	6	Caribou County	ID	Doug Foss	1986	520
325 2/8	49 1/8	49 3/8	39 6/8	6	6	Lemhi County	ID	Mike Benton	1989	520
325 1/8	48 3/8	49 3/8	39 5/8	6	6	Lincoln County	NM	John D. Fitzgibbon	1991	522
325 0/8	47 1/8	47 3/8	35 6/8	7	7	Silver Bow County	MT	Bob Gossack	1977	523
325 0/8	52 4/8	49 5/8	39 4/8	6	6	Catron County	NM	Courtney King	1985	523
325 0/8	44 7/8	51 0/8	45 2/8	6	6	Catron County	NM	Steve McCoy	1988	523
325 0/8	49 7/8	51 1/8	41 0/8	7	7	Rio Arriba County	NM	Gene White	1990	523
324 6/8	47 1/8	46 2/8	42 0/8	7	6	Coconino County	AZ	William S. Acheson	1979	527
324 6/8	45 7/8	45 2/8	37 0/8	6	6	Beaverhead County	MT	Tyler Robinson	1983	527
324 5/8	46 0/8	47 4/8	32 1/8	6	8	Moffat County	CO	Glenn W. Pritchard	1986	529
324 4/8	49 3/8	48 7/8	40 6/8	6	6	Grant County	OR	Chuck Boatman	1982	530
324 4/8	48 3/8	49 2/8	34 6/8	6	6	Petroleum County	MT	Gary Damuth	1986	530
324 4/8	50 1/8	50 2/8	46 7/8	7	8	Musselshell County	MT	Ted Steinke	1988	530
324 3/8	53 2/8	54 7/8	33 7/8	7	6	Summit County	CO	Gordon R. Horn	1986	533
324 2/8	47 5/8	47 4/8	31 0/8	6	6	Hodgson	MAN	Barry Bird	1982	534
324 2/8	52 0/8	51 1/8	37 5/8	6	7	Catron County	NM	Thomas Drumme	1990	534
324 1/8	47 7/8	48 6/8	46 7/8	6	7	Rio Arriba County	NM	Richard Manwell	1986	536
324 1/8	54 2/8	53 3/8	44 1/8	6	7	Apache County	AZ	Rick Mazol	1989	536
324 1/8	53 5/8	55 5/8	34 1/8	6	6	Coconino County	AZ	Phillip C. Dalrymple	1990	536
324 1/8	47 5/8	48 6/8	43 1/8	7	7	Shoshone County	ID	Jerry D. Ely	1991	536
324 0/8	52 0/8	50 0/8	41 4/8	7	6	Catron County	NM	Dave Scott	1991	540
323 7/8	48 7/8	47 2/8	37 1/8	6	6	Granite County	MT	Clint Carlson	1983	541
323 7/8	50 7/8	52 0/8	43 3/8	6	6	Coconino County	AZ	John Stigsell	1987	541
323 7/8	45 1/8	46 2/8	37 3/8	6	6	Phillips County	MT	Todd A. Erickson	1991	541
323 7/8	53 6/8	51 3/8	39 3/8	7	7	Coconino County	AZ	Joseph O. Fogleman	1992	541
323 6/8	48 2/8	51 1/8	43 6/8	6	6	Valley County	ID	Rodney Bremer	1983	545
323 5/8	46 6/8	46 3/8	40 3/8	7	6	Teton County	MT	Ron Granneman	1978	546
323 5/8	47 4/8	48 7/8	35 5/8	6	7	Custer County	ID	John R. Sample	1983	546
323 5/8	52 0/8	53 7/8	42 4/8	6	8	Cascade County	MT	Bill Tesinsky	1983	546
323 5/8	48 0/8	47 6/8	36 7/8	6	6	Taos County	NM	Jeffrey D. Butts	1987	546
323 5/8	50 5/8	51 1/8	37 3/8	7	7	Flathead County	MT	John Hale	1990	546
323 4/8	40 7/8	41 2/8	35 6/8	6	6	Phillips County	MT	Buzz Beto	1983	551
323 4/8	49 4/8	48 6/8	37 6/8	6	6	Missoula County	MT	John W. Zahrte	1987	551
323 4/8	51 5/8	52 0/8	35 0/8	6	6	Spirit River	ALB	Gerald Desjardins	1990	551
323 4/8	44 2/8	47 3/8	37 2/8	6	6	Catron County	NM	Abe Dimas	1992	551
323 3/8	50 6/8	50 1/8	37 7/8	7	6	Gallatin County	MT	Rick Jones	1977	555
323 3/8	50 1/8	51 1/8	38 3/8	6	6	Catron County	NM	Roy L. Hall	1991	555
323 2/8	55 7/8	53 5/8	44 2/8	6	6	Grant County	OR	Andy Day	1982	557
323 2/8	46 7/8	46 4/8	38 7/8	7	8	Catron County	NM	Thomas R. Sansom	1984	557
323 1/8	49 6/8	49 5/8	42 3/8	6	6	Blaine County	ID	Larry Whittaker	1988	559
323 0/8	52 5/8	50 1/8	39 0/8	6	6	Blaine County	ID	Ted Chu	1977	560

SCORE	LENGTH OF R MAIN BEAM L		INSIDE SPREAD	NUMBER OF R POINTS L		AREA	STATE/ PROVINCE	HUNTER'S NAME	DATE	RANK
323 0/8	54 7/8	50 0/8	45 5/8	6	7	Gallatin County	MT	Tim Wells	1983	560
323 0/8	47 4/8	48 3/8	40 0/8	6	6	Grand County	CO	Russell Gross	1985	560
323 0/8	50 4/8	51 0/8	40 0/8	6	6	White Pine County	NV	Paul D. Patterson	1987	560
323 0/8	50 7/8	51 4/8	39 2/8	6	6	Morgan County	UT	Hugh H. Hogle	1991	560
322 7/8	50 6/8	51 0/8	44 3/8	6	7	Phillips County	MT	Ray Hoveskeland	1967	565
322 7/8	48 5/8	46 5/8	36 5/8	6	6	Deer Lodge County	MT	Eddie McGreevey	1977	565
322 7/8	51 3/8	52 2/8	41 4/8	7	7	Coconino County	AZ	Darrell Christensen	1979	565
322 7/8	47 4/8	47 5/8	36 1/8	6	6	Canmore	ALB	David R. Coupland	1982	565
322 6/8	49 2/8	48 5/8	36 4/8	6	6	Rio Arriba County	NM	Santos E. Corriz	1982	569
322 5/8	49 4/8	47 1/8	37 7/8	6	6	Taos County	NM	Jason Kent	1991	570
322 4/8	51 3/8	48 7/8	40 0/8	6	7	Lewis & Clark County	MT	Jerry Biresch	1970	571
322 4/8	48 6/8	49 1/8	36 4/8	6	6	Sublette County	WY	Charles T. Moore II	1988	571
322 3/8	46 7/8	44 3/8	40 1/8	6	6	Coconino County	AZ	Salvatore J. Carlomagno	1991	573
322 2/8	51 5/8	53 1/8	33 0/8	6	6	Colfax County	NM	Tom L. Handy	1986	574
322 2/8	52 4/8	49 7/8	38 2/8	6	6	Catron County	NM	Sam Chavez	1990	574
322 1/8	50 4/8	50 6/8	37 3/8	6	6	Coconino County	AZ	John F. Schultz	1978	576
322 1/8	50 5/8	50 4/8	37 3/8	6	6	Powell County	MT	Gene Coughlin	1982	576
322 1/8	45 6/8	44 3/8	34 3/8	7	8	Fergus County	MT	Ben Starburg	1985	576
322 1/8	47 0/8	47 2/8	40 3/8	6	6	Beaverhead County	MT	Ric Twardoski	1987	576
322 1/8	47 5/8	49 5/8	43 3/8	7	7	Coconino County	AZ	Roger O. Iveson	1990	576
322 1/8	53 1/8	51 5/8	42 2/8	6	8	Rio Arriba County	NM	Michael Herrera	1991	576
322 0/8	50 3/8	50 6/8	36 2/8	7	8	Coconino County	AZ	Dick Hensley	1979	582
322 0/8	46 3/8	48 0/8	36 2/8	6	6	Sandoval County	NM	John McClendon	1983	582
322 0/8	52 6/8	53 0/8	35 0/8	6	6	Moffat County	CO	Guy Love	1984	582
322 0/8	47 2/8	49 0/8	40 6/8	6	6	Pierce County	WA	Dale Kistenmacher	1985	582
322 0/8	48 4/8	49 0/8	34 4/8	6	7	Boggy Creek	MAN	Tom Nebbs	1986	582
322 0/8	52 6/8	53 1/8	41 2/8	6	7	Caribou County	ID	Brian D. Bailey	1991	582
321 7/8	47 7/8	43 6/8	41 7/8	6	6	Taos County	NM	Dr. Dean A. Henbest	1971	588
321 7/8	49 3/8	53 2/8	34 1/8	6	6	Coconino County	AZ	Mike Burm	1981	588
321 7/8	51 0/8	50 5/8	37 7/8	6	6	Teller County	CO	Harry Rathke	1983	588
321 6/8	50 6/8	52 5/8	38 6/8	6	6	Fergus County	MT	Jake Damone	1991	591
321 4/8	45 2/8	56 2/8	39 2/8	5	6	Apache County	AZ	John D. 'Jack' Frost	1986	592
321 3/8	45 6/8	45 6/8	43 3/8	6	6	Gallatin County	MT	Ed Tertelgte	1975	593
321 2/8	46 1/8	48 4/8	40 0/8	6	6	Larimer County	CO	Tom Tietz	1981	594
321 2/8	50 6/8	50 5/8	35 6/8	6	6	Elmore County	ID	Robert M. Egusquiza	1991	594
321 2/8	53 1/8	53 5/8	41 6/8	6	7	Camas County	ID	Steve Wiedmeier	1992	594
321 1/8	48 6/8	50 6/8	38 1/8	6	6	Lincoln County	NM	Jay H. Henley, Sr.	1985	597
321 1/8	43 0/8	45 3/8	36 1/8	8	8	Idaho County	ID	Randy J. Demro	1989	597
321 1/8	46 3/8	46 7/8	34 3/8	6	6	Pierce County	WA	Joe H. Frields	1990	597
321 0/8	46 4/8	46 7/8	46 4/8	7	6	Lincoln County	MT	Steve A. Kluver	1986	600
321 0/8	51 7/8	49 4/8	42 4/8	6	6	Shoshone County	ID	Chax Peterson	1991	600
320 3/8	46 1/8	46 6/8	39 3/8	6	6	Rio Grande County	CO	Bing Kemp	1966	602
320 3/8	49 3/8	50 7/8	36 5/8	7	6	Catron County	NM	Randall S. Madding	1986	602
320 2/8	52 0/8	50 6/8	36 0/8	6	6	Meagher County	MT	Ted Hysell	1983	604
320 2/8	49 4/8	49 6/8	47 6/8	6	6	Shoshone County	ID	Tom J. O'Grady	1986	604
320 2/8	45 1/8	44 2/8	30 6/8	6	6	Garfield County	CO	Jason Adamson	1990	604
320 2/8	47 6/8	45 5/8	44 6/8	6	6	Beaverhead County	MT	Raymond Cote	1991	604
320 1/8	46 2/8	47 7/8	41 3/8	6	6	Madison County	MT	Lee J. Poole	1976	608
320 1/8	48 6/8	48 7/8	38 7/8	6	6	Fergus County	MT	J. Douglas Krings	1979	608
320 1/8	48 1/8	45 1/8	44 3/8	6	7	Albany County	WY	Doug Pope	1979	608
320 1/8	50 1/8	48 4/8	37 1/8	6	6	Lemhi County	ID	Joe Fraser	1980	608
320 1/8	52 6/8	51 1/8	41 1/8	6	6	Yellowstone County	MT	Robert M. Labert	1986	608
320 1/8	50 5/8	49 1/8	46 7/8	6	6	Cibola County	NM	Howard Schreiber	1992	608
320 0/8	50 6/8	53 1/8	39 6/8	6	6	Mineral County	MT	Michael Ruhkala	1980	614
320 0/8	51 4/8	50 5/8	36 6/8	6	6	Huerfano County	CO	Mike Culwell	1984	614
320 0/8	48 7/8	48 1/8	41 0/8	7	6	Grant County	OR	James M. Carter	1985	614
319 7/8	51 7/8	50 2/8	38 1/8	7	8	Socorro County	NM	David Ryles	1977	617
319 7/8	51 7/8	52 2/8	40 5/8	6	6	Hinton	ALB	Blair D. Crites	1979	617
319 7/8	46 3/8	47 6/8	39 7/8	7	6	Otero County	NM	Simon L. Gomez	1986	617
319 4/8	48 4/8	49 0/8	40 2/8	6	6	Pitkin County	CO	Bob Gulman	1975	620
319 4/8	49 5/8	49 6/8	36 4/8	7	6	Clearwater County	ID	Audie Powers	1979	620
319 4/8	50 6/8	52 0/8	41 2/8	6	6	Caribou County	ID	Mark Hill	1980	620
319 3/8	44 2/8	43 2/8	35 4/8	7	7	Crook County	OR	Jeff Carver	1985	623
319 3/8	52 6/8	54 1/8	42 5/8	6	6	Catron County	NM	Travis Gillentine	1987	623
319 3/8	47 5/8	47 1/8	37 1/8	6	6	Fergus County	MT	Edwin Evans	1990	623
319 3/8	47 3/8	48 2/8	39 7/8	6	6	Sublette County	WY	Doulgas Weir/ Glenn Socia	1990	623
319 2/8	45 2/8	46 1/8	35 0/8	6	6	Morgan County	UT	C. Keith Maynes	1987	627
319 1/8	45 2/8	45 0/8	36 3/8	7	7	Rio Arriba County	NM	Dr. O. D. Brown	1986	628
319 0/8	48 7/8	53 2/8	39 6/8	5	6	Catron County	NM	Eddie Howard	1983	629
318 7/8	45 6/8	45 4/8	37 1/8	7	6	Fergus County	MT	Donald R. Hecht	1984	630

SCORE	LENGTH OF MAIN BEAM		INSIDE SPREAD	NUMBER OF POINTS		AREA	STATE/ PROVINCE	HUNTER'S NAME	DATE	RANK
	R	L		R	L					
318 7/8	48 0/8	49 6/8	41 5/8	6	6	Carbon County	UT	Sam Raby	1989	630
318 7/8	48 4/8	49 4/8	34 1/8	6	6	Coconino County	AZ	Eugene E. Hafen	1990	630
318 6/8	48 5/8	48 1/8	42 2/8	6	7	Larimer County	CO	Tony Seahorn	1972	633
318 6/8	52 1/8	51 1/8	39 2/8	7	6	Niobrara County	WY	Donald L. Smith	1973	633
318 6/8	50 1/8	53 6/8	45 0/8	7	6	Coconino County	AZ	Tom Dalrymple	1980	633
318 6/8	47 4/8	47 4/8	39 4/8	6	6	Sanders County	MT	Wayne L. Haines	1982	633
318 6/8	44 3/8	44 2/8	35 2/8	6	6	Bow Valley	ALB	Pat Leiser	1986	633
318 6/8	48 6/8	46 2/8	31 2/8	6	6	Morgan County	UT	Hugh H. Hogle	1988	633
318 6/8	46 6/8	47 5/8	43 2/8	6	6	Converse County	WY	Chris D. Yeoman	1990	633
318 5/8	44 4/8	44 0/8	34 6/8	6	6	Mineral County	CO	David Powell	1969	640
318 5/8	54 0/8	55 7/8	39 7/8	6	6	Beaverhead County	MT	Greg L. Munther	1981	640
318 5/8	49 3/8	49 7/8	37 7/8	6	6	Missoula County	MT	J. Scott Graham	1982	640
318 5/8	47 7/8	49 6/8	43 1/8	6	6	Lincoln County	WY	Randy Ulmer	1990	640
318 5/8	46 7/8	46 7/8	44 3/8	6	7	Sweetwater County	WY	Mark Hamilton	1990	640
318 5/8	49 0/8	50 3/8	43 3/8	6	6	Morgan County	UT	Bob Frank	1991	640
318 4/8	43 7/8	42 6/8	39 4/8	6	6	Bighorn Mountains	WY	Ron Johnson	1975	646
318 4/8	51 1/8	49 4/8	43 0/8	6	6	Shoshone County	ID	Michael R. Whaley	1989	646
318 4/8	46 4/8	48 2/8	47 0/8	6	6	Apache County	AZ	Dave Mortimer	1989	646
318 4/8	51 4/8	50 6/8	38 4/8	7	7	Flathead County	MT	Jeffrey M. Benda	1992	646
318 3/8	51 4/8	49 7/8	33 3/8	6	6	Mineral County	MT	Farrell Cooper	1975	650
318 3/8	52 4/8	51 5/8	41 0/8	7	6	Deer Lodge County	MT	Dennis Neitzke	1980	650
318 3/8	48 1/8	48 1/8	36 5/8	6	6	Sierra County	NM	Jim Ryan	1988	650
318 3/8	51 0/8	51 6/8	34 3/8	6	6	Catron County	NM	Dr. Dale Mansfield	1992	650
318 2/8	45 1/8	45 4/8	36 0/8	6	6	Gunnison County	CO	Brian Newton	1989	654
318 2/8	45 7/8	46 1/8	38 4/8	6	6	Fergus County	MT	Bob Allen	1992	654
318 1/8	48 4/8	47 0/8	34 2/8	7	7	Ravalli County	MT	Rick Twardoski	1984	656
318 1/8	49 3/8	47 1/8	36 7/8	6	6	Uintah County	UT	Everett Burson	1986	656
318 1/8	48 7/8	51 2/8	41 1/8	6	6	Catron County	NM	Delbert Holley	1987	656
318 1/8	52 0/8	52 2/8	35 7/8	7	8	Baker County	OR	John Buck	1987	656
318 0/8	45 6/8	45 2/8	44 4/8	7	8	Bighorn Mountains	WY	Henry 'Hank' Frey	1977	660
318 0/8	45 6/8	48 4/8	46 6/8	6	6	Carbon County	WY	James Blocker	1980	660
317 7/8	45 6/8	45 4/8	45 1/8	6	6	Teton County	MT	Ronald K. Granneman	1974	662
317 7/8	47 6/8	43 3/8	38 5/8	6	6	Park County	WY	Wesley D. Engleman	1983	662
317 7/8	53 0/8	53 7/8	42 5/8	6	6	Flathead County	MT	James Norvell	1986	662
317 7/8	46 2/8	45 4/8	44 1/8	6	6	Clackamas County	OR	Gerald L. Egbert	1987	662
317 7/8	50 6/8	50 1/8	35 5/8	6	6	White Pine County	NV	Michael Scott Laity	1989	662
317 6/8	47 3/8	48 0/8	44 6/8	6	6	Valley County	ID	William R. "Steve" Stephe	1988	667
317 6/8	44 3/8	44 1/8	35 4/8	6	6	Lincoln County	MT	Ron Halvorson	1991	667
317 5/8	47 6/8	47 7/8	42 3/8	6	6	Lemhi County	ID	Lewis Zane Abbott	1981	669
317 5/8	56 6/8	55 5/8	35 3/8	6	6	Grant County	NM	Jimmy Head	1988	669
317 5/8	48 3/8	45 4/8	42 1/8	6	6	Pincher Creek	ALB	John Jacoby	1989	669
317 5/8	49 6/8	49 5/8	40 5/8	6	6	Beaverhead County	MT	Jim Muzynoski	1990	669
317 5/8	43 0/8	43 0/8	37 5/8	6	6	Jackson County	CO	Hal Rogers	1991	669
317 5/8	50 0/8	49 3/8	36 1/8	6	6	Coconino County	AZ	Randy S. Wagner	1992	669
317 4/8	52 0/8	52 3/8	40 2/8	6	6	Custer County	ID	Ed McIntosh	1989	675
317 3/8	49 0/8	48 3/8	40 7/8	6	6	Fremont County	ID	Donald M. Sherick	1982	676
317 3/8	45 1/8	47 1/8	36 4/8	7	7	Boundary County	ID	Walt Dinning	1987	676
317 3/8	51 3/8	50 0/8	37 1/8	6	6	Coconino County	AZ	Jim Norris	1991	676
317 3/8	47 1/8	48 1/8	44 6/8	9	6	Fergus County	MT	Jess Knerr	1992	676
317 2/8	51 4/8	52 6/8	36 4/8	6	6	Coconino County	AZ	Blaine "Bub" Mathews	1991	680
317 2/8	53 2/8	53 1/8	35 0/8	6	6	Coconino County	AZ	Michael Ellena	1992	680
317 1/8	49 0/8	47 0/8	39 7/8	6	6	Catron County	NM	Eddie Claypool	1989	682
317 1/8	49 1/8	47 7/8	35 5/8	6	6	Catron County	NM	Robert Haymaker	1990	682
317 1/8	47 5/8	47 0/8	47 7/8	6	6	Catron County	NM	Rick L. Chukas	1990	682
317 1/8	47 2/8	47 5/8	39 5/8	6	6	Colfax County	NM	Mike Wiley	1990	682
317 1/8	49 1/8	53 0/8	38 7/8	6	7	Coconino County	AZ	Bill Grahlherr	1991	682
317 0/8	46 5/8	47 0/8	42 2/8	6	7	Apache County	AZ	Robert H. Warren	1975	687
317 0/8	51 3/8	51 7/8	39 4/8	6	6	Rio Arriba County	NM	Alfred Vigil	1984	687
317 0/8	48 4/8	43 3/8	41 4/8	6	6	Mineral County	MT	S. Howie Henrikson	1987	687
317 0/8	49 3/8	51 1/8	37 0/8	6	6	Catron County	NM	Lars E. Winquist	1991	687
316 6/8	49 3/8	49 7/8	35 6/8	6	6	Lodgepole	ALB	Lynn M. Kasper	1991	691
316 6/8	47 6/8	48 5/8	35 2/8	6	6	Coconino County	AZ	Joseph O. Fogleman	1991	691
316 5/8	46 1/8	49 3/8	37 5/8	6	7	Morrow County	OR	Bob Lindsay	1989	693
316 5/8	48 7/8	46 5/8	39 7/8	7	7	Coconino County	AZ	John Gurasich	1989	693
316 4/8	49 2/8	48 5/8	39 4/8	6	6	Grant County	OR	A. Corey Heath	1984	695
316 4/8	54 0/8	56 6/8	40 2/8	7	6	Kootenai County	ID	Theodore Costo	1991	695
316 3/8	51 0/8	51 0/8	40 5/8	6	6	Missoula County	MT	Ben L. Jennings	1984	697
316 3/8	52 3/8	51 1/8	38 5/8	6	6	Lewis County	WA	Leonard L. Stolen	1986	697
316 2/8	48 2/8	48 2/8	34 6/8	7	7	Coconino County	AZ	William M. Lanese	1981	699
316 2/8	49 5/8	49 1/8	39 4/8	6	6	Canmore	ALB	Glenn Derovin	1990	699

SCORE	LENGTH OF MAIN BEAM		INSIDE SPREAD	NUMBER OF POINTS		AREA	STATE/ PROVINCE	HUNTER'S NAME	DATE	RANK
	R	L		R	L					
316 1/8	54 0/8	51 0/8	37 7/8	6	6	Valley County	MT	Dan Sturgis	1981	701
316 1/8	44 1/8	47 4/8	39 3/8	6	6	Rio Blanco County	CO	Darrell S. Jones	1987	701
316 0/8	48 4/8	46 0/8	52 7/8	7	6	Deer Lodge County	MT	Bob Gossack	1976	703
316 0/8	46 4/8	48 2/8	40 0/8	6	6	Archuleta County	CO	Loren Hofeldt	1981	703
316 0/8	45 1/8	43 7/8	43 2/8	6	6	Rich County	UT	Robert G. Petersen	1988	703
316 0/8	48 3/8	49 0/8	39 4/8	7	7	Apache County	AZ	Melvin E. Norris	1989	703
316 0/8	44 0/8	45 4/8	36 0/8	6	6	Coconino County	AZ	Earnest D. Stanley	1991	703
315 7/8	51 2/8	51 4/8	43 3/8	6	6	Wasco County	OR	Ivan Duncan	1982	708
315 6/8	47 7/8	48 5/8	38 0/8	6	6	Nez Perce County	ID	Alfred J. Gemrich	1984	709
315 6/8	48 4/8	47 2/8	34 2/8	6	6	Converse County	WY	Arthur Rubel	1987	709
315 6/8	49 1/8	50 5/8	41 4/8	7	8	Converse County	WY	Frank Moore	1989	709
315 6/8	40 0/8	47 7/8	42 4/8	6	6	Caribou County	ID	Coby Tigert	1990	709
315 6/8	49 6/8	56 0/8	31 6/8	6	6	Catron County	NM	John S. Patterson	1992	709
315 5/8	48 6/8	47 6/8	36 3/8	6	6	Gallatin National Forest	MT	Rocky Miller	1981	714
315 5/8	47 0/8	46 3/8	45 1/8	6	6	Lemhi County	ID	Jeffrey T. Shaffer	1990	714
315 5/8	55 2/8	54 1/8	39 4/8	8	6	Coconino County	AZ	David C. Fretz	1992	714
315 4/8	51 7/8	49 0/8	42 6/8	6	6	Wallowa County	OR	Dr. Russell A. Colgan	1976	717
315 4/8	45 2/8	46 3/8	44 4/8	7	6	Harney County	OR	"Ray" L. D. Reimers	1989	717
315 3/8	53 0/8	50 7/8	37 3/8	6	6	Clear Creek County	CO	Gary Christoffersen	1982	719
315 2/8	51 0/8	51 1/8	41 2/8	6	6	Teton County	MT	Ronald K. Granneman	1976	720
315 2/8	50 4/8	52 0/8	40 2/8	6	6	Clark County	ID	Ken Vander Linden	1986	720
315 2/8	46 6/8	45 6/8	41 4/8	6	6	Canmore	ALB	Dennis Francis	1986	720
315 2/8	45 7/8	45 6/8	40 0/8	5	6	Custer County	ID	Edward Allen Mack	1987	720
315 1/8	42 4/8	43 4/8	38 3/8	6	6	Grant County	OR	Rod Curtis	1988	724
315 1/8	50 0/8	47 1/8	43 1/8	6	6	Bear Lake County	ID	Jerry B. Tueller	1991	724
314 6/8	50 0/8	51 3/8	40 0/8	6	6	Catron County	NM	Wayne K. Curtis	1984	726
314 6/8	46 7/8	45 6/8	42 2/8	6	6	Catron County	NM	Dennis Curtis	1986	726
314 6/8	48 3/8	48 1/8	31 0/8	6	6	Mesa County	CO	Parker Leon	1989	726
314 4/8	48 0/8	48 2/8	39 4/8	6	6	Caribou County	ID	Alan E. Christiansen	1982	729
314 4/8	47 7/8	47 6/8	36 0/8	6	6	Moffat County	CO	Dave Holt	1985	729
314 3/8	48 4/8	46 1/8	41 3/8	6	6	Caribou County	ID	Bruce N. Moss	1980	731
314 3/8	48 4/8	52 3/8	35 3/8	6	6	Grant County	NM	Ronald L. Pack, Sr.	1988	731
314 3/8	45 5/8	45 4/8	42 3/8	6	6	Catron County	NM	Bruce Carlisle	1989	731
314 2/8	48 6/8	45 3/8	47 0/8	6	6	Coconino County	AZ	Michael Faherty	1986	734
314 2/8	44 6/8	44 4/8	36 6/8	6	6	Coconino County	AZ	Ron Kirk	1989	734
314 1/8	51 0/8	51 2/8	41 5/8	6	6	Gallatin County	MT	C. W. Smith	1974	736
314 0/8	47 7/8	48 2/8	44 0/8	6	6	Fremont County	ID	Tom Savage	1981	737
314 0/8	46 1/8	45 6/8	36 4/8	6	7	Phillips County	MT	Mark D. Hughes	1982	737
314 0/8	50 3/8	50 1/8	40 4/8	6	6	Catron County	NM	Randall F. Cooley	1983	737
314 0/8	54 3/8	54 4/8	37 0/8	6	5	Coconino County	AZ	James R. Dreves	1985	737
314 0/8	45 6/8	46 4/8	42 4/8	7	7	Bighorn County	WY	Mike Belcourt	1986	737
314 0/8	49 5/8	49 2/8	42 6/8	6	6	Flathead County	MT	Jim Hawkins	1986	737
313 7/8	47 5/8	44 7/8	33 3/8	7	7	Porcupine Hills	ALB	John Archibald	1980	743
313 7/8	49 2/8	47 3/8	44 2/8	7	6	Coconino County	AZ	Don R. Newton	1980	743
313 7/8	44 4/8	44 3/8	34 1/8	6	6	Apache County	AZ	Doug Kleck	1986	743
313 7/8	49 0/8	52 5/8	41 5/8	6	6	Rich County	UT	C. Keith Maynes	1990	743
313 7/8	49 4/8	45 7/8	34 1/8	7	7	Albany County	WY	Bill Gorman	1992	743
313 6/8	47 7/8	47 7/8	36 2/8	6	6	Otero County	NM	Lynn Saxon	1987	748
313 6/8	44 4/8	45 2/8	48 0/8	6	5	Moffat County	CO	Mike Wallers	1991	748
313 5/8	53 3/8	53 2/8	31 4/8	6	7	Coconino County	AZ	Michael John Bylina	1988	750
313 4/8	45 0/8	43 4/8	41 4/8	6	6	Jefferson County	CO	Charles Cater	1976	751
313 4/8	50 5/8	51 0/8	43 4/8	6	6	Grant County	OR	Andy Day	1980	751
313 4/8	51 2/8	52 4/8	45 2/8	6	6	Catron County	NM	Mike Moore	1988	751
313 3/8	42 7/8	42 4/8	34 1/8	6	6	Apache County	AZ	Ronald Mellick	1990	754
313 3/8	47 2/8	47 2/8	37 5/8	6	7	Harney County	OR	Robert M. Choate	1990	754
313 2/8	49 2/8	46 0/8	44 2/8	6	6	Albany County	WY	Jerry Bowen	1979	756
313 2/8	43 4/8	44 1/8	30 4/8	7	7	Park County	MT	Robert Wennerstrom	1985	756
313 2/8	51 2/8	51 2/8	39 6/8	6	6	Bonneville County	ID	Ron Mueller	1986	756
313 1/8	46 1/8	49 3/8	34 0/8	8	7	Chaffee County	CO	Rick D. Montgomery	1986	759
313 1/8	49 5/8	49 1/8	42 4/8	7	6	Glacier County	MT	Rick R. Winkowitsch	1989	759
313 1/8	51 2/8	50 6/8	35 3/8	6	6	Albany County	WY	Mark Stiller	1992	759
313 0/8	48 4/8	47 3/8	46 2/8	6	6	Park County	MT	Charles Milner	1973	762
313 0/8	48 3/8	47 3/8	31 4/8	6	6	Catron County	NM	Steven J. Vittetow	1987	762
313 0/8	56 5/8	55 4/8	39 4/8	6	6	Coconino County	AZ	Vince Dimiceli	1989	762
313 0/8	47 2/8	46 2/8	35 6/8	7	6	Greenlee County	AZ	Charles Steven Williams	1990	762
313 0/8	49 5/8	50 1/8	35 6/8	7	6	Sierra County	NM	Gerald Lambert Lopez	1991	762
312 7/8	46 7/8	50 1/8	43 7/8	6	6	Shoshone County	ID	Harry Barker	1962	767
312 7/8	49 6/8	50 0/8	41 6/8	6	7	Catron County	NM	Lee Braudt	1988	767
312 7/8	45 7/8	46 1/8	31 5/8	7	7	Alder Flats	ALB	John Miller	1990	767
312 7/8	44 4/8	45 3/8	38 3/8	6	6	Valley County	MT	Kenneth Smoker, Jr.	1990	767

SCORE	LENGTH OF MAIN BEAM R	L	INSIDE SPREAD	NUMBER OF POINTS R	L	AREA	STATE/ PROVINCE	HUNTER'S NAME	DATE	RANK
312 7/8	50 1/8	50 2/8	37 1/8	6	6	Catron County	NM	Randall S. Ulmer	1991	767
312 6/8	44 3/8	46 1/8	33 4/8	7	6	Clearwater County	ID	Doyle Anderegg	1975	772
312 6/8	55 2/8	54 0/8	40 4/8	5	5	Cibola County	NM	Mark Webber	1982	772
312 6/8	53 3/8	53 6/8	39 4/8	6	6	Greenlee County	AZ	Dick Hall	1986	772
312 5/8	47 0/8	47 3/8	39 5/8	6	6	Caribou County	ID	Dean Humphreys	1962	775
312 5/8	50 4/8	54 4/8	41 7/8	6	6	Fremont County	ID	Blair R. Jones	1987	775
312 5/8	46 7/8	47 6/8	32 3/8	6	6	Park County	CO	William Elfland	1991	775
312 4/8	51 0/8	51 6/8	42 3/8	9	7	Sanders County	MT	Ron Halvorson	1980	778
312 4/8	46 4/8	49 5/8	40 2/8	6	6	Clearwater County	ID	Steven E. Baxter	1984	778
312 4/8	48 6/8	46 6/8	37 2/8	6	7	Coconino County	AZ	Tony W. Zimbaro	1989	778
312 4/8	51 6/8	51 4/8	38 6/8	7	6	Grant County	OR	James M. Carter	1991	778
312 4/8	53 3/8	51 6/8	35 5/8	6	7	Catron County	NM	Johnny C. Parsons	1992	778
312 3/8	53 5/8	52 0/8	36 1/8	6	6	Socorro County	NM	James C. Hayes	1992	783
312 2/8	46 4/8	48 4/8	49 2/8	7	7	Ravalli County	MT	Dick Robertson	1973	784
312 2/8	44 6/8	44 7/8	38 2/8	6	6	Eagle County	CO	Gary D. Allen	1974	784
312 2/8	48 1/8	48 4/8	36 4/8	6	6	Larimer County	CO	Steve Stumbo	1975	784
312 2/8	50 0/8	49 0/8	35 5/8	7	8	Butte County	ID	Floyd L. Collins, Jr.	1982	784
312 2/8	46 4/8	46 2/8	35 0/8	6	7	Catron County	NM	Billy E. Gourley	1984	784
312 1/8	45 5/8	45 3/8	33 3/8	6	6	Garfield County	UT	Russell Peterson	1984	789
312 1/8	45 2/8	44 4/8	35 3/8	6	6	Catron County	NM	Randy Williams	1985	789
312 1/8	50 2/8	50 4/8	34 7/8	6	6	Lemhi County	ID	Mike S. Szekely	1986	789
312 1/8	48 4/8	47 6/8	36 1/8	6	6	Musselshell County	MT	Bill Krenz	1992	789
312 0/8	48 2/8	48 6/8	37 7/8	6	6	Montrose County	CO	Stanley R. Godfrey	1978	793
312 0/8	49 7/8	49 7/8	39 0/8	6	6	Rio Blanco County	CO	John Richardson	1990	793
311 6/8	47 6/8	47 1/8	37 6/8	6	8	Lewis & Clark County	MT	Douglas L. Conrady	1980	795
311 6/8	51 5/8	52 1/8	38 4/8	6	6	Deschutes County	OR	Gary Scroggins	1988	795
311 5/8	47 0/8	48 7/8	35 1/8	7	7	Larimar County	CO	Roger J. Kabage	1992	797
311 4/8	52 3/8	51 6/8	39 4/8	6	6	Coconino County	AZ	Richard Foss	1977	798
311 4/8	48 7/8	45 7/8	37 2/8	6	6	Bonneville County	ID	Gene H. Dressen	1978	798
311 4/8	46 2/8	45 6/8	38 0/8	6	6	Rio Blanco County	CO	Jack Lambert	1980	798
311 4/8	55 6/8	54 4/8	37 4/8	6	6	Archuleta County	CO	Tim Chavez	1983	798
311 4/8	44 6/8	44 2/8	37 2/8	6	6	Cypress River	MAN	Perry Fleet	1986	798
311 4/8	48 2/8	48 1/8	38 4/8	6	6	Idaho County	ID	Stan Myers	1988	798
311 4/8	48 0/8	49 2/8	34 4/8	6	6	Greenlee County	AZ	Carl L. Plasterer	1990	798
311 3/8	48 4/8	46 5/8	37 3/8	7	7	Sanders County	MT	Rus Willis	1981	805
311 3/8	49 3/8	48 6/8	39 7/8	6	6	Coconino County	AZ	Greg Winn	1991	805
311 3/8	48 2/8	47 5/8	44 3/8	6	8	Catron County	NM	Duane "Corky" Richardson	1992	805
311 2/8	44 5/8	46 2/8	33 6/8	6	6	Park County	CO	Lynn Campbell	1981	808
311 2/8	48 3/8	48 5/8	37 0/8	6	6	Clackamas County	OR	Bill Hensley	1984	808
311 2/8	47 7/8	49 3/8	32 2/8	6	7	Madison County	MT	Jacob Baine	1991	808
311 2/8	50 0/8	49 1/8	35 0/8	6	6	Socorro County	NM	Frank Sanders	1991	808
311 1/8	51 2/8	50 0/8	40 7/8	6	6	Ravalli County	MT	Gary J. Hartman	1989	812
311 1/8	48 6/8	47 6/8	34 5/8	6	6	Flathead County	MT	Ron Krueger	1989	812
311 0/8	51 6/8	50 0/8	41 6/8	6	6	Teton County	WY	Fred Bear	1953	814
311 0/8	51 1/8	49 5/8	47 2/8	8	6	Larimer County	CO	H. Mike Palmer	1983	814
311 0/8	47 3/8	47 4/8	43 6/8	6	6	Beaverhead County	MT	Jerry Strodtman	1985	814
311 0/8	46 0/8	46 0/8	41 0/8	6	6	Mineral County	MT	Robert F. Erickson	1988	814
311 0/8	49 1/8	49 0/8	38 2/8	6	6	Sanders County	MT	Rick Dieterich	1990	814
311 0/8	46 3/8	48 2/8	41 6/8	6	6	Coconino County	AZ	Eddy Broderick	1992	814
310 7/8	55 2/8	53 6/8	53 1/8	6	6	Pitkin County	CO	Bob Gulman	1973	820
310 7/8	45 6/8	45 0/8	36 3/8	6	6	Flathead County	MT	Scott Halama	1986	820
310 6/8	49 5/8	51 2/8	43 4/8	6	6	Lemhi County	ID	Joe Hollifield	1977	822
310 6/8	45 5/8	46 2/8	35 0/8	7	8	Fergus County	MT	Steven J. Nelson	1977	822
310 6/8	45 6/8	47 0/8	36 2/8	6	7	Ravalli County	MT	Alan Lear	1988	822
310 5/8	51 3/8	51 2/8	38 3/8	6	6	Little Belt Mountains	MT	Jim Ekness	1978	825
310 5/8	47 1/8	44 6/8	39 3/8	7	6	Coconino County	AZ	Rick Brewer	1984	825
310 5/8	49 5/8	50 7/8	49 5/8	5	6	Granite County	MT	Shaun Twardoski	1992	825
310 4/8	49 0/8	49 0/8	43 6/8	6	6	La Plata County	CO	Tom Price	1967	828
310 4/8	43 2/8	43 6/8	38 2/8	6	6	Baker County	OR	Billy J. Cruise	1970	828
310 4/8	46 7/8	46 6/8	37 4/8	6	6	Clearwater County	ID	Rory Roby	1981	828
310 4/8	46 1/8	46 3/8	41 0/8	6	6	Valley County	ID	Ron Phillips	1983	828
310 4/8	53 3/8	51 1/8	37 0/8	6	6	Converse County	WY	Dennis Spawn	1986	828
310 4/8	52 2/8	51 2/8	33 2/8	6	7	Apache County	AZ	Steve McInelly	1986	828
310 4/8	45 2/8	45 7/8	42 6/8	6	6	Grant County	OR	Dean P. Pasche	1990	828
310 3/8	49 0/8	51 0/8	39 2/8	8	6	Caribou County	ID	Patrick G. Selfridge	1980	835
310 3/8	43 7/8	46 0/8	36 1/8	6	6	Santa Fe County	NM	Bennie "Buddy" Rhodes, Jr	1990	835
310 2/8	49 4/8	50 0/8	30 0/8	6	6	Phillips County	MT	Daniel Tellefson	1981	837
310 2/8	45 0/8	45 4/8	33 4/8	6	6	Canmore	ALB	Cam Wilson	1984	837
310 2/8	48 2/8	49 7/8	34 6/8	6	6	Coconino County	AZ	Russ Warner	1984	837
310 2/8	45 1/8	43 4/8	39 0/8	6	6	Gallatin County	MT	David Burtch	1986	837

SCORE	LENGTH OF MAIN BEAM R	L	INSIDE SPREAD	NUMBER OF POINTS R	L	AREA	STATE/ PROVINCE	HUNTER'S NAME	DATE	RANK
310 2/8	45 3/8	47 6/8	46 6/8	6	6	Coconino County	AZ	Alan H. Timonen	1992	837
310 1/8	50 3/8	50 4/8	48 3/8	8	5	Idaho County	ID	Roy S. Lathen	1988	842
310 1/8	51 4/8	52 7/8	40 3/8	5	5	Rio Arriba County	NM	Isaac Julian, Sr.	1989	842
310 0/8	51 2/8	50 3/8	38 0/8	6	6	Ravalli County	MT	Bob Sappenfield	1978	844
310 0/8	46 5/8	49 1/8	37 2/8	5	6	Grant County	OR	Andy Day	1987	844
310 0/8	47 1/8	48 7/8	33 2/8	6	8	Clearwater County	ID	Jim Lashly	1990	844
310 0/8	48 6/8	48 7/8	44 2/8	6	7	Grant County	OR	Darin C. Jenison	1992	844
309 7/8	47 2/8	47 3/8	37 3/8	6	7	Baker County	OR	James D. Ward	1983	848
309 6/8	43 1/8	43 4/8	35 0/8	6	6	Routt County	CO	Steve Gorr	1971	849
309 6/8	50 6/8	51 0/8	40 0/8	7	6	Sanders County	MT	Brad Borden	1984	849
309 6/8	48 6/8	50 6/8	43 2/8	6	6	Coconino County	AZ	Robert L. Smith	1986	849
309 6/8	48 3/8	46 5/8	37 0/8	6	6	Park County	MT	Steve Kamps	1987	849
309 6/8	46 2/8	49 2/8	42 3/8	7	6	Yavapai County	AZ	Mark A. Rucker	1991	849
309 5/8	51 0/8	50 6/8	39 7/8	6	6	Flathead County	MT	Paul Roney	1976	854
309 5/8	46 2/8	44 7/8	37 1/8	6	6	Lincoln County	MT	Mike Billingsley	1990	854
309 4/8	44 3/8	44 5/8	30 0/8	6	6	Valley County	MT	Charles Seiler	1976	856
309 4/8	42 6/8	41 7/8	32 6/8	6	6	Lincoln County	MT	Lee S. Lampton	1992	856
309 3/8	47 0/8	47 4/8	35 7/8	6	6	Granite County	MT	Dwayne Garner	1985	858
309 2/8	51 1/8	51 2/8	38 6/8	7	7	Garfield County	CO	Harry Earl Temple	1960	859
309 2/8	44 6/8	47 4/8	44 4/8	5	6	Fremont County	ID	Larry Bauer	1960	859
309 2/8	45 0/8	45 7/8	34 4/8	6	6	Union County	OR	Ron Angell	1981	859
309 2/8	48 0/8	47 6/8	42 2/8	6	6	Sheridan County	WY	George Rogers	1988	859
309 2/8	48 2/8	47 4/8	41 4/8	6	6	Uintah County	UT	Justin Arrowchis	1990	859
309 2/8	45 0/8	44 4/8	44 2/8	5	6	Rio Arriba County	NM	Dr. Leo A. Lucas	1990	859
309 1/8	44 4/8	46 4/8	34 5/8	6	6	Coconino County	AZ	Les Butters	1981	865
309 1/8	48 0/8	46 6/8	39 7/8	6	6	Missoula County	MT	Chad Spicknall	1984	865
309 1/8	49 5/8	50 0/8	37 5/8	6	6	Mora County	NM	Randy Ries	1990	865
309 1/8	48 6/8	50 0/8	41 1/8	6	6	Sandoval County	NM	Chuck Adams	1991	865
309 1/8	50 5/8	48 2/8	42 1/8	6	6	Coconino County	AZ	John Woodruff	1992	865
309 0/8	46 3/8	45 5/8	38 6/8	6	6	Boise County	ID	Steve Groff	1989	870
308 6/8	44 6/8	45 0/8	36 6/8	7	6	Lincoln County	MT	Steve Kluver	1987	871
308 5/8	47 5/8	46 3/8	40 1/8	7	6	Wasco County	OR	Gary Paugh	1984	872
308 5/8	50 2/8	51 2/8	37 5/8	6	6	Taos County	NM	Nicholas J Rowley	1985	872
308 4/8	47 7/8	47 7/8	41 2/8	7	6	Socorro County	NM	Jack W. Bruton	1985	874
308 4/8	48 0/8	48 2/8	39 0/8	6	6	Catron County	NM	Bob A. Gourley	1986	874
308 4/8	45 1/8	47 4/8	40 4/8	6	6	Elmore County	ID	Matt March, Jr.	1987	874
308 4/8	47 6/8	46 6/8	37 7/8	7	7	Elmore County	ID	Anthony L. Mudd	1992	874
308 3/8	49 0/8	50 4/8	38 5/8	7	6	Idaho County	ID	Bill G. Davis	1989	878
308 3/8	48 3/8	47 3/8	37 1/8	6	6	Lincoln County	MT	John C. McDivitt	1992	878
308 3/8	49 5/8	48 4/8	33 3/8	7	7	Missoula County	MT	Joseph J. Simone, Jr.	1992	878
308 2/8	42 4/8	44 0/8	42 4/8	6	6	Kane County	UT	Ron Simmers	1991	881
308 2/8	44 4/8	44 4/8	38 4/8	6	6	Lincoln County	WY	Tom A. Daughetee	1991	881
308 2/8	51 2/8	50 3/8	43 0/8	6	7	Rich County	UT	Hugh H. Hogle	1992	881
308 1/8	51 1/8	50 6/8	42 7/8	6	5	Crook County	OR	Jim Hodson	1983	884
308 1/8	48 3/8	49 4/8	39 1/8	6	6	Coconino County	AZ	Richard D. Tone	1987	884
308 1/8	49 3/8	49 7/8	40 1/8	6	7	Missoula County	MT	Kevin P. Grenier	1990	884
308 0/8	43 4/8	48 0/8	32 6/8	6	6	Shoshone County	ID	Randy Hammond	1983	887
307 7/8	46 5/8	46 3/8	37 5/8	6	6	Ravalli County	MT	Ray Tlamka	1984	888
307 7/8	47 3/8	48 6/8	36 3/8	6	5	Baca County	CO	Max Crocker	1989	888
307 6/8	47 0/8	47 1/8	40 2/8	6	6	Valley County	ID	Neil Thagard	1991	890
307 6/8	44 7/8	46 2/8	49 2/8	6	6	Madison County	MT	Everett W. Ayers, Sr.	1992	890
307 4/8	45 5/8	42 7/8	37 4/8	7	7	Huerfano County	CO	Wilbur F. Lay, Jr.	1974	892
307 4/8	47 7/8	48 0/8	40 4/8	5	6	Caribou County	ID	Charlie Humphreys	1979	892
307 4/8	54 6/8	54 6/8	46 3/8	7	7	Apache County	AZ	Tom David	1985	892
307 4/8	44 0/8	43 7/8	40 4/8	6	5	Gallatin County	MT	Don Syvrud	1985	892
307 4/8	46 7/8	47 1/8	37 2/8	6	6	Teller County	CO	James M. Strampe	1985	892
307 4/8	44 4/8	43 7/8	33 6/8	6	6	Valley County	ID	Brian Hunter Heck	1990	892
307 4/8	47 1/8	48 0/8	34 4/8	6	6	Beaverhead County	MT	Gary Dudden	1991	892
307 3/8	46 2/8	36 4/8	33 3/8	6	6	Garfield County	MT	Jerry L. Molstad	1986	899
307 3/8	48 2/8	47 4/8	36 1/8	6	6	Lemhi County	ID	George C. Engelhardt	1988	899
307 3/8	46 5/8	47 0/8	37 7/8	7	6	Greenlee County	AZ	Clifford White	1989	899
307 3/8	42 4/8	43 3/8	51 7/8	7	7	Park County	CO	Marko Green	1989	899
307 2/8	49 5/8	50 4/8	35 6/8	6	6	Coconino County	AZ	Larry Hines	1981	903
307 2/8	48 6/8	46 1/8	35 1/8	7	7	Bonner County	ID	Brian T. Farley	1982	903
307 2/8	52 5/8	47 0/8	38 1/8	7	8	Idaho County	ID	John Moehrle	1987	903
307 1/8	54 4/8	52 4/8	40 3/8	6	6	Park County	MT	David Thiry	1981	906
307 1/8	47 0/8	47 5/8	43 1/8	6	6	Grant County	OR	George Schiedler	1983	906
307 1/8	50 4/8	51 0/8	42 3/8	6	6	Park County	MT	Robert Ward	1983	906
307 1/8	48 5/8	45 4/8	33 1/8	6	6	Missoula County	MT	Tou Lee	1992	906
307 0/8	51 5/8	50 2/8	35 6/8	6	6	Judith Basin County	MT	Mark A. Petroni	1982	910

Score	Length of Main Beam R	L	Inside Spread	Number of Points R	L	Area	State/ Province	Hunter's Name	Date	Rank
307 0/8	49 3/8	50 6/8	37 0/8	6	6	Apache County	AZ	Melvin Edward Norris	1986	910
307 0/8	53 1/8	52 0/8	38 6/8	6	7	Clearwater County	ID	Ralph L. Albright	1986	910
306 6/8	50 5/8	43 7/8	35 6/8	6	6	Coconino County	AZ	Philip M. Rippey	1988	913
306 6/8	44 7/8	46 0/8	30 2/8	8	6	Fergus County	MT	Roland E. Sanford, Jr.	1988	913
306 6/8	43 0/8	42 5/8	32 4/8	6	6	Sanders County	MT	Jeffrey M. Myny	1991	913
306 5/8	50 2/8	49 1/8	39 7/8	5	5	Granite County	MT	J. Greg Jones	1983	916
306 4/8	42 7/8	43 2/8	43 4/8	5	5	Lemhi County	ID	A. LaVerne Hokanson	1974	917
306 4/8	43 4/8	44 5/8	40 0/8	6	6	Clearwater County	ID	Kim J. Vander Sys	1977	917
306 4/8	46 4/8	47 2/8	37 4/8	6	6	Blaine County	ID	Tom Goicoechea	1982	917
306 4/8	45 6/8	46 3/8	33 6/8	6	6	Valley County	ID	Bob Shaw	1991	917
306 3/8	48 4/8	48 5/8	40 6/8	7	6	Summit County	UT	Clifton B. Johnson	1978	921
306 3/8	45 3/8	47 1/8	32 7/8	6	6	Catron County	NM	Jim R. Wood	1992	921
306 2/8	49 3/8	48 3/8	40 2/8	6	6	Garfield County	UT	Bruce E. Carlisle	1985	923
306 2/8	46 2/8	45 7/8	37 3/8	7	6	Catron County	NM	Sonny Turner	1991	923
306 1/8	48 6/8	46 0/8	34 1/8	6	7	Beaverhead County	MT	Kenneth M. Carlson	1983	925
306 1/8	49 5/8	47 2/8	39 5/8	6	6	Catron County	NM	Martin Plugge	1991	925
306 0/8	45 0/8	44 3/8	36 6/8	6	6	Eagle County	CO	Walt Williams	1979	927
306 0/8	49 2/8	48 7/8	34 2/8	6	6	Catron County	NM	William C. Davis	1986	927
306 0/8	53 2/8	53 2/8	39 4/8	6	6	Ravalli County	MT	Dave L. Fretz	1987	927
306 0/8	48 7/8	48 1/8	39 3/8	7	6	Phillips County	MT	Dave Farnsworth	1991	927
305 7/8	46 5/8	46 6/8	37 7/8	6	6	Grant County	OR	Gregory Stathos	1987	931
305 7/8	46 0/8	46 2/8	39 1/8	7	6	Sheridan County	WY	Randy Lee Reece	1990	931
305 6/8	46 7/8	47 7/8	34 0/8	6	6	Larimer County	CO	Steve Stumbo	1980	933
305 6/8	45 2/8	46 4/8	38 4/8	6	6	Kootenai County	ID	Brent K. Jacobson	1982	933
305 6/8	47 6/8	47 2/8	33 4/8	6	6	Catron County	NM	Randall S. Madding	1984	933
305 6/8	40 1/8	42 0/8	36 4/8	7	6	Gilpin County	CO	Dennis Myer	1985	933
305 6/8	44 5/8	46 1/8	38 2/8	6	6	Lincoln County	WY	Steven J. Vanlerberghe	1987	933
305 6/8	52 7/8	52 7/8	37 0/8	5	5	Catron County	NM	Russell Hull	1989	933
305 5/8	48 6/8	49 6/8	36 3/8	6	6	Archuleta County	CO	Lester Hawkins, Jr.	1989	939
305 4/8	46 7/8	47 5/8	43 6/8	5	6	Clackamas County	OR	Bill Lancaster	1981	940
305 4/8	47 4/8	47 5/8	40 2/8	6	6	Catron County	NM	Stan Rauch	1985	940
305 4/8	48 0/8	48 6/8	37 2/8	6	6	Coconino County	AZ	Wayne Miller	1988	940
305 2/8	50 2/8	51 2/8	39 4/8	6	6	Larimer County	CO	Craig Nelson	1968	943
305 2/8	48 7/8	48 6/8	38 0/8	6	6	Catron County	NM	Glen L. Dillehay	1984	943
305 2/8	47 0/8	45 2/8	38 1/8	7	6	Lincoln County	NM	Henry Vega	1987	943
305 2/8	49 4/8	48 5/8	36 0/8	6	6	Lincoln County	NM	Johnny King	1988	943
305 2/8	48 6/8	49 5/8	40 2/8	6	6	Grant County	OR	Randy Burgess	1990	943
305 2/8	47 6/8	46 5/8	33 5/8	7	6	Granite County	MT	Jeremy J. Sandoz	1992	943
305 1/8	45 1/8	45 5/8	38 4/8	7	7	Fergus County	MT	Gary O. Stewart	1986	949
305 0/8	44 6/8	43 5/8	37 6/8	6	6	Morgan County	UT	Hugh Hogle	1987	950
304 6/8	42 4/8	45 0/8	45 6/8	6	6	Coconino County	AZ	Art Potter	1976	951
304 6/8	49 5/8	50 2/8	43 2/8	7	6	Coconino County	AZ	Jerry Carpenter	1979	951
304 5/8	51 1/8	49 6/8	37 5/8	6	6	Catron County	NM	A. Jerry McBride	1991	953
304 4/8	46 7/8	45 4/8	45 2/8	6	6	Grant County	OR	Clayton Severin	1982	954
304 4/8	52 1/8	52 7/8	39 4/8	6	6	Catron County	NM	Robert W. Chilcutt	1986	954
304 4/8	45 7/8	45 7/8	35 0/8	6	6	Missoula County	MT	Byron Schurg	1989	954
304 3/8	50 6/8	48 1/8	44 1/8	6	6	McKinley County	NM	Rick Collard	1987	957
304 2/8	46 6/8	49 0/8	36 4/8	6	6	Flathead County	MT	Steven C. Street	1980	958
304 2/8	49 5/8	49 6/8	34 4/8	6	6	Sanders County	MT	Ray J. Baenen	1982	958
304 2/8	48 2/8	47 3/8	40 6/8	6	6	Cibola County	NM	Jim Pepper	1983	958
304 2/8	45 2/8	45 5/8	33 4/8	6	6	Douglas County	CO	James Phelps	1990	958
304 2/8	49 7/8	49 6/8	34 2/8	6	5	Routt County	CO	Craig Greenheck	1990	958
304 2/8	45 1/8	43 5/8	35 0/8	6	6	Otero County	NM	James E. Borron	1990	958
304 2/8	55 2/8	53 3/8	32 4/8	6	6	Greenlee County	AZ	Lonnie R. Lashley	1991	958
304 0/8	47 5/8	46 6/8	39 6/8	6	6	Grant County	OR	James E. Hodson	1981	965
304 0/8	50 1/8	48 4/8	37 0/8	5	5	Park County	CO	Ronald King	1981	965
304 0/8	49 3/8	53 4/8	44 2/8	6	6	Cibola County	NM	Wayne L. Mathews	1986	965
304 0/8	48 5/8	48 7/8	37 2/8	6	6	Chouteau County	MT	K. C. Palagi	1986	965
303 7/8	48 6/8	46 0/8	41 7/8	6	6	Pitkin County	CO	Joseph Mendozza	1980	969
303 7/8	43 3/8	43 4/8	41 3/8	6	6	Fergus County	MT	Carson J. Rife	1984	969
303 7/8	46 3/8	44 4/8	37 5/8	6	6	Flathead County	MT	Doug Bronson	1987	969
303 7/8	42 4/8	44 7/8	41 1/8	6	8	Apache County	AZ	Jim Scholes	1991	969
303 6/8	46 2/8	47 7/8	36 2/8	6	6	Eagle County	CO	Tim W. Hulce	1981	973
303 6/8	44 6/8	44 4/8	38 2/8	6	6	Benewah County	ID	Eugene Lewis	1989	973
303 6/8	46 0/8	44 4/8	36 0/8	6	6	Coconino County	AZ	David S. Stone	1990	973
303 5/8	51 7/8	51 0/8	36 3/8	6	6	Grant County	OR	James M. Carter	1987	976
303 5/8	52 1/8	54 2/8	39 3/8	7	6	Pierce County	WA	Joe Harrison Frields	1987	976
303 5/8	49 3/8	48 2/8	35 2/8	6	6	Sandoval County	NM	Gerald Schullo	1988	976
303 5/8	49 7/8	49 5/8	38 1/8	6	6	Catron County	NM	A. Jerry McBride	1988	976
303 4/8	49 1/8	42 1/8	41 0/8	6	6	Grand County	CO	Jim Cleland	1977	980

SCORE	LENGTH OF MAIN BEAM R	L	INSIDE SPREAD	NUMBER OF POINTS R	L	AREA	STATE/ PROVINCE	HUNTER'S NAME	DATE	RANK
303 4/8	44 6/8	45 3/8	36 2/8	6	6	Sierra County	NM	Chuck Wagner	1986	980
303 4/8	48 0/8	47 4/8	38 4/8	6	6	Sheridan County	WY	Dan G. Powers	1991	980
303 4/8	44 2/8	43 4/8	43 6/8	6	6	Idaho County	ID	Glen Burney	1991	980
303 4/8	48 5/8	48 7/8	39 6/8	6	6	Coconino County	AZ	Patrick Fillman	1991	980
303 4/8	43 5/8	43 5/8	40 0/8	6	6	Rio Arriba County	NM	Gene Bishop	1992	980
303 3/8	44 0/8	43 0/8	42 7/8	5	6	Adams County	ID	Rick Mason	1984	986
303 3/8	47 1/8	48 1/8	38 5/8	6	6	Flathead County	MT	Kenneth M. Sharp	1992	986
303 2/8	47 4/8	45 6/8	38 4/8	6	6	Garfield County	CO	Alan Harbin	1980	988
303 2/8	47 1/8	47 0/8	35 4/8	6	6	Park County	WY	James Dinkins	1983	988
303 2/8	49 0/8	50 4/8	34 2/8	6	7	Grant County	OR	James M. Carter	1989	988
303 2/8	46 6/8	46 0/8	38 0/8	6	8	Millard County	UT	Bryon M. Griffiths	1990	988
303 2/8	56 7/8	51 5/8	42 4/8	6	6	Custer County	ID	John W. Heimes	1991	988
303 2/8	47 4/8	48 0/8	35 4/8	6	6	Greenlee County	AZ	Tim E. Downs	1991	988
303 2/8	46 0/8	48 1/8	35 2/8	6	6	Catron County	NM	Ron Madsen	1992	988
303 1/8	45 7/8	46 7/8	35 7/8	6	6	Jackson County	OR	Armone Foulon	1990	995
303 0/8	48 7/8	47 6/8	41 0/8	5	6	Las Animas County	CO	David L. Brady	1983	996
303 0/8	48 0/8	50 7/8	35 2/8	6	6	Fergus County	MT	Mark Robbins	1990	996
303 0/8	48 2/8	50 1/8	37 6/8	8	9	Catron County	NM	L. David Hubler, MD	1990	996
302 7/8	44 6/8	45 6/8	38 5/8	6	6	Swan River	MT	Joe Lawrence	1969	999
302 7/8	43 3/8	45 0/8	41 7/8	7	6	Grant County	OR	Jim Richardson	1990	999
302 6/8	49 4/8	47 4/8	43 0/8	5	6	Apache County	AZ	Gary Preston	1981	1,001
302 6/8	49 1/8	47 0/8	34 0/8	7	7	Converse County	WY	Fred Romero	1992	1,001
302 5/8	45 0/8	46 0/8	42 3/8	6	6	Clear Creek County	CO	Billy E. Corley	1987	1,003
302 5/8	49 2/8	48 7/8	38 7/8	6	6	Beaverhead County	MT	Jack Brilz	1990	1,003
302 4/8	47 7/8	47 2/8	38 5/8	6	6	Eagle County	CO	Roger Rothhaar	1974	1,005
302 4/8	46 4/8	46 2/8	37 0/8	6	6	Beaverhead County	MT	Dennis Rehse	1982	1,005
302 3/8	44 0/8	45 0/8	35 3/8	6	6	Routt County	CO	Mike Newman	1989	1,007
302 3/8	49 2/8	44 3/8	30 7/8	6	6	Coconino County	AZ	Jeffery Duane Hines	1992	1,007
302 2/8	48 7/8	48 7/8	39 0/8	6	6	Grant County	OR	Randy Bonner	1983	1,009
302 2/8	53 3/8	50 3/8	39 6/8	6	6	Coconino County	AZ	G. Henry Strohm	1986	1,009
302 1/8	51 1/8	49 4/8	37 7/8	6	6	Canmore	ALB	David R. Coupland	1984	1,011
302 1/8	44 1/8	44 1/8	35 1/8	6	6	Greenlee County	AZ	Timothy Hall	1985	1,011
302 1/8	48 1/8	46 7/8	37 3/8	6	6	Valley County	ID	Michael S. Moore	1987	1,011
302 1/8	46 6/8	47 0/8	40 1/8	6	7	Beaverhead County	MT	Fred C. Church	1991	1,011
302 0/8	45 0/8	46 6/8	40 0/8	6	6	Archuleta County	CO	Billy Ellis	1977	1,015
302 0/8	50 4/8	49 6/8	38 6/8	6	6	Eagle County	CO	John Schell	1980	1,015
302 0/8	42 3/8	41 6/8	31 0/8	6	6	Routt County	CO	Kevin Stailey	1981	1,015
302 0/8	47 6/8	48 0/8	35 4/8	6	7	Missoula County	MT	Richard W. Talbert	1986	1,015
302 0/8	44 0/8	43 7/8	37 4/8	6	6	Fremont County	WY	Edward A. Dykstra	1988	1,015
302 0/8	44 6/8	45 2/8	34 0/8	6	6	Lemhi County	ID	Buster Williams	1990	1,015
301 7/8	44 2/8	44 2/8	38 3/8	6	6	Larimer County	CO	Adrian H. Farmer, Jr.	1984	1,021
301 6/8	47 2/8	46 2/8	36 0/8	6	6	Missoula County	MT	Guy Leibenguth	1976	1,022
301 6/8	40 6/8	40 5/8	33 6/8	6	6	Yakima County	WA	James Garner	1989	1,022
301 5/8	44 1/8	42 2/8	39 2/8	7	7	Ravalli County	MT	Dick Kerr	1977	1,024
301 5/8	44 0/8	41 2/8	31 5/8	7	6	Grant County	NM	Raymond Albertina	1991	1,024
301 5/8	49 2/8	50 1/8	38 7/8	6	7	Ravalli County	MT	Ned Coorough	1992	1,024
301 4/8	45 1/8	44 6/8	37 0/8	6	6	Lewis & Clark County	MT	Doug Conrady	1979	1,027
301 4/8	47 3/8	44 5/8	41 1/8	6	7	Park County	MT	Donald Lee Ferguson	1988	1,027
301 4/8	45 5/8	44 2/8	42 0/8	6	6	Madison County	MT	Vaughn Ballard	1989	1,027
301 4/8	43 3/8	42 4/8	33 1/8	6	9	Wallowa County	OR	Tim Andrew Collins	1990	1,027
301 4/8	46 0/8	47 0/8	40 2/8	6	6	McKinley County	NM	Ben Gibson	1991	1,027
301 3/8	47 1/8	48 4/8	35 5/8	5	6	Catron County	NM	Timothy C. Junior	1992	1,032
301 1/8	45 0/8	41 2/8	38 4/8	7	6	Teton County	WY	Craig Sorenson	1979	1,033
301 1/8	43 7/8	44 1/8	32 1/8	6	6	Clearwater County	ID	Jim Walters	1981	1,033
301 1/8	47 3/8	45 7/8	37 7/8	6	6	Lincoln County	MT	Paul Buti	1984	1,033
301 0/8	46 2/8	49 6/8	38 4/8	5	6	Sandoval County	NM	Fred J. McDonald	1985	1,036
300 7/8	45 6/8	44 5/8	39 1/8	6	5	Teton County	MT	Bill Schenck	1979	1,037
300 6/8	42 1/8	43 7/8	36 4/8	6	6	Sheridan County	WY	Kerry Struckman	1992	1,038
300 5/8	44 3/8	44 5/8	44 6/8	6	6	Beaverhead County	MT	Monty Moravec	1989	1,039
300 5/8	46 3/8	44 0/8	33 3/8	7	6	Benewah County	ID	Joel L. Emerson	1991	1,039
300 3/8	41 5/8	40 0/8	36 1/8	6	6	Fergus County	MT	Randy Cook	1981	1,041
300 3/8	46 5/8	44 5/8	44 0/8	7	7	Marion County	OR	Ron Bergeron	1986	1,041
300 3/8	47 3/8	48 4/8	30 5/8	6	6	Madison County	MT	Gary Moris	1992	1,041
300 2/8	46 2/8	45 3/8	41 0/8	6	6	McKinley County	NM	Mark Sauters	1987	1,044
300 2/8	45 7/8	46 6/8	38 2/8	5	6	Coconino County	AZ	Bradley Mitchell Irish	1990	1,044
300 2/8	41 0/8	41 2/8	38 2/8	6	6	Petroleum County	MT	Ron Kukus	1991	1,044
300 1/8	45 4/8	47 4/8	39 7/8	6	6	San Miguel County	NM	Lawrence Stiscak	1977	1,047
300 1/8	46 3/8	44 2/8	35 7/8	6	6	Clearwater County	ID	Danny Moore	1985	1,047
300 1/8	46 3/8	44 7/8	36 1/8	6	6	Sandoval County	NM	Bob Young	1990	1,047
300 1/8	43 3/8	44 6/8	38 3/8	6	6	La Plata County	CO	Bob E. Wren	1992	1,047

SCORE	LENGTH OF MAIN BEAM R	L	INSIDE SPREAD	NUMBER OF POINTS R	L	AREA	STATE/ PROVINCE	HUNTER'S NAME	DATE	RANK
300 0/8	45 2/8	44 5/8	47 3/8	6	6	Beaverhead County	MT	Greg L. Munther	1980	1,051
300 0/8	39 5/8	42 0/8	37 4/8	7	6	Coconino County	AZ	Mike Kentera	1985	1,051
300 0/8	47 4/8	46 0/8	40 0/8	6	6	Missoula County	MT	Anthony K Nease	1985	1,051
300 0/8	48 5/8	48 4/8	38 4/8	6	6	Adams County	ID	Robert Dowen	1985	1,051
300 0/8	41 4/8	42 6/8	34 6/8	6	6	Catron County	NM	Ned Smith	1991	1,051
299 7/8	51 0/8	54 0/8	41 0/8	6	7	Fergus County	MT	Charles R. Bowman	1966	1,056
299 7/8	44 4/8	44 0/8	36 3/8	5	5	Routt County	CO	Mark Wuerthele	1987	1,056
299 6/8	53 2/8	53 7/8	44 6/8	6	6	Coconino County	AZ	Michael L. Campbell	1987	1,058
299 6/8	50 4/8	49 2/8	35 6/8	6	6	Flathead County	MT	Ken White	1989	1,058
299 5/8	48 0/8	48 6/8	34 1/8	5	6	Taos County	NM	Bubba Finstad	1987	1,060
299 5/8	45 2/8	44 7/8	43 5/8	6	7	Klamath County	OR	Ron Botsford	1991	1,060
299 3/8	45 2/8	46 2/8	38 3/8	6	6	Gunnison County	CO	Gene Chastain	1985	1,062
299 3/8	42 1/8	42 3/8	42 4/8	6	8	Coconino County	AZ	Tony W. Zimbaro	1992	1,062
299 2/8	47 2/8	46 1/8	34 4/8	6	6	Caribou County	ID	Tex Wolfley	1979	1,064
299 2/8	51 4/8	49 7/8	37 2/8	6	6	Coconino County	AZ	Larry VanLiew	1983	1,064
299 2/8	46 4/8	43 3/8	32 2/8	6	7	Idaho County	ID	Neal Forrester	1989	1,064
299 1/8	44 2/8	41 2/8	32 5/8	6	6	Lincoln County	WY	Richard Peart	1980	1,067
299 1/8	47 0/8	48 1/8	39 5/8	6	6	Madison County	MT	Royce A. Carroll	1988	1,067
299 1/8	51 4/8	50 1/8	38 6/8	7	8	Catron County	NM	Thomas Merritt	1990	1,067
299 1/8	45 2/8	47 6/8	34 1/8	6	7	Catron County	NM	Jules Pacheco	1990	1,067
299 1/8	47 3/8	48 3/8	34 1/8	6	7	Caribou County	ID	Steven Boothe	1992	1,067
299 0/8	42 3/8	43 1/8	33 0/8	6	6	Mineral County	CO	Gary Oden	1976	1,072
299 0/8	45 5/8	46 4/8	37 2/8	6	6	Powell County	MT	Paul Brunner	1979	1,072
299 0/8	46 1/8	47 3/8	42 0/8	6	6	Park County	MT	Joe Skaggs	1988	1,072
299 0/8	45 0/8	46 3/8	40 4/8	6	6	Clearwater County	ID	James L. Tucker	1992	1,072
298 7/8	45 5/8	46 1/8	39 7/8	6	6	Jefferson County	CO	Jerry Grueneberg	1989	1,076
298 6/8	46 3/8	46 3/8	31 5/8	6	7	Mineral County	MT	James Kingsley	1983	1,077
298 6/8	44 2/8	45 5/8	38 0/8	6	6	Gallatin County	MT	Steven P Hopkins	1984	1,077
298 6/8	50 6/8	52 4/8	37 2/8	6	6	Catron County	NM	Wayne Keehart	1986	1,077
298 5/8	55 0/8	56 5/8	38 3/8	5	6	Coconino County	AZ	Kevin Cox	1979	1,080
298 5/8	46 0/8	47 5/8	41 7/8	6	6	Coconino County	AZ	Pete Shepley	1986	1,080
298 5/8	43 3/8	40 0/8	48 6/8	6	6	Gem County	ID	Ron Williams	1988	1,080
298 5/8	42 2/8	42 5/8	44 5/8	6	6	Sandoval County	NM	Robert Woeck	1991	1,080
298 5/8	45 3/8	44 2/8	40 1/8	6	7	Catron County	NM	Sam Thompson	1992	1,080
298 4/8	44 5/8	46 1/8	42 6/8	6	7	Coconino County	AZ	Les Shelton	1991	1,085
298 4/8	48 4/8	46 6/8	36 6/8	6	6	Catron County	NM	Steve Mastagni	1992	1,085
298 1/8	49 7/8	48 0/8	33 1/8	6	6	Park County	WY	Bruce K. Fauskee	1986	1,087
298 1/8	46 2/8	47 1/8	33 3/8	6	6	Iron County	UT	Brad Robinson	1992	1,087
298 0/8	45 6/8	46 4/8	37 0/8	6	6	Caribou County	ID	Dean Monson	1982	1,089
298 0/8	48 6/8	47 2/8	38 6/8	6	6	Delta County	CO	Todd B. Roberts	1992	1,089
298 0/8	40 0/8	41 2/8	42 0/8	6	6	Yakima County	WA	Troy Goben	1992	1,089
297 7/8	44 5/8	46 7/8	31 1/8	7	8	Coconino County	AZ	Mark Vancas	1980	1,092
297 7/8	46 4/8	47 0/8	33 5/8	6	6	Lincoln County	MT	Darryl Lien	1985	1,092
297 7/8	45 4/8	44 2/8	37 7/8	6	7	Clear Creek County	CO	Paul Ray	1988	1,092
297 7/8	46 3/8	45 0/8	37 5/8	6	6	Catron County	NM	Gale A. Hedges	1989	1,092
297 6/8	46 4/8	46 5/8	41 4/8	6	6	Boulder County	CO	Steve Gorr	1969	1,096
297 6/8	48 6/8	50 0/8	38 6/8	6	7	Caribou County	ID	Doug Cushman, Jr.	1981	1,096
297 6/8	45 6/8	43 6/8	37 6/8	6	6	Apache County	AZ	Donata P. Montgomery	1990	1,096
297 5/8	45 4/8	44 2/8	37 5/8	6	6	Caribou County	ID	Tom M. Carter	1990	1,099
297 4/8	45 1/8	41 6/8	43 0/8	6	7	King County	WA	Larry L. Sheward	1984	1,100
297 4/8	41 3/8	42 2/8	34 6/8	6	7	Huerfano County	CO	Esco R. Billings III	1992	1,100
297 3/8	46 1/8	45 2/8	42 3/8	5	7	Fremont County	ID	Thomas W. Savage	1982	1,102
297 3/8	50 2/8	53 2/8	39 7/8	6	6	Taos County	NM	Randal Church	1989	1,102
297 3/8	48 3/8	47 5/8	37 3/8	6	7	Moffat County	CO	Glenn Pritchard	1990	1,102
297 2/8	50 0/8	47 5/8	30 6/8	6	6	Grant County	OR	Joe Copeland	1986	1,105
297 1/8	46 1/8	44 2/8	42 3/8	6	8	Missoula County	MT	David E. Torrey, Jr.	1977	1,106
297 1/8	46 0/8	48 0/8	40 6/8	7	8	Coconino County	AZ	Dave Baker	1979	1,106
297 1/8	43 0/8	42 3/8	39 3/8	6	6	Wainright	ALB	Norman Hookes	1982	1,106
297 1/8	45 0/8	45 3/8	38 3/8	6	6	Granite County	MT	Ralph W. Phillips	1992	1,106
297 0/8	46 4/8	46 0/8	36 2/8	6	6	Wallowa County	OR	Martha J Soeth	1985	1,110
297 0/8	44 4/8	44 3/8	34 0/8	6	6	Rich County	UT	Hugh H. Hogle	1986	1,110
297 0/8	41 6/8	46 5/8	37 2/8	6	6	Rio Arriba County	NM	Patrick Smith	1988	1,110
297 0/8	43 2/8	42 0/8	36 2/8	6	6	Coconino County	AZ	Gary Linendoll	1990	1,110
296 6/8	47 4/8	46 4/8	35 6/8	6	6	Idaho County	ID	Gerald B. Jameson	1987	1,114
296 6/8	50 7/8	51 6/8	40 6/8	6	6	Coconino County	AZ	Jerry W. Lilly	1992	1,114
296 5/8	46 6/8	44 6/8	32 6/8	6	7	Kakwa River	ALB	Wilf Lehners	1990	1,116
296 5/8	48 2/8	52 1/8	44 7/8	6	7	Greenlee County	AZ	Bill Golden	1992	1,116
296 4/8	45 1/8	46 7/8	35 4/8	6	6	Catron County	NM	Randall N. Bostick	1988	1,118
296 4/8	42 5/8	40 7/8	35 6/8	6	6	Park County	WY	John R. Buche	1989	1,118
296 3/8	41 7/8	44 2/8	39 3/8	6	6	Idaho County	ID	Jerry Vega	1985	1,120

SCORE	LENGTH OF MAIN BEAM R	L	INSIDE SPREAD	NUMBER OF POINTS R	L	AREA	STATE/ PROVINCE	HUNTER'S NAME	DATE	RANK
296 3/8	39 3/8	39 1/8	42 7/8	6	6	Sheridan County	WY	Richard M. Young, Jr.	1988	1,120
296 2/8	45 7/8	44 6/8	37 0/8	6	7	Clackamas County	OR	Bill Lancaster	1984	1,122
296 2/8	44 6/8	44 2/8	36 0/8	6	6	Crook County	OR	Rod Curtis	1984	1,122
296 2/8	48 7/8	45 4/8	37 6/8	6	6	Moffat County	CO	Robert L Syvertson, Jr.	1984	1,122
296 2/8	48 4/8	48 0/8	40 2/8	6	6	Catron County	NM	Pete Raynor	1989	1,122
296 2/8	49 2/8	49 1/8	35 2/8	6	6	Canal Flats	BC	Glenn Dreger	1990	1,122
296 2/8	49 4/8	48 1/8	37 2/8	7	6	Coconino County	AZ	Charles Urban	1992	1,122
296 1/8	43 2/8	45 3/8	43 1/8	6	6	Sheridan County	WY	Mike Barrett	1982	1,128
296 1/8	44 3/8	44 3/8	32 1/8	6	6	Wolverine Creek	ALB	Dave Bathke	1990	1,128
296 0/8	44 2/8	45 0/8	39 4/8	6	6	Gallatin County	MT	Bob Savage	1968	1,130
296 0/8	48 7/8	46 6/8	37 6/8	6	6	Bighorn Mountains	WY	Dean Fudge	1979	1,130
296 0/8	40 7/8	41 7/8	28 4/8	8	6	Spruce Woods	MAN	Brian Morash	1981	1,130
296 0/8	44 5/8	44 0/8	33 4/8	6	6	Flathead County	MT	Mark Fopp	1987	1,130
296 0/8	48 7/8	50 6/8	40 2/8	6	5	Lemhi County	ID	David C. Manca	1991	1,130
296 0/8	47 2/8	52 0/8	41 4/8	5	6	Phillips County	MT	Ronald S. Kline	1991	1,130
296 0/8	45 6/8	45 6/8	38 6/8	6	6	Montrose County	CO	Bobby David Tipping	1992	1,130
295 7/8	42 5/8	40 5/8	38 2/8	6	7	Larimer County	CO	Ben Alexander	1972	1,137
295 7/8	44 4/8	43 7/8	38 1/8	6	7	Madison County	MT	Kevin Fogal	1985	1,137
295 6/8	49 6/8	50 0/8	38 4/8	6	6	Bonneville County	ID	Jim Cox	1976	1,139
295 6/8	43 7/8	44 6/8	32 6/8	6	6	Powell County	MT	Bryan C. Anderson	1985	1,139
295 6/8	42 0/8	46 0/8	40 2/8	6	6	Boulder County	CO	Jerry Bryan	1986	1,139
295 6/8	45 5/8	45 3/8	41 0/8	6	6	Gallatin County	MT	H. C. Tysinger, Jr.	1986	1,139
295 4/8	48 0/8	47 1/8	37 0/8	6	6	Custer County	ID	A. Lynn Burton	1982	1,143
295 4/8	46 4/8	45 3/8	42 0/8	6	6	Clearwater County	ID	Jerry Weverka	1988	1,143
295 4/8	46 1/8	45 0/8	39 4/8	6	6	Clackamas County	OR	David L. Winters	1989	1,143
295 3/8	45 2/8	43 6/8	37 1/8	6	6	Catron County	NM	Ricardo Unzueta	1992	1,146
295 3/8	47 5/8	47 7/8	33 7/8	6	6	Socorro County	NM	Doug Aikin	1992	1,146
295 2/8	45 0/8	46 4/8	38 4/8	6	6	Lincoln County	NM	Bart J. Gillan III	1984	1,148
295 2/8	51 3/8	51 3/8	37 0/8	7	6	Kittitas County	WA	Kirk Cresto	1984	1,148
295 2/8	48 4/8	48 4/8	40 6/8	6	6	Catron County	NM	Gary Burnett	1986	1,148
295 2/8	43 4/8	48 4/8	39 6/8	6	5	Catron County	NM	Spencer O. Moore III	1986	1,148
295 2/8	42 5/8	42 0/8	41 4/8	6	6	Clearwater County	ID	Rudy Marmelo, Jr.	1988	1,148
295 2/8	44 4/8	44 1/8	51 1/8	6	6	Pueblo County	CO	Steve Willsey	1991	1,148
295 1/8	43 1/8	42 0/8	39 1/8	6	6	Gallatin County	MT	Tom L. Miller	1986	1,154
295 1/8	42 4/8	44 0/8	36 3/8	6	6	Sublette County	WY	Ronald A. Noble	1989	1,154
295 0/8	51 2/8	49 7/8	38 5/8	7	6	Crook County	OR	Michael Hawkins	1983	1,156
295 0/8	43 7/8	42 7/8	36 6/8	6	6	Catron County	NM	Loyd Street	1988	1,156
294 7/8	42 1/8	41 0/8	46 3/8	6	6	Catron County	NM	John McClendon	1987	1,158
294 7/8	48 4/8	44 5/8	44 3/8	6	6	Coconino County	AZ	Michael Weldon	1988	1,158
294 7/8	41 1/8	40 6/8	38 7/8	6	6	Priddis Creek	ALB	Roger Meyer	1991	1,158
294 7/8	48 6/8	48 6/8	37 3/8	6	6	Coconino County	AZ	Ralph B. Harris	1991	1,158
294 5/8	41 2/8	39 7/8	38 7/8	6	6	Fremont County	CO	William Bowlby	1984	1,162
294 5/8	52 3/8	49 0/8	38 7/8	5	6	Sanders County	MT	Ralph W. Flockerzi	1987	1,162
294 5/8	50 0/8	47 2/8	35 5/8	6	6	Sandoval County	NM	Robert K. Woeck	1992	1,162
294 4/8	46 0/8	45 2/8	40 2/8	6	6	Deer Lodge County	MT	Dale J. Goytowski	1986	1,165
294 4/8	48 3/8	50 0/8	46 4/8	6	6	McKinley County	NM	Eugene Duran	1987	1,165
294 4/8	45 2/8	47 1/8	32 4/8	6	6	Coconino County	AZ	Jesse Smith	1988	1,165
294 4/8	45 2/8	41 5/8	41 6/8	6	7	Grant County	OR	James M. Carter	1990	1,165
294 4/8	46 4/8	45 6/8	39 0/8	6	6	Shoshone County	ID	David V. Wait	1992	1,165
294 3/8	45 0/8	48 4/8	37 1/8	5	7	Saguache County	CO	David A. Larson	1978	1,170
294 3/8	45 1/8	46 0/8	35 1/8	6	6	Socorro County	NM	Eddie Claypool	1988	1,170
294 3/8	45 7/8	44 1/8	44 7/8	6	6	Granite County	MT	Scott A. Breum	1992	1,170
294 3/8	43 2/8	44 1/8	36 7/8	6	6	Lincoln County	WY	Steven B. Julander	1992	1,170
294 2/8	50 2/8	45 6/8	37 0/8	7	6	La Plata County	CO	J. Barry Dyar	1983	1,174
294 2/8	43 5/8	45 4/8	40 2/8	7	6	Apache County	AZ	Fred Clifford	1985	1,174
294 2/8	42 5/8	46 2/8	42 0/8	6	6	Catron County	NM	Billy Barber	1986	1,174
294 2/8	43 7/8	40 7/8	35 2/8	6	6	Otero County	NM	Bruce Bonnet	1990	1,174
294 2/8	48 4/8	48 2/8	38 1/8	7	6	Grand County	CO	Mike Brown	1992	1,174
294 0/8	41 1/8	42 5/8	33 0/8	6	6	Clearwater County	ID	Don Kubasch	1981	1,179
293 7/8	46 3/8	48 0/8	40 5/8	6	6	Gunnison County	CO	Robert C. Goodman	1974	1,180
293 7/8	42 6/8	44 4/8	34 5/8	6	5	Graham County	AZ	Clifford White	1982	1,180
293 7/8	50 4/8	47 5/8	33 5/8	6	6	Phillips County	MT	Mike Mjelstad	1987	1,180
293 7/8	45 5/8	45 4/8	39 5/8	5	5	Idaho County	ID	Michael J. Collins	1990	1,180
293 7/8	48 0/8	48 6/8	37 3/8	6	6	Custer County	ID	Tom Szurgot	1990	1,180
293 7/8	48 3/8	48 3/8	33 3/8	6	6	Missoula County	MT	Pao K. Moua	1990	1,180
293 6/8	47 0/8	45 4/8	37 0/8	6	6	Archuleta County	CO	Eddie Claypool	1985	1,186
293 6/8	43 1/8	46 0/8	46 6/8	6	6	Lemhi County	ID	Ben L. Fahnholz	1987	1,186
293 6/8	49 3/8	48 0/8	38 6/8	6	6	Sheridan County	WY	Gary T. Laya	1988	1,186
293 6/8	50 4/8	52 2/8	31 0/8	6	6	Rio Arriba County	NM	Paul Locey	1990	1,186
293 6/8	48 3/8	47 0/8	45 0/8	6	7	Grant County	OR	Tim L. Hayward	1991	1,186

SCORE	LENGTH OF MAIN BEAM R	L	INSIDE SPREAD	NUMBER OF POINTS R	L	AREA	STATE/ PROVINCE	HUNTER'S NAME	DATE	RANK
293 5/8	42 6/8	43 3/8	39 7/8	6	6	West	MT	Raymond Alt	1962	1,191
293 4/8	49 5/8	50 2/8	42 2/8	6	5	Sheridan County	WY	Mike Barrett	1980	1,192
293 4/8	47 4/8	46 6/8	34 6/8	6	6	Beaverhead County	MT	Dennis Rehse	1981	1,192
293 4/8	50 0/8	46 4/8	33 6/8	6	6	Catron County	NM	Bob Gourley	1984	1,192
293 3/8	46 0/8	45 5/8	37 5/8	6	6	Boise County	ID	David Hale	1983	1,195
293 3/8	46 0/8	45 5/8	30 5/8	6	7	Lemhi County	ID	William C. Shuster	1986	1,195
293 3/8	46 6/8	47 4/8	32 5/8	6	6	Gallatin County	MT	Michael Groulx	1990	1,195
293 3/8	45 1/8	43 0/8	40 1/8	5	6	Morgan County	UT	Pancho McCoy	1992	1,195
293 3/8	46 6/8	46 5/8	36 5/8	6	6	Lewis County	WA	Scott Murray	1992	1,195
293 2/8	47 2/8	47 6/8	39 2/8	6	6	Musselshell County	MT	Dan Acord	1986	1,200
293 2/8	42 6/8	42 6/8	32 4/8	6	6	Flathead County	MT	Larry O. Hadley	1987	1,200
293 2/8	46 6/8	46 6/8	35 6/8	6	6	Navajo County	AZ	Corky Richardson	1990	1,200
293 2/8	47 7/8	47 7/8	36 6/8	6	6	Los Alamos County	NM	Jeffrey M. Bradley	1992	1,200
293 1/8	44 6/8	39 1/8	32 1/8	6	6	Clearwater County	ID	T. LeRoy West	1981	1,204
293 1/8	42 6/8	39 6/8	35 1/8	6	6	Catron County	NM	Butch Allen	1990	1,204
293 0/8	49 0/8	48 4/8	32 4/8	6	6	Beaverhead County	MT	Martin L. Sapp	1988	1,206
293 0/8	42 7/8	44 2/8	40 4/8	6	6	Sandoval County	NM	John Clarence Rector	1990	1,206
293 0/8	42 6/8	45 4/8	40 2/8	8	7	Wallowa County	OR	Dwight Huffman	1990	1,206
293 0/8	44 0/8	44 1/8	38 6/8	6	6	Catron County	NM	Leonard Rohlik	1991	1,206
292 7/8	48 0/8	52 4/8	38 5/8	6	6	Sweet Grass County	MT	Dr. Dale Schlehuber	1986	1,210
292 7/8	46 7/8	46 4/8	40 5/8	6	6	Lincoln County	MT	Dan Bundrock	1989	1,210
292 7/8	41 4/8	41 3/8	38 5/8	6	6	Boulder County	CO	Ron Readmond	1990	1,210
292 7/8	45 5/8	44 1/8	36 1/8	6	6	Petroleum County	MT	Don Davidson	1992	1,210
292 6/8	42 3/8	44 5/8	34 0/8	6	6	Chouteau County	MT	Tom Brady	1987	1,214
292 5/8	43 6/8	42 1/8	34 1/8	7	6	Rio Blanco County	CO	James Raetz	1976	1,215
292 5/8	45 2/8	42 6/8	35 1/8	6	6	Catron County	NM	John Stanley	1987	1,215
292 5/8	41 1/8	41 1/8	33 5/8	6	6	Albany County	WY	Michael Lancaster	1990	1,215
292 5/8	39 2/8	38 5/8	39 7/8	6	7	Colfax County	NM	Dave Holt	1990	1,215
292 4/8	48 0/8	50 4/8	33 4/8	6	6	Sanders County	MT	Doug Gunderson	1978	1,219
292 4/8	43 0/8	43 6/8	40 2/8	6	6	Jackson County	CO	Daniel H. Chaney	1981	1,219
292 4/8	43 1/8	42 1/8	30 0/8	6	6	Strathcona	ALB	Jack Kempf	1984	1,219
292 4/8	46 6/8	46 2/8	34 4/8	6	6	Grant County	OR	Terry J. Caster	1990	1,219
292 4/8	42 4/8	42 0/8	37 0/8	6	6	Morgan County	UT	Brad T. Francis	1991	1,219
292 3/8	44 6/8	40 4/8	35 1/8	6	6	Idaho County	ID	Robert C. Mitchell	1979	1,224
292 3/8	44 6/8	44 2/8	36 3/8	6	6	Ravalli County	MT	Paul Hamilton	1984	1,224
292 2/8	41 2/8	44 4/8	39 6/8	6	6	Idaho County	ID	Richard C. Nichols	1975	1,226
292 2/8	47 5/8	46 1/8	31 4/8	6	6	Mineral County	MT	Kenneth D. Verley	1981	1,226
292 2/8	45 2/8	49 1/8	33 4/8	6	6	Grant County	OR	Robert R. Gedlick	1983	1,226
292 2/8	42 5/8	41 3/8	35 2/8	6	6	Clark County	ID	Billy Burbank III	1988	1,226
292 1/8	44 7/8	47 0/8	34 3/8	6	6	Powell County	MT	Richard W. Malone	1976	1,230
292 1/8	47 5/8	47 0/8	46 7/8	6	6	Coconino County	AZ	Bryant McGee	1980	1,230
292 1/8	49 4/8	48 2/8	39 5/8	6	6	Custer County	ID	James Schrader	1991	1,230
292 1/8	40 3/8	38 4/8	41 4/8	6	6	Park County	WY	Scott Moore	1991	1,230
292 0/8	36 2/8	37 6/8	33 4/8	6	6	Lincoln County	NM	Terence A. Wahlgren	1985	1,234
292 0/8	46 0/8	45 0/8	34 0/8	6	6	Catron County	NM	Brad Blanchard	1989	1,234
292 0/8	43 7/8	43 0/8	36 2/8	6	7	Uintah County	UT	Smiley Arrowchis	1989	1,234
292 0/8	44 6/8	44 6/8	39 0/8	6	6	Coconino County	AZ	Mark J. Dominguez	1991	1,234
291 7/8	45 7/8	45 0/8	46 2/8	6	6	Coconino County	AZ	Dick & Gary Mendenhall	1974	1,238
291 7/8	45 5/8	45 2/8	38 5/8	6	6	Chaffee County	CO	Douglas E. Wilson	1982	1,238
291 7/8	52 7/8	51 5/8	46 1/8	5	6	King County	WA	Ty Martin	1984	1,238
291 7/8	44 2/8	44 0/8	35 7/8	6	6	Saguache County	CO	Dario J. Archuleta	1991	1,238
291 7/8	46 6/8	43 2/8	39 1/8	5	5	Fremont County	WY	Nelson Scherrer	1991	1,238
291 6/8	45 2/8	45 5/8	41 0/8	6	6	Summit County	CO	Howard Moser	1972	1,243
291 6/8	45 4/8	45 1/8	40 0/8	6	6	Gem County	ID	Larry Holmquist	1986	1,243
291 5/8	53 2/8	54 6/8	34 7/8	7	7	Coconino County	AZ	Bruce Ludeke	1989	1,245
291 4/8	45 4/8	43 7/8	38 4/8	6	6	Dolores County	CO	William W. Gurley	1977	1,246
291 4/8	42 2/8	43 4/8	35 2/8	7	6	Garfield County	MT	Gaylord Johnson	1983	1,246
291 4/8	44 2/8	44 6/8	34 4/8	6	6	Sanders County	MT	Matthew J. Dorenkamper	1992	1,246
291 3/8	44 6/8	46 1/8	42 1/8	6	5	Idaho County	ID	Dr. Brian M. Howard	1987	1,249
291 2/8	44 1/8	48 1/8	27 0/8	6	6	Phillips County	MT	Scott L. Augustine	1980	1,250
291 2/8	47 5/8	45 0/8	36 6/8	6	6	Albany County	WY	Oliver P. Williamson	1982	1,250
291 2/8	43 7/8	44 6/8	46 5/8	6	7	Clearwater County	ID	Scott Rabe	1984	1,250
291 2/8	43 6/8	46 7/8	31 4/8	7	6	Gilpin County	CO	Lee L. Florian	1986	1,250
291 2/8	52 1/8	51 4/8	35 4/8	6	6	Clearwater County	ID	Jim Horneck	1987	1,250
291 1/8	43 4/8	41 6/8	35 3/8	7	6	Coconino County	AZ	Tom Jensen	1989	1,255
291 1/8	48 1/8	47 6/8	39 5/8	6	6	Grant County	OR	Dennis McClelland	1991	1,255
291 1/8	46 7/8	47 2/8	30 5/8	6	6	Montrose County	CO	Lannie Ellis	1991	1,255
291 0/8	48 4/8	49 4/8	40 4/8	6	6	Custer County	CO	Douglas R. Jones	1970	1,258
291 0/8	50 2/8	49 1/8	35 0/8	6	6	Elmore County	ID	Gary Briggs	1986	1,258
291 0/8	47 2/8	47 0/8	38 4/8	6	5	Skamania County	WA	Terry Kern	1987	1,258

SCORE	LENGTH OF MAIN BEAM R	LENGTH OF MAIN BEAM L	INSIDE SPREAD	NUMBER OF POINTS R	NUMBER OF POINTS L	AREA	STATE/ PROVINCE	HUNTER'S NAME	DATE	RANK
290 7/8	44 6/8	42 6/8	38 5/8	6	6	Ravalli County	MT	Sheldon M. Jones	1991	1,261
290 6/8	42 4/8	43 0/8	35 6/8	6	6	Park County	WY	William P. Mastrangel	1955	1,262
290 6/8	42 6/8	43 6/8	36 2/8	5	5	Larimer County	CO	Tom Tietz	1979	1,262
290 6/8	41 5/8	41 3/8	38 0/8	6	6	Rio Arriba County	NM	Craig Barrows	1990	1,262
290 6/8	46 2/8	46 5/8	38 6/8	6	7	Coconino County	AZ	Duane "Corky" Richardson	1991	1,262
290 6/8	42 4/8	43 6/8	38 2/8	6	6	Madison County	MT	Randy Brown	1991	1,262
290 5/8	45 2/8	46 6/8	36 7/8	8	8	Greenlee County	AZ	Sonny Turner	1986	1,267
290 5/8	51 7/8	50 0/8	30 3/8	6	7	Coconino County	AZ	John Alfred Musgrove	1989	1,267
290 3/8	49 4/8	48 7/8	36 7/8	6	6	Custer County	ID	Tom Jarvis	1984	1,269
290 3/8	49 2/8	49 2/8	39 5/8	6	6	Sublette County	WY	Joey Gomes	1989	1,269
290 2/8	45 7/8	46 4/8	41 4/8	6	6	Gunnison County	CO	Jack Allen Rasmusson	1982	1,271
290 2/8	42 6/8	44 5/8	40 0/8	6	6	Granite County	MT	Dennis Neitzke	1985	1,271
290 2/8	42 1/8	40 3/8	34 6/8	6	6	Gallatin County	MT	Chris Cey	1991	1,271
290 1/8	45 6/8	44 7/8	38 3/8	6	6	Grant County	OR	James M. Carter	1984	1,274
290 1/8	49 4/8	49 4/8	40 7/8	6	6	McKinley County	NM	Larry Dwyer	1989	1,274
290 0/8	47 2/8	46 4/8	39 0/8	6	6	Phillips County	MT	Cecil I. Tharp	1978	1,276
290 0/8	41 6/8	43 5/8	43 5/8	6	7	Canmore	ALB	David R. Coupland	1980	1,276
290 0/8	45 7/8	42 4/8	35 6/8	6	6	Shoshone County	ID	Larry Rose	1988	1,276
289 7/8	43 0/8	41 0/8	40 3/8	6	6	Boulder County	CO	John Powell	1983	1,279
289 7/8	47 7/8	47 4/8	36 5/8	6	6	Missoula County	MT	Bill Spicknall	1984	1,279
289 7/8	41 5/8	46 3/8	40 3/8	6	6	Mesa County	CO	George P. Sofronas	1986	1,279
289 6/8	45 3/8	45 0/8	35 6/8	6	6	Ravalli County	MT	Dan Smith	1980	1,282
289 6/8	42 3/8	41 6/8	33 0/8	5	6	Rich County	UT	Raymond E. Goff	1989	1,282
289 5/8	42 2/8	42 2/8	38 3/8	6	6	Ravalli County	MT	Michael S. Mitchell	1985	1,284
289 4/8	48 0/8	50 3/8	33 2/8	6	6	Clearwater County	ID	LeRoy West	1983	1,285
289 4/8	48 0/8	46 4/8	41 0/8	6	6	Coconino County	AZ	Fred Searle	1985	1,285
289 4/8	44 5/8	42 0/8	39 2/8	7	7	Grant County	OR	Ray Martin	1988	1,285
289 3/8	43 1/8	43 4/8	38 7/8	5	5	Lewis County	WA	Douglas H. Brandt	1986	1,288
289 3/8	40 4/8	42 0/8	37 3/8	6	7	Valley County	MT	Erik E. Scarpholt	1986	1,288
289 3/8	41 7/8	44 5/8	38 7/8	6	6	Hinsdale County	CO	Kevin W. Bauman	1989	1,288
289 3/8	46 1/8	46 1/8	44 1/8	6	6	Sandoval County	NM	Randy Erickson	1992	1,288
289 2/8	43 7/8	45 3/8	33 0/8	6	6	Converse County	WY	Darin L. Geringer	1989	1,292
289 2/8	48 0/8	50 0/8	34 2/8	6	6	Sandoval County	NM	Danny Lee Reed	1989	1,292
289 2/8	49 2/8	48 0/8	41 4/8	6	6	Pitkin County	CO	James L. Behn	1990	1,292
289 2/8	54 7/8	55 4/8	38 0/8	7	7	Grant County	NM	Adam Jimenez, Jr.	1991	1,292
289 1/8	46 0/8	46 1/8	35 1/8	6	6	Catron County	NM	Paul D. Payne	1986	1,296
289 1/8	46 5/8	45 7/8	38 3/8	6	6	Flathead County	MT	Bill Love	1987	1,296
289 1/8	43 4/8	48 1/8	35 7/8	6	6	Lemhi County	ID	Danny Moore	1988	1,296
289 0/8	51 6/8	50 0/8	38 6/8	6	6	Socorro County	NM	Will Eckelhoff	1991	1,299
288 7/8	44 6/8	45 4/8	38 6/8	6	7	Ravalli County	MT	David Harris Stalling	1992	1,300
288 6/8	53 1/8	52 5/8	34 2/8	5	6	Lane County	OR	Ken Abraham	1986	1,301
288 6/8	43 3/8	44 0/8	31 2/8	6	6	Teton County	MT	Brad Stewart	1992	1,301
288 5/8	46 5/8	44 6/8	39 1/8	6	6	Rio Arriba County	NM	Keith Cheatham	1988	1,303
288 5/8	43 0/8	45 4/8	37 5/8	6	6	Adams County	ID	Randal R. Siemens	1990	1,303
288 5/8	49 6/8	48 5/8	38 3/8	6	6	Sierra County	NM	Bill Elmer	1990	1,303
288 5/8	47 3/8	44 2/8	35 3/8	6	6	Coconino County	AZ	David C. Fretz	1991	1,303
288 4/8	50 2/8	49 2/8	34 4/8	6	6	Lemhi County	ID	Ben L. Fahnholz	1984	1,307
288 4/8	44 5/8	48 3/8	39 4/8	5	6	San Miguel County	NM	Robert B. Lewis	1987	1,307
288 4/8	40 6/8	41 5/8	38 6/8	6	6	Sandoval County	NM	Peter C. Swenson	1990	1,307
288 4/8	44 0/8	45 0/8	44 0/8	6	6	Klickitat County	WA	Tom Gaul	1991	1,307
288 4/8	47 6/8	49 3/8	40 4/8	6	6	Rio Arriba County	NM	Scott Miller	1992	1,307
288 3/8	43 2/8	44 5/8	34 7/8	6	6	Marion County	OR	Daniel Smith	1989	1,312
288 2/8	50 6/8	48 3/8	39 2/8	6	6	Lincoln County	MT	Robert L. Burk	1976	1,313
288 2/8	46 2/8	45 0/8	39 6/8	6	6	Lemhi County	ID	John A. McCarthy	1984	1,313
288 2/8	44 5/8	44 1/8	32 7/8	7	6	Greenlee County	AZ	John C. Jackson	1987	1,313
288 2/8	48 0/8	48 2/8	30 6/8	6	6	Madison County	MT	Ben Manor	1990	1,313
288 0/8	46 4/8	44 4/8	35 0/8	6	6	Albany County	WY	Dan Kolb	1981	1,317
288 0/8	49 2/8	47 7/8	36 0/8	5	6	Carbon County	UT	David A. Justmann	1989	1,317
288 0/8	44 3/8	45 6/8	44 0/8	6	6	Yakima County	WA	Gaylen Bierman	1990	1,317
287 7/8	38 1/8	38 4/8	34 7/8	6	6	Garfield County	CO	Michael J. Reid	1981	1,320
287 6/8	44 0/8	44 0/8	35 4/8	6	6	Idaho County	ID	Ronald Ward	1984	1,321
287 5/8	50 4/8	48 5/8	38 1/8	6	7	Park County	MT	George Kamps	1987	1,322
287 4/8	44 4/8	45 0/8	38 2/8	6	6	Adams County	ID	Gary Kinney	1986	1,323
287 4/8	45 2/8	44 0/8	39 0/8	6	6	Baker County	OR	Larry D. Jones	1987	1,323
287 4/8	43 1/8	41 6/8	36 1/8	6	7	Morgan County	UT	Hal Stauff	1987	1,323
287 4/8	45 4/8	44 5/8	35 6/8	6	6	Phillips County	MT	William P. Kirkman	1987	1,323
287 4/8	42 0/8	41 0/8	37 2/8	6	6	Phillips County	MT	Kenneth E. Ruzicka	1988	1,323
287 3/8	45 2/8	43 2/8	29 3/8	6	7	Bighorn Mountains	WY	Don Dvoroznak	1977	1,328
287 3/8	49 7/8	50 4/8	35 4/8	6	7	Coconino County	AZ	William P. Pate	1979	1,328
287 3/8	51 3/8	50 0/8	44 1/8	6	7	Beaverhead County	MT	Ronnie Everett	1982	1,328

SCORE	LENGTH OF MAIN BEAM R	L	INSIDE SPREAD	NUMBER OF POINTS R	L	AREA	STATE/ PROVINCE	HUNTER'S NAME	DATE	RANK
287 3/8	50 7/8	50 1/8	39 3/8	6	6	Lane County	OR	Charles M. Reich	1991	1,328
287 2/8	41 4/8	41 4/8	29 2/8	6	6	San Isabel National Forest	CO	Richard L. Doman	1977	1,332
287 2/8	50 0/8	50 6/8	35 4/8	6	6	Grand County	CO	Robert Pitt	1978	1,332
287 2/8	42 6/8	41 6/8	32 0/8	6	6	Flathead County	MT	Rod Hickle	1982	1,332
287 2/8	45 6/8	46 7/8	35 6/8	6	6	Sublette County	WY	Ron A. Noble	1987	1,332
287 2/8	40 0/8	41 6/8	36 4/8	7	6	Larimer County	CO	Brent Byram	1989	1,332
287 2/8	46 4/8	46 5/8	32 4/8	5	6	Catron County	NM	Glenn Isler	1991	1,332
287 2/8	42 0/8	41 2/8	38 0/8	6	6	La Plata County	CO	Brook Jobes	1991	1,332
287 2/8	41 6/8	43 6/8	38 6/8	6	6	San Jaun County	CO	WIlliam J. Farrell	1991	1,332
287 2/8	44 1/8	45 6/8	34 0/8	6	6	Sandoval County	NM	Joe H. Campbell	1992	1,332
287 1/8	46 0/8	45 6/8	37 3/8	6	7	Valley County	ID	L. Lombard/C. Rukkala	1980	1,341
287 1/8	44 1/8	44 0/8	32 7/8	6	6	Apache County	AZ	John A. Holcomb	1981	1,341
287 1/8	44 7/8	43 6/8	37 3/8	7	7	Sheridan County	WY	Richard Miller	1987	1,341
287 1/8	48 0/8	49 5/8	37 5/8	6	6	Washakie County	WY	Terry Kuhnert	1991	1,341
287 1/8	44 1/8	44 3/8	41 1/8	6	6	Uinta County	WY	Jason Rooney	1992	1,341
287 0/8	46 2/8	47 2/8	42 6/8	6	5	Three Sisters Mtn.	ALB	David R. Coupland	1986	1,346
286 7/8	42 4/8	42 0/8	40 5/8	6	6	Lewis & Clark County	MT	Stephen Tylinski	1979	1,347
286 7/8	48 2/8	46 4/8	36 7/8	6	6	Valley County	MT	Jim Seiler	1986	1,347
286 7/8	43 0/8	42 6/8	39 1/8	6	7	Fergus County	MT	Robert L. Little, Jr.	1989	1,347
286 7/8	49 2/8	48 0/8	33 7/8	7	6	Coconino County	AZ	Van Clark	1989	1,347
286 7/8	45 2/8	46 1/8	31 5/8	5	5	Park County	MT	George Kamps	1991	1,347
286 6/8	46 5/8	47 0/8	36 2/8	6	6	Valley County	ID	Phil VonBargen	1982	1,352
286 6/8	49 7/8	47 2/8	35 2/8	6	6	Sandoval County	NM	Wilbern Glenn Hitt	1985	1,352
286 6/8	43 7/8	45 4/8	38 2/8	6	6	Mesa County	CO	Brad R. Davidson	1988	1,352
286 6/8	44 0/8	44 6/8	32 4/8	6	5	Petroleum County	MT	Scott Ballem	1992	1,352
286 5/8	42 1/8	42 0/8	39 3/8	6	6	Gallatin County	MT	Arnold Marolf	1977	1,356
286 4/8	43 1/8	44 1/8	39 4/8	6	6	Shoshone County	ID	Donald A. Young	1979	1,357
286 4/8	41 4/8	43 6/8	39 4/8	6	6	Clackamas County	OR	Larry D. Jones	1983	1,357
286 4/8	49 0/8	52 2/8	30 6/8	6	6	Coconino County	AZ	Bob Dooley	1984	1,357
286 4/8	44 0/8	44 2/8	36 0/8	6	6	Morgan County	UT	Robert G. Petersen	1987	1,357
286 4/8	40 5/8	40 5/8	35 6/8	6	6	Ravalli County	MT	Rod Osburn	1989	1,357
286 4/8	47 2/8	46 6/8	34 2/8	6	6	Boise County	ID	Todd Kane	1990	1,357
286 3/8	42 2/8	41 7/8	38 7/8	6	6	Rio Arriba County	NM	Jim Dougherty	1989	1,363
286 2/8	44 6/8	47 6/8	43 6/8	6	6	Uintah County	UT	Larry L. Parker	1990	1,364
286 2/8	44 6/8	44 2/8	38 0/8	6	6	La Plata County	CO	David A. Crom	1991	1,364
286 1/8	44 6/8	44 6/8	41 7/8	6	6	Mineral County	MT	Ken Drake	1981	1,366
286 1/8	46 6/8	49 5/8	38 3/8	6	6	Yakima County	WA	Raymond Gimlin	1984	1,366
286 1/8	41 7/8	41 5/8	40 0/8	6	7	Beaverhead County	MT	Shaun Twardoski	1987	1,366
286 0/8	45 6/8	45 5/8	31 6/8	6	6	Fergus County	MT	Tom Madden	1991	1,369
285 6/8	46 1/8	47 4/8	30 6/8	6	6	Blaine County	ID	Andy Moore	1985	1,370
285 6/8	41 4/8	41 3/8	41 0/8	6	6	Crook County	OR	Scott Stomps	1988	1,370
285 5/8	47 3/8	48 2/8	45 3/8	6	6	Lemhi County	ID	Dennis DesJardins	1969	1,372
285 5/8	42 7/8	39 5/8	44 3/8	6	6	Lemhi County	ID	Larry Cross	1981	1,372
285 5/8	45 3/8	45 1/8	37 3/8	6	7	Missoula County	MT	Paul Pasquariello	1982	1,372
285 5/8	44 4/8	43 6/8	34 3/8	6	6	Taos County	NM	Randal Church	1987	1,372
285 5/8	45 6/8	46 4/8	41 5/8	6	6	Coconino County	AZ	Robert V. Ruiz	1988	1,372
285 5/8	42 1/8	41 1/8	38 3/8	6	6	Larimer County	CO	George Banderia	1989	1,372
285 4/8	42 2/8	38 1/8	40 4/8	6	5	Catron County	NM	Eddie Collins	1986	1,378
285 4/8	43 6/8	44 4/8	41 2/8	6	6	Beaverhead County	MT	Mike Davis	1989	1,378
285 4/8	42 6/8	43 5/8	36 0/8	7	6	Catron County	NM	Les Norman	1990	1,378
285 4/8	46 1/8	39 5/8	40 4/8	7	6	Socorro County	NM	Gilbert Apodaca	1990	1,378
285 3/8	45 4/8	45 7/8	36 1/8	6	6	Umatilla County	OR	Bob Burggraff	1982	1,382
285 3/8	46 5/8	38 4/8	32 5/8	6	6	Caribou County	ID	Craig Hill	1988	1,382
285 3/8	46 3/8	45 5/8	37 1/8	6	6	Mineral County	CO	Douglas A. Ducote, Jr.	1990	1,382
285 3/8	43 2/8	45 4/8	35 5/8	6	6	Grant County	OR	Dean Pasche	1991	1,382
285 2/8	43 2/8	41 5/8	52 0/8	6	6	Albany County	WY	Douglas Cringan	1991	1,386
285 2/8	46 0/8	45 7/8	31 0/8	6	6	Caribou County	ID	John C. Miller	1991	1,386
285 1/8	44 6/8	46 0/8	45 4/8	7	6	Sanders County	MT	Conrad Anderson	1983	1,388
285 0/8	45 4/8	45 2/8	33 4/8	6	6	Fergus County	MT	James Southworth	1980	1,389
285 0/8	40 3/8	44 6/8	33 4/8	6	6	Umatilla County	OR	Ray A. Warren	1982	1,389
285 0/8	47 7/8	47 4/8	37 2/8	5	6	Sandoval County	NM	Robert L. Pagel	1987	1,389
284 7/8	44 2/8	44 7/8	35 7/8	6	6	Lewis & Clark County	MT	Ron Granneman	1977	1,392
284 7/8	43 3/8	42 4/8	44 1/8	6	6	Malheur County	OR	Kent Kemble	1982	1,392
284 7/8	43 0/8	44 1/8	35 1/8	6	7	Catron County	NM	Dean Hamilton	1986	1,392
284 7/8	44 2/8	43 4/8	32 3/8	6	6	Sanders County	MT	Jim Regh, Jr.	1986	1,392
284 6/8	47 5/8	47 7/8	37 4/8	6	6	Marion County	OR	Jack Smith	1984	1,396
284 6/8	43 2/8	43 6/8	43 0/8	6	6	Socorro County	NM	Kenneth M. Thompson	1991	1,396
284 5/8	44 0/8	45 0/8	33 7/8	5	7	Eagle County	CO	Stan Hunt	1981	1,398
284 5/8	41 1/8	40 6/8	37 3/8	6	6	Fergus County	MT	Frank R. Thompson	1991	1,398
284 4/8	46 4/8	40 0/8	40 2/8	6	7	Gallatin National Forest	MT	Dennis Fishbaugher	1981	1,400

Score	Length of Main Beam R	Length of Main Beam L	Inside Spread	Number of Points R	Number of Points L	Area	State/Province	Hunter's Name	Date	Rank
284 4/8	38 0/8	40 0/8	38 4/8	6	6	Garfield County	CO	Bruce Easterly	1985	1,400
284 3/8	44 1/8	43 6/8	46 4/8	7	6	Clearwater County	ID	Neil Hinton	1983	1,402
284 3/8	44 0/8	41 2/8	35 7/8	6	6	Sierra County	NM	Gerald Lambert Lopez	1990	1,402
284 3/8	46 3/8	47 4/8	33 3/8	7	6	Coconino County	AZ	George Toot, Jr.	1990	1,402
284 2/8	45 3/8	45 3/8	41 6/8	6	6	Mineral County	MT	Dwayne Garner	1982	1,405
284 2/8	47 7/8	46 3/8	34 4/8	6	6	Apache County	AZ	Ronald King	1985	1,405
284 2/8	49 3/8	48 0/8	37 2/8	6	6	Coconino County	AZ	John Toot	1990	1,405
284 1/8	50 4/8	49 3/8	37 7/8	5	6	Clear Creek County	CO	Gary Christoffersen	1980	1,408
284 1/8	44 1/8	43 1/8	31 1/8	6	6	Sandoval County	NM	Steve Alderete	1986	1,408
284 1/8	48 2/8	47 2/8	34 5/8	7	6	Apache County	AZ	David N. Brilhart	1989	1,408
284 1/8	44 5/8	44 4/8	37 1/8	7	6	Fergus County	MT	Tom Madden	1990	1,408
284 1/8	50 0/8	44 7/8	45 3/8	7	7	Catron County	NM	Wayne W. Franzen	1992	1,408
284 0/8	49 4/8	46 7/8	42 2/8	6	6	Grant County	OR	Robert Gedlick	1981	1,413
284 0/8	41 3/8	43 6/8	39 4/8	6	7	Clearwater County	ID	Steve Richards	1986	1,413
284 0/8	49 6/8	48 4/8	37 2/8	6	6	Colfax County	NM	John L. Chapman	1989	1,413
284 0/8	45 7/8	48 4/8	34 6/8	6	6	Phillips County	MT	Henry J. Mischel	1990	1,413
283 7/8	47 5/8	47 2/8	33 3/8	6	6	Phillips County	MT	Doug Quilling	1979	1,417
283 7/8	42 6/8	43 5/8	33 5/8	6	6	Adams County	ID	Richard Fletcher	1987	1,417
283 7/8	44 2/8	45 0/8	31 7/8	6	6	Harney County	OR	Craig D. Hawkins	1991	1,417
283 6/8	46 0/8	45 4/8	40 6/8	6	6	Conejos County	CO	Arthur M. Davis	1974	1,420
283 6/8	47 3/8	49 0/8	36 6/8	6	6	Custer County	ID	Donald Johnson	1986	1,420
283 6/8	43 6/8	43 1/8	44 2/8	6	6	Mesa County	CO	Lawrence Clark	1987	1,420
283 6/8	46 2/8	45 1/8	39 0/8	6	6	Eagle County	CO	Keith Scheitzer	1990	1,420
283 5/8	46 6/8	45 6/8	33 7/8	6	6	Hinsdale County	CO	Dennis Pistole	1990	1,424
283 4/8	40 3/8	40 2/8	39 6/8	6	6	Apache County	AZ	Sonny Turner	1985	1,425
283 4/8	49 1/8	47 7/8	39 2/8	6	6	Rio Arriba County	NM	Ray Milligan	1987	1,425
283 4/8	46 6/8	44 7/8	35 2/8	6	6	Park County	MT	Jon Okonek	1990	1,425
283 3/8	42 0/8	44 4/8	31 7/8	6	6	Routt County	CO	Kevin Cole	1990	1,428
283 2/8	44 6/8	40 5/8	32 6/8	6	6	Clearwater County	ID	Jay Deones	1983	1,429
283 2/8	44 6/8	46 0/8	45 4/8	7	6	Lincoln County	NM	Steve Morgan	1986	1,429
283 1/8	50 3/8	48 1/8	31 6/8	6	7	Bighorn Mountains	WY	David Shoop	1979	1,431
283 1/8	41 2/8	40 6/8	38 7/8	6	7	Bergen	ALB	Sandy Watt	1991	1,431
283 0/8	42 7/8	44 5/8	41 0/8	6	6	Baker County	OR	Don Rajnus	1962	1,433
283 0/8	45 1/8	47 5/8	43 2/8	6	6	Grand County	CO	G. Fred Asbell	1973	1,433
283 0/8	48 4/8	46 4/8	36 2/8	6	6	Crook County	OR	Rick V. Herbst	1985	1,433
283 0/8	43 6/8	44 3/8	33 0/8	6	6	La Plata County	CO	David R. Hall	1985	1,433
283 0/8	42 2/8	43 3/8	35 5/8	7	6	Bear Lake County	ID	Barry James Shelton	1989	1,433
282 6/8	39 7/8	40 2/8	42 3/8	6	6	Gallatin County	MT	Gregg L. Welch	1982	1,438
282 6/8	46 4/8	47 3/8	31 0/8	6	6	Colfax County	NM	Melvin Sloan	1990	1,438
282 6/8	45 4/8	45 1/8	31 4/8	6	6	Larimer County	CO	Thomas Langer	1991	1,438
282 6/8	39 3/8	42 7/8	35 6/8	6	6	Jumping Pound Creek	ALB	Archie Nesbitt	1992	1,438
282 5/8	50 0/8	47 2/8	42 1/8	7	6	Gallatin County	MT	Scott L. Koelzer	1979	1,442
282 5/8	47 1/8	44 7/8	39 7/8	6	6	Meagher County	MT	Pete Ecker	1980	1,442
282 5/8	39 2/8	43 7/8	33 3/8	5	6	Valley County	ID	Dennis Gratton	1983	1,442
282 5/8	42 6/8	43 0/8	42 7/8	6	6	Dolores County	CO	Mike Zion	1985	1,442
282 5/8	41 2/8	41 6/8	35 5/8	6	6	Mesa County	CO	Jeffrey Price	1989	1,442
282 5/8	47 0/8	43 4/8	24 3/8	6	6	Sheridan County	WY	Mike Barrett	1990	1,442
282 4/8	32 6/8	39 2/8	36 4/8	6	6	Judith Basin County	MT	Jerome R. Parsons	1981	1,448
282 4/8	46 0/8	45 7/8	42 4/8	7	6	Custer County	ID	Joel C. Lenz	1986	1,448
282 3/8	44 2/8	41 0/8	38 1/8	6	6	Larimer County	CO	Dale E. Wenger	1981	1,450
282 3/8	44 6/8	46 2/8	34 3/8	7	6	Catron County	NM	Todd Zeuske	1987	1,450
282 2/8	42 6/8	43 1/8	39 2/8	6	6	Wallowa County	OR	Neil Summers	1986	1,452
282 2/8	44 6/8	43 3/8	30 6/8	6	6	Harney County	OR	Steven J. Christensen	1990	1,452
282 2/8	39 4/8	38 4/8	34 6/8	6	6	Routt County	CO	Marion A. Heintz	1991	1,452
282 1/8	45 4/8	44 7/8	44 7/8	5	6	Wallowa County	OR	Dale F. Story	1967	1,455
282 1/8	43 7/8	43 4/8	33 3/8	6	6	Teton County	MT	James Dean	1977	1,455
282 1/8	43 3/8	44 2/8	32 3/8	6	6	Sheridan County	WY	Mike Barrett	1983	1,455
282 1/8	40 7/8	41 6/8	40 5/8	7	6	Monterey County	CA	Chuck Adams	1990	1,455
282 1/8	45 4/8	42 5/8	35 1/8	6	6	Coconino County	AZ	Ronald G. Scherer	1990	1,455
282 0/8	53 7/8	53 5/8	34 0/8	6	6	Moffat County	CO	Clark Stokes	1985	1,460
282 0/8	44 0/8	45 0/8	37 0/8	6	6	Otero County	NM	John Bowman	1991	1,460
281 6/8	38 4/8	39 3/8	32 5/8	7	6	Powell County	MT	James L. Tillotson	1980	1,462
281 6/8	40 7/8	42 2/8	42 5/8	6	6	Missoula County	MT	Charles E. Hansen	1982	1,462
281 6/8	41 7/8	42 4/8	37 0/8	7	7	Lincoln County	MT	Mark Wachsman	1982	1,462
281 6/8	43 4/8	45 0/8	38 6/8	6	6	Custer County	ID	Vito Palazzolo	1983	1,462
281 6/8	48 2/8	47 4/8	38 0/8	6	5	Greenlee County	AZ	Joseph Barry	1986	1,462
281 6/8	46 0/8	46 4/8	38 4/8	6	7	San Miguel County	CO	Tony Thomas	1988	1,462
281 6/8	45 3/8	42 3/8	39 5/8	7	6	Wheeler County	OR	Roetta Williams	1990	1,462
281 5/8	44 6/8	45 6/8	39 3/8	6	6	Phillips County	MT	Robert Monhollon	1986	1,469
281 4/8	47 4/8	48 3/8	40 0/8	6	6	Catron County	NM	Randy Lockhart	1991	1,470

SCORE	LENGTH OF MAIN BEAM R	LENGTH OF MAIN BEAM L	INSIDE SPREAD	NUMBER OF POINTS R	NUMBER OF POINTS L	AREA	STATE/ PROVINCE	HUNTER'S NAME	DATE	RANK
281 4/8	48 6/8	49 6/8	30 0/8	6	6	Colfax County	NM	Howard L. Samit	1991	1,470
281 3/8	45 1/8	45 4/8	36 3/8	6	6	Coconino County	AZ	Judy Shelton	1991	1,472
281 3/8	37 5/8	37 0/8	36 1/8	6	6	Gunnison County	CO	Doug McCauley	1992	1,472
281 2/8	43 4/8	44 4/8	35 2/8	6	6	Powell County	MT	John Bottman	1986	1,474
281 1/8	42 4/8	44 1/8	35 6/8	6	6	Larimer County	CO	Gary Galloway	1984	1,475
281 1/8	44 0/8	44 7/8	39 3/8	6	6	Shoshone County	ID	Dean C. Weyen	1988	1,475
281 1/8	41 3/8	42 4/8	37 5/8	7	7	Fergus County	MT	Tom Madden	1989	1,475
281 1/8	45 6/8	43 2/8	41 1/8	5	6	Malheur County	OR	Dennis H. Slagle	1992	1,475
281 0/8	43 2/8	43 4/8	38 0/8	6	6	Lemhi County	ID	A. Marc Whisler	1980	1,479
281 0/8	47 0/8	45 5/8	37 0/8	6	6	Baker County	OR	Robert L. Unruh	1982	1,479
281 0/8	44 4/8	49 0/8	36 6/8	6	6	Moffat County	CO	Lonny Vanatta	1984	1,479
281 0/8	42 6/8	42 1/8	34 2/8	6	6	Sublette County	WY	George E. Hall	1984	1,479
281 0/8	42 5/8	41 3/8	39 2/8	6	6	Lemhi County	ID	William Bullock, Sr.	1984	1,479
281 0/8	51 3/8	52 1/8	37 0/8	5	6	Apache County	AZ	Kendall R. Adair	1991	1,479
280 7/8	43 1/8	42 3/8	32 7/8	6	6	Johnson County	WY	Paul S. Warren	1979	1,485
280 7/8	45 7/8	41 0/8	38 1/8	6	6	Jefferson County	CO	David A. Graham	1991	1,485
280 7/8	42 7/8	43 1/8	33 3/8	6	6	Shoshone County	ID	Harold L. Sterner, Jr.	1991	1,485
280 7/8	46 3/8	44 0/8	34 3/8	6	6	Lemhi County	ID	M. G. Reynolds	1992	1,485
280 6/8	48 5/8	47 0/8	38 2/8	6	6	Summit County	UT	John B. Rice, Jr.	1986	1,489
280 6/8	44 6/8	44 1/8	35 6/8	6	6	Yakima County	WA	Kevin Spencer	1989	1,489
280 5/8	44 2/8	41 4/8	39 3/8	6	6	Coconino County	AZ	Randall S. MacMillan	1990	1,491
280 4/8	46 3/8	44 6/8	34 2/8	6	6	Boise County	ID	Robert D. Dowen	1991	1,492
280 4/8	44 5/8	43 4/8	35 6/8	6	6	Catron County	NM	Bob "Jake" Jacobsen	1992	1,492
280 3/8	49 7/8	49 1/8	37 5/8	5	5	Rocky Mtn. House	ALB	Eugene Lopushinsky	1981	1,494
280 3/8	47 0/8	46 2/8	36 3/8	6	6	Clearwater County	ID	Tony Hyde	1986	1,494
280 2/8	39 2/8	37 3/8	33 6/8	6	5	Routt County	CO	D. F. Holt	1981	1,496
280 2/8	42 4/8	42 1/8	34 2/8	6	6	Beaverhead County	MT	Danny Moore	1987	1,496
280 1/8	44 0/8	40 2/8	38 7/8	6	7	Coconino County	AZ	Scott Kellner	1983	1,498
280 1/8	39 3/8	40 0/8	29 7/8	6	6	Phillips County	MT	Thomas R. Herman	1987	1,498
280 1/8	51 4/8	48 0/8	40 5/8	6	6	Coconino County	AZ	Todd Hinkins	1989	1,498
280 1/8	44 5/8	39 0/8	34 0/8	6	7	Sanders County	MT	Gerry Mercer	1992	1,498
280 0/8	45 4/8	45 3/8	33 6/8	6	6	Rio Blanco County	CO	Rolland M. Esterline	1969	1,502
280 0/8	47 3/8	45 5/8	32 5/8	6	7	Judith Basin County	MT	Ronald Ozbun	1987	1,502
280 0/8	45 6/8	45 0/8	27 4/8	6	6	King County	WA	George Dan Feighner	1987	1,502
280 0/8	43 0/8	42 6/8	41 4/8	6	6	Washington County	ID	Randy Wilkins	1989	1,502
279 7/8	43 6/8	44 0/8	40 2/8	7	6	Valley County	ID	Kenneth A Hyde	1983	1,506
279 6/8	45 7/8	44 2/8	33 0/8	6	6	Valley County	ID	Phil Barton	1989	1,507
279 5/8	41 2/8	42 5/8	41 1/8	6	6	Sheridan County	WY	Mike Barrett	1987	1,508
279 5/8	43 4/8	45 6/8	33 7/8	6	6	Catron County	NM	John Wirth, Jr.	1991	1,508
279 4/8	41 2/8	39 0/8	33 0/8	6	6	Wallowa County	OR	James R. Brackenbury	1970	1,510
279 4/8	46 5/8	45 0/8	40 4/8	6	5	Idaho County	ID	Richard C. Nichols	1973	1,510
279 4/8	41 6/8	40 6/8	33 2/8	6	6	Clearwater County	ID	John Burns, Sr.	1982	1,510
279 3/8	45 6/8	45 1/8	39 1/8	6	6	Phillips County	MT	Dave Zimmer	1983	1,513
279 2/8	45 2/8	46 0/8	34 0/8	6	6	Clearwater County	ID	Don West	1981	1,514
279 2/8	48 7/8	46 5/8	33 6/8	6	5	Clear Creek County	CO	Ken Shelton	1986	1,514
279 2/8	46 2/8	45 6/8	28 4/8	6	6	Phillips County	MT	Bill Rackley	1986	1,514
279 2/8	42 1/8	46 5/8	29 2/8	6	7	Missoula County	MT	Jim B. Bradford	1987	1,514
279 2/8	42 1/8	40 7/8	31 6/8	6	6	Grant County	NM	David H. Walske	1991	1,514
279 1/8	45 2/8	44 6/8	35 5/8	6	6	Coconino County	AZ	Todd B. Rice	1990	1,519
279 0/8	44 6/8	44 5/8	32 4/8	7	6	Las Animas County	CO	Ray Ramirez	1976	1,520
279 0/8	41 1/8	39 5/8	36 6/8	6	6	Caribou County	ID	Randy J. Stephens	1979	1,520
279 0/8	43 2/8	40 4/8	40 4/8	6	6	Cascade County	MT	Rick Holzheimer	1991	1,520
279 0/8	47 1/8	46 0/8	35 4/8	6	6	Coconino County	AZ	Russ Pearson	1991	1,520
279 0/8	45 4/8	44 0/8	40 6/8	6	6	Granite County	MT	Garret Decker	1991	1,520
278 7/8	45 7/8	45 6/8	33 3/8	6	6	Apache County	AZ	Marvin W. Wuertz	1989	1,525
278 6/8	43 5/8	43 7/8	35 2/8	6	6	Cascade County	MT	Norman T. Frusti	1979	1,526
278 6/8	42 3/8	39 0/8	36 4/8	6	6	Park County	MT	George Kamps	1984	1,526
278 6/8	44 0/8	44 6/8	33 2/8	6	6	Sevier County	UT	Dall Dimick	1987	1,526
278 6/8	40 4/8	43 0/8	35 0/8	6	6	Grant County	OR	Dennis Marshall	1989	1,526
278 6/8	46 7/8	45 3/8	38 2/8	6	6	Clearwater County	ID	Bryan Ohlms	1990	1,526
278 6/8	38 6/8	39 4/8	35 2/8	7	7	Phillips County	MT	Lee D. Laeupple	1992	1,526
278 5/8	46 0/8	46 5/8	34 7/8	6	6	Rio Arriba County	NM	Michael J. Cullen	1987	1,532
278 5/8	45 4/8	50 5/8	42 5/8	6	6	Sierra County	NM	David Swisher	1991	1,532
278 4/8	45 4/8	43 4/8	31 4/8	6	6	Cascade County	MT	David Holloway	1983	1,534
278 4/8	42 5/8	42 0/8	38 6/8	6	6	Socorro County	NM	Randall McAfee	1989	1,534
278 4/8	51 2/8	51 1/8	32 4/8	6	7	Navajo County	AZ	William R."Randy" Vaughn	1990	1,534
278 4/8	46 3/8	45 5/8	33 0/8	6	6	Valley County	MT	Myran Gartner	1991	1,534
278 4/8	44 5/8	41 5/8	35 0/8	6	6	Catron County	NM	David L. Willis	1992	1,534
278 0/8	48 2/8	44 3/8	47 0/8	6	6	Lincoln County	MT	Bud Journey	1978	1,539
278 0/8	41 2/8	43 1/8	37 2/8	6	6	Grant County	OR	Clayton Severin	1984	1,539

SCORE	LENGTH OF R MAIN BEAM L		INSIDE SPREAD	NUMBER OF R POINTS L		AREA	STATE/ PROVINCE	HUNTER'S NAME	DATE	RANK
277 7/8	42 2/8	41 7/8	36 3/8	6	6	Beaverhead County	MT	Gary Palmer	1990	1,541
277 6/8	39 0/8	38 6/8	37 0/8	7	7	High River	ALB	Andrew Schrock	1987	1,542
277 6/8	47 2/8	47 6/8	34 4/8	6	6	Big Horn County	WY	Robert Partridge	1992	1,542
277 5/8	47 1/8	45 6/8	38 1/8	6	6	Sandoval County	NM	David V. Collis	1983	1,544
277 4/8	45 2/8	47 4/8	38 0/8	6	6	La Plata County	CO	Andy White	1980	1,545
277 4/8	43 4/8	45 2/8	37 0/8	6	6	Larimer County	CO	Bruce Bowman	1985	1,545
277 4/8	44 3/8	43 3/8	30 0/8	7	7	Caribou County	ID	Royce Brown	1986	1,545
277 3/8	37 7/8	39 2/8	37 3/8	6	6	Greenlee County	AZ	Clifford White	1984	1,548
277 3/8	42 1/8	43 0/8	38 1/8	6	6	Larimer County	CO	Forrest McMichael	1987	1,548
277 3/8	44 0/8	44 5/8	33 2/8	7	6	Lodgepole	ALB	Marvin Dusterhoft	1990	1,548
277 2/8	47 0/8	47 3/8	40 2/8	6	6	Bonneville County	ID	Jerry Clark	1979	1,551
277 2/8	41 1/8	39 7/8	40 2/8	6	7	Fergus County	MT	Ray Lundin	1982	1,551
277 2/8	38 6/8	38 6/8	38 2/8	6	6	Colfax County	NM	Kenny Brice Poulson	1988	1,551
277 2/8	39 4/8	37 3/8	34 0/8	5	6	Clearwater County	ID	Thomas Storr	1989	1,551
277 2/8	42 4/8	43 3/8	37 0/8	6	6	Granite County	MT	Christian L. Frank	1992	1,551
277 1/8	41 7/8	39 3/8	42 5/8	6	6	Clearwater County	ID	Jon Skinner	1988	1,556
277 0/8	43 0/8	43 0/8	31 6/8	6	6	Grant County	OR	Andy Day	1981	1,557
277 0/8	40 4/8	40 3/8	32 0/8	6	6	Cascade County	MT	David Yaeger	1983	1,557
277 0/8	39 0/8	40 3/8	35 4/8	6	6	Flathead County	MT	Jerry L. Wootan	1984	1,557
277 0/8	43 1/8	42 4/8	36 0/8	6	6	Sanders County	MT	Chuck Adams	1985	1,557
276 7/8	46 4/8	46 1/8	38 1/8	6	7	Pitkin County	CO	Byron S. Donahue	1981	1,561
276 7/8	47 6/8	47 2/8	26 5/8	7	6	Rio Arriba County	NM	Michael G. Fierro	1982	1,561
276 7/8	42 2/8	41 3/8	37 1/8	6	6	Benewah County	ID	Greg DesLaurier	1984	1,561
276 7/8	46 1/8	45 4/8	33 5/8	6	6	Grant County	OR	Gary Nyden	1984	1,561
276 6/8	45 0/8	44 1/8	34 4/8	6	6	Lincoln County	MT	Jerry Brown	1982	1,565
276 6/8	45 2/8	45 0/8	36 2/8	6	6	Taos County	NM	Calvin Farner	1986	1,565
276 6/8	42 0/8	45 0/8	35 0/8	6	6	Carbon County	UT	Kenneth D. Evans	1989	1,565
276 6/8	40 7/8	38 0/8	31 4/8	6	6	Larimer County	CO	Todd Johnson	1990	1,565
276 5/8	45 7/8	45 1/8	32 5/8	6	6	Belmont Creek	MT	Max G. Bauer, Jr.	1980	1,569
276 5/8	46 6/8	45 5/8	35 1/8	6	6	Teton County	MT	William McRae	1982	1,569
276 5/8	44 4/8	43 4/8	36 5/8	6	6	Bear Lake County	ID	Troy Hymas	1984	1,569
276 4/8	41 1/8	40 2/8	35 0/8	6	6	Rio Blanco County	CO	Tom O. Milligan	1976	1,572
276 4/8	42 3/8	42 2/8	34 0/8	6	6	Gallatin County	MT	George Kamps	1981	1,572
276 4/8	46 6/8	50 1/8	38 4/8	6	5	Clearwater County	ID	Marvin J. Gerking	1983	1,572
276 4/8	43 0/8	42 4/8	33 4/8	6	6	Shoshone County	ID	Stephen P. Rapier	1983	1,572
276 4/8	39 1/8	37 5/8	36 2/8	6	6	Morgan County	UT	Rob Helfrich	1992	1,572
276 2/8	50 4/8	44 2/8	40 6/8	6	7	Fremont County	ID	Rene' Harrop	1981	1,577
276 2/8	43 5/8	44 2/8	38 4/8	5	6	Sandoval County	NM	Rett Kelly	1987	1,577
276 1/8	42 3/8	38 7/8	41 7/8	6	6	Saguache County	CO	Jerry Woodland	1977	1,579
276 1/8	44 4/8	45 7/8	33 1/8	7	6	Caribou County	ID	Irv Wanlass	1981	1,579
276 0/8	42 2/8	44 6/8	33 4/8	6	6	Teller County	CO	Dr. David B. Johnson	1983	1,581
276 0/8	42 5/8	42 6/8	33 2/8	6	6	Morgan County	UT	Hugh H. Hogle	1989	1,581
276 0/8	41 7/8	41 0/8	30 6/8	6	6	Lincoln County	WY	Rodney L. Dehart	1991	1,581
276 0/8	40 4/8	41 1/8	32 4/8	6	6	Routt County	CO	Charles DeLong	1991	1,581
275 7/8	47 1/8	46 5/8	39 1/8	6	6	Madison County	MT	Edward Wright	1990	1,585
275 6/8	45 6/8	44 2/8	34 0/8	6	6	Valley County	ID	David G. Nagelmann	1986	1,586
275 6/8	48 4/8	48 3/8	36 4/8	6	7	Teton County	MT	Keith Aune	1988	1,586
275 6/8	44 7/8	43 5/8	30 4/8	6	6	Idaho County	ID	Jerry Vega	1989	1,586
275 5/8	42 1/8	43 6/8	38 7/8	6	6	Ravalli County	MT	Rod Osburn	1980	1,589
275 5/8	45 4/8	44 4/8	34 7/8	6	6	Moffat County	CO	Glenn Pritchard	1988	1,589
275 5/8	46 2/8	45 1/8	35 1/8	6	6	Sheridan County	WY	Ron Niziolek	1990	1,589
275 5/8	46 4/8	44 2/8	33 1/8	6	6	Coconino County	AZ	Allen Farnsworth	1990	1,589
275 4/8	35 6/8	40 2/8	33 6/8	6	6	Valley County	MT	Andy Hicks	1983	1,593
275 4/8	48 5/8	48 7/8	34 2/8	6	6	Clackamas County	OR	Rip H. Caswell	1986	1,593
275 2/8	44 0/8	44 3/8	30 6/8	6	6	Missoula County	MT	John A. Reiter	1990	1,595
275 2/8	43 5/8	44 5/8	37 6/8	6	6	Grant County	OR	Tim Hall	1990	1,595
275 1/8	42 6/8	39 6/8	39 7/8	6	6	Bonner County	ID	Ren Hone	1980	1,597
275 1/8	46 6/8	44 6/8	28 7/8	6	6	Idaho County	ID	Hollis Sapp, Jr.	1986	1,597
275 1/8	44 4/8	45 6/8	34 7/8	6	6	Jefferson County	MT	Ron Scharf	1986	1,597
275 1/8	38 1/8	39 1/8	35 6/8	6	7	San Juan County	NM	Gerry J. Johnson	1988	1,597
275 1/8	45 5/8	44 2/8	28 1/8	6	6	Rio Arriba County	NM	Terry Karl	1989	1,597
275 1/8	46 0/8	47 0/8	39 5/8	5	6	Socorro County	NM	Randall C. Barnes	1990	1,597
275 1/8	44 4/8	45 2/8	41 5/8	6	6	Wallowa County	OR	Sam Shuh	1992	1,597
275 0/8	43 1/8	44 6/8	33 0/8	7	6	Garfield County	MT	Frank Kasten	1982	1,604
275 0/8	45 1/8	42 3/8	33 4/8	6	6	Conejos County	CO	Dewey Brown	1982	1,604
275 0/8	45 3/8	45 5/8	38 3/8	6	7	Madison County	ID	Shayne L. Ard	1982	1,604
275 0/8	45 2/8	44 6/8	36 6/8	6	6	Missoula County	MT	Terry See	1985	1,604
274 7/8	43 5/8	43 4/8	37 1/8	6	6	Flathead County	MT	Dean F. Cole	1985	1,608
274 6/8	42 4/8	41 1/8	29 7/8	7	7	Rimbey	ALB	Clifford Hill	1984	1,609
274 6/8	44 0/8	39 6/8	41 4/8	5	5	Navajo County	AZ	Troy Eiffert	1988	1,609

SCORE	LENGTH OF MAIN BEAM R	LENGTH OF MAIN BEAM L	INSIDE SPREAD	NUMBER OF POINTS R	NUMBER OF POINTS L	AREA	STATE/ PROVINCE	HUNTER'S NAME	DATE	RANK
274 6/8	44 0/8	44 3/8	32 4/8	6	6	Union County	OR	Gene Macomb	1990	1,609
274 5/8	39 6/8	40 1/8	35 7/8	6	6	Coconino County	AZ	Paul E. Wells	1992	1,612
274 4/8	44 1/8	43 5/8	37 2/8	5	5	Sandoval County	NM	Dave McInroy	1988	1,613
274 3/8	41 3/8	42 0/8	31 1/8	6	6	Saguache County	CO	Jerry Woodland	1973	1,614
274 3/8	47 1/8	44 7/8	28 7/8	6	6	Cabinet County	MT	Gayle A. Voisine	1992	1,614
274 2/8	42 4/8	42 3/8	40 0/8	6	6	Fremont County	ID	Clarence A. Frickey	1981	1,616
274 2/8	46 4/8	46 6/8	35 6/8	6	6	Blaine County	ID	Larry Newton	1987	1,616
274 2/8	50 3/8	53 6/8	40 4/8	6	5	McKinley County	NM	Malcolm D. Snyder	1991	1,616
274 1/8	42 2/8	43 7/8	38 0/8	7	6	Gallatin County	MT	David F. Gibson	1974	1,619
274 1/8	48 3/8	48 3/8	34 5/8	6	6	Converse County	WY	Jeffrey Rieker	1979	1,619
274 1/8	49 5/8	41 3/8	31 3/8	6	5	Dunn County	ND	Craig Richardson	1989	1,619
274 0/8	43 3/8	43 4/8	31 2/8	6	6	Clearwater County	ID	Jay Deones	1984	1,622
274 0/8	43 0/8	41 4/8	36 0/8	6	6	Grant County	OR	Robert D. Coffey	1986	1,622
273 6/8	48 4/8	49 0/8	33 6/8	6	6	Lemhi County	ID	Greg Munther	1963	1,624
273 6/8	42 1/8	43 3/8	33 0/8	6	6	Broadwater County	MT	Don Lovely	1978	1,624
273 6/8	39 3/8	37 6/8	37 6/8	6	6	Grant County	OR	John Bridgewater	1983	1,624
273 6/8	44 5/8	43 6/8	40 6/8	6	6	Valley County	ID	Tom Scoggin	1990	1,624
273 5/8	48 0/8	47 6/8	40 5/8	6	7	Sublette County	WY	Lyndon W. Henri	1987	1,628
273 5/8	44 6/8	43 1/8	29 5/8	6	6	Beaverhead County	MT	Danny Moore	1988	1,628
273 4/8	43 1/8	43 3/8	32 6/8	6	6	Archuleta County	CO	J.D. "Chip" Davis, Jr.	1990	1,630
273 4/8	44 4/8	42 6/8	31 1/8	8	7	Douglas County	OR	Ken French	1990	1,630
273 4/8	36 1/8	38 0/8	38 2/8	6	6	Mesa County	CO	John J. Ferrara	1990	1,630
273 4/8	41 1/8	42 6/8	39 0/8	6	6	Fremont County	WY	Ken Davis	1991	1,630
273 2/8	46 5/8	47 5/8	31 6/8	6	6	Phillips County	MT	Buddy Lundstrom	1981	1,634
273 2/8	45 5/8	44 3/8	37 6/8	6	6	Coconino County	AZ	Tony W. Zimbaro	1986	1,634
273 2/8	35 1/8	34 4/8	34 4/8	6	6	Elmore County	ID	George Law	1988	1,634
273 2/8	40 0/8	37 3/8	39 4/8	6	6	Custer County	ID	Jerry L. Bowhay	1990	1,634
273 2/8	47 3/8	44 0/8	35 0/8	6	6	Sandoval County	NM	Steve E. Lynch	1991	1,634
273 2/8	44 4/8	43 3/8	32 6/8	6	6	Lane County	OR	Rick Willhite	1992	1,634
273 1/8	42 3/8	41 7/8	39 3/8	6	6	Mora County	NM	Michael J. Maes	1986	1,640
273 0/8	42 2/8	42 1/8	32 6/8	6	6	Sandoval County	NM	George Bennett, Jr.	1984	1,641
273 0/8	41 1/8	40 7/8	37 2/8	6	6	Grant County	OR	Coby Moulton	1987	1,641
273 0/8	48 1/8	46 0/8	34 4/8	6	6	Custer County	ID	Randy Guinn	1987	1,641
273 0/8	47 0/8	46 2/8	37 2/8	6	6	Teton County	MT	Jerry Bianchi	1988	1,641
273 0/8	40 0/8	40 2/8	37 1/8	7	6	Apache County	AZ	John F. Richards	1990	1,641
273 0/8	47 3/8	44 7/8	36 6/8	6	5	Coconino County	AZ	Wiley Burnett	1990	1,641
273 0/8	44 6/8	42 2/8	36 0/8	6	6	Carbon County	WY	Rodney C. Hill	1990	1,641
272 7/8	39 6/8	40 0/8	37 7/8	6	6	Clackamas County	OR	Ed Bensel	1959	1,648
272 7/8	37 1/8	37 1/8	36 0/8	6	6	Rio Blanco County	CO	Dr. Charles Leidheiser	1973	1,648
272 7/8	44 7/8	44 2/8	41 5/8	5	6	Sanders County	MT	Donald R. Read	1991	1,648
272 6/8	51 6/8	48 3/8	31 6/8	7	6	Beaverhead County	MT	Ms. Charlie I. White	1988	1,651
272 6/8	47 0/8	44 6/8	38 0/8	6	6	Catron County	NM	Rick Mann	1991	1,651
272 5/8	44 7/8	42 1/8	36 3/8	6	6	Pitkin County	CO	Robert F. Cutting	1975	1,653
272 5/8	44 0/8	45 1/8	35 7/8	6	6	Baker County	OR	Lloyd V. Christensen	1987	1,653
272 5/8	44 4/8	44 7/8	35 1/8	6	6	Sublette County	WY	John B. Rice, Jr.	1990	1,653
272 5/8	40 5/8	39 4/8	42 5/8	6	6	Greenlee County	AZ	Craig Marietta	1990	1,653
272 4/8	42 5/8	43 7/8	35 6/8	6	6	Grant County	OR	Dean P. Pasche	1981	1,657
272 4/8	42 7/8	41 5/8	33 4/8	6	6	Lincoln County	WY	Peggy Barcak	1987	1,657
272 4/8	40 6/8	39 6/8	36 4/8	6	7	Lincoln County	WY	David McKae	1987	1,657
272 4/8	39 4/8	39 3/8	38 2/8	7	6	Sibbald Flats	ALB	Archie Nesbitt	1989	1,657
272 3/8	41 7/8	39 5/8	35 3/8	6	6	Skagit County	WA	Steve Gorr	1982	1,661
272 3/8	38 0/8	39 6/8	38 5/8	7	6	Teller County	CO	Rick K. Campbell	1987	1,661
272 3/8	44 1/8	42 3/8	40 1/8	6	6	Harney County	OR	Doug Foster	1989	1,661
272 3/8	37 2/8	38 5/8	38 6/8	6	6	Catron County	NM	James F. Welles	1991	1,661
272 2/8	38 6/8	39 4/8	34 4/8	6	6	Idaho County	ID	Stanley D. Miles	1976	1,665
272 2/8	48 0/8	46 5/8	37 2/8	5	5	Saguache County	CO	Kenneth A. Wollermann	1986	1,665
272 2/8	45 2/8	39 3/8	39 6/8	6	5	Morgan County	UT	Don Keady	1992	1,665
272 0/8	43 7/8	44 4/8	38 0/8	6	6	Saguache County	CO	Buster Mize	1968	1,668
272 0/8	45 5/8	45 0/8	37 4/8	6	6	Idaho County	ID	Donald M. Martin	1978	1,668
271 7/8	47 4/8	49 1/8	32 5/8	6	6	Chelan County	WA	Claude E. Gates	1973	1,670
271 6/8	46 4/8	46 5/8	33 6/8	6	6	Sheridan County	WY	Mike Barrett	1985	1,671
271 6/8	41 7/8	43 7/8	32 6/8	6	6	Catron County	NM	Mark D. Barboa	1990	1,671
271 6/8	41 1/8	40 7/8	38 0/8	6	6	Phillips County	MT	Kevin Bertsch	1992	1,671
271 5/8	43 1/8	43 6/8	36 1/8	5	6	Park County	MT	Dennis Vance	1975	1,674
271 5/8	38 5/8	39 5/8	36 1/8	6	6	Larimer County	CO	Kenneth D. Allen	1981	1,674
271 5/8	43 5/8	44 4/8	32 7/8	6	6	Lewis County	WA	Keith Heldreth	1985	1,674
271 4/8	38 4/8	40 6/8	34 2/8	6	6	Mud Creek	ID	Jr. Barnett	1977	1,677
271 4/8	44 4/8	45 6/8	43 0/8	6	5	Caribou County	ID	Preston Phelps	1980	1,677
271 4/8	46 3/8	47 2/8	36 2/8	6	6	Sweetwater County	WY	Vaughn Cross	1981	1,677
271 4/8	45 2/8	46 3/8	36 0/8	6	5	Flathead County	MT	Rick Meyer	1987	1,677

Score	Length of Main Beam R	L	Inside Spread	Number of Points R	L	Area	State/Province	Hunter's Name	Date	Rank
271 4/8	38 5/8	38 7/8	37 4/8	7	7	King County	WA	G. Dan Feighner	1989	1,677
271 3/8	42 7/8	42 5/8	39 7/8	6	6	Rio Arriba County	NM	Bryan Adair	1984	1,682
271 2/8	44 2/8	45 7/8	27 0/8	6	6	Gunnison County	CO	Jeff Helming	1984	1,683
271 2/8	39 5/8	39 5/8	32 2/8	6	6	Rio Arriba County	NM	Lee Braudt	1985	1,683
271 2/8	42 1/8	43 4/8	39 4/8	6	5	Grant County	OR	Don D. Litts	1986	1,683
271 2/8	41 0/8	39 3/8	34 4/8	7	7	Rio Arriba County	NM	Greg Harmsen	1986	1,683
271 2/8	38 6/8	38 3/8	39 5/8	6	6	Sanders County	MT	Z. Kent Sullivan	1988	1,683
271 2/8	39 6/8	39 1/8	34 4/8	6	6	Socorro County	NM	Ted A. Shinn	1990	1,683
271 2/8	51 5/8	45 5/8	34 2/8	6	5	Otero County	NM	Rocky Abney	1991	1,683
271 2/8	45 4/8	46 3/8	35 6/8	5	6	Grand County	CO	Dave Rayfield	1992	1,683
271 1/8	45 1/8	45 6/8	31 3/8	6	6	Rio Arriba County	NM	James A. Waters	1988	1,691
271 1/8	43 3/8	43 4/8	38 3/8	6	6	Lemhi County	ID	David A. Bronson	1991	1,691
271 0/8	48 0/8	47 7/8	34 2/8	6	5	Park County	CO	Victor B. Hines	1981	1,693
271 0/8	41 2/8	41 3/8	33 4/8	6	6	Routt County	CO	Starlene Clayson	1991	1,693
271 0/8	40 6/8	41 0/8	33 0/8	6	6	Las Animas County	CO	Jason Crockett Pettigrew	1992	1,693
270 7/8	38 5/8	38 4/8	34 5/8	6	6	Gallatin National Forest	MT	Steve D. Wing	1979	1,696
270 7/8	37 1/8	42 6/8	31 3/8	6	6	Morgan County	UT	Hugh H. Hogle	1983	1,696
270 7/8	40 5/8	38 5/8	38 5/8	5	5	King County	WA	Ken Gettman	1987	1,696
270 7/8	42 4/8	43 5/8	30 3/8	6	6	Petroleum County	MT	Bryant Shermoe	1989	1,696
270 7/8	42 0/8	41 5/8	35 3/8	6	6	Natrona County	WY	Jeff Kovalick	1990	1,696
270 5/8	38 1/8	39 2/8	36 3/8	6	6	Routt County	CO	Jake Hoeschler	1977	1,701
270 5/8	45 7/8	45 5/8	35 5/8	6	6	Granite County	MT	Michael J. Nielsen	1988	1,701
270 4/8	50 5/8	48 6/8	42 0/8	5	5	King County	WA	Jon Fuller	1985	1,703
270 4/8	44 1/8	45 3/8	35 4/8	6	6	Rio Blanco County	CO	Perry Smith	1989	1,703
270 3/8	40 6/8	40 4/8	36 5/8	6	6	Ravalli County	MT	Wayne Buhler	1982	1,705
270 3/8	46 0/8	46 4/8	36 7/8	6	6	Grant County	OR	Dennis G. Marshall	1986	1,705
270 3/8	43 5/8	42 6/8	34 7/8	6	6	Catron County	NM	Bill Clink	1989	1,705
270 2/8	42 6/8	41 6/8	36 2/8	6	6	Montezuma County	CO	Dwight V. English	1976	1,708
270 2/8	38 6/8	37 0/8	32 2/8	6	6	Blaine County	ID	John Turner	1977	1,708
270 2/8	42 7/8	44 4/8	43 6/8	5	5	Shoshone County	ID	Roy Meyer	1979	1,708
270 2/8	41 0/8	40 4/8	35 4/8	5	6	Simonette River	ALB	Gerald Rogers	1990	1,708
270 1/8	38 1/8	39 1/8	35 5/8	6	6	Powell County	MT	E. Kits Smith	1976	1,712
270 1/8	41 2/8	42 5/8	28 5/8	6	6	Petroleum County	MT	Ken Rustad	1991	1,712
270 1/8	42 7/8	43 1/8	36 1/8	6	5	Catron County	NM	George Morris	1991	1,712
270 1/8	43 6/8	43 6/8	27 7/8	6	6	Conejos County	CO	Jack A. Gardner	1991	1,712
270 0/8	45 6/8	46 5/8	31 2/8	6	6	Coconino County	AZ	James H. Hansen	1981	1,716
270 0/8	48 6/8	47 5/8	32 4/8	6	6	Coconino County	AZ	Wade L. Carstens	1983	1,716
269 7/8	38 2/8	36 6/8	28 1/8	6	6	Bear Lake County	ID	Dennis Burdick	1969	1,718
269 7/8	45 4/8	45 4/8	38 5/8	6	5	Park County	MT	Jay Bosma	1984	1,718
269 7/8	36 2/8	39 4/8	33 3/8	5	6	Rio Blanco County	CO	Brad Murray	1990	1,718
269 7/8	43 3/8	39 0/8	37 4/8	6	7	Daggett County	UT	Michiel D. Watts	1991	1,718
269 6/8	47 4/8	47 5/8	46 2/8	6	5	Idaho County	ID	Edward Keeton	1985	1,722
269 6/8	44 4/8	46 5/8	36 4/8	6	6	Malheur County	OR	Jim Hodson	1986	1,722
269 6/8	43 1/8	45 3/8	35 6/8	6	6	Archuleta County	CO	Floyd Earl Fralish	1990	1,722
269 5/8	41 6/8	42 3/8	35 5/8	6	6	Bonneville County	ID	Mike Taylor	1980	1,725
269 5/8	42 0/8	41 1/8	36 1/8	6	6	Caribou County	ID	Chet Hopkins	1985	1,725
269 5/8	44 4/8	44 1/8	33 1/8	6	6	Park County	MT	George Kamps	1986	1,725
269 4/8	42 7/8	42 4/8	35 6/8	6	7	Pinal County	AZ	Larry P. Matthews	1985	1,728
269 4/8	45 1/8	45 0/8	40 3/8	7	5	Custer County	ID	Bryan R. Sword	1988	1,728
269 4/8	44 4/8	44 2/8	33 7/8	6	7	Huerfano County	CO	Danny Ray	1992	1,728
269 3/8	46 1/8	47 2/8	36 5/8	5	6	Cibola County	NM	Deryl Moore	1986	1,731
269 2/8	44 0/8	43 4/8	34 2/8	6	6	Grant County	NM	Joe F. Apodaca	1990	1,732
269 1/8	41 7/8	42 5/8	34 1/8	6	6	Archuleta County	CO	George Eubank	1989	1,733
269 0/8	48 5/8	44 6/8	39 6/8	5	6	Bighorn Mountains	WY	Dennis A. Phaneuf	1980	1,734
269 0/8	41 3/8	40 5/8	35 6/8	6	6	Idaho County	ID	Larry A. Youngdell	1980	1,734
269 0/8	39 2/8	40 6/8	37 2/8	6	6	Lewis & Clark County	MT	Steven E. Miller	1982	1,734
269 0/8	42 7/8	41 1/8	33 4/8	6	6	Converse County	WY	Jim Young	1982	1,734
269 0/8	35 5/8	35 5/8	33 2/8	6	6	Park County	CO	Jarold Allen Shriver	1988	1,734
269 0/8	39 2/8	38 2/8	39 0/8	7	6	Boise County	ID	Jeffrey S. Stevens	1988	1,734
269 0/8	41 6/8	45 0/8	33 2/8	6	6	Teton County	MT	Don Davidson	1990	1,734
268 7/8	44 0/8	43 4/8	34 7/8	6	6	Judith Basin County	MT	Dan Hassel	1985	1,741
268 7/8	41 6/8	42 2/8	34 3/8	6	6	Sanders County	MT	Craig R. Johnson	1986	1,741
268 6/8	41 3/8	42 5/8	39 4/8	6	6	Park County	CO	Wayne Helming	1983	1,743
268 6/8	44 7/8	43 4/8	35 0/8	6	7	Huerfano County	CO	Lee Moore	1985	1,743
268 5/8	41 7/8	43 1/8	32 2/8	6	6	Hinsdale County	CO	Billy R. Spears	1973	1,745
268 5/8	39 1/8	40 4/8	38 3/8	6	6	Catron County	NM	Scott Miltenberger	1990	1,745
268 5/8	46 2/8	43 3/8	30 1/8	6	6	Coconino County	AZ	Paul M. Rogers	1991	1,745
268 4/8	43 6/8	43 4/8	32 4/8	5	6	Coconino County	AZ	Charles R. Haverin	1984	1,748
268 4/8	49 1/8	48 4/8	33 2/8	5	5	Sandoval County	NM	Roby Grossheim	1988	1,748
268 2/8	45 6/8	42 6/8	35 2/8	6	6	Navajo County	AZ	Julius Fortuna	1983	1,750

SCORE	LENGTH OF MAIN BEAM R	LENGTH OF MAIN BEAM L	INSIDE SPREAD	NUMBER OF POINTS R	NUMBER OF POINTS L	AREA	STATE/ PROVINCE	HUNTER'S NAME	DATE	RANK
268 1/8	39 0/8	40 3/8	30 0/8	7	6	Lincoln County	WY	Troy Miller	1973	1,751
268 1/8	45 2/8	46 0/8	36 5/8	5	6	Gallatin County	MT	William L. Anderson	1982	1,751
268 1/8	44 3/8	44 5/8	34 1/8	6	6	Silver Bow County	MT	Andrew Kuchtyn	1982	1,751
268 1/8	44 4/8	44 2/8	35 1/8	6	6	Grant County	OR	Gary Persinger	1983	1,751
268 1/8	42 5/8	41 0/8	33 7/8	6	6	Caribou County	ID	Max F. Park	1990	1,751
268 0/8	42 3/8	40 5/8	32 6/8	6	5	Baker County	OR	Les Thoreby	1963	1,756
268 0/8	41 7/8	42 2/8	33 3/8	7	6	Idaho County	ID	Richard C. Nichols	1974	1,756
268 0/8	41 0/8	40 7/8	35 2/8	6	6	Colfax County	NM	Peter J. Santi	1991	1,756
267 7/8	45 2/8	43 5/8	41 3/8	6	6	Valley County	ID	Jack St. Germain	1981	1,759
267 7/8	44 2/8	43 6/8	32 7/8	6	6	Los Alamos County	NM	Doug Aikin	1983	1,759
267 7/8	41 4/8	42 0/8	29 4/8	7	6	Phillips County	MT	Dr. Richard L. Lopez	1987	1,759
267 7/8	46 5/8	44 7/8	47 7/8	6	5	Coconino County	AZ	Kenneth Wilson	1989	1,759
267 7/8	40 3/8	39 0/8	41 0/8	6	6	Silver Bow County	MT	Steve Petroni	1990	1,759
267 6/8	43 3/8	47 0/8	39 6/8	6	6	Caribou County	ID	Jerry Baird	1976	1,764
267 6/8	47 3/8	46 2/8	33 2/8	5	5	Rich County	UT	C. Keith Maynes	1989	1,764
267 6/8	40 1/8	39 4/8	31 4/8	7	7	Catron County	NM	Ronald R. Johnson	1990	1,764
267 5/8	42 2/8	42 4/8	33 3/8	6	6	Larimer County	CO	Dennis Worrell	1979	1,767
267 5/8	40 0/8	39 6/8	33 7/8	6	6	Chaffee County	CO	Bruce Long	1985	1,767
267 5/8	35 4/8	36 1/8	39 6/8	6	6	Wallowa County	OR	Peter E. Palmer	1989	1,767
267 4/8	42 2/8	44 4/8	31 6/8	6	6	Gallatin County	MT	Jim Wondzell	1990	1,770
267 3/8	40 4/8	39 3/8	30 3/8	6	6	Ravalli County	MT	Harold Wilson	1977	1,771
267 3/8	38 2/8	47 4/8	33 1/8	5	6	Coconino County	AZ	John C. McClendon	1980	1,771
267 3/8	43 6/8	45 6/8	35 5/8	6	6	Linn County	OR	Michael Hawkins	1982	1,771
267 1/8	42 3/8	42 4/8	33 3/8	6	6	Beaverhead County	MT	Neal Davis	1987	1,774
267 0/8	41 5/8	38 3/8	41 4/8	5	7	Grand County	CO	Noel Feather	1980	1,775
267 0/8	43 2/8	37 7/8	36 1/8	7	6	Teton County	WY	James Yager	1990	1,775
266 6/8	41 0/8	40 4/8	32 6/8	6	6	Lemhi County	ID	Scott Spaeth	1978	1,777
266 6/8	45 5/8	43 2/8	37 4/8	6	6	Apache County	AZ	Tom David	1980	1,777
266 6/8	43 7/8	44 6/8	39 2/8	6	6	Caribou County	ID	Max Park	1981	1,777
266 6/8	42 5/8	42 7/8	29 0/8	6	6	Rio Blanco County	CO	Bill McMahan	1989	1,777
266 5/8	42 1/8	43 7/8	29 5/8	6	6	Chaffee County	CO	Frank A. Morminello	1977	1,781
266 5/8	48 1/8	45 0/8	42 5/8	6	6	Caribou County	ID	Max Park	1982	1,781
266 5/8	43 2/8	43 2/8	31 7/8	6	6	Phillips County	MT	Steve Baeth	1985	1,781
266 5/8	47 0/8	43 2/8	29 7/8	6	5	White Pine County	NV	Gary Wright	1989	1,781
266 5/8	42 7/8	40 7/8	39 5/8	6	6	Sandoval County	NM	Peter F. Woeck II	1991	1,781
266 5/8	44 6/8	42 0/8	36 5/8	6	6	Routt County	CO	Craig Thrasher	1991	1,781
266 5/8	41 2/8	41 5/8	33 3/8	6	6	Mesa County	CO	Jimmy Wayne Birchfield	1991	1,781
266 4/8	36 7/8	37 0/8	30 4/8	6	6	Lewis & Clark County	MT	Laurence F. Crim	1977	1,788
266 4/8	41 7/8	43 1/8	35 2/8	6	6	Gem County	ID	Randy L. Wilkins	1985	1,788
266 4/8	41 5/8	42 2/8	39 4/8	6	6	Missoula County	MT	Steve Byerly	1988	1,788
266 4/8	42 3/8	42 6/8	41 0/8	7	7	Rio Arriba County	NM	Dave Conrad	1992	1,788
266 3/8	45 1/8	45 3/8	31 7/8	6	6	Archuleta County	CO	Mark Lowery	1989	1,792
266 3/8	42 2/8	42 6/8	31 7/8	5	6	Sandoval County	NM	Greg Strait	1989	1,792
266 3/8	41 1/8	43 1/8	36 3/8	5	6	Teller County	CO	James Wolfe	1990	1,792
266 2/8	47 3/8	45 6/8	36 4/8	5	6	La Plata County	CO	Charlie Chrane	1977	1,795
266 2/8	45 7/8	46 6/8	41 2/8	6	6	McKinley County	NM	Robert Stearns	1987	1,795
266 1/8	42 6/8	43 6/8	32 3/8	6	6	Skamania County	WA	James S. Newman	1986	1,797
266 1/8	41 2/8	42 1/8	36 5/8	6	6	Idaho County	ID	Charles E. Groft	1988	1,797
266 0/8	47 1/8	45 7/8	38 6/8	6	6	Sandoval County	NM	Lloyd Baird	1984	1,799
266 0/8	48 5/8	47 5/8	31 0/8	5	6	Douglas County	CO	James Robert Phelps	1986	1,799
265 7/8	40 1/8	40 5/8	36 5/8	6	7	San Miguel County	CO	Bubba Schmidt	1988	1,801
265 7/8	42 4/8	45 0/8	37 7/8	6	6	Coconino County	AZ	Prentiss Chanceller	1988	1,801
265 7/8	43 7/8	47 0/8	30 7/8	6	6	Coconino County	AZ	Cy Hershey	1990	1,801
265 6/8	41 2/8	40 6/8	36 0/8	6	6	Wallowa County	OR	Grainger Hunt	1987	1,804
265 6/8	39 2/8	40 6/8	32 2/8	6	6	Madison County	MT	Richard Ballard	1987	1,804
265 6/8	40 4/8	39 6/8	40 2/8	6	6	Sheridan County	WY	Skip Reilly	1988	1,804
265 6/8	49 4/8	50 3/8	40 4/8	5	5	Boise County	ID	John E. Smith	1988	1,804
265 6/8	39 2/8	39 0/8	28 2/8	6	6	Lincoln County	WY	Donlee L. Jackson	1990	1,804
265 5/8	37 2/8	38 4/8	29 1/8	6	6	Shoshone County	ID	Jeff Jackson	1987	1,809
265 5/8	44 0/8	44 6/8	31 1/8	6	6	Huerfano County	CO	Steve Jeans	1988	1,809
265 5/8	43 4/8	43 4/8	33 3/8	5	5	Mineral County	CO	Greg Ogle	1988	1,809
265 5/8	44 4/8	43 2/8	39 3/8	6	6	Wallowa County	OR	Rick Turner	1990	1,809
265 5/8	45 4/8	44 6/8	29 1/8	6	6	Columbia County	WA	Jess Mings	1992	1,809
265 4/8	43 2/8	42 7/8	32 6/8	6	6	Delta County	CO	Emil C. Frein	1973	1,814
265 4/8	49 4/8	45 5/8	31 6/8	6	6	Dolores County	CO	Scott Roberts	1975	1,814
265 4/8	37 6/8	35 3/8	39 5/8	6	6	Catron County	NM	John D. Smith	1989	1,814
265 1/8	41 2/8	39 2/8	29 1/8	6	7	Mineral County	CO	Rod Wintz	1968	1,817
265 1/8	44 2/8	43 5/8	31 3/8	6	6	Huerfano County	CO	Duane Raspotnik	1989	1,817
265 1/8	40 4/8	40 6/8	39 1/8	5	5	Catron County	NM	Jeffrey Aycock	1990	1,817
265 1/8	42 4/8	44 4/8	28 5/8	6	6	Navajo County	AZ	Steve Johnston	1991	1,817

SCORE	LENGTH OF MAIN BEAM R / L	INSIDE SPREAD	NUMBER OF POINTS R / L	AREA	STATE/ PROVINCE	HUNTER'S NAME	DATE	RANK
265 0/8	44 5/8 43 2/8	30 0/8	6 6	Kittitas County	WA	Eric Seim	1991	1,821
265 0/8	43 0/8 42 1/8	34 4/8	6 6	Petroleum County	MT	Mark Rigotti	1992	1,821
264 7/8	42 5/8 45 5/8	33 1/8	6 6	Coconino County	AZ	Dennis Newman	1973	1,823
264 7/8	39 1/8 42 2/8	33 5/8	6 6	Huerfano County	CO	Michael J. Eutsler	1986	1,823
264 7/8	40 0/8 38 2/8	39 7/8	6 6	Union County	OR	Ellis E. Speer	1986	1,823
264 6/8	38 5/8 37 4/8	32 6/8	6 6	Teton County	WY	Paul Birkholz	1966	1,826
264 6/8	41 4/8 40 5/8	35 4/8	6 6	Pitkin County	CO	Donald Hanford	1981	1,826
264 6/8	43 0/8 44 1/8	36 0/8	5 5	Meagher County	MT	Gary H. Thompson	1981	1,826
264 6/8	41 3/8 41 0/8	36 4/8	6 6	Meagher County	MT	Gene Clark	1982	1,826
264 4/8	44 6/8 45 7/8	34 4/8	7 7	Boise County	ID	Robert Hiller	1969	1,830
264 4/8	38 6/8 39 2/8	33 6/8	6 6	Jefferson County	CO	Darrell Kitzman	1986	1,830
264 4/8	46 3/8 49 6/8	39 2/8	6 6	Sierra County	NM	Guy D. Pointer	1988	1,830
264 4/8	42 3/8 42 1/8	37 0/8	6 6	Lincoln County	NM	Jim Tyler	1988	1,830
264 4/8	42 4/8 43 7/8	36 4/8	5 6	Catron County	NM	Adam Jimenez, Jr.	1989	1,830
264 4/8	42 4/8 42 3/8	30 2/8	6 6	Saguache County	CO	Arthur D. Johnson	1991	1,830
264 3/8	44 2/8 44 4/8	30 7/8	6 6	Coconino County	AZ	Joel R. Youngblood III	1990	1,836
264 3/8	39 4/8 40 1/8	33 5/8	6 6	Huerfano County	CO	Esco R. Billings, III	1991	1,836
264 2/8	41 5/8 43 5/8	27 6/8	6 6	Coconino County	AZ	Randy Breland	1984	1,838
264 2/8	39 7/8 39 3/8	39 6/8	5 5	Catron County	NM	Adam Jimenez Jr.	1986	1,838
264 2/8	43 5/8 43 4/8	38 6/8	6 5	Gunnison County	CO	Mark Asplund	1987	1,838
264 2/8	39 6/8 40 1/8	27 2/8	6 6	Sheridan County	WY	Richard E. Jones	1992	1,838
264 1/8	40 4/8 39 0/8	39 7/8	5 5	Larimer County	CO	Eric Peterson	1982	1,842
264 1/8	39 7/8 38 7/8	31 3/8	6 6	Taos County	NM	Ronald Corvin	1990	1,842
264 0/8	40 1/8 40 5/8	37 0/8	6 6	Valley County	ID	Brian Crook	1989	1,844
263 7/8	46 4/8 46 7/8	39 7/8	6 5	Boise County	ID	Jack Brennan	1964	1,845
263 5/8	40 5/8 39 6/8	34 3/8	6 6	Ouray County	CO	Doug McCauley	1982	1,846
263 4/8	41 5/8 41 4/8	37 4/8	6 6	Caribou County	ID	Wade Dursteler	1988	1,847
263 3/8	38 7/8 38 4/8	33 5/8	6 6	Idaho County	ID	John C. Mitchell	1985	1,848
263 3/8	40 1/8 39 2/8	38 2/8	6 7	Larimer County	CO	B.D. Ramsey	1988	1,848
263 3/8	51 3/8 49 3/8	36 4/8	6 6	Rio Blanco County	CO	Brad Murray	1992	1,848
263 2/8	40 7/8 43 1/8	32 5/8	6 7	Coconino County	AZ	Michael H. Bingham	1982	1,851
263 2/8	45 3/8 43 5/8	34 2/8	6 6	Gallatin County	MT	Bob Fromme	1983	1,851
263 2/8	43 7/8 43 6/8	35 4/8	6 6	Fremont County	WY	Guy LeMonnier, Jr.	1989	1,851
263 2/8	39 2/8 40 7/8	36 0/8	6 6	Ouray County	CO	Dexter G. Efird	1990	1,851
263 2/8	39 4/8 40 4/8	28 2/8	7 7	Petroleum County	MT	Ken Rustad	1990	1,851
263 1/8	43 5/8 42 6/8	35 5/8	6 5	Lewis County	WA	Keith Heldreth	1984	1,856
263 1/8	44 6/8 42 6/8	36 3/8	6 6	Socorro County	NM	Joe Caskey	1986	1,856
263 0/8	41 0/8 41 3/8	36 2/8	6 6	Clear Creek County	CO	Don Bording	1982	1,858
263 0/8	41 7/8 42 6/8	35 2/8	6 6	Los Alamos County	NM	Doug Aikin	1984	1,858
263 0/8	38 7/8 39 4/8	38 6/8	6 6	Grant County	OR	Phillip Koep	1991	1,858
263 0/8	42 2/8 43 7/8	33 4/8	5 6	Silver Bow County	MT	Victor Romano	1992	1,858
262 7/8	37 7/8 36 7/8	34 3/8	6 6	Garfield County	CO	Clifford White	1977	1,862
262 7/8	43 4/8 44 1/8	36 5/8	7 6	Coconino County	AZ	Dr. Van Bennett	1985	1,862
262 6/8	40 5/8 42 1/8	31 6/8	6 6	Archuleta County	CO	David W. Cather	1984	1,864
262 5/8	39 5/8 39 4/8	36 7/8	6 6	Pierce County	WA	David T. Robertson	1985	1,865
262 5/8	41 5/8 39 3/8	34 7/8	6 6	Custer County	ID	Brent McBride	1987	1,865
262 5/8	47 5/8 46 0/8	30 1/8	6 6	Routt County	CO	John Pershing Lundberg	1990	1,865
262 4/8	39 4/8 40 0/8	31 6/8	6 7	Coconino County	AZ	Donald L. Kennedy	1977	1,868
262 4/8	42 6/8 43 4/8	38 4/8	6 6	Flathead County	MT	Chester Fessum	1983	1,868
262 4/8	42 7/8 43 2/8	30 2/8	5 6	Pierce County	WA	Andy Bales	1989	1,868
262 4/8	40 5/8 41 1/8	39 6/8	6 6	Montezuma County	CO	Ron Laird	1991	1,868
262 4/8	38 4/8 38 0/8	39 0/8	6 6	Chaffee County	CO	Joel D. Morgan	1991	1,868
262 3/8	46 1/8 44 5/8	32 6/8	7 6	Rio Arriba County	NM	Ronnie Williams	1986	1,873
262 3/8	43 3/8 43 3/8	32 0/8	7 6	Kakwa River	ALB	Wilf Lehners	1991	1,873
262 2/8	45 0/8 45 3/8	32 6/8	5 5	Grand County	CO	G. Fred Asbell	1979	1,875
262 2/8	41 4/8 40 2/8	37 0/8	5 5	Crook County	OR	Terry A. Luther	1981	1,875
262 0/8	43 4/8 43 6/8	35 4/8	6 6	Chaffee County	CO	Ray Nelson	1981	1,877
262 0/8	42 4/8 42 1/8	37 4/8	6 6	Deer Lodge County	MT	Todd R. Zeuske	1982	1,877
261 7/8	36 6/8 41 3/8	34 7/8	6 6	Coconino County	AZ	Charles Stevenson	1980	1,879
261 7/8	41 1/8 41 0/8	35 7/8	6 6	Clearwater County	ID	Jim Prudhomme	1990	1,879
261 6/8	38 0/8 40 0/8	37 6/8	6 5	Taos County	NM	Dr. D. A. Henbest	1972	1,881
261 6/8	39 4/8 40 2/8	32 4/8	6 6	Delta County	CO	John C. Lamont	1989	1,881
261 5/8	40 0/8 37 2/8	33 5/8	6 6	Rio Blanco County	CO	H. V. McFarland, Jr.	1974	1,883
261 5/8	37 1/8 36 1/8	37 6/8	6 6	Flathead County	MT	Dr. Brad Black	1981	1,883
261 5/8	35 6/8 35 4/8	34 5/8	6 6	Fremont County	ID	Todd J. Frickey	1987	1,883
261 5/8	43 1/8 43 2/8	37 5/8	5 6	Garfield County	CO	Francis J. Dehner	1989	1,883
261 5/8	39 1/8 40 2/8	34 1/8	6 6	Beaverhead County	MT	Eduard Hale	1990	1,883
261 4/8	43 0/8 43 2/8	35 0/8	6 6	Caribou County	ID	Randy K. Guinn	1986	1,888
261 3/8	41 6/8 41 3/8	31 1/8	6 6	Fremont County	ID	Gary Owens	1980	1,889
261 2/8	42 5/8 42 4/8	31 0/8	5 5	Rio Arriba County	NM	Donald N. Lehman	1983	1,890

SCORE	LENGTH OF MAIN BEAM		INSIDE SPREAD	NUMBER OF POINTS		AREA	STATE/ PROVINCE	HUNTER'S NAME	DATE	RANK
	R	L		R	L					
261 2/8	42 4/8	41 3/8	33 4/8	6	6	Costilla County	CO	Timothy L. Walters	1985	1,890
261 2/8	44 6/8	44 1/8	34 0/8	5	5	Cibola County	NM	Duane T. Corley	1986	1,890
261 2/8	46 2/8	44 3/8	37 6/8	6	6	Sheridan County	WY	Mike Barrett	1988	1,890
261 1/8	37 7/8	36 2/8	37 7/8	6	6	Jackson County	CO	Knut A. Paulsen	1975	1,894
261 1/8	44 1/8	43 1/8	36 7/8	6	7	Caribou County	ID	Richard T. Vance	1975	1,894
261 1/8	41 1/8	42 6/8	35 5/8	6	6	Clearwater County	ID	Steve Eiede	1988	1,894
261 1/8	41 5/8	40 6/8	40 2/8	6	7	Lewis & Clark County	MT	Sonny Templeton	1991	1,894
261 0/8	46 6/8	45 6/8	32 4/8	6	5	Saguache County	CO	Irene M. Blaskowski	1990	1,898
261 0/8	46 0/8	45 1/8	36 2/8	6	6	Clearwater County	ID	Don Leedham	1991	1,898
261 0/8	44 2/8	42 6/8	38 6/8	5	5	Sublette County	WY	Kim A. Glasgow	1991	1,898
260 7/8	37 6/8	37 6/8	34 3/8	6	6	Grant County	OR	Colby Moulton	1986	1,901
260 7/8	41 7/8	42 0/8	38 7/8	6	6	Pitkin County	CO	Jim Plett	1987	1,901
260 7/8	41 2/8	41 1/8	31 3/8	6	6	Madison County	MT	Chester Graham	1992	1,901
260 6/8	40 4/8	44 6/8	30 2/8	7	7	Coconino County	AZ	James Casady	1978	1,904
260 6/8	38 0/8	37 3/8	34 0/8	6	6	Converse County	WY	Russell Burghard	1983	1,904
260 6/8	38 0/8	37 5/8	34 2/8	6	6	Clearwater County	ID	Chuck Lynde	1988	1,904
260 6/8	40 2/8	40 2/8	35 6/8	6	6	Beaverhead County	MT	Marvin Hearon	1992	1,904
260 5/8	40 5/8	42 0/8	34 7/8	6	6	Kimberley	BC	Rick Hammond	1986	1,908
260 5/8	38 1/8	38 4/8	38 1/8	6	6	Catron County	NM	Michael J. Bradeen	1990	1,908
260 5/8	40 6/8	40 4/8	34 3/8	6	6	Mineral County	MT	Chris W. Dix	1992	1,908
260 4/8	40 4/8	40 7/8	38 0/8	6	6	Blaine County	ID	Wesley Moore	1986	1,911
260 4/8	40 6/8	40 1/8	34 0/8	6	7	Fergus County	MT	Jerry Knerr	1987	1,911
260 4/8	40 2/8	37 4/8	34 0/8	6	6	Elmore County	ID	Roger W. Atwood	1988	1,911
260 4/8	46 2/8	44 7/8	34 5/8	6	7	Montrose County	CO	David Henkie	1989	1,911
260 3/8	38 4/8	38 7/8	30 7/8	6	6	Madison County	ID	Paul L. Beesley	1979	1,915
260 2/8	41 2/8	41 4/8	37 0/8	6	6	Pitkin County	CO	Wayne MacDonnell	1987	1,916
260 2/8	37 0/8	38 0/8	35 0/8	6	6	Rio Blanco County	CO	Charles R. Clark	1991	1,916
260 1/8	44 1/8	43 2/8	37 5/8	6	6	Catron County	NM	Bob "Jake" Jacobsen	1989	1,918
260 1/8	41 0/8	44 3/8	36 3/8	5	5	Catron County	NM	Jim Eppler	1990	1,918
260 1/8	39 7/8	38 4/8	33 3/8	6	6	Fisher Creek	ALB	Rick Lepp	1991	1,918
260 1/8	42 4/8	44 1/8	35 5/8	5	5	Idaho County	ID	Steven L. DeBauche	1992	1,918
260 0/8	36 4/8	36 4/8	39 5/8	6	6	Grand County	CO	Kevin O'Connell	1981	1,922

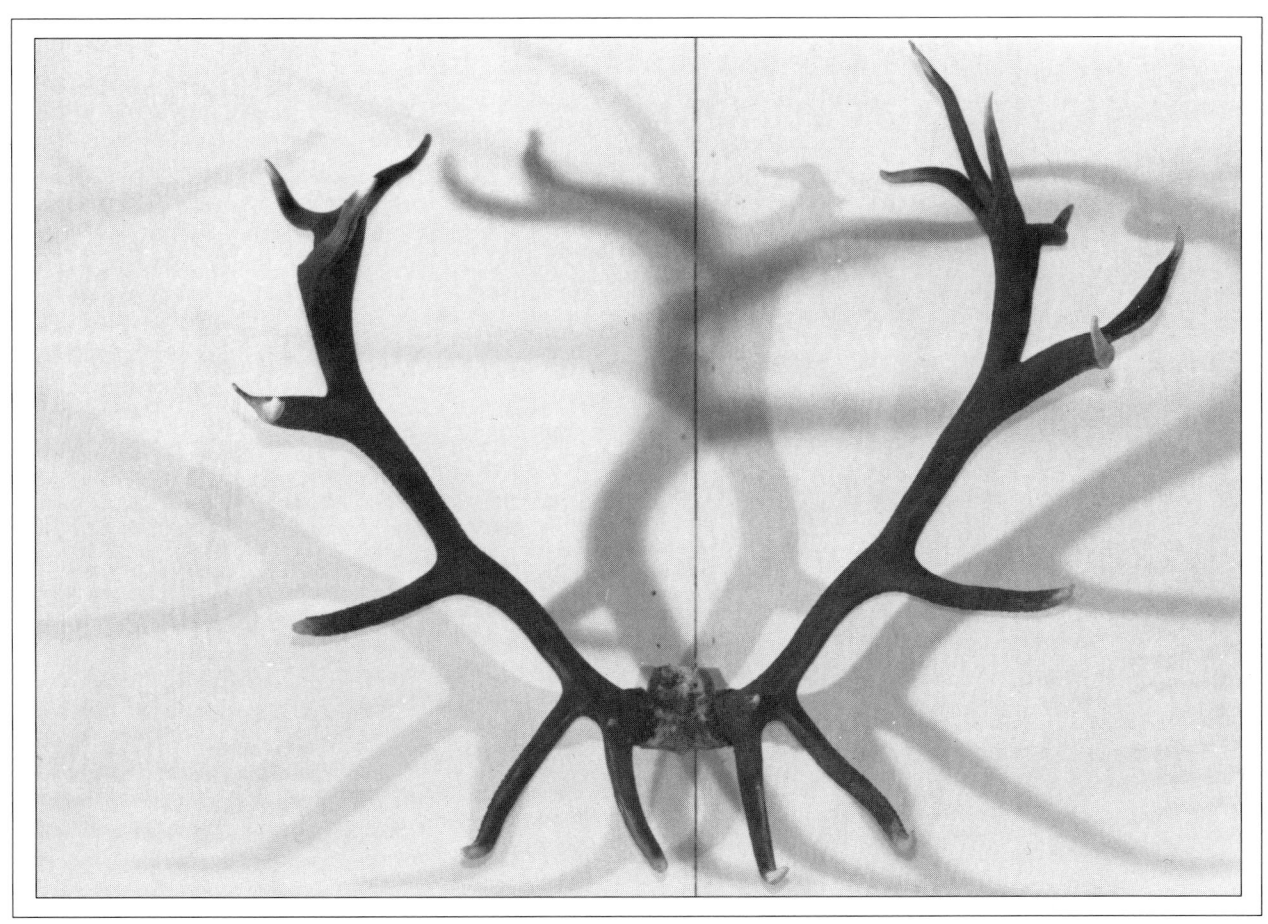

World Record Yellowstone *"American"* Elk (Non-Typical)
Score: 419 5/8
Coconino County, Arizona - 1985
Hunter: James L. Ludvigson

YELLOWSTONE *"AMERICAN"* ELK *(Non-Typical Antlers)*
MINIMUM SCORE 300   *Cervus elaphus nelsoni* and certain related subspecies

SCORE	LENGTH OF R MAIN BEAM L		INSIDE SPREAD	NUMBER OF R POINTS L		AREA	STATE/ PROVINCE	HUNTER'S NAME	DATE	RANK
419 5/8	53 1/8	51 6/8	39 4/8	8	10	Coconino County	AZ	James L. Ludvigson	1985	1
403 0/8	49 0/8	50 2/8	39 0/8	8	9	Powell County	MT	Donald Roberson	1987	2
387 2/8	48 6/8	48 3/8	37 3/8	7	7	Catron County	NM	Robert J. Brooks	1992	3
381 3/8	52 7/8	51 5/8	41 5/8	7	8	Coconino County	AZ	David A. Niemann	1990	4
371 1/8	50 0/8	49 2/8	42 5/8	7	7	Catron County	NM	Eddie Collins	1991	5
370 3/8	53 0/8	54 0/8	47 3/8	8	9	Gila County	AZ	John Bush	1989	6
364 3/8	50 1/8	50 0/8	29 2/8	6	8	Catron County	NM	Wayne K. Curtis	1988	7
361 3/8	45 6/8	45 1/8	39 5/8	8	8	Nez Perce County	ID	Randy Hollibaugh	1989	8
361 0/8	48 6/8	47 2/8	41 2/8	8	7	Flathead County	MT	Chester G. Fossum, Jr.	1992	9
345 4/8	48 0/8	49 4/8	31 6/8	7	7	Coconino County	AZ	Barry Stonehouse	1992	10
342 7/8	52 7/8	51 4/8	38 7/8	7	7	Greenlee County	AZ	Bill Golden	1990	11
335 6/8	43 5/8	40 4/8	42 4/8	9	8	Solano County	CA	Audrey Goodnight	1990	12
335 5/8	45 5/8	42 6/8	40 0/8	8	7	Catron County	NM	Paul T. Horne	1990	13
325 4/8	43 1/8	45 4/8	42 6/8	7	7	Missoula County	MT	G. Thompson/ W. Mitchell	1981	14

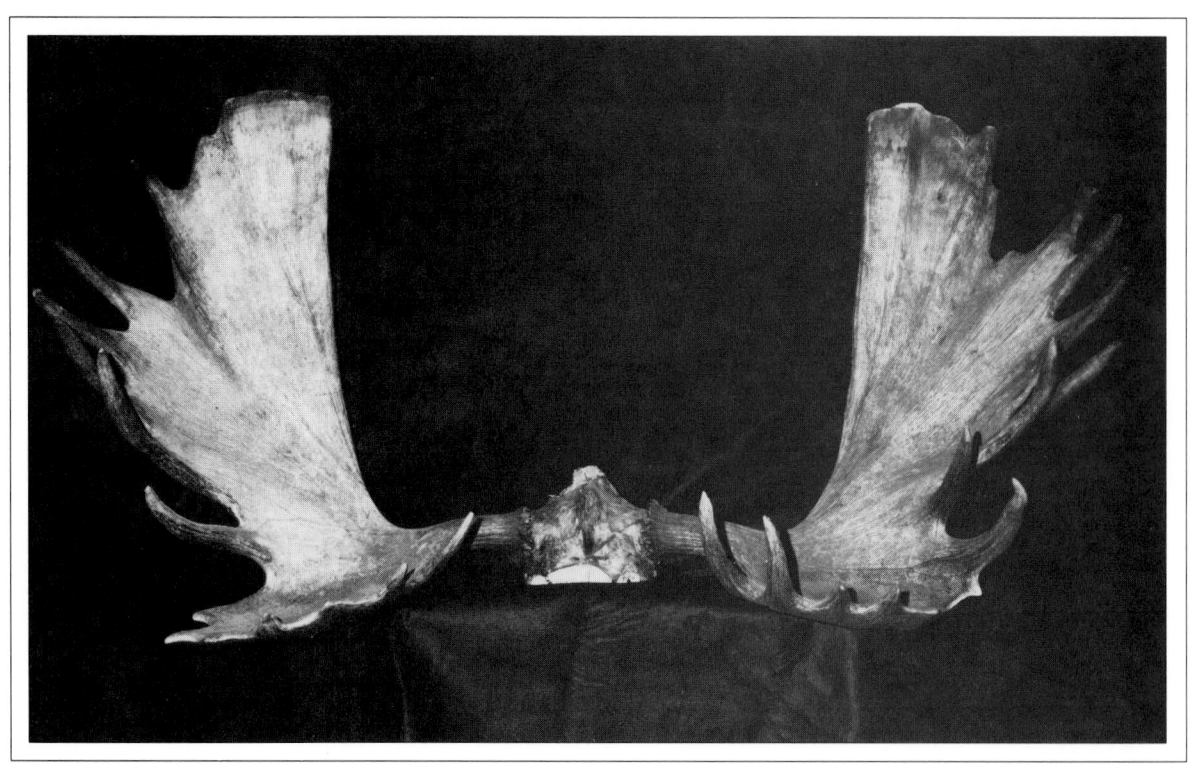

World Record Alaska-Yukon Moose
Score: 248 0/8
Bear Creek, Alaska - 1973
Hunter: Dr. Michael L. Cusack

ALASKA-YUKON MOOSE

MINIMUM SCORE 170

Alces alces gigas

SCORE	GREATEST SPREAD	WIDTH R OF PALM L		NUMBER OF R POINTS L		AREA	STATE/ PROVINCE	HUNTER'S NAME	DATE	RANK
248 0/8	74 0/8	18 6/8	19 2/8	11	11	Bear Creek	AK	Dr. Michael L. Cusack	1973	1
224 3/8	59 5/8	17 0/8	16 4/8	15	13	Lake Iliamna	AK	George Faerber	1974	2
223 7/8	73 7/8	14 2/8	16 0/8	12	11	Kugruk River	AK	Rocky Tope	1978	3
223 1/8	62 5/8	13 3/8	14 2/8	11	11	Sugarloaf Mtn.	AK	James C. Walters	1990	4
222 1/8	67 1/8	20 0/8	15 4/8	13	12	Lower Susitna	AK	Steve McCalmant	1981	5
220 3/8	57 3/8	16 0/8	16 2/8	12	11	Little Delta River	AK	William Wright	1959	6
219 0/8	61 0/8	14 4/8	8 0/8	13	12	Kichatna River	AK	Ronald N. Kolpin	1974	7
217 4/8	71 2/8	13 2/8	12 6/8	10	12	Ugashik River	AK	Gary Hoffer	1986	8
217 3/8	64 1/8	17 0/8	15 0/8	14	15	Moose John River	AK	Mike Parsons	1991	9
215 7/8	63 3/8	13 2/8	12 1/8	15	14	Koyukuk River	AK	Rickie D. Snell	1990	10
215 3/8	71 7/8	13 5/8	12 7/8	11	11	Boston Creek	AK	Charles Harrison	1992	11
214 2/8	57 2/8	14 5/8	17 2/8	11	16	Cheeneetnuk River	AK	Dean Layman	1988	12
213 2/8	62 4/8	18 4/8	15 6/8	9	10	Rainy Pass	AK	Rick Tollison	1978	13
213 1/8	59 7/8	17 3/8	18 1/8	13	12	Mulchatna River	AK	Peter Weatherford	1988	14
212 7/8	65 7/8	13 0/8	17 6/8	9	10	Mulchatna River	AK	Jay Massey	1973	15
212 2/8	62 6/8	14 2/8	15 0/8	12	13	Koyukuk River	AK	Joe Caswell	1991	16
212 1/8	58 3/8	15 0/8	14 6/8	16	15	Brooks Range	AK	Roger Stewart	1985	17
211 2/8	66 6/8	15 0/8	14 4/8	9	9	Anchorage	AK	Dr. Rex Hancock	1961	18
211 2/8	66 6/8	21 3/8	16 0/8	7	9	Meshik River	AK	Art Kragness	1970	18
210 6/8	60 0/8	12 7/8	13 1/8	13	13	New Stuyahok	AK	Thomas Clevenger	1988	20
210 1/8	64 5/8	14 1/8	13 6/8	8	9	Nabesna	AK	Bill Ellis	1965	21
209 6/8	60 5/8	13 2/8	11 3/8	14	14	Koyukuk River	AK	Gerald Weeks	1990	22
209 6/8	69 0/8	13 0/8	14 4/8	9	9	Port Heiden	AK	Margaret Cooley	1966	23
209 1/8	62 7/8	14 6/8	19 4/8	8	9	Susitna River	AK	John D. 'Jack' Frost	1981	24
209 1/8	64 7/8	15 0/8	16 0/8	9	10	Tagagawik River	AK	Bill Grahlherr	1984	24
209 1/8	63 1/8	15 0/8	14 1/8	13	13	Mac Millan River	YUK	David Baldwin	1989	24
208 6/8	63 0/8	13 3/8	13 7/8	9	9	Galena	AK	James McCloskey	1988	27
208 1/8	59 7/8	13 5/8	15 2/8	13	13	Brooks Range	AK	Ted Grover	1985	28

MINIMUM SCORE 170

SCORE	GREATEST SPREAD	WIDTH R OF PALM L		NUMBER OF R POINTS L		AREA	STATE/ PROVINCE	HUNTER'S NAME	DATE	RANK
208 0/8	65 4/8	13 0/8	12 0/8	9	7	Alaska Peninsula	AK	Jack Niles	1970	29
207 5/8	59 1/8	14 3/8	14 2/8	14	15	Coleen River	AK	Lyle Willmarth	1990	30
207 2/8	60 2/8	12 1/8	16 6/8	10	10	Yenlo Mountains	AK	John F. Sumrall	1979	31
206 5/8	62 1/8	12 2/8	13 2/8	12	13	Kotzebue	AK	Bruce A. Moe	1980	32
206 3/8	69 3/8	12 0/8	9 4/8	7	9	Alaska Peninsula	AK	Dr. Charles R. Leidheiser	1974	33
206 2/8	59 4/8	12 5/8	15 2/8	15	14	Kuparuk River	AK	Kurt Lepping	1987	34
206 0/8	65 0/8	12 1/8	14 0/8	12	11	Chulitna River	AK	Rodney Bremer	1988	35
205 7/8	55 1/8	13 1/8	14 0/8	12	10	Inoko River	AK	Jack Smythe	1974	36
205 6/8	70 0/8	15 7/8	13 3/8	9	9	Alaska Peninsula	AK	Dr. Howard Schneider	1982	37
205 6/8	67 6/8	11 6/8	12 0/8	12	9	Kuskokwim River	AK	Jimmy Harkins	1986	37
205 4/8	57 6/8	13 4/8	13 3/8	11	13	Horsetrail Lake	AK	Donald Poole	1979	39
205 2/8	64 0/8	14 0/8	12 7/8	8	12	Alaska Peninsu	AK	Donald B. McIntosh	1969	40
205 1/8	57 7/8	14 2/8	12 4/8	15	13	Telaquana	AK	Mike Mitten	1988	41
204 7/8	60 3/8	14 5/8	15 6/8	10	11	Paxon	AK	Alan Perry	1972	42
204 7/8	68 3/8	14 7/8	14 6/8	7	11	Black Lake	AK	Stanley Winslow	1973	42
204 7/8	58 1/8	15 1/8	15 4/8	12	11	Jim River	AK	Eldon Holm	1990	42
204 4/8	58 0/8	12 6/8	13 0/8	11	11	Chilikadrotna River	AK	Peter Thomas Weatherford	1987	45
204 2/8	61 4/8	13 4/8	12 5/8	10	11	Fairbanks	AK	Keith Jensen	1986	46
203 6/8	66 0/8	11 5/8	12 7/8	13	11	Port Heiden	AK	Jim Dougherty	1968	47
203 3/8	66 7/8	11 0/8	11 7/8	13	12	Seven Mile Lake	AK	Dr. William J. Young, Jr.	1980	48
202 7/8	58 1/8	12 6/8	13 4/8	15	13	Earn Lake	YUK	Dr. R. D. Keeler	1986	49
202 6/8	67 4/8	12 4/8	13 2/8	9	9	Port Heiden	AK	Noel Feather	1973	50
202 4/8	49 6/8	14 2/8	14 4/8	10	12	Brooks Range	AK	Brent Chapman	1978	51
202 4/8	58 2/8	15 2/8	14 1/8	13	12	Chulitna River	AK	Rickie D. Snell	1982	51
202 2/8	62 6/8	12 5/8	13 4/8	9	10	Toolik River	AK	George P. Mann	1987	53
202 0/8	63 1/8	14 2/8	13 5/8	10	8	Moose John River	AK	Kent Brigham	1985	54
201 6/8	59 0/8	11 7/8	13 0/8	13	12	Brooks Range	AK	Mike Rosetti	1985	55
201 2/8	62 4/8	14 1/8	13 2/8	10	10	Rackla Lake	YUK	Paul Hight	1991	56
201 2/8	63 6/8	14 7/8	14 7/8	14	13	Brooks Range	AK	James L. Behn	1991	56
200 7/8	58 5/8	12 5/8	15 0/8	13	13	Wrangell Mtns.	AK	Robert Warpack	1988	58
200 3/8	61 1/8	13 3/8	13 7/8	10	11	Chanuk Creek	AK	Roger O. Wyant	1989	59
200 2/8	64 2/8	14 4/8	14 0/8	10	11	Dog Salmon River	AK	Robert C. Keadle	1972	60
200 2/8	62 2/8	13 1/8	12 7/8	12	12	King Salmon	AK	Ken Slaght	1982	60
200 2/8	60 4/8	13 6/8	11 0/8	12	12	Skentna River	AK	David Bailey	1983	60
199 6/8	52 0/8	12 5/8	12 2/8	10	11	Timberline Lk. Kenai	AK	DeWayne Benton	1984	63
199 3/8	56 1/8	11 2/8	11 2/8	9	9	Nelchina	AK	Henry Wichers	1962	64
199 2/8	58 6/8	14 4/8	14 7/8	12	10	Koyukuk River	AK	Joe Caswell	1990	65
198 7/8	63 7/8	11 1/8	13 0/8	8	10	Gulkana Basin	AK	Thomas L. A. Pucci	1970	66
198 7/8	64 1/8	15 3/8	15 6/8	7	8	Tag River	AK	Thomas E. Rothrock	1991	66
198 4/8	60 2/8	16 0/8	15 4/8	9	10	Arctic Wildlife Refuge	AK	William Gardner Rowell	1981	68
198 2/8	52 2/8	17 0/8	13 4/8	8	10	Nenana River	AK	Dr. Harley Scholz	1973	69
198 1/8	63 5/8	11 3/8	11 6/8	10	12	Rainy Pass	AK	Dr. Henry C. McDonald	1970	70
197 6/8	64 0/8	11 4/8	11 2/8	12	11	King Salmon	AK	Gary L. Petty	1976	71
197 6/8	63 2/8	13 2/8	12 1/8	8	9	Susitina	AK	Mark S Bode	1989	71
197 5/8	59 5/8	12 7/8	12 5/8	9	9	Galena	AK	George Ollert	1988	73
197 4/8	65 4/8	13 0/8	14 5/8	6	9	Ugashik River	AK	Robert Borland	1972	74
197 4/8	61 4/8	10 6/8	12 1/8	8	11	Ugashik Lake	AK	John Wallace	1974	74
197 4/8	59 2/8	11 4/8	15 2/8	12	12	Chulitna River	AK	Rickie D. Snell	1983	74
197 2/8	64 2/8	12 3/8	14 4/8	8	8	Sugar Loaf Mtns.	AK	Jeffrey S. Stevens	1988	77
197 1/8	62 1/8	14 4/8	11 1/8	12	10	Susitna River	AK	Jake Sonnentag	1969	78
197 1/8	59 3/8	19 1/8	13 5/8	11	8	Mac Millan River	YUK	Bob Fromme	1991	78
197 0/8	62 6/8	12 0/8	12 3/8	8	11	King Salmon	AK	Brian L. Heise	1977	80
196 6/8	63 6/8	13 2/8	16 4/8	6	6	Alaska Peninsula	AK	Phillip Durr	1969	81
196 5/8	58 3/8	15 2/8	14 1/8	9	10	Kaktovik	AK	Judy Grooms	1987	82
196 4/8	63 0/8	11 1/8	11 1/8	10	10	Chiliadrotna River	AK	Patrick J. Lefemine	1991	83
196 2/8	58 0/8	11 0/8	11 5/8	8	9	Mulchatna River	AK	Kurt M. Zurawski	1989	84
195 6/8	55 2/8	10 1/8	11 3/8	13	11	Koyukuk River	AK	Mark Hanson	1990	85
195 5/8	52 5/8	11 4/8	11 0/8	12	12	Fairbanks	AK	Rocky Chisholm	1988	86
195 4/8	55 6/8	12 6/8	13 6/8	10	10	Bonnet Plume Lake	YUK	Billy Ellis	1981	87
195 0/8	68 2/8	14 0/8	12 6/8	7	7	Lake Iliamna	AK	Rex William Maurer	1987	88
194 7/8	53 1/8	11 7/8	12 4/8	13	14	Tustumena Lake	AK	Lavern Davidhizar	1980	89
194 6/8	56 6/8	12 2/8	12 3/8	9	9	Juniper Creek	AK	David L. Stull	1991	90
194 4/8	64 0/8	17 5/8	15 3/8	11	7	Alaska Peninsula	AK	Jim Dougherty	1962	91
194 3/8	57 5/8	11 4/8	15 5/8	11	12	Mystery Creek	AK	Joe Kelly	1989	92
194 2/8	61 6/8	12 7/8	13 7/8	7	12	Koyukuk River	AK	Thomas J. Hentrick	1984	93
194 0/8	58 6/8	13 6/8	12 2/8	8	9	Lake Clark	AK	Dr. Gary G. Sauer	1987	94
194 0/8	59 6/8	11 4/8	12 2/8	12	13	Kotzebue	AK	Mark D. Mishinski	1990	94
193 5/8	60 3/8	10 7/8	12 5/8	8	9	Beluga Mtn.	AK	Dennis A. Lundine	1984	96
193 3/8	53 7/8	11 6/8	11 6/8	10	10	Kenai Peninsula	AK	Robert LaFollette	1962	97
193 0/8	52 6/8	13 5/8	12 3/8	8	10	Kateel River	AK	Dennis Tol	1987	98

SCORE	GREATEST SPREAD	WIDTH OF PALM R L	NUMBER OF POINTS R L	AREA	STATE/ PROVINCE	HUNTER'S NAME	DATE	RANK
192 7/8	56 3/8	13 7/8 12 7/8	9 10	Little Tok River	AK	Dennis L. Lattery	1977	99
192 5/8	55 1/8	10 5/8 12 5/8	11 13	Wrangell Mtns.	AK	Loren Willey	1973	100
192 4/8	60 6/8	14 2/8 12 4/8	7 9	Kluane Lake	YUK	Eugene A. Tieman	1973	101
192 4/8	51 0/8	10 6/8 9 2/8	14 12	Fort Richardson	AK	Donald D. Roberts	1984	101
192 4/8	61 4/8	11 3/8 12 0/8	8 10	Kuparuk River	AK	Robert Barrie	1987	101
192 3/8	55 7/8	11 6/8 12 0/8	11 11	Eklutna Lake	AK	Ron C. Harvey	1989	104
192 0/8	52 6/8	14 2/8 16 2/8	8 10	Clarence Lake	AK	John Schoenike	1966	105
192 0/8	69 6/8	10 6/8 13 4/8	7 9	Wood River	AK	Doug Strecker	1981	105
192 0/8	56 4/8	14 0/8 13 3/8	8 9	Koyukuk River	AK	Joe Caswell	1989	105
192 0/8	56 6/8	14 4/8 11 1/8	11 12	Kilik River	AK	John S. Borg	1991	105
191 7/8	57 7/8	16 3/8 14 7/8	8 10	Rainy Pass	AK	Rick Tollison	1977	109
191 6/8	54 6/8	12 3/8 12 2/8	9 12	Brooks Range	AK	Joseph Stanevich	1986	110
191 3/8	57 3/8	14 0/8 14 5/8	8 11	Whitefish Lake	AK	Jim Hoss	1975	111
191 1/8	58 5/8	13 2/8 14 2/8	11 9	Galena	AK	Frank Prata	1988	112
190 6/8	52 4/8	11 3/8 10 3/8	10 11	Ugashik Lake	AK	Dr. William Schultz	1987	113
190 5/8	57 3/8	8 4/8 9 2/8	11 10	Kotzebue	AK	Raymond Lengyel	1990	114
190 4/8	63 6/8	11 0/8 11 1/8	7 7	Mother Goose Lake	AK	Cecil Jarvis	1987	115
190 3/8	57 3/8	13 0/8 13 0/8	12 12	Teslin Lake	YUK	Paul Schafer	1977	116
190 3/8	62 3/8	13 6/8 15 1/8	11 12	Derby Creek	AK	Greg Kempf	1991	116
190 2/8	58 4/8	14 0/8 13 2/8	9 14	Yentna River	AK	Dan Hollingsworth	1978	118
190 2/8	57 0/8	11 6/8 13 2/8	13 12	Anchorage	AK	Paul Persano	1981	118
190 1/8	60 5/8	11 2/8 10 6/8	10 12	Alaska Peninsula	AK	Rick W. Simpson	1979	120
190 0/8	57 4/8	12 4/8 15 1/8	11 11	Lime Village	AK	Jerad Dittrich	1976	121
190 0/8	56 6/8	12 2/8 11 7/8	9 13	Mackenzie Mtns.	NWT	Robert A. Hermann	1992	121
189 0/8	53 6/8	13 1/8 13 1/8	9 13	Alaska Peninsula	AK	Richard T. Vance	1972	123
188 7/8	57 7/8	11 1/8 12 5/8	13 10	Sagaranirktok River	AK	Robert G. Chouinard	1980	124
188 7/8	59 1/8	14 3/8 14 3/8	10 9	Cantwell	AK	John W. Williams	1983	124
188 4/8	63 0/8	11 5/8 12 3/8	8 8	Kenai Peninsula	AK	Dale L. Lofstedt	1969	126
188 2/8	61 2/8	12 3/8 11 0/8	10 9	Upper Dog Salmon River	AK	Robert T. Morgan	1983	127
188 1/8	53 7/8	12 5/8 13 2/8	11 13	Alaska Range	AK	Richard Moran	1991	128
187 7/8	67 7/8	11 4/8 13 4/8	10 11	Jim River	AK	Ernie Dempsey	1981	129
187 7/8	48 1/8	14 4/8 14 4/8	10 13	Watson Lake	YUK	Pete Shepley	1985	129
187 5/8	60 7/8	12 5/8 11 6/8	12 12	Innoko River	AK	Ron Madsen	1989	131
186 6/8	62 0/8	12 1/8 12 2/8	7 6	Ugashik Lake	AK	Richard King	1988	132
186 5/8	53 1/8	12 0/8 12 7/8	10 10	Squirrel River	AK	Randy Martin	1992	133
186 4/8	50 4/8	12 5/8 13 7/8	13 13	Fox Mtn.	YUK	Steve Crooks	1991	134
186 3/8	52 5/8	13 5/8 14 0/8	10 11	Middle Fork	AK	Glen Williams	1969	135
186 3/8	50 7/8	12 4/8 12 7/8	11 12	Hess River	YUK	Russell Thornberry	1987	135
186 3/8	56 7/8	11 1/8 11 3/8	10 10	Mackenzie Mtns.	NWT	Chuck Adams	1990	135
186 2/8	56 2/8	11 2/8 12 4/8	8 8	Cook Inlet	AK	George Moerlein	1961	138
186 2/8	62 6/8	13 2/8 12 2/8	9 9	Kejulik River	AK	John Crump	1981	138
186 1/8	61 5/8	10 6/8 10 7/8	10 9	Cinder River	AK	Glenn Hisey	1976	140
185 7/8	56 5/8	11 2/8 10 7/8	8 9	Susitina Valley	AK	Dan J. Tobin	1984	141
185 7/8	55 1/8	12 2/8 11 0/8	11 11	Kanuti River	AK	Scott R. Nordin	1989	141
185 5/8	56 3/8	14 0/8 14 3/8	7 6	Cantwell	AK	John Eilertson	1983	143
185 4/8	56 4/8	12 0/8 9 4/8	12 11	Fort Richardson	AK	David Dodds	1991	144
185 3/8	57 5/8	10 0/8 9 6/8	10 11	King Salmon	AK	Paul Persano	1982	145
185 0/8	56 0/8	10 6/8 11 6/8	10 11	Squirrel River	AK	James Borron	1992	146
184 7/8	59 7/8	13 1/8 11 5/8	12 10	Susitina Valley	AK	Dan J. Tobin	1988	147
184 6/8	55 6/8	11 3/8 12 4/8	5 10	Cinder River	AK	Francis Hosch	1965	148
184 6/8	59 4/8	15 4/8 13 3/8	7 8	Anaktuvak Pass	AK	Rod Van DeGraaf	1990	148
184 4/8	55 0/8	12 1/8 12 0/8	10 9	Port Heiden	AK	Frank 'Rit' Heller	1974	150
184 4/8	59 6/8	12 0/8 12 2/8	9 15	Eklutna Lake	AK	Steve J. Latz	1986	150
184 3/8	53 5/8	9 4/8 13 4/8	12 13	Palmer	AK	A. H. Stange, Jr.	1962	152
184 3/8	63 3/8	12 4/8 11 0/8	12 8	Mishik River	AK	George Wright	1969	152
184 1/8	59 7/8	11 1/8 13 0/8	10 10	Brooks Range	AK	Kent Devine	1988	154
184 0/8	59 6/8	11 0/8 10 6/8	6 7	Whitefish Lake	AK	George A. Mohr	1982	155
183 6/8	50 4/8	12 5/8 12 1/8	8 8	Nabesna	AK	George Moerlein	1962	156
183 3/8	53 5/8	12 5/8 12 5/8	10 9	Nahanni Butte	NWT	Roy M. Goodwin	1990	157
183 2/8	53 4/8	11 4/8 11 7/8	7 7	Brooks Range	AK	Matt Jones	1990	158
183 0/8	54 6/8	11 1/8 11 2/8	10 10	Alaska Peninsula	AK	Jerry Putnam	1973	159
182 7/8	55 1/8	11 0/8 12 0/8	11 11	Eklutna Lake	AK	K. Edward Atwood	1986	160
182 7/8	52 1/8	12 3/8 11 7/8	8 10	Ivishak River	AK	Ed Strayhorn	1987	160
182 6/8	55 0/8	13 3/8 13 2/8	11 11	Nowetta River	AK	Alan Winger	1988	162
182 5/8	57 5/8	11 2/8 16 1/8	10 10	Little Delta River	AK	Keith R. Clemmons	1957	163
182 5/8	54 5/8	13 5/8 13 2/8	9 8	Juniper River	AK	Dennis Faulkenberry	1986	163
182 4/8	56 0/8	12 0/8 12 0/8	6 7	Fort Richardson	AK	Mark Wojtalik	1988	165
182 2/8	57 4/8	12 2/8 12 6/8	7 8	Nome	AK	Erv Plotz	1979	166
182 1/8	56 5/8	9 7/8 12 0/8	7 9	Toolic	AK	Reggie Spiegelberg	1986	167
182 1/8	56 5/8	9 7/8 11 1/8	12 12	Coleville River	AK	Kurt Lepping	1990	167

MINIMUM SCORE 170

SCORE	GREATEST SPREAD	WIDTH OF PALM R	L	NUMBER OF POINTS R	L	AREA	STATE/ PROVINCE	HUNTER'S NAME	DATE	RANK
182 0/8	59 0/8	12 0/8	11 4/8	10	10	Slope Mountain	AK	Roger Wheelock	1980	169
181 6/8	56 0/8	11 4/8	12 6/8	10	12	Moose Creek	AK	Bill Brown	1991	170
181 4/8	57 2/8	14 3/8	16 6/8	7	9	Port Heiden	AK	Bill L. Carlos	1970	171
181 4/8	55 4/8	12 4/8	12 6/8	6	10	Ft. Yukon	AK	Ron Rockwell	1985	171
181 1/8	57 7/8	9 7/8	10 0/8	10	11	Ugashik Lake	AK	Scott Showalter	1972	173
181 1/8	54 1/8	8 6/8	10 2/8	8	10	King Salmon	AK	Joe Fogleman	1982	173
181 0/8	56 6/8	13 3/8	12 3/8	7	6	Colville River	AK	Kurt Lepping	1986	175
180 7/8	54 1/8	10 6/8	10 3/8	9	11	Earn Lake	YUK	Glen R. Cousins	1978	176
180 5/8	51 3/8	11 1/8	11 2/8	8	9	Port Heiden	AK	Art Heinze	1973	177
180 4/8	57 6/8	12 7/8	11 3/8	10	8	Middle Fork	AK	Norm Goodwin	1969	178
180 2/8	61 4/8	11 6/8	10 2/8	7	10	Alaska Peninsula	AK	Keith Pilz	1976	179
180 2/8	53 6/8	11 0/8	12 1/8	8	10	Lake Clark	AK	Paul L. Fischer	1988	179
179 7/8	56 1/8	11 3/8	11 2/8	9	9	Sugar Loaf Mtn.	AK	James White	1988	181
179 6/8	59 2/8	9 3/8	12 3/8	8	7	Susitna River	AK	Robert Pitt	1968	182
179 6/8	54 2/8	14 3/8	12 6/8	9	9	Tag River	AK	Scott Privette	1986	182
179 6/8	54 6/8	13 2/8	11 0/8	10	10	Wrangel Mtns.	AK	Bret T. Walker	1991	182
179 5/8	53 3/8	11 0/8	11 2/8	11	12	Berry Creek	AK	Larry Jones	1962	185
179 5/8	53 1/8	9 4/8	13 3/8	10	13	Kenai Peninsula	AK	George Moerlein	1969	185
179 4/8	48 2/8	11 0/8	11 2/8	12	12	Kotzebue	AK	Stephen Kotz	1990	187
179 2/8	57 0/8	11 4/8	11 6/8	8	10	Brooks Range	AK	Kurt W. Keskimaki	1989	188
179 1/8	55 7/8	13 1/8	12 0/8	6	7	Fort Yukon	AK	Barry J. Smith	1985	189
179 0/8	53 0/8	13 6/8	13 3/8	8	10	Ft. Richardson	AK	Earl G. Brown	1984	190
178 5/8	52 5/8	10 5/8	11 3/8	12	12	Koyukuk River	AK	Steven M. Stroka	1991	191
178 4/8	55 4/8	13 0/8	11 5/8	10	9	Kuskokwim River	AK	Bill Stonebraker	1980	192
178 3/8	53 7/8	9 6/8	7 2/8	13	9	Tustamena Lake	AK	Lowell Thomas	1973	193
178 1/8	59 1/8	10 1/8	9 5/8	9	7	Cheeneetnuk River	AK	H. R. 'Rusty' Neely	1982	194
177 3/8	61 1/8	10 4/8	10 5/8	6	12	Iliamna	AK	Thad Barnes	1989	195
177 3/8	58 7/8	11 0/8	11 4/8	11	12	Galena	AK	Larry Spiva	1992	195
177 2/8	51 6/8	12 4/8	12 0/8	9	9	Kenai Peninsula	AK	Alan Perry	1971	197
177 2/8	55 0/8	13 7/8	12 1/8	7	12	Whitehorse	YUK	Scott Koelzer	1977	197
177 2/8	60 0/8	10 1/8	10 0/8	8	7	Juniper River	AK	Boyd Holley	1986	197
177 0/8	62 0/8	9 0/8	9 2/8	5	7	Port Heiden	AK	James R. Scott	1966	200
176 6/8	56 6/8	10 4/8	11 4/8	11	11	Brooks Range	AK	Steve Weekly	1990	201
176 5/8	57 3/8	10 1/8	11 0/8	11	10	Crow Pass	AK	Michael J. Schneider	1982	202
176 2/8	54 0/8	10 2/8	10 1/8	11	8	Chugiak	AK	Jerry D. Fletcher	1990	203
176 2/8	55 4/8	9 3/8	9 7/8	9	8	Eklutna Lake	AK	Thomas J. Rutz	1991	203
175 4/8	60 4/8	11 6/8	10 0/8	7	8	Susitna River	AK	David A. Drover	1971	205
175 4/8	50 6/8	11 4/8	11 3/8	9	9	Kuparuk River	AK	Bill Krenz	1984	205
175 3/8	46 3/8	11 3/8	13 1/8	11	15	Kaktovik	AK	Grant Poindexter	1987	207
175 2/8	56 6/8	11 7/8	11 1/8	4	5	Brooks Range	AK	Thomas T. King	1989	208
175 1/8	51 3/8	11 2/8	12 1/8	9	10	Healy	AK	Vic Killian	1991	209
174 6/8	58 6/8	8 0/8	9 6/8	8	8	McCarty Creek	AK	Stanley J. Rogers, Jr.	1972	210
174 5/8	58 1/8	13 3/8	12 3/8	8	8	Koyukuk River	AK	Gerald L. Weeks	1991	211
174 3/8	57 5/8	12 5/8	12 0/8	13	8	Tustamena Lake	AK	Gary Wall	1974	212
174 3/8	52 1/8	11 3/8	12 3/8	9	10	Koyukuk River	AK	Roger Stewart	1982	212
174 2/8	54 6/8	10 0/8	10 0/8	12	9	Delta River	AK	Dr. R. Congdon	1960	214
174 2/8	58 0/8	11 3/8	11 6/8	11	9	Kajulik River	AK	Mike Hedrick	1984	214
173 6/8	49 0/8	9 2/8	10 7/8	10	11	Chistochina River	AK	Larry L. Schweitzer	1982	216
173 6/8	53 6/8	10 6/8	10 4/8	7	6	Colville River	AK	Bob Gulman	1984	216
173 5/8	57 5/8	12 5/8	11 4/8	12	10	Northway	AK	Chuck Adams	1978	218
173 5/8	55 1/8	12 7/8	12 4/8	8	8	Juniper River	AK	Dr. F. D. Elias	1986	218
173 0/8	50 4/8	10 1/8	10 4/8	12	12	Koyukuk River	AK	William E. Lee	1984	220
173 0/8	58 2/8	11 2/8	10 4/8	11	10	Koksitna Drainage	AK	Ron Hopkins	1987	220
172 7/8	49 3/8	14 0/8	12 6/8	12	12	Coldfoot	AK	Danny F. Watson	1988	222
172 5/8	47 1/8	11 0/8	12 0/8	7	7	Brooks Range	AK	John Ribic	1983	223
171 7/8	60 5/8	9 2/8	7 5/8	13	10	Brooks Range	AK	Bruce R. Schoeneweis	1989	224
171 5/8	57 3/8	10 6/8	9 0/8	13	7	Hayes Creek	AK	Keith R. Clemmons	1962	225
171 4/8	49 4/8	10 2/8	10 6/8	12	9	Delta River	AK	Richard R. Cooper	1959	226
171 4/8	57 0/8	10 2/8	10 0/8	10	12	Fish Creek	AK	Doug Keller	1990	226
171 2/8	59 0/8	12 0/8	10 1/8	11	9	Big River Flats	AK	Lonnie Rumley	1988	228
171 1/8	53 3/8	10 4/8	10 2/8	10	12	Tillei Lake	YUK	Roger M. Tyler	1989	229
171 0/8	48 2/8	12 0/8	11 4/8	7	8	Brooks Range	AK	Edward Keltgen	1986	230
171 0/8	45 2/8	11 1/8	8 4/8	8	7	Bonnet Plume Lake	YUK	Stan Rauch	1989	230
170 7/8	58 1/8	12 0/8	10 6/8	8	5	Port Heiden	AK	John E. Lawson	1970	232
170 7/8	48 5/8	11 0/8	9 2/8	9	10	King Salmon River	AK	Bob Sweisthal	1986	232
170 7/8	62 7/8	10 1/8	11 4/8	6	9	Ugashik Lake	AK	Dennis Statham	1989	232
170 6/8	56 0/8	10 0/8	12 1/8	9	8	Ugashik Lake	AK	Dr. Von A. Mitton	1978	235
170 4/8	52 6/8	12 1/8	11 4/8	10	9	Unit 13D	AK	Dayle Paulson	1969	236
170 1/8	50 1/8	10 3/8	11 2/8	9	9	Fort Richardson	AK	Harry Gordon Evans	1989	237
170 0/8	58 2/8	12 2/8	11 5/8	9	10	Zone 4	YUK	Keith Baker	1988	238

World Record Canada Moose
Score: 222 1/8
Cap Chat, Quebec - 1988
Hunter: Charles Roy

CANADA MOOSE

MINIMUM SCORE 135

Alces alces americana and *Alces alces andersoni*

SCORE	GREATEST SPREAD	WIDTH R OF PALM L		NUMBER OF R POINTS L		AREA	STATE/ PROVINCE	HUNTER'S NAME	DATE	RANK
222 1/8	66 1/8	16 1/8	14 7/8	16	15	Cap-Chat	QUE	Charles Roy	1988	1
214 3/8	55 7/8	14 1/8	14 4/8	16	17	Chevis Creek	BC	Wayne Carlton	1988	2
201 4/8	55 2/8	12 4/8	11 4/8	12	12	Mt. Lady Laurier	BC	Peter Halbig	1968	3
201 2/8	60 4/8	11 1/8	11 1/8	12	11	Hutt Twp.	ONT	Fred Robinson	1986	4
198 6/8	56 6/8	16 3/8	16 7/8	15	13	Toad River	BC	Dirk V. Lawyer	1984	5
197 0/8	58 6/8	16 4/8	13 5/8	9	7	Cold Fish Lake	BC	Steve Gorr	1975	6
196 7/8	52 3/8	17 3/8	14 6/8	16	15	Dryden	ONT	Murray Macquarrie	1990	7
196 6/8	48 6/8	16 4/8	15 2/8	12	13	Besa River	BC	Edward Flowerdew	1976	8
196 2/8	59 5/8	14 4/8	13 7/8	10	13	Skeena	BC	Larry Garoutte	1972	9
196 2/8	53 6/8	12 3/8	15 4/8	13	12	Nacht Creek	BC	Scott L. Koelzer	1991	9
194 4/8	55 6/8	13 4/8	14 2/8	11	13	Thunder Bay	ONT	Bob Toderash	1987	11
192 7/8	55 3/8	14 4/8	15 6/8	12	13	Algoma	ONT	Larry Pilon	1989	12
192 6/8	56 6/8	11 5/8	10 5/8	12	13	Cassiar Mtns.	BC	Thomas B. Frye	1978	13
192 3/8	61 1/8	12 3/8	13 6/8	7	8	Thunder Bay	ONT	Ron Mahler	1992	14
191 2/8	51 4/8	13 0/8	12 6/8	12	14	Duck Mountain	MAN	M. Dale Robins	1992	15
190 2/8	55 2/8	15 4/8	16 0/8	9	6	Lake Nipigon	ONT	Ohne Raasch	1991	16
189 3/8	60 3/8	13 2/8	11 2/8	12	11	Sultan	ONT	Michael Wiseman	1989	17
188 5/8	52 5/8	10 0/8	10 6/8	8	8	Sultan	ONT	Mike R. Nowaczyk	1986	18
187 5/8	57 0/8	13 3/8	12 1/8	11	13	Turnagin River	BC	Glenn Hisey	1978	19
187 0/8	50 6/8	12 6/8	11 5/8	13	13	Dibble Lake	ONT	Bruce Zuehlke	1992	20
186 7/8	57 1/8	13 2/8	13 1/8	8	12	Klastline River	BC	Gregory White	1992	21
186 2/8	54 0/8	11 2/8	11 2/8	10	11	Ash Mt.	BC	Pink Atkins	1984	22
186 1/8	53 1/8	14 1/8	13 2/8	11	12	Pitman Lake	BC	Kevin Schmid	1990	23
186 0/8	62 0/8	10 5/8	10 4/8	10	13	St. Gilles	QUE	Michel Aubert	1986	24
185 3/8	54 3/8	11 4/8	11 3/8	13	11	Mossy River	SAS	Jerome J. Huseby	1966	25
184 7/8	58 7/8	11 3/8	11 4/8	9	9	Goat Creek	BC	Atley Lovelace	1974	26
184 6/8	55 7/8	11 7/8	11 5/8	13	8	Blanchard Creek	BC	Ron Johnson	1974	27
184 2/8	49 0/8	12 5/8	13 2/8	11	11	St. Gilles	QUE	Michel Aubert	1985	28
183 4/8	60 6/8	10 4/8	11 5/8	10	9	Terminus Valley	BC	Paul P. Schafer	1975	29
182 7/8	52 5/8	13 6/8	12 2/8	11	6	Christian Falls	BC	Mike Ryan	1990	30
182 4/8	58 4/8	14 6/8	14 3/8	8	9	East Hereford	QUE	Daniel Fecteau	1990	31
182 1/8	50 5/8	11 2/8	11 1/8	10	10	Stanley Creek	BC	Donald L. Pahl	1973	32
181 1/8	51 5/8	12 0/8	11 5/8	12	13	Halfway River	BC	Duane L. Scroggins	1977	33

SCORE	GREATEST SPREAD	WIDTH OF PALM R	WIDTH OF PALM L	NUMBER OF POINTS R	NUMBER OF POINTS L	AREA	STATE/ PROVINCE	HUNTER'S NAME	DATE	RANK
180 2/8	44 6/8	12 4/8	11 4/8	13	14	Lake Lac Seul	ONT	Josef K. Rud	1989	34
180 1/8	47 3/8	11 6/8	11 1/8	12	13	Unit 23	ONT	Paul F. J. Petrie	1985	35
180 0/8	55 4/8	12 0/8	13 0/8	9	10	Algoma	ONT	Larry Pilon	1988	36
179 6/8	50 6/8	11 5/8	13 2/8	11	12	Dease Lake	BC	Robert G. Petersen	1985	37
179 1/8	56 3/8	11 0/8	10 0/8	11	9	Atikokan	ONT	Russ Martin	1987	38
178 5/8	51 2/8	11 1/8	12 6/8	10	10	Kechika River	BC	Scott L. Koelzer	1976	39
178 0/8	46 6/8	11 2/8	11 1/8	10	12	Ketchika Valley	BC	Edd Clack	1991	40
177 2/8	52 2/8	10 7/8	9 0/8	10	8	Thrimble Lake	BC	Chester Schardt	1966	41
177 1/8	56 7/8	12 7/8	12 4/8	7	8	Heyson Twp.	ONT	R. S. Illingworth	1986	42
176 6/8	52 0/8	12 5/8	12 2/8	9	13	Majuba Lake	BC	Glenn Dreger	1990	43
176 3/8	47 7/8	11 2/8	10 4/8	10	10	Algoma	ONT	Edward Broderick	1989	44
176 2/8	57 6/8	9 4/8	10 4/8	9	9	Fallon Twp.	ONT	Frank J. Julling	1987	45
176 0/8	55 2/8	13 6/8	14 2/8	9	14	Long Range Mtns.	NFL	Waldemar D. Maya	1965	46
176 0/8	58 2/8	9 5/8	9 0/8	9	9	Algoma	ONT	Larry Pilon	1987	46
175 4/8	50 6/8	11 2/8	9 6/8	10	10	Moose Lake	BC	Dan Martin	1986	48
175 3/8	51 7/8	11 4/8	11 7/8	8	9	Dease Lake	BC	Bill Coburn	1979	49
175 1/8	50 3/8	12 0/8	11 6/8	10	11	Northern Light Lake	ONT	Ian Robinson	1991	50
175 0/8	52 0/8	10 1/8	10 7/8	9	9	Central	BC	Ronald Lauretti	1973	51
175 0/8	53 4/8	10 4/8	12 0/8	8	10	Kechika River	BC	Paul F. Schafer	1974	51
174 6/8	54 6/8	13 4/8	9 4/8	11	11	Algoma	ONT	Larry Pilon	1990	53
174 5/8	50 5/8	11 3/8	10 7/8	12	11	McConnell Range	BC	Dave Young	1976	54
174 3/8	56 1/8	13 0/8	10 2/8	10	7	Algoma District	ONT	Paul Kovich	1981	55
174 2/8	51 4/8	12 1/8	12 2/8	9	8	Atikokan	ONT	David Williams	1992	56
173 5/8	52 1/8	9 4/8	11 1/8	10	10	Lake Lac Seul	ONT	Josef K. Rud	1990	57
173 2/8	52 6/8	10 6/8	12 3/8	12	10	Red Deer Lake	ALB	Terry Lane	1988	58
172 4/8	59 2/8	10 4/8	9 4/8	11	9	Piscataquis County	ME	Frank White	1989	59
172 2/8	61 4/8	10 2/8	9 5/8	9	8	Lake County	MN	Chuck Schultz	1987	60
172 0/8	50 6/8	11 4/8	11 7/8	10	10	Thutade Lake	BC	Larry Nirk	1975	61
172 0/8	53 0/8	11 2/8	10 2/8	9	7	Timmins	ONT	Carl Doerner	1976	61
172 0/8	48 6/8	11 4/8	11 3/8	11	10	Magone Township	ONT	John L. Burket	1986	61
171 6/8	48 4/8	10 4/8	12 2/8	12	11	S. Branch	NFL	Paul Erdbrink	1966	64
171 5/8	44 1/8	15 5/8	13 1/8	13	11	Cape Anquille Mtns.	NFL	Terrance Estes	1966	65
171 4/8	50 6/8	10 5/8	10 4/8	7	9	Algoma	ONT	David Reinke	1991	66
171 2/8	53 2/8	12 6/8	12 6/8	9	13	Atikokan	ONT	Mark C. Johnson	1987	67
171 0/8	53 4/8	8 3/8	8 5/8	9	8	Gaspe'	QUE	Claude St'Amour	1989	68
170 7/8	49 3/8	10 2/8	10 6/8	9	9	Graham River	BC	Dr. James Shubert	1979	69
170 4/8	44 4/8	10 7/8	12 4/8	13	12	Quibell	ONT	Fred Bear	1945	70
170 2/8	52 0/8	11 3/8	10 0/8	7	10	Tua Lake	BC	Jeff Koelzer	1991	71
169 1/8	50 7/8	12 5/8	12 2/8	9	11	Stikine River	BC	Dave Brousseau	1979	72
168 1/8	45 7/8	12 5/8	11 1/8	13	10	Fort St. John	BC	Duane Hicks	1981	73
168 1/8	48 1/8	11 1/8	11 6/8	5	6	Stone Lake	ONT	D. E. "Babe" Winkelman	1991	73
168 0/8	46 4/8	10 3/8	11 0/8	11	12	Kechika River	BC	Dave Seidelman	1989	75
168 0/8	52 4/8	12 5/8	12 1/8	10	12	Nipigon	ONT	Charles Steven DeLeeuw	1990	75
167 6/8	50 6/8	10 2/8	11 0/8	6	6	Chevis Creek	BC	Wayne Carlton	1989	77
167 0/8	58 4/8	10 7/8	10 7/8	11	11	Argenteuil	QUE	Richard K. Clark	1983	78
166 6/8	48 4/8	9 4/8	9 4/8	9	10	Nipisi Lake	ALB	Lee Hamilton	1991	79
164 4/8	46 4/8	10 6/8	10 3/8	10	9	Woman River	ONT	Jim C. Dehoey	1991	80
164 3/8	47 7/8	10 2/8	10 3/8	9	12	Fort St. John	BC	Chuck Adams	1976	81
164 1/8	49 3/8	12 5/8	11 2/8	12	10	Tweedsmuir Pk.	BC	Glenn St. Charles	1954	82
163 6/8	47 6/8	10 4/8	10 2/8	11	9	Pink Mtn.	BC	Gerald R. Dishion	1987	83
163 3/8	45 1/8	11 1/8	10 2/8	10	10	McKeough Township	ONT	Larry Pilon	1991	84
163 2/8	45 2/8	9 4/8	10 2/8	10	9	Cassiar Mtns.	BC	Harold Boyack	1978	85
163 1/8	50 3/8	10 6/8	10 4/8	9	9	Edmonton	ALB	Pat Marek	1989	86
163 0/8	50 4/8	10 1/8	11 2/8	6	6	Nakanok Lake	BC	Phil Forte	1984	87
163 0/8	54 6/8	9 0/8	8 0/8	10	8	Algoma	ONT	Larry Pilon	1986	87
163 0/8	54 0/8	9 1/8	9 6/8	8	8	Sudbury	ONT	Vite Chomicki	1986	87
163 0/8	51 6/8	12 1/8	12 6/8	7	10	Turtle Mtn.	MAN	Daryl Fisher	1987	87
162 6/8	47 0/8	10 5/8	11 2/8	6	7	Kenora	ONT	John P. Hartman	1991	91
162 4/8	48 0/8	9 0/8	9 0/8	10	11	Kapuskasing	ONT	Ron Alguire	1963	92
162 2/8	50 0/8	12 7/8	11 5/8	9	8	Nakina Lake	BC	Dee C. Steinheiser	1986	93
161 4/8	50 0/8	6 4/8	9 5/8	7	7	Tatla Lake	BC	Bill Nickerson	1985	94
161 2/8	46 6/8	10 0/8	10 1/8	9	9	Schalze River	BC	Dale Snyder	1983	95
161 2/8	40 2/8	10 0/8	9 2/8	11	10	Nakina Lake	BC	Dean Stebner	1988	95
161 1/8	45 5/8	10 5/8	11 6/8	11	11	Lloyds River	NFL	Harold A. Hill	1966	97
160 4/8	46 0/8	10 4/8	10 4/8	10	9	Muskwa River	BC	W. Jay Boynton III	1970	98
160 1/8	50 7/8	10 0/8	9 5/8	9	8	Toad River	BC	Jerry Leair	1986	99
160 0/8	49 2/8	10 0/8	9 6/8	8	9	Matane	QUE	Claude St' Amour	1990	100
160 0/8	47 0/8	11 4/8	11 7/8	10	9	Machion	ONT	Michael J. Goza	1991	100
159 5/8	49 5/8	15 2/8	12 2/8	6	6	Moose Lake	BC	Michael Delfino, Sr.	1988	102
159 1/8	51 7/8	9 5/8	8 7/8	9	8	Gogama	ONT	Jack Richard	1984	103

SCORE	GREATEST SPREAD	WIDTH R OF PALM L		NUMBER OF R POINTS L		AREA	STATE/ PROVINCE	HUNTER'S NAME	DATE	RANK
158 7/8	50 7/8	12 1/8	11 7/8	13	11	Kirkland Lake	ONT	Luther Gordon	1963	104
158 6/8	50 4/8	12 0/8	12 1/8	8	10	Dryden	ONT	Dean J. Smaney	1990	105
158 0/8	49 0/8	8 0/8	8 5/8	7	8	Williams Lake	BC	Gary Swan	1968	106
158 0/8	47 6/8	10 2/8	9 7/8	11	13	Strathcona	ALB	Darrell Stiles	1985	106
157 6/8	47 4/8	10 4/8	9 5/8	7	8	Thunder Bay	ONT	Bill Stringer	1991	108
157 4/8	46 0/8	11 4/8	10 7/8	9	10	Rocky Mtn. House	ALB	Dennis Meyer	1988	109
157 3/8	47 3/8	11 6/8	9 2/8	11	9	St. Louis County	MN	Gus Maxfield	1987	110
156 4/8	48 2/8	10 6/8	9 0/8	8	11	Tsayta Lake	BC	Bob Duncan	1986	111
156 4/8	50 6/8	8 4/8	9 5/8	5	6	Kluachesi Lake	BC	Jerry R. Stutt	1987	111
156 2/8	42 0/8	9 6/8	9 5/8	9	9	AK Hwy. Milepost 163	BC	John Zahrte	1978	113
156 2/8	49 0/8	10 3/8	10 4/8	7	8	Canton De Kondiaronk	QUE	Wayne J. Martin	1991	113
155 6/8	48 6/8	9 5/8	8 7/8	7	9	Maniwaki	QUE	Jay Pitha	1983	115
155 3/8	34 2/8	8 0/8	10 0/8	8	10	Smithers	BC	Chris Vanderhorst	1974	116
155 3/8	48 7/8	8 7/8	9 2/8	9	11	Kapuskasing	ONT	Tom Nowakowski	1980	116
155 2/8	44 0/8	8 2/8	8 2/8	8	6	Algoma	ONT	Dan Bertalan	1991	118
155 1/8	51 5/8	10 3/8	10 4/8	8	9	Algoma District	ONT	Carol Wert	1963	119
154 7/8	49 7/8	10 3/8	11 4/8	8	11	Saddler Pond	NFL	Paul Locey	1982	120
154 7/8	44 3/8	9 5/8	9 4/8	9	9	Duffield Creek	BC	Wayne Johnson	1990	120
154 4/8	48 6/8	12 1/8	11 4/8	10	9	Turtle Mtn.	MAN	Jack Barrows	1992	122
154 2/8	42 4/8	12 0/8	11 4/8	10	10	Temidicamaine	QUE	Guy-Maurice Algier	1987	123
154 1/8	44 3/8	9 7/8	9 7/8	8	11	Thutade Lake	BC	Donald N. Lehman	1973	124
154 0/8	49 2/8	10 0/8	10 3/8	9	8	Jackfish Creek	ONT	Darryl Miller	1987	125
153 5/8	45 3/8	10 6/8	11 2/8	7	12	Lloyds River	NFL	Harold A. Hill	1964	126
153 4/8	45 2/8	9 0/8	7 2/8	8	8		QUE	Bruce R. Wilson	1983	127
152 7/8	42 7/8	9 1/8	9 7/8	10	10	Zone 1	NFL	Harold A. Hill	1961	128
152 4/8	49 0/8	8 0/8	8 3/8	6	6	Gilbault Creek	BC	David V. Collis	1977	129
152 4/8	54 2/8	7 7/8	8 1/8	9	8	McKeough Township	ONT	Larry Pilon	1992	129
152 2/8	49 6/8	11 2/8	10 6/8	5	6	Nakina Lake	BC	Guy Anttila	1982	131
152 0/8	49 2/8	10 7/8	9 7/8	8	6	Devon Twsp.	ONT	Lorne Davis	1991	132
151 6/8	47 6/8	11 5/8	9 6/8	9	10		NFL	Bill Hirst	1960	133
151 6/8	44 0/8	10 6/8	9 4/8	9	9	Duti Lake	BC	Walter J. Sawicki	1972	133
151 5/8	53 3/8	8 7/8	9 6/8	8	6	Stikine River	BC	James A. Farnsworth	1973	135
151 2/8	42 2/8	8 2/8	9 4/8	9	9	Josephburg	ALB	Darwin Hunter	1990	136
150 1/8	48 3/8	8 2/8	10 4/8	8	10	Thunder Bay	ONT	Carl Whittier	1990	137
150 1/8	47 7/8	7 6/8	7 5/8	9	7	Fort McMurray	ALB	Bruce Hendy	1992	137
150 0/8	45 6/8	9 6/8	9 0/8	8	7	Atikokan	ONT	Albert Clement	1991	139
149 6/8	46 2/8	8 5/8	9 3/8	7	7	Little Johnny Lake	BC	Larry D. Jones	1988	140
148 3/8	42 1/8	9 2/8	9 2/8	10	10	S. Branch	NFL	W. P. Hirst	1964	141
148 0/8	47 6/8	9 0/8	9 1/8	9	11	Spray Lakes	ALB	Yves Blanchette	1991	142
147 2/8	48 2/8	8 2/8	7 4/8	9	8	Kenora	ONT	John P. Hartman	1990	143
146 6/8	39 4/8	8 1/8	9 5/8	8	10	King George IV Lake	NFL	Bill Hirst	1966	144
146 3/8	45 3/8	9 2/8	10 2/8	6	9	Ardrossan	ALB	John Visscher	1987	145
146 3/8	45 7/8	8 4/8	10 2/8	8	9	Caramat	ONT	L. Reed Breight	1988	145
146 0/8	46 0/8	8 4/8	8 0/8	9	8	Tarnezell Lake	BC	Dr. Rex Hancock	1960	147
145 7/8	47 5/8	8 5/8	10 0/8	6	6	Kitchener Lake	BC	Randy E. Doyle	1979	148
145 6/8	47 4/8	8 3/8	8 4/8	9	8	Princess Lake	NFL	John Iannuzzo	1967	149
145 4/8	45 4/8	9 1/8	8 3/8	9	8	Tatlatui Lake	BC	G. Fred Asbell	1975	150
145 3/8	48 5/8	9 0/8	8 6/8	9	9	Duck Mts.	MAN	Richard Hay	1986	151
145 2/8	45 0/8	10 0/8	9 4/8	10	8	Morton	MAN	Dennis Olischefski	1988	152
145 1/8	46 3/8	12 4/8	9 5/8	7	8	Trapnarrows Lake	ONT	John A. Schmidt	1985	153
144 6/8	41 6/8	9 4/8	11 0/8	9	11	Dease Lake	BC	Dave Ramsay	1981	154
144 2/8	50 0/8	8 5/8	10 3/8	8	9	Raith	ONT	Gerald D. Young	1983	155
143 6/8	44 0/8	10 0/8	11 1/8	7	6	Lake Nipigon	ONT	Ohne Raasch	1992	156
143 1/8	44 3/8	9 0/8	8 3/8	9	9	Algoma	ONT	Larry Pilon	1985	157
142 3/8	42 5/8	8 6/8	8 1/8	8	8	Hurdman Lake	QUE	Bill Dunn	1987	158
141 6/8	41 2/8	11 4/8	9 5/8	6	9	Sheba Township	ONT	Jerry Boudreault	1987	159
141 3/8	44 5/8	12 1/8	13 0/8	6	4	Penobscot County	ME	Gregory A. Bonecutter, Sr.	1991	160
140 7/8	43 1/8	9 0/8	9 0/8	6	6	Strathcona	ALB	Pat Marek	1985	161
140 2/8	48 2/8	7 0/8	7 2/8	7	7	Princess Lake	NFL	John Musacchia	1966	162
139 7/8	40 5/8	8 2/8	9 0/8	10	10	Edmonton	ALB	Wes Pietz	1991	163
139 5/8	40 7/8	8 0/8	9 0/8	8	8	Fort St. John	BC	Michael R. Traub	1981	164
138 0/8	34 4/8	11 2/8	10 5/8	8	10	St. George Lake	NFL	Bill Carlos	1968	165
137 7/8	41 5/8	8 1/8	10 6/8	7	8	Princess Lake	NFL	Ken Rapp	1966	166
137 6/8	48 0/8	7 0/8	7 4/8	8	7	Algoma	ONT	Edward K. Broderick	1987	167
137 6/8	42 0/8	12 5/8	10 3/8	6	7	Rolette County	ND	Robert J. Benth	1991	167
137 5/8	44 7/8	7 7/8	7 0/8	8	9	Thutade Lake	BC	Kim S Ades	1984	169
135 7/8	43 3/8	7 4/8	7 2/8	7	6	Sangudo	ALB	Allan C. Doell	1983	170
135 4/8	47 2/8	8 3/8	9 0/8	4	7	Sheerway Lake	QUE	Richard A. Sawyer	1985	171
135 4/8	47 0/8	8 2/8	6 4/8	9	6	Kananaskis	ALB	John Visscher	1992	171
135 2/8	41 2/8	11 0/8	12 3/8	9	4	Boissevain	MAN	Hellar Nakonechny	1987	173

World Record Shiras *"Wyoming"* Moose
Score: 185 6/8
Sheridan County, Wyoming - 1987
Hunter: Richard E. Jones

SHIRAS *"WYOMING"* MOOSE

MINIMUM SCORE 115

Alces alces shirasi

SCORE	GREATEST SPREAD	WIDTH OF PALM R	WIDTH OF PALM L	NUMBER OF POINTS R	NUMBER OF POINTS L	AREA	STATE/ PROVINCE	HUNTER'S NAME	DATE	RANK
185 6/8	54 0/8	9 3/8	8 4/8	8	11	Sheridan County	WY	Richard E. Jones	1987	1
180 3/8	48 1/8	10 4/8	11 0/8	10	10	Fremont County	ID	Kenneth K. Fordyce	1983	2
174 7/8	45 1/8	11 5/8	13 5/8	15	13	Caribou County	ID	James Keller	1992	3
174 3/8	48 1/8	13 0/8	15 2/8	14	12	Bonneville County	ID	David C. Cole	1987	4
174 2/8	55 2/8	11 4/8	9 5/8	11	11	Idaho County	ID	Larry Hoff	1991	5
173 6/8	47 4/8	9 2/8	8 3/8	12	13	Teton County	ID	Van W. Shotzman	1988	6
172 0/8	46 6/8	10 4/8	10 0/8	12	11	Madison County	ID	Trent Wood	1983	7
170 2/8	47 2/8	8 6/8	11 4/8	9	10	Madison County	ID	Ron Stacey	1988	8
169 7/8	51 5/8	12 3/8	8 6/8	13	11	Sheridan County	WY	James L. Nealey	1990	9
166 5/8	50 1/8	10 1/8	11 0/8	11	10	Madison County	ID	Dale Johnson	1987	10
166 4/8	45 4/8	10 6/8	13 2/8	9	11	Sheridan County	WY	Don Groskopf	1986	11
165 5/8	47 7/8	10 1/8	8 7/8	11	11	Gallatin County	MT	Albert D. Williams	1986	12
164 7/8	49 3/8	8 6/8	9 6/8	9	10	Idaho County	ID	Oliver E. Robinett	1980	13
164 1/8	41 3/8	13 4/8	13 2/8	14	12	Gallatin County	MT	Larry Schweitzer	1984	14
163 7/8	53 5/8	9 2/8	8 2/8	10	8	Lincoln County	WY	Brad Hugh Jacobs	1990	15
163 6/8	44 6/8	13 1/8	13 4/8	12	10	Lincoln County	WY	Walter Walbridge	1980	16
163 3/8	44 7/8	9 6/8	11 4/8	12	12	Morgan County	UT	Archie Nesbitt	1987	17
161 6/8	47 0/8	11 3/8	11 0/8	9	10	Sheridan County	WY	John D. "Jack" Frost	1988	18
160 6/8	51 6/8	9 3/8	8 0/8	10	8	Bonneville County	ID	Marty George	1986	19
160 4/8	47 0/8	9 3/8	10 0/8	12	9	Weber County	UT	Hugh H. Hogle	1989	20
159 6/8	43 0/8	15 4/8	12 0/8	6	7	Teton County	WY	Daniel B. White	1978	21
159 6/8	45 6/8	9 0/8	9 3/8	11	11	Sweetwater County	WY	Mike Deaton	1992	22
159 1/8	49 5/8	12 7/8	10 7/8	8	10	Gallatin County	MT	Keith Wheat	1960	23
159 0/8	48 0/8	9 4/8	9 5/8	10	8	Sheridan County	WY	Bradley Carl Wichman	1990	24
158 6/8	50 2/8	10 6/8	11 0/8	11	11	Lincoln County	WY	Mike Smith	1976	25
158 1/8	45 5/8	9 1/8	10 5/8	10	10	Wasatch County	UT	Todd Lemley	1992	26
157 1/8	45 3/8	11 6/8	12 1/8	8	8	Bighorn Mountains	WY	Jeffrey L. Welsh	1980	27
155 5/8	47 5/8	10 1/8	10 0/8	9	9	Lemhi County	ID	Bob Johnson	1991	28
154 6/8	45 4/8	11 0/8	10 5/8	10	8	Sheridan County	WY	Jerry Bailey	1992	29
154 5/8	44 1/8	12 1/8	7 6/8	10	13	Caribou County	ID	James F. Dougherty	1992	30
154 4/8	41 4/8	10 0/8	10 6/8	9	9	Cache County	UT	Kirk Peterson	1992	31
154 0/8	49 4/8	9 1/8	8 7/8	8	9	Flathead County	MT	C. P. Mendenhall	1960	32

SCORE	GREATEST SPREAD	WIDTH OF PALM R	WIDTH OF PALM L	NUMBER OF POINTS R	NUMBER OF POINTS L	AREA	STATE/PROVINCE	HUNTER'S NAME	DATE	RANK
154 0/8	45 2/8	9 2/8	9 2/8	10	11	Caribou County	ID	Brett Dee Hymas	1986	32
153 6/8	42 0/8	11 7/8	11 0/8	13	11	Bonneville County	ID	Lonnie Pickens	1988	34
153 4/8	45 4/8	10 0/8	12 6/8	9	11	Deer Lodge County	MT	Terry L. Button	1986	35
152 7/8	46 5/8	10 6/8	9 5/8	10	9	Lincoln County	WY	Franklin W Sheets	1989	36
152 4/8	39 6/8	13 2/8	12 2/8	9	10	Sweetwater County	WY	Patti Pollard	1990	37
151 6/8	43 4/8	10 3/8	8 2/8	12	6	Morgan County	UT	Len Cardinale	1987	38
151 5/8	40 5/8	8 5/8	8 5/8	10	9	Sanders County	MT	Jim Ryan	1989	39
151 3/8	47 1/8	12 4/8	10 4/8	12	9	Rich County	UT	Mike Poynor	1990	40
150 7/8	42 3/8	10 7/8	9 7/8	10	10	Clark County	ID	Joseph E. Packer	1981	41
150 6/8	39 4/8	9 4/8	11 2/8	10	11	Sublette County	WY	Bryan Radakovich	1990	42
150 4/8	48 6/8	9 3/8	8 7/8	9	10	Rich County	UT	Blake Poppleton	1987	43
150 4/8	49 4/8	8 4/8	8 3/8	7	8	Sheridan County	WY	Darrell Cook	1991	43
149 1/8	46 1/8	9 2/8	10 0/8	8	10	Clark County	ID	Spence Settles	1990	45
147 6/8	46 4/8	10 0/8	10 2/8	8	9	Uinta County	WY	Vernon M. Poynor	1989	46
147 4/8	41 2/8	10 0/8	11 3/8	8	10	Sublette County	WY	Michael Beckwith	1985	47
147 2/8	41 6/8	10 6/8	10 2/8	5	8	Madison County	ID	Randy Lee Davison	1987	48
147 2/8	42 4/8	7 7/8	8 3/8	7	5	Sheridan County	WY	Larry Katz	1992	48
147 1/8	43 5/8	7 5/8	8 3/8	8	9	Summit County	UT	Jerry Cross	1979	50
147 1/8	46 3/8	10 1/8	9 6/8	10	9	Lincoln County	WY	Gary Gale	1988	50
147 0/8	45 0/8	11 3/8	9 6/8	9	8	Teton County	WY	Jerry Bowen	1982	52
147 0/8	46 2/8	6 1/8	11 1/8	8	13	Weber County	UT	Matthew G. Hogle	1990	52
146 4/8	44 4/8	7 3/8	7 5/8	6	6	Park County	MT	Randy Cook	1982	54
146 4/8	42 4/8	11 0/8	9 2/8	10	6	Spokane County	WA	Lance B. Cussons	1991	54
146 3/8	45 1/8	9 1/8	9 1/8	8	7	Sheridan County	WY	Cecil Benner	1990	56
146 1/8	40 5/8	10 4/8	8 4/8	9	9	Sheridan County	WY	Dan Barngrover	1989	57
145 1/8	45 1/8	9 4/8	8 2/8	5	6	Beaverhead County	MT	Greg L. Munther	1982	58
144 4/8	43 0/8	11 0/8	10 7/8	9	8	Sublette County	WY	Boyd Andersen	1988	59
144 3/8	47 5/8	8 5/8	10 4/8	9	8	Weber County	UT	Chuck Adams	1987	60
143 2/8	47 6/8	9 3/8	10 0/8	9	7	Idaho County	ID	Stanley Leake	1979	61
143 0/8	47 6/8	13 3/8	8 4/8	9	8	Clark County	ID	Alton Howell	1987	62
142 6/8	40 6/8	9 4/8	9 4/8	8	7	Gallatin County	MT	Stuart J. Georgitis	1986	63
142 5/8	39 5/8	10 2/8	11 0/8	9	10	Lincoln County	WY	Clayton "Karl" Knudsen	1992	64
141 4/8	40 4/8	12 2/8	11 1/8	9	9	Lincoln County	WY	Von K. Merritt	1992	65
141 0/8	41 1/8	9 5/8	9 4/8	8	7	Lincoln County	WY	V. Kay Bangerter	1978	66
140 4/8	44 2/8	11 5/8	12 3/8	8	5	Morgan County	UT	Bruce Carlisle	1988	67
140 2/8	42 2/8	10 5/8	10 6/8	9	6	Lincoln County	WY	Keith Dana	1977	68
139 3/8	42 1/8	8 4/8	7 6/8	5	7	Idaho County	ID	Ray Torrey	1968	69
139 0/8	46 4/8	7 4/8	7 7/8	8	8	Sheridan County	WY	Tom Hlinka	1986	70
139 0/8	42 2/8	9 0/8	9 6/8	9	11	Weber County	UT	Mike Steckel	1991	70
138 4/8	40 6/8	11 4/8	13 2/8	6	7	Teton County	WY	Jerry A. Bodar	1990	72
138 2/8	42 0/8	9 6/8	7 6/8	9	7	Lincoln County	MT	Thomas A. DeShazer	1965	73
137 7/8	47 1/8	9 2/8	11 3/8	7	9	Sublette County	WY	R. H. Siegert	1969	74
137 2/8	42 4/8	10 4/8	9 0/8	8	11	Lincoln County	WY	Robert K. Robinson	1978	75
136 7/8	42 1/8	6 5/8	9 6/8	8	10	Cache County	UT	Larry Cross	1986	76
136 7/8	43 1/8	6 3/8	5 5/8	7	8	Clark County	ID	Gayland Gilson	1987	76
136 0/8	43 2/8	8 6/8	8 2/8	7	7	Sublette County	WY	August S. Gray	1991	78
135 7/8	44 7/8	8 4/8	7 3/8	7	8	Park County	WY	Mike Yonker	1987	79
135 3/8	46 1/8	9 4/8	8 4/8	8	8	Sublette County	WY	Dave Funderburk	1978	80
135 3/8	42 7/8	8 4/8	9 2/8	6	6	Idaho County	ID	Ronald Smith	1986	80
134 7/8	40 5/8	8 0/8	10 2/8	6	8	Lincoln County	MT	Jerry Brown	1982	82
134 4/8	38 6/8	8 1/8	7 5/8	8	9	Lincoln County	MT	Don Davidson	1989	83
133 5/8	44 3/8	8 0/8	9 1/8	7	7	Sheridan County	WY	Duff De Lon	1989	84
133 3/8	45 5/8	10 3/8	7 5/8	9	7	Lincoln County	WY	Mike Johnston	1988	85
133 0/8	41 6/8	8 6/8	7 4/8	10	9	Teton County	WY	Bob Dawson	1988	86
132 2/8	37 6/8	10 3/8	10 6/8	11	9	Lincoln County	WY	Dennis L. Shirley	1988	87
132 1/8	42 1/8	8 5/8	9 1/8	8	8	Lincoln County	WY	Lee Challinor	1982	88
131 6/8	44 0/8	7 6/8	7 7/8	7	7	Lincoln County	WY	Kevin Jackson	1980	89
131 6/8	40 4/8	8 6/8	10 3/8	9	9	Morgan County	UT	Larry Mathis	1989	89
131 2/8	34 4/8	10 6/8	11 0/8	8	8	Bonneville County	ID	Edward Keller	1986	91
131 2/8	43 6/8	9 5/8	7 7/8	9	8	Uinta County	WY	Larry Lee Francis, Jr.	1991	91
130 7/8	39 5/8	8 6/8	9 1/8	9	8	Lincoln County	WY	Dave Cordes	1982	93
130 6/8	46 2/8	7 2/8	7 5/8	6	6	Lincoln County	WY	Ken Allen	1986	94
130 5/8	38 3/8	8 4/8	8 3/8	7	11	Park County	WY	Greg Deatsman	1985	95
129 7/8	39 1/8	8 2/8	10 2/8	9	11	Lincoln County	WY	Bob Tynsky	1987	96
129 7/8	37 1/8	7 0/8	9 7/8	7	9	Sheridan County	WY	Michael L. Graham	1988	96
129 7/8	38 7/8	8 0/8	8 6/8	7	7	Sublette County	WY	Kevin Cross	1989	96
129 5/8	44 5/8	9 0/8	8 5/8	7	7	Weber County	UT	Jamie Roper	1991	99
129 3/8	42 7/8	7 6/8	9 0/8	7	9	Lincoln County	MT	Jerry Brown	1990	100
129 2/8	37 2/8	8 6/8	8 5/8	8	8	Sublette County	WY	Jerrold M. Judkins	1979	101
129 0/8	39 4/8	7 4/8	8 0/8	9	8	Flathead County	MT	Dyrk Eddie	1991	102

SCORE	GREATEST SPREAD	WIDTH R OF PALM L		NUMBER OF R POINTS L		AREA	STATE/ PROVINCE	HUNTER'S NAME	DATE	RANK
129 0/8	45 0/8	8 4/8	6 6/8	7	8	Morgan County	UT	Robert G. Petersen	1992	102
128 1/8	40 5/8	6 4/8	6 0/8	6	6	Teton County	WY	Keith Frick	1984	104
127 4/8	35 0/8	9 6/8	12 0/8	8	8	Lincoln County	WY	Al Bitker	1982	105
127 4/8	36 6/8	7 0/8	7 4/8	7	7	Idaho County	ID	Brad Johnson	1985	105
126 2/8	43 4/8	8 6/8	9 1/8	7	7	Idaho County	ID	Robert Jackson	1990	107
125 5/8	49 3/8	8 2/8	7 7/8	8	7	Weber County	UT	Clark Stokes	1986	108
125 0/8	34 6/8	9 5/8	8 6/8	9	9	Morgan County	UT	C. Danny Butler	1991	109
124 6/8	40 2/8	10 1/8	10 1/8	5	3	Lincoln County	WY	David H. Boland	1977	110
124 0/8	40 4/8	7 4/8	8 4/8	8	6	Fremont County	WY	John Applegate	1977	111
123 7/8	43 3/8	6 3/8	8 0/8	8	8	Uinta County	WY	Pep Brinkerhoff	1986	112
123 4/8	39 6/8	6 4/8	8 3/8	6	7	Madison County	MT	Erwin Clark	1992	113
123 2/8	37 6/8	8 5/8	7 4/8	9	7	Rich County	UT	Richard Ballard	1987	114
123 2/8	35 0/8	8 2/8	8 7/8	9	8	Lincoln County	WY	Ronald D. Halvorson	1988	114
123 1/8	35 7/8	7 6/8	8 0/8	7	8	Weber County	UT	Randall S. Ulmer	1991	116
122 4/8	36 6/8	8 2/8	7 3/8	7	7	Morgan County	UT	Robert K. Paulson	1987	117
122 2/8	41 4/8	7 5/8	8 3/8	7	8	Sublette County	WY	Larry Honeycutt	1990	118
121 4/8	44 2/8	9 4/8	7 5/8	8	5	Lincoln County	WY	Craig P. Mitton	1987	119
121 2/8	39 6/8	7 3/8	7 2/8	9	6	Sublette County	WY	Vern A. Butler	1973	120
120 7/8	42 5/8	6 7/8	7 2/8	5	5	Sublette County	WY	Wade L. Carstens	1982	121
120 6/8	34 6/8	9 2/8	9 4/8	9	8	Caribou County	ID	Chad Doell	1992	122
120 0/8	49 4/8	3 7/8	5 6/8	5	7	Sublette County	WY	Dick Mauch	1959	123
119 7/8	37 1/8	8 2/8	7 7/8	9	7	Teton County	WY	Todd Zeuske	1989	124
119 4/8	40 4/8	7 3/8	7 4/8	4	4	Idaho County	ID	David Wilken	1986	125
119 2/8	39 0/8	7 1/8	7 4/8	8	7	Sheridan County	WY	James T. Dawson	1987	126
119 0/8	35 4/8	7 0/8	8 6/8	8	9	La Barge	WY	Glen Talbott	1980	127
119 0/8	37 0/8	7 2/8	7 2/8	7	7	Summit County	UT	Charles R. Justmann	1989	127
118 6/8	37 0/8	8 7/8	7 3/8	8	8	Park County	WY	Raymond E. Questiaux	1991	129
118 6/8	41 4/8	7 3/8	7 5/8	7	7	Sublette County	WY	Casey Blum	1991	129
118 4/8	40 2/8	6 2/8	6 4/8	7	7	Teton County	WY	Richard Lopez	1988	131
117 5/8	38 5/8	7 5/8	7 1/8	7	6	Uinta County	WY	David Kaden	1982	132
117 5/8	44 3/8	12 0/8	9 2/8	11	3	Cache County	UT	Mark Wright	1985	132
117 5/8	34 1/8	9 4/8	7 6/8	7	7	Caribou County	ID	Randy K. Vranes	1991	132
117 3/8	40 7/8	6 6/8	6 4/8	6	6	Summit County	UT	Mike Christiansen	1988	135
116 7/8	45 1/8	6 0/8	6 0/8	5	5	Jagg Creek	WY	Robert W. Steller	1975	136
116 6/8	42 0/8	8 1/8	7 2/8	6	6	Lincoln County	WY	Kirt Prestwich	1986	137
116 2/8	41 4/8	8 6/8	9 6/8	5	4	Lincoln County	MT	Lee Lampton	1982	138
116 2/8	40 6/8	7 7/8	6 7/8	8	7	Weber County	UT	Todd Hinkins	1990	138
116 0/8	33 6/8	8 3/8	7 6/8	8	7	Lincoln County	WY	Glenn Hisey	1982	140
116 0/8	36 4/8	7 0/8	7 0/8	8	8	Lincoln County	WY	Jack M. Conner	1988	140
115 5/8	36 1/8	8 6/8	7 5/8	8	8	Lincoln County	WY	Cathy Lee Jordan	1983	142
115 5/8	42 7/8	5 5/8	5 6/8	7	6	Duchesne County	UT	Sam Nesi	1987	142
115 1/8	41 1/8	7 7/8	6 3/8	9	4	Sheridan County	WY	Bradley T. Miller	1991	144
115 0/8	36 2/8	7 3/8	7 2/8	7	7	Idaho County	ID	Tom Fliss	1987	145

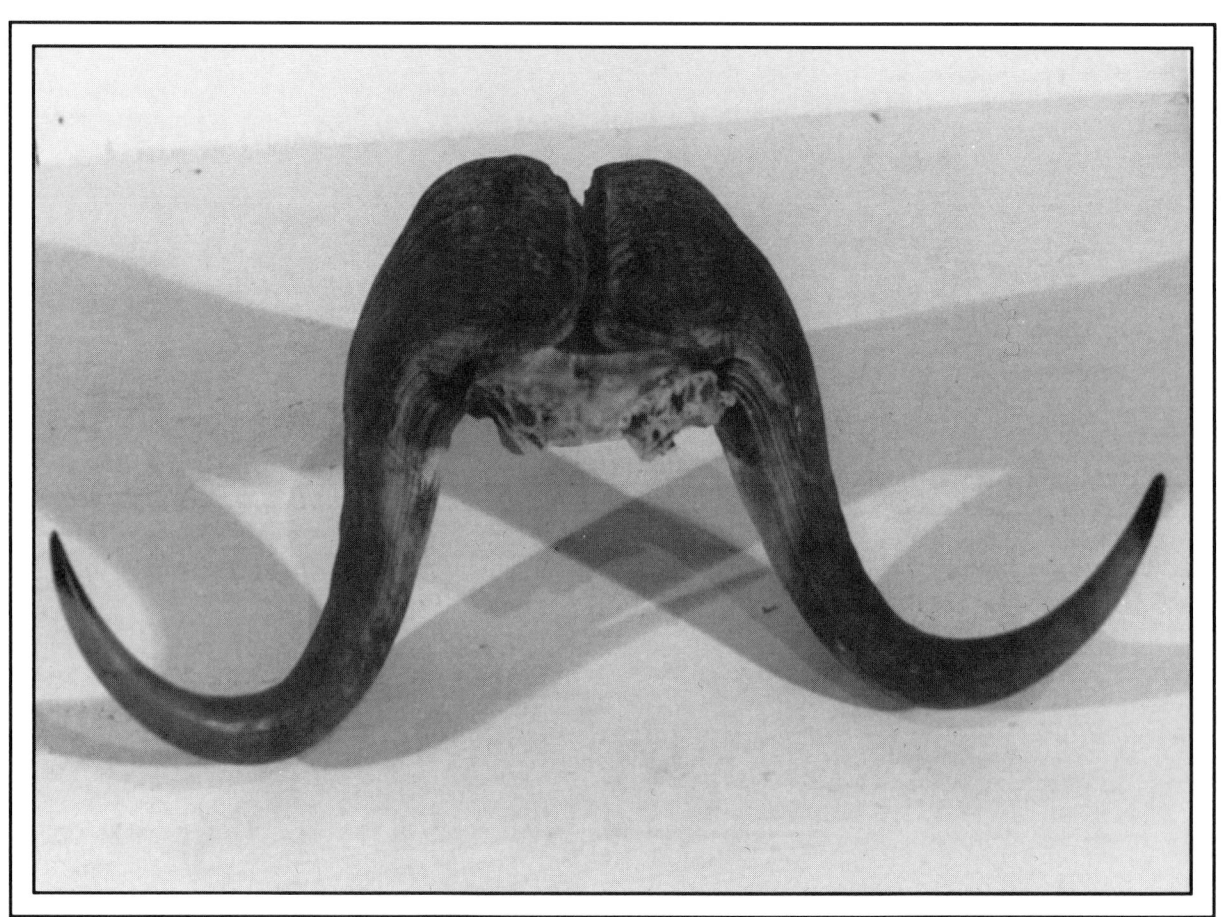

World Record Muskox
Score: 114 2/8
Elice River, Northwest Territories - 1988
Hunter: Steve Munier

Ovibos moschatus
and certain related subspecies

Score	Length of Horn R	L	Circumference of Base R	L	Greatest Spread	Area	State/Province	Hunter's Name	Date	Rank
114 2/8	29 1/8	28 0/8	9 0/8	9 3/8	28 7/8	Ellice River	NWT	Steve Munier	1988	1
114 0/8	27 4/8	27 6/8	9 0/8	8 7/8	30 6/8	Perry Island	NWT	J. T. Smith	1988	2
113 2/8	25 2/8	25 6/8	9 5/8	9 5/8	28 1/8	Kent Penninsula	NWT	Archie Nesbitt	1989	3
111 4/8	26 3/8	26 0/8	9 5/8	9 5/8	25 5/8	Banks Island	NWT	David V.Collis	1985	4
110 6/8	27 1/8	27 2/8	8 5/8	8 4/8	26 3/8	Nunivak Island	AK	Todd A. Sneesby	1988	5
110 6/8	26 6/8	26 0/8	8 7/8	8 7/8	28 5/8	McLoughlin River	NWT	Archie J. Nesbitt	1990	5
110 4/8	27 0/8	27 3/8	9 2/8	9 3/8	26 1/8	Banks Island	NWT	Robert L. Jacobsen	1987	7
110 0/8	28 0/8	27 2/8	8 3/8	8 5/8	26 7/8	Nunivak Island	AK	Richard Moran	1988	8
109 4/8	26 2/8	26 5/8	9 5/8	9 5/8	26 7/8	Banks Island	NWT	Roger Anderson	1986	9
109 4/8	26 1/8	26 0/8	9 4/8	9 5/8	25 5/8	Banks Island	NWT	Larry Hoff	1986	9
109 4/8	25 6/8	25 6/8	9 7/8	9 6/8	25 5/8	Banks Island	NWT	Jim Ryan	1989	9
109 2/8	26 3/8	27 2/8	9 0/8	8 5/8	26 7/8	Nunivak Island	AK	Craig Scarbrough	1988	12
109 2/8	25 4/8	25 4/8	9 2/8	9 2/8	25 6/8	Victoria Island	NWT	Larry Barton	1991	12
108 4/8	26 3/8	28 2/8	9 5/8	9 6/8	27 0/8	Paulatuk	NWT	Ron Kolpin	1981	14
108 2/8	26 4/8	26 6/8	8 7/8	8 2/8	24 5/8	Bluenose Lake	NWT	George P. Mann	1990	15
108 0/8	27 5/8	28 5/8	8 4/8	8 4/8	25 4/8	Nelson Island	AK	Dexter Lemon	1986	16
108 0/8	26 0/8	25 3/8	9 3/8	9 4/8	26 1/8	Perry Island	NWT	Theodore Dzienis	1986	16
107 6/8	25 1/8	27 3/8	9 6/8	9 5/8	27 3/8	Banks Island	NWT	Rusty Neely	1987	18
107 4/8	26 3/8	26 0/8	9 5/8	10 0/8	25 7/8	Banks Island	NWT	John McAteer	1986	19
107 4/8	25 0/8	25 1/8	8 1/8	8 1/8	26 3/8	Nunivak Island	AK	Timothy A. Gleason	1992	19
107 2/8	24 6/8	25 3/8	10 0/8	10 1/8	26 7/8	Victoria Island	NWT	Ray Keenan	1987	21
107 2/8	26 2/8	26 4/8	9 0/8	9 1/8	24 6/8	Banks Island	NWT	Karen K. Jacobsen	1987	21
107 0/8	28 2/8	26 2/8	9 3/8	9 4/8	26 7/8	Banks Island	NWT	Dennis Kamstra	1987	23
106 6/8	25 5/8	26 2/8	8 5/8	9 0/8	27 6/8	Banks Island	NWT	Billy Ellis	1982	24
106 6/8	25 5/8	25 6/8	8 6/8	8 2/8	27 6/8	Nelson Island	AK	Dexter Lemon	1985	24
106 6/8	28 6/8	27 3/8	8 5/8	8 4/8	28 1/8	Nunivak Island	AK	Ernest J. Emmi	1991	24
106 4/8	24 3/8	24 5/8	8 3/8	8 4/8	27 3/8	Nunivak Island	AK	Joseph O. Fogleman	1976	27
106 4/8	26 7/8	27 3/8	8 0/8	8 0/8	27 4/8	Nunivak Island	AK	John D. 'Jack' Frost	1986	27
106 4/8	26 5/8	27 2/8	8 5/8	8 3/8	26 2/8	Nelson Island	AK	Dexter Lemon	1990	27
106 2/8	25 4/8	25 5/8	8 2/8	8 2/8	27 5/8	Kaktovik	AK	Herman Griese	1984	30
106 2/8	26 4/8	25 7/8	7 6/8	8 1/8	27 6/8	Perry River	NWT	Jack Downing	1988	30
105 6/8	25 1/8	25 1/8	9 2/8	9 2/8	26 0/8	Banks Island	NWT	Kirk Westervelt	1986	32
105 6/8	24 2/8	25 1/8	9 1/8	9 1/8	27 2/8	Copper Mines	NWT	Leo F. Neuls	1991	32
105 4/8	26 0/8	25 2/8	8 7/8	8 5/8	28 5/8	Perry Island	NWT	Ronald E. Sanders	1988	34
105 2/8	25 6/8	26 2/8	8 6/8	9 2/8	27 4/8	Victoria Island	NWT	Len Cardinale	1987	35
105 0/8	25 1/8	26 4/8	8 7/8	8 6/8	26 2/8	Kaktovik	AK	Bill Petrovish	1984	36
105 0/8	27 2/8	26 4/8	8 2/8	9 0/8	28 0/8	Nunivak Island	AK	Harvey A. Kolberg	1991	36
104 6/8	24 5/8	25 0/8	9 4/8	9 2/8	25 0/8	Banks Island	NWT	Susan D. Sherer	1986	38
104 4/8	27 2/8	25 4/8	9 2/8	9 2/8	27 2/8	Banks Island	NWT	Dr. Howard Schneider	1985	39
104 4/8	25 4/8	25 2/8	9 0/8	9 1/8	25 4/8	Banks Island	NWT	Ronald L. Sherer	1986	39
104 4/8	24 6/8	25 0/8	9 2/8	9 2/8	26 0/8	Banks Island	NWT	Richard L. Westervelt	1986	39
104 4/8	25 1/8	26 1/8	9 5/8	9 2/8	25 7/8	West Victoria Island	NWT	John Janelli	1987	39
104 0/8	24 3/8	24 6/8	9 6/8	9 5/8	24 4/8	Banks Island	NWT	Larry Hoff	1986	43
104 0/8	24 6/8	25 4/8	8 4/8	8 3/8	26 6/8	Perry River	NWT	Bruce R. Schoeneweis	1990	43
103 2/8	27 0/8	27 0/8	8 1/8	8 2/8	25 5/8	Polatuck	NWT	Erv Plotz	1980	45
103 0/8	22 6/8	23 5/8	8 5/8	8 4/8	26 7/8	Nunivak Island	AK	P.J. Londo	1977	46
102 6/8	25 0/8	27 0/8	8 7/8	8 3/8	29 0/8	Nunivak Island	AK	Jim Voeller	1978	47
102 6/8	24 4/8	24 6/8	9 3/8	9 2/8	26 0/8	Banks Island	NWT	Frank C. Eifert	1987	47
101 6/8	24 3/8	24 5/8	7 7/8	7 7/8	27 3/8	Nunivak Island	AK	Tim Moerlein	1990	49
101 4/8	24 6/8	25 2/8	8 6/8	8 6/8	27 6/8	Nunivak Island	AK	David A. Widby	1983	50
101 4/8	26 4/8	25 1/8	8 3/8	8 6/8	26 3/8	Nunivak Island	AK	Lon E. Lauber	1991	50
101 0/8	25 1/8	25 0/8	8 0/8	8 2/8	26 2/8	Nunivak Island	AK	Edward L. Russell	1984	52
101 0/8	24 7/8	26 4/8	8 0/8	8 2/8	26 0/8	Nunivak Island	AK	Michael J. Lettis	1989	52
100 6/8	24 1/8	25 1/8	7 7/8	7 7/8	24 1/8	Nunivak Island	AK	Dr. Von A. Mitton	1978	54
100 6/8	24 1/8	25 0/8	8 6/8	8 6/8	26 3/8	Victoria Island	NWT	David Richey	1988	54
100 6/8	26 4/8	26 2/8	8 3/8	8 3/8	25 7/8	Nunivak Island	AK	Maxallen D. Jackson	1991	54
100 4/8	25 2/8	26 2/8	7 7/8	7 6/8	28 1/8	Nunivak Island	AK	Bruce J. Werba	1977	57
100 4/8	24 5/8	26 4/8	10 2/8	10 1/8	27 2/8	Banks Island	NWT	Dr. Howard Schneider	1985	57
100 2/8	24 5/8	25 5/8	8 3/8	7 7/8	24 0/8	Nunivak Island	AK	Curt Lynn	1984	59
100 2/8	25 3/8	24 4/8	8 2/8	8 3/8	27 3/8	Nunivak Island	AK	Rex Wright	1992	59
100 0/8	25 0/8	26 4/8	8 4/8	8 3/8	25 1/8	Nunivak Island	AK	Max C. Lyon, Jr.	1991	61
98 4/8	23 4/8	24 2/8	9 0/8	8 5/8	25 7/8	Sachs Harbor	NWT	Dwight Pfeiffer	1989	62
98 2/8	23 5/8	24 1/8	7 3/8	7 5/8	28 3/8	Nunivak Island	AK	Tony Russ	1990	63
97 0/8	24 4/8	24 1/8	8 3/8	8 4/8	28 0/8	Nunivak Island	AK	Michael J. Schneider	1983	64
96 6/8	22 5/8	24 0/8	8 2/8	8 0/8	26 2/8	Nunivak Island	AK	Bob Hammond	1988	65
96 6/8	24 2/8	25 3/8	8 4/8	8 3/8	28 3/8	Nunivak Island	AK	Matt Jones	1992	65
95 4/8	21 0/8	20 6/8	8 0/8	8 2/8	26 2/8	Nunivak Island	AK	Dick Gulman	1978	67
94 4/8	24 5/8	23 6/8	6 6/8	6 6/8	26 7/8	Nunivak Island	AK	C. Vernon Humble	1976	68
94 4/8	21 0/8	22 7/8	9 2/8	9 2/8	25 1/8	South Gjoa Haven	NWT	Gary Bogner	1991	68

World Record Pronghorn
Score: 88 6/8
Raleigh, North Dakota - 1958
Hunter: Archie Malm

SCORE	LENGTH OF HORN R	L	CIRCUMFERENCE OF BASE R	L	GREATEST SPREAD	AREA	STATE/ PROVINCE	HUNTER'S NAME	DATE	RANK
88 6/8	15 6/8	15 7/8	7 2/8	7 0/8	14 2/8	Grant County	ND	Archie Malm	1958	1
86 6/8	16 0/8	15 7/8	6 6/8	6 6/8	8 6/8	Maple Creek	SAS	Jerry Bien	1990	2
85 2/8	16 1/8	16 4/8	6 5/8	6 5/8	13 1/8	Carbon County	WY	Lonny Curtis	1990	3
85 0/8	17 2/8	17 1/8	6 4/8	6 4/8	10 3/8	Moffat County	CO	Judd Cooney	1983	4
84 6/8	16 2/8	16 6/8	6 6/8	6 6/8	8 0/8	Otero County	CO	Larry C. Hansen	1992	5
84 4/8	17 0/8	16 7/8	6 4/8	6 4/8	11 4/8	White Pine County	NV	Harold R. "Bud" Kirk	1988	6
84 2/8	16 0/8	15 6/8	6 3/8	6 3/8	10 0/8	Garfield County	MT	Ron J. Hoaglund	1989	7
84 2/8	15 7/8	15 7/8	7 1/8	7 0/8	9 3/8	Sweetwater County	WY	Kurt D. Olson	1990	7
84 2/8	16 3/8	16 2/8	6 4/8	6 2/8	13 4/8	Goshen County	WY	Gary Korell	1992	7
84 0/8	16 2/8	15 5/8	6 7/8	6 7/8	11 6/8	Perkins County	SD	Spike Jorgensen	1964	10
84 0/8	16 6/8	16 3/8	6 4/8	6 4/8	11 0/8	Catron County	NM	Perry Harper	1991	10
84 0/8	17 1/8	17 1/8	6 5/8	6 5/8	10 6/8	Campbell County	WY	Loy Dean Peters	1992	10
83 6/8	15 4/8	15 2/8	7 3/8	7 3/8	15 2/8	Washoe County	NV	Fred Church	1978	13
83 6/8	15 2/8	15 6/8	6 3/8	6 4/8	11 6/8	Nye County	NV	Rich Sauer	1985	13
83 6/8	16 3/8	16 3/8	7 0/8	7 1/8	10 2/8	Harney County	OR	John S. Hansen	1990	13
83 6/8	15 7/8	15 7/8	6 3/8	6 2/8	11 5/8	Yavapai County	AZ	Roland J. Chooljian	1991	13
83 6/8	17 0/8	17 0/8	6 3/8	6 2/8	8 4/8	Sioux County	NE	Daniel F. Hejl	1991	13
83 4/8	16 1/8	16 1/8	6 2/8	6 1/8	10 7/8	Yavapai County	AZ	Richard S. Jones	1987	18
83 4/8	15 2/8	15 2/8	6 7/8	6 7/8	9 3/8	Campbell County	WY	James N. Monat	1990	18
83 4/8	15 4/8	15 4/8	6 6/8	6 7/8	9 2/8	Moffat County	CO	Larry Adkins	1992	18
83 2/8	15 3/8	15 7/8	6 6/8	6 5/8	8 5/8	Natrona County	WY	Gary L. Miller	1990	21
83 2/8	16 4/8	16 3/8	6 3/8	6 2/8	9 1/8	Catron County	NM	James F. Welles	1991	21
83 0/8	17 0/8	17 0/8	6 0/8	6 0/8	12 3/8	Eddy County	NM	Jim Stell	1984	23
83 0/8	16 6/8	16 6/8	6 1/8	6 0/8	13 6/8	Coconino County	AZ	William P Pate	1985	23
83 0/8	16 4/8	16 4/8	6 5/8	6 4/8	15 7/8	Moffat County	CO	Mike Wallers	1989	23
83 0/8	15 6/8	15 5/8	7 2/8	6 7/8	14 5/8	Washoe County	NV	Daniel R. Brown	1990	23
82 6/8	16 4/8	16 3/8	6 2/8	6 3/8	8 5/8	Sublette County	WY	Michael D. Towne	1987	27
82 6/8	16 1/8	15 5/8	6 6/8	6 4/8	12 6/8	Coconino County	AZ	Kenneth C. Fulk	1988	27
82 6/8	16 2/8	16 1/8	6 5/8	6 4/8	9 0/8	Juab County	UT	David B. Nielsen	1992	27
82 4/8	15 1/8	16 0/8	6 5/8	6 3/8	6 3/8	McLean County	ND	Edward J. Weigel	1966	30
82 4/8	17 1/8	15 4/8	6 4/8	6 4/8	8 5/8	Yavapai County	AZ	Chris Skoczylas	1988	30
82 4/8	15 6/8	15 6/8	6 2/8	6 4/8	9 2/8	Graham County	AZ	Daniel C Hicks	1989	30
82 3/8	16 7/8	16 5/8	6 3/8	6 2/8	17 0/8	Luna County	NM	Ed Lowry	1990	33
82 2/8	15 7/8	15 6/8	7 0/8	6 6/8	12 1/8	Elko County	NV	Monte D. Fuller	1987	34
82 2/8	16 5/8	16 1/8	6 3/8	6 4/8	14 1/8	Dunn County	ND	Peter Braun	1990	34
82 0/8	17 4/8	18 2/8	6 6/8	6 2/8	15 6/8	Guadalupe County	NM	C. E. Foster, Jr.	1961	36
82 0/8	16 3/8	16 2/8	6 3/8	6 4/8	9 6/8	Coconino County	AZ	Fred W. Fernow, Jr.	1981	36
82 0/8	16 4/8	17 0/8	7 0/8	7 0/8	14 4/8	Billings County	ND	Kenneth E. Ruzicka	1987	36
82 0/8	16 0/8	16 0/8	6 3/8	6 2/8	15 0/8	Coconino County	AZ	Mike Kentera	1988	36
81 6/8	15 0/8	15 3/8	6 4/8	6 4/8	11 0/8	Coconino County	AZ	Noel Harris	1988	40
81 4/8	15 4/8	15 1/8	7 0/8	6 7/8	13 1/8	Washoe County	NV	Owen K. Mercer, Jr.	1981	41
81 4/8	16 3/8	16 6/8	6 2/8	5 7/8	13 6/8	Yellowstone County	MT	Robert M. Labert	1984	41
81 4/8	16 5/8	16 5/8	6 2/8	6 2/8	11 3/8	Yavapai County	AZ	James C. Roth	1990	41
81 4/8	15 2/8	15 3/8	6 5/8	6 4/8	10 6/8	Lake County	OR	Jeff Eder	1990	41
81 4/8	16 3/8	16 3/8	6 1/8	6 1/8	8 7/8	Lea County	NM	Mike Cowger	1992	41
81 2/8	15 4/8	15 3/8	7 1/8	7 1/8	6 6/8	Sweetwater County	WY	Clifford Rockhold	1985	46
81 2/8	15 2/8	15 1/8	6 2/8	6 3/8	10 4/8	Sublette County	WY	Ronald J. Clark	1986	46
81 2/8	15 5/8	15 4/8	6 7/8	6 6/8	10 0/8	Jefferson County	ID	Scott Griggs	1987	46
81 2/8	15 7/8	15 2/8	6 2/8	6 1/8	11 7/8	Yavapai County	AZ	Marty Cowie	1988	46
81 2/8	14 6/8	15 0/8	6 5/8	6 5/8	7 4/8	Etzikom	ALB	Rick Livingston	1988	46
81 2/8	16 2/8	16 4/8	6 5/8	6 5/8	13 1/8	Coconino County	AZ	Bob Gourley	1990	46
81 2/8	16 0/8	15 5/8	6 7/8	6 5/8	10 6/8	Catron County	NM	Jim Machac	1992	46
81 0/8	15 7/8	15 6/8	6 7/8	6 6/8	10 7/8	McLean County	ND	James Lahman	1971	53
81 0/8	15 3/8	15 4/8	7 0/8	6 6/8	12 0/8	Ormsby	WY	Richard L. Huber	1978	53
81 0/8	15 4/8	15 4/8	6 6/8	6 6/8	11 6/8	Elko County	NV	Darcy W. Tate	1979	53
81 0/8	14 6/8	16 4/8	6 3/8	6 4/8	10 0/8	Coconino County	AZ	Jim Scott	1984	53
81 0/8	15 5/8	16 6/8	6 3/8	6 3/8	9 2/8	Yavapai County	AZ	Dan Robbins	1986	53
81 0/8	15 2/8	15 1/8	6 4/8	6 4/8	8 3/8	Lassen County	CA	Brian McCoslin	1990	53
81 0/8	16 4/8	16 3/8	6 3/8	6 4/8	8 5/8	Coconino County	AZ	John Lund	1990	53
81 0/8	15 7/8	15 4/8	6 3/8	6 3/8	9 6/8	Orion	ALB	Dan Kilborn	1990	53
81 0/8	16 7/8	17 1/8	6 2/8	6 1/8	6 4/8	Yavapai County	AZ	Walter J. Kellner, Jr.	1991	53
81 0/8	14 6/8	14 6/8	6 4/8	6 6/8	10 5/8	Humboldt County	NV	Scott Tilzey	1992	53
80 6/8	15 5/8	15 5/8	6 3/8	6 2/8	11 6/8	Lincoln County	NM	Robert W. Davis	1959	63
80 6/8	16 4/8	16 4/8	6 6/8	6 6/8	17 2/8	Jackson County	CO	Steve Jackson	1985	63
80 6/8	16 0/8	15 4/8	5 7/8	5 7/8	10 1/8	Converse County	WY	Greg Winters	1989	63
80 6/8	16 0/8	16 0/8	6 1/8	6 2/8	8 4/8	Harney County	OR	Russell Jacobs	1990	63
80 6/8	14 2/8	14 3/8	6 7/8	6 7/8	8 2/8	Albany County	WY	John Buxton	1990	63
80 6/8	15 6/8	15 6/8	7 0/8	7 1/8	10 3/8	Washoe County	NV	Dave Holt	1992	63
80 6/8	15 0/8	15 1/8	6 6/8	6 6/8	12 2/8	Rosebud County	MT	Mike Cummings	1992	63
80 4/8	16 5/8	17 0/8	5 5/8	5 6/8	10 3/8	Humboldt County	NV	Shane E. Evans	1984	70

Score	Length of Horn R	L	Circumference of Base R	L	Greatest Spread	Area	State/ Province	Hunter's Name	Date	Rank
80 4/8	15 0/8	15 0/8	6 4/8	6 4/8	9 7/8	Sweetwater County	WY	Christopher J. Cordes	1986	70
80 4/8	16 3/8	16 0/8	6 3/8	6 2/8	9 0/8	Sweetwater County	WY	Gene McFadden	1987	70
80 4/8	15 3/8	15 3/8	6 6/8	6 6/8	9 2/8	Owyhee County	ID	Shane Gehring	1991	70
80 2/8	14 5/8	14 5/8	7 1/8	7 3/8	8 6/8	Natrona County	WY	Dr. J. A. Martin	1964	74
80 2/8	14 1/8	13 7/8	7 3/8	7 3/8	10 6/8	Butte County	ID	Danny Owens	1974	74
80 2/8	15 4/8	15 3/8	6 6/8	6 6/8	8 7/8	Modoc County	CA	Ed Dowling	1982	74
80 2/8	14 5/8	14 7/8	6 6/8	6 7/8	10 4/8	Yuma County	CO	Mark Sievers	1982	74
80 2/8	16 2/8	16 3/8	6 1/8	5 7/8	17 3/8	Coconino County	AZ	Les Shelton	1985	74
80 2/8	15 7/8	15 6/8	6 4/8	6 4/8	8 4/8	Yavapai County	AZ	Jim Machac	1988	74
80 2/8	16 3/8	14 4/8	6 4/8	6 4/8	11 3/8	Lassen County	CA	Greg Morris	1990	74
80 2/8	15 4/8	15 5/8	6 6/8	6 6/8	11 0/8	Mora County	NM	George P. Mann	1991	74
80 0/8	16 6/8	16 5/8	6 1/8	6 1/8	13 6/8	Albany County	WY	Dave A. Current	1969	82
80 0/8	16 0/8	15 7/8	6 2/8	6 2/8	10 7/8	Washoe County	NV	Kevin S. Wheeler	1983	82
80 0/8	16 4/8	16 2/8	6 4/8	6 4/8	13 0/8	McKinley County	NM	Steve Yearout	1985	82
80 0/8	15 6/8	15 6/8	6 0/8	6 2/8	8 5/8	Coconino County	AZ	Jim Felt	1987	82
80 0/8	15 7/8	16 4/8	6 5/8	6 4/8	14 0/8	Coconino County	AZ	David Bushell	1988	82
80 0/8	16 1/8	15 5/8	6 4/8	6 3/8	9 7/8	Rosebud County	MT	Everett M. Morris	1988	82
80 0/8	14 6/8	15 0/8	7 0/8	7 0/8	8 5/8	Humboldt County	NV	James Puryear	1990	82
80 0/8	14 7/8	14 7/8	6 5/8	6 4/8	13 0/8	Cibola County	NM	Shaun Finch	1990	82
80 0/8	16 3/8	16 3/8	6 1/8	6 1/8	11 0/8	McKenzie County	ND	Travis Wollan	1990	82
79 6/8	15 4/8	14 6/8	7 1/8	7 3/8	9 3/8	Mellette County	SD	John Anderson	1970	91
79 6/8	15 4/8	15 4/8	6 0/8	6 0/8	10 5/8	Washoe County	NV	Mike J. Ellena	1983	91
79 6/8	13 7/8	13 6/8	6 5/8	6 4/8	11 5/8	Modoc County	CA	Dave Masamori	1990	91
79 6/8	15 2/8	15 3/8	6 4/8	6 4/8	12 2/8	Converse County	WY	Roger J. Reynolds	1990	91
79 6/8	16 0/8	15 7/8	6 1/8	6 1/8	14 4/8	McKenzie County	ND	Kevin Caroline	1990	91
79 6/8	15 4/8	15 3/8	6 4/8	6 4/8	11 0/8	Sweetwater County	WY	Keith Dana	1991	91
79 6/8	16 0/8	15 6/8	6 4/8	6 4/8	11 4/8	Dunn County	ND	Vance Vaagen	1991	91
79 6/8	15 3/8	15 2/8	6 5/8	6 5/8	13 5/8	Yavapai County	AZ	Patrick Kirby	1992	91
79 4/8	14 3/8	14 4/8	5 7/8	5 6/8	11 6/8	Mountrail County	ND	Bill Kurry	1976	99
79 4/8	16 4/8	16 0/8	6 3/8	6 4/8	9 0/8	Klamath County	OR	Harold Benson	1977	99
79 4/8	14 4/8	14 4/8	6 3/8	6 3/8	7 5/8	Converse County	WY	Russ Guerndt, Jr.	1985	99
79 4/8	14 1/8	14 0/8	7 2/8	7 2/8	9 2/8	Carbon County	WY	Michael L. Cone	1986	99
79 4/8	15 1/8	15 0/8	6 1/8	6 2/8	12 5/8	Dundy County	NE	Bradley Wiese	1987	99
79 4/8	16 0/8	16 0/8	6 2/8	6 2/8	13 3/8	Dunn County	ND	Terry Buechler	1990	99
79 4/8	15 5/8	15 5/8	6 1/8	6 2/8	10 6/8	Juab County	UT	Julie Robertson	1992	99
79 2/8	14 3/8	14 5/8	6 4/8	6 2/8	9 2/8	Musselshell County	MT	Jon Kowalski	1982	106
79 2/8	15 5/8	15 3/8	6 6/8	6 4/8	9 4/8	Moffat County	CO	Alan Martellaro	1986	106
79 2/8	15 5/8	15 4/8	6 5/8	6 4/8	10 6/8	Washoe County	NV	Kenneth J. Wilkinson	1987	106
79 2/8	15 2/8	15 0/8	6 2/8	6 1/8	8 4/8	Lincoln County	WY	LeRoy Moulding	1987	106
79 2/8	16 1/8	15 5/8	6 2/8	6 1/8	13 6/8	Eddy County	NM	Carl D. Bradford	1987	106
79 2/8	15 0/8	15 4/8	6 5/8	6 5/8	10 4/8	Sublette County	WY	Steven Hill	1990	106
79 2/8	15 3/8	15 2/8	6 6/8	6 6/8	10 7/8	Colfax County	NM	Delbert T. Vigil	1991	106
79 2/8	16 1/8	16 3/8	6 3/8	6 3/8	12 5/8	Washoe County	NV	A. H. "Wilk" Wilkerson	1992	106
79 2/8	15 3/8	15 4/8	6 7/8	7 0/8	11 2/8	Weld County	CO	Kevin Waller	1992	106
79 2/8	16 3/8	15 7/8	6 2/8	6 4/8	11 1/8	Lincoln County	WY	C. R. (Bob) Bolton	1992	106
79 2/8	14 1/8	13 7/8	6 6/8	6 7/8	8 6/8	Moffat County	CO	Steven Vittetow	1992	106
79 2/8	13 5/8	13 6/8	7 0/8	6 5/8	11 0/8	Twin Falls County	ID	Brent L. Compton	1992	106
79 0/8	15 0/8	15 3/8	6 3/8	6 3/8	11 5/8	Washoe County	NV	Tom Thompson	1979	118
79 0/8	15 7/8	15 6/8	6 2/8	6 2/8	12 6/8	Carbon County	WY	Michael Ambur	1982	118
79 0/8	14 7/8	15 0/8	6 3/8	6 2/8	8 5/8	Carbon County	WY	Kim Cooper	1983	118
79 0/8	14 6/8	14 5/8	7 2/8	7 3/8	7 0/8	Sweetwater County	WY	Steve Rueck	1985	118
79 0/8	14 1/8	14 4/8	6 3/8	6 2/8	11 5/8	Millard County	UT	Keith Dana	1988	118
79 0/8	14 6/8	15 0/8	6 5/8	6 4/8	9 4/8	Sweetwater County	WY	Gerry Wolfe	1988	118
79 0/8	15 7/8	15 7/8	6 0/8	6 1/8	9 4/8	Harney County	OR	Jim Nielsen	1990	118
79 0/8	15 0/8	15 0/8	7 4/8	7 3/8	11 2/8	Campbell County	WY	Mike "Pie" Piaskowski	1990	118
79 0/8	16 4/8	17 1/8	6 1/8	6 0/8	8 7/8	Yavapai County	AZ	T. J. Baehre	1991	118
79 0/8	15 0/8	13 6/8	6 6/8	7 1/8	12 2/8	Bennett County	SD	Wayne Johnson	1991	118
78 6/8	16 5/8	16 2/8	6 4/8	6 2/8	7 4/8	Sweetwater County	WY	Mike Holmes	1982	128
78 6/8	14 2/8	14 4/8	7 1/8	7 1/8	12 2/8	Johnson County	WY	Steve Winkey	1982	128
78 6/8	16 1/8	16 3/8	6 3/8	6 3/8	15 4/8	Clark County	ID	Dennis R Marshall	1985	128
78 6/8	15 5/8	15 7/8	6 2/8	6 2/8	9 7/8	Converse County	WY	Tom Glendinning	1988	128
78 6/8	15 6/8	15 7/8	6 2/8	6 1/8	10 1/8	Catron County	NM	Steve Frazier	1991	128
78 6/8	13 4/8	14 0/8	7 0/8	6 7/8	10 5/8	Natrona County	WY	Timothy D. Baer	1991	128
78 6/8	15 7/8	15 7/8	6 2/8	6 1/8	11 0/8	Hudspeth County	TX	Craig B. Baird	1991	128
78 6/8	15 5/8	16 0/8	6 2/8	6 2/8	12 5/8	Humboldt County	NV	Carl W. Rose	1992	128
78 6/8	14 0/8	14 0/8	6 4/8	6 4/8	9 3/8	Sweetwater County	WY	Mark L. Preston	1992	128
78 6/8	14 5/8	14 6/8	6 3/8	6 3/8	10 2/8	Sweetwater County	WY	Mike Barrett	1992	128
78 6/8	15 3/8	15 6/8	6 3/8	6 2/8	10 0/8	McKenzie County	ND	Travis Wollan	1992	128
78 5/8	15 7/8	16 0/8	6 6/8	6 4/8	17 1/8	Washoe County	NV	James P. Mason	1992	139
78 4/8	16 0/8	15 7/8	6 0/8	6 2/8	11 4/8	Chaves County	NM	Dr. D. A. Henbest	1957	140

PRONGHORN

(Continued)

SCORE	LENGTH OF HORN R	LENGTH OF HORN L	CIRCUMFERENCE OF BASE R	CIRCUMFERENCE OF BASE L	GREATEST SPREAD	AREA	STATE/ PROVINCE	HUNTER'S NAME	DATE	RANK
78 4/8	15 1/8	14 7/8	6 5/8	6 5/8	10 0/8	Mountrail County	ND	Bennie J. Burtts	1967	140
78 4/8	14 4/8	14 1/8	6 3/8	6 2/8	10 6/8	Klamath County	OR	Paul D. Lewis	1976	140
78 4/8	13 7/8	14 0/8	6 4/8	6 2/8	8 2/8	Moffat County	CO	Mike Brezonick	1986	140
78 4/8	15 7/8	16 0/8	6 0/8	6 1/8	13 2/8	Coconino County	AZ	Randy McKusick	1988	140
78 4/8	14 1/8	14 6/8	7 0/8	7 1/8	10 2/8	Big Horn County	MT	Ron Johnson	1988	140
78 4/8	15 2/8	15 1/8	6 2/8	6 2/8	9 1/8	Lassen County	CA	Eddie L. Boyd	1989	140
78 4/8	15 0/8	15 2/8	6 3/8	6 2/8	11 0/8	Sweetwater County	WY	Kenneth Stinchcomb	1989	140
78 4/8	14 3/8	14 3/8	7 0/8	6 6/8	7 6/8	Sweetwater County	WY	Mark L. Preston	1989	140
78 4/8	15 3/8	15 0/8	6 2/8	6 4/8	10 3/8	Catron County	NM	Wade Finch	1990	140
78 4/8	16 2/8	16 3/8	5 6/8	5 6/8	14 5/8	Lea County	NM	Jim King	1990	140
78 4/8	15 3/8	15 1/8	6 4/8	6 4/8	9 5/8	Petroleum County	MT	Clark Jenner	1990	140
78 4/8	14 2/8	14 4/8	6 1/8	6 0/8	10 2/8	Medicine Hat	ALB	Dale Fournier	1990	140
78 3/8	14 4/8	14 6/8	6 6/8	6 6/8	15 3/8	Moffat County	CO	Steven J. Lepic	1983	153
78 2/8	17 3/8	17 1/8	5 5/8	5 6/8	14 6/8	Guadalupe County	NM	James L. Henry	1961	154
78 2/8	15 2/8	15 0/8	6 2/8	6 2/8	10 6/8	Wheatland County	MT	Phil Reno	1981	154
78 2/8	16 1/8	16 1/8	6 2/8	6 1/8	6 2/8	Moffat County	CO	Dan Liccardi	1982	154
78 2/8	15 2/8	15 7/8	5 7/8	5 7/8	7 3/8	Moffat County	CO	Ralph L. Albright	1985	154
78 2/8	14 3/8	14 4/8	6 1/8	6 1/8	11 3/8	Cochise County	AZ	Michael John Bylina	1985	154
78 2/8	13 7/8	14 0/8	6 2/8	6 2/8	12 6/8	Sweetwater County	WY	Tom Domson	1986	154
78 2/8	15 7/8	15 7/8	5 7/8	5 6/8	12 2/8	Washoe County	NV	Robert Jenney	1988	154
78 2/8	16 0/8	16 4/8	6 1/8	6 1/8	5 0/8	Klamath County	OR	Chuck Warner	1989	154
78 2/8	16 1/8	15 7/8	6 2/8	6 2/8	13 1/8	Coconino County	AZ	Randy McKusick	1989	154
78 2/8	15 0/8	15 2/8	6 0/8	6 0/8	10 2/8	Socorro County	NM	Glenn W. Isler	1990	154
78 2/8	14 0/8	14 1/8	6 2/8	6 1/8	9 0/8	Socorro County	NM	Mike Van Wormer	1990	154
78 2/8	13 6/8	13 7/8	6 5/8	6 4/8	8 7/8	Natrona County	WY	Jack Conner	1990	154
78 2/8	16 2/8	15 2/8	6 7/8	6 6/8	11 0/8	Sweetwater County	WY	Mark Olson	1991	154
78 2/8	15 6/8	15 5/8	5 7/8	6 0/8	13 5/8	Wayne County	UT	Shane Daley	1991	154
78 2/8	15 0/8	15 3/8	6 1/8	6 0/8	11 2/8	Yavapai County	AZ	Van M. Clark	1992	154
78 2/8	15 1/8	15 2/8	6 3/8	6 3/8	10 2/8	Converse County	WY	Kevin W. Schmieg	1992	154
78 0/8	15 0/8	14 7/8	6 3/8	6 2/8	11 5/8	Lemhi County	ID	Eugene J. Ottonello	1980	170
78 0/8	15 1/8	15 2/8	6 2/8	6 1/8	11 3/8	Stanley County	SD	Rick Ray	1980	170
78 0/8	15 3/8	15 2/8	6 7/8	6 4/8	13 7/8	Moffat County	CO	Tony Seahorn	1980	170
78 0/8	14 4/8	14 5/8	5 7/8	6 0/8	12 4/8	Stanley County	SD	George Hipple	1982	170
78 0/8	14 7/8	14 4/8	6 5/8	6 3/8	7 5/8	Fremont County	WY	Joe E. Nelson	1983	170
78 0/8	16 0/8	16 0/8	6 0/8	6 0/8	12 2/8	Washoe County	NV	Gregg Tanner	1986	170
78 0/8	14 1/8	14 2/8	6 5/8	6 5/8	13 2/8	Moffat County	CO	Calvin Farner	1986	170
78 0/8	14 5/8	14 4/8	5 6/8	6 0/8	10 1/8	Coconino County	AZ	Les Shelton	1990	170
78 0/8	14 6/8	14 1/8	6 7/8	7 1/8	11 6/8	Lincoln County	WY	Marlin Batista	1991	170
78 0/8	15 4/8	15 3/8	6 1/8	6 1/8	12 3/8	Saguache County	CO	Dan Bertalan	1991	170
77 6/8	15 4/8	15 4/8	6 2/8	6 1/8	11 5/8	McKinley County	NM	Lee Burnett	1975	180
77 6/8	15 7/8	15 0/8	6 0/8	5 6/8	10 4/8	Lincoln County	CO	Steve Winkelman	1978	180
77 6/8	14 3/8	14 1/8	6 5/8	6 5/8	6 0/8	Moffat County	CO	Phil Hughes	1983	180
77 6/8	14 0/8	14 0/8	7 0/8	6 5/8	12 1/8	Navajo County	AZ	Pat Nichols	1989	180
77 6/8	15 6/8	15 6/8	5 7/8	5 6/8	13 2/8	Powder River County	MT	Bob Carlson	1989	180
77 6/8	14 1/8	14 5/8	7 1/8	7 1/8	12 5/8	Musselshell County	MT	Wayne Muth	1990	180
77 6/8	14 7/8	14 7/8	6 1/8	6 1/8	10 2/8	Williams County	ND	Jeff Syverson	1990	180
77 6/8	13 1/8	13 4/8	6 6/8	6 7/8	7 5/8	Bighorn County	WY	Terry A. Long	1990	180
77 6/8	15 0/8	15 0/8	6 2/8	6 1/8	8 5/8	Fremont County	WY	Gary Laya	1991	180
77 6/8	15 7/8	15 6/8	6 2/8	6 2/8	12 7/8	Harney County	OR	Michael J. Kaiser	1991	180
77 6/8	14 7/8	14 6/8	5 7/8	5 6/8	11 6/8	Millard County	UT	Jeanie Clements	1992	180
77 6/8	14 7/8	15 0/8	6 1/8	6 1/8	10 7/8	Millard County	UT	Dave Scott	1992	180
77 4/8	15 1/8	15 1/8	6 0/8	6 0/8	8 3/8	Washoe County	NV	Christian J. Coleman	1979	192
77 4/8	15 1/8	15 1/8	6 1/8	6 2/8	13 6/8	Butte County	ID	Ron Johnson	1979	192
77 4/8	15 7/8	16 1/8	5 7/8	5 7/8	12 0/8	Carbon County	WY	Doug Cringan	1983	192
77 4/8	14 7/8	14 5/8	6 1/8	6 2/8	9 2/8	Graham County	AZ	Scott Kellner	1984	192
77 4/8	16 0/8	16 0/8	6 4/8	6 2/8	12 5/8	Washoe County	NV	James Mason	1985	192
77 4/8	14 0/8	14 4/8	6 2/8	6 2/8	11 5/8	Sweetwater County	WY	Dean Simmons	1987	192
77 4/8	15 4/8	15 1/8	6 1/8	6 1/8	12 4/8	McKenzie County	ND	Scott Borchert	1987	192
77 4/8	14 5/8	14 5/8	6 4/8	6 3/8	8 1/8	Moffat County	CO	Robert W. Wilkerson	1988	192
77 4/8	14 7/8	14 7/8	6 2/8	6 2/8	10 6/8	Golden Valley County	ND	Terry Buechler	1988	192
77 4/8	15 4/8	15 2/8	6 4/8	6 3/8	9 6/8	Yavapai County	AZ	Robert M. Dryden	1989	192
77 4/8	16 0/8	16 5/8	6 0/8	6 0/8	10 1/8	Sioux County	NE	Lane Ostendorf	1990	192
77 4/8	14 7/8	14 6/8	6 4/8	6 4/8	8 7/8	Moffat County	CO	Tim Atwater	1991	192
77 4/8	16 2/8	15 4/8	6 3/8	6 3/8	9 2/8	Fremont County	WY	Gary L. Hinaman	1992	192
77 4/8	14 7/8	15 4/8	6 3/8	6 3/8	10 6/8	Duchesne County	UT	Cindy Labrum	1992	192
77 4/8	15 6/8	15 6/8	6 1/8	6 0/8	14 1/8	Lincoln County	WY	Allen D. Sellers	1992	192
77 2/8	16 3/8	16 4/8	6 0/8	6 0/8	10 0/8	Lincoln County	NM	Charles L. Hughes	1960	207
77 2/8	15 0/8	15 1/8	5 7/8	5 7/8	9 0/8	Treasure County	MT	Tom Grunhuvd	1975	207
77 2/8	14 6/8	15 1/8	6 2/8	6 0/8	12 1/8	Sweetwater County	WY	William Dolenc	1978	207
77 2/8	15 4/8	15 2/8	6 1/8	5 1/8	10 4/8	Yavapai County	AZ	Tim Pender	1978	207

SCORE	LENGTH OF HORN R	LENGTH OF HORN L	CIRCUMFERENCE OF BASE R	CIRCUMFERENCE OF BASE L	GREATEST SPREAD	AREA	STATE/ PROVINCE	HUNTER'S NAME	DATE	RANK
77 2/8	15 1/8	15 1/8	6 5/8	6 3/8	8 7/8	Moffat County	CO	Tom States	1981	207
77 2/8	15 6/8	15 4/8	6 1/8	6 0/8	14 4/8	Moffat County	CO	Mike Brust	1982	207
77 2/8	14 0/8	14 2/8	6 7/8	6 6/8	14 0/8	Sweetwater County	WY	David L. Price	1983	207
77 2/8	14 4/8	14 3/8	6 0/8	6 0/8	8 7/8	Mesa County	CO	Bob Black	1983	207
77 2/8	16 3/8	16 3/8	6 3/8	6 3/8	14 1/8	Bowman County	ND	Donald C. Hestekin	1983	207
77 2/8	14 4/8	14 4/8	6 3/8	6 1/8	10 6/8	Custer County	MT	Joe Good	1984	207
77 2/8	14 5/8	14 5/8	6 1/8	6 1/8	10 3/8	Moffat County	CO	David Gunning	1987	207
77 2/8	15 5/8	15 3/8	6 2/8	6 1/8	9 3/8	Rosebud County	MT	Dr. Dale Schlehuber	1987	207
77 2/8	15 0/8	15 2/8	6 1/8	6 1/8	11 1/8	Rosebud County	MT	Gene Welle	1988	207
77 2/8	16 0/8	16 4/8	5 5/8	5 5/8	7 7/8	Humboldt County	NV	Clayton Keister	1989	207
77 2/8	15 7/8	16 0/8	6 2/8	6 1/8	8 6/8	Natrona County	WY	Kenneth D. Sundquist	1989	207
77 2/8	15 0/8	15 0/8	6 2/8	6 3/8	10 7/8	Golden Valley County	ND	Terry Buechler	1989	207
77 2/8	14 0/8	14 0/8	6 6/8	6 5/8	10 6/8	Lassen County	CA	Danny Westberg	1990	207
77 2/8	15 1/8	15 1/8	5 6/8	5 5/8	8 6/8	Harney County	OR	Donald R. Paulsen	1990	207
77 2/8	15 6/8	15 0/8	6 3/8	6 2/8	10 4/8	Yavapai County	AZ	James N. Schmidt	1991	207
77 2/8	14 2/8	14 2/8	6 1/8	6 0/8	10 2/8	Harney County	OR	Ralph Burt	1991	207
77 2/8	14 5/8	14 5/8	7 2/8	7 2/8	10 3/8	Radville	SAS	Ken Paslawski	1991	207
77 2/8	14 2/8	14 2/8	6 5/8	6 6/8	11 3/8	Sweetwater County	WY	Brad Hugh Jacobs	1992	207
77 0/8	14 1/8	15 2/8	6 2/8	6 0/8	9 4/8	Billings County	ND	Jonathan Zieman	1984	229
77 0/8	14 4/8	14 5/8	6 2/8	6 1/8	11 1/8	Rosebud County	MT	Steve Cutright	1987	229
77 0/8	15 2/8	15 1/8	6 0/8	6 0/8	10 5/8	Garfield County	MT	Daryl P. Hinther	1987	229
77 0/8	14 7/8	14 7/8	6 0/8	6 1/8	7 3/8	Sweetwater County	WY	Rod Schmidt	1988	229
77 0/8	15 2/8	15 0/8	6 1/8	6 2/8	8 5/8	Moffat County	CO	Louis Dodaro	1988	229
77 0/8	14 0/8	14 0/8	6 3/8	6 2/8	11 0/8	Cochise County	AZ	Brian Davis	1988	229
77 0/8	14 4/8	15 1/8	5 7/8	5 7/8	11 3/8	Park County	WY	Rocky Deromedi	1988	229
77 0/8	14 2/8	14 3/8	5 7/8	5 7/8	8 0/8	Bare Creek	ALB	Paul Ronald Goodberry	1988	229
77 0/8	14 3/8	14 4/8	6 3/8	6 3/8	15 0/8	Campbell County	WY	Michael H. Albers	1989	229
77 0/8	15 1/8	14 6/8	5 7/8	5 6/8	11 4/8	Washoe County	NV	Jeffrey L. Dodge	1990	229
77 0/8	14 2/8	14 2/8	6 0/8	6 1/8	10 1/8	Mesa County	CO	Darren K. Peacock	1990	229
77 0/8	14 7/8	15 2/8	6 0/8	5 7/8	10 6/8	Millard County	UT	Vee F. Hanks	1990	229
77 0/8	14 7/8	14 4/8	6 3/8	6 3/8	8 4/8	Humboldt County	NV	Mike Fillmore	1992	229
77 0/8	15 0/8	14 7/8	6 2/8	6 2/8	9 3/8	Carbon County	WY	Rod Schmidt	1992	229
77 0/8	15 4/8	15 5/8	6 2/8	6 1/8	9 6/8	Hudspeth County	TX	William R. Fair	1992	229
76 6/8	14 1/8	14 5/8	6 2/8	6 2/8	14 2/8	Fremont County	WY	Jim Puthoff	1969	244
76 6/8	14 6/8	14 6/8	6 3/8	6 3/8	10 5/8	Fremont County	WY	Ron D. Evitt	1982	244
76 6/8	14 2/8	14 2/8	6 1/8	6 0/8	12 4/8	Campbell County	WY	Tony Janssen	1984	244
76 6/8	14 6/8	14 6/8	6 1/8	6 1/8	8 6/8	Converse County	WY	Vito Palazzolo	1984	244
76 6/8	15 5/8	15 7/8	5 7/8	5 7/8	10 2/8	Butte County	ID	Champ Church	1986	244
76 6/8	14 0/8	13 6/8	5 5/8	5 6/8	13 4/8	San Miguel County	CO	Stuart Howard	1986	244
76 6/8	16 7/8	17 1/8	5 7/8	6 0/8	10 6/8	Humboldt County	NV	Lance R. Wodke	1987	244
76 6/8	15 0/8	15 0/8	6 1/8	6 0/8	10 3/8	Dunn County	ND	Ron Bachmeier	1987	244
76 6/8	15 5/8	15 5/8	6 3/8	6 4/8	9 2/8	Fremont County	WY	Dan Chappell	1990	244
76 6/8	14 3/8	13 6/8	6 0/8	6 1/8	13 7/8	Jackson County	CO	Dominic Florian	1990	244
76 6/8	16 2/8	15 7/8	5 7/8	5 7/8	10 7/8	Santa Cruz County	AZ	Jerry A. Clarno	1990	244
76 6/8	15 1/8	14 5/8	6 2/8	6 1/8	8 2/8	Moffat County	CO	Roderick E. Nutter	1991	244
76 6/8	13 5/8	14 1/8	6 5/8	6 5/8	8 3/8	Natrona County	WY	Gary L. Miller	1991	244
76 6/8	14 5/8	15 2/8	6 0/8	6 0/8	10 4/8	Carbon County	WY	Marc D. Hallowell	1991	244
76 6/8	15 1/8	15 1/8	6 5/8	6 4/8	11 7/8	Grant County	NM	John Trewern	1992	244
76 4/8	14 5/8	14 6/8	5 6/8	5 7/8	10 3/8	Lemhi County	ID	Roger W. Atwood	1977	259
76 4/8	14 6/8	14 6/8	6 1/8	6 1/8	12 3/8	Custer County	ID	Juilan Salutregui	1983	259
76 4/8	14 1/8	14 1/8	6 0/8	6 0/8	7 4/8	Converse County	WY	Scott Ames	1983	259
76 4/8	16 0/8	15 7/8	6 2/8	6 2/8	9 2/8	McKinley County	NM	Patrick J. Sharp	1984	259
76 4/8	15 1/8	14 6/8	6 0/8	6 0/8	11 3/8	Carter County	MT	Jamie Byrne	1984	259
76 4/8	14 0/8	14 0/8	6 0/8	6 0/8	14 6/8	Garfield County	MT	Paul Schafer	1984	259
76 4/8	13 6/8	13 6/8	6 6/8	6 6/8	10 3/8	Carbon County	WY	Jerry DeCroo	1985	259
76 4/8	15 2/8	15 2/8	6 1/8	6 1/8	12 1/8	Washoe County	NV	Ken Tavener	1986	259
76 4/8	15 4/8	15 4/8	6 2/8	6 3/8	12 6/8	Coconino County	AZ	Gary D. Davis	1986	259
76 4/8	15 2/8	15 3/8	6 0/8	6 0/8	8 1/8	Clark County	SD	Scott Lindgren	1988	259
76 4/8	13 2/8	12 7/8	6 0/8	6 0/8	11 3/8	Sceptre	SAS	Ron Todd	1988	259
76 4/8	16 0/8	16 1/8	6 1/8	6 0/8	14 4/8	Humboldt County	NV	Dwight Schuh	1989	259
76 4/8	14 1/8	13 7/8	6 3/8	6 7/8	9 5/8	Coconino County	AZ	Dennis Pugh	1990	259
76 4/8	14 2/8	14 7/8	6 1/8	6 2/8	13 5/8	Yavapai County	AZ	Josiah Scott	1990	259
76 4/8	14 2/8	14 4/8	5 7/8	6 0/8	10 2/8	Carter County	MT	Donald Travis	1990	259
76 4/8	15 5/8	15 5/8	6 0/8	6 0/8	8 2/8	Beaverhead County	MT	Neil L. Jacobson	1990	259
76 4/8	15 0/8	15 1/8	6 4/8	6 3/8	11 7/8	Thomas County	NE	Andrew L. Glidden	1990	259
76 4/8	15 4/8	15 4/8	6 0/8	5 7/8	11 0/8	Delta County	CO	Donald E. Liddell	1991	259
76 4/8	14 3/8	14 3/8	6 4/8	6 3/8	11 5/8	Sweetwater County	WY	Randy Downs	1991	259
76 4/8	14 7/8	14 7/8	6 1/8	6 1/8	11 6/8	Fremont County	WY	Gary Laya	1992	259
76 4/8	13 5/8	13 3/8	5 7/8	5 7/8	9 0/8	Converse County	WY	G. Allen Sink	1992	259
76 2/8	14 5/8	14 1/8	6 1/8	6 1/8	10 3/8	Citten	ND	Richard R. Chandler	1972	280

SCORE	LENGTH OF R HORN L		CIRCUMFERENCE R OF BASE L		GREATEST SPREAD	AREA	STATE/ PROVINCE	HUNTER'S NAME	DATE	RANK
76 2/8	14 1/8	14 2/8	6 4/8	6 2/8	10 6/8	Converse County	WY	Jack Cassidy	1980	280
76 2/8	13 6/8	14 1/8	6 2/8	6 2/8	8 5/8	Converse County	WY	Chris Cassidy	1980	280
76 2/8	14 7/8	14 6/8	5 5/8	5 6/8	8 6/8	Blaine County	ID	Champ Church	1980	280
76 2/8	16 3/8	16 1/8	6 0/8	6 1/8	8 5/8	Weston County	WY	David M. Nahrgang	1980	280
76 2/8	16 0/8	15 6/8	5 7/8	6 1/8	11 4/8	Converse County	WY	Jack M. Conner	1981	280
76 2/8	14 3/8	14 3/8	5 6/8	5 7/8	9 2/8	Converse County	WY	Robert R. Vance	1981	280
76 2/8	14 6/8	14 6/8	6 3/8	6 3/8	11 1/8	Moffat County	CO	James Bowerman	1982	280
76 2/8	14 4/8	14 5/8	6 2/8	6 2/8	10 5/8	Sweetwater County	WY	Darrell H. Nations	1982	280
76 2/8	14 4/8	14 5/8	6 0/8	6 0/8	10 2/8	Taos County	NM	Galen G. Roumpf	1983	280
76 2/8	13 4/8	13 7/8	6 4/8	6 2/8	10 6/8	Wallace County	KS	Steve Rugg	1983	280
76 2/8	14 6/8	14 7/8	6 5/8	6 3/8	7 7/8	Sweetwater County	WY	Steve L. Rueck	1984	280
76 2/8	14 6/8	14 7/8	5 7/8	5 6/8	10 6/8	Eddy County	NM	Derek A. Tierney	1986	280
76 2/8	14 0/8	13 6/8	6 2/8	6 1/8	9 1/8	Converse County	WY	David Kugler	1987	280
76 2/8	15 2/8	15 2/8	6 4/8	6 4/8	10 4/8	Hettinger County	ND	Bill Clink	1988	280
76 2/8	14 3/8	14 7/8	6 5/8	6 4/8	11 2/8	Bowman County	ND	Craig Egeland	1988	280
76 2/8	15 2/8	15 2/8	5 7/8	5 7/8	11 3/8	Empress	ALB	Kenneth John Akkermans	1988	280
76 2/8	16 0/8	16 3/8	5 7/8	5 7/8	12 1/8	Lassen County	CA	Gary Bagnaschi	1989	280
76 2/8	15 0/8	15 0/8	5 7/8	5 7/8	11 1/8	Moffat County	CO	Robert M. Fromme	1990	280
76 2/8	15 6/8	15 4/8	6 1/8	6 1/8	16 4/8	Coconino County	AZ	Kevin Shackleford	1990	280
76 2/8	13 4/8	13 6/8	7 3/8	7 2/8	9 3/8	Mountrail County	ND	Lonny G. Waggoner	1990	280
76 2/8	15 0/8	15 0/8	6 2/8	6 3/8	13 4/8	Harney County	OR	Trevin Webster	1990	280
76 2/8	15 2/8	15 1/8	6 0/8	6 0/8	9 5/8	Catron County	NM	Cary Cuba	1991	280
76 2/8	15 0/8	15 0/8	6 3/8	6 2/8	10 1/8	Sweetwater County	WY	William Metz	1991	280
76 2/8	13 5/8	13 5/8	6 5/8	6 5/8	8 4/8	Converse County	WY	William L. Randles	1991	280
76 2/8	14 7/8	14 4/8	6 1/8	6 2/8	9 2/8	Johnson County	WY	Joseph L. Ravis	1991	280
76 2/8	15 0/8	14 6/8	6 4/8	6 3/8	10 4/8	Box Butte County	NE	Myron R. Drumheller	1991	280
76 1/8	17 0/8	17 1/8	6 3/8	6 2/8	22 2/8	Yavapai County	AZ	Rick Anderson	1987	307
76 0/8	15 0/8	14 7/8	6 0/8	6 0/8	14 6/8	Mountrail County	ND	Wayne A. Metcalf	1972	308
76 0/8	14 5/8	14 5/8	6 2/8	6 4/8	13 4/8	Clark County	ID	Kerry Hillman	1977	308
76 0/8	14 7/8	14 3/8	5 6/8	6 1/8	10 0/8	Sweetwater County	WY	John Grady Lee	1983	308
76 0/8	14 2/8	14 2/8	6 1/8	6 1/8	9 3/8	Converse County	WY	Richard Rabe, Jr.	1985	308
76 0/8	14 4/8	14 3/8	6 0/8	6 1/8	9 7/8	Nye County	NV	Paul Campos	1988	308
76 0/8	14 0/8	14 1/8	6 0/8	6 0/8	8 7/8	Yavapai County	AZ	T. J. Baehre	1989	308
76 0/8	14 6/8	14 3/8	6 5/8	6 4/8	10 4/8	Sweetwater County	WY	Lori Kay Stinchcomb	1990	308
76 0/8	14 2/8	13 6/8	6 3/8	6 3/8	11 2/8	Campbell County	WY	James K. Keim	1990	308
76 0/8	15 4/8	15 2/8	6 0/8	5 7/8	12 2/8	Quay County	NM	Tommy C. Jones	1991	308
76 0/8	15 4/8	15 5/8	6 3/8	6 2/8	8 7/8	Milk River	ALB	Daniel Harder	1991	308
76 0/8	15 2/8	15 2/8	6 0/8	6 0/8	12 1/8	Morton County	ND	Gary Hanson	1991	308
76 0/8	14 2/8	14 1/8	6 3/8	6 2/8	9 5/8	Campbell County	WY	Doy K. Curtis	1991	308
76 0/8	15 4/8	15 6/8	5 4/8	5 3/8	13 7/8	Lake County	OR	Donald R. Pritchett	1992	308
76 0/8	13 5/8	13 5/8	6 5/8	6 4/8	9 6/8	Sweetwater County	WY	Justin Miller	1992	308
75 6/8	14 0/8	14 0/8	6 1/8	6 1/8	12 4/8	Sweetwater County	WY	Gene McFadden	1982	322
75 6/8	14 4/8	14 6/8	6 1/8	6 1/8	10 0/8	Natrona County	WY	Jack M. Conner	1982	322
75 6/8	15 2/8	14 6/8	5 7/8	5 7/8	11 1/8	Moffat County	CO	Judd Cooney	1982	322
75 6/8	15 1/8	15 1/8	6 2/8	6 2/8	10 3/8	Converse County	WY	Lonny G. Herrick	1983	322
75 6/8	15 0/8	15 0/8	5 7/8	5 6/8	14 2/8	Sweetwater County	WY	Marty Martin	1986	322
75 6/8	14 1/8	14 0/8	6 2/8	6 2/8	10 4/8	Moffat County	CO	Tom Foss	1987	322
75 6/8	14 2/8	15 2/8	6 6/8	6 6/8	15 2/8	Moffat County	CO	Randy Major/Frank Major	1988	322
75 6/8	13 5/8	14 0/8	6 4/8	6 3/8	6 3/8	Carbon County	WY	David Wiltse	1988	322
75 6/8	15 0/8	15 1/8	5 5/8	5 5/8	9 1/8	Sublette County	WY	Ronell Skinner	1988	322
75 6/8	13 5/8	13 5/8	6 0/8	6 1/8	11 7/8	Coconino County	AZ	Noel Harris	1989	322
75 6/8	14 6/8	14 5/8	6 0/8	5 7/8	9 2/8	Moffat County	CO	Joseph Schwartz	1990	322
75 6/8	15 6/8	15 2/8	6 0/8	5 6/8	10 4/8	Elko County	NV	Paul J. Vietti	1990	322
75 6/8	14 2/8	14 3/8	5 6/8	6 1/8	6 5/8	Carbon County	WY	Clarence E. Faber	1990	322
75 6/8	13 6/8	13 3/8	6 1/8	6 0/8	12 4/8	Sublette County	WY	Mike Lamade	1990	322
75 6/8	15 1/8	15 2/8	5 7/8	5 7/8	9 4/8	Millard County	UT	Dennis L. Shirley	1990	322
75 6/8	15 2/8	15 3/8	6 1/8	6 1/8	12 4/8	Harney County	OR	Gary Nyden	1990	322
75 6/8	12 6/8	12 5/8	6 3/8	6 6/8	7 6/8	Harney County	OR	Eugene F. Martin	1990	322
75 6/8	13 6/8	13 7/8	6 3/8	6 4/8	10 4/8	Converse County	WY	Wayne Sanders	1990	322
75 6/8	14 6/8	15 1/8	5 6/8	5 6/8	8 1/8	Lemhi County	ID	Ben Fahnholz	1991	322
75 6/8	15 1/8	15 3/8	6 0/8	6 0/8	10 7/8	Yavapai County	AZ	Paul Fritzinger	1991	322
75 6/8	15 4/8	15 4/8	5 7/8	5 6/8	10 1/8	Socorro County	NM	Mike Van Wormer	1992	322
75 6/8	15 7/8	16 2/8	6 0/8	6 0/8	6 2/8	Carbon County	WY	Jeff Martin	1992	322
75 6/8	14 0/8	13 7/8	6 6/8	6 5/8	10 4/8	Jenner	ALB	Carter Calliou	1992	322
75 5/8	15 4/8	15 4/8	5 5/8	5 5/8	16 7/8	Dunn County	ND	Allan Lynch	1975	345
75 4/8	12 1/8	12 2/8	5 7/8	6 0/8	8 2/8	Campbell County	WY	Dr. R. F. Helzerman	1960	346
75 4/8	17 2/8	16 4/8	6 0/8	5 6/8	15 0/8	Guadalupe County	NM	M. K. Vance	1962	346
75 4/8	14 7/8	14 7/8	6 0/8	6 0/8	12 0/8	Williams County	ND	Terry L. Halgrimson	1970	346
75 4/8	14 3/8	14 2/8	6 0/8	6 2/8	12 6/8	McLean County	ND	Don Sorge	1970	346
75 4/8	13 3/8	13 4/8	6 6/8	6 7/8	11 6/8	Ormsby	WY	Richard L. Huber	1979	346

SCORE	LENGTH OF R HORN L		CIRCUMFERENCE R OF BASE L		GREATEST SPREAD	AREA	STATE/ PROVINCE	HUNTER'S NAME	DATE	RANK
75 4/8	15 3/8	15 2/8	5 6/8	5 6/8	12 5/8	Fergus County	MT	Don Davidson	1981	346
75 4/8	14 5/8	14 7/8	6 2/8	6 2/8	9 6/8	Klamath County	OR	Larry E. Jones	1982	346
75 4/8	16 0/8	16 0/8	6 0/8	5 7/8	11 0/8	Moffat County	CO	John R. Morris II	1983	346
75 4/8	14 4/8	14 4/8	6 4/8	6 4/8	11 6/8	Coconino County	AZ	Gary Warnica	1983	346
75 4/8	14 0/8	14 0/8	6 2/8	6 2/8	10 0/8	Powder River County	MT	Raleigh D. Buckmaster	1983	346
75 4/8	16 2/8	16 2/8	6 0/8	6 0/8	12 0/8	Coconino County	AZ	Harry M. Weeks	1984	346
75 4/8	14 4/8	14 0/8	6 4/8	6 4/8	12 1/8	Weld County	CO	Lorn Barnica	1984	346
75 4/8	14 6/8	14 6/8	6 0/8	6 0/8	11 1/8	Lassen County	CA	Pete Becker	1985	346
75 4/8	15 1/8	15 2/8	6 0/8	5 7/8	9 3/8	Meagher County	MT	Don Babcock	1986	346
75 4/8	15 0/8	14 4/8	5 6/8	5 7/8	6 7/8	Washoe County	NV	Conrad Stitser	1987	346
75 4/8	14 3/8	14 5/8	5 5/8	5 7/8	12 0/8	Coconino County	AZ	Bill Kerr	1987	346
75 4/8	14 7/8	14 6/8	6 1/8	6 2/8	10 3/8	Cochise County	AZ	Jerry Clarno	1987	346
75 4/8	15 6/8	15 3/8	6 1/8	6 2/8	12 3/8	Humboldt County	NV	G. Todd Brooks	1988	346
75 4/8	15 3/8	15 1/8	6 7/8	6 7/8	7 4/8	Custer County	ID	Matt March	1990	346
75 4/8	13 6/8	13 6/8	6 0/8	6 0/8	10 0/8	Coconino County	AZ	Rick Betten	1991	346
75 4/8	14 4/8	14 0/8	6 0/8	6 0/8	12 7/8	Campbell County	WY	Gene Bremmer	1991	346
75 4/8	14 1/8	14 1/8	6 2/8	6 1/8	10 1/8	Yavapai County	AZ	Jeffrey W. Adams	1992	346
75 4/8	14 2/8	14 2/8	5 7/8	5 6/8	10 2/8	Stanley County	SD	Robert G. Barden	1992	346
75 4/8	13 6/8	13 6/8	6 5/8	6 3/8	9 6/8	Carbon County	WY	Larry Cross	1992	346
75 3/8	15 5/8	15 1/8	6 2/8	6 2/8	18 2/8	Sweetwater County	WY	Don Dvoroznak	1976	370
75 2/8	15 4/8	15 3/8	5 7/8	5 7/8	8 6/8	Burke County	ND	Richard R. Chandler	1971	371
75 2/8	16 1/8	16 6/8	5 6/8	5 5/8	11 2/8	Klamath County	OR	Steve H. Bell	1973	371
75 2/8	14 3/8	14 5/8	6 3/8	6 4/8	9 2/8	Carbon County	WY	Duane Caudle	1980	371
75 2/8	14 5/8	14 5/8	6 2/8	6 2/8	10 2/8	Musselshell County	MT	John Crump	1980	371
75 2/8	13 0/8	13 0/8	7 0/8	7 1/8	10 6/8	Sweetwater County	WY	Charlene Shaw	1985	371
75 2/8	15 0/8	14 4/8	7 0/8	6 6/8	9 2/8	Sweetwater County	WY	Marlene Bowen	1986	371
75 2/8	14 0/8	14 5/8	6 0/8	6 0/8	12 0/8	Coconino County	AZ	David L. Wolf	1986	371
75 2/8	13 7/8	14 0/8	6 5/8	6 4/8	12 5/8	Dunn County	ND	Jeff J. Kostelecky	1987	371
75 2/8	14 1/8	14 0/8	6 2/8	6 2/8	8 5/8	Lea County	NM	Lynn Sims	1987	371
75 2/8	13 7/8	13 6/8	6 4/8	6 5/8	11 2/8	Coconino County	AZ	Johnny Rooker	1988	371
75 2/8	15 6/8	16 0/8	6 3/8	6 2/8	10 7/8	Phillips County	MT	Don Andrews	1988	371
75 2/8	14 4/8	14 4/8	6 3/8	6 3/8	12 3/8	Presidio County	TX	Tommy Culbertson	1988	371
75 2/8	15 0/8	14 5/8	6 2/8	6 3/8	8 7/8	Sweetwater County	WY	Norman Bradley	1989	371
75 2/8	13 7/8	14 0/8	6 0/8	5 7/8	7 1/8	Moffat County	CO	Rickey Phillips	1989	371
75 2/8	13 7/8	14 0/8	6 1/8	6 2/8	12 5/8	Sweetwater County	WY	Harv Dalton	1989	371
75 2/8	15 3/8	15 4/8	5 6/8	5 6/8	11 3/8	Eddy County	NM	Dennis L. Howell	1989	371
75 2/8	14 4/8	14 5/8	6 1/8	6 2/8	9 0/8	Washoe County	NV	Cory Pengelly	1990	371
75 2/8	14 2/8	14 1/8	6 2/8	6 2/8	7 3/8	Sweetwater County	WY	Edward Ferebee	1990	371
75 2/8	15 7/8	15 4/8	5 5/8	5 5/8	6 5/8	Sweetwater County	WY	Ron Serwa	1990	371
75 2/8	14 4/8	14 5/8	6 1/8	6 0/8	12 2/8	Moffat County	CO	Ronald King	1990	371
75 2/8	15 4/8	16 1/8	5 7/8	5 5/8	9 1/8	Harney County	OR	Stanley Miles	1990	371
75 2/8	14 3/8	14 1/8	5 6/8	5 6/8	9 0/8	Billings County	ND	Mark Sowieja	1990	371
75 2/8	14 2/8	14 0/8	6 1/8	6 3/8	9 3/8	Wallace County	KS	Daniel P. Carmen	1990	371
75 2/8	14 3/8	14 4/8	6 3/8	6 3/8	14 4/8	Moffat County	CO	Bud Boker	1991	371
75 2/8	14 3/8	14 3/8	6 1/8	6 0/8	11 3/8	Carbon County	WY	Greg Bonetti	1991	371
75 2/8	13 2/8	13 4/8	6 5/8	6 4/8	12 0/8	Garfield County	MT	Kim Tatman	1991	371
75 2/8	15 1/8	15 0/8	6 6/8	6 5/8	11 1/8	Sioux County	NE	Steve Woitaszewski	1991	371
75 2/8	14 6/8	14 5/8	5 6/8	5 6/8	10 2/8	Catron County	NM	Patrick Kirk	1992	371
75 2/8	13 7/8	15 0/8	6 2/8	6 2/8	10 1/8	Yavapai County	AZ	Roland J. Chooljian	1992	371
75 2/8	15 6/8	15 4/8	6 0/8	6 0/8	9 7/8	Yavapai County	AZ	Don Parks, Jr.	1992	371
75 0/8	14 2/8	14 2/8	6 3/8	6 1/8	10 2/8	Butte County	ID	Ross M. Conlin	1971	401
75 0/8	14 0/8	13 6/8	7 4/8	7 4/8	11 6/8	Sheridan County	ND	Dave Baumiller	1973	401
75 0/8	13 4/8	13 5/8	6 5/8	6 3/8	10 2/8	Campbell County	WY	Mick Larson	1975	401
75 0/8	13 6/8	14 0/8	6 2/8	6 2/8	8 6/8	Bairoil	WY	Mike Ward	1976	401
75 0/8	14 5/8	14 4/8	6 2/8	6 1/8	8 7/8	Humboldt County	NV	Robert Mathews	1977	401
75 0/8	14 2/8	14 1/8	6 3/8	6 3/8	10 1/8	Bairoil	WY	Earl Frye	1980	401
75 0/8	14 0/8	14 0/8	5 5/8	5 6/8	9 7/8	Moffat County	CO	Ronald C. Halpin	1980	401
75 0/8	14 0/8	14 0/8	6 1/8	6 0/8	12 6/8	Wheatland County	MT	Phil Reno	1980	401
75 0/8	13 5/8	14 6/8	6 0/8	6 0/8	13 0/8	Moffat County	CO	Carl Smith	1981	401
75 0/8	15 0/8	14 7/8	6 2/8	6 2/8	9 0/8	Natrona County	WY	Richard A. Schreiber	1982	401
75 0/8	14 5/8	14 5/8	6 0/8	6 0/8	12 1/8	Meagher County	MT	Gene Clark	1984	401
75 0/8	15 5/8	15 3/8	6 0/8	6 0/8	11 6/8	Coconino County	AZ	Jim Scott	1986	401
75 0/8	14 4/8	14 4/8	5 5/8	5 5/8	10 4/8	Converse County	WY	William G. Mason	1986	401
75 0/8	14 4/8	14 4/8	5 6/8	5 6/8	13 5/8	Sweetwater County	WY	Steve Bellis	1988	401
75 0/8	14 6/8	14 6/8	5 6/8	5 6/8	11 2/8	Pueblo County	CO	Freeman Howard	1989	401
75 0/8	14 3/8	14 4/8	6 1/8	6 2/8	9 2/8	Custer County	MT	Marty Penrod	1989	401
75 0/8	12 0/8	12 1/8	6 2/8	6 2/8	9 4/8	Campbell County	WY	Richard Reeb	1990	401
75 0/8	14 4/8	13 6/8	6 0/8	6 0/8	11 2/8	Grant County	NM	Brandon Jones	1991	401
75 0/8	13 6/8	13 5/8	6 2/8	6 1/8	11 7/8	Carbon County	WY	Heather E. Haines	1991	401
75 0/8	13 7/8	13 7/8	6 4/8	6 5/8	12 7/8	Carbon County	WY	Kenneth J. Kahler	1991	401

Score	Length of R Horn L		Circumference R of Base L		Greatest Spread	Area	State/ Province	Hunter's Name	Date	Rank
75 0/8	14 5/8	14 5/8	6 2/8	6 4/8	9 2/8	Fremont County	WY	Joel Nirider	1991	401
75 0/8	13 5/8	13 7/8	6 1/8	6 2/8	12 2/8	Mercer County	ND	Leland A. Mehlhoff	1991	401
75 0/8	15 3/8	15 3/8	5 3/8	5 2/8	9 0/8	Converse County	WY	Robert Brenneman	1991	401
75 0/8	14 1/8	13 7/8	6 3/8	6 3/8	8 6/8	Sweetwater County	WY	James B. White	1992	401
75 0/8	15 0/8	15 0/8	6 2/8	6 1/8	8 3/8	Butte County	ID	L. D. Green	1992	401
75 0/8	15 3/8	15 4/8	6 1/8	6 0/8	9 6/8	Millard County	UT	Terry Costa	1992	401
75 0/8	13 6/8	14 3/8	6 7/8	7 1/8	12 4/8	Moffat County	CO	Glenn W. Pritchard	1992	401
74 6/8	14 3/8	14 3/8	5 5/8	5 5/8	9 5/8	Lemhi County	ID	Kent Merrill	1979	428
74 6/8	13 5/8	13 2/8	7 4/8	7 5/8	11 2/8	Converse County	WY	George A. Zanoni	1980	428
74 6/8	14 4/8	14 5/8	6 3/8	6 1/8	7 0/8	Converse County	WY	Norm Goodwin	1981	428
74 6/8	14 3/8	14 5/8	5 6/8	5 6/8	10 1/8	Fremont County	WY	James R. Mecca	1981	428
74 6/8	14 2/8	14 2/8	6 1/8	6 1/8	9 1/8	Sweetwater County	WY	Pete J Cintorino	1982	428
74 6/8	14 7/8	14 1/8	6 2/8	6 1/8	12 1/8	Moffat County	CO	Richard K. Hess	1982	428
74 6/8	14 1/8	14 1/8	6 0/8	5 7/8	5 7/8	Converse County	WY	Thomas Fleming	1982	428
74 6/8	14 4/8	14 5/8	6 0/8	6 1/8	9 6/8	Converse County	WY	Steve Gorr	1982	428
74 6/8	13 7/8	14 0/8	5 7/8	6 1/8	12 4/8	Carbon County	WY	Len Cardinale	1982	428
74 6/8	14 3/8	14 3/8	6 2/8	6 2/8	8 6/8	Sweetwater County	WY	Mike Denney	1982	428
74 6/8	14 7/8	14 7/8	6 0/8	6 0/8	8 7/8	Humboldt County	NV	Ken Mallory	1983	428
74 6/8	14 0/8	14 1/8	6 0/8	5 7/8	10 3/8	Moffat County	CO	Wallace Hobby	1983	428
74 6/8	14 5/8	14 6/8	6 2/8	6 2/8	9 7/8	Campbell County	WY	Arthur Geltz	1984	428
74 6/8	14 4/8	14 4/8	6 2/8	6 2/8	10 3/8	Moffat County	CO	Susan Bingham Syvertson	1985	428
74 6/8	15 3/8	15 4/8	5 7/8	5 6/8	8 0/8	Fremont County	WY	Joe E. Nelson	1985	428
74 6/8	14 1/8	14 0/8	6 1/8	6 0/8	7 3/8	Sweetwater County	WY	Dennis L. Shirley	1986	428
74 6/8	14 2/8	14 1/8	6 4/8	6 3/8	9 6/8	Sweetwater County	WY	Michael Chaffin	1986	428
74 6/8	14 3/8	14 7/8	6 1/8	6 0/8	10 5/8	Carbon County	WY	Robert L. Hudman	1988	428
74 6/8	14 5/8	14 6/8	5 7/8	5 7/8	10 7/8	Billings County	ND	Pam Baird	1988	428
74 6/8	14 3/8	14 3/8	5 7/8	5 7/8	8 3/8	Converse County	WY	James Erickson	1988	428
74 6/8	13 4/8	13 3/8	6 3/8	6 3/8	11 0/8	Humboldt County	NV	David Stoker	1991	428
74 6/8	14 3/8	14 5/8	6 1/8	6 1/8	11 7/8	Perkins County	SD	Darin Allen Manthie	1991	428
74 6/8	14 7/8	14 6/8	5 7/8	6 0/8	7 2/8	Washoe County	NV	Jim Bradley	1992	428
74 6/8	15 2/8	14 7/8	5 7/8	5 7/8	7 4/8	Washoe County	NV	Charlie Powning	1992	428
74 6/8	13 7/8	14 0/8	6 6/8	6 6/8	7 7/8	Sweetwater County	WY	Robert G. Petersen	1992	428
74 6/8	13 4/8	13 4/8	5 7/8	6 0/8	8 0/8	Converse County	WY	Russell A. Nichols	1992	428
74 6/8	14 6/8	14 5/8	5 7/8	5 7/8	11 1/8	Natrona County	WY	Elmer R. Luce, Jr.	1992	428
74 4/8	14 6/8	14 4/8	6 2/8	6 2/8	12 3/8	Campbell County	WY	William P. Mastrangel	1957	455
74 4/8	15 3/8	15 3/8	6 3/8	6 2/8	11 2/8	Lincoln County	NM	Harvey May	1960	455
74 4/8	14 2/8	14 6/8	6 0/8	6 1/8	12 0/8	Ward County	ND	Bennie Burtts	1964	455
74 4/8	14 1/8	14 0/8	6 6/8	6 5/8	8 7/8	Wheeler County	NE	Lynn M. Briggs	1965	455
74 4/8	13 4/8	13 6/8	7 1/8	7 2/8	8 5/8	Sioux County	NE	Bill Carlos	1969	455
74 4/8	14 0/8	14 2/8	6 4/8	6 4/8	11 5/8	Lyman County	SD	Loran Hills	1970	455
74 4/8	15 4/8	15 2/8	5 6/8	5 6/8	9 7/8	Sweetwater County	WY	Clifford White	1977	455
74 4/8	14 4/8	14 4/8	6 0/8	5 6/8	7 2/8	Logan County	KS	Calvin Henry	1980	455
74 4/8	13 3/8	13 3/8	6 1/8	6 0/8	9 0/8	Moffat County	CO	George Griffiths	1981	455
74 4/8	14 2/8	14 2/8	6 4/8	6 4/8	10 0/8	Baca County	CO	Bill McEndree	1982	455
74 4/8	12 5/8	12 7/8	6 4/8	6 4/8	10 5/8	Arapahoe County	CO	Sid Strzok	1982	455
74 4/8	13 5/8	13 2/8	6 3/8	6 3/8	12 1/8	Moffat County	CO	Dale Drilling	1985	455
74 4/8	14 1/8	14 5/8	6 1/8	6 2/8	14 4/8	Modoc County	CA	George Taylor	1985	455
74 4/8	14 1/8	13 7/8	5 0/8	5 0/8	9 4/8	Converse County	WY	Ronald M. Cook	1985	455
74 4/8	13 3/8	13 3/8	6 5/8	6 5/8	10 0/8	Sweetwater County	WY	Bill Clink	1986	455
74 4/8	13 3/8	13 3/8	6 4/8	6 4/8	7 4/8	Sweetwater County	WY	Glenn Hisey	1986	455
74 4/8	14 3/8	12 7/8	6 4/8	6 4/8	10 2/8	Carbon County	UT	Don R. Logston	1986	455
74 4/8	15 3/8	15 4/8	6 0/8	6 0/8	8 4/8	Washoe County	NV	Timothy P. Wooley	1987	455
74 4/8	14 4/8	14 4/8	6 0/8	6 0/8	10 2/8	Natrona County	WY	James R. McCain	1988	455
74 4/8	14 4/8	14 4/8	6 4/8	6 3/8	8 6/8	Moffat County	CO	Doy K. Curtis	1988	455
74 4/8	15 0/8	14 6/8	5 7/8	5 7/8	6 5/8	Nye County	NV	Jim Loncar	1989	455
74 4/8	14 0/8	13 7/8	5 7/8	5 7/8	8 1/8	Tooele County	UT	Paul H. Laver	1989	455
74 4/8	14 4/8	15 1/8	6 1/8	6 1/8	14 1/8	Washoe County	NV	Darrel Reed	1990	455
74 4/8	13 5/8	14 0/8	6 7/8	6 7/8	11 4/8	Washoe County	NV	Rick Lund	1990	455
74 4/8	14 2/8	14 1/8	5 7/8	6 0/8	8 1/8	Carbon County	WY	Dennis Bader	1990	455
74 4/8	13 4/8	13 3/8	6 2/8	6 1/8	10 4/8	Yavapai County	AZ	Van Clark	1990	455
74 4/8	15 1/8	15 1/8	5 5/8	5 5/8	13 3/8	Millard County	UT	Tom Stephenson	1991	455
74 4/8	14 1/8	14 3/8	6 2/8	6 2/8	6 7/8	Rosebud County	MT	Rick Miller	1991	455
74 4/8	13 5/8	13 3/8	6 7/8	6 2/8	9 0/8	Butte County	SD	Gary English	1992	455
74 4/8	15 0/8	15 0/8	6 0/8	6 1/8	12 3/8	Converse County	WY	A. M. Oakes, Jr.	1992	455
74 2/8	13 4/8	13 7/8	5 5/8	5 5/8	8 1/8	Sweet Grass County	MT	Charles Alkire	1964	485
74 2/8	14 5/8	14 6/8	6 3/8	6 2/8	10 3/8	Sioux County	NE	Wayne Scherbarth	1969	485
74 2/8	14 1/8	14 0/8	6 0/8	6 0/8	9 2/8	Moffat County	CO	Bret Thomas Atkins	1981	485
74 2/8	13 2/8	13 2/8	6 7/8	6 7/8	10 2/8	Converse County	WY	Arnie Roytek	1981	485
74 2/8	14 0/8	14 0/8	6 1/8	6 1/8	11 4/8	Carbon County	WY	Scott A. Smith	1981	485
74 2/8	14 2/8	14 2/8	5 3/8	5 3/8	8 5/8	Moffat County	CO	Rich Padula	1982	485

Score	Length of R Horn L		Circumference R of Base L		Greatest Spread	Area	State/ Province	Hunter's Name	Date	Rank
74 2/8	13 1/8	13 0/8	6 2/8	6 2/8	7 6/8	Sweetwater County	WY	Keith Dana	1983	485
74 2/8	14 6/8	14 7/8	6 0/8	5 7/8	9 1/8	Graham County	AZ	Jeran E Montierth	1983	485
74 2/8	14 4/8	14 3/8	5 7/8	5 7/8	9 5/8	Union County	NM	Keith Cheatham	1983	485
74 2/8	13 3/8	13 5/8	6 1/8	6 0/8	11 7/8	Converse County	WY	John Ellas	1983	485
74 2/8	12 6/8	14 4/8	6 4/8	6 4/8	12 7/8	Crook County	OR	Garry Rodakowski	1986	485
74 2/8	13 4/8	13 4/8	6 1/8	6 0/8	12 2/8	Moffat County	CO	Tim Decker	1987	485
74 2/8	14 6/8	14 7/8	6 0/8	6 0/8	13 1/8	Sweetwater County	WY	Marty Talbott	1987	485
74 2/8	14 5/8	14 4/8	5 6/8	5 7/8	10 0/8	Cochise County	AZ	Jim Tomlin	1987	485
74 2/8	15 4/8	15 6/8	5 7/8	5 7/8	10 4/8	Eddy County	NM	Jimmy King	1987	485
74 2/8	15 3/8	15 4/8	6 5/8	6 6/8	13 0/8	Rosebud County	MT	Ricky L. Miller	1987	485
74 2/8	13 4/8	13 5/8	6 4/8	6 4/8	9 0/8	Sweetwater County	WY	Brenda Hatcher	1988	485
74 2/8	15 4/8	14 7/8	6 1/8	6 3/8	13 0/8	Natrona County	WY	George A. Fenton	1988	485
74 2/8	14 4/8	14 7/8	6 0/8	6 0/8	9 3/8	Natrona County	WY	Gerry C. Stinski	1988	485
74 2/8	14 4/8	14 6/8	6 2/8	6 0/8	11 2/8	Washoe County	NV	Robert D. Jeffers	1990	485
74 2/8	14 6/8	15 0/8	5 6/8	5 5/8	9 2/8	Laramie County	WY	Steve Bellis	1990	485
74 2/8	14 4/8	14 6/8	6 2/8	6 3/8	8 7/8	Rich County	UT	Patrick Hogle	1990	485
74 2/8	15 0/8	15 0/8	6 0/8	6 0/8	10 0/8	Billings County	ND	Todd Winczewski	1990	485
74 2/8	15 0/8	15 0/8	5 7/8	5 6/8	7 7/8	Natrona County	WY	Paul A. Anderson	1990	485
74 2/8	14 0/8	13 5/8	6 3/8	6 3/8	7 6/8	Rich County	UT	Robert G. Petersen	1990	485
74 2/8	12 7/8	12 7/8	6 0/8	6 0/8	12 2/8	Johnson County	WY	Gerald V. Shields	1990	485
74 2/8	14 4/8	14 3/8	5 4/8	5 4/8	8 5/8	Carter County	MT	Jamie Byrne	1990	485
74 2/8	14 2/8	14 5/8	6 2/8	6 0/8	8 2/8	Moffat County	CO	John L. Gardner	1991	485
74 2/8	14 0/8	14 0/8	6 2/8	6 3/8	10 0/8	Moffat County	CO	Michael Dziekan	1991	485
74 2/8	14 1/8	13 6/8	6 3/8	6 3/8	11 6/8	Moffat County	CO	Cary Laman	1991	485
74 2/8	13 7/8	14 0/8	6 4/8	6 2/8	8 2/8	Carbon County	WY	Daniel H. House, Jr.	1991	485
74 2/8	14 0/8	14 1/8	6 2/8	6 2/8	11 0/8	Moffat County	CO	Bruno Ammann	1991	485
74 2/8	14 2/8	14 2/8	5 5/8	5 5/8	9 5/8	Converse County	WY	Gene Mathias	1991	485
74 2/8	15 0/8	14 7/8	5 6/8	5 6/8	7 3/8	Natrona County	WY	Ronald Dean Nelson	1991	485
74 2/8	13 3/8	13 2/8	6 3/8	6 3/8	9 7/8	Laramie County	WY	Jim Krawczyk	1992	485
74 2/8	14 2/8	14 3/8	6 7/8	6 6/8	10 0/8	Natrona County	WY	Gary Morse	1992	485
74 2/8	13 1/8	13 1/8	6 5/8	6 4/8	9 3/8	Weld County	CO	Michael J. McArtor	1992	485
74 1/8	14 6/8	14 4/8	6 0/8	6 1/8	14 7/8	Moffat County	CO	Dennis Heitz	1982	522
74 1/8	14 2/8	14 2/8	6 2/8	6 2/8	14 5/8	Toole County	MT	Ryan Winkowitsch	1991	522
74 0/8	14 1/8	13 7/8	6 2/8	6 2/8	9 5/8	Carbon County	WY	James N. Willcox	1977	524
74 0/8	15 2/8	15 5/8	6 2/8	6 3/8	11 4/8	McKinley County	NM	Alfred J. Herrera	1979	524
74 0/8	14 3/8	14 0/8	6 3/8	6 1/8	11 3/8	Jefferson County	ID	Earl Peterson	1980	524
74 0/8	15 0/8	15 1/8	5 5/8	5 5/8	10 5/8	Wallace County	KS	Mike Gilbert	1980	524
74 0/8	16 0/8	15 4/8	5 6/8	5 4/8	8 6/8	Converse County	WY	Frank Moore	1981	524
74 0/8	13 7/8	13 7/8	6 1/8	6 2/8	10 1/8	Moffat County	CO	Randy Sanburg	1981	524
74 0/8	14 5/8	14 4/8	6 4/8	6 2/8	8 6/8	Valley County	MT	Tom Devlin	1984	524
74 0/8	13 4/8	13 3/8	5 7/8	5 6/8	10 4/8	Sweetwater County	WY	Herb Voyles	1985	524
74 0/8	15 1/8	14 6/8	6 1/8	6 1/8	8 4/8	Moffat County	CO	John Cottrell	1986	524
74 0/8	14 1/8	14 0/8	6 4/8	6 4/8	11 7/8	Billings County	ND	Greg Schafer	1986	524
74 0/8	14 2/8	14 3/8	6 2/8	6 0/8	8 7/8	Klamath County	OR	Randall T. Drabandt	1987	524
74 0/8	14 3/8	14 1/8	6 0/8	5 7/8	8 3/8	Moffat County	CO	Bob Bain	1987	524
74 0/8	15 1/8	15 3/8	6 2/8	6 2/8	10 6/8	Sweetwater County	WY	Jackie Simmons	1988	524
74 0/8	14 0/8	13 6/8	5 6/8	5 5/8	11 3/8	Millard County	UT	John G. Homatas	1988	524
74 0/8	15 0/8	14 4/8	6 4/8	6 4/8	8 7/8	Sweetwater County	WY	Norman Lee Bradley	1990	524
74 0/8	14 1/8	13 5/8	6 6/8	6 4/8	12 1/8	Carbon County	WY	Rod Schmidt	1990	524
74 0/8	15 0/8	14 5/8	5 3/8	5 3/8	8 3/8	Moffat County	CO	Glenn Pritchard	1990	524
74 0/8	14 2/8	14 7/8	5 7/8	5 5/8	8 0/8	Carter County	MT	Mark Frank	1990	524
74 0/8	13 1/8	13 2/8	6 4/8	6 3/8	8 5/8	County of 40 Mile	ALB	Brent Van Maarion	1990	524
74 0/8	14 1/8	14 1/8	6 3/8	6 2/8	12 3/8	Sierra County	NM	Peter La Scala	1991	524
74 0/8	14 5/8	14 7/8	6 5/8	6 5/8	9 5/8	Morgan County	UT	Dallas Smith	1991	524
74 0/8	13 1/8	13 4/8	6 5/8	6 4/8	9 3/8	Niobrara County	WY	Tom J. Bruegger	1991	524
74 0/8	13 4/8	13 4/8	6 1/8	6 1/8	7 2/8	Millard County	UT	Craig Bonham	1992	524
74 0/8	14 1/8	14 3/8	5 7/8	5 7/8	11 1/8	Converse County	WY	Louis Cinquegrano	1992	524
73 6/8	14 0/8	14 0/8	6 1/8	6 2/8	13 7/8	Williams County	ND	Robert Halseth	1967	548
73 6/8	14 2/8	14 0/8	6 2/8	6 2/8	10 4/8	Sweetwater County	WY	Dan Winder	1973	548
73 6/8	13 4/8	13 3/8	5 6/8	5 6/8	10 5/8	Sweetwater County	WY	Ellen Lewis	1978	548
73 6/8	14 4/8	15 0/8	6 0/8	6 0/8	10 0/8	Sweetwater County	WY	Clifford White	1978	548
73 6/8	14 2/8	14 1/8	6 1/8	6 0/8	7 7/8	Converse County	WY	Charles Stephens	1980	548
73 6/8	14 2/8	14 1/8	6 5/8	6 4/8	8 5/8	Converse County	WY	Don Schram	1982	548
73 6/8	14 4/8	14 7/8	6 0/8	5 7/8	9 3/8	Sweetwater County	WY	Larry J. Aksamit	1983	548
73 6/8	13 4/8	13 4/8	6 2/8	6 2/8	12 2/8	Carbon County	WY	Willis P. Duhon, Jr.	1983	548
73 6/8	13 3/8	13 4/8	6 3/8	6 1/8	10 1/8	Natrona County	WY	John Priday	1983	548
73 6/8	12 7/8	12 7/8	7 0/8	6 7/8	10 7/8	Natrona County	WY	Pat McAteer	1984	548
73 6/8	14 7/8	15 0/8	5 6/8	5 6/8	14 0/8	Custer County	MT	Marty Penrod	1984	548
73 6/8	15 1/8	15 0/8	5 7/8	5 7/8	10 3/8	Moffat County	CO	Lonny Vanatta	1985	548
73 6/8	14 6/8	14 4/8	6 0/8	6 0/8	10 6/8	Moffat County	CO	Kurt Keskimaki	1986	548

SCORE	LENGTH OF HORN R	L	CIRCUMFERENCE OF BASE R	L	GREATEST SPREAD	AREA	STATE/ PROVINCE	HUNTER'S NAME	DATE	RANK
73 6/8	13 3/8	13 6/8	6 0/8	6 1/8	8 5/8	Sweetwater County	WY	Ryan Roark	1986	548
73 6/8	14 1/8	13 6/8	6 3/8	6 3/8	10 7/8	McKinley County	NM	Terry L. Sanders	1986	548
73 6/8	14 3/8	14 2/8	6 2/8	6 3/8	8 6/8	Lemhi County	ID	Ben Fahnholz	1987	548
73 6/8	15 4/8	15 1/8	6 0/8	6 1/8	11 1/8	Divide County	ND	Kenneth Engelhart	1987	548
73 6/8	14 2/8	14 1/8	6 1/8	6 1/8	10 6/8	Campbell County	WY	Tamas M. Raday	1988	548
73 6/8	14 7/8	14 6/8	6 2/8	6 2/8	10 4/8	Converse County	WY	Bruce Warburg	1988	548
73 6/8	13 7/8	13 6/8	6 0/8	6 1/8	9 6/8	Campbell County	WY	Nick Hengel	1988	548
73 6/8	14 2/8	14 2/8	5 7/8	5 6/8	11 6/8	Moffat County	CO	Ron Rockwell	1988	548
73 6/8	13 7/8	13 7/8	6 0/8	6 0/8	11 4/8	Converse County	WY	Gary De Smidt	1988	548
73 6/8	14 5/8	15 0/8	6 0/8	6 0/8	11 0/8	Carbon County	WY	Rod Schmidt	1989	548
73 6/8	14 3/8	14 2/8	6 2/8	6 2/8	8 1/8	Washoe County	NV	Gregory G. Koehl	1990	548
73 6/8	14 3/8	14 4/8	6 4/8	6 4/8	8 0/8	Natrona County	WY	Ron Niziolek	1990	548
73 6/8	13 6/8	14 1/8	6 2/8	6 0/8	10 3/8	Moffat County	CO	Ron Serwa	1990	548
73 6/8	14 2/8	14 4/8	5 7/8	5 6/8	9 4/8	Cascade County	MT	Dan Holskey	1990	548
73 6/8	14 1/8	14 1/8	5 6/8	5 7/8	10 3/8	Moffat County	CO	Robert L. Syvertson, Jr.	1991	548
73 6/8	14 7/8	14 5/8	5 5/8	5 5/8	11 2/8	Campbell County	WY	Russ Miller	1991	548
73 6/8	14 1/8	14 1/8	6 1/8	6 0/8	13 2/8	Harney County	OR	Donald R. Paulsen	1991	548
73 6/8	13 7/8	13 7/8	6 1/8	6 1/8	10 7/8	Converse County	WY	Jerry Worley	1991	548
73 6/8	14 6/8	15 0/8	6 1/8	5 7/8	8 1/8	Madison County	MT	Doug Stonebraker	1991	548
73 6/8	14 3/8	14 3/8	5 6/8	5 4/8	10 2/8	Campbell County	WY	Bruce Hudalla	1991	548
73 6/8	15 4/8	15 2/8	5 5/8	5 6/8	8 7/8	Rosebud County	MT	Michael J. Kemp	1991	548
73 6/8	13 4/8	13 4/8	6 1/8	6 1/8	9 0/8	Sheridan County	WY	Gerhard Eimer	1991	548
73 5/8	15 1/8	15 4/8	5 6/8	5 6/8	16 1/8	Hettinger County	ND	Scott Wiseman	1991	583
73 4/8	15 4/8	15 1/8	5 6/8	5 7/8	8 3/8	Moffat County	CO	Henry Wichers	1957	584
73 4/8	16 0/8	16 4/8	5 6/8	5 6/8	15 6/8	Guadalupe County	NM	Jack McCaw	1961	584
73 4/8	15 7/8	16 0/8	5 7/8	5 6/8	10 5/8	Coconino County	AZ	Charles Meriwether	1968	584
73 4/8	13 0/8	12 5/8	6 1/8	6 2/8	9 4/8	Carbon County	WY	John Marolt III	1971	584
73 4/8	13 0/8	12 6/8	6 1/8	6 6/8	10 7/8	McLean County	ND	Roy O. Yunker	1971	584
73 4/8	13 2/8	13 2/8	6 7/8	6 6/8	10 0/8	Moffat County	CO	Curtis Lynn	1972	584
73 4/8	15 4/8	15 4/8	5 3/8	5 3/8	12 4/8	Natrona County	WY	Mel Johnson	1981	584
73 4/8	14 4/8	14 6/8	6 2/8	6 3/8	8 3/8	Natrona County	WY	Kim S. Ades	1982	584
73 4/8	13 0/8	13 4/8	6 3/8	6 3/8	10 6/8	Sublette County	WY	Terry Reach	1982	584
73 4/8	15 0/8	15 2/8	5 6/8	5 7/8	8 4/8	Val Marie	SAS	Allan Sykes	1982	584
73 4/8	15 4/8	15 4/8	6 0/8	6 1/8	13 2/8	Fremont County	WY	Dan Lookingbill	1983	584
73 4/8	13 7/8	14 1/8	6 2/8	6 3/8	8 6/8	Sweetwater County	WY	Jim Dougherty	1983	584
73 4/8	14 0/8	13 7/8	6 3/8	6 2/8	9 6/8	Weston County	WY	Dick Kinder	1983	584
73 4/8	15 2/8	15 3/8	5 3/8	5 3/8	9 4/8	Prowers County	CO	Lloyd M. Brown	1984	584
73 4/8	15 1/8	15 0/8	5 4/8	5 4/8	9 0/8	Coconino County	AZ	Richard Ball	1985	584
73 4/8	13 7/8	14 2/8	6 1/8	6 0/8	9 7/8	Converse County	WY	Leland E. Scott	1985	584
73 4/8	15 2/8	15 4/8	5 4/8	5 3/8	12 6/8	Lassen County	CA	Richard K. Hoppis	1986	584
73 4/8	14 7/8	14 4/8	6 2/8	6 3/8	12 4/8	Garfield County	MT	John Fleharty	1986	584
73 4/8	14 1/8	14 5/8	6 2/8	6 1/8	7 7/8	Moffat County	CO	Roger Gipple	1986	584
73 4/8	13 6/8	14 2/8	6 0/8	6 0/8	8 3/8	Carbon County	WY	Rod Schmidt	1987	584
73 4/8	14 2/8	14 6/8	6 0/8	6 0/8	7 3/8	Jefferson County	ID	Lonnie Gilson	1988	584
73 4/8	14 4/8	14 1/8	6 1/8	6 0/8	9 1/8	Fremont County	WY	Jim Thieme	1988	584
73 4/8	15 0/8	14 7/8	6 1/8	6 0/8	7 4/8	Campbell County	WY	Jim Keim	1988	584
73 4/8	13 6/8	13 5/8	6 0/8	5 7/8	9 2/8	Carbon County	WY	Larry N. Perkins	1990	584
73 4/8	14 2/8	14 1/8	6 1/8	6 1/8	8 1/8	Moffat County	CO	Michael LaVan	1990	584
73 4/8	15 0/8	14 5/8	6 4/8	6 4/8	10 4/8	Millard County	UT	Robert Quayle	1990	584
73 4/8	14 6/8	14 6/8	6 2/8	6 1/8	13 3/8	White Pine County	NV	Patrick Fillman	1991	584
73 4/8	12 5/8	12 6/8	6 7/8	6 7/8	8 1/8	Campbell County	WY	Elroy Thorson	1991	584
73 4/8	13 1/8	13 4/8	6 0/8	6 2/8	12 0/8	Dunn County	ND	Keith Kaste	1991	584
73 4/8	15 4/8	15 4/8	6 0/8	5 7/8	14 2/8	Harney County	OR	Charles L. Boatman	1991	584
73 4/8	14 6/8	14 6/8	5 6/8	5 6/8	12 5/8	Harney County	OR	Roger Bersin	1991	584
73 4/8	14 2/8	14 2/8	6 0/8	5 7/8	7 5/8	Platte County	WY	John Stienmetz	1991	584
73 4/8	15 7/8	15 6/8	5 6/8	5 6/8	12 1/8	Mora County	NM	Doug Aikin	1992	584
73 4/8	14 3/8	14 3/8	6 4/8	6 4/8	7 6/8	Washoe County	NV	Trinidad Guillen	1992	584
73 4/8	13 6/8	13 5/8	6 0/8	6 0/8	12 6/8	Grant County	NM	Senovid Perea	1992	584
73 4/8	15 0/8	15 0/8	5 4/8	5 3/8	10 7/8	Millard County	UT	Steven Jackson	1992	584
73 4/8	13 2/8	13 6/8	5 7/8	6 0/8	9 1/8	Malheur County	OR	Fredrick Johnson	1992	584
73 4/8	14 3/8	14 2/8	5 7/8	6 2/8	8 3/8	Fremont County	WY	Gerald S. O'Dean	1992	584
73 2/8	13 0/8	13 1/8	6 6/8	6 4/8	11 3/8	Fremont County	WY	Chuck Kroll	1952	622
73 2/8	11 3/8	11 7/8	6 3/8	6 3/8	11 1/8	Carter County	MT	Benny F. Padden	1960	622
73 2/8	14 2/8	14 2/8	5 2/8	5 2/8	7 5/8	Fergus County	MT	Wayne Miller	1962	622
73 2/8	14 6/8	14 3/8	6 0/8	6 0/8	9 2/8	Garfield County	MT	Paul Brunner	1976	622
73 2/8	13 5/8	13 3/8	6 2/8	6 1/8	9 5/8	Converse County	WY	Abe White	1980	622
73 2/8	15 2/8	15 2/8	5 5/8	5 5/8	8 3/8	Sweetwater County	WY	Randy Gamble	1982	622
73 2/8	15 2/8	15 0/8	5 4/8	5 5/8	9 4/8	Santa Cruz County	AZ	Tracy G. Hardy	1982	622
73 2/8	13 3/8	13 5/8	6 2/8	6 2/8	13 3/8	Fremont County	WY	Bill Lookingbill	1982	622
73 2/8	13 6/8	13 3/8	6 0/8	6 0/8	12 5/8	Musselshell County	MT	Daniel A. Nielsen	1982	622

SCORE	LENGTH OF R HORN L		CIRCUMFERENCE R OF BASE L		GREATEST SPREAD	AREA	STATE/ PROVINCE	HUNTER'S NAME	DATE	RANK
73 2/8	11 5/8	11 5/8	7 3/8	7 1/8	7 3/8	Siskiyou County	CA	Mike Domeyer	1982	622
73 2/8	13 6/8	13 5/8	6 0/8	5 7/8	9 6/8	Natrona County	WY	James I. Shipley, Jr.	1982	622
73 2/8	12 7/8	13 2/8	5 7/8	6 0/8	11 0/8	Moffat County	CO	Jack Cassidy	1983	622
73 2/8	13 2/8	13 3/8	6 3/8	6 2/8	9 3/8	Moffat County	CO	John W. Rose	1983	622
73 2/8	14 2/8	14 4/8	6 1/8	6 1/8	12 1/8	Moffat County	CO	Paul Locey	1983	622
73 2/8	15 4/8	17 0/8	6 1/8	6 0/8	9 6/8	Coconino County	AZ	Randy Fix	1983	622
73 2/8	13 4/8	14 0/8	5 7/8	6 1/8	10 4/8	Moffat County	CO	Charles B. Lanzarone	1983	622
73 2/8	13 7/8	14 0/8	6 2/8	6 2/8	13 4/8	Fremont County	WY	John Priday	1984	622
73 2/8	14 4/8	14 3/8	6 4/8	6 3/8	8 7/8	Converse County	WY	Lee Jernigan	1984	622
73 2/8	14 2/8	14 4/8	6 1/8	6 1/8	10 0/8	Rosebud County	MT	Greg Munther	1986	622
73 2/8	13 4/8	13 6/8	6 3/8	6 3/8	12 2/8	Moffat County	CO	Evans V. Brewster	1986	622
73 2/8	14 3/8	14 3/8	5 7/8	5 7/8	8 2/8	Converse County	WY	Ron Rockwell	1988	622
73 2/8	14 3/8	15 0/8	5 7/8	5 7/8	10 5/8	Washoe County	NV	Larry Burchard	1990	622
73 2/8	14 4/8	14 2/8	6 2/8	6 1/8	7 7/8	Abbey	SAS	Clarence Hughes	1990	622
73 2/8	14 6/8	14 4/8	6 1/8	6 0/8	11 7/8	Fergus County	MT	Jess Knerr	1990	622
73 2/8	13 1/8	13 2/8	6 1/8	6 0/8	9 7/8	Mountrail County	ND	Don Scofield	1990	622
73 2/8	13 2/8	13 5/8	6 2/8	6 2/8	10 5/8	Campbell County	WY	Russell Guerndt	1990	622
73 2/8	14 4/8	14 3/8	5 6/8	5 6/8	10 3/8	Buffalo	ALB	Roger Meyer	1990	622
73 2/8	13 3/8	12 7/8	6 2/8	6 1/8	9 3/8	Musselshell County	MT	Michael James Songer	1990	622
73 2/8	14 0/8	13 7/8	6 0/8	5 7/8	11 1/8	Sweetwater County	WY	Norman Lee Bradley	1991	622
73 2/8	13 0/8	13 0/8	7 2/8	6 6/8	9 1/8	Converse County	WY	Russ Weakland	1991	622
73 2/8	15 1/8	15 2/8	5 7/8	5 7/8	11 4/8	McKenzie County	ND	John H. Holt	1991	622
73 2/8	14 4/8	14 6/8	5 6/8	5 7/8	10 2/8	Val Marie	SAS	Steve Von Hagen	1991	622
73 2/8	15 3/8	15 1/8	5 7/8	5 6/8	11 6/8	Musselshell County	MT	Keith W. Hice	1991	622
73 2/8	13 6/8	13 6/8	6 1/8	6 1/8	12 0/8	Sweetwater County	WY	Fred R. Trujillo	1992	622
73 2/8	14 7/8	14 2/8	5 7/8	5 7/8	8 0/8	Moffat County	CO	Anthony Harrison	1992	622
73 2/8	15 2/8	15 1/8	6 4/8	6 4/8	7 1/8	Butte County	ID	Troy Dale Green	1992	622
73 2/8	13 7/8	14 0/8	6 1/8	6 1/8	11 3/8	Sweetwater County	WY	Richard L. Gasser	1992	622
73 2/8	16 0/8	15 5/8	5 7/8	5 7/8	10 4/8	Sioux County	NE	Orville J. DeVoss	1992	622
73 2/8	13 1/8	13 0/8	6 2/8	6 2/8	9 4/8	Rosebud County	MT	Michael J. Kemp	1992	622
73 1/8	14 2/8	14 4/8	6 4/8	6 3/8	15 7/8	Rosebud County	MT	Wayne Pearson	1986	661
73 1/8	14 5/8	15 0/8	6 1/8	6 0/8	15 1/8	Sweetwater County	WY	Harvey L. Dalton	1988	661
73 0/8	13 5/8	13 5/8	5 3/8	5 3/8	9 6/8	Harding County	SD	Ted G. Carter	1961	663
73 0/8	12 7/8	12 6/8	6 2/8	6 3/8	11 7/8	Stark County	ND	Ronald D. Hauck	1970	663
73 0/8	15 1/8	14 6/8	6 1/8	6 1/8	7 1/8	Converse County	WY	Ed Coy	1976	663
73 0/8	14 0/8	14 2/8	5 4/8	5 4/8	11 6/8	Moffat County	CO	Fred Cornish	1980	663
73 0/8	14 4/8	13 5/8	6 0/8	5 7/8	8 4/8	Klamath County	OR	Tom Tipton	1981	663
73 0/8	13 7/8	13 7/8	6 3/8	6 2/8	11 0/8	Rosebud County	MT	Dan Helm	1982	663
73 0/8	14 1/8	13 2/8	6 5/8	6 5/8	9 1/8	Sioux County	NE	Dick Kohles	1983	663
73 0/8	13 5/8	13 7/8	5 6/8	5 6/8	7 6/8	Converse County	WY	Edward Oswald	1983	663
73 0/8	13 4/8	13 4/8	6 1/8	6 0/8	11 2/8	Sweetwater County	WY	Marty Stubstad	1985	663
73 0/8	14 1/8	13 7/8	5 5/8	5 5/8	9 6/8	Yavapai County	AZ	Christopher R. Jackson	1985	663
73 0/8	14 7/8	12 6/8	6 0/8	10 1/8	9 1/8	Coconino County	AZ	Todd Rice	1987	663
73 0/8	15 3/8	15 2/8	5 4/8	5 4/8	8 2/8	Blaine County	ID	Bruce McStay	1988	663
73 0/8	13 2/8	13 4/8	6 4/8	6 2/8	10 6/8	Moffat County	CO	Garret Decker	1988	663
73 0/8	16 0/8	16 0/8	5 3/8	5 5/8	12 0/8	Coconino County	AZ	Gary Steinmann	1988	663
73 0/8	15 0/8	15 2/8	5 4/8	5 4/8	11 2/8	Converse County	WY	James Gates	1988	663
73 0/8	14 1/8	14 2/8	6 0/8	6 0/8	10 6/8	Sargent County	ND	Dennis Wheeler	1988	663
73 0/8	14 2/8	14 4/8	6 1/8	5 7/8	11 7/8	Washoe County	NV	Daryl Salley	1989	663
73 0/8	13 5/8	13 7/8	5 7/8	5 7/8	8 6/8	Moffat County	CO	James Phelps	1989	663
73 0/8	14 0/8	13 6/8	6 1/8	6 1/8	8 1/8	Sweetwater County	WY	David Urasky	1989	663
73 0/8	15 0/8	15 1/8	5 6/8	5 6/8	12 0/8	Sublette County	WY	David Seaver	1989	663
73 0/8	14 6/8	14 1/8	6 0/8	6 2/8	10 5/8	Sioux County	NE	David Clancy	1989	663
73 0/8	15 4/8	15 0/8	5 5/8	5 5/8	14 7/8	Washoe County	NV	Jeffrey M. Kovac	1990	663
73 0/8	13 3/8	13 5/8	6 4/8	6 5/8	9 5/8	Fremont County	WY	Gary Laya	1990	663
73 0/8	13 1/8	13 3/8	5 7/8	6 1/8	8 2/8	Millard County	UT	Michael Pietropaolo	1990	663
73 0/8	13 5/8	13 4/8	5 6/8	5 6/8	7 1/8	Lake County	OR	Rodney W. Ferry	1990	663
73 0/8	14 0/8	13 5/8	5 7/8	5 7/8	7 6/8	Natrona County	WY	Greg Downs	1990	663
73 0/8	14 1/8	14 4/8	6 2/8	6 2/8	13 4/8	Lassen County	CA	Stan Xavier	1991	663
73 0/8	15 2/8	15 1/8	6 0/8	6 0/8	9 2/8	Rich County	UT	Hugh H. Hogle	1991	663
73 0/8	13 0/8	13 0/8	6 2/8	6 2/8	8 6/8	Converse County	WY	Wayne Nicholson	1991	663
73 0/8	15 0/8	15 1/8	5 7/8	5 6/8	7 2/8	Sioux County	NE	Dave Wray	1991	663
73 0/8	15 2/8	15 3/8	6 0/8	6 0/8	15 7/8	Washoe County	NV	Gregg Tanner	1992	663
73 0/8	14 1/8	14 2/8	6 6/8	6 5/8	8 1/8	Owyhee County	ID	Sam Wells	1992	663
73 0/8	14 6/8	14 4/8	6 4/8	6 4/8	6 5/8	Twin Falls County	ID	Derek Trent	1992	663
73 0/8	13 4/8	13 4/8	6 5/8	6 6/8	11 2/8	Sweetwater County	WY	Neil E. Hanson	1992	663
72 6/8	14 3/8	14 2/8	6 0/8	6 0/8	8 0/8	Washoe County	NV	Lawrence Heward	1973	697
72 6/8	12 1/8	12 1/8	6 6/8	6 6/8	10 6/8	Natrona County	WY	Dennis Spawn	1974	697
72 6/8	15 1/8	14 6/8	5 6/8	5 7/8	9 2/8	Carbon County	WY	I. C. Benjamin	1976	697
72 6/8	14 0/8	14 1/8	5 6/8	5 7/8	10 7/8	Washoe County	NV	Ritchard E. Golden	1977	697

Score	Length of Horn R	L	Circumference of Base R	L	Greatest Spread	Area	State/ Province	Hunter's Name	Date	Rank
72 6/8	12 1/8	11 6/8	6 7/8	6 7/8	9 1/8	Moffat County	CO	Dwight D. Greenwell	1980	697
72 6/8	13 2/8	13 2/8	6 2/8	6 3/8	12 4/8	Moffat County	CO	Albert Ahlrich	1981	697
72 6/8	13 5/8	13 2/8	5 6/8	5 4/8	7 1/8	Moffat County	CO	Lyle Willmarth	1981	697
72 6/8	14 5/8	14 5/8	5 7/8	5 5/8	8 0/8	Washoe County	NV	Gary Furman	1982	697
72 6/8	13 3/8	13 4/8	6 3/8	6 2/8	11 3/8	Moffat County	CO	Thomas H. States	1982	697
72 6/8	13 4/8	13 6/8	5 7/8	5 7/8	9 5/8	Hettinger County	ND	Jeff Watne	1983	697
72 6/8	14 0/8	13 6/8	6 0/8	6 0/8	7 0/8	Moffat County	CO	Jim Dougherty	1983	697
72 6/8	14 0/8	14 0/8	6 2/8	6 1/8	9 0/8	Converse County	WY	Willis Chapman	1983	697
72 6/8	14 6/8	15 1/8	5 6/8	5 6/8	9 0/8	Duchesne County	UT	Delos W. 'Sonny' Kempton	1984	697
72 6/8	14 0/8	14 1/8	5 7/8	5 7/8	7 1/8	Natrona County	WY	Dorian Gilbert	1985	697
72 6/8	13 7/8	13 7/8	5 7/8	6 0/8	13 5/8	Yavapai County	AZ	Richard S. Jones	1985	697
72 6/8	13 6/8	13 7/8	6 1/8	6 0/8	11 7/8	Washington County	CO	Randy Fassler	1986	697
72 6/8	14 1/8	14 2/8	6 4/8	6 3/8	10 5/8	Fergus County	MT	Daniel R. Vogl	1986	697
72 6/8	12 7/8	12 7/8	6 1/8	6 0/8	10 1/8	Coconino County	AZ	Phillip K. Hugh	1987	697
72 6/8	14 0/8	14 0/8	5 4/8	5 3/8	8 4/8	Wheatland County	MT	Bob Radocy	1988	697
72 6/8	15 0/8	15 0/8	5 7/8	5 6/8	9 2/8	Mountrail County	ND	Todd Boechler	1988	697
72 6/8	14 4/8	15 3/8	6 0/8	6 0/8	10 3/8	Sublette County	WY	Steven Hill	1989	697
72 6/8	14 5/8	14 2/8	6 0/8	6 0/8	8 3/8	Meagher County	MT	D. Mitch Kottas	1989	697
72 6/8	13 7/8	13 7/8	5 7/8	5 6/8	11 0/8	Moffat County	CO	Ralph Compton	1990	697
72 6/8	12 3/8	12 4/8	5 6/8	5 6/8	11 3/8	Moffat County	CO	Gary Biles	1990	697
72 6/8	14 4/8	14 0/8	6 0/8	6 0/8	9 2/8	Moffat County	CO	Dave Palonis	1990	697
72 6/8	13 2/8	13 3/8	6 0/8	6 0/8	13 0/8	Moffat County	CO	Pat Grogan	1990	697
72 6/8	13 7/8	14 0/8	6 0/8	6 1/8	11 7/8	Moffat County	CO	Ron Rockwell	1990	697
72 6/8	14 3/8	14 3/8	5 7/8	5 6/8	6 2/8	Campbell County	WY	Gary DeSmidt	1990	697
72 6/8	14 0/8	13 3/8	5 7/8	5 6/8	9 2/8	Natrona County	WY	Kim Cooper	1990	697
72 6/8	15 3/8	15 2/8	5 6/8	5 6/8	11 6/8	Elko County	NV	Jimmie Rebich	1991	697
72 6/8	15 1/8	15 0/8	5 5/8	5 4/8	13 1/8	Box Elder County	UT	Henry O. Davies	1991	697
72 6/8	14 0/8	13 6/8	6 0/8	5 7/8	8 7/8	Campbell County	WY	Mark Yelken	1991	697
72 6/8	13 6/8	13 6/8	6 0/8	6 0/8	8 0/8	Sheridan County	WY	Michael Briganti	1991	697
72 6/8	14 0/8	14 4/8	6 2/8	6 3/8	8 7/8	Beaverhead County	MT	Neal Davis	1991	697
72 6/8	14 2/8	14 3/8	6 6/8	6 5/8	7 5/8	Crook County	WY	John A. Bogucki	1991	697
72 6/8	14 0/8	14 0/8	5 7/8	6 0/8	9 7/8	Humboldt County	NV	Tim Iveson	1992	697
72 6/8	13 3/8	13 0/8	6 1/8	6 0/8	11 2/8	Sweetwater County	WY	Clayton "Karl" Knudsen	1992	697
72 6/8	13 2/8	13 1/8	6 5/8	6 7/8	13 0/8	Laramie County	WY	Wayne Mackey	1992	697
72 6/8	13 5/8	13 6/8	5 6/8	5 6/8	9 6/8	Crook County	WY	Chuck Mead	1992	697
72 6/8	13 7/8	13 3/8	5 7/8	5 6/8	10 6/8	Weld County	CO	James L. Tatro	1992	697
72 6/8	12 5/8	12 4/8	5 7/8	5 6/8	8 7/8	Converse County	WY	Donald Paul Charpentier	1992	697
72 6/8	13 4/8	13 5/8	6 0/8	6 1/8	11 5/8	Converse County	WY	John W. Flies	1992	697
72 6/8	13 2/8	13 2/8	6 6/8	6 6/8	11 1/8	Slope County	ND	Rick A. Schaeffer	1992	697
72 6/8	14 3/8	14 4/8	6 2/8	6 2/8	8 6/8	Albany County	WY	Jack Satterfield, Jr.	1992	697
72 6/8	14 3/8	14 6/8	5 6/8	5 6/8	9 5/8	Yellowstone County	MT	Tom Wulfekuhle	1992	697
72 4/8	13 6/8	13 5/8	7 0/8	7 3/8	9 4/8	Meade County	SD	Wallace C. Neville	1977	742
72 4/8	14 3/8	14 2/8	6 0/8	6 0/8	8 4/8	Jefferson County	ID	Kenny Peterson	1980	742
72 4/8	15 4/8	15 4/8	5 5/8	5 2/8	9 0/8	Converse County	WY	Joseph F. Scheuerman	1982	742
72 4/8	13 6/8	13 3/8	5 7/8	5 7/8	8 1/8	Natrona County	WY	Gilbert Clement	1983	742
72 4/8	13 7/8	13 6/8	5 5/8	5 4/8	10 4/8	Carbon County	WY	Jerome Deaven	1983	742
72 4/8	13 2/8	13 3/8	6 4/8	6 4/8	11 5/8	Natrona County	WY	Tony Lanzarone	1983	742
72 4/8	13 7/8	14 0/8	5 7/8	5 6/8	8 3/8	Converse County	WY	Lee Jernigan	1983	742
72 4/8	13 1/8	13 1/8	6 0/8	5 7/8	8 2/8	Moffat County	CO	Holt Dougherty	1984	742
72 4/8	15 2/8	14 0/8	6 1/8	6 1/8	11 3/8	Modoc County	CA	Tim Sayer	1986	742
72 4/8	14 6/8	14 3/8	5 7/8	5 7/8	8 2/8	Sweetwater County	WY	Kirby Warnock	1986	742
72 4/8	12 7/8	12 3/8	6 4/8	6 2/8	10 5/8	Lemhi County	ID	Matt March, Jr.	1986	742
72 4/8	13 3/8	13 3/8	6 2/8	6 0/8	9 3/8	Fremont County	WY	John Lemke	1986	742
72 4/8	13 5/8	13 5/8	6 3/8	6 2/8	7 5/8	Moffat County	CO	Terry Weimer	1987	742
72 4/8	13 7/8	13 7/8	6 2/8	6 1/8	9 4/8	Moffat County	CO	Judd Cooney	1987	742
72 4/8	13 6/8	13 4/8	5 7/8	5 7/8	9 5/8	Sweetwater County	WY	Stan Godfrey	1987	742
72 4/8	14 3/8	14 6/8	5 7/8	6 1/8	12 6/8	Petroleum County	MT	D. Mitch Kottas	1987	742
72 4/8	14 1/8	13 1/8	6 3/8	6 3/8	6 3/8	Rosebud County	MT	Vic Riggs	1987	742
72 4/8	15 6/8	15 4/8	6 2/8	6 1/8	15 6/8	Converse County	WY	Frank Moore	1988	742
72 4/8	13 4/8	13 2/8	5 5/8	5 4/8	7 4/8	Navajo County	AZ	Mike D. Meyer	1989	742
72 4/8	14 6/8	14 6/8	6 1/8	6 1/8	10 0/8	Stewart Valley	SAS	Sean Ferguson	1989	742
72 4/8	14 3/8	14 1/8	5 3/8	5 3/8	9 6/8	Yavapai County	AZ	Daniel J. Hellman	1989	742
72 4/8	14 6/8	14 5/8	5 3/8	5 3/8	12 5/8	Las Animas County	CO	Bill Swift	1989	742
72 4/8	15 5/8	15 3/8	5 5/8	5 5/8	8 6/8	Natrona County	WY	Michael Ryan	1989	742
72 4/8	14 0/8	13 6/8	5 7/8	5 6/8	11 0/8	Sweetwater County	WY	Bryan Radakovich	1990	742
72 4/8	14 1/8	13 3/8	6 4/8	6 3/8	10 7/8	Sweetwater County	WY	Ted Williams	1990	742
72 4/8	14 4/8	13 4/8	5 6/8	5 5/8	10 2/8	Natrona County	WY	John Comstock, Jr.	1990	742
72 4/8	14 0/8	14 1/8	5 7/8	6 0/8	5 5/8	Washoe County	NV	Terrie Powning	1991	742
72 4/8	13 5/8	14 2/8	6 3/8	6 3/8	12 2/8	Sweetwater County	WY	George R. Koebel	1991	742
72 4/8	14 2/8	14 0/8	5 7/8	5 7/8	11 4/8	Campbell County	WY	Jim Reints	1991	742

PRONGHORN

SCORE	LENGTH OF R HORN L		CIRCUMFERENCE R OF BASE L		GREATEST SPREAD	AREA	STATE/ PROVINCE	HUNTER'S NAME	DATE	RANK
72 4/8	14 0/8	14 2/8	6 0/8	5 7/8	10 1/8	Natrona County	WY	Gerald Gay	1991	742
72 4/8	13 7/8	14 1/8	5 2/8	5 3/8	8 4/8	Converse County	WY	Bruce R. Schoeneweis	1991	742
72 4/8	15 0/8	15 0/8	5 3/8	5 2/8	6 5/8	Converse County	WY	Kenneth D. Musgrove	1991	742
72 4/8	14 3/8	14 3/8	5 7/8	5 6/8	9 4/8	Sioux County	NE	Steve Leichleiter	1991	742
72 4/8	14 5/8	15 0/8	5 7/8	5 7/8	10 0/8	Rosebud County	MT	Gene A. Welle	1991	742
72 4/8	14 0/8	14 4/8	5 6/8	5 6/8	10 6/8	Stark County	ND	Randy A. Heitz	1991	742
72 4/8	12 6/8	12 7/8	6 2/8	6 4/8	9 3/8	Sioux County	NE	Lyle Prell	1991	742
72 4/8	13 3/8	12 6/8	6 7/8	6 7/8	11 5/8	Rich County	UT	Hal Stauff	1991	742
72 4/8	13 7/8	13 7/8	5 5/8	5 5/8	9 3/8	Elko County	NV	Jeremy Loncar	1992	742
72 4/8	13 3/8	13 3/8	6 7/8	6 5/8	9 6/8	Twin Falls County	ID	Ron Klimes	1992	742
72 2/8	13 5/8	13 5/8	6 2/8	6 1/8	11 1/8	Carbon County	WY	William Scoggin	1953	781
72 2/8	14 0/8	14 0/8	6 0/8	5 7/8	10 4/8	Campbell County	WY	K. K. Knickerbocker	1954	781
72 2/8	13 1/8	13 2/8	6 1/8	6 1/8	7 3/8	Campbell County	WY	Carol Wert	1966	781
72 2/8	13 4/8	13 5/8	5 7/8	5 7/8	10 5/8	Carbon County	WY	Harold Boyack	1972	781
72 2/8	15 1/8	14 7/8	5 5/8	5 4/8	8 6/8	Meade County	SD	John S. Anderson	1973	781
72 2/8	14 3/8	14 3/8	6 0/8	5 7/8	9 5/8	Valley County	MT	Wayne Anderson	1975	781
72 2/8	14 1/8	14 0/8	6 2/8	6 3/8	8 5/8	Moffat County	CO	Glenn Pritchard	1977	781
72 2/8	13 7/8	13 6/8	6 1/8	5 7/8	8 0/8	Carbon County	WY	Arthur Heinze	1977	781
72 2/8	13 7/8	13 6/8	6 0/8	6 0/8	7 2/8	Butte County	ID	Dennis A. Gratton	1978	781
72 2/8	14 3/8	14 4/8	6 1/8	6 0/8	12 3/8	Moffat County	CO	Glenn Pritchard	1979	781
72 2/8	14 3/8	14 6/8	5 4/8	5 4/8	13 0/8	Coconino County	AZ	Terry E. Hansen	1981	781
72 2/8	17 0/8	15 5/8	5 4/8	5 5/8	9 0/8	Klamath County	OR	Richard Howell	1981	781
72 2/8	11 3/8	11 3/8	6 3/8	6 3/8	10 4/8	Humboldt County	NV	Verlyn Owens	1981	781
72 2/8	13 3/8	13 2/8	6 1/8	6 1/8	7 3/8	Moffat County	CO	Wayne A. Jensen	1982	781
72 2/8	13 0/8	12 7/8	6 1/8	6 1/8	6 6/8	Converse County	WY	Thomas Brannagan	1982	781
72 2/8	14 4/8	14 5/8	6 0/8	6 2/8	6 6/8	Carbon County	WY	Kim Cooper	1982	781
72 2/8	14 0/8	13 7/8	6 0/8	6 0/8	7 6/8	Morgan County	CO	Barry Smith	1983	781
72 2/8	13 5/8	13 4/8	5 6/8	5 6/8	8 2/8	Moffat County	CO	Dan Liccardi	1983	781
72 2/8	12 7/8	12 7/8	6 3/8	6 1/8	8 0/8	Converse County	WY	Tim Cassidy	1983	781
72 2/8	13 2/8	13 6/8	6 0/8	5 7/8	10 5/8	Carbon County	WY	Paul Persano	1983	781
72 2/8	13 1/8	13 2/8	6 1/8	6 2/8	10 3/8	Carbon County	WY	Larry Hayes	1983	781
72 2/8	13 5/8	13 7/8	5 6/8	5 5/8	11 5/8	Valley County	MT	David Tofte	1983	781
72 2/8	13 0/8	13 0/8	6 1/8	6 2/8	9 3/8	Carbon County	WY	Robert L. Hudman	1984	781
72 2/8	14 7/8	15 0/8	6 0/8	5 7/8	14 1/8	Campbell County	WY	Mike Ballard	1985	781
72 2/8	14 3/8	14 1/8	6 4/8	6 1/8	10 4/8	Lemhi County	ID	Peter Cintorino	1986	781
72 2/8	13 4/8	13 4/8	6 1/8	6 2/8	10 5/8	Natrona County	WY	J. Bruce Ashcroft	1986	781
72 2/8	14 0/8	14 0/8	5 7/8	6 0/8	11 1/8	Sweetwater County	WY	Dale Hill	1987	781
72 2/8	13 0/8	13 2/8	6 3/8	6 3/8	8 7/8	Jackson County	CO	Bruce Ayers	1987	781
72 2/8	15 0/8	14 6/8	5 4/8	5 4/8	8 2/8	Sweetwater County	WY	Michael Chaffin	1987	781
72 2/8	13 1/8	13 2/8	6 0/8	6 0/8	11 0/8	Carter County	MT	Robert Keith Hacker	1987	781
72 2/8	14 4/8	14 0/8	6 0/8	6 2/8	12 4/8	Moffat County	CO	Richard King	1987	781
72 2/8	12 5/8	12 7/8	6 3/8	6 3/8	12 2/8	Fremont County	WY	Kevin Anderson	1989	781
72 2/8	14 3/8	14 3/8	5 5/8	5 3/8	14 2/8	Yavapai County	AZ	Richard Anderson	1989	781
72 2/8	14 4/8	14 6/8	5 2/8	5 2/8	7 5/8	Rio Grande County	CO	James A. Phillips	1989	781
72 2/8	13 7/8	13 6/8	6 3/8	6 4/8	8 4/8	Moffat County	CO	Scott A. Wilson	1990	781
72 2/8	14 3/8	13 6/8	6 0/8	6 0/8	8 6/8	Billings County	ND	William R. Metzger	1990	781
72 2/8	13 3/8	13 6/8	6 0/8	5 7/8	11 4/8	Catron County	NM	Clifford Armstrong	1991	781
72 2/8	14 0/8	13 7/8	6 4/8	6 2/8	9 5/8	Fremont County	WY	Troy Stone	1991	781
72 2/8	15 0/8	15 3/8	5 5/8	5 6/8	9 5/8	Fox Valley	SAS	Floyd Forster	1991	781
72 2/8	14 2/8	14 2/8	5 7/8	5 6/8	7 1/8	Converse County	WY	Kevin Stier	1991	781
72 2/8	14 3/8	14 3/8	5 6/8	5 7/8	11 0/8	Rosebud County	MT	Robert L. Fraley	1991	781
72 2/8	13 4/8	13 5/8	6 3/8	6 5/8	11 0/8	Moffat County	CO	Wayne Depperschmidt	1992	781
72 2/8	14 2/8	14 0/8	6 4/8	6 3/8	10 3/8	Moffat County	CO	J. Keith Chastain	1992	781
72 2/8	13 2/8	13 2/8	6 3/8	6 1/8	8 2/8	Moffat County	CO	Janet George	1992	781
72 2/8	14 6/8	14 7/8	5 6/8	5 6/8	10 0/8	Campbell County	WY	David Vomela	1992	781
72 2/8	13 1/8	12 4/8	6 0/8	5 7/8	12 1/8	Garfield County	MT	Christopher Downs	1992	781
72 0/8	13 4/8	13 5/8	5 6/8	5 7/8	9 4/8	Perkins County	SD	Ben Clark	1974	827
72 0/8	13 3/8	13 3/8	5 6/8	6 0/8	11 2/8	Sioux County	NE	Richard Koons	1974	827
72 0/8	12 7/8	12 4/8	6 7/8	6 7/8	10 1/8	Bennett County	SD	Donald Pierce	1978	827
72 0/8	13 3/8	13 1/8	5 7/8	5 7/8	10 5/8	Butte County	ID	Mike Ellis	1980	827
72 0/8	14 0/8	14 0/8	5 6/8	5 6/8	14 6/8	Converse County	WY	Jack Cassidy	1981	827
72 0/8	13 3/8	13 2/8	6 1/8	5 7/8	6 2/8	Klamath County	OR	Harold McCraven	1981	827
72 0/8	13 3/8	13 1/8	6 0/8	6 0/8	11 0/8	Natrona County	WY	E. W. Onken	1981	827
72 0/8	13 3/8	13 3/8	5 7/8	5 7/8	10 4/8	Moffat County	CO	Gary Smith	1981	827
72 0/8	13 4/8	14 0/8	6 3/8	6 3/8	9 3/8	Carbon County	WY	Charles A. Vande Hei	1982	827
72 0/8	13 7/8	14 1/8	5 6/8	5 7/8	11 2/8	Carbon County	WY	Michael Beckwith	1982	827
72 0/8	14 3/8	14 2/8	5 5/8	5 5/8	8 6/8	Moffat County	CO	Augie Nicolas	1983	827
72 0/8	13 1/8	13 1/8	6 1/8	6 1/8	8 2/8	Converse County	WY	Tom Flemming	1983	827
72 0/8	14 1/8	13 6/8	5 7/8	5 6/8	12 3/8	McCone County	MT	Gary Rueh	1983	827
72 0/8	14 2/8	14 1/8	5 6/8	5 7/8	10 2/8	Carter County	MT	Dean Irwin	1983	827

(Continued)

SCORE	LENGTH OF R HORN L		CIRCUMFERENCE R OF BASE L		GREATEST SPREAD	AREA	STATE/ PROVINCE	HUNTER'S NAME	DATE	RANK
72 0/8	14 6/8	14 6/8	5 3/8	5 3/8	10 6/8	Tide Lake	ALB	Adrian Erickson	1983	827
72 0/8	14 3/8	14 6/8	5 5/8	5 5/8	10 4/8	Washoe County	NV	C. J. Coleman	1984	827
72 0/8	13 2/8	13 1/8	6 0/8	6 0/8	8 7/8	Moffat County	CO	Lynn Pariso	1985	827
72 0/8	13 6/8	13 3/8	6 2/8	6 2/8	8 1/8	Carbon County	UT	Kenny E. Leo	1986	827
72 0/8	14 5/8	15 0/8	5 5/8	5 5/8	11 6/8	Moffat County	CO	Roger Gipple	1987	827
72 0/8	13 4/8	13 2/8	6 4/8	6 3/8	11 4/8	Box Elder County	UT	Gary E. Craner	1987	827
72 0/8	13 6/8	13 5/8	6 0/8	6 1/8	13 5/8	Rosebud County	MT	Dr. Kevin Brewer	1987	827
72 0/8	14 2/8	14 3/8	5 6/8	5 6/8	7 2/8	Humboldt County	NV	Carl J. Corey	1988	827
72 0/8	14 2/8	14 3/8	5 6/8	5 7/8	12 1/8	Moffat County	CO	Tom Bartholomew	1988	827
72 0/8	13 2/8	13 0/8	6 1/8	6 2/8	8 6/8	Carbon County	WY	Darrus D. Martin	1988	827
72 0/8	13 7/8	13 7/8	5 2/8	5 2/8	9 2/8	Moffat County	CO	M. R. James	1988	827
72 0/8	13 2/8	13 4/8	6 0/8	6 0/8	10 1/8	Grant County	ND	Mark Bogert	1988	827
72 0/8	12 5/8	12 5/8	5 7/8	5 7/8	10 6/8	Wallace County	KS	Roger Potter	1988	827
72 0/8	13 0/8	12 7/8	6 2/8	6 2/8	10 0/8	Klamath County	OR	Bob Baley	1989	827
72 0/8	14 0/8	13 7/8	6 1/8	6 1/8	9 5/8	Campbell County	WY	Dave Vomela	1989	827
72 0/8	13 5/8	13 4/8	6 1/8	6 2/8	7 6/8	Uinta County	WY	Drew Dockstader	1989	827
72 0/8	13 7/8	13 3/8	6 3/8	6 0/8	9 6/8	Uinta County	WY	Scott Dockstader	1989	827
72 0/8	14 4/8	14 3/8	5 7/8	6 0/8	9 1/8	Moffat County	CO	Keith Hensel	1989	827
72 0/8	12 1/8	12 2/8	6 4/8	6 3/8	8 6/8	Carbon County	WY	Dean Stebner	1990	827
72 0/8	12 7/8	12 7/8	6 2/8	6 0/8	10 6/8	Converse County	WY	Kelvin W. Lancaster	1990	827
72 0/8	12 5/8	13 0/8	7 0/8	7 0/8	11 4/8	Rosebud County	MT	Gary C. Wolf	1990	827
72 0/8	14 0/8	14 0/8	5 3/8	5 3/8	11 4/8	Converse County	WY	Roy W. Mackey	1990	827
72 0/8	14 7/8	14 5/8	5 6/8	5 6/8	9 6/8	Elko County	NV	Jimmy Cooney	1991	827
72 0/8	13 2/8	13 2/8	5 6/8	6 0/8	8 6/8	Park County	WY	Craig Childress	1991	827
72 0/8	13 7/8	13 7/8	5 7/8	5 6/8	9 5/8	Sweetwater County	WY	R. E. "Bud" Watson	1991	827
72 0/8	13 7/8	13 7/8	5 5/8	5 5/8	11 4/8	Navajo County	AZ	Charles P. Cooley	1991	827
72 0/8	13 1/8	12 7/8	6 0/8	6 0/8	11 1/8	Laramie County	WY	Gary W. Brimm	1991	827
72 0/8	14 3/8	14 2/8	6 0/8	6 0/8	8 2/8	Sioux County	NE	Gaylen Rogers	1991	827
72 0/8	13 3/8	13 4/8	6 0/8	6 0/8	12 4/8	Washoe County	NV	Gary Wright	1992	827
72 0/8	13 1/8	13 6/8	6 0/8	6 0/8	9 6/8	Union County	NM	Dave Conrad	1992	827
72 0/8	13 4/8	13 7/8	5 6/8	5 6/8	9 3/8	Saguache County	CO	Mark Wuerthele	1992	827
72 0/8	13 4/8	13 6/8	6 5/8	6 4/8	11 6/8	Sioux County	NE	Jim Ritz	1992	827
72 0/8	14 4/8	14 3/8	6 1/8	6 1/8	10 4/8	Converse County	WY	Richard Wheeler	1992	827
71 7/8	15 4/8	16 0/8	6 1/8	6 0/8	16 3/8	Washoe County	NV	Gene A. Jones	1991	874
71 6/8	14 2/8	14 1/8	5 6/8	5 7/8	10 5/8	Klamath County	OR	Jerry Phillips	1977	875
71 6/8	13 5/8	13 3/8	6 1/8	6 0/8	11 0/8	Natrona County	WY	George Kegler	1980	875
71 6/8	14 1/8	14 3/8	5 7/8	5 6/8	14 5/8	Custer County	ID	Gene Nelson	1981	875
71 6/8	14 2/8	14 5/8	5 6/8	5 6/8	10 6/8	Converse County	WY	Ron Spratling	1981	875
71 6/8	13 0/8	13 0/8	5 5/8	5 4/8	8 7/8	Bowman County	ND	Donald C. Hestekin	1982	875
71 6/8	13 1/8	13 1/8	5 4/8	5 4/8	10 6/8	Converse County	WY	Robert R. Vance	1982	875
71 6/8	13 5/8	14 4/8	5 7/8	5 6/8	10 2/8	Carbon County	WY	Don Carter	1983	875
71 6/8	12 5/8	12 7/8	6 3/8	6 1/8	6 6/8	Converse County	WY	Jim Nielsen	1983	875
71 6/8	14 3/8	14 5/8	5 7/8	5 7/8	11 6/8	Fremont County	WY	Jim Walters	1983	875
71 6/8	13 6/8	13 4/8	6 4/8	6 4/8	14 2/8	Converse County	WY	James B. Evans, Jr.	1983	875
71 6/8	14 6/8	14 6/8	5 7/8	5 7/8	10 5/8	Powder River County	MT	Ron Thompson	1983	875
71 6/8	14 5/8	14 1/8	6 2/8	6 1/8	7 4/8	Campbell County	WY	Mike Ingold	1985	875
71 6/8	13 6/8	13 4/8	6 3/8	6 2/8	9 1/8	Sweetwater County	WY	James E. Summerall	1986	875
71 6/8	13 4/8	13 6/8	5 5/8	5 4/8	10 4/8	Moffat County	CO	Denny Williamson	1987	875
71 6/8	14 0/8	13 7/8	5 3/8	5 4/8	8 7/8	Natrona County	WY	Scott Privette	1987	875
71 6/8	13 6/8	14 0/8	5 6/8	5 6/8	12 3/8	Rosebud County	MT	Daniel Hudek	1987	875
71 6/8	13 5/8	14 0/8	6 0/8	6 0/8	8 2/8	Converse County	WY	Frank Moore	1987	875
71 6/8	13 3/8	13 0/8	5 7/8	5 7/8	6 5/8	Lassen County	CA	Tom Devlin	1988	875
71 6/8	14 0/8	14 2/8	5 5/8	5 6/8	10 2/8	Moffat County	CO	David Greenwalt	1988	875
71 6/8	12 1/8	13 7/8	6 0/8	6 0/8	9 5/8	Las Animas County	CO	Bill Swift	1988	875
71 6/8	13 4/8	13 4/8	6 1/8	6 0/8	10 4/8	Cutbank Creek	ALB	Darrell Peters	1988	875
71 6/8	14 4/8	13 6/8	5 4/8	5 7/8	11 1/8	Moffat County	CO	David Travaglio	1989	875
71 6/8	16 0/8	16 2/8	6 1/8	6 0/8	10 6/8	Bowman County	ND	Gene D. Davis	1989	875
71 6/8	13 0/8	12 3/8	6 3/8	6 2/8	8 3/8	Rosebud County	MT	Kent Kaufman	1989	875
71 6/8	14 5/8	14 4/8	5 6/8	5 5/8	9 5/8	Washoe County	NV	George F. Howard	1990	875
71 6/8	14 6/8	14 7/8	6 4/8	6 5/8	19 1/8	Colfax County	NM	Ron Serwa	1990	875
71 6/8	13 6/8	14 1/8	6 1/8	6 1/8	9 4/8	Carbon County	WY	Sam Amberson	1990	875
71 6/8	14 2/8	14 6/8	5 5/8	5 4/8	11 3/8	Lincoln County	WY	Jeff Blain	1990	875
71 6/8	13 5/8	13 6/8	5 6/8	5 5/8	8 4/8	Rosebud County	MT	Jesse Meyer	1990	875
71 6/8	15 5/8	15 7/8	5 1/8	5 2/8	7 4/8	Golden Valley County	ND	Wayne Streitz	1990	875
71 6/8	14 2/8	14 3/8	6 0/8	6 0/8	8 6/8	Fergus County	MT	Ronald Eugene Sanford, Jr	1990	875
71 6/8	14 0/8	13 6/8	5 3/8	5 4/8	10 0/8	Converse County	WY	Tom Mulchay	1990	875
71 6/8	14 6/8	14 4/8	5 4/8	5 4/8	12 3/8	Orion	ALB	Gunter Lemke	1990	875
71 6/8	15 1/8	15 0/8	6 0/8	6 0/8	11 0/8	Hudspeth County	TX	James E. Borron	1990	875
71 6/8	14 3/8	14 3/8	5 5/8	5 5/8	8 0/8	Larimer County	CO	Michael J. McArtor	1991	875
71 6/8	13 6/8	13 7/8	6 3/8	6 3/8	11 2/8	Moffat County	CO	R. Tim Reed	1991	875

MINIMUM SCORE 64

(Continued)

SCORE	LENGTH OF R HORN L		CIRCUMFERENCE R OF BASE L		GREATEST SPREAD	AREA	STATE/ PROVINCE	HUNTER'S NAME	DATE	RANK
71 6/8	13 4/8	13 4/8	5 7/8	5 7/8	9 6/8	Yavapai County	AZ	James Monroe Haines	1991	875
71 6/8	13 5/8	13 4/8	6 3/8	6 4/8	8 2/8	Custer County	ID	Matt March	1991	875
71 6/8	14 1/8	13 5/8	6 3/8	6 3/8	10 7/8	Rich County	UT	Peter E. Paulds, Jr.	1991	875
71 6/8	14 2/8	14 0/8	6 2/8	6 1/8	12 1/8	Converse County	WY	Jack Schatz	1991	875
71 6/8	13 3/8	13 7/8	6 0/8	6 0/8	8 0/8	Campbell County	WY	Dr. Robert Edward Speegle	1991	875
71 6/8	14 1/8	13 7/8	5 7/8	5 7/8	14 7/8	Humboldt County	NV	Tony Reinolds	1992	875
71 6/8	14 4/8	14 0/8	6 0/8	5 7/8	8 5/8	Sweetwater County	WY	Jed R. Ashworth	1992	875
71 6/8	14 2/8	14 3/8	5 7/8	5 6/8	8 5/8	Union County	NM	Jeff Fitts	1992	875
71 6/8	13 2/8	13 1/8	6 4/8	6 1/8	12 2/8	Moffat County	CO	Bruce Eggenberger	1992	875
71 6/8	14 0/8	13 7/8	5 6/8	5 7/8	8 7/8	Rich County	UT	Guy G. Fitzgerald	1992	875
71 6/8	13 7/8	14 0/8	5 7/8	6 0/8	10 6/8	Moffat County	CO	Dave Parri	1992	875
71 6/8	13 3/8	13 0/8	5 4/8	5 7/8	12 6/8	Sublette County	WY	Phil N. Skinner	1992	875
71 6/8	13 5/8	13 7/8	6 3/8	6 3/8	8 6/8	Natrona County	WY	Ed Gawel	1992	875
71 6/8	14 1/8	14 1/8	5 7/8	5 7/8	11 0/8	Buffalo	ALB	Dewain Ollenberger	1992	875
71 6/8	13 4/8	13 3/8	7 0/8	6 4/8	12 4/8	Campbell County	WY	Paul Vomela	1992	875
71 4/8	13 6/8	13 4/8	6 4/8	6 2/8	10 0/8	Carbon County	WY	Bill Scoggin	1957	926
71 4/8	14 7/8	14 7/8	6 0/8	6 2/8	13 5/8	Moffat County	CO	Henry Wichers	1959	926
71 4/8	13 4/8	13 3/8	6 0/8	6 0/8	8 2/8	Tripp County	SD	Dan Smith	1965	926
71 4/8	14 2/8	14 0/8	5 4/8	5 4/8	9 6/8	Carbon County	WY	Jerry Bowen	1976	926
71 4/8	14 1/8	14 0/8	6 2/8	6 3/8	9 1/8	Sweetwater County	WY	Val Jones	1978	926
71 4/8	14 4/8	14 4/8	5 6/8	5 5/8	9 7/8	Albany County	WY	Tom Tietz	1978	926
71 4/8	12 6/8	12 6/8	5 6/8	5 6/8	8 2/8	Carbon County	WY	Ronald J. Wedge	1978	926
71 4/8	13 0/8	13 0/8	6 0/8	5 6/8	9 3/8	Converse County	WY	Mike Burley	1980	926
71 4/8	12 4/8	12 1/8	6 4/8	6 3/8	9 7/8	Carbon County	WY	Bruce Butkiewicz	1980	926
71 4/8	13 1/8	13 6/8	6 1/8	6 2/8	11 4/8	Yavapai County	AZ	Peter C. Knagge	1980	926
71 4/8	13 6/8	13 6/8	6 0/8	6 0/8	6 6/8	Sheridan County	WY	David Shoop	1980	926
71 4/8	12 6/8	12 5/8	5 7/8	5 6/8	10 0/8	Natrona County	WY	David Manthei	1981	926
71 4/8	12 7/8	12 4/8	6 7/8	6 4/8	12 7/8	Carbon County	WY	Dennis Crank	1982	926
71 4/8	15 0/8	15 0/8	5 7/8	5 6/8	10 6/8	Perkins County	SD	H. Melvin Dutton	1982	926
71 4/8	13 0/8	13 0/8	5 6/8	5 7/8	9 4/8	Delta County	CO	Doug McCauley	1983	926
71 4/8	13 3/8	13 4/8	6 2/8	6 1/8	9 2/8	Carbon County	WY	Bob Moore	1983	926
71 4/8	12 6/8	13 0/8	6 0/8	6 1/8	10 0/8	Perkins County	SD	H. Melvin Dutton	1983	926
71 4/8	14 0/8	14 1/8	6 1/8	6 1/8	6 5/8	Grand Forks	ALB	Ian Sangster	1983	926
71 4/8	13 2/8	13 1/8	6 2/8	6 1/8	7 5/8	Converse County	WY	George Hecker	1984	926
71 4/8	12 0/8	14 3/8	6 3/8	6 2/8	8 1/8	Petroleum County	MT	Ben Maughan	1984	926
71 4/8	15 3/8	15 2/8	5 7/8	6 0/8	15 2/8	Moffat County	CO	Richard King	1985	926
71 4/8	13 7/8	13 6/8	6 0/8	5 7/8	9 3/8	Beaverhead County	MT	Ron Oswald	1985	926
71 4/8	14 6/8	14 3/8	5 5/8	5 5/8	12 1/8	Humboldt County	NV	Martin J. Larraneta, Jr.	1986	926
71 4/8	13 0/8	13 0/8	6 2/8	6 0/8	9 1/8	Moffat County	CO	Terry Weimer	1986	926
71 4/8	14 0/8	14 2/8	5 5/8	5 6/8	9 5/8	Sublette County	WY	Jim Carr	1986	926
71 4/8	13 6/8	14 0/8	6 0/8	5 7/8	11 0/8	Converse County	WY	Scott Wilke	1986	926
71 4/8	14 2/8	14 1/8	6 1/8	5 7/8	8 7/8	Mountrail County	ND	Todd W. Boechler	1986	926
71 4/8	14 1/8	14 6/8	5 6/8	5 5/8	8 4/8	Coconino County	AZ	Tim Edwards	1987	926
71 4/8	14 1/8	13 7/8	5 7/8	6 0/8	11 6/8	Moffat County	CO	Mike Ottenbacher	1987	926
71 4/8	12 1/8	12 1/8	6 0/8	6 1/8	9 1/8	Sublette County	WY	Gaylynn Turner	1988	926
71 4/8	14 2/8	14 4/8	6 1/8	6 0/8	10 4/8	Moffat County	CO	Robert A. Hermann	1988	926
71 4/8	13 6/8	13 6/8	6 0/8	6 0/8	10 7/8	Buffalo	ALB	Stuart Sinclair-Smith	1988	926
71 4/8	13 5/8	13 6/8	6 1/8	6 0/8	9 6/8	Moffat County	CO	Michael Magana	1989	926
71 4/8	12 4/8	12 7/8	6 1/8	6 2/8	9 7/8	Moffat County	CO	James VanAlstine	1989	926
71 4/8	13 4/8	13 4/8	6 0/8	5 7/8	9 0/8	Billings County	ND	Micheal Ness	1989	926
71 4/8	13 2/8	14 4/8	5 7/8	5 6/8	10 2/8	Yavapai County	AZ	Richard M Compau	1989	926
71 4/8	14 4/8	14 1/8	5 5/8	5 4/8	11 5/8	Foremost	ALB	Kelly Kerner	1989	926
71 4/8	14 7/8	13 4/8	5 7/8	5 6/8	11 0/8	Jackson County	CO	Lance Barnica	1990	926
71 4/8	14 3/8	13 4/8	5 7/8	5 7/8	9 5/8	Dunn County	ND	Rick Stein	1990	926
71 4/8	13 3/8	13 4/8	6 1/8	6 2/8	9 5/8	Twin Falls County	ID	John Stevens	1991	926
71 4/8	13 1/8	13 4/8	6 2/8	6 2/8	12 7/8	Owyhee County	ID	Steve Stephenson	1991	926
71 4/8	13 7/8	14 0/8	6 0/8	6 0/8	8 6/8	Converse County	WY	Charles R. Cramer	1991	926
71 4/8	13 6/8	14 0/8	6 1/8	6 1/8	9 0/8	Campbell County	WY	Wayne Jossart	1991	926
71 4/8	13 5/8	13 4/8	6 4/8	6 4/8	11 5/8	Converse County	WY	Steve Gorr	1991	926
71 4/8	13 7/8	14 1/8	5 6/8	5 7/8	10 0/8	Lake County	OR	Phillip L. Severson	1992	926
71 4/8	14 6/8	14 2/8	5 7/8	5 1/8	9 0/8	Klamath County	OR	Frank Sanders	1992	926
71 4/8	13 3/8	13 0/8	6 2/8	6 2/8	9 6/8	Carbon County	WY	Jim Kurth	1992	926
71 4/8	14 3/8	14 6/8	5 6/8	5 5/8	12 5/8	County of 40 Mile	ALB	Murray T. Campbell	1992	926
71 3/8	13 2/8	13 6/8	6 7/8	6 4/8	14 5/8	Converse County	WY	Tommy L. Mackey	1990	974
71 2/8	14 4/8	14 2/8	5 7/8	5 7/8	8 1/8	Musselshell County	MT	A. A. Anderson	1960	975
71 2/8	14 3/8	14 5/8	5 4/8	5 4/8	13 1/8	Perkins County	SD	Elwood Patterson	1961	975
71 2/8	15 0/8	15 3/8	5 3/8	5 2/8	9 7/8	Natrona County	WY	Doug Pope	1976	975
71 2/8	14 5/8	14 7/8	5 2/8	5 2/8	12 0/8	McLean County	ND	Leo N. Patch	1977	975
71 2/8	12 7/8	12 6/8	5 7/8	5 7/8	9 1/8	Converse County	WY	G. Merrill Jones	1980	975
71 2/8	14 2/8	13 4/8	6 1/8	6 2/8	8 3/8	Sweetwater County	WY	Terry Walbridge	1980	975

PRONGHORN

SCORE	LENGTH OF R HORN L		CIRCUMFERENCE R OF BASE L		GREATEST SPREAD	AREA	STATE/ PROVINCE	HUNTER'S NAME	DATE	RANK
71 2/8	13 3/8	13 3/8	5 5/8	5 6/8	8 3/8	Natrona County	WY	Hayden Allen, Jr.	1981	975
71 2/8	13 4/8	13 1/8	6 2/8	6 2/8	8 4/8	Sweetwater County	WY	Lyle R. Prell	1981	975
71 2/8	12 3/8	12 3/8	6 4/8	6 5/8	9 6/8	Sargent County	ND	Terry Hopewell	1982	975
71 2/8	13 4/8	13 5/8	6 0/8	5 5/8	12 0/8	Natrona County	WY	Rick Landeis	1983	975
71 2/8	13 0/8	13 2/8	6 2/8	6 2/8	10 7/8	Converse County	WY	Jack M. Conner	1983	975
71 2/8	15 0/8	15 1/8	5 7/8	5 6/8	8 4/8	Washoe County	NV	Robert L. Brooks, Jr.	1984	975
71 2/8	12 2/8	12 1/8	6 0/8	6 0/8	9 5/8	Converse County	WY	Jack M. Conner	1984	975
71 2/8	14 4/8	14 6/8	6 1/8	5 6/8	8 0/8	Powder River County	MT	Steve Kramer	1984	975
71 2/8	13 1/8	12 6/8	5 6/8	6 2/8	11 6/8	Johnson County	WY	Glenn Tappen	1984	975
71 2/8	14 3/8	13 2/8	6 0/8	5 7/8	11 6/8	Hot Springs County	WY	Mike Conner	1985	975
71 2/8	13 4/8	13 4/8	6 1/8	6 0/8	11 6/8	Natrona County	WY	Kelley Swift	1985	975
71 2/8	13 3/8	13 4/8	6 2/8	6 2/8	8 7/8	Sweetwater County	WY	David S. Petrie	1987	975
71 2/8	14 3/8	14 4/8	5 7/8	5 7/8	11 2/8	Tide Lake	ALB	Archie Nesbitt	1987	975
71 2/8	13 2/8	13 1/8	6 4/8	6 3/8	11 3/8	Moffat County	CO	Randy Lamdin	1988	975
71 2/8	13 0/8	13 1/8	5 1/8	5 1/8	11 2/8	White Pine County	NV	Steven P. Newberger	1988	975
71 2/8	13 4/8	13 5/8	6 1/8	6 0/8	8 6/8	Moffat County	CO	Daniel L. Tekavec	1988	975
71 2/8	14 2/8	14 2/8	6 1/8	6 1/8	10 0/8	Converse County	WY	David L. Mosher	1988	975
71 2/8	13 4/8	13 3/8	5 5/8	5 7/8	11 6/8	Modoc County	CA	Gary M. Gentile	1988	975
71 2/8	13 2/8	12 6/8	6 2/8	6 2/8	9 6/8	Lassen County	CA	John Diedrich	1988	975
71 2/8	12 7/8	12 7/8	6 2/8	6 1/8	11 2/8	Natrona County	WY	Michael Ryan	1988	975
71 2/8	13 6/8	13 2/8	5 7/8	5 7/8	9 7/8	Carbon County	WY	Willis Duhon	1989	975
71 2/8	13 3/8	12 6/8	6 1/8	6 0/8	8 1/8	Converse County	WY	Edward W. Vetter	1989	975
71 2/8	12 7/8	13 0/8	6 0/8	6 0/8	9 6/8	Harding County	SD	Daniel Dietrich	1989	975
71 2/8	13 1/8	13 2/8	5 4/8	5 3/8	9 6/8	Socorro County	NM	Jose Romero	1990	975
71 2/8	13 6/8	13 6/8	6 2/8	6 2/8	6 2/8	Moffat County	CO	Michael P. McCarty	1990	975
71 2/8	13 4/8	13 3/8	6 3/8	6 2/8	9 5/8	Uinta County	WY	Earl Sutherland	1990	975
71 2/8	13 4/8	13 1/8	6 2/8	6 2/8	7 6/8	Johnson County	WY	Joe Coleman	1990	975
71 2/8	13 0/8	13 0/8	6 3/8	6 3/8	12 2/8	Forty Mile County	ALB	Darrell Hougen	1990	975
71 2/8	12 7/8	13 2/8	6 0/8	5 7/8	10 7/8	Converse County	WY	Dave Vander Vorst	1990	975
71 2/8	13 5/8	13 1/8	6 0/8	6 1/8	9 2/8	Harding County	SD	Jamie Byrne	1990	975
71 2/8	14 6/8	14 0/8	6 4/8	6 4/8	12 2/8	Washoe County	NV	David Niehaus	1991	975
71 2/8	13 4/8	13 6/8	6 5/8	6 5/8	10 3/8	Converse County	WY	Steve Duranso	1991	975
71 2/8	13 2/8	13 1/8	6 4/8	6 2/8	7 3/8	Rosebud County	MT	Everett M. Morris	1991	975
71 2/8	14 1/8	14 1/8	5 7/8	5 6/8	9 1/8	Moffat County	CO	Ken Assmus	1992	975
71 2/8	14 1/8	13 7/8	5 4/8	5 4/8	9 6/8	Millard County	UT	Jim Fowler	1992	975
71 2/8	13 6/8	13 5/8	5 7/8	6 0/8	8 3/8	Sweetwater County	WY	Brian Kerr	1992	975
71 2/8	14 1/8	14 4/8	6 0/8	5 7/8	5 1/8	Twin Falls County	ID	Vincent Trent	1992	975
71 2/8	13 1/8	13 4/8	6 4/8	6 3/8	11 0/8	Sioux County	NE	Tommy M. Brown	1992	975
71 2/8	14 2/8	14 3/8	5 5/8	5 6/8	8 3/8	Billings County	ND	Jeff Dudgeon	1992	975
71 2/8	13 3/8	13 2/8	6 0/8	6 0/8	8 6/8	Campbell County	WY	Bob Pozner	1992	975
71 2/8	13 3/8	13 3/8	6 2/8	6 1/8	10 1/8	Converse County	WY	Richard Pippenger	1992	975
71 1/8	15 2/8	15 0/8	6 0/8	6 1/8	16 3/8	Modoc County	CA	Richard Wormington	1986	1,022
71 1/8	13 0/8	12 7/8	6 3/8	6 4/8	13 5/8	Carbon County	WY	Randy Long	1988	1,022
71 1/8	13 7/8	13 7/8	5 7/8	5 6/8	14 6/8	Crook County	OR	Clint Hall	1991	1,022
71 0/8	12 7/8	12 7/8	6 1/8	6 1/8	12 6/8	Washoe County	NV	Roger Iveson	1980	1,025
71 0/8	14 0/8	14 1/8	5 6/8	5 7/8	8 3/8	Converse County	WY	Eugene Smith, Jr.	1980	1,025
71 0/8	13 2/8	13 0/8	6 0/8	6 0/8	11 5/8	Converse County	WY	Mike Butler	1981	1,025
71 0/8	13 7/8	13 5/8	6 0/8	6 0/8	7 3/8	Sweetwater County	WY	Vaughn Cross	1981	1,025
71 0/8	14 1/8	14 1/8	5 7/8	5 7/8	13 2/8	Moffat County	CO	Scott Kelley	1981	1,025
71 0/8	14 7/8	14 7/8	5 6/8	5 6/8	8 1/8	Modoc County	CA	Jeff Scheetz	1982	1,025
71 0/8	13 5/8	13 4/8	5 6/8	5 6/8	8 4/8	Converse County	WY	Ted J. Jaycox	1982	1,025
71 0/8	14 4/8	14 5/8	5 5/8	5 4/8	9 3/8	McKenzie County	ND	Mark D. Hughes	1982	1,025
71 0/8	13 1/8	13 4/8	6 4/8	6 4/8	9 6/8	Moffat County	CO	Lance Cussons	1983	1,025
71 0/8	13 3/8	13 3/8	5 7/8	5 7/8	8 1/8	Natrona County	WY	Wade L. Carstens	1983	1,025
71 0/8	14 0/8	14 1/8	6 0/8	6 0/8	9 1/8	Garfield County	MT	Bruce W. Blauvelt	1983	1,025
71 0/8	13 6/8	13 4/8	5 6/8	5 6/8	10 4/8	White Pine County	NV	Simo O. Ahlgren	1984	1,025
71 0/8	14 4/8	14 2/8	5 6/8	5 6/8	9 2/8	Sweetwater County	WY	Earl Kennedy	1986	1,025
71 0/8	13 4/8	13 3/8	6 1/8	6 0/8	8 0/8	Stark County	ND	Daniel W. Johnson	1987	1,025
71 0/8	14 5/8	14 7/8	5 2/8	5 2/8	9 6/8	Moffat County	CO	Bruce Hallowell	1988	1,025
71 0/8	14 5/8	14 6/8	5 7/8	5 7/8	10 2/8	Millard County	UT	Len Cardinale	1988	1,025
71 0/8	13 2/8	13 3/8	5 6/8	5 6/8	9 3/8	Converse County	WY	Ron Foote	1988	1,025
71 0/8	14 0/8	13 5/8	5 6/8	5 6/8	13 1/8	Converse County	WY	Roy G. Burton	1988	1,025
71 0/8	13 5/8	13 4/8	6 4/8	6 2/8	10 2/8	Natrona County	WY	Rickey E. Morse	1989	1,025
71 0/8	15 0/8	14 5/8	5 5/8	5 6/8	8 6/8	Musselshell County	MT	Darren Parker	1989	1,025
71 0/8	14 3/8	14 3/8	5 7/8	5 6/8	11 2/8	Valley County	MT	Ty Milne	1989	1,025
71 0/8	13 2/8	13 2/8	5 4/8	5 5/8	9 5/8	Moffat County	CO	Dennis Newton	1990	1,025
71 0/8	15 3/8	15 0/8	5 5/8	5 5/8	9 2/8	Converse County	WY	Paul Sieg	1990	1,025
71 0/8	13 7/8	13 5/8	6 0/8	6 0/8	7 0/8	Converse County	WY	Jeff Fitts	1991	1,025
71 0/8	13 7/8	14 0/8	5 6/8	5 5/8	11 5/8	Rosebud County	MT	Anthony Hess	1991	1,025
71 0/8	12 7/8	12 7/8	6 2/8	6 1/8	11 3/8	Converse County	WY	J. Todd Payne	1991	1,025

SCORE	LENGTH OF R HORN L		CIRCUMFERENCE R OF BASE L		GREATEST SPREAD	AREA	STATE/ PROVINCE	HUNTER'S NAME	DATE	RANK
71 0/8	13 7/8	13 5/8	5 7/8	6 0/8	10 2/8	Buffalo	ALB	Andy P. Charchun	1991	1,025
71 0/8	13 6/8	13 7/8	5 6/8	5 6/8	9 7/8	Garfield County	MT	Randal R. Mayes	1991	1,025
71 0/8	14 2/8	14 2/8	5 7/8	5 5/8	12 6/8	Converse County	WY	Barry J. Smith	1991	1,025
71 0/8	12 6/8	13 2/8	6 1/8	6 1/8	8 3/8	Moffat County	CO	Marvin Weible	1992	1,025
71 0/8	13 0/8	13 2/8	6 4/8	6 2/8	11 1/8	Fremont County	WY	Tim Downs	1992	1,025
71 0/8	13 1/8	13 0/8	6 0/8	6 0/8	6 6/8	Converse County	WY	Mark Graham	1992	1,025
71 0/8	14 4/8	14 4/8	6 0/8	6 1/8	9 3/8	Malheur County	OR	Rick Martin	1992	1,025
71 0/8	12 7/8	14 0/8	6 1/8	6 1/8	8 4/8	Rosebud County	MT	Donald Kemkes	1992	1,025
71 0/8	14 0/8	14 0/8	5 5/8	5 5/8	9 1/8	Campbell County	WY	Tim Stahman	1992	1,025
71 0/8	14 2/8	14 2/8	5 5/8	5 6/8	7 4/8	Sheridan County	WY	Billy S. Huff	1992	1,025
70 7/8	14 3/8	14 0/8	5 3/8	5 7/8	16 0/8	Clark County	ID	Shane Bird	1988	1,061
70 6/8	14 7/8	15 2/8	5 5/8	5 4/8	10 3/8	Washoe County	NV	Frank M. Davis	1967	1,062
70 6/8	13 2/8	13 2/8	6 3/8	6 2/8	9 6/8	Washoe County	NV	Gordon A. Nicholson	1972	1,062
70 6/8	12 5/8	12 4/8	5 5/8	5 4/8	9 0/8	Natrona County	WY	Bernard R. Giacoletto	1973	1,062
70 6/8	11 2/8	11 2/8	6 0/8	6 0/8	10 1/8	Natrona County	WY	Jerry Zanandrea	1976	1,062
70 6/8	13 4/8	13 6/8	5 7/8	5 6/8	9 7/8	Lemhi County	ID	Alan Monroe	1979	1,062
70 6/8	13 0/8	13 3/8	5 6/8	5 5/8	7 4/8	Stanley County	SD	Rick Ray	1979	1,062
70 6/8	13 6/8	14 0/8	5 4/8	5 3/8	12 1/8	Converse County	WY	Russell Hull	1980	1,062
70 6/8	14 0/8	14 0/8	5 4/8	5 4/8	12 6/8	Converse County	WY	Frank Moore	1980	1,062
70 6/8	14 3/8	14 1/8	5 4/8	5 3/8	12 5/8	Tillard Ranch	WY	Charles A. Myers	1981	1,062
70 6/8	13 4/8	13 4/8	6 2/8	6 2/8	10 1/8	Moffat County	CO	Mike Miller	1981	1,062
70 6/8	15 0/8	15 1/8	5 5/8	5 4/8	10 4/8	Klamath County	OR	Paul D. Lewis	1982	1,062
70 6/8	12 5/8	12 5/8	5 7/8	5 7/8	9 4/8	Converse County	WY	Steve Woodman	1982	1,062
70 6/8	13 7/8	13 7/8	6 0/8	6 1/8	10 4/8	Butte County	ID	Larry A. Wilde	1983	1,062
70 6/8	13 5/8	13 3/8	5 6/8	5 6/8	9 4/8	Converse County	WY	Dan Naccarto	1983	1,062
70 6/8	13 1/8	13 1/8	6 0/8	5 6/8	11 1/8	Natrona County	WY	Don Wilson	1983	1,062
70 6/8	16 2/8	15 4/8	5 1/8	5 1/8	9 6/8	Golden Valley County	ND	Thomas S. Lunski	1983	1,062
70 6/8	13 7/8	13 7/8	5 3/8	5 2/8	9 3/8	Moffat County	CO	Darryl Quidort	1984	1,062
70 6/8	15 1/8	14 6/8	6 1/8	6 0/8	12 7/8	Lassen County	CA	Wayne Goodrich	1985	1,062
70 6/8	12 6/8	14 3/8	5 7/8	5 6/8	11 3/8	Slope County	ND	Todd Seymanski	1985	1,062
70 6/8	14 3/8	14 2/8	5 7/8	5 6/8	11 1/8	Sweetwater County	WY	Craig Boheler	1986	1,062
70 6/8	13 0/8	13 3/8	6 3/8	6 1/8	10 2/8	Jefferson County	ID	Tony Hyde	1986	1,062
70 6/8	14 0/8	13 6/8	5 7/8	5 7/8	7 0/8	Moffat County	CO	Mike Ottenbacher	1986	1,062
70 6/8	13 1/8	13 4/8	6 2/8	6 0/8	11 0/8	Rosebud County	MT	Gary Olsen	1986	1,062
70 6/8	13 0/8	12 6/8	6 4/8	6 4/8	10 0/8	Billings County	ND	Ron Tudahl	1987	1,062
70 6/8	13 0/8	12 6/8	6 4/8	6 3/8	12 2/8	Moffat County	CO	Steven Wilson	1988	1,062
70 6/8	14 2/8	14 2/8	5 4/8	5 3/8	7 4/8	Slope County	ND	Scott Bradac	1988	1,062
70 6/8	14 0/8	14 0/8	5 5/8	5 5/8	11 0/8	Converse County	WY	David M. Ackland, Jr.	1988	1,062
70 6/8	13 7/8	13 7/8	5 5/8	5 4/8	7 1/8	Converse County	WY	Kevin "Krauty" Krautkrame	1988	1,062
70 6/8	12 6/8	12 6/8	6 3/8	6 1/8	8 4/8	Campbell County	WY	Bob Austin	1988	1,062
70 6/8	14 0/8	13 6/8	5 7/8	5 6/8	10 5/8	Moffat County	CO	Wayne Depperschmidt	1989	1,062
70 6/8	13 2/8	13 1/8	5 5/8	5 4/8	9 7/8	Millard County	UT	David B. Nielsen	1989	1,062
70 6/8	13 1/8	13 1/8	6 2/8	6 1/8	7 3/8	Billings County	ND	Al Zeller	1989	1,062
70 6/8	14 0/8	13 4/8	5 6/8	5 6/8	10 4/8	Moffat County	CO	Dan Gillenwater	1989	1,062
70 6/8	13 3/8	13 4/8	6 3/8	6 3/8	8 6/8	Moffat County	CO	Mike Boland	1989	1,062
70 6/8	12 7/8	13 6/8	5 7/8	5 6/8	11 1/8	Hughes County	SD	Lyle Goodall	1989	1,062
70 6/8	14 0/8	14 0/8	6 0/8	6 0/8	7 7/8	Uinta County	WY	Douglas Shelby	1990	1,062
70 6/8	14 2/8	14 2/8	5 7/8	5 7/8	8 4/8	Moffat County	CO	Marvin Cochran	1990	1,062
70 6/8	13 4/8	13 4/8	5 7/8	6 0/8	7 6/8	Moffat County	CO	Dennis Modlin	1990	1,062
70 6/8	12 5/8	13 2/8	6 3/8	6 3/8	9 7/8	Natrona County	WY	Edward J. Brennan	1990	1,062
70 6/8	14 1/8	14 1/8	5 6/8	5 6/8	10 0/8	Modoc County	CA	John Garr	1991	1,062
70 6/8	14 2/8	14 4/8	6 1/8	6 1/8	12 7/8	Meade County	SD	Dan Limmer	1991	1,062
70 6/8	13 2/8	13 3/8	6 1/8	6 1/8	11 2/8	White Pine County	NV	Brett North	1992	1,062
70 6/8	13 6/8	13 4/8	5 7/8	5 7/8	6 6/8	Owyhee County	ID	Brian Hunter Heck	1992	1,062
70 6/8	13 6/8	14 0/8	6 2/8	6 1/8	12 4/8	Carbon County	WY	Boyd Burbank	1992	1,062
70 6/8	14 3/8	14 1/8	5 6/8	5 6/8	11 0/8	Converse County	WY	John North	1992	1,062
70 6/8	12 4/8	12 3/8	5 6/8	5 6/8	7 6/8	Billings County	ND	Jeff Hapala	1992	1,062
70 6/8	13 7/8	13 7/8	5 7/8	6 0/8	8 5/8	Fergus County	MT	Kelly Norskog	1992	1,062
70 6/8	13 2/8	13 1/8	5 6/8	5 5/8	9 5/8	Harding County	SD	John Simpson	1992	1,062
70 5/8	13 0/8	13 0/8	6 0/8	6 0/8	14 1/8	Natrona County	WY	Kim Cooper	1987	1,110
70 4/8	14 1/8	14 2/8	5 6/8	5 5/8	13 6/8	Custer County	MT	Bob Torgerson	1964	1,111
70 4/8	12 3/8	12 3/8	5 7/8	5 6/8	7 5/8	Ward County	ND	Bob Torgerson	1964	1,111
70 4/8	12 5/8	12 4/8	6 0/8	6 0/8	10 5/8	Sweetwater County	WY	Vern A. Butler	1973	1,111
70 4/8	14 2/8	14 1/8	5 5/8	5 4/8	8 2/8	Fall River County	SD	Noel Feather, Jr.	1975	1,111
70 4/8	13 0/8	13 0/8	6 4/8	6 4/8	9 3/8	Clark County	ID	Larry Cross	1977	1,111
70 4/8	14 5/8	14 0/8	6 4/8	6 1/8	9 6/8	Meade County	SD	Floyd McElroy	1977	1,111
70 4/8	13 6/8	13 4/8	6 1/8	6 1/8	11 6/8	Grant County	NE	Albert Kant	1978	1,111
70 4/8	13 2/8	13 1/8	5 4/8	5 3/8	7 5/8	Clark County	ID	Ron Johnson	1980	1,111
70 4/8	13 3/8	13 5/8	6 0/8	6 0/8	13 7/8	Sweetwater County	WY	Victor Organ	1980	1,111
70 4/8	13 0/8	13 1/8	6 1/8	6 1/8	9 1/8	Area 55	WY	Walter Walbridge	1980	1,111

SCORE	LENGTH OF R HORN L		CIRCUMFERENCE R OF BASE L		GREATEST SPREAD	AREA	STATE/ PROVINCE	HUNTER'S NAME	DATE	RANK
70 4/8	13 4/8	13 6/8	5 7/8	5 7/8	11 4/8	Converse County	WY	James D. Miller	1981	1,111
70 4/8	15 0/8	15 0/8	5 3/8	5 3/8	8 7/8	Perkins County	SD	John Pollreisz	1981	1,111
70 4/8	13 7/8	13 5/8	5 6/8	5 6/8	9 1/8	Natrona County	WY	Gordon W. Stone	1981	1,111
70 4/8	13 3/8	13 0/8	6 1/8	6 1/8	9 3/8	Hughes County	SD	Darrel L. Reinke	1982	1,111
70 4/8	14 2/8	14 3/8	5 5/8	5 5/8	8 6/8	Natrona County	WY	Ray Smith	1982	1,111
70 4/8	12 4/8	13 1/8	6 3/8	6 3/8	8 6/8	Moffat County	CO	Janet Schreur	1983	1,111
70 4/8	13 5/8	13 5/8	5 6/8	5 7/8	7 7/8	Converse County	WY	Al Sullivan	1983	1,111
70 4/8	13 1/8	13 1/8	6 2/8	6 0/8	10 4/8	Converse County	WY	Rick Poe	1983	1,111
70 4/8	12 7/8	13 1/8	5 6/8	5 6/8	8 3/8	Moffat County	CO	Gary McCain	1983	1,111
70 4/8	13 4/8	13 4/8	5 7/8	5 6/8	8 2/8	Converse County	WY	Rick Walker	1983	1,111
70 4/8	13 1/8	13 0/8	5 7/8	6 0/8	8 3/8	Moffat County	CO	H. R. 'Rusty' Neely	1984	1,111
70 4/8	13 2/8	13 3/8	6 0/8	6 0/8	8 3/8	Converse County	WY	Anthony Ruggeri	1984	1,111
70 4/8	12 4/8	13 0/8	6 4/8	6 4/8	11 1/8	Converse County	WY	Robin Klemme	1984	1,111
70 4/8	12 1/8	12 3/8	6 0/8	6 0/8	10 6/8	Converse County	WY	John M. McAteer	1984	1,111
70 4/8	13 2/8	13 2/8	6 1/8	6 1/8	11 6/8	Modoc County	CA	Robert L. Smith	1986	1,111
70 4/8	15 1/8	15 7/8	5 6/8	5 5/8	15 0/8	Lassen County	CA	Tom Gordon	1986	1,111
70 4/8	14 3/8	13 0/8	5 7/8	5 7/8	11 3/8	San Miguel County	CO	Bill Wilson	1986	1,111
70 4/8	13 5/8	13 6/8	5 3/8	5 3/8	11 6/8	Moffat County	CO	Glenn Pritchard	1986	1,111
70 4/8	13 1/8	13 2/8	6 0/8	6 0/8	8 3/8	Brewster County	TX	Michael M. Reamy	1986	1,111
70 4/8	13 2/8	12 7/8	6 5/8	6 4/8	9 2/8	Sweetwater County	WY	Brenda Hatcher	1987	1,111
70 4/8	13 3/8	13 2/8	6 4/8	6 4/8	9 7/8	Converse County	WY	Eric Wayne Noble	1987	1,111
70 4/8	13 7/8	13 6/8	5 6/8	5 4/8	11 1/8	Presidio County	TX	K. D. Sandifer	1987	1,111
70 4/8	14 7/8	15 0/8	5 3/8	5 3/8	12 5/8	Sweetwater County	WY	Don Waechtler	1988	1,111
70 4/8	13 2/8	13 2/8	6 0/8	6 0/8	11 0/8	Campbell County	WY	Gary D. Johansen	1988	1,111
70 4/8	13 6/8	13 1/8	5 6/8	6 1/8	6 7/8	Humboldt County	NV	Dr. John F. Lohse	1989	1,111
70 4/8	13 6/8	14 0/8	5 7/8	6 0/8	10 4/8	Washoe County	NV	David A. Heffner	1989	1,111
70 4/8	13 2/8	13 3/8	6 3/8	6 3/8	8 5/8	Carbon County	WY	Robert R. Sherman	1989	1,111
70 4/8	13 6/8	13 6/8	5 7/8	5 7/8	9 3/8	Millard County	UT	Stan Xavier	1989	1,111
70 4/8	14 1/8	14 1/8	5 6/8	5 6/8	13 6/8	Hot Springs County	WY	Jim Fraizer	1989	1,111
70 4/8	13 2/8	13 4/8	6 4/8	6 5/8	11 4/8	Converse County	WY	Clem Grimaldi	1989	1,111
70 4/8	13 2/8	12 7/8	6 0/8	6 0/8	7 6/8	Natrona County	WY	Ohne Raasch	1989	1,111
70 4/8	14 6/8	14 7/8	5 4/8	5 4/8	7 4/8	Bowman County	ND	Nolan A. Johnson	1989	1,111
70 4/8	13 0/8	13 2/8	6 1/8	6 0/8	8 2/8	Moffat County	CO	Steve Overstreet	1990	1,111
70 4/8	13 4/8	13 0/8	6 0/8	6 0/8	8 6/8	Uinta County	WY	Kyle D. Hansen	1990	1,111
70 4/8	12 7/8	12 7/8	6 4/8	6 4/8	8 7/8	Natrona County	WY	Kevin Davis	1990	1,111
70 4/8	14 3/8	14 3/8	6 0/8	6 0/8	11 5/8	Douglas County	NV	Mark Custis	1991	1,111
70 4/8	13 1/8	13 2/8	5 6/8	5 7/8	6 3/8	Moffat County	CO	Kurt W. Keskimaki	1991	1,111
70 4/8	14 1/8	14 0/8	5 4/8	5 2/8	14 0/8	Divide County	ND	Robert M. Brunner	1991	1,111
70 4/8	12 4/8	12 4/8	5 6/8	5 7/8	8 7/8	Golden Valley County	ND	Terry Buechler	1991	1,111
70 4/8	14 3/8	14 3/8	5 5/8	5 6/8	6 4/8	Moffat County	CO	Ken Hoehn	1992	1,111
70 4/8	12 4/8	12 6/8	6 2/8	6 3/8	9 5/8	Fremont County	WY	Lyle R. Prell	1992	1,111
70 4/8	13 6/8	13 6/8	5 5/8	5 4/8	8 4/8	Converse County	WY	Robert Radford	1992	1,111
70 4/8	13 5/8	13 6/8	6 0/8	6 0/8	9 3/8	Fergus County	MT	Jerry Knerr	1992	1,111
70 4/8	14 3/8	14 3/8	5 3/8	5 3/8	14 1/8	McKenzie County	ND	Vernon D. Hahn	1992	1,111
70 2/8	15 2/8	15 4/8	5 4/8	5 3/8	11 5/8	Natrona County	WY	Larry J. Colombo	1970	1,165
70 2/8	12 7/8	12 7/8	6 1/8	6 1/8	12 5/8	Converse County	WY	Edward Coy	1972	1,165
70 2/8	14 0/8	14 0/8	5 6/8	5 6/8	13 7/8	Butte County	ID	Dale Dunn	1973	1,165
70 2/8	12 6/8	13 0/8	6 3/8	6 3/8	9 0/8	Dawes County	NE	Bruce Troester	1973	1,165
70 2/8	12 2/8	12 2/8	5 5/8	5 5/8	9 2/8	Saguache County	CO	Sandra Scheid	1975	1,165
70 2/8	13 2/8	13 4/8	5 6/8	5 6/8	11 0/8	Saguache County	CO	Tom Tietz	1977	1,165
70 2/8	13 6/8	13 6/8	6 6/8	6 4/8	10 6/8	Sweetwater County	WY	Vaughn Cross	1980	1,165
70 2/8	14 2/8	11 7/8	6 1/8	6 1/8	10 0/8	Converse County	WY	Anthony Wells	1980	1,165
70 2/8	13 7/8	13 5/8	6 0/8	6 0/8	9 3/8	Moffat County	CO	Dave Skiff	1981	1,165
70 2/8	13 7/8	13 4/8	6 1/8	6 0/8	14 1/8	Moffat County	CO	Gene Moore	1981	1,165
70 2/8	13 1/8	13 2/8	6 2/8	6 1/8	8 1/8	Natrona County	WY	Jim Plemmons	1981	1,165
70 2/8	14 2/8	14 3/8	5 5/8	5 5/8	9 6/8	Lassen County	CA	B. Jensen/F. Searle	1981	1,165
70 2/8	12 6/8	12 7/8	6 0/8	5 7/8	9 6/8	Carbon County	WY	George Raab	1982	1,165
70 2/8	14 0/8	14 0/8	5 7/8	5 6/8	10 2/8	Converse County	WY	Brad Johnson	1982	1,165
70 2/8	13 6/8	14 1/8	6 1/8	6 0/8	12 2/8	Natrona County	WY	Tim Sturm	1982	1,165
70 2/8	12 4/8	12 4/8	5 5/8	5 7/8	10 6/8	Moffat County	CO	Wendy Decker	1983	1,165
70 2/8	12 2/8	12 2/8	6 0/8	6 0/8	10 3/8	Converse County	WY	Ron Montross	1983	1,165
70 2/8	13 0/8	13 4/8	5 6/8	5 7/8	10 6/8	Moffat County	CO	Rick Kralicek	1983	1,165
70 2/8	13 4/8	13 6/8	5 7/8	5 5/8	9 7/8	Sweetwater County	WY	Judd Cooney	1983	1,165
70 2/8	13 2/8	13 5/8	5 5/8	5 5/8	10 6/8	Converse County	WY	Rocky Chisholm	1983	1,165
70 2/8	13 0/8	13 3/8	5 6/8	5 6/8	11 6/8	Sweetwater County	WY	Michael R. Westvang	1984	1,165
70 2/8	12 6/8	13 2/8	5 7/8	5 7/8	11 1/8	Carbon County	WY	Ken Bean	1984	1,165
70 2/8	13 5/8	13 6/8	6 1/8	5 7/8	10 3/8	McCone County	MT	Frank Kasten III	1984	1,165
70 2/8	13 0/8	12 6/8	6 0/8	6 0/8	12 1/8	Sweetwater County	WY	David Wells	1985	1,165
70 2/8	13 0/8	12 7/8	6 2/8	6 2/8	9 3/8	Converse County	WY	Theodore C. Dzienis	1985	1,165
70 2/8	13 6/8	14 1/8	6 1/8	6 1/8	8 7/8	Powder River County	MT	Stephen J. Jaworski	1985	1,165

SCORE	LENGTH OF R HORN L		CIRCUMFERENCE R OF BASE L		GREATEST SPREAD	AREA	STATE/ PROVINCE	HUNTER'S NAME	DATE	RANK
70 2/8	15 0/8	14 7/8	5 1/8	5 1/8	9 6/8	Las Animas County	CO	Bill Swift	1985	1,165
70 2/8	13 5/8	13 4/8	5 6/8	5 7/8	8 6/8	Sweetwater County	WY	Darren L. Shirley	1986	1,165
70 2/8	13 2/8	13 5/8	6 0/8	6 1/8	8 0/8	Billings County	ND	Randy Bakken	1986	1,165
70 2/8	13 3/8	13 3/8	5 6/8	5 5/8	9 2/8	Carbon County	WY	Duane Hicks	1987	1,165
70 2/8	13 3/8	13 3/8	6 0/8	5 7/8	9 5/8	Converse County	WY	James H. Miller	1987	1,165
70 2/8	13 4/8	14 0/8	6 0/8	6 2/8	10 2/8	Lincoln County	NV	Michael W. Zech	1987	1,165
70 2/8	14 6/8	14 2/8	5 5/8	5 6/8	9 2/8	Humboldt County	NV	Clayton J. Larsen	1988	1,165
70 2/8	13 4/8	13 5/8	6 0/8	5 7/8	11 0/8	Moffat County	CO	Jim Tatro	1988	1,165
70 2/8	13 4/8	12 6/8	5 7/8	5 6/8	11 2/8	Slope County	ND	Todd Seymanski	1988	1,165
70 2/8	14 2/8	14 2/8	5 6/8	5 6/8	8 5/8	Converse County	WY	M. R. James	1988	1,165
70 2/8	14 1/8	14 0/8	5 5/8	5 4/8	10 4/8	Chouteau County	MT	Jack A. Clouse	1988	1,165
70 2/8	14 0/8	13 6/8	6 0/8	6 0/8	9 1/8	Converse County	WY	Joel M. Riotto	1989	1,165
70 2/8	13 1/8	13 2/8	6 0/8	5 7/8	10 7/8	Carbon County	WY	Donald P. Peel	1989	1,165
70 2/8	14 1/8	14 1/8	5 4/8	5 4/8	11 3/8	Petroleum County	MT	Clark Jenner	1989	1,165
70 2/8	14 5/8	15 1/8	5 4/8	5 3/8	7 7/8	Klamath County	OR	Randy Carter	1990	1,165
70 2/8	12 4/8	12 5/8	6 0/8	6 0/8	9 4/8	McKenzie County	ND	Alan Smith	1990	1,165
70 2/8	12 1/8	12 0/8	6 1/8	6 1/8	7 6/8	Campbell County	WY	Craig Boheler	1990	1,165
70 2/8	14 0/8	13 7/8	5 6/8	5 5/8	10 2/8	Carbon County	WY	Tim Cuthriell	1991	1,165
70 2/8	12 4/8	12 4/8	6 2/8	6 0/8	7 5/8	Sweetwater County	WY	Carl G. Esterly	1991	1,165
70 2/8	14 2/8	14 0/8	5 5/8	5 4/8	12 0/8	Coconino County	AZ	Kevin Robinson	1991	1,165
70 2/8	12 5/8	13 1/8	6 2/8	6 2/8	10 5/8	Sublette County	WY	Stephen Kotz	1991	1,165
70 2/8	14 6/8	15 2/8	5 5/8	5 4/8	8 3/8	Converse County	WY	Charles Peters	1991	1,165
70 2/8	14 6/8	14 3/8	6 0/8	5 6/8	10 3/8	Converse County	WY	Roger Brittain	1991	1,165
70 2/8	13 0/8	12 6/8	5 7/8	6 0/8	7 6/8	Niobrara County	WY	Thomas D. Mackowski	1991	1,165
70 2/8	13 6/8	14 2/8	5 7/8	5 6/8	10 0/8	Campbell County	WY	Al Ratajesak	1991	1,165
70 2/8	13 2/8	13 1/8	6 1/8	6 1/8	8 2/8	Converse County	WY	Michael E. Zimmerman	1991	1,165
70 2/8	12 5/8	12 7/8	6 3/8	6 3/8	9 0/8	Converse County	WY	Myron Jochmann	1991	1,165
70 2/8	14 7/8	14 4/8	5 6/8	5 6/8	9 6/8	Sioux County	NE	Steve Neujahr	1991	1,165
70 2/8	15 1/8	14 2/8	5 6/8	5 6/8	11 1/8	McKenzie County	ND	Travis Wollan	1991	1,165
70 2/8	14 6/8	15 0/8	5 5/8	5 5/8	8 1/8	Twin Falls County	ID	John Stevens	1992	1,165
70 2/8	13 7/8	14 2/8	5 7/8	5 6/8	7 6/8	Moffat County	CO	Conrad Anderson	1992	1,165
70 2/8	13 5/8	13 6/8	6 1/8	6 1/8	9 2/8	Natrona County	WY	David L. Willis	1992	1,165
70 2/8	15 5/8	15 4/8	5 2/8	5 3/8	10 5/8	Perkins County	SD	James J. Willard	1992	1,165
70 0/8	13 1/8	13 1/8	6 1/8	6 1/8	13 1/8	Butte County	SD	Wayne Wanhanen	1961	1,224
70 0/8	13 6/8	13 7/8	5 6/8	5 6/8	11 4/8	Garfield County	MT	Paul M. Ramsey	1963	1,224
70 0/8	14 0/8	14 0/8	5 3/8	5 3/8	9 5/8	Harding County	SD	Ira Hilburn	1964	1,224
70 0/8	13 1/8	13 4/8	5 6/8	5 6/8	9 0/8	Morton County	ND	Paul R. Shannon	1971	1,224
70 0/8	13 4/8	13 2/8	6 1/8	6 0/8	12 5/8	Pennington County	SD	Thomas Huitfeldt	1974	1,224
70 0/8	13 1/8	13 2/8	5 7/8	5 6/8	8 2/8	Dawes County	NE	Allan Mintken	1974	1,224
70 0/8	13 4/8	13 7/8	5 4/8	5 5/8	9 0/8	Rio Grande County	CO	Arthur M. Davis	1975	1,224
70 0/8	14 5/8	14 6/8	5 6/8	5 5/8	7 1/8	Humboldt County	NV	Wally Lopey	1981	1,224
70 0/8	12 5/8	12 3/8	5 4/8	5 4/8	7 5/8	Moffat County	CO	Charles A. Nicholas	1981	1,224
70 0/8	13 7/8	13 6/8	5 5/8	5 5/8	12 5/8	Sweetwater County	WY	Gerri Risley	1981	1,224
70 0/8	13 2/8	13 2/8	6 0/8	5 7/8	10 5/8	Natrona County	WY	Mark A. Smith	1981	1,224
70 0/8	13 6/8	13 6/8	5 4/8	5 4/8	8 7/8	White Pine County	NV	Richard Fillman	1982	1,224
70 0/8	13 0/8	13 0/8	5 7/8	5 6/8	12 4/8	Converse County	WY	Steven A. Wolff	1982	1,224
70 0/8	13 6/8	14 1/8	5 7/8	5 7/8	8 1/8	Carbon County	WY	Ron Breitsprecher	1982	1,224
70 0/8	13 0/8	13 4/8	6 0/8	5 7/8	14 0/8	Carbon County	WY	Ron Stacey	1983	1,224
70 0/8	13 7/8	13 6/8	5 4/8	5 5/8	10 3/8	Sargent County	ND	Terry Freehauf	1983	1,224
70 0/8	13 1/8	13 1/8	5 7/8	5 6/8	9 4/8	Converse County	WY	Dean Taylor	1983	1,224
70 0/8	13 5/8	13 5/8	5 7/8	5 5/8	9 2/8	Perkins County	SD	Jeffery Rieker	1983	1,224
70 0/8	13 3/8	12 5/8	6 1/8	6 1/8	8 0/8	Rosebud County	MT	Daniel A. Nielsen	1983	1,224
70 0/8	13 2/8	13 2/8	6 0/8	6 0/8	7 2/8	Custer County	ID	Brad Chilton	1984	1,224
70 0/8	14 5/8	14 0/8	5 6/8	5 6/8	5 7/8	Moffat County	CO	Dale Drilling	1984	1,224
70 0/8	13 4/8	13 4/8	5 5/8	5 4/8	9 4/8	Moffat County	CO	Todd Clyncke	1984	1,224
70 0/8	12 4/8	12 4/8	5 7/8	5 7/8	8 3/8	Converse County	WY	Bill Doemland	1984	1,224
70 0/8	13 4/8	13 4/8	5 4/8	5 3/8	11 6/8	Slope County	ND	Gene D. Davis	1984	1,224
70 0/8	12 0/8	12 0/8	6 1/8	6 0/8	7 4/8	Elko County	NV	Ted Simpson	1985	1,224
70 0/8	13 3/8	13 0/8	6 1/8	6 0/8	8 6/8	Converse County	WY	David Stuhr	1985	1,224
70 0/8	13 0/8	12 7/8	5 4/8	5 3/8	10 1/8	Converse County	WY	Dean Herschede	1985	1,224
70 0/8	13 2/8	13 4/8	6 0/8	6 0/8	9 7/8	Carter County	MT	James Jessen	1985	1,224
70 0/8	14 6/8	15 0/8	5 5/8	5 5/8	14 5/8	Carbon County	WY	David Pawlicki	1986	1,224
70 0/8	13 1/8	13 1/8	5 6/8	5 6/8	7 6/8	Converse County	WY	John Unser	1986	1,224
70 0/8	13 2/8	13 1/8	6 2/8	6 2/8	9 6/8	Moffat County	CO	John Hunter	1987	1,224
70 0/8	13 3/8	13 7/8	6 1/8	6 1/8	9 0/8	Converse County	WY	Bruce Warberg	1987	1,224
70 0/8	14 2/8	14 0/8	5 3/8	5 3/8	9 4/8	Moffat County	CO	Roger Gipple	1988	1,224
70 0/8	14 4/8	14 0/8	5 4/8	5 2/8	9 4/8	Converse County	WY	George A. Zanoni	1988	1,224
70 0/8	14 3/8	14 3/8	5 3/8	5 1/8	11 2/8	Moffat County	CO	Glenn Pritchard	1988	1,224
70 0/8	13 5/8	13 6/8	5 6/8	5 6/8	11 3/8	Dunn County	ND	Rick Regeth	1988	1,224
70 0/8	13 6/8	13 4/8	5 7/8	5 6/8	8 2/8	Sweetwater County	WY	Dennis L. Shirley	1989	1,224

SCORE	LENGTH OF HORN R / L		CIRCUMFERENCE OF BASE R / L		GREATEST SPREAD	AREA	STATE/ PROVINCE	HUNTER'S NAME	DATE	RANK
70 0/8	15 3/8	14 6/8	5 7/8	5 5/8	8 6/8	Custer County	ID	Matt March, Jr.	1989	1,224
70 0/8	13 2/8	13 7/8	5 6/8	5 6/8	7 7/8	Sweetwater County	WY	Larry Norris	1989	1,224
70 0/8	12 2/8	12 5/8	5 7/8	6 0/8	9 3/8	Moffat County	CO	Bob Solimena	1989	1,224
70 0/8	13 6/8	13 7/8	5 6/8	5 4/8	8 4/8	McKenzie County	ND	Michael Lee	1989	1,224
70 0/8	12 5/8	12 2/8	5 6/8	5 6/8	11 5/8	Rosebud County	MT	Shawn A. Wahl	1989	1,224
70 0/8	13 1/8	13 0/8	6 3/8	6 3/8	11 0/8	Harney County	OR	Raymon L. Johnson	1990	1,224
70 0/8	13 0/8	13 0/8	6 2/8	6 2/8	10 1/8	Modoc County	CA	Monty Clemmer	1991	1,224
70 0/8	13 3/8	13 4/8	5 5/8	5 4/8	8 6/8	Butte County	SD	Bryce Lambley	1991	1,224
70 0/8	12 6/8	12 6/8	6 2/8	6 4/8	9 1/8	Campbell County	WY	Robert A. Carman	1991	1,224
70 0/8	12 1/8	12 3/8	6 1/8	6 2/8	10 4/8	Campbell County	WY	Gary R. Shields	1991	1,224
70 0/8	13 7/8	14 1/8	5 7/8	5 7/8	12 0/8	Harney County	OR	Dwight Griffin	1991	1,224
70 0/8	13 2/8	13 1/8	6 0/8	6 3/8	14 6/8	Fremont County	WY	Glen L. Mahlum	1991	1,224
70 0/8	11 7/8	12 0/8	6 1/8	6 0/8	9 6/8	Powder River County	MT	Ronald J. Watt	1991	1,224
70 0/8	14 2/8	14 2/8	5 5/8	5 4/8	11 3/8	Millard County	UT	Steven Bowen Plett	1992	1,224
70 0/8	14 6/8	15 1/8	5 5/8	5 4/8	7 6/8	Moffat County	CO	Steve Barnhill	1992	1,224
70 0/8	12 6/8	12 3/8	6 0/8	6 1/8	8 0/8	Millard County	UT	Clark A. Moss	1992	1,224
69 7/8	13 3/8	12 6/8	6 2/8	6 1/8	15 4/8	Albany County	WY	Vince DiMiceli	1992	1,277
69 6/8	12 6/8	12 6/8	6 6/8	6 6/8	11 4/8	Custer County	ID	Dr. Richard Hagerman	1966	1,278
69 6/8	13 4/8	13 4/8	6 2/8	6 2/8	10 5/8	Carbon County	WY	Maurice Savora	1972	1,278
69 6/8	13 6/8	13 5/8	5 6/8	5 6/8	9 0/8	Ormsby	WY	Edward Pitchkites	1973	1,278
69 6/8	14 6/8	14 6/8	5 2/8	5 2/8	10 2/8	Perkins County	SD	Marvin R. Bohnet	1974	1,278
69 6/8	14 4/8	14 5/8	5 2/8	5 4/8	10 0/8	Meade County	SD	David Martin	1976	1,278
69 6/8	14 0/8	14 2/8	5 2/8	5 0/8	9 0/8	Sublette County	WY	John Kelly	1977	1,278
69 6/8	13 0/8	12 5/8	5 6/8	5 7/8	9 5/8	Carbon County	WY	John L. Craig	1978	1,278
69 6/8	14 5/8	14 5/8	5 3/8	5 3/8	13 4/8	Coconino County	AZ	Robin Underdown	1978	1,278
69 6/8	13 0/8	12 7/8	6 0/8	6 0/8	8 6/8	Arapahoe County	CO	Wayne E. Watson, Sr.	1979	1,278
69 6/8	13 2/8	13 2/8	5 4/8	5 4/8	10 0/8	Arapahoe County	CO	Steve Cosper	1980	1,278
69 6/8	13 3/8	13 5/8	5 1/8	5 1/8	10 4/8	Converse County	WY	Rickey Melde	1981	1,278
69 6/8	13 5/8	13 6/8	5 7/8	5 6/8	9 0/8	Converse County	WY	Jeff Reynolds	1982	1,278
69 6/8	13 6/8	13 7/8	5 6/8	5 5/8	9 7/8	Moffat County	CO	Albert Ahlrich	1982	1,278
69 6/8	14 0/8	13 5/8	6 2/8	6 2/8	8 4/8	Siskiyou County	CA	Scott Walker	1983	1,278
69 6/8	13 6/8	13 6/8	5 4/8	5 3/8	8 4/8	Moffat County	CO	Gary Decker	1983	1,278
69 6/8	13 2/8	13 2/8	5 4/8	5 3/8	10 7/8	Moffat County	CO	Richard Gearhart	1983	1,278
69 6/8	11 7/8	11 6/8	6 2/8	6 2/8	9 4/8	Moffat County	CO	Cathy Lee Jordon	1983	1,278
69 6/8	13 4/8	13 1/8	6 2/8	6 2/8	9 7/8	Moffat County	CO	Galen J. Wertz	1983	1,278
69 6/8	14 0/8	13 2/8	5 6/8	5 6/8	10 0/8	Converse County	WY	Jeff Davis	1983	1,278
69 6/8	13 1/8	13 2/8	5 7/8	5 7/8	10 3/8	Sweetwater County	WY	Michael Chaffin	1985	1,278
69 6/8	14 6/8	15 0/8	5 7/8	6 0/8	13 6/8	Modoc County	CA	Bill Golden	1985	1,278
69 6/8	14 0/8	14 0/8	5 5/8	5 4/8	10 6/8	Powder River County	MT	David Fitton	1985	1,278
69 6/8	13 2/8	13 0/8	5 7/8	6 0/8	10 4/8	Moffat County	CO	Howard Tieden	1986	1,278
69 6/8	13 5/8	13 6/8	5 6/8	5 6/8	10 0/8	McCone County	MT	Mitch Kottas	1986	1,278
69 6/8	12 3/8	12 3/8	5 6/8	5 6/8	8 0/8	Rio Arriba County	NM	Derek Tierney	1987	1,278
69 6/8	12 6/8	12 6/8	6 3/8	6 4/8	10 5/8	Moffat County	CO	Dale Elliott	1987	1,278
69 6/8	13 5/8	13 5/8	6 0/8	6 1/8	13 1/8	Fremont County	WY	Keith L. Frick	1987	1,278
69 6/8	14 7/8	14 6/8	6 0/8	5 7/8	9 5/8	McKinley County	NM	Travis Taylor	1987	1,278
69 6/8	13 6/8	13 4/8	5 3/8	5 3/8	9 2/8	Moffat County	CO	Alvin Tieden	1988	1,278
69 6/8	14 2/8	14 1/8	5 2/8	5 3/8	10 1/8	Converse County	WY	Carolyn S. Zanoni	1988	1,278
69 6/8	13 7/8	14 0/8	5 7/8	5 6/8	13 6/8	Many Berries	ALB	Randy Bernier	1989	1,278
69 6/8	13 3/8	13 4/8	5 1/8	5 1/8	9 4/8	Brewster County	TX	Thomas J. Buxton	1989	1,278
69 6/8	13 6/8	13 6/8	6 1/8	6 1/8	10 4/8	Niobrara County	WY	Jim Jepson	1990	1,278
69 6/8	13 6/8	13 6/8	6 0/8	5 7/8	8 0/8	Campbell County	WY	Mark E. Heberlein	1990	1,278
69 6/8	14 1/8	14 4/8	5 6/8	5 4/8	13 7/8	Fergus County	MT	Kelly Norskog	1990	1,278
69 6/8	15 1/8	15 1/8	5 4/8	5 4/8	10 3/8	Valencia County	NM	Frank Montano	1991	1,278
69 6/8	13 2/8	13 2/8	6 0/8	5 7/8	9 1/8	Natrona County	WY	David J. Steger	1991	1,278
69 6/8	13 5/8	13 4/8	6 0/8	6 0/8	8 4/8	Malheur County	OR	Fredrick J. Johnson	1991	1,278
69 6/8	13 2/8	13 2/8	6 1/8	6 0/8	11 2/8	Larimer County	CO	Randy Brian Snyder	1991	1,278
69 6/8	13 5/8	13 6/8	5 7/8	5 7/8	12 5/8	Converse County	WY	Shirley Jochmann	1991	1,278
69 6/8	13 7/8	14 0/8	5 6/8	5 6/8	10 1/8	Garfield County	MT	Peter J. Mancl	1991	1,278
69 6/8	14 0/8	13 4/8	5 6/8	5 6/8	9 4/8	Beaverhead County	MT	Jim Muzynoski	1991	1,278
69 6/8	13 0/8	13 0/8	6 0/8	6 0/8	7 2/8	Bowman County	ND	Jim Hicks	1991	1,278
69 6/8	12 2/8	12 2/8	6 1/8	6 0/8	9 0/8	Carbon County	WY	Mark Wardlaw	1992	1,278
69 6/8	12 1/8	12 4/8	6 1/8	6 1/8	7 3/8	Converse County	WY	Troy McGinnis	1992	1,278
69 5/8	12 4/8	13 0/8	6 4/8	6 3/8	14 1/8	Powder River County	MT	Daryl E. Jennings	1983	1,323
69 5/8	13 1/8	14 4/8	6 1/8	6 2/8	14 5/8	Moffat County	CO	Wendy Decker	1988	1,323
69 5/8	13 4/8	13 2/8	6 0/8	5 7/8	14 1/8	Daggett County	UT	Steve Dailey	1991	1,323
69 4/8	15 0/8	13 6/8	5 4/8	5 4/8	5 6/8	Rosebud County	MT	Glenn Gibson	1958	1,326
69 4/8	14 4/8	14 2/8	5 2/8	5 2/8	10 6/8	Grant County	NM	Harold W. Groves	1960	1,326
69 4/8	14 4/8	14 2/8	5 5/8	5 4/8	9 4/8	Washoe County	NV	Kenneth D. Allen	1972	1,326
69 4/8	13 2/8	13 0/8	6 0/8	6 0/8	10 6/8	Natrona County	WY	John Benetti	1973	1,326
69 4/8	13 6/8	14 0/8	5 5/8	5 3/8	9 6/8	Washoe County	NV	Jack S. McCracken	1973	1,326

Score	Length of R horn L		Circumference R of Base L		Greatest Spread	Area	State/Province	Hunter's Name	Date	Rank
69 4/8	12 0/8	12 4/8	6 0/8	6 1/8	9 1/8	Meade County	SD	Lelan L. Anderson	1974	1,326
69 4/8	14 3/8	14 4/8	5 5/8	5 3/8	8 4/8	Park County	CO	Ed Zehner	1974	1,326
69 4/8	12 6/8	12 3/8	5 7/8	6 0/8	9 4/8	Lemhi County	ID	Randy J. Stephens	1980	1,326
69 4/8	13 0/8	13 0/8	5 5/8	5 5/8	9 5/8	Jefferson County	ID	Ron Stacey	1981	1,326
69 4/8	12 7/8	12 7/8	6 0/8	6 0/8	9 5/8	Moffat County	CO	Martin James Murrish	1981	1,326
69 4/8	13 6/8	13 4/8	6 5/8	6 6/8	11 0/8	Carbon County	WY	Mike C. Montgomery	1981	1,326
69 4/8	11 5/8	11 6/8	6 4/8	6 4/8	10 5/8	Converse County	WY	Ben Munoz	1981	1,326
69 4/8	13 5/8	14 3/8	6 1/8	5 7/8	11 5/8	Converse County	WY	Dr. James R. Scott	1981	1,326
69 4/8	12 6/8	12 7/8	5 7/8	5 7/8	9 5/8	Bowman County	ND	Ron Cizek	1982	1,326
69 4/8	14 1/8	14 2/8	5 4/8	5 3/8	6 5/8	Converse County	WY	Ronnie Everett	1982	1,326
69 4/8	13 4/8	13 7/8	5 4/8	5 4/8	8 1/8	Moffat County	CO	Rich Humpal	1982	1,326
69 4/8	12 2/8	11 7/8	6 0/8	6 0/8	8 0/8	Beaver County	UT	Joey Leko	1982	1,326
69 4/8	14 0/8	14 0/8	5 6/8	5 5/8	9 6/8	Sweetwater County	WY	Ronnie Williams	1982	1,326
69 4/8	14 0/8	13 7/8	5 2/8	5 3/8	6 1/8	Converse County	WY	Jim Wilbur	1983	1,326
69 4/8	13 4/8	12 4/8	6 1/8	6 1/8	10 5/8	Natrona County	WY	Paul Persano	1984	1,326
69 4/8	12 7/8	13 1/8	5 2/8	5 2/8	7 3/8	Moffat County	CO	Roy V. Roig	1984	1,326
69 4/8	13 6/8	14 7/8	5 7/8	5 7/8	11 6/8	Sweetwater County	WY	Glenn Hisey	1985	1,326
69 4/8	12 6/8	12 5/8	6 0/8	6 1/8	7 3/8	Sweetwater County	WY	Rod Knight	1985	1,326
69 4/8	13 5/8	13 2/8	5 2/8	5 2/8	8 3/8	Converse County	WY	Samuel M. Durham	1985	1,326
69 4/8	13 3/8	13 0/8	5 6/8	5 6/8	13 2/8	Billings County	ND	Pat Caroline	1985	1,326
69 4/8	12 5/8	12 5/8	5 6/8	5 6/8	8 3/8	Uintah County	UT	Rob Johnston	1986	1,326
69 4/8	13 2/8	13 2/8	5 6/8	5 5/8	8 6/8	Sublette County	WY	John Cheese	1987	1,326
69 4/8	13 7/8	13 6/8	5 2/8	5 2/8	10 2/8	Musselshell County	MT	Jeff Matson	1987	1,326
69 4/8	13 2/8	13 2/8	5 7/8	5 6/8	11 4/8	Converse County	WY	John A. Driver	1987	1,326
69 4/8	14 2/8	14 1/8	6 0/8	5 7/8	10 6/8	Carbon County	WY	Steven Perkins	1988	1,326
69 4/8	12 7/8	12 6/8	6 4/8	6 2/8	6 0/8	Moffat County	CO	Dale Drilling	1988	1,326
69 4/8	13 3/8	13 3/8	6 3/8	6 2/8	9 0/8	McKinley County	NM	Gary Isom	1988	1,326
69 4/8	14 1/8	14 1/8	5 1/8	5 1/8	8 4/8	Moffat County	CO	Ron Scherer	1988	1,326
69 4/8	13 3/8	13 5/8	6 0/8	5 7/8	8 6/8	Natrona County	WY	Shawn Kinker	1988	1,326
69 4/8	13 2/8	13 5/8	5 6/8	5 6/8	11 2/8	Carbon County	WY	Lonny Curtis	1988	1,326
69 4/8	12 5/8	12 7/8	6 0/8	5 7/8	11 0/8	Albany County	WY	William Zahradka	1988	1,326
69 4/8	14 7/8	14 4/8	6 2/8	6 2/8	14 1/8	Campbell County	WY	Curt Christensen	1988	1,326
69 4/8	13 4/8	13 0/8	6 3/8	6 2/8	10 6/8	Crook County	WY	David Hinton	1988	1,326
69 4/8	13 0/8	13 0/8	6 2/8	6 1/8	8 4/8	Converse County	WY	Kevin Stier	1988	1,326
69 4/8	12 2/8	12 1/8	6 5/8	6 4/8	11 6/8	Natrona County	WY	Steve Turck	1988	1,326
69 4/8	14 2/8	14 4/8	5 7/8	5 7/8	10 1/8	Buffalo	ALB	Larry Flaata	1988	1,326
69 4/8	13 0/8	13 0/8	5 7/8	5 6/8	11 3/8	Rosebud County	MT	Gene Welle	1989	1,326
69 4/8	14 2/8	13 7/8	5 5/8	5 5/8	9 2/8	Lassen County	CA	Guy Rozar	1990	1,326
69 4/8	12 0/8	11 7/8	6 3/8	6 3/8	10 6/8	Fremont County	WY	David J. Steger	1990	1,326
69 4/8	13 4/8	13 2/8	5 6/8	5 5/8	10 4/8	Moffat County	CO	Eugene Ray, Sr.	1990	1,326
69 4/8	12 6/8	13 6/8	6 0/8	6 1/8	13 5/8	Moffat County	CO	Reggie Spiegelberg	1990	1,326
69 4/8	13 7/8	13 7/8	5 3/8	5 4/8	11 7/8	Lake County	OR	Buck Windom	1990	1,326
69 4/8	12 3/8	12 2/8	6 0/8	6 1/8	9 7/8	Ward County	ND	Glen R. Hauf	1990	1,326
69 4/8	13 0/8	13 1/8	6 0/8	6 1/8	12 2/8	Fremont County	WY	G. R. Pool	1991	1,326
69 4/8	13 6/8	13 5/8	5 5/8	5 5/8	9 4/8	Lincoln County	WY	Bob Grace	1992	1,326
69 4/8	13 1/8	13 3/8	6 0/8	6 0/8	7 5/8	Converse County	WY	Lou Edelis	1992	1,326
69 4/8	13 3/8	13 2/8	5 7/8	5 6/8	11 3/8	Converse County	WY	Rodney L. Hamann	1992	1,326
69 3/8	14 1/8	14 3/8	5 6/8	5 7/8	15 6/8	Deschutes County	OR	William E. Lancaster	1973	1,378
69 2/8	14 2/8	13 7/8	5 4/8	5 4/8	11 6/8	Custer County	ID	Jack Edwards	1960	1,379
69 2/8	13 5/8	13 4/8	5 3/8	5 2/8	6 2/8	Haakon County	SD	Floyd Hauk	1966	1,379
69 2/8	12 3/8	12 1/8	5 6/8	5 6/8	8 0/8	Converse County	WY	Bill Martin	1976	1,379
69 2/8	12 7/8	12 7/8	5 3/8	5 5/8	11 7/8	Converse County	WY	Dr. James L. Emerson	1980	1,379
69 2/8	12 4/8	12 1/8	6 0/8	6 0/8	9 5/8	Morgan County	CO	Filiberto Lopez	1980	1,379
69 2/8	11 6/8	13 5/8	6 1/8	6 1/8	8 6/8	Custer County	ID	Dick Fleming	1981	1,379
69 2/8	13 2/8	14 0/8	5 5/8	5 5/8	11 0/8	Converse County	WY	Gene A. Esch	1981	1,379
69 2/8	13 1/8	13 3/8	5 4/8	5 4/8	7 7/8	Butte County	ID	Garry Gunderson	1981	1,379
69 2/8	12 4/8	13 0/8	5 7/8	5 5/8	11 5/8	Moffat County	CO	Jim Jarvis	1981	1,379
69 2/8	14 3/8	13 7/8	5 7/8	5 6/8	10 4/8	Valencia County	NM	Reggie Spiegelberg	1981	1,379
69 2/8	12 7/8	13 0/8	5 7/8	5 5/8	11 0/8	Sweetwater County	WY	Dean Kendall	1982	1,379
69 2/8	13 2/8	13 6/8	6 2/8	6 2/8	9 5/8	Albany County	WY	Peter Vasek	1982	1,379
69 2/8	12 7/8	13 1/8	5 5/8	5 4/8	8 4/8	Moffat County	CO	Ross Dieffenbaucher	1982	1,379
69 2/8	14 3/8	14 0/8	5 7/8	5 7/8	8 0/8	Moffat County	CO	Les Smith	1983	1,379
69 2/8	14 2/8	13 7/8	6 0/8	6 0/8	8 1/8	Natrona County	WY	Joe M. Skipp	1983	1,379
69 2/8	12 7/8	12 4/8	5 7/8	5 6/8	9 3/8	Converse County	WY	Bruce H. Sabaini	1983	1,379
69 2/8	13 7/8	13 4/8	5 4/8	5 4/8	10 6/8	White Pine County	NV	Patrick Fillman	1984	1,379
69 2/8	14 4/8	14 6/8	5 6/8	5 2/8	10 6/8	Converse County	WY	Donald Jackson	1984	1,379
69 2/8	13 3/8	13 1/8	5 6/8	5 6/8	10 5/8	Converse County	WY	Bob Frank	1984	1,379
69 2/8	13 3/8	12 4/8	6 1/8	6 1/8	12 0/8	McKenzie County	ND	Bill Zahradka	1984	1,379
69 2/8	13 2/8	13 2/8	5 7/8	5 7/8	10 5/8	Carbon County	WY	Steve Bolan	1985	1,379
69 2/8	12 6/8	12 4/8	6 5/8	6 4/8	9 0/8	Moffat County	CO	Casey Veach	1985	1,379

Score	Length of Horn R	Length of Horn L	Circumference of Base R	Circumference of Base L	Greatest Spread	Area	State/ Province	Hunter's Name	Date	Rank
69 2/8	13 0/8	12 7/8	5 6/8	5 4/8	11 2/8	Yavapai County	AZ	Tony W. Zimbaro	1985	1,379
69 2/8	12 1/8	12 0/8	5 7/8	5 7/8	8 4/8	Converse County	WY	Larry L. Fies	1985	1,379
69 2/8	12 1/8	12 0/8	5 7/8	5 7/8	8 4/8	Converse County	WY	Larry L. Fies	1985	1,379
69 2/8	12 5/8	12 7/8	6 1/8	6 0/8	11 1/8	Moffat County	CO	Lynn Ingalsbe	1986	1,379
69 2/8	13 4/8	13 4/8	6 0/8	6 0/8	9 4/8	Moffat County	CO	Gil Gilbertson	1986	1,379
69 2/8	13 4/8	13 3/8	5 5/8	5 5/8	10 4/8	Converse County	WY	Don Schram	1986	1,379
69 2/8	13 4/8	13 5/8	5 5/8	5 5/8	8 3/8	Presidio County	TX	Larry Zimmerman	1986	1,379
69 2/8	13 6/8	14 1/8	6 0/8	5 6/8	9 7/8	Jefferson County	OR	Karen J. Demaris	1987	1,379
69 2/8	13 3/8	13 3/8	5 2/8	5 1/8	9 1/8	Natrona County	WY	Mike Mitten	1987	1,379
69 2/8	13 0/8	13 0/8	5 5/8	5 6/8	11 5/8	Campbell County	WY	Rick Mowles	1987	1,379
69 2/8	13 5/8	12 6/8	5 5/8	5 6/8	10 2/8	Presidio County	TX	Jack F. Demetruk	1987	1,379
69 2/8	12 1/8	12 0/8	5 7/8	5 7/8	8 3/8	Moffat County	CO	John Wagner	1988	1,379
69 2/8	14 4/8	14 3/8	5 6/8	5 6/8	12 6/8	Modoc County	CA	Bill C. Osborne	1988	1,379
69 2/8	14 2/8	13 7/8	5 2/8	5 1/8	10 5/8	Pima County	AZ	Barry Sopher	1988	1,379
69 2/8	13 4/8	13 3/8	5 6/8	5 6/8	8 6/8	Hot Springs County	WY	Dan Wood	1988	1,379
69 2/8	13 3/8	13 3/8	5 6/8	5 5/8	10 0/8	Converse County	WY	Denny Raper	1988	1,379
69 2/8	14 5/8	15 0/8	6 4/8	6 1/8	12 2/8	Sweetwater County	WY	Mike Barrett	1989	1,379
69 2/8	13 7/8	13 6/8	5 7/8	5 7/8	9 3/8	Mountrail County	ND	Brian C. Johnson	1989	1,379
69 2/8	13 3/8	13 0/8	5 5/8	5 5/8	9 7/8	Buffalo	ALB	Steve Mackenzie	1989	1,379
69 2/8	12 0/8	12 2/8	6 2/8	6 2/8	12 1/8	Carbon County	WY	Jeffrey Mueller	1990	1,379
69 2/8	14 4/8	14 4/8	5 7/8	6 0/8	7 2/8	Harding County	SD	Dean Wagner	1990	1,379
69 2/8	13 6/8	13 2/8	5 7/8	5 7/8	13 4/8	Coconino County	AZ	Charles Steven Williams	1990	1,379
69 2/8	11 3/8	11 3/8	6 1/8	6 2/8	6 7/8	Natrona County	WY	Robert E. Ebert	1990	1,379
69 2/8	12 5/8	12 2/8	6 0/8	6 0/8	8 6/8	Converse County	WY	Robert Frank	1990	1,379
69 2/8	13 4/8	13 1/8	5 7/8	6 0/8	11 4/8	Powder River County	MT	John Witschen	1990	1,379
69 2/8	13 0/8	13 1/8	5 5/8	5 5/8	11 2/8	Billings County	ND	Gary W. Heidecker	1990	1,379
69 2/8	13 5/8	13 3/8	6 2/8	6 2/8	12 6/8	Fremont County	WY	Dave Holt	1991	1,379
69 2/8	13 2/8	13 0/8	5 5/8	5 5/8	9 1/8	Natrona County	WY	Carson V. Brown II	1991	1,379
69 2/8	13 1/8	13 3/8	5 6/8	5 5/8	10 4/8	Campbell County	WY	John Shields	1991	1,379
69 2/8	12 0/8	12 0/8	6 0/8	5 6/8	9 2/8	McKenzie County	ND	Benjamin Stewart	1991	1,379
69 2/8	14 1/8	13 6/8	6 2/8	6 0/8	10 2/8	Converse County	WY	John Flies	1991	1,379
69 2/8	11 6/8	11 6/8	6 1/8	6 0/8	11 0/8	Campbell County	WY	Ron Ralston	1991	1,379
69 2/8	14 1/8	14 1/8	6 0/8	5 7/8	7 2/8	Converse County	WY	Wayne Radley	1991	1,379
69 2/8	11 7/8	12 0/8	6 1/8	6 1/8	10 2/8	Moffat County	CO	Don Sousa	1992	1,379
69 2/8	14 2/8	14 0/8	5 4/8	5 4/8	11 2/8	Catron County	NM	Glenn W. Isler	1992	1,379
69 2/8	14 0/8	14 1/8	5 7/8	6 1/8	8 2/8	Lassen County	CA	Randy Jarvis	1992	1,379
69 2/8	13 0/8	12 3/8	6 2/8	6 0/8	7 5/8	Unita County	WY	George Fabian	1992	1,379
69 2/8	12 4/8	12 7/8	6 3/8	6 4/8	9 4/8	Sweetwater County	WY	Mark Grace	1992	1,379
69 2/8	14 6/8	14 3/8	5 4/8	5 4/8	8 2/8	Hettinger County	ND	Scott Wiseman	1992	1,379
69 1/8	13 2/8	14 0/8	5 7/8	5 7/8	15 1/8	Moffat County	CO	Kurt W. Keskimaki	1988	1,440
69 1/8	12 7/8	13 1/8	6 6/8	6 6/8	13 2/8	Sweetwater County	WY	Bill Clink	1992	1,440
69 0/8	12 7/8	13 0/8	5 6/8	5 7/8	8 4/8	Fall River County	SD	Francis R. Tovar	1968	1,442
69 0/8	14 0/8	14 2/8	5 2/8	5 3/8	9 1/8	Mercer County	ND	John J. Willoughby	1977	1,442
69 0/8	13 4/8	13 2/8	5 6/8	5 5/8	8 3/8	Butte County	ID	Larry Roberts	1979	1,442
69 0/8	14 1/8	13 7/8	5 4/8	5 3/8	10 0/8	Carbon County	WY	Grant Poindexter	1980	1,442
69 0/8	14 0/8	14 2/8	5 7/8	5 6/8	8 0/8	Converse County	WY	Don Clark	1981	1,442
69 0/8	13 2/8	13 3/8	5 6/8	5 5/8	11 0/8	Converse County	WY	George Place	1981	1,442
69 0/8	12 5/8	12 4/8	5 6/8	5 6/8	9 5/8	Fremont County	WY	A. E. 'Butch' Whelchel	1981	1,442
69 0/8	12 6/8	12 6/8	5 6/8	5 6/8	12 5/8	Converse County	WY	Jeff Wright	1981	1,442
69 0/8	13 5/8	13 6/8	5 7/8	6 0/8	11 6/8	Washoe County	NV	Dr. Ronald H. Thole	1982	1,442
69 0/8	13 0/8	12 6/8	6 0/8	6 0/8	7 0/8	Park County	CO	Greg Brown	1983	1,442
69 0/8	12 4/8	12 4/8	6 0/8	6 1/8	9 4/8	Moffat County	CO	Burton Arbogast	1983	1,442
69 0/8	13 2/8	13 3/8	5 6/8	5 6/8	11 4/8	Moffat County	CO	Mike Wallers	1983	1,442
69 0/8	13 4/8	13 4/8	6 0/8	6 1/8	10 3/8	Converse County	WY	Michael Nimmer	1983	1,442
69 0/8	13 0/8	13 1/8	6 1/8	6 1/8	9 2/8	Converse County	WY	Lloyd E. Musser	1983	1,442
69 0/8	13 4/8	12 7/8	5 7/8	5 6/8	9 2/8	Converse County	WY	James R. Dreves	1983	1,442
69 0/8	14 1/8	14 0/8	5 4/8	5 4/8	10 1/8	Johnson County	WY	Steve Nolte	1984	1,442
69 0/8	12 7/8	12 5/8	6 0/8	6 1/8	11 2/8	Converse County	WY	Janice Peterman	1984	1,442
69 0/8	13 2/8	13 3/8	5 6/8	5 7/8	13 3/8	Converse County	WY	John L Kosharek	1985	1,442
69 0/8	12 7/8	12 6/8	6 0/8	5 7/8	9 3/8	Campbell County	WY	Bill Heinike	1985	1,442
69 0/8	13 1/8	13 2/8	5 5/8	5 6/8	12 4/8	Carbon County	WY	Richard L. Westervelt	1987	1,442
69 0/8	12 2/8	13 3/8	5 5/8	5 5/8	10 2/8	Moffat County	CO	Harry Torkilson	1987	1,442
69 0/8	14 0/8	14 0/8	5 3/8	5 4/8	7 1/8	Natrona County	WY	Ricky A. Wall	1987	1,442
69 0/8	12 4/8	12 4/8	6 0/8	6 0/8	8 4/8	Moffat County	CO	Brent Newton	1988	1,442
69 0/8	13 2/8	13 2/8	6 0/8	5 6/8	9 4/8	Campbell County	WY	Dennis Klemick	1988	1,442
69 0/8	13 0/8	13 0/8	6 1/8	6 0/8	9 6/8	Converse County	WY	Michael E. Rice	1988	1,442
69 0/8	13 1/8	13 3/8	5 7/8	6 0/8	8 7/8	Converse County	WY	Steve VanZile	1988	1,442
69 0/8	12 7/8	12 7/8	5 7/8	5 6/8	8 5/8	Sweetwater County	WY	Robert G. Petersen	1989	1,442
69 0/8	13 0/8	12 7/8	6 0/8	5 5/8	10 6/8	Modoc County	CA	Cheryl Vermilion	1989	1,442
69 0/8	12 5/8	14 3/8	5 6/8	5 5/8	8 5/8	Navajo County	AZ	Ron Nichols	1989	1,442

Minimum score 64

(Continued)

Score	Length of Horn R L	Circumference of Base R L	Greatest Spread	Area	State/ Province	Hunter's Name	Date	Rank
69 0/8	13 4/8 13 5/8	5 3/8 5 3/8	9 0/8	Converse County	WY	Robert Moon	1989	1,442
69 0/8	12 7/8 12 5/8	5 6/8 5 6/8	9 0/8	Albany County	WY	Gene Welle	1989	1,442
69 0/8	14 0/8 13 6/8	5 4/8 5 4/8	12 0/8	Campbell County	WY	Tippy Clark	1989	1,442
69 0/8	13 2/8 13 2/8	5 7/8 5 7/8	10 3/8	White Pine County	NV	David Brown	1990	1,442
69 0/8	13 3/8 13 1/8	5 4/8 5 3/8	9 1/8	Moffat County	CO	John Morris	1990	1,442
69 0/8	13 7/8 14 0/8	5 7/8 5 7/8	7 4/8	Campbell County	WY	Elroy Thorson	1990	1,442
69 0/8	12 6/8 12 5/8	6 0/8 6 0/8	7 2/8	Converse County	WY	Stan Rauch	1990	1,442
69 0/8	13 5/8 13 3/8	6 0/8 6 0/8	11 1/8	Natrona County	WY	Tony Zirkelbach	1990	1,442
69 0/8	13 2/8 13 3/8	5 5/8 5 6/8	11 3/8	Jenner	ALB	Dale Johnson	1990	1,442
69 0/8	14 3/8 14 0/8	6 2/8 5 7/8	11 4/8	Wallace County	KS	Mike Jenkins	1990	1,442
69 0/8	13 5/8 13 2/8	5 4/8 5 5/8	11 7/8	Carbon County	WY	Karl Knudsen	1991	1,442
69 0/8	12 5/8 12 6/8	5 5/8 5 6/8	10 1/8	Sweetwater County	WY	Patricia C. Sands	1991	1,442
69 0/8	13 3/8 13 2/8	6 0/8 6 0/8	10 4/8	Modoc County	CA	Dave S. Semple	1991	1,442
69 0/8	14 4/8 13 0/8	5 4/8 5 4/8	9 3/8	Natrona County	WY	Gregory L. Reed	1991	1,442
69 0/8	13 6/8 14 0/8	5 6/8 5 6/8	9 7/8	Bowman County	ND	Mark Froelich	1991	1,442
69 0/8	13 6/8 14 1/8	6 1/8 6 2/8	13 5/8	Buffalo County	SD	Darrell Hahn	1991	1,442
69 0/8	13 7/8 13 4/8	5 4/8 5 3/8	12 2/8	Sioux County	NE	Roger Dekok	1991	1,442
69 0/8	13 6/8 13 6/8	5 3/8 5 4/8	7 1/8	Meagher County	MT	D. Mitch Kottas	1991	1,442
69 0/8	14 4/8 14 2/8	5 5/8 5 5/8	9 1/8	Petroleum County	MT	Mark D. Hughes	1991	1,442
69 0/8	14 4/8 15 6/8	5 2/8 5 1/8	9 1/8	Hudspeth County	TX	Kenneth L. Zoller	1991	1,442
69 0/8	12 2/8 12 4/8	6 1/8 6 1/8	9 4/8	Butte County	ID	David Wayne Ary	1992	1,442
69 0/8	12 3/8 12 3/8	6 3/8 6 2/8	6 2/8	Campbell County	WY	Barb Kleve	1992	1,442
69 0/8	13 4/8 13 6/8	5 4/8 5 4/8	9 7/8	Converse County	WY	Larry M. Peterson	1992	1,442
69 0/8	13 0/8 13 1/8	6 0/8 6 0/8	9 4/8	Albany County	WY	Roger Sheaffer	1992	1,442
69 0/8	12 7/8 13 5/8	6 5/8 6 5/8	8 0/8	Campbell County	WY	Jack Savini	1992	1,442
69 0/8	13 6/8 13 6/8	5 3/8 5 3/8	11 3/8	Weston County	WY	Roland Weeg	1992	1,442
69 0/8	13 5/8 13 7/8	5 5/8 5 5/8	10 7/8	Petroleum County	MT	Mark D. Hughes	1992	1,442
68 7/8	14 7/8 14 7/8	5 4/8 5 3/8	16 2/8	Converse County	WY	Fred Wallace	1989	1,498
68 6/8	14 7/8 14 7/8	5 4/8 5 4/8	12 0/8	Sweetwater County	WY	Dr. Fred Mack	1960	1,499
68 6/8	13 2/8 13 4/8	6 1/8 6 1/8	7 4/8	Gallatin County	MT	Robert Savage	1971	1,499
68 6/8	12 3/8 12 4/8	6 4/8 6 2/8	11 0/8	Sweetwater County	WY	Keith Dana	1978	1,499
68 6/8	13 6/8 13 5/8	5 3/8 5 5/8	9 0/8	Park County	MT	George Kamps	1980	1,499
68 6/8	13 0/8 12 7/8	5 7/8 5 4/8	9 0/8	Natrona County	WY	Jim L. McCrory	1981	1,499
68 6/8	12 4/8 12 4/8	5 5/8 5 4/8	7 3/8	Converse County	WY	Donald Schram	1981	1,499
68 6/8	13 0/8 13 2/8	5 7/8 5 7/8	11 6/8	Weld County	CO	Ron Montross	1983	1,499
68 6/8	12 4/8 12 0/8	6 4/8 6 3/8	9 4/8	Crook County	WY	Jim P Hallock	1983	1,499
68 6/8	13 4/8 13 3/8	5 5/8 5 5/8	7 6/8	Converse County	WY	Gary Duncan	1983	1,499
68 6/8	13 3/8 13 5/8	5 1/8 5 1/8	12 2/8	Garfield County	MT	Darwin Frison	1983	1,499
68 6/8	14 0/8 14 0/8	5 3/8 5 2/8	10 6/8	Moffat County	CO	Gary Fritzler	1984	1,499
68 6/8	12 4/8 12 5/8	6 0/8 6 3/8	9 1/8	McKinley County	NM	John W. Rose	1984	1,499
68 6/8	14 3/8 14 3/8	5 4/8 5 4/8	9 4/8	Butte County	SD	Reginald E. Faber, Jr.	1984	1,499
68 6/8	12 6/8 12 4/8	6 0/8 5 7/8	8 2/8	Converse County	WY	Eric Bruce	1984	1,499
68 6/8	14 1/8 14 2/8	6 0/8 5 7/8	15 0/8	Fergus County	MT	James W. Southworth	1984	1,499
68 6/8	13 4/8 14 0/8	5 6/8 5 4/8	11 1/8	Washoe County	NV	Gary Zunino	1985	1,499
68 6/8	13 7/8 13 1/8	6 2/8 6 2/8	11 2/8	Sweetwater County	WY	W.R. "Tony" Dukes	1985	1,499
68 6/8	13 0/8 12 7/8	5 5/8 5 4/8	5 3/8	Sweetwater County	WY	Gary Belvoir	1986	1,499
68 6/8	13 7/8 14 2/8	5 5/8 5 5/8	11 6/8	Washoe County	NV	Gilbert Hernandez	1987	1,499
68 6/8	13 2/8 12 6/8	5 6/8 5 4/8	8 1/8	Custer County	ID	Brian Hunter Heck	1987	1,499
68 6/8	13 2/8 13 4/8	6 5/8 6 4/8	6 1/8	Garfield County	CO	Rory Robie	1987	1,499
68 6/8	12 6/8 12 6/8	6 4/8 6 3/8	11 3/8	Moffat County	CO	Tommy M. Brown	1987	1,499
68 6/8	12 4/8 12 5/8	5 6/8 5 5/8	10 2/8	Converse County	WY	David L. Lundy	1987	1,499
68 6/8	13 7/8 13 5/8	6 1/8 6 0/8	9 3/8	Beaverhead County	MT	Mervin Johnston	1987	1,499
68 6/8	13 4/8 13 7/8	5 6/8 5 5/8	9 6/8	Buffalo	ALB	Lou Carrier	1987	1,499
68 6/8	13 5/8 14 0/8	5 5/8 5 4/8	10 1/8	Buffalo	ALB	Orest Popil	1988	1,499
68 6/8	12 7/8 12 6/8	5 5/8 5 4/8	9 3/8	Medicine Hat	ALB	Owen Telke	1988	1,499
68 6/8	13 1/8 13 2/8	5 5/8 5 5/8	11 0/8	Sublette County	WY	Peter L. Bucklin	1989	1,499
68 6/8	13 0/8 12 6/8	5 7/8 6 0/8	11 3/8	Yavapai County	AZ	Charles P. Cooley	1989	1,499
68 6/8	13 7/8 13 5/8	5 5/8 5 7/8	10 3/8	McCone County	MT	Jaron Schillinger	1989	1,499
68 6/8	13 6/8 14 0/8	5 6/8 5 7/8	10 7/8	Jenner	ALB	Brian J. Ward	1989	1,499
68 6/8	14 0/8 14 2/8	6 4/8 6 2/8	10 5/8	Phillips County	MT	Mike Dunwell	1989	1,499
68 6/8	13 4/8 13 0/8	5 6/8 5 5/8	13 4/8	Wallace County	KS	Larry Buchholz	1989	1,499
68 6/8	13 2/8 13 1/8	5 4/8 5 5/8	7 2/8	Natrona County	WY	R. Ray Wix	1990	1,499
68 6/8	13 1/8 13 2/8	5 3/8 5 4/8	9 6/8	Campbell County	WY	Randy Cook	1990	1,499
68 6/8	14 5/8 14 3/8	5 3/8 5 4/8	9 7/8	Washoe County	NV	Richard Oliver	1991	1,499
68 6/8	12 0/8 11 5/8	6 6/8 6 6/8	10 4/8	Converse County	WY	Bob Arne	1991	1,499
68 6/8	13 1/8 13 0/8	5 7/8 5 7/8	9 1/8	Converse County	WY	Phil Perry	1991	1,499
68 6/8	13 0/8 13 0/8	6 3/8 6 2/8	7 3/8	Campbell County	WY	Allan White	1991	1,499
68 6/8	13 4/8 13 3/8	5 5/8 5 4/8	10 5/8	Campbell County	WY	Dan M. Mooney	1991	1,499
68 6/8	12 2/8 12 4/8	5 6/8 5 6/8	11 0/8	Rosebud County	MT	Craig Gerber	1991	1,499
68 6/8	13 3/8 13 7/8	6 0/8 6 1/8	11 2/8	Fergus County	MT	Chris G. Sanford	1991	1,499

SCORE	LENGTH OF HORN R	L	CIRCUMFERENCE OF BASE R	L	GREATEST SPREAD	AREA	STATE/ PROVINCE	HUNTER'S NAME	DATE	RANK
68 6/8	13 6/8	13 5/8	5 6/8	5 5/8	8 0/8	Washoe County	NV	Anthony L. Mudd	1992	1,499
68 6/8	13 0/8	12 7/8	6 1/8	6 1/8	8 6/8	Humboldt County	NV	Erik L. Self	1992	1,499
68 6/8	14 0/8	13 7/8	6 0/8	5 5/8	9 4/8	Sweetwater County	WY	Jeffrey J. Petersen	1992	1,499
68 6/8	13 1/8	13 0/8	5 1/8	5 1/8	8 1/8	Moffat County	CO	David Joyce	1992	1,499
68 6/8	12 7/8	12 6/8	6 1/8	6 0/8	9 1/8	Carbon County	WY	Mark Alan Bartkoski	1992	1,499
68 6/8	12 5/8	12 3/8	6 0/8	5 7/8	7 1/8	Manyberries	ALB	John Visscher	1992	1,499
68 4/8	13 4/8	13 0/8	5 4/8	5 5/8	8 6/8	Tripp County	SD	Spike Jorgensen	1965	1,547
68 4/8	14 1/8	14 1/8	5 2/8	5 1/8	12 3/8	Lincoln County	NM	James H. Simmons	1966	1,547
68 4/8	12 6/8	12 2/8	6 5/8	6 5/8	12 1/8	McLean County	ND	Tom O'Connell	1970	1,547
68 4/8	14 1/8	14 0/8	5 4/8	5 2/8	10 5/8	Johnson County	WY	David Collis	1975	1,547
68 4/8	12 6/8	12 7/8	6 0/8	6 0/8	9 4/8	Billings County	ND	Dean Nevland	1975	1,547
68 4/8	12 6/8	12 4/8	5 6/8	5 7/8	9 3/8	Converse County	WY	Ron Carpenter	1976	1,547
68 4/8	13 0/8	12 7/8	5 5/8	6 0/8	8 3/8	Lincoln County	WY	Preston C. Phelps	1977	1,547
68 4/8	13 7/8	13 4/8	5 6/8	5 5/8	13 1/8	Logan County	CO	Tony Seahorn	1978	1,547
68 4/8	13 7/8	14 0/8	6 0/8	5 7/8	12 4/8	McKinley County	NM	James M. Finn	1979	1,547
68 4/8	14 1/8	14 1/8	5 4/8	5 5/8	10 5/8	Butte County	ID	Clifton Robinson	1979	1,547
68 4/8	13 3/8	13 2/8	5 5/8	5 5/8	13 0/8	Carbon County	WY	Dale Gauthier	1980	1,547
68 4/8	13 0/8	12 5/8	5 7/8	5 7/8	10 3/8	Moffat County	CO	Ron Bolinger	1981	1,547
68 4/8	13 6/8	13 5/8	5 0/8	5 0/8	8 4/8	Natrona County	WY	Dan Skolaski	1981	1,547
68 4/8	13 5/8	13 4/8	5 4/8	5 3/8	12 1/8	Converse County	WY	Richard Stokke	1981	1,547
68 4/8	12 6/8	13 3/8	5 7/8	6 0/8	9 1/8	Converse County	WY	Charles O. Boggs	1982	1,547
68 4/8	14 1/8	13 7/8	5 5/8	5 6/8	8 6/8	Eddy County	NM	Jim Stell	1982	1,547
68 4/8	13 6/8	14 0/8	5 4/8	5 5/8	13 2/8	Converse County	WY	Harold Leslie	1982	1,547
68 4/8	13 4/8	13 5/8	5 3/8	5 3/8	13 3/8	Converse County	WY	Kent Brigham	1982	1,547
68 4/8	12 4/8	13 0/8	6 3/8	6 1/8	8 6/8	Carbon County	WY	Willis Duhon	1982	1,547
68 4/8	12 7/8	13 0/8	6 0/8	6 0/8	9 6/8	Natrona County	WY	Roger Smith	1982	1,547
68 4/8	12 3/8	12 1/8	6 2/8	6 3/8	10 3/8	Natrona County	WY	Steve Turck	1982	1,547
68 4/8	12 7/8	12 7/8	5 5/8	5 4/8	10 6/8	Moffat County	CO	Len Cardinale	1983	1,547
68 4/8	13 4/8	13 4/8	5 2/8	5 1/8	10 5/8	Sweetwater County	WY	Dean Dolenc	1983	1,547
68 4/8	13 3/8	13 6/8	5 5/8	5 4/8	7 2/8	Sioux County	NE	Chuck Starr	1983	1,547
68 4/8	13 6/8	13 6/8	5 2/8	5 3/8	7 6/8	Logan County	KS	Lynn Freese	1984	1,547
68 4/8	13 6/8	13 6/8	5 6/8	5 4/8	11 2/8	Converse County	WY	Marty Horn	1984	1,547
68 4/8	13 6/8	14 5/8	5 4/8	5 4/8	11 2/8	Converse County	WY	Joe Guth	1984	1,547
68 4/8	12 2/8	12 3/8	6 0/8	6 0/8	10 7/8	Campbell County	WY	John 'Jack' Cordes	1984	1,547
68 4/8	12 0/8	12 0/8	5 5/8	5 5/8	8 2/8	Moffat County	CO	Robert Syvertson, Sr.	1985	1,547
68 4/8	13 6/8	13 6/8	5 7/8	5 7/8	11 5/8	Coconino County	AZ	Jesse E. Smith	1985	1,547
68 4/8	12 0/8	11 5/8	5 5/8	5 5/8	9 6/8	Converse County	WY	Steve Woodman	1985	1,547
68 4/8	12 3/8	12 5/8	5 6/8	5 7/8	10 5/8	Campbell County	WY	Thomas R. Dvorak	1985	1,547
68 4/8	13 4/8	13 2/8	5 4/8	5 4/8	9 4/8	WMU 151	ALB	Allen Avery	1985	1,547
68 4/8	13 0/8	13 0/8	5 6/8	5 7/8	10 7/8	Campbell County	WY	Donald Ace Morgan	1986	1,547
68 4/8	12 0/8	12 4/8	5 7/8	5 7/8	9 0/8	Billings County	ND	Rick Froehlich	1986	1,547
68 4/8	12 4/8	12 2/8	5 6/8	5 5/8	9 0/8	Moffat County	CO	Mike Callaway	1987	1,547
68 4/8	12 5/8	12 5/8	5 7/8	5 6/8	12 7/8	Sweetwater County	WY	David Breakfield	1987	1,547
68 4/8	13 3/8	12 7/8	5 7/8	5 4/8	9 4/8	Slope County	ND	Terry Buechler	1987	1,547
68 4/8	13 1/8	13 2/8	5 3/8	5 3/8	11 6/8	Moffat County	CO	Tim Cuthriell	1988	1,547
68 4/8	14 1/8	14 1/8	5 7/8	5 7/8	11 2/8	Carbon County	WY	Raymond R. Robison	1988	1,547
68 4/8	13 0/8	13 0/8	5 4/8	5 4/8	6 2/8	Moffat County	CO	Steve Barnhill	1988	1,547
68 4/8	13 5/8	13 6/8	5 5/8	5 5/8	11 1/8	Converse County	WY	Mick Cochrane	1988	1,547
68 4/8	13 4/8	13 6/8	6 0/8	6 0/8	10 4/8	Campbell County	WY	Al Haugestuen	1988	1,547
68 4/8	13 1/8	13 1/8	5 5/8	5 5/8	11 6/8	Klamath County	OR	Steve Tandy	1989	1,547
68 4/8	14 2/8	14 3/8	5 5/8	5 5/8	9 6/8	Buffalo	ALB	Glenn Moir	1989	1,547
68 4/8	13 4/8	13 2/8	5 6/8	5 4/8	10 0/8	Washoe County	NV	Linda Manion	1990	1,547
68 4/8	13 2/8	13 1/8	5 6/8	5 6/8	9 4/8	Moffat County	CO	Cheryl Ray	1990	1,547
68 4/8	13 1/8	13 2/8	5 6/8	5 4/8	13 6/8	Manyberries	ALB	Ken Maier	1990	1,547
68 4/8	12 3/8	12 0/8	6 1/8	5 5/8	7 5/8	Moffat County	CO	Mark Petersen	1991	1,547
68 4/8	13 2/8	13 0/8	5 4/8	5 3/8	13 1/8	Campbell County	WY	Marlene Odahlen-Hinz	1991	1,547
68 4/8	11 7/8	11 7/8	6 2/8	6 0/8	8 2/8	Campbell County	WY	Jon Lammle	1991	1,547
68 4/8	13 4/8	13 2/8	5 6/8	5 4/8	8 5/8	Custer County	ID	John R. Sample	1991	1,547
68 4/8	13 7/8	14 0/8	5 6/8	5 4/8	9 0/8	Petroleum County	MT	Theodore J. Poper	1991	1,547
68 4/8	13 1/8	13 2/8	6 1/8	5 6/8	11 4/8	Converse County	WY	Michael L. Hoft	1991	1,547
68 4/8	13 0/8	12 1/8	5 7/8	5 7/8	7 6/8	Musselshell County	MT	Scott A. Silverness	1991	1,547
68 4/8	13 0/8	13 0/8	5 7/8	5 6/8	9 5/8	Johnson County	WY	Mike Neilson	1992	1,547
68 4/8	12 6/8	12 7/8	6 1/8	5 7/8	8 3/8	Beaverhead County	MT	Terry Barkell	1992	1,547
68 3/8	13 2/8	13 2/8	5 5/8	5 5/8	13 3/8	Carbon County	WY	Robert Pitt	1974	1,604
68 3/8	12 5/8	12 7/8	5 7/8	5 7/8	14 6/8	Moffat County	CO	Sam Godfrey	1988	1,604
68 2/8	12 4/8	12 4/8	6 2/8	6 0/8	11 6/8	Moffat County	CO	Burl Duckworth	1958	1,606
68 2/8	12 6/8	12 6/8	5 7/8	5 5/8	10 5/8	Harding County	SD	Chet Wohlhueter	1963	1,606
68 2/8	13 5/8	13 3/8	5 3/8	5 2/8	8 7/8	Morton County	ND	Fred F. Heer	1973	1,606
68 2/8	13 2/8	13 2/8	5 6/8	6 0/8	9 1/8	Sweetwater County	WY	Charles Bartlett	1978	1,606
68 2/8	13 0/8	12 5/8	5 6/8	5 5/8	8 1/8	Thomas County	NE	Harold L. Bowman	1978	1,606

SCORE	LENGTH OF R HORN L		CIRCUMFERENCE R OF BASE L		GREATEST SPREAD	AREA	STATE/ PROVINCE	HUNTER'S NAME	DATE	RANK
68 2/8	13 1/8	13 1/8	5 3/8	5 2/8	9 5/8	Saguache County	CO	Doy K. Curtis	1978	1,606
68 2/8	13 6/8	14 2/8	5 5/8	5 4/8	7 2/8	Lemhi County	ID	Richard Dewey	1978	1,606
68 2/8	12 4/8	12 5/8	6 2/8	6 3/8	11 4/8	Fremont County	WY	Bob Freese	1978	1,606
68 2/8	13 5/8	13 2/8	5 6/8	5 4/8	8 4/8	Fremont County	WY	Will Yeates	1978	1,606
68 2/8	12 1/8	11 7/8	5 6/8	5 7/8	8 0/8	Lemhi County	ID	Larry Cross	1979	1,606
68 2/8	14 1/8	13 7/8	5 5/8	6 0/8	7 5/8	Coconino County	AZ	Jim Ellis	1979	1,606
68 2/8	13 6/8	13 7/8	6 2/8	6 2/8	8 6/8	Sweetwater County	WY	Dean Kendall	1980	1,606
68 2/8	12 6/8	12 6/8	6 0/8	6 1/8	7 3/8	Sweetwater County	WY	Ed Budge	1981	1,606
68 2/8	13 0/8	13 0/8	6 0/8	5 5/8	9 0/8	Natrona County	WY	William E. Ehrman	1981	1,606
68 2/8	12 3/8	12 4/8	5 6/8	5 6/8	8 0/8	Moffat County	CO	Barry J. Smith	1981	1,606
68 2/8	13 0/8	13 0/8	5 7/8	5 6/8	6 7/8	Natrona County	WY	Rodger Warwick	1981	1,606
68 2/8	12 6/8	12 6/8	5 4/8	5 5/8	10 0/8	Natrona County	WY	R. G. Williams	1981	1,606
68 2/8	12 0/8	12 2/8	5 6/8	5 6/8	8 0/8	Converse County	WY	Butch Crawford	1982	1,606
68 2/8	14 1/8	13 7/8	5 4/8	5 4/8	13 1/8	Converse County	WY	Donald Schram	1982	1,606
68 2/8	11 7/8	12 1/8	6 1/8	6 1/8	9 3/8	White Pine County	NV	Tony S. Whitten	1983	1,606
68 2/8	14 6/8	14 6/8	5 2/8	5 1/8	10 6/8	Saguache County	CO	Steve Van Treese	1983	1,606
68 2/8	12 7/8	12 6/8	5 4/8	5 4/8	9 4/8	Sublette County	WY	Terry Wright	1983	1,606
68 2/8	13 3/8	13 1/8	5 4/8	5 4/8	11 1/8	Weld County	CO	Dennis Schweitzer	1983	1,606
68 2/8	13 5/8	13 5/8	5 4/8	5 4/8	10 4/8	Bingham County	ID	Doug Foss	1983	1,606
68 2/8	13 1/8	12 7/8	5 7/8	5 6/8	11 7/8	Wallace County	KS	Darren Collins	1983	1,606
68 2/8	13 5/8	13 1/8	5 3/8	5 3/8	10 3/8	Hughes County	SD	Darrel L. Reinke	1984	1,606
68 2/8	13 1/8	13 3/8	5 6/8	5 6/8	11 3/8	Carbon County	WY	Ron Breitsprecher	1984	1,606
68 2/8	14 3/8	14 6/8	6 1/8	5 7/8	11 1/8	Fremont County	WY	Thomas E. Axthelm	1984	1,606
68 2/8	12 2/8	13 2/8	5 3/8	5 4/8	6 7/8	Converse County	WY	Al Sullivan	1984	1,606
68 2/8	12 4/8	12 7/8	6 3/8	6 2/8	8 6/8	Natrona County	WY	Ray L. Harbin	1985	1,606
68 2/8	14 0/8	13 6/8	5 4/8	5 4/8	10 5/8	Carter County	MT	Juanita Byrne	1985	1,606
68 2/8	12 3/8	12 6/8	5 4/8	5 7/8	9 2/8	White Pine County	NV	Carlos Hernandez	1987	1,606
68 2/8	13 1/8	13 2/8	5 7/8	5 7/8	8 4/8	Jenner	ALB	Jack Kempf	1987	1,606
68 2/8	13 3/8	13 4/8	5 4/8	5 4/8	10 3/8	Dawson County	MT	Dave Athas	1987	1,606
68 2/8	14 0/8	14 0/8	5 4/8	5 4/8	12 1/8	Sweetwater County	WY	Marvin L. Temme	1988	1,606
68 2/8	13 5/8	13 7/8	5 5/8	5 5/8	9 3/8	Meagher County	MT	Gene Clark	1988	1,606
68 2/8	13 3/8	13 4/8	6 0/8	5 6/8	6 7/8	Converse County	WY	Morris Karski	1989	1,606
68 2/8	13 2/8	13 2/8	5 4/8	5 4/8	9 6/8	Park County	MT	Steve Kamps	1989	1,606
68 2/8	12 5/8	13 0/8	5 3/8	5 3/8	8 0/8	Morton County	ND	Mike Fischer	1989	1,606
68 2/8	14 2/8	14 5/8	5 6/8	5 6/8	13 0/8	Garfield County	MT	Ken Davidson	1989	1,606
68 2/8	12 5/8	13 1/8	5 7/8	5 5/8	11 7/8	Campbell County	WY	Allen Jackson	1989	1,606
68 2/8	11 2/8	11 1/8	6 0/8	6 1/8	11 2/8	Moffat County	CO	Richard C. Green	1990	1,606
68 2/8	13 2/8	13 4/8	5 3/8	5 2/8	8 5/8	Moffat County	CO	Lonny Vanatta	1990	1,606
68 2/8	13 3/8	13 2/8	5 4/8	5 3/8	9 0/8	Carter County	MT	Lewis E. Hartenstine	1990	1,606
68 2/8	12 4/8	12 3/8	5 5/8	5 5/8	13 0/8	Natrona County	WY	James V. Siebels	1990	1,606
68 2/8	11 3/8	11 4/8	5 6/8	5 6/8	8 6/8	Cypress	ALB	Dan David	1990	1,606
68 2/8	11 7/8	12 2/8	6 0/8	5 6/8	9 1/8	Converse County	WY	Len Elie	1990	1,606
68 2/8	13 3/8	13 4/8	5 5/8	5 4/8	13 4/8	Campbell County	WY	Troy C. Christensen	1991	1,606
68 2/8	13 7/8	14 1/8	5 6/8	5 5/8	11 7/8	Slope County	ND	Gene D. Davis	1991	1,606
68 2/8	13 2/8	13 2/8	5 4/8	5 4/8	8 1/8	Converse County	WY	John S. Lewis III	1991	1,606
68 2/8	12 4/8	12 3/8	5 6/8	5 6/8	8 7/8	Campbell County	WY	Dave Vomela	1991	1,606
68 2/8	13 6/8	14 1/8	5 7/8	5 6/8	13 5/8	Campbell County	WY	Ken Rimer	1991	1,606
68 2/8	13 0/8	12 7/8	6 1/8	6 0/8	9 1/8	Moffat County	CO	Jeffrey C. Fretz	1992	1,606
68 2/8	13 5/8	13 2/8	5 5/8	5 4/8	11 0/8	Campbell County	WY	Vernon Kleve	1992	1,606
68 2/8	13 2/8	12 6/8	5 6/8	5 7/8	12 1/8	Converse County	WY	Johnnie R. Walters	1992	1,606
68 2/8	12 4/8	13 1/8	6 0/8	5 7/8	9 1/8	Manyberries	ALB	Gary Goulet	1992	1,606
68 2/8	13 2/8	13 2/8	5 6/8	5 5/8	8 0/8	Fremont County	WY	Reggie Scheierman	1992	1,606
68 2/8	13 4/8	13 3/8	5 7/8	5 6/8	12 4/8	MD Cypress	ALB	David Moore	1992	1,606
68 0/8	13 0/8	13 2/8	5 6/8	5 5/8	10 1/8	Ziebach County	SD	Jim Glines	1934	1,664
68 0/8	14 1/8	13 0/8	5 4/8	5 6/8	7 7/8	Campbell County	WY	Reinhold L. Lind	1961	1,664
68 0/8	13 4/8	13 4/8	5 4/8	5 4/8	7 5/8	Carbon County	WY	Bill Cunningham	1963	1,664
68 0/8	14 0/8	13 6/8	5 2/8	5 3/8	8 0/8	Morton County	ND	Roy D. Russell, Jr.	1967	1,664
68 0/8	11 4/8	11 3/8	5 7/8	5 6/8	7 3/8	Burke County	ND	Allen L. Nelson	1974	1,664
68 0/8	13 0/8	13 0/8	5 7/8	5 7/8	9 6/8	Saguache County	CO	David Scheid	1974	1,664
68 0/8	12 4/8	12 5/8	5 6/8	5 5/8	10 6/8	Custer County	ID	Gary Schaffner	1975	1,664
68 0/8	13 0/8	13 3/8	5 5/8	5 4/8	9 7/8	Clark County	ID	Ron Parish	1977	1,664
68 0/8	13 5/8	13 3/8	5 6/8	5 6/8	10 3/8	Humboldt County	NV	Vic Christison	1978	1,664
68 0/8	13 2/8	12 7/8	6 1/8	6 0/8	10 1/8	Sweetwater County	WY	Jack Riddle	1979	1,664
68 0/8	12 2/8	12 4/8	5 6/8	5 5/8	8 4/8	Natrona County	WY	Todd James	1980	1,664
68 0/8	13 6/8	12 3/8	5 6/8	5 5/8	7 2/8	Moffat County	CO	Judd Cooney	1981	1,664
68 0/8	14 1/8	14 1/8	5 4/8	5 1/8	6 7/8	Lassen County	CA	Junior Morris	1982	1,664
68 0/8	13 4/8	13 6/8	5 6/8	5 6/8	13 4/8	Sweetwater County	WY	Sy Gilliland	1982	1,664
68 0/8	13 2/8	13 3/8	5 5/8	5 4/8	11 0/8	Fremont County	WY	Everett A. Boss	1982	1,664
68 0/8	13 2/8	13 2/8	5 7/8	5 6/8	10 1/8	Converse County	WY	Bill Frodl	1982	1,664
68 0/8	12 7/8	12 5/8	4 7/8	4 7/8	14 1/8	Moffat County	CO	Keith R. Hardy	1983	1,664

PRONGHORN

MINIMUM SCORE 64

(Continued)

Score	Length of Horn R	Length of Horn L	Circumference of Base R	Circumference of Base L	Greatest Spread	Area	State/Province	Hunter's Name	Date	Rank
68 0/8	12 2/8	12 7/8	5 7/8	6 0/8	6 7/8	Natrona County	WY	E. Michael Onken	1983	1,664
68 0/8	13 1/8	13 1/8	5 6/8	5 5/8	9 0/8	Converse County	WY	William Kobart	1983	1,664
68 0/8	13 6/8	13 7/8	5 5/8	5 5/8	12 2/8	Converse County	WY	David P. Lindman	1983	1,664
68 0/8	13 1/8	13 2/8	5 7/8	5 6/8	7 5/8	Albany County	WY	Adrian H. Farmer, Jr.	1983	1,664
68 0/8	14 0/8	14 1/8	5 2/8	5 4/8	12 4/8	Coconino County	AZ	Dean Zuern	1984	1,664
68 0/8	12 6/8	12 0/8	6 0/8	5 7/8	10 1/8	Converse County	WY	Michael Murphy	1984	1,664
68 0/8	13 5/8	13 6/8	6 0/8	6 0/8	15 4/8	Sweetwater County	WY	Bill Clink	1985	1,664
68 0/8	13 4/8	13 5/8	5 6/8	5 5/8	8 6/8	Sweetwater County	WY	Robert L Kampen	1985	1,664
68 0/8	13 3/8	13 4/8	5 1/8	5 2/8	6 5/8	Natrona County	WY	Joe Brant	1985	1,664
68 0/8	13 0/8	13 1/8	5 7/8	5 7/8	9 4/8	Natrona County	WY	Dave James	1985	1,664
68 0/8	12 3/8	12 5/8	5 4/8	5 4/8	11 5/8	Natrona County	WY	David Bouchard	1985	1,664
68 0/8	14 0/8	13 6/8	6 3/8	6 2/8	14 6/8	Converse County	WY	Frank Moore	1985	1,664
68 0/8	12 3/8	12 4/8	6 2/8	6 2/8	9 0/8	Converse County	WY	Mark Slaughter	1986	1,664
68 0/8	13 0/8	13 1/8	6 0/8	6 1/8	9 4/8	Keya Paha County	NE	Rory Swim	1987	1,664
68 0/8	13 5/8	13 2/8	5 5/8	5 6/8	8 5/8	Converse County	WY	Jimmy R. Speer	1987	1,664
68 0/8	12 6/8	12 6/8	6 1/8	6 1/8	8 6/8	Converse County	WY	Dan Bertalan	1987	1,664
68 0/8	13 7/8	13 6/8	5 5/8	5 3/8	11 0/8	Washoe County	NV	Bill Fuller	1988	1,664
68 0/8	13 7/8	13 7/8	5 5/8	5 4/8	10 3/8	Butte County	ID	Andy Moore	1988	1,664
68 0/8	12 6/8	12 7/8	5 7/8	5 7/8	8 5/8	Moffat County	CO	Randy Gipple	1988	1,664
68 0/8	12 6/8	12 7/8	5 6/8	5 5/8	9 5/8	Natrona County	WY	Nolan C. Fowles	1988	1,664
68 0/8	13 1/8	13 2/8	5 3/8	5 3/8	9 1/8	Moffat County	CO	Rich McNutt	1988	1,664
68 0/8	13 4/8	13 6/8	5 4/8	5 4/8	10 3/8	Moffat County	CO	Dennis Wehling	1989	1,664
68 0/8	12 7/8	12 7/8	5 6/8	5 5/8	9 2/8	Garfield County	MT	Bruce Balerud	1989	1,664
68 0/8	12 4/8	12 2/8	6 4/8	6 2/8	8 2/8	Campbell County	WY	Thomas J. Buchner	1989	1,664
68 0/8	12 1/8	12 3/8	5 2/8	5 4/8	11 0/8	Sargent County	ND	Richard G. Olson	1989	1,664
68 0/8	15 4/8	15 3/8	4 7/8	4 7/8	8 4/8	Powder River County	MT	John A. Stuver	1989	1,664
68 0/8	12 3/8	12 3/8	5 6/8	5 6/8	10 2/8	Moffat County	CO	Mike Lamade	1990	1,664
68 0/8	12 6/8	12 4/8	5 6/8	5 6/8	8 1/8	Moffat County	CO	John Brassard	1990	1,664
68 0/8	12 5/8	12 6/8	5 7/8	5 6/8	7 0/8	Delta County	CO	James C. Lake	1990	1,664
68 0/8	13 5/8	14 0/8	5 4/8	5 5/8	7 5/8	Johnson County	WY	L. Dan Neebe	1990	1,664
68 0/8	12 4/8	12 5/8	5 6/8	6 0/8	6 7/8	Converse County	WY	Paul J. Ganzen	1990	1,664
68 0/8	13 3/8	13 3/8	5 6/8	5 6/8	10 3/8	Chouteau County	MT	K. C. Palagi	1990	1,664
68 0/8	13 2/8	12 7/8	5 6/8	5 7/8	7 6/8	Campbell County	WY	Timothy Hammes	1990	1,664
68 0/8	12 3/8	11 5/8	5 6/8	5 6/8	8 3/8	Slope County	ND	Dennis Moritz	1990	1,664
68 0/8	12 3/8	12 5/8	6 0/8	6 0/8	9 1/8	Moffat County	CO	Ronald Dinger	1991	1,664
68 0/8	12 5/8	12 5/8	5 5/8	5 5/8	11 2/8	Fremont County	WY	Jerry A. Bodar	1991	1,664
68 0/8	11 2/8	11 0/8	5 6/8	5 6/8	10 1/8	Natrona County	WY	Scott D. Baer	1991	1,664
68 0/8	13 0/8	13 7/8	5 4/8	5 5/8	8 5/8	Thomas County	NE	Matt Gideon	1991	1,664
68 0/8	12 0/8	12 1/8	6 5/8	6 4/8	10 3/8	Converse County	WY	Derek Goto	1991	1,664
68 0/8	13 5/8	13 2/8	5 7/8	5 6/8	10 1/8	Sheridan County	WY	Marty Krohn	1991	1,664
68 0/8	13 3/8	13 5/8	5 6/8	5 6/8	8 4/8	Bowman County	ND	Kendall Bauer	1991	1,664
68 0/8	13 1/8	13 0/8	6 0/8	5 6/8	9 3/8	Sioux County	NE	Alton Schroeder	1991	1,664
68 0/8	13 7/8	14 0/8	5 5/8	5 5/8	7 1/8	Ward County	ND	Russel Jon Hardy	1991	1,664
68 0/8	12 4/8	12 2/8	6 2/8	6 3/8	9 2/8	Converse County	WY	Jeff Reynolds	1991	1,664
68 0/8	13 6/8	13 7/8	5 6/8	5 6/8	9 0/8	Washoe County	NV	David Schopper	1992	1,664
68 0/8	13 4/8	13 4/8	5 7/8	6 0/8	9 5/8	Carbon County	WY	Steven R. Hohensee	1992	1,664
68 0/8	13 2/8	13 3/8	5 7/8	5 7/8	9 7/8	Owyhee County	ID	DeLoy Desaro	1992	1,664
68 0/8	13 6/8	13 2/8	5 6/8	6 0/8	9 6/8	Campbell County	WY	Ken Rimer	1992	1,664
67 6/8	12 3/8	12 4/8	5 6/8	5 5/8	9 0/8	McHenry County	ND	Darryl Ablestad	1967	1,729
67 6/8	12 6/8	12 4/8	6 2/8	6 0/8	11 3/8	McHenry County	ND	Jim Budeau	1968	1,729
67 6/8	13 4/8	13 4/8	5 5/8	5 5/8	11 2/8	Logan County	CO	Loren Johnston	1968	1,729
67 6/8	13 3/8	13 2/8	5 2/8	5 5/8	10 1/8	Fremont County	WY	Doris Clark	1970	1,729
67 6/8	14 0/8	13 1/8	5 0/8	5 0/8	13 4/8	Butte County	ID	Craig L. Hansen	1974	1,729
67 6/8	12 4/8	12 6/8	5 5/8	5 5/8	11 1/8	Carbon County	WY	James Beeson	1976	1,729
67 6/8	14 0/8	14 0/8	5 2/8	5 2/8	11 1/8	Park County	WY	Fred W. Achilles	1978	1,729
67 6/8	13 7/8	13 6/8	5 2/8	5 2/8	8 5/8	Moffat County	CO	Dave Skiff	1980	1,729
67 6/8	11 2/8	11 2/8	5 6/8	5 5/8	8 1/8	Converse County	WY	Ron Carpenter	1980	1,729
67 6/8	11 6/8	11 7/8	5 6/8	5 5/8	8 6/8	Carbon County	WY	Bob Funke	1980	1,729
67 6/8	13 1/8	13 2/8	5 4/8	5 2/8	9 7/8	Sweetwater County	WY	Jerry Giovannoni	1980	1,729
67 6/8	13 6/8	13 2/8	5 6/8	5 6/8	11 4/8	Natrona County	WY	David Stejskal	1980	1,729
67 6/8	13 5/8	12 6/8	5 5/8	5 4/8	10 4/8	Custer County	ID	Gerard J. Krauth	1981	1,729
67 6/8	13 7/8	13 6/8	5 6/8	5 5/8	9 2/8	Rio Arriba County	NM	Jose R. Montalvo	1982	1,729
67 6/8	13 4/8	13 6/8	5 4/8	5 4/8	11 7/8	Moffat County	CO	Robert L. Kinser	1982	1,729
67 6/8	14 5/8	14 1/8	4 6/8	4 7/8	9 7/8	Carbon County	WY	Bill Nation	1982	1,729
67 6/8	13 5/8	13 5/8	5 3/8	5 2/8	8 0/8	Beaverhead County	MT	L. C. Trimber	1982	1,729
67 6/8	12 2/8	12 1/8	5 7/8	5 7/8	11 4/8	Moffat County	CO	Mike Ward	1982	1,729
67 6/8	12 2/8	12 6/8	5 4/8	5 4/8	11 7/8	Converse County	WY	Joe Ed McCray	1982	1,729
67 6/8	12 3/8	13 1/8	5 2/8	5 2/8	12 2/8	Larimer County	CO	William Shuster	1983	1,729
67 6/8	13 3/8	13 3/8	5 4/8	5 3/8	8 7/8	Converse County	WY	Roger Schmitt	1983	1,729
67 6/8	14 0/8	13 6/8	5 3/8	5 2/8	9 5/8	Las Animas County	CO	Edward F. Bryan, Jr.	1983	1,729

SCORE	LENGTH OF R HORN L		CIRCUMFERENCE R OF BASE L		GREATEST SPREAD	AREA	STATE/ PROVINCE	HUNTER'S NAME	DATE	RANK
67 6/8	14 2/8	14 3/8	5 7/8	6 0/8	11 1/8	Hettinger County	ND	Mike Schiwal	1984	1,729
67 6/8	13 0/8	13 0/8	5 6/8	5 6/8	11 5/8	Natrona County	WY	Kirk H. Soulliere	1985	1,729
67 6/8	14 4/8	14 4/8	5 3/8	5 2/8	8 0/8	Carbon County	WY	Bob Boyle	1985	1,729
67 6/8	12 6/8	12 6/8	6 1/8	6 1/8	7 6/8	Sweetwater County	WY	Dean Lawyer	1986	1,729
67 6/8	13 4/8	13 5/8	6 2/8	6 0/8	9 6/8	Mountrail County	ND	Kevin Ohlhauser	1986	1,729
67 6/8	13 3/8	13 4/8	5 4/8	5 5/8	6 4/8	Tom Green County	TX	Terry Turney	1986	1,729
67 6/8	12 1/8	12 2/8	6 2/8	6 2/8	11 6/8	Converse County	WY	Martin Scott Campbell	1987	1,729
67 6/8	13 3/8	13 2/8	5 6/8	5 6/8	10 5/8	Sublette County	WY	Randy Tolman	1987	1,729
67 6/8	13 0/8	13 0/8	5 5/8	5 4/8	7 6/8	Medicine Hat	ALB	James Pike	1987	1,729
67 6/8	13 6/8	13 2/8	5 4/8	5 5/8	9 1/8	Moffat County	CO	Carol Ashurst	1988	1,729
67 6/8	12 3/8	12 4/8	5 6/8	5 6/8	12 2/8	Converse County	WY	Larry Crouch	1988	1,729
67 6/8	12 4/8	12 4/8	5 4/8	5 4/8	9 5/8	Sweetwater County	WY	Mark Perqande	1989	1,729
67 6/8	13 5/8	14 0/8	5 2/8	5 3/8	9 3/8	Campbell County	WY	Robert F. Synder	1989	1,729
67 6/8	12 7/8	13 3/8	6 4/8	5 4/8	8 6/8	Campbell County	WY	Charles Smith	1989	1,729
67 6/8	12 7/8	13 2/8	5 4/8	5 3/8	10 5/8	Hudspeth County	TX	Melvin Sloan	1990	1,729
67 6/8	12 0/8	12 0/8	6 1/8	6 0/8	12 6/8	Weld County	CO	Kenneth W. Ayers	1991	1,729
67 6/8	14 0/8	14 5/8	5 6/8	5 5/8	10 1/8	Natrona County	WY	Michael Running	1991	1,729
67 6/8	13 1/8	12 0/8	5 6/8	5 5/8	9 0/8	Yavapai County	AZ	Gary French	1991	1,729
67 6/8	12 6/8	12 6/8	5 7/8	5 6/8	9 2/8	Campbell County	WY	Joe Gohres	1991	1,729
67 6/8	13 3/8	13 0/8	5 5/8	5 5/8	10 4/8	Converse County	WY	James C. Gates	1991	1,729
67 6/8	12 4/8	12 6/8	5 7/8	5 7/8	8 7/8	Perkins County	SD	James S. Bidwell	1991	1,729
67 6/8	13 4/8	13 2/8	5 4/8	5 4/8	6 1/8	Beaverhead County	MT	Curtis A. Green	1991	1,729
67 6/8	13 7/8	13 6/8	5 5/8	5 6/8	6 4/8	Owyhee County	ID	David R. Heck	1992	1,729
67 6/8	13 0/8	13 0/8	5 7/8	5 5/8	12 4/8	Converse County	WY	Carolyn Siebrasse Zanoni	1992	1,729
67 6/8	12 5/8	12 3/8	5 7/8	5 7/8	9 3/8	Natrona County	WY	Kim Cooper	1992	1,729
67 6/8	13 1/8	13 1/8	6 0/8	6 0/8	9 2/8	Bowman County	ND	Gene Welle	1992	1,729
67 4/8	13 4/8	13 5/8	5 3/8	5 2/8	13 3/8	Cherry County	NE	Marlin Wells	1967	1,777
67 4/8	13 7/8	13 7/8	5 3/8	5 2/8	10 1/8	Oregon Basin	WY	John Pruszyski	1973	1,777
67 4/8	13 3/8	13 2/8	5 4/8	5 4/8	9 0/8	Meade County	SD	Jim Bohls	1974	1,777
67 4/8	14 2/8	14 0/8	5 2/8	5 1/8	8 5/8	Jackson County	CO	Robert Souza	1974	1,777
67 4/8	12 4/8	12 5/8	5 4/8	5 4/8	11 6/8	Converse County	WY	Bob Jensen	1976	1,777
67 4/8	13 6/8	13 4/8	5 6/8	5 4/8	11 7/8	Natrona County	WY	Steve Turck	1976	1,777
67 4/8	13 1/8	13 5/8	5 4/8	5 4/8	8 2/8	Converse County	WY	James E. Boland	1979	1,777
67 4/8	13 0/8	13 1/8	5 2/8	5 4/8	13 3/8	Natrona County	WY	Clifford G. James	1980	1,777
67 4/8	12 6/8	12 5/8	5 6/8	5 6/8	10 0/8	Converse County	WY	Bruce Sanders	1980	1,777
67 4/8	12 5/8	12 0/8	6 1/8	5 6/8	9 1/8	Moffat County	CO	Robert L. Wright	1981	1,777
67 4/8	13 5/8	13 4/8	5 4/8	5 4/8	10 1/8	Converse County	WY	Ron Breitsprecher	1981	1,777
67 4/8	14 1/8	13 0/8	5 6/8	5 6/8	10 2/8	Lemhi County	ID	Daniel A. Davis	1981	1,777
67 4/8	14 2/8	14 4/8	5 4/8	5 3/8	7 4/8	Carbon County	WY	Mike Fortman	1982	1,777
67 4/8	11 6/8	12 6/8	5 5/8	5 4/8	8 1/8	Moffat County	CO	Ken Keller	1983	1,777
67 4/8	13 0/8	13 2/8	5 3/8	5 3/8	6 5/8	Custer County	CO	Rohn L. Garnhart	1983	1,777
67 4/8	12 3/8	12 4/8	5 4/8	5 4/8	9 1/8	Converse County	WY	Roberta Byerly	1983	1,777
67 4/8	13 0/8	13 1/8	5 6/8	5 5/8	9 0/8	Converse County	WY	Jon Arneson	1983	1,777
67 4/8	14 1/8	14 0/8	5 4/8	5 4/8	9 7/8	Converse County	WY	Gary Hunsicker	1983	1,777
67 4/8	12 4/8	12 6/8	6 3/8	6 1/8	8 4/8	Converse County	WY	Jim Hodson	1984	1,777
67 4/8	12 3/8	12 4/8	6 0/8	5 7/8	9 0/8	Sweetwater County	WY	Craig Richardson	1984	1,777
67 4/8	13 0/8	12 6/8	5 6/8	5 6/8	11 0/8	Bowman County	ND	Mark Delong	1984	1,777
67 4/8	13 4/8	13 3/8	5 4/8	5 4/8	10 3/8	Campbell County	WY	Rick Gilley	1984	1,777
67 4/8	13 2/8	13 5/8	5 4/8	5 2/8	11 3/8	Johnson County	WY	Edward Carmichael	1984	1,777
67 4/8	13 4/8	13 4/8	5 4/8	5 4/8	12 0/8	Phillips County	MT	Ken Ruzicka	1984	1,777
67 4/8	13 1/8	13 1/8	5 6/8	5 6/8	9 2/8	Sweetwater County	WY	Kevin J. Slovak	1985	1,777
67 4/8	13 0/8	13 0/8	6 2/8	6 3/8	9 4/8	Billings County	ND	Ronald M. Bachmeier	1985	1,777
67 4/8	13 0/8	12 7/8	5 3/8	5 3/8	8 3/8	Converse County	WY	Len Cardinale	1985	1,777
67 4/8	12 7/8	12 6/8	5 3/8	5 2/8	9 0/8	Converse County	WY	Burt Thompson, Jr.	1985	1,777
67 4/8	12 3/8	12 7/8	5 5/8	5 5/8	9 6/8	Converse County	WY	Thomas Vitale	1985	1,777
67 4/8	12 1/8	12 0/8	5 7/8	6 0/8	9 2/8	Sweetwater County	WY	Chris Switzer	1986	1,777
67 4/8	13 7/8	12 7/8	5 6/8	5 6/8	8 3/8	McKenzie County	ND	David Tofte	1986	1,777
67 4/8	11 3/8	11 3/8	6 3/8	6 2/8	9 0/8	Lemhi County	ID	C. Richard Wenger	1987	1,777
67 4/8	12 5/8	12 5/8	5 5/8	5 5/8	8 6/8	Billings County	ND	Ivan Bachamp	1987	1,777
67 4/8	11 7/8	11 7/8	5 6/8	5 6/8	10 0/8	Daggett County	UT	L. Scot Jenkins	1987	1,777
67 4/8	12 4/8	12 4/8	5 7/8	5 7/8	9 7/8	Yellowstone County	MT	Jack S. Esterly, Jr.	1987	1,777
67 4/8	13 3/8	13 2/8	5 2/8	5 2/8	8 4/8	Moffat County	CO	E. Damon Handley	1988	1,777
67 4/8	12 6/8	12 6/8	5 5/8	5 5/8	10 4/8	Natrona County	WY	Paul Jayson	1988	1,777
67 4/8	12 2/8	12 2/8	5 6/8	5 7/8	7 5/8	Converse County	WY	J. G. "Rusty" Watson	1988	1,777
67 4/8	10 7/8	11 2/8	6 1/8	6 0/8	8 0/8	Converse County	WY	Rick Simonson	1988	1,777
67 4/8	12 2/8	12 2/8	5 1/8	5 2/8	8 2/8	Weston County	WY	Keith Gould	1988	1,777
67 4/8	13 4/8	12 1/8	5 6/8	5 6/8	8 3/8	Moffat County	CO	Todd Weiszbrod	1989	1,777
67 4/8	12 3/8	12 2/8	5 5/8	5 6/8	10 5/8	Moffat County	CO	James "Boomer" Hayden	1989	1,777
67 4/8	12 0/8	12 0/8	5 5/8	5 4/8	8 6/8	Moffat County	CO	James A. Davison	1990	1,777
67 4/8	12 7/8	12 7/8	5 6/8	5 5/8	7 7/8	Chaffee County	CO	Joel Morgan	1990	1,777

MINIMUM SCORE 64   *(Continued)*

Score	Length of R HORN	L	Circumference R OF BASE	L	Greatest Spread	Area	State/ Province	Hunter's Name	Date	Rank
67 4/8	13 3/8	13 3/8	5 4/8	5 3/8	12 0/8	Clark County	ID	Tom Thiel	1990	1,777
67 4/8	12 7/8	14 2/8	6 0/8	6 0/8	10 4/8	Lake County	OR	Rick D. Breckel	1990	1,777
67 4/8	14 0/8	13 7/8	5 5/8	5 5/8	8 1/8	Walsh	ALB	David R. Coupland	1990	1,777
67 4/8	12 3/8	12 4/8	6 0/8	6 0/8	12 1/8	Rosebud County	MT	Scott Propst	1990	1,777
67 4/8	13 2/8	13 0/8	6 1/8	5 7/8	9 2/8	Johnson County	WY	Brian R. Potter	1990	1,777
67 4/8	13 2/8	13 0/8	5 3/8	5 2/8	6 4/8	Outram	SAS	Garry Leslie	1990	1,777
67 4/8	12 4/8	12 4/8	6 0/8	5 7/8	8 0/8	Converse County	WY	Greg McTee	1990	1,777
67 4/8	13 5/8	13 6/8	5 4/8	5 4/8	12 2/8	Meagher County	MT	D. Mitch Kottas	1990	1,777
67 4/8	12 5/8	12 3/8	6 3/8	5 6/8	7 4/8	Natrona County	WY	Mark D. Christopherson	1991	1,777
67 4/8	13 6/8	12 4/8	5 5/8	5 4/8	9 4/8	Malheur County	OR	Dave Seida	1991	1,777
67 4/8	12 5/8	12 2/8	6 0/8	5 7/8	12 1/8	Fremont County	WY	Lyle Prell	1991	1,777
67 4/8	14 1/8	13 3/8	5 3/8	5 4/8	11 2/8	Campbell County	WY	Edwin John Durushia	1991	1,777
67 4/8	13 5/8	13 2/8	5 7/8	5 7/8	12 1/8	Madison County	MT	Jim Powell	1991	1,777
67 4/8	13 4/8	13 4/8	5 4/8	5 4/8	8 2/8	Harding County	SD	John R. Simpson	1991	1,777
67 4/8	12 4/8	13 0/8	6 0/8	6 0/8	8 1/8	Converse County	WY	Peter F. Woech	1991	1,777
67 4/8	12 5/8	13 0/8	6 1/8	6 1/8	9 0/8	Weld County	CO	Michael J. McArtor	1992	1,777
67 4/8	13 6/8	14 0/8	5 4/8	5 4/8	13 4/8	Owyhee County	ID	Frank Sanders	1992	1,777
67 4/8	13 0/8	13 3/8	5 6/8	5 4/8	12 2/8	Owyhee County	ID	Jay D. King	1992	1,777
67 3/8	13 1/8	13 2/8	5 7/8	5 5/8	13 3/8	Carbon County	WY	Steve Stumbo	1975	1,839
67 2/8	12 1/8	12 1/8	6 0/8	5 5/8	11 6/8	Carbon County	WY	Dennis Behn	1974	1,840
67 2/8	12 7/8	13 0/8	5 2/8	5 2/8	6 4/8	Musselshell County	MT	Scott L. Koelzer	1976	1,840
67 2/8	13 7/8	14 0/8	5 4/8	5 4/8	9 2/8	Campbell County	WY	Larry Tiner	1978	1,840
67 2/8	12 6/8	13 1/8	5 7/8	5 7/8	9 5/8	Sweetwater County	WY	Blair Smith	1978	1,840
67 2/8	11 5/8	11 5/8	5 0/8	5 0/8	9 2/8	Converse County	WY	Eugene Smith, Jr.	1979	1,840
67 2/8	13 1/8	13 0/8	5 4/8	5 5/8	9 2/8	Converse County	WY	Ronald J. Collier	1980	1,840
67 2/8	13 5/8	13 1/8	5 5/8	5 5/8	10 3/8	Humboldt County	NV	Jeff Purcell	1980	1,840
67 2/8	13 3/8	13 4/8	5 5/8	5 4/8	10 2/8	Converse County	WY	John Zawaski	1980	1,840
67 2/8	12 6/8	12 6/8	5 3/8	5 3/8	12 3/8	Converse County	WY	Al Gross	1981	1,840
67 2/8	13 7/8	13 7/8	5 4/8	5 4/8	11 2/8	Converse County	WY	Wayne W. Wagner	1981	1,840
67 2/8	13 1/8	13 2/8	5 2/8	5 1/8	9 4/8	Pueblo County	CO	Mitchell McMahon	1982	1,840
67 2/8	14 1/8	12 7/8	5 4/8	5 4/8	10 6/8	Moffat County	CO	Steven Neal	1982	1,840
67 2/8	13 4/8	13 4/8	5 4/8	5 3/8	8 2/8	Wallace County	KS	Steve Rugg	1982	1,840
67 2/8	13 6/8	12 3/8	6 1/8	6 1/8	9 6/8	White Pine County	NV	Larry T. Gilbertson	1983	1,840
67 2/8	11 7/8	12 0/8	5 7/8	5 7/8	9 4/8	Bowman County	ND	Greg Braun	1983	1,840
67 2/8	14 3/8	14 2/8	5 4/8	5 4/8	12 0/8	Perkins County	SD	Vilas Schoenfelder	1983	1,840
67 2/8	13 0/8	12 4/8	6 0/8	5 6/8	7 3/8	Converse County	WY	Larry Crooks	1983	1,840
67 2/8	13 1/8	12 7/8	5 5/8	5 6/8	11 5/8	Converse County	WY	Gary Holtz	1983	1,840
67 2/8	12 5/8	12 3/8	5 3/8	5 4/8	11 7/8	Meade County	SD	Steve D. Krier	1983	1,840
67 2/8	13 0/8	13 0/8	5 5/8	5 5/8	8 1/8	Hettinger County	ND	Brian Scherr	1983	1,840
67 2/8	12 0/8	12 2/8	5 7/8	6 1/8	7 3/8	Campbell County	WY	William Heineke	1984	1,840
67 2/8	13 1/8	13 1/8	4 5/8	4 7/8	11 7/8	Moffat County	CO	Glenn Pritchard	1984	1,840
67 2/8	12 0/8	12 1/8	5 6/8	5 5/8	7 7/8	Converse County	WY	Ron Rockwell	1984	1,840
67 2/8	12 4/8	12 3/8	6 0/8	6 0/8	12 0/8	Sweetwater County	WY	John Cheese	1985	1,840
67 2/8	13 2/8	13 2/8	5 4/8	5 2/8	7 2/8	Moffat County	CO	John E. Axelson	1985	1,840
67 2/8	13 3/8	12 6/8	5 4/8	5 4/8	7 6/8	Moffat County	CO	Kurt Keskimaki	1985	1,840
67 2/8	12 4/8	12 4/8	5 6/8	5 6/8	8 3/8	Moffat County	CO	James A. Davison	1985	1,840
67 2/8	13 1/8	12 7/8	5 7/8	5 6/8	9 3/8	Carbon County	WY	Richard L. Westervelt	1985	1,840
67 2/8	13 7/8	13 7/8	5 6/8	5 5/8	11 1/8	Converse County	WY	David Jerome	1985	1,840
67 2/8	12 5/8	12 5/8	5 3/8	5 3/8	9 0/8	Converse County	WY	William Doemland	1985	1,840
67 2/8	13 2/8	13 2/8	5 1/8	5 1/8	8 4/8	Campbell County	WY	Richard Andre	1985	1,840
67 2/8	13 2/8	13 1/8	5 7/8	5 6/8	11 0/8	Converse County	WY	Craig James Stransky	1985	1,840
67 2/8	12 5/8	12 7/8	6 1/8	5 6/8	13 5/8	Converse County	WY	John May	1986	1,840
67 2/8	12 4/8	12 3/8	6 0/8	5 7/8	10 1/8	Valley County	MT	Bryan Erickson	1986	1,840
67 2/8	12 7/8	12 7/8	6 0/8	5 6/8	8 5/8	Converse County	WY	Gregory White	1986	1,840
67 2/8	12 4/8	12 2/8	6 2/8	6 2/8	10 0/8	Converse County	WY	Richard Crawford	1986	1,840
67 2/8	13 6/8	13 7/8	4 7/8	5 0/8	9 3/8	Chouteau County	MT	Wayne Arnold	1986	1,840
67 2/8	11 3/8	12 4/8	5 6/8	5 6/8	9 2/8	Blaine County	ID	Wesley Moore	1988	1,840
67 2/8	12 4/8	12 7/8	5 4/8	5 4/8	9 5/8	Bingham County	ID	Reggie N. Scheierman	1988	1,840
67 2/8	11 4/8	11 6/8	6 1/8	6 0/8	7 6/8	McKenzie County	ND	Bill Kelly	1988	1,840
67 2/8	13 0/8	12 7/8	5 5/8	5 5/8	7 1/8	Converse County	WY	Carmine Agostine	1988	1,840
67 2/8	14 1/8	13 7/8	5 4/8	5 3/8	14 5/8	Suffield	ALB	Jay Brown	1988	1,840
67 2/8	13 2/8	13 1/8	5 7/8	6 0/8	10 6/8	Petroleum County	MT	Leamon D. Ferrell	1988	1,840
67 2/8	12 4/8	12 6/8	5 7/8	5 6/8	9 5/8	Moffat County	CO	Barry Rich	1989	1,840
67 2/8	12 2/8	12 5/8	5 4/8	5 3/8	8 7/8	Converse County	WY	Jason W. Zebrowski	1989	1,840
67 2/8	13 1/8	13 4/8	5 6/8	5 5/8	7 2/8	Campbell County	WY	Robin D. Johnson	1989	1,840
67 2/8	11 1/8	11 3/8	6 2/8	6 1/8	10 1/8	Custer County	MT	Mark L. Frank	1989	1,840
67 2/8	13 2/8	13 2/8	5 6/8	5 6/8	10 1/8	Billings County	ND	Jeff Brigham	1989	1,840
67 2/8	13 2/8	13 0/8	5 3/8	5 3/8	9 3/8	Converse County	WY	David A. Widby	1990	1,840
67 2/8	12 7/8	13 2/8	6 0/8	5 7/8	10 4/8	Harney County	OR	Richard Wright	1990	1,840
67 2/8	13 2/8	12 7/8	6 3/8	6 3/8	14 0/8	Natrona County	WY	Kurt W. Keskimaki	1990	1,840

Score	Length of Horn R	Length of Horn L	Circumference of Base R	Circumference of Base L	Greatest Spread	Area	State/Province	Hunter's Name	Date	Rank
67 2/8	12 2/8	12 5/8	5 5/8	5 4/8	11 0/8	Sweetwater County	WY	Dave Holt	1990	1,840
67 2/8	13 2/8	13 1/8	5 3/8	5 5/8	9 6/8	Sheridan County	WY	Tom Hlinka	1990	1,840
67 2/8	13 3/8	13 3/8	5 6/8	5 4/8	8 5/8	Wallace County	KS	Roger Potter	1990	1,840
67 2/8	13 5/8	13 5/8	5 6/8	5 4/8	9 0/8	Harding County	SD	Marty Adams	1990	1,840
67 2/8	12 7/8	13 1/8	5 7/8	5 6/8	7 1/8	Owyhee County	ID	Jesse M. Frandsen	1991	1,840
67 2/8	12 5/8	12 4/8	5 5/8	5 5/8	9 4/8	Sweetwater County	WY	Mark Petersen	1991	1,840
67 2/8	12 0/8	12 7/8	6 2/8	6 1/8	7 6/8	Converse County	WY	Ed Defibaugh	1991	1,840
67 2/8	13 3/8	13 3/8	5 6/8	5 6/8	9 2/8	Campbell County	WY	William J. McGrath	1991	1,840
67 2/8	11 5/8	11 7/8	5 7/8	5 6/8	8 7/8	McKenzie County	ND	Mark D. Hughes	1991	1,840
67 2/8	13 2/8	13 1/8	5 6/8	5 5/8	11 0/8	Campbell County	WY	Tom Griffin	1991	1,840
67 2/8	13 0/8	13 1/8	6 2/8	6 2/8	12 2/8	Carbon County	WY	Levi Nelson	1991	1,840
67 2/8	12 4/8	12 6/8	5 6/8	5 6/8	7 0/8	Butte County	SD	Larry Kracht	1991	1,840
67 2/8	13 4/8	13 2/8	5 5/8	5 5/8	9 7/8	Moffat County	CO	Garry Woodman	1992	1,840
67 2/8	13 3/8	13 3/8	5 2/8	5 2/8	12 1/8	Bowman County	ND	David Brag	1992	1,840
67 2/8	13 1/8	13 3/8	5 0/8	5 0/8	11 2/8	Converse County	WY	Scott McCormack	1992	1,840
67 2/8	13 3/8	12 6/8	6 2/8	6 1/8	6 6/8	Rosebud County	MT	John W. Offord	1992	1,840
67 0/8	12 7/8	12 7/8	5 6/8	5 4/8	10 2/8	Butte County	SD	David Lind	1961	1,907
67 0/8	13 0/8	13 2/8	5 5/8	5 5/8	10 6/8	McLean County	ND	Harold Janssen	1971	1,907
67 0/8	13 0/8	12 4/8	6 0/8	6 0/8	10 4/8	Campbell County	WY	Gerald L. Egbert	1975	1,907
67 0/8	11 0/8	11 0/8	6 6/8	6 4/8	8 3/8	Converse County	WY	Eddie Hayden	1978	1,907
67 0/8	12 6/8	12 4/8	6 1/8	6 0/8	11 2/8	Converse County	WY	Kenneth L. Stoneburner	1978	1,907
67 0/8	12 7/8	12 7/8	5 5/8	5 5/8	7 2/8	Converse County	WY	Alton Gross	1980	1,907
67 0/8	11 5/8	11 5/8	6 0/8	6 0/8	9 0/8	Weld County	CO	Dennis Schweitzer	1980	1,907
67 0/8	12 3/8	12 2/8	5 5/8	5 6/8	8 7/8	Sheridan County	WY	Travis Adsit	1981	1,907
67 0/8	12 6/8	13 0/8	5 5/8	5 6/8	10 7/8	Natrona County	WY	Robert Arvey	1981	1,907
67 0/8	11 6/8	11 6/8	5 6/8	5 6/8	9 1/8	Converse County	WY	Richard Smith	1981	1,907
67 0/8	13 7/8	14 0/8	5 7/8	5 7/8	10 5/8	Converse County	WY	Robert A. Christensen	1982	1,907
67 0/8	12 2/8	12 1/8	5 6/8	5 6/8	9 3/8	Converse County	WY	Howard Holmes	1982	1,907
67 0/8	13 7/8	14 1/8	5 2/8	5 2/8	10 7/8	Lassen County	CA	Don Rossiter	1983	1,907
67 0/8	15 0/8	14 7/8	5 2/8	5 2/8	11 2/8	Yavapai County	AZ	Michael John Bylina	1983	1,907
67 0/8	12 2/8	12 4/8	7 0/8	7 0/8	9 7/8	Converse County	WY	Eric Ames	1983	1,907
67 0/8	13 5/8	14 0/8	5 3/8	5 3/8	11 3/8	Natrona County	WY	Charles Lanzarone	1983	1,907
67 0/8	12 7/8	12 5/8	5 6/8	5 5/8	11 0/8	Broadwater County	MT	Bob A. Closson	1983	1,907
67 0/8	12 5/8	12 5/8	5 3/8	5 1/8	10 6/8	Converse County	WY	Thomas L. Hughes	1983	1,907
67 0/8	12 3/8	12 3/8	5 5/8	5 5/8	8 4/8	Carbon County	WY	Raymond R. Robison	1984	1,907
67 0/8	12 5/8	12 4/8	5 5/8	5 4/8	10 3/8	Custer County	ID	Matt March, Jr.	1984	1,907
67 0/8	13 4/8	13 3/8	5 2/8	5 3/8	11 2/8	Sweetwater County	WY	Cliff Wiseman	1985	1,907
67 0/8	13 1/8	12 7/8	5 4/8	5 4/8	7 6/8	Sweetwater County	WY	Chuck Ashton	1985	1,907
67 0/8	12 5/8	12 5/8	5 4/8	5 3/8	9 2/8	Modoc County	CA	Anthony R. Dipino	1986	1,907
67 0/8	13 6/8	14 0/8	5 4/8	5 4/8	9 5/8	Carbon County	WY	Rod Schmidt	1986	1,907
67 0/8	12 4/8	12 3/8	6 2/8	6 2/8	7 7/8	Campbell County	WY	Keith Olson	1986	1,907
67 0/8	13 5/8	13 3/8	6 0/8	6 1/8	10 6/8	Mountrail County	ND	Charles LeRohl	1986	1,907
67 0/8	13 5/8	13 5/8	5 4/8	5 3/8	10 7/8	Modoc County	CA	Rick Holbrook	1987	1,907
67 0/8	12 4/8	12 2/8	6 0/8	6 0/8	11 4/8	Moffat County	CO	Grant Adkisson	1987	1,907
67 0/8	13 4/8	14 0/8	5 5/8	5 4/8	9 2/8	Uinta County	WY	Dave Murray	1987	1,907
67 0/8	13 4/8	13 7/8	5 1/8	5 2/8	6 7/8	Natrona County	WY	Doug Anderson	1987	1,907
67 0/8	13 0/8	12 6/8	6 0/8	6 0/8	11 5/8	Converse County	WY	Jack C. Staley, Jr.	1987	1,907
67 0/8	12 5/8	12 5/8	5 4/8	5 4/8	12 2/8	Fergus County	MT	Jess Knerr	1987	1,907
67 0/8	13 1/8	12 6/8	5 6/8	5 6/8	7 6/8	Moffat County	CO	James Libra	1988	1,907
67 0/8	13 4/8	13 4/8	5 5/8	5 4/8	9 2/8	Moffat County	CO	Terry Weimer	1988	1,907
67 0/8	13 2/8	13 3/8	5 6/8	5 5/8	11 1/8	Butte County	ID	Edward F. Keeton	1988	1,907
67 0/8	12 4/8	12 5/8	5 5/8	5 4/8	10 1/8	Natrona County	WY	Charles Lanzarone	1988	1,907
67 0/8	14 2/8	14 4/8	5 2/8	5 1/8	6 5/8	Converse County	WY	Jay Deones	1988	1,907
67 0/8	13 4/8	13 3/8	5 6/8	5 6/8	10 7/8	Rio Grande County	CO	Arthur G. Garcia	1988	1,907
67 0/8	13 5/8	13 4/8	5 5/8	5 6/8	8 5/8	Eddy County	NM	Jess Stuart	1988	1,907
67 0/8	13 4/8	13 6/8	5 7/8	6 0/8	11 4/8	Sublette County	WY	Tony Litts	1989	1,907
67 0/8	13 4/8	13 0/8	5 2/8	5 2/8	8 5/8	Richland County	MT	Douglas A. Lang	1989	1,907
67 0/8	12 6/8	12 7/8	5 5/8	5 5/8	10 4/8	Moffat County	CO	Dennis M. Hayden	1989	1,907
67 0/8	12 3/8	11 7/8	6 3/8	6 4/8	11 4/8	Converse County	WY	James C. Gates	1989	1,907
67 0/8	12 2/8	12 4/8	5 6/8	5 6/8	8 5/8	Garfield County	MT	Glen Prestegaard	1989	1,907
67 0/8	12 2/8	12 2/8	6 0/8	6 0/8	10 4/8	Converse County	WY	Arthur Wirsing, Jr.	1989	1,907
67 0/8	12 5/8	12 6/8	6 0/8	6 0/8	8 2/8	Moffat County	CO	Chuck Leidheiser	1990	1,907
67 0/8	13 7/8	13 7/8	5 4/8	5 3/8	10 7/8	Moffat County	CO	Bob Radocy	1990	1,907
67 0/8	11 5/8	12 5/8	5 5/8	5 7/8	10 3/8	Sweetwater County	WY	Kurt Zurawski	1990	1,907
67 0/8	14 7/8	14 4/8	5 7/8	5 6/8	10 7/8	Rich County	UT	Robert K. Paulson	1990	1,907
67 0/8	12 3/8	12 3/8	6 0/8	5 7/8	8 1/8	McKenzie County	ND	Terry Sivertson	1990	1,907
67 0/8	13 1/8	13 1/8	5 4/8	5 3/8	11 0/8	Rosebud County	MT	Sherrill McNalley	1990	1,907
67 0/8	12 2/8	12 1/8	6 1/8	6 1/8	8 7/8	Converse County	WY	Gerry Smarelli	1990	1,907
67 0/8	12 6/8	13 4/8	5 7/8	5 6/8	11 2/8	McKenzie County	ND	Burnell Sammons	1990	1,907
67 0/8	13 5/8	14 6/8	4 7/8	5 0/8	11 2/8	Hudspeth County	TX	Ernest M. Elbert, Jr.	1990	1,907

SCORE	LENGTH OF R HORN L		CIRCUMFERENCE R OF BASE L		GREATEST SPREAD	AREA	STATE/ PROVINCE	HUNTER'S NAME	DATE	RANK
67 0/8	13 3/8	13 2/8	5 4/8	5 2/8	11 3/8	Harding County	SD	William J. Bushong	1991	1,907
67 0/8	13 4/8	13 1/8	6 0/8	5 7/8	12 5/8	Owyhee County	ID	Terry Bennett	1991	1,907
67 0/8	13 2/8	13 0/8	5 6/8	5 6/8	9 6/8	Natrona County	WY	Eugene Damron	1991	1,907
67 0/8	13 0/8	13 0/8	6 1/8	5 7/8	9 6/8	Converse County	WY	Gary M. Funk	1991	1,907
67 0/8	12 0/8	12 1/8	6 0/8	6 0/8	9 4/8	Campbell County	WY	Jerry Hinz	1991	1,907
67 0/8	14 2/8	15 0/8	5 3/8	5 2/8	7 7/8	Converse County	WY	Kathy Strecker	1991	1,907
67 0/8	11 2/8	12 1/8	5 7/8	6 0/8	9 2/8	Natrona County	WY	Jeffrey Johnson	1991	1,907
67 0/8	13 6/8	14 0/8	5 3/8	5 2/8	9 3/8	Converse County	WY	Lou Edelis	1991	1,907
67 0/8	12 7/8	12 5/8	5 5/8	5 5/8	9 0/8	Converse County	WY	Michael J. Kennedy	1991	1,907
67 0/8	12 4/8	13 0/8	5 5/8	5 4/8	9 0/8	Moffat County	CO	Richard Davis	1992	1,907
67 0/8	12 6/8	12 4/8	6 1/8	6 2/8	11 6/8	Carbon County	WY	Willis Duhon	1992	1,907
67 0/8	13 0/8	13 1/8	5 4/8	5 4/8	11 3/8	Garfield County	MT	Rick Stinson	1992	1,907
67 0/8	12 4/8	13 0/8	6 1/8	6 0/8	9 1/8	Converse County	WY	Robert K. Woeck	1992	1,907
67 0/8	13 6/8	13 7/8	5 7/8	6 0/8	10 1/8	Madison County	MT	Mark Stonebraker	1992	1,907
66 7/8	13 3/8	14 3/8	5 3/8	5 5/8	15 4/8	Campbell County	WY	Joseph Strasser, Jr.	1981	1,975
66 6/8	14 4/8	14 2/8	5 3/8	5 4/8	13 5/8	Converse County	WY	Roland Gravenkemper	1955	1,976
66 6/8	13 3/8	13 1/8	5 7/8	5 7/8	8 4/8	Campbell County	WY	Pete Erickson	1967	1,976
66 6/8	12 4/8	12 4/8	5 6/8	5 6/8	10 3/8	Butte County	SD	Dr. William L. Lee	1974	1,976
66 6/8	12 6/8	12 6/8	5 6/8	5 5/8	10 0/8	Butte County	SD	Charles C. Tippton, Jr.	1974	1,976
66 6/8	14 1/8	13 2/8	5 5/8	5 4/8	10 6/8	Wallace County	KS	David Stevenson	1975	1,976
66 6/8	12 7/8	12 7/8	5 4/8	5 4/8	9 4/8	Natrona County	WY	Mel Johnson	1978	1,976
66 6/8	13 1/8	13 0/8	5 4/8	5 2/8	11 6/8	Johnson County	WY	Frederick A. Suran	1978	1,976
66 6/8	11 6/8	11 3/8	5 4/8	5 3/8	9 6/8	Carbon County	WY	Ed Downard	1980	1,976
66 6/8	12 5/8	12 7/8	5 6/8	5 6/8	8 0/8	Natrona County	WY	James R. Kilgore	1980	1,976
66 6/8	12 2/8	12 2/8	5 7/8	5 7/8	7 4/8	Converse County	WY	Carl W. Van Ryswyk	1980	1,976
66 6/8	13 0/8	13 0/8	5 3/8	5 4/8	7 4/8	Moffat County	CO	Tim Chastain	1981	1,976
66 6/8	13 0/8	13 0/8	5 7/8	5 6/8	7 7/8	Blaine County	ID	Champ Church	1981	1,976
66 6/8	13 3/8	14 3/8	5 3/8	5 3/8	11 4/8	Natrona County	WY	Dean Hamilton	1981	1,976
66 6/8	14 0/8	11 3/8	5 2/8	5 2/8	10 7/8	Converse County	WY	Lee Jernigan	1981	1,976
66 6/8	11 7/8	11 5/8	5 5/8	5 6/8	9 0/8	Converse County	WY	Charlie Kroll	1981	1,976
66 6/8	12 2/8	12 3/8	5 7/8	5 6/8	8 0/8	Clark County	ID	Richard K. Russell	1981	1,976
66 6/8	12 1/8	12 0/8	5 4/8	5 5/8	10 4/8	Converse County	WY	John S. Shields	1983	1,976
66 6/8	14 1/8	14 2/8	5 1/8	5 0/8	12 2/8	Moffat County	CO	Rick Stockburger	1983	1,976
66 6/8	13 1/8	13 2/8	5 3/8	5 4/8	9 2/8	Converse County	WY	Gene Gilmer	1983	1,976
66 6/8	12 6/8	12 7/8	5 5/8	5 5/8	11 7/8	Converse County	WY	Spencer Wilker	1983	1,976
66 6/8	13 2/8	12 6/8	5 7/8	5 6/8	9 2/8	Converse County	WY	Randy Dittmer	1984	1,976
66 6/8	13 7/8	14 0/8	5 6/8	5 6/8	12 7/8	McKenzie County	ND	Mitch Griebel	1984	1,976
66 6/8	12 7/8	12 5/8	6 2/8	5 7/8	11 4/8	Campbell County	WY	Robert Finelli	1984	1,976
66 6/8	14 4/8	14 0/8	5 2/8	5 3/8	10 1/8	Rio Arriba County	NM	Michael M. Hawkes	1985	1,976
66 6/8	12 5/8	12 6/8	6 0/8	5 6/8	10 7/8	Converse County	WY	Jack Leggo	1985	1,976
66 6/8	12 4/8	12 7/8	5 4/8	5 4/8	9 4/8	Carbon County	WY	Kim Cooper	1985	1,976
66 6/8	12 7/8	12 7/8	5 5/8	5 5/8	10 4/8	Natrona County	WY	Rickey E. Morse	1986	1,976
66 6/8	12 4/8	12 6/8	5 6/8	5 5/8	9 4/8	Fergus County	MT	Charles B. Vogl	1986	1,976
66 6/8	13 7/8	13 1/8	5 4/8	5 4/8	11 5/8	Petroleum County	MT	Stan Colton	1986	1,976
66 6/8	12 2/8	12 5/8	5 6/8	5 4/8	7 4/8	Sweetwater County	WY	Winston Parkinson	1987	1,976
66 6/8	12 4/8	12 6/8	6 0/8	5 7/8	9 5/8	Laramie County	WY	Robert S. Simms, Jr.	1987	1,976
66 6/8	13 0/8	12 5/8	5 6/8	5 6/8	9 0/8	Petroleum County	MT	Mark D. Hughes	1987	1,976
66 6/8	13 0/8	12 7/8	5 3/8	5 3/8	12 5/8	Tide Lake	ALB	Archie Nesbitt	1988	1,976
66 6/8	13 1/8	12 4/8	5 1/8	5 1/8	10 0/8	Carbon County	WY	Ray Dierking	1989	1,976
66 6/8	12 3/8	12 1/8	5 7/8	5 7/8	9 6/8	Moffat County	CO	Bruno Ammann	1989	1,976
66 6/8	13 4/8	13 4/8	5 3/8	5 3/8	7 0/8	Campbell County	WY	Gary D. Johansen	1989	1,976
66 6/8	12 1/8	12 6/8	6 4/8	6 3/8	11 3/8	Sioux County	NE	Victor Reese	1989	1,976
66 6/8	12 6/8	12 5/8	6 1/8	6 1/8	8 2/8	Ward County	ND	Russel Goodwin	1989	1,976
66 6/8	13 3/8	13 0/8	5 4/8	5 4/8	9 6/8	Buffalo	ALB	Larry Mandseth	1989	1,976
66 6/8	12 7/8	12 7/8	5 4/8	5 3/8	11 1/8	Meagher County	MT	Gene Clark	1989	1,976
66 6/8	12 7/8	13 0/8	5 4/8	5 4/8	7 6/8	Washoe County	NV	Scott Jones	1990	1,976
66 6/8	12 7/8	12 5/8	5 3/8	5 4/8	8 4/8	Moffat County	CO	Roy M. Goodwin	1990	1,976
66 6/8	12 1/8	12 4/8	5 7/8	5 7/8	9 3/8	Natrona County	WY	Douglas R. Hahn	1990	1,976
66 6/8	12 5/8	12 1/8	6 2/8	6 1/8	9 0/8	Natrona County	WY	Nelson Beane	1990	1,976
66 6/8	13 5/8	13 7/8	5 6/8	5 4/8	9 6/8	McKenzie County	ND	Cecil I. Tharp	1990	1,976
66 6/8	13 2/8	13 4/8	5 4/8	5 4/8	11 6/8	Rosebud County	MT	Harvey McNalley	1990	1,976
66 6/8	12 1/8	13 0/8	5 3/8	5 3/8	7 6/8	Catron County	NM	Rick Forrest	1991	1,976
66 6/8	14 3/8	13 4/8	5 0/8	5 0/8	11 4/8	Tooele County	UT	Michael Tim McIntyre	1991	1,976
66 6/8	13 1/8	13 2/8	5 2/8	5 3/8	10 0/8	Coconino County	AZ	Duane "Corky" Richardson	1991	1,976
66 6/8	13 4/8	13 4/8	5 6/8	5 6/8	8 4/8	Bowman County	ND	Sheldon D. Snyder	1991	1,976
66 6/8	12 5/8	11 6/8	6 0/8	6 1/8	10 7/8	Campbell County	WY	John Tregembo	1991	1,976
66 6/8	13 2/8	13 4/8	5 4/8	5 4/8	13 1/8	Sioux County	NE	Tom Tobiasson	1991	1,976
66 6/8	12 6/8	12 6/8	5 5/8	5 5/8	8 4/8	Golden Valley County	ND	Les Tomanek	1991	1,976
66 6/8	13 3/8	13 3/8	5 4/8	5 2/8	10 0/8	Lewis & Clark County	MT	Mike Saulter	1991	1,976
66 6/8	13 4/8	13 6/8	5 1/8	5 1/8	8 5/8	Saguache County	CO	Ronnie Ellington	1992	1,976

SCORE	LENGTH OF R HORN L		CIRCUMFERENCE R OF BASE L		GREATEST SPREAD	AREA	STATE/ PROVINCE	HUNTER'S NAME	DATE	RANK
66 6/8	13 6/8	13 5/8	5 1/8	5 3/8	7 3/8	Pima County	AZ	Robert Forrest	1992	1,976
66 6/8	13 3/8	13 5/8	5 4/8	5 5/8	12 2/8	Owyhee County	ID	Bryce Moore	1992	1,976
66 6/8	11 4/8	11 7/8	6 0/8	6 0/8	10 4/8	Malheur County	OR	Phillip T. Staton	1992	1,976
66 6/8	13 5/8	13 4/8	5 6/8	5 6/8	10 1/8	Butte County	SD	Mike R. Erickson	1992	1,976
66 6/8	11 6/8	11 6/8	6 0/8	6 0/8	8 6/8	Natrona County	WY	Joseph A. Romeu	1992	1,976
66 6/8	11 6/8	11 6/8	6 3/8	6 2/8	6 6/8	Campbell County	WY	Gary Wobig	1992	1,976
66 5/8	13 3/8	13 3/8	5 5/8	5 4/8	14 6/8	Moffat County	CO	Stan Manuel	1988	2,037
66 4/8	12 0/8	12 0/8	5 5/8	5 4/8	12 0/8	Fremont County	WY	Fred Bear	1955	2,038
66 4/8	13 6/8	13 4/8	5 4/8	5 4/8	11 2/8	Guadalupe County	NM	Paul Link	1962	2,038
66 4/8	12 6/8	12 2/8	6 0/8	6 0/8	8 2/8	Stark County	ND	Dennis A. Schneider	1965	2,038
66 4/8	13 4/8	13 7/8	5 4/8	5 4/8	6 5/8	Harding County	SD	Richard Bolyard	1974	2,038
66 4/8	13 4/8	13 7/8	5 4/8	5 4/8	8 6/8	Valley County	MT	Tom Solem	1979	2,038
66 4/8	12 4/8	12 7/8	5 4/8	5 4/8	8 4/8	Dawes County	NE	Jerry Dennis	1980	2,038
66 4/8	13 0/8	13 0/8	5 6/8	5 4/8	9 0/8	Converse County	WY	Ronald J. Collier	1981	2,038
66 4/8	13 4/8	13 3/8	5 6/8	6 0/8	9 5/8	Fremont County	WY	Everett A. Boss	1981	2,038
66 4/8	13 0/8	13 0/8	5 6/8	5 5/8	7 2/8	Converse County	WY	Andy Tkach	1981	2,038
66 4/8	12 3/8	12 3/8	5 4/8	5 4/8	12 2/8	Moffat County	CO	Bill Yessa	1981	2,038
66 4/8	13 1/8	11 7/8	5 7/8	5 7/8	9 0/8	Siskiyou County	CA	Doug Walker	1982	2,038
66 4/8	12 4/8	12 7/8	5 7/8	5 6/8	10 0/8	Power County	ID	Robert Bennett	1982	2,038
66 4/8	13 6/8	14 1/8	6 2/8	6 4/8	13 3/8	Bowman County	ND	Curt Wells	1982	2,038
66 4/8	12 6/8	12 7/8	5 4/8	5 4/8	7 4/8	Moffat County	CO	Dennis J. Erkinger	1982	2,038
66 4/8	13 1/8	13 1/8	5 5/8	5 5/8	12 6/8	McCone County	MT	Dan Sturgis	1982	2,038
66 4/8	12 4/8	13 1/8	5 6/8	5 4/8	11 1/8	Moffat County	CO	Chris Cassidy	1983	2,038
66 4/8	12 3/8	12 4/8	6 1/8	5 7/8	12 4/8	Moffat County	CO	Toni R. Roberts	1983	2,038
66 4/8	13 0/8	12 6/8	5 6/8	5 6/8	8 4/8	Converse County	WY	Steve Byerly	1983	2,038
66 4/8	12 1/8	12 1/8	5 7/8	5 4/8	9 1/8	Natrona County	WY	Arthur S. Wert	1983	2,038
66 4/8	12 5/8	12 3/8	5 6/8	5 4/8	8 1/8	McKenzie County	ND	James R. Greutman	1983	2,038
66 4/8	12 5/8	12 4/8	6 0/8	6 0/8	10 1/8	Carbon County	WY	James D. Davis	1983	2,038
66 4/8	12 5/8	12 5/8	5 7/8	5 4/8	9 2/8	Converse County	WY	Gary White	1983	2,038
66 4/8	11 7/8	12 0/8	5 5/8	5 5/8	6 5/8	Moffat County	CO	Tim Decker	1984	2,038
66 4/8	12 6/8	13 0/8	5 3/8	5 6/8	9 5/8	Carbon County	WY	Paul Kniss	1984	2,038
66 4/8	12 2/8	12 3/8	5 7/8	5 6/8	12 1/8	Campbell County	WY	Mark S. Presta	1984	2,038
66 4/8	13 1/8	13 2/8	5 3/8	5 3/8	12 2/8	Converse County	WY	Charles E Gose	1984	2,038
66 4/8	12 6/8	12 6/8	5 6/8	5 3/8	10 1/8	Johnson County	WY	Jerry Leair	1984	2,038
66 4/8	13 3/8	13 4/8	5 2/8	5 2/8	10 0/8	Moffat County	CO	Reina Kemp	1985	2,038
66 4/8	12 7/8	13 4/8	5 4/8	5 3/8	10 0/8	Tooele County	UT	Scott Anderson	1985	2,038
66 4/8	11 7/8	11 6/8	5 5/8	5 5/8	9 7/8	Musselshell County	MT	Brian Acton	1985	2,038
66 4/8	12 0/8	12 2/8	5 2/8	5 2/8	9 2/8	Yellowstone County	MT	Jim Forwood	1986	2,038
66 4/8	12 7/8	12 3/8	5 6/8	5 5/8	10 3/8	Stark County	ND	Howard Sharp	1987	2,038
66 4/8	12 7/8	12 7/8	5 6/8	5 6/8	8 0/8	Campbell County	WY	Nick Hengel	1987	2,038
66 4/8	11 3/8	12 6/8	6 0/8	5 7/8	9 4/8	Jefferson County	ID	Richard Beesley	1988	2,038
66 4/8	12 3/8	12 3/8	6 0/8	6 0/8	8 2/8	Moffat County	CO	Barry J. Smith	1988	2,038
66 4/8	13 0/8	13 1/8	5 5/8	5 6/8	8 4/8	Converse County	WY	Paul Mehnert	1988	2,038
66 4/8	11 5/8	11 4/8	5 4/8	5 3/8	10 0/8	Power County	ID	Frank W. Sparkman	1988	2,038
66 4/8	13 0/8	13 0/8	5 4/8	5 3/8	9 2/8	Garfield County	MT	Bill Helphrey	1988	2,038
66 4/8	12 7/8	12 7/8	5 4/8	5 4/8	12 1/8	Converse County	WY	Harold Osborne	1988	2,038
66 4/8	12 4/8	12 5/8	5 5/8	5 3/8	8 6/8	Natrona County	WY	Mike Kistler	1989	2,038
66 4/8	12 7/8	12 7/8	5 5/8	5 6/8	14 5/8	McKenzie County	ND	Wayne R. Streitz	1989	2,038
66 4/8	13 1/8	13 1/8	5 4/8	5 4/8	10 2/8	Many Berries	ALB	John Visscher	1989	2,038
66 4/8	12 5/8	10 6/8	6 2/8	6 1/8	10 0/8	Campbell County	WY	Larry Honeycutt	1989	2,038
66 4/8	12 2/8	12 7/8	5 5/8	5 5/8	11 1/8	Las Animas County	CO	William D. Yirka	1990	2,038
66 4/8	12 0/8	11 7/8	5 4/8	5 4/8	8 1/8	Sweetwater County	WY	Ronald E. Hergott	1990	2,038
66 4/8	13 4/8	12 0/8	6 2/8	6 0/8	11 4/8	Rosebud County	MT	Robert Bartlett	1990	2,038
66 4/8	13 6/8	13 5/8	5 2/8	5 0/8	10 3/8	Morton County	ND	Mark W. Bogert	1990	2,038
66 4/8	12 4/8	12 4/8	6 1/8	6 0/8	6 7/8	Lincoln County	WY	Mark Grace	1991	2,038
66 4/8	12 5/8	11 7/8	5 7/8	5 6/8	12 4/8	Moffat County	CO	Cecil D. Richburg	1991	2,038
66 4/8	13 6/8	13 7/8	5 0/8	5 1/8	7 6/8	Converse County	WY	Matt Curry	1991	2,038
66 4/8	13 6/8	13 7/8	5 4/8	5 3/8	7 2/8	Beaverhead County	MT	Terry Barkel	1991	2,038
66 4/8	12 3/8	12 5/8	6 4/8	6 4/8	8 6/8	Sioux County	NE	Mike Morrow	1991	2,038
66 4/8	13 0/8	13 1/8	5 4/8	5 3/8	8 6/8	Converse County	WY	Richard Peloquin	1991	2,038
66 4/8	13 2/8	13 1/8	5 6/8	5 5/8	5 6/8	Uinta County	WY	Carol Ann Fitzgerald	1992	2,038
66 4/8	12 3/8	12 4/8	5 6/8	5 6/8	9 2/8	Stanley County	SD	Dan Dietrich	1992	2,038
66 3/8	12 5/8	13 0/8	5 7/8	5 6/8	13 3/8	Natrona County	WY	Richard Iverson	1981	2,093
66 3/8	13 0/8	12 6/8	5 7/8	5 6/8	13 1/8	Coconino County	AZ	Scott Kellner	1983	2,093
66 3/8	14 4/8	13 6/8	5 6/8	5 6/8	16 5/8	Millard County	UT	Bob McGill, Jr.	1990	2,093
66 2/8	12 7/8	13 0/8	5 3/8	5 3/8	8 7/8	McLean County	ND	Robert Freeberg	1967	2,096
66 2/8	12 5/8	12 6/8	5 5/8	5 4/8	9 2/8	Carbon County	WY	Steve Gorr	1971	2,096
66 2/8	12 1/8	12 1/8	6 3/8	6 4/8	11 5/8	Converse County	WY	Denny Behn	1979	2,096
66 2/8	13 3/8	13 2/8	5 6/8	5 4/8	11 1/8	Natrona County	WY	Don Schram	1980	2,096
66 2/8	11 4/8	11 4/8	5 6/8	5 6/8	8 3/8	Natrona County	WY	Billy Ellis	1981	2,096

Score	Length of Horn R	Length of Horn L	Circumference of Base R	Circumference of Base L	Greatest Spread	Area	State/ Province	Hunter's Name	Date	Rank
66 2/8	12 4/8	12 5/8	5 7/8	5 5/8	9 0/8	Campbell County	WY	William F. Heineke	1981	2,096
66 2/8	13 0/8	12 7/8	5 5/8	5 4/8	8 7/8	Campbell County	WY	Pat Mitchell	1981	2,096
66 2/8	12 5/8	12 4/8	5 5/8	5 5/8	10 1/8	Lincoln County	WY	Lonnie Smith	1981	2,096
66 2/8	11 6/8	12 1/8	5 7/8	5 6/8	8 4/8	Moffat County	CO	Earl Stout	1981	2,096
66 2/8	11 7/8	12 0/8	5 5/8	5 5/8	10 7/8	Moffat County	CO	Warren P. Uhl	1981	2,096
66 2/8	11 4/8	11 4/8	6 7/8	6 6/8	7 7/8	Converse County	WY	Albert R. Taylor	1982	2,096
66 2/8	12 4/8	12 4/8	5 7/8	6 0/8	9 2/8	Bowman County	ND	Dean Albertson	1982	2,096
66 2/8	11 3/8	11 4/8	5 6/8	5 6/8	8 4/8	Converse County	WY	David Hell	1982	2,096
66 2/8	11 6/8	11 5/8	6 0/8	6 0/8	12 6/8	Sioux County	NE	Melvin L. Rein	1982	2,096
66 2/8	13 1/8	12 7/8	5 5/8	5 4/8	9 7/8	Meagher County	MT	D. Mitch Kottas	1982	2,096
66 2/8	12 6/8	13 1/8	5 5/8	5 6/8	9 1/8	Lemhi County	ID	Richard C. Nichols	1982	2,096
66 2/8	10 7/8	11 0/8	6 3/8	6 2/8	8 6/8	Moffat County	CO	Ray Ryan	1983	2,096
66 2/8	13 6/8	13 4/8	5 5/8	5 5/8	8 1/8	Weston County	WY	Pat Graham	1983	2,096
66 2/8	12 6/8	12 4/8	5 5/8	5 3/8	10 0/8	Converse County	WY	Michael Arneson	1983	2,096
66 2/8	12 3/8	12 3/8	5 4/8	5 4/8	8 5/8	Campbell County	WY	Joseph Strasser, Jr.	1984	2,096
66 2/8	12 3/8	13 0/8	5 4/8	5 4/8	8 3/8	Crook County	WY	Terry Walton	1984	2,096
66 2/8	13 3/8	13 3/8	5 4/8	5 4/8	10 2/8	Washoe County	NV	Ralph L Albright	1985	2,096
66 2/8	13 0/8	12 4/8	5 5/8	5 5/8	11 5/8	Fremont County	WY	David Dickson	1985	2,096
66 2/8	13 0/8	13 0/8	5 5/8	5 6/8	9 3/8	Moffat County	CO	Randy Lamdin	1986	2,096
66 2/8	12 0/8	12 1/8	5 5/8	5 5/8	9 7/8	Converse County	WY	John Rook	1986	2,096
66 2/8	12 4/8	12 6/8	5 6/8	5 6/8	11 0/8	Box Elder County	UT	Bob Richardson	1986	2,096
66 2/8	12 3/8	11 6/8	6 0/8	5 6/8	10 2/8	Valley County	MT	Gerald Polesky	1986	2,096
66 2/8	12 6/8	13 4/8	5 6/8	5 5/8	10 3/8	Grand Forks	ALB	Paul Deme	1986	2,096
66 2/8	14 0/8	14 4/8	5 3/8	5 4/8	11 0/8	Converse County	WY	Roger L. Hensley	1987	2,096
66 2/8	12 4/8	12 3/8	5 6/8	5 4/8	9 4/8	Converse County	WY	Gary Lee Gregg	1987	2,096
66 2/8	13 4/8	13 4/8	5 4/8	5 3/8	9 6/8	Converse County	WY	Michael Murphy	1987	2,096
66 2/8	12 5/8	12 6/8	5 5/8	5 5/8	8 7/8	Albany County	WY	James Rapp	1988	2,096
66 2/8	12 2/8	12 0/8	5 6/8	5 5/8	8 4/8	Moffat County	CO	Michael L. Callaway	1988	2,096
66 2/8	12 5/8	13 3/8	5 5/8	5 4/8	11 4/8	Daggett County	UT	Steve Dailey	1988	2,096
66 2/8	14 1/8	14 1/8	4 7/8	5 0/8	8 2/8	Humboldt County	NV	Mike Williams	1989	2,096
66 2/8	11 7/8	12 0/8	6 2/8	6 2/8	8 5/8	Converse County	WY	James W. Casto, Jr.	1989	2,096
66 2/8	14 1/8	13 5/8	5 4/8	5 4/8	10 7/8	Rosebud County	MT	Keith D. Kemkes	1989	2,096
66 2/8	12 2/8	12 4/8	5 1/8	5 1/8	10 1/8	Converse County	WY	James Bragg	1989	2,096
66 2/8	12 6/8	12 6/8	5 1/8	5 1/8	4 6/8	Converse County	WY	Jack Dellger	1989	2,096
66 2/8	13 3/8	13 2/8	5 6/8	5 5/8	10 2/8	Sweetwater County	WY	Donald R. Williamson	1989	2,096
66 2/8	13 0/8	13 4/8	5 3/8	5 2/8	6 1/8	Sweetwater County	WY	Steve Brockmann	1990	2,096
66 2/8	12 5/8	13 1/8	5 7/8	5 6/8	9 3/8	Custer County	ID	Doug Burkman	1990	2,096
66 2/8	13 4/8	13 5/8	5 0/8	5 1/8	10 4/8	Harney County	OR	Don R. Davidson	1990	2,096
66 2/8	12 2/8	12 2/8	5 4/8	5 4/8	9 3/8	Weston County	WY	James P. Landwehr	1990	2,096
66 2/8	13 0/8	13 1/8	5 4/8	5 4/8	7 1/8	Powder River County	MT	John McCarthy	1990	2,096
66 2/8	12 7/8	12 4/8	5 2/8	5 3/8	9 0/8	Uintah County	UT	F. Jeffrey Peterson	1991	2,096
66 2/8	12 0/8	12 2/8	5 2/8	5 2/8	7 7/8	Converse County	WY	Russell A. Nichols	1991	2,096
66 2/8	14 5/8	14 5/8	5 2/8	5 1/8	8 3/8	Converse County	WY	James Saunoris	1991	2,096
66 2/8	13 0/8	12 6/8	5 6/8	5 6/8	10 4/8	Petroleum County	MT	Debbie Jenner	1991	2,096
66 2/8	11 6/8	12 0/8	6 1/8	6 4/8	11 7/8	Rosebud County	MT	Mark A. Schwartznau	1991	2,096
66 2/8	12 4/8	12 1/8	5 5/8	5 5/8	9 3/8	Converse County	WY	Russ Tye	1991	2,096
66 2/8	13 5/8	13 4/8	5 6/8	5 5/8	9 6/8	Sioux County	NE	Orville J. DeVoss	1991	2,096
66 2/8	12 6/8	12 7/8	6 0/8	6 1/8	11 2/8	Powder River County	MT	Edwin John Durushia	1991	2,096
66 2/8	12 2/8	12 2/8	5 5/8	5 5/8	8 5/8	Moffat County	CO	Betty Gulman	1992	2,096
66 2/8	12 5/8	12 5/8	5 2/8	5 2/8	8 7/8	Moffat County	CO	Joe Prueher	1992	2,096
66 2/8	12 3/8	12 5/8	6 1/8	6 0/8	9 3/8	Crook County	WY	Dean A. Ransbottom	1992	2,096
66 2/8	12 3/8	12 0/8	5 7/8	5 7/8	9 5/8	Campbell County	WY	Janet J. Wilk	1992	2,096
66 1/8	12 6/8	12 4/8	6 0/8	5 7/8	14 3/8	Carbon County	WY	Willis Duhon	1985	2,153
66 1/8	13 3/8	13 2/8	5 7/8	5 6/8	15 0/8	Platte County	WY	Derek Long	1990	2,153
66 0/8	12 0/8	12 0/8	5 5/8	5 4/8	11 1/8	Rock County	NE	Mac Forbes	1967	2,155
66 0/8	12 5/8	12 5/8	6 1/8	5 6/8	8 2/8	Sublette County	WY	Frank D. Prentup	1976	2,155
66 0/8	12 7/8	12 7/8	5 2/8	5 2/8	9 0/8	Stewart Valley	SAS	Daniel N. Rayner	1976	2,155
66 0/8	12 6/8	12 6/8	6 0/8	6 1/8	11 6/8	Mountrail County	ND	Wade F. Williamson	1976	2,155
66 0/8	14 4/8	14 3/8	5 5/8	5 3/8	7 6/8	Butte County	ID	Richard B. Harvey	1978	2,155
66 0/8	13 0/8	12 4/8	5 7/8	5 6/8	8 3/8	Converse County	WY	Pat Walker	1978	2,155
66 0/8	12 0/8	11 7/8	6 1/8	5 7/8	8 5/8	Natrona County	WY	Daniel Carlson	1980	2,155
66 0/8	10 6/8	11 0/8	5 5/8	5 6/8	7 1/8	Stanley County	SD	Brian Fox	1980	2,155
66 0/8	11 4/8	12 0/8	5 7/8	5 7/8	8 4/8	Moffat County	CO	William T. Shoemaker	1980	2,155
66 0/8	13 0/8	13 2/8	5 3/8	5 3/8	11 6/8	Johnson County	WY	Denny Ennis	1981	2,155
66 0/8	11 4/8	11 4/8	5 5/8	5 4/8	7 4/8	Converse County	WY	Ronald Grzybowski	1981	2,155
66 0/8	13 0/8	13 3/8	5 2/8	5 1/8	9 5/8	Natrona County	WY	Dan Kolb	1981	2,155
66 0/8	11 0/8	10 2/8	5 4/8	5 3/8	7 7/8	Moffat County	CO	Gail Martin	1981	2,155
66 0/8	12 3/8	12 2/8	6 0/8	6 2/8	8 7/8	Lassen County	CA	Ronald R. Mayfield	1981	2,155
66 0/8	12 4/8	11 5/8	5 4/8	5 3/8	8 7/8	Weld County	CO	Mike Nobe	1982	2,155
66 0/8	12 4/8	12 3/8	6 0/8	5 7/8	14 4/8	Yavapai County	AZ	Jeff W. Elmer	1982	2,155

431

SCORE	LENGTH OF R HORN L		CIRCUMFERENCE R OF BASE L		GREATEST SPREAD	AREA	STATE/ PROVINCE	HUNTER'S NAME	DATE	RANK
66 0/8	13 1/8	13 1/8	5 4/8	5 3/8	11 1/8	Lemhi County	ID	Ben Fahnholz	1983	2,155
66 0/8	13 4/8	13 5/8	5 7/8	5 6/8	12 2/8	Carbon County	WY	Jim Hodson	1983	2,155
66 0/8	13 0/8	13 1/8	5 0/8	5 0/8	9 4/8	Moffat County	CO	Jerry Lotspeich	1983	2,155
66 0/8	13 2/8	12 4/8	5 5/8	5 5/8	10 3/8	Converse County	WY	David S. Bunce	1983	2,155
66 0/8	12 7/8	12 5/8	5 5/8	5 4/8	6 6/8	Converse County	WY	Roger Wintle	1983	2,155
66 0/8	13 1/8	13 2/8	5 2/8	5 4/8	11 2/8	Converse County	WY	David Baldwin	1983	2,155
66 0/8	11 5/8	11 6/8	6 0/8	6 0/8	11 1/8	Converse County	WY	Reggie Spiegelberg	1983	2,155
66 0/8	12 5/8	12 5/8	5 2/8	5 6/8	11 2/8	Converse County	WY	Jon Thomas	1983	2,155
66 0/8	12 5/8	13 0/8	5 4/8	5 4/8	7 0/8	Washoe County	NV	Randall T. Harris	1984	2,155
66 0/8	11 6/8	11 0/8	6 0/8	5 7/8	9 1/8	Converse County	WY	Jeff Wagstaff	1984	2,155
66 0/8	13 5/8	13 4/8	5 2/8	5 1/8	11 6/8	Carbon County	WY	Kirk Westervelt	1985	2,155
66 0/8	12 5/8	12 6/8	5 2/8	5 3/8	9 6/8	Garfield County	MT	T. Anthony Brock	1985	2,155
66 0/8	13 2/8	13 4/8	5 2/8	5 0/8	10 4/8	Perkins County	SD	Michael P. Brust	1985	2,155
66 0/8	13 0/8	13 0/8	6 0/8	6 0/8	10 3/8	Crook County	WY	Pink Atkins	1985	2,155
66 0/8	12 3/8	12 4/8	5 2/8	5 2/8	9 4/8	Slope County	ND	Tim Belland	1985	2,155
66 0/8	12 4/8	12 4/8	5 7/8	5 6/8	10 2/8	Sweetwater County	WY	Harv Dalton	1986	2,155
66 0/8	13 4/8	13 4/8	5 3/8	5 2/8	10 2/8	Converse County	WY	Larry Hesterly	1986	2,155
66 0/8	12 6/8	12 6/8	5 7/8	5 7/8	6 1/8	Moffat County	CO	John Lupi	1987	2,155
66 0/8	12 0/8	12 0/8	5 7/8	5 7/8	9 2/8	Moffat County	CO	Bob Rennels	1987	2,155
66 0/8	13 2/8	13 2/8	5 2/8	5 2/8	10 1/8	Carbon County	WY	Kirk Westervelt	1987	2,155
66 0/8	12 6/8	12 2/8	5 4/8	5 4/8	11 3/8	Custer County	ID	Paul A. Dupuis	1987	2,155
66 0/8	11 6/8	12 1/8	6 0/8	5 7/8	8 7/8	Moffat County	CO	Randy Lamdin	1987	2,155
66 0/8	13 2/8	13 4/8	5 1/8	5 1/8	8 2/8	Clark County	ID	Max Lewis	1988	2,155
66 0/8	12 5/8	12 5/8	5 4/8	5 3/8	8 7/8	Sweetwater County	WY	Scott Sanders	1988	2,155
66 0/8	13 1/8	13 1/8	5 5/8	5 6/8	8 3/8	Washoe County	NV	Dr. Lawrence L. Heward	1988	2,155
66 0/8	13 2/8	13 1/8	5 0/8	5 2/8	5 4/8	Converse County	WY	Harold M. Burton	1988	2,155
66 0/8	12 2/8	12 2/8	5 4/8	5 4/8	7 4/8	Converse County	WY	Donald L. Nelson	1988	2,155
66 0/8	10 3/8	15 0/8	7 4/8	7 0/8	14 0/8	Rosebud County	MT	Gail Martin	1988	2,155
66 0/8	12 3/8	12 2/8	5 6/8	5 6/8	11 0/8	Sweetwater County	WY	Craig Boheler	1989	2,155
66 0/8	12 7/8	13 4/8	5 4/8	5 4/8	11 5/8	Bowman County	ND	Kendell Bauer	1989	2,155
66 0/8	11 0/8	11 5/8	6 1/8	6 0/8	10 7/8	Converse County	WY	Richard Gustafson	1989	2,155
66 0/8	11 5/8	11 5/8	5 7/8	5 7/8	7 2/8	Blaine County	ID	Brian Hunter Heck	1990	2,155
66 0/8	14 2/8	13 2/8	5 6/8	5 5/8	7 1/8	Carbon County	WY	Jim Finn	1990	2,155
66 0/8	13 4/8	13 4/8	6 1/8	6 0/8	14 2/8	Corson County	SD	Bill Soyland	1990	2,155
66 0/8	12 5/8	12 4/8	5 5/8	5 4/8	10 6/8	Moffat County	CO	Joe Vincent	1990	2,155
66 0/8	13 3/8	13 0/8	5 6/8	5 6/8	7 0/8	Custer County	SD	Craig Fuhrmann	1990	2,155
66 0/8	12 2/8	12 6/8	5 3/8	5 3/8	9 4/8	Weston County	WY	Greg Seymour	1990	2,155
66 0/8	13 2/8	13 2/8	5 4/8	5 3/8	11 0/8	Campbell County	WY	Richard F. Nelson	1991	2,155
66 0/8	12 7/8	12 7/8	5 7/8	5 6/8	12 1/8	Harding County	SD	Chad Barth	1991	2,155
66 0/8	13 2/8	13 2/8	5 7/8	5 5/8	10 5/8	Weston County	WY	Mark R. Batterson	1991	2,155
66 0/8	11 4/8	11 3/8	5 6/8	5 6/8	9 6/8	Converse County	WY	John E. Wencley	1991	2,155
66 0/8	13 7/8	14 0/8	5 6/8	5 5/8	10 6/8	Rich County	UT	Carol B. Hogle	1992	2,155
65 7/8	13 4/8	13 6/8	5 0/8	5 0/8	13 7/8	Haakon County	SD	Ward McCaughey	1971	2,213
65 7/8	13 0/8	13 0/8	5 3/8	5 3/8	14 3/8	Natrona County	WY	Dennis Keyser	1978	2,213
65 6/8	13 2/8	13 5/8	5 1/8	5 1/8	10 6/8	Lincoln County	NM	Frank W. Evans	1960	2,215
65 6/8	13 0/8	13 0/8	5 4/8	5 3/8	6 7/8	Rock County	NE	Del Austin	1964	2,215
65 6/8	13 1/8	13 1/8	6 1/8	5 5/8	11 2/8	Campbell County	WY	Russell Wright	1966	2,215
65 6/8	12 5/8	12 2/8	5 6/8	5 7/8	11 0/8	Perkins County	SD	Gerald Bentson	1968	2,215
65 6/8	11 4/8	11 7/8	5 3/8	5 4/8	9 2/8	McCone County	MT	Charles M. Carlson	1970	2,215
65 6/8	11 2/8	11 6/8	7 0/8	6 5/8	12 4/8	Natrona County	WY	Bill Emery	1974	2,215
65 6/8	12 4/8	12 3/8	5 6/8	5 6/8	10 1/8	Carter County	MT	John Fleharty	1981	2,215
65 6/8	12 2/8	12 6/8	5 7/8	5 6/8	4 7/8	Yavapai County	AZ	Oscar Dale Porter	1981	2,215
65 6/8	12 1/8	12 0/8	6 1/8	6 0/8	8 3/8	Weld County	CO	Larry Gann	1981	2,215
65 6/8	11 6/8	11 4/8	5 5/8	5 5/8	12 6/8	Converse County	WY	Tom Kayser	1981	2,215
65 6/8	11 6/8	11 6/8	8 2/8	8 2/8	10 7/8	Moffat County	CO	Ray Ryan	1982	2,215
65 6/8	13 4/8	13 2/8	5 5/8	5 4/8	8 5/8	Campbell County	WY	Robert Erickson	1982	2,215
65 6/8	12 4/8	12 4/8	5 4/8	5 4/8	11 4/8	Converse County	WY	Steven A. Janik	1982	2,215
65 6/8	12 6/8	12 6/8	5 4/8	5 4/8	12 1/8	Clark County	ID	Ron Stacey	1982	2,215
65 6/8	12 6/8	12 4/8	5 6/8	5 7/8	8 6/8	Johnson County	WY	James Kaszynski	1982	2,215
65 6/8	13 0/8	12 6/8	5 7/8	6 0/8	11 7/8	Converse County	WY	Steve Miller	1982	2,215
65 6/8	13 2/8	13 1/8	5 2/8	5 1/8	7 2/8	Converse County	WY	Larry Noland	1982	2,215
65 6/8	13 7/8	14 0/8	5 2/8	5 2/8	11 4/8	Sweetwater County	WY	Matt March, Jr.	1983	2,215
65 6/8	13 2/8	12 7/8	5 4/8	5 2/8	8 0/8	Lemhi County	ID	Larry Cross	1983	2,215
65 6/8	12 6/8	13 0/8	5 2/8	5 5/8	7 2/8	Carbon County	WY	Mike Schuchard	1983	2,215
65 6/8	14 6/8	14 4/8	5 1/8	5 1/8	9 7/8	Natrona County	WY	William W. Onken	1983	2,215
65 6/8	12 3/8	12 3/8	5 2/8	5 1/8	7 0/8	Campbell County	WY	Jeff Deline	1983	2,215
65 6/8	12 5/8	12 3/8	5 1/8	5 2/8	9 7/8	Converse County	WY	Robert M. Sweisthal, Jr.	1983	2,215
65 6/8	11 6/8	12 2/8	5 4/8	5 4/8	9 0/8	Converse County	WY	Joe Trinceri	1983	2,215
65 6/8	11 7/8	11 7/8	5 5/8	5 6/8	10 4/8	Sioux County	NE	Kevin Langan	1983	2,215
65 6/8	12 1/8	12 1/8	5 5/8	5 5/8	10 3/8	Moffat County	CO	Stephen Mikkelsen	1984	2,215

Score	Length of R horn L		Circumference R of Base L		Greatest Spread	Area	State/ Province	Hunter's Name	Date	Rank
65 6/8	12 5/8	12 5/8	5 3/8	5 2/8	6 7/8	Converse County	WY	R. Tim Reed	1984	2,215
65 6/8	12 5/8	12 2/8	5 6/8	5 3/8	8 0/8	Weston County	WY	Gary D. Johansen	1984	2,215
65 6/8	13 2/8	13 2/8	5 2/8	5 2/8	10 4/8	Converse County	WY	Gene A. Welle	1984	2,215
65 6/8	12 2/8	13 3/8	5 7/8	5 7/8	6 7/8	Moffat County	CO	Gary Spangenberg	1985	2,215
65 6/8	12 2/8	12 0/8	5 5/8	5 4/8	8 7/8	Natrona County	WY	Kurt Keskimaki	1985	2,215
65 6/8	11 3/8	11 3/8	6 0/8	6 0/8	8 6/8	Converse County	WY	Dick Gambrel	1985	2,215
65 6/8	12 2/8	12 4/8	5 5/8	5 5/8	10 0/8	Converse County	WY	Mark Folk	1985	2,215
65 6/8	11 5/8	11 6/8	5 6/8	5 6/8	7 0/8	Yuma County	CO	Larry Bishop	1986	2,215
65 6/8	13 2/8	13 6/8	5 2/8	5 2/8	9 1/8	Mercer County	ND	Howell J. Flowers	1986	2,215
65 6/8	12 6/8	12 5/8	5 4/8	5 5/8	8 5/8	Carbon County	WY	Larry Hayes	1986	2,215
65 6/8	13 2/8	13 0/8	4 6/8	4 7/8	11 4/8	Presidio County	TX	Kenny N. Heath	1986	2,215
65 6/8	13 0/8	13 3/8	5 4/8	5 2/8	7 3/8	Moffat County	CO	Douglas Burton	1987	2,215
65 6/8	12 4/8	12 4/8	5 6/8	5 6/8	9 2/8	Moffat County	CO	Ed Vallee	1987	2,215
65 6/8	14 2/8	13 4/8	5 2/8	5 3/8	11 4/8	Campbell County	WY	Jim Keim	1987	2,215
65 6/8	13 5/8	13 2/8	5 6/8	5 6/8	6 7/8	Sweetwater County	WY	Christopher J. Cordes	1988	2,215
65 6/8	12 0/8	11 5/8	5 4/8	5 4/8	6 3/8	Moffat County	CO	Bob Dawson	1988	2,215
65 6/8	12 6/8	13 2/8	5 4/8	5 4/8	6 7/8	Moffat County	CO	Neal Kelly	1988	2,215
65 6/8	12 4/8	12 3/8	4 7/8	5 0/8	6 6/8	Converse County	WY	James Lawless Sullivan	1988	2,215
65 6/8	13 2/8	13 0/8	5 4/8	5 4/8	12 2/8	Converse County	WY	David L. Fuller	1988	2,215
65 6/8	12 4/8	12 5/8	5 7/8	6 0/8	9 2/8	Converse County	WY	Tom Siebeneck	1988	2,215
65 6/8	14 1/8	14 1/8	5 2/8	5 2/8	11 1/8	McCone County	MT	Dan Sturgis	1988	2,215
65 6/8	12 6/8	11 6/8	5 6/8	5 7/8	7 4/8	Converse County	WY	Chad Rabe	1988	2,215
65 6/8	13 0/8	13 0/8	5 3/8	5 3/8	8 6/8	Campbell County	WY	Daniel "Boone" Bell	1989	2,215
65 6/8	11 1/8	11 5/8	5 5/8	5 4/8	9 6/8	Campbell County	WY	Jeffrey W. Murray	1989	2,215
65 6/8	13 0/8	13 0/8	5 3/8	5 2/8	7 7/8	Natrona County	WY	Gary L. Morse	1989	2,215
65 6/8	12 1/8	11 7/8	5 5/8	5 5/8	7 5/8	Converse County	WY	Donald Travis	1989	2,215
65 6/8	12 0/8	12 0/8	5 7/8	5 7/8	8 7/8	Campbell County	WY	Dave Grabow	1989	2,215
65 6/8	12 4/8	12 3/8	5 2/8	5 4/8	8 1/8	Moffat County	CO	John Weiss	1990	2,215
65 6/8	12 6/8	12 7/8	5 4/8	5 5/8	9 0/8	Sweetwater County	WY	Ken Maynard	1990	2,215
65 6/8	13 6/8	13 5/8	5 2/8	5 3/8	7 4/8	Lemhi County	ID	Stanley Leake	1990	2,215
65 6/8	13 3/8	13 2/8	5 1/8	5 0/8	6 7/8	Converse County	WY	Rich Fait	1990	2,215
65 6/8	12 7/8	12 6/8	5 2/8	5 1/8	11 7/8	Moffat County	CO	Thomas P. Bartholomew	1991	2,215
65 6/8	13 5/8	13 4/8	5 3/8	5 2/8	9 7/8	Custer County	ID	Robert D. Dowen	1991	2,215
65 6/8	12 7/8	12 7/8	5 6/8	5 6/8	6 1/8	Converse County	WY	Larry C. Osborne	1991	2,215
65 6/8	11 5/8	11 7/8	5 7/8	5 6/8	10 4/8	Natrona County	WY	Mark Owsley	1991	2,215
65 6/8	11 5/8	12 1/8	5 5/8	5 4/8	9 0/8	Moffat County	CO	Dennis Hayden	1992	2,215
65 6/8	13 3/8	13 7/8	5 3/8	5 3/8	11 7/8	Tooele County	UT	Dean Leland Smith	1992	2,215
65 6/8	12 7/8	12 6/8	5 3/8	5 2/8	8 7/8	McKenzie County	ND	Mark D. Hughes	1992	2,215
65 6/8	12 4/8	12 5/8	5 4/8	5 4/8	7 7/8	Converse County	WY	Wayne A. Grasseth	1992	2,215
65 6/8	13 6/8	13 5/8	5 4/8	5 2/8	10 7/8	Moffat County	CO	Kevin Synder	1992	2,215
65 5/8	11 6/8	11 3/8	6 0/8	5 7/8	11 7/8	Converse County	WY	Darwood J. "Doug" Anderso	1990	2,281
65 4/8	12 0/8	12 0/8	5 4/8	5 4/8	8 4/8	Butte County	SD	Alden Hobbs	1958	2,282
65 4/8	12 3/8	12 2/8	5 5/8	5 4/8	7 0/8	Natrona County	WY	Clarence J. Grandt	1973	2,282
65 4/8	11 6/8	11 6/8	5 7/8	5 6/8	11 0/8	Natrona County	WY	Pat Inman	1973	2,282
65 4/8	12 2/8	12 2/8	5 5/8	5 4/8	9 6/8	Carbon County	WY	G. Fred Asbell	1974	2,282
65 4/8	12 0/8	11 7/8	5 4/8	5 0/8	9 1/8	Johnson County	WY	Charles Jahnke	1979	2,282
65 4/8	12 1/8	12 1/8	5 3/8	5 2/8	9 4/8	Converse County	WY	Robert V. Anderson	1981	2,282
65 4/8	13 5/8	13 1/8	5 2/8	5 2/8	11 3/8	Natrona County	WY	Jack H. Williams	1981	2,282
65 4/8	13 2/8	12 2/8	5 6/8	5 7/8	8 7/8	Johnson County	WY	Fred Thanel	1982	2,282
65 4/8	12 6/8	12 7/8	5 4/8	5 2/8	13 5/8	Converse County	WY	Melvin R. Wells	1983	2,282
65 4/8	12 7/8	13 1/8	5 0/8	5 0/8	6 6/8	Converse County	WY	Terry Wobig	1983	2,282
65 4/8	12 6/8	12 6/8	5 1/8	5 1/8	8 3/8	Custer County	ID	Dwight Rollins	1984	2,282
65 4/8	13 4/8	13 3/8	5 5/8	5 5/8	9 2/8	White Pine County	NV	Bob Price	1984	2,282
65 4/8	12 1/8	12 2/8	5 4/8	5 3/8	9 7/8	Converse County	WY	Don Schram	1984	2,282
65 4/8	13 3/8	13 4/8	5 2/8	5 3/8	6 7/8	Natrona County	WY	Gregory R. Bonetti	1984	2,282
65 4/8	11 7/8	11 4/8	5 7/8	5 6/8	9 5/8	Converse County	WY	Ron Hopkins	1984	2,282
65 4/8	12 5/8	12 4/8	5 7/8	5 6/8	8 5/8	Moffat County	CO	Win Knechtel	1985	2,282
65 4/8	12 0/8	12 0/8	6 0/8	6 0/8	8 5/8	Moffat County	CO	Randy Lamdin	1985	2,282
65 4/8	12 7/8	13 1/8	5 0/8	5 0/8	11 1/8	Converse County	WY	Daniel R Sowders	1985	2,282
65 4/8	13 0/8	13 0/8	5 0/8	5 1/8	8 2/8	Converse County	WY	Gerry Rubalcaba	1985	2,282
65 4/8	12 5/8	12 3/8	5 4/8	5 4/8	12 0/8	Glasscock County	TX	Courtney King	1985	2,282
65 4/8	11 6/8	12 4/8	5 2/8	5 3/8	11 2/8	Hettinger County	ND	Bill Clink	1986	2,282
65 4/8	13 1/8	13 1/8	5 6/8	5 6/8	11 2/8	Campbell County	WY	Dan R. Kohl	1986	2,282
65 4/8	12 0/8	12 2/8	5 3/8	5 3/8	9 0/8	Converse County	WY	James S. Saunoris	1986	2,282
65 4/8	12 5/8	12 2/8	5 6/8	5 7/8	9 1/8	McKenzie County	ND	Mark D. Hughes	1987	2,282
65 4/8	12 2/8	12 4/8	5 7/8	5 6/8	7 4/8	Converse County	WY	George Ollert	1987	2,282
65 4/8	12 5/8	12 5/8	5 2/8	5 2/8	12 0/8	Natrona County	WY	Robert L. Perkins	1987	2,282
65 4/8	12 1/8	12 1/8	5 3/8	5 4/8	9 4/8	Carbon County	WY	Steve J. Turner	1988	2,282
65 4/8	14 1/8	13 7/8	5 1/8	5 2/8	8 3/8	Converse County	WY	Leonard Kohan	1988	2,282
65 4/8	13 1/8	12 7/8	5 3/8	5 3/8	8 2/8	Converse County	WY	Tom Prosser	1988	2,282

Score	Length of R Horn L		Circumference R of Base L		Greatest Spread	Area	State/ Province	Hunter's Name	Date	Rank
65 4/8	13 2/8	13 2/8	5 2/8	5 3/8	6 2/8	Converse County	WY	Randy E. Doyle	1988	2,282
65 4/8	13 1/8	13 4/8	5 5/8	5 4/8	12 3/8	Millard County	UT	Bob Spina	1989	2,282
65 4/8	12 3/8	12 1/8	5 0/8	5 0/8	12 1/8	Campbell County	WY	Jay Riewestahl	1989	2,282
65 4/8	12 3/8	12 2/8	5 4/8	5 4/8	8 5/8	Moffat County	CO	Fred Richter	1990	2,282
65 4/8	13 7/8	14 0/8	5 3/8	5 3/8	6 7/8	Converse County	WY	Ron Voigt	1990	2,282
65 4/8	13 0/8	12 0/8	5 4/8	5 3/8	9 6/8	Washoe County	NV	Audrey Hanson	1991	2,282
65 4/8	12 6/8	13 2/8	5 2/8	5 2/8	10 2/8	Washoe County	NV	Michael Bradeen	1991	2,282
65 4/8	12 4/8	12 4/8	5 3/8	5 3/8	7 7/8	Sioux County	NE	Neil R. Blohm	1991	2,282
65 4/8	12 3/8	12 3/8	6 0/8	6 3/8	9 5/8	Campbell County	WY	Thomas Hlinka	1991	2,282
65 4/8	13 4/8	13 5/8	5 3/8	5 4/8	8 1/8	Sioux County	NE	Tom Rutt	1991	2,282
65 4/8	13 6/8	14 0/8	5 3/8	5 1/8	10 2/8	Sioux County	NE	Ivan Buss	1991	2,282
65 4/8	13 1/8	13 2/8	5 0/8	5 0/8	10 3/8	Modoc County	CA	Wayne Piersol	1992	2,282
65 4/8	13 4/8	13 1/8	5 0/8	5 0/8	10 2/8	Coconino County	AZ	George R. Richardson	1992	2,282
65 4/8	12 6/8	12 3/8	5 2/8	5 2/8	12 3/8	Converse County	WY	Patricia Stewart	1992	2,282
65 4/8	12 6/8	12 5/8	5 4/8	5 4/8	9 6/8	Harding County	SD	Gene M. Hove	1992	2,282
65 4/8	13 2/8	13 2/8	5 7/8	5 5/8	11 0/8	Harding County	SD	Marty Adams	1992	2,282
65 3/8	10 6/8	10 4/8	5 6/8	5 7/8	11 3/8	Pennington County	SD	Dean Nevland	1970	2,327
65 3/8	10 3/8	11 2/8	5 5/8	5 4/8	11 3/8	Moffat County	CO	Harry Campagnola	1982	2,327
65 2/8	11 6/8	12 3/8	6 0/8	5 7/8	10 1/8	Moffat County	CO	Henry Wichers	1958	2,329
65 2/8	12 0/8	11 7/8	6 2/8	6 2/8	10 3/8	Clark County	ID	Larry Cross	1978	2,329
65 2/8	13 4/8	13 3/8	4 7/8	4 7/8	11 0/8	Natrona County	WY	Mark Smith	1978	2,329
65 2/8	11 7/8	12 2/8	6 0/8	5 7/8	12 6/8	Natrona County	WY	Greg L. Pope	1979	2,329
65 2/8	14 6/8	13 6/8	5 4/8	5 4/8	9 2/8	Johnson County	WY	D. Collis/R. Smith	1979	2,329
65 2/8	12 4/8	11 7/8	6 0/8	5 5/8	11 3/8	Petroleum County	MT	Danny Moore	1980	2,329
65 2/8	13 0/8	13 1/8	5 5/8	5 3/8	12 1/8	Converse County	WY	Robert King	1980	2,329
65 2/8	13 0/8	13 0/8	5 2/8	5 2/8	9 4/8	Converse County	WY	Jim Keim	1981	2,329
65 2/8	13 3/8	13 4/8	5 6/8	5 6/8	10 7/8	Converse County	WY	William Pyle	1981	2,329
65 2/8	12 2/8	12 6/8	5 4/8	5 4/8	9 5/8	Converse County	WY	Hank Sisil	1981	2,329
65 2/8	12 4/8	12 1/8	5 5/8	5 5/8	8 3/8	Valley County	MT	Leith S. Wimmer	1982	2,329
65 2/8	14 1/8	14 0/8	4 7/8	4 5/8	8 7/8	Fergus County	MT	Don Davidson	1982	2,329
65 2/8	13 1/8	13 3/8	5 4/8	5 3/8	10 2/8	Converse County	WY	Richard C. Martell	1982	2,329
65 2/8	11 2/8	11 2/8	6 1/8	6 1/8	9 2/8	Lemhi County	ID	Blair G. Fisher	1982	2,329
65 2/8	12 1/8	12 0/8	6 0/8	5 7/8	9 6/8	Butte County	ID	Doug Ramsey	1983	2,329
65 2/8	12 0/8	12 1/8	5 6/8	5 6/8	10 5/8	Natrona County	WY	Vincent Cina	1983	2,329
65 2/8	12 4/8	12 3/8	5 5/8	5 3/8	10 2/8	Moffat County	CO	Gene E. Smith	1983	2,329
65 2/8	11 2/8	11 1/8	5 6/8	5 6/8	9 1/8	Converse County	WY	Ken Horton	1983	2,329
65 2/8	12 5/8	12 3/8	6 0/8	6 0/8	10 4/8	Sweetwater County	WY	Bryan Radakovich	1984	2,329
65 2/8	12 0/8	12 3/8	5 2/8	5 2/8	8 5/8	Lemhi County	ID	Larry Cross	1984	2,329
65 2/8	11 2/8	11 4/8	5 7/8	5 6/8	9 4/8	Carbon County	WY	Dick Bean	1984	2,329
65 2/8	12 7/8	13 2/8	6 0/8	6 1/8	8 6/8	Sweetwater County	WY	Evan Bellville	1986	2,329
65 2/8	12 1/8	12 0/8	5 4/8	5 4/8	9 3/8	Clark County	ID	Jay Parke	1987	2,329
65 2/8	12 1/8	12 1/8	5 4/8	5 4/8	8 7/8	Santa Cruz County	AZ	Dallas Smith	1987	2,329
65 2/8	12 1/8	12 2/8	5 6/8	5 5/8	13 0/8	Moffat County	CO	Pat Grogan	1987	2,329
65 2/8	12 3/8	12 0/8	5 3/8	5 3/8	11 4/8	Coconino County	AZ	Dan Robbins	1987	2,329
65 2/8	13 0/8	12 6/8	5 4/8	5 3/8	8 7/8	Converse County	WY	George A. Zanoni	1987	2,329
65 2/8	11 2/8	11 4/8	6 2/8	6 2/8	10 1/8	Crook County	WY	Robert Thompson	1987	2,329
65 2/8	13 1/8	12 7/8	5 3/8	5 3/8	9 5/8	Natrona County	WY	Paul A. Anderson	1989	2,329
65 2/8	12 3/8	12 5/8	5 4/8	5 3/8	8 3/8	Sioux County	NE	Gary L. Mason	1990	2,329
65 2/8	13 0/8	12 7/8	5 3/8	5 2/8	11 5/8	Empress	ALB	David E. Powell	1990	2,329
65 2/8	12 4/8	12 3/8	5 6/8	5 6/8	10 0/8	Rosebud County	MT	Tim Finley	1990	2,329
65 2/8	13 2/8	12 7/8	5 5/8	5 4/8	9 5/8	Campbell County	WY	Alan Solley	1991	2,329
65 2/8	12 6/8	12 6/8	5 4/8	5 3/8	7 7/8	McKenzie County	ND	Joel Beck	1991	2,329
65 2/8	12 2/8	12 2/8	5 4/8	5 4/8	11 2/8	Converse County	WY	Robert Webster	1991	2,329
65 2/8	13 3/8	12 5/8	5 4/8	5 5/8	7 3/8	Washoe County	NV	Allen Davis	1992	2,329
65 2/8	11 1/8	11 0/8	5 7/8	5 6/8	9 0/8	Sweetwater County	WY	Craig Boheler	1992	2,329
65 2/8	13 5/8	13 2/8	6 0/8	5 4/8	11 6/8	Clark County	ID	Mark Sherick	1992	2,329
65 2/8	12 4/8	12 1/8	5 6/8	5 6/8	8 7/8	Converse County	WY	Ken Gettman	1992	2,329
65 0/8	13 2/8	13 3/8	5 0/8	4 7/8	10 2/8	Lincoln County	NM	Ben Evans	1962	2,368
65 0/8	12 6/8	12 6/8	5 2/8	5 3/8	12 6/8	McLean County	ND	John Zahrte	1974	2,368
65 0/8	12 4/8	12 2/8	5 4/8	6 1/8	8 3/8	Albany County	WY	Robert Gorge	1979	2,368
65 0/8	12 6/8	12 6/8	5 6/8	5 5/8	12 5/8	Converse County	WY	Joseph Hopwood	1980	2,368
65 0/8	12 2/8	12 2/8	5 6/8	5 6/8	10 0/8	Moffat County	CO	Lyle Willmarth	1980	2,368
65 0/8	11 2/8	11 2/8	6 2/8	6 1/8	7 7/8	Converse County	WY	David E. Smith	1982	2,368
65 0/8	12 3/8	12 3/8	5 7/8	6 0/8	9 3/8	Converse County	WY	Mark R. Mussey	1982	2,368
65 0/8	13 2/8	13 0/8	5 5/8	5 4/8	9 5/8	Bowel Tower	ALB	Chris Kearing	1982	2,368
65 0/8	11 7/8	12 2/8	5 6/8	5 6/8	10 3/8	Converse County	WY	Darrell A. Bendel	1982	2,368
65 0/8	13 4/8	13 0/8	5 3/8	5 3/8	8 6/8	Converse County	WY	Kathy Kelly	1982	2,368
65 0/8	12 4/8	12 6/8	5 2/8	5 2/8	10 6/8	Albany County	WY	Claude Oppegard	1982	2,368
65 0/8	13 0/8	13 1/8	5 4/8	5 2/8	9 4/8	Sweetwater County	WY	Joe Dombovy	1983	2,368
65 0/8	12 0/8	12 2/8	5 4/8	5 2/8	10 7/8	Carbon County	WY	Steven Bins	1983	2,368

Score	Length of R horn L		Circumference R of base L		Greatest Spread	Area	State/ Province	Hunter's Name	Date	Rank
65 0/8	12 4/8	12 1/8	5 3/8	5 2/8	11 4/8	Carbon County	WY	Dan McPherson	1983	2,368
65 0/8	12 5/8	12 4/8	5 3/8	5 2/8	7 1/8	Slope County	ND	Ed Steidler	1983	2,368
65 0/8	12 0/8	12 0/8	6 0/8	6 0/8	11 4/8	Converse County	WY	Gary R. Shields	1983	2,368
65 0/8	12 1/8	12 2/8	5 6/8	5 6/8	8 2/8	Moffat County	CO	Reggie Spiegelberg	1983	2,368
65 0/8	13 4/8	14 0/8	5 6/8	5 4/8	10 0/8	Sweetwater County	WY	Kevin Jackson	1983	2,368
65 0/8	12 3/8	12 3/8	5 2/8	5 2/8	11 6/8	Cochise County	AZ	Dennis R Ward	1984	2,368
65 0/8	11 7/8	11 6/8	5 3/8	5 3/8	8 7/8	Garfield County	MT	Loren Blossom	1984	2,368
65 0/8	13 7/8	14 2/8	5 0/8	5 1/8	10 4/8	Rosebud County	MT	Daniel A. Nielson	1984	2,368
65 0/8	11 6/8	12 1/8	6 1/8	5 7/8	11 2/8	Carbon County	WY	James Smith	1985	2,368
65 0/8	13 3/8	13 5/8	5 4/8	5 4/8	9 0/8	McHenry County	ND	Kevin Ohlhauser	1985	2,368
65 0/8	12 0/8	12 2/8	6 1/8	6 0/8	9 0/8	Grassy Lake	ALB	Sam Kadoyama	1985	2,368
65 0/8	12 0/8	11 5/8	5 4/8	5 4/8	10 7/8	Converse County	WY	B. J. Higley, Sr.	1986	2,368
65 0/8	14 6/8	14 1/8	6 2/8	6 0/8	13 4/8	Petroleum County	MT	Brad Borden	1986	2,368
65 0/8	11 7/8	11 7/8	5 6/8	5 6/8	9 3/8	Natrona County	WY	Louis Strahler	1987	2,368
65 0/8	12 1/8	12 1/8	5 6/8	5 6/8	10 3/8	Converse County	WY	Gary L. Fischer	1988	2,368
65 0/8	12 2/8	12 2/8	5 3/8	5 3/8	8 1/8	Converse County	WY	Dean K. Reidt	1988	2,368
65 0/8	13 3/8	13 4/8	5 4/8	5 3/8	9 4/8	Malheur County	OR	Charles R. Bagent	1988	2,368
65 0/8	11 3/8	11 3/8	6 1/8	6 2/8	11 0/8	Moffat County	CO	Cecil O. Richburg	1988	2,368
65 0/8	13 3/8	13 4/8	5 1/8	5 2/8	9 4/8	Dunn County	ND	Don Paul	1988	2,368
65 0/8	13 0/8	12 5/8	5 5/8	5 4/8	8 1/8	Crook County	WY	John Papenfuss	1989	2,368
65 0/8	11 6/8	12 0/8	5 6/8	5 6/8	8 2/8	Carbon County	WY	Cecilia M. Watts	1990	2,368
65 0/8	12 1/8	11 6/8	5 6/8	5 6/8	8 4/8	Wildhorse	ALB	Dave Gerber	1990	2,368
65 0/8	11 7/8	11 7/8	6 0/8	6 0/8	11 0/8	Moffat County	CO	Kenneth Thompson	1991	2,368
65 0/8	12 6/8	12 4/8	5 5/8	5 4/8	8 6/8	Natrona County	WY	Jerry E. Burt	1991	2,368
65 0/8	13 2/8	13 1/8	5 1/8	5 1/8	9 3/8	Lincoln County	WY	Bob Grace	1991	2,368
65 0/8	12 7/8	12 6/8	5 4/8	5 2/8	10 1/8	Campbell County	WY	Robert A. Deems	1991	2,368
65 0/8	12 3/8	12 4/8	5 5/8	5 5/8	8 1/8	Converse County	WY	Walter H. Kennedy	1991	2,368
65 0/8	12 0/8	12 1/8	5 0/8	5 0/8	10 6/8	Converse County	WY	Larry L. Haines	1991	2,368
65 0/8	12 5/8	12 6/8	5 2/8	5 1/8	9 0/8	Bighorn County	MT	Terry Selph	1991	2,368
65 0/8	12 0/8	12 2/8	5 4/8	5 4/8	9 5/8	Converse County	WY	Gary R. Trumpy	1991	2,368
65 0/8	11 7/8	11 5/8	6 2/8	6 0/8	9 3/8	Campbell County	WY	Steve Ashley	1991	2,368
65 0/8	12 3/8	12 2/8	5 6/8	5 5/8	12 2/8	Rosebud County	MT	Everett "Eb" Morris	1992	2,368
64 7/8	12 5/8	12 5/8	6 4/8	6 3/8	16 4/8	Washoe County	NV	Robert Reed	1988	2,413
64 6/8	12 5/8	12 6/8	5 3/8	5 2/8	9 4/8	Perkins County	SD	Richard Bolyard	1975	2,414
64 6/8	12 5/8	12 7/8	5 2/8	5 3/8	7 7/8	Area 34	WY	John Dykes	1975	2,414
64 6/8	11 3/8	11 4/8	5 6/8	5 6/8	8 7/8	Johnson County	WY	James E. Taylor	1975	2,414
64 6/8	12 3/8	12 4/8	5 3/8	5 2/8	12 2/8	Lemhi County	ID	Dale Johnson	1977	2,414
64 6/8	11 6/8	11 6/8	6 0/8	6 1/8	7 3/8	Natrona County	WY	James E. Hodson	1979	2,414
64 6/8	12 0/8	11 6/8	5 7/8	5 7/8	6 6/8	Sweetwater County	WY	Silas Risely	1980	2,414
64 6/8	10 5/8	10 5/8	5 5/8	5 6/8	8 0/8	Converse County	WY	Papa Al Walther	1980	2,414
64 6/8	12 2/8	12 5/8	5 6/8	5 6/8	8 1/8	Converse County	WY	James H. Cox	1981	2,414
64 6/8	12 3/8	12 2/8	5 4/8	5 4/8	11 5/8	Converse County	WY	James K. Keim	1982	2,414
64 6/8	12 3/8	12 5/8	5 4/8	5 4/8	9 2/8	Converse County	WY	A. M. Oakes, Jr.	1982	2,414
64 6/8	12 1/8	11 4/8	5 3/8	5 3/8	10 3/8	Sweetwater County	WY	Bryan Radakovich	1982	2,414
64 6/8	12 6/8	13 1/8	5 0/8	5 2/8	10 5/8	Butte County	ID	William A. Burns	1983	2,414
64 6/8	12 0/8	11 6/8	6 0/8	5 6/8	10 0/8	Carbon County	WY	Paul Bowers	1983	2,414
64 6/8	13 4/8	13 5/8	5 0/8	5 0/8	8 4/8	Converse County	WY	Robert D Hankins	1984	2,414
64 6/8	13 1/8	13 0/8	5 6/8	5 4/8	13 0/8	Converse County	WY	Steve Woodman	1984	2,414
64 6/8	12 2/8	12 3/8	5 2/8	5 2/8	8 5/8	Johnson County	WY	Cecil Benner	1984	2,414
64 6/8	11 5/8	12 0/8	5 5/8	5 5/8	11 0/8	Converse County	WY	Rocky Chisholm	1984	2,414
64 6/8	11 1/8	11 2/8	6 0/8	6 0/8	8 5/8	Converse County	WY	Roy Goodwin	1984	2,414
64 6/8	12 2/8	12 5/8	5 3/8	5 2/8	8 3/8	Converse County	WY	John W. Dillon	1984	2,414
64 6/8	12 0/8	11 7/8	5 5/8	5 5/8	9 6/8	White Pine County	NV	Eugene W McNutt	1985	2,414
64 6/8	12 7/8	13 0/8	4 7/8	4 6/8	9 3/8	Moffat County	CO	Gary Oden	1985	2,414
64 6/8	12 1/8	12 1/8	5 3/8	5 2/8	9 5/8	Converse County	WY	Leonard J. Emmen	1985	2,414
64 6/8	11 7/8	11 7/8	5 7/8	5 6/8	8 5/8	Weston County	WY	Loren J. Liedl	1985	2,414
64 6/8	11 4/8	11 3/8	5 7/8	5 7/8	8 0/8	Converse County	WY	John M. Negley	1985	2,414
64 6/8	12 5/8	12 5/8	5 2/8	5 2/8	11 4/8	Converse County	WY	Rodney D. Johnson	1985	2,414
64 6/8	12 4/8	12 5/8	5 5/8	5 4/8	11 3/8	Rosebud County	MT	Greg L. Munther	1985	2,414
64 6/8	11 7/8	11 7/8	5 7/8	5 6/8	9 0/8	Garfield County	MT	John Fleharty	1985	2,414
64 6/8	12 0/8	12 1/8	5 3/8	5 3/8	7 3/8	Billings County	ND	Howard Sharp	1985	2,414
64 6/8	13 3/8	13 4/8	5 4/8	5 2/8	9 2/8	Converse County	WY	Floyd Horton	1986	2,414
64 6/8	12 4/8	12 4/8	5 4/8	5 4/8	9 4/8	Sweetwater County	WY	Ron Books	1987	2,414
64 6/8	11 6/8	11 2/8	6 2/8	6 3/8	11 2/8	Natrona County	WY	Richard Tudor	1987	2,414
64 6/8	11 5/8	11 4/8	5 5/8	5 5/8	11 1/8	Presidio County	TX	Gary J. Oden	1987	2,414
64 6/8	13 2/8	13 2/8	5 2/8	5 2/8	6 7/8	Blaine County	ID	Danny Moore	1988	2,414
64 6/8	11 4/8	11 3/8	5 7/8	5 7/8	9 3/8	Moffat County	CO	Mark Balavender	1988	2,414
64 6/8	12 4/8	12 5/8	5 1/8	5 1/8	7 0/8	Converse County	WY	Matt Curry	1988	2,414
64 6/8	12 5/8	12 4/8	5 3/8	5 3/8	3 4/8	Converse County	WY	William L. Ewald	1988	2,414
64 6/8	12 0/8	12 1/8	5 3/8	5 1/8	9 4/8	Converse County	WY	Ronald E. Marion	1988	2,414

SCORE	LENGTH OF R HORN L		CIRCUMFERENCE R OF BASE L		GREATEST SPREAD	AREA	STATE/ PROVINCE	HUNTER'S NAME	DATE	RANK
64 6/8	12 6/8	13 2/8	5 4/8	5 2/8	11 1/8	Unitah County	UT	Everett Burson	1988	2,414
64 6/8	12 5/8	12 7/8	5 4/8	5 5/8	9 2/8	Jenner	ALB	Neil Ostermayer	1988	2,414
64 6/8	12 2/8	13 4/8	5 2/8	5 2/8	11 1/8	Sublette County	WY	Dr. David Samuel	1989	2,414
64 6/8	12 6/8	12 6/8	5 2/8	5 3/8	8 2/8	Natrona County	WY	Jerry Novak	1989	2,414
64 6/8	12 2/8	12 3/8	5 2/8	5 1/8	9 1/8	Rosebud County	MT	Donald A. Kemkes	1989	2,414
64 6/8	11 6/8	11 7/8	5 7/8	5 7/8	8 7/8	Campbell County	WY	Terry Williams	1989	2,414
64 6/8	13 3/8	14 5/8	5 1/8	5 1/8	11 0/8	Slope County	ND	Tim Belland	1989	2,414
64 6/8	10 3/8	11 1/8	5 7/8	5 7/8	7 4/8	Converse County	WY	Dennis C. Faulkenberry	1990	2,414
64 6/8	11 4/8	11 7/8	5 7/8	5 7/8	10 0/8	Converse County	WY	William L. Doolittle	1990	2,414
64 6/8	12 4/8	12 2/8	5 2/8	5 3/8	11 2/8	Converse County	WY	Tony Naismith	1990	2,414
64 6/8	11 7/8	11 6/8	5 1/8	5 2/8	10 3/8	Jackson County	SD	Barry W. Scholes	1991	2,414
64 6/8	12 4/8	12 5/8	5 1/8	5 0/8	10 5/8	Morton County	ND	John Finck	1991	2,414
64 6/8	12 0/8	11 6/8	5 2/8	5 2/8	8 6/8	Converse County	WY	Larry Sylvester	1991	2,414
64 6/8	13 0/8	13 0/8	5 0/8	5 1/8	10 7/8	Converse County	WY	Jerome A. Wallenfang, Jr.	1991	2,414
64 6/8	13 4/8	13 2/8	5 6/8	5 6/8	17 0/8	Slope County	ND	Rydell Becker	1991	2,414
64 6/8	12 6/8	12 7/8	5 1/8	5 0/8	8 3/8	Converse County	WY	Norman Roy	1991	2,414
64 6/8	13 6/8	12 5/8	5 6/8	5 5/8	8 6/8	Harding County	SD	Marty Adams	1991	2,414
64 6/8	12 1/8	12 2/8	5 4/8	5 4/8	8 1/8	Petroleum County	MT	Richard Gensch	1991	2,414
64 6/8	12 5/8	12 6/8	5 6/8	5 6/8	8 6/8	Butte County	SD	Jim Thompson	1992	2,414
64 6/8	12 0/8	12 1/8	5 4/8	5 4/8	6 6/8	Converse County	WY	Alex McClelland	1992	2,414
64 6/8	13 1/8	12 2/8	5 6/8	5 5/8	11 5/8	Buffalo	ALB	Darryl Kublik	1992	2,414
64 4/8	12 2/8	11 5/8	5 5/8	5 5/8	7 2/8	Harding County	SD	Floyd Hauk	1959	2,472
64 4/8	12 1/8	12 0/8	4 7/8	4 7/8	9 3/8	Stanley County	SD	Ned E. Fogle	1965	2,472
64 4/8	10 7/8	10 7/8	6 2/8	6 2/8	9 2/8	Cherry County	NE	Jack Joseph	1970	2,472
64 4/8	13 3/8	13 4/8	5 4/8	5 4/8	9 6/8	Mineral County	NV	Gordon Diehl	1974	2,472
64 4/8	11 2/8	12 0/8	5 5/8	5 2/8	7 2/8	Carbon County	WY	Art Heinze	1976	2,472
64 4/8	13 4/8	13 1/8	5 0/8	5 0/8	12 2/8	Washoe County	NV	Roger O. Iveson	1979	2,472
64 4/8	12 7/8	12 3/8	5 1/8	5 1/8	6 0/8	Jefferson County	ID	Doug M. Chase	1980	2,472
64 4/8	12 1/8	12 0/8	5 1/8	5 2/8	7 5/8	Converse County	WY	John D. Davis	1980	2,472
64 4/8	11 6/8	11 2/8	6 0/8	5 6/8	8 7/8	Jones County	SD	Kenneth Kuchta	1980	2,472
64 4/8	13 1/8	13 0/8	5 2/8	5 0/8	9 1/8	Natrona County	WY	Carl W. Waggle	1981	2,472
64 4/8	12 4/8	12 4/8	5 2/8	5 2/8	13 3/8	Moffat County	CO	Harvey Grady	1981	2,472
64 4/8	13 0/8	12 7/8	5 2/8	5 2/8	10 2/8	Natrona County	WY	Harry A. Ulrich	1981	2,472
64 4/8	12 6/8	13 0/8	5 2/8	5 1/8	8 3/8	Converse County	WY	Bob Whitton	1981	2,472
64 4/8	12 3/8	12 0/8	5 5/8	5 4/8	10 0/8	Moffat County	CO	Mary Ann Madrigal	1982	2,472
64 4/8	13 3/8	12 6/8	5 6/8	5 6/8	10 6/8	Klamath County	OR	Richard D. Howell	1982	2,472
64 4/8	12 1/8	12 4/8	5 7/8	6 0/8	9 3/8	Natrona County	WY	Joseph Guerra	1982	2,472
64 4/8	11 5/8	11 5/8	5 5/8	5 5/8	6 6/8	Converse County	WY	Larry Lendman	1982	2,472
64 4/8	10 5/8	11 2/8	6 1/8	6 2/8	7 5/8	Wallace County	KS	Doug Wilson	1982	2,472
64 4/8	12 1/8	12 3/8	5 5/8	5 4/8	6 3/8	Harding County	SD	Chuck Bame	1983	2,472
64 4/8	11 7/8	11 6/8	4 7/8	4 7/8	8 5/8	Butler	WY	Timmy Glass	1983	2,472
64 4/8	12 1/8	12 2/8	5 7/8	5 7/8	10 3/8	Converse County	WY	Randy Rhoads	1984	2,472
64 4/8	12 5/8	12 4/8	5 5/8	5 4/8	7 6/8	Converse County	WY	Steve D. Munier	1984	2,472
64 4/8	12 4/8	12 6/8	5 7/8	5 6/8	8 4/8	Converse County	WY	Wayne Miller	1984	2,472
64 4/8	12 4/8	12 6/8	5 2/8	5 2/8	7 0/8	Washoe County	NV	Michael Davis	1985	2,472
64 4/8	12 0/8	11 5/8	5 4/8	5 4/8	9 0/8	Hettinger County	ND	William D. Helphrey	1986	2,472
64 4/8	11 5/8	11 5/8	5 6/8	5 5/8	8 7/8	Ward County	ND	Michael Dene Karna	1986	2,472
64 4/8	12 5/8	12 4/8	5 0/8	4 6/8	7 0/8	Moffat County	CO	Doug Beck	1987	2,472
64 4/8	13 2/8	13 3/8	5 0/8	5 0/8	8 5/8	Natrona County	WY	Michael G. McCarthy	1987	2,472
64 4/8	11 4/8	11 5/8	5 5/8	5 4/8	10 2/8	Moffat County	CO	Jack Van Vianen	1988	2,472
64 4/8	13 6/8	13 5/8	5 1/8	5 1/8	5 4/8	Butte County	ID	Clifton Robinson	1988	2,472
64 4/8	11 5/8	11 3/8	5 5/8	5 5/8	8 2/8	Converse County	WY	Steve Williams	1988	2,472
64 4/8	13 0/8	13 1/8	5 3/8	5 2/8	7 6/8	Converse County	WY	Gretchen Burton	1988	2,472
64 4/8	12 5/8	12 3/8	5 2/8	5 1/8	9 7/8	Campbell County	WY	Eric Wayne Noble	1988	2,472
64 4/8	13 4/8	13 4/8	5 2/8	5 4/8	9 4/8	Musselshell County	MT	Carl E. Nelsen	1988	2,472
64 4/8	13 2/8	13 0/8	5 3/8	5 3/8	10 2/8	Sweetwater County	WY	Len Cardinale	1989	2,472
64 4/8	12 6/8	12 6/8	5 7/8	5 5/8	11 7/8	Natrona County	WY	Larry Crouch	1989	2,472
64 4/8	11 6/8	12 0/8	5 4/8	5 3/8	11 3/8	Tompkins	SAS	Clarence R. Hughes	1989	2,472
64 4/8	12 4/8	12 6/8	5 5/8	5 3/8	8 3/8	Moffat County	CO	Mark Livingston	1990	2,472
64 4/8	13 6/8	13 6/8	5 2/8	5 0/8	9 6/8	Moffat County	CO	Mike Knight	1990	2,472
64 4/8	13 0/8	13 2/8	5 6/8	5 4/8	13 1/8	Fremont County	WY	Stanley Bocian	1990	2,472
64 4/8	12 5/8	12 7/8	5 4/8	5 2/8	8 5/8	Sioux County	NE	James D. Bourn	1990	2,472
64 4/8	13 1/8	13 0/8	5 4/8	5 2/8	11 1/8	Converse County	WY	Robert Oxley	1990	2,472
64 4/8	12 2/8	12 2/8	5 1/8	5 0/8	7 2/8	Laramie County	WY	Craig Boheler	1991	2,472
64 4/8	12 5/8	12 3/8	4 7/8	4 6/8	10 7/8	Converse County	WY	David DiPaolo	1991	2,472
64 4/8	11 4/8	11 4/8	5 4/8	5 4/8	6 6/8	Weston County	WY	Chuck Mead	1991	2,472
64 4/8	13 0/8	13 4/8	5 1/8	5 1/8	9 0/8	Bowman County	ND	Dennis Moritz	1991	2,472
64 4/8	11 4/8	11 4/8	5 6/8	5 7/8	9 2/8	Converse County	WY	William Siebeneck	1991	2,472
64 4/8	13 5/8	11 5/8	5 6/8	5 5/8	7 7/8	Malheur County	OR	Glenn W. Abbott	1992	2,472
64 4/8	13 4/8	12 4/8	5 2/8	5 2/8	13 6/8	Converse County	WY	John Leo Hojan	1992	2,472

SCORE	LENGTH OF R HORN L		CIRCUMFERENCE R OF BASE L		GREATEST SPREAD	AREA	STATE/ PROVINCE	HUNTER'S NAME	DATE	RANK
64 4/8	12 7/8	12 6/8	5 5/8	5 4/8	8 4/8	Phillips County	MT	Kevin Bertsch	1992	2,472
64 4/8	12 1/8	12 3/8	5 6/8	5 6/8	11 2/8	Stark County	ND	Mark Carter	1992	2,472
64 3/8	13 5/8	13 3/8	4 7/8	5 0/8	14 2/8	Carbon County	WY	David T. Funderburk	1978	2,523
64 3/8	11 3/8	11 5/8	6 1/8	6 1/8	12 2/8	Harney County	OR	Stanley Miles	1988	2,523
64 2/8	12 0/8	12 2/8	5 6/8	5 7/8	10 6/8	Harding County	SD	Rodney Foster	1965	2,525
64 2/8	11 5/8	12 2/8	5 4/8	5 3/8	9 3/8	Butte County	SD	Donald V. Friberg	1968	2,525
64 2/8	12 4/8	12 5/8	5 2/8	5 3/8	9 0/8	Stanley County	SD	George Hipple	1971	2,525
64 2/8	12 0/8	11 7/8	6 1/8	5 7/8	7 0/8	Ormsby	WY	Frank C. Rathje	1973	2,525
64 2/8	12 7/8	12 6/8	5 7/8	5 4/8	10 6/8	Perkins County	SD	Greg Larsen	1977	2,525
64 2/8	12 1/8	13 3/8	5 3/8	5 3/8	10 3/8	Natrona County	WY	Richard Aylward	1980	2,525
64 2/8	11 2/8	10 7/8	5 4/8	5 4/8	9 7/8	Moffat County	CO	Jeff Ollinger	1980	2,525
64 2/8	12 2/8	12 3/8	5 4/8	5 7/8	10 4/8	Converse County	WY	David E. Smith	1980	2,525
64 2/8	12 3/8	12 4/8	5 6/8	5 6/8	10 6/8	Carbon County	WY	Ervin Wagner	1980	2,525
64 2/8	12 6/8	12 6/8	5 4/8	5 3/8	8 6/8	Park County	WY	John Sides	1981	2,525
64 2/8	11 7/8	11 6/8	5 7/8	5 7/8	10 7/8	Custer County	ID	Robert J. Mayton	1981	2,525
64 2/8	13 5/8	13 1/8	5 2/8	5 3/8	15 1/8	Converse County	WY	Michael Smith	1981	2,525
64 2/8	12 0/8	11 7/8	5 0/8	5 1/8	6 3/8	Moffat County	CO	Dave Ellis	1982	2,525
64 2/8	11 6/8	11 7/8	5 4/8	5 5/8	9 1/8	Natrona County	WY	Douglas R. Parrott	1982	2,525
64 2/8	12 2/8	11 7/8	5 4/8	5 3/8	11 0/8	Moffat County	CO	George T. Kili	1982	2,525
64 2/8	13 1/8	12 0/8	5 4/8	5 4/8	11 1/8	Moffat County	CO	Gregory White	1982	2,525
64 2/8	12 4/8	12 4/8	5 4/8	5 4/8	9 3/8	Jefferson County	ID	C. Eugene Jordan	1983	2,525
64 2/8	12 7/8	12 6/8	5 5/8	5 4/8	7 2/8	Converse County	WY	David Arndt	1983	2,525
64 2/8	12 6/8	12 2/8	5 3/8	5 3/8	8 5/8	Sublette County	WY	Dennis L. Shirley	1983	2,525
64 2/8	11 6/8	11 6/8	5 2/8	5 2/8	11 3/8	Moffat County	CO	Dan Liccardi	1984	2,525
64 2/8	12 4/8	12 5/8	5 2/8	5 2/8	9 0/8	Converse County	WY	Donald W Malina	1984	2,525
64 2/8	11 2/8	10 7/8	5 6/8	5 4/8	10 6/8	Converse County	WY	Jason S. Miller	1984	2,525
64 2/8	12 1/8	12 2/8	5 5/8	5 4/8	6 7/8	Phillips County	MT	Dyrk Eddie	1984	2,525
64 2/8	13 0/8	13 0/8	5 2/8	5 2/8	11 2/8	Converse County	WY	Bill Sande	1984	2,525
64 2/8	14 0/8	14 3/8	4 6/8	4 6/8	12 0/8	Eddy County	NM	Noble Sinclair	1984	2,525
64 2/8	12 5/8	12 6/8	5 4/8	5 4/8	11 4/8	Sweetwater County	WY	Craig Boheler	1985	2,525
64 2/8	10 6/8	10 7/8	5 7/8	5 7/8	11 3/8	Dunn County	ND	Scott Lang	1985	2,525
64 2/8	12 4/8	13 0/8	5 3/8	5 2/8	6 6/8	Converse County	WY	Dennis Dunn	1985	2,525
64 2/8	12 4/8	12 4/8	5 0/8	4 6/8	6 6/8	Converse County	WY	Mark Labarbera	1985	2,525
64 2/8	11 7/8	12 1/8	5 3/8	5 2/8	8 3/8	Campbell County	WY	Richard Sapp	1985	2,525
64 2/8	13 1/8	13 1/8	5 4/8	5 3/8	12 5/8	Custer County	MT	James R. Thibault	1985	2,525
64 2/8	11 7/8	12 3/8	5 4/8	5 4/8	9 7/8	Converse County	WY	Floyd Rettler	1985	2,525
64 2/8	12 2/8	11 6/8	5 7/8	5 7/8	9 3/8	Stark County	ND	Scott Borchert	1986	2,525
64 2/8	12 0/8	12 2/8	5 6/8	6 0/8	11 2/8	Moffat County	CO	Fred Wallace	1987	2,525
64 2/8	13 2/8	13 4/8	5 2/8	5 2/8	9 3/8	McKenzie County	ND	Brent Perdue	1987	2,525
64 2/8	12 4/8	12 7/8	6 4/8	6 2/8	10 6/8	Billings County	ND	Robert Shannon	1987	2,525
64 2/8	11 1/8	11 0/8	5 6/8	5 6/8	9 4/8	Moffat County	CO	Steven Tisdale	1988	2,525
64 2/8	13 4/8	13 6/8	5 4/8	5 3/8	10 0/8	Carbon County	WY	Dave Gerhardt	1988	2,525
64 2/8	12 7/8	13 2/8	5 0/8	4 7/8	9 2/8	Moffat County	CO	John Axelson	1988	2,525
64 2/8	12 5/8	12 6/8	5 5/8	5 6/8	8 6/8	Converse County	WY	Marcel Kulas	1988	2,525
64 2/8	12 4/8	12 4/8	5 1/8	5 1/8	10 7/8	Moffat County	CO	Gary Fischer	1989	2,525
64 2/8	13 6/8	13 5/8	5 4/8	5 3/8	9 5/8	Rosebud County	MT	Steve Anderson	1989	2,525
64 2/8	12 6/8	12 6/8	5 2/8	5 1/8	8 3/8	Sheridan County	WY	Benjamin A. Dorward	1989	2,525
64 2/8	13 0/8	12 7/8	5 2/8	5 2/8	9 6/8	Moffat County	CO	Roy "Butch" Goodwin, Jr.	1990	2,525
64 2/8	12 3/8	12 2/8	5 3/8	5 4/8	8 6/8	Natrona County	WY	Roger L. Hendricks	1990	2,525
64 2/8	12 4/8	12 4/8	5 0/8	5 0/8	6 7/8	Powder River County	MT	Edwin John Durushia	1990	2,525
64 2/8	11 6/8	11 6/8	6 0/8	6 1/8	9 6/8	Powder River County	MT	Rick Simonson	1990	2,525
64 2/8	11 6/8	11 6/8	5 6/8	5 7/8	9 0/8	Bowman County	ND	Gene Welle	1991	2,525
64 2/8	13 0/8	12 7/8	5 1/8	5 2/8	10 3/8	Campbell County	WY	Larry Streiff	1991	2,525
64 2/8	11 0/8	11 2/8	6 0/8	6 0/8	7 5/8	Johnson County	WY	Robert M. Larson	1991	2,525
64 2/8	13 1/8	13 3/8	5 0/8	5 1/8	7 7/8	Washoe County	NV	Bill G. Davis	1992	2,525
64 2/8	12 6/8	12 6/8	5 1/8	5 1/8	9 1/8	Moffat County	CO	Charlie Hanawalt	1992	2,525
64 2/8	12 3/8	13 6/8	5 5/8	5 4/8	13 6/8	Converse County	WY	Anthony DiChiara	1992	2,525
64 2/8	12 7/8	12 3/8	5 2/8	5 1/8	7 7/8	Sioux County	NE	Lane L. Ostendorf	1992	2,525
64 0/8	12 4/8	12 4/8	5 0/8	5 0/8	8 6/8	Campbell County	WY	Carol Wert	1964	2,579
64 0/8	12 6/8	12 5/8	5 2/8	5 2/8	8 6/8	Lincoln County	NM	Harold Groves	1966	2,579
64 0/8	12 6/8	12 6/8	5 3/8	5 4/8	7 1/8	Natrona County	WY	Bernard Giacoletto	1970	2,579
64 0/8	12 1/8	12 1/8	6 1/8	6 0/8	11 3/8	Natrona County	WY	Mike Massa	1971	2,579
64 0/8	12 7/8	12 7/8	5 1/8	5 2/8	9 0/8	Sioux County	NE	Clyde M. Storie	1971	2,579
64 0/8	11 6/8	12 4/8	5 5/8	5 5/8	11 7/8	Harding County	SD	Roger Moul	1972	2,579
64 0/8	13 2/8	13 3/8	5 3/8	5 2/8	12 4/8	Harding County	SD	DeWayne Yantes	1973	2,579
64 0/8	11 7/8	12 0/8	5 6/8	5 6/8	11 4/8	Moffat County	CO	Dennis Behn	1981	2,579
64 0/8	12 1/8	12 2/8	5 5/8	5 6/8	8 0/8	Sweetwater County	WY	Mark Chapman	1981	2,579
64 0/8	13 0/8	13 1/8	5 1/8	5 1/8	10 7/8	Converse County	WY	Todd Schulz	1981	2,579
64 0/8	12 0/8	12 1/8	5 4/8	5 6/8	7 2/8	Natrona County	WY	Jim Smith	1982	2,579
64 0/8	12 3/8	12 0/8	5 3/8	5 3/8	10 3/8	Carbon County	WY	Ron Stacey	1982	2,579

Score	Length of R horn L		Circumference R of Base L		Greatest Spread	Area	State/ Province	Hunter's Name	Date	Rank
64 0/8	12 2/8	11 7/8	5 4/8	5 3/8	10 3/8	Converse County	WY	Richard Samson	1983	2,579
64 0/8	12 3/8	12 2/8	5 2/8	5 3/8	9 1/8	McCone County	MT	Mike Elsbernd	1983	2,579
64 0/8	11 7/8	13 1/8	5 6/8	5 4/8	10 6/8	Niobrara County	WY	Elgie D. Rewey	1983	2,579
64 0/8	12 3/8	12 5/8	5 4/8	5 4/8	14 0/8	Carbon County	WY	Kim S. Brockhoff	1984	2,579
64 0/8	12 5/8	12 5/8	5 4/8	5 4/8	12 2/8	Converse County	WY	Dicky Newberry	1984	2,579
64 0/8	12 4/8	12 5/8	5 1/8	5 1/8	9 4/8	Corson County	SD	Richard D. Hansen	1984	2,579
64 0/8	12 7/8	12 0/8	5 6/8	5 5/8	8 1/8	Campbell County	WY	Frank S McClain	1984	2,579
64 0/8	12 2/8	12 0/8	5 4/8	5 3/8	9 1/8	White Pine County	NV	David W Taylor	1985	2,579
64 0/8	12 6/8	12 6/8	5 1/8	5 0/8	8 1/8	Converse County	WY	Randy Johnson	1985	2,579
64 0/8	12 2/8	12 2/8	5 5/8	5 6/8	8 3/8	Natrona County	WY	Gary C. Cargill	1985	2,579
64 0/8	11 5/8	11 5/8	6 5/8	6 3/8	15 3/8	McKinley County	NM	Robert Allen Stearns	1985	2,579
64 0/8	11 7/8	12 1/8	5 5/8	5 6/8	8 7/8	Ward County	ND	Michael Dene Karna	1985	2,579
64 0/8	13 0/8	13 5/8	5 4/8	5 3/8	9 4/8	Washoe County	NV	David Powning	1986	2,579
64 0/8	11 7/8	12 1/8	5 4/8	5 5/8	11 2/8	Converse County	WY	Bill Doemland	1986	2,579
64 0/8	12 3/8	12 0/8	5 5/8	5 5/8	11 0/8	Moffat County	CO	Dennis J. Modlin	1987	2,579
64 0/8	13 3/8	13 2/8	5 4/8	5 1/8	11 0/8	Natrona County	WY	Gary L. Morse	1987	2,579
64 0/8	12 4/8	12 6/8	5 2/8	5 2/8	7 6/8	Moffat County	CO	Rex Blackwell	1988	2,579
64 0/8	13 2/8	13 3/8	4 7/8	4 7/8	7 0/8	Sublette County	WY	Earl Butts	1988	2,579
64 0/8	11 5/8	11 0/8	5 7/8	5 7/8	10 1/8	Campbell County	WY	Randy Deones	1988	2,579
64 0/8	11 7/8	11 7/8	5 5/8	5 4/8	11 5/8	Converse County	WY	Brad Holm	1988	2,579
64 0/8	12 2/8	12 1/8	5 5/8	5 4/8	10 4/8	Converse County	WY	Tom Nelson	1988	2,579
64 0/8	13 4/8	13 4/8	5 4/8	5 4/8	9 6/8	Converse County	WY	William Chaplin	1988	2,579
64 0/8	11 3/8	11 6/8	5 2/8	5 2/8	11 2/8	Johnson County	WY	Mike Renn II	1988	2,579
64 0/8	12 7/8	12 3/8	5 1/8	5 1/8	11 3/8	Rosebud County	MT	Ed Morris	1989	2,579
64 0/8	12 3/8	12 3/8	5 5/8	5 4/8	9 0/8	Morgan County	CO	Tim Bradley	1989	2,579
64 0/8	13 7/8	13 7/8	5 2/8	5 3/8	7 2/8	Converse County	WY	Randy Doyle	1989	2,579
64 0/8	12 4/8	12 4/8	5 6/8	5 5/8	10 7/8	Many Berries	ALB	Dale Peters	1989	2,579
64 0/8	13 0/8	12 3/8	5 3/8	5 3/8	7 0/8	McKenzie County	ND	Joe Hoffart	1989	2,579
64 0/8	12 2/8	12 3/8	5 2/8	5 1/8	9 6/8	Park County	CO	Daniel J. Lee	1990	2,579
64 0/8	13 2/8	13 3/8	5 4/8	5 5/8	8 3/8	Billings County	ND	John Serna	1990	2,579
64 0/8	13 2/8	13 4/8	5 4/8	5 4/8	10 0/8	Converse County	WY	Dick H. Fischer	1990	2,579
64 0/8	11 6/8	11 5/8	5 3/8	5 3/8	9 1/8	Campbell County	WY	Sheldon Showalter	1990	2,579
64 0/8	12 1/8	12 2/8	5 3/8	5 4/8	8 5/8	Campbell County	WY	Dave Vomela	1990	2,579
64 0/8	13 7/8	12 3/8	5 6/8	5 5/8	7 6/8	Converse County	WY	Mark Graham	1990	2,579
64 0/8	12 1/8	12 4/8	5 3/8	5 4/8	7 7/8	Converse County	WY	James Gorczynski	1990	2,579
64 0/8	11 5/8	11 4/8	6 1/8	6 2/8	8 7/8	Natrona County	WY	Russell A. Nichols	1990	2,579
64 0/8	12 0/8	12 0/8	6 0/8	5 7/8	11 1/8	Campbell County	WY	John Keenan	1990	2,579
64 0/8	11 6/8	13 5/8	5 6/8	5 5/8	5 3/8	Sioux County	NE	Richard W. Waller	1990	2,579
64 0/8	12 2/8	12 4/8	5 4/8	5 5/8	8 2/8	Sioux County	NE	Michael A. Ellingson	1990	2,579
64 0/8	12 4/8	12 4/8	6 0/8	5 6/8	9 6/8	Elko County	NV	Kurt W. Carpenter	1991	2,579
64 0/8	12 6/8	13 1/8	5 5/8	5 4/8	8 6/8	Campbell County	WY	Randy Springborn	1991	2,579
64 0/8	12 3/8	12 1/8	5 3/8	5 4/8	6 2/8	Converse County	WY	Donald L. Mott	1991	2,579
64 0/8	12 5/8	12 5/8	5 2/8	5 2/8	11 6/8	Converse County	WY	H. B. (Pat) Clark	1991	2,579
64 0/8	13 3/8	13 4/8	5 1/8	5 2/8	7 2/8	Bowman County	ND	Owen L. Wentz	1991	2,579
64 0/8	12 2/8	12 1/8	5 4/8	5 4/8	10 6/8	Converse County	WY	Rodney L. Eckberg	1991	2,579
64 0/8	12 1/8	12 1/8	5 3/8	5 2/8	6 6/8	Sioux County	NE	Ron Suponchick	1991	2,579
64 0/8	12 0/8	11 7/8	5 4/8	5 4/8	10 0/8	Moffat County	CO	John C. (Jack) Culpepper	1992	2,579
64 0/8	11 4/8	11 3/8	5 4/8	5 5/8	8 1/8	Moffat County	CO	Dennis E. Lerum	1992	2,579
64 0/8	13 3/8	13 5/8	5 3/8	5 4/8	10 0/8	Bowman County	ND	Renee Welle	1992	2,579
64 0/8	12 4/8	12 6/8	5 5/8	5 4/8	9 5/8	Rosebud County	MT	Rick Miller	1992	2,579

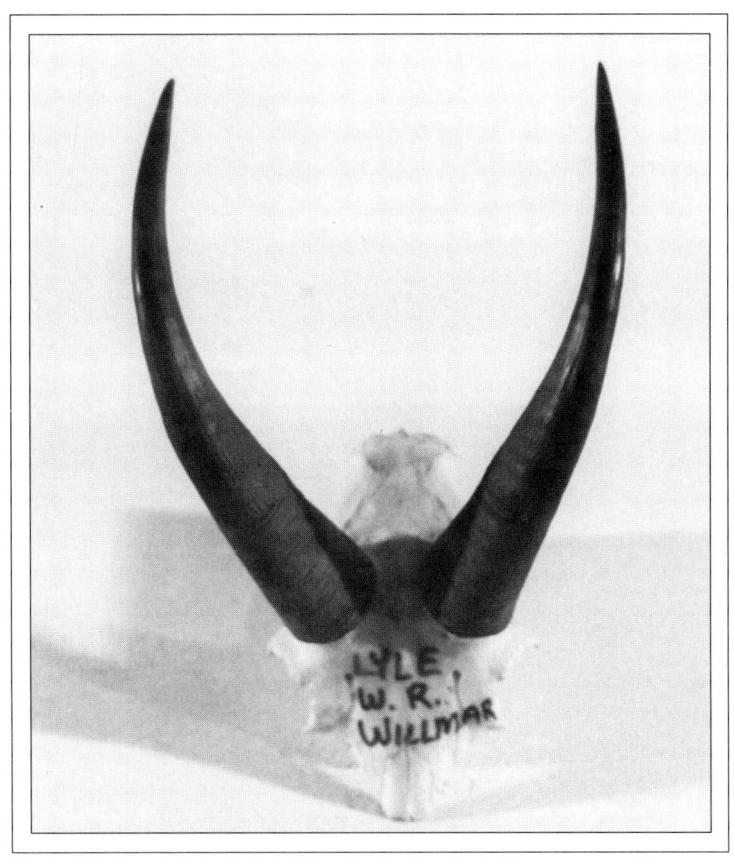

World Record Rocky Mountain Goat
Score: 52 4/8
Park County, Colorado - 1988
Hunter: Lyle K. Willmarth

SCORE	**LENGTH OF R HORN L**		**CIRCUMFERENCE R OF BASE L**		**GREATEST SPREAD**	**SEX**	**AREA**	**STATE/ PROVINCE**	**HUNTER'S NAME**	**DATE**	**RANK**

ROCKY MOUNTAIN GOAT

MINIMUM SCORE 40   *Oreamnos americanus americanus*
and related subspecies

SCORE	R HORN	L	R BASE	L	GREATEST SPREAD	SEX	AREA	STATE/PROVINCE	HUNTER'S NAME	DATE	RANK
52 4/8	11 3/8	11 2/8	5 7/8	5 7/8	8 1/8	M	Park County	CO	Lyle K. Willmarth	1988	1
51 4/8	10 5/8	10 2/8	5 6/8	5 5/8	7 4/8	M	Wrangell	AK	C. Wayne Treadway	1988	2
51 0/8	9 6/8	9 6/8	5 7/8	6 0/8	7 4/8	M	Terrace	BC	Dave Ramsay	1982	3
50 2/8	10 7/8	10 6/8	5 3/8	5 3/8	5 6/8	M	Ketchikan	AK	Kurt Kuehl	1989	4
50 0/8	10 2/8	10 1/8	5 7/8	5 6/8	5 4/8	M	Kittitas County	WA	Bob Haugen	1971	5
50 0/8	10 5/8	10 2/8	5 5/8	5 5/8	7 0/8	M	Snohomish County	WA	Edward M. Beitner	1984	5
50 0/8	10 2/8	10 2/8	5 4/8	5 4/8	6 3/8	M	Wrangell	AK	Bob Fromme	1987	5
50 0/8	10 2/8	10 2/8	5 4/8	5 5/8	10 2/8	M	Klastline River	BC	Gregory White	1992	5
49 6/8	9 1/8	9 1/8	5 6/8	5 6/8	7 6/8	M	Tesla Lake	BC	Peter Halbig	1970	9
49 6/8	9 5/8	9 6/8	5 5/8	5 5/8	6 2/8	M	Gallatin County	MT	Clark Kelly III	1990	9
49 4/8	10 0/8	10 0/8	5 4/8	5 4/8	6 1/8	M	Custer County	SD	William G. Chipman	1991	11
49 2/8	9 7/8	9 6/8	5 5/8	5 4/8	7 6/8	M	King County	WA	Jerry Solie	1978	12
49 2/8	10 4/8	10 5/8	5 2/8	5 3/8	7 1/8	M	Snohomish County	WA	Jonathon L. Bogle	1987	12
49 2/8	9 3/8	9 4/8	5 6/8	5 6/8	7 1/8	M	Taku River	BC	Jerry Davis	1991	12
49 2/8	9 4/8	9 3/8	5 6/8	5 6/8	6 6/8	M	Utah County	UT	Dennis L. Dobson	1992	12
49 0/8	9 5/8	9 4/8	5 1/8	5 0/8	7 6/8	M	Whatcom County	WA	Courtney Salmonsen	1974	16
49 0/8	9 1/8	9 1/8	5 5/8	5 5/8	7 0/8	M	Snohomish County	WA	Dick Smethurst	1975	16
49 0/8	9 0/8	9 0/8	5 6/8	5 6/8	6 7/8	M	Bennett Lake	BC	Jack Stephen	1982	16
49 0/8	10 2/8	10 3/8	5 3/8	5 3/8	6 0/8	M	Cleveland Penn.	AK	Kurt Kuehl	1990	16
48 6/8	10 0/8	9 4/8	5 5/8	5 5/8	7 6/8	M	Hedley	BC	Ernest Popoff	1981	20
48 4/8	9 5/8	9 5/8	5 5/8	5 5/8	7 3/8	M	Clallam County	WA	Dr. Charles F. Raab	1967	21
48 4/8	9 1/8	9 1/8	5 5/8	5 5/8	5 6/8	M	Terrace	BC	Dave Ramsay	1979	21
48 2/8	9 3/8	9 4/8	5 6/8	5 5/8	6 6/8	M	Seebe	ALB	Chris Kroll	1962	23
48 2/8	9 3/8	9 2/8	5 6/8	5 5/8	7 2/8	M	Crown Mountain	AK	Harold W. Jacobson	1973	23
48 2/8	9 7/8	9 2/8	5 7/8	5 7/8	6 4/8	M	Chaffee County	CO	Marvin Clyncke	1978	23

SCORE	LENGTH OF R HORN L		CIRCUMFERENCE R OF BASE L		GREATEST SPREAD	SEX	AREA	STATE/ PROVINCE	HUNTER'S NAME	DATE	RANK
48 2/8	9 1/8	8 7/8	5 4/8	5 4/8	5 3/8	M	Kittitas County	WA	Jim Pavack	1983	23
48 2/8	9 3/8	9 3/8	5 4/8	6 6/8	6 6/8	M	Kittitas County	WA	L. T. Spring	1986	23
48 2/8	9 3/8	9 2/8	5 3/8	5 4/8	7 0/8	M	Telegraph Creek	BC	Al Schroeder	1987	23
48 2/8	9 5/8	9 5/8	5 6/8	5 6/8	7 2/8	M	Jefferson County	WA	G. A. "Toby" Hart	1987	23
48 2/8	9 4/8	9 4/8	5 5/8	5 4/8	6 0/8	M	Natlude Lake	BC	Darrell Yetter	1988	23
48 2/8	9 7/8	9 7/8	5 0/8	5 1/8	6 1/8	M	Snohomish County	WA	Mathew Hayvaz	1991	23
48 0/8	9 4/8	9 7/8	5 5/8	5 5/8	7 4/8	M	Kitchener Lake	BC	Walt Sawicki	1975	32
48 0/8	9 6/8	10 0/8	5 5/8	5 5/8	6 2/8	M	Firesteel River	BC	John H. Kaykendall	1978	32
48 0/8	9 5/8	9 5/8	5 2/8	5 4/8	5 4/8	M	Snohomish County	WA	Gerry J. Lamarre	1978	32
48 0/8	9 3/8	9 3/8	5 3/8	5 2/8	6 7/8	M	Snohomish County	WA	Greg A. McTee	1986	32
47 6/8	9 2/8	9 2/8	5 5/8	5 4/8	7 0/8	M	Terminus Mtn.	BC	Paul P. Schafer	1975	36
47 6/8	9 5/8	9 3/8	5 5/8	5 6/8	6 4/8	M	Thuodadi Lake	BC	Phil Bauer	1978	36
47 6/8	9 5/8	9 7/8	5 3/8	5 3/8	6 6/8	M	Clallam County	WA	Wayne Haag	1979	36
47 6/8	9 3/8	9 3/8	5 4/8	5 4/8	7 3/8	M	Bonneville County	ID	Darrus D. Martin	1985	36
47 6/8	9 3/8	9 3/8	5 4/8	5 4/8	6 7/8	M	Jefferson County	WA	Donald Phipps	1992	36
47 6/8	9 3/8	9 3/8	5 4/8	5 4/8	7 4/8	M	Hope	AK	Demitrios N. Deoudes	1992	36
47 4/8	9 4/8	9 4/8	5 4/8	5 4/8	5 6/8	M	Jefferson County	WA	Bob Dierick	1976	42
47 4/8	9 6/8	9 6/8	5 3/8	5 3/8	7 1/8	M	Stalk Lake	BC	Chester J. Thompson	1977	42
47 4/8	9 5/8	9 3/8	5 4/8	5 4/8	6 2/8	M	Gallatin County	MT	Mark Ness	1984	42
47 4/8	9 7/8	9 5/8	5 1/8	5 1/8	6 7/8	M	Skagit County	WA	Steve Kempf	1987	42
47 4/8	9 3/8	9 3/8	5 3/8	5 3/8	7 4/8	M	Spencer Glacier	AK	Lon Lauber	1989	42
47 2/8	9 4/8	9 3/8	5 3/8	5 4/8	6 2/8	M	Kennedy Springs	MT	Don Leondorf	1964	47
47 2/8	8 6/8	8 7/8	5 3/8	5 4/8	6 2/8	M	Kittitas County	WA	Arnold L. Deckwa	1969	47
47 2/8	9 2/8	9 2/8	6 2/8	6 2/8	7 5/8	M	Kenai Peninsula	AK	John Moline	1971	47
47 2/8	9 5/8	9 5/8	5 2/8	5 2/8	7 0/8	M	Alsek River	AK	F. Wyatt Cook	1976	47
47 2/8	9 1/8	9 2/8	5 4/8	5 4/8	6 6/8	M	Cassier Inlet	BC	Peter L. Halbig	1984	47
47 2/8	8 7/8	9 0/8	5 4/8	5 4/8	6 4/8	M	Clear Creek County	CO	Don Stiles	1984	47
47 2/8	9 4/8	9 5/8	5 3/8	5 3/8	6 2/8	M	Lewis & Clark County	MT	Doug Getz	1985	47
47 2/8	10 0/8	9 5/8	5 1/8	5 1/8	7 2/8	M	Ravalli County	MT	Ray Tlamka	1985	47
47 2/8	9 2/8	9 2/8	5 3/8	5 3/8	5 5/8	M	Mitchell Mtn.	BC	Vincent Pisani	1986	47
47 2/8	9 7/8	10 0/8	5 2/8	5 2/8	6 3/8	M	Clear Creek County	CO	Richard A. Devrous, Jr.	1990	47
47 2/8	10 1/8	9 7/8	5 2/8	5 2/8	6 6/8	M	Ravalli County	MT	Shaun Twardoski	1992	47
47 0/8	9 3/8	9 3/8	5 3/8	5 4/8	7 2/8	M	Olympic Peninsula	WA	William V. Mishler	1968	58
47 0/8	9 1/8	9 1/8	5 2/8	5 2/8	5 6/8	M	Lemhi County	ID	Eugene E. Farmer	1972	58
47 0/8	9 1/8	9 1/8	5 5/8	5 5/8	6 4/8	M	Mason County	WA	Bob Brandfas	1976	58
47 0/8	9 3/8	9 0/8	5 5/8	5 5/8	6 6/8	M	Kenai Mtn.	AK	Rick Tollison	1978	58
47 0/8	9 2/8	9 3/8	5 5/8	5 4/8	6 0/8	M	Chaffee County	CO	Calvin Farner	1981	58
47 0/8	10 1/8	10 1/8	5 1/8	5 1/8	6 5/8	M	La Plata County	CO	Mark Wuerthele	1987	58
46 6/8	9 2/8	9 2/8	5 3/8	5 4/8	6 1/8	M	Haines	AK	Lowell Marylin	1962	64
46 6/8	9 3/8	9 3/8	5 2/8	5 2/8	7 0/8	M	Cordova	AK	Dwane J. Sykes	1973	64
46 6/8	9 2/8	9 3/8	5 4/8	5 4/8	6 2/8	M	Clallam County	WA	Dean Cook	1978	64
46 6/8	9 0/8	9 0/8	5 3/8	5 2/8	6 3/8	M	Stalk Lakes	BC	Walt Krom	1979	64
46 6/8	8 2/8	9 5/8	5 6/8	5 6/8	6 3/8	M	Kittitas County	WA	Robert J. Fischer	1981	64
46 6/8	10 0/8	10 1/8	5 3/8	5 4/8	6 0/8	M	Clearwater County	ID	Timothy A. Hyde	1986	64
46 6/8	9 2/8	9 0/8	5 3/8	5 3/8	6 6/8	M	Babine Range	BC	Don St. Jean	1987	64
46 6/8	9 7/8	9 4/8	5 2/8	5 2/8	6 4/8	M	Bonneville County	ID	Coby Tigert	1989	64
46 6/8	8 3/8	8 4/8	5 3/8	5 3/8	6 4/8	M	Todagin Mtn.	BC	Len Cardinale	1990	64
46 4/8	9 1/8	8 7/8	5 3/8	5 3/8	7 1/8	M	Clallam County	WA	Thos. J. Smith	1969	73
46 4/8	9 6/8	9 0/8	5 4/8	5 4/8	7 2/8	M	Day Harbor	AK	William L. Ruby	1970	73
46 4/8	10 0/8	9 7/8	5 2/8	5 1/8	7 4/8	M	Thuodadi Lake	BC	Gary Petee	1979	73
46 4/8	9 3/8	9 4/8	5 2/8	5 3/8	6 6/8	M	Olympic Peninsula	WA	Gerald Egbert	1980	73
46 4/8	9 2/8	9 1/8	5 4/8	5 4/8	5 6/8	M	Chaffee County	CO	Ken McIntosh	1983	73
46 4/8	9 1/8	9 0/8	5 4/8	5 4/8	6 7/8	M	Jefferson County	WA	Greg Tedlund	1986	73
46 4/8	8 3/8	8 2/8	5 5/8	5 5/8	6 0/8	M	Chaffee County	CO	Todd Clyncke	1987	73
46 4/8	8 4/8	9 6/8	5 5/8	5 4/8	7 6/8	M	Chouteau County	MT	Robert Lucas	1988	73
46 4/8	9 0/8	8 7/8	5 5/8	5 5/8	6 0/8	M	Kodiak Island	AK	Roger Stewart	1989	73
46 4/8	8 6/8	8 6/8	5 3/8	5 3/8	6 6/8	M	Atlin	BC	Gary M. Martin	1990	73
46 4/8	9 0/8	9 0/8	5 2/8	5 2/8	5 5/8	M	Bella Coola	BC	Barry McCay	1990	73
46 4/8	8 4/8	9 3/8	5 5/8	5 6/8	7 1/8	M	Moose Pass	AK	Craig Scarbrough	1990	73
46 4/8	8 5/8	8 6/8	5 3/8	5 4/8	7 2/8	M	Kodiak Island	AK	Lon E. Lauber	1992	73
46 2/8	9 2/8	9 5/8	5 2/8	5 3/8	6 5/8	M	Lewis & Clark County	MT	W. J. Fuller	1958	86
46 2/8	9 1/8	9 1/8	5 2/8	5 3/8	6 2/8	M	Lemhi County	ID	Ray Torrey	1967	86
46 2/8	9 4/8	9 3/8	5 1/8	5 1/8	5 5/8	M	Kittitas County	WA	Keith E. Anyan	1978	86
46 2/8	8 7/8	8 6/8	5 3/8	5 3/8	6 3/8	M	Terrace	BC	Bill Coburn	1979	86
46 2/8	9 3/8	9 3/8	4 4/8	4 5/8	6 3/8	M	Snohomish County	WA	Fred Collins	1980	86
46 2/8	9 5/8	9 7/8	5 2/8	5 2/8	7 3/8	M	Berners Bay	AK	Noel Feather	1982	86
46 2/8	9 1/8	9 0/8	5 3/8	5 3/8	6 3/8	M	Smithers	BC	Robert M. Fromme	1990	86
46 2/8	9 1/8	8 7/8	5 3/8	5 3/8	6 5/8	M	Clear Creek County	CO	Kurt W. Keskimaki	1991	86
46 2/8	8 3/8	9 2/8	5 4/8	5 4/8	7 1/8	M	Kodiak Island	AK	Mark A. Pfost	1992	86
46 0/8	9 3/8	9 4/8	5 2/8	5 2/8	6 6/8	M	Whidbey Bay	AK	George Moerlein	1964	95

Score	Length of R Horn L		Circumference R of Base L		Greatest Spread	Sex	Area	State/ Province	Hunter's Name	Date	Rank
46 0/8	8 5/8	8 5/8	5 0/8	5 0/8	6 2/8	M	Boise County	ID	Jerry E. Burt	1971	95
46 0/8	8 7/8	9 0/8	5 4/8	5 4/8	7 6/8	M	Kenai Peninsula	AK	Roger D. Morris	1971	95
46 0/8	9 1/8	9 3/8	5 1/8	5 1/8	6 2/8	M	Clear Creek County	CO	Kurt Keskimaki	1979	95
46 0/8	8 7/8	9 0/8	5 4/8	5 4/8	6 5/8	M	Kechika Range	BC	Roger Stewart	1980	95
46 0/8	9 2/8	9 2/8	5 2/8	5 2/8	6 6/8	M	Clear Creek County	CO	David Skiff	1981	95
46 0/8	9 3/8	9 3/8	5 2/8	5 1/8	5 7/8	M	Chouteau County	MT	Kay Davidson	1984	95
46 0/8	9 0/8	9 0/8	5 2/8	5 1/8	6 5/8	M	Kenai Peninsula	AK	Robert D. Warpack	1985	95
46 0/8	9 1/8	9 1/8	5 1/8	5 2/8	8 2/8	M	Spencer Glacier	AK	Matt Jones	1990	95
46 0/8	9 1/8	9 2/8	5 3/8	5 3/8	7 0/8	M	Jefferson County	WA	David K. Olson	1991	95
45 6/8	8 5/8	8 5/8	5 3/8	5 3/8	7 3/8	M	Skagway	AK	Rick Furniss	1972	105
45 6/8	8 5/8	8 5/8	5 2/8	5 2/8	6 4/8	M	Jefferson County	WA	John Lund	1978	105
45 6/8	9 0/8	8 7/8	5 1/8	5 1/8	5 4/8	M	Stalk Lakes	BC	John Stadler	1980	105
45 6/8	8 6/8	9 0/8	5 1/8	5 2/8	6 7/8	M	Cordova	AK	Gary A. Twigg	1980	105
45 6/8	9 1/8	9 1/8	5 2/8	5 2/8	6 4/8	M	Duti Lake	BC	W. C. MacCarty III	1981	105
45 6/8	9 3/8	9 4/8	5 2/8	5 2/8	5 3/8	M	Mount Jeldness	BC	Gerald Bond	1982	105
45 6/8	8 7/8	9 1/8	5 3/8	5 3/8	7 0/8	M	Todagin Mtn.	BC	Reggie Spiegelberg	1984	105
45 6/8	9 6/8	9 6/8	5 0/8	5 1/8	6 2/8	M	Clearwater County	ID	Mike VonLindern	1984	105
45 6/8	8 4/8	8 7/8	5 3/8	5 3/8	7 6/8	M	Atlin	BC	Harrison O'Conner	1985	105
45 6/8	9 0/8	8 5/8	5 1/8	5 0/8	7 0/8	M	Snohomish County	WA	Norman Ward	1987	105
45 6/8	8 7/8	8 6/8	5 2/8	5 1/8	6 2/8	M	Kittitas County	WA	William R. Kinnan	1991	105
45 4/8	9 2/8	9 3/8	5 3/8	5 3/8	6 0/8	M	Lemhi County	ID	A. LaVerne Hokanson	1968	116
45 4/8	8 7/8	8 7/8	5 2/8	5 1/8	8 1/8	M	Kenai Peninsula	AK	Dean Lust	1969	116
45 4/8	8 7/8	8 6/8	5 2/8	5 2/8	6 6/8	M	McCarthy Glacier	AK	John F. Sumrall	1974	116
45 4/8	9 0/8	8 7/8	5 2/8	5 2/8	6 0/8	M	Bonner County	ID	Dean A. Cox	1979	116
45 4/8	8 7/8	9 0/8	5 2/8	5 3/8	6 2/8	M	Kenai Peninsula	AK	Chris Kempf	1981	116
45 4/8	9 3/8	9 2/8	5 1/8	5 2/8	6 3/8	M	Jefferson County	WA	Gary R. Fountain	1987	116
45 4/8	8 7/8	8 6/8	5 2/8	5 2/8	6 4/8	M	Wrangell	AK	David Schuelke	1988	116
45 4/8	8 4/8	8 4/8	5 2/8	5 2/8	5 5/8	M	Snohomish County	WA	Timothy T. Neal	1988	116
45 2/8	8 6/8	8 7/8	5 5/8	5 4/8	7 4/8	M	Telegraph Creek	BC	Troy M. Miller	1968	124
45 2/8	9 3/8	9 0/8	5 2/8	5 2/8	6 5/8	M	Kenai Mtn.	AK	Robert Borland	1970	124
45 2/8	9 5/8	9 4/8	5 0/8	5 0/8	7 1/8	M	Lemhi County	ID	D. Kittredge/R. Torrey	1973	124
45 2/8	8 3/8	8 5/8	5 1/8	5 2/8	6 2/8	M	Kechika River	BC	Paul Brunner	1974	124
45 2/8	8 5/8	8 5/8	5 3/8	5 3/8	5 3/8	M	Kittitas County	WA	Jim Novak	1974	124
45 2/8	8 6/8	8 7/8	5 2/8	5 4/8	6 2/8	M	Jefferson County	WA	Larry Ramsey	1978	124
45 2/8	9 4/8	10 1/8	5 0/8	5 0/8	7 6/8	M	Valdez	AK	Kevin Chelf	1984	124
45 2/8	9 1/8	9 3/8	5 0/8	5 0/8	5 5/8	M	Snohomish County	WA	Douglas H. Brandt	1988	124
45 2/8	8 7/8	8 7/8	5 3/8	5 2/8	7 0/8	M	Valdez	AK	Rickie D. Snell	1990	124
45 0/8	9 3/8	9 1/8	5 3/8	5 3/8	5 5/8	M	Flathead County	MT	Jack Whitney	1962	133
45 0/8	9 0/8	9 1/8	5 0/8	5 0/8	6 3/8	M	Boise County	ID	Bradley H. Jolley	1972	133
45 0/8	9 4/8	9 3/8	5 0/8	5 0/8	7 1/8	M	Lemhi County	ID	G. Yasuda/R. White	1973	133
45 0/8	8 7/8	8 7/8	4 7/8	5 0/8	5 6/8	M	Jefferson County	WA	Edward H. Boyle	1974	133
45 0/8	9 2/8	9 6/8	5 2/8	5 2/8	7 2/8	M	Lemhi County	ID	Donald J. Keady	1976	133
45 0/8	8 6/8	9 0/8	5 2/8	5 2/8	6 4/8	M	Kenai Peninsula	AK	Eugene Smith, Jr.	1976	133
45 0/8	8 2/8	8 2/8	5 4/8	5 3/8	5 3/8	M	Big Sheep Creek	BC	Gerald Bond	1981	133
45 0/8	9 2/8	9 1/8	5 2/8	5 2/8	6 1/8	M	English Bay	AK	Maxallen D. Jackson	1982	133
45 0/8	8 1/8	8 2/8	5 2/8	5 2/8	6 4/8	M	Moricetown	BC	Don St. Jean	1985	133
45 0/8	9 2/8	9 2/8	5 2/8	5 2/8	5 5/8	M	La Plata County	CO	Jeffrey Yehl	1986	133
45 0/8	8 7/8	8 7/8	5 3/8	5 2/8	5 6/8	M	Kodiak Island	AK	Patricia Stewart	1989	133
45 0/8	9 1/8	9 2/8	5 2/8	5 2/8	6 3/8	M	Park County	WY	Jon E. Umphlett	1990	133
45 0/8	9 0/8	8 7/8	5 2/8	5 2/8	6 6/8	M	Bonneville County	ID	Randy K. Vranes	1990	133
45 0/8	9 5/8	9 4/8	4 7/8	4 7/8	6 2/8	M	Clear Creek County	CO	Sherwin Van Kooten	1990	133
45 0/8	9 1/8	9 1/8	5 2/8	5 2/8	6 6/8	M	Blaine County	ID	James Deitrick	1991	133
45 0/8	10 4/8	10 3/8	4 4/8	4 5/8	10 1/8	F	Bonneville County	ID	Mike Yantis	1992	133
44 6/8	8 6/8	8 5/8	5 1/8	5 1/8	0/8	M	Kittitas County	WA	Les Turner	1967	149
44 6/8	8 4/8	8 4/8	5 2/8	5 2/8	4 7/8	M	Snohomish County	WA	Kelly King	1977	149
44 6/8	8 7/8	8 6/8	5 1/8	5 1/8	6 1/8	M	Fox River	AK	John F. Sumrall	1977	149
44 6/8	8 7/8	8 6/8	5 2/8	5 3/8	6 7/8	M	Park County	WY	Scott Steere	1982	149
44 6/8	9 1/8	9 1/8	5 1/8	5 1/8	6 6/8	M	Valdez	AK	Rick D. Snell	1991	149
44 4/8	9 7/8	9 7/8	4 3/8	4 3/8	8 5/8	F	Cold Fish Lake	BC	K. K. Knickerbocker	1957	154
44 4/8	8 7/8	9 0/8	5 1/8	5 1/8	6 4/8	M	Kenai Peninsula	AK	Larry Jones	1969	154
44 4/8	8 5/8	8 5/8	5 1/8	5 2/8	6 1/8	M	Kittitas County	WA	David L. Smartt	1972	154
44 4/8	8 6/8	8 5/8	5 1/8	5 1/8	6 6/8	M	Stalk Lakes	BC	Richard J. Crowder	1977	154
44 4/8	10 1/8	10 2/8	4 4/8	4 4/8	8 5/8	F	Stock Creek	BC	Jay Deones	1978	154
44 4/8	9 0/8	9 0/8	4 7/8	4 7/8	6 6/8	M	Murky Lake	BC	Chuck Adams	1979	154
44 4/8	8 1/8	8 2/8	5 2/8	5 1/8	5 7/8	M	Jefferson County	WA	David P. Sanford	1981	154
44 4/8	9 2/8	9 2/8	5 2/8	5 2/8	5 5/8	M	Idaho County	ID	Darrell Howard	1982	154
44 4/8	10 2/8	10 1/8	4 3/8	4 3/8	7 6/8	F	Thatade Lake	BC	Jerry Baek	1984	154
44 4/8	9 2/8	9 3/8	4 6/8	4 5/8	7 7/8	M	Chugach Mtns.	AK	Darryl Quidort	1985	154
44 4/8	9 0/8	9 1/8	5 0/8	5 0/8	6 2/8	M	Atlin	BC	Tom Tietz	1985	154
44 4/8	8 5/8	8 5/8	5 1/8	5 1/8	6 4/8	M	Chugach Mtns.	AK	Gary White	1986	154

SCORE	LENGTH OF R HORN L		CIRCUMFERENCE R OF BASE L		GREATEST SPREAD	SEX	AREA	STATE/ PROVINCE	HUNTER'S NAME	DATE	RANK
44 4/8	9 1/8	9 2/8	5 0/8	5 0/8	5 7/8	M	Chaffee County	CO	Tim Cuthriell	1987	154
44 4/8	9 0/8	8 5/8	5 0/8	5 0/8	6 5/8	M	Mason County	WA	Dan Howell	1987	154
44 4/8	9 2/8	8 6/8	5 3/8	5 3/8	5 6/8	M	Custer County	SD	Vilas Schoenfelder	1988	154
44 4/8	8 6/8	8 5/8	5 1/8	5 1/8	5 3/8	M	Todagin Mtn.	BC	Craig Reichmuth	1989	154
44 4/8	8 5/8	8 5/8	5 2/8	5 2/8	6 7/8	M	Hyland Lake	YUK	Gregory White	1989	154
44 4/8	9 0/8	9 0/8	5 0/8	5 1/8	5 4/8	M	Kittitas County	WA	Jim Charlton	1989	154
44 4/8	9 2/8	9 4/8	5 0/8	5 0/8	6 7/8	M	Madison County	MT	Steve Rhodes	1989	154
44 4/8	9 2/8	9 1/8	4 7/8	4 7/8	6 6/8	M	Summit County	CO	Steve Fausel	1990	154
44 4/8	8 7/8	8 5/8	5 2/8	5 2/8	5 7/8	M	Custer County	SD	R. Craig Oberle	1990	154
44 4/8	9 0/8	8 7/8	5 2/8	5 1/8	7 0/8	M	Jefferson County	WA	Steve Brown	1990	154
44 4/8	8 5/8	8 6/8	5 2/8	5 2/8	6 1/8	M	Kodiak Island	AK	Larry Spiva	1992	154
44 4/8	8 0/8	9 0/8	5 5/8	5 5/8	6 3/8	M	Carbon County	MT	Chris G. Sanford	1992	154
44 2/8	8 5/8	8 5/8	5 1/8	5 0/8	5 6/8	M	Kenai Lake	AK	James R. Carr	1973	178
44 2/8	8 6/8	9 0/8	5 1/8	5 1/8	6 5/8	M	Cold Fish Lake	BC	Dennis Behn	1975	178
44 2/8	7 7/8	7 6/8	5 1/8	5 2/8	5 2/8	M	King County	WA	Ronald A. Carpenter	1977	178
44 2/8	8 3/8	8 6/8	5 1/8	5 1/8	7 0/8	M	Todagin Lake	BC	Stanley D. Moore	1978	178
44 2/8	9 0/8	8 7/8	5 1/8	5 2/8	6 7/8	M	Custer County	SD	Kent D. Keenlyne	1981	178
44 2/8	8 0/8	8 0/8	5 5/8	5 4/8	6 2/8	M	Tutachi Lake	BC	Ray Keenan	1987	178
44 2/8	9 2/8	9 2/8	5 0/8	5 0/8	6 1/8	M	Gallatin County	MT	Phil Auble	1987	178
44 2/8	9 2/8	9 4/8	5 0/8	5 0/8	6 2/8	M	Clear Creek County	CO	Elmer R. Luce, Jr.	1990	178
44 0/8	7 4/8	9 0/8	5 4/8	5 4/8	6 0/8	M	Clallam County	WA	Virgil T. Cole, Jr.	1973	186
44 0/8	8 5/8	8 4/8	5 0/8	5 0/8	5 3/8	M	Chelan County	WA	Steve Gorr	1975	186
44 0/8	8 4/8	8 3/8	4 6/8	4 6/8	4 0/8	M	Snohomish County	WA	Steve Gorr	1978	186
44 0/8	8 6/8	8 6/8	5 1/8	5 1/8	5 2/8	M	Clear Creek County	CO	Lee Kline	1978	186
44 0/8	9 3/8	9 4/8	4 6/8	4 6/8	6 4/8	M	Valley County	ID	Jack Barrett	1980	186
44 0/8	7 6/8	7 7/8	5 3/8	5 3/8	5 6/8	M	Duti Lake	BC	Mike Morgan	1981	186
44 0/8	8 5/8	8 6/8	5 2/8	5 1/8	5 7/8	M	Idaho County	ID	Randy Ulmer	1982	186
44 0/8	9 0/8	9 2/8	5 0/8	5 0/8	6 6/8	M	Lake Tatlatui	BC	Rick Gilley	1983	186
44 0/8	9 6/8	6 3/8	5 7/8	5 7/8	7 5/8	M	Kenai Peninsula	AK	Michael R. Traub	1983	186
44 0/8	9 1/8	8 7/8	5 3/8	5 2/8	5 6/8	M	Lincoln County	MT	Jerry Brown	1983	186
44 0/8	8 4/8	8 3/8	4 7/8	4 7/8	6 5/8	M	Cordova	AK	James A. Davison	1985	186
44 0/8	8 7/8	8 7/8	5 1/8	5 1/8	6 6/8	M	Clark County	ID	Brent Poulter	1985	186
44 0/8	8 7/8	9 0/8	4 7/8	4 7/8	5 7/8	M	Snohomish County	WA	Stan Hansen	1985	186
44 0/8	8 4/8	9 1/8	5 1/8	5 1/8	5 7/8	M	Snohomish County	WA	Mark Knaus	1987	186
43 6/8	8 4/8	8 4/8	5 1/8	5 0/8	5 4/8	M	Kittitas County	WA	Joe Walker	1967	200
43 6/8	9 3/8	9 4/8	4 6/8	4 4/8	7 3/8	F	Duti River	BC	Walter J. Sawicki	1976	200
43 6/8	8 2/8	8 3/8	5 1/8	5 2/8	6 3/8	M	Park County	WY	Pat McAteer	1979	200
43 6/8	8 7/8	8 7/8	5 0/8	5 0/8	6 7/8	M	Bonner County	ID	Howard W. Holmes	1983	200
43 6/8	8 5/8	8 6/8	5 1/8	5 1/8	5 3/8	M	Chaffee County	CO	Doug Beck	1988	200
43 6/8	8 4/8	8 4/8	4 6/8	4 6/8	5 7/8	M	Kittitas County	WA	Greg "Wild Horse" Willett	1989	200
43 4/8	8 7/8	8 7/8	4 7/8	4 7/8	6 0/8	M	Lake County	MT	Jack J. Whitney	1969	206
43 4/8	8 7/8	9 1/8	5 1/8	5 1/8	5 1/8	M	Lemhi County	ID	Joe Becker	1977	206
43 4/8	8 7/8	8 6/8	5 0/8	5 0/8	5 1/8	M	Kittitas County	WA	Glen Berry	1979	206
43 4/8	8 0/8	8 2/8	5 0/8	5 0/8	6 5/8	M	Ice Mtn.	BC	Larry Streiff	1979	206
43 4/8	8 5/8	8 5/8	4 7/8	4 7/8	6 2/8	M	Kitchener Lake	BC	James Saunoris	1983	206
43 4/8	8 3/8	8 5/8	5 1/8	5 2/8	5 6/8	M	Chaffee County	CO	Dan Eastin	1983	206
43 4/8	8 6/8	8 6/8	5 1/8	5 1/8	5 6/8	M	Chaffee County	CO	Don Bording	1983	206
43 4/8	9 1/8	9 2/8	4 4/8	4 4/8	7 0/8	F	Inklin River	BC	Dee C. Steinheiser	1986	206
43 4/8	9 0/8	8 7/8	4 7/8	4 7/8	6 1/8	M	Clear Creek County	CO	Daniel L. Tekavec	1986	206
43 4/8	10 4/8	10 1/8	4 3/8	4 3/8	6 2/8	F	Clear Creek County	CO	Donald Ace Morgan	1989	206
43 4/8	9 6/8	9 6/8	4 4/8	4 3/8	7 6/8	F	Ealue Lake	BC	Dave Hannas	1990	206
43 4/8	8 3/8	8 3/8	5 2/8	5 2/8	5 6/8	M	Park County	MT	Steve Kamps	1991	206
43 2/8	10 0/8	10 0/8	4 2/8	4 2/8	8 0/8	F	Tutaday Lake	BC	Larry Alma	1982	218
43 2/8	8 4/8	8 3/8	5 0/8	5 0/8	7 4/8	M	Telegraph Creek	BC	Jamie Byrne	1990	218
43 2/8	9 0/8	9 0/8	5 1/8	5 0/8	5 4/8	M	Ewilka Peak	BC	Larry D. Jones	1990	218
43 0/8	10 5/8	8 7/8	5 1/8	5 1/8	4 6/8	M		BC	Vic Clarkson	1960	221
43 0/8	10 0/8	10 0/8	4 4/8	4 4/8	6 2/8	F	Kittitas County	WA	Richard L. Thrasher	1968	221
43 0/8	10 1/8	10 2/8	3 7/8	3 7/8	8 0/8	F	Haines	AK	Roger O. Iveson	1972	221
43 0/8	8 7/8	8 2/8	5 0/8	5 0/8	7 3/8	M	Lemhi County	ID	Gregory D. Dodson	1977	221
43 0/8	9 0/8	9 0/8	5 1/8	5 1/8	5 2/8	M	Lemhi County	ID	Larry Nirk	1977	221
43 0/8	8 4/8	8 5/8	4 7/8	4 7/8	6 5/8	M	Mason County	WA	Andrew E. Appleby	1982	221
43 0/8	9 3/8	9 4/8	4 5/8	4 5/8	5 5/8	M	Custer County	ID	Larry A. Wilde	1983	221
43 0/8	8 0/8	8 1/8	5 0/8	5 1/8	6 6/8	M	Kittitas County	WA	Lance B. Cussons	1986	221
43 0/8	9 0/8	8 6/8	5 1/8	5 0/8	5 5/8	M	Keele River	NWT	Jim Ryan	1990	221
43 0/8	8 3/8	8 4/8	5 0/8	5 0/8	5 5/8	M	Border Lake	BC	Dean Stebner	1990	221
43 0/8	8 2/8	8 2/8	4 7/8	4 7/8	4 0/8	M	Pierce County	WA	Howard L. Harding	1990	221
43 0/8	8 1/8	8 1/8	5 1/8	5 1/8	5 4/8	M	Kittitas County	WA	John R. Sample	1991	221
42 6/8	9 7/8	9 7/8	4 3/8	4 3/8	7 6/8	F	Lake County	MT	Jack Whitney	1965	233
42 6/8	8 2/8	8 7/8	5 0/8	5 0/8	6 0/8	M	Chaffee County	CO	Chuck Hutton	1979	233
42 6/8	9 0/8	7 3/8	5 5/8	5 4/8	6 3/8	M	Chaffee County	CO	Duke Prentup	1979	233

SCORE	LENGTH OF R HORN L		CIRCUMFERENCE R OF BASE L		GREATEST SPREAD	SEX	AREA	STATE/ PROVINCE	HUNTER'S NAME	DATE	RANK
42 6/8	9 7/8	9 7/8	4 0/8	4 0/8	9 2/8	F	Knik Glacier	AK	Gary G. Wall	1985	233
42 6/8	8 4/8	8 5/8	4 7/8	4 7/8	6 2/8	M	Jefferson County	WA	Kevin Boyle	1986	233
42 6/8	9 4/8	9 3/8	4 3/8	4 3/8	6 7/8	F	Park County	CO	Corey Clyncke	1989	233
42 6/8	8 5/8	8 6/8	5 0/8	5 0/8	6 7/8	M	Jefferson County	WA	Gary Worth	1989	233
42 4/8	8 4/8	9 0/8	5 2/8	5 1/8	5 0/8	M	Chelan County	WA	G. H. Malinoski	1964	240
42 4/8	8 5/8	8 6/8	4 7/8	4 6/8	4 4/8	M	Goat Area 12	WA	James F. Miller	1977	240
42 4/8	8 5/8	8 6/8	4 6/8	4 6/8	5 4/8	M	Custer County	ID	Jim Wilson	1989	240
42 4/8	8 7/8	8 6/8	5 0/8	4 7/8	4 7/8	M	Custer County	ID	Kirk Westervelt	1989	240
42 4/8	8 7/8	9 2/8	5 0/8	4 7/8	6 7/8	M	Custer County	ID	David R. Anderson	1991	240
42 4/8	8 6/8	7 5/8	5 2/8	5 2/8	7 1/8	M	Park County	WY	Rob Marosok	1992	240
42 4/8	8 4/8	7 5/8	5 3/8	5 3/8	5 7/8	M	San Juan County	CO	Dennis L. Howell	1992	240
42 4/8	8 3/8	8 3/8	4 6/8	4 7/8	5 3/8	M	Howser Creek	BC	Alan Bressanutti	1992	240
42 2/8	7 6/8	8 2/8	5 0/8	5 0/8	5 4/8	M	Kleena Kleene	BC	William P. Mastrangel	1956	248
42 2/8	8 5/8	9 0/8	4 7/8	4 7/8	5 7/8	M	Terminus Mtn.	BC	Paul P. Schafer	1976	248
42 2/8	10 3/8	10 4/8	4 0/8	4 0/8	9 2/8	F	Kenai Peninsula	AK	Gilbert M. W. Smith	1976	248
42 2/8	8 3/8	8 5/8	4 7/8	5 0/8	5 2/8	M	Snohomish County	WA	Eric A. Olson	1979	248
42 2/8	8 1/8	8 1/8	5 1/8	5 0/8	5 1/8	M	Snohomish County	WA	Thomas E. Tipton	1985	248
42 2/8	9 0/8	9 0/8	4 3/8	4 3/8	7 3/8	F	Inklin River	BC	Dean Stebner	1987	248
42 2/8	8 1/8	8 1/8	4 7/8	4 7/8	7 2/8	M	Turnagain Pass	AK	Craig E. Scarbrough	1988	248
42 2/8	7 6/8	7 6/8	5 1/8	5 0/8	5 3/8	M	Snohomish County	WA	Jim Cowgill	1988	248
42 2/8	8 4/8	8 4/8	4 7/8	4 6/8	5 6/8	M	Park County	CO	Marvin Clyncke	1989	248
42 2/8	8 3/8	8 2/8	4 7/8	5 0/8	6 3/8	M	Eastman Mtn.	BC	Ron Serwa	1990	248
42 0/8	7 2/8	8 2/8	5 1/8	5 1/8	7 0/8	M	Taylor Lake	BC	Bill Brown	1957	258
42 0/8	8 4/8	8 5/8	5 0/8	5 0/8	5 7/8	F	Swan Range	MT	Jack Whitney	1960	258
42 0/8	8 4/8	8 4/8	4 5/8	4 5/8	6 1/8	M	Lemhi County	ID	Frank N. Hough	1968	258
42 0/8	8 4/8	8 5/8	4 6/8	4 6/8	5 3/8	M	Lewis & Clark County	MT	Don Davidson	1978	258
42 0/8	9 4/8	9 4/8	4 0/8	4 0/8	6 1/8	F	Snohomish County	WA	Joseph R. St. Charles	1980	258
42 0/8	9 6/8	9 6/8	4 2/8	4 2/8	6 3/8	F	Chouteau County	MT	Terry Albrecht	1981	258
42 0/8	9 3/8	9 4/8	4 0/8	4 1/8	7 3/8	F	Todagin Mtns.	BC	Neil Summers	1985	258
42 0/8	8 3/8	8 2/8	4 7/8	5 0/8	5 4/8	M	Ravalli County	MT	Jon Cusker	1987	258
42 0/8	8 1/8	8 3/8	4 7/8	4 7/8	6 5/8	M	Park County	CO	Doug Rininger	1990	258
41 6/8	8 1/8	8 0/8	4 7/8	4 7/8	6 3/8	F	Lord River	BC	Dr. R. Congdon	1958	267
41 6/8	8 1/8	8 1/8	4 7/8	4 6/8	5 6/8	M	Beaverhead County	MT	Mike Bartz	1976	267
41 6/8	9 1/8	9 1/8	4 3/8	4 3/8	5 3/8	F	Snohomish County	WA	Scott McDermott	1980	267
41 6/8	9 4/8	9 4/8	4 2/8	4 1/8	6 2/8	F	Snohomish County	WA	Steve Novy	1981	267
41 6/8	8 2/8	8 2/8	4 6/8	4 6/8	5 6/8	M	Jefferson County	WA	Richard Van Calcar	1983	267
41 6/8	7 6/8	7 5/8	4 7/8	4 7/8	5 5/8	M	Lawson Lake	BC	David Baldwin	1984	267
41 6/8	7 3/8	7 6/8	5 1/8	5 1/8	5 0/8	M	Snohomish County	WA	Jack Williams	1984	267
41 6/8	8 3/8	8 3/8	4 7/8	4 7/8	5 3/8	M	Jefferson County	WA	Steve Wyman	1984	267
41 6/8	8 6/8	8 7/8	4 6/8	4 7/8	5 5/8	M	La Plata County	CO	Sid Strzok	1986	267
41 6/8	8 3/8	8 3/8	4 7/8	4 6/8	6 2/8	M	Clear Creek County	CO	Tony Snow	1988	267
41 6/8	8 0/8	8 7/8	5 0/8	5 0/8	5 7/8	M	Chaffee County	CO	Ron Sniff	1992	267
41 4/8	10 2/8	10 2/8	4 0/8	4 0/8	10 1/8	F	Takia River	BC	William L. Sullivan	1966	278
41 4/8	8 1/8	8 1/8	4 6/8	4 7/8	5 4/8	M	Summit County	CO	Wayne Depperschmidt	1979	278
41 4/8	9 5/8	9 6/8	3 6/8	3 5/8	7 2/8	F	Snohomish County	WA	Steve Wait	1981	278
41 4/8	9 3/8	9 1/8	4 1/8	4 1/8	7 1/8	F	Whatcom County	WA	Adam Redford	1981	278
41 4/8	9 4/8	9 4/8	4 2/8	4 2/8	10 0/8	F	Atlin Lake	BC	Ty Harpain	1989	278
41 4/8	8 2/8	8 2/8	4 7/8	5 0/8	6 0/8	M	La Plata County	CO	Dale Struble	1990	278
41 4/8	8 4/8	8 5/8	4 4/8	4 5/8	7 5/8	M	Prince William Sound	AK	John D. "Jack" Frost	1990	278
41 4/8	7 5/8	8 2/8	5 1/8	5 1/8	5 6/8	M	Clear Creek County	CO	Lonny Vanatta	1992	278
41 2/8	9 7/8	9 6/8	4 2/8	4 2/8	6 4/8	F	Crazy Mountains	MT	Glenn Gibson	1957	286
41 2/8	8 3/8	8 3/8	4 3/8	4 3/8	5 1/8	F	Kittitas County	WA	Dennis Dunn	1973	286
41 2/8	8 3/8	8 2/8	4 6/8	4 6/8	5 3/8	M	Teton County	MT	Edwin Evans	1983	286
41 2/8	9 2/8	9 2/8	4 2/8	4 2/8	6 1/8	F	Rusty Creek	BC	Ronald Montross	1984	286
41 2/8	8 2/8	8 2/8	4 7/8	4 6/8	6 0/8	M	Pierce County	WA	Dale Holpainen	1986	286
41 2/8	9 3/8	9 3/8	3 7/8	3 7/8	8 1/8	F	Chugach Mtns.	AK	Richard Moran	1988	286
41 2/8	7 7/8	7 7/8	4 7/8	4 7/8	5 3/8	M	Snohomish County	WA	Dale Drilling	1988	286
41 2/8	8 4/8	8 4/8	4 6/8	4 5/8	6 0/8	M	Chaffee County	CO	Larick Spencer	1990	286
41 2/8	8 2/8	8 2/8	4 6/8	4 6/8	7 0/8	M	Otter Tail Creek	BC	Vaughn D. Ballard	1991	286
41 2/8	8 3/8	8 3/8	4 6/8	4 7/8	5 6/8	M	Summit County	CO	Dominic Florian	1992	286
41 0/8	8 6/8	8 5/8	4 2/8	4 2/8	7 0/8	M	Penticton	BC	Bill Brown	1958	296
41 0/8	8 7/8	9 0/8	4 4/8	4 4/8	5 5/8	F	Snohomish County	WA	Bud Peck	1960	296
41 0/8	10 0/8	10 0/8	3 6/8	3 7/8	6 2/8	F	Holly Creek	BC	Jim Jackson	1964	296
41 0/8	9 2/8	9 3/8	3 7/8	3 7/8	10 0/8	F	Valdez	AK	Jim Jarvis	1979	296
41 0/8	8 7/8	9 0/8	4 0/8	3 7/8	5 7/8	F	Snohomish County	WA	Mark S. Jacobs	1980	296
41 0/8	8 1/8	8 1/8	4 6/8	4 6/8	5 7/8	M	Clallam County	WA	Russ Spaulding	1981	296
41 0/8	8 1/8	7 4/8	4 7/8	4 7/8	6 4/8	M	Bennett Lake	BC	Dave Richardson	1982	296
41 0/8	9 1/8	9 1/8	4 0/8	4 0/8	6 1/8	F	Snohomish County	WA	Richard Kobel	1984	296
41 0/8	7 7/8	8 0/8	4 6/8	4 6/8	4 6/8	M	Bonner County	ID	Linda Leake	1984	296
41 0/8	8 3/8	8 2/8	4 5/8	4 5/8	6 1/8	M	Park County	CO	Scott George	1990	296

Score	Length of R Horn L		Circumference R of Base L		Greatest Spread	Sex	Area	State/ Province	Hunter's Name	Date	Rank
41 0/8	9 5/8	9 3/8	4 2/8	4 2/8	6 4/8	F	Clear Creek County	CO	John Borlang	1991	296
40 6/8	8 3/8	8 3/8	4 6/8	4 6/8	5 2/8	M	Boise County	ID	Ronald L. Sherer	1970	307
40 6/8	7 3/8	7 2/8	4 7/8	4 6/8	6 1/8	M	Kitchener Lake	BC	Walt Krom	1971	307
40 6/8	8 0/8	7 7/8	4 5/8	4 5/8	6 0/8	M	Kenai Lake	AK	Dennis Lattery	1973	307
40 6/8	8 6/8	8 5/8	4 6/8	4 6/8	5 5/8	M	Park County	WY	Jeff Umphlett	1979	307
40 6/8	9 1/8	9 1/8	4 1/8	4 1/8	5 4/8	F	Kittitas County	WA	Roger Pitman	1980	307
40 6/8	9 0/8	9 0/8	4 3/8	4 4/8	6 2/8	F	San Juan County	CO	Bill McEwen	1984	307
40 6/8	9 2/8	9 1/8	4 1/8	4 1/8	5 6/8	F	Kittitas County	WA	L. James Bailey	1984	307
40 6/8	8 1/8	8 5/8	4 4/8	4 5/8	6 3/8	M	Clallam County	WA	Dave Kanters	1988	307
40 6/8	9 0/8	8 7/8	4 2/8	4 2/8	6 6/8	F	Mt. Hunter	BC	Dennis Kamstra	1990	307
40 6/8	9 2/8	9 3/8	4 1/8	4 1/8	5 5/8	F	Clear Creek County	CO	Dave Culter	1990	307
40 6/8	8 2/8	8 2/8	4 6/8	4 7/8	5 2/8	M	Golden	BC	Jeffrey W. Murray	1992	307
40 4/8	9 0/8	8 3/8	4 1/8	4 1/8	7 5/8	F	Little Johnstone Bay	AK	Ray Uhl	1965	318
40 4/8	8 7/8	8 6/8	4 1/8	4 1/8	6 4/8	F	Smithers	BC	Chris Vanderhorst	1974	318
40 4/8	9 4/8	9 5/8	3 7/8	4 0/8	10 3/8	F	Kenai Mtn.	AK	David E. Smith	1976	318
40 4/8	8 6/8	8 4/8	4 2/8	4 2/8	4 7/8	F	Kittitas County	WA	Kirk Cresto	1981	318
40 4/8	7 3/8	8 4/8	5 0/8	5 0/8	6 6/8	M	Cordova	AK	Ray Ryan	1986	318
40 4/8	6 6/8	8 7/8	5 3/8	5 2/8	6 7/8	M	La Plata County	CO	John Gardner	1986	318
40 4/8	8 1/8	8 1/8	4 5/8	4 5/8	4 7/8	M	Snohomish County	WA	Gregg Welch	1987	318
40 2/8	7 6/8	7 3/8	4 5/8	4 5/8	5 5/8	M	Boise County	ID	Jack Arbaugh	1975	325
40 2/8	8 5/8	8 4/8	4 0/8	4 0/8	5 7/8	F	Kittitas County	WA	Bob McClure	1977	325
40 2/8	7 2/8	7 2/8	4 5/8	4 5/8	5 3/8	M	Tustemena Glacier	AK	Lloyd M. Minerich	1988	325
40 2/8	9 0/8	8 7/8	4 1/8	4 1/8	6 0/8	F	Clear Creek County	CO	Wes Heiland	1991	325
40 0/8	8 7/8	8 7/8	4 2/8	4 2/8	6 6/8	F	Chaffee County	CO	Wayne Spencer	1973	329
40 0/8	8 3/8	8 2/8	4 5/8	4 6/8	6 1/8	M	Lemhi County	ID	Marvin Tye	1973	329
40 0/8	8 3/8	8 3/8	4 1/8	4 1/8	5 1/8	F	Snohomish County	WA	Albert A. Rinaldi, Jr.	1974	329
40 0/8	7 5/8	7 5/8	4 6/8	4 6/8	5 0/8	M	Cordova	AK	Ray P. Noregaard	1975	329
40 0/8	9 1/8	9 1/8	4 1/8	4 1/8	6 7/8	F	Kitchener Lake	BC	John Dmytryka	1976	329
40 0/8	9 4/8	9 2/8	4 2/8	4 1/8	7 5/8	F	Cimari Valley	ID	Robert Frank	1976	329
40 0/8	8 3/8	8 2/8	4 5/8	4 5/8	4 7/8	M	Lemhi County	ID	H. R. 'Rusty' Neely	1976	329
40 0/8	8 5/8	8 5/8	4 3/8	4 2/8	6 1/8	F	Summit County	CO	Michael Beckwith	1978	329
40 0/8	8 7/8	8 5/8	4 1/8	4 1/8	5 5/8	F	Kittitas County	WA	Wilton Viall	1984	329
40 0/8	9 3/8	9 2/8	4 1/8	4 1/8	6 0/8	F	La Plata County	CO	Daniel Willems	1988	329
40 0/8	9 0/8	8 7/8	4 1/8	4 2/8	6 4/8	F	Bonneville County	ID	Tab R. Mendenhall	1989	329
40 0/8	7 5/8	7 6/8	4 6/8	4 6/8	6 3/8	M	Clear Creek County	CO	Monty Ace Morgan	1990	329
40 0/8	8 7/8	9 0/8	3 6/8	3 6/8	7 0/8	F	Kynck Inlet	BC	Steve Schmid	1990	329

World Record Bighorn Sheep
Score: 191 3/8
El Paso County, Colorado - 1983
Hunter: Gene Moore

BIGHORN SHEEP

MINIMUM SCORE 140

Ovis canadensis canadensis
and certain related subspecies

SCORE	LENGTH OF R HORN L		CIRCUMFERENCE R OF BASE L		GREATEST SPREAD	AREA	STATE/ PROVINCE	HUNTER'S NAME	DATE	RANK
191 3/8	42 3/8	42 2/8	15 5/8	15 4/8	24 0/8	El Paso County	CO	Gene Moore	1983	1
190 2/8	39 4/8	39 4/8	16 4/8	16 3/8	20 4/8	Canmore	ALB	Brian Eloschuk	1982	2
186 1/8	38 2/8	37 1/8	15 5/8	15 3/8	20 7/8	Canmore	ALB	Cornel Yarmoloy	1982	3
184 1/8	38 4/8	38 7/8	15 5/8	15 5/8	21 1/8	Pigeon Mtn.	ALB	Guy Woods	1985	4
184 0/8	39 1/8	37 7/8	15 3/8	15 1/8	20 2/8	Canmore	ALB	Al Schroeder	1989	5
183 7/8	38 3/8	38 6/8	15 4/8	15 5/8	24 5/8	Deer Lodge County	MT	Jerry Parsons	1986	6
183 7/8	36 6/8	37 1/8	15 0/8	15 0/8	22 0/8	Clear Creek County	CO	Ray Alt	1988	6
183 4/8	40 3/8	41 1/8	15 5/8	15 6/8	23 3/8	Lincoln County	MT	Paul Schafer	1983	8
183 4/8	38 4/8	39 0/8	16 1/8	16 0/8	19 6/8	Ravalli County	MT	Jim Chinn	1986	8
183 2/8	40 4/8	39 2/8	14 7/8	14 7/8	21 6/8	El Paso County	CO	Bob Renner	1979	10
182 7/8	38 2/8	38 5/8	15 3/8	15 3/8	22 6/8	El Paso County	CO	Fred Church	1989	11
182 0/8	39 6/8	39 6/8	15 0/8	15 0/8	22 4/8	Sanders County	MT	John T. Beyer	1990	12
181 5/8	38 1/8	34 4/8	16 2/8	16 2/8	23 0/8	Canmore	ALB	Paul Inzanti	1984	13
181 1/8	38 1/8	39 0/8	14 3/8	14 3/8	21 6/8	Clear Creek County	CO	Gary Renfro	1982	14
180 7/8	37 3/8	38 4/8	15 4/8	15 4/8	22 1/8	Granite County	MT	Alden Gregory Beard	1992	15
180 3/8	37 6/8	36 5/8	15 2/8	15 2/8	19 5/8	San Miguel County	NM	Ronald D. Rod	1992	16
180 1/8	37 4/8	37 3/8	15 2/8	15 2/8	22 7/8	Clear Creek County	CO	Charles W. Hanawalt	1990	17
179 3/8	39 4/8	38 3/8	14 4/8	14 2/8	22 1/8	El Paso County	CO	Doy K. Curtis	1977	18

445

Score	Length of Horn R	Length of Horn L	Circumference of Base R	Circumference of Base L	Greatest Spread	Area	State/ Province	Hunter's Name	Date	Rank
179 3/8	38 1/8	37 4/8	15 7/8	15 7/8	21 0/8	Mineral County	MT	Craig Thomas	1985	18
179 2/8	37 6/8	37 4/8	14 4/8	14 3/8	21 6/8	El Paso County	CO	Thomas H. States	1982	20
178 6/8	35 2/8	35 0/8	16 3/8	16 3/8	19 6/8	Mt. Livingston	ALB	Jim Smetaniuk	1982	21
178 5/8	38 4/8	37 5/8	15 4/8	15 3/8	23 0/8	Park County	MT	Mike Mahlman	1983	22
177 7/8	34 6/8	34 1/8	16 2/8	16 4/8	22 0/8	Fergus County	MT	Rob Lucas	1988	23
177 6/8	34 6/8	36 0/8	15 6/8	15 6/8	25 1/8	El Paso County	CO	John Diedrich	1990	24
176 3/8	37 3/8	39 0/8	14 6/8	14 4/8	22 0/8	Sweet Grass County	MT	Ray Alt	1968	25
176 2/8	37 2/8	38 0/8	14 4/8	14 3/8	22 1/8	Clear Creek County	CO	Dominic Florian	1989	26
176 1/8	35 3/8	37 4/8	15 4/8	15 3/8	24 4/8	El Paso County	CO	Tony Seahorn	1977	27
176 1/8	39 4/8	38 1/8	14 7/8	15 2/8	22 2/8	Phillips County	MT	Ty Milne	1991	27
176 0/8	35 2/8	36 2/8	15 2/8	15 2/8	23 5/8	El Paso County	CO	Gary Eastwood	1982	29
175 2/8	35 2/8	33 0/8	15 4/8	15 2/8	25 2/8	Lake County	OR	Stephen Herrera	1989	30
175 1/8	39 5/8	39 6/8	15 2/8	15 2/8	19 4/8	Canmore	ALB	Dave Addie	1985	31
174 0/8	35 2/8	35 4/8	16 0/8	16 2/8	21 3/8	Wind Ridge	ALB	Dirk Kieft	1984	32
173 7/8	35 1/8	37 0/8	15 1/8	15 3/8	20 7/8	Sanders County	MT	Bart Schleyer	1987	33
173 6/8	32 6/8	34 0/8	16 1/8	16 1/8	19 1/8	Canmore	ALB	Michael Ukrainetz	1983	34
173 4/8	38 0/8	38 0/8	15 0/8	15 0/8	23 5/8	Cougar Canyon	ALB	Curt Lynn	1983	35
172 6/8	35 6/8	36 4/8	14 3/8	14 3/8	22 0/8	El Paso County	CO	Duane Imhoff	1982	36
171 7/8	38 3/8	35 2/8	14 5/8	14 5/8	22 0/8	Canmore	ALB	Chuck Adams	1985	37
171 7/8	37 1/8	37 2/8	15 4/8	15 3/8	22 2/8	Canmore	ALB	Merlyn Howg	1990	37
171 6/8	34 6/8	33 4/8	15 3/8	15 2/8	21 4/8	Clear Creek County	CO	Lonny Vanatta	1988	39
170 7/8	37 2/8	37 1/8	14 6/8	14 6/8	21 1/8	Mora County	NM	Dave McInroy	1991	40
170 5/8	33 3/8	33 4/8	14 1/8	14 1/8	21 0/8	Clear Creek County	CO	Robert L. Syvertson, Jr	1989	41
170 5/8	36 1/8	37 2/8	14 3/8	14 4/8	21 5/8	Beaverhead County	MT	Jerry Allen	1991	41
170 0/8	35 6/8	36 2/8	14 2/8	14 3/8	22 2/8	Clear Creek County	CO	Troy Cunningham	1988	43
169 7/8	32 2/8	38 3/8	14 5/8	14 7/8	22 4/8	Fergus County	MT	Terry L. Selph	1990	44
169 6/8	35 2/8	34 6/8	14 4/8	14 4/8	23 0/8	Clear Creek County	CO	Janet George	1989	45
169 2/8	33 2/8	33 6/8	14 5/8	14 6/8	21 4/8	Clear Creek County	CO	Barry J. Smith	1992	46
169 0/8	33 2/8	35 2/8	14 3/8	14 2/8	20 2/8	Cougar Canyon	ALB	Paul Schwengler	1980	47
169 0/8	34 0/8	35 2/8	15 6/8	15 7/8	21 6/8	Canmore	ALB	Dave Gerber	1989	47
168 7/8	37 0/8	36 1/8	16 0/8	16 1/8	29 4/8	Chouteau County	MT	Mark L. Gilkey	1990	49
168 1/8	32 2/8	32 7/8	15 0/8	14 7/8	20 5/8	Saguache County	CO	Simon Aragi	1990	50
168 0/8	33 6/8	33 6/8	15 1/8	15 0/8	20 6/8	Custer County	CO	Jennings Cress	1977	51
167 6/8	36 3/8	36 1/8	14 6/8	14 6/8	21 1/8	N. Sask. River	ALB	Larry Jones	1962	52
167 6/8	34 4/8	35 0/8	15 4/8	15 4/8	22 2/8	Sanders County	MT	Robert L. Borden	1983	52
167 6/8	32 3/8	35 1/8	14 7/8	15 0/8	20 0/8	Canmore	ALB	Ken Madsen	1984	52
167 6/8	35 1/8	32 3/8	14 4/8	14 4/8	20 5/8	Idaho County	ID	Bill Fisk	1991	52
167 4/8	31 4/8	32 0/8	15 4/8	15 3/8	22 2/8	Clear Creek County	CO	Reggie Spiegelberg	1988	56
167 3/8	33 4/8	35 3/8	15 2/8	15 2/8	21 6/8	Canmore	ALB	Gregory Koehl	1989	57
167 1/8	34 1/8	34 4/8	14 2/8	14 5/8	22 4/8	Lincoln County	MT	Ron Bain	1974	58
167 1/8	38 5/8	32 4/8	15 4/8	15 6/8	19 0/8	Blaine County	MT	Ed Evans	1990	58
166 7/8	31 4/8	34 7/8	14 7/8	14 6/8	21 5/8	Clear Creek County	CO	Thomas J. Hoffman	1986	60
166 5/8	33 5/8	33 6/8	15 4/8	15 4/8	21 6/8	Canmore	ALB	Mike Traub	1988	61
166 2/8	32 6/8	36 2/8	14 6/8	14 6/8	20 7/8	County of Bighorn	ALB	Jeff B. Davis	1991	62
166 0/8	33 2/8	32 2/8	14 7/8	14 7/8	19 7/8	Jefferson County	CO	Robert Sorrell	1977	63
165 7/8	36 1/8	37 0/8	13 4/8	13 3/8	19 3/8	Kananaskis	ALB	Richard G. Perrett	1980	64
165 5/8	31 4/8	36 1/8	14 6/8	14 6/8	21 4/8	Clear Creek County	CO	Kurt Keskimaki	1984	65
165 3/8	33 7/8	34 4/8	13 7/8	13 6/8	19 4/8	Saguache County	CO	Tom Sieverding	1987	66
164 7/8	38 0/8	37 3/8	14 3/8	14 4/8	20 1/8	Yakima County	WA	Albert Rinaldi, Jr.	1973	67
164 5/8	32 3/8	32 6/8	15 6/8	15 6/8	21 7/8	Larimer County	CO	Dennis Campbell	1989	68
164 4/8	35 6/8	37 6/8	13 4/8	13 5/8	24 5/8	Columbia County	WA	Jack Sandvig	1981	69
163 7/8	34 3/8	32 4/8	14 7/8	14 7/8	22 6/8	Teller County	CO	Dale Struble	1987	70
163 6/8	35 3/8	35 3/8	15 2/8	15 3/8	23 1/8	Lincoln County	MT	Paul Brunner	1983	71
163 5/8	32 0/8	30 3/8	14 1/8	14 0/8	21 2/8	Clear Creek County	CO	Jim Lake	1990	72
163 4/8	31 7/8	30 5/8	14 1/8	14 0/8	19 1/8	Saguache County	CO	David Hall	1990	73
163 3/8	34 1/8	34 4/8	15 6/8	15 7/8	20 6/8	Canmore	ALB	John Visscher	1986	74
163 2/8	34 6/8	34 0/8	15 5/8	15 5/8	22 3/8	Fremont County	WY	Randy Nelson	1984	75
163 1/8	33 4/8	33 1/8	14 7/8	14 7/8	23 0/8	Chaffee County	CO	Roger Stewart	1976	76
163 0/8	36 3/8	36 3/8	13 7/8	13 7/8	22 0/8	Lake County	MT	Steve Gorr	1973	77
162 7/8	32 4/8	32 7/8	14 2/8	14 2/8	22 2/8	Clear Creek County	CO	Lyle Willmarth	1982	78
162 7/8	33 3/8	34 2/8	14 7/8	15 0/8	22 3/8	Canmore	ALB	Thomas J. Hoffman	1985	78
162 5/8	33 4/8	34 1/8	14 7/8	15 0/8	21 5/8	Canmore	ALB	Jordon Ohrn	1988	80
162 3/8	31 6/8	33 5/8	13 6/8	13 7/8	19 7/8	Greenlee County	AZ	James Bradley Miller	1990	81
162 2/8	37 6/8	34 6/8	13 7/8	14 0/8	23 0/8	Lemhi County	ID	Arne Vetrhus	1988	82
162 1/8	30 6/8	33 5/8	15 0/8	15 1/8	23 7/8	Park County	CO	Wayne Depperschmidt	1977	83
162 1/8	31 6/8	31 5/8	14 4/8	14 4/8	22 0/8	Clear Creek County	CO	Linda Strong	1990	83
162 0/8	34 1/8	33 1/8	13 4/8	13 4/8	20 1/8	Park County	WY	Tom Stoffel, Jr.	1990	85
161 7/8	36 0/8	35 3/8	14 0/8	14 0/8	20 3/8	Canmore	ALB	Chris Kempf	1986	86
161 5/8	33 6/8	32 5/8	13 0/8	13 0/8	18 0/8	Canmore	ALB	Ron Layden	1991	87
161 1/8	33 4/8	33 5/8	15 6/8	15 5/8	20 4/8	Custer County	MT	Joe Frazier	1984	88

Score	Length of R horn L		Circumference R of base L		Greatest Spread	Area	State/ Province	Hunter's Name	Date	Rank
161 0/8	36 3/8	33 7/8	13 7/8	13 7/8	24 4/8	Kittitas County	WA	Rick Kobel	1985	89
160 5/8	31 1/8	32 6/8	14 3/8	14 3/8	21 1/8	Fremont County	WY	Daniel S. Fritz	1982	90
160 5/8	35 7/8	34 6/8	14 5/8	14 2/8	21 6/8	Canmore	ALB	John D. 'Jack' Frost	1984	90
160 5/8	35 5/8	33 4/8	14 2/8	14 1/8	20 6/8	Catron County	NM	Barry Dyar	1986	90
160 2/8	30 0/8	30 0/8	14 7/8	14 6/8	17 7/8	Saguache County	CO	Jim Ryan	1988	93
160 2/8	31 6/8	32 2/8	13 6/8	14 0/8	19 0/8	Saguache County	CO	Tim Cuthriell	1991	93
160 1/8	33 0/8	33 1/8	15 2/8	15 0/8	19 7/8	Canmore	ALB	Jordon Ohrn	1991	95
159 3/8	31 4/8	34 5/8	15 0/8	15 0/8	19 1/8	Canmore	ALB	David R. Coupland	1982	96
158 5/8	30 1/8	30 0/8	15 4/8	15 3/8	21 5/8	Park County	CO	Marvin Clyncke	1977	97
158 3/8	30 2/8	27 3/8	14 4/8	14 4/8	20 4/8	Fremont County	CO	John Quick	1974	98
158 3/8	31 7/8	31 0/8	14 4/8	14 2/8	24 2/8	Lake County	CO	Wayne Lucero	1981	98
158 3/8	34 4/8	34 5/8	15 0/8	15 0/8	21 1/8	Park County	WY	Terry Constable	1988	98
158 3/8	32 3/8	32 6/8	15 5/8	15 4/8	21 4/8	Saguache County	CO	John L. Gardner	1990	98
158 0/8	32 6/8	37 0/8	14 0/8	14 1/8	19 6/8	Canmore	ALB	Jeff Gaudry	1981	102
157 5/8	32 0/8	29 5/8	14 5/8	14 4/8	21 1/8	Larimer County	CO	Glen Vlass	1991	103
157 2/8	33 0/8	31 0/8	13 3/8	13 2/8	19 0/8	Fremont County	CO	Steve Gorr	1973	104
156 7/8	32 5/8	32 4/8	13 4/8	13 4/8	19 4/8	Fergus County	MT	Jay Almas	1988	105
156 5/8	31 1/8	34 2/8	14 5/8	14 5/8	23 4/8	El Paso County	CO	Barry J. Smith	1983	106
156 1/8	32 4/8	29 7/8	13 4/8	13 4/8	22 4/8	Harney County	OR	James Schrader	1987	107
156 1/8	29 4/8	32 7/8	14 0/8	14 1/8	19 5/8	Park County	WY	Terry Sieveke	1991	107
155 6/8	33 6/8	33 2/8	13 0/8	13 0/8	17 1/8	Canmore	ALB	William O. Dudley	1985	109
155 4/8	31 0/8	34 4/8	14 2/8	14 2/8	21 0/8	Canmore	ALB	Barry Dyar	1985	110
155 2/8	30 0/8	30 6/8	14 5/8	14 5/8	21 3/8	Clear Creek County	CO	Garret Decker	1990	111
154 7/8	32 0/8	31 7/8	15 0/8	15 0/8	21 1/8	El Paso County	CO	Lee Kline	1976	112
154 4/8	31 7/8	32 7/8	13 5/8	13 6/8	19 0/8	Kittitas County	WA	Rick Vandergiessen	1984	113
154 4/8	30 6/8	31 2/8	14 6/8	14 6/8	20 5/8	Chaffee County	CO	Ray Nelson	1986	113
154 3/8	34 5/8	34 4/8	15 0/8	14 6/8	25 0/8	Sanders County	MT	John Voelker	1980	115
154 0/8	33 4/8	32 0/8	14 3/8	14 5/8	20 1/8	Jefferson County	CO	Dennis Behn	1974	116
153 2/8	28 7/8	26 7/8	14 6/8	15 0/8	20 0/8	Saguache County	CO	Steve Van Treese	1982	117
153 2/8	31 7/8	29 3/8	15 0/8	14 7/8	19 0/8	Park County	WY	William J. Gartland	1982	117
152 2/8	31 6/8	32 2/8	14 5/8	14 5/8	19 3/8	Canmore	ALB	Jay Brown	1991	119
151 1/8	31 3/8	31 4/8	15 1/8	15 2/8	21 2/8	Cougar Creek	ALB	Archie Nesbitt	1983	120
151 0/8	34 6/8	33 0/8	13 6/8	13 6/8	22 1/8	Park County	WY	Larry L. Schweitzer	1984	121
150 6/8	29 2/8	29 4/8	14 6/8	14 6/8	19 3/8	Saguache County	CO	David 'Jake' Powell	1985	122
150 6/8	30 1/8	31 1/8	13 6/8	13 7/8	21 5/8	Lemhi County	ID	Scott Woodland	1988	122
150 6/8	30 4/8	30 4/8	13 5/8	13 7/8	22 7/8	Owyhee County	ID	Stan Godfrey	1992	122
150 4/8	29 5/8	29 7/8	15 0/8	14 6/8	20 6/8	Park County	WY	James R. Dreves	1988	125
150 3/8	31 3/8	33 2/8	13 4/8	13 4/8	18 6/8	Kittitas County	WA	Duane Fink	1984	126
150 1/8	28 4/8	29 3/8	15 4/8	15 3/8	18 0/8	Clear Creek County	CO	Calvin Farner	1990	127
149 4/8	31 2/8	29 2/8	15 0/8	14 7/8	19 3/8	Canmore	ALB	Larry Vayro	1989	128
149 3/8	30 0/8	26 5/8	13 6/8	13 6/8	24 6/8	Lake County	OR	Don Rajnus	1982	129
149 3/8	32 0/8	29 7/8	15 2/8	15 2/8	18 0/8	Canmore	ALB	Warren Witherspoon	1986	129
149 2/8	30 0/8	28 6/8	15 0/8	14 7/8	20 3/8	El Paso County	CO	Mark Heiland	1989	131
148 7/8	29 1/8	31 6/8	14 4/8	14 5/8	20 5/8	Canmore	ALB	Kent Hillard	1990	132
148 2/8	30 6/8	29 6/8	14 5/8	14 5/8	21 4/8	Park County	CO	Roland D. Cameron	1979	133
147 6/8	30 0/8	29 2/8	15 5/8	15 5/8	20 1/8	El Paso County	CO	Glenn R. Kuklick	1988	134
147 4/8	27 6/8	24 2/8	15 6/8	15 7/8	20 2/8	Saguache County	CO	Charles Grumley	1988	135
147 3/8	30 3/8	31 4/8	14 2/8	14 2/8	17 7/8	Canmore	ALB	Don Ferguson	1981	136
147 2/8	30 2/8	32 0/8	14 3/8	13 7/8	20 3/8	Eagle County	CO	Joe Theaman	1989	137
147 2/8	28 7/8	34 1/8	13 3/8	13 3/8	23 4/8	Park County	WY	Jamie Byrne	1991	137
147 1/8	29 7/8	30 0/8	13 6/8	13 7/8	19 6/8	Lake County	CO	G. Fred Asbell	1979	139
147 0/8	30 6/8	30 0/8	13 3/8	13 3/8	21 3/8	El Paso County	CO	Sherman Spoelstra	1983	140
145 5/8	29 4/8	30 3/8	13 2/8	13 2/8	19 3/8	Canmore	ALB	Oran Hirsch	1979	141
145 5/8	30 1/8	29 6/8	15 2/8	15 3/8	18 4/8	Lemhi County	ID	Dale Johnson	1985	141
145 1/8	29 3/8	30 6/8	14 6/8	14 4/8	20 5/8	Trout Creek	ALB	Chad Lenz	1992	143
144 5/8	29 3/8	29 0/8	14 5/8	14 4/8	20 4/8	Clear Creek County	CO	Rob Firth	1988	144
143 5/8	28 2/8	28 1/8	13 4/8	13 4/8	20 6/8	Clear Creek County	CO	Otho Hobbs	1991	145
142 6/8	26 1/8	28 7/8	14 0/8	14 0/8	19 2/8	Teller County	CO	Steve Barnhill	1990	146
142 0/8	30 7/8	30 7/8	13 2/8	13 2/8	21 0/8	Clear Creek County	CO	Jeff Reynolds	1989	147
141 6/8	25 6/8	27 4/8	14 4/8	14 7/8	19 2/8	Chaffee County	CO	Ron Breitsprecher	1978	148
141 5/8	31 0/8	30 5/8	13 3/8	12 7/8	18 6/8	Park County	WY	Kurt H. Eisenach	1988	149
141 4/8	29 1/8	27 3/8	13 3/8	13 3/8	21 0/8	Adams County	CO	Jim Usrey	1976	150
141 2/8	30 7/8	29 1/8	12 6/8	12 5/8	18 6/8	Chaffee County	CO	Tom Tietz	1984	151
141 0/8	27 4/8	28 2/8	13 5/8	13 6/8	21 0/8	Park County	CO	Dan Tekavec	1980	152
141 0/8	28 0/8	28 0/8	14 1/8	14 1/8	19 2/8	Fremont County	WY	Jerry W. Mathewes	1983	152
140 7/8	27 6/8	33 3/8	14 1/8	14 0/8	19 6/8	Kittitas County	WA	Stan Hansen	1984	154
140 4/8	28 6/8	28 6/8	14 1/8	14 1/8	19 1/8	Valley County	ID	Michael Schlegel	1987	155
140 0/8	30 5/8	27 7/8	13 4/8	13 5/8	23 6/8	Kittitas County	WA	Martin Sapp	1990	156

World Record Dall Sheep
Score: 171 0/8
Chugach Mountains, Alaska
Hunter: Tony Russ

DALL SHEEP

Minimum score 120

Ovis dalli dalli and Ovis dalli kenaiensis

Score	Length of R Horn L		Circumference R of Base L		Greatest Spread	Area	State/ Province	Hunter's Name	Date	Rank
171 0/8	42 1/8	42 5/8	14 2/8	13 6/8	22 6/8	Chugach Mtns.	AK	Tony Russ	1988	1
166 4/8	41 1/8	40 7/8	13 3/8	13 3/8	26 2/8	East Fork	AK	Braun Kopsack	1990	2
164 5/8	40 6/8	41 3/8	13 3/8	13 5/8	28 4/8	Nahanni Butte	NWT	Gary Laya	1986	3
162 3/8	38 7/8	39 0/8	12 4/8	12 4/8	22 6/8	Delta River	AK	Dr. Russell Congdon	1960	4
162 0/8	38 6/8	37 0/8	13 4/8	13 7/8	22 3/8	Chugach Mtns.	AK	Richard Moran	1991	5
160 6/8	39 6/8	37 6/8	13 2/8	13 2/8	22 7/8	Nahanni Butte	NWT	Lonny Vanatta	1986	6
160 4/8	39 2/8	40 2/8	13 7/8	13 4/8	23 5/8	Nahanni Butte	NWT	Joseph D. Maddock	1989	7
159 2/8	40 1/8	40 5/8	12 6/8	12 5/8	26 3/8	Mackenzie Mtns.	NWT	Jerry Bowen	1990	8
158 2/8	38 0/8	38 0/8	13 4/8	13 6/8	27 2/8	Knik River	AK	Tony Russ	1989	9
157 6/8	38 3/8	39 7/8	12 2/8	12 2/8	26 6/8	Brooks Range	AK	Kurt Lepping	1988	10
157 4/8	38 6/8	38 6/8	12 7/8	12 7/8	24 2/8	Eagle River	AK	David Litchfield	1988	11
157 1/8	39 1/8	40 2/8	12 3/8	12 3/8	24 3/8	Nahanni Butte	NWT	Tom Tietz	1987	12
157 1/8	38 0/8	35 1/8	13 0/8	13 1/8	22 0/8	Chugach Mtns.	AK	Calvin W. Hall	1991	12
157 0/8	35 4/8	35 4/8	13 6/8	14 0/8	21 2/8	Chitina Glacier	AK	Roger Morris	1973	14
155 5/8	36 3/8	35 0/8	12 6/8	12 6/8	19 5/8	Mackenzie Mtns.	NWT	Bob Renner	1983	15
155 1/8	37 1/8	37 2/8	13 4/8	13 4/8	25 7/8	Rams Head Mountain	NWT	Ron Breitsprecher	1981	16
155 1/8	36 6/8	35 7/8	13 2/8	13 2/8	19 5/8	Liard Range	NWT	John E. Haefeli	1988	16
155 1/8	39 2/8	37 7/8	12 6/8	12 6/8	25 5/8	East Fork	AK	Braun Kopsack	1989	16
155 1/8	40 4/8	37 3/8	12 5/8	12 5/8	25 5/8	Alaska Range	AK	Ed Hull	1990	16
154 7/8	35 2/8	34 7/8	14 1/8	14 1/8	21 4/8	Mackenzie Mtns.	NWT	Mike Barrett	1983	20
154 7/8	37 3/8	36 6/8	12 6/8	12 6/8	22 3/8	Kenai Mtns.	AK	Lon E. Lauber	1992	20
154 6/8	35 6/8	37 2/8	13 0/8	13 2/8	20 6/8	Chugach Mtns.	AK	Rick Tollison	1979	22
154 6/8	33 2/8	38 2/8	13 4/8	13 4/8	25 3/8	Brooks Range	AK	Kurt Lepping	1987	22
153 5/8	35 1/8	36 6/8	13 3/8	13 3/8	21 6/8	Nahanni Butte	NWT	E. Damon Handley	1989	24
153 3/8	37 5/8	37 4/8	13 1/8	13 1/8	26 4/8	Divide Lake	NWT	Stanley Walchuk, Jr.	1984	25
153 3/8	36 5/8	36 4/8	13 3/8	13 3/8	23 5/8	Chugach Mtns.	AK	Nathan Callis	1986	25
153 2/8	37 6/8	33 0/8	13 2/8	13 2/8	20 4/8	Rams Head Mountain	NWT	Dennis Schweitzer	1981	27
153 2/8	36 6/8	37 0/8	13 0/8	13 0/8	24 5/8	Keele River	NWT	Ron Serwa	1988	27
152 6/8	37 1/8	36 5/8	13 1/8	13 1/8	30 0/8	Wrangell Mtns.	AK	Ray Torrey	1973	29
152 5/8	38 6/8	39 3/8	12 3/8	12 4/8	31 2/8	Keele River	NWT	Thomas J. Hoffman	1986	30
152 4/8	33 0/8	34 0/8	12 6/8	12 6/8	18 5/8	Mackenzie Mtns.	NWT	Al Reay	1982	31
152 2/8	37 0/8	36 2/8	12 5/8	12 5/8	23 4/8	Kuskokwim Mtn.	AK	Kenneth R. Wallenberg	1978	32
152 0/8	37 0/8	37 0/8	12 4/8	12 4/8	27 4/8	Wrangell Mtns.	AK	Dr. Rex Hancock	1962	33
152 0/8	31 3/8	34 3/8	12 4/8	12 7/8	20 6/8	Brooks Range	AK	Calvin Farner	1988	33
151 6/8	35 7/8	35 1/8	13 5/8	13 5/8	28 0/8	Chugach Mtns.	AK	John D. 'Jack' Frost	1984	35
151 6/8	40 1/8	35 7/8	12 3/8	12 4/8	23 1/8	Matanuska River	AK	Tony Russ	1990	35
151 2/8	36 6/8	36 6/8	12 6/8	12 6/8	26 4/8	Johnson River	AK	Larry Jones	1963	37
151 2/8	36 4/8	36 4/8	13 7/8	13 6/8	23 4/8	Tonsona Creek	AK	Bruce Stephens	1974	37
151 2/8	35 5/8	36 1/8	13 2/8	13 0/8	25 0/8	Rainy Pass	AK	Roger Stewart	1978	37
151 0/8	35 4/8	34 4/8	13 3/8	13 5/8	27 3/8	Mackenzie Mtns.	NWT	Mike Barrett	1986	40
150 3/8	36 1/8	36 2/8	12 4/8	12 5/8	24 2/8	Mountain River	NWT	George Flournoy	1985	41
150 2/8	37 5/8	33 3/8	12 4/8	12 2/8	19 7/8	Brooks Range	AK	James A. Baker	1971	42
150 1/8	37 4/8	37 1/8	12 3/8	12 3/8	18 6/8	Mackenzie Mtns.	NWT	Robert L. Kampen	1988	43
149 6/8	40 0/8	34 2/8	12 3/8	12 3/8	22 4/8	Keele River	NWT	Jim Ryan	1990	44
149 3/8	37 1/8	34 4/8	13 2/8	13 2/8	25 7/8	Wrangell Mtns.	AK	J. Barry Dyar	1984	45
149 1/8	34 1/8	34 4/8	13 4/8	13 5/8	21 3/8	Eklutna Lake	AK	Steven J. Latz	1988	46
149 0/8	34 7/8	35 3/8	13 3/8	13 3/8	23 3/8	Keele River	NWT	Thomas J. Hoffman	1985	47
149 0/8	37 4/8	37 0/8	12 0/8	11 6/8	22 1/8	Nahanni Butte	NWT	Robert Pyne	1989	47
148 6/8	37 6/8	38 0/8	12 2/8	12 2/8	22 5/8	Nahanni Butte	NWT	Bill Grammer	1986	49
148 6/8	35 1/8	38 5/8	12 1/8	12 1/8	22 0/8	Nahanni Butte	NWT	Gary M. Martin	1992	49
148 4/8	35 7/8	35 3/8	13 2/8	13 2/8	26 6/8	Brooks Range	AK	Randy Butler	1979	51
148 4/8	31 4/8	35 4/8	13 6/8	13 6/8	25 0/8	Mackenzie Mtns.	NWT	Dyrk Eddie	1986	51
148 3/8	33 4/8	35 1/8	13 3/8	13 3/8	24 2/8	Atigun Pass	AK	Maxallen D. Jackson	1984	53
148 0/8	38 3/8	35 5/8	12 6/8	12 7/8	28 1/8	Delta	AK	Mike Hedrick	1988	54
147 6/8	35 1/8	35 1/8	12 4/8	12 6/8	19 7/8	Tlogotsho Range	NWT	Archie Nesbitt	1986	55
147 6/8	35 0/8	35 0/8	13 2/8	13 3/8	24 0/8	Chugach Mtns.	AK	Richard Moran/Lon Lauber	1989	55
147 5/8	35 0/8	35 3/8	12 6/8	12 7/8	22 5/8	Dadina Glacier	AK	Roger O. Wyant	1990	57
147 4/8	34 6/8	35 4/8	12 0/8	12 0/8	21 5/8	Mackenzie Mtns.	NWT	Paul Brunner	1982	58
147 3/8	34 4/8	35 1/8	13 0/8	13 0/8	20 0/8	DeLong Mtns.	AK	Carl E. Brent	1991	59
147 2/8	35 2/8	35 4/8	12 5/8	12 5/8	25 2/8	Mackenzie Mtns.	NWT	Janice J. Traub	1987	60
147 2/8	35 5/8	35 1/8	12 2/8	12 2/8	22 6/8	Eklutna Lake	AK	John McCullough	1988	60
147 1/8	35 5/8	32 2/8	12 0/8	12 0/8	20 3/8	Chugach Mtns.	AK	Lon E. Lauber	1990	62
147 0/8	36 0/8	36 2/8	12 4/8	12 4/8	25 1/8	Nahanni Butte	NWT	Jim Arnold	1988	63
147 0/8	34 7/8	35 1/8	13 0/8	12 7/8	21 7/8	Chugach Mtns.	AK	Tony Russ	1992	63
146 6/8	35 0/8	34 4/8	12 2/8	12 3/8	23 5/8	Liard Range	NWT	Dennis Dunn	1984	65
146 5/8	36 3/8	35 0/8	11 6/8	11 5/8	21 0/8	Liard Range	NWT	Ron Rockwell	1983	66
146 4/8	33 4/8	34 2/8	12 0/8	12 2/8	25 7/8	Delta River	AK	Elisha Gray	1958	67
146 2/8	33 4/8	32 6/8	11 5/8	11 4/8	17 6/8	Nahanni Butte	NWT	Barry J. Smith	1989	68
145 6/8	29 0/8	36 6/8	12 5/8	12 6/8	24 1/8	Brooks Range	AK	Maxallen D. Jackson	1989	69
145 4/8	33 1/8	37 7/8	11 6/8	11 6/8	21 2/8	Brooks Range	AK	John D. 'Jack' Frost	1982	70

Score	Length of R horn L		Circumference R of base L		Greatest Spread	Area	State/ Province	Hunter's Name	Date	Rank
145 2/8	35 1/8	35 5/8	12 3/8	12 4/8	25 5/8	Talkeetna Mtns.	AK	Jay Deones	1980	71
145 1/8	32 2/8	33 1/8	13 4/8	13 7/8	23 5/8	Wood River	AK	Art Young	1923	72
145 1/8	34 5/8	35 0/8	13 2/8	13 2/8	25 5/8	DoDo Mtn.	NWT	Tom D. Slusser	1990	72
145 0/8	33 5/8	33 5/8	13 0/8	13 0/8	25 5/8	Mt. Ibex	YUK	Martin Hanson	1957	74
144 5/8	34 5/8	35 2/8	13 0/8	13 0/8	23 1/8	Mt. Hayes	AK	Keith R. Clemmons	1962	75
144 2/8	33 1/8	33 3/8	12 5/8	12 4/8	21 6/8	Liard Range	NWT	Richard W. Sage	1986	76
144 1/8	33 3/8	36 4/8	12 3/8	13 0/8	25 4/8	Delta Management	AK	John W. Williams	1978	77
143 6/8	35 0/8	35 2/8	13 0/8	12 7/8	25 0/8	Chistochina River	AK	Capt. Leonard Mackler	1977	78
143 4/8	35 0/8	34 2/8	12 5/8	12 6/8	22 4/8	Nahanni Butte	NWT	Dirk Lawyer	1985	79
143 3/8	35 0/8	34 5/8	12 0/8	12 2/8	19 4/8	Endicott Mountains	AK	Dwane J. Sykes	1968	80
143 2/8	31 0/8	35 2/8	12 4/8	12 4/8	23 6/8	Mackenzie Mtns.	NWT	Paul Schafer	1983	81
143 1/8	32 0/8	32 5/8	13 3/8	13 3/8	21 4/8	Chugach Mtns.	AK	Glenn R. L. Schmidt	1977	82
143 0/8	36 0/8	34 6/8	11 4/8	11 4/8	21 2/8	Nahanni Butte	NWT	Lee Veldhouse	1983	83
142 2/8	33 4/8	36 2/8	11 5/8	11 5/8	24 3/8	Post River	AK	Rick Tollison	1978	84
142 2/8	33 1/8	33 1/8	12 4/8	12 5/8	27 4/8	Brooks Range	AK	Larry E. Townsend	1991	84
142 0/8	28 1/8	33 5/8	12 1/8	12 0/8	22 1/8	Atigun Pass	AK	Maxallen D. Jackson	1980	86
141 6/8	32 0/8	32 4/8	12 0/8	12 1/8	20 2/8	Mackenzie Mtns.	NWT	Reggie Spiegelberg	1982	87
141 5/8	31 7/8	32 0/8	13 0/8	13 0/8	26 2/8	MacKenzie Mtns.	NWT	Chuck Adams	1985	88
141 0/8	35 6/8	36 6/8	11 5/8	11 5/8	22 0/8	Ptarmigan Pass	AK	Ralph Ertz	1977	89
141 0/8	31 4/8	31 6/8	13 6/8	13 6/8	20 2/8	Eklutna Lake	AK	Craig Scarbrough	1989	89
140 7/8	33 3/8	34 2/8	13 0/8	13 0/8	23 3/8	Wrangel Mtns.	AK	Mike Renfro	1987	91
140 5/8	32 4/8	31 5/8	12 4/8	12 4/8	23 7/8	Liard River	NWT	Greg Munther	1984	92
140 1/8	34 3/8	34 4/8	11 7/8	11 7/8	20 4/8	Nahanni Butte	NWT	Fred C. Church	1990	93
139 6/8	33 1/8	33 3/8	12 5/8	12 5/8	17 7/8	Chugach Mtns.	AK	John Sarvis	1988	94
139 6/8	33 7/8	33 5/8	12 5/8	12 6/8	25 3/8	Wrangel Mtns.	AK	Bret T. Walker	1991	94
139 4/8	33 0/8	33 2/8	12 3/8	12 3/8	21 7/8	Chugach Mtns.	AK	Tom S. Lenort	1990	96
139 1/8	34 2/8	34 7/8	12 3/8	12 3/8	27 7/8	Tok	AK	Gardner Rowell	1991	97
139 0/8	37 2/8	32 6/8	11 7/8	12 0/8	26 4/8	Talkeetna Mtns.	AK	Rusty Hayes	1975	98
138 6/8	31 4/8	32 4/8	11 4/8	11 4/8	21 3/8	Brooks Range	AK	DeWayne J. Benton	1987	99
138 4/8	32 6/8	34 0/8	12 6/8	12 5/8	22 6/8	Chitina	AK	Robert Ewers	1972	100
138 0/8	29 3/8	35 5/8	12 4/8	12 4/8	26 7/8	Hula Hula River	AK	Paul Persano	1985	101
137 4/8	31 2/8	31 2/8	13 2/8	13 3/8	18 5/8	Mackenzie Mtns.	NWT	William R. VyVyan	1990	102
137 2/8	34 2/8	32 0/8	11 2/8	11 1/8	21 1/8	Liard Range	NWT	Tom Taylor	1992	103
136 5/8	30 0/8	31 1/8	12 1/8	12 1/8	23 2/8	Brooks Range	AK	Jim Ryan	1986	104
136 0/8	32 2/8	32 2/8	12 1/8	12 1/8	23 7/8	Brooks Range	AK	Ken Vorisek	1990	105
135 1/8	34 0/8	33 5/8	11 4/8	11 4/8	23 0/8	Alaska Range	AK	Richard Moran	1988	106
135 0/8	31 2/8	31 2/8	12 0/8	11 7/8	23 6/8	Liard Range	NWT	Mark Checki	1988	107
134 6/8	33 4/8	33 2/8	11 3/8	11 3/8	21 7/8	Nahanni Butte	NWT	Linda Strong	1987	108
134 5/8	32 1/8	33 0/8	11 1/8	11 2/8	20 6/8	Nahanni Butte	NWT	Jerry Leair	1990	109
133 2/8	32 0/8	31 6/8	11 7/8	11 6/8	21 2/8	Nabesna River	AK	George A. Moerlein	1983	110
133 2/8	30 0/8	31 0/8	11 2/8	11 3/8	24 2/8	Mackenzie Mtns.	NWT	Dean Stebner	1989	110
133 0/8	30 6/8	30 4/8	12 4/8	12 5/8	27 1/8	Wrangell Mtns.	AK	George A. Moerlein	1971	112
132 7/8	32 0/8	32 1/8	11 6/8	11 6/8	21 0/8	Mackenzie Mts.	NWT	Stan Godfrey	1988	113
132 6/8	30 2/8	30 4/8	12 5/8	12 5/8	18 2/8	Brooks Range	AK	Robert Warpack	1986	114
131 6/8	31 5/8	31 1/8	12 5/8	12 5/8	17 6/8	Wrangell Mtns.	AK	John Sarvis	1985	115
131 4/8	30 7/8	31 7/8	11 3/8	11 1/8	21 4/8	Nahanni Butte	NWT	Ralph L. Albright	1990	116
130 7/8	32 6/8	28 5/8	12 4/8	12 4/8	20 6/8	Talkeetna Mtns.	AK	John L. Wozniak	1984	117
130 0/8	30 2/8	30 6/8	11 4/8	11 4/8	20 6/8	Liard Range	NWT	John Borlang	1986	118
128 0/8	31 2/8	31 4/8	11 2/8	11 3/8	24 0/8	Wrangell	AK	Gilbert M. W. Smith	1977	119
127 0/8	29 7/8	29 3/8	11 2/8	11 1/8	21 2/8	Sheep Creek	AK	Ray Uhl, Jr.	1968	120
125 7/8	31 6/8	31 3/8	10 4/8	10 4/8	21 1/8	Alaska Range	AK	Larry Jones	1969	121
125 0/8	29 1/8	29 1/8	11 2/8	11 2/8	17 4/8	Liard Range	NWT	Todd Henck	1988	122
123 3/8	30 1/8	30 0/8	11 0/8	11 0/8	24 2/8	Kongakut River	AK	Stan Parkerson	1984	123
121 6/8	30 4/8	30 4/8	10 2/8	10 2/8	22 6/8	Alaska Range	AK	Lon E. Lauber	1988	124
121 1/8	27 3/8	28 2/8	10 7/8	10 6/8	21 4/8	Brooks Range	AK	Thomas Chadwick	1984	125
120 5/8	29 1/8	29 4/8	11 4/8	11 5/8	21 0/8	Attigun Pass	AK	Steve Herrera	1991	126

World Record Desert Sheep

Score: 176 7/8
Pima County, Arizona - 1990
Hunter: Mark D. Morris

DESERT SHEEP

MINIMUM SCORE 140

Ovis canadensis nelsoni and certain related subspecies

Score	Length of R Horn L		Circumference R of Base L		Greatest Spread	Area	State/ Province	Hunter's Name	Date	Rank
176 7/8	36 3/8	35 2/8	15 2/8	15 1/8	19 6/8	Pima County	AZ	Mark D. Morris	1990	1
175 0/8	35 5/8	36 5/8	14 7/8	14 7/8	22 5/8	Graham County	AZ	Jim Ryan	1989	2
167 1/8	34 5/8	34 2/8	14 7/8	14 7/8	23 5/8	Maricopa County	AZ	Peter C. Knagge	1985	3
166 6/8	28 6/8	34 4/8	14 5/8	14 5/8	21 7/8	San Bernardino County	CA	Jim Ryan	1988	4
166 2/8	36 1/8	36 5/8	14 2/8	14 2/8	22 2/8	Graham County	AZ	Max T. Hinton	1987	5
164 2/8	32 4/8	31 6/8	15 3/8	15 3/8	21 1/8	Maricopa County	AZ	Chuck Meacham	1984	6
163 4/8	33 5/8	33 1/8	14 7/8	14 5/8	23 3/8	Mohave County	AZ	Gary Steinmann	1986	7
163 1/8	34 6/8	35 5/8	15 4/8	15 4/8	22 3/8	Clark County	NV	Fred Church	1984	8
162 1/8	34 2/8	33 3/8	14 3/8	14 2/8	20 2/8	Mohave County	AZ	Darell Lee Christensen	1987	9
157 5/8	32 3/8	33 4/8	13 1/8	13 2/8	21 7/8	Yuma County	AZ	Barry Sopher	1985	10
157 3/8	30 4/8	31 5/8	14 2/8	14 2/8	22 3/8	Lincoln County	NV	James R. Puryear	1984	11
156 3/8	32 7/8	31 4/8	14 3/8	14 6/8	26 2/8	Nye County	NV	Jerry Vega	1987	12
155 7/8	30 5/8	30 2/8	14 4/8	14 4/8	25 7/8	Nye County	NV	David Powning	1984	13
155 5/8	31 6/8	33 7/8	15 1/8	15 2/8	20 0/8	Sonora	MEX	Thomas J. Hoffman	1985	14
154 1/8	30 5/8	31 2/8	14 0/8	14 1/8	22 7/8	Nye County	NV	Richard J. Panelli	1985	15
154 0/8	31 6/8	30 0/8	13 5/8	13 7/8	22 7/8	Mohave County	AZ	Ward Villamor	1989	16
153 7/8	31 2/8	31 3/8	15 2/8	15 4/8	19 6/8	Maricopa County	AZ	Brad L. Siefarth	1979	17
153 6/8	34 0/8	31 6/8	13 5/8	12 5/8	19 2/8	Yuma County	AZ	Jeffery Stevens	1990	18
152 1/8	30 0/8	30 3/8	14 7/8	14 5/8	19 1/8	Mohave County	AZ	Pete Shepley	1986	19
151 3/8	32 3/8	34 6/8	12 6/8	12 1/8	21 2/8	Clark County	NV	Gilbert Hernandez	1985	20
148 7/8	31 4/8	30 5/8	14 4/8	14 3/8	27 2/8	Mohave County	AZ	Randy Ulmer	1991	21
146 0/8	28 6/8	28 6/8	13 0/8	13 3/8	19 4/8	Yuma County	AZ	Mark F. Vancas	1990	22
145 1/8	28 6/8	28 3/8	13 7/8	13 7/8	20 4/8	Lincoln County	NV	San Stiver	1980	23
142 6/8	26 1/8	26 5/8	12 5/8	12 5/8	21 5/8	Lincoln County	NV	Kurt W. Keskimaki	1991	24
141 2/8	27 0/8	29 2/8	13 2/8	13 2/8	19 0/8	Mohave County	AZ	Chuck Adams	1986	25

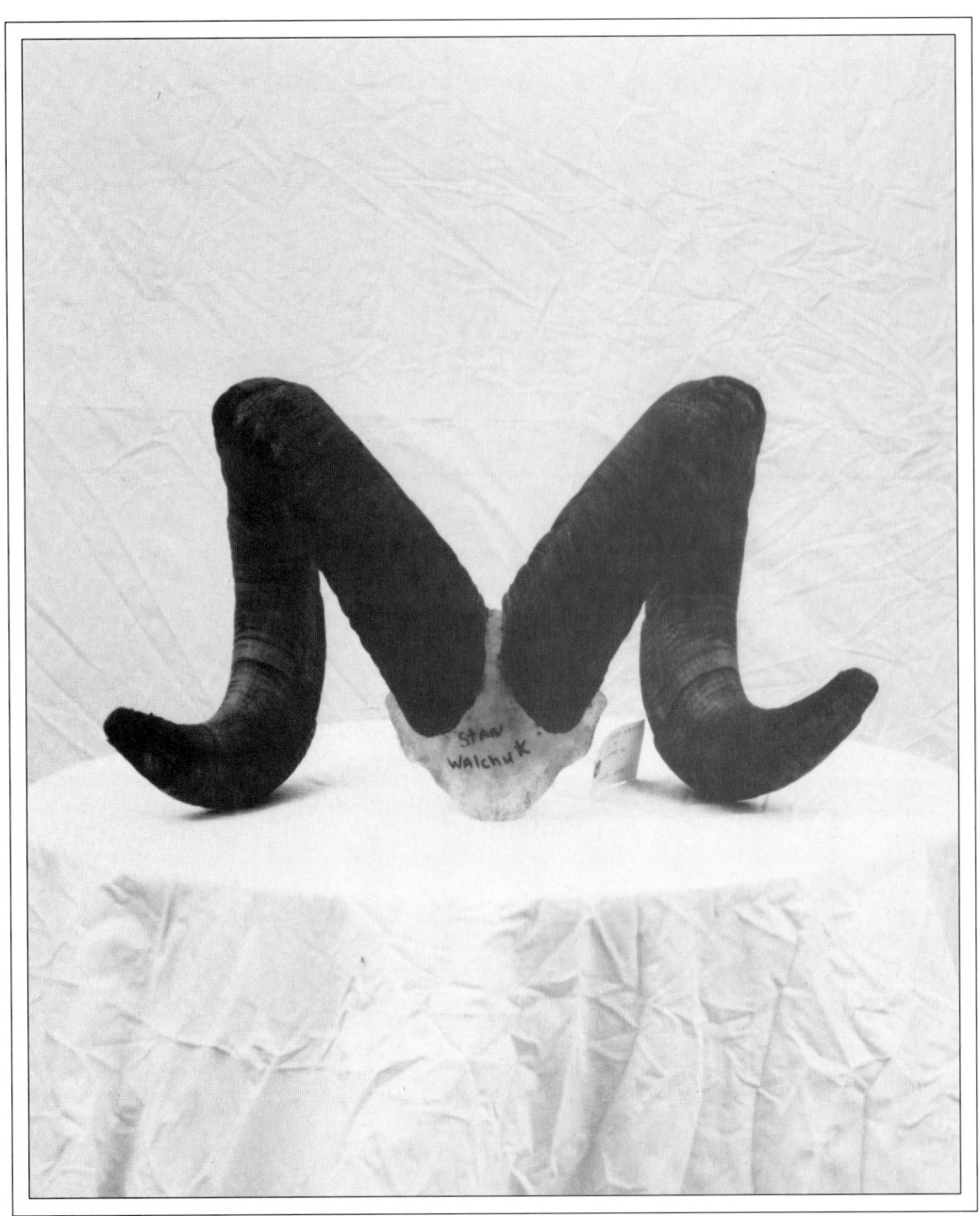

World Record Stone Sheep
Score: 174 2/8
Testa River, British Columbia - 1992
Hunter: Stanley Walchuk, Jr.

STONE SHEEP

Ovis dalli stonei

SCORE	LENGTH OF HORN R	LENGTH OF HORN L	CIRCUMFERENCE OF BASE R	CIRCUMFERENCE OF BASE L	GREATEST SPREAD	AREA	STATE/ PROVINCE	HUNTER'S NAME	DATE	RANK
174 2/8	41 1/8	42 1/8	12 4/8	12 4/8	22 0/8	Tetsa River	BC	Stanley Walchuk, Jr.	1992	1
165 3/8	39 5/8	41 6/8	13 0/8	13 1/8	23 4/8	MacMillan River	YUK	Lonny Vanatta	1989	2
163 1/8	39 2/8	35 5/8	14 0/8	14 0/8	22 4/8	Racing River	BC	Archie Nesbitt	1989	3
162 5/8	34 5/8	35 2/8	14 2/8	14 4/8	21 2/8	Muskwa River	BC	Thomas J. Hoffman	1987	4
160 1/8	38 7/8	38 2/8	13 0/8	13 0/8	26 2/8	Todagin Mtn.	BC	Bob Renner	1987	5
160 0/8	39 2/8	38 6/8	13 0/8	13 0/8	26 1/8	Todagin Mtn.	BC	Ken Scheer	1990	6
158 4/8	36 0/8	39 2/8	12 5/8	12 6/8	22 0/8	Ram Mtn.	BC	Mike Traub	1991	7
158 2/8	37 6/8	38 0/8	13 4/8	13 4/8	23 6/8	Todagin Mtn.	BC	Randy De Biasio	1992	8
158 1/8	40 4/8	38 3/8	12 4/8	13 1/8	27 0/8	Cold Fish Lake	BC	Fred Bear	1957	9
157 6/8	35 2/8	38 6/8	12 5/8	12 5/8	23 1/8	Todagin Lake	BC	Mickey McDonald	1991	10
157 4/8	37 5/8	37 3/8	13 3/8	13 3/8	25 0/8	Todagin Mtn.	BC	Bruce Ambler	1991	11
157 1/8	36 2/8	35 5/8	13 4/8	13 4/8	21 0/8	Trygue Lake	BC	Walt Krom	1979	12
156 7/8	37 2/8	37 7/8	13 4/8	13 5/8	25 6/8	Todagin Mtn.	BC	Len Cardinale	1990	13
156 1/8	37 1/8	39 0/8	13 0/8	13 2/8	24 0/8	Mount Armstrong	YUK	J. Bradley Thurston	1987	14
156 0/8	38 3/8	37 5/8	13 0/8	12 7/8	27 4/8	Todagin Mtn.	BC	Lee Veldhouse	1984	15
155 2/8	38 1/8	37 1/8	13 1/8	13 2/8	26 6/8	Todagin Mtn.	BC	Reggie Spiegelberg	1984	16
155 1/8	36 6/8	36 3/8	13 2/8	13 2/8	21 6/8	Telegraph Creek	BC	Jamie Byrne	1990	17
154 3/8	35 6/8	36 3/8	13 2/8	13 3/8	25 3/8	Todagin Creek Mtn.	BC	Roy Lynch	1983	18
154 2/8	38 0/8	34 4/8	12 7/8	12 7/8	21 3/8	Todagin Mtn.	BC	Stanley R. Godfrey	1991	19
154 1/8	38 0/8	39 2/8	14 0/8	14 0/8	24 1/8	Kechika River	BC	Paul Brunner	1974	20
154 1/8	35 7/8	34 6/8	13 3/8	13 3/8	23 5/8	Cassiar Mtns.	BC	Calvin Farner	1986	20
154 1/8	36 7/8	36 4/8	13 0/8	13 0/8	23 6/8	Todagin Mtn.	BC	Dennis Palmer	1991	20
153 1/8	36 1/8	34 2/8	13 6/8	13 6/8	20 6/8	Kechika River	BC	John D. 'Jack' Frost	1985	23
152 3/8	30 6/8	33 4/8	13 4/8	13 4/8	24 2/8	Tucho Lake	BC	Chuck Adams	1985	24
151 4/8	33 2/8	33 0/8	13 2/8	13 2/8	20 3/8	Racing River	BC	Pete Shepley	1985	25
151 4/8	38 5/8	37 7/8	12 3/8	12 3/8	22 7/8	Mac Millan River	YUK	Bob Fromme	1991	25
151 2/8	35 7/8	34 7/8	13 3/8	13 3/8	24 1/8	Todagin Mtn.	BC	Craig Kohorst	1991	27
150 7/8	35 4/8	36 1/8	13 2/8	13 2/8	22 7/8	Todagin Creek	BC	Rick Paquette	1990	28
150 3/8	36 1/8	33 2/8	13 3/8	13 1/8	19 6/8	Toad River	BC	Jim Ryan	1987	29
150 3/8	28 0/8	36 5/8	13 4/8	13 3/8	23 6/8	Todagin Mtn.	BC	Bill Nickerson	1987	29
149 1/8	35 4/8	35 3/8	13 2/8	13 1/8	21 6/8	Terminus Mtn.	BC	Paul P. Schafer	1975	31
148 3/8	34 0/8	35 7/8	13 0/8	13 1/8	28 0/8	Todagin Mtn.	BC	Al Klopfenstein	1977	32
148 1/8	36 3/8	33 6/8	12 4/8	14 0/8	21 5/8	Tetachi Lake	BC	Robert Pyne	1987	33
147 7/8	35 7/8	30 0/8	13 3/8	13 3/8	28 0/8	Tatogga Lake	BC	Eric Hoglund	1979	34
146 4/8	35 5/8	35 3/8	13 0/8	13 3/8	27 1/8	Atlin	BC	Tom Tietz	1985	35
145 7/8	34 4/8	34 7/8	13 0/8	13 0/8	22 1/8	Todagin Mtn.	BC	Lee Kline	1983	36
145 6/8	33 1/8	33 7/8	12 5/8	12 5/8	21 4/8	Todagin Lake	BC	Thomas J. Hoffman	1985	37
145 6/8	33 7/8	33 5/8	12 6/8	12 6/8	18 6/8	Todagin Mtn.	BC	Alan Bressanutti	1992	37
143 5/8	33 0/8	34 5/8	12 3/8	12 4/8	19 0/8	Christian Falls	BC	Jim Ryan	1990	39
142 2/8	33 6/8	34 2/8	12 2/8	12 1/8	22 1/8	Todagin Mtn.	BC	David Hooper	1977	40
140 5/8	35 0/8	34 7/8	12 1/8	12 0/8	23 3/8	Turnagin River	BC	Maxallen D. Jackson	1984	41
140 4/8	32 5/8	32 7/8	12 5/8	12 7/8	21 4/8	Todagin Creek Mtn.	BC	Dennis McCarthy	1983	42
126 4/8	27 3/8	31 1/8	11 6/8	11 6/8	19 2/8	Todagin Mtn.	BC	Don St. Jean	1987	43

APPENDIX

BOWHUNTING

BIG GAME

RECORDS

BOWHUNTER'S BIG GAME RECORDS

POPE AND YOUNG CLUB

Under the heading of North American Big Game are included the following with the minimum point score requirements (Boone & Crockett scoring system) as revised January, 1993.

To be eligible for entry into the Pope and Young Records and awards, the trophy must equal or exceed the score listed on the Minimum List and must have been taken by the individual or persons who are entering it, entirely by means of the Bow and Arrow under the Club's Rules of Fair Chase. A Trophy Award Citation will be issued to each qualifying entry.

Cougar taken in any area where a bounty provision of any type is allowed are not eligible for entry in Pope and Young Club Records, or for Record Class Citations.

Southern Boundary of North America to be defined as the Southern Boundary of Mexico.

MINIMUM POINT SCORE REQUIREMENTS

Alaska Brown Bear	20	* Mule Deer, Non-Typical	160 (16)
Black Bear	18	Whitetail Deer, Typical	125
Grizzly Bear	19	Whitetail Deer, Non-Typical	150 (15)
Polar Bear	20	Roosevelt's (Olympic) Elk	225
Bison	100	Yellowstone (Wapiti) Elk	260
* Barren Ground Caribou	325	Yellowstone Elk, Non-Typical	300 (20)
* Mountain Caribou	300	Rocky Mountain Goat	40
* Quebec-Labrador Caribou	325	Alaska-Yukon Moose	170
* Woodland Caribou	220	Canada Moose	135
Cougar	13 8/16	Wyoming Moose	115
Columbian Blacktail Deer	90	Muskox	90
Columbian Blacktail Deer Non-Typical	110 (9)	Pronghorn	64
Sitka Blacktail Deer	75	Bighorn Sheep	140
Coues' Deer, Typical	65	Dall's (White) Sheep	120
Coues' Deer, Non-typical	75 (7)	Desert Bighorn Sheep	140
* Mule Deer, Typical	145	Stone's Sheep	120

* Velvet entries are accepted in these categories, the above minimums apply.

Revised January, 1993

HOW TO ENTER A TROPHY

FOR AN ANIMAL to qualify for entry into the Pope and Young Club's records, it must equal or exceed established minimum score requirements and must have been legally taken by a bowhunter under the rules detailed on the Fair Chase Affidavit.

Successful hunters need not be members of the Pope and Young Club to enter their trophies. The Club's records are open to any bowhunter taking an eligible big game animal.

Each trophy must be scored by an official measurer of either the Pope and Young or Boone and Crockett Club. Before any trophy can be officially measured, 60 days must have passed since the date of kill. During this "drying period," the trophy should be stored at room temperature without any modifications and without the attachment of any items designed to prevent normal drying. All successful hunters must complete and submit a scoring form and a signed Fair Chase Affidavit.

Each record-class entry must be accompanied by a minimum of three photos showing the left side, right side and frontal view. If possible, a site-of-kill photo showing the entire animal is to be provided. Color or black and white prints, including clear Polaroid shots, are acceptable; however, color transparencies may not be submitted.

At present an entry fee of $25.00 (U.S. funds) is required for each trophy being submitted for record book entry. Personal checks or money orders, payable to the Pope and Young Club, are acceptable. Volunteer measurers do not receive a fee for scoring the trophy.

To obtain the name, address and telephone number of the nearest official measurer, bowhunters may write or call:

Pope and Young Club
P. O Box 548
Chatfield, MN 55923
(507) 867-4144

POPE & YOUNG CLUB
NORTH AMERICAN BIG GAME TROPHY SCORING FORM
BOWHUNTING
BIG GAME ————————— RECORDS

BEAR

KIND OF BEAR _____

SEX _____

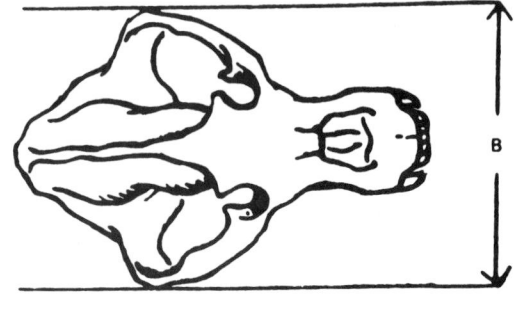

SEE OTHER SIDE FOR INSTRUCTIONS		Measurements
A. Greatest Length Without Lower Jaw (Measured in Sixteenths)		
B. Greatest Width (Measured in Sixteenths)		
TOTAL AND FINAL SCORE		

Exact locality where killed		(County)	(State)
Date killed	By whom killed		
Present owner		Phone ( )	
Address			
Guide's Name and Address			

REMARKS (Mention any abnormalities)

Were dogs used in conjunction with the pursuit and harvest of this animal? YES _____ NO _____

If yes, the following statements apply:
1. I was present on the hunt at the time the dogs were released to pursue this animal.
2. If electric collars were attached to any of the dogs, <u>at no time</u> from the beginning of the chase until the harvest of this animal were receivers used in the pursuit and harvest.

If you answered yes and if conditions #1 or #2 do not apply, please explain on separate sheet.

_____ _____
(HUNTERS SIGNATURE) (DATE)

• •

I certify that I have measured the above trophy on_____19_____
at (address)_____ City _____
State_____ Zip Code_____ and that these measurements and data are, to the best
of my knowledge and belief, made in accordance with the instructions given.
Witness:_____ Signature_____
(To Measurer's Signature)   Pope & Young Club Official Measurer

_____

MEASURER (Print)

_____

ADDRESS

_____
CITY   STATE   ZIP

INSTRUCTIONS

All measurements must be made with a flexible steel tape to the nearest one-sixteenth of an inch.

Official measurements cannot be taken for at least sixty days after the animal was killed. Photographs of right side, left side, and front of skull are required.

A. Greatest Length is measured between perpendiculars to the long axis of the skull WITHOUT the lower jaw and EXCLUDING malformations. (Normal teeth are included)

B. Greatest Width is measured between perpendiculars at right angles to the long axis.

All adhering flesh, membrane and cartilage must be completely removed before official measurements are taken.

Photographs: All entries **must** include photographs of the trophy. A right side, left side and front view photograph is required for all skulls. A photograph of the entire animal, preferably at the site of kill, is requested if at all possible. The front view is best taken from above at a 45° angle.

Drying Period: To be eligible for entry in the Pope & Young Records, a trophy must first have been stored under normal room temperature and humidity for at least 60 days after date of kill. No trophy will be considered which has in any way been altered from its natural state.

All flesh and membrane **must** be completely removed from skull prior to measuring.

> **IF DOGS ARE USED, THE HUNTER MUST BE PRESENT AT THE TIME THE DOGS ARE RELEASED**

THIS SCORING FORM MUST BE ACCOMPANIED BY A SIGNED POPE & YOUNG FAIR CHASE AFFIDAVIT, 3 PHOTOS OF SKULL, AND A RECORDING FEE OF $25.00.

BOWHUNTING

BIG GAME   RECORDS

BISON

SEX

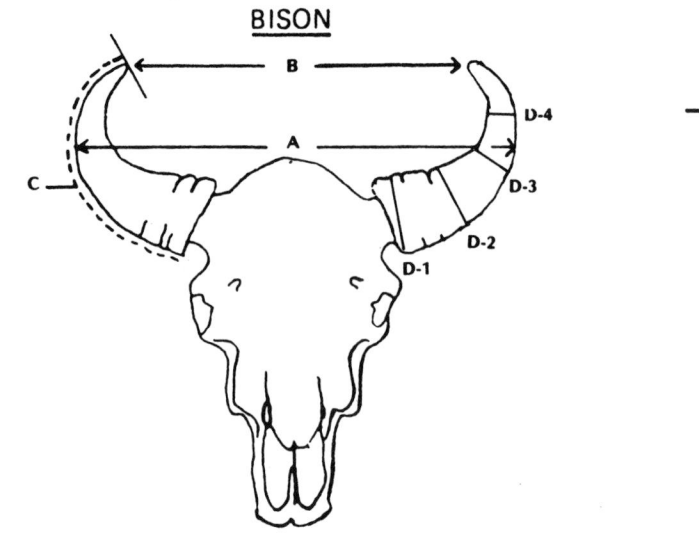

SEE OTHER SIDE FOR INSTRUCTIONS		Supplementary Data	Column 1	Column 2	Column 3
			Right Horn	Left Horn	Difference
A	Greatest Spread				
B	Tip to Tip Spread				
C	Length of Horn				
D-1	Circumference of Base				
D-2	Circumference at First Quarter	(this measurement taken at _____ inches from base)			
D-3	Circumference at Second Quarter	(this measurement taken at _____ inches from base)			
D-4	Circumference at Third Quarter	(this measurement taken at _____ inches from base)			
TOTALS					

ADD	Column 1		Exact locality where killed	(County)	(State)
	Column 2		Date killed	By whom killed	
TOTAL			Present owner	Phone ( )	
SUBTRACT Column 3			Address		
FINAL SCORE			Guide's Name and Address		
			Remarks: (Mention any abnormalities)		

I certify that I have measured the above trophy on _____ 19_____
at (address)_____ City _____
State _____ Zip Code_____ and that these measurements and data are, to the best
of my knowledge and belief, made in accordance with the instructions given.
Witness:_____ Signature_____
(To Measurer's Signature)
Pope & Young Club Official Measurer

MEASURER (Print)

ADDRESS

CITY   STATE   ZIP

INSTRUCTIONS

Measurements must be made with a flexible steel tape to the nearest one-eighth of an inch. To simplify addition, please enter fractional figures in **eighths.** Official measurements cannot be taken for at least sixty days after the day the animal was killed. **Please submit photographs [see below].**

A. **Greatest Spread** is measured between perpendiculars at right angles to the center line of the skull.

B. **Tip to Tip Spread** is measured between tips of horns.

C. **Length of Horn** is measured from lowest point on under side over outer curve to a point in line with tip. Use a straight edge, perpendicular to horn axis, to end the measurement, if necessary.

D-1 Circumferernce of Base is measured at right angles to axis of horn. **DO NOT** follow irregular edge of horn. The line of measurement must be entirely on horn material, not the jagged edge often noted. Circumference measurements must be taken with a steel tape.

D-2-3-4 Divide measurement C of **LONGER** horn by four, mark **BOTH** horns at these quarters even though other horn is shorter, and measure circumference at these marks. Mark quarters by starting from base only.

Photographs: All entries must include photographs of the trophy. A right side, left side and front view photograph is required of the horns. A photograph of the entire animal, preferably at the site of kill, is requested if at all possible.

Drying Period: To be eligible for entry in the Pope & Young Records, a trophy must first have been stored under normal room temperature and humidity for at least 60 days after date of kill. No trophy will be considered which has in any way been altered from its natural state.

THIS SCORING FORM MUST BE ACCOMPANIED BY A SIGNED POPE & YOUNG FAIR CHASE AFFIDAVIT, 3 PHOTOS OF HORNS, AND A RECORDING FEE OF $25.00.

POPE & YOUNG CLUB
NORTH AMERICAN BIG GAME TROPHY SCORING FORM
BOWHUNTING

CARIBOU

BIG GAME RECORDS

KIND OF CARIBOU_____

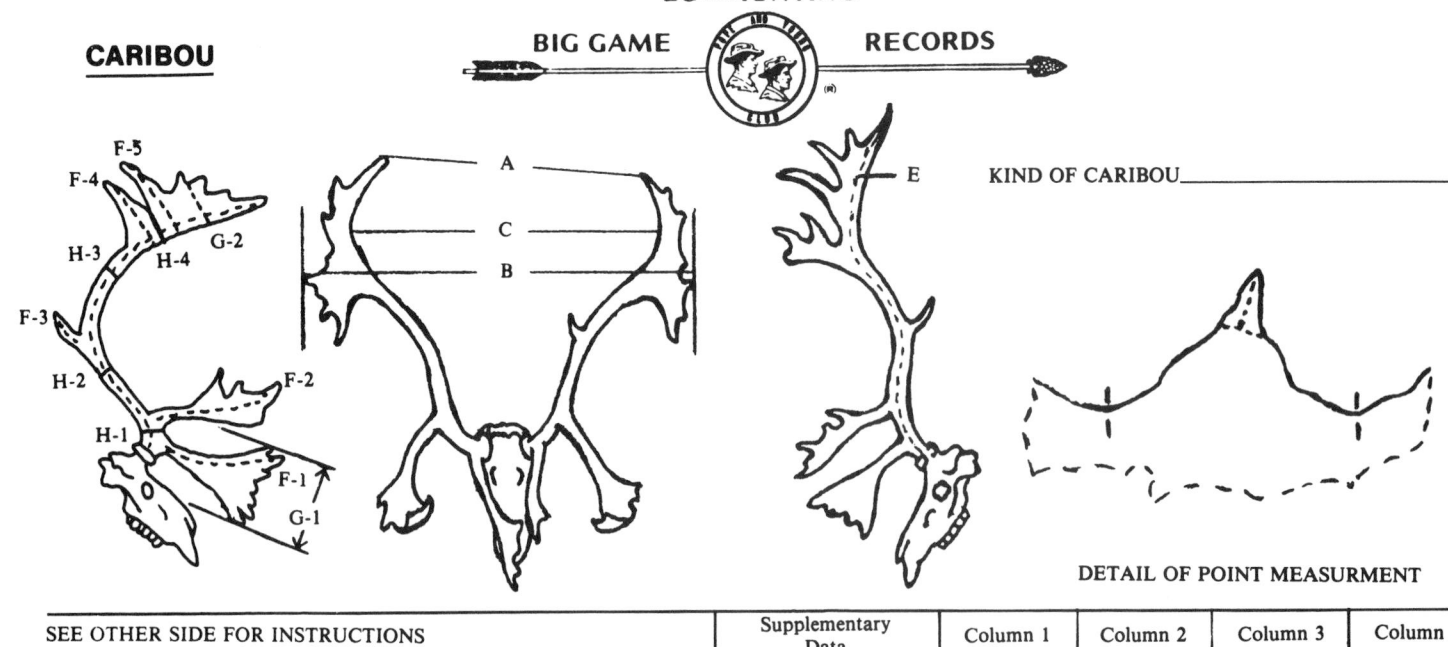

DETAIL OF POINT MEASUREMENT

SEE OTHER SIDE FOR INSTRUCTIONS		Supplementary Data	Column 1	Column 2	Column 3	Column 4
			Spread Credit	Right Antler	Left Antler	Difference
A.	Tip to Tip Spread					
B.	Greatest Spread					
C.	Inside Spread of MAIN BEAMS	Spread credit may equal but not exceed length of longer antler				
D.	Number of Points on Each Antler excluding brows					
	Number of Points on Each Brow					
E.	Length of Main Beam					
F-1	Length of Brow Palm or First Point					
F-2	Length of Bez or Second Point					
F-3	Length of Rear Point, if present					
F-4	Length of Second Longest Top Point					
F-5	Length of Longest Top Point					
G-1	Width of Brow Palm					
G-2	Width of Top Palm					
H-1	Circumference at Smallest Place Between Brow and Bez Points					
H-2	Circumference at Smallest Place Between Bez and Rear Point, if present					
H-3	Circumference at Smallest Place Before First Top Point					
H-4	Circumference at Smallest Place Between Two Longest Top Palm Points					
TOTALS						

ADD	Column 1		Exact locality where killed	
	Column 2		Date killed	By whom killed
	Column 3		Present owner	Phone ( )
TOTAL			Address	
SUBTRACT Column 4			Guide's Name and Complete Address	
FINAL SCORE			REMARKS (Mention any abnormalities)	

I certify that I have measured the above trophy on _____ 19_____

at (address)_____ City _____

State _____ Zip Code_____ and that these measurements and data are, to the best

of my knowledge and belief, made in accordance with the instructions given.

Witness: _____ Signature_____

(To Measurer's Signature)

Pope & Young Club Official Measurer

_____

MEASURER (Print)

_____

ADDRESS

_____

CITY   STATE   ZIP

INSTRUCTIONS

Measurements must be made with a flexible steel tape or steel cable to the nearest one-eighth of an inch. To simplify addition, please enter fractional figures in **eighths.** Official measurements cannot be taken for at least sixty days after the day the animal was killed. **Please submit photographs (see below).**

A. **Tip to Tip Spread** is measured between tips of Main Beams.

B. **Greatest Spread** is measured between perpendiculars at right angles to the center line of the skull at widest part whether across main beams or points.

C. **Inside Spread of Main Beams** is measured at right angles to the center line of the skull at the widest point between main beams. Enter this measurement again in ''Spread Credit'' column if it is less than or equal to the length of longer antler; if longer, enter longer antler length for Spread Credit.

D. **Number of Points on Each Antler.** To be counted a point, a projection must be at least one-half inch long and this length must exceed the breadth at the point of measurement. The length may be measured to any location - at least one-half inch from the tip - at which the length of the point exceeds its breadth. Beam tip is counted as a point but not measured as a point. There are no ''abnormal'' points on caribou.

E. **Length of Main Beam** is measured from lowest outside edge of burr over outer curve to the most distant point of what is, or appears to be, the main beam. The point of beginning is that point on the burr where the center line along the outer curve of the beam intersects the burr.

F-1-2-3. Length of Points. The lengths of these points are measured from nearest edge of beam on the shortest line over outer curve to tip. To determine nearest edge (top edge) of beam, lay the tape along the outer curve of the beam so that the top edge of the tape coincides with the tip edge of the beam on both sides of the point. Draw line along top edge of tape. This line will be base line from which point is measured.

F-4-5. The length of these points are measured from the tip of the point to the top of the beam, then at right angle to the LOWER EDGE of beam. The second longest Top Point **cannot** be a point branch of the Longest Top Point.

G-1 Width of Brow is measured in a straight line from top edge to lower edge, as illustrated, with measurement line at right angle to main axis of brow. A spike brow is credited with a 1/8 inch width.

G-2 Width of Top Palm is measured from midpoint of lower rear edge of main beam to midpoint of a dip between points, at widest part of palm. The line of measurement begins and ends at mid-points of palm edges, which gives credit for palm thickness.

H-1-2-3-4. Circumferences - If rear point is missing, take H-2 and H-3 measurements at smallest place between bez and first top point. A steel tape must be used to take circumference measurements (a cable cannot be used for these measurements).

Photographs: All entries must include photographs of the trophy. A right side, left side and front view photograph is required for all antlers. A photograph of the entire animal, preferably at the site of kill, is requested if at all possible.

Drying Period: To be eligible for entry in the Pope & Young Records, a trophy must first have been stored under normal room temperature and humidity for at least 60 days after date of kill. No trophy will be considered which has in any way been altered from its natural state.

THIS SCORING FORM MUST BE ACCOMPANIED BY A SIGNED
POPE & YOUNG FAIR CHASE AFFIDAVIT, 3 PHOTOS OF ANTLERS, AND A
RECORDING FEE OF $25.00.

BIG GAME   RECORDS

COUGAR   SEX _____

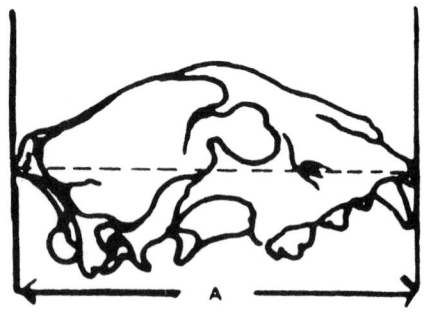

SEE OTHER SIDE FOR INSTRUCTIONS		Measurements
A. Greatest Length Without Lower Jaw (Measured in Sixteenths)		
B. Greatest Width (Measured in Sixteenths)		
TOTAL AND FINAL SCORE		

Exact locality where killed	(County)	(State)
Date killed	By whom killed	
Present owner		Phone ( )
Address		
Guide's Name and Address		

REMARKS (Mention any abnormalities)

Were dogs used in conjunction with the pursuit and harvest of this animal?   YES _____ NO _____

If yes, the following statements apply:

     1. I was present on the hunt at the time the dogs were released to pursue this animal.

     2. If electric collars were attached to any of the dogs, <u>at no time</u> from the beginning of the chase until the harvest of this animal were receivers used in the pursuit and harvest.

If you answered yes and if conditions #1 or #2 do not apply, please explain on separate sheet.

_____   _____
(HUNTERS SIGNATURE)   (DATE)

• •

I certify that I have measured the above trophy on _____ _____ 19_____

at (address)_____ City _____

State _____ Zip Code_____ and that these measurements and data are, to the best

of my knowledge and belief, made in accordance with the instructions given.

Witness:_____   Signature_____
         (To Measurer's Signature)   Pope & Young Club Official Measurer

_____

MEASURER (Print)

_____

ADDRESS

_____

CITY   STATE   ZIP

INSTRUCTIONS

All measurements must be made with a flexible steel tape to the nearest one-sixteenth of an inch.

Official measurements cannot be taken for at least sixty days after the animal was killed. Photographs of right side, left side, and front of skull are required.

A. Greatest Length is measured between perpendiculars to the long axis of the skull WITHOUT the lower jaw and EXCLUDING malformations. (Normal teeth are included)

B. Greatest Width is measured between perpendiculars at right angles to the long axis.

All adhering flesh, membrane and cartilage must be completely removed before official measurements are taken.

Photographs: All entries **must** include photographs of the trophy. A right side, left side and front view photograph is required for all skulls. A photograph of the entire animal, preferably at the site of kill, is requested if at all possible. The front view is best taken from above at a 45° angle.

Drying Period: To be eligible for entry in the Pope & Young Records, a trophy must first have been stored under normal room temperature and humidity for at least 60 days after date of kill. No trophy will be considered which has in any way been altered from its natural state.

All flesh and membrane **must** be completely removed from skull prior to measuring.

> ### IF DOGS ARE USED, THE HUNTER MUST BE PRESENT AT THE TIME THE DOGS ARE RELEASED

THIS SCORING FORM MUST BE ACCOMPANIED BY A SIGNED POPE & YOUNG FAIR CHASE AFFIDAVIT, 3 PHOTOS OF SKULL, AND A RECORDING FEE OF $25.00.

BIG GAME   RECORDS

KIND OF DEER _____

TYPICAL MULE AND BLACKTAIL DEER

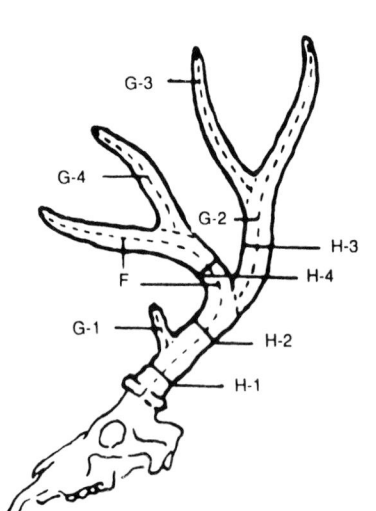

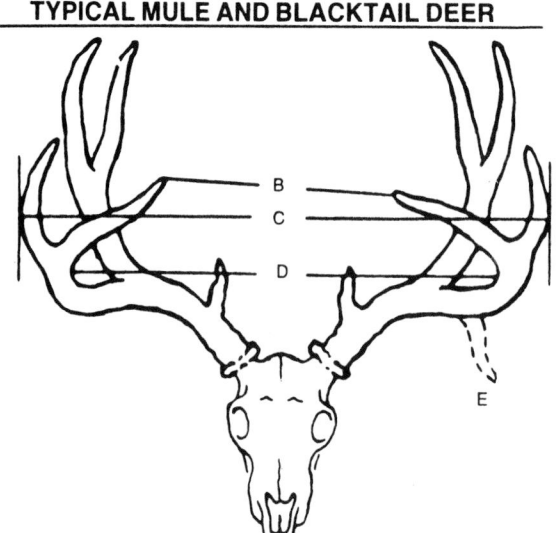

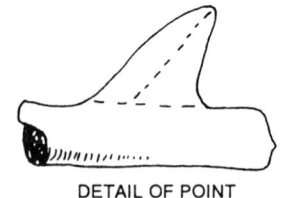

DETAIL OF POINT
MEASUREMENT

Abnormal Points	
Right	Left

Total To E

SEE OTHER SIDE FOR INSTRUCTIONS		Supplementary Data		Column 1	Column 2	Column 3	Column 4
		R	L	Spread Credit	Right Antler	Left Antler	Difference
A.	Number of Points on Each Antler						
B.	Tip to Tip Spread						
C.	Greatest Spread						
D.	Inside Spread of MAIN BEAMS	Spread credit may equal but not exceed length of longer antler					
E.	Total of Lengths of all Abnormal Points						
F.	Length of Main Beam						
G-1	Length of First Point, if present						
G-2	Length of Second Point						
G-3	Length of Third Point						
G-4	Length of Fourth Point, if present						
H-1	Circumference at Smallest Place Between Burr and First Point						
H-2	Circumference at Smallest Place Between First and Second Points						
H-3	Circumference at Smallest Place Between Main and Second Points						
H-4	Circumference at Smallest Place between Second and Fourth Points						
TOTALS							

ADD	Column 1		Exact locality where killed		(County)		(State)
	Column 2		Date killed	By whom killed			
	Column 3		Present owner			Phone ( )	
Total			Address				
SUBTRACT Column 4			Guide's name and Complete Address				
FINAL SCORE			Remarks: (Mention any abnormalities)				

I certify that I have measured the above trophy on_____19_____
at (address)_____ City_____
State_____ Zip Code_____ and that these measurements and data are, to the best
of my knowledge and belief, made in accordance with the instructions given.
Witness:_____ Signature_____
        (To Measurer's Signature)   Pope & Young Club Official Measurer

_____

MEASURER (Print)

_____

ADDRESS

_____

CITY   STATE   ZIP

INSTRUCTIONS

Measurements must be made with a flexible steel tape or steel cable to the nearest one-eighth of an inch. To simplify addition, please enter fractional fitures in **eighths**. Official measurements cannot be taken for at least sixty days after the animal was killed. **Please submit photographs (see below).**

A. Number of Points on each antler. To be counted a point, a projection must be at least one inch long AND at some location, at least one inch from the tip, the length of the projection must exceed its width. **Beam tip is counted as a point but not measured as a point.**

B. Tip to Tip Spread is measured between tips of main beams.

C. Greatest Spread is measured between perpendiculars at right angles to the center line of the skull at widest part whether across main beams or points.

D. Inside Spread on Main Beam is measured at right angles to the center line of the skull at widest point between main beams. Enter this measurement again in "Spread Credit" column if it is less than or equal to the length of longer antler; if longer, enter longer antler length for spread credit.

E. Total of Length of all Abnormal Points. Abnormal points are generally considered to be those non-typical in shape or location. Sketch all abnormal points on antler illustration (front of form) showing location and approximate size. Measure in usual manner and enter in appropriate blanks.

F. Length of Main Beam is measured from lowest outside edge of burr over outer curve to the most distant point of the main beam. The point of beginning is that point on the burr where the center line along the outer curve of the beam intersects the burr.

G-1-2-3-4. Length of Normal Points. Normal points are the brow (or first) and the upper and lower forks as shown in illustration. They are measured from nearest edge of beam over outer curve to tip. To determine nearest edge (top edge) of beam, lay the tape along the outer curve of the beam so that the top edge of the tape coincides with the top edge of the beam on both sides of the point. Draw line along top of tape. This line will be base line from which point is measured.

H-1-2-3-4. Circumferences - If first point is missing, take H-1 and H-2 at smallest place between burr and second point. If third point is missing, take H-3 halfway between the base and tip of second point. If the fourth is missing, take H-4 halfway between the second point and tip of main beam. Circumference measurements must be taken with a steel tape (a cable cannot be used for these measurements).

Photographs: All entries must include photograhs of the trophy. A right side, left side and front view photograph is required for all antlers. A photograph of the entire animal is requested if at all possible.

Drying Period: To be eligible for entry in the Pope & Young Records, a trophy must first have been stored under normal room temperature and humidity for at least 60 days. No trophy will be considered which has in any way been altered from its natural state.

THIS SCORING FORM MUST BE ACCOMPANIED BY A SIGNED
POPE & YOUNG FAIR CHASE AFFIDAVIT, 3 PHOTOS OF ANTLERS, AND A
RECORDING FEE OF $25.00

POPE & YOUNG CLUB
NORTH AMERICAN BIG GAME TROPHY SCORING FORM
BOWHUNTING

BIG GAME ⟶ **RECORDS**

NON-TYPICAL MULE DEER

DETAIL OF POINT MEASUREMENT

ABNORMAL

Points Line E	
R	L

Total To E		

SEE OTHER SIDE FOR INSTRUCTIONS

		Supplementary Data		Column 1	Column 2	Column 3	Column 4
A.	Number of Points on Each Antler	R	L	Spread Credit	Right Antler	Left Antler	Difference
B.	Tip to Tip Spread						
C.	Greatest Spread						
D.	Inside Spread of MAIN BEAMS		Spread credit may equal but not exceed length of longer antler				
E.	Total of Lengths of all Abnormal Points						
F	Length of Main Beam						
G-1	Length of First Point, if present						
G-2	Length of Second Point						
G-3	Length of Third Point, if present						
G-4	Length of Fourth Point, if present						
H-1	Circumference at Smallest Place Between Burr and First Points						
H-2	Circumference at Smallest Place Between First and Second Points						
H-3	Circumference at Smallest Place Between Main Beam and Third Point						
H-4	Circumference at Smallest Place Between Second and Fourth Points						
TOTALS							

ADD	Column 1		Exact locality where killed		(County)		(State)
	Column 2		Date killed		By whom killed		
	Column 3		Present owner			Phone ( )	
TOTAL			Address				
SUBTRACT Column 4			Guide's Name and Complete Address				
Result			REMARKS: (Mention any abnormalities)				
Add Line E Total							
FINAL SCORE							

I certify that I have measured the above trophy on _____ 19_____

at (address)_____ City _____

State _____ Zip Code_____ and that these measurements and data are, to the best

of my knowledge and belief, made in accordance with the instructions given.

Witness:_____ Signature_____

(To Measurer's Signature)   Pope & Young Club Official Measurer

_____

MEASURER (Print)

_____

ADDRESS

_____

CITY   STATE   ZIP

INSTRUCTIONS

Measurements must be made with a flexible steel tape or steel cable to the nearest one-eighth of an inch. To simplify addition, please enter fractional figures in **eighths**. Official measurements cannot be taken for at least sixty days after the day the animal was killed. **Please submit photographs [see below].**

A. Number of Points on each antler. To be counted a point, a projection must be at least one inch long AND at some location, at least one inch from the tip, the length of the projection must exceed its width. **Beam tip is counted as a point but not measured as a point.**

B. Tip to Tip Spread is measured between tips of main beams.

C. Greatest Spread is measured between perpendiculars at right angles to the center line of the skull at widest part whether across main beams or points.

D. Inside Spread on Main Beam is measured at right angles to the center line of the skull at widest point between main beams. Enter this measurement again in "Spread Credit" column if it is less than or equal to the length of longer antler; if longer. enter longer antler length for spread credit.

E. Total of Length of all Abnormal Points. Abnormal points are generally considered to be those non-typical in location. Measure in usual manner and enter in appropriate blanks.

F. Length of Main Beam is measured from lowest outside edge of burr over outer curve to the most distant point of the main beam. The point of beginning is that point on the burr where the center line along the outer curve of the beam intersects the burr.

G-1-2-3-4. Length of Normal Points. Normal points project from the top of the main beam as shown in illustration. They are measured from nearest edge of beam over outer curve to tip. To determine nearest edge (top edge) of beam, lay the tape along the outer curve of the beam so that the top edge of the tape coincides with the top edge of the beam on both sides of the point. Draw line along top of tape. This line will be base line from which point is measured.

H-1-2-3-4. Circumferences. If first point is missing, take H-1 and H-2 at smallest place between burr and second point. If G-4 is missing, take H-4 halfway between G-3 and tip of main beam. Circumference measurements must be taken with a steel tape (a cable cannot be used for these measurements).

Photographs: All entries must include photographs of the trophy. A right side, left side and front view photograph is required for all antlers. A photograph of the entire animal, preferably at the site of kill, is requested if at all possible.

Drying Period: To be eligible for entry in the Pope & Young Records, a trophy must first have been stored under normal room temperature and humidity for at least 60 days after date of kill. No trophy will be considered which has in any way been altered from its natural state.

THIS SCORING FORM MUST BE ACCOMPANIED BY A SIGNED POPE & YOUNG FAIR CHASE AFFIDAVIT, 3 PHOTOS OF ANTLERS, AND A RECORDING FEE OF $25.00.

BIG GAME  RECORDS

KIND OF DEER _____

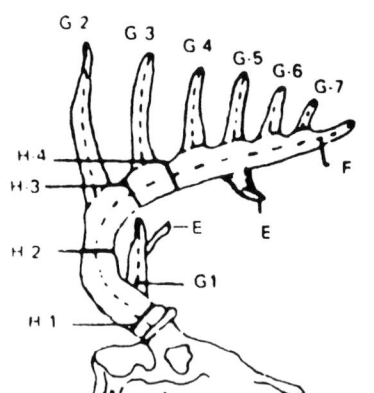

TYPICAL
WHITETAIL AND COUES DEER

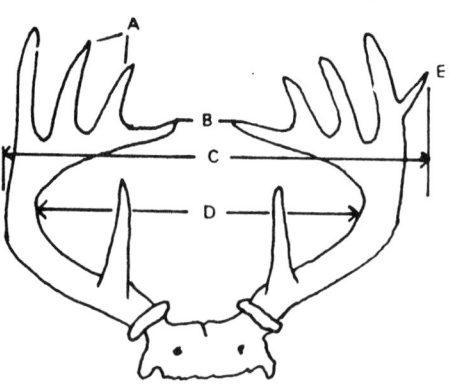

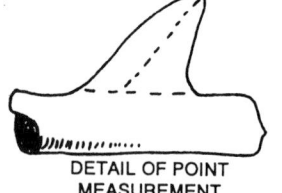

DETAIL OF POINT
MEASUREMENT

Abnormal Points	
Right	Left

Total To E

SEE OTHER SIDE FOR INSTRUCTIONS		Supplementary Data		Column 1	Column 2	Column 3	Column 4
		R	L	Spread Credit	Right Antler	Left Antler	Difference
A.	Number of Points on Each Antler						
B.	Tip to Tip Spread						
C.	Greatest Spread						
D.	Inside Spread of MAIN BEAMS	Spread credit may equal but not exceed length of longer antler					
E.	Total of Lengths of all Abnormal Points						
F.	Length of Main Beam						
G-1	Length of First Point, if present						
G-2	Length of Second Point						
G-3	Length of Third Point						
G-4	Length of Fourth Point, if present						
G-5	Length of Fifth Point, if present						
G-6	Length of Sixth Point, if present						
G-7	Length of Seventh Point, if present						
H-1	Circumference at Smallest Place Between Burr and First Point						
H-2	Circumference at Smallest Place Between First and Second Points						
H-3	Circumference at Smallest Place Between Second and Third Points						
H-4	Circumference at Smallest Place between Third and Fourth Points Or half way between Third point and Beam Tip if Fourth Point is missing						
TOTALS							

	Column 1		Exact locality where killed	(County)	(State)
ADD	Column 2		Date killed	By whom killed	
	Column 3		Present owner	Phone ( )	
	Total		Address		
SUBTRACT Column 4			Guide's name and Complete Address		
FINAL SCORE			Remarks: (Mention any abnormalities)		

I certify that I have measured the above trophy on_____ 19_____
at (address)_____ City_____
State_____ Zip Code_____ and that these measurements and data are, to the best
of my knowledge and belief, made in accordance with the instructions given.
Witness:_____ Signature_____
(To Measurer's Signature)   Pope & Young Club Official Measurer

_____
MEASURER (Print)

_____
ADDRESS

_____
CITY   STATE   ZIP

INSTRUCTIONS

Measurements must be made with a flexible steel tape or steel cable to the nearest one-eighth of an inch. To simplify addition, please enter fractional figures in **eighths.** Official measurements cannot be taken for at least sixty days after the day the animal was killed. **Please submit photographs (see below).**

A. Number of Points on each antler. To be counted a point, a projection must be at least one inch long AND at some location at least one inch from the tip, the length of the projection must exceed its width. **Beam tip is counted as a point but not measured as a point.**

B. Tip to Tip Spread is measured between tips of main beams.

C. Greatest Spread is measured between perpendiculars at right angles to the center line of the skull at widest part whether across main beams or points.

D. Inside Spread on Main Beam is measured at right angles to the center line of the skull at widest point between main beams. Enter this measurement again in "Spread Credit" column if it is less than or equal to the length of longer antler; if longer, enter longer antler length for spread credit.

E. Total of Length of all Abnormal Points. Abnormal points are generally considered to be those non-typical in location. Sketch all abnormal points on antler illustration (front of form) showing location and approximate size. Measure in usual manner and enter in appropriate blanks.

F. Length of Main Beam is measured from lowest outside edge of burr over outer curve to the most distant point of the main beam. The point of beginning is that point on the burr where the center line along the outer curve of the beam intersects the burr.

G-1-2-3-4-5-6-7. Length of Normal Points. Normal points project from the top of the main beam as shown in illustration. They are measured from nearest edge of beam over outer curve to tip. To determine nearest edge (top edge) of beam, lay the tape along the outer curve of the beam so that the top edge of the tape coincides with the top edge of the beam on both sides of the point. Draw line along top of tape. This line will be base line from which point is measured.

H-1-2-3-4. Circumferences. If first point is missing, take H-1 and H-2 at smallest place between burr and second point. If G-4 is missing, take H-4 halfway between G-3 and tip of main beam. Circumference measurements must be taken with a steel tape (a cable cannot be used for these measurements).

Photographs: All entries must include photographs of the trophy. A right side, left side and front view photograph is required for all antlers. A photograph of the entire animal, preferably at the site of kill, is requested if at all possible.

Drying Period: To be eligible for entry in the Pope & Young Records, a trophy must first have been stored under normal room temperature and humidity for at least 60 days after date of kill. No trophy will be considered which has in any way been altered from its natural state.

THIS SCORING FORM MUST BE ACCOMPANIED BY A SIGNED POPE & YOUNG FAIR CHASE AFFIDAVIT, 3 PHOTOS OF ANTLERS, AND A RECORDING FEE OF $25.00.

BOWHUNTING

BIG GAME   RECORDS

KIND OF DEER _____

NON-TYPICAL WHITETAIL AND COUES' DEER

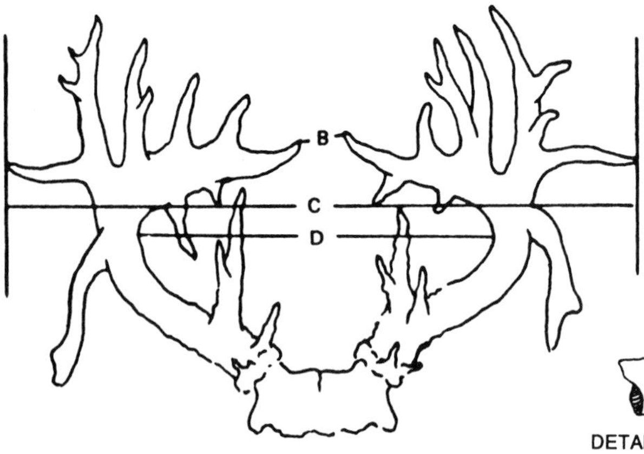

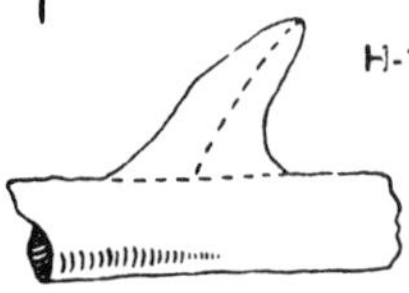

G-2 G-3
G-4
G-5
G-6
E E
H-4
H-3 E
G-1
H-2 E F
E
H-1
E

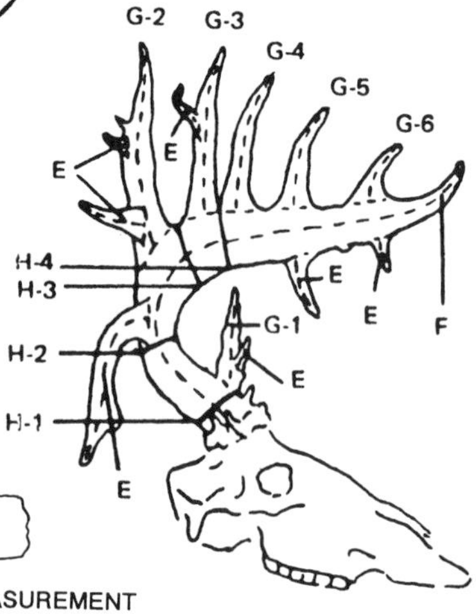

ABNORMAL

Points Line E	
R	L

Total To E

DETAIL OF POINT MEASUREMENT

SEE OTHER SIDE FOR INSTRUCTIONS		Supplementary Data		Column 1	Column 2	Column 3	Column 4
		R	L	Spread Credit	Right Antler	Left Antler	Difference
A.	Number of Points on Each Antler						
B.	Tip to Tip Spread						
C.	Greatest Spread						
D.	Inside Spread of MAIN BEAMS		Spread credit may equal but not exceed length of longer antler				
E.	Total of Lengths of all Abnormal Points						
F	Length of Main Beam						
G-1	Length of First Point, if present						
G-2	Length of Second Point						
G-3	Length of Third Point						
G-4	Length of Fourth Point, if present						
G-5	Length of Fifth Point, if present						
G-6	Length of Sixth Point, if present						
G-7	Length of Seventh Point, if present						
H-1	Circumference at Smallest Place Between Burr and First Points						
H-2	Circumference at Smallest Place Between First and Second Points						
H-3	Circumference at Smallest Place Between Second and Third Points						
H-4	Circumference at Smallest Place Between Third and Fourth Points or half way between Third Point and Beam Tip if Fourth Point is missing						
TOTALS							

ADD	Column 1		Exact locality where killed	(County)	(State)
	Column 2		Date killed	By whom killed	
	Column 3		Present owner	Phone ( )	
	TOTAL		Address		
	SUBTRACT Column 4		Guide's Name and Complete Address		
	Result		REMARKS: (Mention any abnormalities)		
	Add Line E Total				
	FINAL SCORE				

I certify that I have measured the above trophy on _____ 19_____
at (address)_____ City _____
State_____ Zip Code _____ and that these measurements and data are, to the best
of my knowledge and belief, made in accordance with the instructions given.
Witness: _____ Signature_____
        (To Measurer's Signature)   Pope & Young Club Official Measurer

MEASURER (Print) _____

ADDRESS _____

CITY	STATE	ZIP

INSTRUCTIONS

Measurements must be made with a flexible steel tape or steel cable to the nearest one-eighth of an inch. To simplify addition, please enter fractional figures in **eighths**. Official measurements cannot be taken for at least sixty days after the day the animal was killed. **Please submit photographs (see below).**

A. Number of Points on each antler. To be counted a point, a projection must be at least one inch long AND at some location, at least one inch from the tip, the length of the projection must exceed its width. **Beam tip is counted as a point but not measured as a point.**

B. Tip to Tip Spread is measured between tips of main beams.

C. Greatest Spread is measured between perpendiculars at right angles to the center line of the skull at widest part whether across main beams or points.

D. Inside Spread on Main Beam is measured at right angles to the center line of the skull at widest point between main beams. Enter this measurement again in "Spread Credit" column if it is less than or equal to the length of longer antler: if longer, enter longer antler length for spread credit.

E. Total of Length of all Abnormal Points. Abnormal points are generally considered to be those non-typical in location. Measure in usual manner and enter in appropriate blanks.

F. Length of Main Beam is measured from lowest outside edge of burr over outer curve to the distant point of the main beam. The point of beginning is that point on the burr where the center line along the outer curve of the beam intersects the burr.

G. 1-2-3-4-5-6-7. Length of Normal Points. Normal points project from the top of the main beam as shown in illustration. They are measured from nearest edge of beam over outer curve to tip. To determine nearest edge (top edge) of beam, lay the tape along the outer curve of the beam so that the top edge of the tape coincides with the top edge of the beam on both sides of the point. Draw line along top of tape. This line will be base line from which point is measured.

H-1-2-3-4. Circumferences. If first point is missing, take H-1 and H-2 at smallest place between burr and second point. If G-4 is missing, take H-4 halfway between G-3 and tip of main beam. Circumference measurements must be taken with a steel tape (a cable cannot be used for these measurements).

Photographs: All entries must include photographs of the trophy. A right side, left side and front view photograph is required for all antlers. A photograph of the entire animal, preferably at the side of kill, is requested if al all possible.

Drying Period: To be eligible for entry in the Pope & Young Records, a trophy must first have been stored under normal room temperature and humidity for at least 60 days after date of kill. No trophy will be considered wihich has in any way been altered from its natural state.

THIS SCORING FORM MUST BE ACCOMPANIED BY A SIGNED POPE & YOUNG FAIR CHASE AFFIDAVIT, 3 PHOTOS OF ANTLERS, AND A RECORDING FEE OF $25.00.

BOWHUNTING

BIG GAME ➤ ⊙ **RECORDS** ➤

ROOSEVELT'S ELK

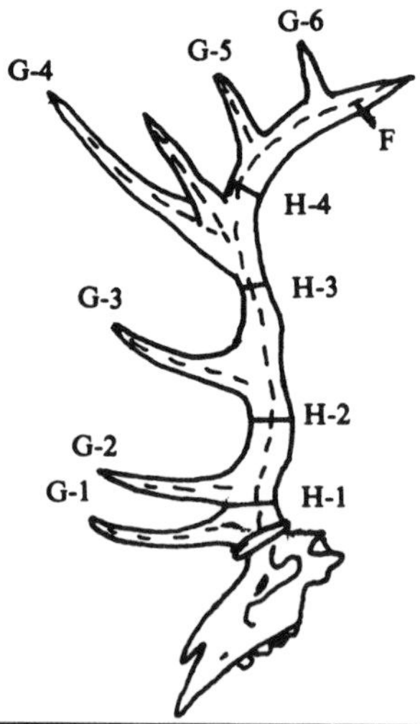

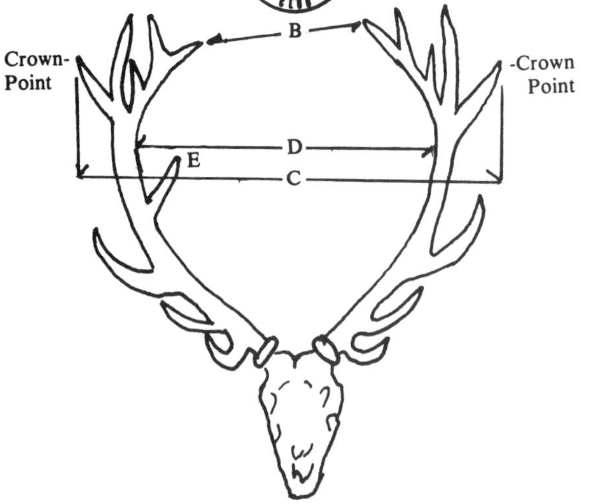

Crown Points	
Right	Left
Total	

Abnormal Points	
Right	Left
Total to E	

	Supplementary Data		Column 1	Column 2	Column 3	Column 4
SEE OTHER SIDE FOR INSTRUCTIONS	R	L	Spread Credit	Right Antler	Left Antler	Difference
A. Number of Points on Each Antler						
B. Tip to Tip Spread						
C. Greatest Spread						
D. Inside Spread of MAIN BEAMS	Spread credit may equal but not exceed length of longer antler					
E. Total of Lengths of All Abnormal Points						
F. Length of Main Beam						
G-1. Length of First Point, if present						
G-2. Length of Second Point						
G-3. Length of Third Point						
G-4. Length of Fourth (Royal) Point						
G-5. Length of Fifth Point, if present						
G-6. Length of Sixth Point, if present						
G-7. Length of Seventh Point, if present						
H-1. Circumference at Smallest Place Between First and Second Points						
H-2. Circumference at Smallest Place Between Second and Third Points						
H-3. Circumference at Smallest Place Between Third and Fourth Points						
H-4. Circumference at Smallest Place Between Fourth and Fifth Points						
TOTALS						

ADD	Column 1	
	Column 2	
	Column 3	
TOTAL		
SUBTRACT Column 4		
Result		
Add Crown Point Total		
Final Score		

Exact locality where killed   (County)   (State)

Date killed   By whom killed

Present Owner   Phone ( )

Address

Guide's Name and Address

REMARKS (Mention any abnormalities)

I certify that I have measured the above trophy on _____ 19_____

at (address)_____ City _____

State_____ Zip Code_____ and that these measurements and data are, to the best

of my knowledge and belief, made in accordance with the instructions given.

Witness:_____ Signature_____
　　　　　　　(To Measurer's Signature)

Pope & Young Club Official Measurer

_____

MEASURER (Print)

_____

ADDRESS

_____

CITY　　　　　　　　　STATE　　　　　　　　　ZIP

INSTRUCTIONS

Measurements must be made with a flexible steel tape or steel cable to the nearest one-eighth of an inch. To simplify addition, please enter fractional figures in **eighths**. Official measurements cannot be taken for at least sixty days after the day the animal was killed. **Please submit photographs (see below)**.

A.　Number of Points on each antler. To be counted a point, a projection must be at least one inch long AND at some location, at least one inch from the tip, the length of the projection must exceed its width. **Beam tip is counted as a point but not measured as a point.**

B.　Tip to Tip Spread is measured between tips of main beams.

C.　Greatest Spread is measured between perpendiculars at right angles to the center line of the skull at widest part whether across main beams or points.

D.　Inside Spread of Main Beam is measured at right angles to the center line of the skull at widest point between main beams. Enter this measurement again in "Spread Credit" column if it is less than or equal to the length of longer antler; if longer, enter longer antler length for spread credit.

E.　Total of Length of all Abnormal Points. Abnormal points are generally considered to be those non-typical in location on or below G-3. Sketch all abnormal points on antler illustration (front of form) showing location and approximate size. Measure in usual manner and enter in appropriate blanks.

Total Length of Crown Points. Crown points are any points projecting from the main beam or from another point on or above G-4 that are **NOT** typical in shape and location. Sketch these points on the form, enter their individual lengths in the crown point box. Then transfer the total to the score as provided.

F.　Length of Main Beam is measured from lowest outside edge of burr over outer curve to the most distant point of the main beam. The point of beginning is that point on the burr where the center line along the outer curve of the beam intersects the burr.

G-1-2-3-4-5-6-7. Length of Normal Points. Normal points project from the top or front of the main beam in the general pattern illustrated. They are measured from the nearest edge of main beam over outer curve to tip. Record point length in appropriate blanks.

H-1-2-3. Circumference. If first point is missing, take H-1 and H-2 at smallest place between burr and second point. A steel tape must be used to take circumference measurements (a cable can not be used for these measurements).

H-4 Circumference. Take H-4 between G-4 and what appears to be the typical G-5 point. The H-4 score should not be unduly influenced by the presence of crown points. If the typical G-5 point is missing, take H-4 halfway between G-4 and beam tip.

Photographs: All entries must include photographs of the trophy. A right side, left side and front view photograph is required for all antlers. A photograph of the entire animal, preferably at the site of kill, is requested if at all possible.

Drying Period: To be eligible for entry in the Pope & Young Records, a trophy must first have been stored under normal room temperature and humidity for at least 60 days after date of kill. No trophy will be considered which has in any way been altered from its natural state.

THIS SCORING FORM MUST BE ACCOMPANIED BY A SIGNED
POPE & YOUNG FAIR CHASE AFFIDAVIT, 3 PHOTOS OF ANTLERS, AND A
RECORDING FEE OF $25.00.

POPE & YOUNG CLUB
NORTH AMERICAN BIG GAME TROPHY SCORING FORM
BOWHUNTING
BIG GAME RECORDS

YELLOWSTONE ELK

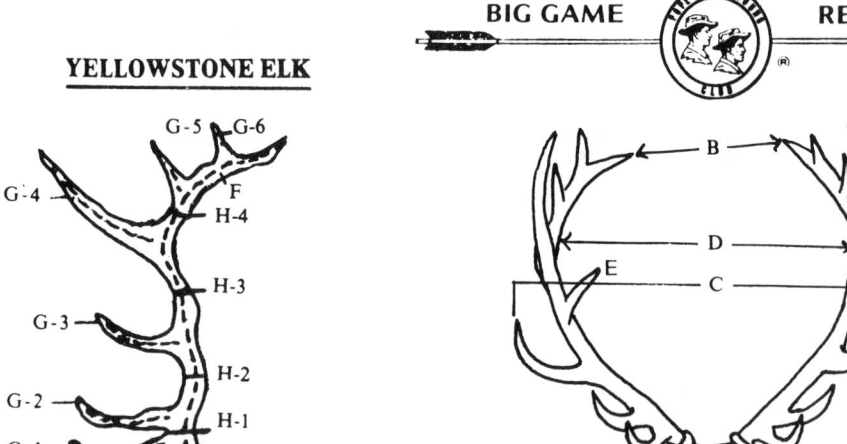

DETAIL OF POINT MEASUREMENT

Abnormal Points	
Right	Left
Total to E	

SEE OTHER SIDE FOR INSTRUCTIONS	Supplementary Data		Column 1	Column 2	Column 3	Column 4
	R	L	Spread Credit	Right Antler	Left Antler	Difference
A. Number of Points on Each Antler						
B. Tip to Tip Spread						
C. Greatest Spread						
D. Inside Spread of MAIN BEAMS	Spread credit may equal but not exceed length of longer antler					
E. Total of Lengths of all Abnormal Points						
F. Length of Main Beam						
G-1. Length of First Point						
G-2. Length of Second Point						
G-3. Length of Third Point						
G-4. Length of Fourth Point						
G-5. Length of Fifth Point, if present						
G-6. Length of Sixth Point, if present						
G-7. Length of Seventh Point, if present						
H-1. Circumference at Smallest Place Between First and Second Points						
H-2. Circumference at Smallest Place Between Second and Third Points						
H-3. Circumference at Smallest Place Between Third and Fourth Points						
H-4. Circumference at Smallest Place Between Fourth and Fifth Points						
TOTALS						

ADD	Column 1	
	Column 2	
	Column 3	
TOTAL		
SUBTRACT Column 4		
FINAL SCORE		

Exact locality where killed _____ (County) _____ (State)

Date killed _____ By whom killed _____

Present owner _____ Phone ( )

Address _____

Guide's Name and Complete Address _____

REMARKS (Mention any abnormalities) _____

I certify that I have measured the above trophy on _____ 19_____
at (address)_____ City _____
State _____ Zip Code _____ and that these measurements and data are, to the best
of my knowledge and belief, made in accordance with the instructions given.
Witness:_____ Signature_____
　　　　　　(To Measurer's Signature)　　　　Pope & Young Club Official Measurer

_____
MEASURER (Print)

_____
ADDRESS

_____
CITY　　　　　　　　STATE　　　　　ZIP

INSTRUCTIONS

Measurements must be made with a flexible steel tape or steel cable to the nearest one-eighth of an inch. To simplify addition, please enter fractional figures in **eighths.** Official measurements cannot be taken for at least sixty days after the day the animal was killed. **Please submit photographs [see below].**

A. Number of Points on each antler. To be counted a point, a projection must be at least one inch long AND at some location, at least one inch from the tip, the length of the projection must exceed its width. **Beam tip is counted as a point but not measured as a point.**

B. Tip to Tip Spread is measured between tips of main beams.

C. Greatest Spread is measured between perpendiculars at right angles to the center line of the skull at widest part whether across main beams or points.

D. Inside Spread on Main Beam is measured at right angles to the center line of the skull at widest point between main beams. Enter this measurement again in ''Spread Credit'' column if it is less than or equal to the length of longer antler; if longer, enter longer antler length for spread credit.

E. Total of Length of all Abnormal Points. Abnormal points are generally considered to be those non-typical in location. Sketch abnormal points on antler illustration (front of form) showing location and approximate size. Measure in usual manner and enter in appropriate blanks.

F. Length of Main Beam is measured from lowest outside edge of burr over outer curve to the distant point of the main beam. The point of beginning is that point on the burr where the center line along the outer curve of the beam intersects the burr.

G-1-2-3-4-5-6-7. Length of Normal Points. Normal points project from the top or front of the main beam as shown in illustration. They are measured from nearest edge of beam over outer curve to tip. To determine nearest edge (top edge) of beam, lay the tape along the outer curve of the beam so that the top edge of the tape coincides with the top edge of the beam on both sides of the point. Draw line along top of tape. This line will be base line from which point is measured.

H-1-2-3-4. Circumferences. If first point is missing, take H-1 at smallest place between burr and second point. If G-5 is missing, take H-4 halfway between G-4 and beam tip. A steel tape must be used to take circumference measurements (a cable cannot be used for these measurements).

Photographs: All entries must include photographs of the trophy. A right side, left side and front view photograph is required for all antlers. A photograph of the entire animal, preferably at the site of kill, is requested if at all possible.

Drying Period: To be eligible for entry in the Pope & Young Records, a trophy must first have been stored under normal room temperature and humidity for at least **60 days** after date of kill. No trophy will be considered which has in any way been altered from its natural state.

THIS SCORING FORM MUST BE ACCOMPANIED BY A SIGNED POPE & YOUNG FAIR CHASE AFFIDAVIT, 3 PHOTOS OF ANTLERS, AND A RECORDING FEE OF $25.00.

POPE & YOUNG CLUB
NORTH AMERICAN BIG GAME TROPHY SCORING FORM
BOWHUNTING
BIG GAME — RECORDS

NON-TYPICAL
YELLOWSTONE ELK

DETAIL OF POINT MEASUREMENT

ABNORMAL	
Points Line E	
H	L

Total To E

SEE OTHER SIDE FOR INSTRUCTIONS		Supplementary Data		Column 1	Column 2	Column 3	Column 4
		R	L	Spread Credit	Right Antler	Left Antler	Difference
A. Number of Points on Each Antler							
B. Tip to Tip Spread							
C. Greatest Spread							
D. Inside Spread of MAIN BEAMS		Spread credit may equal but not exceed length of longer antler					
E. Total of Lengths of all Abnormal Points							
F. Length of Main Beam							
G-1. Length of First Point							
G-2. Length of Second Point							
G-3. Length of Third Point							
G-4. Length of Fourth Point							
G-5. Length of Fifth Point, if present							
G-6. Length of Sixth Point, if present							
G-7. Length of Seventh Point, if present							
H-1. Circumference at Smallest Place Between First and Second Points							
H-2. Circumference at Smallest Place Between Second and Third Points							
H-3. Circumference at Smallest Place Between Third and Fourth Points							
H-4. Circumference at Smallest Place Between Fourth and Fifth Points							
TOTALS							

ADD	Column 1	
	Column 2	
	Column 3	
	TOTAL	
	SUBTRACT Column 4	
	Result	
	Add Line E Total	
	FINAL SCORE	

Exact locality where killed _____ (County) _____ (State)

Date killed _____ By whom killed _____

Present owner _____ Phone ( )

Address _____

Guide's Name and Complete Address _____

REMARKS (Mention any abnormalities)

POPE & YOUNG CLUB
NORTH AMERICAN BIG GAME TROPHY SCORING FORM
BOWHUNTING
BIG GAME **RECORDS**

MOOSE

KIND OF MOOSE

_____

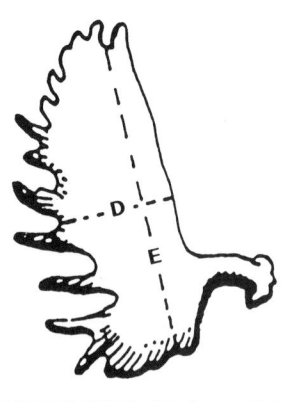

UNDER SURFACE OF ANTLER

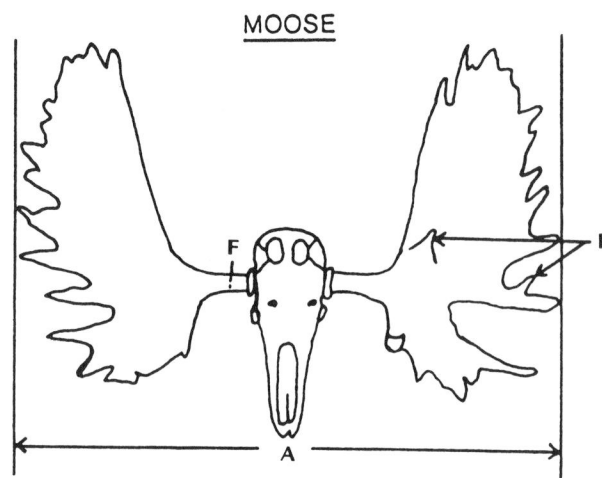

DETAIL OF POINT MEASUREMENT

SEE OTHER SIDE FOR INSTRUCTIONS	Column 1	Column 2	Column 3	Column 4
A. Greatest Spread		Right Antler	Left Antler	Difference
B. Number of Abnormal Points on Both Antlers				
C. Number of Normal Points				
D. Width of Palm				
E. Length of Palm including Brow Palm				
F. Circumferrence of Beam at Smallest Place				
TOTALS				

ADD					
	Column 1		Exact locality where killed	(County)	(State)
	Column 2		Date killed	By whom killed	
	Column 3		Present owner		Phone ( )
	Total		Address		
SUBTRACT Column 4			Guide's Name and Address		
FINAL SCORE			REMARKS: (Mention any abnormalities)		

I certify that I have measured the above trophy on _____ 19_____
at (address)_____ City _____
State _____ Zip Code_____ and that these measurements and data are, to the best
of my knowledge and belief, made in accordance with the instructions given.
Witness:_____ Signature_____
　　　　　(To Measurer's Signature)　　　　　　　　 Pope & Young Club Official Measurer

_____
MEASURER (Print)

_____
ADDRESS

_____
CITY　　　　　　　　　 STATE　　　　　　　 ZIP

INSTRUCTIONS

Measurements must be made with a flexible steel tape or steel cable to the nearest one-eighth of an inch. To simplify addition, please enter fractional figures in **eighths.** Official measurements cannot be taken for at least sixty days after the day the animal was killed. **Please submit photographs [see below].**

A. Greatest Spread is measured between perpendiculars in a straight line at a right angle to the center line of the skull.

B. Number of Abnormal Points on Both Antlers - Abnormal points are those originating from normal points or from the upper or lower palm surface, or from the inner edge of palm (see illustration). Abnormal points must be at least one inch long, with length exceeding width at one inch or more of length.

C. Number of Normal Points - Normal points originate from the outer edge of palm. To be counted a point, a projection must be at least one inch long, with the length exceeding width at one inch or more of length.

D. Width of Palm is taken in contact with the under surface of palm, at a right angle to the length of palm measurement line. The line of measurement should begin and end at the midpoint of the palm edge, which give credit for the desirable character of palm thickness.

E. Length of Palm including Brow Palm is taken in contact with the surface along the under side of the palm, **parallel** to the inner edge, from dips between points at the top to dips between points (if present) at the bottom. If a bay is present, measure across the open bay if the proper line of measurement **parallel to inner edge,** follows this path. The line of measurement should begin and end at the midpoint of the palm edge, which give credit for the desirable character of palm thickness.

F. Circumference of Beam at smallest place is taken as illustrated.

Photographs: All entries must include photographs of the trophy. A right side, left side and front view photograph is required of the antlers. A photograph of the entire animal, preferably at the site of kill, is requested if at all possible.

Drying Period: To be eligible for entry in the Pope & Young Records, a trophy must first have been stored under normal room temperature and humidity for at least 60 days after date of kill. No trophy will be considered which has in any way been altered from its natural state.

THIS SCORING FORM MUST BE ACCOMPANIED BY A SIGNED POPE & YOUNG FAIR CHASE AFFIDAVIT, 3 PHOTOS OF ANTLERS, AND A RECORDING FEE OF $25.00.

MUSKOX

SEX _____

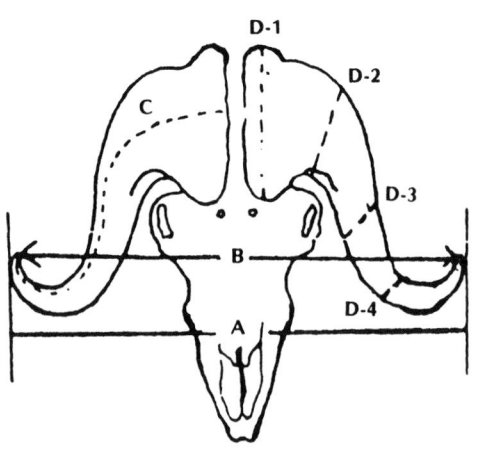
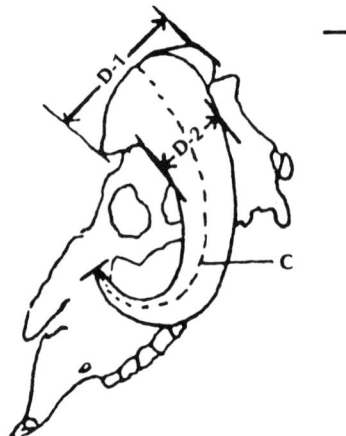

SEE OTHER SIDE FOR INSTRUCTIONS		Supplementary Data	Column 1	Column 2	Colum
			Right Horn	Left Horn	Differe
A.	Greatest Spread				
B.	Tip to Tip Spread				
C.	Length of Horn				
D-1	Width of Boss				
D-2	Width at First Quarter	(this measurement taken at_____ inches from base)			
D-3	Circumference at Second Quarter	(this measurement taken at_____ inches from base)			
D-4	Circumference at Third Quarter	(this measurement taken at_____ inches from base)			
TOTALS					

ADD	Column 1		Exact locality where killed		(County)	(State)
	Column 2		Date killed	By whom killed		
TOTAL			Present owner		Phone ( )	
SUBTRACT Column 3			Address			
FINAL SCORE			Guide's Name and Address			
			REMARKS: (Mention any abnormalities)			

I certify that I have measured the above trophy on_____19_____

at (address)_____City_____

State_____Zip Code_____and that these measurements and data are, to the best

of my knowledge and belief, made in accordance with the instructions given.

Witness:_____Signature_____

         (To Measurer's Signature)   Pope & Young Club Official Measurer

_____

MEASURER (Print)

_____

ADDRESS

_____

CITY   STATE   ZIP

INSTRUCTIONS

Measurements must be made with a flexible steel tape or steel cable, and adjustable calipers to the nearest one-eight of an inch. To simplify addition, please enter fractional figures in **eighths**. Official measurements cannot be taken for at least sixty days after the animal was killed. **Please submit photographs (see below).**

A. Greatest Spread is measured between perpendiculars at right angles to the center line of the skull.

B. Tip to Tip Spread is measured between tips of horns.

C. Length of Horn is measured along center of upper horn surface, staying within curve of horn as illustrated, to a point in line with tip. Attempt to free the connective tissue between the horns at the center of the boss to determine the lowest point of horn material on each side, near the top center of the skull. Hook the tape under the lowest point of the horn and measure the length of horn, with the measurement line maintained in the center of the upper surface of horn following the converging lines to the horn tip.

D-1 Width of Boss is measured with calipers at greatest width of base, with measurement line forming a right angle with horn axis. It is often helpful to measure D-1 before c, marking the midpoint of the boss as the correct path of C.

D-2-3-4 Divide measurement C of **LONGER** horn by four. Starting at base, mark **BOTH** horns at these quarters (even though other horn is shorter). Then, using calipers, measure width of the horn at D-2, making sure the measurement is perpendicular to the surface of horn excluding boss material. Circumferences are then measured at D-3 and D-4, with measurements being taken at right angles to horn axis.

Photographs: All entries must include photographs of the trophy. A right side, left side and front view photograph is required of the horns. A photograph of the entire animal, preferable at the site of kill, is requested if at all possible.

Drying Period: To be eligible for entry in the Pope & Young Records, a trophy must first have been stored under normal room temperature and humidity for at least 60 days after date of kill. No trophy will be considered which has in any way been altered from its natural state.

THIS SCORING FORM MUST BE ACCOMPANIED BY A SIGNED POPE & YOUNG FAIR CHASE AFFIDAVIT, 3 PHOTOS OF HORNS, AND A RECORDING FEE OF $25.00.

POPE & YOUNG CLUB
NORTH AMERICAN BIG GAME TROPHY SCORING FORM
BOWHUNTING
BIG GAME · **RECORDS**

PRONGHORN

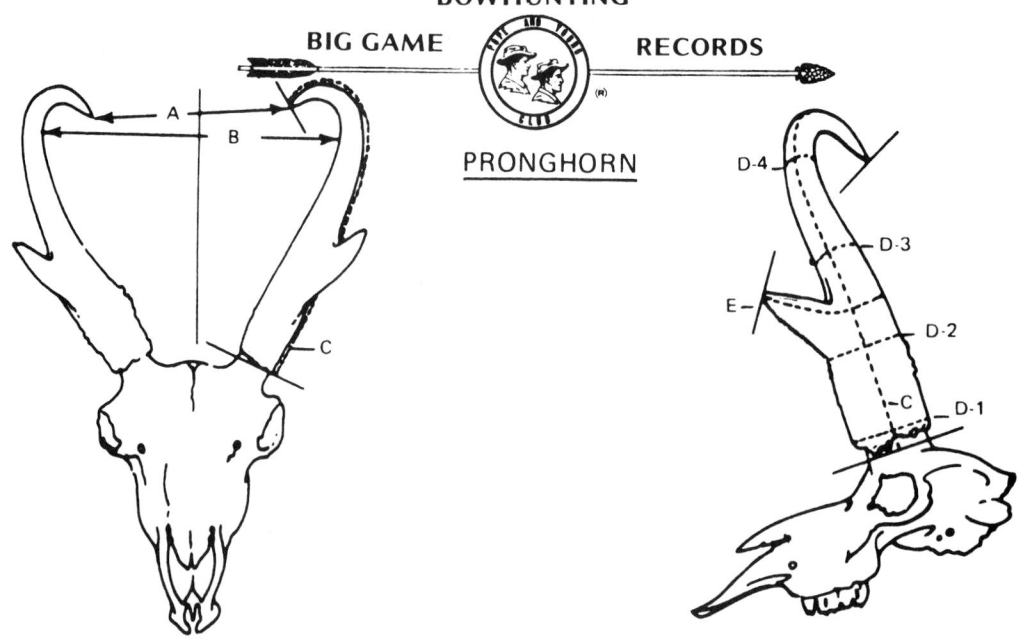

SEE OTHER SIDE FOR INSTRUCTIONS	Supplementary Data	Column 1	Column 2	Column
		Right Horn	Left Horn	Differen
A. Tip to Tip Spread				
B. Inside Spread of Main Beams				
If Inside Spread of Main Beams exceeds longer horn length, enter difference.				
C. Length of Horn				
D-1 Circumference of Base				
D-2 Circumference at First Quarter (this measurement taken at _____ inches from base)				
D-3 Circumference at Second Quarter (this measurement taken at _____ inches from base)				
D-4 Circumference at Third Quarter (this measurement taken at _____ inches from base)				
E. Length of Prong				
TOTALS				

ADD	Column 1		Exact locality where killed		(County)	(State)
	Column 2		Date killed	By whom killed		
TOTAL			Present owner		Phone ( )	
SUBTRACT Column 3			Address			
FINAL SCORE			Guide's name and Complete Address			
			REMARKS: (Mention any abnormalities)			

I certify that I have measured the above trophy on _____ 19_____

at (address)_____ City _____

State_____ Zip Code_____ and that these measurements and data are, to the best

of my knowledge and belief, made in accordance with the instructions given.

Witness:_____ Signature_____
(To Measurer's Signature)   Pope & Young Club Official Measurer

_____
MEASURER (Print)

_____
ADDRESS

_____
CITY   STATE   ZIP

INSTRUCTIONS

Measurements must be made with a flexible steel tape or steel cable to the nearest one-eighth of an inch. To simplify addition, please enter fractional figures in **eighths.** Official measurements cannot be taken for at least sixty days after the day the animal was killed. **Please submit photographs (see below).**

A. Tip to Tip Spread measured between tip of horns.

B. Inside Spread of Main Beams measured at right angles to the center line of the skull at widest point between main beams.

C. Length of horn is measured on the outside curve, so the line taken will vary with different heads, depending on the direction of the curvature. Measure along the center of the outer curve from tip of horn to a point in line with the lowest edge of the base.

D-1 Measure around base of horn at right angles to long axis. Tape must be in contact with the lowest circumference of the horn in which there are no serrations.

D-2-3-4. Divide measurement of LONGER horn by four; **measuring from the base,** mark **BOTH** horns at these quarters even though one horn is shorter and measure circumferences at these marks. Note D-3 **must** be taken above the prong. If D-3 falls on or below the prong then take this measurement immediately **above** the prong. Should D-2 land on the swelling of the prong, take D-2 measurement **immediately below** swelling of prong. If adjustments are made for swelling of prong on D-2 or D-3 measurement, note these adjustments in "REMARKS" section. Circumference measurements must be taken with a steel tape (a cable cannot be used for these measurements).

E. Length of Prong - Measure from the tip of the prong along the upper edge of the outer side to the horn; thence, around the horn to a point at the rear of the horn where a straight edge across the back of both horns touches the horn. This measurement around the horn from the base of the prong should be taken at right angles to the long axis of the horn.

Photographs: All entries must include photographs of the trophy. A right side, left side and front view photograph is required of the horns. A photograph of the entire animal, preferably at the site of kill, is requested if at all possible.

Drying Period: To be eligible for entry in the Pope & Young Records, a trophy must first have been stored under normal room temperature and humidity for at least 60 days after date of kill. No trophy will be considered which has in any way been altered from its natural state.

THIS SCORING FORM MUST BE ACCOMPANIED BY A SIGNED POPE & YOUNG FAIR CHASE AFFIDAVIT, 3 PHOTOS OF HORNS, AND A RECORDING FEE OF $25.00.

POPE & YOUNG CLUB
NORTH AMERICAN BIG GAME TROPHY SCORING FORM
BOWHUNTING
BIG GAME   **RECORDS**

ROCKY MOUNTAIN GOAT

SEX _____

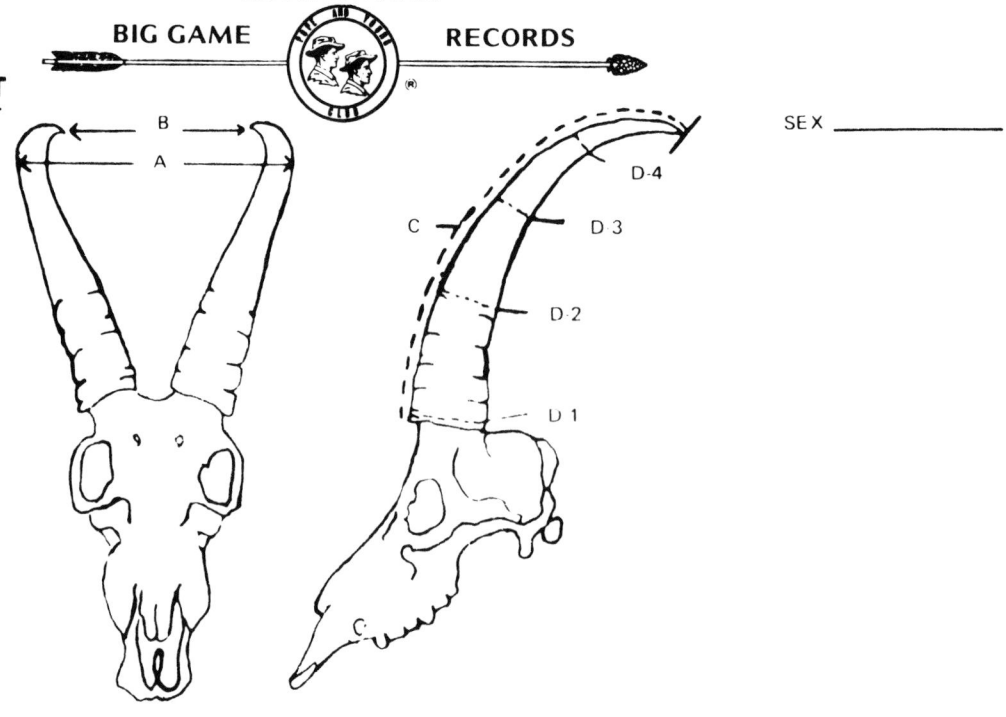

SEE OTHER SIDE FOR INSTRUCTIONS		Supplementary Data	Column 1	Column 2	Column 3
			Right Horn	Left Horn	Difference
A. Greatest Spread					
B. Tip to Tip Spread					
C. Length of Horn					
D-1. Circumference of Base					
D-2. Circumference at First Quarter	(this measurement taken at _____ inches from base)				
D-3. Circumference at Second Quarter	(this measurement taken at _____ inches from base)				
D-4. Circumference at Third Quarter	(this measurement taken at _____ inches from base)				
TOTALS					

ADD	Column 1		Exact locality where killed		(County)		(State)
	Column 2		Date killed	By whom killed			
TOTAL			Present owner			Phone ( )	
SUBTRACT Column 3			Address				
FINAL SCORE			Guide's Name and Address				
			REMARKS (Mention any abnormalities)				

I certify that I have measured the above trophy on _____ 19_____
at (address)_____ City _____
State _____ Zip Code_____ and that these measurements and data are, to the best
of my knowledge and belief, made in accordance with the instructions given.
Witness:_____ Signature_____
    (To Measurer's Signature)
                              Pope & Young Club Official Measurer

MEASURER (Print) _____

ADDRESS _____

CITY _____ STATE _____ ZIP

INSTRUCTIONS

Measurements must be made with a flexible steel tape to the nearest one-eighth of an inch. To simplify addition, please enter fractional figures in **eighths.** Official measurements cannot be taken for at least sixty days after the day the animal was killed. **Please submit photographs |see below|.**

A. **Greatest Spread** is measured between perpendiculars at right angles to the center line of the skull.

B. **Tip to Tip Spread** is measured between tips of horns.

C. **Length of Horn** is measured from lowest point in front over outer curve to a point in line with tip.

D-1. **Circumference of Base** is measured at right angles to axis of horn. **DO NOT** FOLLOW IRREGULAR EDGE OF HORN. Circumference measurements must be taken with a steel tape.

D-1-2-3-4. Divide measurement C of LONGER horn by four, mark **BOTH** horns at these quarters even though other horn is shorter, and measure circumference at these marks. Mark quarters by starting from base only. Circumference measurements must be taken with a steel tape.

Photographs: All entries must include photographs of the trophy. A right side, left side and front view photograph is required of the horns. A photograph of the entire animal, preferably at the site of kill, is requested if at all possible.

Drying Period: To be eligible for entry in the Pope & Young Records, a trophy must first have been stored under normal room temperature and humidity for at least 60 days after date of kill. No trophy will be considered which has in any way been altered from its natural state.

THIS SCORING FORM MUST BE ACCOMPANIED BY A SIGNED
POPE & YOUNG FAIR CHASE AFFIDAVIT, 3 PHOTOS OF HORNS, AND A
RECORDING FEE OF $25.00.

POPE & YOUNG CLUB
NORTH AMERICAN BIG GAME TROPHY SCORING FORM
BOWHUNTING
BIG GAME   RECORDS

SHEEP

KIND OF SHEEP

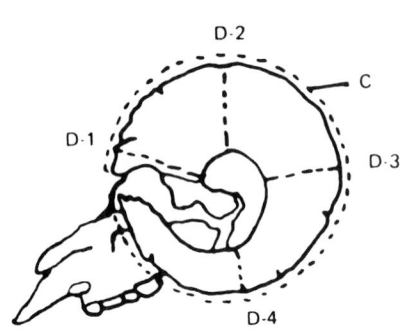

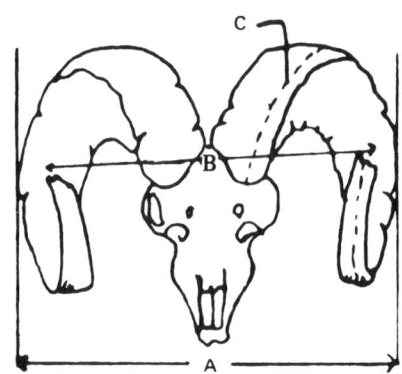

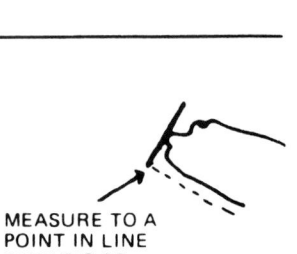

MEASURE TO A
POINT IN LINE
WITH TIP OF
HORN

SEE OTHER SIDE FOR INSTRUCTIONS		Supplementary Data	Column 1	Column 2	Column 3
A.	Greatest Spread (Is often Tip to Tip Spread)		Right Horn	Left Horn	Difference
B.	Tip to Tip Spread (If Greatest Spread, Enter again here)				
C.	Length of Horn				
D-1.	Circumference of Base				
D-2.	Circumference at First Quarter (this measurement taken at _____ inches from base)				
D-3.	Circumference at Second Quarter (this measurement taken at _____ inches from base)				
D-4.	Circumference at Third Quarter (this measurement taken at _____ inches from base)				
TOTALS					

ADD	Column 1		Exact locality where killed	(County)	(State)
	Column 2		Date killed	By whom killed	
TOTAL			Present owner	Phone ( )	
SUBTRACT Column 3			Address		
FINAL SCORE			Guide's Name and Address		
			REMARKS (Mention any abnormalities)		

I certify that I have measured the above trophy on _____ 19_____
at (address)_____ City _____
State _____ Zip Code_____ and that these measurements and data are, to the best
of my knowledge and belief, made in accordance with the instructions given.
Witness:_____ Signature_____
(To Measurer's Signature)

Pope & Young Club Official Measurer

_____

MEASURER (Print)

_____

ADDRESS

_____
CITY   STATE   ZIP

INSTRUCTIONS

Measurements must be made with a flexible steel tape to the nearest one-eighth of an inch. To simplify addition, please enter fractional figures in **eighths.** Official measurements cannot be taken for at least sixty days after the day the animal was killed. **Please submit photographs [see below].**

A. **Greatest Spread** is measured between perpendiculars at right angles to the center line of the skull.

B. **Tip to Tip Spread** is measured between tips of horns.

C. **Length of Horn** measured from lowest point in front on outer curve to a point in line with tip. **DO NOT** press tape into depressions. The low point of the outer curve of the horn is considered to be the low point of the frontal portion of the horn, situated above and slightly medial to the eye socket, (not on the outside edge of the horn). Use a straight edge, perpendicular to horn axis, to end measurement on "broomed" horns.

D-1 Circumferrence of Base measured at right angles to axis of horn. **DO NOT** follow irregular edge of horn. The line of measurement must be entirely on horn material, not the jagged edge often noted.

D-2-3-4 Divide measurement C of **LONGER** horn by four, mark **BOTH** horns at these quarters even though other horn is shorter, and measure circumferences at these marks. Mark quarters by starting from base only.

Photographs: All entries must include photographs of the trophy. A right side, left side and front view photograph is required of the horns. A photograph of the entire animal, preferably at the site of kill, is requested if at all possible.

Drying Period: To be eligible for entry in the Pope & Young Records, a trophy must first have been stored under normal room temperature and humidity for at least 60 days after date of kill. No trophy will be considered which has in any way been altered from its natural state.

THIS SCORING FORM MUST BE ACCOMPANIED BY A SIGNED POPE & YOUNG FAIR CHASE AFFIDAVIT, 3 PHOTOS OF HORNS, AND A RECORDING FEE OF $25.00.

BOWHUNTING

BIG GAME

RECORDS

POPE & YOUNG CLUB
P.O. BOX 548
CHATFIELD, MN 55923

FAIR CHASE AFFIDAVIT

To be entered into the Pope & Young Club Records, the animal must meet the minimum scoring requirements, and must be taken in complete compliance with the controlling game laws and the Rules of Fair Chase. The term "Fair Chase" shall not include the taking of animals under the following conditions:

1. Helpless in a trap, deep snow or water, or on ice.
2. From any power vehicle or power boat.
3. While confined behind fences as on game farms, etc.
4. By "Jacklighting" or shining at night.
5. By the use of any tranquilizers or poisons.
6. By the use of any power vehicles or power boat for herding or driving animals, including use of aircraft to land alongside or to communicate with or direct a hunter on the ground.
7. By the use of electronic devices for attracting, locating or pursuing game, or guiding the hunter to such game, or by the use of a bow or arrow to which any electronic device is attached.
8. Any other condition considered by the Board of Directors as unsportsmanlike.

SPECIAL NOTE: For the purpose of the Pope & Young Club, a bow shall be defined as a longbow, recurve bow or compound bow that is hand-held and hand-drawn, and that has no mechcanical device to enable the hunter to lock the bow at full or partial draw. Other than energy stored by the drawn bow, no device to propel the arrow will be permitted. A letoff of sixty-five (65) percent on a compound bow is the maximum allowed.

SEARCH & RECOVERY: Was the animal recovered on the same day as hit? **YES ☐ NO* ☐**
(check one)

* If "NO", give COMPLETE DETAILS
of recovery on back, **[COMMENTS]**, or on a separate sheet.

Falsification of the Fair Chase Affidavit is grounds for dismissal from the Pope & Young Club. Falsification will cause the entry to be rejected, no future entries accepted and all past entries dropped from the Pope & Young Club records for the individual falsifying the affidavit. In addition to the requirements of this affidavit, by submitting this entry the applicant agrees that the sole decision of acceptance of this entry belongs to the Board of Directors and its discretionary decision is in all respects final.

I,_____attest that my_____
                    (print)   (species)
was taken entirely by the means of BOW & ARROW, and in complete compliance with the controlling game laws and the rules of Fair Chase.

WE THE UNDERSIGNED, DECLARE THAT THE FOREGOING STATEMENTS ARE TRUE TO THE BEST OF OUR KNOWLEDGE AND BELIEF:

_____   _____
              Hunter's Signature   Date

• •

_____   _____
Witness to verification of bow kill, Signature of witness   (please print name)
(Does not have to be Eye Witness)

_____   _____
        Address of witness   City   State   Zip

THIS FORM MUST BE COMPLETELY FILLED OUT!
REVISED MARCH, 1989

Please complete the following form as it relates to the harvest of this trophy. This information is used by the Pope & Young Club to provide an overall view of the nature of hunts for the various North American big game animals for which we maintain records.

1. **SPECIES**_____ **SEX**_____

2. **HUNTER INFORMATION:** Age_____ Sex _____Years of bowhunting experience_____

3. **HUNT INFORMATION:** Guide ☐ ☐ Date of Kill_____,_____,_____
                              yes no   month   day   year

   WEATHER CONDITIONS AT TIME OF KILL: Clear ☐ Cloudy ☐ Rain ☐ Snow ☐ Other_____
   Time_____ a.m. p.m. Temperature_____

4. **DISTANCE OF SHOT:** (if more than one shot, write distance of each arrow in appropriate box)
   #1._____yds. #2._____yds. #3._____yds. #4._____yds.

   For the next four questions, place an X in the space corresponding to each arrow, e.g., if arrow #1 and #3 were both broadside, record your entry as follows: **Broadside**
                                   EXAMPLE   ☒ ☐ ☒ ☐
                                                 1 2 3 4

   ANGLE OF THE SHOT:

	Rear Quartering	Front Quartering	Rear	Front	Above
Broadside					
☐ ☐ ☐ ☐	☐ ☐ ☐ ☐	☐ ☐ ☐ ☐	☐ ☐ ☐ ☐	☐ ☐ ☐ ☐	☐ ☐ ☐ ☐
1 2 3 4	1 2 3 4	1 2 3 4	1 2 3 4	1 2 3 4	1 2 3 4

   WHERE ARROW STRUCK ANIMAL:

Chest	Paunch	Rump	Leg	Head	Other_____
☐ ☐ ☐ ☐	☐ ☐ ☐ ☐	☐ ☐ ☐ ☐	☐ ☐ ☐ ☐	☐ ☐ ☐ ☐	☐ ☐ ☐ ☐
1 2 3 4	1 2 3 4	1 2 3 4	1 2 3 4	1 2 3 4	1 2 3 4

5. **STYLE OF HUNTING:** Bait ☐   Stalk ☐   Still ☐   Tree Stand ☐   Ground Blind ☐   Calling ☐ Dogs ☐
                               (Stalk - spotting animal first then moving in: Still - locating animal by moving)

6. **NUMBER OF MEMBERS** IN YOUR HUNTING PARTY WHEN ANIMAL WAS HARVESTED_____

7. **NUMBER OF DAYS** HUNTING DURING THE SEASON FOR THIS SPECIES_____

8. **NUMBER OF ARROWS** SHOT DURING THE SEASON AT THIS SPECIES_____

9. **NUMBER OF ANIMALS** OF THIS SPECIES SEEN DURING THE SEASON_____

10. **TYPE OF BOW:** Longbow ☐   Recurve ☐   Compound ☐ **% Letoff**_____ Draw Weight_____ lbs.

   TYPE OF QUIVER: Hip ☐ Back ☐ Bow ☐ Other (specify)_____**Quiver size** (number of arrows)_____

   TYPE OF BROADHEAD: Fixed blade (no insert) ☐   Fixed blade (with insert) ☐   Replaceable Blade ☐
   Other_____ **Number of blades**_____

   TYPE OF ARROWS: Wood ☐   Glass ☐   Aluminum ☐   Other (specify)_____ Length_____

11. **COMMENTS:**

The Club's initial awards banquets were in Chicago. A display featuring Del Austin's World Record (non-typical) whitetail, "Mossy Horns," recipient of the first Ishi Award, was the focus of attention at the 1964 gathering (top photo). Another whitetail, Mel Johnson's World Record (typical) "Beanfield Buck," earned the second Ishi Award (above center). The Club's namesakes, Dr. Saxton Pope (left) and Arthur Young (right), are pictured above and on the facing page.

POPE AND YOUNG HISTORY

DURING THE EARLY DAYS of modern bowhunting, much of the public and some state fish and game department personnel had a difficult time accepting the fact that hunting with the bow and arrow was an effective method of harvesting North American big game animals.

It was in these early years that a growing number of determined bowhunters set out to prove their worth to their many skeptics. Not only did these bowhunters have to prove the capability of their equipment, they also had to establish and maintain high ethical standards of sportsmanship and to create a good image in the eyes of a watchful public.

At this time when bowhunters were struggling to earn the respect of other hunters and fish and game departments, while working hard to secure special archery seasons nationwide, a small group of dedicated bow and arrow hunters, led by Glenn St. Charles of Seattle, united to form the Pope and Young Club. Its dual purpose was to record for posterity outstanding specimens of North American big game taken with the hunting bow and to prove the effectiveness of bows and arrows.

An offshoot of the National Field Archery Association's Hunting Activities Committee of the late 1950s, the Club was founded in Washington State in early 1961 and later that same year the first pictoral folder — the forerunner to this record book — containing the P & Y Records was published. An awards banquet, attended by 30 people, was held in Chicago the following January. Incorporation followed in 1963 and a year later some 75 members and guests gathered in Chicago for another awards banquet. The first Ishi Award was presented at this time and the number of registered entries as of 1964 totaled 402. The Club's bylaws were approved in 1966, paving the way for the first election of officers in 1967. The formative years had passed; the Club's future was assured.

From its modest beginning with a mere handful of dedicated individuals, the Pope and Young Club has grown to become recognized and admired worldwide for its philosophy of selective, fair chase hunting and for its strong support of sound wildlife conservation principles. In essence, the Pope and Young Club of today is comprised of thousands of bowhunters who promote the highest ethical bowhunting practices and who maintain a time tested record-keeping system that has established the national standard for trophy class big game. It continues to lead by example as one century ends and another dawns.

Past and Present Club Officers

President
Glenn St. Charles *Dec 1967 - Aug 1972*
Larry Bamford *Aug 1972 - Aug 1975*
George Moerlein *Aug 1975 - Apr 1976*
Jim Dougherty *Apr 1976 - Apr 1984*
G. Fred Asbell *Apr 1984 -*

First Vice President
Fred Bear *Dec 1967 - Aug 1970*
Larry Bamford *Aug 1970 - Aug 1972*
Norm Goodwin *Aug 1972 - Aug 1974*
George Moerlein *Aug 1974 - Aug 1975*
None *Aug 1975 - Apr 1976*
John Culpepper *Apr 1976 - Apr 1978*
Paul Shannon *Apr 1978 - Apr 1980*
Charlie Kroll *Apr 1980 - Apr 1984*
Marvin Clyncke *Apr 1984 - Apr 1988*
Rick Grooms *Apr 1988 - Apr 1989*
M. R. James *Apr 1990 -*

Second Vice President
Dr. Dean Henbest *Dec 1967 - Aug 1970*
Dr. Rex Hancock *Aug 1970 - Aug 1972*
George Moerlein *Aug 1972 - Aug 1974*
Norm Goodwin *Aug 1974 - Apr 1976*
Doug Kittredge *Apr 1976 - Apr 1978*
Charlie Kroll *Apr 1978 - Apr 1980*
Paul Shannon *Apr 1980 - Apr 1982*
Scott Showalter *Apr 1982 - Apr 1984*
(Note: This office was eliminated by a vote of the membership, effective April 1984.)

Third/Second Vice President
Charles A. Young *Jan 1970 - Apr 1980*
Frank "Duke" Prentup *Apr 1980 - Apr 1982*
Rick Grooms *Apr 1982 - Apr 1988*
Glenn Hisey *Apr 1988 - Apr 1990*
Naomi Torrey-Simmons *Apr 1990 - Apr 1992*
Stan Rauch *Apr 1992 -*
(Note: With elimination of the original Second Vice President position in 1984, the 3rd Vice President's office representing the Associate membership was renamed Second Vice President.)

Past and Present Club Officers

Executive Secretary
Charlie Kroll *Dec 1967 - Apr 1969*
Jim Dougherty *Apr 1969 - Jul 1970*
Dick Mauch *Jul 1970 - Aug 1972*
Doug Walker *Aug 1972 - Apr 1974*
Scott Showalter *Apr 1974 - Jan 1975*
Carl M. Hulbert *Jan 1975 - Jun 1976*
Naomi Torrey-Simmons *Jul 1976 - Sep 1989*
Glenn Hisey *Sept 1989 -*

Treasurer
Carl M. Hulbert *Dec 1967 - Jun 1976*
Naomi Torrey-Simmons *Jul 1976 - May 1987*
Donald Ace Morgan *May 1987 -*

Directors
Richard Cooley *Dec 1967 - Aug 1970*
Doug Walker *Dec 1967 - Aug 1970*
G. H. Malinoski *Dec 1967 - Aug 1972*
George Moerlein *Dec 1967 - Aug 1972, Apr 1984 - Mar 1992*
Fred Bear *Aug 1970 - Apr 1978*
Peter Halbig *Aug 1970 - Aug 1974*
Dick Mauch *Aug 1972 - Aug 1976*
Wayne Trimm *Aug 1972 - Apr 1976*
Lowell Eddy, M.D. *Aug 1974 - Apr 1976*
Ray Torrey *Apr 1976 - Oct 1983*
Marvin Clyncke *Apr 1976 - Apr 1984*
Len Cardinale *Apr 1976 - Apr 1978*
G. Fred Asbell *Apr 1978 - Apr 1984*
Frank "Rit" Heller *Apr 1978 - Apr 1990*
Scott Showalter *Apr 1984 - Apr 1988, Apr 1990 -*
Art Kragness *Apr 1984 - Apr 1986*
M. R. James *Apr 1986 - Apr 1990*
Ron Sherer *Apr 1988 -*
Bill Krenz *Apr 1990 -*
Larry Streiff *Apr 1992 -*

Past President Directors
Glenn St. Charles *Aug 1972 - Apr 1975*
George Moerlein *Apr 1976 - Apr 1984*
Jim Dougherty *Apr 1984 -*

Past and Present Club Officers

Records Committee Chairman
Glenn St. Charles *Jan 1961 - Feb 1968*
Dick Mauch *Feb 1968 - Aug 1972*
Doug Walker *Aug 1972 - Apr 1974*
Scott Showalter *Apr 1974 - Dec 1980*
Ray Torrey *Jan 1981 - Oct 1983*
C. Randall Byers *Nov 1983 -*

Membership Chairman
Dr. Dean Henbest *Dec 1967 - May 1969*
Larry Bamford *May 1969 - Sept 1972*
Scott Showalter *Sep 1972 - Jan 1975*
Harv Ebers *Jan 1975 -*

Conservation Committee Chairman
Dr. Lowell Eddy *Feb 1975 - Apr 1976*
Wayne Trimm *Feb 1975 - Apr 1976*
Charlie Kroll *Mar 1977 - Apr 1989*
Dr. Dave Samuel *Apr 1989 -*
(Board Position Mar 1992)

*C*irca 1972 Pope and Young Club Officers. Front row: Chuck Young, Larry Bamford, Glenn St. Charles, George Moerlein. Second row: Dick Mauch, Fred Bear, Doug Walker, Carl Hulbert, Norm Goodwin.

POPE & YOUNG CLUB
Official Measurers

ALABAMA
Dennis Campbell, Adamsville
David L. Crockett, Birmingham
Keith Guyse, Elmore
Dr. G. Merrill Jones, Huntsville
Rett Kelly, Wetumpka
Douglas Schofield, Montgomery
T. H. Tanner, Semmes
James Thornhill, Sr., Montgomery
Eugene Widder, Jackson
Stephen Joe Zolczynski, Spanish Fort

ALASKA
Bob Boutang, Fairbanks
Carl E. Brent, Kotzebue
Ronald L. Deis, Anchorage
Wayne DiSarro, Willow
Ralph Ertz, Anchorage
Dennis Goldbach, Fairbanks
George Hronkin, Glennallen
Dennis Lattery, Eagle River
George Moerlein, Anchorage
Don Nickel, Kenai
Don Poole, Soldotna
Edward Russell, Anchorage
Ted H. Spraker, Soldotna
David Widby, Anchorage

ARIZONA
Marty Allred, Safford
George Steven Blackett, Mesa
Rodger L. Bruce, Phoenix
Jerry A. Clarno, Tucson
Michael Cupell, Glendale
Thomas Dalrymple, Tucson
Jimmie Engelmann, Tucson
Joseph Foglemann, Laveen
Jay Gates III, Kingman
James C. Scott, Tucson
Richard Tone, Gilbert
David Wolf, Flagstaff

ARKANSAS
Cliff Beaver, Compton
Michael E. Cartwright, Calico Rock
James DeSpain, Manila
Dave Ensminger, Little Rock
Jack Johnson, Dierks
Joseph W. Moody, Lonoke
Doyle Shook, Jr., Little Rock
Carl Turpin, Clarksville
Craig Uyeda, Little Rock

CALIFORNIA
Michael J. Bradeen, Grass Valley
Rocky Chisholm, Orange
Jim Cox, Salinas
South Cox, Windsor
Ronald Crouch, Visalia
Robert Dawson, Bonita
Paul Farina, Santa Clara
Robert Frost, Lincoln
Scott Hargrove, Camarillo
Gary Hoffer, Madera
Guy Hooper, Eureka
Ronald Hopkins, Garden Grove
Jack Kenyon, San Bruno
Gary Maytum, Palmdale
Jerry Maytum, Palmdale
Robert C. Solimena, Concord
Naomi Simmons, Grizzly Flats
Deborah Tellez, Pleasanton
Doug Walker, Squaw Valley
Clifford White, Paradise
Rodney York, North Fork

COLORADO
Frank Alameno, Rifle
G. Fred Asbell, Longmont
Bob Black, Grand Junction
Ronald Breitsprecher, Fort Collins
Hal Burdick, Colorado Springs
Marvin Clyncke, Boulder
Judd Cooney, Pagosa Springs
Gary Day, Greeley
Paul Dickson, Ft. Collins
James Finn, Bayfield
Bill Goosman, Meeker
Dr. Nicholas J. Gray, Clifton
Jack Jonas, Denver
Lee Kline, Loveland
Bill Marchand, Grand Junction
Doug McCauley, Olathe
Michael B. Moline, Broomfield
Glenn W. Pritchard, Craig
Ronald Rockwell, Aurora
Barry J. Smith, Hot Sulphur Springs
Ronald Sniff, Pueblo
Gregg Stults, Wray
Leo R. Suazo II, Littleton
John Jay Verzuh, Grand Junction
Don Waechtler, Glenwood Springs
Ed Wiseman, Moffat

CONNECTICUT
Barry Rich, Vernon
Bernard Sippin, Monroe
Gary Vincent, Plainville

DELAWARE
William Jones, Dover
Kenneth Reynolds, Dover

FLORIDA
Timothy Breault, Panama City
David Collis, Bradenton
Donald Lee Francis, Tallahassee
William Frankenberger, High Springs
Stanley Kirkland, Lynn Haven
Charles Kroll, Gainesville
Phil Palmer, Havana

GEORGIA
David M. Carlock, Gainesville
William Cooper, Tifton
Oscar Dewberry, Bainbridge
Dave Grabow, Kennesaw
R. Larry Marchinton, Athens
Dan Marshall, Thomson
Bob Monroe, Sapelo Island

Richard Whittington, Fort Valley

HAWAII
W. T. Yoshimoto, Honolulu

IDAHO
John Anderson, Boise
Roger Atwood, Rexburg
Steven Atwood, Arco
C. Randall Byers, Moscow
Christian Chaffin, Boise
Phil Cooper, Pocatello
Larry Cross, Preston
Larry Hlavaty, Soda Springs
Frank Hough, McCammon
Dr. Brad L. Johnson, Lewiston
Stanley Leake, Bayview
Michael Lewis, Fruitland
Matt March, Jr., Eagle
Harvey J. McNeel, Coeur d'Alene
Gary R. "Sam" McNeill, Lewiston
Kenneth E. Ruzicka, Mountain Home
Michael Schlegel, McCall
Ronald Sherer, Eagle
Tad Sherman, Boise
Randy Stephens, Soda Springs
Roger Stewart, Post Falls
William Vanderhoef, Boise

ILLINOIS
Fred W. Achilles, Oswego
Thomas Beissel, Oregon
Patrick Cebuhar, Canton
Richard Dewey, Pleasant Hill
Robert Erb, Rockford
Dwayne R. Etter, Macomb
Bert W. Everett, Jr., Hillsboro
Jared K. Garver, Jonesboro
Robert A. Gorge, Elk Grove Village
Keith J. Graham, Carlinville
Larry D. Grant, Godfrey
Art Heinze, Rock Falls
Melvin Johnson, Metamora
Mike Kistler, Brownstown
Michael Kottkamp, Irvington
John Kube, Petersburg
Thomas Micetich, Olney
Kenneth D. Neal, Paris
Mark E. Pittman, Danville
Gary Rogers, Highland Park
Glen Sanderson, Champaign
Carl Spaeth, Zion
J. James Stewart III, Hebron
Joseph Burke Sullivan, Timewell
Steven R. Tice, Rochester
Jeffrey VerSteeg, Springfield

Kevin Edward Weeks, Grafton
Gary L. Wilford, Westville
Steven Wolff, South Holland

INDIANA
William Bean, Winamac
John Bogucki, North Liberty
Jon L. Bronnenberg, Warren
Don Castrup, Newburgh
Donald L. Clark, Angola
Philip Hawkins, Franklin
Paul Bradley Herndon, Brownstown
Arthur Kragness, Merrillville
Larry Lawson, Anderson
Mike Mounts, Owensville
Gregory Raatz, Fremont
Thomas Rothrock, Terre Haute

IOWA
Duane C. Baumler, Decorah
Larry Briney, Cedar Rapids
Douglas Clayton, Council Bluffs
Paul "Buck" Farni, Durango
Robert Filbrandt, Dows
Kevin Freymiller, Des Moines
Lee Gladfelter, Boone
Rick Grooms, Bloomfield
Guy Hempey, Sioux City
Ronald Howing, Wallingford
William Lee Knight, Plano
Stephen James Manary, Iowa City
Michael McKenna, Salix
Joseph Meder, Solon
Thomas Oldfather, Elk Run Heights
David Schrody, DDS, Clinton
Thomas L. Tucker, Knoxville
Ervin Wagner, Des Moines
LaVerne Woock, Shell Rock

KANSAS
Tommie Berger, Dodge City
Tom Bowman, Wakefield
Michael Gilbert, Garden City
Jim Hays, Ellsworth
Wally Hayward, Jr., Kansas City
Bill Hlavachick, Pratt
Leonard Hopper, Gem
Gary Hunsicker, Topeka
Raymond A. Kirk, Meriden
Ronald Little, Hutchinson
Michael McFadden, Lawrence
Gerald J. McKinney, Parsons
Kent Montei, Pratt
Tom Mosher, Emporia
Todd Murray, Partridge
David Rogers, El Dorado

Maloy Rollins, Winfield
Keith Sexson, Emporia
Scott Showalter, Garden City
Michael Sohm, Otis
Steven G. Sorensen, Valley Center
Odie Sudbeck, Seneca
Tom Swan, Mound City
Charles Swank, Great Bend
Larry Thomas, Baxter Springs
Marvin D. Whitehead, Fredonia
Daniel Willems, Windom
Greg Wright, Wichita

KENTUCKY
Roy Wayne Biddle, Falmouth
Joseph Bland, Finchville
Karl W. Brantley, Marion
Eugene Culver, New Haven
David D. Haley, Elkton
Robert L. Hegge, Jr., Williamstown
Gregory Ison, Cornettsville
John Phillips, Williamstown
Michael Roberts, Bagdad
Larry Ross, Elkton
Dale Weddle, Nancy
Charles Wilkins, La Center

LOUISIANA
J. W. Farrar, Monroe
Joe Herring, Baton Rouge
Robert Kimble, Minden
David Moreland, Baton Rouge
Tommy L. Ramage, Bastrop
Kerney Sonnier, Opelousas
Reggie Wycoff, Ferriday

MAINE
Jean Arsenault, Rumford
Don Cote, Eustis
Terrence H. Estes, Winslow
Harvey L. Libby, Gorham
Edgar Simonton, Union

MARYLAND
Gyongyver "Kitty" Beuchert,
Hughesville
Robert Beyer, Mt. Airy
Richard O. Cook, Bel Air
Hillard Hayzlett, Hagerstown
Edwin Obrecht, Jr., Owings Mills
Al Sullivan, Dunkirk
H. W. Voigt, College Park
Paul Wigfield, Salisbury

MASSACHUSETTS
Richard Christoforo, Revere

Roy Goodwin, Northbridge
Richard LaBlue, Adams
David J. Lamoreaux, North Oxford
John Rovedo, Bellingham
Richard Scorzafava, Granville

MICHIGAN
Wayne H. Andersen, Ludington
Gary Bandrow, Sterling Heights
Gary C. Berger, Houghton Lake
Bob Bouck, Rock
Clarence Bowers, Jr., Albion
Cameron Cogsdill, Milford
James Dean, Williamsburg
Ned Fogle, Lansing
James Howard Hammill, Crystal Falls
Julie M. Hammill, Crystal Falls
LeRoy L. Hansen, Greenville
Larry Hayes, Delton
Leland Holbrook, Petoskey
Lewis Johnson, Grayling
Raymond J. Kastura, Saginaw
Lyle C. Kelley, Drummond Island
Dan M. LaRose, Bloomfield Hills
Jack Menges, Three Rivers
Tony Naismith, Swartz Creek
Joseph Newmyer, Walled Lake
Thomas A. O'Brien, Dryden
John Olmer, Yale
Frank Rinella, Twin Lake
Larry Robinson, Lupton
Mitch Rompola, Traverse
Harry W. Squibb, Grand Ledge
Joseph L. Vincent, Fenton
David J. Wellman, Bark River
John Wencley, Metamora
Glenn Williams, Dearborn

MINNESOTA
Dr. Eugene Altiere, Duluth
Darwin Arndt, Madelia
Chuck Bailey, Luverne
H. Neil Becker, Plymouth
David Boland, Chatfield
David Brandenburger, Dayton
Ron Carlson, Mahtomedi
Ronald D. Court, Rice
Rodney Dehart, International Falls
Keith David Edberg, Forest Lake
James M. Eidson, Owatonna
James Gorden, Deer River
Glenn E. Hisey, Chatfield
Kevin Hisey, Chatfield
Douglas E. Huderle, East Grand Forks
Floyd B. Johnson, Alvarado
Willie Johnson, Oslo

Ronald Kienholz, Dilworth
Curtis Kozitka, Detroit Lakes
Sharon Larsen, Arden Hills
Ron Mackedanz, Kandiyohi
Thomas E. Miller, Kilkenny
Craig R. Pierce, Lewiston
Dean Reidt, Cottage Grove
Larry Streiff, Rochester
Dean Westby, Plymouth

MISSISSIPPI
Randy Breland, Avon
Larry Castle, Kilmichael
Dan Cotton, Macon
J. Dale Hale, Isola
Don Lewis, Brookhaven
Jim McCrory, Greenwood
Bobby Wilson, Smithville

MISSOURI
Larry Abraham, Nevada
Charles Dwayne Allen, Neosho
Don Barnes, Hannibal
Marc Bowen, Blue Springs
Jim Braithwait, Williamsburg
John Detjen, Frankfort
Dale Dortch, Ozark
Jim Fitzgerald, New Boston
Roy Grimes, St. Charles
Roger Hensley, Nevada
Randall Herberg, Glencoe
James Holdenried, Jr., St. Louis
Daniel L. Johnson, Blue Springs
Bill Kohne, Sullivan
Martin Marks, Meadville
Joe Ed McCray, Fulton
Anthony Mihalevich, Kirksville
Charles A. Myers, Greenfield
Kenneth R. Perry, Holts Summit
Wayne Porath, Columbia
Jim Pyland, Kansas City
Joe Ream, Unionville
Dale H. Ream, Jr., Unionville
Donald Roper, Farmington
John Schulz, Columbia
Carl Schwarz, St. Louis
Paul Schwarz, St. Louis
Gerald Wayne Webber, Unionville

MONTANA
Jerry Brown, Libby
R. Bruce Campbell, Lakeside
Kevin Charles Conners, Belgrade
James Cross, Kalispell
G. L. "Buck" Damone, Lewistown
Neal Davis, Dillon

Mark George DeLong, Billings
Frank H. Dodge, Jr., Hamilton
Bryan J. Erickson, Glasgow
John Fleharty, Lewistown
Dwayne C. Garner, Missoula
Bernie Hildebrand, Miles City
M. R. James, Kalispell
Fred King, Bozeman
Scott Koelzer, Three Forks
James Liebelt, Fort Peck
Vern Lindquist, Glendive
John Morris, II, Bozeman
Stan Rauch, Victor
Jack Reneau, Missoula
Robert Savage, Bozeman
Mark Schwartznau, Huson
David Sorensen, Harlowton
Graham S. Taylor, Great Falls
Dr. Barry Wensel, Whitefish
Dr. C. Gene Wensel, Stevensville
Philip Wright, Missoula
Vincent Yannone, Clancy
Harley Yeager, Simms
Lewis Yearout, Great Falls

NEBRASKA
Thomas E. Day, Omaha
Daniel E. Evasco, Beatrice
Donald Goracke, Burr
Denny C. Graham, Holdrege
Lee Hansen, Superior
David J. Hinton, North Platte
Jack Joseph, Valentine
Richard Mauch, Bassett
Donald Ace Morgan, Kearney
Russell A. Mort, Nebraska City
George Nason, North Platte
James Newman, Fremont
Dan Rochford, North Platte
Harvey Suetsugu, Alliance
Bruce Trindle, Norfolk
Bradley L. Wiese, Benkelman
Steve Woitaszewski, Lincoln

NEVADA
Fred Church, Reno
Chris J. Coleman, Carson City
Gilbert Hernandez, Elko
Paul Podborny, Ely
David Snyder, Las Vegas
Dennis Spawn, Las Vegas
Gregg Tanner, Fallon
George Tsukamoto, Sparks
Mike Wickersham, Las Vegas

NEW HAMPSHIRE
Kevin M. Bowles, Fremont
William Earle, Portsmouth
Reginald Moore, Keene

NEW JERSEY
Emanuele J. Barone, Kinnelon
David Burke, Egg Harbor
Len Cardinale, Belleville
David Chanda, Long Valley
Daniel M. Ferrigno, Atlantic City
John Janelli, Union City
Cindy Kuenstner, Robbinsville
Robert Lund, Belvidere
James McCloskey, Jr., Lawrenceville
Susan Predl, Hampton
Richard Santomauro, Wall
Fred Snyder, Sicklerville

NEW MEXICO
Douglas J. Aikin, Los Alamos
R. Grant Clawson, Ramah
Roy Cogburn, Jr., Albuquerque
Tom David, Albuquerque
Dan P. Fleming, Bosque Farms
Volney Howard, Jr., Las Cruces
Ronald W. Madsen, Albuquerque
Steven G. Richards, Alamogordo
Terry Sanders, Albuquerque
Lynn Saxon, Hobbs
Patrick J. Sharp, Gallup
Bob Stevens, Farmington
George L. Taulman, Taos
James S. Willems, Farmington

NEW YORK
David Baldwin, Patchogue
John Borlang, Hudson Falls
Merritt Compton, Trumansburg
Brian Dam, Vernon
Bob Estes, Caledonia
Nelson Harrington, Delmar
Donald W. Hunt, Nichols
Collins Kellogg, Croghan
Richard Kent, Farmingville
Phil Liddle, Schoharie
John McAteer, Manorville
Carl Pepi, Mt. Vernon
Bob A. Sandwick, Saranac Lake
Peter Synyard, Farmington
Jon P. Thomas, Staten Island
Robert L. Turk, Silver Creek
Victor Zarnock, Pearl River

NORTH CAROLINA
Denton O. Baumbarger, Burlington

Ramon Bell, Stokesdale
Jim Edwards, Colerain
Harlan T. Hall, Burlington
Donald A. Hayes, State Road
J. Scott Osborne, Sanford
Michael H. Seamster, Providence
Terry Sharpe, Hamlet
David Eugene Stepp, Hendersonville

NORTH DAKOTA
Warren Buss, Fargo
Wes Cumings, Garrison
Dane Eider, Bismarck
Tim Finley, Oberon
Scott Lang, Bismarck
James McKenzie, Mandan
John Plesuk, Minot
Craig Richardson, Williston
Paul Shannon, Bismarck
Cecil I. Tharp, Williston

OHIO
George W. Bauer, West Union
Dana Booghier, Springfield
Mark Buehrer, Leipsic
Barry Cooper, Galena
David M. Couch, Russellville
Lloyd Culbertson, New Marshfield
Roger Davis, Newbury
Mike Dickess, Ironton
Jack E. Henderson, Barnesville
Tom Hentrick, Kettering
Thomas L. Hughes, Chillicothe
Harold L. Knowlton, Mansfield
William Lee, Jr., Kettering
Jeffrey McKnight, Waterville
Richard Meier, Columbus
Gerald E. Meyer, Millfield
George R. Mitchell, Urbana
Mike Moutoux, Killbuck
John Myers, Toledo
Ronald Perrine, Sr., Xenia
Mike Serio, Cincinnati
Elbert Todd, Cambridge
Thomas Wagner, Bryan
James R. Williamson, Richmond

OKLAHOMA
Jontie W. Aldrich, Coweta
Deveral Bridges, Chandler
Donald E. Campbell, Ponca City
Sonny Charboneau, Wagoner
Tracy L. Daniel, Ponca City
Jim Dougherty, Tulsa
James Edwards, Stonewall
Wade A. Free, Forgan

Richard T. Hatcher, Edmond
Richard Hoar, Broken Arrow
David Jilge, Prague
Eric Kitchell, Pond Creek
Ron Masters, Stillwater
Randy Rains, Stillwater
Steven A. Schmid, Tulsa
Rod Smith, Duncan
Dawn Tomlins, Norman

OREGON
Glenn W. Abbott, Sandy
Robert Bouret, Portland
Eldon "Buck" Buckner, Baker City
Terry Constable, Gresham
Ben R. Cook, Troutdale
Elvin Hawkins, Medford
Larry Jones, Springfield
Charles Lynde, Clackamas
Gary Madison, Prineville
Dale Marcy, Medford
Stanley Miles, Corvallis
Donald Rajnus, Malin
Charles Sarrett, LaGrande
Eugene Smith, Jr., Joseph
John Stone, Lebanon
Thomas Tipton, Roseburg

PENNSYLVANIA
Thomas P. Bartholomew, Greenville
George H. Block, Eighty Four
Glenn L. Bowers, Dillsburg
Timothy O. Bowers, Dillsburg
Randy R. Caspersen, Glenmore
Edward T. Clark, Austin
Kelly Cooper, Picture Rocks
Ed Defibaugh, Venus
Albert C. Dewald, Grove City
Gregory D. Dodson, Langhorne
Phillip Durr, McKees Rocks
Carl Graybill, Jr., Harrisburg
Darrell W. Grove, Norwood
Michael J. Hardison, Uniontown
Frank "Rit" Heller, Reading
Steven Homyack, Jr., DMD, Reinholds
Dennis E. Jones, Ligonier
Perry G. Klein, Ridgway
Charles Kohler, Butler
Timothy A. Marks, Milroy
Barry K. Moore, Ligonier
William Nordby, Rural Valley
Mark Parker, Selinsgrove
Harry E. Richards, New Florence
Michael W. Schmit, Fleetwood
Jacob F. Serfass, Jr., Gouldsboro
Thomas Slusser, Bloomsburg

Roland J. Trombetto, New Enterprise
Lorraine Yocum, Oil City

SOUTH CAROLINA
David Baumann, Bonneau
Robert Gooding, Greenwood

SOUTH DAKOTA
Paul Anderson, Crooks
Jerry Curry, Rapid City
Robert A. Fraser, Brandon
Larry Fredrickson, Chamberlain
A. Dean Gretschmann, Pierre
Eldon Hagen, Sioux Falls
Danny Havens, Lead
Roger Heupel, Aberdeen
Thomas Kuck, Aberdeen
R. Craig Oberle, Mellette
Ron Pesek, Yankton
Arthur H. Richardson, Custer
Joseph John Rieger, Aberdeen
Paul Sieg, Watertown

TENNESSEE
Lewis "Buddy" Adkisson, Talbott
Norman Bates, Thompson's Station
Clarence Coffey, Crossville
Tom Grimsley, Jackson
Larry Marcum, Nashville
Robert McGuire, Johnson City
Thomas Pinkston, Cordova
Robert Ripley, Talbott

TEXAS
Viron Barbay, Lufkin
Earle Bateman III, Fischer
Joseph W. Carroll, Katy
Randolph Coleman, San Antonio
Ronald Collier, Austin
James Paul Ellis, Midland
Edwin Foreman, Orangefield
Eugene R. Fuchs, Ingram
Earl Griffith, Marble Falls
Mickey W. Hellickson, Carrizo Springs
Douglas R. Johnson, Lubbock
James Lewis, Cedar Hill
David H. Lott, Jr., Dallas
T. A. Low IV, Brenham
James H. Miller, Canadian
A. M. Oakes, Jr., Conroe
Dean Oatman, Adkins
Robert L. Oliver, Abilene
Glenn A. Parker, Houston
Ronnie Parsons, Lubbock
Mike Ramage, Spur
Suzan Ramage, Spur

Randal A. Reeves, Spring
Ray Roussett, Jr., Huntsville
Garth Stokes, Texarkana
Ed Strayhorn, Austin
Robert D. Sweisthal, Spring
Dane Widner, Odessa
Ken Witt, Burleson

UTAH
Dave Baierline, West Valley
William Bradwisch, Farmington
Bruce Carlisle, Orem
Todd Scott Hinkins, Orangeville
Merlin Killpack, Ogden
Bill Krenz, Sandy
Kenny Leo, Price
H. Wayne Ludington, Helper
Jerry Mason, Brigham City
David B. Nielsen, American Fork
Robert S. Price, St. George
Brad W. Robinson, Enoch
Dennis Shirley, Elk Ridge

VERMONT
Ronald L. Boucher, Wallingford
Karl J. Gunzer, Jr., Pawlet
Thomas Mohan, Brandon

VIRGINIA
Robert Byrne, Haymarket
Stephen Capel, Powhatan
Max Carpenter, Dayton
William MacCarty III, MD, South
Boston
Robert H. Mayer, Petersburg
William Harold Nesbitt, Woodbridge
Dennis Scott, Hopewell
C. D. Tarter, Wytheville
Mack Walls, Marion

WASHINGTON
Rob Allen, Bellevue
Larry R. Carey, Spokane
Mike Casey, Puyallup
Barbara Cook, Bremerton
John Cook III, North Bend
Dean H. Cook, Jr., Bremerton
Lance B. Cussons, Yakima
Jack Davis, Mt. Vernon
Donne Durst, Port Orchard
John Durst, Port Orchard
Gerald Egbert, Vancouver
Mark Allen Frame, Belfair
Toni J. Hage, Bremerton
Toby Hart, Hoquiam
Larry Jensen, Maple Valley

Rick Kobel, Enumclaw
Henry T. Kohler, Spokane
Kevin C. Krause, Port Orchard
Larry C. Lack, Sequim
Arlen Lipper, Dupont
Gail Martin, Walla Walla
Robert Mayton, Aberdeen
Greg McTee, Snohomish
Rick Morgan, Seattle
Jack Schwabland, Seattle
Michael Shane, Spokane
Charles B. Smith, Kettle Falls
Russ Spaulding, Forks
Glenn St. Charles, Seattle
Jay St. Charles, Kent
Karen St. Charles, Kent
Robert Trask, Silverdale
Wayne Van Zwoll, Bridgeport
Tim J. Wiggins, Auburn

WEST VIRGINIA
Thomas Allen, Elkins
Larry Berry, MacArthur
Greg Bonecutter, Sr., Letart
John D. Edman, Washington
James Evans, Fairmont
Jim Farren, Malden
Allan C. Glasscock, Petersburg
James Hill, Parkersburg
Ray W. Knotts, French Creek

WISCONSIN
Steven Ashley, Hudson
Patrick Barwick, West Allis
Dave Bathke, Franklin
Michael Beaufeaux, Rhinelander
Thomas Bloomingdale, Mequon
Jim Carrig, Limeridge
Richard A. Case, Ontario
Jack Cook, Mondovi
Craig Cousins, Milltown
John F. Davis, Minocqua
Gregory A. Fish, Pepin
Donald Fisher, Eastman
Clark Gallup, Stoddard
Thomas M. Gehl, Racine
Stan Godfrey, Whitewater
William Grosskreutz, Greenbush
Larrie Hazen, Mt. Hope
Jim Hjort, Eau Claire
Craig Hollman, Abbotsford
J. Robert Hults, Germantown
Lester Jass, Janesville
Michael J. Kaufmann, Birnamwood
Arlyn Loomans, Rhinelander
Terry A. G. Moline, Eau Claire

James Nikolopoulos, Milwaukee
Jim Nowakowski, Marinette
David O'Brien, Dresser
Thomas Orlikowski, Stevens Point
Robert L. Pagel, Marion
Michael Piaskowski, Green Bay
Ken J. Rimer, Hudson
John Romans, New Berlin
Curtis J. Rotering, Waumandee
Bruce Scheehle, Milton
Richard Schreiber, Portage
Maynard Schultz, Hudson
Steve Sirianni, Wausau
Dick Strait, Siren
Brian Tessmann, Waukesha
Walter White, Cable

WYOMING
Chuck Anderson, Jr., Laramie
Mike Barrett, Dayton
Jerry R. Bowen, Wheatland
Steve Brockmann, Cheyenne
Mark Chapman, Rock Springs
Gary Cole, Newcastle
Lonny L. Curtis, Baggs
Keith Dana, Rock Springs
Vic Dana, Green River
Robert H. Hanson, Cody
George Johnson, Buffalo
G. Richard "Dick" Keeney, Casper
Pat McAteer, Casper
Lyle Prell, Story
Ronell Skinner, Bedford
Reg Smith, Clearmont
James C. Vance, Cheyenne
George K. Warner, Sheridan
James Willcox, Rawlins

CANADA

ALBERTA
David Coupland, Calgary
Albert England, Lloydminster
Brian Fode, Bow Island
John Graham, Edmonton
Duane Hicks, Edmonton
Gunter Lemke, Calgary
Duane Nelson, Glenwood
Dave Richardson, Calgary
Steve K. Swinhoe, Fort McMurray
Ryk Visscher, Edmonton
Brent Watson, Grande Prairie

BRITISH COLUMBIA
Gordon Calam, Comox
Douglas Clinkenbeard, Smithers
Bill Dear, Nelson
Bob Dunlop, Prince George
Robert Frew, Montrose
Peter Halbig, 100 Mile House
Larry Henriet, Sparwood
William G. Hills, Cranbrook
Peter Martinson, Terrace
Robert Petrie, Kamloops
John J. Rodeman, Victoria
Ken Scheer, Abbotsford

MANITOBA
Delmar Bamford, Foxwarren
Randall Joseph Bean, Winnipeg
Vince Chrichton, Winnipeg
Dwain Davies, Dauphin
L. Greg Fehr, Gladstone
Ronald Larche, Winnipeg
Gil Rodger, Brandon
Chris Switzer, Swan River
Eugene Syrotiuk, Moosehorn

NEW BRUNSWICK
Mike Bowling, Saint John
William G. Hanson, Westfield
Danny C. Mott, Saint John

NEWFOUNDLAND
W. Charles Banfield, Deer Lake
Gerard R. Beaulien, Deer Lake
Larry A. Smith, Stephenville

NOVA SCOTIA
Allan Joseph Gallant, Mt. Uniacke
Walter L. Hingley, Halifax

ONTARIO
David T. Beaudry, Ear Falls
Carl Doerner, Waterloo
Ronald Patrick Frank, Capreol
Rolly Hasner, Sudbury
John W. Horner, Gloucester
Fred Law, Cambridge
Jack Leggo, Inglewood
Don J. McVittie, Huntsville
Richard M. Poulin, Nepean
Fred Robinson, Callander
Ian Robinson, Thunder Bay
Herb Scherer, Sault Ste. Marie
Darrel Sidney, Dryden

QUEBEC
Guy Maurice Algier, St. Sabine

Alex Davidson, Sawyerville
Michel Jerome, La Sarre

SASKATCHEWAN
Howard Hanson, Mankota
Allan Hill, Moose Jaw
John Kuzma, Norquay
Wayne Leonhardt, Saskatoon
Archie Lovelace, Pilot Butte
Frank Mosley, Estevan

MEXICO

Jose Trevino, Chihuahua

EUROPE

Pascal Perrin, Paris

FISH AND GAME DEPARTMENTS

Alabama Department of Game and Fish
64 North Union Street
Montgomery, AL 36130
(205) 261-3486

Alaska Department of Fish and Game
P. O. Box 3-2000
Juneau, AK 99802
(907) 465-4100

Arizona Game and Fish Department
2222 West Greenway Road
Phoenix, AZ 85023
(602) 789-3350

Arkansas Game and Fish Commission
2 Natural Resources Drive
Little Rock, AR 72205
(501) 223-6300

California Department of Fish and Game
1416 Ninth Street
Sacramento, CA 95814
(916) 445-3531

Colorado Department of Natural Resources
1313 Sherman, Room 718
Denver, CO 80203
(303) 866-3311

Connecticut Department of Environmental Protection
165 Capitol Avenue
Hartford, CT 06106
(203) 566-5599

Delaware Division of Fish and Wildlife
P. O. Box 1401
Dover, DE 19903
(302) 736-4431

Florida Game and Freshwater Fish Commission
620 South Meridan Street
Tallahassee, FL 32399
(904) 488-1960

Georgia Department of Natural Resources
205 Butler Street
Atlanta, GA 30334
(404) 656-4994

Hawaii Division of Aquatic Resources
Room 325, 1151 Punchbowl Street
Honolulu, HI 96813
(808) 548-4000

Idaho Fish and Game Department
600 South Walnut Street
P. O. Box 25
Boise, ID 83703
(208) 334-3700

Illinois Department of Conservation
524 South Second Street
Springfield, IL 62701
(217) 782-6302

Indiana Division of Fish and Wildlife
607 State Office Building
Indianapolis, IN 46204
(317) 232-4080

Iowa Department of Natural Resources
Wallace State Office Building
East Ninth and Grand Avenue
Des Moines, IA 50319
(515) 281-5145

Kansas Fish and Game Commission
RR 2, Box 54A
Pratt, KS 67124
(316) 672-5911

Kentucky Department of Fish and Wildlife
1 Game Farm Road
Frankfort, KY 40601
(502) 564-3400

Louisiana Department of Wildlife and Fisheries
P. O. Box 98000
Baton Rouge, LA 70898
(504) 765-2800

Maine Department of Inland Fisheries and Wildlife
284 State Street, Station 41
Augusta, ME 04333
(207) 289-2766

Maryland Department of Natural Resources
Tawes State Office Building
580 Taylor Avenue
Annapolis, MD 21401
(301) 974-3990

Massachusetts Department of Fisheries and Wildlife
100 Cambridge Street
Boston, MA 02202
(617) 727-3151

Michigan Department of Fisheries and Wildlife
P. O. Box 30028
Lansing, MI 48909
(517) 373-1220

Minnesota Department of Natural Resources
Division of Fish and Wildlife
500 Lafayette Road
St. Paul, MN 55155
(612) 296-6157

Mississippi Department of Wildlife Conservation
P. O. Box 451
Jackson, MS 39205
(601) 362-9212

Missouri Department of Conservation
P. O. Box 180
Jefferson City, MO 65102
(314) 751-4115

Montana Department of Fish and Wildlife
1420 East Sixth
Helena, MT 59620
(406) 444-2535

Nebraska Game and Parks Commission
2200 North 33rd Street
P. O. Box 30370
Lincoln, NE 68503
(402) 464-0641

Nevada Department of Wildlife
P. O. Box 10678
Reno, NV 89520
(702) 89520
(702) 789-0500

New Hampshire Fish and Game Department
2 Hazen Drive

Concord, NH 03301
(603) 271-3421

New Jersey Division of Fish, Game and Wildlife
401 East State Street CN402
Trenton, NJ 08625
(609) 292-2695

New Mexico Game and Fish Department
Villagra Building, Box 25112
Santa Fe, NM 87504
(505) 827-7899

New York Department of Fish and Wildlife
50 Wolf Road
Albany, NY 12233
(518) 457-5690

North Carolina Wildlife Resources Commission
Archdale Bldg., 512 North Salisbury Street
Raleigh, NC 27611
(919) 733-3391

North Dakota State Game and Fish Department
100 North Bismarck Expressway
Bismarck, ND 58501
(701) 221-6300

Ohio Department of Natural Resources
Division of Wildlife
Fountain Square
Columbus, OH 43224
(614) 265-6565

Oklahoma Department of Wildlife Conservation
Game Division
1801 North Lincoln
Oklahoma City, OK 73152
(405) 521-3851

Oregon Department of Fish and Wildlife
P. O. Box 59
Portland, OR 97207
(502) 299-5551

Pennsylvania Game Commission
2001 Elmerton Avenue
Harrisburg, PA 17110
(717) 787-4250

Rhode Island Department of Environmental
Management
22 Hayes Street
Providence, RI 02908
(401) 277-2774

South Carolina Wildlife and Marine Resources
Department
Rembert C. Dennis Building
P. O. Box 167
Columbia, SC 29202
(803) 734-3888

South Dakota Game, Fish and Parks
445 East Capitol
Pierre, SD 57501
(605) 773-3485

Tennessee Wildlife Resources Agency
Ellington Agricultural Center
P. O. Box 40747
Nashville, TN 37204
(615) 781-6500

Texas Parks and Wildlife Department
4200 Smith School Road
Austin, TX 78744
(512) 389-4800

Utah Department of Natural Resources
1596 West North Temple
Salt Lake City, UT 84116
(801) 538-4700

Vermont Fish and Wildlife Department
103 South Main Street
Waterbury Complex
Waterbury, VT 05676
(802) 244-7331

Virginia Department of Game and Inland Fisheries
4010 South Broad Street
P. O. Box 11104
Richmond, VA 23230
(804) 367-1000

Washington Department of Wildlife
600 Capitol Way North
Olympia, WA 98501
(206) 753-5700

West Virginia Department of Natural Resources
1900 Kanawha Blvd. East
Charleston, WV 25305
(304) 348-2754

Wisconsin Department of Natural Resources
P. O. Box 7921
Madison, WI 53707
(608) 266-2621

Wyoming Game and Fish Department

5400 Bishop Blvd.
Cheyenne, WY 82006
(307) 777-7735

Alberta Department of Forestry, Lands and Wildlife
Main Floor North Tower
Petroleum Plaza
9945 108th Street
Edmonton, Alberta T5K 2G6
(403) 427-6733

British Columbia Ministry of Environment
Fish and Wildlife Branch
780 Blanchard Street
Victoria, British Columbia V8V 1X5
(604) 387-9299

Manitoba Department of Natural Resources
Wildlife Branch
1495 St. James Court
Winnipeg, Manitoba R3H 0W9
(204) 945-7752

New Brunswick Bureau of Natural Resources
Fish and Wildlife Branch
P. O. Box 6000
Fredricton, New Brunswick E3B 4X5
(506) 453-2440

Newfoundland Department of Culture
Wildlife Division
P. O. Box 8750
St. Johns, Newfoundland A1C 5 7
(709) 772-5585

Northwest Territories Department of Renewable
Resources
Legislative Building
Yellowknife, Northwest Territories X1A 2C6
(403) 873-7760

Nova Scotia Department of Lands and Forests
Wildlife Division
136 Exhibition Street
Kentville, Nova Scotia B4N 4E5
(902) 424-5935

Ontario Ministry of Natural Resources
Wildlife Branch
Room 1-73, MacDonald Block
900 Bay Street
Toronto, Ontario M7A 2C3

(416) 965-4251
Prince Edward Island Community and Cultural Affairs
P. O. Box 2000
Charlottetown, Prince Edward Island C1A 7N8
(902) 368-4683

Quebec Department of Recreation, Hunting and
Fishing
P. O. Box 2200
150 East St. Cyrille
Quebec City, Quebec G1R 4Y1
(418) 643-2207

Saskatchewan Parks and Renewable Resources
Wildlife Branch
3211 Albert Street
Regina, Saskatchewan S4S 5W6
(306) 787-2930

Yukon Department of Renewable Resources
Wildlife Branch
P. O. Box 2703
Whitehorse, Yukon Territory Y1A 2C6
(403) 667-5715